FEMINISMS

revised edition

FEMINISMS

an anthology | *edited by*

of literary | **robyn r. warhol**

theory and | *and*

criticism | **diane price herndl**

rutgers university press • new brunswick, new jersey

Third paperback printing, 2010

Library of Congress Cataloging-in-Publication Data

Feminisms : an anthology of literary theory and criticism / edited by
    Robyn R. Warhol and Diane Price Herndl. — 2nd ed.
        p.   cm.
    Includes bibliographical references and index.
    ISBN 0-8135-2388-5. — ISBN 0-8135-2389-3 (pbk.)
    1. Feminist literary criticism.   2. Feminism and literature.
3. Women and literature.   I. Warhol, Robyn R.   II. Price Herndl,
Diane, 1959– .
PN98.W64F366   1997
809'.89287—dc20

                                                                96-31072
                                                                CIP

CONTENTS

CONFLICTS

BODY

GAZE

DESIRE

HISTORY

CLASS

MEN

AUTOBIOGRAPHY

ABOUT *FEMINISMS*

The introduction to the first edition of *Feminisms*, published in 1991, began with the statement that "self-consciousness is one hallmark of contemporary literary scholarship, and feminist criticism is no exception. Indeed, being explicit about the referents of one's pronouns, the origins of one's projects, and the position from which one speaks has become very common among feminists; beginning a book with a personal anecdote is practically obligatory. There are good reasons for this: feminism holds that 'the personal *is* political,' and as feminists we believe that the traditional academic boundaries between professional and personal experience ought to be undermined."

In *Who Stole Feminism?*, her 1994 diatribe against academic feminists, Christina Hoff Sommers quotes from the second paragraph of our introduction: "'We' are Robyn and Diane; we speak as white middle-class heterosexual American feminist academics in our early thirties (to cover a number of the categories feminist criticism has lately been emphasizing as significant to one's reading and speaking position: race, class, sexual orientation, nationality, political positioning, education-level, and age). Colleagues at the University of Vermont since 1989, we two have found that we share passionate interests in fiction, feminism and quiltmaking.'" Sommers quotes us in order to criticize the convention of self-disclosure in feminist criticism, but a telltale mistake shows that she never bothered to read past the first page of our introduction: she calls the book "*Feminism*," instead of *Feminisms*. The error is more than merely typographical; it reveals a fundamental misunderstanding behind many recent attacks on feminist criticism and theory. Detractors like Sommers assume that "feminism" is a monolithic, prescriptive, conformist stance—that it is singular. The purpose of this anthology is, as it was in 1991, to dispel that error by demonstrating the multiplicity of perspectives and approaches called feminist literary theory and criticism.

As our first introduction explained, we began this project as an alternative to using photocopied readings packets for feminist courses in literary studies. Today as in the late 1980s, most collections of feminist theory are either interdisciplinary (leaving little room for a diversity of approaches to literature and cultural studies) or are short, containing twelve to fifteen essays that either represent a particular methodology or are focused on a specific subject. When such anthologies do attempt to represent a variety of methodological approaches, their limited space prevents any attempt at real comprehensiveness. Generally, if an anthology focuses on French feminist theories, it excludes Anglo-American approaches; if it brings together work on writings by women of color, it leaves out "mainstream" subjects; if it aspires to represent a broad spectrum of perspectives, it usually saves room for one or two voices to speak for issues of "race" or "postcolonialism" and perhaps one to speak for "sexual orientation." Given the constraints of expense and space in such books, these editorial decisions make perfect sense.

Since its first appearance, *Feminisms* has remained the largest collection of complete essays and book chapters representing feminist literary criticism. The first edition contained work by fifty-three different critics; by eliminating duplications and substituting some shorter essays for longer ones by the same authors, we have raised the number of critics represented in the second edition to sixty-six. In the second edition as in the first, *Feminisms* takes advantage of its larger scale to draw upon the collective insights of other anthologies, bringing together as many current strains of feminist literary theory as possible. This book aspires to give a wide-angle view of what is going on in feminist literary studies in the United States today. Even a book reproducing sixty-five essays has limits, though; this introductory chapter explains the principles we followed in making our selections.

Our title, *Feminisms: An Anthology of Literary Theory and Criticism*, sets out some of the parameters of our goals. As Christina Hoff Sommers failed to notice, we've used the plural form "feminisms," rather than "feminism," to acknowledge the diversity of motivation, method, and experience among feminist academics. While the multiplicity of approaches and assumptions inside the movement can lead to conflict and competition, it can also be the source of vitality and genuine learning. Such diversity—if fostered, as it has been in some feminist thought—can be a model for cultural heterogeneity. Indeed, conflict itself can be fruitful, as we have emphasized by adding sections on "Conflicts" and "Practice" to this new edition. Our title underscores our commitment to diversity within feminism. By choosing this approach, we take just one of the many positions available within the movement; some feminists do take more aggressive, competitive stances than the one we are adopting here. Our purpose, though, is not to model a single "feminist" critical perspective: we have tried to put together a collection that can be tailored to fit a number of different pedagogical purposes for courses in literary and cultural studies.

Although feminisms are multiple, feminists do share certain beliefs, which we see as the common denominators among the sixty-five essays reprinted here. Feminist critics generally agree that the oppression of women is a fact of life, that gender leaves its traces in literary texts and on literary history, and that feminist literary criticism plays a worthwhile part in the struggle to end oppression in the world outside of texts. When they turn their attention to social history, most feminists agree that oppression of ethnic and racial minorities, gay men and lesbians, and working-class people is closely tied to the oppression of women. Of course, not all feminist critics ground their work in material history. But even when they focus on such comparatively abstract matters as discourse, aesthetics, or the constitution of subjectivity, feminists are always engaged in an explicitly political enterprise, always working to change existing power structures both inside and outside academia. Its overtly political nature is perhaps the single most distinguishing feature of feminist scholarly work. Of course, as feminists have long insisted, all scholarly work is political, but not all scholars are as forthright about their politics as feminists are.

Perhaps the most important development in the five years that have passed since we edited the first *Feminisms* is a widening acknowledgment that feminist studies have been too much the domain of white, middle-class, straight women who share much of the cultural privilege of their male counterparts. As we surveyed the field to update the table of contents, we were glad that we had not "ghettoized" the voices of women of color or of lesbians in sections of their own; instead, we had distributed selections by nonmainstream theorists throughout the volume. Still, we have acted upon the need to increase their representation in the second edition. We also have included essays by straight, middle-class, white feminists who interrogate their own identity positioning, rather than taking their perspective as universally representative of "women." This edition includes many essays that work through the common assertion that race, sexual orientation, and class always inflect understandings of gender.

Attention to gender is another rubric by which feminist criticism can usually be identified. But "gender" is a debatable term: some writers use it to mean biological sex (male/female), whereas others insist upon making a distinction between biology and culture. The latter theorists argue that masculinity and femininity are not predetermined by the body itself, but are constructed within culture. To borrow a vivid illustration of this distinction from Susan Brownmiller: It is female (just as it is male) to grow hair on the legs and in the armpits, but in the United States it is deemed feminine (but not masculine) to shave that hair off. The "female," then, is a matter of sex, the "feminine" a matter of culture. Some feminists depend upon this distinction as a key to combating "essentialism," or a deterministic view that "biology is destiny." Others embrace the biological facts of femaleness (for example, childbearing, lactation, and menstruation) as potentially liberatory for women, encouraging women to celebrate difference from the male "norm" rather than to discount or denigrate it. Still others (especially those whose work is grounded in the French language, which uses *féminine* to mean both "female" and "feminine") resist the binary opposition of sex and gender, arguing that the cultural differences are, after all, instilled on the basis of biological givens. More recently, some feminists have also begun to argue, conversely, that sex itself is historically constructed, and that the male/female distinction is as dependent upon cultural assumptions as the masculine/feminine divide. All of these versions of what "gender" means are represented in *Feminisms*, and all are brought to bear here upon literary studies.

We conceive "literary theory and criticism" as the realm of what is taught today in American departments of English. Broadly speaking, we define that realm as "texts." Hence, each of our entries addresses gender-related issues in the study of texts, which may be drawn from traditional "high-culture" literature, from such recently emerging genres as diaries or letters, or from popular forms such as dime-store romance and Hollywood film. This new edition adds a section on "Gaze" to show how feminist film theory has influenced literary criticism. The first four sections of the book—"Institutions," "Canon," "Practice," and "Conflicts"—address the definitions of "literature and criticism" directly, inquiring into the role feminism has played in the task of reshaping the entire field.

Literary studies are not what they were when feminist criticism entered the scene twenty-five years ago. Indeed, at that time few people were questioning the received definitions of either "literature" or "literary studies," but today both terms demand explanation. One major change brought about chiefly by feminist criticism has been the increasingly interdisciplinary nature of literary studies. Influenced by and participating in Women's Studies, feminists have brought new vitality to the study of literature by introducing to it research done in such fields as sociology, anthropology, history, religion, psychology, political science, law, and communications. Signs of all these disciplines' influence abound in the primarily literary essays reprinted here.

The book is thus designed for use in courses on criticism and on women in literature, but it is addressed to many other audiences outside the classroom as well. Because this collection seeks to answer such basic questions as "What is feminist literary theory?" and "What does it mean to do feminist criticism?" it is directed at curious nonfeminist academics as well as at feminists outside of academia looking for correspondences between their own political action and academically applied theory. We have assumed some knowledge of literary history on our readers' part, but we have been careful in our introductions to each section to define terms that are specific to feminism or to literary theory. We hope this will be the book an interdisciplinary reading group could use as an introduction to feminist literary studies, or the book a feminist teacher could hand to the student, colleague, or friend who says "I like what you're saying about literature and about writing—what can I read to learn more about it?" We hope, too, that *Feminisms* will serve specialists in feminist criticism as a manageable repository of often-quoted and innovative essays representing multiple feminist positions.

We are both feminist teachers, committed to using feminist pedagogy in the classroom. Neither of us is politically reconciled to the position of authority that leading a class discussion—or editing this anthology—implies. Just as we encourage our students to question us and our assumptions, we invite our readers to question this book's assumptions, its inclusions and exclusions, and its organization. Some of our friends ridiculed us for adopting the quilt metaphor for *Feminisms*, calling it a feminist cliché. We don't deny that, but we find the metaphor useful nevertheless. This patchwork is not the only way these essays could have been pieced together; nor is this material the only selection we could have made.

SELECTING THE PIECES OF *FEMINISMS*

The concept of *Feminisms*, based as it is upon multiplicity, depends, as we have said, upon accepting heterogeneity within feminist literary studies. This does not mean that we, as editors, position ourselves as "pluralists," or as theorists who think that "anything goes." As independent critics, each of us agrees with some of the pieces in this collection, and each disapproves of others. (Since Diane's work tends to be more "historicist" than Robyn's, Robyn's more "discourse"-oriented than Diane's; and since Diane's work has roots in psychoanalytic theory while Robyn's is influenced by structuralist narratology, the essays Diane likes are not always the same as the ones Robyn likes.) We do, however, believe that each essay here represents a viable—and important—voice in contemporary feminist literary studies, one that should be heard. Still, we recognize that the diversity of views represented here sometimes leads to irreconcilable logical conflicts. There is no way to force these many voices into a unison performance, or even—in some cases—to make them harmonize. For this reason, we have chosen not to evaluate individual positions in our introductions to each section of the book. We were very much amused by the reviewer who objected to our reticence about our own positions as a "boutique" approach to feminist criticism; she said we treated the various feminisms as "each its own little shop in the great American intellectual mall." We recognize ourselves in the caricature, because shopping is perhaps the only thing we enjoy doing together more than quilting. However, we stand by our decision not to evaluate individual entries.

Rather than poking holes in each writer's argument or declaring any winners in the debate, our section introductions try to take every entry on its own terms, summarizing briefly what each author has to say and showing the relation each piece holds to the others in its section. In taking this descriptive stance, rather than a prescriptive or evaluative one, we are choosing to avoid what James J. Sosnoski calls "intellectual machismo" (in his essay reprinted in "Institutions"), the kind of power-posturing that prompts endless arguments and inevitably leads either to hegemony or to a paralytic standoff. We are interested in promoting the forward movement of feminist activism, a movement we believe can only occur where difference commands attention, not dismissal or negativism.

Although all the selections in this edition appear in chronological order within sections, we are resisting any temptation to impose a "progress" model on the development of feminist criticism over the past fifteen years. The order within sections is not intended to imply that the final essays have issued the final word on the question. We do not subscribe to what Olivia Frey has called "literary Darwinism," or a notion that the fittest approaches will survive by eliminating their weaker competitors. We have avoided editorial determinations of "political correctness" (which is, we believe, a fabrication attributable to the New Right in its campaign to discredit progressive academics, including feminists); we do not want to be the arbiters of feminist taste. Our vision of feminist criticism is not as a marketplace where the distinguished individual will rise in importance through special achievement by providing a better mousetrap than the next gal, nor even as a consumer-driven shopping mall, where fashion rules. We see it instead as a collective effort, able to absorb and benefit from conflict within the collective. We have left out some movements within feminist criticism that were current in the mid-1970s but that no longer enter the discussions being held today: myth criticism is one example of a formerly popular approach that is not represented in *Feminisms*. While this could suggest that we view these positions as weaker competitors, our intent rather is to give a wide-ranging picture of feminist criticism today. We have therefore tried to focus on questions that are still current, debates that are still going on in the mid-1990s.

In choosing these previously published essays and book chapters, we followed two basic principles. First, we wanted to reproduce as many as possible of those theoretical statements within feminist criticism that have been repeatedly cited, disputed, and invoked in work written through the 1980s. We have tried to include essays that have, themselves, sparked their own critical debates. Our second principle of selection was to print interesting essays that represent as many current approaches as possible, regardless of the writers' institutional prominence or fame. These guidelines have resulted in a conglomeration of scholars at many different stages of their careers, though we have, in all cases, selected critics who are still actively pursuing research. We have, in several cases, reprinted essays written early in the careers of critics who have been consistently productive; we do not mean for the pieces here by Myra Jehlen, Jane Marcus, Bonnie Zimmerman, Luce Irigaray, Julia Kristeva, Laura Mulvey, Jane Gallop, Judith Fetterley, Judith Lowder Newton, Annette Kolodny, Shoshana Felman, or Sandra M. Gilbert and Susan Gubar, for example, to obscure the importance of work they have done since. Indeed, we hope these selections will prompt readers to look into the writers' later productions.

Having said all this, we do recognize the paradox inherent in setting up what could be seen as a "canon" of feminist criticism. By their nature and function, critical anthologies, like literary anthologies, create canons (as Jane Gallop has argued in *Around 1981* [1991]); when they become the basis for syllabi, collections come to define the fields they seek to introduce. While the canonization effect is probably to some degree unavoidable, we have tried our best to subvert it. We hope the diversity of our selections and their organization into sections will emphasize our assertion that this volume does not intend to propose a totalizing definition of feminist criticism, but rather to present various feminisms, a significant number of voices and approaches functioning alongside other feminisms in the academy today.

Those pieces we selected are—with only a few exceptions—uncut; most articles and book chapters appear here in their original forms. We felt it was important for readers to get as full as possible an idea of the rhetorical thrust of each piece, even though that meant we had space for fewer entries than we might have included, had we used excerpts as does Maggie Humm in her interdisciplinary collection, *Modern Feminisms* (1992). Selections from books appearing in *Feminisms* are not meant as substitutes for the whole works; we hope readers will follow through on the citations in our section introductions. In a few cases we did excerpt parts of book chapters to accommodate constraints of space and of resources available from our press.

The financial constraints upon *Feminisms* have been real and reflect a serious issue facing feminist scholars at work today: How can feminist criticism reject marketplace ethics while still working within the marketplace of the competitive publishing industry? As more and more publishing houses are consolidated or bought by major multinational corporations, even the relatively autonomous university presses are forced to conform, to some extent, to the norms they establish. These norms are increasingly those of the corporate, rather than the academic, world (in the 1990s, the distinction is beginning to blur, anyway). We have been astonished at the range of fees university presses charge for permission to reprint scholarly work, from nothing more than a credit line to over a thousand dollars. Even more dismaying was our realization that some presses will agree to reduce the price for permission only if authors are willing to waive their part of the profits the fees represent. We remain grateful to the many scholars whose fame would warrant hefty fees but who generously donated their work to the first edition of *Feminisms*. For the present edition, we have sought to include essays by important scholars who were left out of the first edition because their publishers asked for higher permissions fees than we could pay. In some cases this has meant that we include essays that may not be the most prominent or even the most representative piece of a critic's work, but we stand by the scholarly value of every entry.

To keep the size of the volume within economically feasible limits—and to give it a measure of coherence within diversity—we have narrowed the subject matter of the essays to include chiefly British and North American literature of the nineteenth and twentieth centuries. In doing so, we repeat the gesture of Gilbert and Gubar's 1985 *Norton Anthology of Literature by Women*, which (as many have argued) grants disproportionate space to the same periods and nations we feature here. References to certain writers (Charlotte Brontë, Virginia Woolf, Toni Morrison, and Alice Walker) and certain genres (the romance, autobiography, the novel) occur repeatedly here, partly because of our personal interest in those subjects, but partly also to provide various viewpoints on the same material. This choice means that we have omitted important feminist criticism on earlier periods and on literature written in languages other than English. In reprinting pieces from Hélène Cixous, Shoshana Felman, Jane Gallop, Luce Irigaray, and Julia Kristeva, however, we have made some exceptions for writers who have particularly influenced the American critical scene.

In making selections from each critic's corpus, we favored theoretical over purely critical pieces. We looked for works by critics who were explicit about their premises and methods, and who illustrated their theories with specific reference to texts. Of course, the diversity of *Feminisms* means that there are exceptions to this rule, too—Kristeva, Cixous, and Irigaray, for instance, write theory without much recourse to practical criticism. But we have steered clear of essays that apply criticism to texts without some self-consciousness about the theories they are using, because we wanted to highlight the process and thought behind the practice of feminist literary study.

THE PATTERN OF *FEMINISMS*

We have made a few references here to "Anglo-American" and "French" feminisms, a distinction that will be clearer to those who have read the essays and section introductions in this volume, but that bears some explanation here. In the most general terms, French feminism proceeds from the psychoanalytic premises of Freud and Lacan, and adopts or adapts the deconstructive methods of Jacques Derrida. It is poststructuralist in that it focuses on discourse and on the constructedness of subjectivity and of representation. By contrast, Anglo-American feminism is generally more interested in history. That can mean literal history (accounts of the lived experience of people in the world), or literary history, or both. Anglo-American feminism tends to focus more than does French feminism on the interaction of texts with the extratextual world they simultaneously address and represent.

This simple differentiation between the two is, of course, too schematic; Anglo-American feminists often concern themselves with discourse, French feminists with the world outside of texts. When applied to the essays in this volume, especially, the distinction between French and Anglo-American feminisms becomes blurred. The essays here reveal the many intersections between theories, and show how feminist writers have used various theoretical approaches to understand the mechanisms through which gender operates within texts. We have tried to avoid privileging either approach.

Just as critics can be categorized by identifying their approach as "French" or "Anglo-American," so too can scholars who narrate the history of feminist criticism be divided into two general groups: One approach is to contrast French and Anglo-American feminism with each other, coming down on the French side (as Toril Moi does in *Sexual/Textual Politics* [1985]) or the Anglo-American side (as Janet Todd does in *Feminist Literary History* [1988]). The other way of talking about feminist criticism is to put French and Anglo-American modes together and narrate their development as a series of "moments" or "phases," as Elaine Showalter does in our section on "Practice." Though some sections of *Feminisms* are dominated by critics working in the French mode ("Desire," "Gaze," and "Body," in particular) and others contain chiefly Anglo-American work (especially "Canon," "Practice," "Conflicts," "Reading," "Ethnicity," and "Class"), we do not wish to reinforce oppositions between the two modes. Indeed, as the essays written since the late 1980s reveal, the argument over which mode is superior has abated as the divisions between them have blurred.

As we tried not to assign national labels to the critics we have reprinted, we also have avoided designating them by methodology. Traditionally, anthologies of criticism are arranged either chronologically or by type of criticism (and, in such collections, "feminist criticism" or "gender theory" is usually represented by just one section, including feminist criticism alongside queer theory and masculinity studies). We found that to try to describe any piece in this collection according to its method (to say, for instance, that something is "Marxist" or "deconstructionist" or "semiotic" criticism) would be greatly to oversimplify and misrepresent the complexity of what each of these feminist critics is doing. We include pieces that represent all the major theoretical orientations within current feminist criticism, including psychoanalytic, Marxist, Foucauldian, Bakhtinian, narratological, reader-response, postcolonialist, gay studies/queer theory, race-centered, cultural studies, deconstructionist, and "personal criticism" approaches, and yet we would be hard pressed to designate any piece in the anthology by a singular label. Most of these authors combine theoretical approaches in their work; some of them practice an eclecticism that defies categorization. We decided, therefore, to organize the book around a group of concepts that keep coming up in contemporary feminist critical debates.

Each of these concepts—resembling what Raymond Williams has called "keywords"—represents the topic of lively discussions among feminists through the 1980s and into the mid-1990s. Some keywords that might have been included on such a list fifteen years ago are not here ("archetype" and "chauvinism" come to mind), because the debates that centered on them seem to have closed down. The keywords we did choose come from a long list of current possibilities, including "domesticity," "imperialism," "lesbian," "authority," "the subject," "text," "femininity," even "woman" (for a more complete list, see the "Alternative Arrangements"). All of these concepts—and many others—come up more than once among the selections we have made for this volume. The ideal collection of feminist criticism would devote sections to each of them.

This piece of patchwork is organized into fourteen blocks or sections, each one focusing on a single keyword. The introduction to each section explains how we construe its central concept, shows what the relation of each essay to that concept is (from our point of view), and identifies the basic theoretical and methodological assumptions behind each essay's argument. Most pieces could just as easily fit into several other sections of the book; to facilitate discussion of how the issues intersect, we have provided an index suggesting alternative organizations for this material.

The organization of *Feminisms* is ultimately arbitrary—in that way, the volume most strikingly resembles a quilt. We have cut out and stitched together pieces of criticism, and we have laid them out in a pattern that imposes a sense of coherence the pieces themselves might not have fallen into of their own accord. Like the components of a quilt, however, those pieces all maintain their own integrity. Pulled together, the pieces acquire a new form and new function. We hope our readers will be critical, actively considering the value not just of individual pieces, but of the governing design. We hope, too, that readers who become newly acquainted with these pieces will be moved to go back to the bolts from which they have been cut, to acquire a comfortable familiarity with all the material of feminist criticism and theory.

—RRW & DPH

ACKNOWLEDGMENTS FOR THE FIRST EDITION

In this collaboration, we have come to rely a great deal on each other, but without the help of many other people, *Feminisms* could never have happened. We are particularly grateful for the financial support from the University of Vermont Women's Studies program, directed by Joan Smith. That grant, together with the material support that came through Virginia Clark, Chair of the English Department at UVM, enabled us to finish the project in half the time we thought it would take.

Ed White, our research assistant, deserves special appreciation for the rigor and efficiency of the work he did for us. We could ask on Monday for a list of every article ever published in a particular category of feminist criticism, and it would be in our hands by Wednesday. Without his hard work, resourcefulness, and insight, the correspondence and research necessary to a project of this scale would have been unmanageable.

We are grateful, too, to the undergraduate work-study students who helped us with correspondence and manuscript preparation, Willow Older and Mary Thompson. We extend our thanks to Sandy Greiner and Kim McMeekin, who provided willing and efficient secretarial support.

Several people read drafts of our introductions, making suggestions that affected the way we were thinking about what we were doing. For these contributions, we would like to thank Helena Michie, Beth Kowaleski Wallace, Philippe Carrard, and especially Carl Herndl.

Many of the scholars represented in this volume were instrumental in making it possible for us to use their work; our thanks go to Dale Bauer, Catharine R. Stimpson, Annette Kolodny, Jane Marcus, Nancy Armstrong, Myra Jehlen, Gayatri Chakravorty Spivak, Sidonie Smith, Bonnie Zimmerman, Leslie Rabine, Susan Stanford Friedman, Paul Lauter, Linda Kauffman, and Sue Lanser. Their enthusiasm sustained us in sometimes trying circumstances.

Polly Mitchell at the Shelburne Museum was very kind in giving us an afternoon to browse through their quilt collection to find our cover art.

Leslie Mitchner, our editor at Rutgers, cannot be thanked enough for her support, her guidance, and her passion for this project. The rest of the staff at the

Press—Dina Bednarczyk, Adaya Henis, Marilyn Campbell, Stephen D. Maikow-
ski, Barbara Kopel, and John Romer, have been super.

Finally, we'd like to dedicate this book to our students, past and present.

—Robyn R. Warhol and Diane Price Herndl
Burlington, Vermont
January 1991

ACKNOWLEDGMENTS FOR THE REVISED EDITION

For this second edition, we'd like to acknowledge the miracles of e-mail, telephones, FAX machines, and airplanes, which made it possible to collaborate at a three-thousand-mile distance, but we'd also like to thank many people.

We'd particularly like to thank our assistants Jill Nebeker and Dawn Vernooy, whose hard and scrupulous work in doing research, secretarial work, permissions work, and manuscript preparation made the whole project possible. Like Ed White before her, Jill provided long, detailed bibliographies on a moment's notice and labored long on the first drafts of contributors' notes; she was also invaluable in offering feedback as the first student to read the new edition cover to cover. Dawn copied, numbered, and organized the whole manuscript, and kept track of the permissions correspondence. We would also like to thank New Mexico State University for providing the funding to hire the two of them.

Several people generously provided us with ideas for revising this edition, in person, through reviews, and by e-mail; we'd like to thank Helena Michie, Shirley Geok-lin Lim, Sherry Linkon, Cheryl Torsney, Irene Goldman, Nancy Goldstein, Miriam Fuchs, C. M. Jackson-Houston, and especially Marilyn Edelstein for their excellent suggestions. We couldn't follow all of them, but they were extremely helpful at a point when we were looking for some fresh ideas.

Without Leslie Mitchner's continuing support and friendship, we wouldn't be doing a revised edition—we are, once again, thankful for her support, enthusiasm, and help with this project. We also appreciate the hard work of the staff at Rutgers University Press—Anne Hegeman, Marlie Wasserman, and Judith Nagata—and our diligent copyeditor, Adaya Henis.

We are grateful to our families for their support—Carl Herndl, Tom Streeter, and especially Seth Warhol-Streeter.

Finally, as before, we dedicate this edition to our students, from whom we just keep learning.

DIANE PRICE HERNDL AND ROBYN R. WARHOL
Las Cruces, New Mexico, and Burlington, Vermont
July 1996

FEMINISMS

institutions

W e begin this anthology with "Institutions" rather than a category like "The Self" or "The Personal" as a way of highlighting the emphasis in current feminisms on the group, the community, and the systemic nature of women's oppression. In fact, recent work in feminism has begun to show how concepts like "self" or "personal" are themselves constructed within institutions. Institutions establish orderliness, rules, sameness; feminism questions whether that orderliness and sameness has been at the expense of the differences represented by women. The essays in this section explore how women's "otherness" from established patterns has caused their exclusion from various structures of power.

This section could, perhaps, have been called "Otherness"; each of the essays here focuses on how women's difference necessarily disrupts and disturbs the orderliness imposed by male-dominated systems. "Otherness" is itself almost always a matter of institutional definition; insuring homogeneity is often one of the most important tasks of the institution. Difference is excluded, overlooked, forced back into conformity with an artificial norm, or suppressed.

Feminists began this analysis from the outside, as people who had themselves been excluded from and oppressed by educational, religious, and governmental institutions. They tried to understand how oppression had become institutionalized, how it functioned, and how it could be changed. Barbara Ehrenreich and Deirdre English's *Complaints and Disorders: The Sexual Politics of Sickness* (1973) examined the medical establishment and its complicity with sexist norms; Phyllis Chesler did the same for the practice of psychiatry in *Women and Madness* (1972); Nancy Chodorow, in *The Reproduction of Mothering* (1978), and Adrienne Rich, in *Of Woman Born: Motherhood as Institution and Experience* (1976), studied sexist norms in childraising, family structures, and the construction of "compulsory heterosexuality"; Mary Daly's *Beyond God the Father* (1973) and *The Church and the Second Sex* (1975) questioned the institutional sexism of religion; Catharine MacKinnon has, in *Feminism Unmodified* (1987) and *Toward a Feminist Theory of the State* (1989), examined women's relation to the law and the state; the field of feminist pedagogy has questioned how sexism affects the classroom and the educational system. These examples represent only a fraction of the feminist critique of institutions, and of the influential work that came together to form the new academic field of Women's Studies.

Feminist *literary* criticism has been a part of this challenge, questioning the most basic institutions of literary studies: how we evaluate literature, how we constitute knowledge about it, how its study is determined by the structure of the academy, and how it is separated from other disciplines. From these questions have come serious critiques of how literature is taught, why it is taught, and who teaches it. Literary study has been dramatically changed in the last two and a half decades, largely as a result of the feminist critique of it *as* an institution.

One could argue that all the essays in this anthology are focused on some kind of institution; certainly, the next three sections (on "Canon," "Practice," and "Conflicts") are direct questionings of some aspects of the literary/academic enterprise. The essays in this section, though, take on these questions directly as issues of institutionality; literary criticism, literary history, academic evaluation, and feminist criticism itself are examined here as systems per se. They explore the construction, maintenance, and functioning of literary studies and/in the academy. All five of these essays explore literary institutions in relation to some other cultural system: criticism, the history of Western thought, psychoanalysis, literary history, medical discourse, and academic advancement.

Shoshana Felman examines the impact that Western, dichotomized thinking has had on literary criticism and women in "Women and Madness: The Critical Phallacy" (1975). Felman uses Jacques Derrida's analysis of the way that oppositional thinking dominates Western culture (understanding things in relation to their opposites, and imposing hierarchy upon the resulting oppositions, for example, man/woman, sane/insane, speech/silence, same/other) to show that traditional ways of defining woman always subordinate her in the opposition; she is man's "Other" and is therefore what he is not—insane and silent. Felman examines the impact of this opposition upon the critical institution when women begin to speak out, to declare that their point of view is sane; she begins her analysis with two books on women and madness: Chesler's *Women and Madness* and Luce Irigaray's *Speculum de l'autre femme* (1974), part of which is reproduced in our section called "Gaze." If woman is, by definition, both made and silent, Felman asks, "how can the woman as such be speaking in [these books]? Who is speaking here, and who is asserting the otherness of the woman?" Although she cannot answer these two questions in this essay, she does point out that they represent the "major theoretical challenge of all contemporary thought," especially feminist thought. Felman turns from this central problem to a corollary one: how the classification of woman as other, insane, and silent makes its appearance in literary criticism. She uses a story by Balzac, "Adieu," and two critical essays on it to illustrate that readings of realism systematically exclude both women and madness. Traditional literary critique is blind to women, she argues; it is unable to theorize or visualize otherness. Her illustration reveals the difficult task facing the feminist critic: how to work against and from the outside of linguistic and critical institutions so that she will no longer be defined as mad, silent, Other, and invisible.

In that they have themselves become an institution within feminist criticism, Sandra M. Gilbert and Susan Gubar embody that difficult task. Their monumental first book, *The Madwoman in the Attic* (1979), challenges the institution of British and American literary history by focusing exclusively on the work of women writers. With other practitioners of gynocriticism (see Elaine Showalter in "Practice" for a definition of this term she coined), they have recently been taken to task for limiting their view to middle- and upper-class white women authors, but within those limits they treat a broad range of genres. The fragment of the second chapter of *Madwoman* reproduced here, from "Infection in the Sentence: The Woman Writer and the Anxiety of Authorship," can give only a faint indication of the entire work's scale. Over seven hundred pages long, the collaboratively written study elaborates a model of a women's literary tradition through scores of readings of texts by female authors who have been more or less accepted as "great" writers, ranging from works as obscure as Jane Austen's juvenilia to such generally acknowledged masterpieces as *Middlemarch*. As our sample indicates, the authors allude to points established in their previous chapters (here, the mentions of Snow White refer back to a close reading performed in chapter 1) to build their theory of the links among nineteenth-century women writers' texts. Like Showalter, they analyze women writers' relation to their literary foremothers in order to "reveal the extraordinary strength of women's literary accomplishments" against daunting odds.

To do so, they must defy the institution of male-centered literary criticism. The first section of the chapter reprinted here outlines Gilbert and Gubar's enormously influential revision of Harold Bloom's Freudian theory of "the anxiety of influence" among authors. Gilbert and Gubar are quick to point out that Bloom's examples—like Freud's—are all male, and that his theory can neither be adopted nor reversed to account for authors working in the female subculture (which is, for Gilbert and Gubar as for Showalter, a historical given). Women authors, they argue, experience "the anxiety of authorship," doubly explicable as a feminine version of Bloom's theory and as women authors' individual and collective response to the pervasive Western metaphor of "literary paternity," that is, the idea that the author stands in a fatherly relation to the text. "Based on the woman's socially determined sense of her own biology," the anxiety makes its way into women's texts in recurring patterns of themes, forms, and motifs. The excerpt from the chapter places women's anxiety about disease and about their bodies in historical context, links it to authorial anxiety, and begins sketching out strategies some nineteenth-century writers use to express and to overcome their sense of "infection in the sentence," as Emily Dickinson called it. The balance of the chapter, with typical Gilbert-and-Gubar scope, brings the theory to bear upon authors from Aphra Behn to H.D., from Jane Austen to Virginia Woolf, from George Eliot to Charlotte Perkins Gilman.

Literary criticism takes place within and is part of a larger institution: the academy. James J. Sosnoski, in "A Mindless Man-driven Theory Machine: Intellectuality, Sexuality, and the Institution of Criticism" (1989), examines criticism as a product of educational and competitive career-oriented systems. Within a structure in which hiring, tenure, and promotion are based on competition, critical debates are not supposed to be a matter of cooperation and collaboration, but must be competitive. Literature departments must be able to distinguish among candidates or to provide some grounds on which to make personnel decisions, and those grounds often take the form of a comparison to some ideal career path, what Sosnoski calls the "Magister Implicatus," a model of the literary career that is consistently modeled on famous men's lives. These institutional pressures to compete, and the related critical institution itself, turn error—or holding a mistaken notion—into what he calls "falsificity": a state equivalent to sinfulness, deserving of punishment. Sosnoski argues that "in the institution of criticism, critical arguments which are judged false are judged so not on purely logical grounds, but on the grounds that they are 'sham, counterfeit, bogus or fake' discourses and therefore punishable." He argues for a new way of thinking about criticism that does not depend on truthfulness and falsehood—but on intuition and feeling, a new critical institution based not on competitiveness but on cooperation and collaboration. One could say that Gilbert and Gubar's joint career as scholars exemplifies feminisms' ability to rise to Sosnoski's challenge.

In recent years, the feminist critique of institutions has taken a slightly different, self-reflexive turn. Feminists have begun to question one another and themselves, to examine their methods, goals, and alliances—and their own exclusions and oppressions of others. Barbara Christian's "The Highs and the Lows of Black

Feminist Criticism" (1990) is a meditation on the relationship between female literary critics and the language(s) they use to establish their places within the academic institution. Christian speaks of her personal history as a woman whose "formal schooling" took her "from kindergarten in the black Virgin Islands through a Ph.D. at white Columbia," and muses on the way education trains us to categorize cultural experience as "high" (Greek and Latin, Western philosophy, teacherly authority) or "low" ("sweat, calypso, long talk and plenty voices"). While Christian credits the women's movement of the 1960s and 1970s with altering the institution of literary criticism ("We have asked why some forms are not considered literature—for example, the diary, the journal, the letter. . . . We have developed women's studies programs."), she criticizes feminist studies for their tendency, as she sees it, to "homogenize the world of our Sisters, to fix ourselves in boxes and categories through jargon, theory, abstraction." Christian offers a model for thinking about the black feminist critic's relationship to her work, not as either "high" or "low," but as "both-and"; she also offers an alternative mode of literary-critical prose style, incorporating Black English and personal details in a formal piece of writing. She alludes, in her list of experiences in "the middle world," to her influential 1987 essay, "The Race for Theory," in which she had questioned the applicability of literary theory to African-American literary studies. In the present essay, she focuses more exclusively on the relationship of the woman critic to theory as an institution.

With Helena Michie's "Confinements: The Domestic in the Discourses of Upper-Middle-Class Pregnancy" (1996), we turn from academia to a set of institutions that shape contemporary women's lives. Michie employs the notion of the "domestic carceral"—a trope articulated by Paul Morrison to describe the way a Jane Austen heroine is figuratively imprisoned at home—to do a feminist analysis of how pregnancy gets talked about at hospitals and in the popular press. Her questions about the "discourse of pregnancy" echo the work of historian Michel Foucault, who theorized the structure of discipline and punishment in modern Western culture. Foucault has shown how prisons, for example, shifted from dark and forbidding dungeons to seemingly open "panoptic" spaces, where prisoners are always visible to their guards. What looks like a humane improvement turns out to have a sinister side. Whether the jailer is watching or not, the prisoner knows he *could* be; hence the prisoner guards himself, internalizing the disciplinary gaze. Michie follows Foucauldian reasoning to examine the darker side of upbeat contemporary writing about pregnancy and childbirth. Casting a feminist literary-critical eye upon the ubiquitous guidebook for middle-class pregnancy, *What to Expect When You're Expecting* (1984), Michie shows that the overt reassurances of the book are double-edged, serving to discipline and control the pregnant female reader as much as to support her. This pregnancy manual, itself an institution of sorts, takes its place alongside the other institutions that frame the experience of middle-class pregnancy—the hospital, the home—as both a "public" and "private" event. Michie's essay shows how feminist critical methods can extend beyond the literary realm to illuminate the workings of institutions in the world at large.

—RRW & DPH

WOMEN AND MADNESS
the critical phallacy

(1975)

Silence gives the proper grace to women.

SOPHOCLES, *AJAX*

Dalila: In argument with men a woman ever
  Goes by the worse, whatever be her cause.
Samson: For want of words, no doubt, or lack of breath!

MILTON, *SAMSON AGONISTES*

I. WOMAN AS MADNESS

Is it by chance that hysteria (significantly derived, as is well known, from the Greek word for "uterus") was originally conceived as an exclusively *female* complaint, as the lot and *prerogative* of women? And is it by chance that even today, between women and madness, sociological statistics establish a privileged relation and a definite correlation? "Women," writes Phyllis Chesler, in her book *Women and Madness*, "Women more than men, and in greater numbers than their existence in the general population would predict, are involved in 'careers' as psychiatric patients" [p. xxii]. How is this sociological fact to be analyzed and interpreted? What is the nature of the relationship it implies between women and madness? Supported by extensive documentation, Phyllis Chesler proposes a confrontation between objective data and the subjective testimony of women: laced with the voices of women speaking in the first person—literary excerpts from the novels and autobiographies of woman writers, and word-for-word interviews with female psychiatric patients—the book derives and disputes a "female psychology" conditioned by an oppressive and patriarchal male culture. "It is clear that for a woman to be healthy she must 'adjust' to and accept the behavioral norms for her sex even though these kinds of behavior are generally regarded as less socially desirable. . . . The ethic of mental health is masculine in our culture" [pp. 68–69]. "The *sine qua non* of 'feminine' identity in patriarchal society is the violation of the incest taboo, i.e., the initial and continued 'preference' for Daddy, followed by the approved falling in love and/or marrying of powerful father figures" [p. 138]. From her initial family upbringing throughout her subsequent development, the social role assigned to the woman is that of *serving* an image, authoritative and central, of man: a woman is first and foremost a daughter/a mother/a wife. "What we consider 'madness,' whether it appears in women or in men, is either the acting out of the devalued female role or the total or partial rejection of one's sex-role stereotype" [p. 56].

In contrast to the critical tendency currently in fashion in Europe, through which a certain French circle has allied itself philosophically with the controversial indictments of the English "anti-psychiatry" movement, Phyllis Chesler, although protesting in turn against psychiatry as such, in no way seeks to bestow upon madness the romanticized glamor of political protest and of social and cultural contestation: "It has never been my intention to romanticize madness, or to confuse it with political or cultural revolution" [p. xxiii]. Depressed and terrified women are not about to seize the means of production and reproduction: quite the opposite of rebellion, madness is the impasse confronting those whom cultural conditioning has deprived of the very means of protest or self-affirmation. Far from being a form of contestation, "mental illness" is a *request for help*, a manifestation both of cultural impotence and of political castration. This socially defined help-needing and help-seeking behavior is itself part of female conditioning, ideologically inherent in the behavioral pattern and in the dependent and helpless role assigned to the woman as such.

It is not the material, social, and psychological female condition, but rather the very *status of womanhood* in Western *theoretical* discourse which concerns Luce Irigaray in her recently published book, *Speculum de l'autre femme*. In contrast to Phyllis Chesler, Luce Irigaray interrogates not the empirical voice of women and their subjective testimony, but the key theoretical writings of men—fundamental texts in philosophy and in psychoanalysis—which, in one way or another, involve the concept of femininity. Her study focuses on the text of Freud's (fictive) lecture entitled "On Femininity" and on the feminine metaphors in Plato's myth of the Cave. A psychoanalyst herself, Luce Irigaray adopts the traditional feminist critique of the male-centered orientation and of the anti-feminine bias in psychoanalytical theory; but her elaboration and consolidation of these classical feminist arguments is derived from the current philosophical methods of thinking developed in France by Jacques Derrida and others in their attempt to work out a general critical "deconstruction" of Western metaphysics. According to Derrida's radicalization of the Nietzschean and Heideggerian critiques of traditional philosophy, Western metaphysics is based on the totalitarian principle of so-called "logocentrism," that is, on the repressive predominance of "logos" over "writing," on the privileged status of the present and the consequent valorization of presence. This *presence-to-itself* of a *center* (given the name of Origin, God, Truth, Being, or Reason) centralizes the world through the authority of its self-presence and subordinates to itself, in an agonistic, hierarchical manner, all the other cognizable elements of the same epistemological (or ontological) system. Thus, the metaphysical logic of dichotomous oppositions which dominates philosophical thought (Presence/ Absence, Being/Nothingness, Truth/Error, Same/ Other, Identity/Difference, etc.) is, in fact, a subtle mechanism of hierarchization which assures the unique valorization of the "positive" pole (that is, of a *single* term) and, consequently, the repressive subordination of all "negativity," the mastery of difference as such. It is by thus examining the mere illusion of duality and the repressive way in which the polarity Masculine/Feminine functions in

Western thought so as to privilege a unique term, that Luce Irigaray proceeds to develop her critical argument. Theoretically subordinated to the concept of masculinity, the woman is viewed by the man as *his* opposite, that is to say, as *his* other, the negative of the positive, and not, in her own right, different, other, Otherness itself. Throughout the Platonic metaphors which will come to dominate Western discourse and to act as a vehicle for meaning, Luce Irigaray points out a latent design to exclude the woman from the production of speech, since the woman, and the Other as such, are philosophically subjugated to the logical principle of Identity—Identity being conceived as a solely *masculine* sameness, apprehended as *male* self-presence and consciousness-to-itself. The possibility of a thought which would neither spring from nor return to this masculine Sameness is simply unthinkable. Plato's text thus establishes the repressive systematization of the logic of identity: the privilege of "oneness," of the reproduction of likeness, of the repetition of sameness, of literal meaning, analogy, symmetry, dichotomous oppositions, teleological projects.

Freud, who for the first time freed thought from a certain conception of the present and of presence-to-oneself, whose notions of deferred action, of the unconscious, of the death instinct, and of the repetition compulsion radically undermine the classical logic of identity, remains, nevertheless, himself a prisoner of philosophy when he determines the nature of sexual difference in function of the *a priori* of sameness, that is, of the male phallus. Female sexuality is thus described as an absence (of the masculine presence), as lack, incompleteness, deficiency, envy with respect to the only sexuality in which value resides. This symmetrical conception of otherness is a theoretical blindness to the woman's actual Difference, which is currently asserting itself, and asserting precisely its claim to a new kind of logic and a new type of theoretical reasoning.

A question could be raised: if "the woman" is precisely the Other of any conceivable Western theoretical locus of speech, how can the woman as such be speaking in this book? Who is speaking here, and who is asserting the otherness of the woman? If, as Luce Irigaray suggests, the woman's silence, or the repression of her capacity to speak, are constitutive of philosophy and of theoretical discourse as such, from what theoretical locus is Luce Irigaray herself speaking in order to develop her own theoretical discourse about the woman's exclusion? Is she speaking the language of men, or the silence of women? Is she speaking as a woman, or *in place of* the (silent) woman, *for* the woman, *in the name of* the woman? Is it enough to be a woman in order to *speak as* a woman? Is "speaking as a woman" a fact determined by some biological *condition* or by a strategic, theoretical *position*, by anatomy[1] or by culture? What if "speaking as a woman" were not a simple "natural" fact, could not be taken for granted? With the increasing number of women and men alike who are currently choosing to share in the rising fortune of female misfortune, it has become all too easy to be a speaker "*for* women." But what does "speaking *for* women" imply? What is "to speak *in the name of* the woman?" What, in a general manner, does "speech in the name of" mean? Is it not a precise repetition of the oppressive gesture of *representation*, by means of which, throughout the history of logos, man has reduced the woman to the status of a silent and subordinate object, to something inherently *spoken for*? To "speak in the name of," to "speak *for*," could thus mean, once again, to appropriate and to silence. This important theoretical question about the status of its own discourse and its own "representation" of women, with which any feminist thought has to cope, is not thought out by Luce Irigaray, and thus remains the blind spot of her critical undertaking.

In a sense, the difficulty involved in any feminist enterprise is illustrated by the complementarity, but also by the incompatibility, of the two feminist studies which we have just examined: the works of Phyllis Chesler and Luce Irigaray. The interest of Chesler's book, its overwhelming persuasive power as an outstanding clinical document, lies in the fact that it does *not* speak *for* women: it lets women speak for themselves. Phyllis Chesler accomplishes thus the first symbolical step of the feminist revolution: she *gives voice to* the woman. But she can only do so in a pragmatic, empirical way. As a result, the book's theoretical contribution, although substantial, does not go beyond the classical feminist thought concerning the socio-sexual victimization of women. On the other side of the coin, Irigaray's book has the merit of perceiving the problem on a theoretical level, of trying to think the feminist question through to its logical ends, reminding us that women's oppression exists not only in the material, practical organization of economic, social, medical, and political structures, but also in the very foundations of logos, reasoning, and articulation—in the subtle linguistic procedures and in the logical processes through which meaning itself is produced. It is not clear, however, that statement and utterance here coincide so as to establish actual feminine difference, not only on the thematic, but also on the rhetorical level: although the otherness of the woman is here fully assumed as the subject of the statement, it is not certain whether that otherness can be taken for granted as positively occupying the un-thought-out, problematical locus *from which* the statement is being *uttered*.

In the current attempt at a radical questioning and a general "deconstruction" of the whole range of cultural codes, feminism encounters the major theoretical challenge of all contemporary thought. The problem, in fact, is common to the revaluation of madness as well as to the contention of women: how can one speak from the place of the Other? How can the woman be thought about outside of the Masculine/Feminine framework, *other* than as opposed to man, without being subordinated to a primordial masculine model? How can madness, in a similar way, be conceived outside of its dichotomous opposition to sanity, without being subjugated to reason? How can difference as such be thought out as *non-subordinate* to identity? In other words, how can thought break away from the logic of polar oppositions?

In light of these theoretical challenges, and in keeping with the feminist questioning of psychoanalytical and philosophical discourse, it could be instructive to examine the ideological effects of the very production of meaning in the language of literature and in its critical exegesis. We therefore propose here to undertake a reading of a text by Balzac which deals with the woman as well as with madness and to examine the way in which this text, and its portrayal of feminine madness, has been traditionally perceived and commented upon. The text—entitled "Adieu"—is a short story first published in 1830, and later included by Balzac in the volume of *Philosophical Studies* of the *Comédie humaine*.

II. THE REALISTIC INVISIBLE

The story is divided into three parts. The first describes a mysterious domain into which have inadvertently wandered two lost hunters: Philippe de Sucy, a former colonel, and his friend d'Albon, a magistrate. Anxious to find out where they are, they turn to two women, the only human beings in the vicinity, but their questions meet only silence: one of the women, Geneviève, turns out to be a deaf-mute, and the other, an aphasic madwoman whose entire vocabulary consists of the word "adieu." On hearing this word, Philippe faints, recognizing in the madwoman his former mistress Countess Stéphanie de Vandières, who had accompanied him to Russia during the Napoleonic Wars but whom he has not seen again since their separation on the banks of the Berezina River and whose trace he has ever since been unable to recover.

The second part is a flashback to the war episode. Among the collapsing masses of the retreating French army, Stéphanie and Philippe are fighting against unbearable cold, inhuman exhaustion and debilitating hunger, in the midst of the snowy plains. Philippe heroically shields Stéphanie in the hope of crossing the Berezina and of thus reaching and having her reach the safety of the other side, free from the Russian threat. But when it turns out that only two places are left on the life raft, Philippe leaves them to Stéphanie and her husband, the Count of Vandières, sacrificing himself for the latter. The Count, however, never reaches the other side: in a violent jolt during the crossing, he is swept overboard and killed. Stéphanie cries out to Philippe, "Adieu!": it is to be her last lucid word before she loses her reason. For two years thereafter, she continues to be dragged along by the army, the plaything of wretched riffraff. Mad and cast off like an animal, she is discovered one day after the end of the war by her uncle, an elderly doctor, who takes her in and sees to her needs.

The third part describes the combined efforts of the two men—the doctor having been joined by Philippe—to save and to cure Stéphanie. Stéphanie, on seeing Philippe, fails to recognize him: her continuous repetition of the word "adieu" implies no understanding and bears no relation to conscious memory. At the sight of the "stranger" (Philippe), she runs away like a frightened animal. Following the advice of the doctor, Philippe learns how to "tame" Stéphanie by giving her sugar cubes, thus accustoming her to his presence. Philippe still hopes that Stéphanie will some day recognize him. Driven to despair, however, by the long wait, Philippe decides to hasten Stéphanie's recognition of him by subjecting her to a psychodrama designed to restore her memory: he artificially creates a replica of the Russian plains and of the Berezina River; using peasants disguised as soldiers, he theoretically reconstructs and replays before the madwoman's eyes the exact scene of their wartime separation. Stéphanie is thus indeed cured: overwhelmed, she recognizes Philippe, smiles to him, repeats once again "adieu"; but at that very instant she dies.

A current pocket edition of this amazing story (recently published by Gallimard in the "Folio" collection) insures, in two different ways, its critical presentation: the text is preceded and followed by pedagogical commentary—a Preface by Pierre Gascar and a "Notice" by Philippe Berthier—which are supposed to "explain" it and "situate" its importance. It is striking that, of the three chapters which constitute this short story—the discovery of the madwoman in the myste-rious domain, the war scene, and the scene of the cure—*both* commentators dis-cuss only one: the chapter depicting the war. The main plot, which consists of the story of a woman's madness (episodes I and III), is somehow completely ne-glected in favor of the subplot (episode II), a historical narrative whose function is to describe the events which preceded and occasioned the madness. The "ex-plication" thus excludes two things: the madness and the woman. Viewed through the eyes of the two academic critics, "Adieu" becomes a story about the suffering of men in which the real protagonists are none but "the soldiers of the Grand Army." The "Préface" indeed makes a great point of praising Balzac for "the realism, unprecedented in the history of literature, with which the war is here depicted" [p. 9]:[2] "by showing us, in 'Adieu,' the soldiers of the Grand Army haggard, half dead with hunger and cold, draped in rags, surging toward the pontoon bridge thrown across the Berezina, he [Balzac] deals with the myth of military grandeur . . . a blow whose repercussions extend well beyond the post-Napoleonic era" [pp. 10–11]. This supposedly "objective" reading of what is called Balzac's "realism" in fact screens out and disguises an ideological pattern of textual amputations and cuts, in which only a *third* of the text is brought to the reader's attention. "Indeed," concedes the Preface's author, "these scenes do not take up much room in . . . "Adieu," where most of the action occurs subse-quent to the historic events which they symbolize. *But they suffice to* give the war its true countenance" [p. 12]. As for the author of the "Notice," he does not even seek to justify the arbitrary, disproportionate cuts underiving his "explication"—by putting forward a *truth* "which suffices": "the *true* countenance of the war. In line with the academic tradition of "selected passages," he proposes, simply and "innocently," literally to *cut up* the text, to *extract* the second chapter, and truly materialize the operation of ideological extirpation with a serene pedagogical con-fidence: "the second chapter, *which can be isolated from the work* as was the story of Goguelat from the *Country Doctor* (cf. our edition of this novel in Folio) marks the appearance in Balzac's work of the theme of the wartime disappearance of an officer who comes back many years later" [p. 266]. The story is here explic-itly summed up as being exclusively that of a man: that of "the wartime disap-pearance of *an officer* who comes back many years later." It is, therefore, by no means surprising to see the author of the "Notice" taken aback by the fact—to him incomprehensible—that in its second version this text could have been, as he puts it, "oddly entitled" *A Woman's Duty* [p. 265]. Evident in an abandoned title, but in the text neither seen nor heard, the woman does not belong to the realm of the "explicable"; her claim to commentary is solely an inexplicable piece of knowledge, an unusable article of erudition.

It is just in this manner that the institution of literary criticism pronounces its expert, professional discourse, without even noticing the conspicuousness of its flagrant misogyny. To the *sociological* sexism of the educational system corre-sponds, in this case, the naive, though by no means innocent, sexism of the ex-egetical system of *literary analysis*, of the academic and pedagogical fabrication of "literary" and critical discourse. By guiding the reader, through the extirpation of "explicable" facts, to the "correct" perception, to the literal, "proper," so-called "objective" level of textual interpretation, academic criticism conditions the very norms of "legibility." Madness and women, however, turn out to be the two outcasts of the establishment of readability. An ideological conditioning of literary and critical discourse, a political orientation of reading thus affirms itself, not so much through the negative treatment of women as through their total neglect, their pure and simple *omission*. This critical oversight, which appears as a *systematic* blindness to significant facts, functions as a censorship mechanism, as a symbolic eradication of women from the world of literature. It is therefore essential to examine the theoretical presuppositions which permit and sanction this kind of blindness.

We have seen that what is invoked so as to authorize the arbitrariness of the curtailment of the text is the critical concept of Balzac's "realism": the realism of *war,* "unprecedented"—as the Preface puts it—"in the history of literature." In the context of this manly realism, the woman is relegated to non-existence, since she is said to partake of the "unreal": "Beside the Berezina . . . Stéphanie's carriage, blocked among hordes of French soldiers savage with hunger and shock, becomes the *unwonted, almost unreal element* in which the whole absurdity of the situation bursts out" [pp. 11–12]. What, then, is this "realism" the critic here ascribes to Balzac, if not the assumption, not shared by the text, that what happens to men is more important, and/or more "real," than what happens to women? A subtle boundary line, which gives itself as a "natural frontier," is thus traced, in the critical vocabulary, between the realm of the "real" and that of the "unreal," between the category of "realism" and that of the so-called "supernatural": "While Colonel Chabert contains no *supernatural* elements . . . 'Adieu' allots a great deal of space to psychic phenomena, with Stéphanie's madness, and even to parapsychic phenomena, with her death. . . . It is noteworthy . . . that Balzac's short stories . . . devote infinitely more space to the *supernatural*, to the presence of the *invisible* . . . than do his novels. . . . In these four stories where it exists side by side with the most striking *realism, the marvellous* is in fact only represented by the *state of semi-unreality* which the main characters attain through the horror of their ordeal. We here come across . . . the romantic conception of the transfiguring power of suffering" [p. 14–17]. The "supernatural," as everyone knows, cannot be rationally explained and hence should not detain us and does not call for *thought*. Flattened out and banalized into the "edifying conclusion" [p. 17] of the beneficent power of suffering, Stéphanie's madness is *not problematic*, does not deserve to detain us, since it is but a "state of semi-unreality." Realism thus postulates a conception of "nature" and of "reality" which seeks to establish itself, tautologically, as "natural" and as "real." Nothing, indeed, is less neutral than this apparent neutrality; nothing is less "natural" than this frontier which is supposed to separate "the real" from "the unreal" and which in fact delimits only the inside and the outside of an ideological circle: an inside which is *inclusive* of "reason" and men, i.e., "reality" and "nature"; and an outside which is *exclusive* of madness and women, i.e., the "supernatural" and the "unreal." And since the supernatural is linked, as the critic would have it, to "the presence of the invisible" [p. 16], it comes as no surprise to find the woman predestined to be, precisely, *the realistic invisible*, that which realism as such is inherently unable to see.

> It is the whole field of a problematic, which defines and structures the invisible as its definite outside—excluded from the domain of visibility and defined as excluded by the existence and the structure of the problematic field

> itself. . . . The invisible is defined by the visible as *its* invisible, *its* prohibited sight. . . . To see this invisible . . . requires something quite different from a sharp or attentive eye, it takes an *educated eye*, a revised, renewed way of looking, itself produced by the effect of a "change of terrain" reflected back upon the act of seeing. [Louis Althusser, *Lire le Capital*, I (Paris: Maspero, 1968), pp. 26–28; translation mine; Althusser's italics]

With a "revised" way of looking, "educated" by the "change of terrain" brought about by the feminist interrogation, let us now attempt to reread Balzac's text and to reinterpret its relation to the woman as well as to madness.

III. "SHE? WHO?"

From the very beginning the woman in this text stands out as a problem. The opening pages present the reader with a series of abstract questions concerning a female identity: the two lost hunters are trying to situate themselves, to ascertain the identity of the woman they have just glimpsed in the unknown place into which they have wandered: "Where the devil are we? . . . She, who? . . . Where are we? What is that house? Whose is it? Who are you? Do you live here? . . . But who is this lady? . . . She? Who? . . . " [pp. 148, 156, 159, 164].

The reader, too, cannot get his bearings: deluged with questions, at the same time deprived systematically of information, not really knowing *who* is speaking, much less about whom, he is in turn as *lost* in the text as the two protagonists are in geographical space. The text thus originates in the *loss* of the very conditions of localization and identification, in a general state of confusion from which, in an almost anonymous manner, a recurrent question emerges: "She? Who?" The feminine pronoun preceding any proper denomination, the ambiguous question preceding any informative clarification, this preliminary inquiry takes on an abstractly emphatic and allegorical character, and seems to situate from the start the textual problematic within a systematic search for the nature of feminine identity. From the beginning, however, the question reaches a dead end: addressed to the women themselves, the query meets only silence, since both women here are deprived of the ability to speak. Addressed to others, the question obtains only distant and hypothetical answers: "But who is this lady? . . . It is presumed that she comes from Moulins . . . she is said to be mad. . . . I wouldn't guarantee you the truth of these rumors" [p. 164].

The allegorical question "She? Who?" will thus remain unanswered. The text, nonetheless, will play out the question to its logical end, so as to show in what way it *precludes* any answer, in what way the question is set as a trap. The *very lack of the answer will* then write itself as a *different* question, through which the original question will find itself dislocated, radically shifted and transformed.

"She? Who?" The women cannot respond: mad, they do not understand the men's questions. Nor do the rational men understand the senseless words of the women. But the women, though mad, understand each other. The doctor thus interprets the friendship that seems to unite Stéphanie and the peasant Geneviève: "Here . . . she has found another creature she seems to get along with. It's an idiot peasant-woman. . . . My niece and this poor girl are in a way united by the invisible chain of their common destiny, and by the feeling that causes their madness" [p. 196]. Understanding occurs in this text only on one side or the other of the boundary line which, separating silence from speech, distinguishes madness from reason. It is nonetheless striking that the dichotomy Reason/Madness, as well as Speech/Silence, exactly coincides in this text with the dichotomy Men/Women. Women as such are associated both with madness and with silence, whereas men are identified with prerogatives of discourse and of reason. In fact, men appear not only as the possessors, but also as the dispensers, of reason, which they can at will mete out to—or take away from—others. While Philippe and the doctor undertake to "restore Stéphanie's reason," the magistrate, on the other hand, brags: "If you should ever bring a suit to court, *I would make you lose it, even if reason were a hundred per cent on your side*" [p. 150]. The three men in the story in fact symbolically represent—by virtue of their professions: magistrate, doctor, soldier—the power to *act upon* others' reason, in the name of the law, of health, or of force.

With respect to the woman's madness, man's reason reacts by trying to *appropriate* it: in the first place, by claiming to "understand" it, but with an external understanding which reduces the madwoman to a spectacle, to an *object* which can be *known* and *possessed*. "Go on, Sir, leave her alone," the doctor recommends to Philippe, "I know how to live with the dear little creature, I *understand* her madness, I *spy upon* her gestures, I am in on her secrets" [pp. 208–209]. To "spy on" in order to "know"; to "tame" in order to "cure": such are the methods used by masculine reason so as to *objectify* feminine madness, thereby mastering it. If the madwoman is throughout the story seen as and compared to an animal, this pervasive metaphor tells us less about Stéphanie's delirium than about the logic of her therapists. For the object is precisely to capture the animal and to tame it. Thus we see the symbolic import of the initial hunting scene. A metaphorical parody of the episode of the war and of its martial logic ("'Come on, deputy, forward! Double time! Speed up . . . march over the ruts. . . . Come on, march! . . . If you sit down, you're lost'" [pp. 147, 151]), the opening scene of the hunt already symbolically prefigures Philippe's attitude toward Stéphanie: "Come on," cries Philippe from the very first, not yet knowing whom he is talking about, but integrating as a matter of course the woman into his hunter's mentality; "Come on, let's run after the white and black lady! Forward!" [p. 157]. But the hunter's chase will here be but the measure of the flight of his prey.

If masculine reason thus constitutes a scheme to capture and master, indeed, metaphorically *rape* the woman, by the same token, Stéphanie's madness is not contingent on but directly related to her femininity: consisting, precisely, in its loss. Several times Philippe, in fact, explicitly defines Stéphanie's madness as the loss of her womanhood. When the doctor advises him to tame her by feeding her pieces of sugar, Philippe sadly answers: "*When she was a woman*, she had no taste for sweets" [p. 202]. And again, in a burst of sorrow, Philippe cries: "I die a little more every day, every minute! My love is too great! I could bear everything if only, in her madness, she had kept some *semblance of femininity*" [p. 208]. Madness, in other words, is precisely what makes a woman *not a woman*. But what is a "woman"? Woman is a "name," denied in fact to Geneviève in the same way as it is denied to Stéphanie: "Then *a woman*, if such a *name* can be applied to the *undefinable being* who got up from under the bushes, pulled on the cow by its rope" [p. 159]. "Woman" is consequently a "definable being"—chained to a "definition" itself implying a model, a definition commanded by a *logic of resemblance*. Even in the war scene, Stéphanie had already lost her "femininity." "[When] all rolled around herself, *she really resembled nothing....* Was this that *charming woman*, the *glory of her lover*, the *queen of the Parisian ballrooms?* Alas! even the eyes of her most devoted friend could perceive *nothing feminine* left in that heap of linens and rags" [p. 180]. If a "woman" is strictly, exactly, "what *resembles* a woman" ("she really resembled nothing... nothing feminine left"), it becomes apparent that "femininity" is much less a "natural" category than a rhetorical one, analogical and metaphorical: a metaphorical category which is explicitly bound, as perceived by Philippe, to a sociosexual stereotype, to the "definable" role of the mistress— "the queen of the Parisian ballrooms." Of course, the "queen" here implies a king; the literal, *proper* meaning of metaphorical femininity, paradoxically enough, turns out to be a masculine property: the "queen of the Parisian ballrooms," "that charming woman," is above all "*The glory of her lover.*" "Woman," in other words, is the exact metaphorical measure of the narcissism of man.

The Masculine thus turns out to be the universal equivalent of the opposition: Masculine/Feminine. It is insofar as Masculinity conditions Femininity as its universal equivalent, as what determines and measures its value, that the textual paradox can be created according to which the woman is "madness," while at the same time "madness" is the very "absence of womanhood." The woman is "madness" to the extent that she is Other, *different* from man. But "madness" is the "absence of womanhood" to the extent that "womanhood" is what precisely resembles the Masculine universal equivalent, in the polar division of sexual roles. If so, the woman is "madness" since the woman is *difference;* but "madness" is "non-woman" since madness is the *lack of resemblance*. What the narcissistic economy of the Masculine universal equivalent tries to eliminate, under the label "madness," is nothing other than *feminine difference*.

III. THE THERAPEUTIC FALLACY

Such is the male narcissistic principle on which the system of reason, with its therapeutic ambition, is based. For, to "restore Stéphanie's reason" signifies, precisely, to reinstate her "femininity": to make her *recognize man*, the "lover" whose "glory" she ought to be. "I'm going to the Bons-Hommes," says Philippe, "to see her, speak to her, *cure* her.... Do you think the poor woman would be able to *hear me* and *not recover her reason?*" [p. 197]. In Philippe's mind, "to recover her reason" becomes synonymous with "to hear *me*." "The cure of the madman," writes Michel Foucault, "is in the reason of the other—his own reason being but the very truth of his madness" [*Histoire de la folie à l'âge classique* (Paris: Gallimard, 1972), p. 540; translation mine]. Stéphanie's cure is in Philippe's reason. The "recovery" of her reason must thus necessarily entail an act of recognition.

> "She doesn't recognize me," cried the colonel in despair.
> "Stéphanie! it's Philippe, your Philippe, Philippe!" [pp. 200–201]
> "Her; not to recognize me, and to run away from me," repeated the colonel. [p. 201]

> "My love," he said, ardently kissing the countess' hands, "I am Philippe." "Come," he added, . . . "Philippe is not dead, he is here, you are sitting on his lap. You are my Stéphanie, and I am your Philippe." "Adieu," she said, "adieu." [p. 207]

Stéphanie's recovery of her "reason," the restoration of her femininity as well as of her identity, depends then, in Philippe's eyes, on her specular recognition of *him*, on her *reflection* of his own name and of his own identity. If the question of female identity remains in the text unanswered, it is simply because it is *never* truly asked: in the guise of asking, "She? Who?", Philippe is in fact always asking "I? Who?"—a false question, the answer to which he believes he knows in advance: "It's Philippe." The question concerning the woman is thereby transformed into the question of a guarantee for men, a question through which nothing is questioned, whose sole function is to insure the validity of its predefined answer: "You are *my* Stéphanie." The use of the possessive adjective makes explicit the act of appropriation focused here on the *proper* names. But it is from Stéphanie's own mouth that Philippe must obtain his proper name, his guarantee of the propriety of his own identity, and of hers: Stéphanie = Philippe, "You are my Stéphanie, and I am your Philippe." In Philippe's eyes, Stéphanie is viewed above all as an object, whose role is to insure, by an interplay of reflections, his own self-sufficiency as a "subject," to serve as a mediator in his own specular relationship with himself. What Philippe pursues in the woman is not a face, but a mirror, which, reflecting his image, will thereby *acknowledge* his narcissistic *self-image*. "Women," writes Virginia Woolf, "have served all these centuries as looking-glasses possessing the magic and delicious power of reflecting the figure of man at twice its natural size." Philippe, as it turns out, desires not *knowledge* of Stéphanie herself but her *acknowledgement* of him: his therapeutic design is to restore her not to *cognition*, but to *recognition*.

To this demand for recognition and for the restoration of identity through language, through the authority of proper names, Stéphanie opposes, in the figure of her madness, the dislocation of any transitive, communicative language, of "propriety" as such, of any correspondence or transparency joining "names" to "things," the blind opacity of a lost signifier unmatched by any signified, the pure recurrent difference of a word detached from both its meaning and its context.

> "Adieu," she said in a soft harmonious voice, but whose melody, impatiently perceived by the expectant hunters, seemed to divulge not the slightest feeling or the least idea. [p. 163]
>
> "Adieu, adieu, adieu!" she said, without her soul's conferring any perceptible inflection upon the word. [p. 200]

To this automatic repetition of senselessness and difference, Philippe in turn will oppose another type of repetition designed precisely to restore resemblance and identity: in order to cure Stéphanie, in order to restore to her demented, dislocated language its nominative and communicative function, he decides to *re-produce* the primal scene of the "adieu" and thus to *re-present* theatrically the errant signifier's lost significance, its proper *signifié*. Without her knowledge, Stéphanie will literally be forced to play herself, to return to her "proper" role.

Through the theatrical set-up, everything will end up making sense: and, with all difference thus erased, re-presentation necessarily will bring about the desired re-cognition.

> The baron [de Sucy] had, inspired by a dream, conceived a plan to restore the countess' reason. . . . He devoted the rest of the autumn to the preparation of this immense enterprise. A small river flowed through his park, where in, the winter, it flooded an extensive marsh which *resembled* . . . the one running along the right bank of the Berezina. The village of Satou, set on a hill, added the final touch to *put this scene of horror in its frame*. . . . The colonel gathered a troop of workers to dig a canal which would represent the voracious river. . . . Thus aided by his memory, Philippe succeeded in *copying* in his park the riverbank where General Elbé had built his bridges. . . . The colonel assembled pieces of debris *similar* to what his fellow sufferers had used to construct their raft. He ravaged his park, in an effort to *complete the illusion* on which he pinned his last hopes. . . . In short, he had forgotten nothing that could reproduce the most horrible of all scenes, and he reached his goal. Toward the beginning of December, when the snow had blanketed the earth with a white coat, he *recognized* the Berezina. This false Russia was of such appalling truth that several of his comrades *recognized* the scene of their former sufferings. Monsieur de Sucy kept the secret of this tragic *representation*. [pp. 209–10]

The cure succeeds. However, so as to fulfill perfectly her "Woman's Duty," to play her role correctly in this theater of the identical, to recognize specularly and reflect perfectly Philippe's "identity," Stéphanie herself must disappear: she has to *die* as *Other*, as a "subject" in her own right. The tragic outcome of the story is inevitable, inscribed as it is from the outset in the very logic of representation inherent in the therapeutic project. Stéphanie will die; Philippe will subsequently commit suicide. If, as ambiguous as it is, the cure turns out to be a murder, this murder, in its narcissistic dialectic, is necessarily suicidal,[3] since, killing Stéphanie in the very enterprise of "saving" her,[4] it is also his own image that Philippe strikes in the mirror.

Through this paradoxical and disconcerting ending, the text subverts and dislocates the logic of representation which it has dramatized through Philippe's endeavor and his failure. Literature thus breaks away from pure representation: when transparency and meaning, "reason" and "representation" are regained, when madness ends, so does the text itself. Literature, in this way, seems to indicate its impuissance to dominate or to recuperate the madness of the signifier from which it speaks, its radical incapacity to master its own signifying repetition, to "tame" its own linguistic difference, to "represent" identity or truth. Like madness and unlike representation, literature can signify but not *make sense*.

Once again, it is amazing to what extent academic criticism, completely unaware of the text's irony, can remain blind to what the text says about itself. It is quite striking to observe to what extent the logic of the unsuspecting "realistic" critic can reproduce, one after the other, all of Philippe's delusions, which the text deconstructs and puts in question. Like Philippe, the "realistic" critic seeks representation, tries, by means of fiction, to reproduce "the real thing," to reconstruct, minutely and exhaustively, the exact historical Berezina scene. Like

Philippe, the "realistic" critic is haunted by an obsession with proper names—identity and reference—sharing the same nostalgia for a transparent, transitive, communicative language, where everything possesses, unequivocally, a single meaning which can be consequently mastered and made clear, where each name "represents" a thing, where each signifier, properly and adequately, corresponds both to a signified and to a referent. On the critical as well as on the literary stage, the same attempt is played out to appropriate the signifier and to reduce its differential repetition; we see the same endeavor to do away with difference, the same policing of identities, the same design of mastery, of *sense-control*. For the "realistic" critic, as for Philippe, the readable is designed as a stimulus not for knowledge and cognition, but for acknowledgement and *re-cognition*, not for the *production* of a question, but for the *reproduction* of a foreknown answer—delimited within a pre-existing, pre-defined horizon, where the "truth" to be discovered is reduced to the natural status of a simple *given*, immediately perceptible, directly "representable" through the totally intelligible medium of transparent language. Exactly in the same way as Philippe, the commentators of "Adieu" are in turn taken in by the illusory security of a specularly structured act of recognition. Balzac's text, which applies as much to the "realistic" critic as to Philippe, can itself be read as a kind of preface to its own "Préface," as an ironic reading of its own academic reading.

For, what Philippe *misrecognizes* in his "realistic" recognition of the Berezina is, paradoxically enough, the *real*: the real not as a convergence of reflections, as an effect of mirroring focalization, but as a radically de-centering resistance; the real as, precisely, Other, the unrepresentable as such, the ex-centric residue which the specular relationship of vision cannot embrace.

Along with the illusions of Philippe, the "realistic" critic thus repeats, in turn, his allegorical act of murder, his obliteration of the Other: the critic also, in his own way, *kills the woman*, while killing, at the same time, the question of the text and the text as a question.

But, here again, as in Philippe's case, the murder is incorporated in an enterprise which can be seen as "therapeutic." For in obliterating difference, in erasing from the text the disconcerting and ex-centric features of a woman's madness, the critic seeks to "normalize" the text, to banish and eradicate all trace of violence and anguish, of scandal or insanity, making the text a reassuring, closed retreat whose balance no upheaval can upset, where no convulsion is of any consequence. "To drive these phantoms firmly back into their epoch, to close it upon them, by means of a historical narrative, this seems to have been the writer's intent" ["Préface," p. 8]. By reducing the story to a recognition scheme, familiar, snug and canny, the critic, like Philippe, "cures" the text, precisely of that which in it is incurably and radically uncanny.

From this paradoxical encounter between literature's critical irony and the uncritical naïveté of its critics, from this confrontation in which Balzac's text itself seems to be an ironic reading of its own future reading, the question arises: how *should* we read? How can a reading lead to something other than recognition, "normalization," and "cure"? How can the critical project, in other words, be detached from the therapeutic projection?

This crucial theoretical question, which undermines the foundations of traditional thought and whose importance the feminist writings have helped to bring out, pinpoints at the same time the difficulty of the woman's position in today's critical discourse. If, in our culture, the woman is by definition associated with madness, her problem is how to break out of this (cultural) imposition of madness *without* taking up the critical and therapeutic positions of reason: how to avoid speaking both as *mad* and as *not mad*. The challenge facing the woman today is nothing less than to "re-invent" language, to *re-learn how to speak*: to speak not only against, but outside of the specular phallogocentric structure, to establish a discourse the status of which would no longer be defined by the phallacy of masculine meaning. An old saying would thereby be given new life: today more than ever, changing our minds—changing *the* mind—is a woman's prerogative.

NOTES

1. Freud has thus pronounced his famous verdict on women: "Anatomy is destiny." But this is precisely the focus of the feminist contestation.

2. Quotations from the "Préface," the "Notice" and from Balzac's text are my translations; page numbers refer to the Gallimard/Folio edition; in all quoted passages, italics mine unless otherwise indicated.

3. This suicidal murder is, in fact, a repetition, not only of Philippe's military logic and his attitude throughout the war scene, but also of a specific previous moment in his relationship with Stéphanie. Well before the story's end, Philippe had already been on the point of killing Stéphanie, and himself with her, having, in a moment of despair, given up the hope of her ever recognizing him. The doctor, seeing through Philippe's intentions, had then saved his niece with a perspicacious lie, playing precisely on the specular illusion of the proper name: " 'You do not know then,' went on the doctor coldly, hiding his horror, 'that last night in her sleep she said, "Philippe! " 'She named me,' cried the baron, letting his pistols drop" [p. 206].

4. Here again, the ambiguous logic of the "savior," in its tragic and heroic narcissism, is prefigured by the war scene. Convinced of his good reason, Philippe characteristically, *imposes* it, by force, on others, so as to "save" them; but ironically and paradoxically, he always saves them in spite of *themselves*: "'Let us save her in spite of herself!' cried Philippe, sweeping up the countess" [p. 182].

WORKS CITED

Balzac, Honoré de. *Adieu (Colonel Chabert, El Verdugo, Adieu, Requisitionnaire)*. Ed. Patrick Berthier. Paris : Gallimard/Folio , 1974.
Chesler, Phyllis. *Women and Madness*. New York: Avon Books, 1973.
Irigaray, Luce. *Speculum de l'autre femme*. Paris: Minuit, 1974.

SANDRA M. GILBERT AND SUSAN GUBAR

INFECTION IN THE SENTENCE

the woman writer and the anxiety of authorship

(1979)

> The man who does not know sick women does not know women.
> —S. WEIR MITCHELL

> I try to describe this long limitation, hoping that with such power as is now mine, and such use of language as is within that power, this will convince any one who cares about it that this "living" of mine had been done under a heavy handicap. . . .
> —CHARLOTTE PERKINS GILMAN

> A Word dropped careless on a Page
> May stimulate an eye
> When folded in perpetual seam
> The Wrinkled Maker lie
> Infection in the sentence breeds
> We may inhale Despair
> At distances of Centuries
> From the Malaria—
>
> —EMILY DICKINSON

> I stand in the ring
> in the dead city
> and tie on the red shoes
> . . . .
> They are not mine,
> they are my mother's,
> her mother's before,
> handed down like an heirloom
> but hidden like shameful letters.
>
> —ANNE SEXTON

What does it mean to be a woman writer in a culture whose fundamental definitions of literary authority are, as we have seen, both overtly and covertly patriarchal? If the vexed and vexing polarities of angel and monster, sweet dumb Snow White and fierce mad Queen, are major images literary tradition offers women, how does such imagery influence the ways in which women attempt the pen? If the Queen's looking glass speaks with the King's voice, how do its perpetual kingly admonitions affect the Queen's own voice? Since his is the chief voice she hears, does the Queen try to sound like the King, imitating his tone, his inflections, his phrasing, his point of view? Or does she "talk back" to him in her own vocabulary, her own timbre, insisting on her own viewpoint? We believe these are basic questions feminist literary criticism—both theoretical and practical—must answer, and consequently they are questions to which we shall turn again and again, not only in this chapter but in all our readings of nineteenth-century literature by women.

That writers assimilate and then consciously or unconsciously affirm or deny the achievements of their predecessors is, of course, a central fact of literary history, a fact whose aesthetic and metaphysical implications have been discussed in detail by theorists as diverse as T. S. Eliot, M. H. Abrams, Erich Auerbach, and Frank Kermode.[1] More recently, some literary theorists have begun to explore what we might call the psychology of literary history—the tensions and anxieties, hostilities and inadequacies writers feel when they confront not only the achievements of their predecessors but the traditions of genre, style, and metaphor that they inherit from such "forefathers." Increasingly, these critics study the ways in which, as J. Hillis Miller has put it, a literary text "is inhabited . . . by a long chain of parasitical presences, echoes, allusions, guests, ghosts of previous texts."[2]

As Miller himself also notes, the first and foremost student of such literary psychohistory has been Harold Bloom. Applying Freudian structures to literary genealogies, Bloom has postulated that the dynamics of literary history arise from the artist's "anxiety of influence," his fear that he is not his own creator and that the works of his predecessors, existing before and beyond him, assume essential priority over his own writings. In fact, as we pointed out in our discussion of the metaphor of literary paternity, Bloom's paradigm of the sequential historical relationship between literary artists is the relationship of father to son, specifically that relationship as it was defined by Freud. Thus Bloom explains that a "strong poet" must engage in heroic warfare with his "precursor," for, involved as he is in a literary Oedipal struggle, a man can only become a poet by somehow invalidating his poetic father.

Bloom's model of literary history is intensely (even exclusively) male, and necessarily patriarchal. For this reason it has seemed, and no doubt will continue to seem, offensively sexist to some feminist critics. Not only, after all, does Bloom describe literary history as the crucial warfare of fathers and sons, he sees Milton's fiercely masculine fallen Satan as *the* type of the poet in our culture, and he metaphorically defines the poetic process as a sexual encounter between a male poet and his female muse. Where, then, does the female poet fit in? Does she want to annihilate a "forefather" or a "foremother"? What if she can find no models, no precursors? Does she have a muse, and what is its sex? Such questions are inevitable in any female consideration of Bloomian poetics.[3] And yet, from a feminist perspective, their inevitability may be just the point; it may, that is, call our attention not to what is wrong about Bloom's conceptualization of the dynamics of Western literary history, but to what is right (or at least suggestive) about his theory.

For Western literary history *is* overwhelmingly male—or, more accurately, patriarchal—and Bloom analyzes and explains this fact, while other theorists have ignored it, precisely, one supposes, because they assumed literature had to be male. Like Freud, whose psychoanalytic postulates permeate Bloom's literary psychoanalyses of the "anxiety of influence," Bloom has defined processes of interaction that his predecessors did not bother to consider because, among other reasons, they were themselves so caught up in such processes. Like Freud, too, Bloom has insisted on bringing to consciousness assumptions readers and writers do not ordinarily examine. In doing so, he has clarified the implications of the psychosexual and sociosexual contexts by which every literary text is surrounded, and thus the meanings of the "guests" and "ghosts" which inhabit texts themselves. Speaking of Freud, the feminist theorist Juliet Mitchell has remarked that "psychoanalysis is not a recommendation *for* a patriarchal society, but an analysis of one."[4] The same sort of statement could be made about Bloom's model of literary history, which is not a recommendation for but an analysis of the patriarchal poetics (and attendant anxieties) which underlie our culture's chief literary movements.

For our purposes here, however, Bloom's historical construction is useful not only because it helps identify and define the patriarchal psychosexual context in which so much Western literature was authored, but also because it can help us distinguish the anxieties and achievements of female writers from those of male writers. If we return to the question we asked earlier—where does a woman writer "fit in" to the overwhelmingly and essentially male literary history Bloom describes?—we find we have to answer that a woman writer does *not* "fit in." At first glance, indeed, she seems to be anomalous, indefinable, alienated, a freakish outsider. Just as in Freud's theories of male and female psychosexual development there is no symmetry between a boy's growth and a girl's (with, say, the male "Oedipus complex" balanced by a female "Electra complex") so Bloom's male-oriented theory of the "anxiety of influence" cannot be simply reversed or inverted in order to account for the situation of the woman writer.

Certainly if we acquiesce in the patriarchal Bloomian model, we can be sure that the female poet does not experience the "anxiety of influence" in the same way that her male counterpart would, for the simple reason that she must confront precursors who are almost exclusively male, and therefore significantly different from her. Not only do these precursors incarnate patriarchal authority (as our discussion of the metaphor of literary paternity argued), they attempt to enclose her in definitions of her person and her potential which, by reducing her to extreme stereotypes (angel, monster) drastically conflict with her own sense of her self—that is, of her subjectivity, her autonomy, her creativity. On the one hand, therefore, the woman writer's male precursors symbolize authority; on the other hand, despite their authority, they fail to define the ways in which she experiences her own identity as a writer. More, the masculine authority with which they construct their literary personae, as well as the fierce power struggles in which they engage in their efforts of self-creating, seem to the woman writer directly to contradict the terms of her own gender definition. Thus the "anxiety of influence" that a male poet experiences is felt by a female poet as an even more primary "anxiety of authorship"—a radical fear that she cannot create, that because she can never become a "precursor" the act of writing will isolate or destroy her.

This anxiety is, of course, exacerbated by her fear that not only can she not fight a male precursor on "his" terms and win, she cannot "beget" art upon the (female) body of the muse. As Juliet Mitchell notes, in a concise summary of the implications Freud's theory of psychosexual development has for women, both a boy and a girl, "as they learn to speak and live within society, want to take the father's [in Bloom's terminology the precursor's] place, and *only the boy will one day be allowed to do so.* Furthermore both sexes are born into the desire of the mother, and as, through cultural heritage, what the mother desires is the phallus-turned-baby, *both* children desire to be the phallus for the mother. Again, *only the boy can fully recognize himself in his mother's desire.* Thus *both* sexes repudiate the implications of femininity," but the girl learns (in relation to her father) "that her subjugation to the law of the father entails her becoming the representative of 'nature' and 'sexuality,' a chaos of spontaneous, intuitive creativity."[5]

Unlike her male counterpart, then, the female artist must first struggle against the effects of socialization which makes conflict with the will of her (male) precursors seem inexpressibly absurd, futile, or even—as in the case of the Queen in "Little Snow White"—self-annihilating. And just as the male artist's struggle against his precursor takes the form of what Bloom calls revisionary swerves, flights, misreadings, so the female writer's battle for self-creation involves her in a revisionary process. Her battle, however, is not against her (male) precursor's reading of the world but against his reading of *her.* In order to define herself as an author she must redefine the terms of her socialization. Her revisionary struggle, therefore, often becomes a struggle for what Adrienne Rich has called "Revision—the act of looking back, of seeing with fresh eyes, of entering an old text from a new critical direction . . . an act of survival."[6] Frequently, moreover, she can begin such a struggle only by actively seeking a *female* precursor who, far from representing a threatening force to be denied or killed, proves by example that a revolt against patriarchal literary authority is possible.

For this reason, as well as for the sound psychoanalytic reasons Mitchell and others give, it would be foolish to lock the woman artist into an Electra pattern matching the Oedipal structure Bloom proposes for male writers. The woman writer—and we shall see women doing this over and over again—searches for a female model not because she wants dutifully to comply with male definitions of her "femininity" but because she must legitimize her own rebellious endeavors. At the same time, like most women in patriarchal society, the woman writer does experience her gender as a painful obstacle, or even a debilitating inadequacy; like most patriarchally conditioned women, in other words, she is victimized by what Mitchell calls "the inferiorized and 'alternative' (second sex) psychology of women under patriarchy."[7] Thus the loneliness of the female artist, her feelings of alienation from male predecessors coupled with her need for sisterly precursors and successors, her urgent sense of her need for a female audience together with her fear of the antagonism of male readers, her culturally conditioned timidity about self-dramatization, her dread of the patriarchal authority of art, her anxiety about the impropriety of female invention—all these phenomena of "inferiorization" mark the woman writer's struggle for artistic self-definition and differentiate her efforts at self-creating from those of her male counterpart.

As we shall see, such sociosexual differentiation means that, as Elaine

Showalter has suggested, women writers participate in a quite different literary subculture from that inhabited by male writers, a subculture which has its own distinctive literary traditions, even—though it defines itself *in relation to* the "main," male-dominated, literary culture—a distinctive history.[8] At best, the separateness of this female subculture has been exhilarating for women. In recent years, for instance, while male writers seem increasingly to have felt exhausted by the need for revisionism which Bloom's theory of the "anxiety of influence" accurately describes, women writers have seen themselves as pioneers in a creativity so intense that their male counterparts have probably not experienced its analog since the Renaissance, or at least since the Romantic era. The son of many fathers, today's male writer feels hopelessly belated; the daughter of too few mothers, today's female writer feels that she is helping to create a viable tradition which is at last definitively emerging.

There is a darker side of this female literary subculture, however, especially when women's struggles for literary self-creation are seen in the psychosexual context described by Bloom's Freudian theories of patrilineal literary inheritance. As we noted above, for an "anxiety of influence" the woman writer substitutes what we have called an "anxiety of authorship," an anxiety built from complex and often only barely conscious fears of that authority which seems to the female artist to be by definition inappropriate to her sex. Because it is based on the woman's socially determined sense of her own biology, this anxiety of authorship is quite distinct from the anxiety about creativity that could be traced in such male writers as Hawthorne or Dostoevsky. Indeed, to the extent that it forms one of the unique bonds that link women in what we might call the secret sisterhood of their literary subculture, such anxiety in itself constitutes a crucial mark of that subculture.

In comparison to the "male" tradition of strong, father-son combat, however, this female anxiety of authorship is profoundly debilitating. Handed down not from one woman to another but from the stern literary "fathers" of patriarchy to all their "inferiorized" female descendants, it is in many ways the germ of a disease or, at any rate, a disaffection, a disturbance, a distrust, that spreads like a stain throughout the style and structure of much literature by women, especially—as we shall see in this study—throughout literature by women before the twentieth century. For if contemporary women do now attempt the pen with energy and authority, they are able to do so only because their eighteenth- and nineteenth-century foremothers struggled in isolation that felt like illness, alienation that felt like madness, obscurity that felt like paralysis to overcome the anxiety of authorship that was endemic to their literary subculture. Thus, while the recent feminist emphasis on positive role models has undoubtedly helped many women, it should not keep us from realizing the terrible odds against which a creative female subculture was established. Far from reinforcing socially oppressive sexual stereotyping, only a full consideration of such problems can reveal the extraordinary strength of women's literary accomplishments in the eighteenth and nineteenth centuries.

Emily Dickinson's acute observations about "infection in the sentence," quoted in our epigraphs, resonate in a number of different ways, then, for women writers, given the literary woman's special concept of her place in literary psychohistory. To begin with, the words seem to indicate Dickinson's keen consciousness that, in the purest Bloomian or Millerian sense, pernicious "guests" and "ghosts" inhabit all literary texts. For any reader, but especially for a reader who is also a writer, every text can become a "sentence" or weapon in a kind of metaphorical germ warfare. Beyond this, however, the fact that "infection in the sentence *breeds*" suggests Dickinson's recognition that literary texts are coercive, imprisoning, fever-inducing; that, since literature usurps a reader's interiority, it is an invasion of privacy. Moreover, given Dickinson's own gender definition, the sexual ambiguity of her poem's "Wrinkled Maker" is significant. For while, on the one hand, "we" (meaning especially women writers) "may inhale Despair" from all those patriarchal texts which seek to deny female autonomy and authority, on the other hand "we" (meaning especially women writers) "may inhale Despair" from all those "foremothers" who have both overtly and covertly conveyed their traditional authorship anxiety to their bewildered female descendants. Finally, such traditional, metaphorically matrilineal anxiety ensures that even the maker of a text, when she is a woman, may feel imprisoned within texts—folded and "wrinkled" by their pages and thus trapped in their "perpetual seam[s]" which perpetually tell her how she *seems*.

Although contemporary women writers are relatively free of the infection of this "Despair" Dickinson defines (at least in comparison to their nineteenth-century precursors), an anecdote recently related by the American poet and essayist Annie Gottlieb summarizes our point about the ways in which, for all women, "Infection in the sentence breeds":

> When I began to enjoy my powers as a writer, I dreamt that my mother had me sterilized! (Even in dreams we still blame our mothers for the punitive choices our culture forces on us.) I went after the mother-figure in my dream, brandishing a large knife; on its blade was writing. I cried, "Do you know what you are doing? You are destroying my femaleness, my *female power*, which is important to me *because of you!*"[9]

Seeking motherly precursors, says Gottlieb, as if echoing Dickinson, the woman writer may find only infection, debilitation. Yet still she must seek, not seek to subvert, her "*female power*, which is important" to her because of her lost literary matrilineage. In this connection, Dickinson's own words about mothers are revealing, for she alternately claimed that "I never had a mother," that "I always ran Home to Awe as a child. . . . He was an awful Mother but I liked him better than none," and that "a mother [was] a miracle."[10] Yet, as we shall see, her own anxiety of authorship was a "Despair" inhaled not only from the infections suffered by her own ailing physical mother, and her many tormented literary mothers, but from the literary fathers who spoke to her—even "lied" to her— sometimes near at hand, sometimes "at distances of Centuries," from the censorious looking glasses of literary texts.

It is debilitating to be *any* woman in a society where women are warned that if they do not behave like angels they must be monsters. Recently, in fact, social scientists and social historians like Jessie Bernard, Phyllis Chesler, Naomi Weisstein, and Pauline Bart have begun to study the ways in which patriarchal socialization literally makes women sick, both physically and mentally.[11] Hysteria, the disease with which Freud so famously began his investigations into the dynamic connections between *psyche* and *soma,* is by definition a "female disease," not so much because it takes its name from the Greek word for womb, *hyster* (the organ which was in the nineteenth century supposed to "cause" this emotional disturbance), but because hysteria did occur mainly among women in turn-of-the-century Vienna, and because throughout the nineteenth century this mental illness, like many other nervous disorders, was thought to be caused by the female reproductive system, as if to elaborate upon Aristotle's notion that femaleness was in and of itself a deformity.[12] And, indeed, such diseases of maladjustment to the physical and social environment as anorexia and agoraphobia did and do strike a disproportionate number of women. Sufferers from anorexia—loss of appetite, self-starvation—are primarily adolescent girls. Sufferers from agoraphobia—fear of open or "public" places—are usually female, most frequently middle-aged housewives, as are sufferers from crippling rheumatoid arthritis.[13]

Such diseases are caused by patriarchal socialization in several ways. Most obviously, of course, any young girl, but especially a lively or imaginative one, is likely to experience her education in docility, submissiveness, self-lessness as in some sense sickening. To be trained in renunciation is almost necessarily to be trained to ill health, since the human animal's first and strongest urge is to his/her *own* survival, pleasure, assertion. In addition, each of the "subjects" in which a young girl is educated may be sickening in a specific way. Learning to become a beautiful object, the girl learns anxiety about—perhaps even loathing of—her own flesh. Peering obsessively into the real as well as metaphoric looking glasses that surround her, she desires literally to "reduce" her own body. In the nineteenth century, as we noted earlier, this desire to be beautiful and "frail" led to tight-lacing and vinegar-drinking. In our own era it has spawned innumerable diets and "controlled" fasts, as well as the extraordinary phenomenon of teenage anorexia.[14] Similarly, it seems inevitable that women reared for, and conditioned to, lives of privacy, reticence, domesticity, might develop pathological fears of public places and unconfined spaces. Like the comb, stay-laces, and apple which the Queen in "Little Snow White" uses as weapons against her hated stepdaughter, such afflictions as anorexia and agoraphobia simply carry patriarchal definitions of "femininity" to absurd extremes, and thus function as essential or at least inescapable parodies of social prescriptions.

In the nineteenth century, however, the complex of social prescriptions these diseases parody did not merely urge women to act in ways which would cause them to become ill; nineteenth-century culture seems to have actually admonished women to *be* ill. In other words, the "female diseases" from which Victorian women suffered were not always byproducts of their training in femininity; they were the goals of such training. As Barbara Ehrenreich and Deirdre English have shown, throughout much of the nineteenth century "Upper- and upper-middle-class women were [defined as] 'sick' [frail, ill]; working-class women were [defined as] 'sickening' [infectious, diseased]." Speaking of the "lady," they go on to point out that "Society agreed that she was frail and sickly," and consequently a "cult of female invalidism" developed in England and America. For the products of such a cult, it was, as Dr. Mary Putnam Jacobi wrote in 1895, "considered natural and almost laudable to break down under all conceivable varieties of strain—a winter dissipation, a houseful of servants, a quarrel with a female friend, not to speak of more legitimate reasons. . . . Constantly considering their nerves, urged to consider them by well-intentioned but short-sighted advisors, [women] pretty soon become nothing but a bundle of nerves."[15]

Given this socially conditioned epidemic of female illness, it is not surprising to find that the angel in the house of literature frequently suffered not just from fear and trembling but from literal and figurative sicknesses unto death. Although her hyperactive stepmother dances herself into the grave, after all, beautiful Snow White has just barely recovered from a catatonic trance in her glass coffin. And if we return to Goethe's Makarie, the "good" woman of *Wilhelm Meister's Travels* whom Hans Eichner has described as incarnating her author's ideal of "contemplative purity," we find that this "model of selflessness and of purity of heart . . . this embodiment of *das Ewig-Weibliche,* suffers from migraine headaches."[16] Implying ruthless self-suppression, does the "eternal feminine" necessarily imply illness? If so, we have found yet another meaning for Dickinson's assertion that "Infection in the sentence breeds." The despair we "inhale" even "at distances of centuries" may be the despair of a life like Makarie's, a life that *"has no story."*

At the same time, however, the despair of the monster-woman is also real, undeniable, and infectious. The Queen's mad tarantella is plainly unhealthy and metaphorically the result of too much storytelling. As the Romantic poets feared, too much imagination may be dangerous to anyone, male or female, but for women in particular patriarchal culture has always assumed mental exercises would have dire consequences. In 1645 John Winthrop, the governor of the Massachusetts Bay Colony, noted in his journal that Anne Hopkins "has fallen into a sad infirmity, the loss of her understanding and reason, which had been growing upon her divers years, by occasion of her giving herself wholly to reading and writing, and had written many books," adding that "if she had attended her household affairs, and such things as belong to women . . . she had kept her wits."[17] And as Wendy Martin has noted:

> in the nineteenth century this fear of the intellectual woman became so intense that the phenomenon . . . was recorded in medical annals. A thinking woman was considered such a breach of nature that a Harvard doctor reported during his autopsy on a Radcliffe graduate he discovered that her uterus had shrivelled to the size of a pea.[18]

If, then, as Anne Sexton suggests (in a poem parts of which we have also used here as an epigraph), the red shoes passed furtively down from woman to woman are the shoes of art, the Queen's dancing shoes, it is as sickening to be a Queen who wears them as it is to be an angelic Makarie who repudiates them. Several passages in Sexton's verse express what we have defined as "anxiety of authorship" in the form of a feverish dread of the suicidal tarantella of female creativity:

> All those girls
> who wore red shoes,
> each boarded a train that would not stop.
>
> . . . . .

> They tore off their ears like safety pins.
> Their arms fell off them and became hats.
> Their heads rolled off and sang down the street.
> And their feet—oh God, their feet in the market place—
> . . . the feet went on. The feet could not stop.
>
> . . . . .
>
> They could not listen.
> They could not stop.
> What they did was the death dance.
> What they did would do them in.

Certainly infection breeds in these sentences, and despair: female art, Sexton suggests, has a "hidden" but crucial tradition of uncontrollable madness. Perhaps it was her semi-conscious perception of this tradition that gave Sexton herself "a secret fear" of being "a reincarnation" of Edna Millay, whose reputation seemed based on romance. In a letter to DeWitt Snodgrass she confessed that she had "a fear of writing as a woman writes," adding, "I wish I were a man—I would rather write the way a man writes."[19] After all, dancing the death dance, "all those girls/ who wore the red shoes" dismantle their own bodies, like anorexics renouncing the guilty weight of their female flesh. But if their arms, ears, and heads fall off, perhaps their wombs, too, will "shrivel" to "the size of a pea"?

In this connection, a passage from Margaret Atwood's *Lady Oracle* acts almost as a gloss on the conflict between creativity and "femininity" which Sexton's violent imagery embodies (or dis-embodies). Significantly, the protagonist of Atwood's novel is a writer of the sort of fiction that has recently been called "female gothic," and even more significantly she too projects her anxieties of authorship into the fairy-tale metaphor of the red shoes. Stepping in glass, she sees blood on her feet, and suddenly feels that she has discovered:

> The real red shoes, the feet punished for dancing. You could dance, or you could have the love of a good man. But you were afraid to dance, because you had this unnatural fear that if you danced they'd cut your feet off so you wouldn't be able to dance. . . . Finally you overcame your fear and danced, and they cut your feet off. The good man went away too, because you wanted to dance.[20]

Whether she is a passive angel or an active monster, in other words, the woman writer feels herself to be literally or figuratively crippled by the debilitating alternatives her culture offers her, and the crippling effects of her conditioning sometimes seem to "breed" like sentences of death in the bloody shoes she inherits from her literary foremothers.

Surrounded as she is by images of disease, traditions of disease, and invitations both to disease and to dis-ease, it is no wonder that the woman writer has held many mirrors up to the discomforts of her own nature. As we shall see, the notion that "Infection in the sentence breeds" has been so central a truth for literary women that the great artistic achievements of nineteenth-century novelists and poets from Austen and Shelley to Dickinson and Barrett Browning are often both literally and figuratively concerned with disease, as if to emphasize the effort with which health and wholeness were won from the infectious "vapors" of despair and fragmentation. Rejecting the poisoned apples her culture offers her, the woman writer often becomes in some sense anorexic, resolutely closing her mouth on silence (since—in the words of Jane Austen's Henry Tilney—"a woman's only power is the power of refusal"[21]), even while she complains of starvation. Thus both Charlotte and Emily Brontë depict the travails of starved or starving anorexic heroines, while Emily Dickinson declares in one breath that she "had been hungry, all the Years," and in another opts for "Sumptuous Destitution." Similarly, Christina Rossetti represents her own anxiety of authorship in the split between one heroine who longs to "suck and suck" on goblin fruit and another who locks her lips fiercely together in a gesture of silent and passionate renunciation. In addition, many of these literary women become in one way or another agoraphobic. Trained to reticence, they fear the vertiginous openness of the literary marketplace and rationalize with Emily Dickinson that "Publication— is the Auction/ Of the Mind of Man" or, worse, punningly confess that "Creation seemed a mighty Crack—/ To make me visible."[22]

As we shall also see, other diseases and dis-eases accompany the two classic symptoms of anorexia and agoraphobia. Claustrophobia, for instance, agoraphobia's parallel and complementary opposite, is a disturbance we shall encounter again and again in women's writing throughout the nineteenth century. Eye "troubles," moreover, seem to abound in the lives and works of literary women, with Dickinson matter-of-factly noting that her eye got "put out," George Eliot describing patriarchal Rome as "a disease of the retina," Jane Eyre and Aurora Leigh marrying blind men, Charlotte Brontë deliberately writing with her eyes closed, and Mary Elizabeth Coleridge writing about "Blindness" that came because "Absolute and bright,/ The Sun's rays smote me till they masked the Sun."[23] Finally, aphasia and amnesia—two illnesses which symbolically represent (and parody) the sort of intellectual incapacity patriarchal culture has traditionally required of women—appear and reappear in women's writings in frankly stated or disguised forms. "Foolish" women characters in Jane Austen's novels (Miss Bates in *Emma,* for instance) express Malapropish confusion about language, while Mary Shelley's monster has to learn language from scratch and Emily Dickinson herself childishly questions the meanings of the most basic English words: "Will there really be a 'Morning'?/ Is there such a thing as 'Day'?"[24] At the same time, many women writers manage to imply that the reason for such ignorance of language—as well as the reason for their deep sense of alienation and inescapable feeling of anomie—is that they have *forgotten* something. Deprived of the power that even their pens don't seem to confer, these women resemble Doris Lessing's heroines, who have to fight their internalization of patriarchal strictures for even a faint trace memory of what they might have become.

"Where are the songs I used to know,/ Where are the notes I used to sing?" writes Christina Rossetti in "The Key-Note," a poem whose title indicates its significance for her. "I have forgotten everything/ I used to know so long ago."[25] As if to make the same point, Charlotte Brontë's Lucy Snowe conveniently "forgets" her own history and even, so it seems, the Christian name of one of the central characters in her story, while Brontë's orphaned Jane Eyre seems to have lost (or symbolically "forgotten") her family heritage. Similarly, too, Emily Brontë's Heathcliff "forgets" or is made to forget who and what he was; Mary Shelley's monster is "born" without either a memory or a family history; and Elizabeth Barrett Browning's Aurora Leigh is early separated from—and thus induced to "forget"—her "mother land" of Italy. As this last example suggests, however, what all these characters and their authors really fear they have forgotten is precisely that aspect of their lives which has been kept from them by patriarchal poetics: their matrilineal heritage of literary strength, their "female power" which, as Annie Gottlieb wrote, is important to them *because of* (not in spite of) their mothers. In order, then, not only to understand the ways in which "Infection in the sentence breeds" for women but also to learn how women have won through disease to artistic health we must begin by redefining Bloom's seminal definitions of the revisionary "anxiety of influence." In doing so, we will have to trace the difficult paths by which nineteenth-century women overcame their "anxiety of authorship," repudiated debilitating patriarchal prescriptions, and recovered or remembered the lost foremothers who could help them find their distinctive female power. . . .

NOTES

Epigraphs: *Doctor on Patient* (Philadelphia: Lippincott, 1888), quoted in Ilza Veith, *Hysteria: The History of a Disease* (Chicago: University of Chicago Press, 1965), pp. 219–20; *The Living of Charlotte Perkins Gilman* (New York: Harper and Row, 1975; first published 1935), p. 104; J. 1261 in *The Poems of Emily Dickinson*, ed. Thomas Johnson, 3 vols. (Cambridge, Mass.: The Belknap Press of Harvard University Press, 1955: all subsequent references are to this edition); "The Red Shoes," *The Book of Folly* (Boston: Houghton Mifflin, 1972), pp. 28–29.

1. In "Tradition and the Individual Talent," Eliot of course considers these matters; in *Mimesis* Auerbach traces the ways in which the realist includes what has been previously excluded from art; and in *The Sense of an Ending* Frank Kermode shows how poets and novelists lay bare the literariness of their predecessors' forms in order to explore the dissonance between fiction and reality.

2. J. Hillis Miller, "The Limits of Pluralism, III: The Critic as Host," *Critical Inquiry* (Spring 1977): 446.

3. For a discussion of the woman writer and her place in Bloomian literary history, see Joanne Feit Diehl, "'Come Slowly—Eden': An Exploration of Women Poets and their Muse," *Signs* 3, no. 3 (Spring 1978): 572–87. See also the responses to Dichl in *Signs* 4, no. 1 (Autumn 1978): 188–96.

4. Juliet Mitchell, *Psychoanalysis and Feminism* (New York: Vintage, 1975), p. xiii.

5. Ibid., pp. 404–05.

6. Adrienne Rich, "When We Dead Awaken: Writing as Re-Vision," in *Adrienne Rich's Poetry*, ed. Barbara Charlesworth Gelpi and Albert Gelpi (New York: Norton, 1975), p. 90.

7. Mitchell, *Psychoanalysis and Feminism*, p. 402.

8. See Elaine Showalter, *A Literature of Their Own* (Princeton: Princeton University Press, 1977).

9. Annie Gottlieb, "Feminists Look at Motherhood," *Mother Jones* (November 1976): 53.

10. *The Letters of Emily Dickinson*, ed. Thomas Johnson, 3 vols. (Cambridge, Mass.: The Belknap Press of Harvard University Press, 1958). 2: 475; 2: 518.

11. See Jessie Bernard, "The Paradox of the Happy Marriage," Pauline B. Bart, "De-

pression in Middle-Aged Women," and Naomi Weisstein, "Psychology Constructs the Female," all in Vivian Gornick and Barbara K. Moran, ed., *Woman in Sexist Society* (New York: Basic Books, 1971). See also Phyllis Chesler, *Women and Madness* (New York: Doubleday, 1972), and—for a summary of all these matters—Barbara Ehrenreich and Deidre English, *Complaints and Disorders: The Sexual Politics of Sickness* (Old Westbury: The Feminist Press, 1973).

12. In *Hints on Insanity* (1861) John Millar wrote that "Mental derangement frequently occurs in young females from Amenorrhoea, especially in those who have any strong hereditary predisposition to insanity," adding that "an occasional warm hipbath or leeches to the pubis will . . . be followed by complete mental recovery." In 1873, Henry Mauldsey wrote in *Body and Mind* that "the monthly activity of the ovaries . . . has a notable effect upon the mind and body; wherefore it may become an important cause of mental and physical derangement." See especially the medical opinions of John Millar, Henry Maudsley, and Andrew Wynter in *Madness and Morals: Ideas on Insanity in the Nineteenth Century*, ed. Vieda Skultans (London and Boston: Routledge and Kegan Paul, 1975), pp. 230–35.

13. See Marlene Boskind-Lodahl, "Cinderella's Stepsisters: A Feminist Perspective on Anorexia Nervosa and Bulimia," *Signs* 2, no. 2 (Winter 1976): 342–56; Walter Blum, "The Thirteenth Guest," (on agoraphobia), in *California Living, The San Francisco Sunday Examiner and Chronicle* (17 April 1977): 8–12; Joan Archart-Treichel, "Can Your Personality Kill You?" (on female rheumatoid arthritis, among other diseases), *New York* 10, no. 48 (28 November 1977): 45: "According to studies conducted in recent years, four out of five rheumatoid victims are women, and for good reason: The disease appears to arise in those unhappy with the traditional female-sex role."

14. More recent discussions of the etiology and treatment of anorexia are offered in Hilde Bruch, M.D., *The Golden Cage: The Enigma of Anorexia Nervosa* (Cambridge, Mass.: Harvard University Press, 1978), and in Salvador Minuchin, Bernice L. Rosman, and Lester Baker, *Psychosomatic Families: Anorexia Nervosa in Context* (Cambridge: Harvard University Press, 1978).

15. Quoted by Ehrenreich and English, *Complaints and Disorders*, p. 19.

16. Eichner, "The Eternal Feminine," Norton Critical Edition of *Faust*, p. 620.

17. John Winthrop, *The History of New England from 1630 to 1649*, ed. James Savage (Boston, 1826), 2: 216.

18. Wendy Martin, "Anne Bradstreet's Poetry: A Study of Subversive Piety," *Shakespeare's Sisters*, ed. Gilbert and Gubar, pp. 19–31.

19. "The Uncensored Poet: Letters of Anne Sexton," *Ms.* 6, no. 5 (November 1977): 53.

20. Margaret Atwood, *Lady Oracle* (New York: Simon and Schuster, 1976), p. 335.

21. See *Northanger Abbey*, chapter 10: "You will allow, that in both [matrimony and dancing], man has the advantage of choice, woman only the power of refusal."

22. See Dickinson, *Poems*, J. 579 ("I had been hungry, all the Years"), J. 709 ("Publication—is the Auction"), and J. 891 ("To my quick ear the Leaves—conferred"); see also Christina Rossetti, "Goblin Market."

23. See Dickinson, *Poems*, J. 327 ("Before I got my eye put out"), George Eliot, *Middlemarch*, book 2, chapter 20, and M. E. Coleridge, "Doubt," in *Poems by Mary E. Coleridge*, p. 40.

24. See Dickinson, *Poems*, J. 101.

25. *The Poetical works of Christina C. Rossetti*, 2 vols. (Boston: Little Brown, 1909), 2: 11.

JAMES J. SOSNOSKI

A MINDLESS MAN-DRIVEN THEORY MACHINE

intellectuality, sexuality, and the institution of criticism

(1989)

> A male perspective, assumed to be 'universal' has dominated fields of knowledge.
>
> > GAYLE GREEN AND COPPÉLIA KAHN, *MAKING A DIFFERENCE*

> I should hope eventually for the erection of intelligent standards of criticism.
>
> > JOHN CROWE RANSOM, 'CRITICISM, INC.'

> To be signed with a woman's name doesn't necessarily make a piece of writing feminine. It could quite well be masculine writing, and conversely, the fact that a piece of writing is signed with a man's name does not in itself exclude femininity.
>
> > HÉLÈNE CIXOUS, 'CASTRATION OR DECAPITATION?'

> The male machine is a special kind of being, different from women, children, and men who don't measure up. He is functional, designed mainly for work. He is programmed to tackle jobs, override obstacles, attack problems, overcome difficulties, and always seize the offensive. He will take on any task that can be presented to him in a competitive framework, and his most important positive reinforcement is victory. . . . this ideology makes competition the guiding principle of moral and intellectual, as well as economic, life. It tells us that the general welfare is served by the self-interested clash of ambitions and ideas.
>
> > MARC FEIGEN FASTEAU, *THE MALE MACHINE*

This is an essay about the tie between the institutional construction of intellectuality and the social construction of sexuality. Let me start with error.

Knowing that we do not know is knowledge. And further, knowing that what one thought one knew is no longer believable is the most significant form of knowing. Just as problems, in some sense, precede solutions and questions precede answers, so not-knowing, including not-knowing-one-does-not-know, precedes knowing. This is the precondition upon which an intellectual comes to know. She acknowledges that a problem remains a problem, that an answer does not answer. She acknowledges that she is in error. For her, paradoxically, being in error is not being wrong. Error, in this case, is heuristic. By contrast, the traditional critic, formed by a long anti-intellectual past, insists that what he already thinks will suffice. This is an essay about his willingness not to know.

Indeed, to err is human. We use many words for this contingency. Realizing the inevitability of changing our minds, we speak of making mistakes, being incorrect, finding ourselves wrong, and ridding ourselves of falsehoods. In each case, we offer reasons for changing what we believe, think and/or do. And what would the world be like if we didn't? Cultures change because persons attempt to alter unwelcome states of affairs, to transform errors into questions, to make right what was wrong, to rethink what is false. To be human is to err. Only fools believe they know more than they do not know. This is an essay about resisting change by restricting error.

Error is the state of believing what is untrue, wrong, incorrect, or mistaken. Living with error is not a simple state of affairs. Our use of the word encompasses and often combines a wide range of faults. 'Error' implies 'deviation from truth, accuracy, correctness, right.'[1] It is the broadest term in the following comparisons. On one side of the semantic spectrum, error is understood as 'a blunder, a slip, a *faux pas*, a boner.' These are 'mistakes.' The word 'mistake' suggests an error resulting from 'carelessness, inattention, misunderstanding.' It does not strongly imply wrong-doing. 'Incorrect' mostly means not correct. Since correctness refers to 'adherence to conventionality' (correct behavior), incorrect suggests little more than deviation from convention. It is a comment upon how accurate, precise, or exact one is in performing some predesigned task. 'Wrong,' on the other hand, in its primary sense, means 'not morally right or just; sinful; wicked; immoral' and, in a derived sense, 'not in accordance with an established standard, previous arrangement, given intention.' If you are wrong, it is because you 'oppress, persecute, aggrieve, or abuse someone.' Wrongs are offenses that should be punished. At the other end of the spectrum of error from a mistake is the word 'false,' the most abstract and legal sense of error. 'False,' whose root sense is 'deception,' primarily means 'not true' (as in the phrase 'a false argument,' *WNWD*). Falsehood refers to 'anything that is not in essence that which it purports to be.' When deception is involved, the synonyms for 'false' are 'sham,' 'counterfeit,' 'bogus,' and 'fake.' Given such contrasting ideas of error, it would seem that, when persons are incorrect, it is not because they are sinful; that, when statements are false, it is not because they are immoral. In the institution of criticism, however, these terms appear to be conflated in judgments that incorrect statements are wrong because they are false. This is an essay about a particular conflation of error termed 'falsification.'

In this essay, I focus upon the institutional use of the word 'false' as a term paired with 'true.' In particular, I focus upon the judgment that critical arguments are 'false' as opposed to 'true.' The distinction between an unsound and a sound argument is the only condition upon which literary study as a discipline can be said to 'accumulate knowledge.' Hence, 'falsification,' 'falsifiability,' 'verification,' and 'verifiability' are crucial theoretical concerns. Since, in practice, verification is the result of falsification, I will focus upon the latter.[2] In literary studies, falsification is a judgment that takes the general form of the utterance: 'Professor X is "mistaken/incorrect/wrong" when he . . . ' Correlatively, the falsifiability of critical discourse is the condition of possibility for grades, ranks, publications.[3] These uses of the concept false depend upon a belief upon which, in turn, the institution of criticism depends: that a claim about a text can be proven false. Since this belief is an idealization of inquiry and therefore an abstraction of it, I have coined the term 'falsificity' to identify the particular conflation of errors upon which the institution of criticism is based. In short, falsificity is the principle that it is logically wrong (and therefore culpable and punishable) to mistake the incorrect for the correct. I use the term 'wrong' in glossing 'falsificity' to emphasize that, in the institution of criticism, critical arguments which are judged false are judged so not on purely logical grounds but on the grounds that they are 'sham, counterfeit, bogus, or fake' discourses and therefore punishable. False arguments are construed as discourses 'not in essence what they purport to be,' that is, not logical. Since they are proffered as criticism, they are instances of counterfeit discourses. According to the principle of falsificity, to submit as criticism a discourse that is not logical is wrong and hence to be punished—to be marked by an 'F,' to be cast out of editorial houses, to be denied an award. My critique of this principle is that it encourages critics to disagree with each other in ways that do not especially differ from familial quarreling wherein the keeper of the Logos is the Father who chastises his children. This is a paper about the construction of intellectuality as a competitive quarreling.

In this essay, I shall not only try to show that, far from being an impersonal, detached, logical judgment, falsification is a rationalization of academic competition, but, more significantly, that it is a device for maintaining the patriarchal *status quo*. Ordinarily, the identification of error leads to useful changes. (Problems are resolved; thus, a negative state of affairs is changed.) But, paradoxically, changes in a 'system' can be prohibited by defining alternatives to it as errors. (It's wrong, so don't do it!) In the institution of criticism, for example, one is instructed to avoid false arguments, that is, to avoid illogic. This instruction seems thoroughly plausible until one recognizes that, in literary study, the identification of falsehood (illogic) reflects the social construction of the feminine as 'man's specular Other'[4] and thus maintains the patriarchal *status quo*. This is an essay about the oppression of women.

Error can be heuristic. But, falsificity makes error a punishable form of wrongdoing. When we consider that it is a central theoretical assumption in a patriarchal institution hierarchically structured by competition, it can be described as a 'mindless, man-driven theory machine' designed to stamp out alternatives to the system it regulates by regarding them as merely feminine.

THE CONSTRUCTION OF INTELLECTUALITY IN THE INSTITUTION OF CRITICISM

The phrase 'traditional literary criticism' refers to a multitude of critics who differ widely among themselves. It is, nonetheless, a useful phrase because it designates a common form of argumentation. Nor is this an accident of history. The critics who have worked in the 'modern American university,' which, Laurence Veysey argues in his *The Emergence of the American University*, took its shape shortly after the turn of the century, are trained in a common form of argumentation.[5] It is structured by an informal logic whose first articulator was Aristotle. In it, claims are supported by evidence and therefore can be verified. It is requisite in this tradition for critics to discriminate between correct and incorrect readings. For example, in A *Handbook to Literature*, the most widely used of its kind, we read of argumentation that 'its purpose is to convince a reader or hearer by establishing the truth or falsity of a proposition.'

Traditional argumentation has long-standing protocols. Most literary students trained in it, have been formed by its scholasticism. Dissertations, for example, follow a pattern reminiscent of the treatises of medieval theologians: 'Most rhetoricians recognized five parts for the usual argumentative discourse: *exordium, narratio, confirmatio* or *probatio, refutatio,* and *peroratio.*'[6] Before a traditional critic proves his own case ('confirmatio'), he gives the history of preceding arguments ('narratio') and afterward refutes the likely objections ('refutatio'). Traditional papers, if only in the first footnote, still begin with reviews of the scholarship, most of which is falsified in order to set the stage for the author's view. Footnotes—many of which, as Stephen Nimis points out, have no logical relationship to the argument they footnote[7]—are either formulaic gestures toward verification ('confirmatio') or falsification ('refutatio').

To our post-modern sensibilities, the theory of falsification that provides a basis for traditional criticism is recognizably 'modern.' As I implied above, in this essay the term 'modern' refers to the historical period characterized by the infusion of 'discipline' (in Foucault's sense) into the structure of Western society. By the late nineteenth century, an intellectualized conception of discipline led institutions of higher learning to reorganize along 'disciplinary' lines, which, in turn, led to a significant structural change that produced what is often called the modern or new American university. In Veysey's terms, the rise of the professions led to the development of disciplines of study which led to the creation of departments to house them. For the most part, the organization of a newly formed study as a discipline was modelled on the successful institutionalization of scientific research. Literary studies followed this pattern. Before the turn of the century philology gave literary study the disciplined appearance of a science of literature. Then, literary history did. New Criticism gives us a more recent legacy of attempts to reformulate literary studies as a discipline. The overt intention of New Critical theory, in classics like 'The Intentional *Fallacy*' (my emphasis) or *Theory of Literature*, was to make literary criticism objective, reliable, verifiable, and so on.

But, it is the fact that *men* endeavored to make criticism a discipline along scientific lines that most interests me here. Though women have argued for literary study as a science, the 'canonical' theoretical statements have been made by men. The unselfconscious 'maleness' of their insistence upon a science of criticism is notable. As Gayle Greene and Coppélia Kahn remind us, 'a male perspective, assumed to be "universal," has dominated fields of knowledge.'[8] Literary criticism is no exception. Consider the following remarks of I. A. Richards, John Crowe Ransom, and René Wellek.

Richards wished to put literary criticism on the solid footing of a discipline. As Elmer Borklund points out, he began his career 'by virtually dismissing the entire critical tradition' prior to him.[9]

> A few conjectures, a supply of admonitions, many acute isolated observations, some brilliant guesses, much oratory and applied poetry, inexhaustible confusion, a sufficiency of dogma, no small stock of prejudices, whimsies and crochets, a profusion of mysticism, a little genuine speculation, sundry stray inspirations, pregnant hints and *aperçus*; of such as these, it may be said without exaggeration, is extant critical theory composed.[10]

Simultaneously, in America, John Crowe Ransom took a similar view, but couched it in business terms, unwittingly reflecting the extent to which universities had become corporations.

> Professors of literature are learned but not critical men. . . . Nevertheless, it is from the professors of literature, in this country the professors of English for the most part, that I should hope eventually for the erection of intelligent standards of criticism. It is their business.
>
> Criticism must become more scientific, or precise and systematic, and this means that it must be developed by the collective and sustained effort of learned persons—which means that its proper seat is in the universities. . . . Rather than occasional criticism by amateurs, I should think the whole enterprise might be seriously taken in hand by professionals. Perhaps I use a distasteful figure, but I have the idea that what we need is Criticism, Inc., or Criticism, Ltd.[11]

Welleck believed that we were still recovering from 'a disaster.' For him, literary criticism, which was 'taken over by politically oriented journalism' during the nineteenth century, became 'degraded to something purely practical, serving temporal ends.' 'The critic,' he laments, 'becomes a middleman, a secretary, even a servant, of the public.'[12] A decade after the publication of *Theory of Literature*, he complained that literary scholars were too much on the defensive:

> Our whole society is based on the assumption that we know what is just, and our science on the assumption that we know what is true. Our teaching of literature is actually also based on aesthetic imperatives, even if we feel less definitely bound by them and seem much more hesitant to bring these assumptions out into the open. The disaster of the 'humanities' as far as they are concerned with the arts and literature is due to their timidity in making the very same claims which are made in regard to law and truth. Actually we do make these claims when we teach *Hamlet* or *Paradise Lost* rather than Grace Metalious. . . . But we do so shamefully, apologetically, hesitatingly. There is, contrary to frequent assertions, a very wide agreement on the great classics: the main canon of literature. There is an insuperable gulf between really great art and very bad art: between say 'Lycidas' and a poem on the leading page of the *New York Times*, between Tolstoy's *Master and Man* and a story in *True Confessions*. (pp. 17–18)

He goes on to defend the possibility not only of correct interpretations but also of correct evaluations. Pointing out that, though the complexity of art might make interpretation difficult,

> this does not mean that all interpretations are equally right, that there is no possibility of differentiating between them. There are utterly fantastic

interpretations, partial, distorted interpretations. We may argue about Bradley's or Dover Wilson's or even Ernest Jones' interpretation of *Hamlet*, but we know that Hamlet was no woman in disguise. The concept of adequacy of interpretation leads clearly to the concept of the correctness of judgment. Evaluation grows out of understanding; correct evaluation out of correct understanding. There is a hierarchy of viewpoints implied in the very concept of adequacy of interpretation. Just as there is correct interpretation, at least as an ideal, so there is correct judgment, good judgment. (p. 18)

For Wellek, the only factor that could keep literary criticism from being a 'secretary' to the public was falsification. That we could correctly understand that 'Hamlet was no woman in disguise' would allow us to make the 'good judgment' that *True Confessions* was degrading. For Wellek, the study of literature was *Literaturwissenschaft*, 'systematic knowledge.'

In retrospect, it is remarkable still that the main opponents to New Criticism in the 1960s did not question the view that literary criticism, even though it could not muster exacting objectivity, should be modelled on the sciences. They regarded New Criticism as not scientific enough. Northrop Frye, in his 'Polemical Introduction' to *Anatomy of Criticism*, outflanks the New Critics by arguing the case for a science of Literature rather than for a scientific method of interpretation. E. D. Hirsch's *Validity in Interpretation* critiques the theory of 'the intentional fallacy' by arguing that we can validly determine intention. In the 1960s, when anti–New Critical ferment began, system and method were, nonetheless, privileged terms. The most wide-scale attempt to make criticism into a science belonged to a movement that would have supplanted New Criticism by making its 'scientific' tendencies explicit, namely, structuralism. It is now an often-told tale how structuralism engendered post-structuralism.

To post-structuralist or post-modernist critics, whose intellectual formation is deeply indebted to feminism,[13] traditional or modern theories of criticism are phallo/logocentric.

> Imagine someone (a kind of Monsieur Teste in reverse) who abolishes within himself all barriers, all classes, all exclusions, not by syncretism but by simple discard of that old specter: *logical contradiction*; who mixes every language, even those said to be incompatible; who silently accepts every charge of illogicality, of incongruity; who remains passive in the face of Socratic irony (leading the interlocutor to the supreme disgrace: *self-contradiction*) and legal terrorism (how much penal evidence is based on a psychology of consistency!) Such a man would be the mockery of our society: court, school, asylum, polite conversations would cast him out: who endures contradiction without shame? Now this antihero exists. . . .[14]

For the most part, modern criticism is based on the notion that readings can be objective, impersonal and detached, that there is a discipline of literary criticism. Though traditional critics differ widely in their assumptions about interpretation, when contrasted with post-modern critics, they appear similar in their logocentrism. Working within this system, modern critics contend that their readings are demonstrable because textual or contextual evidence can show that rival readings are not logically supported. Since readings that are accepted as 'true' at an earlier moment in time can at a later date be shown to be 'false,' the engine of this system is falsification. New readings supplant old readings. This is a familiar pattern to anyone studying literature. Most critics strive to come up with 'new' readings, and, in order to do so, have to clear their paths by falsifying the previously accepted ones.

In other words, what characterizes modern literary criticism is a principle of falsificity.

INTELLECTUAL SEXUALITY IN THE INSTITUTION OF CRITICISM

Literary criticism is a career. Burton Bledstein tells us in *The Culture of Professionalism* that the idea of a career emerged concomitantly with the rise of the professions in the nineteenth century in contrast to 'a random series of jobs, projects, or businesses providing a livelihood.'[15] It changed the lives of *men* because it articulated *their* aspirations as ambitions (emphasis mine). It involved 'a preestablished total pattern of organized professional activity, with upward movement through recognized preparatory stages, and advancement based on merit bearing honor.' Modern literary criticism was conceived during this period. Like professionals elsewhere, critics make their career patterns discernible in their *curriculum vitae* which require them to list chronologically 'preparatory stages,' 'advancement' in employment, 'honors,' and 'merit'—which, in their case, is signalled by increasing success in placing their work with prestigious publishers. What Bledstein calls a 'vertical' movement characterizes the careers of successful professional critics. For critics, an outstanding career is one in which they earn higher and higher salaries in a succession of jobs at increasingly prestigious institutions. Since the mid-nineteenth century, professional success has been imaged as climbing a ladder of institutional status:

> New expectations displayed themselves in a new style. In a social environment now offering vocational alternatives, young men could criticize, calculate, envision a ladder of advancement, and act with some measure of impunity toward their less flexible elders. Above all, young men could begin thinking in vertical rather than horizontal imagery. They mean, very literally, to move up and away. (p. 176)

Bledstein describes the shift in the sense of the purposefulness of a man's life during the nineteenth century as a shift away from a belief in a 'calling' to a choice of a 'career,' a shift easily discerned in the changing ways ministers, lawyers, doctors, and educators spoke about their professions. A 'calling' was not the choice of an individual, but a career most certainly was. Bledstein's remark that a career was a choice for 'young men' leaves unspoken that women were still 'called.'

The shift Bledstein describes was hierarchically and competitively configured not merely as a change in status and roles provoked by analogies to ladders and races, but also as a change in the social construction of masculinity provoked by images of gentlemen.

> The inner intensity of the new life oriented toward a career stood in contrast

to that of the older learned professional life of the eighteenth and early nineteenth centuries. In the earlier period such external attributes of gentlemanly
behavior as benevolence, duty, virtue, and manners circumscribed the professional experience. Competence, knowledge, and preparation were less important in evaluating the skills of the professional than were dedication to the
community, sincerity, trust, permanence, honorable reputation, and righteous
behavior. The qualifying credentials of the learned professionals were honesty, decency and civility. (p. 173)

The career professional, by contrast, thought in terms of advancement. The
nineteenth-century gentleman gave way to the twentieth-century businessman,
who prospered in 'a competitive society in which unrestrained individual self-
determination undermined traditional life styles' (p. 174). He is the prototype of
the persona Marc Feigen Fasteau calls 'the male machine.'

> The male machine is a special kind of being, different from women, children,
> and men who don't measure up. He is functional, designed mainly for work.
> He is programmed to tackle jobs, override obstacles, attack problems, over-
> come difficulties, and always seize the offensive. He will take on any task
> that can be presented to him in a competitive framework, and his most im-
> portant positive reinforcement is victory. . . . this ideology makes competition
> the guiding principle of moral and intellectual, as well as economic, life. It
> tells us that the general welfare is served by the self-interested clash of am-
> bitions and ideas.[16]

Bledstein remarks that in the development of nineteenth-century professionalism ambitious men were instrumental in 'structuring our discipline according
to a distinct vision—the vertical one of career' (p. ix). From this point of view,
the development of literary study matches Bledstein's delineation of the relationship between the growth of the university and the rise of professionalism. To become a literary scholar is to be professionalized, a social process involving the
introjection of an 'intellectual competitiveness.' The 'masculine' qualities of exemplary male professors were imitated and became the traits of an idealized career profile. Exemplary male professors became 'role-models' for success within
the structure of the academy, a phenomenon which shaped the field of literary
study as we now know it.[17] We are the heirs of 'roles' that are explicitly designed
for the new gentleman, the businessman.

The history of literary study, for instance, can be understood as the collective
biography of exemplary *male* figures: George Marsh, Francis March, Francis
Child, Ulrich von Wilamowitz-Moellendorf, Gustave Lanson, I. A. Richards, John
Crowe Ransom, Cleanth Brooks, and so on. The criss-crossing movement of their
careers influenced the newly developing field of literary study. Its historical development is, in most respects, an account of these critical 'movements' which
are usually associated with key men who inspired schools of thought. Figures like
Child, Brooks, and Lanson are historically significant because they became exemplary figures. These men were 'exemplary' because in doing what they believed ought to be done, they became examples for others. Modern literary study
developed as a profession to the extent that the manner in which a particular man
studied literature was widely imitated, to the extent that a man's way of 'doing'

criticism or scholarship became a trait in the composite profile of the ideal professor of literature. Invariably, men were the models underlying the ideal profile
of the scholar/critic at specific junctures in the development of literary studies.
Over time, this idealized career profile became a composite of masculine traits
derived from the superimposition of the portrayals of exemplary male scholars.
Women working in the academy, in order to succeed in their careers, had to acquire these traits. As Hélène Cixous reminds us, a discourse 'signed with a
woman's name doesn't necessarily make a piece of writing feminine. It could
quite well be masculine writing.'[18]

Nowadays, to be a professional critic authorized by the institution of criticism
still requires submission to an idealized career profile whose masculinity derives
from male models. Since this profile is nowhere made explicit as such and *in toto*,
I call it the 'Magister Implicatus' to personify and thus concretize the sum total
of performances now demanded for accreditation as a professional critic.[19] He is
the image we see when we look in the distorted mirror of our resumés. As we
currently know him, the Magister Implicatus is a personification of an ideal male
career. At present, he stands for the professionalization of the male scholar from
the very first examination through various forms of discipline to the final authorization of his work. He is the unified personification of the ways professional
critics are taught to portray themselves in official documents—*vitae*, grant applications, course descriptions, and so on.

In his traditional and modern persona, the Magister's power enables or disables
any member of the institution who introjects him. He punishes by making us
believe we have failed, do not deserve tenure, have not published enough. He
is the monster in the male machine, the instrument of self-discipline and self-
abnegation. In his traditional guise, he is the personification of the patriarchal institution, the site for training, disciplining, schooling men. He professionalizes the
amateur. He governs through our introjection of what the desired outcome of any
performance must be if it is to be rewarded. It is his male interests that are served
when critics serve their institutions by believing those beliefs that hold it together. An emotional bond to him is a bond to the patriarchal institution. In serving him, one serves it, often while believing he has one's best interests in mind.

The Magister Implicatus is the ghostly patriarchal figure who haunts our job
descriptions, our textbooks, our examination committees, and other quarters of
the institution of literary criticism. Not surprisingly, given the history of the institution of criticism, his profile is masculine. Because careers allow for professional advances along a ladder of institutional success (degrees, salaries, ranks and
so on), the Magister through his exemplariness inspires critics to compete with
one another for awards.

It is upon this one trait of the Magister Implicatus, his competitiveness, that I
wish to focus your attention.

FALSIFICITY IS INEXTRICABLY LINKED TO COMPETITIVENESS

In the present academy, competitiveness and falsificity are inextricably bound together. Critics are judged according to the extent to which they have successfully argued. The merit of their arguments is measured by the degree to which

they have falsified their rival's claims and the degree to which their own arguments are deemed falsifiable. 'And merit is, of course, determined by competition. How else?'[20] The success of a critic is therefore inextricably linked with the extent to which he competes with rival critics.

Competition is usually defined as 'a striving for the same object, position, prize, etc., usually in accordance with certain fixed rules' (*WNWD*). Rule-governed striving is the generating principle of career success. Each juncture of the career path presents to the careerist a goal for which he must compete—a grade, a degree, a job, a promotion, a grant, and so on. In every case, the competitor is judged on the merit of his critical arguments. Hence, if we consider that arguments displace earlier arguments through falsification, then the successful competitor is the successful falsifier. Falsification and competitiveness are inextricable in this system.

As Helen E. Longino points out, 'Competition always involves a contest among individuals seeking the same thing when not all can obtain it.'[21] Some competitions, she argues, are based upon the availability of a single prize. As in a race, there is only one first 'prize.' As a consequence, the differences in abilities of the contestants is the salient factor. Such competitions are staged to establish who is 'the best' in a particular performance. There are many examples in literary criticism—competing for a job, a grant, an award. In other competitions the scarcity of the 'object' sought (the reward) creates a 'survival of the fittest' contest and the 'game' has to be played until winners are determined. In literary criticism, competing for publications, jobs, promotions, and salaries has the structure of a 'win/lose' (vs. 'prize') competition. In this type of competition the salient factor is not necessarily ability but perserverance, fortitude, endurance, doggedness, and so on.

When we look at literary criticism as an institution through the lens of competition, that is, when we study the ways in which critical argumentation has been institutionalized as a competition, a peculiar distortion of critical inquiry comes to light. In order to decide between winners and losers in the various career games we all play, administrators, in choosing to focus upon the success of critical arguments, force critics to reify their understanding. Knowledge, as Pierre Bourdieu argues, becomes 'symbolic capital.'[22] What we know has to be quantifiable, measurable and therefore cumulative. We might say that insights have to be converted into information in order to be accumulated. In this system, the goal of criticism is to 'accumulate knowledge,' hence the critic who has accumulated the most knowledge gets the most rewards. Central to this system is falsification.

Let's take a simple example. Jack believes that 'X' is the meaning of poem '1.' He argues his case on the grounds of the beliefs 'A, B, and C' which he takes to be factual. Jill believes that 'y' is the meaning of poem '1.' She argues her case on the grounds of 'a, d, and q.' What are Jack's options? Well, obviously, he could agree. He could say, 'I was mistaken in believing B and C.' If he does so, he admits his reading is false and is no longer eligible for an institutional reward. False arguments are not rewarded. So, in order to maintain his reading, Jack has to say either that d and q are irrelevant or that not-d and not-q are the facts. In other words, to survive the competition among readers, he must maintain his beliefs, otherwise he admits to error and loses status or merit.

In his *Psychology of Intelligence*, Jean Piaget terms the form of intellection I have just described 'assimilation,' namely, the tendency to assimilate all new experiences into the cognitive frameworks one already possesses. He contrasts this mode of intellection to 'accommodation,' wherein inquirers allow new experiences to 'break down' the frameworks they are accustomed to using.[23] It can be safely said that the institution of criticism encourages assimilation. It does not help your career to go around explaining how you are in error.

Considering that the institution of criticism encourages assimilation and therefore falsification as the cognitive strategies best suited to the accumulation of knowledge (information), we might, recalling Cixous's use of 'the proper,' term this cognitive style 'appropriation.'[24] Appropriation is the acquisition of knowledge understood as an entity (identities, samenesses, that is, information); it is the assimilation of concepts into a governing framework. Appropriation is an arrogation, confiscation, seizure of concepts. Ideas can be owned and sold at will. They are proper-ties. A contrasting mode of intellection, like intuition, a term I prefer to the term 'insight,'[25] often involves the in-appropriate, the disconcerting, and so on. Inappropriate because painful, humiliating; disconcerting in forcing one to change one's beliefs. Moreover, intuitions are not appropriatable and thus nothing gets accumulated. Intuitions are unspecifiable.[26] Intuitions are multiple, diverse, *ad hoc*, diffuse, etc. Whereas logical problems have single solutions, intuited problems have plural solutions and often appear illogical.

For post-moderns, thankfully, the veracity of criticism is not a matter of logic. Thought is not single, unified, centered, present. Though I cannot rehearse postmodern critiques of logocentrism here, I believe that I am not alone in thinking that texts do not provide a factual ground to interpretive claims, that writers and readers are discursive subjects who cannot be codified, that distinctions between correct and incorrect are purely conventional, that truth is a signifier like all others. In short, in post-modern theorizing, the very possibility of falsification is thoroughly undermined as a worthwhile intellectual endeavor.

If falsification does not lead to knowledge, then why do we continue to accept it? Obviously, it serves some other purpose. In the case of traditional criticism, the purpose is to regulate competition. Competition always requires rules. Falsification is the governing rule. Thus, modern criticism is no more than a competition governed by an arbitrary rule interpreted by those institutionally empowered to do so. Falsificity is a mechanism of a disciplinary apparatus to regulate competition. In an academic context, 'regulation of competition' refers to the rules that govern the attribution of merit to critical performances. Every competition has to have fixed rules to ensure the result that someone will win. Falsification is a regulating mechanism in the sense that it is like tagging the person who is 'it.' Falsifying reminds one of the fiction boys use in childhood wargames—when an enemy is shot, the victor shouts, 'you're dead!,' moving on to surprise the next opponent. Falsification is a similar device used by successful competitors to establish their progress (over the corpses of rival critics) along the way to winning. In critical games, though rationalized as a reward for possessing 'the best idea' among one's opponents, the competition is for a grade, a degree, a job, a publication, a promotion, a grant, an appointment. The awarding of these prizes in no way guarantees the value of the inquiry. Another irony in this system is that, whereas rules—like falsification—are designed to regulate, to keep under control the aggression involved, they have the effect of increasing it. Falsification, though construed as a regulator, functions only as a measurement of the logicality and frequency of successful counter-claims; hence, it has the effect of multiplying falsifications.

This system intensifies competition and leads to what I call intellectual machismo, the tendency toward an exaggerated expression of competition for the acquisition and appropriation of ideas. It is an exercise of power. In this sense, it is an instance of domination. The instigator, the person who picks the fight, confirms his sense that he is better than his rival often by creating a situation in which the rival, taken by surprise, is overwhelmed. In this scenario knowledge is power. Oddly, since it is an intellectually trivial pursuit, this wargame has the character of a parlor game. The machismic critic scores by knowing the most recent article, the exact date, the most stinging review, the precise reference, the received opinion, and so on. A side effect of these games is that it becomes impossible for the critic whose intellectual style is machismic to admit error. It is regarded as a fault, an embarrassment. This is a ridiculous posture. Ironically, the machismic intellectual, by telling what is obviously a kind of lie, places himself in a ludicrous position if he wishes finally to reach some understanding. Nevertheless, the machismic intellectual's discourse is permeated by utterances like 'Professor X is wrong.' Because, in the institution of criticism, falsification is bound up with the notion of 'wrong-doing,' intellectual machismo has a Rambo effect. The heroic critic is obligated morally to rescue thinkers from the prisons of illogic, to stand up to illogic when no one else cares. He is armed to the teeth with falsifications. Nothing but his self-esteem is left in his wake. He is the supreme falsifier, appropriator, assimilator.

Assimilation, the hallmark of appropriation, mechanizes falsification. When undertaken aggressively, it becomes a machine that falsifies everything in its path. The machine is a simple idea-mower, a handy procrustean mechanism. The machismic intellectual already has a set of beliefs to encompass his world. When he encounters someone else's belief, one of two events occur. Either, the announced belief squares with his own and can be assimilated as a confirmation of what he already believes, in which case verification occurs as a kind of negative falsification (we're right, so they're wrong). Or, as is more often the case, the announced belief does not square with his and is assimilated into his belief system as an error. In the latter instance, the Ramboist (this is, after all, a school of thought that needs a name) finds counter-evidence in his stock of beliefs, or identifies a lapse in logic, or invokes an authority (someone who believes what he believes). In short, since he cannot assimilate a belief that is inconsistent with his belief system, it enters his framework as a false belief. In his Ramboistic wargames, critical arguments are not distinguishable from quarrels. Quarreling is 'a dispute or disagreement, especially one marked by anger and deep resentment' and 'implies heated verbal strife' that 'often suggests continued hostility as a result' (WNWD).

Though arguments are said to be logical, dispassionate, detached, impersonal, objective and so on, and in this sense, can be regarded culturally as 'masculine,' looked at closely, especially in the light of a critique of falsification, they are difficult to distinguish from quarrels. Oddly, the more one examines arguments (intellectual masculinity), the more one finds quarrels (intellectual effeminateness). Similarly, the more one looks at intuition and the confession of error, etc. (intellectual femininity), the more it looks like a strong, incisive, powerful mode of knowing (intellectual virility).

INTELLECTUAL COMPASSION, COMMITMENT, COLLABORATION, CONCURRENCE, AND COMMUNITY

Literary criticism is intellectual work. Unlike work-for-profit, the success of which can be enhanced by competition, intellectual work requires compassion, commitment, collaboration, concurrence, and community. I list these as alternatives to the components of traditional criticism I have critiqued. In this section, I try to articulate my intuitions about them. I admit at the outset that not all of them are obvious alternatives to a competitive system. Collaboration is clearly an alternative to competition, compassion to machismo, intellectual community to scholarly individualism. Once I supply the phrase for which the term stands, it becomes clear that commitment-to-the-public-welfare is an alternative aspiration to self-interested careerism. Concurrence, however, is not the obvious alternative to appropriation. Consequently, in what follows I write about concurrence inchoately, hoping to stir further discussion.

Let me begin with the need for intellectual compassion. Compassion is ordinarily understood as 'sorrow for the sufferings or troubles of another' (*WNWD*) and can be related to the kind of empathy that is necessary for a commitment to collaborative concurrence about painful problems relevant to a community.[27] I contrast it with intellectual machismo. Intellectual compassion allows one intellectual to enter imaginatively into the problems of another. Collaboration depends upon the ability of one intellectual to enter into the pain or suffering that another is attempting to resolve. This contrasts to the kind of intellectual antagonism that competition spawns, which interferes with the resolution of problems.

Problems are not equivalent to puzzles. A problem is frustrating, painful, and difficult; it calls for the articulation of many questions. Each question differs, and therefore questioning requires the breaking down of preconceived frameworks because of the difficulty of formulating the problem in a way that does not simply appropriate it. Collaborative inquiry is not an instance of differing perspectives ultimately coming together in a unified framework. Instead, it seeks intellectual concurrence (rather than appropriation). Concurrence, by which I mean an agreement to join intellectual forces to get something done, is a plausible alternative to appropriation only on the condition that the differences among the researchers are allowed free play. In this form of collaboration, researchers are invited into the group not because they represent the same point of view but because they represent different and even incompatible points of view. Since getting-at-my-truth no longer governs the inquiry, quarrels are abandoned while concurrence is sought because any idea that helps solve the problem helps. Removing contradictions or inconsistencies from one's discourse is less important than resolving the cultural conflicts we call racism, elitism or sexism. Concurrence of this sort is desirable in literary research.[28]

Literary criticism calls for intellectual collaboration. The form of critical collaboration I have been advocating converges upon the apprehension of a problem and the critics involved band together to seek solutions to it. This form of collaboration in literary criticism occurs when a group of differing intellectuals, bound together by the acknowledgment of a textual/cultural problem, concur about a possible reading of it. By concurring, they do not seek conformity; they seek the coincidences among their differences. In this collaboration, concurrences about the problem and the solution are transpersonal. This does not necessarily imply a common ideal or *telos* holding the group together. Intellectual compassion and care hold the group together. In this form of collaboration, intellectual subject positions are not configured competitively. Differences are crucial. Reading is not an appropriation by an individual; it is the political concurrence of a group.

Inescapably, collaboration is the heart of the practice of literary study, despite the patriarch's insistence upon individualistic readings. How do we therefore explain that we rarely acknowledge it? Maria C. Lugones and Elizabeth V. Spelman note that:

> The desire to excel, the desire to avoid obscurity, and the desire for distinction become definitive of a competitive attitude in a context of opposition and they come, in their turn, to be shaped by this context. For at the heart of the desire to excel in the context of opposition, is the desire to excel not merely in some non-comparative sense, but to excel over others, to better them. . . . The overriding preoccupation is with standing out against the performances of others. . . .
>
>   A competitor qua competitor sustains quite a different conception of herself and others than she would if she were engaged in activities in which it is appropriate to think about other humans as needy or as collaborators.[29]

As they remind us, competition is 'essentially self-centered' (p. 237). It makes 'one's own success and well-being . . . impossible without someone else's failure and/or misery' (p. 241). But, they argue, there is an alternative to the politics of competition—communal excelling.[30]

Collaboration takes place within the polis, the aggregate of communities. An intellectual community is a concurrence of intellectuals. Intellectual communities engender different and sometimes competing collaborations. As Lugones and Spelman write,

> There are contexts in which the desire to avoid obscurity and the desire for excellence are not only compatible with but necessary ingredients of projects that are properly communal. In those cases these desires are incompatible with an individualistic conception of excellence and of the participants in the project. (p. 238)

Though the word 'community' includes the word 'unity,' communities are not unities. Obviously, a notion of community can be deconstructed by pointing out that it implies an essential, central, unity, that it implies the 'presence' of some entity.[31] My concern here is not so much with the aberrations of a metaphysics of presence but with the naive assumption that communities are in fact unities. I do not mean to suggest by privileging the word 'community' that every individual in a community communes, that is, moves through the understanding of common goals and ideals toward identity, sameness. Though the word unfortunately suggests some kind of entity that is unified, it is possible to think of a community as a theatre in which intellectual 'play' is dramatized. In this play, the dramatis personae, each with distinct characteristics uniquely performed, act together toward a resolution of a problem. This is a play of differences that concurrently respond to a problem differentially perceived.[32] In this play, critics enjoy differing subject positions and their characters change, that is, they exchange subject positions. The bond of an intellectual community is intellectual compassion, the imaginative entry into another's problem.

In the terms now under discussion, critical inquiry is the compassionate accommodation of difference. Such inquiries are, by this definition, collaborative. But, to be housed in universities, collaborative inquirers (research groups), must, in some sense, *share* problems with communities. And, ultimately, communities of intellectuals can only legitimize themselves in the institution of criticism to the extent that they inquire into problems characterizing the various public spheres that make up our cultural formation.[33] These are not individualizing possibilities and considering them brings us circuitously back to a consideration of 'theory' (but not a man-driven one). Although falsification cannot and should not be recuperated by post-modern critics, in the context of communal inquiry, it seems foolish, if not impossible, to try to do without the heuristic value of error since problems are related to errors, and to inquire requires error and the breaking apart of preconceptions. Inquiries are written (or, in a grammatological sense, inscribed) as questions. Just as texts are intertexts that encompass myriad cultural formations, so inquiries are texts. Knowing this is theorizing.

Theorizing is not necessarily making theories. Theory-making is patriarchal. Theory is often used as a weapon. Theory is an effective instrument of falsification. And so on. But systematic theories that feed into competitive schemes are only the husk of theorizing. It is in the understanding of a problem through differing intuitions of it that theorizing occurs. Out of these intuitions arises a more general view of critical performance than is available to the solitary scholar. Competition obscures this phenomenon. In a competition among critics, theories become machines of falsification. They are used to refute the assumptions of rival critics. But in a communal inquiry, theorizing is informed by intellectual compassion and arises out of the urgency to end the pain associated with a specific problem. In that endeavor, performances must be made as effective as possible. Theorizing helps.

The precondition of possibility for intellectual compassion, commitment, collaboration, concurrence, and community is the de-masculinization of the Magister Implicatus. Why quarrel?

NOTES

I would like to thank my colleagues Ann Ardis, Dale Bauer, Art Casciato, Susan Jarratt, Kristina Straub, Andy Lakritz of Miami University and Patricia Harkin of Akron University for their intellectual compassion. Because of the intellectual community their concurrence occasions, what I have written is, in most respects, collaborative.

1. All of the quotes in this paragraph are references to *Webster's New World Dictionary,* hereafter cited as *WNWD.* I have used this dictionary simply because it compares semantically related terms.

2. Though this theorem comes from the philosophy of science (Popper 1968: 40), it applies to literary criticism whose disciplinary orientation mimics the institutionalization of scientific research.

3. To give the grade 'F' presupposes that the discourse so assigned is false. The same principle pertains to any grade below 'A+.' This system of 'grading' also pertains to ranking and the unqualified or qualified acceptance or rejection of papers submitted for publication.

4. This is an extension of Luce Irigaray's thematic in Irigaray 1985.

5. Veysey 1965. In this essay, I conflate the terms 'traditional' and 'modern' in a sense that combines Foucault's (1977) delineation of the period of our history dominated by 'discipline' and Lyotard's (1984) suggestion that we are 'post-modern' because the conditions of knowledge production have radically changed. In this context, the reliance on various kinds of warranting in informal logic which Toulmin (1972) sees as the defining characteristic of university studies called disciplines fits well into the notion of 'modern' as the logocentric world-view under critique by 'post-moderns.'

6. Corbett 1971: 303.

7. His essay, which is written in English, is ironically entitled, 'Das Fussnoten: das Fundament der Wissenschaft.' It is ironic that a classicist should write this article, since his is among the most heavily footnoted of all fields.

8. Greene and Kahn 1985: 1–2.

9. Borklund 1977: 440.

10. Richards 1925: 6.

11. Ransom 1968: 328–9.

12. Wellek 1967: 3.

13. While deconstruction seems to reign in the news of our profession, post-modern feminism is far more vital. Indeed, post-modern criticism is inconceivable without feminism. Far more important than the deconstruction of literary texts is the politicization of literary study, a project in which feminists have led the way.

14. Barthes 1975: 3.

15. Bledstein 1976: 172.

16. Fasteau 1975: 1.

17. In this section I take an admittedly general look at some aspects of our collective past that can be understood as the historical conditions of the career profile of the literary scholar/critic. Most of my remarks are based on research conducted by the Group for Research into the Institutionalization and Professionalization of Literary Studies (GRIP). Many of the papers published in *The GRIP Report* involve brief historical accounts of exemplary academic figures: George Marsh, Francis Marsh, Francis Child, Ulrich von Wilamowitz-Moellendorf, Gustave Lanson, Cleanth Brooks, and so on. The GRIP collaboration is sponsored by the Society for Critical Exchange, a national organization dedicated to collaborative work in literary theory.

18. Cixous 1981: 52.

19. This paragraph summarizes an essay entitled 'The Magister Implicatus: a configuration of orthodoxy,' originally published in *The GRIP Report*, a revised version of which is included in a volume of GRIP essays under consideration for publication.

20. Longino, 'The ideology of competition,' in Miner and Longino 1987: 253. For detailed discussions of competition and women, see Miner and Longino 1987.

21. Ibid.: 250.

22. Bourdieu 1979: 171–83.

23. Piaget 1963: 8.

24. I draw on Cixous's distinction between the 'proper' and the 'gift' because it succinctly captures the relationship between knowledge and social institutions.

25. I earlier used the term 'insight' in place of the term 'intuition' for rhetorical reasons. Also, for reasons that will become apparent later, I define intuition not in the traditional way as 'the immediate knowing of something without the conscious use of reasoning' (*WNWD*), but as the instantaneous accommodation of unspecifiable differences.

26. I use 'intuition' in roughly Michael Polanyi's sense of 'insight' (Polanyi 1958: 90–1). In his account of intelligence, he focuses upon 'tacit knowledge' which is so complex that it cannot be articulated because the particulars arc unspecifiable. Unlike Polanyi, however, I regard the 'unspecifiability' of insight as owing to the relationship between our short- and long-term memories.

27. See Lugones and Spelman 1987 for a detailed discussion of compassion. My use of the term, suggested to me by their essay, differs from theirs.

28. Unlike scientific theories, literary theories are not paradigms for research. Whereas in paradigmatic research theories govern the formulation of questions in the search for sameness, in literary research groups many, even contradictory, theorems can be used in search of differences that might precipitate concurrences. See David Shumway and James Sosnoski, 'Critical protocols,' *The GRIP Report*, vol. 2 (Research in Progress Circulated by the Society for Critical Exchange, 1984).

29. Lugones and Spelman 1987: 236–7.

30. I agree with Lugones and Spelman that competition has its political usefulness and support their contention that groups competing collectively for the welfare of the public can be beneficial. As they point out, while competition is akin to excelling, communal excelling is not destructive in the way that an individual's competing in self-interested ways is. For them, the crucial difference is that in communal excelling, self-interest is regulated by the interests of the group.

31. I am thinking here of Jean-Luc Nancy's work on community in his *La Communauté Désoeuvrée* (1986).

32. One of the topics in Laclau and Mouffe 1985 is the possibility of differences in political action.

33. Without a strong relationship to public spheres, 'intellectuals' are vulnerable to elitism. This is as true of an intellectual who works in a university as it is of any other.

WORKS CITED

Barthes, Roland 1975. *The Pleasure of the Text*. Trans. Richard Miller. New York: Hill and Wang.

Belsey, Catherine 1980. *Critical Practice*. London and New York: Methuen.

Bledstein, Burton J. 1976. *The Culture of Professionalism*. New York: W. W. Norton.

Borklund, Elmer 1977. *Contemporary Literary Critics*. New York: St. Martin's Press.

Bourdieu, Pierre 1979. *Outline of a Theory of Practice*. Ed. Jack Goody, trans. Richard Nice. Cambridge: Cambridge University Press.

Cixous, Hélène 1981. 'Castration or decapitation?' Trans. Annette Kuhn. *Signs: Journal of Women in Culture and Society* 7.1 (Autumn): 41–55.

Corbett, Edward P. J. 1971. *Classical Rhetoric for the Modern Student*. New York: Oxford University Press.

Fasteau, Marc Feigen 1975. *The Male Machine*. New York: Dell Publishing Co.

Foucault, Michel 1977. *Discipline and Punish: The Birth of the Prison*. Trans. Alan Sheridan. New York: Vintage.

Frye, Northrop 1957. *Anatomy of Criticism: Four Essays*. Princeton: Princeton University Press.

Greene, Gayle and Kahn, Coppélia 1985. *Making a Difference: Feminist Literary Criticism.* London and New York: Methuen.

Hirsch, Jr., E. D. 1967. *Validity in Interpretation.* New Haven: Yale University Press.

Irigaray, Luce 1985. *Speculum of the Other Woman.* Trans. Gillian G. Gill. Ithaca: Cornell University Press.

Jardine, Alice and Smith, Paul (eds.) 1987. *Men in Feminism.* London and New York: Methuen.

Laclau, Ernesto and Mouffe, Chantal 1985. *Hegemony and Socialist Strategy.* London: Verso.

Lugones, Maria C. and Spelman, Elizabeth V. 1987. 'Competition, compassion and community: models for a feminist ethos,' in Miner and Longino 1987.

Lyotard, Jean-François 1984. *The Postmodern Condition: A Report on Knowledge.* Trans. Geoff Bennington and Brian Massumi. Minneapolis: University of Minnesota Press.

Miner, Valerie and Longino, Helen E. 1987. *Competition: A Feminist Taboo.* New York: The Feminist Press at The City University of New York.

Moi, Toril 1985. *Sexual/Textual Politics: Feminist Literary Theory.* London and New York: Methuen.

Nancy, Jean-Luc 1986. *La Communauté Désoeuvrée.* Paris: Christian Bougois.

Nimis, Stephen 1984. 'Fussnoten: das Fundament der Wissenschaft.' *Arethusa*, 17.2 (Fall): 105–34.

Piaget, Jean 1963. *The Psychology of Intelligence.* Paterson, New Jersey: Littlefield, Adams.

Polanyi, Michael 1958. *Personal Knowledge.* Chicago: University of Chicago Press.

Popper, Karl R. 1968. *The Logic of Scientific Discovery.* New York: Harper and Row.

Ransom, John Crowe 1968. 'Criticism, Inc.,' in *The World's Body.* Baton Rouge: Louisiana State University Press.

Richards, I. A. 1925. *Principles of Literary Criticism.* New York: Harcourt, Brace and World.

Toulmin, Stephen 1972. *Human Understanding: The Collective Use and Evolution of Concepts.* Princeton: Princeton University Press.

Veysey, Laurence R. 1965. *The Emergence of the American University.* Chicago: University of Chicago Press.

Wellek, René 1967. *Concepts of Criticism.* New Haven: Yale University Press.

Wellek, René and Warren, Austin 1956. *Theory of Literature.* New York: Harcourt, Brace and World.

THE HIGHS AND THE LOWS
OF BLACK FEMINIST CRITICISM

(1990)

In her essay, "In Search of Our Mothers' Gardens," Alice Walker asked the questions, "What is *my* literary tradition? Who are the black women artists who preceded me? Do I have a ground to stand on?" Confronted by centuries of Afro-American women who, but for an exceptional few, lived under conditions antithetical to the creation of Art as it was then defined, how could she claim a creative legacy of foremothers, women who after all had no access to the pen, to paints, or to clay? If American cultural history was accurate, singing was the only art form in which black women participated.

But Walker turned the *idea* of Art on its head. Instead of looking high, she suggested, we should look low. On that low ground she found a multitude of artist-mothers—the women who'd transformed the material to which they'd had access into their conception of Beauty: cooking, gardening, quilting, storytelling. In retrieving that low ground, Walker not only reclaimed her foremothers, she pointed to a critical approach. For she reminded us that Art, and the thought and sense of beauty on which it is based, is the province not only of those with a room of their own, or of those in libraries, universities and literary Renaissances—that *creating* is necessary to those who work in kitchens and factories, nurture children and adorn homes, sweep streets or harvest crops, type in offices and manage them.

In the early seventies when anyone asked me, "What do you think you're doing anyway? What is this Black Feminist Literary Critic thing you're trying to become?" I would immediately think of Alice's essay.

Like any other critic, my personal history has much to do with what I hear when I read. Perhaps because I am from the Caribbean, Alice's *high* and *low* struck chords in me. I'd grown up with a sharp division between the "high" thought, language, behavior expected in school and in church, and the "low" language that persisted at home and in the yards and the streets.

> *In school:* Proper English, Romanesque sentences, Western philosophy, jargon and exegesis; boys always before girls, lines and lines; "My Country 'Tis of Thee," the authority of the teacher.
> *In church:* Unintelligible Latin and Greek, the canon, the text; the Virgin Mary and the nuclear family; priests always before nuns; Gregorian chant and tiptoeing.

At home: Bad English, raunchy sayings and stories, the intoning of toasts; women in the kitchen, the parlor *and* the market; kallaloo, loud supper talk, cousins, father, aunts, godmothers.

In the yards: Sashaying and bodies, sweat, calypso, long talk and plenty voices; women and men bantering, bad words, politics and bambooshaying.

What is real? The high, though endured, was valued. The low, though enjoyed, was denigrated even by the lowest of the low.

As I read *Jane Eyre*, I wondered what women dreamt as they gazed at men and at the sea. I knew that women as well as men gazed. My mother and aunts constantly assessed men's bodies, the sea's rhythm. But Charlotte Brontë was in print. She had a language across time and space. I could not find my mother's language, far less her attitude, in any books, despite the fact that her phrasing was as complex and as subtle as Charlotte's.

Because of the 1950s (which for me was not the Eisenhower years but rather the Civil Rights movement, rhythm 'n' blues, and the works of James Baldwin), because of the 1960s (which for me was not the Free Speech Movement and the Weathermen, but rather SNCC, SEEK, the Black Muslims, Aretha and the Black Arts Movement), the *low* began to be valued by some of us. Yet there remained the high and the low for many black women. Camouflaged by the rhetoric of the period, we were, on high ground, a monolithic Harriet Tubman or a silent Queen of Africa; on low ground, we were creaming sapphires or bourgeois bitches.

But what were *we* saying, writing? By the early seventies, I knew some black women had written, I'd read Phillis Wheatley, Gwendolyn Brooks, and Lorraine Hansberry. I'd heard poets like Nikki Giovanni and June Jordan read. I'd known women in my childhood and adolescence who'd written stories. Yet I had never, in my years of formal schooling from kindergarten in the black Virgin Islands through a Ph.D. at white Columbia, heard even the name of *one* black woman writer. That women writers were studied, I knew. I'd had courses in which Jane Austen, George Elliot, Emily Dickinson, and Virginia Woolf appeared like fleeting phantoms. I knew the university knew that black writers existed. My professors bristled at the names of Richard Wright and James Baldwin and barely acknowledged Langston Hughes and Ralph Ellison.

But what of black women writers? No phantoms, no bristlings—not even a mention. Few of us knew they wrote; fewer of us cared. In fact, who even perceived of us, as late as the early 1970s, as writers, artists, thinkers? Why should anyone want to know what we thought or imagined? What could we tell others, far less show them, that they did not already know? After all, weren't we, as Mister taunts Celie, "black," "pore," woman, and therefore "nothing at all"?

Of course we were telling stories, playing with language, speculating and specifying, reaching for wisdom, transforming the universe in our image.

Who but us would end a harrowing tale with these words to her tormentors?

Frado has passed from their memories as Joseph from the butler's but she will never cease to track them *till* beyond mortal vision. (Harriet Wilson, *Our Nig*)

Who but us could use the image of a Plum Bun for the intersection of racism and sexism in this country? (Jessie Fauset, *Plum Bun*)

Who but us could begin her story with this comment?

Now, women forget all those things they don't want to remember and remember everything they don't want to forget. The dream is the truth. Then they act and do things accordingly. (Zora Neale Hurston, *Their Eyes Were Watching God*)

Who but us could lovingly present women poets in the kitchen? (Paule Marshall, *Poets in the Kitchen*)

Who but us could tell how it was possible to clean the blood off [our] beaten men and yet receive abuse from the victim? (Toni Morrison, *The Bluest Eye*)

Who but us could chant:
momma/momma/mammy/nanny/granny/
woman/mistress/sista luv
(June Jordan, "Trying to Get Over")

But who knew that we knew? Even those of us who were telling stories or writing did not always see ourselves as artists of the word. And those of us who did know our genius were so rejected, unheard that we sometimes became crazy women crying in the wind or silenced scarecrows. Who could answer us but us?

For us did need us if only to validate that which we knew, we knew. The publications of first novels, Toni Morrison's *The Bluest Eye*, Alice Walker's *The Third Life of Grange Copeland*, June Jordan's *His Own Where*, heralded the decade of the seventies. While their novels were barely acknowledged in 1970, the movement of women all over the world was highlighted by American women who had some access to the Big Capital Media. Inspired though sometimes disappointed, by movements of people of color, of blacks in the United States, of liberation struggles of "underdeveloped" nations, some American women began to seek themselves as women and to protest the truncated definition of woman in this society. In this context the literature of women, the critical responses of women were published as never before during a decade when many others were asserting that *The* Movement was dead.

For those of us who came out of the sixties, the vision of women moving all over the world was not solely a claiming of our rights but also the rights of all those who had been denied their humanity. In the space created for us by our foremothers, by our sisters in the streets, the houses, the factories, the schools, we were now able to speak and to listen to each other, to hear our own language, to refine and critique it across time and space, through the written word. For me that dialogue *is* the kernel of what a black feminist literary critic tries to do. We listen to those of us who speak, write, read, to those who have written, to those who may write. We write to those who write, read, speak, may write, and we try to hear the voiceless. We are participants in a many-voiced palaver of thought/feeling, image/language that moves us to *move*—toward a world where, like Alice Walker's revolutionary petunias, all of us can bloom.

We found that in order to move beyond prescribed categories we had to "rememory"—reconstruct our past. But in the literary church of the sixties, such an appeal to history was anathema. Presiding at the altar were the new critic priests, for whom the text was God, unstained by history, politics, experience, the world. Art for them was artifact. So, for example, the literature of blacks could not be literature, tainted as it was by what they called sociology. To the side of the altar were the pretenders, the political revolutionaries and new philosophers for whom creative works were primarily a pretext to expound their own ideas, their world programs. For both groups, women were neither the word nor the world, though sometimes we could be dots on some i's, muses or furies in the service of the text or the idea.

We found that we could not talk to either group unless we talked their talk, which was specialized, abstract—on high ground. So we learned their language only to find that its character had a profound effect on the questions we thought, the images we evoked, and that such thinking recalled a tradition beyond which we had to move if *we* were to be included in any authentic dialogue.

Because language is one (though not the only) way to express what one knows/ feels even when one doesn't know one knows it, because storytelling *is* a dynamic form of remembering/re-creating, we found that it was often in the relationship between literatures and the world that re-visioning occurred. It is often in the poem, the story, the play, rather than in Western philosophical theorizing, that feminist thought/feeling evolves, challenges and renews itself. So our Sisterbonding was presented and celebrated in novels like *Sula*, our body/spirit/erotic in works like *The Color Purple*, our revision of biography in works like *Zami*. It has often been through our literatures that women have renamed critical areas of human life: mothering, sexuality, bodies, friendship, spirituality, economics, the process of literature itself. And it was to these expressions that many of us turned in order to turn to ourselves as situated in a dynamic rather than a fixed world. For many of us such a turning led us to universities where words, ideas, are, were supposed to be nurtured and valued.

And—ah, here's the rub.

As a result of that gravitation, we *have* moved to excavate the past and restore to ourselves the words of many of our foremothers who were buried in the rumble of distorted history. We have questioned the idea of great works of literature, preferences clearly determined by a powerful elite. We have asked why some forms are not considered literature—for example, the diary, the journal, the letter. We have built journals and presses through which the works of women might be published. We have developed women's studies programs. Using our stories and images, we have taught our daughters and sons about ourselves, our sisters, brothers, and lovers about our desires. And some of us have shared a palaver with our writers/readers that prompts us all to re-vision ourselves.

Yet even as we moved, the high, the low persisted, in fact moved further and further apart. For we now confronted the revelations we always knew, that there is both a She and there are many she's. And that sometimes, in our work we seemed to reduce the *both-and* to *either-or*. That revelation made itself strongly felt in the exclusion that women of color protested when Woman was defined, in the rejection that many working-class women experienced when Woman was described. The awareness that we too seek to homogenize the world of our Sisters, to fix ourselves in boxes and categories through jargon, theory, abstraction, is upon us.

Why so? Has our training led us back to the high ground that has rejected us, our education to the very language that masked our existence? So often feminist literary discussion seems riveted on defining Woman in much the same way that Western medieval scholars tried to define God. Why is it that rather than acknowledge that we are both-and, we persist in seeking the either-or. Might that be because the either-or construction, the either-or deconstruction, is so embedded in our education? Might it be because that language, whether it moves us anywhere or not, is recognized, rewarded as brilliant, intellectual, high, in contrast to the low, vulgar, ordinary language of most creative writers and readers? Is it that we too are drawn to the power that resides on the high ground?

Even as we turned to our literatures, in which language is not merely an object but is always situated in a context, in which the pleasure and emotion of language are as important as its meaning, we have gravitated toward a critical language that is riddled with abstraction and is as distanced as possible from the creative work, and from pleasure. I sometimes wonder if we critics read stories and poems, or, if as our language indicates, our reading fare is primarily that of other critics and philosophers? Do we know our own literatures? Why, for example, does it appear that white feminist critics have abandoned their contemporary novelists? Where is the palaver among them? Or are Freud, Lacan, Barthes, Foucault, Derrida inevitably more appealing? Why are we so riveted on male thinkers, preferably dead and European? Why is it that in refuting essence, we become so fixed on essence? To whom are we writing when we write? Have we turned so far round that we have completed our circle? Is it that we no longer see any connections between the emotion/knowing language of women's literature, the many-voiced sounds of our own language and the re-visioning we seek?

Now when I think of Alice's *high* and *low*, I feel a new meaning. Because I am a black literary/feminist critic, I live in a sharp distinction between the high world of lit crit books, journals, and conferences, the middle world of classrooms and graduate students, and the low world of bookstores, kitchens, communities, and creative writers.

> *In the high world*: Discourse, theory, the canon, the body, the boys (preferably Lacan, Derrida, and Foucault) before the girls; linguistics, the authority of the critic, the exclusion of creative writings.
>
> *In the middle world*: Reading the texts, sometimes of creative writers; negotiating between advancement and appreciation; tropes, research, discourse; now I understand my mother; narrative strategies. What does it mean? The race for theory.
>
> *In the low world*: Stories, poems, plays. The language of the folk. Many bodies—the feeling as one with June, Alice, Toni.

> I sure know what she's talking about.
> I don't want to hear that.
> Her words move me.
> That poem changed my life.
>
> I dream like that.
> That's really disturbing.

> God—that's beautiful.
> Perhaps I'm not so crazy after all.
> I want to write too.
> Say what?

Much, of course, can be learned by all of us from all of us who speak, read, write, including those of us who look high. But as we look high, we might also look low, lest we devalue women in the world even as we define *Woman*. In ignoring their voices, we may not only truncate our movement but we may also limit our own process until our voices no longer sound like women's voices to anyone.

CONFINEMENTS:

The Domestic in the Discourses of Upper-Middle-Class Pregnancy

(1996)

About two years ago, in my seventh month of pregnancy, and halfway through my semester-long course on Jane Austen and Charlotte Brontë—these serve as my calendars and my aids to memory—I found myself teaching a Foucauldian reading of *Northanger Abbey*,[1] trying and failing to explain Paul Morrison's concept of the "domestic carceral" to my students. The class, largely made up of women deeply invested in the euphoric marriage plot and a sense of the ever-expanding domestic spaces it created for women's sexual and social triumph, resisted for the full ninety minutes Morrison's interrogation of the politics of home.

In *Northanger Abbey* the heroine, Catherine Moreland, an avid reader of gothic novels, finds herself in the bedroom of a dark castle owned by the father of the man she loves. Like the gothic heroines upon whom she models herself, she cautiously explores her surroundings, finding, as it happens, a large cabinet, which, according to gothic convention, should contain something crucial to the gothic plot: a mysterious document, probably a will or a confession, or perhaps even a body. Catherine opens the cabinet with some difficulty; it is, to all appearances, empty. As she fumbles for a secret drawer, however, her hand closes on a rolled-up manuscript. Just as she is about to read the document, her candle is snuffed by a gust of wind. Terrified, Catherine retreats to bed. The next morning, Catherine reads the manuscript by the light of day:

> Her greedy eye glanced rapidly over a page. She started at its import. Could it be possible, or did not her senses play her false?—An inventory of linen, in coarse and modern characters, seemed all that was before her! If the evidence of sight might be trusted, she held a washing-bill in her hand.[2]

The deflation from the gothic to the domestic brings not only comfort but shame. Catherine feels "humbled to the dust" that she could have imagined that a room so "modern, so habitable," could have contained anything like the horrors she had imagined for herself the previous night. The room, then, with its modern furniture, its domestic comforts, acts as a visual guarantee against the incursion of the past and of the gothic. Drained of its gothic possibilities the room simply signifies benignly the concept of home.

The humor and the moral of the scene both depend on the contrast between the gothic and the domestic, between the horror of the trunk that holds the dead body and the mundanity of the trunk that holds laundry. Feminist critics have argued in fact that, for women at least, this is no simple opposition, and that the laundry list and the laundry which represent both locus and the method of female oppression are as dangerous to the well-being of a heroine as the ghost or the dead body.[3] The laundry list, as a sign not only of domestic duty but of surveillance, of the listing and categorization of "dirty linen," threatens the female body from a number of directions. The fact that the laundry list belongs to the future husband of our heroine's future sister-in-law also suggests a double or triple entanglement in the marriage plot which itself becomes sign and method of surveillance.

The phrase "domestic carceral" points to women's imprisonment in the home and in the marriage plot and away from a teleology which sees home and marriage as benign alternatives to a gothic world of ghosts, robbers, and rapists who come in from outside. The phrase begins to explain a series of cultural truths which bear the uneasy and contradictory status of proverbs and surprises: most accidents happen at home; a woman is more likely to be physically attacked by her husband than by a stranger.

It was these truths I took with me in my brief walk across the street to Methodist Hospital where I, like so many other women of my social class and stage of pregnancy, was attending a series of "birthing classes" preparatory to my delivery. This was to be an especially interesting day; our class was to take a tour of Methodist Hospital's famous and heavily advertised homelike "birthing suites," complete with Jacuzzis, cherry furniture, and pull-out couches for the expectant father.

Trailing behind our childbirth educator, we paused at the threshold of one particular room to admire its many and resplendent domestic accoutrements: the armoire, the rocking chair, the chintz-covered sofa, the private bath. If the room looked a little like a motel, it was the kind of motel which looks most like home. If it didn't look exactly like my home, or any home that one might visit, it looked—except of course for the I.V. stand and the fetal monitor snuggled against the wall and in between the pieces of matching furniture—like the home one might have if one were, say, a cleaner and neater person.

One brave man broke the hush of desire provoked in us by the room and by the specter of the perfect birth by which it was inhabited. "What," he asked, "actually happens during delivery?" Our leader paused dramatically before pushing a button on the cherry bedstead, and the room began to move. First, the bed, creaking like the door of a medieval castle, began slowly to fold up until its head was perpendicular to the floor and the foot had moved back to form the seat of a high and narrow chair. Next, a panel in the ceiling opened and metal equipment began first to unfold and then to descend. As the equipment locked noiselessly into place, part of it was revealed to be a huge surgical lamp which lowered itself to within about a foot of the now-rumpled surface of the bed. Finally, the nurse opened the door of the armoire to produce a pair of huge black metal stirrups, which she proceeded to attach to slits at the foot of the bed. The living room was now an operating room oddly crowded with remnants from the showroom of

Ethan Allen or its perhaps more appropriately named Houston counterpart, Finger's.

As the gothic apparatus descended, my first thought was to flee the scene. I looked around at the other expectant parents for confirmation of a sudden almost overwhelming fear. They seemed to me impressed, cheerful, absolutely at home with it all. I was edging towards the door when the nurse announced the next stop on the tour: "Next we'll have a look at where you'll be taken if, God forbid, something should go wrong," she said, knocking on what I can now swear was the imitation cherry. "Let's go look at where you'll go if you have a cesarian." She ushered us down a narrow hallway whose plum wallpaper gave way suddenly to greenish tile. "The rooms on that side look like normal hospital rooms, nothing special about them," the nurse explained. "Do you have any questions or comments except 'please God, don't let it be me?'"

Was I the only one praying for the green tile and the "normal operating room"? Was I the only one who never wanted to snuggle down in that nightmare of a trick bed or to give birth in a room where everything folded out, up, or down in the process of turning into something else? I think I was the only one who muttered "Foucault" to my husband as the two of us slunk back past the peaches, plums, and cherries of the birthing suite and back to Rice, where two days later I was able, with the help of the folding bed, for the first time to explain the domestic carceral to my students.

The point of this anecdote as I tell it here is to outline a methodological problem involving the place of the reproductive female body in our culture. The birthing suite and the liberal culture of pregnancy management in which it is embedded offer the promise of safety, domesticity, and control. The birthing suite itself, with its overt visual references to home and to the nexus of comforts which that word however problematically suggests, serves as the topographical centerpiece to the happy story of female autonomy. By replicating home in the hospital, the birthing suite keeps terror at bay. The irony of the hospital-as-home is, of course, twofold. The closets of the birthing suites, unlike the cabinet in *Northanger Abbey*, are, in fact, filled with the gothic apparatus of medicine; the birthing suite only looks like home. More importantly, however, the hospital-as-home depends, as does the parody in *Northanger Abbey*, on an uneasy vision of the home as safe place; in this respect, the gestures of homeliness, whether they succeed or fail in their referentiality, point to the dangers which lurk in and indeed define so many American homes: poverty, abuse, malnutrition, patriarchy. One cannot escape the discipline of the body by invoking the site of that discipline: it is at home, after all, that women embark on diets, read the magazines which produce the desire for that dieting, shave their legs and tease their hair, do or do not have sex, and painfully negotiate the conflicting demands of femininity.

Despite increasing feminist awareness of the dangers associated with home, much feminist and protofeminist discussion of pregnancy and childbirth derives its power and its idiom from a deeply middle-class and heterosexual ideal of domesticity. The remainder of this chapter will look at two exemplary sites of that idiom: the discourse of the home birth movement, and the rhetoric of the contemporary pregnancy advice book. In the first section I will look at how and at what cost home gets constructed as a place of safety and autonomy for women, while in the second, through a close reading of one bestselling advice book, I look at how home becomes both site and instrument of the policing of pregnant women.

In much of the literature of the home birth movement, as well as in feminist and protofeminist accounts of home birth in more general contexts, home functions as a synecdoche for female autonomy; it becomes the place not only of comfort but of power and freedom. As Sheila Kitzinger puts it:

> An overwhelming advantage of home birth is that you control the territory in which birth takes place, and those helping you are guests in your home. You can move around just as you want, eat and drink, take a bath, or go out for a walk—do whatever you feel like doing.[4]

Home functions in this enabling fantasy as a place of free choice over one's body, a context safe for the exercise of will, body, and desire. The power of the fantasy lies in its sometimes explicit, always implicit contrast to the scene of the hospital, where, as numerous feminist writers on childbirth point out, a woman routinely hands over power to the institution. The romanticization of home as a place of security may well be as premature as it is—more on this later—nostalgic; according to Pamela S. Eakins's study of women who chose home birth, most "(w)omen selecting to give birth outside the hospital were not as interested in maintaining the comforts of home as they were in avoiding the 'stark and regimented' hospital environment."[5] In other words, home itself is a relative value.

Despite the instability of home as signifier, many feminist books on childbirth are structured by a now familiar history, a narrative of devolution from the halcyon days of home births attended by midwives to the medicalized and doctor-controlled present. The shift in this first narrative typically takes place somewhere at the beginning of the nineteenth century when the professionalization of medicine allowed doctors to ban midwives from the bedsides of birthing women.[6] This framing and defining historical narrative can also be condensed to fit the span of one woman's lifetime; Jessica Mitford's *The American Way of Birth* begins with the story of her four increasingly medicalized experiences of childbirth, the first and most fondly remembered of which took place at home.[7] Whatever the chronological scope of the framing narrative, the move from home to hospital is a crucial structural element in the devolution of Western obstetrics. Mirror narratives of recuperation and evolution begin with unsatisfactory hospital births and move toward a home or more homelike birth; this kind of narrative, which we see for example in Nancy Wainer Cohen and Lois J. Estner's study of cesarian deliveries, *Silent Knife*, seeks literally to undo the dubious progress of obstetrics and to recapture some ordinary or natural state.[8]

Central to this devolutionary narrative is an embedded history of the revalencing of home and hospital with respect to safety and danger. While at different historical moments, for different populations,[9] the hospital has signified safety for the birthing woman, in feminist analyses the hospital figures as a place of physical and psychological danger, a place where unnecessary interventions threaten a woman's health, life, and sense of well-being. Home and hospital, then, become, in the debates between feminists and the medical profession, sites, not only of contested notions of safety, but of referential exchange, where the term "danger" shifts from one location to the other. The marshaling of statistics in support of either position is a murky business, partly because proponents of home birth want only, for obvious reasons, to count planned home births, while official statistics include all births taking place in a noninstitutional setting.[10] Ann Oakley, in her rich and informative feminist history of pregnancy, *The Captured Womb*, does not even try to untangle the numbers produced by different claims; in an otherwise exhaustively detailed analysis, she remarks only that "the argument about the relative safety of domiciliary and institutional confinement still flourishes in the 1980s. Just as important as the statistics of mortality themselves is the matter of what people make of them."[11]

Analysis of the safety of home birth, then, becomes quickly embedded in an analysis of the rhetoric of both sides of the debate and ultimately, I would argue, in the rhetorical status of home.

Kitzinger and others are quick to point out the degree to which medical culture has, for affluent women at least, co-opted the rhetoric of home and autonomy in their advertisements and particularly in their birthing suites. As Kitzinger notes:

> Decor and furnishings are an insufficient guide to attitudes. There are hospitals where women are offered flowery curtains, patchwork quilts, a special birthing bed or chair, and soft music, where all this is merely a facade for interventionist obstetric practice. In a commercial system, where medical care is another commodity competing in the open market, some hospitals provide these pleasant rooms to persuade women not to have their babies at home, in out-of-hospital birthing centers, or in rival hospitals. (*YB* 169)

Barbara Katz Rothman, in her analysis of various elements of what she calls "natural birth," sees birthing suites with their "flowered linen, photomurals on the walls, and candle-lit postpartum dinners," as competing with home birth through appropriation of the signs of domesticity.[12] While Kitzinger, Rothman, and others are rightly suspicious of hospitals' imitation of "home," they do not take their suspicion a step further into the rhetoric of home itself. They do not mention, for example, that most people's homes are in fact themselves inadequate approximations of the domestic ideal made visible by hospital birthing suites. The problematic nature of the domestic ideal is revealed through a paradox in the statistics about the social class of women who give birth at home. Home births are by far the most common in three groups with very different relations to medical culture: upper-middle-class college educated women who plan a home birth because of a feminist or protofeminist critique of medical ideology; conservative and/or religious women who come from patriarchal family structures which emphasize the privacy of the family and the supervision of the father, and poor and/or extremely young women who have had little prenatal care.[13] The teleologies of these women's births meet at home, or rather, in a series of very different homes with different relations, among other things, to privacy, safety, and power. While I am, of course, not arguing that home is, for middle-class women, exempt from the forces of institutional power—as I hope I make clear in the concluding section of this chapter—"home" might be an especially fraught term for a teenage unwed mother trying to hide her pregnancy from her family by delivering in the bathroom.

While only a small percentage of middle-class women choose home birth, home is nonetheless an important site in much of the contemporary literature about childbirth. Advice literature about pregnancy and childbirth constructs, by definition, a domestic site of information as an alternative to the doctor's or midwife's office. Framed sometimes as resistant and sometimes as a supplement to visits to the doctor's office and to the medical management of pregnancy, these books emphasize a woman's access to information within the confines of her own domestic space. They also of course have things to say *about* home and its role in pregnancy and birth: these books routinely make suggestions about diet, furnishing, sex, and clothing, helping and/or coercing women to reconfigure their relations to domestic spaces and activities.

While much recent work on advice literature has focused on the construction of normative femininity through the body, there has so far been very little emphasis on the relation of these books to notions of home and domestic space. Nancy Armstrong, in her introduction to the collection *The Ideology of Conduct*, points to but does not explore the double valence of home in the phrase "domestic surveillance," which she uses to describe the historical function of conduct books.[14] The term simultaneously suggests a surveillance *of* and *from* the home, a literal internalization of disciplinary norms.

The policing of and from the home by advice books directed at middle-class women works as a more subtle alternative to the more literal policing of the working-class home and the working class pregnant mother within the home. That tradition becomes most visible, although it does not begin, with the implementation of home visitation for pregnant women in England at the beginning of the twentieth century. Ann Oakley sees the spread of home visitation as an indication of a paradigm shift in which the state was newly envisioned as having a stake in the health of pregnant women and in antenatal care. The advice book, aimed at a more affluent audience than home visitation, similarly uses the home as a place for education into cultural ideologies of pregnancy, with this difference: it does its work in the name of autonomy and choice.

As my reading of the bestselling advice book *What to Expect When You're Expecting* will suggest, this manual is deeply invested in constructing a middle-class heterosexual domestic space for the education of women into pregnancy.[15] The woman sitting on the cover in a rocking chair is not, interestingly enough, taking care of a baby or preparing either the baby's room or the healthy food upon which the book is so insistent; instead, she sits in the rocker, an open book in her hand, reflecting, perhaps, on something she has just read. The message of the cover is clear; the book in the mother's lap literally precedes the baby; its presence signifies a prepared pregnancy as surely as a plump baby would signify a successful birth. The book represents the baby in two senses: first iconically, as it renders what is inside the mother's body both visible and visual, and second, in a more traditionally political sense, where the book represents the baby by becoming its advocate. To be pregnant here is to read, to be pregnant with knowledge about pregnancy. The book has entered and constructed the home, has come to rest upon and has all but entered the mother's body as it announces its necessary role in the project of bodily reconstruction.

Sometimes called "the Yuppie Bible of Pregnancy," *What to Expect When You're Expecting* by Arlene Eisenberg, Heidi Eisenberg Nurkoff, and Sandy Eisenberg Hathaway is a resolutely upbeat book organized simultaneously by two competing structures: a developmental narrative which takes the reader from the first through the last weeks of pregnancy, and a question and answer format. Every sign of its intended audience, from the blonde woman rocking on the cover, to its continual invocation of the husband of the expectant mother, to its assumptions about restaurants, indicates that it is targeting a white, upper-middle-class heterosexual audience. The book routinely imagines and invokes a white married woman with money to spend on babysitters, vacations, and eating out.

What to Expect does exhibit certain crucial markers of the specifically feminist self-help book with its roots in the women's health movement of the 1960s and 1970s. Its many diagrams of the female body in various stages of pregnancy, its familiar and experiential tone, and its rhetorical insistence on choice and variation suggest ancestral ties to books like *Our Bodies, Ourselves* which derive from an explicitly feminist project. The later text's use of the concept of autonomy is, however, deeply imbricated in a literally developmental narrative which climaxes at the time of labor and delivery. Like much feminist, protofeminist, and just plain yuppie material on pregnancy, *What to Expect* largely confines the idea of choice to the last few weeks of pregnancy, to the "choice" of various kinds of labor and delivery.

My reading of *What to Expect* focusses on those months before labor and delivery where the concept of the mother's autonomy is entirely absent as the book both enacts and prescribes a constant surveillance of her behaviors. The mother's every move, whether it be taking a bite of dessert or choosing underpants, is carefully inspected, calibrated, and quantified with respect to the baby inside her.[16]

Nowhere is this inspection more evident than in the book's repeated and sometimes repetitive discussions of food and eating. Although the book is reassuring on the subject of X rays, alcohol, and even drugs in the first chapter, food is fraught with danger to the baby. Indeed, the rhetoric of the book positions the baby as the person eating, the mother as a conduit. The introduction to the section on the "Best-Odds Diet" subtitled "Make Every Bite Count" explains:

> You've got only nine months of meals and snacks with which to give your baby the best possible start in life. Make every one of them count. Before you close your mouth on a forkful of food, consider, "Is this the best I can give my baby?" If it will benefit your baby, chew away. If it'll benefit only your sweet tooth or appease your appetite, put your fork down. (76)

This passage sets up two patterns which will recur throughout the book. The first has to do with a particular reproductive calendar which emphasizes the temporal limitation and places the onus of producing a healthy child on the nine months of pregnancy. The warning that the expectant mother has "only nine months" to give the baby a "healthy start" privileges pregnancy over parenting and the fetus over the child. Moreover, it replicates in its rhetorical idiom the "biological clock" which ticks anxiously below the surface of most advice books to professional women and links the discourse of pregnancy to the discourse on infertility. Even pregnancy, which, the book admits in other sections, may seem interminable to the mother, becomes translated into the idiom of time pressure. In fact, *What to Expect* is not extreme with respect to this collapsed calendar; several pregnancy manuals, most notably Janice Graham's *Your Pregnancy Companion*, begin before pregnancy, or with the period of two weeks or so when women are actually pregnant but do not yet know it. This period, is, according to Graham, especially fraught with danger to the developing fetus. As she explains in her introduction, where she collapses the two periods mentioned above:

> The idea of "preconception health" is still very new, but the concept is rooted in the belief that many problems occur before most women even realize they are pregnant. . . . In these weeks, the embryo is in its most rapid state of development: all the fetal organs are forming and virtually millions of cells are dividing and differentiating. And during this critical stage of fetal growth and development, it is believed that the healthier a mother's body, life-style, and environment are, the lower the risk that something will go wrong.[17]

As the calendar gets pushed back the onus on the mother becomes greater. Characteristically, this burden is invoked in the name of reassurance: " . . . you can't imagine how planning ahead can make for an easier pregnancy psychologically; there is so much less to worry about or brood over when you know you've provided a pristine environment for your unborn baby from day one" (*YPC* 4).

The second emerging pattern in the passage from *What to Expect* has to do with an opposition between the baby and the expectant mother. Like other tensions in the book, this one surfaces most acutely in the discourse around food. The passage positions the baby's health against the mother's "appetites." While for economically disadvantaged women this battle will take place over illegal drugs, particularly over crack, the yuppie mother is represented as working through this problem over food.

While there is some mention of a possible of problems associated with alcohol in an introductory section on Fetal Alcohol Syndrome, alcoholics and "heavy drinkers" are excised from the text early on by being referred to counseling or to Alcoholics Anonymous. Although alcohol does reappear on several occasions in the month-by-month accounts which make up the body of the book, it is usually relegated to a dependent clause in discussions of *What to Expect*'s more vexing consumable—food. The long and detailed section on eating out begins "For most pregnant women it isn't substituting Perrier for the two martinis that poses a challenge at business lunches (or when dining out after hours); it's trying to put together a meal that's nutritionally sound from a menu of cream sauces, elegant but empty starches, and tempting sweets" (159). That "most pregnant women" do not go out to expensive business lunches seems too obvious to mention here; "most pregnant women," even those with good jobs, are not regularly confronted with the agonizing choice between "elegant but empty starches" and nutritionally sound meals. By placing the problem of alcohol during pregnancy in the context of the two-martini lunch, the authors manage oddly enough both to trivialize the issue of alcohol abuse and effectively to police all drinking of alcoholic beverages. By speaking only parenthetically about the problem, they suggest that the prohibition on alcohol has been so efficiently internalized that it needs no more discussion. Again, this has a disorientingly double effect, demonizing women who cannot dismiss alcohol from their lives in one dependent clause by suggesting that it is not a problem for "most women," and stressing the impossibility of any discussion of how much alcohol is too much.

The opposition between mother and fetus actually places the latter in the position of monitor. Although agency is not ascribed to the fetus in this process, its very helplessness turns it into a branch of the police; its agency, in fact, derives from its inability to act. This conflict is rhetorically resolved by the disappearance of the mother's body; every forkful of food is imagined as going directly to the fetus. When confronted with the problem of resisting Grandma's special brownies, for example, the expectant mother is advised to say something like "I'm sorry, but baby's too young to eat brownies." The very identification of mother as grandmother places the fetus in the role of fully imagined and resisting personhood. The disappearance of the mother also oddly suggests that the pregnancy is in fact over; the phrase, "Is this the best I can give my baby?" evokes a child already outside the womb, a child who is "fed" in a more literal sense. The reproductive calendar, then, contracts even further as the baby is represented as being in some sense *already born*.

If the baby polices implicitly, the father is imagined as doing so explicitly. In the section entitled "Fathers Are Expectant Too," the authors discuss the husband's role in the wife's diet. Although a subtitle warns the father, "Don't Be Too Preachy," the husband/father is clearly expected to enforce good eating habits:

> If she slips, nagging will only help her to fall faster and farther. Remind, don't remonstrate. Prod her conscience, don't try to become it. Signal her quietly when in public, rather than making a pointed announcement to all within earshot about her ordering her chicken breaded and fried. Most important, do it with a sense of humor and a lot of love. (326)

The threat of falling with which this paragraph begins brings us back to what seems clearly to be a sexualized image of "appetite" in the paragraph I quoted earlier. While it would be too simple to see eating simply as a code for sex here or elsewhere, the fall into desire of all sorts is a terrible specter and an efficient way of enforcing control. It is especially interesting to contrast the hysteria of the opening sentence with the reassuring passage on literal falling, where the authors reassure women who stumble in the street how well protected the fetus is and how little chance there is of actual harm even from the most spectacular accident.

The images of privacy and publicity which structure this paragraph are especially open to a rereading through the domestic carceral. While the fear expressed toward the end of the passage is humiliation in public, it seems clear that in private the husband can feel freer to correct his wife's food choices. Home becomes in effect a house of correction, a place where a husband can, by implication, be "pointed" in his criticism of his wife's tastes in chicken.

The emphasis on the dangers of leaving one's house are apparent in the emphasis on guidelines for "eating out." The reader is repeatedly warned about the issue of control in restaurants. Desserts, for example, should probably not even be attempted outside the home. Although the best-odds diet permits fruit and unsweetened whipped cream on the side, women are told to wait and to "indulge in sugar-free best-odds treats when you get home." Home, it seems, also has a national dimension. A boxed inset helpfully lists national cuisines in order of healthiness: American and Continental, not surprisingly, top the list. In a truly startling moment of xenophobia, the reader is instructed to avoid Chinese, Japanese, German, and Mexican food. No mention is made of the fact that millions of healthy babies are born each year to mothers who eat only the cuisine of these particular countries and that for several of these countries the infant mortality rate, to use only one measure of postnatal health, is considerably better than it is in the United States.

What to Expect's concern with food is, of course, inextricably linked to issues of weight gain and body image in pregnancy. While, again, the overt message is reassuring and indeed celebratory of the pregnant body, the underlying message is more anxious. The authors first tackle the issue of appropriate weight gain in response to the following "question": "I only gained one pound in my first trimester. My friend, who's also pregnant, gained six. What's enough, and what's too much?" The structure of the answer is absolutely typical of the anxious doublespeak which pervades *What to Expect*:

> Weight gain that is just enough for one woman may be too much or too little for another. The extremely underweight woman is probably doing her baby a favor by gaining six pounds (as long as they're gained by eating highly nutritious food) in the first trimester, or doing him or her an injustice by gaining only one. The obese mother-to-be, on the other hand, is doing no one a favor by gaining weight rapidly, and can probably afford to gain only one pound (or even none) in the first trimester (as long as she eats adequate amounts of nutritious foods) without jeopardizing her baby's health. For the woman who is average, however, six pounds is probably too much and one is not enough. Two to four would be just right. (122)

The passage begins, like so many others in this text, with a cheery relativism and the implication that one should not compare oneself to other women. Pregnancy, according to this narrative, is an individual matter; no one can set the standards for any one else—except, of course, the expert answerer of questions. The tone of the paragraph follows a downward spiral through a series of parentheses, qualifications, warnings, and aberrations, until the average woman is admonished in the final sentence. Since the questions are, in fact, made up by the authors, it is interesting that they choose a negative example—negative at least for the "average woman." As the tone becomes darker, the scale of what is appropriate narrows, and the difference between one and two pounds, one bleary morning misreading, one forbidden cupcake, swells to become, as it were, pregnant with meaning. Since the hypothetical woman asking the question does not tell us whether she is "seriously underweight" or "obese," she and the reader are admonished with the "average"; since if she were underweight or obese she would be aberrant in any case, this hypothetical woman is rendered abnormal in some sense through any of the passages' calculations: she is either, it seems, obese, in which case her original weight was a problem, or "average," in which case she has gained too little. I emphasize the arithmetic of this answer only because these are no-win equations whose application can only have an anxiety-producing effect. Even wading through the inverted syntax and the parentheses—not to mention the arithmetic—is difficult. The inevitable result ratifies the anxiety of calculation.

Also remarkable in this passage are the allusions to doing someone—first the baby and then, in the case of the obese woman, anyone at all—"a favor." This, of course, gets us back to the language of body image and sexuality. The woman herself is never named as one of the people receiving or not receiving the "favor"; in the case of the obese woman the "no one" seems to point to a third person, to the husband or father. The authors do reply specifically to a question about the relation of the wife's weight gain to her sexual attractiveness. Interestingly, this occurs in the section on expectant fathers and the question is posed in the voice of the husband: "As petty as this might seem, I'm afraid my wife's going to get fat and flabby with pregnancy, and stay that way afterward." The answer is in many ways a canny one which opens with a statement about the primacy of the baby over both husband and wife: "If it were in your wife's obstetrical interest to gain 50 pounds with a pregnancy you . . . would have no option, of course, but to accept fat and flab as the price of a healthy baby" (325). Having set up this possibility, this straw man of a flabby woman, the authors proceed to knock it down to size. Moderate weight gain of 30 pounds or so, they explain, will not produce flab and will ensure the wife's "speediest return to slenderness after childbirth" (325). The section goes on to exhort husbands to help keep their wives from temptation. By giving the husbands a role in the process of fighting flab—a gesture typical of liberal feminism's desire to integrate men into all aspects of the pregnancy process—they also apportion responsibility and blame.

The question of responsibility is articulated through a collapsing of boundaries, not only between mother and fetus but between mother and father. Fathers are expected by the authors to share in some of the physical sacrifices of pregnancy; they should learn to eat steamed vegetables and should themselves abstain from drinking alcohol. When offered a drink at a party, an expectant father should reply, "No thanks, we're pregnant." The "we," figured here as a sign of support, is, of course, also a symptom of a systematic appropriation of the reproductive body. The pregnant body, so resistant to forces from outside the family, knows no boundaries within it. Father collapses into mother who in turn collapses into fetus. The subjectivity of the mother is eroded from both the inside and the outside.

The disappearance of the mother's body is a key moment in Rosalind Petchesky's productive analysis of the rhetoric of Right-to-Life movements. In her reading of their most effective piece of propaganda, the film *The Silent Scream*, she notes the repeated presentation of the fetus without the visual context of the mother's body.[18] *The Silent Scream* returns again and again to the image of the free-floating fetus, unconnected to the outside world and to the body which sustains it. The rhetoric of liberal advice culture, with its benign gestures toward working women and its repeated invocations of female autonomy during the process of birth and labor, produces a fetus and a pregnancy eerily reminiscent of the one at the visual and emotional center of Right-to-Life propaganda. Ironically, that advice culture, with its multiple investments in home, produces a homeless fetus, a baby without walls as the surveillance of the female body erases that body in the very act of inspection, rendering it not so much invisible as transparent. As we look at the diagrams of fetal development which, for example, begin every new chapter, every new monthly installment of *What to Expect*, as we are told to eat, sleep, and exercise for the fetus, we are implicitly being told to look through the body of the pregnant woman.

The transparent pregnant body, spectacularly permeable to the gaze, must itself be fixed within the boundaries of home. Although it may be held up for publicity, its place is essentially private; its confinement within the domestic makes it legible according to a series of culturally sanctioned codes. While the word "confinement" has slipped out of the discourse of contemporary pregnancy and childbirth, it leaves its traces in the domestic carceral, and in the elaborate culture of advice, surveillance, and admonition which mark off the "private" sphere.

NOTES

1. Paul Morrison, "Enclosed in Openness, *Northanger Abbey* and the Domestic Carceral," *Texas Studies in Language and Literature* 23:1 (Spring 1991), 1–23.

2. Jane Austen, *Northanger Abbey* (New York: Oxford University Press, 1971), 137.

3. Sandra M. Gilbert and Susan Gubar, *The Madwoman in the Attic* (New Haven: Yale University Press, 1980)

4. Sheila Kitzinger, *Your Baby, Your Way: Making Pregnancy Decisions and Birth Plans* (New York: Pantheon, 1987), 165.

5. Pamela S. Eakins, "Out-of-Hospital Birth," in *The American Way of Birth*, Eakins, ed. (Philadelphia: Temple University Press, 1986), 223.

6. For various narratives along this line see Barbara Ehrenreich and Dierdre English, *For Their Own Good: 150 Years of the Experts' Advice to Women* (New York: Anchor, 1979); Ann Dally, *Women Under the Knife: A History of Surgery* (London: Hutchinson Radius, 1991); and Karen Michaelson and contributors, *Childbirth in America: An Anthropological Perspective* (New York: Bergin and Garvey, 1987).

7. Jessica Mitford, *The American Way of Birth* (New York: Dutton, 1992), chapter 1.

8. Nancy Wainer Cohen and Lois J. Estner, *Silent Knife: Cesarian Prevention and Vaginal Birth after Cesarian (VBAC)* (New York: Bergin and Garvey, 1983), xv–xx.

9. For example, Carolyn Fishel Sargent, in *Maternity, Medicine, and Power: Reproductive Decisions in Urban Benin* (Berkeley: University of California Press, 1989), notes that many urban women in her study see the hospital as a safer alternative to home birth, and hospitals as more helpful in relieving suffering (51).

10. See Michaelson, 28, and Barbara Katz Rothman, "Awake and Aware, or False Consciousness," in Shelly Romalis, ed. *Childbirth: Alternatives to Medical Control* (Austin: University of Texas Press, 1981).

11. Ann Oakley, *The Captured Womb: A History of the Medical Care of Pregnant Women* (Oxford: Basil Blackwell, 1984), 33.

12. Rothman, 172.

13. For a discussion of populations giving or planning to give birth at home, see Michaelson, 28, and Romalis, 171–72.

14. Nancy Armstrong and Leonard Tennenhouse, eds., *The Ideology of Conduct: Essays on Literature and the History of Sexuality* (New York: Methuen, 1987).

15. Arlene Eisenberg, Heidi Eisenberg Murkoff, and Sandee Eisenberg Hathaway, *What to Expect When You're Expecting* (New York: Workman, 1984, 1988).

16. The decision to use the term "baby" or "fetus" is, of course, a fraught one laden with and productive of a series of assumptions. We have chosen, when applicable, to echo

the choice of the author we are discussing. When we are not discussing a particular author or point of view, we have chosen to use "fetus" until the moment of birth.

17. Janice Graham, *Your Pregnancy Companion* (New York: Pocket Books, 1991), 3.

18. Rosalind Pollack Petchesky, "Foetal Images: The Power of Visual Culture in the Politics of Reproduction," in Michelle Stanworth, ed., *Reproductive Technologies: Gender Motherhood and Medicine* (Oxford: Basil Blackwell, 1987), 36–57.

canon

O ne of the axioms of traditional literary study has been that "great literature" represents "universal" experiences. But as more women and people
of diverse ethnic and class backgrounds have begun to study literature, that notion has come into question. What had appeared universal to the once homogeneous group that studied literature and defined what was "great" as well—a
group almost entirely composed of white upper- and upper-middle-class males—
does not seem so to the now heterogeneous group. What had once been taken
for purely "aesthetic" choices about which literary texts would be included on
course syllabi, in anthologies, on graduate and undergraduate examinations, have
begun to be questioned as political and social choices.

The "canon" of literature—those literary works recognized as "great" or at least
recognized as worthy to be read and studied in an academic setting—was never
as codified as its religious namesake. As Lillian S. Robinson points out in her essay, "Treason Our Text," the canon's lack of definition makes challenging it difficult. There was never an official council set up to determine what books would
and would not be read. There are instead many diverse, complex mechanisms
for creating a canon of "authentic" literature (authenticity being one of the standard rubrics of canonicity): individual professors, faculty examination and editorial committees, publishing houses and scholarly journals. The nebulousness of
these mechanisms was for many years taken to be proof of the choices' merit—
surely, since so many readers *independently* determined a work's merit or lack of
it, that judgment was accurate, right?

Feminist critics began exploring just how connected, in fact, those apparently
independent groups were: The individual professor read the journals, received
the catalogs of the publishing houses, and sat on those faculty committees; the
faculty committees were the advisory boards to the journals and to the publishing houses; the publishing houses kept in print the books that the individual professors kept ordering for their courses. And most of those individuals making
judgments were white upper- and upper-middle-class men. "Independent" judgments, indeed.

Judgment, of course, is at the center of the question of canonicity. What makes
literature "great"? What makes it worth studying in a university? What makes it
worth reading at all? Early feminist critics found that their answers to these questions were not the same ones that they had been taught in graduate school. Is
the purpose of literature to examine "universal" or individual, diverse experiences? Should we value "representative" or "aesthetic" language? What makes
an experience "universal"? What guides our choice of what *is* aesthetic? As
women readers found so-called minor women writers whose work was more moving, exciting, and representative of *their* experience than that of supposedly major writers, they began to question the standards of literary taste and to question
the grounds on which those standards were based.

In "What Has Never Been: An Overview of Lesbian Feminist Literary Criticism" (1981), Bonnie Zimmerman links sexuality to these questions of taste and
universality: "Lesbian literary criticism," she argues, "simply restates what feminists already know, that one group cannot name itself 'humanity' or even
'woman.' She calls for an expansion of the feminist literary canon to include more
works by lesbian writers, and suggests that lesbian critics actively seek to discover
more as yet unknown works by lesbian writers, reread the so-called great canon

of literature from a lesbian perspective, and elaborate a lesbian perspective, an agenda that presaged the broader feminist literary-critical projects of the 1980s. Zimmerman also examines what could be called the "canon" of feminist *criticism*, to argue that the most influential feminist projects of the 1970s were themselves based on heterosexist assumptions and suppressed or overlooked lesbian writers and texts.

But while Zimmerman would like to expand the feminist canon itself, of more importance to her is the development of a unique critical perspective or "at the very least, determining whether or not such a perspective is possible." The challenges for critics trying to make that determination parallel many of those that make expansion of the literary canon difficult: The long-standing silence of lesbian voices in literature and in the academy obscures the lesbian tradition, and the complexity of defining "lesbian"—is it strictly a sexual term, or does it mean more loosely "woman-identified"?—makes defining a "lesbian text"—one by a lesbian writer? one that depicts lesbian experience?—an important, but perhaps limiting, act. Zimmerman calls for reforms of lesbian feminist criticism that outline many of the reforms that would come about in 1980s feminist criticism at large: greater attention to the specificity of a text's relation to history and place, and a firmer acceptance of differences among women (not just the differences between women and men).

Joanna Russ, in her 1983 book, *How to Suppress Women's Writing*, explicitly connects exclusion from the literary canon with difference. As Russ sees it, people are profoundly threatened by difference and are apt to characterize it as inferiority; the threat offered by women's writing, she shows, was effectively suppressed for decades. Russ delineates the variety of critical positions that seem to be arguments about quality but that are in fact arguments about difference. Such arguments are sometimes a matter of ignorance, but sometimes a matter of genuine bad faith; the "Glotologs" who make them often do not even recognize what they are doing (Glotologs are the creatures she describes in a science-fiction-inspired prologue who revel in exclusion). In the chapters reprinted here, "Anomalousness" and "Aesthetics," she examines how the lack of literary context for women's writing can be self-perpetuating, because it can continue to make women's writings seem too "different" to include in the canon of literature. In other chapters, she reveals how critical issues of quality have been used to question the validity of writings by women, from the authenticity of their authorship ("She didn't write it" or "She had help"), to the validity of what they write about and what they produce ("She wrote it, but look at what she wrote about," "She isn't really an artist, and it isn't really art"). Russ argues that we must dispel the notion of absolute values when it comes to judging literary value; as she puts it, "when we all live in the same culture, then it will be time for one literature."

Lillian S. Robinson identifies the task of denying absolute values as both the opportunity and the challenge of feminist criticism in "Treason Our Text: Feminist Challenges to the Literary Canon" (1983). Although challenges to the canon frequently proceed on a case-by-case basis, arguing that this or that woman author deserves to be read because she is "as good as" currently accepted writers, many feminist critics nonetheless advocate opening the whole question of literary value itself. Robinson recognizes the dilemma that the conflict between these two kinds of challenges creates: "What is involved here is more like the *agony* of

feminist criticism, for it is the champions of women's literature who are torn between defending the quality of their discoveries and radically redefining quality
itself." Robinson goes on to argue that in undertaking such a complicated and
conflicted project, feminist critics must examine their own politics, lest they make
the exclusionary mistakes they criticize in others; a vague "pluralism" or "populism without the politics of populism" is not enough. Feminist critics must, she
argues, undertake a thorough study of aesthetics to avoid a "reverse discrimination" when putting together their own anthologies and syllabi.

Paul Lauter examines precisely these politics of feminist criticism in "Caste,
Class, and Canon" (1987; a revised version of his 1981 essay of the same name).
After questioning the use of New Critical technique in some feminist criticism, he asks, "Is the *form* of criticism value-free? . . . How is canon—that is,
selection—related to, indeed a function of, critical technique?" To answer these
questions, Lauter examines first a body of literature not often studied,
working-class writing. What he finds is that it is unlikely to be studied because it
does not conform to the criteria validated by New Critical technique—innovative or complex language and form, an individual creator—but must be explored
in terms of its function or use. Lauter moves from this analysis to a question of
why some feminist critics still employ New Critical techniques when the political implications of New Criticism are so antithetical to a feminist undertaking.
He argues that since, in the feminist revision of the canon, "the work of criticism
and of political action most fully converge," feminist critics cannot rely on solely
"literary" criteria, because such criteria are never value-free, and can never be
innocently used. Instead, feminist criticism calls for an evaluation of culture, the
role literature plays in that culture, and the role that criticism plays in making
the world better and our lives fuller.

Nelly McKay's "Reflections of Black Women Writers: Revising the Literary
Canon" (1987), stands as a case study of the questions Russ, Robinson, and
Lauter raise. In this essay, she reviews the history of African-American women
writers to show how they "have consistently provided for themselves and
others . . . a rendering of the black woman's place in the world in which she lives,
as she shapes and defines that from her own impulses and actions." These writers, almost all of whom were neglected for decades or even centuries, reveal a
very different "American experience" and a different literary tradition from that
encountered in anthologies of American literature, and different even from that
revealed in writings by African-American men. McKay provides the context in
which contemporary African-American writers like Alice Walker or Toni Morrison
do not have to appear "anomalous" and sets out the political and social bases for
their aesthetics. The inclusion of these writers in the American canon, she argues, "makes more complete the reality of the multi-faceted American experience." Along with Zimmerman, Russ, Robinson, and Lauter, McKay provides a
critique of the notion of "universality" and the myth of "purely aesthetic" judgments of literature.

—DPH & RRW

BONNIE ZIMMERMAN

WHAT HAS NEVER BEEN

an overview of lesbian feminist literary criticism

(1 9 8 1)

In the 1970s, a generation of lesbian feminist literary critics came of age. Some, like the lesbian professor in Lynn Strongin's poem, "Sayre,"[1] had been closeted in the profession; many had "come out" as lesbians in the women's liberation movement. As academics and as lesbians, we cautiously began to plait together the strands of our existence: teaching lesbian literature, establishing networks and support groups, and exploring assumptions about a lesbian-focused literary criticism. Beginning with nothing, as we thought, this generation quickly began to expand the limitations of literary scholarship by pointing to what had been for decades "unspeakable"—lesbian existence—thus phrasing, in novelist June Arnold's words, "what has never been."[2] Our process has paralleled the development of feminist literary criticism—and, indeed, pioneering feminist critics and lesbian critics are often one and the same. As women in a male-dominated academy, we explored the way we write and read from a different or "other" perspective. As lesbians in a heterosexist academy, we have continued to explore the impact of "otherness," suggesting dimensions previously ignored and yet necessary to understand fully the female condition and the creative work born from it.

Lesbian critics, in the 1980s, may have more questions than answers, but the questions are important not only to lesbians, but to all feminists teaching and criticizing literature. Does a woman's sexual and affectional preference influence the way she writes, reads, and thinks? Does lesbianism belong in the classroom and in scholarship? Is there a lesbian aesthetic distinct from a feminist aesthetic? What should be the role of the lesbian critic? Can we establish a lesbian "canon" in the way in which feminist critics have established a female canon? Can lesbian feminists develop insights into female creativity that might enrich all literary criticism? Different women, of course, answer these questions in different ways, but one set of assumptions underlies virtually all lesbian criticism: that a woman's identity is not defined only by her relation to a male world and male literary tradition (as feminist critics have demonstrated), that powerful bonds between women are a crucial factor in women's lives, and that the sexual and emotional orientation of a woman profoundly affects her consciousness and thus her creativity. Those critics who have consciously chosen to read as lesbians argue that this perspective can be uniquely liberating and can provide new insights into life and literature because it assigns the lesbian a specific vantage point from which to criticize and analyze the politics, language, and culture of patriarchy:

> We have the whole range of women's experience and the other dimension too, which is the unique viewpoint of the dyke. This extra dimension puts us a step outside of so-called normal life and lets us see how gruesomely abnormal it is. . . . [This perspective] can issue in a world-view that is distinct in history and uniquely liberating.[3]

The purpose of this essay is to analyze the current state of lesbian scholarship, to suggest how lesbians are exercising this unique world view, and to investigate some of the problems, strengths, and future needs of a developing lesbian feminist literary criticism.[4]

One way in which this unique world view takes shape is as a "critical consciousness about heterosexist assumptions."[5] Heterosexism is the set of values and structures that assumes heterosexuality to be the only natural form of sexual and emotional expression, "*the* perceptual screen provided by our [patriarchal] cultural conditioning."[6] Heterosexist assumptions abound in literary texts, such as feminist literary anthologies, that purport to be open-minded about lesbianism. When authors' biographies make special note of husbands, male mentors, and male companions, even when that author was primarily female-identified, but fail to mention the female companions of prominent lesbian writers—that is heterosexism. When anthologists ignore historically significant lesbian writers such as Renée Vivien and Radclyffe Hall—that is heterosexism. When anthologies include only the heterosexual or nonsexual works of a writer like Katherine Philips or Adrienne Rich who is celebrated for her lesbian or homoemotional poetry—that is heterosexism. When a topically organized anthology includes sections on wives, mothers, sex objects, young girls, aging women, and liberated women, but not lesbians—that is heterosexism. Heterosexism in feminist anthologies—like the sexism of androcentric collections— serves to obliterate lesbian existence and maintain the lie that women have searched for emotional and sexual fulfillment only through men—or not at all.

Lesbians have also expressed concern that the absence of lesbian material in women's studies journals such as *Feminist Studies, Women's Studies,* and *Women and Literature* indicates heterosexism either by omission or by design. Only in 1979 did lesbian-focused articles appear in *Signs* and *Frontiers.* Most lesbian criticism first appeared in alternative, non-establishment lesbian journals, particularly *Sinister Wisdom* and *Conditions,* which are unfamiliar to many feminist scholars. For example, *Signs's* first review article on literary criticism by Elaine Showalter (1975) makes no mention of lesbianism as a theme or potential critical perspective, not even to point out its absence. Annette Kolodny, in the second review article in *Signs* (1976), does call Jane Rule's *Lesbian Images* "a novelist's challenge to the academy and its accompanying critical community," and further criticizes the homophobia in then-current biographies, calling for "candor and sensitivity" in future work.[7] However, neither this nor subsequent review articles familiarize the reader with "underground" sources of lesbian criticism, some of which had appeared by this time, nor do they explicate lesbianism as a literary theme or critical perspective. Ironically, more articles on lesbian literature have appeared in traditional literary journals than in the women's studies press, just as for years only male critics felt free to mention lesbianism. Possibly, feminist critics continue to feel that they will be identified as "dykes," thus invalidating their work.

The perceptual screen of heterosexism is also evident in most of the acclaimed works of feminist literary criticism. None of the current collections of essays—such as *The Authority of Experience* or *Shakespeare's Sisters*—includes even a token article from a lesbian perspective. Ellen Moers's *Literary Women*, germinal work as it is, is homophobic as well as heterosexist. Lesbians, she points out, appear as monsters, grotesques, and freaks in works by Carson McCullers, Djuna Barnes (her reading of *Nightwood* is at the very least questionable), and Diane Arbus, but she seems to concur in this identification rather than call it into question or explain its historical context. Although her so-called defense of unmarried women writers against the "charge" of lesbianism does criticize the way in which this word has been used as a slur, she neither condemns such antilesbianism nor entertains the possibility that some women writers were, in fact, lesbians. Her chapter on "Loving Heroinism" is virtually textbook heterosexism, assuming as it does that women writers only articulate love for men.[8] Perceptual blinders also mar *The Female Imagination* by Patricia Meyers Spacks which never uses the word "lesbian" (except in the index) or "lover" to describe either the "sexual ambiguity" of the bond between Jane and Helen in *Jane Eyre*, nor Margaret Anderson's relationship with a "beloved older woman." Furthermore, Spacks claims that Gertrude Stein, "whose life lack[ed] real attachments" (a surprise to Alice B. Toklas), also "denied whatever is special to women" (which lesbianism is not?).[9] This latter judgment is particularly ominous because heterosexuals often have difficulty accepting that a lesbian, especially a role-playing "butch," is in fact a woman. More care is demonstrated by Elaine Showalter who, in *A Literature of Their Own*, uncovers the attitudes toward lesbianism held by nineteenth-century writers Eliza Lynn Linton and Mrs. Humphrey Ward. However, she does not integrate lesbian issues into her discussion of the crucial generation of early twentieth-century writers (Virginia Woolf, Vita Sackville-West, Dorothy Richardson, and Rosamond Lehmann among others; Radclyffe Hall is mentioned, but not *The Well of Loneliness*), all of whom wrote about sexual love between women. Her well-taken point that modern British novelists avoid lesbianism might have been balanced, however, by a mention of Maureen Duffy, Sybille Bedford, or Fay Weldon.[10] Finally, Sandra Gilbert and Susan Gubar's *The Madwoman in the Attic* does not even index lesbianism; the lone reference made in the text is to the possibility that "Goblin Market" describes "a covertly (if ambiguously) lesbian world." The authors' tendency to interpret all pairs of female characters as aspects of the self sometimes serves to mask a relationship that a lesbian reader might interpret as bonding or love between women.[11]

Lesbian critics, who as feminists owe much to these critical texts, have had to turn to other resources, first to develop a lesbian canon, and then to establish a lesbian critical perspective. Barbara Grier, who, as Gene Damon, reviewed books for the pioneering lesbian journal *The Ladder*, laid the groundwork for this canon with her incomparable, but largely unknown *The Lesbian in Literature: A Bibliography*.[12] Equally obscure was Jeanette Foster's *Sex Variant Women in Literature*, self-published in 1956 after having been rejected by a university press because of its subject matter. An exhaustive chronological account of every reference to love between women from Sappho and Ruth to the fiction of the fifties, *Sex Variant Women* has proven to be an invaluable starting point for lesbian readers and scholars. Out of print almost immediately after its publication and lost to all but a few intrepid souls, it was finally reprinted by Diana Press in 1975.[13] A further resource and gathering point for lesbian critics was the special issue on lesbian writing and publishing in *Margins*, a review of small press publications, which appeared in 1975, the first issue of a literary journal devoted entirely to lesbian writing. In 1976, its editor, Beth Hodges, produced a second special issue, this time in *Sinister Wisdom*.[14] Along with the growing visibility and solidarity of lesbians within the academic profession, and the increased availability of lesbian literature from feminist and mass-market presses, these two journal issues propelled lesbian feminist literary criticism to the surface.[15]

The literary resources available to lesbian critics form only part of the story, for lesbian criticism is equally rooted in political ideology. Although not all lesbian critics are activists, most have been strongly influenced by the politics of lesbian feminism. These politics travel the continuum from civil rights advocacy to separatism; however, most, if not all, lesbian feminists assume that lesbianism is a healthy lifestyle chosen by women in virtually all eras and all cultures, and thus strive to eliminate the stigma historically attached to lesbianism. One way to remove this stigma is to associate lesbianism with positive and desirable attributes, to divert women's attention away from male values and toward an exclusively female communitas. Thus, the influential Radicalesbians' essay, "The Woman-Identified Woman," argues that lesbian feminism assumes "the primacy of women relating to women, of women creating a new consciousness of and with each other. . . . We see ourselves as prime, find our centers inside of ourselves."[16] Many lesbian writers and critics have also been influenced profoundly by the politics of separatism which provides a critique of heterosexuality as a political institution rather than a personal choice, "because relationships between men and women are essentially political, they involve power and dominance."[17] As we shall see, the notion of "woman-identification," that is, the primacy of women bonding with women emotionally and politically, as well as the premises of separatism, that lesbians have a unique and critical place at the margins of patriarchal society, are central to much current lesbian literary criticism.

Unmasking heterosexist assumptions in feminist literary criticism has been an important but hardly primary task for lesbian critics. We are more concerned with the development of a unique lesbian feminist perspective or, at the very least, determining whether or not such a perspective is possible. In order to do so, lesbian critics have had to begin with a special question: "When is a text a 'lesbian text' or its writer a 'lesbian writer'"?[18] Lesbians are faced with this special problem of definition: presumably we know when a writer is a "Victorian writer" or a "Canadian writer." To answer this question, we have to determine how inclusively or exclusively we define "lesbian." Should we limit this appellation to those women for whom sexual experience with other women can be proven? This is an almost impossible historical task, as many have noted, for what constitutes proof? Women have not left obvious markers in their private writings. Furthermore, such a narrow definition "names" lesbianism as an exclusively sexual phenomenon which, many argue, may be an inadequate construction of lesbian experience, both today and in less sexually explicit eras. This sexual definition of lesbianism also leads to the identification of literature with life, and thus can be an overly defensive and suspect strategy.

Nevertheless, lesbian criticism continues to be plagued with the problem of definition. One perspective insists that

> desire must be there and at least somewhat embodied. . . . That carnality distinguishes it from gestures of political sympathy for homosexuals and from affectionate friendships in which women enjoy each other, support each other, and commingle their sense of identity and well-being.[19]

A second perspective, which might be called a school, claims, on the contrary, that "the very meaning of lesbianism is being expanded in literature, just as it is being redefined through politics."[20] An articulate spokeswoman for this "expanded meaning" school of criticism is Adrienne Rich, who offers a compelling inclusive definition of lesbianism:

> I mean the term *lesbian continuum* to include a range—through each woman's life and throughout history—of woman-identified experience; not simply the fact that a woman has had or consciously desired genital experience with another woman. If we expand it to embrace many more forms of primary intensity between and among women, including the sharing of a rich inner life, the bonding against male tyranny, the giving and receiving of practical and political support . . . we begin to grasp breadths of female history and psychology which have lain out of reach as a consequence of limited, mostly clinical, definitions of "lesbianism."[21]

This definition has the virtue of deemphasizing lesbianism as a static entity and of suggesting interconnections among the various ways in which women bond together. However, all inclusive definitions of lesbianism risk blurring the distinctions between lesbian relationships and non-lesbian female friendships, or between lesbian identity and female-centered identity. Some lesbian writers would deny that there are such distinctions, but this position is reductive and of mixed value to those who are developing lesbian criticism and theory and who may need limited and precise definitions. In fact, reductionism is a serious problem in lesbian ideology. Too often, we identify lesbian and woman, or feminist; we equate lesbianism with any close bonds between women or with political commitment to women. These identifications can be fuzzy and historically questionable, as, for example, in the claim that lesbians have a unique relationship with nature or (as Rich also has claimed) that all female creativity is lesbian. By so reducing the meaning of lesbian, we have in effect eliminated lesbianism as a meaningful category.

A similar problem arises when lesbian theorists redefine lesbianism politically, equating it with strength, independence, and resistance to patriarchy. This new political definition then influences the interpretation of literature: "If in a woman writer's work a sentence refuses to do what it is supposed to do, if there are strong images of women and if there is a refusal to be linear, the result is innately lesbian literature."[22] The concept of an "innately" lesbian perspective or aesthetic allows the critic to separate lesbianism from biographical content which is an essential development in lesbian critical theory. Literary interpretation will, of course, be supported by historical and biographical evidence, but perhaps lesbian critics should borrow a few insights from new criticism. If a text lends itself to a lesbian reading, then no amount of biographic "proof" ought to be necessary to establish it as a lesbian text.[23] Barbara Smith, for example, interprets Toni Morrison's *Sula* as a lesbian novel, regardless of the author's affectional preference. But we need to be cautious about what we call "innately" lesbian. Why is circularity or strength limited to lesbians, or, similarly, why is love of nature or creativity? It is certainly not evident that women, let alone lesbians, are "innately" anything. And, although it might require a lesbian perspective to stress the dominant relationship between Nel and Sula ("All that time, all that time, I thought I was missing Jude"), it is difficult to imagine a novel so imbued with heterosexuality as lesbian.

Almost midway between the inclusive and exclusive approaches to a definition of lesbianism lies that of Lillian Faderman in her extraordinary overview, *Surpassing the Love of Man: Romantic Friendship and Love Between Women From the Renaissance to the Present*. Faderman's precise definition of lesbianism provides a conceptual framework for the four hundred years of literary history explored by the text:

> "Lesbian" describes a relationship in which two women's strongest emotions and affections are directed toward each other. Sexual contact may be a part of the relationship to a greater or lesser degree, or it may be entirely absent. By preference the two women spend most of their time together and share most aspects of their lives with each other.[24]

Broader than the exclusive definition of lesbianism—for Faderman argues that not all lesbian relationships may be fully embodied—but narrower than Rich's "lesbian continuum," this definition is both specific and discriminating. The book is slightly marred by a defensive, overexplanatory tone, caused, no doubt, by her attempt to neutralize the "intense charge of the word *lesbian*"; note, for example, that this charged word is omitted from the title.[25] Furthermore, certain problems remain with her framework, as with any that a lesbian critic or historian might establish. The historical relationship between genital sexuality and lesbianism remains unclear, and we cannot identify easily lesbianism outside a monogamous relationship. Nevertheless, despite problems in definition that may be inherent in lesbian studies, the strength of *Surpassing the Love of Men* is partially the precision with which Faderman defines her topic and chooses her texts and subjects.

This problem of definition is exacerbated by the problem of silence. One of the most pervasive themes in lesbian criticism is that woman-identified writers, silenced by a homophobic and misogynistic society, have been forced to adopt coded and obscure language and internal censorship. Emily Dickinson counseled us to "tell all the truth / but tell it slant," and critics are now calculating what price we have paid for slanted truth. The silences of heterosexual women writers may become lies for lesbian writers, as Rich warns: "a life 'in the closet' . . . [may] spread into private life, so that lying (described as *discretion*) becomes an easy way to avoid conflict or complication."[26] Gloria T. Hull recounts the moving story of just such a victim of society, the black lesbian poet Angelina

Weld Grimké, whose "convoluted life and thwarted sexuality" marked her slim output of poetry with images of self-abnegation, diminution, sadness, and the wish for death. The lesbian writer who is working class or a woman of color may be particularly isolated, shackled by conventions, and, ultimately, silenced "with [her] real gifts stifled within."[27] What does a lesbian writer do when the words cannot be silenced? Critics are pointing to the codes and strategies for literary survival adopted by many women. For example, Willa Cather may have adopted her characteristic male persona in order to express safely her emotional and erotic feelings for other women.[28] Thus, a writer some critics call antifeminist or at least disappointing may be better appreciated when her lesbianism is taken into account. Similarly, many ask whether Gertrude Stein cultivated obscurity, encoding her lesbianism in order to express hidden feelings and evade potential enemies. Or, on the other hand, Stein may have been always a declared lesbian, but a victim of readers' (and scholars') unwillingness or inability to pay her the close and sympathetic attention she requires.[29]

The silence of "Shakespeare's [lesbian] sister" has meant that modern writers have had little or no tradition with which to nurture themselves: Feminist critics such as Moers, Showalter, and Gilbert and Gubar have demonstrated the extent and significance of a female literary tradition, but the lesbian writer developed her craft alone (and perhaps this is the significance of the title of *the* lesbian novel about novel writing, *The Well of Loneliness*). Elly Bulkin's much-reprinted article on lesbian poetry points out that lesbian poets "have their work shaped by the simple fact of their having begun to write without knowledge of such history and with little or no hope of support from a woman's and/or lesbian writing community."[30] If white women can at least imagine a lesbian literature, the black lesbian writer, as Barbara Smith demonstrates, is even more hampered by the lack of tradition: "Black women are still in the position of having to 'imagine,' discover and verify Black lesbian literature because so little has been written from an avowedly lesbian perspective."[31] Blanche Wiesen Cook points out further that all lesbians are affected by this absence of tradition and role models, or the limiting of role models to Hall's Stephen Gordon. She also reminds us that our lesbian foremothers and networks were not simply lost and forgotten; rather, our past has been "erased," obliterated by the actions of a hostile society.[32]

It would appear then that lesbian critics are faced with a set of problems that make our work particularly delicate and problematic, requiring caution, sensitivity, and flexibility as well as imagination and risk. Lesbian criticism begins with the establishment of the lesbian text: the creation of language out of silence. The critic must first define the term "lesbian" and then determine its applicability to both writer and text, sorting out the relation of literature to life. Her definition of lesbianism will influence the texts she identifies as lesbian, and, except for the growing body of literature written from an explicit lesbian perspective since the development of a lesbian political movement, it is likely that many will disagree with various identifications of lesbian texts. It is not only *Sula* that may provoke controversy, but even the "coded" works of lesbian writers like Gertrude Stein. The critic will need to consider whether a lesbian text is one written by a lesbian (and if so, how do we determine who is a lesbian?), one written about lesbians (which might be by a heterosexual woman or a man), or one that expresses a lesbian "vision" (which has yet to be satisfactorily outlined). But despite the problems raised by definition, silence and coding, and absence of tradition, lesbian critics have begun to develop a critical stance. Often this stance involves peering into shadows, into the spaces between words, into what has been unspoken and barely imagined. It is a perilous critical adventure with results that may violate accepted norms of traditional criticism, but which may also transform our notions of literary possibility.

One of the first tasks of this emerging lesbian criticism has been to provide lesbians with a tradition, even if a retrospective one. Jane Rule, whose *Lesbian Images* appeared about the same time as *Literary Women*, first attempted to establish this tradition.[33] Although her text is problematic, relying overly much on biographical evidence and derivative interpretations and including some questionable writers (such as Dorothy Baker) while omitting others, *Lesbian Images* was a milestone in lesbian criticism. Its importance is partially suggested by the fact that it took five years for another complete book—Faderman's—to appear on lesbian literature. In a review of *Lesbian Images*, I questioned the existence of a lesbian "great tradition" in literature, but now I think I was wrong.[34] Along with Rule, Dolores Klaich in *Woman Plus Woman* and Louise Bernikow in the introduction to *The World Split Open* have explored the possibility of a lesbian tradition,[35] and recent critics such as Faderman and Cook in particular have begun to define that tradition, who belongs to it, and what links the writers who can be identified as lesbians. Cook's review of lesbian literature and culture in the early twentieth century proposes "to analyze the literature and attitudes out of which the present lesbian feminist works have emerged, and to examine the continued denials and invalidation of the lesbian experience."[36] Focusing on the recognized lesbian networks in France and England that included Virginia Woolf, Vita Sackville-West, Ethel Smythe, Gertrude Stein, Radclyffe Hall, Natalie Barney, and Romaine Brooks, Cook provides an important outline of a lesbian cultural tradition and an insightful analysis of the distortions and denials of homophobic scholars, critics, and biographers.

Faderman's *Surpassing the Love of Men*, like her earlier critical articles, ranges more widely through a literary tradition of romantic love between women (whether or not one calls that "lesbian") from the sixteenth to the twentieth centuries. Her thesis is that passionate love between women was labeled neither abnormal nor undesirable—probably because women were perceived to be asexual—until the sexologists led by Krafft-Ebing and Havelock Ellis "morbidified" female friendship around 1900.

Although she does not always clarify the dialectic between idealization and condemnation that is suggested in her text, Faderman's basic theory is quite convincing. Most readers, like myself, will be amazed at the wealth of information about women's same-sex love that Faderman has uncovered. She rescues from heterosexual obscurity Mary Wollstonecraft, Mary Wortley Montagu, Anna Seward, Sarah Orne Jewett, Edith Somerville, "Michael Field," and many others, including the Scottish schoolmistresses whose lesbian libel suit inspired Lillian Hellman's *The Children's Hour.* Faderman has also written on the theme of same-sex love and romantic friendship in poems and letters of Emily Dickinson; in novels by Henry James, Oliver Wendell Holmes, and Henry Wadsworth Longfellow; and in popular magazine fiction of the early twentieth century.[37]

Faderman is preeminent among those critics who are attempting to establish a lesbian tradition by rereading writers of the past previously assumed to be heterosexual or "spinsters." As songwriter Holly Near expresses it: "Lady poet of great acclaim/ I have been misreading you/ I never knew your poems were meant for me."[38] It is in this area of lesbian scholarship that the most controversy—and some of the most exciting work—occurs. Was Mary Wollstonecraft's passionate love for Fanny Blood, recorded in *Mary, A Fiction*, lesbian? Does Henry James dissect a lesbian relationship in *The Bostonians*? Did Emily Dickinson address many of her love poems to a woman, not a man? How did Virginia Woolf's relationships with Vita Sackville-West and Ethel Smythe affect her literary vision? Not only are some lesbian critics increasingly naming such women and relationships "lesbian," they are also suggesting that criticism cannot fail to take into account the influence of sexual and emotional orientation on literary expression.

In the establishment of a self-conscious literary tradition, certain writers have become focal points both for critics and for lesbians in general, who affirm and celebrate their identity by "naming names," establishing a sense of historical continuity and community through the knowledge that incontrovertibly great women were also lesbians. Foremost among these heroes (or "heras") are the women who created the first self-identified lesbian feminist community in Paris during the early years of the twentieth century. With Natalie Barney at its hub, this circle included such notable writers as Colette, Djuna Barnes, Radclyffe Hall, Renée Vivien, and, peripherally, Gertrude Stein. Contemporary lesbians—literary critics, historians, and lay readers—have been drawn to their mythic and mythmaking presence, seeing in them a vision of lesbian society and culture that may have existed only once before—on the original island of Lesbos.[39] More interest, however, has been paid to their lives so far than to their art. Barnes's portraits of decadent, tormented lesbians and homosexuals in *Nightwood* and silly, salacious ones in *The Ladies Almanack* often prove troublesome to lesbian readers and critics.[40] However, Elaine Marks's perceptive study of French lesbian writers traces a tradition and how it has changed, modified by circumstance and by feminism, from the Sappho of Renée Vivien to the amazons of Monique Wittig.[41]

The problem inherent in reading lesbian literature primarily for role modeling is most evident with Hall—the most notorious of literary lesbians—whose archetypal "butch," Stephen Gordon, has bothered readers since the publication of *The Well of Loneliness*. Although one critic praises it as "the standard by which all subsequent similar works are measured," most contemporary lesbian feminists would, I believe, agree with Faderman's harsh condemnation that it "helped to wreak confusion in young women."[42] Such an extraliterary debate is not limited to lesbian novels and lesbian characters; I am reminded of the intense disappointment expressed by many feminists over George Eliot's disposal of Dorothea Brooke in *Middlemarch*. In both cases, the cry is the same: why haven't these writers provided us with appropriate role models? Cook may be justified in criticizing Hall for creating a narrow and debilitating image for lesbians who follow, but my reading of the novel (and that of Catharine Stimpson in an excellent study of the lesbian novel) convinces me that both Hall's hero and message are highly complex.[43] In looking to writers for a tradition, we need to recognize that the tradition may not always be a happy one. Women like Stephen Gordon exist alongside characters like Molly Bolt, in Rita Mae Brown's *Rubyfruit Jungle*, but lesbians may also question whether or not the incarnation of a "politically correct" but elusive and utopian mythology provides our only appropriate role model.

As with Hall, many readers and critics are strongly antipathetic to Stein, citing her reactionary and antifeminist politics and her role-playing relationship with Alice B. Toklas. However, other critics, by carefully analyzing Stein's actual words, establish, convincingly to my reading, that she did have a lesbian and feminist perspective, calling into question assumptions about coding and masculine role playing. Cynthia Secor, who is developing an exciting lesbian feminist interpretation of Stein, argues that her novel *Ida* attempts to discover what it means to be a female person, and that the author profited from her position on the boundaries of patriarchal society: "Stein's own experience as a lesbian gives her a critical distance that shapes her understanding of the struggle to be one's self. Her own identity is not shaped as she moves into relation with a man." Similarly, Elizabeth Fifer points out that Stein's situation encouraged her to experiment with parody, theatricality, role playing, and "the diversity of ways possible to look at homosexual love and at her love object." Dierdre Vanderlinde finds in *Three Lives* "one of the earliest attempts to find a new language in which to say, 'I, woman-loving woman, exist.'" Catharine Stimpson places more critical emphasis on Stein's use of masculine pronouns and conventional language, but despite what may have been her compromise, Stimpson feels that female bonding in Stein provides her with a private solution to woman's mind–body split.[44]

Along with Stein, Dickinson's woman-identification has drawn the most attention from recent critics, and has generated considerable controversy between lesbian and other feminist critics. Faderman insists that Dickinson's love for women must be considered homosexual, and that critics must take into account her sexuality (or affectionality). Like most critics who accept this lesbian identification of Dickinson, she points to Susan Gilbert Dickinson as Emily's primary romantic and sexual passion. Both Faderman and Bernikow thus argue that Dickinson's "muse" was sometimes a female figure as well as a male.[45] Some of this work can be justifiably criticized for too closely identifying literature with life; however, by altering our awareness of what is *possible*—namely, that Dickinson's poetry was inspired by her love for a woman—we also can transform our response to the poetry. Paula Bennett daringly suggests that Dickinson's use of crumbs, jewels, pebbles, and similar objects was an attempt to create "clitoral imagery." In a controversial paper on the subject, Nadean Bishop argues forcefully that the poet's marriage poems must be reread in light of what she considers to have been Dickinson's consummated sexual relationship with her sister-in-law.[46]

The establishment of a lesbian literary tradition, a "canon," as my lengthy discussion suggests, has been the primary task of critics writing from a lesbian feminist perspective. But it is not the only focus to emerge. For example, lesbian critics, like feminist critics in the early seventies, have begun to analyze the images, stereotypes, and mythic presence of lesbians in fiction by or about lesbians. Bertha Harris, a major novelist as well as a provocative and trailblazing critic, considers the lesbian to be the prototype of the monster and "the quintessence of all that is female; and female enraged . . . a lesbian is . . . that which has been unspeakable about women."[47] Harris offers this monstrous lesbian as a female archetype who subverts traditional notions of female submissiveness, passivity, and virtue. Her "tooth-and-claw" image of the lesbian is ironically similar to that of Ellen Moers, although from a lesbian rather than heterosexual point of view. But the very fact that Moers presents the lesbian-as-monster in a derogatory context and Harris in a celebratory one suggests that there is an important dialectic between how the lesbian articulates herself and how she is articulated and objectified by others. Popular culture, in particular, exposes the objectifying purpose of the lesbian-as-monster image, such as the lesbian vampire first created by Joseph Sheridan LeFanu's 1871 ghost story "Carmilla," and revived in early 1970s "B" films as a symbolic attack on women's struggle for self-identity.[48] Other critics also have analyzed the negative symbolic appearance of the lesbian in literature. Ann Allen Shockley, reviewing black lesbian characters in American fiction, notes that "within these works exists an undercurrent of hostility, trepidation, subtlety, shadiness, and in some instances, ignorance culling forth homophobic stereotypes."[49] Homophobic stereotypes are also what Judith McDaniel and Maureen Brady find in abundance in recent commercial fiction (such as *Kinflicks, A Sea Change, Some Do,* and *How to Save Your Own Life*) by avowedly feminist novelists. Although individuals might disagree with McDaniel and Brady's severe criticism of specific novels, their overall argument is unimpeachable. Contemporary feminist fiction, by perpetuating stereotyped characters and themes (such as the punishment theme so dear to pre-feminist lesbian literature), serves to "disempower the lesbian."[50] Lesbian, as well as heterosexual, writers present the lesbian as Other, as Julia Penelope Stanley discovered in prefeminist fiction: "The lesbian character creates for herself a mythology of darkness, a world in which she moves through dreams and shadows."[51] Lesbian critics may wish to avoid this analysis of the lesbian as Other because we no longer wish to dwell upon the cultural violence done against us. Yet this area must be explored until we strip these stereotypes of their inhibiting and dehumanizing presence in our popular culture and social mythology.

Lesbian critics have also delved into the area of stylistics and literary theory. If we have been silenced for centuries and speak an oppressor's tongue, then liberation for the lesbian must begin with language. Some writers may have reconciled their internal censor with their speech by writing in code, but many critics maintain that modern lesbian writers, because they are uniquely alienated from the patriarchy, experiment with its literary style and form. Julia Penelope Stanley and Susan Wolfe, considering such diverse writers as Virginia Woolf, Gertrude Stein, Kate Millett, and Elana Dykewoman, claim that "a feminist aesthetic, as it emerges out of women's evolution, grounds itself in female consciousness and in the unrelenting language of process and change."[52] In this article, the authors do not call their feminist aesthetic a lesbian feminist aesthetic, although all the writers they discuss are, in fact, lesbians. Susan Wolfe later confronted this fact: "Few women who continue to identify with men can risk the male censure of 'women's style,' and few escape the male perspective long enough to attempt it."[53] Through examples from Kate Millett, Jill Johnston, and Monique Wittig, she illustrates her contention that lesbian literature is characterized by the use of the continuous present, unconventional grammar, and neologism; and that it breaks boundaries between art and the world, between events and our perceptions of them, and between past, present, and the dream world. It is, as even the proponents of this theory admit, highly debatable that all lesbian writers are modernists, or that all modernists are lesbians. If Virginia Woolf wrote in non-linear, stream-of-consciousness style because she was a lesbian (or "woman-identified") how does one explain Dorothy Richardson whose *Pilgrimage*, despite one lesbian relationship, is primarily heterosexual? If both Woolf and Richardson can be called "feminist" stylists, then how does one explain the nonlinear experimentation of James Joyce or Alain Robbe-Grillet, for example? The holes that presently exist in this theory should not, however, detract from the highly suggestive overlap between experimental and lesbian writers. Nor should we ignore the clear evidence that many contemporary, self-conscious lesbian writers (such as Wittig, Johnston, Bertha Harris, and June Arnold) are choosing an experimental style as well as content.

This development of a self-conscious lesbian literature and literary theory in recent years has led a number of critics to investigate the unifying themes and values of current literature. Such an attempt has been made by Elly Bulkin, who traces the various sources of contemporary lesbian poetry, analyzes "the range of lesbian voices," and advises feminist teachers how to teach lesbian poetry. Mary Carruthers, in asking why so much contemporary feminist poetry is also lesbian, observes that the "lesbian love celebrated in contemporary women's poetry requires an affirmation of the value of femaleness, women's bodies, women's sexuality—in women's language."[54] Jane Gurko and Sally Gearhart compare contemporary lesbian and gay male literature, attempting to discern to what extent one or the other transforms heterosexual ideology. They claim that, unlike gay male literature, lesbian literature "does express a revolutionary model of sexuality which in its structure, its content, and its practice defies the fundamental violent assumptions of patriarchal culture."[55] There is a danger in this attempt to establish a characteristic lesbian vision or literary value system, one that is well illustrated by this article. In an attempt to say this is what defines a lesbian literature, we are easily tempted to read selectively, omitting what is foreign to our theories. Most contemporary lesbian literature does embrace a rhetoric of nonviolence, but this is not universally true; for example, M. F. Beal's *Angel Dance* is a lesbian hard-boiled detective novel and Monique Wittig's *Le Corps lesbien* is infused with a violent eroticism that is, nonetheless, intensely non-patriarchal. Violence, role playing, disaffection, unhappiness, suicide, and self-hatred, to name a few "taboo" subjects, all exist within the lesbian culture, and a useful criticism will have to effectively analyze these as *lesbian* themes and issues, regardless of ideological purity.

Lesbian feminist criticism faces a number of concerns that must be addressed as it grows in force and clarity. Among these concerns is the fact that this criticism is dominated by the politics of lesbian separatism. This is exemplified by the following statement from *Sinister Wisdom*, a journal that has developed a consistent and articulate separatist politics, that

> 'lesbian consciousness' is really a point of view, a view from the boundary. And in a sense every time a woman draws a circle around her psyche, saying 'this is a room of *my own*,' and then writes from within that 'room, she's inhabiting lesbian consciousness.[56]

The value of separatism which, I believe, has always provided the most exciting theoretical developments in lesbian ideology, is precisely this marginality: lesbian existence "on the periphery of patriarchy."[57] Separatism provides criticism, as it did for lesbian politics, a cutting edge and radical energy that keeps us moving forward rather than backward either from fear or complacency. Those critics who maintain a consciously chosen position on the boundaries (and not one imposed by a hostile society) help to keep lesbian and feminist criticism radical and provocative, preventing both from becoming another arm of the established truth. At the same time, however, it is essential that separatist criticism does not itself become an orthodoxy, and thus repetitive, empty, and resistant to change. Lesbian criticism, as Kolodny has argued about feminist criticism, has more to gain from resisting dogma than from monotheism.[58] Understandably, those critics and scholars willing to identify themselves publicly as lesbians also have tended to hold radical politics of marginality. Exposing one's self to public scrutiny as a lesbian may in fact entail marginality through denial of tenure or loss of job, and those lesbians willing to risk these consequences usually have a political position that justifies their risk. However, to me it seems imperative that lesbian criticism develop diversity in theory and approach. Much as lesbians, even more than heterosexual feminists, may mistrust systems of thought developed by and associated with men and male values, we may, in fact, enrich our work through the insights of Marxist, structuralist, semiotic, or even psychoanalytic criticism. Perhaps "male" systems of thought are incompatible with a lesbian literary vision, but we will not know until we attempt to integrate these ideas into our work.[59]

Similarly, lesbian criticism and cultural theory in general can only gain by developing a greater specificity, historically and culturally. We have tended to write and act as if lesbian experience—which is perceived as that of a contemporary, white, middle-class feminist—is universal and unchanging. Although most lesbians know that this is not the case, we too often forget to apply rigorous historical and cross-cultural tools to our scholarship. Much of this ahistoricity occurs around the shifting definitions of lesbianism from one era and one culture to another. To state simply that Wollstonecraft "was" a lesbian because she passionately loved Fanny Blood, or Susan B. Anthony was a lesbian because she wrote amorous letters to Anna Dickinson, without accounting for historical circumstances, may serve to distort or dislocate the actual meaning of these women's lives (just as it is distorting to *deny* their love for women). There are also notable differences among the institution of the *berdache* (the adoption by one sex of the opposite gender role) in Native American tribes; *faute de mieux* lesbian activity tolerated in France (as in Colette's *Claudine* novels); idyllic romantic friendships (such as that of the famous Ladies of Llangollen); and contemporary self-conscious lesbianism. I do believe that there is a common structure—a lesbian "essence"—that may be located in all these specific historical existences, just as we may speak of a widespread, perhaps universal, structure of marriage or the family. However, in each of these cases—lesbianism, marriage, the family—careful attention to history teaches us that differences are as significant as similarities, and vital information about female survival may be found in the different ways in which women have responded to their historical situation. This tendency toward simplistic universalism is accompanied by what I see as a dangerous development of biological determinism and a curious revival of the nineteenth-century feminist notion of female (now lesbian) moral superiority—that women are uniquely caring and superior to inherently violent males. Although only an undertone in some criticism and literature, any such sociobiological impulse should be questioned at every appearance.

The denial of meaningful differences among women is being challenged, particularly around the issue of racism. Bulkin has raised criticisms about the racism of white lesbian feminist theory. She has written that

> if I can put together—or think someone else can put together—a viable piece of feminist criticism or theory whose base is the thought and writing of white women/lesbians and expect that an analysis of racism can be tacked on or dealt with later as a useful addition, it is a measure of the extent to which I partake of that white privilege.[60]

Implicit in the criticism of Bulkin and other antiracist writers is the belief that lesbians, because of our experience of stigma and exclusion from the feminist mainstream, ought to be particularly sensitive to the dynamic between oppression and oppressing. White lesbians who are concerned about eradicating racism in criticism and theory have been greatly influenced as well by the work of several black lesbian feminist literary critics, such as Gloria T. Hull, Barbara Smith, and Lorraine Bethel.[61] Such concern is not yet present over the issue of class, although the historical association of lesbianism with upper-class values has often been used by left-wing political groups and governments to deny legitimacy to homosexual rights and needs. Lesbian critics studying the Barney circle, for example, might analyze the historical connections between lesbianism and class status. Lesbian critics might also develop comparisons among the literatures of various nationalities because the lesbian canon is of necessity cross-national. We have barely explored the differences between American, English, French, and German lesbian literature (although *Surpassing the Love of Men* draws some distinctions), let alone non-Western literature. The paucity of lesbian scholars trained in these literatures has so far prevented the development of a truly international lesbian literary canon.

As lesbian criticism matures, we may anticipate the development of ongoing and compelling political and practical concerns. At this time, for example, lesbians are still defining and discovering texts. We are certainly not as badly off as we were in the early seventies when the only lesbian novels in print were *The Well of Loneliness, Rubyfruit Jungle,* and Isabel Miller's *Patience and Sarah.* However, texts published prior to 1970 are still difficult to find, and even *The Well of Loneliness* is intermittently available at the whim of publishers. Furthermore, the demise of Diana Press and the apparent slowdown of Daughters (two of the most active lesbian publishing houses) leaves many major works unavailable, possibly forever. As the boom in gay literature subsides, teachers of literature will find it very difficult to unearth teachable texts. Scholars have the excellent Arno Press series, *Homosexuality: Lesbians and Gay Men in Society, History, and Literature,* but, as Faderman's monumental scholarship reveals, far more lesbian literature exists than anyone has suspected. This literature needs to be unearthed, analyzed, explicated, perhaps translated, and made available to readers.

As lesbian critics, we also need to address the exclusion of lesbian literature from not merely the traditional, but also the feminist canon. Little lesbian litera-ture has been integrated into the mainstream of feminist texts, as evidenced by what is criticized, collected, and taught. It is a matter of serious concern that les-bian literature is omitted from anthologies or included in mere token amounts, or that critical works and Modern Language Association panels still exclude les-bianism. It may as yet be possible for heterosexual feminists to claim ignorance about lesbian literature; however, lesbian critics should make it impossible for that claim to stand much longer.

Lesbianism is still perceived as a minor and somewhat discomforting variation within the female life cycle, when it is mentioned at all. Just as we need to inte-grate lesbian material and perspectives into the traditional and feminist canons, we might also apply lesbian theory to traditional literature. Feminists have not only pointed out the sexism in many canonical works, but have also provided cre-ative and influential rereadings of these works; similarly lesbians might contrib-ute to the rereading of the classics. For example, *The Bostonians,* an obvious text, has been reread often from a lesbian perspective, and we could reinterpret D. H. Lawrence's antifeminism or Doris Lessing's compromised feminism (particularly in *The Golden Notebook)* by relating these attitudes to their fear of or discomfort with lesbianism. Other texts or selections of texts—such as Rossetti's "Goblin Market" or the relationship between Lucy Snowe and Ginevra Fanshawe in *Villette*—might reveal a subtext that could be called lesbian. Just as few texts es-cape a feminist re-vision, few might invade a lesbian transformation.

This last point—that there is a way in which we might "review" literature as lesbians—brings me to my conclusion. In a brief period of a few years, critics have begun to demonstrate the existence of a distinct lesbian aesthetic, just as femi-nists have outlined elements of a female aesthetic. Certain components of this aesthetic or critical perspective are clear:

> Perhaps lesbian feminist criticism [or literature, I would add] is a political or
> thematic perspective, a kind of imagination that can see beyond the barriers
> of heterosexuality, role stereotypes, patterns of language and culture that may
> be repressive to female sexuality and expression.[62]

A lesbian artist very likely would express herself differently about sexuality, the body, and relationships. But are there other—less obvious—unifying themes, ideas, and imagery that might define a lesbian text or subtext? How, for example, does the lesbian's sense of outlaw status affect her literary vision? Might lesbian writing, because of the lesbian's position on the boundaries, be characterized by a particular sense of freedom and flexibility or, rather, by images of violently im-posed barriers, the closet? Or, in fact, is there a dialectic between freedom and imprisonment unique to lesbian writing? Do lesbians have a special perception of suffering and stigma, as so much prefeminist literature seems to suggest? What about the "muse," the female symbol of literary creativity: do women writers cre-ate a lesbian relationship with their muse as May Sarton asserts? If so, do those writers who choose a female muse experience a freedom from inhibition because of that fact, or might there be a lack of creative tension in such a figurative same-sex relationship? I feel on solid ground in asserting that there are certain topics and themes that define lesbian culture, and that we are beginning to define a lesbian symbolism. Lesbian literature may present a unified tradition of thematic concerns such as that of unrequited longing, a longing of almost cosmic totality because the love object is denied not by circumstance or chance, but by necessity. The tension between romantic love and genital sexuality takes a particular form in woman-to-woman relationships, often articulated through musings on the difference between purity and impurity (culminating in Colette's study of variant sexuality, *The Pure and the Impure*). Lesbian literature approaches the theme of development or the quest in a manner different from that of men or heterosexual women. Lesbian literature, as lesbian culture in general, is particularly flexible on issues of gender and role identification; even *The Well of Loneliness* hints at the tragedy of rigid gender roles. Because of this flexibility, lesbian artists and writers have always been fascinated with costuming, because dress is an external manifestation of gender roles lesbians often reject.[63] As we read and reread literature from a lesbian perspective, I am confident we will continue to expand our understanding of the lesbian literary tradition and a lesbian aesthetic.

This essay has suggested the vigor of lesbian criticism and its value to all feminists in raising awareness of entrenched heterosexism in existing texts, clarifying the lesbian traditions in literature through scholarship and reinterpretation, pointing out barriers that have stood in the way of free lesbian expression, explicating the recurring themes and values of lesbian literature, and exposing the dehumanizing stereotypes of lesbians in our culture. Many of the issues that face lesbian critics—resisting dogma, expanding the canon, creating a non-racist and non-classist critical vision, transforming our readings of traditional texts, and exploring new methodologies—are the interests of all feminist critics. Because feminism concerns itself with the removal of limitations and impediments in the way of female imagination, and lesbian criticism helps to expand our notions of what is *possible* for women, then all women would grow by adopting for themselves a lesbian vision. Disenfranchised groups have had to adopt a double-vision for survival; one of the political transformations of recent decades has been the realization that enfranchised groups—men, whites, heterosexuals, the middle class—would do well to adopt that double-vision for the survival of us all. Lesbian literary criticism simply restates what feminists already know, that one group cannot name itself "humanity" or even "woman": "We're not trying to become part of the old order misnamed 'universal' which has tabooed us; we are transforming the meaning of 'universality.'"[64] Whether lesbian criticism will survive depends as much upon the external social climate as it does upon the creativity and skill of its practitioners. If political attacks on gay rights and freedom grow; if the so-called Moral Majority wins its fight to eliminate gay teachers and texts from the schools (it would be foolhardy to believe they will exempt universities); and if the academy, including feminist teachers and scholars, fails to support lesbian scholars, eradicate heterosexist values and assumptions, and incorporate the insights of lesbian scholarship into the mainstream; then current lesbian criticism will probably suffer the same fate as did Jeanette Foster's *Sex Variant Women* in the fifties. Lesbian or heterosexual, we will all suffer from that loss.

NOTES

An earlier version of this paper was presented at the first annual convention of the National Women's Studies Association, Lawrence, Kansas, May 1979.

1. Lynn Strongin, "Sayre," in *Rising Tides: Twentieth-Century American Women Poets*, ed. Laura Chester and Sharon Barba (New York: Washington Square Press, 1973), p. 317.

2. June Arnold, "Lesbian Fiction," Special Issue on Lesbian Writing and Publishing, *Sinister Wisdom* 2 (Fall 1976): 28.

3. Sandy Boucher, "Lesbian Artists," Special Issue on Lesbian Art and Artists, *Heresies* 3 (Fall 1977): 48.

4. This survey is limited to published and unpublished essays in literary criticism that present a perspective either sympathetic to lesbianism or those explicitly lesbian in orientation. It is limited to *literature* and to theoretical articles (not book reviews). The sexual preference of the authors is, for the most part, irrelevant; this is an analysis of lesbian feminist *ideas*, not authors. Although the network of lesbian critics is well developed, some major unpublished papers may have escaped my attention.

5. Elly Bulkin, "'Kissing Against the Light': A Look at Lesbian Poetry," *Radical Teacher* 10 (December 1978): 8. This article was reprinted in *College English* and *Women's Studies Newsletter*; an expanded version is available from the Lesbian-Feminist Study Clearinghouse, Women's Studies Program, University of Pittsburgh, Pittsburgh, Pennsylvania 15260.

6. Julia Penelope [Stanley], "The Articulation of Bias: Hoof in Mouth Disease," paper presented at the 1979 convention of the National Council of Teachers of English, San Francisco, November 1979, pp. 4–5. On the same panel, I presented a paper on "Heterosexism in Literary Anthologies," which develops some of the points of this paragraph.

7. Annette Kolodny, "Literary Criticism: Review Essay," *Signs* 2, no. 2 (Winter 1976): 416, 419.

8. Ellen Moers, *Literary Women: The Great Writers* (Garden City, N.Y.: Doubleday & Co., 1976), pp. 108–9, 145.

9. Patricia Meyer Spacks, *The Female Imagination* (New York: Avon Books, 1975), pp. 89, 214, 363.

10. Elaine Showalter, *A Literature of Their Own: British Women Novelists From Brontë to Lessing* (Princeton: Princeton University Press, 1977), pp. 178, 229, 316.

11. Sandra M. Gilbert and Susan Gubar, *The Madwoman in the Attic: The Woman Writer and the Nineteenth-Century Literary Imagination* (New Haven: Yale University Press, 1979), p. 567. Regarding another issue—their analysis of Emily Dickinson's poem no. 1722— Nadean Bishop says, "It is hard to fathom how Sandra Gilbert and Susan Gubar could take this erotic representation of lesbian love-making to be an 'image of the chaste moon goddess Diana,' who does not have hand or tender tongue or inspire incredulity." See Nadean Bishop, "Renunciation in the Bridal Poems of Emily Dickinson," paper presented at the National Women's Studies Association, Bloomington, Indiana, 16–20 May 1980. One other major critical study, Judith Fetterley's *The Resisting Reader: a Feminist Approach to American Fiction* (Bloomington: Indiana University Press, 1978), is uniquely sensitive to lesbianism in its interpretation of *The Bostonians*.

12. Gene Damon, Jan Watson, and Robin Jordan, *The Lesbian in Literature: A Bibliography* (1967; reprinted., Reno, Nev.: Naiad Press, 1975).

13. Jeannette Foster, *Sex Variant Women in Literature* (1956; reprinted, Baltimore: Diana Press, 1975). See also, Karla Jay, "The X-Rated Bibliographer: A Spy in the House of Sex," in *Lavender Culture*, ed. Karla Jay and Allen Young (New York: Harcourt Brace Jovanovich, 1978), pp. 257–61.

14. Beth Hodges, ed., Special Issue on Lesbian Writing and Publishing, *Margins* 23

(August 1975). Beth Hodges, ed., Special Issue on Lesbian Literature and Publishing, *Sinister Wisdom* 2 (Fall 1976).

15. In addition, networks of lesbian critics, teachers, and scholars were established through panels at the Modern Language Association's annual conventions and at the Lesbian Writers' Conference in Chicago, which began in 1974 and continued for several years. Currently, networking continues through conferences, journals, and other institutionalized outlets. The Lesbian-Feminist Study Clearinghouse reprints articles, bibliographies, and syllabi pertinent to lesbian studies. See note 5 for the address. The Lesbian Herstory Archives collects all material documenting lesbian lives past or present; their address is P.O. Box 1258, New York, New York 10001. *Matrices*, "A Lesbian-Feminist Research Newsletter," is a network of information about research projects, reference materials, calls for papers, bibliographies, and so forth. There are several regional editors; the managing editor is Bobby Lacy, 4000 Randolph, Lincoln, Nebraska 68510.

16. Radicalesbians, "The Woman-Identified Woman," in *Radical Feminism*, ed. Anne Koedt, Ellen Levine, and Anita Rapone (New York; Quadrangle, 1973). This article is extensively reprinted in women's studies anthologies.

17. Charlotte Bunch, "Lesbians in Revolt," in *Lesbianism and the Women's Movement*, ed. Nancy Myron and Charlotte Bunch (Baltimore: Diana Press, 1975), p. 30.

18. Susan Sniader Lanser, "Speaking in Tongues: *Ladies Almanack* and the Language of Celebration," *Frontiers* 4, no. 3 (Fall 1979): 39.

19. Catharine R. Stimpson, "Zero Degree Deviancy: A Study of the Lesbian Novel," *Critical Inquiry* 8, no. 2 (1981): 363–79.

20. Barbara Smith, "Toward a Black Feminist Criticism," *Conditions: Two* 1, no. 2 (October 1977): 39. It is sometimes overlooked that Smith's pathbreaking article on black feminist criticism is also a lesbian feminist analysis.

21. Adrienne Rich, "Compulsory Heterosexuality and Lesbian Existence," *Signs* 5, no. 4 (Summer 1980): 648–49.

22. Bertha Harris, quoted by Smith, "Toward a Black Feminist Criticism," p. 33.

23. Supportive historical and biographical information about women writers can be found in a number of recent articles, in addition to those cited elsewhere in this paper. See, for example, Judith Schwarz, "*Yellow Clover*: Katherine Lee Bates and Katherine Coman," pp. 59–67; Josephine Donovan, "The Unpublished Love Poems of Sarah Orne Jewett," pp. 26–31; and Margaret Cruikshank, "Geraldine Jewsbury and Jane Carlyle," pp. 60–64, all in Special Issue on Lesbian History, *Frontiers* 4, no. 3 (Fall 1979).

24. Lillian Faderman, *Surpassing the Love of Men: Romantic Friendship and Love Between Women From the Renaissance to the Present* (New York: William Morrow and Co., 1981), pp. 17–18.

25. Adrienne Rich, "'It Is the Lesbian in Us . . . ,'" in *On Lies, Secrets, and Silence* (New York: W. W. Norton & Co., 1979), p. 202.

26. Rich, "Women and Honor: Some Notes on Lying (1975)," in *On Lies, Secrets, and Silence*, p. 190.

27. Gloria T. Hull, " 'Under the Days': The Buried Life and Poetry of Angelina Weld Grimké," The Black Women's Issue, *Conditions: Five* 2, no. 2 (Autumn 1979): 23, 20.

28. Joanna Russ, "To Write 'Like a Woman': Transformations of Identity in Willa Cather," paper presented at the MLA convention, in San Francisco, December 1979. On coding in other writers, see also Ann Cothran and Diane Griffin Crowder, "An Optical Thirst for Invisible Water: Image Structure, Codes and Recoding in Colette's *The Pure and the Impure*," paper presented at the MLA convention, New York, December 1978; and Annette Kolodny, "The Lady's Not For Spurning: Kate Millett and the Critics," *Contemporary Literature* 17, no. 4: 541–62.

29. Two male critics—Edmund Wilson and Robert Bridgman—first suggested the connection between Stein's obscurity and her lesbianism. Jane Rule in *Lesbian Images* and

Dolores Klaich in *Woman Plus Woman* (see note 35) both follow their analysis. Cynthia Secor has argued that Stein did declare her lesbianism in her writing ("Can We Call Gertrude Stein a Non-Declared Lesbian Writer?") in a paper presented at the MLA convention, San Francisco, December 1979. For more on Stein, see note 44.

30. Bulkin, "'Kissing Against the Light,'" p. 8.

31. Smith, "Toward a Black Feminist Criticism," p. 39.

32. Blanche Wiesen Cook, "'Women Alone Stir My Imagination': Lesbianism and the Cultural Tradition," *Signs* 4, no. 4 (Summer 1979): 718–39. A curious example of contemporary denial of lesbianism—the obliteration of the lesbian tradition such as it is—is found in Judith Hallett, "Sappho and Her Social Context: Sense and Sensuality," *Signs* 4, no. 3 (Spring 1979): 447–64. Sappho, of course, personifies "lesbian existence," indeed lesbian *possibility*, as well as female poetic creativity. Hallett, however, essentially denies Sappho's love for women with her conclusion that "she did not represent herself in her verses as having expressed homosexual feelings physically." One might certainly argue that no other possible interpretation can exist for Sappho's "He is more than a hero" (Mary Barnard's translation). Eva Stigers, in "Romantic Sensuality, Poetic Sense: A Response to Hallett on Sappho" (same issue, pp. 464–71), contends that Sappho "chose female homosexual love as the vehicle because lesbian love offered the most receptive setting for romantic *eros*." This interpretation may more accurately reflect the perspective of the nineteenth-century romantic poets who rediscovered Sappho. However, Stiger's argument that Sappho used lesbian love to create an alternate world in which male values are not dominant and in which to explore the female experience provides a starting point for a feminist analysis of Sappho's influence on her modern lesbian followers. A fine exposition of this "Sappho model" in French lesbian literature is provided by Elaine Marks in her essay "Lesbian Intertextuality" (see note 41).

33. Jane Rule, *Lesbian Images* (Garden City, N.Y.; Doubleday & Co., 1975).

34. Bonnie Zimmerman, "The New Tradition," *Sinister Wisdom* 2 (Fall 1976): 34–41.

35. Dolores Klaich, *Woman Plus Woman: Attitudes Toward Lesbianism* (New York: William Morrow and Co., 1974); Louise Bernikow, *The World Split Open: Four Centuries of Women Poets in England and America, 1552–1950* (New York: Vintage Books, 1974).

36. Cook, "Women Alone Stir My Imagination," p. 720.

37. See Lillian Faderman's articles: "The Morbidification of Love Between Women by Nineteenth-Century Sexologists," *Journal of Homosexuality* 4, no. 1 (Fall 1978): 73–90; "Emily Dickinson's Letters to Sue Gilbert," *Massachusetts Review* 18, no. 2 (Summer 1977): 197–225; "Emily Dickinson's Homoerotic Poetry," *Higginson Journal* 18 (1978): 19–27; "Female Same-Sex Relationships in Novels by Longfellow, Holmes, and James," *New England Quarterly* 60, no. 3 (September 1978): 309–32; and "Lesbian Magazine Fiction in the Early Twentieth Century," *Journal of Popular Culture* 11, no. 4 (Spring 1978): 800–17.

38. Holly Near, "Imagine My Surprise," on *Imagine My Surprise!* (Redwood Records, 1978).

39. See Klaich, chap. 6. Also, see Bertha Harris, "The More Profound Nationality of their Lesbianism: Lesbian Society in Paris in the 1920's," *Amazon Expedition* (New York: Times Change Press, 1973), pp. 77–88; and Gayle Rubin's Introduction to Renée Vivien's: *A Woman Appeared to Me*, trans. Jeanette Foster (Reno, Nev.: Naiad Press, 1976).

40. For example, see Lanser, "Speaking in Tongues."

41. Marks, "Lesbian Intertextuality," in *Homosexualities and French Literature*, ed. George Stambolian and Elaine Marks (Ithaca, N.Y.: Cornell University Press, 1979), pp. 353–77.

42. Lillian Faderman and Ann Williams, "Radclyffe Hall and the Lesbian Image," *Conditions: One* 1, no. 1 (April 1977): 40; and Sybil Korff Vincent, "Nothing Fails Like Success: Radclyffe Hall's *The Well of Loneliness*," unpublished paper.

43. Stimpson, "Zero Degree Deviancy."

44. Cynthia Secor, "*Ida*, A Great American Novel," *Twentieth-Century Literature* 24, no. 1

(Spring 1978): 99; Elizabeth Fifer, "Is Flesh Advisable: The Interior Theater of Gertrude Stein," *Signs* 4, no. 3 (Spring 1979): 478; Dierdre Vanderlinde, "Gertrude Stein: Three Lives," paper presented at MLA convention, San Francisco, December 1979, p. 10; and Catharine Stimpson, "The Mind, and Body and Gertrude Stein," *Critical Inquiry* 3, no. 3 (Spring 1977): 489–506. Like Stimpson on Stein, Lanser, in "Speaking in Tongues," suggests that Djuna Barnes in *Ladies Almanack* "writes through the lesbian body, celebrating not the abstraction of a sexual preference, but female sexuality and its lesbian expression."

45. Lillian Faderman and Louise Bernikow, "Comment on Joanne Feit Diehl's 'Come Slowly—Eden,'" *Signs* 4, no. 1 (Autumn 1978): 188–95. For another perspective on woman as muse, see my paper, " 'The Dark Eye Beaming': George Eliot, Sara Hennell and the Female Muse" (presented at MLA convention, "George Eliot and the Female Tradition," 1980); and Arlene Raven and Ruth Iskin, "Through the Peephole: Toward a Lesbian Sensibility in Art," *Chrysalis* no. 4, pp. 19–31. Contemporary lesbian interpretations of Dickinson were anticipated by Rebecca Patterson in *The Riddle of Emily Dickinson* (Boston: Houghton Mifflin, 1951).

46. Paula Bennett, "The Language of Love: Emily Dickinson's Homoerotic Poetry," *Gai Saber* 1, no. 1 (Spring 1977): 13–17; Bennett, "Emily Dickinson and the Value of Isolation," *Dickinson Studies* 36 (1979): 13–17; Bennett's paper presented at the MLA, 1979; and Bishop, "Renunciation in the Bridal Poems."

47. Bertha Harris, *"What we mean to say:* Notes Toward Defining the Nature of Lesbian Literature," *Heresies* 3 (Fall 1977): 7–8. Also, Harris, "The Purification of Monstrosity: The Lesbian as Literature," paper presented at the MLA convention, New York, December 1974.

48. Bonnie Zimmerman, "'Daughters of Darkness': Lesbian Vampires," *Jump Cut* no. 24–25 (March 1981): 23–24. See also, Jane Caputi, "'Jaws': Fish Stories and Patriarchal Myth," *Sinister Wisdom* 7 (Fall 1978): 66–81.

49. Ann Allen Shockley, "The Black Lesbian in American Literature: An Overview," *Conditions: Five* 2: no. 2 (Autumn 1979): 136.

50. Maureen Brady and Judith McDaniel, "Lesbians in the Mainstream: Images of Lesbians in Recent Commercial Fiction," *Conditions: Six* 2, no. 3 (Summer 1980): 83.

51. Julia Penelope Stanley, "Uninhabited Angels: Metaphors for Love," *Margins* 23 (August 1975): 8.

52. Julia Penelope Stanley and Susan J. Wolfe, "Toward a Feminist Aesthetic," *Chrysalis,* no. 6, p. 66.

53. Susan J. Wolfe, "Stylistic Experimentation in Millett, Johnston, and Wittig," paper presented at the MLA convention, New York, December 1978, p. 3. On lesbian stylistics, see Lanser, "Speaking in Tongues"; and Martha Rosenfield, "Linguistic Experimentation in Monique Wittig's *Le Corps lesbien*," paper presented at the MLA convention, 1978.

54. Mary Carruthers, "Imagining Women: Notes Toward a Feminist Poetic," *Massachusetts Review* 20, no. 2 (Summer 1979): 301.

55. Jane Gurko and Sally Gearhart, "The Sword and the Vessel Versus the Lake on the Lake: A Lesbian Model of Nonviolent Rhetoric," paper presented at the MLA convention, 1979, p. 3.

56. Harriet Desmoines, "Notes for a Magazine 11," *Sinister Wisdom* 1, no. 1 (July 1976): 29.

57. Wolfe, "Stylistic Experimentation," p. 16.

58. Annette Kolodny, "Dancing Through the Minefield: Some Observations on the Theory, Practice, and Politics of a Feminist Literary Criticism," *Feminist Studies* 6, no. 1 (Spring 1980): 1–25; in *Feminisms*, 2nd ed., under "Practice."

59. For example, a panel at the 1980 MLA convention (Houston), "Literary History and the New Histories of Sexuality," presented gay and lesbian perspectives on contemporary French philosophies.

60. Elly Bulkin, "Racism and Writing: Some Implications for White Lesbian Critics," *Sinister Wisdom* 13 (Spring 1980): 16.

61. See Lorraine Bethel, "'This Infinity of Conscious Pain': Zora Neale Hurston and the Black Female Literary Tradition" and Gloria T. Hull, "Researching Alice Dunbar Nelson: A Personal and Literary Perspective," both in *All the Women Are White, All the Blacks Are Men, But Some of Us Are Brave: Black Women's Studies,* ed. Gloria T. Hull, Patricia Bell Scott, and Barbara Smith (Old Westbury, N.Y.: Feminist Press, 1982); and Cheryl Clarke et al., "Conversations and Questions: Black Women on Black Women Writers," *Conditions: Nine* 3, no. 3 (1983): 88–137.

62. Judith McDaniel, "Lesbians and Literature," *Sinister Wisdom* 2 (Fall 1976): 2.

63. Susan Gubar, "Blessings in Disguise: Cross-Dressing as Re-Dressing for Female Modernists," *Massachusetts Review* 22, no. 3 (1981): 477–508.

64. Elly Bulkin, "An Interview with Adrienne Rich: Part II," *Conditions: Two* (1977): 58.

ANOMALOUSNESS

(1983)

She didn't write it.

She wrote it, but she shouldn't have.

She wrote it, but look what she wrote about.

She wrote it, but "she" isn't really an artist and "it" isn't really serious, of the right genre—i.e., really art.

She wrote it, but she wrote only one of it.

She wrote it, but it's only interesting / included in the canon for one, limited reason.

She wrote it, but there are very few of her.

Here are some anthologies and academic lists, chosen at random, which may aid in seeing how few of her there are.

The Golden Treasury, edited by F. T. Palgrave in 1861, was reedited by Oscar Williams in 1961.[1] Palgrave declares his intention to include only lyrics by writers not living in 1855, "lyric" being defined as "some single thought, feeling, or situation." Williams, who has both added poets to the periods Palgrave covers and brought the anthology up to 1955, says that Palgrave's "own definition of the lyrical as unity of feeling or thought" has been kept as a "determinant of choice," although both standards are flexible enough to include, for Palgrave, Shelley's "To a Skylark" and Keats' "Ode to Autumn"; and for Williams, Eliot's "The Journey of the Magi," Auden's "In Memory of W. B. Yeats," and Lindsay's "The Congo." Palgrave includes four women: Anna Letitia Barbauld, Jane Elliott, Lady Anne Lindsay, and Lady Carolina Nairne, all active mainly in the eighteenth century; the latter three were Scotswomen. Each is represented by one selection. Palgrave did not include either Aphra Behn or Anne Finch, Countess of Winchilsea, although some of their works certainly fall within his definition of the lyric. Nor, in his introduction, does he mention the then-famous Elizabeth Barrett Browning as one of the living poets who "will no doubt claim and obtain their place among the best." Emily Brontë (died 1848) is neither mentioned nor included. Palgrave also omitted Donne, Blake, and Traherne, all added by Williams.

In order to count the percentage of women included in this anthology, I have omitted all poets dead before 1650. The assumption that no women dead before

1650 wrote anything at all is questionable (see Epilogue), but since it's very probably an assumption Palgrave and Williams would make (as would other anthologists) there's no need to load the figures. It's probably fair to assume that Williams would not include Palgrave's female lyricists but impossible to tell which of the male poets he would likewise delete; I will therefore give both sets of figures: Williams' female choices are 8 percent of the total number of poets in the anthology; the addition of Palgrave's choices raises the total to 11 percent.

Of Williams' fourteen women additions, six are nineteenth-century poets: Emily Brontë, Christina Rossetti, Emily Dickinson, Alice Meynell, Elizabeth Barrett Browning, and (surprisingly) George Eliot. There are no seventeenth- or eighteenth-century additions to Palgrave's four. The remaining eight are twentieth-century figures: Leonie Adams, Elizabeth Bishop, Ruth Herschberger, Esther Matthews, Edna St. Vincent Millay, Marianne Moore, Elinor Wylie, and Gene Derwood. The only women represented by more than two selections apiece are Gene Derwood (seven), Emily Dickinson (eight), and Edna Millay (eleven). Elizabeth Barrett Browning is represented by two of the *Sonnets from the Portuguese*, and Christina Rossetti and Dante Gabriel Rossetti each by two poems. If we compare female poets represented by more than two selections with male poets similarly represented, there are three women out of a total of sixty, or 5 percent. (Only one of these women is not a twentieth-century poet.) To recall Van Gerven, "Since . . . only contemporary women poets are represented in any number, it becomes clear that a woman must be extraordinary to outlive her generation—And that a man need not."[2]

In *A Treasury of Great Poems*, Louis Untermeyer includes Aphra Behn and Anne Finch, Countess of Winchilsea (whom Williams excludes). Untermeyer's twentieth-century choices (except for Millay) differ entirely from Williams', yet he ends up with much the same percentage of women poets as Williams does (if we subtract Palgrave's choices): 8.6 percent of the total. This figure holds, by the way, either with or without the inclusion of both editors' twentieth-century male and female choices.

In Auden and Pearson's far less idiosyncratic *Poets of the English Language* (which ends with Yeats), 5 percent of the authors listed are women. (Again I have considered 1650 as a rough beginning date.) Anne Bradstreet is present, but Aphra Behn and Elizabeth Barrett Browning are absent, although in evidence are such male figures as John Byrom, Henry Alabaster, and John Wolcot. In all three anthologies there are sections of anonymous ballads, but no speculation that the authorship of some of these may have been female, although an Elizabethan scholar, Frederick O. Waage, notes "the strong tendency of all social ballads to vindicate covertly their women."[3] I would certainly hesitate to attribute a later ballad like "Once I wore my apron low" to male authorship, and even among the earlier ones there are some which suggest not only female authorship but female revenge— for example, "May Colvin." (Here the false young man who has drowned six women attempts to drown a seventh, but wants her to take off her clothes, which are too costly to rot in the sea. Pretending modesty, she bids him to turn his back and when he does, throws *him* into the sea, triumphantly telling him to keep company with the women he's drowned.)

To turn again to the graduate reading list of the University of Washington's Department of English (for August 1977), we find no women from 1660 to 1780, four female novelists (but no poets) in nineteenth-century England, and in the United States (up to 1900) four women. The twentieth-century list includes one female novelist, Virginia Woolf, and, out of an elective selection of seven novelists, one black man (Ralph Ellison) and one white woman (Doris Lessing). Out of a similar elective selection of eight poets, two are (white) women: Larkin and Rich. Counting again from about 1660, the number of women is about 6 percent. In an earlier list (1968), Chopin, Chesnutt, and Bradstreet do not appear, but Edith Wharton (invisible in 1977) does. In both lists, Cotton Mather appears but not Margaret Fuller; in 1977 Rochester, William Cowper, and William Collins but not Mary Wollstonecraft. Missing also are Aphra Behn, Fanny Burney, Elizabeth Barrett, and Christina Rossetti; and to give my own very partial list of twentieth-century omissions: Willa Cather (Ernest Hemingway is represented by three selections), Dorothy Richardson, Djuna Barnes, Katherine Mansfield, Carson McCullers, Isak Dinesen, Marianne Moore, Zora Neale Hurston, Elizabeth Bishop, and so on and so on.

What is so striking about these examples is that although the percentage of women included remains somewhere between 5 percent and 8 percent, the personnel change rather strikingly from book to book; Aphra Behn appears and vanishes, Anne Bradstreet is existent or nonexistent according to whom you read, Elizabeth Barrett Browning and Emily Brontë bob up and down like corks, Edith Wharton is part of English literature in 1968 and banished to the outer darkness in 1977—and yet there are always enough women for that 5 percent and never quite enough to get much past 8 percent. It recalls the proportion of female entries (about 7 percent) in those freshman textbooks, chosen not as selections of great literature but in order to teach freshmen to read and write: "the ratio of women writers . . . was fairly constant: about 7%."[4]

In a study of courses given by the Department of English of the women's college she once attended, Elaine Showalter finds (of the writers listed in courses past the freshman year) 17 women out of 313, or just about 5 percent. But which 5 percent? Showalter writes:

> In the twenty-one courses beyond the freshman level . . . there were . . . such [male] luminaries as William Shenstone, James Barrie, and Dion Boucicault; and . . . Lady Mary Wortley Montagu, Anne Bradstreet, Mrs. Centlivre, Fanny Burney, Jane Austen, Charlotte and Emily Brontë, George Eliot, Margaret Fuller, Emily Dickinson, Sarah Orne Jewett, Lady Gregory, Virginia Woolf, Dorothy Richardson, Marianne Moore, Gertrude Stein, and Djuna Barnes.

She adds: "The *Norton Anthology* . . . includes 169 men and 6 women,"[5] $3^1/_2$ percent and 11.6 percent. Average: 7 percent.

Showalter talks of imbalance, but what bothers me is the constancy of the imbalance despite the changes in personnel. For example, Showalter's English Department includes many more women than the University of Washington list; yet in the former case the percentage of women is lower, not higher, than in the latter. It seems that when women are brought into a reading list, a curriculum, or an anthology, men arrive, too—let the number of men drop and the women mysteriously disappear.

Nonetheless, as Van Gerven says:

the inclusion of only the most extraordinary women [but not only the most extraordinary men] . . . distorts the relevance of those few women . . . who remain. Since women are so often thus isolated in anthologies . . . they seem odd, unconventional, and therefore, a little trivial.

She adds:

When Dickinson, or any woman poet for that matter, is isolated from all writing in her own and succeeding generations, she appears bizarre, extraneous. . . . Since women writers are thus isolated, they often do not fit into the literary historian's "coherent view of the total literary culture." . . . As each succeeding generation of women . . . is excluded from the literary record, the connections between women . . . writers become more and more obscure, which in turn simply justifies the exclusion of more and more women on the grounds that they are anomalous—they just don't fit in.[6]

Pollution of quality via anomalousness is similar to *pollution of agency via abnormality.* Thus R. P. Blackmur, writing of Emily Dickinson, can speak of:

[her] private and eccentric . . . relation to the business of poetry. She was neither a professional poet nor an amateur; she was a private poet who wrote indefatigably as other women cook or knit . . . [driven] to poetry instead of antimacassars. Neither her personal education nor the habit of her society . . . gave her the least inkling that poetry is a rational and objective art.[7]

Thus Dickinson's *anomalousness* as a poet, in part referable to her lack of proper education, leads to an assertion of her personal eccentricity (pollution of agency via abnormality) which along with a re-categorizing of Dickinson as not-a-poet and her work as equivalent to antimacassars, converges on the final judgment; her poetry is not what poetry ought to be. Blackmur wrote in 1937, but what he said is not far from the *Commercial Advertiser* review of 1891:

Extreme hunger often causes strange visions. That this hermitess never satisfied, perhaps never could satisfy, her craving for human companionship, may have first brought her into her strangely visionary state. Upon the theme of human love she becomes absurdly, if not blasphemously, intemperate.[8]

Again pollution of agency is given as the reason for the defects in Dickinson's work, nor are the defects very different: she is "driven" and "hungry," *therefore* not "rational" or temperate. In both accounts she appears as totally isolated, a "private" poet or a "hermitess" whose talent came from nowhere and bore no relation to anything. Yet according to other sources this anomalous being can be placed squarely in a public literary tradition, influenced by it and influencing it in turn. Moers writes:

Dickinson had been reading about Mrs. Browning in Kate Field's memorial tribute . . . in the September 1861 *Atlantic Monthly* just as, earlier that year, she had read of Julia Ward Howe's . . . abridgment of George Sand's autobio-

graphy... hundreds of phrases of Dickinson's ... suggest she had the whole
of *Aurora Leigh* almost by heart.... Dickinson named Mrs. Browning as mentor; she referred often in her letters to her poems, and to the portraits that
friends had sent her.

Moers adds: "Browning scholars do not mention it." And, "Among... [some]
Dickinsonians ... the literary relationship is treated with shocked prurience."
(She is referring to John Evangelist Walsh's *The Hidden Life of Emily Dickinson*,
published in 1971.) According to Moers, Dickinson read little, despite her "single
year... at Mount Holyoke." She knew Emerson "well ... perhaps a little
Thoreau and Hawthorne; but she pretended, at least, not to have read a line of
Whitman, no Melville, no Poe, no Irving...." But she read:

> and re-read... Helen Hunt Jackson and Lydia Maria Child, and Harriet
> Beecher Stowe, and Lady Georgina Fullerton, and Dinah Maria Craik, and
> Elizabeth Stuart Phelps, and Rebecca Harding Davis, and Harriet Prescott
> Spofford, and Francesca Alexander, and Mathilda Mackarness and everything
> that George Eliot ... ever wrote.

Helen Hunt Jackson "correctly valued Emily Dickinson's poetry and urged her
to publish."[9]

As for those whom Dickinson influenced, Amy Lowell wrote "Sisters" in 1925,
affirming Dickinson as an "older sister."[10] Rich's "I Am in Danger—Sir" calls
Dickinson her ancestor.[11] Juhasz, herself a poet, calls Dickinson "the great woman
poet to serve as foremother" and goes on to quote from Lowell's "Sisters," Lynn
Strongin's "Emily Dickinson Postage Stamp" (1972), and her own "The Poems
of Women" (1973).[12] Van Gerven speculates about Dickinson's possible influence
on other women poets.[13]

As for other connections between literary women, Moers' *Literary Women* is a
mine of cross-references: if Dickinson read Elizabeth Barrett Browning, the latter "had read it all" [fiction by women] and once said that on her tombstone
should be written *Ci-gît* the greatest novel reader in the world" (p. 61). She corresponded with Harriet Beecher Stowe. Charlotte Brontë went to London, exhibiting "an awkwardness and timidity in literary society that have become
legendary"—except with Harriet Martineau (p. 64). George Eliot corresponded
with Stowe. Jane Austen read Sarah Harriet Burney, Mrs. Jane West, Anna Maria
Porter, Mrs. Anne Grant, Elizabeth Hamilton, Laetitia Matilda Hawkins, Helen
Maria Williams "and the rest of the women writers of her day." She studied Maria
Edgeworth and Fanny Burney (pp. 66–67). Nor were all the associations literary.
George Eliot knew Barbara Leigh Smith (founder of the Association for Promot-
ing the Employment of Women) (p. 28); Charlotte Brontë knew the feminist
Mary Taylor; Mrs. Gaskell knew Bessie Parks and read Mrs. Tonna; Harriet
Beecher Stowe,wrote the introduction to the 1844 edition of Mrs. Tonna's *Works*
(p. 39). George Sand reviewed *Uncle Tom's Cabin* with "All honor and respect to
you, Madame Stowe" (p. 55), while George Eliot's famous letter about *Daniel
Deronda* and anti-Semitism in England was addressed to Stowe, "whom she honored as her predecessor" (p. 59). Pairings of student with literary mentor are cited
by Moers: Willa Cather and Sarah Orne Jewett, Jean Rhys and Charlotte Brontë,

Carson McCullers and Isak Dinesen, Nathalie Sarraute, and Ivy Compton-Burnett (p. 68). Elizabeth Barrett and Miss Mitford were correspondents (Flush was a gift from Mitford to her friend), and both wished to send their books, "tied together in a parcel for courage to the great Madame Sand." Miss Barrett wrote, "I would give anything to have a letter from her, though it smelt of cigar. And it would, of course!" (pp. 82–83). Mrs. Browning later visited Mme. Sand twice, despite her husband's objections. There are other surprising influences Moers finds; George Eliot on Gertrude Stein, for example (pp. 98–99). As for single novels, *Consuelo* was read by Charlotte Brontë, Mary Taylor said it was worth learning French to read it, and Willa Cather kept Sand's portrait over her mantelpiece into the 1930s (p. 289). (Moers does not mention along with George Eliot's *Armgart* Isak Dinesen's Pellegrina Leoni, but there may be a connection there, too.) Moers also traces the enormous influence of Mrs. Radcliffe (her books turn up, among other places, in *Shirley*—pp. 192–193) and the even greater influence of *Corinne* (which turns up everywhere). She also finds, in women's works, repeated themes which a synopsis could only travesty.

In some other places studies are beginning to be made of the connections between women artists. For example, Virginia Woolf knew that Geraldine Jewsbury knew Jane Carlyle, but her essay on the two of them gives the impression that Jewsbury was otherwise isolated.[14] A recent issue of *Heresies*, however, links as "intimates" Geraldine Jewsbury, Charlotte Cushman, Fanny Kemble, Harriet Hosmer, and several other women artists. There is the circle around Natalie Barney in the twenties. (Barney complains vigorously of the "artificial Renée [Vivien] whom Colette presents in *Ces Plaisirs*!")[15] Nor are all these networks among artists; Blanche Wiesen Cook documents the female support groups surrounding the married Crystal Eastman (who, "surrounded by men who shared her work" had "a feminist support group as well") and the homosexual Jane Addams and Lillian Wald, "involved almost exclusively with women." She also describes the extent to which these relationships between women, whether sexual or not, have been ignored by historians. When the relationships are homosexual (as in the case of Mount Holyoke president, Mary E. Woolley, who lived for years with her lover, the chairwoman of the English Department), it is understandable that "the historical evidence was juggled." Cook provides some examples of the astounding lengths to which historians will go to explain away the obvious.[16] But surely Emily Dickinson's admiration for Elizabeth Barrett is not socially tabooed. Yet Moers can observe, "Among most Dickinsonians the literary relationship is treated with embarrassment" and "Browning scholars . . . do not mention it." And elsewhere:

> Scholarship has averted its refined and weary eyes from the female fiction that Austen's letters inform us was her daily sustenance in the years she became one of the greatest writers in the language.

And again Moers complains that the "stability and integrity" of Mrs. Radcliffe's Gothic heroines have been made to vanish from modern view by:

> what was done with the figure by the male writers who followed Mrs. Radcliffe. For most of them . . . the Gothic heroine was quintessentially a de-

fenseless victim, a weakling . . . whose sufferings are the source of her erotic fascination. [Moers suggests elsewhere that the proper model for Emily in *The Mysteries of Udolpho* is not de Sade's female victims but Katharine Hepburn in *The African Queen*.][17]

From Dolores Palomo I find also that the refined eyes of scholarship condemn "one half to two thirds of the fiction printed in the eighteenth century" as minor, mediocre, or salacious—that is, the fiction written by women.[18]

Thus the female tradition in literature has been either ignored, derided, or even (as with Mrs. Radcliffe's property-minded heroines) taken over and replaced. Why? Here is one possible answer, not aesthetic but political (by Judith Long Laws, a psychologist):

> Tokenism is . . . found whenever a dominant group is under pressure to share privilege, power, or other desirable commodities with a group which is excluded. . . . tokenism advertises a promise of mobility which is severely restricted in quantity. . . . the Token does not become assimilated into the dominant group, but is destined for permanent marginality.[19]

Here is another: Novelist Samuel Delany has argued that outside of specifically social situations (like cocktail parties), Americans are trained to "see" a group in which men predominate to the extent of 65 percent to 75 percent as half male and half female. In business and on the street, groups in which women actually number 50 percent tend to be seen as being *more* than 50 percent female.[20] It is not impossible that some similar, unconscious mechanism controls the number of female writers which looks "proper" or "enough" to anthologists and editors. (I am reminded of the folk wisdom of female academics, one of whom whispered to me before a meeting at which we were the only women present, "Don't sit next to me or they'll say we're taking over.")

There are three elements here: a promise, numerical restrictions, and permanent marginality. We have seen the restrictions on the quantity of visibility allowed women writers: that 5 to 8 percent representation. Quality can be controlled by denial of agency, pollution of agency, and false categorizing. I believe that the *anomalousness* of the woman writer—produced by the double standard of content and the writer's isolation from the female tradition—is the final means of ensuring permanent marginality. In order to have her "belong" fully to English literature, the tradition to which she belongs must also be admitted. Other writers must be admitted along with their tradition, written and unwritten. Speech must be admitted. Canons of excellence and conceptions of excellence must change, perhaps beyond recognition. In short, we have a complete collapse of the original solution to the problem of the "wrong" people creating the "right" values. When this happens, the very idea that some people *are* "wrong" begins to fade. And that makes it necessary to recognize what has been done to the "wrong" people and why. And that means recognizing one's own complicity in an appalling situation. It means anger, horror, helplessness, fear for one's own privilege, a conviction of personal guilt, and what for professional intellectuals may be even worse, a conviction of one's own profound stupidity. It may mean fear of retaliation. It means knowing that *they* are watching *you*. Imagine a middle-aged, white, male professor (the typical sort in the profession) asked to let into the Sacred Canon of Literature the following:

> call me
> roach and presumptuous
> nightmare on your white pillow. . . .
> (Audre Lorde, "The Brown Menace or Poem to the Survival of Roaches"[21])

Anger is hard to take. But there are worse things. Imagine our professor confronted with a long, elegant, comic poem about impotence, masturbation, and premature ejaculation. Here is Canto 9:

> In vain th' inraged Youth essay'd
> To call its [his penis'] fleeting vigor back.
> No motion 'twill from Motion take;
> Excess of Love his Love betray'd:
> In vain he Toils, in vain Commands;
> The Insensible fell weeping in his Hand.[22]

The above is from Aphra Behn's "The Disappointment." Of those who are not ignored completely, dismissed as writing about the "wrong" things, condemned for (whatever passes for) impropriety (that year), described as of merely technical interest (on the basis of a carefully selected few worst works), falsely categorized as other than artists, condemned for writing in the wrong genre, or out of genre, or simply joked about, or blamed for what has, in fact, been deleted from or misinterpreted out of their work by others, it is still possible to say, quite sincerely:

She wrote it, but she doesn't fit in.

Or, more generously: *She's wonderful, but where on earth did she come from?*

NOTES

1. *F. T. Palgrave's The Golden Treasury of the Best Songs and Lyrical Poems: Centennial Edition*, ed. Oscar Williams (New York: New American Library, 1961), pp. viii, ix, xi.

2. Claudia Ven Gerven, "Lost Literary Traditions: A Matter of Influence," MS., p. 2.

3. Frederick O. Waage, "Urban Broadsides of Renaissance England," *Journal of Popular Culture* 11, no. 3 (Winter 1977): 736.

4. Jean S. Mullen, "Freshman Textbooks," *College English* 34 (1972): 79.

5. Elaine Showalter, "Women and the Literary Curriculum," *College English* 32, no. 8 (May 1971): 856.

6. Van Gerven, "Lost Literary Traditions," pp. 2–3, 5–6.

7. Cited by Suzanne Juhasz, *Naked and Fiery Forms: Modern American Poetry by Women: A New Tradition* (New York: Harper & Row, 1976), p. 11.

8. *Ibid., p.* 9.

9. Moers, *Literary Women*, pp. 83, 85–86, 87, 91–92.

10. Juhasz, *Naked and Fiery Forms*, p. 7.

11. Van Gerven, "Lost Literary Traditions," p. 4.

12. Juhasz, *Naked and Fiery Forms*, pp. 7–9.

13. Van Gerven, "Lost Literary Traditions," p. 5.

14. Virginia Woolf, "Geraldine and Jane," in *The Second Common Reader,* pp. 167–81.

15. Natalie Barney, "Natalie Barney on Renée Vivien," trans. Margaret Porter, *Heresies* 3 (Fall 1977): 71.

16. Blanche Wiesen Cook, "Female Support Networks and Political Activism," *Chrysalis* 3 (1977): 45–46.

17. Moers, *Literary Women*, pp. 87, 66, 208, 211.

18. Personal interview with Dolores Palomo, summer 1978.

19. Judith Long Laws, "The Psychology of Tokenism: An Analysis," *Sex Roles* I: 1 (1975): 51.

20. Samuel Delany, "To Read the Dispossessed," in *The Jewel-hinged Jaw* (New York: Berkley, 1978), p. 261.

21. Audre Lorde, *The New York Head Shop and Museum* (Detroit: Broadside, 1974), p. 48.

22. In *By a Woman Writt,* ed. Joan Goulianos (Baltimore: Penguin, 1974), p. 92.

AESTHETICS

(1983)

The re-evaluation and rediscovery of minority art (including the cultural minority of women) is often conceived as a matter of remedying injustice and exclusiveness through doing justice to individual artists by allowing their work into the canon, which will thereby be more complete, but fundamentally unchanged. Sometimes it's also stressed that the erasing of previous injustice will encourage new artists of the hitherto "wrong" groups and thus provide art with more artists who will provide new (or different) material—and that all of this activity will enrich, but not change, the canon of art itself.

But in the case of women, what has been left out? "Merely," says Carolyn Kizer, "the private lives of one half of humanity."[1]

These lives are not lived in isolation from the private and public lives of the other half. Here is Jean Baker Miller describing what happens when the lives of half a community are omitted from the consciousness of the other half:

> Some of the areas of life denied by the dominant group are . . . projected onto all subordinate groups. . . . But other parts of experience are so necessary that they cannot be projected very far away. One must *have* them nearby, even if one can still deny *owning* them. These are the special areas delegated to women.

She adds:

> . . . when . . . women move out of their restricted place, they threaten men in a very profound sense with the need to reintegrate many of the essentials of human development. . . . These things have been warded off and become doubly fearful because they look as if they will entrap men in "emotions," weakness, sexuality, vulnerability, helplessness, the need for care, and other unsolved areas.

And:

> Inevitably the dominant group is the model for "normal human relationships." It then becomes normal to treat others destructively and to derogate

them, to obscure the truth of what you are doing by creating false explanations . . . to keep on doing these things, one need only behave "normally."[2]

A mode of understanding life which wilfully ignores so much can do so only at the peril of thoroughly distorting the rest. A mode of understanding literature which can ignore the private lives of half the human race is not "incomplete"; it is distorted through and through. Feminist criticism of the early 1970s began by pointing out the simplest of these distortions, that is, that the female characters of even our greatest realistic "classics" by male writers are often not individualized portraits of possible women, but creations of fear and desire. At best, according to Lillian Robinson:

> . . . the problem is . . . [whether] the author, in showing what goes on in a heroine's mind, is showing us anything like the mind of an actual human female. . . . I am amazed at how many writers have chosen to evade it by externalizing the psychological situation, using "objective" images that convey the pattern or content of a woman's thought without actually entering into it. . . . Emma Bovary and Anna Karenina, to name two eminently successful literary creations, are realized for us in this way.[3]

Some literary creations are not so successful or so innocuous, from Dickens' incapacity to portray women alone or in solely female society to Hemingway's misogynistic daydreams. I am thinking especially of Dickens' Bella Wilfer in *Our Mutual Friend*, vain and pretty, who flirts (quite reasonably) with her father, then applies the same manner to her younger sister (which is not reasonable) and then—alone—flirts (impossibly) with her mirror. Women speaking of mirrors and prettiness make it all too clear that even for pretty women, mirrors are the foci of anxious, not gratified, narcissism. The woman who knows beyond a doubt that she is beautiful exists aplenty in male novelists' imaginations; I have yet to find her in women's books or women's memoirs or in life. Women spend a lot of time looking in mirrors, but the "compulsion to visualize the self" is a phrase Moers uses of women in her chapter on Gothic freaks and horrors; the compulsion is a constant check on one's (possible) beauty, not an enjoyment of it. Dickens' error is simple; how could he have observed the Bellas of his world alone or heard their thoughts? So he simply extends public behavior into a private situation. Here is Annis Pratt, on that incarnation of the eternal feminine, Molly Bloom:

> It is difficult not to feel about Molly Bloom on her chamberpot what Eldridge Cleaver must feel about Jack Benny's Rochester, but a good critic will not withdraw her attention from a work which is resonant and craftsmanlike even if it is chauvinistic.[4]

Robinson, answering Pratt in the same issue of the same journal, refuses to take so mild a position:

> sexual stereotypes serve *somebody's* interest. . . . I believe only a feminist knows what Molly Bloom is really about and can ask the questions that will demonstrate the real functioning of sexual myth in Joyce's novel.[5]

In the same issue, Dolores Barracano Schmidt performs this investigation in an essay on "The Great American Bitch," calling this twentieth-century character who appears in men's novels:

> more myth than reality, a fabrication used to maintain the *status quo*. She is a figure about whom a whole cluster of values and taboos clings: women's fight for equality was a mistake . . . women are not equipped for civilization. . . . by being so thoroughly hateful the Great American Bitch of fiction reinforces the sexist view.[6]

Another feminist critic, Cynthia Griffin Wolff, generalizes:

> The definition [in literature] of women's most serious problems and the proposed solutions . . . are . . . covertly tailored to meet the needs of fundamentally *masculine* problems. . . . women appear in literature . . . as conveniences to the resolution of masculine dilemmas.

One of Wolff's examples is the opposition of "virtuous" to "sensuous" woman, a projection of a male split in feeling and value which "relieves . . . [the man] from the difficulties of trying to unite two forces of love." (The "sensuous" woman, as Wolff points out, is not one who desires men but one who is desired by them.) She goes on:

> men may appear stereotypically . . . but the stereotype [e.g., the Warrior] is usually a fantasied solution to an essentially masculine problem. . . . Moreover, there is a . . . significant body of literature which recognizes the limitations of some of these masculine stereotypes [e.g., *The Red Badge of Courage*]. There is no comparable body of anti-stereotype literature about women. . . . Even women writers . . . seem to adopt them.[7]

Judith Fetterley offers even more telling examples:

> . . . when I look at a poem like "The Solitary Reaper" . . . I do not find my experience in it at all. Rather I find that the drama of the poem depends upon a contrast between the male subject as conscious, creative knower and the unknowing female object of his contemplation; it is my wordless, artless, natural and utterly unself-conscious song which has provided the male speaker/poet with the opportunity to define himself as knower. . . . [in "To His Coy Mistress"] the complexity of the speaker's situation, which is the subject of the poem, is modest compared to the complexity of the mistress's position . . . [which is] the essence of *my* relation to the poem.

Elsewhere she states one of the central problems of feminist criticism:

> What happens to one's definition of aesthetic criteria . . . when one is confronted by a literature which does not support the self but assaults it[?][8]

Vonda McIntyre answers:

> Right now a lot of literary and film "classics" are unbearable . . . because of

the underlying [sexist] assumptions. In a few generations I think they will be either incomprehensible or so ridiculous as to be funny.[9]

And Ellen Cantarow, looking into her college textbook, finds that next to Pope's line, "Most women have no Characters at all," she once wrote: "SPEAKER TONE DEFINE." She asks:

> Where in my notes was that other girl, the girl who once raged at being taken for "a typical Wellesley *girl*?" . . . [there was] intense self-hatred. . . . education at Wellesley . . . didn't just belie our life experience as girls . . . it nullified that experience, rendered it invisible. . . . we lived in a state of schizophrenia that we took to be normal.[10]

A more explicit, systematic rejection of the canon and the standards that support it can be found in the field of art—a rejection I believe parallel to that going on in a more piecemeal fashion in literature. For example, Mary Garrard asks:

> Why is our art history . . . full of virtuous reversals in which a virile, heroic, or austere style suddenly and dramatically replaces a feminine, lyrical, or luxurious one—David over Fragonard, Caravaggio over Salviati, clean international Modern Gropius over wickedly ornamental Sullivan or Tiffany?[11]

Valerie Jaudon and Joyce Kozloff answer:

> The prejudice against the decorative has a long art history and is based on hierarchies: fine art above decorative art, Western art above non-Western art, men's art above women's art . . . "high art" [means] man, mankind, the individual man, individuality, humans, humanity, the human figure, humanism, civilization, culture, the Greeks, the Romans, the English, Christianity, spiritual transcendence, religion, nature, true form, science, logic, creativity, action, war, virility, violence, brutality, dynamism, power, and greatness.
>
> In the same texts other words are used repeatedly in connection with . . . "low art": Africans, Orientals, Persians, Slovaks, peasants, the lower classes, women, children, savages, pagans, sensuality, pleasure, decadence, chaos, anarchy, impotence, exotica, eroticism, artifice, tattoos, cosmetics, ornaments, decoration, carpets, weaving, patterns, domesticity, wallpaper, fabrics, and furniture.

The rest of Jaudon and Kozloff's essay consists of quotations from artists and art historians arranged under such headings as "War and Virility," "Purity in Art as a Holy Cause," and a particularly damning section expressing "the desire for unlimited personal power," which the authors call "Autocracy."[12]

Such associations of art with virility, quality with size, and authenticity with self-aggrandizement appear in literature, too. (One of the strangest conversations I ever had was with a male colleague who stated that Chekhov could not be a "great" artist because he never wrote anything "full-length." In some confusion—apparently short stories and novellas didn't count—I mentioned the plays. These, it seemed, didn't count either; "They're much shorter than novels," said my colleague.) Here is Adrienne Rich, pointing out that the "masterpieces" we have been taught to admire are not merely flawed, but that they may not even mean what we have been taught they mean. In "The Ninth Symphony of Beethoven Understood at Last as a Sexual Message" Rich begins with "A man in terror of impotence," goes on to describe the music as:

> music of the entirely
> isolated soul
> yelling at Joy from the tunnel of the ego
> music without the ghost
> of another person in it. . . .

What is the man trying to say? Something he would keep back if he could, "bound and flogged" with "chords of Joy." The real situation behind all this pounding?

> . . . everything is silence and the
> beating of a bloody fist
> upon a splintered table.[13]

If the canon is an attempt to shore up the *status quo*, if the masterpieces don't mean what they pretend to mean, then artists must throw away the rules altogether in favor of something else. "Their musty rules of unity, and God knows what besides, if they meant anything," says Aphra Behn, but she goes no further.[14] Rich does, stating:

> in pretending to stand for "the human," masculine subjectivity tries to force us to name our truths in an alien language, to dilute them; we are constantly told that the "real" problems . . . are those men have defined, that the problems we need to examine are trivial, unscholarly, nonexistent. . . .
>
> Any woman who has moved from the playing-fields of male discourse into the realm where women are developing our own descriptions of the world, knows the extraordinary sense of shedding . . . someone else's baggage, of ceasing to translate. It is not that thinking becomes easy, but that the difficulties are intrinsic to the work itself, rather than to the environment. . . . [15]

In "ceasing to translate," the "wrong" people begin to make not only good, but genuinely experimental art. Several contemporary women's theater groups have thrown away not only the unities but the lights, the proscenium, the elaborate impressiveness, the "primitivism," and the assault-on-the-audience that marked the theatrical "experiments" of the 1960s. Contemporaneously with the reappearance of feminism, these women's groups have instead created a version of Epic Theater (though nobody's noticed): much narrative, constantly changing characters, many incidents (personal and historical), direct (and sympathetic) commentary to the audience, and the reenactment, sometimes in mime, rather than the here-and-now "hot" acting, of important scenes. These performances are, to my mind, more genuinely experimental than what passed for experimental theater in the 1960s, just as Baldwin's non-fiction is not only beautiful but genuinely experimental in comparison (for example) with much Joyce- or Nabokov-derived modern work. We have been trained to regard certain kinds of art (especially the violent, the arcane, and the assaultive) as "experimental." But there's all the difference in the world between studying oxidation and producing loud noises with gunpowder. The former leads somewhere; the latter (analogous to rock groups' raising the ante with decibelage, luridness, and violence) does not.

There are genuine experiments happening in women's writing. According to Suzanne Juhasz, "In the late sixties and early seventies an explosion of poetry by women occurred. . . . " She goes on, concluding that women are being forced to create new poetic forms, since:

> If the woman poet wants . . . to link her particular experiences with larger universals . . . she can call upon only a percentage of her own experiences. Much of what she knows does not link up to universals because the universals presently in existence are based upon masculine experience, masculine norms.

One way of dealing with the norms of what is or is not universal is to ignore them and relate particulars to particulars. This leads to writing (as Juhasz puts it) in the vernacular and not in Latin. It also leads to rejection slips as she finds out:

> Recently I received rejection slip from a well-meaning editor who, while admitting the "necessary" nature of my poems, took issue with the fact that my poems "said it all." "Try more denotation, synecdoche, metonymy, suggestion," he said. Yet I and many feminist poets do not want to treat poetry as a metalanguage that needs to be decoded.[16]

Julia Penelope, also, notes the critics' annoyance when "works . . . make the function of the critic obsolete. The . . . work . . . (is) immediately available to the reader, and there is no need for the . . . intervention of the critic as guide or explicator."[17] Noting that the epigram is, by tradition, inferior to the epic, Johasz quotes with delight some of Alta's short poems, for example:

> if you won't make love to me, at least
> get out of my dreams!

Here's another, by black poet Pat Parker, to white women:

> SISTER! your foot's smaller
> but it's still on my neck.

Juhasz finally abandons the idea of the canon altogether:

> a poem works if it lives up to itself. Such a definition contains no built-in ranking system.[18]

And here is Woolf's opinion of the canon:

> They [the children] knew what he liked best—to be forever walking up and down, up and down, with Mr. Ramsay, and saying who had won this, who had won that, who was a "first-rate man" . . . who was "brilliant but . . . fundamentally unsound," who was "undoubtedly the ablest fellow in Bailliol." . . . That was what they talked about.[19]

But if we throw out the linear hierarchy, are we to do without standards altogether? Here is Juhasz again:

> Yet a poem can work and not be good. It can be dull or ordinary, or superficial. A *good* poem works *powerfully* and *accurately* to communicate between poet and reader or listener.[20] [Italics mine]

But which reader? Which listener? The techniques for mystifying women's lives and belittling women's writing that I have described work by suppressing context: writing is separated from experience, women writers are separated from their tradition and each other, public is separated from private, political from personal—all to enforce a supposed set of absolute standards. What is frightening about black art or women's art or Chicago art—and so on—is that it calls into question the very idea of objectivity and absolute standards:

This is a good novel.

Good *for what*?

Good *for whom*?

One side of the nightmare is that the privileged group will not recognize that "other" art, will not be able to judge it, that the superiority of taste and training possessed by the privileged critic and the privileged artist will suddenly vanish.

The other side of the nightmare is not that what is found in the "other" art will be incomprehensible, but that it will be all too familiar. That is:

Women's lives are the buried truth about men's lives.

The lives of people of color are the buried truth about white lives.

The buried truth about the rich is who they take their money from and how.

The buried truth about "normal" sexuality is how one kind of sexual expression has been made privileged, and what kinds of unearned virtue and terrors about identity this distinction serves.

There are other questions: why is "greatness" in art so often aggressive? Why does "great" literature have to be long? Is "regionalism" only another instance of down-grading the vernacular? Why is "great" architecture supposed to knock your eye out at first view, unlike "indigenous" architecture, which must be appreciated slowly and with knowledge of the climate in which it exists? Why is the design of clothing—those grotesque and sometimes perilously fantastic anatomical-social-role-characterological ideas of the person—a "minor" art? Because it has a use? In admiring "pure" (i.e., useless) art, are we not merely admiring Veblenian conspicuous consumption, like the Mandarin fingernail? In Eve Merriam's recent play *The Club* it became clear that masculine and feminine body-language are very different; gestures socially recognizable as "male" lay claim to as much space as possible, while comparable "female" gestures are self-protective, self-referential, and take up as little space as possible.

Male reviewers, astonished at a play in which the members of a nineteenth-century men's club *and* the club's black waiter *and* its boy in buttons *and* its piano player were all played by women, praised the actresses for their success in imitating men without making any attempt to hide their own female anatomy. In her autobiography Judy Chicago comments:

> when the women "acted out" walking down the street and being accosted by men, everyone seemed able to "take on" the characteristics of the tough swagger, of men "coming on." It was as if they knew the words so well.[21]

Male reviewers understood the point of hearing sexist jokes and songs of the period performed by women, but it took a female reviewer (in *Harper's Bazaar,* I think) to see that the final effect of seeing women in the habiliments of power was utter confusion as to what roles belonged to whom. She called this disappearance of the link between gender and sexual physiology the labels washing off the bottles; I came out of the theater saying, "But what *is* 'women'?" Perhaps this isn't the effect the play had on men, or perhaps male reviewers were not being honest. I think it would be unlikely if a play like this had an identical effect on women and on men.

In art, are we (in fact) trained to admire body language? An obviously aggressive or forceful technique? Loudness? These questions are being asked and dealt with. But they cannot be (and are not being) dealt with by assuming one absolute center of value.

In everybody's present historical situation, there can be, I believe, no single center of value and hence no absolute standards. That does not mean that assignment of values must be arbitrary or self-serving (like my students, whose defense of their poetry is "I felt it"). It does mean that for the linear hierarchy of good and bad it becomes necessary to substitute a multitude of centers of value, each with its own periphery, some closer to each other, some farther apart. The centers have been constructed by the historical facts of what it is to be female or black or working class or what-have-you; when we all live in the same culture, then it will be time for one literature. But that is not the case now. Nor is there one proper "style." There are many kinds of English (including Anglo-Indian) and before determining whether (for example) Virginia Woolf "writes better than" Zora Neale Hurston, it might be a good idea to decide who is addressing the mind's ear and who the mind's eye, in short, *what* English we're talking about. One is a kind of Latin, sculptured, solid, and distinct, into which comes the vernacular from time to time; the other is literary-as-vernacular: fluid, tone-shifting, visually fleeting, with the (impossible) cadences of the mind's ear constantly overriding the memory of the physical ear. (Woolf often writes sentences too long for any but the most experienced actor to speak as a single breath-unit.) If the one kind of English is too slow and too eternally set, is not the other kind too facile, too quick, always a little too thin?

There used to be an odd, popular, and erroneous idea that the sun revolved around the earth.

This has been replaced by an even odder, equally popular, and equally erroneous idea that the earth goes around the sun.

In fact, the moon and the earth revolve around a common center, and this commonly-centered pair revolves with the sun around another common center, except that you must figure in all the solar planets here, so things get complicated. Then there is the motion of the solar system with regard to a great many other objects, e.g., the galaxy, and if at this point you ask *what does the motion of the earth really look like from the center of the entire universe,* say (and where are the Glotolog?), the only answer is:

that it doesn't.

Because there isn't.

NOTES

1. Carolyn Kizer, "Pro Femina," in *No More Masks*, ed. Ellen Bass and Florence Howe (Garden City: Doubleday, 1973), p. 175.

2. Jean Baker Miller, *Toward a New Psychology of Women* (Boston: Beacon Press, 1975), pp. 47, 120, 8.

3. Lillian S. Robinson, "Who's Afraid of a Room of One's Own?" in *The Politics of Literature: Dissenting Essays on the Teaching of English*, ed. Louis Kampf and Paul Lauter (New York: Random House, 1973), pp. 376–77.

4. Annis Pratt, "The New Feminist Criticism," *College English* 32, no. 8 (May 1971): 877.

5. Lillian S. Robinson, "Dwelling in Decencies: Radical Criticism and the Feminist Perspective," *College English* 32, no. 8 (May 1971): 884–87.

6. Dolores Barracano Schmidt, "The Great American Bitch," *College English* 32, no. 8 (May 1971): 904.

7. Cynthia Griffin Wolff, "A Mirror for Men: Stereotypes of Women in Literature," in *Woman: An Issue*, ed. Edwards et al., pp. 207–8, 217.

8. Judith Fetterley, MLA convention, December 1975, pp. 8–9.

9. McIntyre, *Khatru*, p. 119.

10. Ellen Cantarow, "Why Teach Literature?" in *The Politics of Literature*, ed. Kampf and Lauter, pp. 57–61.

11. Mary D. Garrard, "Feminism: Has It Changed Art History?" *Heresies* 4 (1978): 60.

12. Valerie Jaudon and Joyce Kozloff, "Art Hysterical Notions of Progress and Culture," *Heresies* 4 (1978): 38–42.

13. Adrienne Rich, *Poems Selected and New: 1950–1974* (New York: W. W. Norton, 1975), pp. 205–6.

14. In *By a Woman Writt*, ed. Goulianos, p. 99.

15. Adrienne Rich, "Conditions for Work: The Common World of Women," *Heresies* 3 (1977): 53–54.

16. Juhasz, *Naked and Fiery Forms*, pp. 139, 178–79.

17. Julia Penelope (Stanley), "Fear of *Flying*?", *Sinister Wisdom* 2 (1976): 59.

18. Juhasz, *Naked and Fiery Forms*, pp. 185, 201.

19. Virginia Woolf, *To the Lighthouse* (New York: Harcourt, Brace & World, 1927), p. 15.

20. Juhasz, *Naked and Fiery Forms*, p. 201.

21. Judy Chicago, *Through the Flower: My Life as a Woman Artist* (Garden City: Doubleday, 1975), p. 127.

TREASON OUR TEXT

feminist challenges to the literary canon

(1983)

> Successful plots have often had gunpowder in them. Feminist critics
> have gone so far as to take treason to the canon as our text.[1]
>
> JANE MARCUS

THE LOFTY SEAT OF CANONIZED BARDS (POLLOK, 1827)

As with many other restrictive institutions, we are hardly aware of it until we
come into conflict with it; the elements of the literary canon are simply absorbed
by the apprentice scholar and critic in the normal course of graduate education,
without anyone's ever seeming to inculcate or defend them. Appeal, were any
necessary, would be to the other meaning of "canon," that is, to established standards of judgment and of taste. Not that either definition is presented as rigid
and immutable—far from it, for lectures in literary history are full of wry references to a benighted though hardly distant past when, say, the metaphysical poets were insufficiently appreciated or Vachel Lindsay was the most modern poet
recognized in American literature. Whence the acknowledgment of a subjective
dimension, sometimes generalized as "sensibility," to the category of taste.
Sweeping modifications in the canon are said to occur because of changes in collective sensibility, but individual admissions and elevations from "minor" to "major" status tend to be achieved by successful critical promotion, which is to say,
demonstration that a particular author does meet generally accepted criteria of
excellence.

The results, moreover, are nowhere codified: they are neither set down in a
single place, nor are they absolutely uniform. In the visual arts and in music, the
cold realities of patronage, purchase, presentation in private and public collections, or performance on concert programs create the conditions for a work's canonical status or lack of it. No equivalent set of institutional arrangements exists
for literature, however. The fact of publication and even the feat of remaining
in print for generations, which are at least analogous to the ways in which pictures and music are displayed, are not the same sort of indicators; they represent
less of an investment and hence less general acceptance of their canonicity. In
the circumstances, it may seem somewhat of an exaggeration to speak of "the"

literary canon, almost paranoid to call it an institution, downright hysterical to characterize that institution as restrictive. The whole business is so much more informal, after all, than any of these terms implies, the concomitant processes so much more gentlemanly. Surely, it is more like a gentlemen's agreement than a repressive instrument—isn't it?

But a gentleman is inescapably—that is, by definition—a member of a privileged class and of the male sex. From this perspective, it is probably quite accurate to think of the canon as an entirely gentlemanly artifact, considering how few works by non-members of that class and sex make it into the informal agglomeration of course syllabi, anthologies, and widely commented-upon "standard authors" that constitutes the canon as it is generally understood. For, beyond their availability on bookshelves, it is through the teaching and study—one might even say the habitual teaching and study—of certain works that they become institutionalized as canonical literature. Within that broad canon, moreover, those admitted but read only in advanced courses, commented upon only by more or less narrow specialists, are subjected to the further tyranny of "major" versus "minor."

For more than a decade now, feminist scholars have been protesting the apparently systematic neglect of women's experience in the literary canon, neglect that takes the form of distorting and misreading the few recognized female writers and excluding the others. Moreover, the argument runs, the predominantly male authors in the canon show us the female character and relations between the sexes in a way that both reflects and contributes to sexist ideology—an aspect of these classic works about which the critical tradition remained silent for generations. The feminist challenge, although intrinsically (and, to my mind, refreshingly) polemical, has not been simply a reiterated attack, but a series of suggested alternatives to the male-dominated membership and attitudes of the accepted canon. In this essay, I propose to examine these feminist alternatives, assess their impact on the standard canon, and propose some directions for further work. Although my emphasis in each section is on the substance of the challenge, the underlying polemic is, I believe, abundantly clear.

THE PRESENCE OF CANONIZED FOREFATHERS (BURKE, 1790)

Start with the Great Books, the traditional desert-island ones, the foundation of courses in the Western humanistic tradition. No women authors, of course, at all, but within the works thus canonized, certain monumental female images: Helen, Penelope, and Clytemnestra, Beatrice and the Dark Lady of the Sonnets, Bérénice, Cunégonde, and Margarete. The list of interesting female characters is enlarged if we shift to the Survey of English Literature and its classic texts; here, moreover, there is the possible inclusion of a female author or even several, at least as the course's implicit "historical background" ticks through and past the Industrial Revolution. It is a possibility that is not always honored in the observance. "*Beowulf* to Virginia Woolf" is a pleasant enough joke, but though lots of surveys begin with the Anglo-Saxon epic, not all that many conclude with *Mrs. Dalloway*. Even in the nineteenth century, the pace and the necessity of mass omissions may mean leaving out Austen, one of the Brontës, or Eliot. The analogous overview of American literary masterpieces, despite the relative brevity and modernity of the period considered, is likely to yield a similarly all-male pantheon; Emily Dickinson may be admitted—but not necessarily—and no one else even comes close.[2] Here again, the male-authored canon contributes to the body of information, stereotype, inference, and surmise about the female sex that is generally in the culture.

Once this state of affairs has been exposed, there are two possible approaches for feminist criticism. It can emphasize alternative readings of the tradition, readings that reinterpret women's character, motivations, and actions and that identify and challenge sexist ideology. Or it can concentrate on gaining admission to the canon for literature by women writers. Both sorts of work are being pursued, although, to the extent that feminist criticism has defined itself as a subfield of literary studies—as distinguished from an approach or method—it has tended to concentrate on writing by women.

In fact, however, the current wave of feminist theory began as criticism of certain key texts, both literary and paraliterary, in the dominant culture. Kate Millett, Eva Figes, Elizabeth Janeway, Germaine Greer, and Carolyn Heilbrun all use the techniques of essentially literary analysis on the social forms and forces surrounding those texts.[3] The texts themselves may be regarded as "canonical" in the sense that all have had significant impact on the culture as a whole, although the target being addressed is not literature or its canon.

In criticism that is more strictly literary in its scope, much attention has been concentrated on male writers in the American tradition. Books like Annette Kolodny's *The Lay of the Land* and Judith Fetterley's *The Resisting Reader* have no systematic, comprehensive equivalent in the criticism of British or European literature.[4] Both of these studies identify masculine values and imagery in a wide range of writings, as well as the alienation that is their consequence for women, men, and society as a whole. In a similar vein, Mary Ellmann's *Thinking About Women* examines ramifications of the tradition of "phallic criticism" as applied to writers of both sexes.[5] These books have in common with one another and with overarching theoretical manifestos like *Sexual Politics* a sense of having been betrayed by a culture that was supposed to be elevating, liberating, and one's own.

By contrast, feminist work devoted to that part of the Western tradition which is neither American nor contemporary is likelier to be more even-handed. "Feminist critics," declare Lenz, Greene, and Neely in introducing their collection of essays on Shakespeare, "recognize that the greatest artists do not necessarily duplicate in their art the orthodoxies of their culture; they may exploit them to create character or intensify conflict, they may struggle with, criticize, or transcend them."[6] From this perspective, Milton may come in for some censure, Shakespeare and Chaucer for both praise and blame, but the clear intention of a feminist approach to these classic authors is to enrich our understanding of what is going on in the texts, as well as how—for better, for worse, or for both—they have shaped our own literary and social ideas.[7] At its angriest, none of this reinterpretation offers a fundamental challenge to the canon as *canon*; although it posits new values, it never suggests that, in the light of those values, we ought to reconsider whether the great monuments are really so great, after all.

SUCH IS ALL THE WORLDE HATHE CONFIRMED AND AGREED UPON, THAT IT IS AUTHENTIQUE AND CANONICAL (T. WILSON, 1553)

In an evolutionary model of feminist studies in literature, work on male authors is often characterized as "early," implicitly primitive, whereas scholarship on female authors is the later development, enabling us to see women—the writers themselves and the women they write about—as active agents rather than passive images or victims. This implicit characterization of studies addressed to male writers is as inaccurate as the notion of an inexorable evolution. In fact, as the very definition of feminist criticism has come increasingly to mean scholarship and criticism devoted to women writers, work on the male tradition has continued. By this point, there has been a study of the female characters or the views on the woman question of every major—perhaps every known—author in Anglo-American, French, Russian, Spanish, Italian, German, and Scandinavian literature.[8]

Nonetheless, it is an undeniable fact that most feminist criticism focuses on women writers, so that the feminist efforts to humanize the canon have usually meant bringing a woman's point of view to bear by incorporating works by women into the established canon. The least threatening way to do so is to follow the accustomed pattern of making the case for individual writers one by one. The case here consists in showing that an already recognized woman author has been denied her rightful place, presumably because of the general devaluation of female efforts and subjects. More often than not, such work involves showing that a woman already securely established in the canon belongs in the first rather than the second rank. The biographical and critical efforts of R. W. B. Lewis and Cynthia Griffin Wolff, for example, have attempted to enhance Edith Wharton's reputation in this way.[9] Obviously, no challenge is presented to the particular notions of literary quality, timelessness, universality, and other qualities that constitute the rationale for canonicity. The underlying argument, rather, is that consistency, fidelity to those values, requires recognition of at least the few best and best-known women writers. Equally obviously, this approach does not call the notion of the canon itself into question.

WE ACKNOWLEDGE IT CANONLIKE, BUT NOT CANONICALL (BISHOP BARLOW, 1601)

Many feminist critics reject the method of case-by-case demonstration. The wholesale consignment of women's concerns and productions to a grim area bounded by triviality and obscurity cannot be compensated for by tokenism. True equity can be attained, they argue, only by opening up the canon to a much larger number of female voices. This is an endeavor that eventually brings basic aesthetic questions to the fore.

Initially, however, the demand for wider representation of female authors is substantiated by an extraordinary effort of intellectual reappropriation. The emergence of feminist literary study has been characterized, at the base, by scholarship devoted to the discovery, republication, and reappraisal of "lost" or undervalued writers and their work. From Rebecca Harding Davis and Kate Chopin through Zora Neale Hurston and Mina Loy to Meridel LeSueur and Rebecca West, reputations have been reborn or remade and a female counter-canon has come into being, out of components that were largely unavailable even a dozen years ago.[10]

In addition to constituting a feminist alternative to the male-dominated tradition, these authors also have a claim to representation in "the" canon. From this perspective, the work of recovery itself makes one sort of *prima facie* case, giving the lie to the assumption, where it has existed, that aside from a few names that are household words—differentially appreciated, but certainly well known—there simply has not been much serious literature by women. Before any aesthetic arguments have been advanced either for or against the admission of such works to the general canon, the new literary scholarship on women has demonstrated that the pool of potential applicants is far larger than anyone has hitherto suspected.

WOULD AUGUSTINE, IF HE HELD ALL THE BOOKS TO HAVE AN EQUAL RIGHT TO CANONICITY... HAVE PREFERRED SOME TO OTHERS? (W. FITZGERALD, TRANS. WHITAKER, 1849)

But the aesthetic issues cannot be forestalled for very long. We need to understand whether the claim is being made that many of the newly recovered or validated texts by women meet existing criteria or, on the other hand, that those criteria themselves intrinsically exclude or tend to exclude women and hence should be modified or replaced. If this polarity is not, in fact, applicable to the process, what are the grounds for presenting a large number of new female candidates for (as it were) canonization?

The problem is epitomized in Nina Baym's introduction to her study of American women's fiction between 1820 and 1870:

> Reexamination of this fiction may well show it to lack the esthetic, intellectual and moral complexity and artistry that we demand of great literature. I confess frankly that, although I have found much to interest me in these books, I have not unearthed a forgotten Jane Austen or George Eliot or hit upon the one novel that I would propose to set alongside *The Scarlet Letter*. Yet I cannot avoid the belief that "purely" literary criteria, as they have been employed to identify the best American works, have inevitably had a bias in favor of things male—in favor of, say, a whaling ship, rather than a sewing circle as a symbol of the human community.... While not claiming any literary greatness for any of the novels ... in this study, I would like at least to begin to correct such a bias by taking their content seriously. And it is time, perhaps—though this task lies outside my scope here—to reexamine the grounds upon which certain hallowed American classics have been called great.[11]

Now, if students of literature may be allowed to confess to one Great Unreadable among the Great Books, my own *bête noire* has always been the white whale; I have always felt I was missing something in *Moby-Dick* that is clearly there for many readers and that is there for me when I read, say, Aeschylus or Austen. So I find Baym's strictures congenial, at first reading. Yet the contradictory nature of the position is also evident on the face of it. Am I or am I not being invited to construct a (feminist) aesthetic rationale for my impatience with *Moby-Dick*? Do Baym and the current of thought she represents accept "esthetic, intellectual and moral complexity and artistry" as the grounds of greatness, or are they challenging those values as well?

As Myra Jehlen points out most lucidly, this attractive position will not bear close analysis: "[Baym] is having it both ways, admitting the artistic limitations of the women's fiction . . . and at the same time denying the validity of the rulers that measure these limitations, disdaining any ambition to reorder the literary canon and, on second thought, challenging the canon after all, or rather challenging not the canon itself but the grounds for its selection."[12] Jehlen understates the case, however, in calling the duality a paradox, which is, after all, an intentionally created and essentially rhetorical phenomenon. What is involved here is more like the *agony* of feminist criticism, for it is the champions of women's literature who are torn between defending the quality of their discoveries and radically redefining literary quality itself.

Those who are concerned with the canon as a pragmatic instrument rather than a powerful abstraction—the compilers of more equitable anthologies or course syllabi, for example—have opted for an uneasy compromise. The literature by women that they seek—as well as that by members of excluded racial and ethnic groups and by working people in general—conforms as closely as possible to the traditional canons of taste and judgment. Not that it reads like such literature as far as content and viewpoint are concerned, but the same words about artistic intent and achievement may be applied without absurdity. At the same time, the rationale for a new syllabus or anthology relies on a very different criterion: that of truth to the culture being represented, the *whole* culture and not the creation of an almost entirely male white elite. Again, no one seems to be proposing—aloud—the elimination of *Moby-Dick* or *The Scarlet Letter,* just squeezing them over somewhat to make room for another literary reality, which, joined with the existing canon, will come closer to telling the (poetic) truth.

The effect is *pluralist, at best,* and the epistemological assumptions underlying the search for a more fully representative literature are strictly empiricist: by including the perspective of women (who are, after all, half-the-population), we will know more about the culture as it actually was. No one suggests that there might be something in this literature itself that challenges the values and even the validity of the previously all-male tradition. There is no reason why the canon need speak with one voice or as one man on the fundamental questions of human experience. Indeed, even as an elite white male voice, it can hardly be said to do so. Yet a commentator like Baym has only to say "it is time, perhaps . . . to reexamine the grounds," *while not proceeding to do so,* for feminists to be accused of wishing to throw out the entire received culture. The argument could be more usefully joined, perhaps, if there *were* a current within feminist criticism that went beyond insistence on representation to consideration of precisely how inclusion of women's writing alters our view of the tradition. Or even one that suggested some radical surgery on the list of male authors usually represented.

After all, when we turn from the construction of pantheons, which have no *prescribed* number of places, to the construction of course syllabi, then something does have to be eliminated each time something else is added, and here ideologies, aesthetic and extra-aesthetic, do necessarily come into play. Is the canon and hence the syllabus based on it to be regarded as the compendium of excellence or as the record of cultural history? For there comes a point when the proponent of making the canon recognize the achievement of both sexes has to put up or shut up; either a given woman writer is good enough to replace some male writer on the prescribed reading list or she is not. If she is not, then either she should replace him anyway, in the name of telling the truth about the culture, or she should not, in the (unexamined) name of excellence. This is the debate that will have to be engaged and that has so far been broached only in the most "inclusionary" of terms. It is ironic that in American literature, where attacks on the male tradition have been most bitter and the reclamation of women writers so spectacular, the appeal has still been only to pluralism, generosity, and guilt. It is populism without the politics of populism.

TO CANONIZE YOUR OWNE WRITERS (POLIMANTERIA, 1595)

Although I referred earlier to a feminist counter-canon, it is only in certain rather restricted contexts that literature by women has in fact been explicitly placed "counter" to the dominant canon. Generally speaking, feminist scholars have been more concerned with establishing the existence, power, and significance of a specially female tradition. Such a possibility is adumbrated in the title of Patricia Meyer Spacks's *The Female Imagination*; however, this book's overview of selected themes and stages in the female life-cycle as treated by some women writers neither broaches nor (obviously) suggests an answer to the question whether there is a female imagination and what characterizes it.[13]

Somewhat earlier, in her anthology of British and American women poets, Louise Bernikow had made a more positive assertion of a continuity and connection subsisting among them.[14] She leaves it to the poems, however, to forge their own links, and, in a collection that boldly and incisively crosses boundaries between published and unpublished writing, literary and anonymous authorship, "high" art, folk art, and music, it is not easy for the reader to identify what the editor believes it is that makes women's poetry specifically *"women's."*

Ellen Moers centers her argument for a (trans-historical) female tradition upon the concept of "heroinism," a quality shared by women writers over time with the female characters they created.[15] Moers also points out another kind of continuity, documenting the way that women writers have read, commented on, and been influenced by the writings of other women who were their predecessors or contemporaries. There is also an unacknowledged continuity between the writer and her female reader. Elaine Showalter conceives the female tradition, embodied particularly in the domestic and sensational fiction of the nineteenth century, as being carried out through a kind of subversive conspiracy between author and audience.[16] Showalter is at her best in discussing this minor "women's fiction."

Indeed, without ever making a case for popular genres as serious literature, she bases her arguments about a tradition more solidly on them than on acknowledged major figures like Virginia Woolf. By contrast, Sandra Gilbert and Susan Gubar focus almost exclusively on key literary figures, bringing women writers and their subjects together through the theme of perceived female aberration —in the act of literary creation itself, as well as in the behavior of the created persons or personae.[17]

Moers's vision of a continuity based on "heroinism" finds an echo in later feminist criticism that posits a discrete, perhaps even autonomous "women's culture." The idea of such a culture has been developed by social historians studying the "homosocial" world of nineteenth-century women.[18] It is a view that underlies, for example, Nina Auerbach's study of relationships among women in selected novels, where strong, supportive ties among mothers, daughters, sisters, and female friends not only constitute the real history in which certain women are conceived as living but function as a normative element as well.[19] That is, fiction in which positive relations subsist to nourish the heroine comes off much better, from Auerbach's point of view, than fiction in which such relations do not exist.

In contrast, Judith Lowder Newton sees the heroines of women's fiction as active, rather than passive, precisely because they do live in a man's world, not an autonomous female one.[20] Defining their power as "ability" rather than "control," she perceives "both a preoccupation with power and subtle power strategies" being exercised by the women in novels by Fanny Burney, Jane Austen, Charlotte Brontë, and George Eliot. Understood in this way, the female tradition, whether or not it in fact reflects and fosters a "culture" of its own, provides an alternative complex of possibilities for women, to be set beside the pits and pedestals offered by all too much of the Great Tradition.

CANONIZE SUCH A MULTIFARIOUS GENEALOGIE OF COMMENTS (NASHE, 1593)

Historians like Smith-Rosenberg and Cott are careful to specify that their generalizations extend only to white middle- and upper-class women of the nineteenth century. Although literary scholars are equally scrupulous about the national and temporal boundaries of their subject, they tend to use the gender term comprehensively. In this way, conclusions about "women's fiction" or "female consciousness" have been drawn or jumped to from considering a body of work whose authors are all white and comparatively privileged. Of the critical studies I have mentioned, only Bernikow's anthology, *The World Split Open*, brings labor songs, black women's blues lyrics, and anonymous ballads into conjunction with poems that were written for publication by professional writers, both black and white. The other books, which build an extensive case for a female tradition that Bernikow only suggests, delineate their subject in such a way as to exclude not only black and working-class authors but any notion that race and class might be relevant categories in the definition and apprehension of "women's literature." Similarly, even for discussions of writers who were known to be lesbians, this aspect of the female tradition often remains unacknowledged; worse yet, some of the books that develop the idea of a female tradition are openly homophobic, employing the word "lesbian" only pejoratively.[21]

Black and lesbian scholars, however, have directed much less energy to polemics against the feminist "mainstream" than to concrete, positive work on the literature itself. Recovery and reinterpretation of a wealth of unknown or undervalued texts has suggested the existence of both a black women's tradition and a lesbian tradition. In a clear parallel with the relationship between women's literature in general and the male-dominated tradition, both are by definition part of women's literature, but they are also distinct from and independent of it.

There are important differences, however, between these two traditions and the critical effort surrounding them. Black feminist criticism has the task of demonstrating that, in the face of all the obstacles a racist and sexist society has been able to erect, there is a continuity of black women who have written and written well. It is a matter of gaining recognition for the quality of the writing itself and respect for its principal subject, the lives and consciousness of black women. Black women's literature is also an element of black literature as a whole, where the recognized voices have usually been male. A triple imperative is therefore at work: establishing a discrete and significant black female tradition, then situating it within black literature and (along with the rest of that literature) within the common American literary heritage.[22] So far, unfortunately, each step toward integration has met with continuing exclusion. A black women's tradition has been recovered and revaluated chiefly through the efforts of black feminist scholars. Only some of that work has been accepted as part of either a racially mixed women's literature or a two-sex black literature. As for the gatekeepers of American literature in general, how many of them are willing to swing open the portals even for Zora Neale Hurston or Paule Marshall? How many have heard of them?

The issue of "inclusion," moreover, brings up questions that echo those raised by opening the male-dominated canon to women. How do generalizations about women's literature "as a whole" change when the work of black women is not merely added to but fully incorporated into that tradition? How does our sense of black literary history change? And what implications do these changes have for reconsideration of the American canon?

Whereas many white literary scholars continue to behave as if there were no major black woman writers, most are prepared to admit that certain well-known white writers were lesbians for all or part of their lives. The problem is getting beyond a position that says either "so *that's* what was wrong with her!" or, alternatively, "it doesn't matter who she slept with—we're talking about literature." Much lesbian feminist criticism has addressed theoretical questions about *which* literature is actually part of the lesbian tradition, all writing by lesbians, for example, or all writing by women about women's relations with one another. Questions of class and race enter here as well, both in their own guise and in the by now familiar form of "aesthetic standards." Who speaks for the lesbian community: the highly educated experimentalist with an unearned income or the naturalistic working-class autobiographer? Or are both the *same kind* of foremother, reflecting the community's range of cultural identities and resistance?[23]

A CHEAPER WAY OF CANON-MAKING IN A CORNER (BAXTER, 1639)

It is not only members of included social groups, however, who have challenged the fundamentally elite nature of the existing canon. "Elite" is a literary as well as a social category. It is possible to argue for taking all texts seriously as texts without arguments based on social oppression or cultural exclusion, and popular genres have therefore been studied as part of the female literary tradition. Feminists are not in agreement as to whether domestic and sentimental fiction, the female Gothic, the women's sensational novel functioned as instruments of expression, repression, or subversion, but they have successfully revived interest in the question as a legitimate cultural issue.[24] It is no longer automatically assumed that literature addressed to the mass female audience is necessarily bad because it is sentimental, or for that matter, sentimental because it is addressed to that audience. Feminist criticism has examined without embarrassment an entire literature that was previously dismissed solely because it was popular with women and affirmed standards and values associated with femininity. And proponents of the "continuous tradition" and "women's culture" positions have insisted that this material be placed beside women's "high" art as part of the articulated and organic female tradition.

This point of view remains controversial within the orbit of women's studies, but the real problems start when it comes into contact with the universe of canon formation. Permission may have been given the contemporary critic to approach a wide range of texts, transcending and even ignoring the traditional canon. But in a context where the ground of struggle—highly contested, moreover—concerns Edith Wharton's advancement to somewhat more major status, fundamental assumptions have changed very little. Can Hawthorne's "d——d mob of scribbling women" *really* be invading the realms so long sanctified by Hawthorne himself and his brother geniuses? Is this what feminist criticism or even feminist cultural history means? Is it—to apply some outmoded and deceptively simple categories—a good development or a bad one? If these questions have not been raised, it is because women's literature and the female tradition tend to be evoked as an autonomous cultural experience, not impinging on the rest of literary history.

WISDOME UNDER A RAGGED COATE IS SELDOME CANONICALL (CROSSE, 1603)

Whether dealing with popular genres or high art, commentary on the female tradition usually has been based on work that was published at some time and was produced by professional writers. But feminist scholarship has also pushed back the boundaries of literature in other directions, considering a wide range of forms and styles in which women's writing—especially that of women who did not perceive themselves as writers—appears. In this way, women's letters, diaries, journals, autobiographies, oral histories, and private poetry have come under critical scrutiny as evidence of women's consciousness *and expression*.

Generally speaking, feminist criticism has been quite open to such material, recognizing that the very conditions that gave many women the impetus to write made it impossible for their culture to define them as writers. This acceptance has expanded our sense of possible forms and voices, but it has challenged our received sense of appropriate style. What it amounts to is that if a woman writing in isolation and with no public audience in view nonetheless had "good"— that is, canonical—models, we are impressed with the strength of her text when she applies what she has assimilated about writing to her own experiences as a woman. If, however, her literary models were chosen from the same popular literature that some critics are now beginning to recognize as part of the female tradition, then she has not got hold of an expressive instrument that empowers her.

At the Modern Language Association meeting in 1976, I included in my paper the entire two-page autobiography of a participant in the Summer Schools for Women Workers held at Bryn Mawr in the first decades of the century. It is a circumstantial narrative in which events from the melancholy to the melodramatic are accumulated in a serviceable, somewhat hackneyed style. The anonymous "Seamer on Men's Underwear" had a unique sense of herself both as an individual and as a member of the working class. But was she a writer? Part of the audience was as moved as I was by the narrative, but the majority was outraged at the piece's failure to meet the criteria—particularly, the "complexity" criteria— of good art.

When I developed my remarks for publication, I wrote about the problems of dealing with an author who is trying too hard to write elegantly, and attempted to make the case that clichés or sentimentality need not be signals of meretricious prose and that ultimately it is honest writing for which criticism should be looking.[25] Nowadays, I would also address the question of the female tradition, the role of popular fiction within it, and the influence of that fiction on its audience. It seems to me that, if we accept the work of the professional "scribbling woman," we have also to accept its literary consequences, not drawing the lines at the place where that literature may have been the force that enabled an otherwise inarticulate segment of the population to grasp a means of expression and communication.

Once again, the arena is the female tradition itself. If we are thinking in terms of canon formation, it is the alternative canon. Until the aesthetic arguments can be fully worked out in the feminist context, it will be impossible to argue, in the general marketplace of literary ideas, that the novels of Henry James ought to give place—a *little* place, even—to the diaries of his sister Alice. At this point, I suspect most of our male colleagues would consider such a request, even in the name of Alice James, much less the Seamer on Men's Underwear, little more than a form of "reverse discrimination"—a concept to which some of them are already overly attached. It is up to feminist scholars, when we determine that this is indeed the right course to pursue, to demonstrate that such an inclusion would constitute a genuinely affirmative action for all of us.

The development of feminist literary criticism and scholarship has already proceeded through a number of identifiable stages. Its pace is more reminiscent of the survey course than of the slow processes of canon formation and revision, and it has been more successful in defining and sticking to its own intellectual turf, the female counter-canon, than in gaining general canonical recognition for Edith

Wharton, Fanny Fern, or the female diarists of the Westward Expansion. In one sense, the more coherent our sense of the female tradition is, the stronger will be our eventual case. Yet the longer we wait, the more comfortable the women's literature ghetto—separate, apparently autonomous, and far from equal—may begin to feel.

At the same time, I believe the challenge cannot come only by means of the patent value of the work of women. We must pursue the questions certain of us have raised and retreated from as to the eternal verity of the received standards of greatness or even goodness. And, while not abandoning our new-found female tradition, we have to return to confrontation with "the" canon, examining it as a source of ideas, themes, motifs, and myths about the two sexes. The point in so doing is not to label and hence dismiss even the most sexist literary classics, but to enable all of us to apprehend them, finally, in all their human dimensions.

NOTES

1. Jane Marcus, "Gunpowder Treason and Plot," talk delivered at the School of Criticism and Theory, Northwestern University, colloquium "The Challenge of Feminist Criticism," November 1981. Seeking authority for the sort of creature a literary canon might be, I turned, like many another, to the *Oxford English Dictionary*. The tags that head up the several sections of this essay are a by-product of that effort rather than of any more exact and laborious scholarship.

2. In a survey of 50 introductory courses in American literature offered at 25 U.S. colleges and universities, Emily Dickinson's name appeared more often than that of any other woman writer: 20 times. This frequency puts her in a fairly respectable twelfth place. Among the 61 most frequently taught authors, only 7 others are women; Edith Wharton and Kate Chopin are each mentioned 8 times, Sarah Orne Jewett and Anne Bradstreet 6 each, Flannery O'Connor 4 times, Willa Cather and Mary Wilkins Freeman each 3 times. The same list includes 5 black authors, all of them male. Responses from other institutions received too late for compilation only confirmed these findings. See Paul Lauter, "A Small Survey of Introductory Courses in American Literature," *Women's Studies Quarterly* 9 (Winter 1981): 12. In another study, 99 professors of English responded to a survey asking which works of American literature published since 1941 they thought should be considered classics and which books should be taught to college students. The work mentioned by the most respondents (59 citations) was Ralph Ellison's *Invisible Man*. No other work by a black appears among the top 20 that constitute the published list of results. Number 19, *The Complete Stories of Flannery O'Connor*, is the only work on this list by a woman. (*Chronicle of Higher Education*, September 29, 1982). For British literature, the feminist claim is not that Austen, the Brontës, Eliot, and Woolf are habitually omitted, but rather that they are by no means always included in courses that, like the survey I taught at Columbia some years ago, had room for a single nineteenth-century novel. I know, however, of no systematic study of course offerings in this area more recent than Elaine Showalter's "Women in the Literary Curriculum," *College English* 32 (May 1971): 855–62.

3. Kate Millett, *Sexual Politics* (Garden City, N.Y.: Doubleday, 1970); Eva Figes, *Patriarchal Attitudes* (New York: Stein & Day, 1970); Elizabeth Janeway, *Man's World, Woman's Place: A Study in Social Mythology* (New York: William Morrow, 1971); Germaine Greer, *The Female Eunuch* (New York: McGraw-Hill, 1971); Carolyn G. Heilbrun, *Toward a Recognition of Androgyny* (New York: Harper & Row, 1974). The phenomenon these studies represent is discussed at greater length in a study of which I am a co-author; see Ellen Carol DuBois,

Gail Paradise Kelly, Elizabeth Lapovsky Kennedy, Carolyn W. Korsmeyer, and Lillian S. Robinson, *Feminist Scholarship: Kindling in the Groves of Academe* (Urbana: University of Illinois Press, 1985).

4. Annette Kolodny, *The Lay of the Land: Metaphor as Experience and History in American Life and Letters* (Chapel Hill: University of North Carolina Press, 1975); Judith Fetterley, *The Resisting Reader: A Feminist Approach to American Fiction* (Bloomington: Indiana University Press, 1978).

5. Mary Ellmann, *Thinking About Women* (New York: Harcourt, Brace & World, 1968).

6. Carolyn Ruth Swift Lenz, Gayle Greene, and Carol Thomas Neely, eds. *The Woman's Part: Feminist Criticism of Shakespeare* (Urbana: University of Illinois Press, 1980), p. 4. In this vein, see also Juliet Dusinberre, *Shakespeare and the Nature of Woman* (London: Macmillan, 1975); Irene G. Dash, *Wooing, Wedding, and Power: Women in Shakespeare's Plays* (New York: Columbia University Press, 1981).

7. Sandra M. Gilbert, "Patriarchal Poetics and the Woman Reader: Reflections on Milton's Bogey," *PMLA* 93 (May 1978): 368–82. The articles on Chaucer and Shakespeare in *The Authority of Experience: Essays in Feminist Criticism*, ed. Arlyn Diamond and Lee R. Edwards (Amherst: University of Massachusetts Press, 1977), reflect the complementary tendency.

8. As I learned when surveying fifteen years' worth of *Dissertation Abstracts* and MLA programs, much of this work has taken the form of theses or conference papers rather than books and journal articles.

9. See R. W. B. Lewis, *Edith Wharton: A Biography* (New York: Harper & Row, 1975); Cynthia Griffin Woolf, *A Feast of Words: The Triumph of Edith Wharton* (New York: Oxford University Press, 1977); see also Marlene Springer, *Edith Wharton and Kate Chopin: A Reference Guide* (Boston: G. K. Hall, 1976).

10. See, for instance, Rebecca Harding Lavis, *Life in the Iron Mills* (Old Westbury, N.Y.: Feminist Press, 1972), with a biographical and critical Afterword by Tillie Olsen; Kate Chopin, *The Complete Works*, ed. Per Seyersted (Baton Rouge: Louisiana State University Press, 1969); Alice Walker, "In Search of Zora Neale Hurston," *Ms*, March 1975, pp. 74–75; Robert Hemenway, *Zora Neale Hurston* (Urbana: University of Illinois Press, 1978): Zora Neale Hurston, *I Love Myself When I Am Laughing and Also When I Am Looking Mean and Impressive* (Old Westbury: Feminist Press, 1979), with introductory material by Alice Walker and Mary Helen Washington; Carolyn G. Burke, "Becoming Mina Loy," *Women's Studies* 7 (1979): 136–50; Meridel LeSueur, *Ripening* (Old Westbury: Feminist Press, 1981); on LeSueur, see also Mary McAnally, ed., *We Sing Our Struggle: A Tribute to Us All* (Tulsa, Okla.: Cardinal Press, 1982); *The Young Rebecca: Writings of Rebecca West, 1911–1917*, selected and introduced by Jane Marcus (New York: Viking Press, 1982).

The examples cited are all from the nineteenth and twentieth centuries. Valuable work has also been done on women writers before the Industrial Revolution. See Joan Goulianos, ed., *By a Woman Writt: Literature from Six Centuries By and About Women* (Indianapolis: Bobbs-Merrill, 1973); Mary R. Mahl and Helene Koon, eds., *The Female Spectator: English Women Writers before 1800* (Bloomington: Indiana University Press, 1977).

11. Nina Brown, *Woman's Fiction: A Guide to Novels by and about Women in America, 1820–70* (Ithaca: Cornell University Press, 1978), pp. 14–15.

12. Myra Jehlen, "Archimedes and the Paradox of Feminist Criticism," *Signs* 6 (Summer 1981): 592; also this volume pages 191–212.

13. Patricia Meyer Spacks, *The Female Imagination* (New York: Alfred A. Knopf, 1975).

14. *The World Split Open: Four Centuries of Women Poets In England and America, 1552–1950*, ed. and intro. Louise Bernikow (New York: Vintage Books, 1974).

15. Ellen Moers, *Literary Women: The Great Writers* (Garden City, N.Y.: Doubleday, 1976).

16. Elaine Showalter, *A Literature of Their Own: British Women Novelists from Brontë to Lessing* (Princeton, N.J.: Princeton University Press, 1977).

17. Sandra M. Gilbert and Susan Gubar, *Madwoman in the Attic: The Woman Writer and the Nineteenth-Century Literary Imagination* (New Haven, Conn.: Yale University Press, 1979).

18. Carroll Smith-Rosenberg, "The Female World of Love and Ritual: Relations Between Women in Nineteenth-Century America," *Signs* (Fall 1975): 1–30; Nancy F. Cott, *The Bonds of Womanhood: "Woman's Sphere" in New England, 1780–1830* (New Haven, Conn.: Yale University Press, 1977).

19. Nina Auerbach, *Communities of Women: An Idea in Fiction* (Cambridge, Mass.: Harvard University Press, 1979). See also Janet M. Todd, *Women's Friendship in Literature* (New York: Columbia University Press, 1980); Louise Bernikow, *Among Women* (New York: Crown, 1980).

20. Judith Lowder Newton, *Women, Power, and Subversion: Social Strategies in British Fiction* (Athens: University of Georgia Press, 1981).

21. On the failings of feminist criticism with respect to black and lesbian writers, see Barbara Smith, "Toward a Black Feminist Criticism," *The New Feminist Criticism*, ed. Elaine Showalter (New York: Pantheon, 1985), pp. 168–85; Mary Helen Washington, "New Lives and New Letters: Black Women Writers at the End of the Seventies," *College English* 43 (January 1981): 1–11; Bonnie Zimmerman, "What Has Never Been: An Overview of Lesbian Feminist Literary Criticism," in *Feminisms*, rev. ed., under "Canon."

22. See, e.g., Smith, "Toward a Black Feminist Criticism"; Barbara Christian, *Black Women Novelists: The Development of a Tradition, 1892–1976* (Westport, Conn.: Greenwood Press, 1980); Erlene Stetson, ed., *Black Sister: Poetry by Black American Women, 1764–1980* (Bloomington: Indiana University Press, 1981); Gloria Hull, "Black Women Poets from Wheatley to Walker," in *Sturdy Black Bridges: Visions of Black Women in Literature*, ed. Roseann P. Bell et al. (Garden City, N.Y.: Anchor Books, 1979); Mary Helen Washington, "Introduction: In Pursuit of Our Own History," *Midnight Birds: Stories of Contemporary Black Women Writers* (Garden City, N.Y.: Anchor Books, 1980); the essays and bibliographies in *But Some of Us Are Brave: Black Women's Studies*, ed. Gloria Hull, Patricia Bell Scott, and Barbara Smith (Old Westbury: Feminist Press, 1982).

23. See Zimmerman, "What Has Never Been"; Adrienne Rich, "Jane Eyre: Trials of a Motherless Girl," *Lies, Secrets, and Silence: Selected Prose, 1966–1978* (New York: W. W. Norton, 1979); Lillian Faderman, *Surpassing the Love of Men: Romantic Friendship and Love Between Women from the Renaissance to the Present* (New York: William Morrow, 1981); the literary essays in *Lesbian Studies*, ed. Margaret Cruikshank (Old Westbury, N.Y.: Feminist Press, 1982).

24. Some examples on different sides of the question are: Ann Douglas, *The Feminization of American Culture* (New York: Alfred A. Knopf, 1976); Elaine Showalter, A *Literature of Their Own* and her article "Dinah Mulock Craik and the Tactics of Sentiment: A Case Study in Victorian Female Authorship," *Feminist Studies* 2 (May 1975): 5–23; Katherine Ellis, "Paradise Lost: The Limits of Domesticity in the Nineteenth-Century Novel," *Feminist Studies* 2 (May 1975): 55–65.

25. Lillian S. Robinson, "Working/Women/Writing," *Sex, Class, and Culture* (Bloomington: Indiana University Press, 1978), p. 252.

CASTE, CLASS, AND CANON

(1981/87)

〜〜〜〜〜〜〜〜〜〜〜〜〜〜〜〜〜〜〜〜〜〜〜〜〜〜〜〜

I

I want to consider two problems in this essay, problems which—as I shall try to show—are closely related, although they may not at first glimpse appear to be. One problem, as my title suggests, involves the "canon" of literature—that is, the works from the past that we continue to read, teach, and write about. I am less concerned here with describing the history or features of a canon, or proposing alternatives to the canons we have inherited, than in exploring some of the factors that have continued to shape it. In particular, I want to consider how "class" and "caste," especially as they emerge in the work of literary analysis, shape canon. Examining the relationships of class, caste, and canon will, I believe, aid in understanding what we might mean by "feminist criticism," the second problem I wish to address. To frame that problem somewhat differently, how does—does?—the project of feminist criticism differ from other forms of literary analysis, and especially the formalisms rooted in the work of the New Critics? Can the question of the canon serve as a lens to help focus the project of feminist criticism?

I want to begin with an experience I had at the 1980 National Women's Studies Association convention during a session on the practice of feminist literary criticism. A group of young critics, all women, described to the audience how they met regularly at a library centrally located in their city, how they prepared and discussed various texts, and how they aided each other in developing their critical skills and range. They then handed out a poem and read it aloud, each one taking one section, and began discussing it by having each member of the group present a short statement about it. Then the audience was invited to join in the discussion. It seems like a reasonable process, and I am sure that—especially for those living in relatively isolated areas—it felt like the rushing of falls in the desert. But as the session wore on I found myself getting more and more restive, indeed rather irritated.

I tried to trace my growing anger. It seemed to derive from the dynamic of the panel itself; it had, I thought, to do with the *form* of criticism, almost all close analysis of text. I found myself, reluctantly, painfully, being drawn back into the tortured style of graduate-school competition: "can you top this?" As much macho as mind filled the room. Was this feminist criticism? I began to wonder: is the *form* of criticism value-free? Is critical technique simply a tool, like trigonometry? Well, is trigonometry value-free?

There was a second problem, the poem under consideration. As might be guessed, the poem was one from Adrienne Rich's *The Dream of a Common Language*. I want to be very clear about my comment here: I respect Adrienne Rich's poetry very much, and I particularly like that book. I think the poem that was under discussion quite a good poem indeed. But I remembered Deborah Hilty's questioning such a focus in a paper she prepared for a Midwest Modern Language Association conference. Why was it, she asked, that such panels always seem to take up poems by Adrienne Rich? Why not Judy Grahn or Susan Griffin? Or Vera Hall? or Malvina Reynolds? Or Gwendolyn Brooks? Adrienne Rich, by the way, was among the first to ask precisely that question.

Those two questions—about the technique of criticism and the subject for analysis—led, in turn, to a third question: what connection existed between the selection of the poem and the kind of criticism, really the kind of response, being undertaken? Or, to put it another way, how is *canon*—that is, selection—related to, indeed a *function of,* critical technique? That is the fundamental question I want to consider here—the relationship of style in criticism to the canon of literature. But before I address that question specifically, I want simply to outline the nest of questions implicit in the central one:

—Can the canon significantly change if we retain essentially the same critical techniques and priorities?

—Where do the techniques of criticism come from? Do they fall from the sky? Or do they arise out of social practice? And if the latter, from what social practice?

—Out of what social practice, from what values, did close analysis of complex texts arise?

—Do we perpetuate those values in pursuing the critical practice derived from them?

—Does such critical practice effectively screen from our appreciation, even our scrutiny, other worlds of creativity, of art?

—Are there other worlds of art out there whose nature, dynamics, values we fail to appreciate because we ask the wrong questions, or don't know what questions to ask? Or maybe shouldn't simply be asking questions?

Such questions clearly enough reveal the drift of my argument. But to summarize it: I think the literary canon as we have known it is a product in significant measure of our training in a male, white, bourgeois cultural tradition, including in particular the formal techniques of literary analysis. And further, that other cultural traditions provide alternate views about the nature and function of art, and of approaches to it. Indeed, if our concern is to change the canon "radically"—that is, at its roots—as distinct from grafting on to it a few odd branches, we must look at the full range of these alternate traditions. This argument holds, I believe, whether one is concerned with working-class art, the art of minority groups, or much of the art of women. For in significant ways, all "marginalized" groups have experiences and traditions distinct from those of the dominant majority. In this paper I focus initially on working-class and black traditions, both for their inherent interest and also because they provide us with revealing perspectives on women's art as well as on feminist criticism.

II

Raymond Williams' distinction between "working-class" and "bourgeois" culture provides a useful starting point:

> . . . a culture is not only a body of intellectual and imaginative work; it is also and essentially a whole way of life. The basis of a distinction between bourgeois and working-class culture is only secondarily in the field of intellectual and imaginative work. . . . The crucial distinguishing element in English life since the Industrial Revolution is not language, not dress, not leisure—for these indeed will tend to uniformity. The crucial distinction is between alternative ideas of the nature of social relationship.
>
> "Bourgeois" is a significant term because it marks that version of social relationship which we usually call individualism: that is to say, an idea of society as a neutral area within which each individual is free to pursue his own development and his own advantage as a natural right. . . . [Both] this idea [of service] and the individualistic idea can be sharply contrasted with the idea that we properly associate with the working class: an idea which, whether it is called communism, socialism, or cooperation regards society neither as neutral nor as protective, but as the positive means for all kinds of development, including individual development.[1]

Writing from a British perspective, Williams perhaps underestimates the significance of works of imagination in defining "working-class culture": "It is not proletarian art, or council houses, or a particular use of languages; it is, rather, the basic collective idea, and the institutions, manners, habits of thought and intentions which proceed from this."[2] But his fundamental point is critical to understand: while broad areas of the culture are common to the working class and the bourgeoisie, there remains a "crucial distinction . . . between alternative ideas of the nature of social relationship." This distinction significantly explains differing "institutions, manners, habits of thought and intentions." Distinct cultures also help shape ideas about the nature of art, its functions, the processes of its creation, the nature of the artist and of the artist's social role.

There is nothing very mysterious about this: people whose experiences of the world significantly differ, whose material conditions of life, whose formal and informal training, whose traditions, sometimes even whose language, differ—and especially people whose understanding of their own life-chances and opportunities, their "place"—differ will think about things differently, will talk about things differently, will value at least some things differently, will express themselves *to* different people *in* different ways and *about* different experiences, at least in some measure.

But that is all very abstract. We need to be somewhat more specific about differences between working-class and bourgeois art and literature. Unfortunately, there are relatively few cultural, and particularly literary, analyses of working-class materials (at least in Western practice). Martha Vicinus' *The Industrial Muse*[3] is a unique full-length study, but confined to Great Britian; Dan Tannacito examines the poetry of Colorado miners around the turn of this century;[4] an article of mine provides bibliographical and some theoretical approaches to working-class women's literature;[5] Lawrence Levine brilliantly explores the historical relationships between black culture and consciousness.[6] Even from this limited number of analyses certain features of working-class or "popular"[7] art emerge clearly. First, working-class art often is produced in group situations, rather than in the privacy of a study—or garret—and it is similarly experienced in the hall, the church, the work-site, the quilting bee, the picket line. It thus emerges from the experiences of a particular group of people facing particular problems in a particular time. Much of it is therefore not conceived as timeless and transcendent; rather, it might be called "instrumental." As Tannacito puts it, "the value of the Colorado miners' poetry derived exclusively from the use made of the poems by their audience. The audience was an immediate one. The objective [in writing] was inseparable from those goals" toward which the workers' lives directed them. Vicinus points out that working-class artists, themselves persuaded of the power of literature to "influence people's behavior," aimed to "persuade readers to adopt particular beliefs." Some recommended the bourgeois values embodied in the culture of what they thought of as their "betters." Others, despairing of social and political change, devoted their work to reassuring readers that their lives, debased as they might have become, still had value, and to providing at least some entertainment and consolation in an oppressive world. Many wrote to help change the status quo. Their work, Vicinus says, aimed "to arouse and focus social tension in order to channel it toward specific political actions." By "clarifying" or making vivid economic, social, and political relationships between working people and those who held power, they helped to "shape individual and class consciousness" and to "imbue a sense of class solidarity that encouraged working people to fight for social and political equality."

Tannacito provides a number of instances of the ways in which the miner poets tried to accomplish such goals. Poems of "praise," for example, explicitly tried to link heroic deeds of the past with the contemporary workers' community. Other poems sought to inspire specific forms of struggle, job actions, voting, boycotts. Miner poets, like working-class artists generally, wrote about the world they and their readers shared: the job, oppression by bosses, the militia and the scabs, a heritage of common struggle. They saw art not as a means for removing people from the world in which they lived—however desirable that might seem—nor as a device for producing "catharsis" or "stasis." Rather, art aimed to inspire consciousness about and actions within the world, to make living in that world more bearable, to extend experiences of that world, indeed to enlarge the world working people could experience. Thus, even as sophisticated an example of working-class fiction as Tillie Olsen's "Tell Me a Riddle" centrally concerns the problem of inspiring a new generation with the values, hopes, and images that directed the actions and aspirations of an earlier generation and that lie buried under the grit produced by forty years of daily life. Or consider how Morris

Rosenfeld renders the experience of time-discipline in his work as a pants presser:

> The Clock in the workshop,—it rests not a moment;
> It points on, and ticks on: eternity—time;
> Once someone told me the clock had a meaning,—
> In pointing and ticking had reason and rhyme. . . .
> At times, when I listen, I hear the clock plainly;—
> The reason of old—the old meaning—is gone!
> The maddening pendulum urges me forward
> To labor and still labor on.
> The tick of the clock is the boss in his anger.
> The face of the clock has the eyes of the foe.
> The clock—I shudder—Dost hear how it draws me?
> It calls me "Machine" and it cries [to] me "Sew"![8]

Rosenfeld is concerned to capture, and to mourn, the passing in a particular historical moment of an older, less time-disciplined order of work, as well as the degradation of the worker to the status of machine. The poem gives names and pictures to the experiences that Rosenfeld and his fellow-workers encountered in moving from the shtetl to the sweatshops of the new world.

Working-class art thus functions to focus consciousness and to develop ideology, but it can also play a variety of other roles. Songs were used, especially by black slaves and nominally free laborers, to set the pace of work in a group and, at the same time, to relieve the tension and pent-up feelings born of oppressive labor. Leaders lined out a rhythm for hoeing, chopping, lifting bales, for rowing boats. At the same time, the songs spoke realistically about the shared labor, and more covertly, perhaps, about those exacting it.[9] Similarly, sorrow songs or spirituals served not only to express grief and to sustain hope in slavery, but they were also used as signals to prepare for escapes from it (see Levine, pp. 30–31). Similarly, during the Civil Rights movement of the 1950s and 1960s, what were originally church hymns underwent conversion to marching songs and sometimes means for triumphing over one's jailers.

Clearly, the conception of the functions of art are here very different from those propounded, say, by Aristotle, or Milton, or Coleridge—or formalist criticism, as I shall indicate in a moment. It is not, however, only conception or function which differ, but also form and technique, and even the manner of creation of much working-class art. In characterizing the distinctive qualities of the song styles of black slaves, Levine emphasizes "its overriding antiphony, its group nature, its pervasive functionality, its improvisational character, its strong relationship in performance to dance and bodily movements and expression. . . . " (p. 6). Some of these qualities are peculiar to styles derived from West African roots, but some are characteristic of other working-class cultures. New songs are often based upon old ones, and there is less concern with the unique qualities of art than with building variations upon tunes, themes, and texts well known in the community. For example, songs like "Hold the Fort" and "We Are Building a Strong Union," which began as gospel hymns, went through a series of metamorphoses in order to serve the needs of a diverse sequence of worker's organizations—in the case of the former, including the British transport workers, the Knights of Labor, and the Industrial Workers of the World. The Wobbly poet Joe Hill constructed some of his best-known songs as take-offs on Salvation Army hymns. The spiritual "Oh, Freedom" became one of the most popular songs of the Civil Rights movement; as the movement's militance increased, many singers changed the song's refrain from "Before I be a slave/ I be buried in my grave/ and go home to my Lord/ And be free" to "Before . . . grave/ And I'll fight for my right/ To be free."

In many ways, working-class art, like other elements in working-class life, is highly traditional; certainly innovative form is not a primary consideration and "make it new" a slogan which would be viewed with some suspicion. Similarly, working-class poetry and song, especially, but also tales and stories are often built around repeated elements—refrains, formulae, commonly-accepted assumptions about characters. Language, too, is often simpler, sometimes commonplace, certainly less "heightened" than that of "high-culture" verse. Many of these characteristics are common to literary forms rooted in oral art—made necessary by the exigencies of memory and improvisation. Some may arise from the artist's desire to avoid a fancy vocabulary unfamiliar to the audience, or esoteric images and allusions. Thus a poem like Rosenfeld's carefully works with materials as familiar to his readers as gaberdine was to him.

In some respects, as well, these characteristics are derived from the communal character of the creation of certain working-class art forms. One old former slave describes the creation of a "spiritual" in a pre-Civil War religious meeting in these words:

> I'd jump up dar and den and hollar and shout and sing and pat, and dey would all cotch de words and I'd sing it to some old shout song I'd heard 'em sing from Africa, and dey'd all take it up and keep at it, and keep a-addin' to it, and den it would be a spiritual.[10]

In such situations, the individual creator is generally less significant than the group; or, rather, to the extent that individuals are creators, they shape a common stock to new group purposes without diminishing or expropriating that common stock. The song leader in church is not asked to provide new hymns (much less copyright old ones) and would be looked at with suspicion if she did so. She is asked to reinvigorate a hymn that is known, perhaps to add something especially appropriate for the occasion.[11] The jazz musician may be admired for a new melody, but probably more important—at least until recently—is the ability to ring variations on melodies the listeners know and follow. I am emphasizing here the "folk," communal elements of working-class art, in some degree at the expense of art produced by self-conscious individual working-class artists. I do so because an approach through people's culture helps to focus certain distinctive qualities of working-class art, certain "centers of gravity," not so easily seen if one concentrates on the productions of separate artists. Yet, obviously, a continuum exists between songs, poems, and tales which are, so to speak, common property and works created primarily by individual imaginations.

But what is critical here is precisely the relationship between individual and community. Levine, for example, directly connects the *form* of the spiritual with the underlying social reality of black slave life:

> Just as the process by which the spirituals were created allowed for simultaneous individual and communal creativity, so their very structure provided simultaneous outlets for individual and communal expression. The overriding antiphonal structure of the spirituals—the call and response pattern which Negroes brought with them from Africa and which was reinforced in America by the practice of lining out hymns—placed the individual in continual dialogue with his community, allowing him at one and the same time to preserve his voice as a distinct entity and to blend it with those of his fellows.[12]

I would carry the argument in a slightly different direction by suggesting that one center of gravity of working-class art is its high level of integration of creator and audience. Works often have their origin, as well as their being, in situations which do not absolutely distinguish active performer/artist from passive audience. Or when the distinction is relatively clearer, the artist's "product" is offered *not* primarily for its *exchange* value (money for that song or painting), but for its *use* in the lives of the people to whom it is directed. A moving example is provided by the Kentucky mountain songs sung at the funeral of "Jock" Yablonski and recorded with great majesty in the film *Harlan County, U.S.A.*

In a larger sense, all working-class art (perhaps all art[13]) must be explored precisely in terms of its *use*. Partly that is a function of marginality itself: the struggle for existence and dignity necessarily involves all available resources, including art. But partly, I think, this phenomenon is explained by the fundamental character of working-class culture, what Williams called "solidarity." It is not simply a slogan or an abstraction that happens to appeal to many people who work. It is, rather, a way of describing the culture of people who have been pushed together into workplaces and communities where survival and growth enforce interdependence. In this context, the work of the artist—while it may in some respects be expressive and private—remains overwhelmingly functional in his or her community. And an approach to it cannot strip it of this context without ripping away its substance.

My argument began from the premise that the conditions of life of working-class people have produced ideas about social relationships crucially distinct from those of the bourgeoisie. This distinction shaped differing institutions, manners, and ideas about culture and art. In order to approach working-class culture, then, we must begin not with presuppositions about what literature *is* and is *not*, or what is valuable in it or not, but rather by asking in what forms, on what themes, in what circumstances, and to what *ends* do working people speak and sing and write and signify to each other. We must, in other words, discover the distinctive rules and measures of working-class art and thus the critical strategies and tools appropriate to them.

"Are you saying," someone might object, "that the rules and measures—the critical tools—we now possess are invalid, somehow biased or irrelevant?" Here, indeed, is the nub of the matter. For we do approach culture with certain presuppositions, frameworks, touchstones which we learn and which we learn to valorize. I have tried here to state as neutrally as I can certain of the qualities and origins of working-class art. I have not tried to lay a spiritual like "Roll, Jordan" or a poem like Rosenfeld's alongside, say, Donne's "A Valediction: forbidding mourning" in order to evaluate one in relation to another, or all against some "universal" standard of measurement. For the central issue is not which is "better," but what we mean by "better." And I am sure it is clear by now that I believe such standards of judgment, which shape the canon, to be rooted in assumptions derived from class and caste about the techniques, qualities, and especially the functions of art.

I do not want to be misleading here: I do not believe that somewhere out there is a working-class poet, ignored through bourgeois prejudice, who actually wrote better metaphysical poems than Donne or more singular odes than Shelley. No more do I think that a factory organized along truly socialist lines will be more "efficient" and "productive" than a capitalist factory; capitalists often find means to do rather well what it is they want to do—in this case to squeeze as much profit from workers as they can. But that does not necessarily make for a humane, safe, creative, or socially responsible workplace. The goals are different; the values and thus the priorities different. On the other hand, it has been demonstrated that there are forgotten black and white women writers who wrote fiction as good in traditional terms as that of many of the white men with whom we are familiar. As Williams pointed out, there are vast shared areas of culture. My main point, however, is that if there probably are no working-class metaphysical poets, neither did Donne write verses for "Roll, Jordan." And if "Roll, Jordan" does not demonstrate the fine elaboration of complex language to be found in "A Valediction," it is also the fact that none of Donne's poems—not all of them together I daresay—has served to sustain and inspire so many thousands of oppressed people. What, finally, is art about?

III

Mr. Allen Tate had an answer for us. "Good poetry," he writes in "Tension in Poetry," "is a unity of all the meanings from the furthest extremes of intension and extension. . . . the meaning of poetry is its 'tension,' the full organized body of all the extension and intension that we can find in it."[14] In the same essay he attacks Edna St. Vincent Millay's "Justice Denied in Massachusetts," a poem written in gloomy reaction to the execution of Sacco and Vanzetti.

> Let us abandon then our gardens and go home
> And sit in the sitting-room.
> Shall the larkspur blossom or the corn grow under this cloud?
> Sour to the fruitful seed
> Is the cold earth under this cloud,
> Fostering quack and weed, we have marched upon but cannot conquer;
> We have bent the blades of our hoes against the stalks of them.
>
> Let us go home, and sit in the sitting-room.
> Not in our day
> Shall the cloud go over and the sun rise as before,
> Beneficent upon us
> Out of the glittering bay,
> And the warm winds be blown inward from the sea
> Moving the blades of cord
> With a peaceful sound.

"These lines," Tate claims, "are mass language: they arouse an affective state in one set of terms, and suddenly an object quite unrelated to those terms gets the benefit of it." The Millay poem, he continues,

> is no doubt still admired, by persons to whom it communicates certain feelings about social justice, by persons for whom the lines are the occasion of feelings shared by them and the poet. But if you do not share those feelings, as I happen not to share them in the images of desiccated nature, the lines and even the entire poem are impenetrably obscure.[15]

It once occurred to me that Tate might be using "obscure" in a Pickwickian sense, for whatever one might think of the Millay poem it seems rather less obscure than Tate's critique. But then, from his point of view, "communication in poetry" is a fallacy. The poet is "not responsible to society for a version of what it thinks it is or what it wants." The poet is responsible to his conscience. And he (the pronoun remains Tate's) is responsible "for the virtue proper to him as poet, for his special *arête* for the mastery of a disciplined language which will not shun the full report of reality conveyed to him by his awareness: he must hold, in Yeats' great phrase, 'reality and justice in a single thought.'"[16] Elsewhere Tate approvingly quotes I. A. Richards to the effect that poetry is "complete knowledge": "The order of completeness that it achieves in the great works of the imagination is not the order of experimental completeness aimed at by the positivist sciences. . . . For the completeness of *Hamlet* is not of the experimental order, but of the experienced order; it is, in short, of the mythical order."[17]

Given this self-contained idea of poetry, it is not surprising that formalist critics like Tate should develop techniques emphasizing intense analysis of a poem's language and its "tensions." Or that they should conceive the primary task of the "man of letters" as preserving "the integrity, the purity, and the reality of language wherever and for whatever purpose it may be used." "He must," Tate goes on to explain, approach this task "through the letter—the letter of the poem, the letter of the politician's speech, the letter of the law; for the use of the letter is in the long run our one indispensable test of the actuality of our experience."[18] How different this conservative, monitory role from that staked out for the American Scholar by Emerson. Besides, is it really necessary to talk about the taste of rotting fruit to test its actuality? However that might be, Tate's ultimate vision of the "man of letters" asserts an even weightier function:

> . . . the duty of the man of letters is to supervise the culture of language, to which the rest of culture is subordinate, and to warn us when our language is ceasing to forward the ends proper to man. The end of social man is communion in time through love, which is beyond time.[19]

The man of letters thus stands a priest of language, linking society and culture with the transcendent.

But why devote such attention to these ideas, or once again pillory an often abused guru of the New Criticism? Has not criticism passed beyond the exegetical stage? In theory, it has. In practice, however, and especially in the common practice of the *classroom*, the dominant mode of procedure remains exploring the "furthest extremes of intension and extension" we may find in a text. And the texts we prefer are, on the whole, those which invite such *explication*. One or another version of formalism remains, in short, the meat and potatoes of what men—and women—of letters stir up for our students and readers. And while Tate's ecclesiastical trappings may have been doffed as rather too quaint and burdensome, something of the incense lingers in the justification for what we do. Thus it seems to me important to ask what social and political values generate the forms of criticism and its justifications we find in Tate and his fellows.

There is a second, perhaps more fundamental reason for examining Tate's ideas. He and his New Critical peers were the first generation to pose what became, and still is, the dominant paradigm of academic criticism. I want to suggest that, regardless of form, academic criticism in the past half century has retained a common set of social and political roots and a consistent function. An image may help flesh this assertion. In *Invisible Man* Ellison pictures a statue of the "Founder," his hands holding the edges of a veil, which covers the face of the black youth kneeling before him. The speaker of the book comments that it is never clear whether the Founder is lifting the veil from the boy's face, or holding it ever more firmly in its place. That ambiguous image may stand for the academic critic; is he (I want to retain the overwhelmingly appropriate pronoun) offering enlightenment by lifting the veil or holding the student in a kind of darkness?

In feminist pedagogy a distinction has developed between two forms of teaching: one, which often involves the display of a specialized vocabulary, has the tendency to overwhelm students, paralyzing them before the erudition of the teacher; another, seen as developing from the equalitarian ideals of feminism, tries to legitimize the student's own responses to a text, to history, to experience as the starting points for analysis and thus understanding. To be sure, it has often been easy to overstate this distinction between—in crude shorthand—lecturer as authority and discussion leader as participant, to convert pedagogical tendencies into behavioral absolutes; indeed, to elevate difference in style into fiercely-held educational principles. For all that rhetoric has burdened us with inflation of difference, the differences remain, more perhaps as foci or what I have called "centers of gravity" than as differences in kind. Analogous "centers of gravity" can, I think, be charted in criticism. Is the objective result of criticism to help readers formulate, understand, and develop their own responses? To open a text to a common reader? Or is it to make the reader feel excluded from the critical enterprise, sense his or her own responses to a work as essentially irrelevant to the process of its exploration? The latter result has, it seems to me, the concomitant effect—or, perhaps I should say, underlying motive—of confirming the position, the cultural power, of the critic himself—even while, as was historically the case in the 1920s and 1930s, the real social authority of the class from which "men of letters" were drawn was being eroded. In fact, I want to argue, the major project of criticism as it developed from patriarchs like Tate was the confirmation of the authoritative position, at least with respect to culture, of the Man of Letters and his caste. And while the *forms* of criticism have changed—from New Criticism to structuralism to poststructuralism—the *functions* of academic criticism seem to me to have remained constant, related primarily to the status, power, and careers of critics.[20]

There is, furthermore, an awful logic to the changes in form that derives precisely from the persistence of function. At the beginning, formal analysis did—as it still can—help illuminate texts. And as differing kinds of analyses developed, these too added to the illumination, albeit with increasing marginality. But a law of diminishing returns necessarily begins to operate with the thirtieth explication of "A Valediction," or the eighteenth lick of ice-cream, and the eye of the beholder starts to shift from the qualities of the text to the qualities of the comment, from the poet to the critic; with the exhaustion of the ways of looking at a pigeon, we begin to observe the antics of the pigeon-watchers. And thus emerges a speculative criticism claiming equality with the literary texts, once the objects to be illuminated, and framed in a language increasingly impenetrable to the common reader. The project of such criticism *is* its politics.

This is not to say that academic critics are by character and inclination conscious elitists; my point is not, in any case, characterological. The very momentum, not to say corpulence, of academic criticism hides its political origins. But in sad fact, cultural institutions move in the directions established by their initial political impetus unless or until they are redirected by the intervention of a new political force—like the social and cultural movements of the 1960s and 1970s. Thus, to understand contemporary academic criticism we must examine its roots and its values as these appear in their rudimentary form.

These values emerge into severe profile from Tate's account of the limitations of Southern literature:

> But the abolition of slavery did not make for a distinctively Southern literature. We must seek the cause of our limitations elsewhere. It is worth remarking, for the sake of argument, that chattel slavery is not demonstrably a worse form of slavery than any other upon which an aristocracy may base its power and wealth. That *African* chattel slavery was the worst groundwork conceivable for the growth of a great culture of European pattern, is scarcely at this day arguable. . . . The distance between white master and black slave was unalterably greater than that between white master and white serf after the destruction of feudalism. The peasant *is* the soil. The Negro slave was a barrier between the ruling class and the soil. If we look at aristocracies in Europe, say in eighteenth-century England, we find at least genuine social classes, each carrying on a different level of the common culture. But in the Old South, and under the worse form of slavery that afflicts both races today, genuine social classes do not exist. The enormous "difference" of the Negro doomed him from the beginning to an economic status purely: he has had much the same thinning influence upon the class above him as the anonymous city proletariat has had upon the culture of industrial capitalism. . . .
>
> The white man got nothing from the Negro, no profound image of himself in terms of the soil. . . . But the Negro, who has long been described as a responsibility, got everything from the white man. The history of French culture, I suppose, has been quite different. The high arts have been grafted upon the peasant stock. We could graft no new life upon the Negro; he was too different, too alien.[21]

It is not my intent to comment upon the less than genteel racism, the abysmal cultural chauvinism, or even the simple historical ignorance of this passage. But it does make amply clear the elitist soil in which Tate's formalist ideas of poetry and the "man of letters" are rooted. The New Criticism is the fruit—strange fruit—of such plants. But that metaphor is rather too easy. In plain fact, criticism which makes all-important the special languages that specially-trained critics share with specially-cultivated poets is finally a means for defending special privilege. It is a version of what Raymond Williams calls the "dominative" use of language.

Meridel LeSueur, who studied with Tate and others at the University of Minnesota, has a different way of drawing the connection between the politics and the critical style of these men of letters:

> It was just like being bitten every morning by a black spider—paralysis set in. They taught the structure of the short story this way: you run around Robin Hood's barn, have two or three conclusions, and then come to a kind of paralysis. Ambiguity is a very seductive idea.[22]

The paralysis of ambiguity in a world crying for change fits well with "Reactionary Essays on Poetry and Ideas."

I am not suggesting that formalist critics are necessarily racists or political reactionaries in their personal outlooks. Or that every formalist move necessarily builds higher the bulwarks of bourgeois culture. But it seems to me natural to suspect a project with such roots. And thus (returning at last to the nest of questions I raised many pages back) to propose that, indeed, critical tactics carry with them rather more ideological baggage than we might at first have suspected.

In the opening section of *Stealing the Language: The Emergence of Women's Poetry in America* (1986), Alicia Ostriker has analyzed how that ideology operated to marginalize women poets. She cites, among other documents, John Crowe Ransom's essay on Millay,[23] which nicely illustrates how the formalist aesthetic principles Ransom shared with Tate worked in practice. Ransom writes:

> Man distinguishes himself from woman by intellect, but he should keep it feminized. He knows he should not abandon sensibility and tenderness, though perhaps he has generally done so. . . . But the problem does not arise for a woman. Less pliant, safer as a biological organism, she remains fixed in her famous attitudes, and is indifferent to intellectuality. I mean, of course, comparatively indifferent; more so than a man. (p. 78)

Thus, from Ransom's point of view, Millay's is a lesser "vein of poetry," "spontaneous, straightforward in diction," with "transparently simple" structures and "immediate" effects (pp. 103–5). Indeed, a good deal of Ransom's essay is devoted to showing how, in effect, Millay's "excitingly womanlike" poems display little analyzable "intention" or "extension," and thus are not intellectually challenging. It seems to me clear how in these works patriarchy and racism emerge into critical categories and a methodology that helped place the work of most white women and black writers behind the veil.

Perhaps the final step in the elevation of this critical tradition into orthodoxy was that taken by Lionel Trilling. Tate and Ransom were in some sense defensive, protecting what remained of the privilege of the "man of letters" and his class against the incursions of the crowd, and often cloaking their political sentiments with the mantle of cultural appraisal. Trilling, by contrast, mounts an offensive by situating matters of critical opinion precisely at "the dark and bloody crossroads where literature and politics meet." By so doing, he converts the question of canon into a question of political judgment and moral values. He is thus able to train on that already "bloody crossroads" the devastating weapons of Cold-War rhetoric. His method is perhaps best illustrated in his two-part essay "Reality in America."[24]

Between the writing of the first section of the essay (*Partisan Review,* January–February, 1940) and the second (*The Nation,* April 20, 1946) intruded, among other things, the Second World War, the Holocaust, the first A-bombs, and—perhaps most important to its point—the emergence of the Cold War and the beginnings of anticommunist hysteria in the United States. Part I is primarily an attack on the literary taste and cultural values of V. L. Parrington. Nina Baym has complained that in his search for the "essence" of American culture Trilling offers no *aesthetic* basis for his literary preferences; nor does he present any "notion of culture more valid than Parrington's."[25] While it is true that in this part of the essay Trilling does not develop his aesthetic standards, he displays a clear preference for artists who, in his view, "contain a large part of the dialectic [of cultural struggle or debate] within themselves, their meaning and power lying in their contradictions. . . . " Indeed, Trilling goes on, in the freighted, redundant language of thirties' political debate, "they contain within themselves . . . the very essence of the culture, and the sign of this is that they do not submit to serve the ends of any one ideological group or tendency" (p. 20). The nonpartisanship of artists, their refusal to "submit" to any "group," to "serve" any ideology, here becomes the flag of their cultural significance, an idea which certainly held sway for much of the quarter century following Trilling's presentation of it in, can we say "ironically," *Partisan.* How artists differ from the rest of us in embodying the contradictions of our culture, Trilling does not say; in any case, as later becomes clear, his point is to mark out, like Tate, the difference between how "true" artists and critics think and how "the modern crowd thinks when it decides to think" (p. 28).

To be sure, as Baym points out, Trilling's rhetoric masks the real partisanship of a writer like Hawthorne, even while it provides one basis for devaluing the work, say, of Harriet Beecher Stowe. To detach ourselves from Trilling's judgments, his canon, it has not proved sufficient to demonstrate that Hawthorne and Stowe were both, in their differing ways, partisan; rather, I think, we have had to bring into question his idea that detachment from ideology or "tendency" is a necessary artistic virtue, much less a philosophically credible notion.

But non-partisanship is finally rather a negative criterion of value in art. In part II of the essay, as Bruce Spear has shown, Trilling does indeed present a crucial line of aesthetic defense for his canon, symbolized by Henry James, whom he poses against Theodore Dreiser and his defenders.[26] James, he claims, "was devoted to an extraordinary moral perceptiveness," powerfully aware of "tragedy, irony, and multitudinous distinctions"; but above all, James' work shows "electric qualities of mind, through a complex and rapid imagination and with a kind of authoritative immediacy" (pp. 22, 25). By contrast, Trilling tells us, even Dreiser's defenders acknowledge that his ideas are often unformed, his moral perceptions crude, and his style, above all his style, clumsy. It is in style, finally, that Trilling locates quality: "The great novelists have usually written very good prose, and what comes through even a bad translation is exactly the power of mind that made the well-hung sentence of the original text. In literature style is so little the mere clothing of thought—need it be insisted on at this late date?—that we may say that from the earth of the novelist's prose spring his characters, his ideas, and even his story itself" (p. 27). The failure of Dreiser's liberal defenders— Charles Beard, Granville Hicks, Edward Berry Burgum, and above all F. O. Matthiessen—at least according to Trilling, derives precisely from that form of "progressive" politics which places a concern for "realism" and usefulness above "electric qualities of mind." Or, rather,

> The liberal judgment of Dreiser and James goes back of politics, goes back to the cultural assumptions that make politics. We are still haunted by a kind of political fear of the intellect which Tocqueville observed in us more than a century ago. American intellectuals, when they are being consciously American or political, are remarkably quick to suggest that an art which is marked by perception and knowledge, although all very well in its way, can never get us through gross dangers and difficulties. And their misgivings become the more intense when intellect works in art as it ideally should, when its processes are vivacious and interesting and brilliant. (p. 23)

With his sliding "we"s and "us"s, his use of "political" and "American" as disparagements, his erection of James upon a mound of melioratives, Trilling is attempting to obliterate the fundamental distinction between, on the one hand, suspicion of art that is predominantly artful, precious, self-enclosed, and, on the other, gross anti-intellectualism. But for us, what his argument comes to is this: intellect displayed in brilliance of style displaces whatever other criteria might be posed for the evaluation of art.

With this argument we have returned to our central issue: the relationship of canon and critical practice, the "crossroads" of literature and politics. What Trilling is about in this essay is hanging round the necks of Dreiser's defenders (and James' doubters) not only his crudities of style, but his presumably consequent anti-Semitism, his late religiosity, his later conversion to communism. In short, as Spear convincingly documents, Trilling is deeply engaged in a struggle over cultural politics, in particular with Matthiessen. The stake was not merely one's preference for the style, the subjects, or even the values of James or Dreiser— even if that constituted the universe of choice. At stake was whether there would be room in the canon, in legitimate critical discourse, in the American university or, indeed, polity for the kinds of political commitments Matthiessen and other progressives tried to maintain, and which they recognized, along with his many failings, in Dreiser. Trilling's victory, and it was that, at least then, placed at the center of literary value, and thus of literary study, those figures like James who best exemplified his ideas of complexity of imagination and brilliance of surface, who displayed in their prose the cultural "tensions" Trilling took to exemplify American intellectual history. What he accomplished, or rather what his accomplishment represents, was at once the legitimation of textual analysis by critics sensitive to the electric qualities of the Jameses as the correct form of literary study and the exiling of those forms of cultural analysis used by "progressives" from Parrington to Matthiessen to the outskirts of literary, indeed political, respectability. To think like them, to write like Dreiser, to acknowledge one's ideology, to be partisan was not merely vulgar; it had become by 1946 a sign that you were a cultural risk, unsafe to be determining the texts from which tomorrow's intellectual leaders would draw their images of the world.

IV

By this long and perhaps burdensome route we return to that room in Lawrence, Kansas, that panel on feminist criticism, and maybe even my growing anger. For I came to that panel with the more or less the ideas I've outlined. It seemed to me that while there are broad shared areas, the social experiences and the cultures of women and men diverge at significant points. I do not have ready terms like "individualism" and "solidarity," to characterize the distinct organizing principles, but it seemed quite plain that significantly diverse experiences will produce significantly diverse cultural forms, among men and women, just as among blacks and whites, working people and bourgeoisie. And that, therefore, the application to women's art of principles and standards derived almost exclusively from the study of men's art will tend to obscure, even hide, and certainly undervalue what women have created. Indeed, the application of critical standards and tactics derived from white, male—not to say racist and elitist—culture not only obscures female accomplishment, on the one side, but reinforces the validity of those critical standards and what they represent, on the other. Thus I thought that panel's project was grafting Adrienne Rich's poem onto Allen Tate's stock—to borrow a Tate metaphor—rather than joining the dialogue in which *The Dream of a Common Language* and *The Common Woman* poems both participate. It is not that the panelists shared Tate's and Ransom's values; rather, in pursuing their techniques, the panel seemed to me to reinforce the structures of academic elitism.

I hope this will not be misconstrued into an odd shorthand report like "Lauter says there's a peculiar female sensibility and that criticism is male, so feminists should be doing something else, as yet unspecified." I do *not* know if there is such a thing as a female sensibility. "Sensibility" is a psychological category and is approachable, I think, only through individuals. I am talking not of sensibility but of *culture,* which is a social category. It cannot be used to predict individual behavior, but it is critical to understanding how we perceive, indeed what we look at, as well as how we conceive the structures of language we call works of art.

Formalist critics, I am suggesting, are trapped within their culture, restricted in what they look at and by who looks. Why? First, because they have derived much of their cultural data from a narrow base, largely art composed by white Western men (as Tate's comment on southern culture reveals). They have not adequately considered art from outside that tradition, except, as it were, after the fact, after they had donned their theoretical spectacles. Also these spectacles have been ground by the social and economic pressures which characteristically mold the residents of academe. For criticism is not solely a pure activity of mind, an expression of altruism directed toward revealing truth, or even the play of intellect upon the surfaces of language. It may upon occasion be these. It will also in some measure be an ideology constructed in order to insure and enhance the social and economic position of the critic and his class—even occasionally, now, "her" class. To put it another way, the connection we have seen of New Critical methodology with reactionary politics is no accident, nor is the obscurity of, say, *Diacritics*. An adequate theory of criticism can only be developed by fully considering the art produced by women, by working people, and by national minorities; further, such art needs to be understood in light of its own principles, not simply in terms and categories derived from so-called "high culture," or on the basis of the imperatives imposed by careerism or reigning institutional priorities.

Thus the first task in the project of feminist criticism seems to me the recovery of lost works by women, and the restoration of the value of disdained genres. In part a restorative literary history is required simply for the sake of intellectual honesty. But more important, as I have suggested, is the imperative for broadening the "text milieu" from which we derive critical and historical propositions. Now this task has considerably been advanced in the last decade, as witness, on the one hand, the publications of feminist and university presses and, on the other, the recent issuance of Gilbert and Gubar's *Norton Anthology of Literature by Women* and the new *Heath Anthology of American Literature* (two volumes). But the work is by no means complete nor, for a number of reasons, is it likely soon to be. For example, women writers of early and mid-nineteenth-century America are known to most readers, even most academics, mainly secondhand, through such useful studies as Nina Baym's.[27] In fact, writers of substance like Caroline Kirkland, Lydia Maria Child, and Alice Cary are seldom read, in part because their books have not until recently been reissued for over a hundred years,[28] in part because they have not been given the legitimation of academic study even to the degree that someone as marginal as William Gilmore Simms has been. Most important, the modern outlook, and particularly modern criticism, has been out of sympathy with the sensibilities displayed in the work of such authors. I shall have more to say about that in a moment. Suffice it here to say it is unlikely that the deep obscurity in which women writers from Sherwood Bonner to Zitkala-Sa are hidden is peculiarly an American phenomenon, thus I doubt whether we are close to the end of the process of rediscovery.

More certainly, even, we are far from establishing the distinctive qualities of the art of these and many better known women writers. This seems to me the second major task of feminist criticism. Studies like those by Baym, Barbara Christian, Elaine Showalter, and Sandra Gilbert and Susan Gubar[29] are only among some of the better-known works devoted to establishing thematic and formal connections among women writers. A parallel task is defining the distinctive thematic and formal characteristics of particular women writers. Elizabeth Ammon's examination of the structure of Jewett's *The Country of the Pointed Firs*[30] provides an especially useful example because it implicitly questions received norms about the structure of short fictions and suggests that Jewett used a distinct, and perhaps gender-linked form.

There is, of course, a certain dialectic between the rediscovery of works and an adequate account of characteristics that link them to other texts. In reevaluating the work of Caroline Kirkland, Judith Fetterley has suggested that *A New Home, Who'll Follow* is in essence a series of elaborated letters and that the letter form represented for women a halfway house between the privacy of correspondence and the public act of authorship, an act seen by many in the early nineteenth century as unseemly for women. That suggestion took on for me powerful implications as I reread Sarah Grimké's *Letters on the Equality of the Sexes* and Lydia Maria Child's *Letters from New-York*, thought about the letter form adopted by Margaret Fuller in the last years of her life, and finally focused (thanks particularly to two of my students, Ellen Louise Hart and Katie King) on the implications of such precedents on the major form of Emily Dickinson's (self-) "publication"—letters:

> This is my letter to the World
> That never wrote to Me . . .

It would at this point claim too much to propose correspondence as constituting a fundamental model for many American nineteenth-century women of letters, but as we come to know more about these writers that may, indeed, be one conclusion. I mention this hypothesis as one illustration of how the dialectic between rediscovery of texts and definition of characteristic themes and forms operates. It also leads us toward two additional objectives in the project of feminist criticism.

These I would describe as decentering male texts, on the one hand, and moving female texts from the margins of culture to the core. Decentering male texts (including phallocentric criticism) was in many respects the initial concern of the earliest feminist critics. It took two forms: first, studies of the images of women, often absurd or vile, projected in widely-respected work by male writers. Second, and in these days of theoretical sophistication too often condescended to, were works like Kate Millett's pioneering and courageous *Sexual Politics* (1970). It need hardly be said that the work of decentering male-centered culture as it is expressed in language, syntax, form, and institutional configuration remains a major concern of current feminist criticism. Indeed, the major contribution of contemporary French feminist writing may be in this area. What is surprising, perhaps, is how persistent phallocentric historical models have remained despite the accumulated weight of contrary evidence.

A vivid illustration of how male-centered literary history continues to obscure the work of women writers was provided by Leslie Fiedler in an essay called "Literature and Lucre," featured in the *New York Times Book Review* (May 31, 1981), and reprinted in one of Fiedler's recent books. Fiedler pictures the history of the novel in America as a struggle between "high Art and low," between "those writers among us who aspire to critical acclaim and an eternal place in libraries" and "the authors of 'best sellers.'" The former, "sophisticated novelists," include Charles Brockden Brown, Poe, Hawthorne, and Melville, all male, as Fiedler points out. The latter tradition, "a series of deeply moving though stylistically undistinguished fictions . . . begins with Susanna Rowson's *Charlotte Temple*, reaches a nineteenth-century high point with Harriet Beecher Stowe's *Uncle Tom's Cabin* and a twentieth-century climax with Margaret Mitchell's *Gone With the Wind*."

This spurious battle of the sexes, and the image of the failed artist which supposedly emerges from it, can be sustained only by ignoring huge parts of American literary history. For example, Fiedler proclaims that "only in the last decade of this century did it become possible, first in fact, then in fiction, for a novelist highly regarded by critics (Norman Mailer is an example) to become wealthy long before his death. . . . " This is patrifocal history with a vengeance, since it altogether ignores Edith Wharton, Willa Cather, and Ellen Glasgow, not to speak of Stowe, E. D. E. N. Southworth (who was much praised by contemporary critics), Jewett, Mary Austin, and even William Dean Howells. Most of these women novelists, among others, were and still are "highly regarded by critics," and did very well from their writing. But more to the point, bringing them up altogether explodes the theory, or perhaps myth, Fiedler wishes to float, that in America writers have either been (until our generation) successful *or* artistic:

> . . . both primary and secondary literature in the United Stares, the novels and poems of which we are most proud and the critical autobiographical [sic] works written on them, reflect the myth of the "serious" writer as an alienated male, condemned to neglect and poverty by a culture simultaneously commercialized and feminized.

Since the women novelists don't fit this nice theory, "we" need to ignore them. And also ignore the fact that writers like Melville and Hawthorne indeed aspired to popularity and were enraged by what they took to be the failure of their audience to appreciate them.

Nor is it at all clear as Fiedler makes out that Stowe, for example, was not artistic as well as successful. On the contrary, recent studies have documented her artistry. In linking her to Rowson and Mitchell, Fiedler is trying to stigmatize her with the unstated labels, familiar from critics like Tate, of "sentimental" and "mass market." "Sentimental" and "mass" are terms, like "regional," "popular," "minor," which have been undergoing reexamination[31] since it became clear they were used to bury much of value on specious assumptions, like the proposition that the suppression of feelings, even tears, is a more legitimate basis for fiction than their display.[32] In short, the problem with Fiedler's theory is that it begins with a truncated set of data, examines them from a dazzlingly parochial angle of vision, and, not surprisingly, concludes by reenforcing the artistic centrality of the traditional male texts which have constituted the canon.

Moreover, the myth of the unappreciated artist itself requires a differing analysis. Myths constitute metaphorical ideologies. Here, the problem for American male writers is construed as the frailty of his audience. It might equally well be posed as the obstinate refusal of many male novelists to take that dominantly female audience seriously. In concluding her second series of stories entitled *Clovernook* (1853), Alice Cary deftly questions the motives of those who, as Fiedler puts it, aspire to "an eternal place in libraries":

> In our country, though all men are not "created equal," such is the influence of the sentiment of liberty and political equality, that:
>
> > "All thoughts, all passions, all delights,
> > Whatever stirs this mortal frame,"
>
> may with as much probability be supposed to affect conduct and expectation in the log cabin as in the marble mansion; and to illustrate this truth, to dispel that erroneous belief of the necessary baseness of the "common people" which the great masters in literature have in all ages labored to create, is a

purpose and an object in our nationality to which the finest and highest genius may wisely be devoted; but which may be effected in a degree by writings as unpretending as these reminiscences of what occurred in and about
the little village where I from childhood watched the pulsations of surrounding hearts.[33]

Cary's comment not only raises questions about the values of the literary "masters," but suggests the importance of an alternative standard embodied in the
"unpretending . . . reminiscences" of her village which she—and, indeed, many
American women writers—presents.

And that comment brings me to the last part of the project of feminist criticism upon which I wish to touch: the effort to move the work of women from
the margins toward the center of culture. Here, the work of criticism and of political action most fully converge. For in the first instance, it was not the work of
critics that refocused attention on the distinctive concerns of women writers, any
more than black aestheticians initially established the conditions for recognizing
the traditions of African-American composition. On the contrary, it was the movements for social, economic, and political change of the 1960s and 1970s that challenged long-held assumptions about what was significant as subject matter for
literary art by challenging the assumptions about what was significant for people.
Meridel LeSueur once described how her story "Annunciation," which deals with
pregnancy, was turned down by editors demanding fighting and fornicating. That
may stand as a symbol of my point here: it will *not* be on the basis solely of "literary" criteria that the days and works of women—any more than of other
marginalized groups—will be established at the center of cultural concern.

In California, the school system in cooperation with certain universities has
launched an ambitious "Literature Project" designed to reinvigorate the teaching of English at the secondary level. Part of that effort has involved the creation
of model curricula, including what are called "core" and "extended" readings.
One model thematic unit is titled "Journey to Personal Fulfillment." The "core"
readings are these: Dickens, *Great Expectations*; Twain, *Huckleberry Finn* and *Life
on the Mississippi*; Shaw, *Pygmalion*; Cather, "Paul's Case"; Kafka, "The Hunger
Artist"; Auden, "The Unknown Citizen"; Eliot, "The Hollow Men"; and
Whitman, "The Ox-Tamer." These selections suggest that an old canard still
lives: "Choose works that interest the boys; the girls will read anything." That
reflection is reenforced by considering that among the "extended readings" are
Jane Eyre, *Wuthering Heights*, E. B. Browning's *Sonnets from the Portuguese*, the autobiographies of Mme. Curie and Helen Keller, and Alice Walker's "African Images." Further, one might wonder, in a state in which Latinos, Asian-Americans,
American Indians, and Blacks will shortly constitute a majority, whether all of
these works together constitute any adequate portrait of journeys to "personal
fulfillment." I do not cite this instance to mock the very concerned people working in this important project. On the contrary, I think we need to admire and
support their efforts, even as we criticize them. But it will not be critical practice alone that will shift what is perceived and treated as "core." To be sure, as
literary people we need to reexamine hierarchies of taste as expressed in subject
matter, genre, language and imagery, as well as in conceptions of literary function and audience.[34] Still, there is little more than can be done to establish the

literary equality of the work of the Brontës and Twain. It will be our work as political people, rather, as citizens of real communities, that will be critical to achieving the axial transformation to which we aspire. Revolution is not, finally, in and of the word alone.

Nor should this come as a surprise. It is a commonplace of scholarship informed by a working-class perspective—often honored, I must admit, in the breach—that the point is not to describe the world, but to change it. So it must be, I think, with feminist criticism: it cannot be neutral, simply analytic, formal. It need always to be asking how its project is changing the world, reconstructing history as well as consciousness, so that the accomplishments of women can be fully valued and, more important, so that the lives of women and men can more fully be lived.

NOTES

This essay originally appeared, in somewhat different form, in *A Gift of Tongues: Critical Challenges in Contemporary American Poetry*, ed. Marie Harris and Kathleen Aguero (Athens: University of Georgia Press, 1987), pp. 57–82. I want to express my appreciation for the creativity and support of the editors. Portions of the essay also appear as "The Two Criticisms: Structure, Lingo and Power in the Discourse of Academic Humanists," in my own *Canons and Contexts* (New York: Oxford University Press, 1991).

1. Raymond Williams, *Culture and Society, 1780–1950* (New York: Harper Torchbooks, 1966), pp. 325–326.

2. *Ibid.*, p. 327.

3. Martha Vicinus, *The Industrial Muse* (New York: Barnes and Noble, 1974); see, especially, pp. 1–3.

4. Dan Tannacito, "Poetry of the Colorado Miners: 1903–1906," *Radical Teacher*, #15 (March 1980), pp. 1–8. Appended to Tannacito's article is a small anthology of miners' poetry.

5. Paul Lauter, "Working-Class Women's Literature—An Introduction to Study," *Women in Print, I*, ed. Ellen Messer-Davidow and Joan Hartman (New York: Modern Language Association, 1982), pp. 109–34.

6. Lawrence Levine, *Black Culture and Black Consciousness: Afro-American Folk Thought from Slavery to Freedom* (New York: Oxford University Press, 1977). See also Anthony Heilbut, *The Gospel Sound* and Peter Guralnick, *Sweet Soul Music* (New York: Harper and Row, 1986).

7. I am distinguishing between "working-class," "folk," or "popular" (peoples') culture and what Dwight MacDonald characterized as "mass culture." Popular culture, what people who share class (or ethnicity and race) produce in communicating with one another, can be separated from what is produced as a commodity, generally at the lowest common denominator, for consumption by masses of people. To be sure, the distinction is not always clear-cut, but it is worth seeking.

8. Quoted by Herbert G. Gutman, *Work, Culture, and Society in Industrializing America* (New York: Knopf, 1976), pp. 23–24, from Melech Epstein, *Jewish Labor in the United States* (New York: Trade Union Sponsoring Committee, 1950), pp. 290–291.

9. See John W. Blassingame, *The Slave Community* (New York: Oxford University Press, 1972), pp. 49–59.

10. Jeanette R. Murphy, "The Survival of African Music in America," *Popular Science Monthly*, LV (Sept. 1899), 662; quoted by Blassingame, op. cit., pp. 27–28.

11. See "The Burning Struggle: The Civil Rights Movement," an interview with Bernice Johnson Reagon, *Radical America*, 12 (11–12/78), 18–20.

12. *Black Culture and Black Consciousness*, p. 33; cf. p. 207.

13. The usual distinctions between "poetry" and "propaganda," or between "fine arts" and "crafts" hinge on the issue of function. Modern critics have, in one form or another, generally assumed that "poetry is its own excuse for being" and that a poem should "not mean, but be." This is not the place to argue such claims. I don't find them particularly convincing, though it is obvious enough that art can have differing functions in different cultures. Let it suffice here to assert that viewing working-class culture from the standpoint of such assumptions will fatally mislead the critic.

14. Allen Tate, "Tension in Poetry," *Essays of Four Decades* (Chicago: The Swallow Press, 1968), p. 64.

15. *Ibid.*, p. 58.

16. "To Whom is the Poet Responsible?" *Essays of Four Decades*, p. 27.

17. "Literature as Knowledge," *Essays of Four Decades*, p. 104.

18. "The Man of Letters in the Modern World," *Essays of Four Decades*, p. 14.

19. *Ibid.*, p. 16.

20. In rereading this, it seems to me that I have made it sound like all academic critics are centers of independent power. Clearly, people in academe respond to institutional priorities, corporate definitions of appropriate career tracks. Indeed, most teachers and literary scholars are the victims of established modes of performance rather than their creators. It is not my intention to blame the victims but rather to make clear the source of that victimization. Cf. "The Two Criticisms," in *Canons and Contents*.

21. *Reactionary Essays on Poetry and Ideas* (Freeport, NY: Books for libraries, 1968), pp. 154–157.

22. The comment was quoted in a press release connected with the publication of her collection *Ripening* (Old Westbury, NY: The Feminist Press, 1982).

23. "The Poet as Woman," *The World's Body* (New York: Scribner's, 1938).

24. The essay was printed as a single unit in *The Liberal Imagination* (New York: Viking Press, 1950). I shall be quoting from the Anchor Books edition (Garden City: Doubleday, 1954), pp. 15–32.

25. "Melodramas of Beset Manhood: How Theories of American Fiction Exclude Women Authors," *The New Feminist Criticism*, ed. Elaine Showalter (New York: Pantheon, 1985), p. 68.

26. In the following paragraphs I am deeply indebted to two fine essays by Bruce Spear of the University of California, Santa Cruz. They are "Cold War Aesthetics: Edmund Wilson, Lionel Trilling, and F. O. Matthiessen" and "The Late Work of F. O. Matthiessen: Criticism, Politics, and Spirit."

27. *Woman's Fiction: A Guide to Novels by and about Women in America, 1820–70* (Ithaca: Cornell University Press, 1978).

28. Steps toward changing the absolute unavailability of texts were taken when Indiana University Press issued Judith Fetterley's collection of early- and mid-nineteenth-century American women writers, Rutgers University Press began to issue its excellent series of reprints of the work of writers like Child, Rose Terry Cooke, and Cary, and Oxford University Press began to issue the Schomburg series of works by black women writers. Still, little of Child, Fanny Fern, or Sarah Josepha Hale is accessible. Only one work by Rebecca Harding Davis is available, "Life in the Iron Mills," first restored in an edition from The Feminist Press and now enshrined in some anthologies of American literature. Only within the last few years have works by Elizabeth Stuart Phelps become available; and even some of H. B. Stowe's texts are unavailable in paperback. Nor is there any edition of the work of the most widely published black woman writer of the nineteenth century, Frances Ellen Watkins Harper, though Frances Foster is attempting to remedy that. Still, other minority

works, by men as well as by women, remain to be reprinted—or, as in the case of nineteenth-century autobiographies in Spanish, printed for the first time.

29. Barbara Christian, *Black Women Novelists: The Development of a Tradition, 1892–1976* (Westport, CT: Greenwood Press, 1980); Elaine Showalter, *A Literature of Their Own: British Women Novelists from Brontë to Lessing* (Princeton: Princeton University Press, 1977); Sandra M. Gilbert and Susan Gubar, *The Madwoman in the Attic: The Woman Writer and the Nineteenth-Century Literary Imagination* (New Haven: Yale University Press, 1979).

30. "Going in Circles: The Female Geography of Jewett's *Country of the Pointed Firs*," *Studies in the Literary Imagination,* 16 (Fall 1983), esp. 85–89.

31. See, for example, Jane Tompkins, *Sensational Designs* (New York: Oxford University Press, 1988).

32. See, for example, Baym, *Woman's Fiction*, pp. 25, 144.

33. Alice Cary, *Clovernook, or Recollections of Our Neighborhood in the West, Second Series* (New York: Redfield, 1853), pp. 363–364.

34. My own effort in this direction is represented by "The Literatures of America—A Comparative Discipline," prepared for a Soviet-American conference on minority literatures in the United States, University of Pennsylvania, July, 1985, and printed in *Canons and Contexts* (1991).

REFLECTIONS ON BLACK WOMEN WRITERS
revising the literary canon
(1 9 8 7)

There is no doubt that black women as writers have made drastic inroads into
the American literary consciousness since the beginning of the 1970s, and the film
success of Alice Walker's *The Color Purple* has indeed placed the entire group
within a new dimension in the national consciousness. Aside from its merits (or
demerits) as book and/or movie, *The Color Purple* is important for what its popularity means in terms of the recognition it compels for the works of black women.
Thousands, perhaps millions, of people who had not, until now, ever heard the
name of Alice Walker, and countless others who had, but who were able to ignore her (although she had been publishing fiction and poetry since the late
1960s), have seen and will see the film—learn her name, and respond to her work,
whether they acknowledge its richness, or see it as a misrepresentation of the
black experience. Above the din of the controversy that *The Color Purple* has
sparked inside and outside of the black community, many will discover something new about the experiences of black women in America. For what black
women as writers have consistently provided for themselves and others has been
a rendering of the black woman's place in the world in which she lives, as she
shapes and defines that from her own impulses and actions.

Before *The Color Purple* the only comparable achievement for a black woman
writer was made by Lorraine Hansberry's *A Raisin in the Sun*, which was first
staged in 1959. This play, for which Hansberry won the New York Drama Critics
Circle Award of "Best Play of the Year," over Tennessee Williams's *Sweet Bird of
Youth*, Archibald MacLeish's *JB*, and Eugene O'Neill's *A Touch of the Poet*, made
her not only the youngest American, the first woman, and the first black person
to achieve that honor, but also the first black woman to have her work produced
on Broadway. *A Raisin in the Sun*, seen by millions of Americans on stage, screen,
and television, has been translated into more than thirty languages and produced
on all continents of the globe. It foreshadowed the emergence of a new movement in black theater, a new place in letters for black women writers, and opened
one artistic door onto the large stage of the Civil Rights Movement of the 1960s
and 1970s.

A Raisin in the Sun is not autobiographical. Lorraine Hansberry came from a
black middle-class family which had long overcome the problems faced by the
characters in her play. But if Hansberry was economically removed from the

dilemma of the Youngers, the family she writes about, she was nevertheless emotionally attached to the issues she explored through them, issues that remained at the core of the lives of the majority of black people in America in the 1950s. The experiences of her dramaturgical family were part of the collective three-hundred-year-old consciousness of what it meant to be born black in America. In giving several of the key roles in her play to women, she had also followed in the footsteps of her less well-known earlier sisters who had sought to write out of their black female awareness and point of view on that reality.

At the center of *Raisin* is that most memorable Mama: Lena Younger, whose grandeur takes vengeance for all the black mammies previously presented in American literature. For black women in American literature, from the beginning, have been depicted as either sexually loose and therefore tempters of men, or obedient and subservient mammies, loving and tender to the white children they raised and forever faithful to the owners they served. Lena Younger defies more than two hundred years of such stereotyping of black women, and turns black female strength, too often maligned by everyone else, into the means by which her son Walter shapes his emerging manhood. Lorraine Hansberry was not the first black woman who gave us such a positive image of black women, but she was the first in her own time whose voice reached as wide an audience as hers did. Her achievement opened a wider way for the black women writers who came after her.

What is significant in the Lena Younger image in *Raisin* for the purposes of this paper is that she is the central force that holds her family together, that she has no ambivalences regarding the inherent human worth and dignity of herself and those whom she loves, and that speaking from inside of her own experiences, she demonstrates that the black struggle to transcend dwarfs the victimization that would otherwise have destroyed black people a long time ago. And while Mama Younger stands as the force at the center of her family, there are also the other women in that drama whose roles are fully as important as her own: daughter Beneatha, who wants to be a doctor so that she will be able to heal sick and broken black bodies, but whose sophisticated cynicism meets with the stern rebuke of her mother; and Ruth, Walter's wife, whose concerns for the welfare and well-being of her children precipitates a family controversy over abortion that belies the notion that poor and/or black people produce babies without consideration for what happens after they arrive. Years later, when Ruth will tell Travis and his siblings stories about their grandmother, or when Beneatha recalls her young adulthood and the conflicts she had with her mother, the scripts to those narratives will bear no resemblances to the majority of those concerning black mothers and/or women that appear in the literature written by black men or white men or women.

Since the success of *A Raisin in the Sun* the names of an impressive number of black women writers have become fairly well known to large numbers of Americans, and at the same time new and different images of black women have emerged from their pens. But while it is accurate to give credit to Hansberry's success as foreshadowing the contemporary wider recognition of black women writers and critics, the momentum it signaled had its beginnings more than two hundred years earlier. The history of the creative efforts of black women in America began with the beginnings of literacy, in 1746 with Lucy Terry's "Bars

Fight," a poem about an Indian raid on the white settlement of Deerfield, Massachusetts, and continued with Phillis Wheatley's *Poems on Various Subjects, Religious and Moral* in 1773. Terry's and Wheatley's extant works confirm that black women in the eighteenth century had literary voices which they made bold to use, while black women of the nineteenth century, building on what preceded them, authenticated their voices by speaking to local and national issues that had direct impact on the lives of black people. From Sojourner Truth, abolitionist and feminist, who could neither read nor write but whose words were recorded by others, to Jarena Lee, evangelist, who documented the hundreds of miles she logged across the country preaching and teaching and saving souls, to Maria Stewart, the first woman in the country to make a profession of the public lecture circuit, and Anna Julia Cooper and Frances Watkins Harper, whose feminist, antiracist writings are as contemporary as today, we know that these women spoke loud and clear in celebration of the positive characteristics of human life, and in strong criticism of racial and gender oppression. This history assures us that black women have not ever been artistically or critically silent, even though for most of the past their voices went largely ignored by those who did not wish to hear them. In their own voices, black women have always confirmed and authenticated the complexity of the black American female experience, and in so doing have debunked the negative stereotypes that others created of them while denying them audience for their words. Now, finally admitted to a larger hearing than they ever previously enjoyed, both past and present black female literary voices combine to alter the historical nature of the discourse and to play a prominent role in revising the canon from which they were long excluded.

There is no need here to again recite the history of the stereotyping of black women in American literature by others than themselves. That has been adequately done by several critics.[1] It is important, however, to note that the efforts to reverse the negative images of black women in literature began as early as these women began to find an opportunity to write: with the slave narratives, fiction, poetry, and nonfiction prose of the nineteenth century. The spoken words of women like Sojourner Truth, and the writings of other women like Stewart, Cooper, and Watkins Harper, among others, were primary in the struggle against slavery and the abuses of women, especially of black women. Their boldness and assertiveness define these women as a highly intelligent, morally outraged group in a struggle against white injustice to blacks and male dominance of women.

In the earliest known novel by a black woman, *Our Nig or Sketches from the Life of a Free Black* (1859), by Harriet Wilson, the abused heroine, Frado, is a hardworking, honest child of mixed racial parentage who is caught in a web of white hatred and cruelty. Frado is neither an immoral woman nor a mammy, the most frequent of the stereotypes of black women in that time, and Wilson uses her characterization of the helpless child to emphasize the unfairness of a social structure that permitted individuals to treat black people in a less-than-human fashion. In writing this novel, Wilson, of whom not a great deal is known, was the flesh-and-blood example of the rebel against the treatment she outlined in her book. As such, she provided another concrete example of black women's estimation of their self-worth. For one thing, she explicitly wrote her narrative as a means of earning money to take care of herself and her ailing son. Wilson, who lived in Boston and other areas of New England, and who sets her work in that geographical location, took advantage of the tradition of the sentimental female novel, which at that time enjoyed enormous popularity. The form of her book—the epigraphs, style, and structure of the narrative—shows that she was well aware of many of the conventions of novel writing at the time, and that she considered them valuable to plead the case, not of the poor white heroine who eventually achieves a good marriage and a happy home, as they did in the white female novels, but of an abused black child and woman who was unable to realize the goals of white protagonists. Wilson, deserted by her husband, was sufficiently self-assured to imagine that writing held the possibilities of a vocation for her.

But the slave narrative, not fiction, was the mode that dominated the earliest Afro-American attempts at literature, which through its existence revised the nature of the American "Self." Until recently, most of the attention to this body of work has focused on the writings of men, with *The Narrative of Frederick Douglass, An American Slave, Written by Himself* receiving the majority of the plaudits. It is now recognized that the female slave narrative deserves attention for its own sake—for its unique contributions to the genre. The narrative of Harriet Jacobs, in particular, *Incidents in the Life of a Slave Girl*, published in 1861 under the name of Linda Brent, is a stunning literary success, equal in every way to the preeminent male slave narrative. Jacobs, a South Carolina slave who became a fugitive at age twenty-seven, told a story that brilliantly deconstructs the meaning of the female slave experience in relationship to that of her male counterpart and the white world around her. The literary prowess she displayed in her careful delineation of the sexual harassment she suffered from her owner, her masterly circumvention of his intentions toward her, her patience and determination to free herself and her children, and her understanding of the differences between psychological and physical freedom make her tale a female classic. As an early narrative by a black woman, one of the most significant contributions that *Incidents* makes to the history is its identification of the existence of and effectiveness of a woman's community in which black and white, slave and free women sometimes joined forces to thwart the brutal plans of masters against helpless slave women. In Harriet Wilson's *Our Nig*, the cruel stepmother of the fairy-tale convention is replaced by the cruel mistress and her equally cruel daughter, while the men in the story, sympathetic to Frado, are ineffective against the wickedness of the female members of their family. On the contrary, Jacobs, who hides in the crawl space of her grandmother's house for seven years in real life, is assisted in this effort by a number of women until she can safely escape. Similarly, other black women's slave narratives pay tribute to the roles that women play as models and inspiration in their struggle to rise above oppression. The "sisterhood" of black women and the peculiarity of relations between black and white women that appears in later black women's literature were already well documented in the black female slave narrative tradition.

If the slave narrative as a genre revised the concept of the American self, then, as a separate body of work, the narratives written by slave women are especially important for their revisionist elements in relationship to the narratives of ex-slave men and the American female experience in the autobiographical accounts of white women. We are indebted to Frances Foster's study, "'In Respect to Females . . . ': Differences in the Portrayals of Women by Male and Female Narrators," for alerting us to the implications of gender in slave narratives a few years ago.[2] Of necessity, the experiences of white women in the age of the "cult of true womanhood" were very separate from those of black slave women, but slave men and women also had different perceptions of their common condition. In the narratives of ex-slave men, for instance, slave women appear completely helpless and fully exploited. Much of this is identified as the result of their sexual vulnerability, and the women are pictured as victims without recourse to means of protecting or of defending themselves. Images of these women on auction blocks, stripped to their waists, their children having been sold away from them—all because of the licentiousness of their masters—are among those that abound in the literature. In Douglass's narrative, for instance, he is painstaking in his descriptions of the beatings slave women were often given. His accounts of the sounds of the whips against their flesh and the flow of the blood from their backs are graphic. On the other hand, in telling their own stories, ex-slave women did not concentrate on the sexual exploitation they suffered. They did not deny it, but they made it clear that there were other elements in their lives which were important to them as well. In short, they saw themselves as more than victims of rape and seduction. As Foster points out, when they wrote, they not only wanted to witness to the atrocities of slavery, but also to celebrate their hard-won escapes. Their stories show them to be strong, courageous, dignified, and spirited in spite of the world in which they were forced to live. They depicted themselves as complex human beings with a desire to engage in discourse that took the breadth of their experiences into consideration. In writing, they were no longer secondary characters in someone else's script, but heroines in their own creations. As noted earlier, these black women writers focused less on individual performance and more on the positive roles that engaged women. They allotted time to the value of family relationships, not only to beatings and mutilations by slave masters. As they related their stories, ex-slave women took control of their narratives in much the same way as they took control of the circumstances that enabled them to survive and escape captivity.

Jacobs's narrative provides a good example of this mode. While she tells us of her dilemma with her master, the focus of *Incidents* is largely on her attempts to become free and to free her children. She demonstrates that she had power over her master while she was concealed in her grandmother's house, and she used this power to lead him to believe that she had left the state. She further tells us of her success in finding employment after her escape, and of the happy union she had with her children in the North. Her self-confidence was never destroyed by the abuses of slavery, and her self-esteem remained strong through the difficulties of her escape. Taking up where Foster left off, other critics have noted, from textual evidence in *Incidents*, how well Jacobs understood the meaning of freedom in her dealings with northern whites, especially in her contacts with women. Associated with both the feminist and abolitionist movements. she analyzed her situation and wrote perceptively of the racism of white feminists. Like Wilson, she made use of the sentimental tradition in women's fiction, but skillfully subverted that tradition for her own purposes. It is interesting that both Wilson and Jacobs rejected the convention of marriage and the happy ending of popular white female fiction. There are several less fully developed ex-slave women narratives, but all are equally confirming in their assertion of the positive identity of their authors. Among them we have Elizabeth Keckley, a seamstress who later made a successful living by tending the wardrobes of presidential first ladies in Washington; Susie King Taylor, a woman of many talents, from laundress to schoolteacher; and Amanda Berry Smith, a preacher. All wrote, not only to expose the evils that had been done to them, but also to demonstrate their abilities to gain physical and psychological liberty by transcending those evils.

The poetry, fiction, and nonfiction prose of black women to come out of the latter part of the nineteenth century wage open warfare against racism and gender oppression, on one hand, and on the other, encourage and castigate blacks in an effort to promote the "uplift" of the race. As other critics have often noted, the novels by black men and women with the mulatto heroine were often an appeal to whites for the elimination of atrocities, based on racial prejudices, against blacks, especially in the face of the evidences of the extent of blood co-mingling between the races. Barbara Christian has done an excellent exploration of the range of the intentions of Frances Watkins Harper, for instance, who was responsible for the publication of some eleven volumes of poetry, religious in tone and mainly directed toward the less fortunate, in her effort to "make songs for the people," who spoke out and wrote overtly scathing essays against white racism and sexism. She wrote a novel as well, *Iola LeRoy, Shadows Uplifted* (1892), with a mulatta heroine who revises this type of protagonist as she appears in novels such as William Wells Brown's *Clotel; or The President's Daughter* (1853). Unlike the tragic character whom Brown and others portray, Harper's heroine, given a chance to escape from her race, chooses to marry an Afro-American and dedicate her life to helping unfortunate black people. Anna Julia Cooper, who wrote no fiction, used didactic prose in *A Voice from the South: By a Black Women of the South,* not only to admonish white Americans for their injustices against other Americans, but to celebrate the achievements of black women and to sternly reproach the shortcomings of black men, particularly when those failings diminished the value of what black women strove to achieve.

A much neglected black female voice that spans the period between the end of the nineteenth century and the activities of the Harlem Renaissance of the 1920s is that of Alice Dunbar Nelson, who for a short time was married to the famous Paul Laurence Dunbar. Her importance to the history of Afro-American letters continues to be eclipsed by his. But the recent publication of Dunbar Nelson's diary, *Give Us Each Day, The Diary of Alice Dunbar-Nelson,* edited by Gloria Hull, has added an important work to the corpus of black women's writings. While twentieth-century black women's autobiographies have often proved to be frustrating documents because of their lack of openness, and the tendency of the authors to avoid private disclosures, this diary reveals the side of Dunbar Nelson that would otherwise remain unknown to the world. Dunbar Nelson, who was born in 1875 and died in 1935, like many of the writers of that era, was middle-class, educated, and highly sophisticated, a journalist as well as short-story writer, dramatist, and poet. In the ease with which she handled more than one literary form, she belongs to a group that includes women like Georgia Johnson and Angelina Grimké, both poets and dramatists, whose pens made known that black women were involved not only with the practical problems of education and economics for black people, but also with the creation of art and literature. Most of these women earned a living by teaching, the only respectable profession that was open to them, but one that was also in line with their ideas of service to others. Especially as dramatists, Dunbar Nelson, Johnson, and Grimké, addressed many of the social problems facing the black community, and agitated for changes to alter them. Racism of all kinds, including lynching, were topics of their plays, and these women went as far as to take up the issue of poor women and the need for birth control education in the struggle against poverty and ignorance.

On the opposite side of the coin of achievement, from Dunbar Nelson's diary we learn some details of how women of her standing coped with many of the problems that confronted them in their private lives, away from the long days and busy schedules which make their histories as impressive as they are. Space does not permit an accounting of the financial difficulties which she faced for almost all of her life, or the strength and creativity she put into protecting her public image from the chaos of her private world. Suffice it to say that she worried a great deal over an accumulation of debts; that a fear of bouncing checks is one of the themes in the book; and that she was a woman who could pawn her jewelry to pay her water bill, and go immediately from that second task to address a meeting of wives of professional white men, dressed like a "certified check." From the diary too, there is further confirmation of the strength of the women's community which female slave narrators introduced into the literature. Not only did Dunbar Nelson live in a family in which women were pre-eminent, regardless of the men who entered their lives at different times, but her world outside of her family was peopled by women like Mary McLeod Bethune and Nannine Burroughs, famous educators, in addition to the Club Women and the writers and artists of her time.

Dunbar Nelson and the women who appear in her diary are complex figures who do not fit the stereotypes of black women of their day in the literature of others. They were exciting and strong, but they were also very human in the ways in which they responded to experience. They worked, laughed, loved, cried, and survived because they were tough-minded and respected themselves and others. They transgressed the boundaries of the expectations of women in that day, and created themselves in their own images. In respect to what she discloses of their private lives, Dunbar Nelson's diary is extremely important in the process of the revision of the literary images of ambitious upwardly mobile black women of the early part of the century.

The 1920s were the years in which black culture flourished as it has not done before in America, and the center of the activity was in Harlem, New York City. Following on the heels of the large black migration from a rural to an urban environment that began early in the century, and an increase in the West Indian and African populations in the country, the artistic and scholarly communities, as a group, set themselves to the task of defining the black experience in as positive a way as they could. It is now common knowledge that Jessie Fauset, black woman poet and novelist, in her role as W. E. B. Du Bois's assistant at the *Crisis* (one of the most important journals of the time), was instrumental in bringing all of the important writers of the period into public view. In addition, Fauset was the only member of the group to publish three novels between the early 1920s and early 1930s. She, along with Nella Larsen, author of two novels in the late 1920s, have received less attention as writers than their male counterparts because of a perception that their works belong the genteel tradition of the novel of manners. That condition is moving toward rapid change, however, as contemporary black women critics re-evaluate the writings of women before the 1960s; as co-operative publishers make out-of-print texts available for classroom use; and teachers and professors in Women's Studies and Afro-American and other literature courses make use of them.

Not all the women who came of age in the 1920s or who were associated with the Harlem Renaissance emerged then or did their best work in that period. Dorothy West, novelist, short fiction writer, and journalist, and Pauli Murray, family chronicler, poet, and civil rights activist, were young women attracted to the verve of the cultural movement, but whose work appeared later in the 1930s and 1940s. The most illustrious of the women in the later-blooming group to have had an association with the Renaissance was Zora Neale Hurston. In the early 1970s, her work was rediscovered, and it did more than any single writer's work to mobilize the energy of contemporary black women critics. Hurston arrived in New York from Florida by way of Baltimore and Washington, D.C., in 1925, after having won a prize for short fiction published in *Opportunity* magazine. Before her mature work in the 1930s and 1940s she continued to write short stories, earned herself a degree in anthropology from Columbia University, did fieldwork in the South and the West Indies, and was a colorful figure among the Harlem literati. In her time she received only minor praise for her work, and long before her death in 1960 she was forgotten by most of the literary world and derided by those who remembered her. In the early 1970s, her now-acclaimed novel, *Their Eyes Were Watching God* (1937), retrieved her name from oblivion and set the wheels rolling for the new black feminist criticism of the 1970s and 1980s. In relationship to black literature until then, this novel turned aside from the literature of protest against racism and racial discrimination to explore the inner dynamics of black culture, and to introduce, as heroine, the ordinary, uneducated black woman in search of a self-defined identity. Taking place almost entirely within the black community, *Their Eyes* explores primal relations between black men and women as they had never been done before. Here are rural people without concern for "social uplift," but whose lives are rich with a heritage that has fostered black survival for generations. Janie, her central character, is the first black feminist heroine in the fictional canon. At the same time, the folklore in all of her books makes Hurston's work an important source of information far beyond the boundaries of literature. Unfortunately, her other works have often been adjudged "lesser" than *Their Eyes*, even by her most ardent supporters. This too is a judgment that may well be revised in the near future, as at least one other novel of hers, *Moses, Man of the Mountain* (1939), a black folk rendition of the biblical myth, has finally begun to attract critical attention. Her autobiography, *Dust Tracks on a Road*, is a problematical text from the point of view of its concealments and evasions. But again, new studies in black women's autobiographies suggest that such concealments are a prominent convention in the tradition. As black women's autobiography stands, Hurston may not be the exception most people now think she is. However, had she written nothing of importance other than *Their Eyes Were Watching God*, her place in history would still be fully assured. She did indeed change the nature of the black female heroine in American literature.

From the end of the nineteenth century through the conclusion of the 1940s, the women mentioned above were among those who produced works that were representative of the kinds of writings that black women were engaged in for the first part of the century. Although, except for rare exceptions, they never received the public recognition they deserved, they wrote. They were ambitious, versatile in what they could do, and very productive. As nineteenth-century black women writers had done before them, they continued to explore racism and gender oppression in their writings, especially in fiction and autobiography. Because they were working within the black tradition of protest against white racism, they handled this issue more overtly than they tended to do with gender oppression, especially as that existed within the black community. Since most of these writers were members of the intellectual middle class as well, they also gave a good deal of attention to the "progress" of black people as a whole, an idea that tended to place white middle-class values in a position of superiority in relationship to values inherent in Afro-American culture. In the autobiographical literature of the period the emphasis was on the level of achievement women had made in education and economic independence, although many narratives focused on the ways in which these women worked to "elevate" young women and children, mainly by rescuing them from lives of poverty and immorality and leading them to paths of industry and morality. Hurston, as noted above, unlike many of the writers in her time, deviated from popular black trends and looked backward to the black folk culture for the materials of her art. As a result, she often incurred the anger of her peers, who felt that her stance in applauding the inner vitality of that culture and her lack of attention to the deprivations of racism worked at cross purposes to their goals. They felt that her position undermined their efforts to force social change since it diluted their efforts to present a united front in confronting the white world.

Between 1940 and the beginning of the 1960s there was a good deal of creative activity on the part of black women writers. In 1949 Gwendolyn Brooks received the Pulitzer Prize for poetry, and became the first black American to be so honored. Brooks, whose work began appearing in 1945, continues to be a poet with enormous energy. Her excursions away from poetry produced a novel, *Maud Martha*, in 1953, and an autobiographical narrative that resembles a prose poem, *Report from Part One*, in 1972. Brooks's work, until 1970, though highly stylized, turned to face the plight of urban blacks in her home city of Chicago. Life on the segregated South Side, with its many disadvantages, was the subject of her prizewinning poetry. Her poetry did for blacks in this urban ghetto what Langston Hughes had earlier done for their counterparts in Harlem. In her novel she examined the inner thoughts of a young woman who is not pretty by conventional standards, or dynamic, or specially gifted, but who has the confidence in herself to seek her happiness. Since 1970, Brooks's work has taken on a decided black militant posture.

A number of other writers made important contributions to the literature of black women during these decades. Particularly deserving of special mention are Margaret Alexander Walker, another prizewinning novelist and poet; Adrienne Kennedy, playwright; Alice Childress, playwright and fiction writer; and Ann Petry, journalist, short-story writer, and author of three novels. After some years of neglect, Petry is experiencing a return to acclaim with the 1985 re-publication of her best-known work, *The Street*, originally issued in 1943. In this novel, written in the naturalistic mode, the heroine, Lutie Johnson, bright, beautiful, ambitious, hard-working, and a single mother, is defeated by the hostile environment of the ghetto, represented by a Harlem street. In choosing to use the conventions that she did, Petry creates a character who, unlike most black women's heroines, is alienated from all the support systems available to poor black people; the church, extended family, and a network of friends. Other works of the period emphasize the distressing results of racism on black life, but most demonstrate that survival is possible when their protagonists make use of black support institutions. Especially missing in this novel is the community of women that had for so long been a mainstay in the conventions of black women's fiction.

The 1950s ended on a note of great promise for black American women writers, and in spite of the politics of white racism and of gender, and the sexism of many black men, the rising tide of the Civil Rights Movement was helpful to many of these writers. While Lorraine Hansberry's play received the most outstanding acclaim of all in 1959, there were other women who came to public view with less fanfare, but who were of no less importance to the tradition. One such was Paule Marshall, whose novel *Brown Girl, Brownstones*, was the first black narrative to probe the sensibilities of an American-born adolescent girl of West Indian parents. Marshall, since then, has built her literary career around the interconnections blacks of West Indian heritage feel with white western civilization in the United States. For although most of the Islands were colonized by different European countries, African residuals remained stronger in them than among American blacks, largely because the populations in the islands contained a majority of African descendants. In her second novel, *The Chosen Place, The Timeless People*, published a decade after *Brown Girl*, Marshall's heroine is a West Indian woman who, after several years of living in England, returns to her island home to battle the ills of imperialism there. In *Praise Song For the Widow*, her 1983 work, she examines the recovery of "roots" by a middle-aged West Indian American woman on a journey back to her West Indian past. This is a theme that Marshall, a first-generation American with a West Indian background, seems to find fruitful to pursue. Between her novels she has produced a number of short stories as well, most of them with some "island" flavor.

Writers like Gwendolyn Brooks, Margaret Walker, Alice Childress, Paule Marshall, and Ann Petry continue to be productive in the 1980s. Within the last three decades, however, a remarkable number of new writers have joined their company, many of whom have produced an astonishing volume of writings. Those of us who have been privileged to follow the careers of writers Toni Morrison, whose first novel was *The Bluest Eye* (1970), Alice Walker, since her novel *The Third Life of Grange Copeland* (1970), and Maya Angelou, whose first volume of autobiography was called *I Know Why the Caged Bird Sings* (1970), are aware of how large the output has been in a short time. All of these women have produced multiple volumes of fiction, poetry, autobiography, and essays. Even the newest writers to emerge, like Ntozake Shange and Gloria Naylor, who did not publish until the beginning of the 1980s, have been prolific.

The literature of black women of the 1960s, 1970s, and 1980s follows in the tradition of the earlier times, but is also very different from what went before. Previously, in the slave narrative tradition and the fiction, autobiography, and drama, black women worked hard to debunk the negative stereotypes that other writers had imposed on them. In some instances what they produced were counterstereotypes that depicted black women as strong, and always overcoming hardships. The writers of the present generation see no need to perpetuate only those images, and are now exploring all aspects of black women's experiences— their weaknesses and failings, as well as their strengths and ability to transcend race and gender oppression. Writing from inside of their own experiences, and the knowledge of the experiences of black women for more than three hundred years in America, they examine the innate humanity of the characters they portray—characters who embody qualities that make them neither flawless hero-ines, immoral individuals, or helpless victims. A good example of this reconcilia-tion of human traits shows up in Toni Morrison's first novel, in which a young black girl, driven insane in her quest for the white western ideal of female beauty—blue eyes—is balanced by the second black girl who understood and re-jected the self-destructiveness inherent in a black woman's identifying with such an ideal. In like manner, the conflicts between black men and women that Alice Walker exposes in *Grange Copeland* and other novels are more than an accounting of how brutal some black men can be to their women, but rather a search for the roots of that brutality as a means toward reconciliation between the embattled sexes. Morrison, Walker, and dozens of other new black women writers are "prophets for a new day," in which black American women writers are demand-ing honor in their own country.

The hallmark of contemporary black women's writings is the impulse toward an honest, complicated, and varied expression of the meaning of the black woman's experiences in America. There is little effort to conceal the pain, and just as little to create the ideal, but a great deal to reveal how black women in-corporate the negative and positive aspects of self and external reality into an identity that enables them to meet the challenges of the world in which they must live. Not all black women are strong and enduring, yet a core of resistance to emotional and physical oppression, and a will to discover the path to survival and beyond, resides even in those works in which these women do not transcend. As I noted earlier, a long history of black women and the art-of-words exists, and the literature of black America, in its oral and written contexts, has been within the province of its women from the beginning of the American experience. The work of the writers has been ongoing, and has included every branch of the liter-ary family. From the perceived utility of the slave narrative of antebellum days to the more highly crafted and sophisticated forms of the present time, black women have told their own stories both as a way of self-confirmation and a means of correcting the erroneous white and male record of their inner reality. Black women writers project a dynamic "I" into the canon, one that makes more com-plete the reality of the multi-faceted American experience.

NOTES

1. For a detailed but concise history of this stereotyping see Barbara Christian, *Black Women Novelists* (Westport, Conn.: Greenwood Press, 1980), 3–34.

2. Frances Foster, "'In Respect to Females . . . ': Differences in the Portrayals of Women by Male and Female Narrators," *Black American Literature Forum* 15, no. 2 (Summer 1981), 66–70.

WORKS CITED

Bambara, Toni Cade. *Gorilla, My Love*. New York: Vintage, 1972.

———. *The Salt Eaters*. New York: Vintage, 1980.

———. *The Sea Birds Are Still Alive*. New York: Vintage, 1977.

Brooks, Gwendolyn. *Maud Martha*. New York: Popular Library, 1953.

Butler, Octavia. *Clay's Ark*. New York: St. Martin's Press, 1984.

———. *Kindred*. New York: Simon & Schuster, 1979.

———. *Mind of My Mind*. New York: Doubleday, 1977.

———. *Patternmaster*. New York: Doubleday, 1976.

———. *Survivor*. New York: Doubleday, 1978.

———. *Wild Seed*. New York: Doubleday, 1980.

Chase-Ribound, Barbara. *Sally Hemings*. New York: Viking Press, 1979.

Childress, Alice. *Like One of the Family: Conversations from a Domestic's Life*. Brooklyn: Independence, 1956.

———. *A Short Walk*. New York: Coward, McCann & Geoghegan, 1979.

Cliffe, Michele. *Abeng*. New York: The Crossing Press, 1984.

Fauset, Jessie Redmond. *The Chinaberry Tree*. New York: Frederick A. Stokes Co., 1931.

———. *Comedy, American Style*. New York: Frederick A. Stokes Co., 1932.

———. *Plum Bun*. New York: Frederick A Stokes Co., 1927.

———. *There Is Confusion*. New York: Boni & Liveright, 1924.

Guy, Rosa. *Bird at My Window*. Philadelphia: Lippincott, 1966.

———. *A Measure of Time*. New York: Holt, Rinehart, & Winston, 1983.

———. *Ruby*. New York: Viking Press, 1976.

Harper, Frances E. W. *Iola Leroy, or Shadows Uplifted*. Philadelphia: Garrigues Brothers, 1892.

Hopkins, Pauline Elizabeth. *Contending Forces: A Romance Illustrative of Negro Life, North and South*. Boston: Colored Co-Operative Publishing Co., 1900.

Hunter, Kristin. *God Bless the Child*. New York: Scribner's, 1964. Reprint, New York: Bantam, 1970.

———. *The Lakestown Rebellion*. New York: Scribner's, 1978.

———. *The Landlord*. New York: Scribner's, 1966. Reprint, New York: Avon, 1970.

———. *The Survivors*. New York: Scribner's, 1975.

Hurston, Zora Neale. *Jonah's Gourd Vine*. Philadelphia: Lippincott, 1934.

———. *Moses, Man of the Mountain*. Philadelphia: Lippincott, 1939.

———. *Mules and Men*. Philadelphia: J. P. Lippincott, 1935.

———. *Seraph on the Suwanee*. New York: Scribner's Sons, 1948.

———. *Tell My Horse*. 1938. Reprint, Berkeley: Turtle Island, 1981.

———. *Their Eyes Were Watching God*. Philadelphia: Lippincott, 1937.

Jones, Gayl. *Corregidora*. New York: Random House, 1975.

———. *Eva's Man*. New York: Random House, 1976.

———. *White Rat*. New York: Random House, 1977.

Kincaid, Jamaica. *Annie John*. New York: Farrar, Straus & Giroux, 1985.

———. *At the Bottom of the River*. New York: Farrar, Straus & Giroux, 1978.

Larsen, Nella. *Passing*. New York: A. Knopf, 1929.

———. *Quicksand*. New York: A. Knopf, 1928.

Lee, Andrea. *Sarah Phillips*. New York: Random House, 1984.

Marshall, Paule. *Brown Girl, Brownstones*. New York: Random House, 1959.

———. *The Chosen Place, The Timeless People*. New York: Harcourt Brace Jovanovich, 1969.

———. *Praise Song For the Widow*. New York: Putnam, 1983.

Meriwether, Louise M. *Daddy Was a Number Runner*. Englewood Cliffs, N.J.: Prentice Hall, 1970. New York: Pyramid, 1971.

Morrison, Toni. *The Bluest Eye*. New York: Holt, Rinehart, & Winston, 1970. Reprint, New York: Pocket Books, 1972.

——. *Song of Solomon*. New York: Knopf, 1977.

——. *Sula*. New York: Knopf, 1973.

——. *Tar Baby*. New York: Knopf, 1981.

Naylor, Gloria. *Linden Hills*. New York: Ticknor & Fields, 1985.

——. *The Women of Brewster Place*. Penguin Books, 1982.

Petry, Ann. *Country Place*. Boston: Houghton Mifflin Co., 1947.

——. *The Narrows*. Boston: Houghton Mifflin Co., 1953.

——. *The Street*. Boston: Houghton Mifflin Co., 1946.

Shange, Ntozake. *Betsy Brown*. New York: St. Martin's Press, 1985.

——. *Sassafrass, Cypress and Indigo*. New York: St. Martin's Press, 1982.

Shockley, Ann Allen. *The Black and the White of It*. Florida: Naiad Press, 1980.

——. *Loving Her*. New York: Avon, 1974.

——. *Say Jesus and Come to Me*. New York: Avon, 1982.

Sutherland, Ellease. *Let the Lion Eat Straw*. New York: New American Library, 1979.

Walker, Alice. *The Color Purple*. New York: Harcourt Brace Jovanovich, 1982.

——. *In Love and Trouble*. New York: Harcourt Brace Jovanovich, 1973.

——. *Meridian*. New York: Harcourt Brace Jovanovich, 1976.

——. *The Third Life of Grange Copeland*. New York: Harcourt Brace Jovanovich, 1970.

——. *You Can't Keep a Good Woman Down*. New York: Harcourt Brace Jovanovich, 1981.

Walker, Margaret. *Jubilee*. Boston: Houghton Mifflin Co., 1966. Reprint, New York: Bantam, 1975.

West, Dorothy. *The Living is Easy*. Boston: Houghton Mifflin Co., 1948.

Wilson, Harriet H. *Our Nig; or, Sketches from the Life of a Free Black in a Two-Story White House, North, Showing that Slavery's Shadows Fall Even There*. Boston: George C. Rand & Avery, 1859; 2nd edition, New York: Vintage Books, 1983.

Wright, Sarah. *This Child's Gonna Live*. New York: Delacorte, 1969. New York: Dell, 1971.

practice

T o the extent that "theory" and "practice" are usually understood as opposed terms, it may seem a little perverse to set out a section that attempts to theorize the practice of feminist criticism, but in many ways, it is the explicit purpose of these essays to challenge that opposition. Insofar as it can be said to be an opposition, though, "practice" in the way we are using it here refers to an analysis of a specific literary text—discussing what it means, how it got produced, what it is worth; "theory," on the other hand, is an analysis of doing criticism—examining what our assumptions are, how our questions get formulated, where our values come from.

The separation of theory and practice can be traced back at least as far as Aristotle, who set out a three-part model of human activity in which *theoria* corresponds to the pursuit of eternal truths through thought, *praxis* is the exercise of an art or technical subject, and *poiesis* is the making of things. For Aristotle, then, *praxis* always follows, and is secondary to, *theoria*. A more modern idea of *praxis*, Karl Marx's, has been more influential in recent critical theory. For Marx, *praxis* corresponds more to habitual actions, to "human sensuous activity," and theory follows these actions in an attempt to understand what they really mean. In other words, the role of theory for Marx is not to define the actions that humans will pursue, but to explain those in which humans already take part.

The essays in this section address questions concerning what it means to practice feminist criticism. In some cases, the authors follow an Aristotelian model in which they hope that practice will follow from their theory, while others follow a more Marxist understanding of the relation between practice and theory, trying to theorize feminist criticism based on the practice of it. By contrast, Deborah McDowell challenges the opposition between theory and practice itself. In all these essays, though, the writers are addressing the questions of how we *do* feminist criticism, and what it means to do it the way we do. Closely related to these questions, though, is the whole question of the relation of feminist criticism to theory: Is feminism a theoretical field? should it be?

Annette Kolodny, in "Dancing Through the Minefield: Some Observations on the Theory, Practice, and Politics of a Feminist Literary Criticism" (1980), sets out three "crucial propositions"—that literary history is itself a fiction, that we are taught to interpret texts by applying certain learned paradigms, and that we must examine the biases informing our critical methods and judgment. These ideas have remained central to American feminist critical practice. She goes on to explore what it means for a feminist critic to act on these assumptions; she sees these critical practices as having very definite results and dangers. Kolodny's metaphoric minefield—the academic ground laid with hazards that could destroy the feminist scholar if she treads too heavily—is her warrant for a methodology of pluralism, of choosing freely among the many reading strategies literary theory makes available. Kolodny's argument suggests that the primary task of criticism is to do readings, or find meanings for texts, and she contends that feminist criticism must embrace the possibility that multiple valid readings can be performed on any given work. Similarly open is Kolodny's view of literary value, as she cautions feminist critics against unquestioningly accepting canonized notions of "good" and "bad" literature. Finally, she also explicitly links the practice of feminist criticism to the practices of feminist activism, suggesting that there cannot be a separation between them, that "ideas are important *because* they determine the ways we live, or want to live, in the world."

Myra Jehlen's complex and influential "Archimedes and the Paradox of Feminist Criticism" (1981) raises the problem of practicing feminist theory. Arguing that the real power of feminism comes in its "rethinking" of many of the central assumptions of Western culture—like the oppositions between intuition and reason, heart and head, even male and female—Jehlen asks us to think through where our questioning of these foundations leaves us to stand. She sees the moves among feminist scholars to create an "alternative context" in which women are central, and not marginal, however, as not really challenging the "male universe" but as leaving it intact: separate and essentially unchanged by feminist challenges. She suggests that "we have been, perhaps, too successful" in setting the study of women apart; "our female intellectual community," she argues, "becomes increasingly cut off even as it expands." For this reason, she questions the advisability of concentrating exclusively on literature written by women. She also begins to ask how "ideological" and "appreciative" criticism might come together in a feminist study of men's and women's texts. What can we do, she asks, with texts that are already admittedly biased, for which, in fact, bias is in many ways the appeal? Is there a relationship between judging the literary work's political position and appreciating its artistry? The problem at the heart of feminist criticism, she argues, is that "if we . . . want to address our whole culture" we will have to "deal with what we do not like but recognize as nonetheless valuable, serious, good."

Working through the example of nineteenth-century American sentimental fiction, Jehlen explores what the critic should do when her aesthetic values—her sense of what is good—conflict with her ideological values—her sense of what promotes women's equality. She advocates neither rereading the literary text as "really" meaning what we hope it will mean (promoting its "universality"), nor refusing to read it because it disagrees with what we want it to mean. Instead, she argues that all literature—whether written by men or by women, whether ideologically congenial or hostile—must be read in its historical specificity, to illuminate the ways in which all literary visions are contingent. This kind of "radical comparativism," she suggests, would allow one to "join the contradiction" between aesthetic and ideological values to "tap its energy," rather than to deny that the contradiction exists. As a kind of practice to illustrate this theory, Jehlen compares Samuel Richardson to American sentimental writers in an historicist analysis.

In "A Criticism of Our Own: Autonomy and Assimilation in Afro-American and Feminist Literary Theory" (1989), Elaine Showalter chronicles the differences among feminist critical practices and among the theoretical movements they represent. Since the publication of her influential "Feminist Criticism in the Wilderness" in 1981, Showalter has been one of the primary historians of feminist criticism, proposing categories in which to place all the varieties of feminist projects, and explaining the evolution of those categories within a chronological framework. "A Criticism of Our Own" outlines the dominant feminist methodologies of the 1980s.

Showalter shows that African-American literary criticism and feminist criticism can be seen as having evolved through parallel stages "in our confrontations with the Western literary tradition." Both began "in a separatist cultural aesthetics, born out of participation in a protest movement"; both then moved "to a middle stage of professionalized focus on a specific text-milieu in an alliance with academic literary theory"; and both have recently arrived at "an expanded and pluralistic critical field of expertise on sexual or racial difference." In the case of feminist criticism, Showalter builds upon her earlier versions of its history to delineate six kinds of projects: (1) androgynist poetics, dedicating to effacing gender differences; (2) the feminist critique of male culture; (3) a Female Aesthetic celebrating women's culture; (4) gynocritics, or the study of the tradition(s) of women's writing; (5) gynesic, or poststructuralist feminist criticism, focusing on "the feminine" as a category within culture; and (6) gender theory, which Showalter defines as "the comparative study of sexual difference." Her essay enumerates influential books and essays in each of these approaches, and attends to figures in such fields as philosophy, psychology, and anthropology whose work has had a significant impact on feminist literary theory and practice.

At the end of her essay, Showalter declares that "there is an urgent necessity to affirm the importance of black and female thinkers, speakers, readers, and writers. The Other Woman may be transparent or invisible to some; but she is very vivid, important, and necessary to us." The urgency and necessity of looking to and *listening* to thinkers who are *both* black and female is at the heart of Deborah McDowell's essay, "Recycling: Race, Gender and the Practice of Theory" (1992), and at the heart of much feminist literary theory in the 1990s. Showalter parallels the evolution of African-American criticism and feminist criticism in the 1980s; one could argue that the history of criticism in the 1990s will show the convergence of the two. Indeed, one of the most dramatic changes in the field of feminist theory occurred during the late eighties and early nineties, when feminist theorists of color began to show how central and important racial questions are to gender questions, and how crucial questions of gender are to questions of race.

Like Showalter, McDowell is constructing a history of feminist criticism in "Recycling"; but she also points out that we are constructing that history of literary theory in our actual practice of theory, and examines the role of black women in this construction of/constructed history. She is concerned especially with the problem that "what has been written *about* black feminist thinking eclipses a more constructive, perhaps a more empowering focus on what has been written *by* black feminists," and looks at how black women are often left out of (white) feminist theory as well as out of (male) African-American theory. Too often, she points out, feminist theory is taken to mean white feminist theory; calls to "account" for the experiences of women of color in feminist theory, then she argues, amount to a "maternalistic" stance on the part of white feminists toward women of color. The perception that feminist theory equals whiteness leads to another tension, one between theory and practice: "The strain . . . to 'theorize,' on the one hand, and to recognize material 'differences,' on the other, has created a tension within academic feminist discourse (read *white*). That tension is often formulated as a contrast, if not a contest, between 'theory' and 'practice-politics.'" In African-American theory, she argues, too often theory is itself gendered male, and practice is gendered female.

McDowell addresses these dilemmas facing African-American feminist critics by asking first for us to examine whether black women are marginalized because they do not "do" theory (as some have asserted), or whether they are already marginalized by the theory that is practiced; she then questions the dichotomy of theory and practice altogether. She suggests that it would be more productive, instead of assuming that poststructuralism and black feminist criticism are opposed, to look at the ways that there are very important overlaps between the two. She concludes by arguing that we are misconstruing what counts as theory, and need to look at the material conditions of academic, institutional life to see how defining theory is itself an ideological act. (For a related argument, see Margaret Homans's essay in "Body," which suggests that our definition of "theory" is too narrow to account for the difference that comprises the way African-American women theorize.)

Cordelia Chávez Candelaria, in "The 'Wild Zone' Thesis as Gloss in Chicana Literary Study" (1993), like McDowell, raises the question of how feminist criticism can take into account both racial and gender oppression, without subsuming one under the other. She suggests using the anthropological theory of the "wild zone," "a separate political and cultural space that women inhabit," to take into account the material differences of women's experiences in feminist literary criticism. She argues that the "wild zone" thesis both identifies and allows for a central paradox in writing about Chicana experience, recognizing both an unrestricted, embodied sense of an unimposed sense of identity and a restricted, patriarchal identity that is imposed, an understanding of female identity which she connects to the French feminist theories of Julia Kristeva and Alice Jardine. This understanding of the specificity of gender, she argues, allows the critic to engage in "gender-specific analysis without denying the importance of ethnic- or race-specific or class-specific analyses"; it encourages the analysis of gender without privileging it over race or class, allowing the analyses to exist side by side. Turning to the work of several contemporary Chicana writers—Estela Portrillo-Trambley, Denise Chávez, and Sandra Cisneros—Candelaria argues that the idea of the "wild zone" allows us to see how their stories are configured by place "in terms of thematic *zones* that interconnect experience and imagination."

—DPH & RRW

DANCING THROUGH THE MINEFIELD

some observations on the theory, practice, and politics of a feminist literary criticism

(1980)

Had anyone the prescience, ten years ago, to pose the question of defining a "feminist" literary criticism, she might have been told, in the wake of Mary Ellmann's *Thinking About Women*,[1] that it involved exposing the sexual stereotyping of women in both our literature and our literary criticism and, as well, demonstrating the inadequacy of established critical schools and methods to deal fairly or sensitively with works written by women. In broad outline, such a prediction would have stood well the test of time, and, in fact, Ellmann's book continues to be widely read and to point us in useful directions. What could not have been anticipated in 1969, however, was the catalyzing force of an ideology that, for many of us, helped to bridge the gap between the world as we found it and the world as we wanted it to be. For those of us who studied literature, a previously unspoken sense of exclusion from authorship, and a painfully personal distress at discovering whores, bitches, muses, and heroines dead in childbirth where we had once hoped to discover ourselves, could—for the first time—begin to be understood as more than "a set of disconnected, unrealized private emotions."[2] With a renewed courage to make public our otherwise private discontents, what had once been "felt individually as personal insecurity" came at last to be "viewed collectively as structural inconsistency"[3] within the very disciplines we studied. Following unflinchingly the full implications of Ellmann's percipient observations, and emboldened by the liberating energy of feminist ideology—in all its various forms and guises—feminist criticism very quickly moved beyond merely "expos[ing] sexism in one work of literature after another,"[4] and promised, instead, that we might at last "begin to record new choices in a new literary history."[5] So powerful was that impulse that we experienced it, along with Adrienne Rich, as much "more than a chapter in cultural history": it became, rather, "an act of survival."[6] What was at stake was not so much literature or criticism as such, but the historical, social, and ethical consequences of women's participation in, or exclusion from, either enterprise.

The pace of inquiry these last ten years has been fast and furious—especially after Kate Millett's 1970 analysis of the sexual politics of literature[7] added a note of urgency to what had earlier been Ellmann's sardonic anger—while the diversity of that inquiry easily outstripped all efforts to define feminist literary criticism as either a coherent system or a unified set of methodologies. Under its wide umbrella, everything has been thrown into question: our established canons, our aesthetic criteria, our interpretive strategies, our reading habits, and, most of all, ourselves as critics and as teachers. To delineate its full scope would require nothing less than a book—a book that would be outdated even as it was being composed. For the sake of brevity, therefore, let me attempt only a summary outline.

Perhaps the most obvious success of this new scholarship has been the return to circulation of previously lost or otherwise ignored works by women writers. Following fast upon the initial success of the Feminist Press in reissuing gems such as Rebecca Harding Davis's 1861 novella, *Life in the Iron Mills*, and Charlotte Perkins Gilman's 1892 "The Yellow Wallpaper," published in 1972 and 1973, respectively,[8] commercial trade and reprint houses vied with one another in the reprinting of anthologies of lost texts and, in some cases, in the reprinting of whole series. For those of us in American literature especially, the phenomenon promised a radical reshaping of our concepts of literary history and, at the very least, a new chapter in understanding the development of women's literary traditions. So commercially successful were these reprintings, and so attuned were the reprint houses to the political attitudes of the audiences for which they were offered, that many of us found ourselves wooed to compose critical introductions, which would find in the pages of nineteenth-century domestic and sentimental fictions, some signs of either muted rebellions or overt radicalism, in anticipation of the current wave of "new feminism." In rereading with our students these previously lost works, we inevitably raised perplexing questions as to the reasons for their disappearance from the canons of "major works," and we worried over the aesthetic and critical criteria by which they had been accorded diminished status.

This increased availability of works by women writers led, of course, to an increased interest in what elements, if any, might comprise some sort of unity or connection among them. The possibility that women had developed either a unique, or at least a related tradition of their own, especially intrigued those of us who specialized in one national literature or another, or in historical periods. Nina Baym's recent *Woman's Fiction: A Guide to Novels by and about Women in America, 1820–1870*[9] demonstrates the Americanists' penchant for examining what were once the "best-sellers" of their day, the ranks of the popular fiction writers, among which women took a dominant place throughout the nineteenth century, while the feminist studies of British literature emphasized instead the wealth of women writers who have been regarded as worthy of canonization. Not so much building upon one another's work as clarifying, successively, the parameters of the questions to be posed, Sydney Janet Kaplan, Ellen Moers, Patricia Meyer Spacks, and Elaine Showalter, among many others, concentrated their energies on delineating an internally consistent "body of work" by women that might stand as a female countertradition. For Kaplan, in 1975, this entailed examining women writers' various attempts to portray feminine consciousness and self-consciousness, not as a psychological category, but as a stylistic or rhetorical device.[10] That same year, arguing essentially that literature publicizes the private, Spacks placed her consideration of a "female imagination" within social and historical frames, to conclude that, "for readily discernible historical reasons women have characteristically concerned themselves with matters more or less peripheral to male concerns," and she attributed to this fact an inevitable difference in the literary emphases and subject matters of female and male writers.[11] The next year, Moers's *Literary Women: The Great Writers* focused on the pathways of literary influence that linked the English novel in the hands of women.[12] And, finally, in 1977, Showalter took up the matter of a "female literary tradition in the English novel from the generation of the Brontës to the present day" by arguing that, because women in general constitute a kind of "subculture within the framework of a larger society," the work of women writers, in particular, would thereby demonstrate a unity of "values, conventions, experiences, and behaviors impinging on each individual" as she found her sources of "self-expression relative to a dominant [and, by implication, male] society."[13]

At the same time that women writers were being reconsidered and reread, male writers were similarly subjected to a new feminist scrutiny. The continuing result—to put ten years of difficult analysis into a single sentence—has been nothing less than an acute attentiveness to the ways in which certain power relations—usually those in which males wield various forms of influence over females—are inscribed in the texts (both literary and critical), that we have inherited, not merely as subject matter, but as the unquestioned, often unacknowledged *given* of the culture. Even more important than the new interpretations of individual texts are the probings into the consequences (for women) of the conventions that inform those texts. For example, in surveying selected nineteenth- and early twentieth-century British novels which employ what she calls "the two suitors convention," Jean E. Kennard sought to understand why and how the structural demands of the convention, even in the hands of women writers, inevitably work to imply "the inferiority and necessary subordination of women." Her 1978 study, *Victims of Convention*, points out that the symbolic nature of the marriage which conventionally concludes such novels "indicates the adjustment of the protagonist to society's value, a condition which is equated with her maturity." Kennard's concern, however, is with the fact that the structural demands of the form too often sacrifice precisely those "virtues of independence and individuality," or, in other words, the very "qualities we have been invited to admire in" the heroines.[14] Kennard appropriately cautions us against drawing from her work any simplistically reductive thesis about the mimetic relations between art and life. Yet her approach nonetheless suggests that what is important about a fiction is not whether it ends in a death or a marriage, but what the symbolic demands of that particular conventional ending imply about the values and beliefs of the world that engendered it.

Her work thus participates in a growing emphasis in feminist literary study on the fact of literature as a social institution, embedded not only within its own literary traditions, but also within the particular physical and mental artifacts of the society from which it comes. Adumbrating Millett's 1970 decision to anchor her "literary reflections" to a preceding analysis of the historical, social, and economic contexts of sexual politics,[15] more recent work—most notably Lillian Robinson's—begins with the premise that the process of artistic creation "consists not of ghostly happenings in the head but of a matching of the states and processes of symbolic models against the states and processes of the wider world."[16] The power relations inscribed in the form of conventions within our literary inheritance, these critics argue, reify the encodings of those same power relations in the culture at large. And the critical examination of rhetorical codes becomes, in their hands, the pursuit of ideological codes, because both embody either value systems or the dialectic of competition between value systems. More often than not, these critics also insist upon examining not only the mirroring of life in art, but also the normative impact of art on life. Addressing herself to the popular art available to working women, for example, Robinson is interested in understanding not only "the forms it uses," but, more importantly, "the myths it creates, the influence it exerts." "The way art helps people to order, interpret, mythologize, or dispose of their own experience," she declares, may be "complex and often ambiguous, but it is not impossible to define."[17]

Whether its focus be upon the material or the imaginative contexts of literary invention; single texts or entire canons; the relations between authors, genres, or historical circumstances; lost authors or well-known names, the variety and diversity of all feminist literary criticism finally coheres in its stance of almost defensive rereading. What Adrienne Rich had earlier called "re-vision," that is, "the act of looking back, of seeing with fresh eyes, of entering an old text from a new critical direction,"[18] took on a more actively self-protective coloration in 1978, when Judith Fetterley called upon the woman reader to learn to "resist" the sexist designs a text might make upon her—asking her to identify against herself, so to speak, by manipulating her sympathies on behalf of male heroes, but against female shrew or bitch characters.[19] Underpinning a great deal of this critical rereading has been the not-unexpected alliance between feminist literary study and feminist studies in linguistics and language-acquisition. Tillie Olsen's commonsense observation of the danger of "perpetuating—by continued usage—entrenched, centuries-old oppressive power realities, early-on incorporated into language,"[20] has been given substantive analysis in the writings of feminists who study "language as a symbolic system closely tied to a patriarchal social structure." Taken together, their work demonstrates "the importance of language in establishing, reflecting, and maintaining an asymmetrical relationship between women and men."[21]

To consider what this implies for the fate of women who essay the craft of language is to ascertain, perhaps for the first time, the real dilemma of the poet who finds her most cherished private experience "hedged by taboos, mined with false-namings."[22] It also explains the dilemma of the male reader who, in opening the pages of a woman's book, finds himself entering a strange and unfamiliar world of symbolic significance. For if, as Nelly Furman insists, neither language use nor language acquisition are "gender-neutral," but are, instead, "imbued with our sex-inflected cultural values";[23] and if, additionally, reading is a process of "sorting out the structures of signification,"[24] in any text, then male readers who find themselves outside of and unfamiliar with the symbolic systems that constitute female experience in women's writings, will necessarily dismiss those systems as undecipherable, meaningless, or trivial. And male professors will find no reason to include such works in the canons of "major authors." At the same time, women writers, coming into a tradition of literary language and conventional forms already appropriated, for centuries, to the purposes of male expression, will be forced virtually to "wrestle" with that language in an effort "to remake it as a language adequate to our conceptual processes."[25] To all of this, feminists concerned with the politics of language and style have been acutely attentive. "Language conceals an invincible adversary," observes French critic Hélène Cixous, "because it's the language of men and their grammar."[26] But equally insistent, as in the work of Sandra M. Gilbert and Susan Gubar, has been the understanding of the need for *all* readers—male and female alike—to learn to penetrate the otherwise unfamiliar universes of symbolic action that comprise women's writings, past and present.[27]

To have attempted so many difficult questions and to have accomplished so much—even acknowledging the inevitable false starts, overlapping, and repetition—in so short a time, should certainly have secured feminist literary criticism an honored berth on that ongoing intellectual journey which we loosely term, in academia, "critical analysis." Instead of being welcomed onto the train, however, we've been forced to negotiate a minefield. The very energy and diversity of our enterprise have rendered us vulnerable to attack on the grounds that we lack both definition and coherence; while our particular attentiveness to the ways in which literature encodes and disseminates cultural value systems calls down upon us imprecations echoing those heaped upon the Marxist critics of an earlier generation. If we are scholars dedicated to rediscovering a lost body of writings by women, then our finds are questioned on aesthetic grounds. And if we are critics, determined to practice revisionist readings, it is claimed that our focus is too narrow, and our results are only distortions or, worse still, polemical misreadings.

The very vehemence of the outcry, coupled with our total dismissal in some quarters,[28] suggests not our deficiencies, however, but the potential magnitude of our challenge. For what we are asking be scrutinized are nothing less than shared cultural assumptions so deeply rooted and so long ingrained that, for the most part, our critical colleagues have ceased to recognize them as such. In other words, what is really being bewailed in the claims that we distort texts or threaten the disappearance of the great Western literary tradition itself[29] is not so much the disappearance of either text or tradition but, instead, the eclipse of that particular *form* of the text, and that particular *shape* of the canon, which previously reified male readers' sense of power and significance in the world. Analogously, by asking whether, as readers, we ought to be "really satisfied by the marriage of Dorothea Brooke to Will Ladislaw? of Shirley Keeldar to Louis Moore?" or whether, as Kennard suggests, we must reckon with the ways in which "the qualities we have been invited to admire in these heroines [have] been sacrificed to structural neatness,"[30] is to raise difficult and profoundly perplexing questions about the ethical implications of our otherwise unquestioned aesthetic pleasures. It is, after all, an imposition of high order to ask the viewer to attend to Ophelia's sufferings in a scene where, before, he had always so comfortably kept his eye fixed firmly on Hamlet. To understand all this, then, as the real nature of the challenge we have offered and, in consequence, as the motivation for the often overt hostility we've aroused, should help us learn to negotiate the minefield, if not with grace, then with at least a clearer comprehension of its underlying patterns.

The ways in which objections to our work are usually posed, of course, serve to obscure their deeper motivations. But this may, in part, be due to our own reticence at taking full responsibility for the truly radicalizing premises that lie at the theoretical core of all we have so far accomplished. It may be time, therefore, to redirect discussion, forcing our adversaries to deal with the substantive issues and pushing ourselves into a clearer articulation of what, in fact, we are about. Up until now, I fear, we have only piecemeal dealt with the difficulties inherent in challenging the authority of established canons and then justifying the excellence of women's traditions, sometimes in accord with standards to which they have no intrinsic relation.

At the very point at which we must perforce enter the discourse—that is, claiming excellence or importance for our "finds"—all discussion has already, we discover, long ago been closed. "If Kate Chopin were *really* worth reading," an Oxford-trained colleague once assured me, "she'd have lasted—like Shakespeare"; and he then proceeded to vote against the English department's crediting a women's studies seminar I was offering in American women writers. The canon, for him, conferred excellence; Chopin's exclusion demonstrated only her lesser worth. As far as he was concerned, I could no more justify giving English department credit for the study of Chopin than I could dare publicly to question Shakespeare's genius. Through hindsight, I've now come to view that discussion as not only having posed fruitless oppositions, but also as having entirely evaded the much more profound problem lurking just beneath the surface of our disagreement. That is, that the fact of canonization puts any work beyond questions of establishing its merit and, instead, invites students to offer only increasingly more ingenious readings and interpretations, the purpose of which is to validate the greatness already imputed by canonization.

Had I only understood it for what it was then, into this circular and self-serving set of assumptions I might have interjected some statement of my right to question why *any* text is revered and my need to know what it tells us about "how we live, how we have been living, how we have been led to imagine ourselves, [and] how our language has trapped as well as liberated us."[31] The very fact of our critical training within the strictures imposed by an established canon of major works and authors, however, repeatedly deflects us from such questions. Instead, we find ourselves endlessly responding to the *riposte* that the overwhelmingly male presence among canonical authors was only an accident of history—and never intentionally sexist—coupled with claims to the "obvious" aesthetic merit of those canonized texts. It is, as I say, a fruitless exchange, serving more to obscure than to expose the territory being protected and dragging us, again and again, through the minefield.

It is my contention that current hostilities might be transformed into a true dialogue with our critics if we at last made explicit what appear, to this observer, to constitute the three crucial propositions to which our special interests inevitably give rise. They are, moreover, propositions which, if handled with care and intelligence, could breathe new life into now moribund areas of our profession: (1) Literary history (and with that, the historicity of literature) is a fiction; (2) insofar as we are taught how to read, what we engage are not texts but paradigms; and, finally, (3) that since the grounds upon which we assign aesthetic value to texts are never infallible, unchangeable, or universal, we must reexamine not only our aesthetics but, as well, the inherent biases and assumptions informing the critical methods which (in part) shape our aesthetic responses. For the sake of brevity, I won't attempt to offer the full arguments for each but, rather, only sufficient elaboration to demonstrate what I see as their intrinsic relation to the potential scope of and present challenge implied by feminist literary study.

1. *Literary history (and, with that, the historicity of literature) is a fiction.* To begin with, an established canon functions as a model by which to chart the continu-

ities and discontinuities, as well as the influences upon and the interconnections between works, genres, and authors. That model we tend to forget, however, is of our own making. It will take a very different shape, and explain its inclusions and exclusions in very different ways, if the reigning critical ideology believes that new literary forms result from some kind of ongoing internal dialectic within preexisting styles and traditions or if, by contrast, the ideology declares that literary change is dependent upon societal development and thereby determined by upheavals in the social and economic organization of the culture at large.[32] Indeed, whenever in the previous century of English and American literary scholarship one alternative replaced the other, we saw dramatic alterations in canonical "wisdom."

This suggests, then, that our sense of a "literary history" and, by extension, our confidence in a "historical" canon, is rooted not so much in any definitive understanding of the past, as it is in our need to call up and utilize the past on behalf of a better understanding of the present. Thus, to paraphrase David Couzens Hoy, it becomes "necessary to point out that the understanding of art and literature is such an essential aspect of the present's self-understanding that this self-understanding conditions what even gets taken" as comprising that artistic and literary past. To quote Hoy fully, "this continual reinterpretation of the past goes hand in hand with the continual reinterpretation by the present of itself."[33] In our own time, uncertain as to which, if any, model truly accounts for our canonical choices or accurately explains literary history, and pressured further by the feminists' call for some justification of the criteria by which women's writings were largely excluded from both that canon and history, we suffer what Harold Bloom has called "a remarkable dimming" of "our mutual sense of canonical standards."[34]

Into this apparent impasse, feminist literary theorists implicitly introduce the observation that our choices and evaluations of current literature have the effect either of solidifying or of reshaping our sense of the past. The authority of any established canon, after all, is reified by our perception that current work seems to grow, almost inevitably, out of it (even in opposition or rebellion) and is called into question when what we read appears to have little or no relation to what we recognize as coming before. So, were the larger critical community to begin to seriously attend to the recent outpouring of fine literature by women, this would surely be accompanied by a concomitant researching of the past, by literary historians, in order to account for the present phenomenon. In that process, literary history would itself be altered: works by seventeenth-, eighteenth-, or nineteenth-century women, to which we had not previously attended, might be given new importance as "precursors" or as prior influences upon present-day authors; while selected male writers might also be granted new prominence as figures whom the women today, or even yesterday, needed to reject. I am arguing, in other words, that the choices we make in the present inevitably alter our sense of the past that led to them.

Related to this is the feminist challenge to that patently mendacious critical fallacy that we read the "classics" in order to reconstruct the past "the way it really was," and that we read Shakespeare and Milton in order to apprehend the meanings that they intended. Short of time machines or miraculous resurrections, there is simply no way to know, precisely or surely, what "really was," what

Homer intended when he sang, or Milton when he dictated. Critics more acute than I have already pointed up the impossibility of grounding a reading in the imputation of authorial intention because the further removed the author is from us, so too must be her or his systems of knowledge and belief, points of view, and structures of vision (artistic and otherwise).[35] (I omit here the difficulty of finally either proving or disproving the imputation of intentionality because, inescapably, the only appropriate authority is unavailable: deceased.) What we have really come to mean when we speak of competence in reading historical texts, therefore, is the ability to recognize literary conventions which have survived through time—so as to remain operational in the mind of the reader—and, where these are lacking, the ability to translate (or perhaps transform?) the text's ciphers into more current and recognizable shapes. But we never really reconstruct the past in its own terms. What we gain when we read the "classics," then, is neither Homer's Greece nor George Eliot's England *as they knew it* but, rather, an approximation of an already fictively imputed past made available, through our interpretive strategies, for present concerns. Only by understanding this can we put to rest that recurrent delusion that the "continuing relevance" of the classics serves as "testimony to perennial features of human experience."[36] The only "perennial feature" to which our ability to read and reread texts written in previous centuries testifies is our inventiveness—in the sense that all of literary history is a fiction which we daily re-create as we reread it. What distinguishes feminists in this regard is their desire to alter and extend what we take as historically relevant from out of that vast storehouse of our literary inheritance and, further, feminists' recognition of the storehouse for what it really is: a resource for remodeling our literary history, past, present, and future.

2. *Insofar as we are taught how to read, what we engage are not texts but paradigms.* To pursue the logical consequences of the first proposition leads, however uncomfortably, to the conclusion that we appropriate meaning from a text according to what we need (or desire) or, in other words, according to the critical assumptions or predispositions (conscious or not) that we bring to it. And we appropriate different meanings, or report different gleanings, at different times—even from the same text—according to our changed assumptions, circumstances, and requirements. This, in essence, constitutes the heart of the second proposition. For insofar as literature is itself a social institution, so, too, reading is a highly socialized—or learned—activity. What makes it so exciting, of course, is that it can be constantly relearned and refined, so as to provide either an individual or an entire reading community, over time, with infinite variations of the same text. It *can* provide that, but, I must add, too often it does not. Frequently our reading habits become fixed, so that each successive reading experience functions, in effect, normatively, with one particular kind of novel stylizing our expectations of those to follow, the stylistic devices of any favorite author (or group of authors) alerting us to the presence or absence of those devices in the works of others, and so on. "Once one has read his first poem," Murray Krieger has observed, "he turns to his second and to the others that will follow thereafter with an increasing series of preconceptions about the sort of activity in which he is indulging. In matters of literary experience, as in other experiences," Krieger concludes, "one is a virgin but once."[37]

For most readers, this is a fairly unconscious process, and not unnaturally, what we are taught to read well and with pleasure, when we are young, predisposes us to certain specific kinds of adult reading tastes. For the professional literary critic, the process may be no different, but it is at least more conscious. Graduate schools, at their best, are training grounds for competing interpretive paradigms or reading techniques: affective stylistics, structuralism, and semiotic analysis, to name only a few of the more recent entries. The delight we learn to take in the mastery of these interpretive strategies is then often mistakenly construed as our delight in reading specific texts, especially in the case of works that would otherwise be unavailable or even offensive to us. In my own graduate career, for example, with superb teachers to guide me, I learned to take great pleasure in *Paradise Lost,* even though as both a Jew and a feminist, I can subscribe neither to its theology nor to its hierarchy of sexual valuation. If, within its own terms (as I have been taught to understand them), the text manipulates my sensibilities and moves me to pleasure—as I will affirm it does—then, at least in part, that must be because, in spite of my real-world alienation from many of its basic tenets, I have been able to enter that text through interpretive strategies which allow me to displace less comfortable observations with others to which I have been taught pleasurably to attend. Though some of my teachers may have called this process "learning to read the text properly," I have now come to see it as learning to effectively manipulate the critical strategies which they taught me so well. Knowing, for example, the poem's debt to epic conventions, I am able to discover in it echoes and reworkings of both lines and situations from Virgil and Homer; placing it within the ongoing Christian debate between Good and Evil, I comprehend both the philosophic and the stylistic significance of Satan's ornate rhetoric as compared to God's majestic simplicity in Book III. But, in each case, an interpretive model, already assumed, had guided my discovery of the evidence for it.[38]

When we consider the implications of these observations for the processes of canon formation and for the assignment of aesthetic value, we find ourselves locked in a chicken-and-egg dilemma, unable easily to distinguish as primary the importance of *what* we read as opposed to *how* we have learned to read it. For, simply put, we read well, and with pleasure, what we already know how to read; and what we know how to read is to a large extent dependent upon what we have already read (works from which we've developed our expectations and learned our interpretive strategies). What we then choose to read—and, by extension, teach and thereby "canonize"—usually follows upon our previous reading. Radical breaks are tiring, demanding, uncomfortable, and sometimes wholly beyond our comprehension.

Though the argument is not usually couched in precisely these terms, a considerable segment of the most recent feminist rereadings of women writers allows the conclusion that, where those authors have dropped out of sight, the reason may be due not to any lack of merit in the work but, instead, to an incapacity of predominantly male readers to properly interpret and appreciate women's texts—due, in large part, to a lack of prior acquaintance. The fictions which women compose about the worlds they inhabit may owe a debt to prior, influential works by other women or, simply enough, to the daily experience of the writer herself or, more usually, to some combination of the two. The reader coming upon such fiction, with knowledge of neither its informing literary traditions nor its real-world contexts, will thereby find himself hard-pressed, though he may recognize the words on the page, to competently decipher its intended meanings. And this is what makes the recent studies by Spacks, Moers, Showalter, Gilbert and Gubar, and others so crucial. For, by attempting to delineate the connections and interrelations that make for a female literary tradition, they provide us invaluable aids for recognizing and understanding the unique literary traditions and sex-related contexts out of which women write.

The (usually male) reader who, both by experience and by reading, has never made acquaintance with those contexts—historically, the lying-in room, the parlor, the nursery, the kitchen, the laundry, and so on—will necessarily lack the capacity to fully interpret the dialogue or action embedded therein; for, as every good novelist knows, the meaning of any character's action or statement is inescapably a function of the specific situation in which it is embedded.[39] Virginia Woolf therefore quite properly anticipated the male reader's disposition to write off what he could not understand, abandoning women's writings as offering "not merely a difference of view, but a view that is weak, or trivial, or sentimental because it differs from his own." In her 1929 essay on "Women and Fiction," Woolf grappled most obviously with the ways in which male writers and male subject matter had already preempted the language of literature. Yet she was also tacitly commenting on the problem of (male) audience and conventional reading expectations when she speculated that the woman writer might well "find that she is perpetually wishing to alter the established values [in literature]—to make serious what appears insignificant to a man, and trivial what is to him important."[40] "The 'competence' necessary for understanding [a] literary message . . . depends upon a great number of codices," after all; as Cesare Segre has pointed out, to be competent, a reader must either share or at least be familiar with, "in addition to the code language . . . the codes of custom, of society, and of conceptions of the world"[41] (what Woolf meant by "values"). Males ignorant of women's "values" or conceptions of the world will necessarily, thereby, be poor readers of works that in any sense recapitulate their codes.

The problem is further exacerbated when the language of the literary text is largely dependent upon figuration. For it can be argued, as Ted Cohen has shown, that while "in general, and with some obvious qualifications . . . all literal use of language is accessible to all whose language it is . . . figurative use can be inaccessible to all but those who share information about one another's knowledge, beliefs, intentions, and attitudes."[42] There was nothing fortuitous, for example, in Charlotte Perkins Gilman's decision to situate the progressive mental breakdown and increasing incapacity of the protagonist of "The Yellow Wallpaper" in an upstairs room that had once served as a nursery (with barred windows, no less). But the reader unacquainted with the ways in which women traditionally inhabited a household might not have taken the initial description of the setting as semantically relevant; and the progressive infantilization of the adult protagonist would thereby lose some of its symbolic implications. Analogously, the contemporary poet who declares, along with Adrienne Rich, the need for "a whole new poetry beginning here" is acknowledging that the materials available for symbolization and figuration from women's contexts will necessarily differ from those that men have traditionally utilized:

Vision begins to happen in such a life
as if a woman quietly walked away
from the argument and jargon in a room
and sitting down in the kitchen, began turning in her lap
bits of yarn, calico and velvet scraps,

pulling the tenets of a life together
with no mere will to mastery,
only care for the many-lived, unending
forms in which she finds herself.[43]

What, then, is the fate of the woman writer whose competent reading community is composed only of members of her own sex? And what, then, the response of the male critic who, on first looking into Virginia Woolf or Doris Lessing, finds all of the interpretive strategies at his command inadequate to a full and pleasurable deciphering of their pages? Historically, the result has been the diminished status of women's products and their consequent absence from major canons. Nowadays, however, by pointing out that the act of "interpreting language is no more sexually neutral than language use or the language system itself," feminist students of language, like Nelly Furman, help us better understand the crucial linkage between our gender and our interpretive, or reading, strategies. Insisting upon "the contribution of the . . . reader [in] the active attribution of significance to formal signifiers,"[44] Furman and others promise to shake us all—female and male alike—out of our canonized and conventional aesthetic assumptions.

3. *Since the grounds upon which we assign aesthetic value to texts are never infallible, unchangeable, or universal, we must reexamine not only our aesthetics but, as well, the inherent biases and assumptions informing the critical methods which (in part) shape our aesthetic responses.* I am, on the one hand, arguing that men will be better readers, or appreciators, of women's books when they have read more of them (as women have always been taught to become astute readers of men's texts). On the other hand, it will be noted, the emphasis of my remarks shifts the act of critical judgment from assigning aesthetic valuations to texts and directs it, instead, to ascertaining the adequacy of any interpretive paradigm to a full reading of both female and male writing. My third proposition—and, I admit, perhaps the most controversial—thus calls into question that recurrent tendency in criticism to establish norms for the evaluation of literary works when we might better serve the cause of literature by developing standards for evaluating the adequacy of our critical methods.[45] This does not mean that I wish to discard aesthetic valuation. The choice, as I see it, is not between retaining or discarding aesthetic values; rather, the choice is between having some awareness of what constitutes (at least in part) the bases of our aesthetic responses and going without such an awareness. For it is my view that insofar as aesthetic responsiveness continues to be an integral aspect of our human response system—in part spontaneous, in part learned and educated—we will inevitably develop theories to help explain, formalize, or even initiate those responses.

In challenging the adequacy of received critical opinion or the imputed excellence of established canons, feminist literary critics are essentially seeking to discover how aesthetic value is assigned in the first place, where it resides (in the text or in the reader), and, most importantly, what validity may really be claimed by our aesthetic "judgments." What ends do those judgments serve, the feminist asks; and what conceptions of the world or ideological stances do they (even if unwittingly) help to perpetuate? In so doing, she points out, among other things, that any response labeled "aesthetic" may as easily designate some immediately experienced moment or event as it may designate a species of nostalgia, a yearning for the components of a simpler past, when the world seemed known or at least understandable. Thus the value accorded an opera or a Shakespeare play may well reside in the viewer's immediate viewing pleasure, or it may reside in the play's nostalgic evocation of a once-comprehensible and ordered world. At the same time, the feminist confronts, for example, the reader who simply cannot entertain the possibility that women's worlds are symbolically rich, the reader who, like the male characters in Susan Glaspell's 1917 short story, "A Jury of Her Peers," has already assumed the innate "insignificance of kitchen things."[46] Such a reader, she knows, will prove himself unable to assign significance to fictions that attend to "kitchen things" and will, instead, judge such fictions as trivial and as aesthetically wanting. For her to take useful issue with such a reader, she must make clear that what appears to be a dispute about aesthetic merit is, in reality, a dispute about the *contexts of judgment*; and what is at issue, then, is the adequacy of the prior assumptions and reading habits brought to bear on the text. To put it bluntly: we have had enough pronouncements of aesthetic valuation for a time; it is now our task to evaluate the imputed norms and normative reading patterns that, in part, led to those pronouncements.

By and large, I think I've made my point. Only to clarify it do I add this coda: when feminists turn their attention to the works of male authors which have traditionally been accorded high aesthetic value and, where warranted, follow Olsen's advice that we assert our "right to say: this is surface, this falsifies reality, this degrades,"[47] such statements do not necessarily mean that we will end up with a diminished canon. To question the source of the aesthetic pleasures we've gained from reading Spenser, Shakespeare, Milton, and so on, does not imply that we must deny those pleasures. It means only that aesthetic response is once more invested with epistemological, ethical, and moral concerns. It means, in other words, that readings of *Paradise Lost* which analyze its complex hierarchal structures but fail to note the implications of gender within that hierarchy; or which insist upon the inherent (or even inspired) perfection of Milton's figurative language but fail to note the consequences, for Eve, of her specifically gender-marked weakness, which, like the flowers to which she attends, requires "propping up"; or which concentrate on the poem's thematic reworking of classical notions of martial and epic prowess into Christian (moral) heroism but fail to note that Eve is stylistically edited out of that process—all such readings, however useful, will no longer be deemed wholly adequate. The pleasures we had earlier learned to take in the poem will not be diminished thereby, but they will become part of an altered reading attentiveness.

These three propositions I believe to be at the theoretical core of most current feminist literary criticism, whether acknowledged as such or not. If I am correct in this, then that criticism represents more than a profoundly skeptical stance toward all other preexisting and contemporaneous schools and methods, and more than an impassioned demand that the variety and variability of women's literary expression be taken into full account, rather than written off as caprice and exception, the irregularity in an otherwise regular design. It represents that locus in literary study where, in unceasing effort, female self-consciousness turns in upon itself, attempting to grasp the deepest conditions of its own unique and multiplicitous realities, in the hope, eventually, of altering the very forms through which the culture perceives, expresses, and knows itself. For, if what the larger women's movement looks for in the future is a transformation of the structures of primarily male power which now order our society, then the feminist literary critic demands that we understand the ways in which those structures have been—and continue to be—reified by our literature and by our literary criticism. Thus, along with other "radical" critics and critical schools, though our focus remains the power of the word to both structure and mirror human experience, our overriding commitment is to a radical alteration—an improvement, we hope—in the nature of that experience.

What distinguishes our work from those similarly oriented "social consciousness" critiques, it is said, is its lack of systematic coherence. Pitted against, for example, psychoanalytic or Marxist readings, which owe a decisive share of their persuasiveness to their apparent internal consistency as a system, the aggregate of feminist literary criticism appears woefully deficient in system, and painfully lacking in program. It is, in fact, from all quarters, the most telling defect alleged against us, the most explosive threat in the minefield. And my own earlier observation that, as of 1976, feminist literary criticism appeared "more like a set of interchangeable strategies than any coherent school or shared goal orientation," has been taken by some as an indictment, by others as a statement of impatience. Neither was intended. I felt then, as I do now, that this would "prove both its strength *and* its weakness,"[48] in the sense that the apparent disarray would leave us vulnerable to the kind of objection I've just alluded to; while the fact of our diversity would finally place us securely where, all along, we should have been: camped out, on the far side of the minefield, with the other pluralists and pluralisms.

In our heart of hearts, of course, most critics are really structuralists (whether or not they accept the label) because what we are seeking are patterns (or structures) that can order and explain the otherwise inchoate; thus, we invent, or believe we discover, relational patternings in the texts we read which promise transcendence from difficulty and perplexity to clarity and coherence. But, as I've tried to argue in these pages, to the imputed "truth" or "accuracy" of these findings, the feminist must oppose the painfully obvious truism that what is attended to in a literary work, and hence what is reported about it, is often determined not so much by the work itself as by the critical technique or aesthetic criteria through which it is filtered or, rather, read and decoded. All the feminist is asserting, then, is her own equivalent right to liberate new (and perhaps different) significances from these same texts; and, at the same time, her right to choose which features of a text she takes as relevant because she is, after all, asking new and different questions of it. In the process, she claims neither definitiveness nor structural completeness for her different readings and reading systems, but only their usefulness in recognizing the particular achievements of woman-as-author and their applicability in conscientiously decoding woman-as-sign.

That these alternate foci of critical attentiveness will render alternate readings or interpretations of the same text—even among feminists—should be no cause for alarm. Such developments illustrate only the pluralist contention that, "in approaching a text of any complexity . . . the reader must choose to emphasize certain aspects which seem to him crucial" and that, "in fact, the variety of readings which we have for many works is a function of the selection of crucial aspects made by the variety of readers." Robert Scholes, from whom I've been quoting, goes so far as to assert that "there is no single 'right' reading for any complex literary work," and, following the Russian formalist school, he observes that "we do not speak of readings that are simply true or false, but of readings that are more or less rich, strategies that are more or less appropriate."[49] Because those who share the term "feminist" nonetheless practice a diversity of critical strategies, leading, in some cases, to quite different readings, we must acknowledge among ourselves that sister critics, "having chosen to tell a different story, may in their interpretation identify different aspects of the meanings conveyed by the same passage."[50]

Adopting a "pluralist" label does not mean, however, that we cease to disagree; it means only that we entertain the possibility that different readings, even of the same text, may be differently useful, even illuminating, within different contexts of inquiry. It means, in effect, that we enter a dialectical process of examining, testing, even trying out the contexts—be they prior critical assumptions or explicitly stated ideological stances (or some combination of the two)—that led to the disparate readings. Not all will be equally acceptable to every one of us, of course, and even those prior assumptions or ideologies that are acceptable may call for further refinement and/or clarification. But, at the very least, because we will have grappled with the assumptions that led to it, we will be better able to articulate *why* we find a particular reading or interpretation adequate or inadequate. This kind of dialectical process, moreover, not only makes us more fully aware of what criticism is, and how it functions; it also gives us access to its future possibilities, making us conscious, as R. P. Blackmur put it, "of what we have done," "of what can be done next, or done again,"[51] or, I would add, of what can be done differently. To put it still another way: just because we will no longer tolerate the specifically sexist omissions and oversights of earlier critical schools and methods does not mean that, in their stead, we must establish our own "party line."

In my view, our purpose is not and should not be the formulation of any single reading method or potentially procrustean set of critical procedures nor, even less, the generation of prescriptive categories for some dreamed-of nonsexist literary canon.[52] Instead, as I see it, our task is to initiate nothing less than a playful pluralism responsive to the possibilities of multiple critical schools and methods, but captive of none, recognizing that the many tools needed for our analysis will necessarily be largely inherited and only partly of our own making. Only by employing a plurality of methods will we protect ourselves from the temptation of so oversimplifying any text—and especially those particularly offensive to us—that we render ourselves unresponsive to what Scholes has called "its various systems of meaning and their interaction."[53] Any text we deem worthy of our critical attention is usually, after all, a locus of many and varied kinds of (personal, thematic, stylistic, structural, rhetorical, etc.) relationships. So, whether we tend to treat a text as a *mimesis*, in which words are taken to be re-creating or representing viable worlds; or whether we prefer to treat a text as a kind of equation of communication, in which decipherable messages are passed from writers to readers; and whether we locate meaning as inherent in the text, the act of reading, or in some collaboration between reader and text—whatever our predilection, let us not generate from it a straitjacket that limits the scope of possible analysis. Rather, let us generate an ongoing dialogue of competing potential possibilities—among feminists and, as well, between feminist and nonfeminist critics.

The difficulty of what I describe does not escape me. The very idea of pluralism seems to threaten a kind of chaos for the future of literary inquiry while, at the same time, it seems to deny the hope of establishing some basic conceptual model which can organize all data—the hope which always begins any analytical exercise. My effort here, however, has been to demonstrate the essential delusions that inform such objections: If literary inquiry has historically escaped chaos by establishing canons, then it has only substituted one mode of arbitrary action for another—and, in this case, at the expense of half the population. And if feminists openly acknowledge ourselves as pluralists, then we do not give up the search for patterns of opposition and connection—probably the basis of thinking itself; what we give up is simply the arrogance of claiming that our work is either exhaustive or definitive. (It is, after all, the identical arrogance we are asking our nonfeminist colleagues to abandon.) If this kind of pluralism appears to threaten both the present coherence of and the inherited aesthetic criteria for a canon of "greats," then, as I have earlier argued, it is precisely that threat which, alone, can free us from the prejudices, the strictures, and the blind spots of the past. In feminist hands, I would add, it is less a threat than a promise.

What unites and repeatedly invigorates feminist literary criticism, then, is neither dogma nor method but, as I have indicated earlier, an acute and impassioned *attentiveness* to the ways in which primarily male structures of power are inscribed (or encoded) within our literary inheritance; the consequences of that encoding for women—as characters, as readers, and as writers; and, with that, a shared analytic *concern* for the implications of that encoding not only for a better understanding of the past, but also for an improved reordering of the present and future as well. If that *concern* identifies feminist literary criticism as one of the many academic arms of the larger women's movement, then that *attentiveness*, within the halls of academe, poses no less a challenge for change, generating, as it does, the three propositions explored here. The critical pluralism that inevitably follows upon those three propositions, however, bears little resemblance to what Robinson has called "the greatest bourgeois theme of all, the myth of pluralism, with its consequent rejection of ideological commitment as 'too simple' to embrace the (necessarily complex) truth."[54] Only ideological commitment could have gotten us to enter the minefield, putting in jeopardy our careers and our livelihood. Only the power of ideology to transform our conceptual worlds, and the inspiration of that ideology to liberate long-suppressed energies and emotions, can account for our willingness to take on critical tasks that, in an earlier decade, would have been "abandoned in despair or apathy."[55] The fact of differences among us proves only that, despite our shared commitments, we have nonetheless refused to shy away from complexity, preferring rather to openly disagree than to give up either intellectual honesty or hard-won insights.

Finally, I would argue, pluralism informs feminist literary inquiry not simply as a description of what already exists but, more importantly, as the only critical stance consistent with the current status of the larger women's movement. Segmented and variously focused, the different women's organizations neither espouse any single system of analysis nor, as a result, express any wholly shared, consistently articulated ideology. The ensuing loss in effective organization and political clout is a serious one, but it has not been paralyzing; in spite of our differences, we have united to *act* in areas of clear mutual concern (the push for the Equal Rights Amendment is probably the most obvious example). The trade-off, as I see it, has made possible an ongoing and educative dialectic of analysis and proferred solutions, protecting us thereby from the inviting traps of reductionism and dogma. And so long as this dialogue remains active, both our politics and our criticism will be free of dogma—but never, I hope, of feminist ideology, in all its variety. For, "whatever else ideologies may be—projections of unacknowledged fears, disguises for ulterior motives, phatic expressions of group solidarity" (and the women's movement, to date, has certainly been all of these, and more)—whatever ideologies express, they are, as Geertz astutely observes, "most distinctively, maps of problematic social reality and matrices for the creation of collective conscience." And despite the fact that "ideological advocates . . . tend as much to obscure as to clarify the true nature of the problems involved," as Geertz notes, "they at least call attention to their existence and, by polarizing issues, make continued neglect more difficult. Without Marxist attack, there would have been no labor reform; without Black Nationalists, no deliberate speed."[56] Without Seneca Falls, I would add, no enfranchisement of women, and without "consciousness raising," no feminist literary criticism nor, even less, women's studies.

Ideology, however, only truly manifests its power by ordering the sum of our actions.[57] If feminist criticism calls anything into question, it must be that dog-eared myth of intellectual neutrality. For, what I take to be the underlying spirit, or message, of any consciously ideologically premised criticism—that is, that ideas are important *because* they determine the ways we live, or want to live, in the world—is vitiated by confining those ideas to the study, the classroom, or the pages of our books. To write chapters decrying the sexual stereotyping of women in our literature, while closing our eyes to the sexual harassment of our women students and colleagues; to display Katharine Hepburn and Rosalind Russell in our courses on "The Image of the Independent Career Women in Film," while managing not to notice the paucity of female administrators on our own campus; to study the women who helped make universal enfranchisement a political reality, while keeping silent about our activist colleagues who are denied promotion or tenure; to include segments on "Women in the Labor Movement" in our American studies or women's studies courses, while remaining willfully ignorant of the department secretary fired for her efforts to organize a clerical workers' union; to glory in the delusions of "merit," "privilege," and "status" which accompany campus life in order to insulate ourselves from the millions of women who labor in poverty—all this is not merely hypocritical; it destroys both the spirit and the meaning of what we are about. It puts us, however unwittingly, in the service of those who laid the minefield in the first place. In my view, it is a fine thing for many of us, individually, to have traversed the minefield; but that happy circumstance will only prove of lasting importance if, together, we expose it for what it is (the male fear of sharing power and significance with women) and de-activate its components, so that others, after us, may literally dance through the minefield.

NOTES

"Dancing Through the Minefield" was the winner of the 1979 Florence Howe Essay Contest, which is sponsored by the Women's Caucus of the Modern Language Association.

Some sections of this essay were composed during the time made available to me by a grant from the Rockefeller Foundation, for which I am most grateful.

1. Mary Ellman, *Thinking About Women* (New York: Harcourt Brace Jovanovich, Harvest, 1968).

2. See Clifford Gertz, "Ideology as a Cultural System," in his *The Interpretation of Cultures: Selected Essays* (New York: Basic Books, 1973), p. 232.

3. Ibid., p. 204.

4. Lillian S. Robinson, "Cultural Criticism and the *Horror Vacui,*" *College English* 33, no. 1 (1972); reprinted as "The Critical Task" in her *Sex, Class, and Culture* (Bloomington: Indiana University Press, 1978), p. 51.

5. Elaine Showalter, *A Literature of Their Own: British Women Novelists From Brontë to Lessing* (Princeton: Princeton University Press, 1977), p. 36.

6. Adrienne Rich, "When We Dead Awaken: Writing as Re-Vision," *College English* 34, no. 1 (October 1972); reprinted in *Adrienne Rich's Poetry,* ed. Barbara Charlesworth Gelpi and Albert Gelpi (New York: W. W. Norton Co., 1975), p. 90.

7. Kate Millett, *Sexual Politics* (Garden City, N.Y.: Doubleday and Co., 1970).

8. Rebecca Harding Davis, *Life in the Iron Mills,* originally published in *The Atlantic Monthly,* April 1861; reprinted with "A Biographical Interpretation" by Tillie Olsen (New York: Feminist Press, 1972). Charlotte Perkins Gilman, "The Yellow Wallpaper," originally published in *The New England Magazine,* May 1892; reprinted with an Afterword by Elaine R. Hedges (New York: Feminist Press, 1973).

9. Nina Baym, *Woman's Fiction: A Guide to Novels by and about Women in America, 1820–70* (Ithaca: Cornell University Press, 1978).

10. In her *Feminine Consciousness in the Modern British Novel* (Urbana: University of Illinois Press, 1975), p. 3, Sydney Janet Kaplan explains that she is using the term "feminine consciousness" "not simply as some general attitude of women toward their own femininity, and not as something synonymous with a particular sensibility among female writers. I am concerned with it as a literary device: a method of characterization of females in fiction."

11. Patricia Meyer Spacks, *The Female Imagination* (New York: Avon Books, 1975), p. 6.

12. Ellen Moers, *Literary Women: The Great Writers* (Garden City, N.Y.: Doubleday and Co., 1976).

13. Showalter, *A Literature of Their Own,* p. 11.

14. Jean E. Kennard, *Victims of Convention* (Hamden, Conn.: Archon Books, 1978), pp. 164, 18, 14.

15. See Millett, *Sexual Politics,* pt. 3, "The Literary Reflection," pp. 235–361.

16. The phrase is Geertz's, "Ideology as a Cultural System," p. 214.

17. Lillian Robinson, "Criticism—and Self-Criticism," *College English* 36, no. 4 (1974) and "Criticism: Who Needs It?" in *The Uses of Criticism,* ed. A. P. Foulkes (Bern and Frankfurt: Lang, 1976); both reprinted in *Sex, Class, and Culture,* pp. 67, 80.

18. Rich, "When We Dead Awaken," p. 90.

19. Judith Fetterley, *The Resisting Reader: A Feminist Approach to American Fiction* (Bloomington: Indiana University Press, 1978).

20. Tillie Olsen, *Silences* (New York: Delacorte Press/Seymour Lawrence, 1978), pp. 239–40.

21. See Cheris Kramer, Barrie Thorne, and Nancy Henley, "Perspectives on Language and Communication," Review Essay in *Signs* 3, no. 3 (Summer 1978): 646.

22. See Adrienne Rich's discussion of the difficulty in finding authentic language for her experience as a mother in her *Of Woman Born* (New York: W. W. Norton and Co., 1976), p. 15.

23. Nelly Furman, "The Study of Women and Language: Comment on Vol. 3, no. 3" in *Signs* 4, no. 1 (Autumn 1978): 184.

24. Again, my phrasing comes from Geertz, "Thick Description: Toward an Interpretive Theory of Culture" in his *Interpretation of Cultures: Selected Essays* (New York: Basic Books, 1972), p. 9.

25. Julia Penelope Stanley and Susan W. Robbins, "Toward a Feminist Aesthetic," *Chrysalis*, no. 6 (1977): 63.

26. Hélène Cixous, "The Laugh of the Medusa," trans. Keith Cohen and Paula Cohen, *Signs* 1, no. 4 (Summer 1976): 87.

27. In *The Madwoman in the Attic: The Woman Writer and the Nineteenth-Century Literary Imagination* (New Haven: Yale University Press, 1979), Sandra M. Gilbert and Susan Gubar suggest that women's writings are in some sense "palimpsestic" in that their "surface designs conceal or obscure deeper, less accessible (and less socially acceptable) levels of meaning" (p. 73). It is, in their view, an art designed "both to express and to camouflage" (p. 81).

28. Consider, for example, Paul Boyers's reductive and inaccurate generalization that "what distinguishes ordinary books and articles about women from feminist writing is the feminist insistence on asking the same questions of every work and demanding ideologically satisfactory answers to those questions as a means of evaluating it," in his "A Case Against Feminist Criticism," *Partisan Review* 43, no. 4 (1976): 602. It is partly as a result of such misconceptions that we have the paucity of feminist critics who are granted a place in English departments which otherwise pride themselves on the variety of their critical orientations.

29. Ambivalent though he is about the literary continuity that begins with Homer, Harold Bloom nonetheless somewhat ominously prophesies "that the first true break . . . will be brought about in generations to come, if the burgeoning religion of Liberated Woman spreads from its clusters of enthusiasts to dominate the West," in his *A Map of Misreading* (New York: Oxford University Press, 1975), p. 33. On p. 36, he acknowledges that while something "as violent [as] a quarrel would ensue if I expressed my judgment" on Robert Lowell and Norman Mailer, "it would lead to something more intense than quarrels if I expressed my judgment upon . . . the 'literature of Women's Liberation.'"

30. Kennard, *Victims of Convention*, p. 14.

31. Rich, "When We Dead Awaken," p. 90.

32. The first is a proposition currently expressed by some structuralists and formalist critics; the best statement of the second probably appears in Georg Lukacs, *Writer and Critic* (New York: Grosset and Dunlap, 1970), p. 119.

33. David Couzens Hoy, "Hermeneutic Circularity, Indeterminacy, and Incommensurability," *New Literary History* 10, no. 1 (Autumn 1978): 166–67.

34. Bloom, *Map of Misreading*, p. 36.

35. John Dewey offered precisely this argument in 1934 when he insisted that a work of art "is recreated every time it is esthetically experienced. . . . It is absurd to ask what an artist 'really' meant by his product: he himself would find different meanings in it at different days and hours and in different stages of his own development." Further, he ex-

plained, "It is simply an impossibility that any one today should experience the Parthenon as the devout Athenian contemporary citizen experienced it, any more than the religious statuary of the twelfth century can mean, esthetically, even to a good Catholic today just what it meant to the worshipers of the old period," in *Art as Experience* (New York: Capricorn Books, 1958), pp. 108–109.

36. Charles Altieri, "The Hermeneutics of Literary Indeterminacy: A Dissent from the New Orthodoxy," *New Literary History* 10, no. 1 (Autumn 1978): 90.

37. Murray Krieger, *Theory of Criticism: A Tradition and Its System* (Baltimore: The Johns Hopkins University Press, 1976), p. 6.

38. See Stanley E. Fish, "Normal Circumstances, Literal Language, Direct Speech Acts, the Ordinary, the Everyday, the Obvious, What Goes without Saying, and Other Special Cases," *Critical Inquiry* 4, no. 4 (Summer 1978): 627–28.

39. Ibid., p. 643.

40. Virginia Woolf, "Women and Fiction," *Granite and Rainbow: Essays* (London: Hogarth, 1958), p. 81.

41. Cesare Segre, "Narrative Structures and Literary History," *Critical Inquiry* 3, no. 2 (Winter 1976): 272–73.

42. Ted Cohen, "Metaphor and the Cultivation of Intimacy," *Critical Inquiry* 5, no. 1 (Autumn 1978): 9.

43. From Adrienne Rich's "Transcendental Etude" in her *The Dream of a Common Language: Poems 1974–1977* (New York: W. W. Norton and Co., 1978), pp. 76–77.

44. Furman, "The Study of Women and Language," p. 184.

45. "A recurrent tendency in criticism is the establishment of false norms for the evaluation of literary works," notes Robert Scholes in his *Structuralism in Literature: An Introduction* (New Haven: Yale University Press, 1974), p. 131.

46. For a full discussion of the Glaspell short story which takes this problem into account, please see my "A Map for Re-Reading: Or, Gender and the Interpretation of Literary Texts," *New Literary History* 11 (1980): 451–67.

47. Olsen, *Silences*, p. 45.

48. Annette Kolodny, "Literary Criticism," Review Essay in *Signs* 2, no. 2 (Winter 1976): 420.

49. Scholes, *Structuralism in Literature*, pp. 144–45. These comments appear within his explication of Tzvetan Todorov's theory of reading.

50. I borrow this concise phrasing of pluralistic modesty from M. H. Abrams's "The Deconstructive Angel," *Critical Inquiry* 3, no. 3 (Spring 1977): 427. Indications of the pluralism that was to mark feminist inquiry were to be found in the diversity of essays collected by Susan Koppelman Cornillon for her early and ground-breaking anthology, *Images of Women in Fiction: Feminist Perspectives* (Bowling Green, Ohio: Bowling Green University Popular Press, 1972).

51. R. P. Blackmur, "A Burden for Critics," *The Hudson Review* 1 (1948): 171. Blackmur, of course, was referring to the way in which criticism makes us conscious of how art functions; I use his wording here because I am arguing that that same awareness must also be focused on the critical act itself. "Consciousness," he avers, "is the way we feel the critic's burden."

52. I have earlier elaborated my objection to prescriptive categories for literature in "The Feminist as Literary Critic," Critical Response in *Critical Inquiry* 2, no. 4 (Summer 1976): 827–28.

53. Scholes, *Structuralism in Literature*, pp. 151–52.

54. Lillian Robinson, "Dwelling in Decencies: Radical Criticism and the Feminist Perspective," *College English* 32, no. 8 (May 1971); reprinted in *Sex, Class, and Culture*, p. 11.

55. "Ideology bridges the emotional gap between things as they are and as one would have them be, thus insuring the performance of roles that might otherwise be abandoned

in despair or apathy," comments Geertz in "Ideology as a Cultural System," p. 205.

56. Ibid., pp. 220, 205.

57. I here follow Fredric Jameson's view in *The Prison-House of Language: A Critical Account of Structuralism and Russian Formalism* (Princeton: Princeton University Press, 1974), p. 107, that: "Ideology would seem to be that grillwork of form, convention, and belief which orders our actions."

ARCHIMEDES AND THE PARADOX OF FEMINIST CRITICISM

(1981)

I

Feminist thinking is really *re*thinking, an examination of the way certain assumptions about women and the female character enter into the fundamental assumptions that organize all our thinking. For instance, assumptions such as the one that makes intuition and reason opposite terms parallel to female and male may have axiomatic force in our culture, but they are precisely what feminists need to question—or be reduced to checking the arithmetic, when the issue lies in the calculus.

Such radical skepticism is an ideal intellectual stance that can generate genuinely new understandings; that is, reconsideration of the relation between female and male can be a way to reconsider that between intuition and reason and ultimately between the whole set of such associated dichotomies: heart and head, nature and history. But it also creates unusual difficulties. Somewhat like Archimedes, who to lift the earth with his lever required someplace else on which to locate himself and his fulcrum, feminists questioning the presumptive order of both nature and history—and thus proposing to remove the ground from under their own feet—would appear to need an alternative base. For as Archimedes had to stand somewhere, one has to assume something in order to reason at all. So if the very axioms of Western thought already incorporate the sexual teleology in question, it seems that, like the Greek philosopher, we have to find a standpoint off this world altogether.

Archimedes never did. However persuasively he established that the earth could be moved from its appointed place, he and the lever remained earthbound and the globe stayed where it was. His story may point another moral, however, just as it points to another science able to harness forces internally and apply energy from within. We could then conclude that what he really needed was a terrestrial fulcrum. My point here, similarly, will be that a terrestrial fulcrum, a standpoint from which we can see our conceptual universe whole but which nonetheless rests firmly on male ground, is what feminists really need. But perhaps because being at once on and off a world seems an improbable feat, the prevailing perspectives of feminist studies have located the scholar one place or the other.

Inside the world of orthodox and therefore male-oriented scholarship, a new category has appeared in the last decade, the category of women. Economics textbooks now draw us our own bell curves, histories of medieval Europe record the esoterica of convents and the stoning of adulterous wives, zoologists calibrate the orgasmic capacities of female chimpanzees. Indeed, whole books on "women in" and "women of" are fast filling in the erstwhile blanks of a questionnaire—one whose questions, however, remain unquestioned. They never asked before what the mother's occupation was, now they do. The meaning of "occupation," or for that matter of "mother," is generally not at issue.

It is precisely the issue, however, for the majority of feminist scholars who have taken what is essentially the opposite approach; rather than appending their findings to the existing literature, they generate a new one altogether in which women are not just another focus but the center of an investigation whose categories and terms are derived from the world of female experience. They respond to the Archimedean dilemma by creating an alternative context, a sort of female enclave apart from the universe of masculinist assumptions. Most "women's studies" have taken this approach and stressed the global, structural character of their separate issues. Women are no longer to be seen as floating in a man's world but as a coherent group, a context in themselves. The problem is that the issues and problems women define from the inside as global, men treat from the outside as insular. Thus, besides the exfoliation of reports on the state of women everywhere and a certain piety on the subject of pronouns, there is little indication of feminist impact on the universe of male discourse. The theoretical cores of the various disciplines remain essentially unchanged, their terms and methods are as always. As always, therefore, the intellectual arts bespeak a world dominated by men, a script that the occasional woman at a podium can hardly revise. Off in the enclaves of women's studies, our basic research lacks the contiguity to force a basic reconsideration of all research, and our encapsulated revisions appear inorganic (or can be made to appear inorganic) to the universal system they mean to address. Archimedes' problem was getting off the world, but ours might be getting back on.

For we have been, perhaps, too successful in constructing an alternative footing. Our world apart, our female intellectual community, becomes increasingly cut off even as it expands. If we have little control over being shunted aside, we may nonetheless render the isolation of women's scholarship more difficult. At least we ought not to accept it, as in a sense we do when we ourselves conflate feminist thought with thinking about women, when we remove ourselves and our lever off this man's world to study the history or the literature, the art or the anatomy of women alone. This essay is about devising a method for an alternative definition of women's studies as the investigation, from women's viewpoint, of everything, thereby finding a way to engage the dominant intellectual systems directly and organically: locating a feminist terrestrial fulcrum. Since feminist thinking is the thinking of an insurgent group that in the nature of things will never possess a world of its own, such engagement would appear a logical necessity.

Logical but also contradictory. To a degree, any analysis that rethinks the most basic assumptions of the thinking it examines is contradictory or at least contrary, for its aim is to question more than to explain and chart. From it we learn not so much the intricacies of how a particular mode of thinking works as the essential points to which it can be reduced. And nowhere is such an adversary rather than appreciative stance more problematical than it is in literary criticism. This is my specific subject here, the perils and uses of a feminist literary criticism that confronts the fundamental axioms of its parent discipline.

What makes feminist literary criticism especially contradictory is the peculiar nature of literature as distinct from the objects of either physical or social scientific study. Unlike these, literature is itself already an interpretation that it is the critic's task to decipher. It is certainly not news that the literary work is biased; indeed that is its value. Critical objectivity enters in only at a second level to provide a reliable reading, though even here many have argued that reading too is an exercise in creative interpretation. On the other hand, while biologists and historians will concede that certain a priori postulates affect their gathering of data, they always maintain that they have tried to correct for bias, attempting, insofar as this is ever possible, to discover the factual, undistorted truth. Therefore expositions of subjectivity are always both relevant and revelatory about the work of biologists and historians. But as a way of judging the literary work per se, exposing its bias is essentially beside the point. Not that literature, as the New Critics once persuaded us, transcends subjectivity or politics. Paradoxically, it is just because the fictional universe is wholly subjective and therefore ideological that the value of its ideology is almost irrelevant to its literary value. The latter instead depends on what might be thought of as the quality of the *apologia*, how successfully the work transforms ideology into ideal, into a myth that works to the extent precisely that it obscures its provenance. Disliking that provenance implies no literary judgment, for a work may be, from my standpoint, quite wrong and even wrongheaded about life and politics and still an extremely successful rendering of its contrary vision. Bad ideas, even ideas so bad that most of humanity rejects them, have been known to make very good literature.

I am not speaking here of what makes a work attractive or meaningful to its audience. The politics of a play, poem, or story may render it quite unreadable or, in the opposite case, enhance its value for particular people and situations. But this poses no critical issue, for what we like, we like and can justify that way; the problem, if we as feminists want to address our whole culture, is to deal with what we do not like but recognize as nonetheless valuable, serious, good. This is a crucial problem at the heart of feminism's wider relevance. No wonder we have tried to avoid it.

One way is to point out that "good" changes its definition according to time and place. This is true, but not true enough. Perhaps only because we participate in this culture even while criticizing it, we do (most of us) finally subscribe to a tradition of the good in art and philosophy that must sometimes be a political embarrassment—and what else could it be, given the entire history of both Western and Eastern civilizations and their often outright dependence on misogyny? Nor is it true enough, I believe, to argue that the really good writers and thinkers unconsciously and sometimes consciously rejected such misogyny. As couched in the analogous interpretation of Shylock as hero because Shakespeare could not really have been anti-Semitic, this argument amounts to second-guessing writers and their works in terms of a provincialism that seems especially hard to maintain in these linguistically and anthropologically conscious times. For such provincialism not only assumes that our view of things is universal and has always been the substance of reality but also that all other and prior representations were insubstantial. So when Shakespeare depicted bastards as scheming subversives, Jews as merchants of flesh, and women as hysterics, he meant none of it but was only using the local idiom. What he meant, thereby demonstrating his universality, was what we mean.

I want to suggest that we gain no benefit from either disclaiming the continuing value of the "great tradition" or reclaiming it as after all an expression of our own viewpoint. On the contrary, we lose by both. In the first instance, we isolate ourselves into irrelevance. In the second—denying, for example, that Shakespeare shared in the conventional prejudices about women—we deny by implication that there is anything necessarily different about a feminist outlook. Thus, discovering that the character of Ophelia will support a feminist interpretation may appear to be a political reading of *Hamlet*, but, in fact, by its exegetical approach it reaffirms the notion that the great traditions are all-encompassing and all-normative, the notion that subsumes women under the heading "mankind."

It seems to me perfectly plausible, however, to see Shakespeare as working within his own ideology that defined bastards, Jews, and women as by nature deformed or inferior, and as understanding the contradictions of that ideology without rejecting its basic tenets—so that, from a feminist standpoint, he was a misogynist—and as being nonetheless a great poet. To be sure, greatness involves a critical penetration of conventions but not necessarily or even frequently a radical rejection of them. If, in his villains, Shakespeare revealed the human being beneath the type, his characterization may have been not a denial of the type but a recognition of the complexity of all identity. The kingly ambition of the bastard, the "white" conscience of the Moor, the father love of the Jew, the woman's manly heart: these complexities are expressed in the terms of the contemporary ideology, and in fact Shakespeare uses these terms the more tellingly for not challenging them at the root.

But the root is what feminists have to be concerned with: what it means not to be a good woman or a bad one but to be a woman at all. Moreover, if a great writer need not be radical, neither need a great radical writer be feminist—but so what? It was only recently that the great Romantic poets conned us into believing that to be a great poet was to tell *the* absolute truth, to be the One prophetic voice for all Mankind. As the philosophy of the Other, feminism has had to reject the very conception of such authority—which, by extension, should permit feminist critics to distinguish between appreciative and political readings.

We should begin, therefore, by acknowledging the separate wholeness of the literary subject, its distinct vision that need not be ours—what the formalists have told us and told us about: its integrity. We need to acknowledge, also, that to respect that integrity by not asking questions of the text that it does not ask itself, to ask the text what questions to ask, will produce the fullest, richest reading. To do justice to Shelley, you do not approach him as you do Swift. But doing justice can be a contrary business, and there are aspects of the text that, as Kate Millett demonstrated,[1] a formalist explication actively obscures. If her intentionally tangential approach violated the terms of Henry Miller's work, for example, it also revealed aspects of the work that the terms had masked. But she would not claim,

I think, that her excavation of Miller's underlying assumptions had not done damage to his architecture.

The contradiction between appreciation and political analysis is not peculiar to feminist readings, but those who encountered it in the past did not resolve it either. In fact, they too denied it, or tried to. Sartre, for instance, argued in *What Is Literature?* that a good novel could not propound fascism. But then he also recognized that "the appearance of the work of art is a new event which cannot *be explained* by anterior data."[2] More recently, the Marxist Pierre Macherey has hung on the horns of the same dilemma by maintaining that the literary work is tied inextricably to the life that produces it, but, although not therefore "independent," it is nonetheless "autonomous" in being defined and structured by laws uniquely proper to it.[3] (I cite Sartre and Macherey more or less at random among more or less left-wing critics because theirs is a situation somewhat like that of feminists, though less difficult, many would argue, in that they already have a voice of their own. Perhaps for that reason, the position of black critics in a world dominated by whites would more closely resemble that of women. But at any rate, the large category to which all these belong is that of the literary critic who is also and importantly a critic of her/his society, its political system, and its culture.)

My point is simply that there is no reason to deny the limits of ideological criticism, its reduction of texts that, however, it also illuminates in unique ways. As feminists at odds with our culture, we are at odds also with its literary traditions and need often to talk about texts in terms that the author did not use, may not have been aware of, and might indeed abhor. The trouble is that this necessity goes counter not only to our personal and professional commitment to all serious literature but also to our training as gentlemen and scholars, let alone as Americans, taught to value, above all, value-free scholarship.

Doubtless the possibility of maintaining thereby a sympathetic appreciative critical posture is one of the attractions of dealing only or mainly with women's writings. With such material, ironically, it is possible to avoid political judgment altogether, so that the same approach that for some represents the integration into their work of a political commitment to women can serve Patricia Meyer Spacks to make the point that "criticism need not be political to be aware."[4] She means by this that she will be able to recognize and describe a distinct female culture without evaluating either it or its patriarchal context politically. Of course she understands that all vision is mediated, so that the very selection of texts in which to observe the female imagination is judgment of a kind. But it is not ideological or normative judgment; rather it is an "arbitrary decision" that "reflects the operations of [her] imagination," a personal point of view, a "particular sensibility" with no particular political outlook. The important thing is that her "perception of the problems in every case derived from her reading of the books; the books were not selected to depict preconceived problems."

Spacks seeks in this way to disavow any political bias; but even critics who have chosen a woman-centered approach precisely for its political implications reassure us about their analytical detachment. Ellen Moers stipulates in her preface to *Literary Women* that "the literary women themselves, their language, their concerns, have done the organizing of this book." At the same time she means the book to be "a celebration of the great women who have spoken for us all."[5] Her choice of subject has thus been inspired by feminist thinking, but her approach remains supposedly neutral for she has served only as an informed amanuensis. The uncharacteristic naïveté of this stance is enforced, I think, by Moers's critical ambivalence—her wish, on the one hand, to serve a feminist purpose, and her sense, on the other, that to do so will compromise the study as criticism. So she strikes a stance that should enable her to be, like Spacks, aware but not political. Since in posing a question one already circumscribes the answer, such analytical neutrality is a phantom, however; nor was it even Spacks's goal. Her method of dealing with women separately but traditionally, treating their work as she would the opus of any mainstream school, suits her purpose, which is to define a feminine aesthetic transcending sexual politics. She actively wants to exclude political answers. Moers, seeking to discover the feminist in the feminine, is not as well served by that method; and Elaine Showalter's explicitly feminist study, *A Literature of Their Own,*[6] suggests that a political criticism may require something like the methodological reverse.

Showalter wrote her book in the hope that it would inspire women to "take strength in their independence to act in the world" and begin to create an autonomous literary universe with a "female tradition" as its "center." Coming at the end of the book, these phrases provide a resonant conclusion, for she has shown women writing in search of a wholeness the world denies them and creating an art whose own wholeness seems a sure ground for future autonomy. But if, in an effort to flesh out this vision, one turns back to earlier discussions, one finds that there she has depicted not actual independence but action despite dependence—and not a self-defined female culture either, but a subculture born out of oppression and either stunted or victorious only at often-fatal cost. Women, she writes at the beginning of the book, form such a "subculture within the framework of a larger society," and "the female literary tradition comes from the still-evolving relationships between women writers and their society." In other words, the meaning of that tradition has been bound up in its dependence. Now, it seems to me that much of what Showalter wants to examine in her study, indeed much of what she does examine, resolves itself into the difference for writers between acting independently as men do and resisting dependence as women do. If her conclusion on the contrary conflates the two, it is because the approach she takes, essentially in common with Spacks and Moers, is not well suited to her more analytical goals.

Like theirs, her book is defined territorially as a description of the circumscribed world of women writers. *A Literature of Their Own* is thus "an attempt to fill in the terrain between [the Austen peaks, the Brontë cliffs, the Eliot range, and the Woolf hills] and to construct a more reliable map from which to explore the achievements of English women novelists." The trouble is that the map of an enclosed space describes only the territory inside the enclosure. Without knowing the surrounding geography, how are we to evaluate this woman's estate, whose bordering peaks we have measured anyway, not by any internal dimensions, but according to those of Mount Saint Dickens and craggy Hardy? Still less can one envision the circumscribed province as becoming independently global—hence probably the visionary vagueness of Showalter's ending. Instead of a territorial metaphor, her analysis of the world of women as a subculture suggests to me a more fluid imagery of interacting juxtapositions the point of which would be to represent not so much the territory as its defining borders. Indeed, the fe-male territory might well be envisioned as one long border, and independence for women not as a separate country but as open access to the sea.

Women (and perhaps some men not of the universal kind) must deal with their situation as a *pre*condition for writing about it. They have to confront the assump-tions that render them a kind of fiction in themselves in that they are defined by others, as components of the language and thought of others. It hardly matters at this prior stage what a woman wants to write; its political nature is implicit in the fact that it is she (a "she") who will do it. All women's writing would thus be congenitally defiant and universally characterized by the blasphemous argument it makes in coming into being. And this would mean that the autonomous indi-viduality of a woman's story or poem is framed by engagement, the engagement of its denial of dependence. We might think of the form this necessary denial takes (however it is individually interpreted, whether conciliatory or assertive) as analogous to genre, in being an issue, not of content, but of the structural formu-lation of the work's relationship to the inherently formally patriarchal language which is the only language we have.

Heretofore, we have tended to treat the anterior act by which women writers create their creativity as part of their lives as purely psychological, whereas it is also a conceptual and linguistic act: the construction of an enabling relationship with a language that of itself would deny them the ability to use it creatively. This act is part of their work as well and organic to the literature that results. Since men (on the contrary) can assume a natural capacity for creation, they be-gin there, giving individual shape to an energy with which they are universally gifted. If it is possible, then, to analyze the writings of certain men indepen-dently—not those of all men, but only of those members of a society's ruling group whose identity in fact sets the universal norm—this is because their writ-ings come into existence independent of prior individual acts. Women's litera-ture begins to take its individual shape before it is properly literature, which suggests that we should analyze it inclusive of its *ur*-dependence.

In fact, the criticism of women writers has of late more and more focused on the preconditions of their writing as the inspiration not only of its content but also of its form. The writer's self-creation is the primary concern of Sandra Gil-bert and Susan Gubar's *The Madwoman in the Attic*,[7] whose very title identifies glo-bal (therefore mad) denial as the hot core of women's art. This impressive culmination of what I have called the territorial approach to feminist criticism does with it virtually everything that can be done. In the way of culminations, it delivers us then before a set of problems that cannot be entirely resolved in its terms but that Gilbert and Gubar have uncovered. My earlier questioning can thus become a question: What do we understand about the world, about the whole culture, from our new understanding of the woman's sphere within it? This question looks forward to a development of the study of women in a universal context, but it also has retrospective implications for what we have learned in the female context.

Gilbert and Gubar locate the female territory in its larger context and examine the borders along which the woman writer defined herself. Coming into being—an unnatural being, she must give birth to herself—the female artist commits a double murder. She kills "Milton's bogey" and the specter Virginia Woolf called the "angel in the house," the patriarch and his wife, returning then to an empty universe she will people in her own image. Blasphemy was not until the woman artist was, and the world of women writers is created in sin and extends to a horizon of eternal damnation. For all women must destroy in order to create.

Gilbert and Gubar argue with erudition and passion, and their projection of the woman writer has a definitive ring. It also has a familiar and perhaps a contradictory ring. The artist as mad defiant blasphemer or claustrophobic deviant in a society that denies such a person soulroom is a Romantic image that not only applies also to men but does so in a way that is particularly invidious to women, even more stringently denying them their own identities than earlier ideologies did. That there be contradiction is only right, for when Blake hailed Satan as the hero of *Paradise Lost,* he cast heroism in a newly contradictory mold. Satan is archfiend and Promethean man, individualistic tyrant and revolutionary, architect and supreme wrecker of worlds. It should not be surprising that he is also at once the ultimate, the proto-exploiter of women, and a feminist model. But it does complicate things, as Gilbert and Gubar recognized: Mary Shelley found, in Milton, cosmic misogyny to forbid her creation—and also the model for her rebellion. But then, was her situation not just another version of the general Romantic plight, shared with her friends and relatives, poet-blasphemers all?

No, because she confronted a contradiction that superseded and preceded theirs; she was additionally torn and divided, forbidden to be Satan by Satan as well as by God, ambivalent about being ambivalent. If Satan was both demon and hero to the male poets, he offered women a third possibility, that of Byronic lover and master, therefore a prior choice: feminist assertion or feminine abandon. Here again, women had to act before they could act, choose before they could choose.

But it is just the prior choosing and acting that shape the difference between women's writing and men's that no study of only women's writing can depict. So, for instance, Gilbert and Gubar suggest that the monster in Mary Shelley's *Frankenstein* embodies in his peculiar horror a peculiarly female conception of blasphemy. It may well be, but I do not think we can tell by looking only at *Frankenstein.* At the least we need to go back and look at Satan again, not as a gloss already tending toward *Frankenstein* but as an independent term, an example of what sinful creation is—for a man. Then we need to know what it was for Mary Shelley's fellow Romantics. We might then see the extra dimension of her travail, being able to recognize it because it was extra—outside the requirements of her work and modifying that work in a special way. To reverse the frame of reference, if male critics have consistently missed the woman's aspect of *Frankenstein,* it may be only in part because they are not interested. Another reason could be that in itself the work appears as just another individual treatment of a common Romantic theme. Put simply, then, the issue for a feminist reading of *Frankenstein* is to distinguish its female version of Romanticism: an issue of relatedness and historicity. Women cannot write monologues; there must be two in the world for one woman to exist, and one of them has to be a man.

So in *The Madwoman in the Attic,* building on *Literary Women* and *A Literature of Their Own,* feminist criticism has established the historical relativity of the gender definitions that organize this culture; the patriarchal universe that has always represented itself as absolute has been revealed as man-tailored to a masculine purpose. It is not nature we are looking at in the sexual politics of literature, but history: we know that now because women have rejected the natural order of yin and yang and lived to tell a different tale. I have been arguing that, to read this tale, one needs ultimately to relate it to the myths of the culture it comments on. The converse is also true; in denying the normative universality of men's writing, feminist criticism historicizes it, rendering it precisely, as "men's writing." On the back cover of *The Madwoman in the Attic* Robert Scholes is quoted as having written that "in the future it will be embarrassing to teach Jane Austen, Mary Shelley, the Brontës, George Eliot, Emily Dickinson, and their sisters without consulting this book." Not so embarrassing, one would like to add, as it should be to teach Samuel Richardson, Percy Bysshe Shelley, Charles Dickens, William Makepeace Thackeray, Walt Whitman, and their brothers without consulting a feminist analysis.

Indeed, in suggesting here that women critics adopt a method of radical comparativism, I have in mind as one benefit the possibility of demonstrating thereby the contingency of the dominant male traditions as well. Comparison reverses the territorial image along with its contained methodology and projects instead, as the world of women, something like a long border. The confrontations along that border between, say, *Portrait of a Lady* and *House of Mirth*, two literary worlds created by two gods out of one thematic clay, can light up the outer and most encompassing parameters (perimeters) of both worlds, illuminating the philosophical grounds of the two cosmic models, "natures" that otherwise appear unimpeachably absolute. This border (this no-man's land) might have provided Archimedes himself a standpoint. Through the disengagements, the distancings of comparative analyses, of focusing on the relations between situations rather than on the situations themselves, one might be able to generate the conceptual equivalent of getting off this world and seeing it from the outside. At the same time, comparison also involves engagement by requiring one to identify the specific qualities of each term. The overabstraction of future visions has often been the flip side of nonanalytical descriptions of the present viewed only in its own internal terms. To talk about then and now as focuses of relations may be a way of tempering both misty fantasies and myopic documentations.

Thus the work of a woman—whose proposal to be a writer in itself reveals that female identity is not naturally what it has been assumed to be—may be used comparatively as an external ground for seeing the dominant literature whole. Hers is so fundamental a denial that its outline outlines as well the assumption it confronts. And such comparison works in reverse, too, for juxtaposed with the masculinist assumption we can also see whole the feminist denial and trace its limits. Denial always runs the risk of merely shaping itself in the negative image of what it rejects. If there is any danger that feminism may become trapped, either in winning for women the right to be men or in taking the opposite sentimental tack and celebrating the feminine identity of an oppressed past as ideal womanhood, these extremes can be better avoided when women's assumptions too can be seen down to their structural roots—from the other ground provided by men's writing.

Lest it appear that I am advocating a sort of comparison mongering, let me cite as a model, early blazing a path we have not followed very far, a study that on the surface is not at all comparative. Millett's *Sexual Politics* was all about comparison, however, about the abysses between standpoints, between where men stood to look at women and where women stood to be looked at. Facing these two at the book's starting point was Millett's construction of yet another lookout where a feminist might stand. As criticism per se, *Sexual Politics* may be flawed by its simplifying insistence on a single issue. But as ideological analysis, as model illuminator and "deconstructor," it remains our most powerful work. It is somewhat puzzling that, since then, so little has been written about the dominant literary culture whose ideas and methods of dominance were Millett's major concerns.[8] It may be that the critical shortcomings of so tangential an approach have been too worrisome. Certainly it is in reading the dominant "universal" literature that the contradictions of an ideological criticism become most acute. There are many ways of dealing with contradictions, however, of which only one is to try to resolve them. Another way amounts to joining a contradiction— engaging it not so much for the purpose of overcoming it as to tap its energy. To return one last time to the fulcrum image, a fulcrum is a point at which force is transmitted—the feminist fulcrum is not just any point in the culture where misogyny is manifested but one where misogyny is pivotal or crucial to the whole. The thing to look for in our studies, I believe, is the connection, the meshing of a definition of women and a definition of the world. And insofar as the former is deleterious, the connection will be contradictory; indeed, as the literary examples that follow suggest, one may recognize a point of connection by its contradictions. It will turn out, or I will try to show, that contradictions just such as that between ethical and aesthetic that we have tried to resolve away lest they belie our argument frequently are our firmest and most fruitful grounds. The second part of this essay will attempt to illustrate this use of contradiction through the example of the American sentimental novel, a kind of women's writing in which the contradiction between ideology and criticism would appear well-nigh overwhelming.

II

The problem is all too easily stated: the sentimental novels that were best-sellers in America from the 1820s to the 1870s were written and read mostly by women, constituting an oasis of women's writing in an American tradition otherwise unusually exclusively male. But this oasis holds scant nourishment; in plain words, most of the women's writing is awful. What is a feminist critic to do with it? It is not that as a feminist she must praise women unthinkingly, but there is little point either in her just contributing more witty summaries of improbable plots and descriptions of impossible heroines to enliven the literary histories. There hardly needs a feminist come to tell us that E. D. E. N. Southworth's cautionary tales are a caution; and as to whether Susan Warner's *Wide Wide World* does set "an all-time record for frequency of references to tears and weeping,"[9] there are others already counting. We might do best, with Elizabeth Hardwick, to simply let it alone. In her collection of more or less unknown women's writings,[10] Hardwick selected works that were commendable in their own rights and discarded most of what she read as "so bad I just had to laugh—I wasn't even disappointed. The tradition was just too awful in the nineteenth century."

Still, there it is, the one area of American writing that women have dominated and defined ostensibly in their own image, and it turned out just as the fellows might have predicted. It is gallant but also a little ingenuous of Hardwick to point out that men's sentimental writing was just as bad. For Hawthorne, whose *cri de coeur* against the "damned mob of scribbling women" still resonates in the hearts of his countrymen, did not invent the association between sentimentality and women. The scribbling women themselves did, ascribing their powers to draw readers deep into murky plots and uplift them to heavenly visions to the special gifts of a feminine sensibility. If there is no question of celebrating in the sentimentalists "great women who have spoken for us all," it seems just as clear that they spoke as women to women, and that, if we are to criticize the place of women in this culture, we need to account for the very large place they occupied—and still do; the sentimental mode remains a major aspect of literary commerce, still mostly written and read by women.

Although at bottom either way presents the same contradiction between politics and criticism, the sentimental novel would seem, therefore, to flip the problems encountered in *A Literature of Their Own, Literary Women*, and *The Madwoman in the Attic*. The issue there was to uncover new aspects of works and writers that had more or less transcended the limitations of the patriarchal culture—or failed and found tragedy. Inspired by their example, one had nonetheless to temper admiration with critical distance. Here the difficulty lies instead in tempering rejection with a recognition of kinship, kinship one is somewhat hesitant to acknowledge in that it rests on a shared subordination in which the sentimental novel appears altogether complicitous. For the sentimentalists were prophets of compliance, to God the patriarch as to his viceroys on earth. Their stories are morality dramas featuring heroines prone at the start to react to unjust treatment by stamping their feet and weeping rebellious tears, but who learn better and in the end find happiness in "unquestioning submission to authority, whether of God or an earthly father figure or society in general." They also find some more substantial rewards, Mammon rising like a fairy godmother to bestow rich husbands and fine houses. Conformity is powerful, and Henry Nash Smith's explication of it all has a definitive clarity: "The surrender of inner freedom, the discipline of deviant impulses into rapturous conformity, and the consequent achievement of both worldly success and divine grace merge into a single mythical process, a cosmic success story."[11] If that success is ill-gotten by Smith's lights, it can only appear still more tainted to a feminist critic whose focus makes her acutely aware that the sweet sellout is a woman and the inner freedom of women her first sale. With overgrown conscience and shrunken libido, the sentimental heroine enumerating her blessings in the many rooms of her husband's mansion is the prototype of that deformed angel Virginia Woolf urged us to kill.

To kill within ourselves, that is. Thus we return to the recognition of kinship that makes it necessary to understand the sentimentalists not only the way critics generally have explained them but also as writers expressing a specifically female response to the patriarchal culture. This is a controversial venture that has resulted thus far in (roughly defined) two schools of thought. One of these starts from Hawthorne's charge that the popular novels usurped the place of serious literature. The title of Ann Douglas's *Feminization of American Culture*[12] announces her thesis that the sentimentalists exploited a literary Gresham's law to debase the cultural currency with their feminine coin. But gold is at least hoarded, while this bad money devalued outright Hawthorne's and Melville's good. A tough, iconoclastic, and individualistic masculine high culture, the potential worthy successor of the tough Puritan ethos, was thus routed from the national arena by a conservative femininity that chained the arts to the corners of hearths and to church pews. Henceforth, and still today, a stultifying mass culture has emasculated the American imagination. Douglas does not blame women for this, for she sees them as themselves defined by their society. Even in the exploitation of their destructive power, she thinks, they meant well; nor would she wish for an equivalently simpleminded macho replacement to the feminized culture. But the implied alternative is nonetheless definitely masculine—in a good way, of course: strong, serious, and generously accepting of women who have abjured their feminine sensibilities. Not a hard thing to do, for if the choice is between Susan Warner and Melville, why were we not all born men?

That choice, however, is just the problem, its traditional limits generated by the Archimedean bind of trying to think about new issues in the old terms, when those terms do not merely ignore the new issues but deny them actively and thus force one instead into the old ways, offering choices only among them. The terms here are masculine and feminine as they participate in clusters of value that interpret American history and culture. It has been generally understood among cultural and social historians that the creative force in America is individualistic, active . . . masculine. Perhaps to a fault: Quentin Anderson would have liked the American self less imperially antisocial,[13] and before him Leslie Fiedler worried that its exclusive masculinity excluded heterosexual erotic love.[14] These analysts of American individualism do not necessarily come to judge it the same way, but they define it alike and alike therefore project as its logical opposition conformity, passive compliance, familialism . . . femininity. Huck Finn and Aunt Polly. The critical literature has until now mostly concentrated on Huck Finn, and *The Feminization of American Culture* completes the picture by focusing on Aunt Polly.

In the sense that its features are composed from real facts, "Aunt Polly" may well be a true picture. But her position in the composite American portrait, opposed in her trite conventionality to "his" rugged individualism, is not a function of facts alone but also of an interpretive scheme secured by a set of parallel dichotomies that vouch for one another: Aunt Polly is to Huck as feminine is to masculine; feminine is to masculine as Aunt Polly is to Huck. Only if we pull these apart will we be able to question the separate validity of either.

Potentially even more radically, Nina Baym[15] sets out to reconsider the component terms of the generally accepted dichotomy in the nineteenth century between female conformity and manly individualism, between female social conservatism and masculine rebellion. Representing the other school of thought about sentimentalism, this one in line with recent historical reconsideration of such ridiculed women's movements as temperance and revivalism, she argues that the women novelists too had their reasons. She answers Smith's accusation that the novels' "cosmic success story" pointed an arch-conservative moral by suggesting that for disenfranchised and property-deprived women to acquire wealth, social status, and some measure of control over their domestic environment could be considered a radical achievement, as ruling a husband by virtue of virtue might amount to subversion. As she sees it, "The issue [for the women in the novels] is power and how to live without it." They do not run their society and never hope to, so, short of revolution, no direct action can be taken. Even from their state of total dependence, however, these women can rise to take practical charge of their lives and acquire a significant measure of power by implementing the conservative roles to which the patriarchal society has relegated them. In this light, what Smith terms their "ethos of conformity" takes on another aspect and almost becomes a force for change, all depending on how you look at it.

Which is precisely the problem of this essay, emerging here with unusual clarity because both Smith and Baym approach the material ideologically. Even their descriptions, let alone their interpretations, show the effects of divergent standpoints. Consider how each summarizes the typical sentimental plot. Smith reports that *Wide Wide World* is the tale of "an orphan exposed to poverty and psychological hardships who finally attains economic security and high social status through marriage."[16] Baym reads the same novel as "the story of a young girl who is deprived of the supports she had rightly or wrongly depended on to sustain her throughout life and is faced with the necessity of winning her own way in the world" (p. 19). The second account stresses the role of the girl herself in defining her situation, so that the crux of her story becomes her passage from passivity to active engagement. On the contrary, with an eye to her environment and its use of her, Smith posits her as passive throughout, "exposed" at first, in the end married. Clearly this is not a matter of right or wrong readings but of a politics of vision.

It is as a discussion of the politics of vision that *Woman's Fiction* is perhaps most valuable. Baym has set out to see the novels from a different perspective, and indeed they look different. The impossible piety of the heroine, for instance, Baym views as an assertion of her moral strength against those who consider her an empty vessel, lacking ego and understanding and in need of constant supervision. Typically the heroine starts out sharing this view, taking herself very lightly and looking to the world to coddle and protect her. With each pious stand she takes over the course of the novel, she becomes more self-reliant, until by the end she has "developed a strong conviction of her own worth" (p. 19) and becomes a model for female self-respect. Thus, the heroine's culminating righteousness and its concomitant rewards, that from one viewpoint prove the opportunistic virtues of submission, indicate to Baym a new and quite rare emergence of female power manifested in the avalanche of good things with which the story ends. To Smith those cornucopia endings are the payoff for mindless acquiescence, sweets for the sweet ruining the nation's palate for stronger meat. For Douglas they are a banquet celebrating the women's takeover; a starving Melville is locked out. But for Baym the comfort in which the heroine rests at last is her hard-earned just reward, the sentimental cult of domesticity representing a pragmatic feminism aimed primarily at establishing a place for women under their own rule.

In that spirit, she sees a more grown-up kind of sense than do most critics in the novels' prudishness, pointing out that, when they were written, the Richardsonian model they otherwise followed had become a tale of seduction. The women novelists, she suggests, were "unwilling to accept . . . a concept of woman as inevitable sexual prey" (p. 26); in a world where sexual politics hardly offered women a democratic choice, they preferred to eschew sex altogether rather than be raped. Here again, point of view is all. One recalls that Fiedler had a more ominous reading. According to him, the middle-class ladies who wrote the sentimental fiction had "grown too genteel for sex" but, being female, they still yearned "to see women portrayed as abused and suffering, and the male as crushed and submissive in the end";[17] so they desexed their heroes by causing them to love exceptionally good girls with whom sex was unthinkable.

Without sharing Fiedler's alarm over the state of American manhood, one has to concede that the sentimental novel, with its ethereal heroines and staunchly buttoned heroes, was indeed of a rarefied spirituality. That its typical plot traced, instead of physical seduction, the moral regeneration and all-around strengthening of erstwhile helpless women would appear all to the good; it is surely an improvement for women to cease being portrayed as inevitable victims. But the fact is that the sentimental heroines, perhaps rich as models, are rather poor as characters. Those inner possibilities they discover in becoming self-sufficient seem paradoxically to quench any interior life, so that we nod in both senses of the word when such a heroine "looks to marry a man who is strong, stable and safe." For, "she is canny in her judgment of men, and generally immune to the appeal of a dissolute suitor. When she feels such attraction, she resists it" (p. 41). Quite right, except we actually wish she would not: do we then regret the fragile fair who fell instantly and irrevocably in an earlier literature, or the "graceful deaths that created remorse in all one's tormentors" (p. 25) and in the story some sparks of life?

Baym is well aware of the problem and offers two possible analyses. In the first place, she says, the women novelists never claimed to be writing great literature. They thought of "authorship as a profession rather than a calling, as work and not art. Often the women deliberately and even proudly disavowed membership in an artistic fraternity." So they intentionally traded art for ideology, a matter of political rather than critical significance. "Yet," she adds (and here she is worth quoting at length because she has articulated clearly and forcefully a view that is important in feminist criticism),

> I cannot avoid the belief that "purely" literary criteria, as they have been employed to identify the best American works, have inevitably had a bias in favor of things male—in favor, say of whaling ships rather than the sewing circle as a symbol of the human community; in favor of satires on domineering mothers, shrewish wives, or betraying mistresses rather than tyrannical fathers, abusive husbands, or philandering suitors; displaying an exquisite compassion for the crises of the adolescent male, but altogether impatient with the parallel crises of the female. While not claiming literary greatness for any of the novels introduced in this study, I would like at least to begin to correct such a bias by taking their content seriously. And it is time, perhaps—though this task lies outside my scope here—to reexamine the grounds upon which certain hallowed American classics have been called great. (pp. 14–15)

On the surface this is an attractive position, and, indeed, much of it is unquestionably valid; but it will not bear a close analysis. She is having it both ways, admitting the artistic limitations of the women's fiction ("I have not unearthed a forgotten Jane Austen or George Eliot, or hit upon even one novel that I would propose to set alongside *The Scarlet Letter*" [p. 14]) and at the same time denying the validity of the criteria that measure those limitations; disclaiming any ambition to reorder the literary canon, and, on second thought, challenging the canon after all—or rather challenging not the canon itself but the grounds for its selection.

There is much reason to reconsider these grounds, and such reconsideration should be one aim of an aggressive feminist criticism. But it has little to do with the problem at hand—the low quality of the women's fiction—that no reconsideration will raise. True, whaling voyages are generally taken more seriously than sewing circles, but it is also true that Melville's treatment of the whale hunt is a more serious affair than the sentimentalists' treatment of sewing circles. And the latter, when treated in the larger terms of the former, do get recognized—for example, Penelope weaving the shroud for Ulysses surrounded by her suitors, or, for that matter, the opening scene of *Middlemarch* in which two young girls quibble over baubles, situations whose resonance not even the most misogynist reader misses.

The first part of the explanation, that the women did not take *themselves* seriously, seems more promising. Baym tells us that they "were expected to write specifically for their own sex and within the tradition of their woman's culture rather than within the Great Tradition"; certainly, "they never presented themselves as followers in the footsteps of Milton or Spenser, seekers after literary immortality, or competitors with the male authors of their own time who were aiming at greatness" (p. 178). With this we come closer to the writing itself and therefore to the sources of its intrinsic success or failure. I want to stress intrinsic here as a way of recalling the distinction between a work as politics—its external significance—and as art. So when seeking to explain the intrinsic failures of the sentimentalists, one needs to look beyond their politics, beyond their relationships with publishers, critics, or audiences, to their relationship to writing as such. Melville wrote without the support of publishers, critics, and audiences—indeed, despite their active discouragement—so those cannot be the crucial elements. He did, however, have himself, he took himself seriously; as Whitman might have said, he *assumed* himself.

Now, no woman can assume herself because she has yet to create herself, and this the sentimentalists, acceding to their society's definition, did not do. To the extent that they began by taking the basic order of things as given, they forswore any claim on the primary vision of art[18] and saw themselves instead as interpreters of the established ethos, its guardians, or even, where needed, its restorers. My point is that, for all their virtual monopoly of the literary marketplace, the women novelists, being themselves conceived by others, were conceptually totally dependent. This means dependent on Melville himself and on the dominant culture of which he, but not they, was a full, albeit an alienated or even a reviled, member. His novel in the sentimental mode could take on sentimentalism because he had an alternative world on which to stand: himself. And although no one would wish on a friendly author the travail that brought forth *Pierre*, there it is nonetheless, the perfect example of what no woman novelist conceiving of herself not as an artist or maker but as a "professional"—read practitioner, implementor, transmitter, follower of a craft—could ever have written. *Pierre* does not know how to be acquiescently sentimental, it can only be *about* sentimentalism. The issue is self-consciousness, and in self-consciousness, it is self. With the example of Melville, we might then reconsider the relationship of the rebel to conventions. The rebel has his conventional definition too—that is, his is one possible interpretation of the conventions—so that he stands fully formed within the culture, at a leading edge. On the other hand, in this society women stand outside any of the definitions of complete being; hence perhaps the appeal to them of a literature of conformity and inclusion—and the extraordinary difficulty, but for the extraordinary few, of serious writing.

Indeed, Baym's defense of the women novelists, like that generally of the lesser achievement of women in any art, seems to me finally unnecessary. If history has treated women badly, it is entirely to be expected that a reduced or distorted female culture, one that is variously discouraged, embittered, obsessively parochial, or self-abnegating, will show it. There is little point then in claiming more than exists or in looking to past achievement as evidence of future promise: at this stage of history, we have the right, I think, simply to assert the promise.

If there is no cause for defensiveness, moreover, it does have its cost. In the case of the sentimental novel, for instance, too much apologia can obscure the hard question Baym implies but does not quite articulate, to wit, why are the ways in which the sentimental novel asserts that women can succeed precisely the ways that it fails as literature? *Is its ideological success tied to its artistic failure?* Is its lack of persuasiveness as art in some way the result of the strong ideological argument it makes for female independence? The issue, it seems, is not merely neglecting art for the sake of politics but actively sacrificing it. Which brings the discussion back to the Douglas thesis that since the sentimentalists universalized (Americanized) a debased feminine culture, the more powerful the women (authors and heroines both), the worse the literature and thereby the consequences for the whole culture. The great appeal of this argument is that it confronts squarely the painful contradiction of women becoming powerful not by overcoming but by exploiting their impotence.

I would like to suggest another possible explanation. The contradiction between the art and the politics of the sentimental novel arises, not surprisingly, at the point where the novelists confronted the tradition in which they were working and, for political reasons, rejected it formally: when they refused to perpetuate the image of the seduced and abandoned heroine and substituted in her stead the good girl who holds out to the happy (bitter or boring) end. The parent tradition is that of the novel of sensibility as it was defined in *Clarissa*. But before *Clarissa*, Richardson wrote *Pamela*, probably the prototype of the female "cosmic success story." Pamela begins powerless and ends up in charge, rewarded for her tenacious virtue (or her virtuous tenacity) by a commodious house, a husband, and all those same comforts of upper middle-class life that crowned the goodness of America's sentimental heroines. Indeed, *Pamela* had helped set up their new world, being the first novel actually printed here—by Benjamin Franklin, who understood both romance and commerce and knew how well they could work together. So did Pamela, of course, a superb pragmatist who not only foils a seducer but also turns him into a very nice husband. She is perhaps not so finely tuned or morally nice as her sentimental descendants, but she is quite as careful and controlled, as certain of her values, as unwilling to be victimized—and ultimately as triumphant. In contrast, Clarissa is helplessly enamored, seduced, destroyed. She is also the more interesting character and *Clarissa* the more complex story—can it be that weak victimized women make for better novels?

In the first part of this discussion, I made the point that the madness into which women artists are characterized as driven by social constraints needs to be compared with the similar state often attributed to male artists. The same need arises here, for male protagonists too are generally defeated, and, of course, Clarissa's seducer Lovelace dies along with her. But he is neither weak (in the helpless sense that she is) nor victimized; nor (to name doomed heroes at random) is Stendhal's Julien Sorel or Melville's Pierre. There is certainly no surprise in the contrast as such; we expect male characters to be stronger than female. The juxtaposition, however, may be suggesting something not already so evident: that as the distinctive individual identity of a male character typically is generated by his defiance, so that of a female character seems to come from her vulnerability, which thus would be organic to the heroine as a novelistic construct.

It seems reasonable to suppose that the novel, envisioning the encounter of the individual with his world in the modern idiom, posits as one of its structuring assumptions (an assumption that transcends the merely thematic, to function formally) the special form that sexual hierarchy has taken in modern times. The novel, we know, is organically individualistic: even when it deals with several equally important individuals, or attacks individualism itself, it is always about the unitary self versus the others. Moreover, it is about the generation, the becoming, of that self. I want to suggest that this process may be so defined as to require a definition of female characters that effectively precludes their becoming autonomous, so that indeed they would do so at the risk of the novel's artistic life.

Pamela represents the advent of a new form to deal with such new problems of the modern era as the transformation of the family and the newly dynamic mode of social mobility. *Pamela* works these out very well for its heroine, but there is something wrong in the resolution. Pamela's triumph means the defeat of Mr. B., who in his chastened state can hardly be the enterprising, potent entrepreneur that the rising middle class needs him to be. Her individualism has evolved at the cost of his; later Freud would develop a special term for such misadventures, but Richardson must already have known that this was not the way it should be.

At any rate, he resolved this difficulty in his next work simply by raising the social status of his heroine. Since she was a servant, Pamela's quest for independent selfhood necessarily took a public form. To affirm her value and remain in possession of her self, Pamela had to assert her equality publicly; to claim herself, she had, in effect, to claim power. But as an established member of the powerful class, Clarissa is in full possession of its perquisites, notably that of being taken as honorably marriageable by the lords of her world. Though it is true that her family's greed for yet more wealth and status precipitates her crisis, the problems she faces are really not those of upward mobility. Standing at the other end of that process, she is profoundly unhappy with its results and with the internal workings of her society. Her story is about the conflict within, the problems that arise inside the middle-class world; and its marvelously suited theater for exploring these is the self within.

In thus locating itself inside the life of its dominant class, the novel only followed suit after older genres. But what is peculiar to this genre is that it locates the internal problems of its society still deeper inside, inside the self. Richardson's earlier novel had retained an older conception more like that of Defoe, identifying the self externally—hence *Pamela*'s interpretation of romance as commerce. *Clarissa*, on the contrary, now treats commerce in the terms of romance. Pamela had projected her inner world outward and identified her growth as a character with the extension of her power. But this approach tends to vitiate the distinction between the private self and the world out there that is the powerful crux of middle-class identity. *Clarissa* takes that distinction as its theme, and the locale of the novel henceforth is the interior life. I want to propose the thesis that this interior life, *whether lived by man or woman, is female*, so that women characters define themselves and have power only in this realm. Androgyny, in the novel, is a male trait enabling men to act from their male side and feel from their female side.

One common feminist notion is that the patriarchal society suppresses the interior lives of women. In literature, at least, this does not seem altogether true, for indeed the interior lives of female characters are the novel's mainstay. Instead, it is women's ability to act in the public domain that novels suppress, and again Richardson may have shown the way. *Pamela* developed its heroine by reducing its hero (in conventional terms). This compensation was, in fact, inevitable as long as the characters defined themselves the same way, by using and expanding the individualistic potency of the self. Since by this scheme Pamela would be less of a person and a character if she were less active, she had to compete with Mr. B. to the detriment of one of them—to the detriment also of conjugal hierarchy and beyond that, of their society, whose resulting universal competitiveness must become dangerously atomizing and possibly centrifugal. In a middle-class society, however, the family unit is meant to generate coherence, in that the home provides both a base and a terminus for the competitive activity of the marketplace. The self-reliant man necessarily subsumes his family, chief among them his wife, to his own identity; it is in the middle-class society above all that a man's home is his castle. But how can this subsuming be accomplished without denying identity to women altogether and thus seriously undermining their potency as helpmates as well? The problem lies in retaining this potency, that can come only from individualism, without suffering the consequences of its realization in individualistic competition. Tocqueville particularly admired the way this problem had been resolved in America. Women in the New World were free, strong, and independent, but they *voluntarily* stayed home. In other words, their autonomy was realized by being freely abandoned, after which, of course, they ceased to exist as characters—witness their virtual absence from the American novel.

The European novelist, at least the English and the French, either less sanguine about the natural goodness of middle-class values or more embattled with older norms, saw that this voluntary subjugation could be problematical. If women too are people, and people are individualists, might they not rebel? If they succeeded in this, social order would crumble; indeed, they could not succeed because they did not have the power. But the possibility, arising from the most basic terms of middle-class thought and also doomed by the very prevalence of that thought, emerged as the central drama of the modern imagination. It is precisely the drama of the suppressed self, the self who assumes the universal duty of self-realization but finds its individual model in absolute conflict with society. Then as it becomes the more heroically individualistic, the more self-realized, the more it pushes toward inevitable doom. If there is a tragic dimension to the novel, it is here in the doomed encounter between the female self and the middle-class world. This is the encounter Gilbert and Gubar have observed and attributed, too exclusively I think, to women. The lack of a comparative dimension can tend to obscure the distinction between representation and reality, to fuse them so that the female self simply is woman, if woman maligned. But, as Flaubert might have pointed out, many a male novelist has represented at least part of himself as female.

Which is not to suggest that European novelists were champions of women's rights. Their interest lay rather in the metaphorical potential of the female situation to represent the great Problem of modern society, the reconciliation of the private and the public realms, once the cornerstone of the new social and economic order has been laid in their alienation. Such reconciliation is problematical in that the self, granted its freedom, may not willingly accept social control; it may insist on its separate and other privacy, on the integrity of its interior vision. Clarissa wants to be and do otherwise than her world permits, and with that impulse, her inner self comes into view. It grows as she becomes less and less able to project her will, or rather as the incursions against her private self become more ferocious. Who, and what, Clarissa is finally *is* that private world.

I want to stress that in championing her alienated private self, the novel is not taking the side of real women, or even of female characters as female. Recent praise of *Clarissa* as a feminist document, or vindications of its heroine's behavior against her patriarchal oppressors, have not dealt clearly enough with the fact that her creator was a patriarch. If nonetheless he envisioned his heroine in terms with which feminists may sympathize, it is, I believe, because he viewed her as representing not really woman but the interior self, the female interior self in all men—in all men, but especially developed perhaps in writers, whose external role in this society is particularly incommensurate with their vision, who create new worlds but earn sparse recognition or often outright scorn in this one.

It is in this sense, I think, that Emma Bovary was Flaubert, or Anna Karenina, Tolstoy, or Isabel Archer, James. But the way Dorothea Brooke was George Eliot reveals the edge of this common identification between author and heroine, for Eliot, though herself a successful woman, cannot envision Dorothea as equally so.[19] One might suppose that she at least could have imagined her heroine, if not triumphant like Julien Sorel, acting out her doom rather than accepting it. It is one thing for male novelists to assume that women are incapable of effective action, but that women do so as well is more disturbing. I am suggesting that George Eliot was compelled by the form of her story to tell it as she did, that the novel as a genre precludes androgynously heroic women while and indeed *because* it demands androgynous heroes. In other words, the novel demands that the hero have an interior life and that this interior life be metaphorically female. The exterior life, on the other hand, is just as ineluctably male (and the novel has its share of active, manly women). These identifications are not consciously made as being convenient or realistic, in which case they would be vulnerable to conscious change. They are assumed, built into the genre as organic and natural; for, if action were either male or female, we would be back with the potentially castrating Pamela. She, however, bent her considerable force to enter the middle class, endorsing its values wholeheartedly. A similarly active Clarissa, an effective and militant Dorothea, must threaten the entire order of things.

The novel is critical, it examines and even approves the rebellions of Clarissa and Dorothea, but only after signaling its more basic acceptance of an order it locates, beyond political attack, in nature itself. Julien Sorel's alienation, however Napoleonic his aspirations, is associated throughout with the female part of his character; his sensitivity, his inability to accept the life and values his father offers him, these are repeatedly described as feminine traits, and the final act that destroys him bespeaks his feminine nature, much to the dismay of his male friends. In the mirror world of this and other novels, femaleness is not conservative but potentially revolutionary. At the same time, it is by cultural definition incapable of active fulfillment. In taking woman as metaphor for the interior life, then, and—far from suppressing her—expanding hers almost to the exclusion of any other life, the novel both claimed its interior, individualistic, alienated territory and placed the limits of that territory within the structures of the middle-class world it serves. George Eliot could have made Dorothea strong only by challenging these structures or by accepting them and depicting her as manly, thereby telling another story, perhaps *The Bostonians*. And no more than this latter would that story have challenged the conventional notions of feminine and masculine.

There is a third possibility for the novel, which is to return to *Pamela* and close down the alienated interior realm by having Dorothea act not out of internal impulses but in response to social dictates. This is what the sentimental novel does, its heroines realizing themselves in society actively but in full accord with its values and imperatives. This solution to the subversive threat posed by female individualism amounts to reversing the Richardsonian development from *Pamela* to *Clarissa*. We have a precise representation of that reversal—wrought, one is tempted to think, in deference to the greater solidity of the middle-class ethic in this country—in the first American novel, *Charlotte Temple* (1791). Its author, Susanna Rowson, copies the contemporary fashion of *Clarissa*-like stories but then, apparently thinking the better of such downbeat endings, tacks on a *Pamela* conclusion. Charlotte Temple, the disastrously fragile English heroine of the story, is carried off by a soldier en route to America; no sooner carried off than pregnant, no sooner pregnant than abandoned, no sooner abandoned than wandering the icy roads in winter in slippers and a thin shawl. She is charitably taken in to a hospitable fireside only to pass away, leaving an innocent babe and much remorse all around. At this point, however, with one perfectly satisfactory ending in place, Susanna Rowson adds a second.

While neglecting Charlotte, her faithless lover Montraville has fallen in love with New York's most desirable belle, Julia Franklin, an orphaned heiress who is "the very reverse of Charlotte Temple." Julia is strong, healthy, and of independent means and spirit. Her guardian entertains "too high an opinion of her prudence to scrutinize her actions so much as would have been necessary with many young ladies who were not blest with her discretion." Though Montraville has behaved badly toward the hapless Charlotte, he seems to be capable of a New World redemption. Overcome by guilt at Charlotte's death, he fights a duel to avenge her honor and is dangerously wounded but, more fortunate than Lovelace, is nursed back to health by the discreet Julia. A representative of the new American womanhood, far too sensible to be tempted by rakes, far too clear about the uses of romantic love ever to separate it from marriage, Julia has accomplished the "Pamela" reform. She marries Montraville, and he becomes one of New York's most upright (and affluent) citizens, the fallen seducer risen a husband through the ministrations of a woman who is not merely good but also strong—strong, of course, in being all that she should be. Thus in Julia Franklin the private and the public selves are one, and the novel, with no relation between them to explore and therefore no way or need to envision the private, comes to a speedy end. About Charlotte a far better novel could have and has been written, but about Julia really nothing but exemplary tales for young girls and their spinster aunts. Pioneer mother of sentimental heroines, she deeds them an ability to take care of themselves (by taking care) that Baym rightly applauds from a feminist viewpoint but that effectively does them in as literature. This implies a possibility no less drastic than that the novel, evolved to deal with the psychological and emotional issues of a patriarchal society, may not permit a feminist interpretation.

The possibility that an impotent feminine sensibility is a basic structure of the novel, representing one of the important ways that the novel embodies the basic structures of this society, would suggest more generally that the achievement of female autonomy must have radical implications not only politically but also for the very forms and categories of all our thinking. Yet as students of this thinking, we are not only implicated in it but many of us committed to much of it. Literary criticism especially, because it addresses the best this thinking has produced, exposes this paradox in all its painful complexity—while also revealing the extraordinary possibility of our seeing the old world from a genuinely new perspective.

This analysis of novelistic form has been speculative, of course, a way of setting the issues of women's writing in the context of the whole literature in order to illustrate the uses of a comparative viewpoint as an alternative footing at the critical distance needed for re-vision. It has also been an exercise in joining rather than avoiding the contradiction between ideological and appreciative criticism on the supposition that the crucial issues manifest themselves precisely at the points of contradiction. As a method this has further implications I cannot pursue here. Let me suggest only that to focus on points of contradiction as the places where we can see the whole structure of our world most clearly implies the immanent relativity of all perception and knowledge. Thus, what appears first as a methodological contradiction, then becomes a subject in itself, seems finally to be shaping something like a new epistemology. But then, it is only right that feminism, as rethinking, rethink thinking itself.

NOTES

For their numerous helpful suggestions and suggestive objections, I am grateful to Sacvan Bercovitch, Rachel Blau DuPlessis, Carolyn Heilbrun, Evelyn Keller, Helene Moglen, Sara Ruddick, Catharine Stimpson, and Marilyn Young.

1. Kate Millett, *Sexual Politics* (Garden City, N.Y.: Doubleday & Co., 1970).

2. Jean-Paul Sartre, *What Is Literature?* (New York: Harper Colophon, 1965), p. 40; emphasis in original.

3. Pierre Macherey, *Pour une Théorie de la production littéraire* (Paris: Librairie François Maspero, 1966), pp. 66–68.

4. Patricia Meyer Spacks, *The Female Imagination* (New York: Avon Books, 1976), pp. 5, 6.

5. Ellen Moers, *Literary Women: The Great Writers* (Garden City, N.Y.: Doubleday & Co., 1976), p. xvi.

6. Elaine Showalter, *A Literature of Their Own: British Women Novelists from Brontë to Lessing* (Princeton, N.J.: Princeton University Press, 1977), pp. 11–12, 319.

7. Sandra Gilbert and Susan Gubar, *The Madwoman in the Attic: The Woman Writer and the Nineteenth-Century Literary Imagination* (New Haven, Conn.: Yale University Press, 1979). The chapter referred to at some length in this discussion is chap. 7, "Horror's Twin: Mary Shelley's Monstrous Eve."

8. I want to cite two works, one recently published and one in progress, that do deal with the traditions of male writing. Judith Fetterley in *The Resisting Reader: A Feminist Approach to American Fiction* (Bloomington: Indiana University Press, 1978) writes that women should "resist the view of themselves presented in literature by refusing to believe what they read, and by arguing with it, begin to exercize the male ideas and attitudes they have absorbed." Lee Edwards in her *Psyche as Hero: Female Heroism and Fictional Form* (Middletown, Conn.: Wesleyan University Press, 1984) expresses the somewhat different but related purpose of reclaiming language and mythology for women. My objections to both these approaches will be clear from the essay. Let me add here only that I also find them nonetheless extremely suggestive and often persuasive.

9. Henry Nash Smith, "The Scribbling Women and the Cosmic Success Story," *Critical Inquiry* 1 no. 1 (September 1974): 49–70.

10. Elizabeth Hardwick, *Rediscovered Fiction by American Women* (New York: Arno Press, 1978).

11. Smith, p. 51.

12. Ann Douglas, *The Feminization of American Culture* (New York: Avon Books, 1978).

13. Quentin Anderson, *The Imperial Self* (New York: Alfred A. Knopf, Inc., 1971).

14. Leslie Fiedler, *Love and Death in the American Novel* (New York: Delta Books, 1966).

15. Nina Baym, *Woman's Fiction: A Guide to Novels by and about Women in America, 1820–70* (Ithaca, N.Y.: Cornell University Press, 1978). Page numbers indicated in text.

16. Smith, p. 49.

17. Fiedler, pp. 259–60.

18. I am aware that this analysis assumes a modern psychology of art, that "creation" has not always been the artist's mission, or tacit acceptance of the established ethos considered fatal. But we are here speaking of the nineteenth century, not of all time; and writers who did not challenge their society's values would also not have questioned its fundamental construction of artistic identity as individualistic and as authentically creative.

19. For an illuminating discussion of this phenomenon—of women novelists being unable to imagine female characters as strong as themselves—see Carolyn Heilbrun, "Women Writers and Female Characters: The Failure of Imagination," in *Reinventing Womanhood* (New York: W. W. Norton & Co., 1979), pp. 71–92.

A CRITICISM OF OUR OWN

autonomy and assimilation in afro-american and feminist literary theory

(1989)

~~~~~~

THE OTHER WOMAN

In the summer of 1985, I was one of the speakers at the annual conference on literary theory at Georgetown University. On the first morning, a distinguished Marxist theorist was introduced, and as he began to read his paper, there appeared from the other side of the stage a slender young woman in a leotard and long skirt who looked like a ballet dancer. Positioning herself a few feet from the speaker, she whirled into motion, waving her fingers and hands, wordlessly moving her lips, alternating smiles and frowns. There were murmurs in the audience; what could this mean? Was it a protest against academic conferences? A Feifferesque prayer to the muse of criticism? A celebratory performance of the Althusserian two-step? Of course, as we soon realized, it was nothing so dramatic or strange. Georgetown had hired this young woman from an organization called Deaf Pride to translate all the papers into sign language for the hearing-impaired.

Yet from the perspective of the audience, this performance soon began to look like a guerrilla theatre of sexual difference which had been staged especially for our benefit. After the first ten minutes, it became impossible simply to *listen* to the famous man, immobilized behind the podium. Our eyes were drawn instead to the nameless woman, and to the eloquent body language into which she mutely translated his words. In this context, her signs seemed uncannily feminine and Other, as if we were watching a Kristevan ambassador from the semiotic, or the ghost of a Freudian hysteric back from the beyond. Anna O. is alive and well in Georgetown!

The feminist implications of this arrangement were increasingly emphasized, moreover, throughout the first day of the conference, because, although the young woman reached ever more dazzling heights of ingenuity, mobility, and grace, not one of the three white male theorists who addressed us took any notice of her presence. No one introduced her; no one alluded to her. It was as if they could not see her. She had become transparent, like the female medium of the symbolists who, according to Mary Ann Caws, "served up the sign, conveying it with fidelity, patience, and absolute personal silence. She herself was patiently ruled out."[1]

Sitting in the audience that first morning, I wondered what would happen when *I* was introduced as the fourth speaker. I had wild fantasies that Georgetown would provide a bearded male interpreter who would translate my paper into the rhetoric of deconstruction. (It turned out that there were two young women who alternated the task of interpretation. This does not seem to be a man's job.) I wondered too how I should speak from the position of power as the "theorist" when I also identified with the silent, transparent woman? The presence of the other woman was a return of the repressed paradox of female authority, the paradox Jane Gallop describes as fraudulence: "A woman theoretician is already an exile; expatriated from her *langue maternelle*, she speaks a paternal language; she presumes to a fraudulent power."[2] The translator seemed to represent not only the *langue maternelle*, the feminine other side of discourse, but also the Other Woman of feminist discourse, the woman outside of academia in the "real world," or the Third World, to whom a Feminist critic is responsible, just as she is responsible to the standards and conventions of criticism.[3] Gayatri Chakravorty Spivak has reminded us that she must always be acknowledged in our work: "Who is the other woman? How am I naming her? How does she name me?"[4]

At the Georgetown conference, my awareness of the Other Woman was shared by the other women on the program; all of us, in our presentations, introduced the interpreter, and changed our lectures in order to work with her presence. Yet the only male speaker who took notice of the interpreter was Houston Baker. By the time he spoke on the second day, Baker had learned enough sign language to produce a virtuoso translation of the beginning of his own talk, and to work with the translator in a playful duet.

The Georgetown conference was not the first time that Afro-American and feminist critics have found ourselves on the same side of otherness, but it was certainly one of the most dramatic. For those of us who work within "oppositional" or cultural criticisms—black, socialist, feminist, or gay—questions of the critic's double consciousness, double audience, and double role come with the territory and arise every day. They are not just the sort of global questions Terry Eagleton poses in *Literary Theory*, as to whether an analysis of the Lacanian imaginary can help welfare mothers, but more mundane problems of ethnicity and ethics: how we will answer the mail, how we will conduct ourselves in the classroom or on the podium, and how we will act not only in symbolic relationships but also in real encounters with constituencies inside and outside of academia.

In this essay, I briefly sketch out the parallel histories of Afro-American and feminist literary criticism and theory over the past twenty-five years, in order to learn from our mutual experience in relation to the dominant culture. This may seem like a strange moment for such a project. In both feminist and Afro-American criticism, the Other Woman, the silenced partner, has been the black woman, and the role played by black feminist critics in bridging the two schools is controversial. While black and white feminists have objected to the sexism of black literary history, black women have also challenged the racism of feminist literary history. Black male writers have protested against the representation of black men in the fiction of Afro-American women novelists, and Ishmael Reed's latest novel, *Reckless Eyeballing* (1986), imagines a violent vengeance on feminists in general and black feminist writers in particular.

Yet this record of misunderstanding obscures what I think are the strong and important connections between the two kinds of cultural criticism; we have much to gain by a dialogue.[5] Both feminist and Afro-American criticism have brought together personal, intellectual, and political issues in our confrontations with the Western literary tradition. We have both followed traditional patterns in the institutionalization of critical movements, from our beginnings in a separatist cultural aesthetics, born out of participation in a protest movement; to a middle stage of professionalized focus on a specific text-milieu in an alliance with academic literary theory; to an expanded and pluralistic critical field of expertise on sexual or racial difference. Along with gay and post-Colonial critics, we share many critical metaphors, theories, and dilemmas, such as the notion of a double-voiced discourse, the imagery of the veil, the mask, or the closet; and the problem of autonomy versus mimicry and civil disobedience.

In abandoning marginal territories of our own for places in the poststructuralist critical wilderness, do black and feminist critics also risk exchanging authenticity for imitation, and self-generated critical models for what Lisa Jardine calls Designer Theory? If we oppose the idea that women should have the exclusive franchise on "gender" or blacks the franchise on "race," what can be the distinguishing idiom or role of the black or feminist critic, and how do we identify the place from which we speak? Can we make the compromises necessary for acceptance by the mainstream, and still work for a criticism of our own? Or is the dream of an alternative criticism which is "simultaneously subversive and self-authenticating" the most utopian of all sub-cultural fantasies?[6]

THE BLACK CRITICAL REVOLUTION

In a splendidly argued essay called "Generational Shifts and the Recent Criticism of Afro-American Literature," Houston Baker has drawn on the work of Thomas Kuhn and Lewis Feuer to account for the transformations within Afro-American criticism from the 1950s to the early 1980s. He suggests that intergenerational conflict and the pressures of ascendant class interests can explain the movement towards alliance with the mainstream.[7] While Baker's essay is the most important and coherent account we have of the black critical revolution, his concept of the "generational shift" still raises a number of problems. First of all, critics cannot be assigned to generations with any precision, since, as David Riesman reminds us, people "are not born in batches, as are pancakes, but are born continuously."[8] The shifts within the critical fields, moreover, cannot be seen simply in generational terms, since in the humanities, intelligent people often transform and revise their theoretical positions in the light of new ideas, rather than stubbornly clinging to their original paradigms unto death. Within feminist criticism, indeed, the tendency of such writers as Toril Moi to construct rigid binary oppositions of feminist thought without regard for the complex permutations and exchanges within feminist discourse today, ignores the historical contexts in which ideas began, and the process of self-criticism and revision which has kept them sharp.[9]

A second problem with Baker's essay, and with Afro-American critical history in general, is that it does not take sufficient account of gender, and of the role of black women in shaping both literary and critical discourse. In using a number of his categories, then, I have tried to rethink them as well in the light of black feminist writing.

Before the Civil Rights Movement, criticism of Afro-American literature was dominated by "integrationist poetics"—skepticism about a unified black consciousness, and the ambition to have black writers merge with the mainstream of the American literary tradition. This view was articulated in the 1940s and 1950s by such male writers and scholars as Richard Wright, Arthur P. David, and Sterling Brown, who denied any specificity to "Negro writing" and insisted that black literature should measure up to and be judged by the standards of the dominant critical community. As Davis wrote in an introduction to *The Negro Caravan* in 1941, "the Negro writes in the forms evolved in English and American literature. . . . The editors considered Negro writing to be American writing, and literature by American Negroes to be a segment of American literature."[10] Since black Americans were promised equal rights under such legislation as the 1954 Supreme Court decision, so too, integrationist critics hoped, "Negro writing" would win an equal place in American literary culture. Meanwhile, they argued, black writers "must demand a single standard of criticism," and reject any special consideration on the basis of race. The occasional success of a writer like Ralph Ellison was taken to prove that a serious black artist would be recognized.

Yet integrationist poetics rested on the optimistic and deluded belief that a "single standard of criticism" could respond equitably and intelligently to Afro-American writing, that the "single" standard could be universal, rather than a cultural straitjacket based on the limited and exclusive literary values of an elite.[11] In practice, black writing was often viewed by white critics using the excuse of integrationist poetics as inferior or flawed. Moreover, even when black male writers won recognition, novels by black women such as Ann Petry's *The Street* (1946) and Gwendolyn Brooks's *Maud Martha* (1953) were marginalized by the black and white male literary communities. As Mary Helen Washington has argued, the "real 'invisible man' of the 1950s was the black woman."[12]

Integrationist poetics, however, was challenged in the 1960s by the new political ideology which Stokely Carmichael christened "Black Power." Calling for racial leadership and identity, and for a rejection of the racist standards masked as equality offered by white society, Black Power generated the cultural forms of the Black Arts movement, led by Afro-American writers, artists, and intellectuals such as Amiri Baraka (LeRoi Jones), Larry Neal, Addison Gayle, Jr., and Stephen Henderson. These leaders of the black male intelligentsia insisted on the uniqueness and authenticity of black expression, especially in folk forms and music, and rejected the idea that a uniform standard of criticism derived from white culture could be adequate to the interpretation and evaluation of Black Art. Indeed, Black Art proposed "a radical reordering of the Western cultural aesthetic . . . a separate symbolism, mythology, critique, and iconology."[13] The term "negritude," originating in Paris, the Caribbean, and Francophone Africa, celebrated the existence of a unique black artistic consciousness transcending nationality. Via the concept of negritude, as Melvin Dixon has explained, a "generation of blacks dispersed through the world reclaimed a part of their identity as members of the African diaspora."[14]

In the United States, the Black Aesthetic attempted to produce "a distinctive code for the creation and evaluation of black art."[15] "Blackness" itself became an ontological and critical category for assessing Afro-American literature. Stephen Henderson, one of the major theorists of the Black Aesthetic, argued that the black poem must not be considered in isolation, as the New Critics had maintained, but as a verbal performance in the fullest contexts of the "Black Experience," the "complex galaxy of personal, social, institutional, historical, religious, and mythical meanings that affect everything we say or do as Black people sharing a common heritage."[16] Its value could be determined only by the black interpretive community which shared the "Soul Field" of Afro-American culture.

Thus the Black Aesthetic offered the possibility of an autonomous and coherent black literary-critical discourse, not merely imitative of or parasitic on the white tradition, but in possession of its own roots, themes, structures, terms, and symbols from Afro-American culture. Moreover, the theoretical privileging of the black interpretive community gave the individual black critic a kind of cultural authority that enabled him or her to rise within the profession. As Baker notes, the predication of blackness as a "distinct and positive category of existence . . . was not only a radical political act designed to effect the liberation struggles of Afro-America, but also a bold critical act designed to break the interpretive monopoly on Afro-American expressive culture that had been held from time immemorial by a white liberal-critical establishment that set 'a single standard of criticism.'"[17]

The importance of the Black Aesthetic in the establishment of Afro-American literature cannot be overestimated. But to many black intellectuals, the Black Aesthetic also appeared narrow, chauvinistic, mystical, and theoretically weak. If only black critics were qualified by virtue of their racial experience to interpret black literature, they feared, it would remain ghettoized forever.

In practice, too, the theoretical privileging of the revolutionary black artist and the black critical imagination was open to charges of sexism; the major texts of the Black Aesthetic ignored or patronized women's imaginative and critical writing, just as the Black Power movement, in Stokely Carmichael's other notorious phrase, defined the position of women as "prone."[18] By 1970, beginning with the publication of Toni Morrison's *The Bluest Eye*, black feminist writers and critics began to make their voices heard within the literary community. Alice Walker was teaching courses on black women writers at Wellesley and the University of Massachusetts in the early 1970s, and leading others such as Toni Cade Bambara in "looking for Zora"—carrying out the quest for Zora Neale Hurston, who had been ignored by male critics of the Black Aesthetic, as the literary and critical foremother of the black female literary tradition. Black feminist critics such as Barbara Smith, Mary Helen Washington, Gloria Hull, and Barbara Christian raised important questions about the place of women within the Afro-American literary canon, and within the decade, some male theorists of the Black Aesthetic, including Stephen Henderson and Amiri Baraka, reconsidered their earlier positions. "When Black women discovered a political context that involved both race and gender," Henderson wrote in the introduction to Mari Evans's *Black Women Writers* (1983), "Our history in this country took a special turn, and our literature made a quantum leap toward maturity and honesty."

Yet even when the question of sexism was addressed, there were blatant theoretical weaknesses in the Black Aesthetic. Their concept of "race" was romantic and ideological; they ignored new developments within literary criticism. As Houston Baker concludes:

> The defensive inwardness of the Black Aesthetic—its manifest appeal to a racially-conditioned, revolutionary, and intuitive standard of critical judgment—made the new paradigm an ideal instrument of vision for those who wished to usher into the world new and *sui generis* Afro-American objects of investigation. Ultimately, though, such introspection could not answer the kinds of theoretical questions occasioned by the entry of these objects into the world. In a sense, the Afro-American literary-critical investigator had been given—through a bold act of the critical imagination—a unique literary tradition but no distinctive theoretical vocabulary with which to discuss this tradition.[19]

The political collapse of the Black Power movement, the advent of women's liberation, and the impact of European literary theory in the United States, all led to the demise of the Black Aesthetic. It was succeeded in the late 1970s by a new wave of young black intellectuals, benefitting from the academic prestige the Black Aesthetic had won for black writing, yet skeptical of the cultural claims of the Black Arts movement, and opposed to its separatist policies and poetics. Trained in such deconstructionist centers as Cornell and Yale, these critics sought to establish a "sound theoretical framework for the study of Afro-American literature," by situating it within the discourse of poststructuralist literary theory. Instead of seeing themselves primarily as spokesmen for art in the black community, with the mission of helping to create a revolutionary black literary consciousness in American society, they defined themselves as Afro-American specialists in the theoretical community, with the goal of rendering "major contributions to contemporary theory's quest to 'save the text.'"[20]

Among the central critical texts of the generation Houston Baker calls the "reconstructionists" are two major anthologies, *Afro-American Literature: The Reconstruction of Instruction* (1979), edited by Robert B. Stepto and Dexter Fisher; and *Black Literature and Literary Theory* (1984), edited by Henry Louis Gates, Jr. Stepto's "Introduction" to *Afro-American Literature* argues for a mixture of formal and cultural approaches to the black literary text, which is still seen as the object of a black critical practice, and as the primary subject of a sophisticated and formalized Afro-American pedagogy. *Afro-American Literature*, published by the Modern Language Association, represented the intersection of Afro-American studies and the English department. It suggested ways that black or white teachers of American literature could learn to be competent readers of Afro-American writing.

Gates's anthology goes considerably further, and could easily be subtitled "the reconstruction of deconstruction." Dedicated to the memories of Charles Davis and Paul de Man, *Black Literature and Literary Theory* presents itself in its structure, themes, and rhetoric, as a "two-toned" critical discourse, poised between black studies and the Yale School. Gates defines his textual territory as African, Caribbean, and Afro-American literatures, and his purpose as the application of contemporary literary theory to black literature. The anthology begins with Gates's own dazzling manifesto of black deconstruction, "Criticism in the Jungle." Like Ishmael Reed's *Mumbo Jumbo* (1972), a central novel in Gates's canon of black literature, which provides the epigraph to the essay, the title itself is double-voiced. Gates parodies or signifies upon Geoffrey Hartman's manifesto of rhetorical criticism, *Criticism in the Wilderness*, published in 1980; he alludes ironically to a stereotyped image of primitive and exotic African origins (cf. Vachel Lindsay's "The Congo") and thus literalizes the "sacred jungle" of Hartman's text; and he slyly suggests that black theory must make its way not only in the indeterminate heart of darkness and in the pan-African cultural jungle (the home of the "signifying monkey" and the Tar Baby), but also in the far more dangerous blackboard jungle of professional critical debate.

Gates sees his mission as one of saving the black text from the political and ideological contexts which have repressed its signifying systems, in treating it more as sociology, anthropology, or a document of the black experience, than as art. If the black tradition is to move "into the mainstream of critical debate in the profession," it must free itself from polemic and apply the lessons of formalism, structuralism, and poststructuralism. Gates is a bold and confident spokesman for this new program:

> The black literary tradition now demands, for sustenance and for growth, the sorts of reading which it is the especial province of the literary critic to render; and these sorts of reading will all share a fundamental concern with the nature and functions of figurative language as manifested in specific texts. No matter to what ends we put our readings, we can never lose sight of the fact that a text is not a fixed "thing" but a rhetorical structure which functions in response to a complex set of rules. It can never be related satisfactorily to a reality outside itself merely in a one-to-one relation.[21]

Two major problems came to the fore, however, in the reconstructionist project. First, who is qualified to be a critic of black literature? Second, can black criticism appropriate white or Western literary theory without sacrificing its hard-won independence and individuality? In the earlier phases of black criticism, black critics were first the reluctant or de facto partisans of "Negro writing" and then the passionate advocates of "black literature." During the phase of the Black Aesthetic, black artists and intellectuals who had become frustrated by the condescension or indifference of the white literary establishment toward Afro-American writing staked their own claim to a privileged critical authority within the black cultural tradition. With the early reconstructionist phase, however, the emphasis on the blackness of the ideal critic was abandoned in the interests of establishing black literature in the canon, and replaced by a focus on professional expertise. For Stepto and Fisher in 1979, the teacher of Afro-American literature need no longer be black, and blackness is no guarantee of authority in deciphering the text. Rather, the teacher must be trained to read the "ingrained cultural metaphors," "coded structures," and "poetic rhetoric" of the Afro-American text.[22]

By 1984, as Gates asserts, the "critic of black literature" no longer needs to have a special relationship to Afro-American culture, or a commitment to social change, obligations which saddle the critical project of reading black literature well with an impossible sociological burden. Instead the critic of black literature is an intellectual specialist who writes "primarily for other critics of literature."[23] Moreover, the critic of black literature can no longer be a mere amateur, either an ordinary reader, a practicing artist, or an untheoretical teacher, but must come from the professional community of poststructuralist literary critics, trained in the difficult new methodologies and theories of reading, and fluent in their terms.

The retreat from the populism of the Black Aesthetic could scarcely be more emphatic. Houston Baker, himself a critic who has tried to mediate between the cultural anthropology of the Black Aesthetic and poststructuralism, and whose essay on Ralph Ellison is included in *Black Literature and Literary Theory*, links the rise of black poststructuralism to the rise of black professionals in academia "whose class status . . . and privileges are . . . contingent upon their adherence to accepted (i.e., white) standards. . . . " With the decline of a mass black audience for critical or political discourse in the aftermath of the 1960s, Baker argues, a "class-oriented professionalism among Afro-American literary critics" has led to a "sometimes uncritical imposition upon Afro-American culture of literary theories borrowed from prominent white scholars."[24] While Baker maintains that reconstructionist critics impose such theories without a rigorous analysis of their ethnocentrism, Gates, as we have seen, believes that the black literary tradition itself "demands" to be read in these sophisticated theoretical ways, for "sustenance and growth"—that is, in order to maintain a critical growth curve within academia that gives it parity with the dominant tradition of Dante, Milton, Holderlin, and Rousseau.

In a more telling critique than these sociological objections, however, Baker further protests that Gates simplifies and distorts the theories of the Black Aestheticians, and that he creates a semiotic circle around literature that cuts literary language off from the verbal behavior of Afro-American culture and that isolates the black text from the complex cultural systems that give meaning to its words. Gates's response is to challenge the idea of a unified black subject in terms taken from poststructuralism. Both in his introduction and in his own essay on Ellison and Reed, Gates emphasizes this critique of the "transcendent black subject, integral and whole, self-suffcient and plentiful, the 'always already' black signified, available for literary representation in received Western forms as would be the water dippered from a deep and dark well."[25]

Yet despite his critical rhetoric, Gates is not completely prepared to abandon either the politics of black presence or a vividly particularized sense of Afro-American culture and the black vernacular; and there are a number of contradictions and tensions in his essay pointing towards a different, if repressed, desire. He refers frequently to a "signifying black difference" produced by the process of applying literary theory to the black text, as if the black text were so powerful a catalyst that its combination with deconstruction explosively "changes both the received theory and received ideas about the text."[26] Moreover, his anonymous expert, the "critic of black literature," sometimes merges with a more personal and specific black critic struggling to represent a "black self" in ethnocentric Western languages that make blackness a figure of absence and negation. This black critic speaks in the Afro-American idiom "which makes the black tradition our very own," as well as in the professional idiom of Ithaca or New Haven.[27]

These conflicts between academic centrality and a black tradition and "criticism of our own" became even more pronounced with the newest critical wave. Most recently, the black critic and the critic of black literature have been joined by the Third-World critic and the critic of Third-World literature, whose subject is "the curious dialectic between formal language use and the inscription of meta-phorical racial differences."[28] Metaphorical? Yes, according to the leading figure and theorist in this group, once again Henry Louis Gates, Jr., who edited a special issue of the journal *Critical Inquiry* called "'Race,' Writing, and Difference" in autumn 1985: "Race, as a meaningful criterion within the biological sciences, has long been recognized to be a fiction. When we speak of 'the white race' or 'the black race,' 'the Jewish race' or 'the Aryan race,' we speak in biological mis-nomers, and more generally, in metaphors."[29] As Anthony Appiah points out, "apart from the visible morphological characteristics of skin, hair, and bone, by which we are inclined to assign people to the broadest racial categories— black, white, yellow—," current genetic research proves that there are few biological characteristics of "race."[30] Apart from these unimportant "gross differences," the kind of positive black racial identity advocated by W. E. B. DuBois, involving a common language, history, and tradition, is thus wholly unscientific, and "must go" (p. 27). At the mitochondrial or cellular level, according to Appiah, race has little to do with biological differences between people. What we are talking about, then, is a linguistic construct.

While some black critics, like Houston Baker, might observe that "the shift to the common ground of subtle academic discourse is . . . ultimately unhelpful in a world where New York taxi drivers scarcely ever think of mitochondria before refusing to pick me up,"[31] the move to "race" as a fundamental rhetorical cat-egory in the study of writing and the shaping of critical theory would seem to be the manifest destiny of black criticism, giving it an unlimited access to Third World, colonial, and Western literature, and granting it a primary term like "class" in Marxist criticism. One of the major advantages of the category of "race" is that it problematizes the dominant as well as the Other, and provides a way of talking about "Western" or "white" genres and forms. Moreover, the emphasis on "race" is a brilliant solution to the problem of establishment indifference to the black literary tradition. If black criticism requires expertise in the black text, there will be a lot of important "other critics of literature" who will never qualify. There is no way to compel Jacques Derrida to read Toni Morrison or Ishmael Reed. But when the subject is the rhetorical inscription of "race," Derrida can legitimately be brought inside the hermeneutic circle of Third-World criticism, with a politi-cal essay on South Africa, while it would be very hard to include him in the reconstructionist project except as a mentor.

From another perspective, however, the shift to "race" also marks an obvious swerve away from Afro-American criticism. The quotation marks around "race" signal not only the questioning of racial essentialism, but also the effacement of black identity and an Afro-American literary canon. The very small number of Afro-American literary critics in the volume itself is striking. In a follow-up is-sue, which became part of the book version published by the University of Chi-cago Press, there were additional pieces by Jane Tompkins, Christopher Miller, and Tzvetan Todorov, and a debate between two South African critical activists and Derrida. Most of these essays are extremely good, and several are even bril-liant; what is disturbing about the issue is not the quality of the criticism, but the implications of the fact that the first issue of *Critical Inquiry* edited by a black critic and devoted to the question of race and writing has a list of contributors virtually indistinguishable from any other issue of *Critical Inquiry*. The most unusual part of the issue is the ad section at the back, where books by Trudier Harris, Sunday Anozie, and Hortense Spillers, among others, are featured. The reader of the volume must wonder whether the installation of "race" will displace the study of black literature, and reinstitute a familiar canon, now seen from the perspective of the racial trope. It's troubling, too, that while gender is given some rhetorical attention as a fundamental category of critical analysis in Gates's introduction, and has been a central concern of both his and Houston Baker's recent work, in this volume the responsibility for dealing with gender is almost entirely delegated to the female contributors.[32] And finally, it's revealing that after a vigorous critique and rebuttal of Tzvetan Todorov's contribution to the debate, Gates still believes that the counter-cultural critic must use the language of the dominant since it is the only one Todorov will even pay mild attention to: "Todorov can't even hear us, Houston, when we talk his academic talk; how he gonna hear us if we 'talk *that* talk,' the talk of the black idiom?"[33] In the female vernacular of my own past, or as my mother used to say, why talk to the wall? Why does it still matter so much to be heard by the tone-deaf masters of European theory when other and larger audiences want to listen?

These aspects of the volume are particularly disturbing since in his introductory essay, Gates announces a significant shift in his own thinking, away from his defiant reconstructionist stance to a recognition of the dangers of assimilation, and a renewed emphasis on the cultural grounding of black literature: "I once thought it our most important gesture to *master* the canon of criticism, to *imitate* and *apply* it, but I now believe that we must turn to the black tradition itself to develop theories of criticism indigenous to our literatures." Gates now warns of the dangers in black poststructuralism and the need for Third-World critics to "analyze the language of contemporary criticism itself, recognizing especially that hermeneutic systems are not universal, color-blind, apolitical, or neutral. . . . To attempt to appropriate our own discourses by using Western theory uncritically is to substitute one mode of neocolonialism for another."[34]

THE FEMINIST CRITICAL REVOLUTION

The debates within Afro-American criticism and theory have many parallels within the feminist critical community, and indeed the genealogies of black and feminist criticism are strikingly similar in many respects. For the sake of emphasizing these parallels, and for convenience of reference, I have given names to the various phases and modes which make up the complex totality of feminist literary criticism; but it should be understood that none of these approaches has the exact historical and political specificity that may be claimed by some of the stages of Afro-American criticism. None of these overlapping phases has been superseded or discredited, and in general each has undergone considerable change through a vigorous internal debate.

Before the Women's Liberation Movement, criticism of women's writing took the form of an *androgynist poetics*, denying the uniqueness of a female literary consciousness, and advocating a single or universal standard of critical judgment which women writers had to meet. The women's movement of the late 1960s initiated both a *feminist critique* of male culture and a *Female Aesthetic* celebrating women's culture. By the mid-1970s, academic feminist criticism, in league with interdisciplinary work in women's studies, entered a new phase of *gynocritics*, or the study of women's writing. With the impact of European literary and feminist theory in the late 1970s, *gynesic* or poststructuralist feminist criticism, dealing with "the feminine" in philosophy, language, and psychoanalysis, became an important influence on the field as a whole. And in the late 1980s, we are seeing the rise of *gender theory*, the comparative study of sexual difference.

In contrast to black criticism, where integrationist poetics is at least currently unacceptable, androgynist poetics continues to have many partisans among women writers, creating an apparent conflict between writers and critics that the media have relished. It disturbed many feminist critics, including myself, when Gail Godwin and Cynthia Ozick attacked the *Norton Anthology of Literature by Women* on the grounds that the creative imagination is sexless and that the concept of a female literary tradition was insulting to women who (like Godwin) regard themselves as disciples of Joseph Conrad. I think it unlikely that black writers will raise similar objections to the forthcoming *Norton Anthology of Black Literature*, edited by the indefatigable and phenomenal Skip Gates.

Nevertheless, androgynist poetics, which can be an unexamined misogyny that demands a spurious "universality" from women's writing, as integrationist poetics did from black writers, as well as a form of feminine self-hatred, also speaks for genuinely serious and permanent concerns within feminist criticism. The androgynist position was articulated early on by Mary Ellmann in *Thinking About Women* (1969), which wittily deconstructed the pernicious effects of thinking by sexual analogy; and by Carolyn Heilbrun in *Toward a Recognition of Androgyny* (1973), which argued that "our future salvation lies in a movement away from sexual polarization and the prison of gender."[35] Among contemporary American writers, Joyce Carol Oates is probably the most persuasive representative of this position. In an essay entitled "(Woman) Writer: Theory and Practice" (1986), Oates protests the category of "woman" or "gender" in art: "Subject-matter is culture-determined, not gender-determined. And the imagination, in itself genderless, allows us all things."

Since the 1970s, however, while acknowledging the writer's need to feel free of labels, most feminist critics have rejected the concept of the genderless "imagination," and have argued from a variety of perspectives that the imagination cannot escape from the unconscious structures and strictures of gender identity. These arguments may emphasize the impossibility of separating the imagination from a socially, sexually, and historically positioned self, as in Sandra Gilbert's sensible insistence that "what is finally written is, whether consciously or not, written by the whole person. . . . If the writer is a woman who has been raised as a woman—and I daresay only a very few biologically anomalous human females have *not* been raised as women—how can her sexual identity be split off from her literary energy? Even a denial of her femininity. . . would surely be significant to an understanding of the dynamics of her aesthetic creativity."[36] A more systematic feminist critique of the woman writer's unified and sexless "imagination" comes from Lacanian psychoanalysis, which describes the split in the female subject within language. In a psycholinguistic world structured by father-son resemblance and by the primacy of male logic, woman is a gap or a silence, the invisible and unheard sex. In contrast to the "writer only" problems of androgynist poetics, therefore, most feminist critics insist that the way to contend with patriarchal bias against women is not to deny sexual difference but to dismantle gender hierarchies. Not sexual difference itself, but rather its meaning within patriarchal ideology—"division, oppression, inequality, interiorized inferiority for women"—must be attacked.[37]

The first break with androgynist poetics was the affirmation of womanhood as a positive factor in literary experience. As in the development of a Black Aesthetic, the Female Aesthetic evolved during the early years of the women's liberation movement as a radical response to a past in which the assumed goal for women's literature had been a smooth passage into a neuter and "universal" aesthetic realm. Instead the Female Aesthetic maintained that women's writing expressed a distinct female consciousness, that it constituted a unique and coherent literary tradition, and that the woman writer who denied her female identity restricted or even crippled her art. At the same time, a feminist critique of androcentric literature and criticism examined the "misogyny of literary practice: the stereotyped images of women in literature as angels or monsters, the . . . textual harassment of women in classic and popular male literature, and the exclusion of women from literary history."[38]

Virtually all of the romantic and invigorating images of independence that characterized the Black Aesthetic have their counterpart in the Female Aesthetic as well. In contrast to the hegemony of what it characterized as the arid and elitist "methodolatry" of patriarchal criticism, the Female Aesthetic proposed the empowerment of the common woman reader (indeed we could also see here a conjunction of Women's Liberation with what Terry Eagleton has called the Reader's Liberation Movement), and the celebration of an intuitive female critical consciousness in the interpretation of women's texts. In striking parallels to the Black Aesthetic, the Female Aesthetic also spoke of a vanished nation, a lost motherland; of the female vernacular or Mother Tongue; and of a powerful but neglected women's culture. In her introduction to an anthology of international women's poetry, for example, Adrienne Rich put forth the compelling hypothesis of a female diaspora:

> The idea of a common female culture—splintered and diasporized among the male cultures under and within which women have survived—has been a haunting though tentative theme of feminist thought over the past few years. Divided from each other through our dependencies on men—domestically, tribally, and in the world of patronage and institutions—our first need has been to recognize and reject these divisions, the second to begin exploring all that we share in common as women on this planet.[39]

This phase of intellectual rebellion, gynocentrism, and critical separatism was a crucial period in the experience of women who had always played subordinate roles as dutiful academic daughters, research assistants, second readers, and faculty wives. Through the Female Aesthetic, women experimented with efforts to inscribe a female idiom in critical discourse and to define a feminist critical stylistics based on women's experience. In "Toward a Feminist Aesthetic" (1978), Julia Penelope Stanley and Susan J. Wolfe (Robbins) proposed that "the unique perceptions and interpretations of women require a literary style that reflects, captures, and embodies the quality of our thought," a "discursive, conjunctive style instead of the complex, subordinating, linear style of classification and distinction."[40]

French feminist writing of the same period, although it came out of radically different intellectual sources, also produced the concept of *écriture féminine*, analyzing women's style as a writing-effect of rupture and subversion in avant-garde literature, available to both men and women, but connected or analogous to female sexual morphology. The French feminist project of "writing the body" is a particularly strong and revolutionary effort to provide women's writing with an authority based in women's genital and libidinal difference from men. While the French critique of phallocentrism takes very different paths in the work of Hélène Cixous, Luce Irigaray, and Julia Kristeva, all explore the possibility of a concentric feminine discourse. Whether clitoral, vulval, vaginal, or uterine; whether centered on semiotic pulsions, childbearing, or jouissance, the feminist theorization of female sexuality/textuality, and its funky audacity in violating patriarchal taboos by unveiling the Medusa, is an exhilarating challenge to phallic discourse.

Yet the Female Aesthetic also had serious weaknesses. As many feminist critics sharply noted, its emphasis on the importance of female biological experience came dangerously close to sexist essentialism. Its efforts to establish a specificity of female writing through the hypothesis of a women's language, a lost motherland, or a cultural enclave, could not be supported by scholarship. The initial identification with the Amazon as a figure of female autonomy and creativity (in the work of Monique Wittig and Ti-Grace Atkinson, among others), and with lesbian separatism as the correct political form for feminist commitment, was both too radical and too narrow for a broadly based critical movement. The concepts of female style or *écriture féminine* described only one avant-garde mode of women's writing, and many feminists felt excluded by a prescriptive stylistics that seemed to privilege the non-linear, experimental, and surreal. Insofar as the Female Aesthetic suggested that only women were qualified to read women's texts, feminist criticism ran the risk of ghettoization. Finally, the essentialism of the universal female subject and the female imagination was open to charges of racism, especially since black women's texts were rarely cited as examples. As black women and others within the women's movement protested against the inattention to racial and class differences between women, the idea of a common women's culture had to be re-examined.

Gynocritics, which developed alongside the Female Aesthetic in the 1970s, has been an effort to resolve some of these problems. It identified women's writing as a central subject of feminist criticism, but rejected the concept of an essential female identity and style. In an essay called "Feminist Criticism in the Wilderness" (1981), a response to Geoffrey Hartman whose title now seems feeble compared to the brilliant riposte of Skip Gates, I argued against feminist fantasies of a wild zone of female consciousness or culture outside of patriarchy, declaring instead that "there can be no writing or criticism outside of the dominant culture." Thus both women's writing and feminist criticism were of necessity "a double-voiced discourse embodying both the muted and the dominant, speaking inside of both feminism and criticism."[41]

Instead gynocriticism has focused on the multiple signifying systems of female

literary traditions and intertextualities. In studying women's writing, feminist critics have challenged and revised the prevailing styles of critical discourse, and
asked whether theories of female creativity could be developed instead from
within the female literary tradition itself. Influenced by the interdisciplinary field
of women's studies, they have brought to their reading of women's texts theories
and terms generated by the work of such feminist scholars as the historian Carroll
Smith-Rosenberg, the psychologist Carol Gilligan, and the sociologist Nancy
Chodorow, whose enormously influential study, *The Reproduction of Mothering*
(1978), revised Freudian psychoanalysis and British object-relations psychology
to emphasize the pre-Oedipal phase as the key factor in the construction of gender identity.

The work of Smith-Rosenberg, Chodorow, and Gilligan has led to a wide range
of studies in philosophy, social history, and religion endorsing what are called
"matriarchal values" of nurturance, caring, non-violence, and connectedness, and
urging their adoption by society as a whole. Feminist critics have used metaphors
of this idealized maternity both in the quest for a strong literary matrilineage, and
in the rejection of the adversary method in critical discourse. In a famous and
moving essay, Alice Walker has described black women writers' "search for our
mother's gardens," tracing the suppressed creativity of black women under slavery and poverty to non-verbal art forms.[42] In sharp contrast to the Oedipal poetics of aggression, competition, and defense put forth by Harold Bloom, some
American feminist critics have postulated a pre-Oedipal "female poetics of affiliation," dependent on the daughter's bond with the mother, in which intergenerational conflict is replaced by female literary intimacy, generosity, and continuity.
Joan Lidoff, Judith Kegan Gardiner, and Elizabeth Abel are among the feminist
critics who see women's fluid ego boundaries affecting plot and genre conventions, blurring the lines between lyric and narrative, between realism and romance. Here the Female Aesthetic and postmodernism join in a celebration of
heterogeneity, dissolving boundaries, and *différence*.

Although I can hardly claim to be an innocent bystander on the subject of
gynocriticism, I would argue that over the past decade it has been sufficiently
large, undogmatic, and flexible to have accommodated many theoretical revisions
and criticisms, and it has been enormously productive. In a relatively short period of time, gynocritics has generated a vast critical literature on individual
women writers, persuasive studies of the female literary tradition from the Middle
Ages to the present in virtually every national literature, and important books on
what is called "gender and genre": the significance of gender in shaping generic
conventions in forms ranging from the hymn to the Bildungsroman. Nevertheless, many of the original gynocritical theories of women's writing were based primarily on nineteenth-century English women's texts, so that a black feminist
critic such as Hortense Spillers sees "the gynocritical themes of recent feminist
inquiry" as separate from a "black women's writing community."[43] Only in recent years has attention to black women's writing begun to address and redress
this issue.

A pivotal text of gynocritics is Sandra Gilbert and Susan Gubar's monumental
study *The Madwoman in the Attic* (1979). Gilbert and Gubar offer a detailed revisionist reading of Harold Bloom's theory of the anxiety of influence, transforming his Freudian paradigm of Oedipal struggle between literary fathers and sons

into a feminist theory of influence which describes the nineteenth-century woman writer's anxieties within a patriarchal literary culture. Strongly influenced by the work of Gilbert and Gubar, the theoretical program of gynocritics by the 1980s has been marked by increasing attention to "the analysis of female talent grappling with a male tradition," both in literature and criticism, a project that defined both the female literary text and the feminist critical text as the sum of its "acts of revision, appropriation, and subversion," and its differences of "genre, structure, voice, and plot."[44] Gynocritics had derived much of its strength from its self-reflexive properties as a double-voiced mode of women's writing; the anxieties of the nineteenth-century woman writer were much like those of the modern Feminist critic attempting to penetrate literary theory, the most defended bastion of patriarchal prose. Now, as Feminist critics began to profit from their labors and to enjoy some prestige and authority within the profession of literary studies, questions of the complicity between the feminist critical talent and the male critical tradition became acute, and the acts of theoretical revision, appropriation, and subversion in gynocritics itself became the source of a troubling, sometimes obsessive and guilty, self-consciousness.

About this time, too, as reports on the French feminists began to appear in women's studies journals, and as their work became available to American readers through translation, a new group of feminist critics entered the field, primarily through departments of French and Comparative Literature. They saw post-Saussurean linguistics, psychoanalysis, semiotics, and deconstruction as the most powerful means to understanding the production of sexual difference in language, reading, and writing, and they wrote in a language accessible chiefly to other literary critics, rather than to a wider audience. Following the work of Jacques Derrida, Jacques Lacan, Hélène Cixous, Luce Irigaray, and Julia Kristeva, Franco-American feminist critics focused on what Alice Jardine calls "gynesis": the exploration of the textual consequences and representations of "the feminine" in Western thought. Deconstruction has paid little attention to women writers individually or as a group; "for Derrida and his disciples," Jardine notes, "the question of how women might accede to subjecthood, write texts or acquire their own signatures, are *phallogocentric* questions."[45] Some poststructuralist feminist critics thus maintain that "feminist criticism should avoid 'the women's literature ghetto' . . . and return to confrontation with 'the' canon."[46] While gynocritics looks at the patrilineage and matrilineage of the female literary *work*, poststructuralist feminist criticism views the literary *text* as fatherless and motherless; its feminist subjectivity is a product of the reading process. From a gynesic perspective, moreover, disruptions in discourse constitute disruptions of the patriarchal system.

Gynesic criticism has been a major intellectual force within feminist discourse, but the gynesic project has also raised a number of problems. First of all, as black poststructuralism has questioned the transcendent black self, however, so poststructuralist feminist criticism has had to wrestle with the paradox of fundamental theoretical affiliations that undermine the very notion of female subjectivity. Other modes of feminist criticism have had the empowerment of the female subject as a specific goal. Within the Female Aesthetic, female consciousness was celebrated as an interpretive guide; within gynocritics, the woman critic could use her own confrontation with the male critical tradition and her own experience of writing as a guide to understanding the situation of the woman writer. But if women are the silenced and repressed Other of Western discourse, how can a Feminist theorist speak *as* a woman about women or anything else? As Shoshana Felman asks, "If 'the woman' is precisely the Other of any conceivable Western theoretical focus of speech, how can the woman as such be speaking in this book? Who is speaking here, and who is asserting the otherness of the woman?"[47] Kaja Silverman also admits that "the relationship of the female subject to semiotic theory is . . . necessarily an ambivalent one. The theory offers her a sophisticated understanding of her present cultural condition, but it also seems to confine her forever to the status of one who is to be seen, spoken, and analyzed."[48] The rhetorical problems of expressing a black male self to which Gates briefly alludes in "Criticism in the Jungle" are much less disabling than the burden, inherent in a gynesic feminist criticism heavily and necessarily dependent on psychoanalytic theory, of speaking from the feminine position of absence, silence, and lack.

Furthermore, while poststructuralist feminists have played a significant role within poststructuralism as translators and advocates, as well as critics, of the European male theorists, the male feminists who have participated in gynesis, with some outstanding exceptions (such as Neil Hertz, Stephen Heath, and Andrew Ross) have tended to present themselves as metacritical masters of the feminine rather than as students of women's writing, or critics of masculinity. When the Australian critic Ken Ruthven (sometimes called the Crocodile Dundee of male feminism) observes in his book *Feminist Literary Studies: An Introduction*, that "the female 'problematic' is too important to be left in the hands of anti-intellectual feminists," and could be subjected to much more rigorous metacritical inspection by impartial men like himself, it's difficult not to be suspicious. Since, when you come right down to it, Ruthven argues, feminist criticism is "just another way of talking about books," and he is a guy who "makes a living talking about books," it would be churlish (or girlish) to try to keep him out of the conversation.[49] In other cases, as I have learned from sad experience, "male feminists" do not even bother to read the feminist critical texts they are allegedly responding to, since they always already know what women think. Poststructuralism and feminism are a familiar and almost obligatory critical couple in the 1980s, but they are still having to work at their relationship.

Finally, some recent discussions of what they call "Anglo-American" feminist criticism by poststructuralist feminists have been startlingly *ad feminam* and harsh, introducing a tone of acrimony into what we had hoped was a mutual, if pluralistic, enterprise, and eliciting equally intemperate attacks on "theory" in defensive response. Certainly there are real issues at stake in the theoretical debates, as well as struggles for what Evelyn Fox Keller has called epistemic power in the feminist critical arena. But the polarization of feminist discourse along dualistic lines seems particularly unfortunate at a moment when there is such a lively exchange of ideas. While *The Madwoman in the Attic* has yet to be translated into French, gynesic criticism has been widely read by American feminist critics; it has modified American work in gynocritics, and vice-versa. It is not exceptional that Sandra Gilbert, for example, should have edited the first English translation of Cixous's work and Catherine Clément's *La Jeune Née*, or on the other hand, that Barbara Johnson is currently working on black women writers. The complex heterogeneities of contemporary feminist discourse cannot be reduced to hierarchal oppositions.

The latest and most rapidly growing mode of feminist criticism is gender theory, corresponding to the Third-World critic's focus on "race." Within American feminist scholarship, the term "gender" is used to mean the social, cultural, and psychological constructs imposed upon biological sexual difference. Like "race" or "class," "gender" is a fundamental or organic social variable in all human experience. Within gender theory, the object of feminist criticism undergoes another transformation; unlike the emphasis on women's writing that informs gynocritics, or on the signification of "the feminine" within gynesis, gender theory explores ideological inscription and the literary effects of the sex/gender system: "that set of arrangements by which the biological raw material of human sex and procreation is shaped by human social intervention."[50]

The interest in gender theory is not confined to feminist criticism, but has also appeared in feminist thought in the fields of history, anthropology, philosophy, psychology, and science. In "Anthropology and the Study of Gender," Judith Shapiro argues that the goal of feminist research is not to focus on "women," and thus to reify female marginalization, but rather "to integrate the study of gender differences into the central pursuits of the social sciences."[51] In the natural sciences, the path-breaking work of Evelyn Fox Keller, Ruth Bleier, and Donna Haraway has analyzed "the critical role of gender ideology in mediating between science and social forms."[52] The most searching analysis of gender as a historical concept has been carried out by Joan W. Scott; in an essay called "Gender: A Useful Category of Historical Analysis," Scott outlines three goals of gender theory: to substitute the analysis of social constructs for biological determinism in the discussion of sexual difference; to introduce comparative studies of women and men into the specific disciplinary field; and to transform disciplinary paradigms by adding gender as an analytic category.[53]

What are the advantages of gender theory for feminist criticism? Most significantly, gender theory insists that all writing, not just writing by women, is gendered. To define the objective of feminist criticism as an analysis of gender in literary discourse completely opens the textual field. It also provides a way of uncovering the implicit assumptions about gender in literary theory that pretends to be neutral or gender-free. Secondly, the term "gender," like race, problematizes the dominant. Gender theory promises to introduce the subject of masculinity into feminist criticism, and to bring men into the field as students, scholars, theorists, and critics. It has already opened feminist criticism to include the consideration of male homosexuality, both through the pioneering work of Eve Kosofsky Sedgwick and through writing by gay men. Third, the addition of gender as a fundamental analytic category within literary criticism moves feminist criticism from the margin to the center, and has revolutionary transformative potential for the ways that we read, think, and write. Thinking in terms of gender is a constant reminder of the other categories of difference that structure our lives and texts, just as theorizing gender emphasizes the connections between feminist criticism and other minority critical revolutions.

As with Third-World criticism, however, it is too soon to be certain how these possibilities will work out. One danger is that men will continue to read "gender" as a synonym for "femininity," and pontificate about the representation of women without accepting the risks and opportunities of investigating masculinity, or analyzing the gender subtexts of their own critical practice. Another danger, seemingly paradoxical but actually related, is that gender will become a postfeminist term that declares the study of women, and women's writing, obsolete, or what Ruthven denounces as "separatist." The most troubling risk is that gender studies will depoliticize feminist criticism, that men will declare an interest in what one of my colleagues recently called "gender and power," while refusing to call themselves feminists. Even Ronald Reagan and Sylvester Stallone, after all, are interested in gender and power; in some respects, as Joan Scott acknowledges, the term "gender" seems to transcend the politics of feminism, and to promise a "more neutral and objective" scholarly perspective, certainly one more acceptable to men, than the focus on "women."[54] Despite the risks, however, none of these outcomes is inevitable. Gender can be an important expansion of our work, rather than a displacement or depoliticization, if it is defined within a feminist framework that remains committed to the continuing struggle against sexism, racism, and homophobia.

REPETITION AND DIFFERENCE

Where do we go from here? The parallels between Afro-American and feminist criticism show how problematic the idea of a unified "black" or "female" self has become. Whether it is the linguistic skepticism of poststructuralism, or our acknowledgment of the differences between women that stops us, Feminist critics today can no longer speak as and about women with the unself-conscious authority of the past. The female subject, we are told, is dead, a position instead of a person. Our dilemma has even reached the pages of the *New Yorker*; in Tama Janowitz's short story "Engagements," a graduate student in feminist criticism at Yale takes notes as her distraught professor tells of being severely attacked for trying to talk about "women" and "female identity" at a Poetics of Gender conference.[55] Without a claim to subjectivity or group identity, how can we have a feminist criticism of our own?

Black and Third-World critics haunted by the messages of poststructuralism are now facing the same dilemma. Is there a critic-position as well as a subject-position? Gates asks whether "the critic of black literature acquires his or her identity parodically, as it were, in the manner of the parrot," but hopefully concludes that "we are able to achieve difference through repetition" by looking at a different critical object.[56] Homi Bhabha addresses the issue in the contexts of colonialist discourse, citing "mimicry" as a form of "civil disobedience within the discipline of civility: signs of spectacular resistance."[57] In *Ce Sexe qui n'en est pas un*, Luce Irigaray too locates the subversive force of Feminist discourse in a playful mimesis, a mimicry both of phallocentric discourse which exceeds its logic, and of the feminine position within that system. Yet playing with mimesis cannot offer us authority except in individual star turns, especially if the dominant culture wants to play with your mesis too. And in mimicking the language of the dominant, how can we guarantee that mimicry is *understood* as ironic—as civil disobedience, camp, or feminist difference rather than as merely derivative?

Feminist criticism can't afford to settle for mimicry, or to give up the idea of female subjectivity, even if we accept it as a constructed or metaphysical one. To paraphrase Baker, men's clubs hardly ever think of metaphysics before they keep women out; we need what Gayatri Spivak calls a "strategic essentialism" to combat patriarchy.[58] Neither can we abandon our investigation of women's literary history, or give up the belief that through careful reading of women's texts we will develop a criticism of our own that is both theoretical and feminist. This is a task worth pursuing for its intellectual challenge and for its contribution to a truly inclusive theory of literature, rather than for its "defense" of women's creative gifts. The goal Virginia Woolf envisioned for feminist writers and critics in 1928, to labor in poverty and obscurity for the coming of Shakespeare's sister, no longer seems meaningful or necessary. Our enterprise does not stand or fall by proving some kind of parity with male literary or critical "genius"; even assuming that a female Shakespeare or a female Derrida would be recognized, to question the very idea of "genius" is part of Woolf's legacy to us.

Despite our awareness of diversity and deconstruction, feminist critics cannot depend on gynesic ruptures in discourse to bring about social change. During a period when many of the meager gains of the civil rights and women's movements are being threatened or undone by Reaganism and the New Right, when, indeed, there is a backlash against what the Bennetts and Blooms see as too *much* black and female power in the university, there is an urgent necessity to affirm the importance of black and female thinkers, speakers, readers, and writers. The Other Woman may be transparent or invisible to some; but she is still very vivid, important, and necessary to us.

NOTES

Thanks for helpful suggestions on drafts of this paper to members of the School for Criticism and Theory at Dartmouth College, and also to Skip Gates, Houston Baker, Brenda Silver, Marianne Hirsch, Evelyn Fox Keller, Valerie Smith, Daryl Dance, and English Showalter.

1. Mary Ann Caws, "The Conception of Engendering, the Erotics of Editing," in *The Poetics of Gender*, ed. Nancy K. Miller (New York: Columbia U. P., 1986), pp. 42–63. This episode is all the more ironic in the light of the successful protest in spring 1988 by deaf students of Gallaudet College in Washington.

2. Jane Gallop, *The Daughter's Seduction: Feminism and Psychoanalysis* (Ithaca: Cornell U. P., 1982), pp. 126–27.

3. In this paper I need to make distinctions between a generic feminist criticism, practiced by a feminist critic of either sex; "Feminist" criticism practiced by women; and male feminist criticism, practiced by men.

4. Gayatri Chakravorty Spivak, "French Feminism in an International Frame," *Yale French Studies* 62 (1981): 184. See also Jane Gallop, "Annie Leclerc Writing a Letter, with Vermeer," *The Poetics of Gender*, p. 154.

5. For a stimulating example of how such critical cross-fertilization might take place, see Craig Werner, "New Democratic Vistas: Toward a Pluralistic Genealogy " in *Studies in Black American Literature*, II, ed. Joe Weixlmann and Chester Fontenot (Greenwood, Florida: Penkevill Press, 1986), pp. 47–83.

6. See Jonathan Dollimore, "Shakespeare, Cultural Materialism and the New Historicism," *Political Shakespeare: New Essays in Cultural Materialism*, ed. Jonathan Dollimore and Alan Sinfield (Ithaca: Cornell U. P., 1985), p. 15.

7. Houston A. Baker, Jr., "Generational Shifts and the Recent Criticism of Afro-American Literature," *Black American Literature Forum* 15 (Spring 1981): 3–21. My discussion of Afro-American literary theory is profoundly indebted to Baker's essay, and to my discussions with him about parallels to feminist criticism.

8. Quoted in Werner Sollers, *Beyond Ethnicity* (Cambridge: Harvard U.P., 1986), p. 209.

9. See Toril Moi, *Sexual/Textual Politics* (London and New York: Methuen, 1985).

10. Arthur P. Davis, Ulysses Lee, and Sterling Brown, eds., *The Negro Caravan* (New York: Dryden Press, 1941). Through the 1950s, Davis and other Afro-American critics envisioned the eventual disappearance of the social conditions that produced identifiably "Negro" literature.

11. See Baker, "Generational Shifts," pp. 3–4. The term "integrationist poetics" comes from his essay.

12. Mary Helen Washington, "Rage and Silence in *Maud Martha*," in *Black Literature and Literary Theory*, ed. Henry Louis Gates, Jr. (New York and London: Methuen, 1984), p. 258.

13. Larry Neal, "The Black Arts Movement," in *The Black Aesthetic*, ed. Addison Gayle, Jr. (New York: Doubleday, 1971), p. 272.

14. Melvin Dixon, "Rivers Remembering Their Source," in *The Reconstruction of Instruction*, ed. Robert Stepto and Dexter Fisher (New York: MLA, 1979), pp. 25–26.

15. Baker, "Generational Shifts," p. 6.

16. Stephen Henderson, "The Forms of Things Unknown," in his book *Understanding the New Black Poetry* (New York: Morrow, 1973), p. 41.

17. Baker, "Generational Shifts," p. 9.

18. See Barbara Smith, "Toward a Black Feminist Criticism," in *The New Feminist Criticism*, ed. Elaine Showalter (New York: Pantheon, 1985), pp. 168–87; Deborah McDowell, "New Directions for Black Feminist Criticism," in *The New Feminist Criticism*, pp. 186–99; and Mary Helen Washington, "New Lives and New Letters: Black Women Writers at the End of the Seventies," *College English* 43 (Jan. 1981): 1–11.

19. Baker, "Generational Shifts," p. 10.

20. Baker, "Generational Shifts," p. 12; and Henry Louis Gates, Jr., "Criticism in the Jungle," *Black Literature and Literary Theory*, p. 9.

21. Gates, "Jungle," pp. 5, 8.

22. Robert B. Stepto, quoted in Baker, "Generational Shifts," p. 12.

23. Gates, "Jungle" p. 8. By 1987, Gates had drastically changed this formulation: "No matter what theories we seem to embrace, we have more in common with each other than we do with any other critic of any other literature. We write for each other and for our own contemporary writers" (*Figures in Black*, New York: Oxford U. P., 1987, p. xxii).

24. Baker, "Generational Shifts," p. 11.

25. Henry Louis Gates, Jr., "The Blackness of Blackness: A Critique of the Sign and the Signifying Monkey," *Black Literature and Literary Theory*, p. 297.

26. Gates, "Jungle," p. 9.

27. Gates, "Jungle," p. 8.

28. Gates, "Introduction," *Critical Inquiry*, vol. 12, no. 1 (Autumn 1985): 6.

29. Gates, "Writing, 'Race,' and the Difference It Makes," *Critical Inquiry*, vol. 12, no. 1 (Autumn 1985): 5, 6.

30. Anthony Appiah, "The Uncompleted Argument: Du Bois and the Illusion of Race," *Critical Inquiry*, vol. 12, no. 1 (Autumn 1985): 21–22.

31. Houston A. Baker, Jr., "Caliban's Triple Play," *Critical Inquiry*, vol. 13, no. 1 (Autumn 1986): 186.

32. The exception is Sander L. Gilman, who contributed a controversial essay on race and female sexuality.

33. Henry Louis Gates, Jr., "Talkin' That Talk," *Critical Inquiry*, vol. 13, no. 1 (Autumn 1986): 210.

34. Gates, "Introduction," pp. 13, 15.

35. Carolyn G. Heilbrun, *Toward a Recognition of Androgyny* (New York: Harper Colophon Books, 1973), p. ix.

36. Sandra Gilbert, "Feminist Criticism in the University," in *Criticism in the University*, ed. Gerald Graff and Reginald Gibbons (Evanston: Northwestern U. P., 1985), p. 117.

37. Michèle Barrett, *Women's Oppression Today: Problems in Marxist Feminist Analysis* (London: Villiers, 1980), pp. 112–13.

38. Elaine Showalter, "The Feminist Critical Revolution," in *The New Feminist Criticism*, p. 5.

39. *The Other Voice* (New York: Morrow, 1975), p. xvii.

40. Adrienne Rich, "Toward a Feminist Aesthetic," *Chrysalis* 6 (1978): 59, 67.

41. Showalter, "Feminist Criticism in the Wilderness," in *The New Feminist Criticism*, p. 266.

42. Alice Walker, *In Search of Our Mothers' Gardens* (San Diego: Harcourt, Brace, Jovanovich, 1983).

43. Hortense Spillers, *Conjuring*, ed. Spillers and Marjorie Pryse (Bloomington: Indiana U. P., 1985), p. 261.

44. Elizabeth Abel, "Introduction," *Writing and Sexual Difference* (Chicago: U. of Chicago Press, 1982), p. 2.

45. Alice Jardine, "Pre-Texts for the Transatlantic Feminist," *Yale French Studies* 62 (1981): 225; and *Gynesis: Configurations of Women and Modernity* (Ithaca: Cornell U. P., 1985), pp. 61–63.

46. Gayle Greene and Coppélia Kahn, "Feminist Scholarship and the Social Construction of Woman," in Green and Kahn, eds., *Making a Difference: Feminist Literary Criticism* (London: Methuen, 1985), pp. 24–27.

47. Shoshana Felman, "Woman and Madness: The Critical Phallacy," *Diacritics* 5 (1975): 10; see also this volume, pp. 7–20.

48. Kaja Silverman, *The Subject of Semiotics* (New York: Oxford U. P., 1983), p. viii.

49. Ken Ruthven, *Feminist Literary Studies: An Introduction* (Cambridge: Cambridge U. P., 1985), p. 6.

50. Gayle Rubin, "The Traffic in Women," in Rayna Rapp Reiter, ed., *Toward an Anthropology of Women* (New York: Monthly Review Press, 1975), p. 165.

51. Judith Shapiro, "Anthropology and the Study of Gender," in *A Feminist Perspective in the Academy*, ed. Elizabeth Langland and Walter Gove (Chicago: U. of Chicago Press, 1983), p. 112.

52. Evelyn Fox Keller, *Reflections on Gender and Science* (New Haven: Yale U. P., 1985), p. 3.

53. Joan W. Scott, "Gender: A Useful Category of Historical Analysis," *American Historical Review* 5 (November 1986).

54. Scott, "Gender," p. 1065.

55. Reprinted in Tama Janowitz, *Slaves of New York* (New York: Crown, 1986).

56. Gates, "Jungle," p. 10.

57. Homi Bhabha, "Signs Taken for Words," *Critical Inquiry*, vol. 12, no. 1 (Autumn 1985): 162.

58. See Gayatri Chakravorty Spivak, *In Other Worlds: Essays in Cultural Politics* (London and New York: Routledge, 1987).

RECYCLING

race, gender, and the
practice of theory

(1992)

> The old patterns, no matter how cleverly rearranged to imitate progress, still condemn us to cosmetically altered repetitions of the same old exchanges.
>
> —AUDRE LORDE

> History, I contend, is the present—we, with every breath we take, every move we move, are History—and what goes around, comes around.
>
> —JAMES BALDWIN

> To exist historically is to perceive the events one lives through as part of a story later to be told.
>
> —ARTHUR DANTO

> This was not a story to pass on.
>
> —TONI MORRISON

To speak of "historical knowledge" is to stage or enter a vigorous debate between those who see "history" and "knowledge" as ontological givens and those who don't. I identify with those who don't, with those who recognize that, despite its basis in a verifiable then and thereness, often complete with concrete facts and recognizable personages, history is a fantastical and slippery concept, a making, a construction.[1] I side with those who see history, to invoke the current lingua franca, as a "contested terrain," although it often functions to repress and contain the conflicts and power asymmetries that define the sociopolitical field.

That contemporary students of culture and its institutions have by and large willingly adjusted their assumptions and altered their practices to fit these axioms, is a salutary development. But I share Renato Rosaldo's fear that in our zeal to establish historical contingency, to show that *everything* is constructed, human beings tend to "lose their specific gravity, their weight, and their density, and begin to float." We would do well to heed Rosaldo's warning against the dangers of declaring historical knowledge constructed and simply ending the discussion there, for we must "show in historical perspective, however difficult that is, "how it was constructed, by whom, and with what consequences."[2]

Here, I want to take some liberties with time and construe the present moment as the future's past in order to determine what "historical knowledge" of "literary theory" we are constructing at this moment and with what consequences to what specific bodies. In other words, how are we telling the history or story of recent theoretical developments? Who are the principals in that story? What are the strategies of its employment? How does it reconstitute timeworn structures and strategies of dominance? Recode familiar hierarchical relations?

As with most everyone else today, at least nominally, I am keenly interested in how race and gender figure into the objects of our critical inquiry, and in this matter of criticism's history, I am specifically and especially interested in where *black American women* and their discourses enter into the record (or not). I agree with Hortense Spillers that "in a very real sense, black American women are invisible to various public discourse, and the state of invisibility for them has its precedent in an analogy on any patriarchal symbolic mode that we might wish to name."[3] But what interests me here is their "visible" invisibility within Anglo-American feminism and Afro-American literary criticism. The laudable project to restore black American women to sight is often rent asunder or, at best, stalled by the far more powerful imperatives of historical legacy and contemporary social design. As Evan Watkins notes, "How we tell ourselves the history of recent theoretical developments . . . takes place in [that] shady zone between the boundaries of intellectual work and social situation, and attempts to resolve its tensions,"[4] but, as I hope to show, those tensions are not so easily resolved.

What follows is not a singular narrative, but rather, a few miscellaneous examples—call them "case studies"—about black feminist thinking that are rapidly assuming a structural relevance and significance that can no longer be ignored. One could raise at least two serious objections here. The first is that a focus on what has been written *about* black feminist thinking eclipses a more constructive, perhaps a more empowering focus on what has been written *by* black feminists.

In her review of Patricia Hill Collins's *Black Feminist Thought*, for example, Farah Griffin commended Collins for moving black feminism "to a new level" by spending "little time castigating white feminists or black men for their failures in regard to black women." She praises Collins for focusing instead "on an exploration and analysis of thought produced by black women themselves. In so doing, she reinforces their status as subjects and agents of history."[5] While I would dispute Griffin's perception that the work of black feminists has been, to this point, determinedly other-directed, I regard her implied call for a necessary shift of focus and address *within* the work of black feminism absolutely essential. But such a shift is, alone, insufficient, for it ignores the often unequally positioned sites of knowledge production and their influence on how and if the work of black feminists is read, on how and if it is read in a way that restructures, not simply annexes, knowledge in ceaseless reflex acts.

One could raise a second objection, and that is that my focus is too strictly and narrowly academicist, and curiously so, if we consider that although its main address is now the UNIVERSITY, black feminist thinking does not stake its origins or find its shelter there, and even when academia is its central site, it strives to extend its borders beyond.[6] While the focus is narrow, its implications and imperatives for the organization and construction of historical knowledge are much broader. The hierarchies and orders of value this construction encodes help to resituate African-American women and other "women of color" in a narrative that underwrites a familiar sociocultural contract, the terms of which are often silent, the print of which is often fine.

As we know, in the emplotment or narrativization of history, much depends on familiar vocabularies of reference, on the circulation of names, of proper names, and some names are more proper than others.[7] I want to talk briefly about the circulation of one name—Sojourner Truth—and the knowledge that name helps to construct about black feminist thinking within the general parameters of feminist discourse.[8]

UNCOVERING TRUTH, OR COLORING "FEMINIST THEORY"

In the opening chapter of her study *Am I That Name? Feminism and the Category of "Women" in History,* Denise Riley begins with a reference to Sojourner Truth and her famous and much-quoted question—"Ain't I a Woman?"—posed before the 1851 Women's Rights Convention in Akron, Ohio. Riley supposes that, in the current historical moment, Sojourner "might well—except for the catastrophic loss of grace in wording—issue another plea: 'Ain't I a Fluctuating Identity?'" The temptation here is simply to find the humor in Riley's rewriting and move on, except that to do so is to miss the sociocultural assumptions that constellate around it, assumptions that escape the boundaries of Truth's time to project themselves boldly in our own.

Riley's move to appropriate Sojourner Truth introduces a subtle racial marker that distinguishes between Truth's original words and Riley's modernization that displaces them. That modernization allegorizes a common, if sometimes muted, assumption about black women and their language found in much contemporary literary-critical discussion. That assumption is that black women, and I should add, women of color more generally, need a new language, a language in the service of a theory, preferably a poststructuralist theory, signaled in this context by the term *fluctuating identity.*[9]

To trace the move from Sojourner Truth's "Ain't I a Woman?" to Riley's "Ain't I a Fluctuating Identity?" is to plot, in effect, two crucial stages in a historical narrative of academic feminism's coming of age. Following this evolutionary logic, academic feminist discourse can be said to have "grown out of," or to have outgrown, an attachment to what Riley terms that "blatant[ly] disgrace[ful]" and "transparently suspicious" category—"Woman." That category happens to be personified by Sojourner's rhetorical and declarative question. Riley concedes that Sojourner represents one move in a necessary "double move" of feminist theory which recognizes that "both a concentration on and a refusal of the identity of 'woman' are essential to feminism."[10]

Constance Penley makes essentially the same point in *The Future of an Illusion.* Whereas in Riley's study Sojourner marks the point of departure, in Penley's she marks the point of closure. In the last two pages of the final chapter, she walks on to take a bow with Jacques Lacan. His "notorious bravura"—"the woman does not exist"—is counterposed to Sojourner Truth's "Ain't I a Woman?" Echoing Riley, Penley explains this counterposition as "two ideas or strategies . . . vitally important to feminism," though they might appear completely at odds. Penley classifies the one strategy—represented by Lacan, Althusser, and Derrida—as "epistemological" and "metaphysical"; the other, represented by Sojourner Truth as "political." That Truth's declarative question—"Ain't I a Woman?"—might be read as "political" *and* "epistemological" simultaneously seems not to have occurred to Penley, partly because she manipulates both these categories—consciously or not, to conform to an already polarized and preconceived understanding.[11]

Is it purely accidental that, in these two essays, Sojourner Truth comes to represent the politics but not the poetics that feminism needs? Is hers a purely neutral exemplarity? Agreeing with Gayatri Spivak that "it is at those borders of discourse where metaphor and example seem arbitrarily *chosen* that ideology breaks through,"[12] I would argue that Sojourner is far from an arbitrary example. Possible intentions notwithstanding, Sojourner Truth is useful in this context both to a singular idea of academic feminism, in general, and, in particular, to recent controversies within that discourse over the often uneasy relations between epistemology and politics. Black women figure prominently in both the general and particular dimensions; in the former, by their absence; in the latter, by their complicated presence.

The belief that feminism and whiteness form a homogeneous unity has long persisted, along with the equally persistent directive to feminist theorists to "account" in their discourses for the experiences of women of color. The unexamined assumption that white feminist discourse bears a special responsibility to women of color helps to maintain the perception that feminism equates with whiteness and relates maternalistically to women of color.

Such assumptions are implied in the recently published *Feminist Theory in Practice and Process*. In "Naming the Politics of Theory," one section of the introduction, the editors challenge "feminist theory . . . to recognize the myriad forms of black women's race, gender, and class politics and to envision theories that encompass these lived realities and concrete practices."[13] Elizabeth Spelman's observation is useful here: "It is not white middle class women who are different from other women, but all other women who are different from them."[14]

That difference has become magnified and has assumed an even greater urgency since academic feminism, like all discursive communities on the contemporary scene, has accepted the constructive challenge to take its processes into self-conscious account; that is, since it has accepted the challenge to "theorize" about the work it does and the claims it makes. The strain to fulfill both requirements—to "theorize," on the one hand, and to recognize material "differences," on the other, has created a tension within academic feminist discourse (read *white*). That tension is often formulated as a contrast, if not a contest, between "theory" and "practice-politics" respectively.

I must rush to add that race (here, read *black*) and gender (here, read *female*) are not the only stigmatized markers on the practice-politics side of the border between theory and practice, for they trade places in a fluid system of interchangeability with differences of nationality, sexuality, and class.[15] The now quiescent French-American feminist theory debate—illustrated most controversially in Toril Moi's *Sexual/Textual Politics*—provides one example of what I mean. Moi clumps Anglo-American, black, and lesbian women on the practice-politics-criticism side of the border; French women, on the theory side. After blasting the claims of Anglo-American feminist criticism, Moi then turns to answer those who well "might wonder why [she has] said nothing about black or lesbian (or black lesbian) feminist criticism in America. . . . The answer is simple: this book purports to deal with the theoretical aspects of feminist criticism. So far, lesbian and/or black feminist criticism have presented exactly the same *methodological* and *theoretical* problems as the rest of Anglo-American feminist criticism" (emphasis in text). Moi adds, "This is not to say that black and lesbian criticism have no . . . importance," but that importance is not co be "found at the level of *theory* . . . but the level of *politics*."[16]

In the context of these critical developments, the use of "Sojourner Truth" projects myriad meanings needed to perform the work of distinction and differentiation in the culture of academe. To begin with, as a metonym for "black woman," the name can be read as a mark of racial difference and distinction within "feminist theory," which points up its internal conflicts and ambivalence over the relative merits and value of "political" discourse. That racial difference is frequently hidden in itineraries represented as "purely" (and thus neutrally?) epistemological, is evident in the following summary by Jane Flax: "Feminist theorists have tried to maintain *two* different epistemological positions. The first is that the mind, the self, and knowledge are socially constituted, and what we can know depends on our social practices and contexts. The second is that feminist theorists can uncover truths about the whole as it 'really is.' Those who support the second position reject many post-modern ideas and must depend upon certain assumptions about truth and the knowing subject."[17]

The assumptions about Truth examined so far—both explicit and implied—cast her categorically in that second position, despite the fact that the short text of the "Ain't I a Woman?" speech is a compressed but powerful analysis and critique of the social practices within the context of slavery that depend on biases of class and race to construct an idea of universal or True Womanhood. She challenged that dominant knowledge, offering and authorizing her experiences under slavery as proof of its underlying illogicality.

The "truth" that Truth knows, then, is not reducible to a mere statement turned slogan that acts as theory's Other, or theory's shadow side. The politics contained within *that* epistemology, within that way of knowing Truth, must be interrogated and the foundations on which it rests laid bare. When we remember the full content and context of Sojourner Truth's speech, as well as its degrading aftermath, those foundations are sharply exposed.

After Truth delivered the speech, which turns on references to her body and its exploitation during slavery as a reproductive machine, one Dr. T. W. Strain alleged that she was a man. To prove that she wasn't, Truth bared her breasts.[18] The scene concludes with Truth's fixity in the body and, thus, effectively, in her distance from the "proper" white feminists enlisted to "verify" her sex. Her recuperation in these modern contexts forges a symbolic connection with that prior history, a conjunctive relationship to that past. It is precisely this earlier scene of verification that is being symbolically reenacted today. The demand in this present context is not to bare the breasts to verify womanhood but to bare the evidence that would verify knowledge that "black womanhood" is a discursive formation fluctuating in time.

But the selection of Sojourner Truth as metonym raises still other problems that connect to the relation between the symbolic and the social, the relation between the present and the past. The fact that Sojourner Truth was illiterate and that the words by which we know her were transcribed by stenographic reporters or admiring white friends has only begun to be interrogated with any complexity. Recent work by Nell Irvin Painter has begun to engage the nexus of paradoxes, ironies, and contradictions of these transcriptions and to inquire into why, until recently, Sojourner Truth, a "naive rather than an educated persona, seems to have better facilitated black women's entry into American memory" than any of her educated black female contemporaries. Painter's point is obviously not that only lettered or tutored black women should have facilitated that memory but that Sojourner Truth as figure keeps alive the "disparities of power and distinctions between European and Euro-Americans and natives, domestic and foreign."[19]

As a sign to a rematerializing critical discourse of its sins of omission around race, the utterance of Sojourner Truth or any other metonym for black woman seems to perform for some an absolution of critical guilt; but the utterance is all. "Sojourner"—or any other metonym for black woman—is one of which no more need be said. Truth's experiences beyond popularized clichés are not fully addressed. She is useful simply as a name to drop in an era with at least nominal pretensions to interrogating race and the difference it makes in critical discussion.

But the repetition of Sojourner's name makes no *real* difference. In dominant discourses it is a symbolic gesture masking the face of power and its operations in the present academic context. As a figure summoned from the seemingly safe and comfortable distance of a historical past, Sojourner Truth is removed from the present social context and can thus act symbolically to absorb, defuse, and deflect its conflicts. However, "Sojourner Truth" stirs up far more controversy than it settles, preventing any easy resolution of feminism's conflicts. The name contains locked within it the timeless and unchanging knowledge (the very definition of "truth") of race and gender embedded in Western philosophy that now find their way, like the return of the repressed, into the organization of knowledge in contemporary academe.

The repeated invocation of "Ain't I a Woman?"—detached from historical context—neither captures its immediacy for Truth's time nor reactivates it for our own. Correspondingly, the repeated invocation of "Sojourner Truth" functions not to document a moment in a developing discourse but to freeze that moment in time. Such a chronopolitics operates not so much as history but as an interruption of history, at least as black women might figure in it, a phenomenon not unlike Hegel's description of Africa as outside the "real theatre of History," of "no historical part of the World." "It has no movement or development to exhibit. . . . What we properly understand by Africa, is the Unhistorical, Undeveloped Spirit, still involved in the conditions of mere nature, and which has to be presented . . . on the threshold of the World's history."[20]

The proposition that Black feminist discourse is poised on the threshold of "Theory's" history has predictable consequences. Not least, this view helps to reconstitute the structures and strategies of dominance, even in work that strives zealously in an opposite and oppositional direction.

GENDERING AFRICAN-AMERICAN THEORY

We can observe such strategies of dominance in *Gender and Theory*, a recent anthology edited by Linda Kauffman. Kauffman tries studiously to prevent a reproduction of the simplistic divisions and antagonisms between black and white, male and female, "theory" and "politics." She explains in her introduction that while the title—*Gender and Theory*—posits a couple . . . the essays are arranged to permit men to respond to the essays by women and vice versa. That "structure is designed . . . to draw attention to such dichotomies in order to displace them by dissymmetry and dissonance."[21] Despite that goal, these very oppositions are evident nonetheless.

In fact, we could argue that if theory is often to "practice-politics" what Europe is to America, what white is to black, what straight is to gay, in Kauffman's anthology, theory is to practice what black male is to black female. This reductive accounting has entered the contemporary critical record and has constructed black women as categorically resistant to theory. To be sure, some black women have indeed helped to foster this perception and to encourage the metonymic strategy of choosing the name of any black woman to summarize the critical position of all.[22]

"Race" in Kauffman's anthology is constructed once again as synonymous with "blackness." Barbara Christian's "The Race for Theory" and Michael Awkward's response, "Appropriative Gestures: Theory and Afro-American Literary Criticism," are placed at the very end of the volume and thus apart from the preceding pairs of essays, none of which interrogates the racial inflections of "gender and theory." The racial opposition coordinates with a gendered opposition between male and female and a gendered opposition between theory and practice.

The question Kauffman poses in her introduction—"In what ways are Afro-American theory and Afro-American feminism complementary, and what ways are they antagonistic?"—gets answered in the two concluding essays: "Afro-American theory" is gendered male and Afro-American feminism is gendered female, and they function effectively as structural polarities. Such a seemingly innocent structure has already quickly decided its conclusion: Michael Awkward's response to Barbara Christian calls for a "theory" to her "practice."

One of the strengths of Awkward's response to Christian lies in its implicit recognition that poststructuralist theory cannot be homogenized, nor can it stand synecdochically for all theory. Although it is clear that he thinks Christian has missed the theoretical mark, he asserts that Barbara Smith's "Toward a Black Feminist Criticism" was "essentially a theoretical statement" "if not [a] post-structuralist discussion of critical practice and textual production." Smith's essay, he goes on to say, "theorizes despite its lack of a clearly informed awareness of deconstruction, reader-response theory, [and] semiotics."

Here, Awkward's vocabulary—"if not" and "lack of"—essentially negates whatever value he initially assigns to Smith's essay, which is structured as the negative of the positive—poststructuralism, the sole frame of reference. In an uncritical assertion of the synonymity between black women writers and "black women" as critics, Awkward offers a cautionary note: "If this field [black women's literature] is to continue to make inroads into the canon, if it is to gain the respect it doubtlessly deserves as an ideologically rich literary tradition, within an increasingly theoretical academy, it will require that its critics continue to move beyond description and master the discourse of contemporary theory."[23] If, as Awkward suggests, "black women's literature still does not assume the prominent place in courses and criticism" that it merits, I would ask whether that marginality can be explained exclusively by the lack of theorizing on the part of black women or rather whether that marginalization is often structured into the very theories that Awkward wants black women to master. Again, my point should not be read as a simplistic rejection of theory, as it is narrowly associated with poststructuralist projects, but as a call for a more searching examination of the processes and procedures of marginalizing any historically subjugated knowledge.

Awkward's essay does more than close Kauffman's volume; it performs a kind of closure, or functions as a kind of "final word," which extends far beyond the boundaries of the collection, *Gender and Theory*. He leaves intact the clichéd and unstudied distinctions between "theory" and "practice," represented by Paul de Man and Barbara Christian, respectively. It is paradoxical and ironic that an essay that privileges poststructuralist theory and extols de Man, relies on an uncritical construction of theory as an autonomous entity with semantic stability and immanent properties that separate it from practice. It is all the more ironic that such a dichotomy should dominate in an essay that valorizes a body of theory that emerged to blur such inherited and unmediated oppositions. But such dichotomies mark a difference and issue a set of limits—social limits—with implications that extend beyond the academic realm. In identifying with Paul de Man, Awkward consolidates his own critical authority against Barbara Christian's, making theory a province shared between men.

NOTES TOWARD A COUNTERHISTORY

Where might we go from here? I would start with the forthright assertion that the challenge of any discourse identifying itself as black feminist is not necessarily or most immediately to vindicate itself as theory but to resist the theory-practice dichotomy as at once too broad and too simple to capture the range and diversity of contemporary critical projects, including the range and diversity in the contributions of black women to that discourse. A far more valuable and necessary project would proceed from the commonplace assumption that no consideration of *any* intellectual project is complete without an understanding of the process of that project's formation. And thus any responsible accounting of the work of black women in literary studies would have to provide a history of its emergence and to consider that emergence first on its own terms.

Of course, part of the historical accounting of recent critical production is well under way, but unfortunately it leaves questions of the relations between race and critical discourse largely unexplored. A counterhistory, a more urgent history, would bring theory and practice into a productive tension that would force a reevaluation of each side. But that history could not be written without considering the determining, should I say the overdetermining, influences of institutional life out of which all critical utterances emerge.

It follows, then, that we would have to submit to careful scrutiny the past two decades, which witnessed the uncanny convergence and confluence of significant historical moments, all contributing to the present shape and contours of literary studies. These are: the emergence of a second renaissance of black women writing to public acclaim; a demographic shift that brought the first generation of black intellectuals into the halls of predominantly white, male, and elitist institutions; the institutionalization and decline of Afro-American studies and Women's Studies; and the rising command in the United States academy of poststructuralism, regarded as a synonym for theory.

Our historical narrative would have to dramatize the process by which deconstruction came to stand synecdochically for poststructuralist theory, its dominion extending from the pages of arcane journals of critical theory to the pages of such privileged arbiters of culture as the *New York Times Magazine* and *New York Review of Books*, to the less illustrious pages of *Time* and *Newsweek*.[24] The analysis would have to explore how deconstruction became associated as much with an ideological position as a revitalizing and energetic intellectual project at roughly the same time that a few black women, following Barbara Smith's challenge, began to articulate a position identified as black feminist criticism. Smith focused on recuperating the writings of black women for critical examination and establishing reading strategies attentive to the intersections of gender, race, and class in their work.[25]

If we were to isolate the salient terms of black feminist criticism and poststructuralist theory for this historical narrative, they might run as follows:

1) While black feminist criticism was asserting the significance of black women's experience, poststructuralism was dismantling the authority of experience.

2) While black feminist criticism was calling for nonhostile interpretations of black women's writings, poststructuralism was calling interpretation into question.

3) While black feminist criticism required that these interpretations be grounded in historical context, deconstruction denied history any authoritative value and truth claims, and read context as just another text.

4) While the black woman as author was central to the efforts of black feminist writers to construct a canon of new as well as unknown black women writers, poststructuralism had already rendered such efforts naive by asking, post-Foucault, "What Is an Author?" (1969) and trumpeting post–Roland Barthes, "The Death of the Author" (1968).

5) While black feminist critics and Afro-Americanists more generally were involved in recuperating a canon of writers, a critical vocabulary emerged that subordinated texts and traditions to textuality.

But the salient terms of these admittedly tendentious synopses would also have to reveal some useful correspondences. Both black feminist criticism and deconstruction see the regulation and exclusion of the marginal as essential to maintaining hegemonic structures. Both describe the structural and hierarchical relations between the margins and the center. Our narrative might then pause to ponder how these two reading strategies came to be perceived as antithetical. How their specific *units* of critical interest came to be polarized and assigned an order of intellectual value that drew on a racist and sexist schema with heavy implications and investments in the sociopolitical arrangements of our time.

CHOOSING SIDES

What viable position can be taken in this context? We might begin to assert a provisional conclusion: When the writings of black women and other critics of color are excluded from the category of theory, it must be partly because theory has been reduced to a very particular practice. Since that reduction has been widely accepted, a great many ways of talking about literature have been excluded and a variety of discursive moves and strategies disqualified, in Terry Eagleton's words, as "invalid, illicit, noncritical."[26]

The value of Eagleton's discussion of literary theory lies mainly in its understanding of how critical discourse is institutionalized. In that process, the power arrogated to some to police language, to determine that "certain statements must be excluded because they do not conform to what is acceptably sayable," cannot be denied.[27] The critical language of black women is represented, with few exceptions, as outside the bounds of the acceptably sayable and is heard primarily as an illicit and noncritical variety of critical discourse defined in opposition to theory. Its definition and identity continue to be constructed in contemporary critical discourses, all of which must be recognized, distinguished, and divided from each other in the academy's hierarchical system of classifying and organizing knowledge. To be sure, the discourses that exist at any given historical juncture compete with each other for dominance and meaning, compete with each other for status as knowledge, but we must be constantly on guard for what Biodun Jeyifo is right to term a *misrecognition* of theory, although this misrecognition has "achieved the status of that naturalization and transparency to which all ideologies aspire and which only the most hegemonic achieve."[28]

Given this *misrecognition* of theory and the privileged status it enjoys, even in moments of embattlement, it is readily understandable why some black feminists and other women of color in the academy would argue for the rightful *recognition* of their work as theory. While I would not presume to speak for or issue directives to "women of color," which would, in any case, assume a false and coherent totality, I openly share my growing skepticism, about the tactical advantages of this position.

I am far more interested, for the moment, in joining the growing number of critics—many of them Third World—who have begun to ask the difficult questions about the material conditions of institutional life and to view theory, in its narrow *usages* (rather than in any intrinsic properties to be assigned to it), as an ideological category associated with the politically dominant. It is important that such a statement *not* be read as a resistance to "theory," but one that inquires into why that category is so reductively defined, and especially why its common definitions exclude so many marginalized groups within the academy. Such is Barbara Christian's point in "The Race for Theory," although in their rush to contain her inquiry, critics missed those aspects of value in her critique.

The question that Christian raises about the reassertions of racially coded territorial assumptions and imperatives implied in the distinction between theory and practice are echoed in the writings of a growing number of students of minority and postcolonial discourses. For example, Rey Chow addresses the problem of "the asymmetrical structure between the 'West' as dominating subject and the 'nonWest' or 'Third World' as the oppressed 'other.'" She argues that "contrary to the absolute difference that is often claimed *for* the 'Third World' . . . the work of a twentieth-century Chinese intellectual foretells much that is happening in the contemporary 'Western' theoretical scene."[29] Chow's observations go far beyond and far deeper than a plea for a liberal pluralist position here, beyond a plea for "equal time." Neither she, nor the growing number of Third World intellectuals who have begun to interrogate the uses to which theory has been put for the past twenty years, is so naive as to suggest that the power of theory's gravitational field can be so simply and reactively resisted. Most of us know that the debate over the uses and abuses of theory, formulated as such, followed by a growing demand to choose sides, is sterile and boring. But more importantly, it diverts us from the more difficult pursuit of understanding how theory has been *made* into an exclusively Western phenomenon inextricably attached to the view that it does not and cannot exist outside a Western orbit.

That view is especially apparent in what Edward Said refers to as a "maddening new critical shorthand" that "makes us no less susceptible to the dangers of received authority from canonical works and authors than we ever were. We make lackluster references to Nietzsche, Freud, Lacan as if the name alone carried enough value to override any objection or to settle any quarrel."[30] Said's list of names requires others who are said to embody the most popular terms of critical opprobrium. I am concerned to note that often these are the names of black American women. Their assignment to the political, the empirical, the historical camps helps to construct an identity, a subjectivity for black feminist thinking among the general critical discourses of our time. That identity has so far been anything but fluctuating. It has been solidly fixed to a reference schemata and a racial stigmata that we have seen before.

NOTES

This is a slightly altered version of a talk presented at the Commonwealth Center for Literary and Cultural Change, University of Virginia, as a part of a general symposium, "Is Knowledge Gendered?" and a specific panel on "Race and Gender in the Teaching of Historical Knowledge." I thank Susan Fraiman and Rick Livingston for helpful comments and suggestions.

My epigraphs are drawn from Audre Lorde, "Age, Race, Class & Sex," in *Sister Outsider: Essays and Speeches by Audre Lorde* (Trumansburg, N.Y., 1984); James Baldwin, *The Evidence of Things Not Seen* (New York, 1985); Arthur C. Danto, *Narration and Knowledge* (New York, 1985); and Toni Morrison, *Beloved* (New York, 1987).

1. While certainly not peculiar to this, this philosophy of history has long been prevalent in the writings of African-Americans, especially in the historical, or documentary, fiction produced so insistently for the past twenty years. Random examples would include John A. Williams's two metahistorical novels *The Man Who Cried I Am* and *Captain Blackman* (1972), in both of which history is a suspicious text constructed by paramilitary conspirato-

rial agents. Other examples include Ishmael Reed's *Flight to Canada* (1976) and Sherley Anne Williams's *Dessa Rose,* derived from her short story "Meditations on History." For a discussion of history and documentation in African-American fiction see Barbara Foley's "The Afro-American Documentary Novel" in her *Telling the Truth: The Theory and Practice of Documentary Fiction* (Ithaca, 1986). The charge that history is a construction of the imagination has been articulated in such "nonfiction" as Hayden White's *Tropics of Discourse, The Content of the Form: Narrative Discourse and Historical Representation* (Baltimore, 1987) and *Metahistory* (Baltimore, 1973).

2. Renato Rosaldo, "Others of Invention: Ethnicity and its Discontents," *Voice Literary Supplement,* Feb. 1990, p. 27.

3. Hortense Spillers, "Interstices: A Small Drama of Words," in *Pleasure and Danger: Exploring Female Sexuality,* ed. Carole Vance (New York, 1984), p. 74.

4. Evan Watkins, "The Self-Evaluations of Critical Theory," *Boundary 2,* 12–13 (1984): 359–78.

5. Farah Griffin, *Women's Review of Books* 8 (Feb. 1991): 14.

6. As efforts to fix origins are vain and subject to the desires and needs of those in a given historical moment, I propose no definitive boundaries here, but the speeches of Sojourner Truth and Maria Stewart would have to figure prominently in any narrative of the origins of black feminist thinking. For a discussion of the wider reaches of black feminist thinking, see Patricia Hill Collins's discussion of the implied audiences in her recent book *Black Feminist Thought.* "I explicitly wrote for a broader readership than a strictly faculty or graduate student audience" and avoided "academic jargon" so as to make the "ideas in my book accessible to a wider community" ("The State of the Art," *Women's Review of Books* 8 [Feb. 1991]: 23). See also bell hooks, who described her book *Ain't I a Woman?* (Boston, 1981) as written primarily with an audience in mind of black women who worked at the phone company. She accepted their challenge to "write a book that would make our lives better, one that would make other people understand the hardships of being black and female. It was different to be writing in a context where my ideas were not seen as separate from real people and real lives" ("*Ain't I a Woman?* Looking Back," in *Talking Back: Thinking Feminist, Thinking Black* [Boston, 1989], p. 152).

7. For a discussion of the use of charismatic names to legitimate critical arguments, see Martin Jay, "Name Dropping or Dropping Names? Modes of Legitimation in the Humanities," in *Theory between the Disciplines,* ed. M. Kreiswirth and M. Cheetham.

8. For a discussion of Sojourner Truth as "standard exhibit in modern liberal historiography," see Phyllis Marynick Palmer's "White Women / Black Women: The Dualism of Female Identity and Experience in the United States," *Feminist Studies* 9 (1983): 151–69.

9. Rather than attempt to provide an extensive inventory here, let me call attention to certain benchmark statements from women of color about the injunction to theorize. In her controversial essay "The Race for Theory," Barbara Christian discusses the pressures she feels to "produce a black feminist literary theory as if [she] were a mechanical man" in *Gender and Theory,* ed. Linda Kauffman [London and New York, 1989], p. 227). Gloria Anzaldúa notes that "what passes for theory these days is forbidden territory" for women of color, which makes is "*vital* that we occupy theorizing space," even as we understand that "what is considered theory in the dominant academic community is not necessarily what counts as theory for women of color" (Introduction, *Making Face, Making Soul / Haciendo Caras: Creative and Critical Perspectives by Women of Color* [San Francisco, 1990], p. xxv).

10. Denise Riley, "*Am I That Name?" Feminism and the Category of "Women" in History* (Minneapolis, 1988), p. 1. By her admission, Riley's is a concession to pragmatism. She maintains that "it is compatible to suggest that 'women' don't exist—while maintaining a politics of 'as if they existed'—since the world behaves as if they unambiguously did" (p. 112).

11. Constance Penley, *The Future of an Illusion: Film, Feminism, and Psychoanalysis* (Minneapolis, 1989), p. 179.

12. Gayatri Spivak, "The Politics of Interpretation" in W. J. T. Mitchell, *The Politics of Interpretation* (Chicago, 1982), p. 346.

13. *Feminist Theory in Practice and Process*, ed. Micheline R. Malson et al. (Chicago, 1989), p. 7.

14. Elizabeth Spelman, *Inessential Woman: Problems of Exclusion in Feminist Thought* (Boston, 1988), p. 162.

15. In a perceptive and persuasive essay Judith Roof argues that "while the materialist commitment to gender and the economic" are defined as "'analysis,' a racial or lesbian commitment is defined differently, as anachronistically political—'liberationist'—as activism instead of analysis." She asks, "Why for this moment are gender and class cerebral and race and sexual orientation experiential?" ("All Analogies Are Faulty: The Fear of Intimacy in Feminist Criticism," in *A Lure of Knowledge: Lesbian Sexuality and Theory*, New York, 1991).

16. Toril Moi, *Sexual/Textual Politics* (London and New York, 1985).

17. Jane Flax, *Thinking Fragments: Psychoanalysis, Feminism, and Post-Modernism in the Contemporary West* (Berkeley, 1990), p. 140.

18. For a brilliant discussion of this scene and of the materiality in which black women were embedded more generally, see Haryette Mullen, "'Indelicate Subjects': African-American Women's Subjectivity," *Subversions*, Winter 1991, pp. 1–7. See also Valerie Smith's "Black Feminist Theory and the Representation of the 'Other,'" in *Changing Our Own Words: Essays on Criticism, Theory, and Writing by Black Women*, ed. Cheryl Wall (New Brunswick, N.J., 1989), pp. 38–57; see also this volume pp. 311–325. There, Smith discusses tendencies prevalent in the discourses of Anglo-American feminist and male Afro-Americanists to invoke the experiences of black women who become fetishized Others. She also links this association of black women as embodied Others to "classic Western philosophy as well as to nineteenth-century cultural ideas and ideals of womanhood. Such ideas of womanhood excluded slave women who were pinned in the body and therefore associated with animal passions and slave labor" (p. 45).

19. Nell Irvin Painter, "Sojourner Truth in Life and Memory: Writing the Biography of an American Exotic," *Gender and History* 2 (1990): 3–16. Painter traces the evolution of Sojourner Truth as historical legend and how the dominant representations of her, in both her time and ours, reflect various power asymmetries and hierarchies.

20. Georg W. F. Hegel, "Geographical Basis of History," in *The Philosophy of History*, trans. J. Sibree (New York, 1991), p. 99.

21. *Gender and Theory*, ed. Linda Kauffman (New York, 1989), p. 2.

22. Such a perception derives in large part from the wasteful battle waged on the pages of *New Literary History* 18 (1987). See Joyce Ann Joyce, "The Black Canon: Reconstructing Black American Literary Criticism"; Henry Louis Gates, Jr., "'What's Love Got to Do with It?': Critical Theory, Integrity, and the Black Idiom"; Houston A. Baker, Jr., "In Dubious Battle"; and Joyce Ann Joyce, "Who the Cap Fit': Unconsciousness and Unconscionableness in the Criticism of Houston A. Baker, Jr., and Henry Louis Gates, Jr." Christian's "The Race for Theory" added significantly to that perception.

23. Michael Awkward, "Appropriative Gestures: Theory and Afro-American Literary Criticism," in Kauffman, *Gender and Theory*, p. 243.

24. Jonathan Arac, Wlad Godzich, and Wallace Martin described the spread of deconstruction in their preface to *The Yale Critics* (Minneapolis, 1987). In his estimation, "critics doing the new work most respected by a professionally authoritative screening group have drawn heavily from the Yale critics. In thirty-five essays that recently reached the Editorial Committee of *PMLA*, the American critics most cited were Miller . . . de Man, Bloom, Hartman and Derrida." Yet another and related sign of their powerful sway, Martin

observed, was deconstruction's spread "from elite private institutions to public institutions," embracing "much more of the United States" and enrolling much "broader student bodies."

25. Barbara Smith, "Toward a Black Feminist Criticism."

26. Terry Eagleton, *Literary Theory: An Introduction* (Minneapolis, 1983), p. 203.

27. Ibid.

28. Biodun Jeyifo, "Literary Theory and Theories of Decolonization." Unpublished manuscript. Also see his "On Eurocentric Critical Theory: Some Paradigms from the Texts and Sub-Texts of Post-Colonial Writing," in Helen Tiffin and Stephen Slemon, eds., *After Europe: Critical Theory, Post-Colonial Writing* (Sydney, 1989).

29. Rey Chow, "'It's You, and Not Me': Domination and 'Othering' in Theorizing the 'Third World,'" in *Coming to Terms: Feminism, Theory, Politics*, ed. Elizabeth Week (New York, 1989), p. 161.

30. Edward Said, *The World, the Text, and the Critic* (New York, 1983).

THE "WILD ZONE" THESIS AS GLOSS IN CHICANA LITERARY STUDY

(1993)

One of the difficulties faced in the feminist project undertaken by women of color in the United States[1] has been to avoid privileging gender over race because Chicanos and other men of color are themselves members of politically and economically subordinated classes. Yet, to recognize the compound oppression referred to as "double" or "triple" jeopardy (Millman and Kanter 1975; Candelaria 1978; Melville 1980) of Chicanas, Latinas, and other women of color demands recognition of the additional burden of gender for women as it is interpreted within political hierarchies in all patriarchal societies. One approach to addressing the tension between race and gender, both that experienced in material political reality and that evident in U.S. American analytical feminist discourse, is suggested by an influential essay in *Perceiving Women* (1975), a book on the anthropology of gender written by anthropologists Edwin and Shirley Ardener to analyze their ethnographic field experiences. In it, they describe as a "wild zone" the separate political and cultural space that women inhabit in the societies they studied.

In the societies described by the Ardeners, that space was perceived to derive from certain physiological circumstances which then became defined and affected by societal and cultural responses to those circumstances. Because among humans only women produce ova, experience gestation, childbirth, and how it feels to suckle an infant born of one's body, within historical time this physiology was interpreted and described socioculturally by the societies the Ardeners researched, and it has been throughout history, in a variety of ways (e.g., as saintliness, nurturance, docility, weakness, mental deficiency, and other now established stereotypes of femininity). Civilization's (that is, the patriarchy's) elaborate social conventions and political systems based on learned gender difference are traceable in large measure to the physiology of sexuality and the acquired stereotypes of femininity and masculinity. Even when women have been revered for specific, discrete attributes like maternity, traits that have been generalized metonymically to all women and to essential femaleness, these gendered identities subordinate women as a class to the definitions of male-wielded power and patriarchal institutions. The Mexicano/Chicano cultural archetypes of the Virgin of Guadalupe, La Malinche, La Llorona, and La Adelita exemplify this stereotypification (Candelaria 1980; Limón 1990; Peréz 1991).

The Ardener "wild zone" thesis posits that women's experience has evolved distinct female-identified cultures necessarily marginalized within, and simultaneously outside of, the dominant male-identified patriarchy. The thesis asserts that:

> The real problem is that all world-structures are totalitarian in tendency. . . . The englobed structure [of femaleness] is totally "muted" [i.e., both marginalized and silent] in terms of the englobing one. There is then an absolute equality of world-structures in this principle, for we are talking of their self-defining and reality-reducing features. *Dominance* occurs when one structure blocks the power of actualization of the other, so that it has no "freedom of action." . . . [T]he articulation of world-structures does not rest only in their production base but at all levels of communication: that a structure is also a kind of language of many semiological elements, which specify all actions by its power of definition. (E. Ardener 1975, 252)

The citation stresses that "dominance" of one structure over an/other produces disproportionate socioeconomic (i.e., production base) and cultural (i.e., language and semiotic) effects. The interwoven connection between social norms and individual identity that results in patriarchal dominance over women in turn produces a greater distance between female *desire* and actual choice—between personal identity and the sociocultural power to begin even to approximate the actualization of that identity.

The Ardeners labelled women's separate space as a "zone" to denote both its *physiology-derived* bounded space, as well as to capture the idea of the learned, *stereotype-derived* female space defined by the dominant structure. (Analogous examples include climate zones which typify areas identified by actual, geography-derived characteristics, and traffic parking zones which illustrate areas designated according to abstract ideas [like stereotypes] arbitrarily circumscribed.) To distinguish women's space from the societal hegemony that contains it, the Ardeners applied the term "wild" to suggest an emphatic pristine nature (of geography, physiology, and sexuality) free of the inscribed assumptions and definitions of traditional patriarchal civilization. Although the sign *wild* might be considered problematic because of its perceived pejorative connotations, it is intended to be understood as continuing the feminist project's recuperation of reductive, distorting anthropomorphic labels (e.g., bitch, spinster, witch, dyke) according to feminist-defined primary values of proto-herstory and originary women's experience. Accordingly, "wildness" and "wilderness" not only express conditions of nature in a non-technologized unconquered state, but they also describe certain required conditions and activities of life-generating experience (e.g., sexuality and emotion) in organized society.

The "wild zone" thesis thus identifies a fundamental paradox of female identity: on the one hand, a distinct female experiential, cultural space derived from an unrestricted ("wild") existence unmediated by inimical, imposed definitions of identity, and on the other the restricted women-space defined by and located within the englobing historical patriarchy without recognition of women's human potential or achievement. To Kristeva (1981) and other intellectual descendants of Lacan (1986), this paradox is explained by the historical power of the patriarchy to define language and to subsume within itself the evolved significations of language thus invalidating concepts based on any "real" or "true" categories of "woman" and "femininity." To Jardine (1985) and what she calls the "fundamental feminist gesture" within both Lacanian concepts *and* the political materialist categories identified with U.S. feminism, this paradox is explained by focusing on the "space" between masculinized perceptions (whether perpetuated by men or women) and the Other, "*a space coded as feminine*" [her italics] within her theory of "*gynesis*—the putting into discourse of 'woman'" (1985, 25).

The "wild zone" schema, with the theoretical nuances and anthropological observations contained in *Perceiving Women* only briefly outlined in this essay, offers a gloss on the partially divergent view of Kristeva and Jardine, a gloss that apprehends validity in both viewpoints contingent upon the function of the discourse. The "wild zone" schema acknowledges the legitimacy of questions regarding the idea of *an essential woman-ness* and the critique that dismantles such an idea, but it simultaneously recognizes that a crucial consequence of patriarchy is the persistent *and empowered* "perceiving" of "women" in essential(ist) terms. Further, the schema provides a useful perspective on the fundamental paradox of female identity (and that of other disempowered classes). As politically subordinated subjects, women (and other marginalized political subordinates) must, for survival, know and practice the dominant patriarchal discourse and conventions. But equally manifest is that for survival and maintenance of an unmediated, affirmative identity of self and class, women and other marginalized groups develop an/other culture and discourse—one not required for the survival of, and therefore largely unavailable to, the empowered members of the dominant class. The central point here is that *the power of the patriarchy itself* impedes and frequently precludes members of the dominant class from perceiving, understanding, or accessing "wild zone" values and codes, or what Kolodny has identified as gender inflections outside the canonized norms of patriarchy (1985, 47–50). The empowered statuses and valorized identities of dominant class members—that is, their power—both bind them to the hegemonic order and also blind them from either apprehending or comprehending the separate experience and values of the disempowered classes.

To return to the issue presented in this essay's introduction—the privileging of gender over race given that Chicanos and other men of color are themselves members of subordinate classes—the "wild zone" again offers a useful gloss for reading the Chicana/Latina experience in the United States. The "wild zone" facilitates the examination of gender as a discrete attribute because its very conceptualization is based on a recognition of multiple and distinct *cultures* of experience that develop from such fundamental categories as gender, race, and ethnicity, as well as according to political-economic categories of class and wealth distribution (Candelaria, "Multicultural Wild Zone," 1989). This is salient to Chicana studies (and other studies of politically oppressed groups) for it encourages gender-specific analysis without denying the importance of ethnic- or race-specific or class-specific analyses. Unlike traditional academic studies by Chicanos and non-Chicanos which uncritically focus primarily on male-defined subsets of the patriarchy, the "wild zone" thesis encourages the examination of gender as a subject of critique within the analysis of ideology, power, and culture without privileging it over the defining attributes of other categories of identity.

The conceptualization of an affirmative culture and discourse originating in the "wild zone" distinct from, but also in relation to, the hegemonic culture comple-ments and enhances other conceptualizations of supra/subordinate societal rela-tionships. Du Bois' idea of "double consciousness," for example, recognizes the requirement for political minorities within a culturally different polity to be flu-ent in the language and social behaviors of the supraordinate "masters" even as they develop their own group-affirming idioms (1965). Freire, too, describes a "bi-furcated vision" that political minorities possess as "victims" of dominant/domi-nating structures whose public rhetoric articulates principles and ideals remote from their "concrete victimization" (1970). Beauvoir's "second sex" idea of fe-male gender reflects a similar perspective that defines women and womanhood in relation to the patriarchy, men, and the *droit du seigneur* (the right of the mas-ter) (1949). Emphasizing the important dimension of the subjective conscious-ness of particular individuals or classes, these conceptualizations focus on "minority" subjectivity in relation to the culture of dominance. The "wild zone" idea problematizes that dimension, as Bakhtin does in his reading of the mul-tiple codes of medieval folk culture (1964), by emphasizing the collective culture(s) from which individuals and classes emerge. Further, it focuses on the interactive dynamics of relationship, on the nexus between private and public spheres and between power and disempowerment, and on evolving social forms and patterns.

Another utility of the "wild zone" concept is its forefronting of the substance and affirmative aspects of marginalized cultures. By identifying Chicanas, for in-stance, as part of a zone of experience and power inaccessible to the agents of patriarchal power or to those lacking critical awareness of the patriarchy, the au-thority of Chicana expression in language and other mediums of creativity is de-fined from *within* Chicana experience and not solely *in relation* to the dominating political hegemonies, public or private. This is crucial both in Chicana/o studies and in policy-making arenas for it neutralizes the often voiced reluctance by both women and men to focus on the needs, desires, achievements, and oppressions of women-identified Chicanas (and other women of color) in order to avoid di-minishing issues of race, ethnicity, and class. The very terms of its definition as a space among others underscores the "wild zones'" explicit acknowledgment of the authority, but not superiority, of a multiplicity of other zones of experience, idea, and culture.

Conceptualization of the "wild zone" also complements other descriptions of Chicana-identified creative expression. Literary scholar Rosaura Sánchez, for ex-ample, in "The History of Chicanas: Proposal for a Materialist Perspective" calls for "subject-identified" analysis; that is, analysis that valorizes the Chicana subject's "multiple subjectivities" of gendered identity, ethnoracial experience, and material class situation (1990, 5–23). Similarly, historian Emma Peréz in "Sexuality and Discourse: Notes from a Chicano Survivor" calls for perspectives that seek to comprehend from inside *un sitio y una lengua* of the subject (1991, 161). Implicit in both of these appeals is a recognition of the distinctly separate experiential and political space of Chicanas and other women *as subjects*; in the Ardeners' thesis, the subject-identified "wild zone" asserts both the appropriate-ness *and necessity* of gender-specific interrogation in the research and study of all peoples of color.

As the feminist/ethnic studies revisionary project of the past two decades has demonstrated, Chicana/Latina and other women writers have struggled for centuries to express and assert the validity of womanspace and the textured zone of women's experience. In America at least as far back as Sor Juana in the seventeenth century we find vigorous protest against the accepted hegemonic principle of "silencing women" in her era. Her carefully reasoned and impassioned analysis in *La Repuesta* argued that the effect of barring women from access to formal education resulted in the total disempowerment of women in society. Later women writers of the Americas have echoed Sor Juana by tracing a similar link between gender and genre, between female experience and its expression in literature, the arts, and other discourses.

Examples of these tracings from the "wild zone" include the majority of contemporary Chicana writers. Significantly, many of them have chosen to configure their stories with images and themes of place—that is, in terms of thematic *zones* that interconnect experience and imagination. Sometimes that configuration centers on the geography of birthplace and homeland; sometimes its center is the home and personal surroundings. Whatever the center of origin, these external spaces also serve to inscribe aspects of the interior dimensions and private spaces of Chicana experience. Three noteworthy illustrations of these inscriptions are writings by Estela Portillo-Trambley, Denise Chávez, and Sandra Cisneros.

Estela Portillo-Trambley, one of the first women to gain prominence within contemporary Chicana/o letters (receiving the Quinto Sol Award in 1972), integrates issues of woman-identity and feminism with figures of place in her fiction and drama. For instance, her short story, "The Paris Gown" (1973), highlights in its very title one of the world's premier cosmopolitan cities. More important to a reading of the narrative is that the plot's feminist rite of passage depends for its thematics on the contrast of French and Mexican landscapes and the cultures both places represent in the imagination of the young Theresa, the niece of the story's protagonist, Clotilde, whose life is told in flashback. Paris and Europe represent freedom and choice to Clotilde as she tells her story decades later to her visiting niece, whereas Mexico and home mean suppression under the stifling authority of her father, of the future husband arranged for her, and of the machismo she sees pervading the society of her birth. By inscribing her protagonist's personal desires and choices in terms broader than her private psychology, in the spatial and political dichotomy of place and culture, Portillo-Trambley's narrative expresses one aspect of the paradox of gendered identity described above and usefully glossed by the "wild zone" thesis.

Less dichotomous in its emblematic use of place is *Rain of Scorpions* (1975), the title novella of Portillo-Trambley's first published collection of short fiction. Employing the techniques of naturalism, the author underscores the omnipotence of land, nature, and industrial corporations over the people of Smelter-town, a symbolically drawn industrial town situated between "two propitious mountains where long ago Cabeza de Baca had ciphered the name of El Paso del Norte" (136). The narrative juxtaposes the socioeconomic struggles of the town's downtrodden workers with the personal struggle of Lupe, an earth-mother figure seeking to discover her selfhood and, in the process, to recover her feminine power, particularly over Fito, the veteran who returned from Vietnam with one leg missing but with his political conscience activated. Ever present in the people's lives is the awesomeness of nature with its demanding beauty, its unpredictable weather, and the ubiquitous animals—elements drawn together in the conclusion when the flooding rains arrive along with the deluge of scorpions. Even though the town's smelter is a site of industrial pollution and corporate exploitation, Portillo-Trambley makes it clear (sometimes heavy-handedly) that the smelter and the ore derive from the land that preceded it, and the land's primacy and originary power invests it with spiritual energy. Like the land's precedent spiritual power Lupe's compassion is linked specifically to her womanhood in attributes associated with recuperative "wild zone" definitions of subjectivity.

Denise Chávez's and Sandra Cisneros' work also frequently underscore place, especially home and geography, as metaphor. They share with Portillo-Trambley the portrayal of compelling female figures whose characterizations are closely related to their physical environments. Stylistically, their most well-known titles resemble in their use of short narrative and vignette the major works of several important literary antecedents: Kate Chopin's *Bayou Folk* (1894), Sherwood Anderson's *Winesburg, Ohio* (1919), and Tomas Rivera's *Y no se lo trago la tierra* (1971). The continuity between these titles and Chávez's and Cisneros' extends beyond narrative sketches yoked around a central narrator, for they also portray a similar terrain of psychological alienation and sociopolitical subordination. They share as well a heightened interest in writing the protagonist's self as simultaneous product observer, antagonist, and embodiment of place—whether bayou, Winesburg, or la tierra.

Chávez's *The Last of the Menu Girls* (1986), a collection of short stories, is united by its New Mexico settings and female perspectives. All of the seven stories in *Menu Girls* present the girlhood experiences and imaginings of Rocio Esquibel, the "menu girl" of the collection's title story. Although plots of the stories collectively focus on Rocio's personal development and emergent writer's consciousness, Chávez etches her personality—and that of many of the other characters—through meticulous attention to the specifics of her surroundings. The closing lines of "Compadre," the last story in the book, exemplify this concern with place. To the query, "What do you write?" Rocio responds offhandedly "Oh, about people. New Mexico. You know, everything" (1986, 190). Her mother then intrudes, characteristically, into the conversation with a long monologue that captures much of the essence of the preceding stories: " . . . I say, Rocio, just write about this little street of ours, it's only one block long, but there's so many stories. Too many stories! . . . but why write about this street? Why not just write about 325? That's our house! Write about 325 and that will take the rest of your life . . . " (1986, 190).

The Last of the Menu Girls constitutes the author's realization of this advice, for it chronicles the lives, images, events, speech, and human relations of that street and its houses, yards, secret hiding spots, and special landmarks as remembered by the protagonist.

In the title story, "The Last of the Menu Girls," recipient of the 1985 Puerto del Sol Fiction Award, Rocio's character emerges through her exploration of Altavista Memorial Hospital where she works as a menu taker for the patients. Her encounter of the hospital's offices, patient rooms, corridors, smells, and sounds, along with her reaction to the other employees and patients give texture to her natural inquisitiveness and keen observation, just as her part-time job loosens sharp memories of her Great Aunt Eutilia's dying in the Esquibel home a few summers before. Similarly, in "Willow Game" the unnamed narrator we know to be Rocio recalls a pivotal feature of her girlhood, the trees that punctuated her neighborhood and which serve in her adult mind as landmarks of her rite of passage to maturity. As in the other stories which capture the particulars of place, Chávez here painstakingly describes the trees in their physical spaces: "The Apricot tree was bound by the channelway that led to the Main Street ditch"; "the Willow stump remained underneath the window of my old room" (1986, 43, 49) in order to emphasize the persistence of place in triggering memory: "[Today] I walked outside and the same experience repeated itself" (1986, 50). Like Portillo-Trambley in "Paris Gown," Chávez forefronts concrete places interconnected with psychological and cultural perceptions to show both how the interconnected zones shape her characters' lives and imaginations and also how they persist as catalysts of memory and idea.

In similar fashion, Sandra Cisneros unites *The House on Mango Street* (1983), a series of vignettes and short stories, by attentive focus to the scenic details of her main character's Chicago home. The book, which won the 1985 Before Columbus Book Award, is written with a concreteness and vitality that captures the density and rush of the city, external and visible, as well as the interior traffic of her protagonist Esperanza's feelings and imaginings. Whether recounting the people and occasions that are the subject of the chapters entitled "Boys and Girls," "The Earl of Tennessee," and "Minerva Writes Poems," or telling of the yearning and adolescent angst that gird the chapters "Linoleum Roses," "Born Bad," and "Burns in the Attic," Esperanza defines herself in relation to her memories of her childhood living on the move in the houses on Mango, Keeler, Paulina, and Loomis Streets. As important, her later recollection of the houses and the meaning of all the urban places of her girlhood elicits a sociopolitical sense of community in the adult chronicler actually writing the book. Her memories also locate a positive relation between her adolescent desire for a room of her own and her writerly need for solitude and introspection.

Cisneros' third book, *My Wicked Wicked Ways* (1987), a volume of poetry, contains similarly strong references to geography and physical space. Two of the volume's four sections are titled with place names: "I: 1200 South/2100 West," referring to Chicago's street numbers, and "III: Other Countries," relating to the poet's European travels. In addition, she introduces two of the sections with epigraphs (one by poet Gwendolyn Brooks, Cisneros' mentor; the other from *The Three Marás*) that explicitly allude to place. Especially graphic in communicating idea and feeling through tropes of physical place are the poems "Six Brothers," "Twister Hits Houston," "By Way of Explanation," "Men Asleep," and all the pieces in section III. "Six Brothers," for example, contrasts the "earthbound" speaker's search for ancestral roots in palpable places, "castles maybe" or "a Sahara city," with her father's ambitious hope for his family's successful future as achievers of illustrious careers (1987, 24–25). In "Men Asleep" the speaker casts her sad yearning for intimacy deeper than the flesh in terms of place, by describing past lovers "who go room into room into room,/ who shut themselves like doors,/ who would not let me in" (1987, 89). Like *Mango Street* and Chávez's *Menu Girls*, these poems give voice to a self-expression firmly bound to home and to homeland, to hearth and to earth, and authorizes the literary page itself with a fresh discovered territory within the "wild zone" of her woman-identified identity.

Many other talented Chicana writers and artists[2] have indicated a pressing interest in the geography of Aztlan, in the multiple Mexican American crossroads of the U.S., in the rich cultural and political outgrowths of other known territories as metaphors of "wild zone" consciousness. These expressions of creativity are part of the feminist project undertaken by women of color in the United States (see note 1) and, while offering woman-identified perspectives of Chicana experience, clearly do not privilege gender over race or ethnicity. Rather, they depict areas of a subject-identified "wild zone" thereby "putting" Chicanas "into [the] discourse of women" (Jardine 1985) in its multiple meanings.

NOTES

1. I refer specifically to the *United States* to delimit this paper as much as possible to feminism considered within the context of American political power and patriarchal hierarchies and not within the philosophical and psychological theories of French (anti)feminist discourse—particularly that posited by and derived from Lacan, Derrida, Kristeva, Cixous, and Irigaray—even though I recognize the salience of that discourse. My intention is to suggest a presumptive rationale for an activist ethnic feminism in response to the increased impact of the reactionary counter-discourse of such high profile, popular culture mouthpieces as for example, Dinesh D'Souza, Linda Chavez, Camille Paglia et al. These ultra-conservatives seek to subvert the radical multicultural project of expanding U.S. education and politics with an inclusive curriculum.

2. Among them are Gloria Anzaldúa, whose *Borderlands: The New Mestiza=La Frontera* (1987) argues with passion that Chicana identity cannot be separated from land base and place, and Angela De Hoyos, whose *Chicano Poems for the Barrio* (1975) examines oppression in urban barrios by showing how the land "belongs" to no one even though it must be respected as if it "belong[s] to all." Poets Lorna Dee Cervantes, Carmen Tafolla, Gina Valdes, and Bernice Zamora; novelist Isabela Rios; and essayist Silvia Lizarraga have also written nuanced treatments of the interactive dynamics of place and psyche and space and politics. Among visual artists, muralist Judith Baca and painter Carmen Lomas Garza are two Chicanas who express a similar theme in their work.

WORKS CITED

Anzaldúa, Gloria. *Borderlands: The New Mestiza=La Frontera*. San Francisco: Spinsters/Aunt Lute, 1987.

Ardener, Edwin. "Belief and the Problem of Women." In *Perceiving Women*, ed. Shirley Ardener. London: Malaby Press, 1975.

Ardener, Shirley, ed. *Perceiving Women*. London: Malaby Press, 1975.

Bakhtin, Mikhail M. *Rabelais and His World*. Trans. Helene Iswolsky. Bloomington: Indiana University Press, 1964.

Candelaria, Cordelia Chávez. "Women in the Academy." *Rendezvous: Journal of Arts and Letters*. 13 (1978) 9-18.

——. "La Malinche, Feminist Prototype." *Frontiers: A Journal of Women Studies*. 5 (1989) 1–16.

――. "The Multicultural 'Wild Zone' of Ethnic-identified American Literatures." In *Multiethnic Literatures of the United States: Critical Introductions and Classroom Resources*, ed. Cordelia Chávez Candelaria, i–xiv. Boulder: University of Colorado Press, 1989.

Chávez, Denise. *The Last of the Menu Girls*. Houston: Arte Público Press. 1986.

Cisneros, Sandra. *The House on Mango Street*. Houston: Arte Público Press, 1983.

――. *My Wicked Wicked Ways*. Bloomington: Third Woman Press, 1987.

de Beauvoir, Simone. *The Second Sex*. Trans. H.M. Parshley. New York: Vintage, 1974 [c. 1949].

Du Bois, W. E. B. *The Souls of the Black Folk: The Negro Classics*. New York: Knopf, 1965.

Jardine, Alice A. *Gynesis: Configurations of Woman and Modernity*. Ithaca: Cornell University Press, 1985.

Kolodny, Annette. "A Map for Rereading: Gender and the Interpretation of Literary Texts." In *The New Feminist Criticism*, ed. Elaine Showalter, pp. 46–62. New York: Pantheon, 1985.

Kristeva, Julia. "Women's Time." Trans. Alice Jardine and Harry Blake. *Signs: Journal of Women in Culture and Society*. 7 (May 1981) 55–69; see also this volume pp. 860–879.

Lacan, Jaques. "The Agency of the Letter and the Unconscious, or Reason Since Freud." Trans. Alan Sheridan. In *Critical Theory Since 1965*, ed. Hazard Adams and Leroy Searle, 738–754. Tallahassee: Florida State University Press, 1986.

Limón, José. "La Llorona, the Third Legend of Greater Mexico: Cultural Symbols, Women, and the Political Unconscious." In *Between Borders: Essays on Mexican Chicana History*, ed. Adelaida R. Del Castillo, 399–432. Encino: Floricanto Press, 1990.

Melville, Margarita, ed. *Twice a Minority: Mexican American Women*. St. Louis: C.V. Mosby, 1980.

Millman, Marcia, and Rosabeth Moss Kanter, eds. *Another Voice: Feminist Perspectives on Social Life and Social Science*. New York: Doubleday, 1975.

Peréz, Emma. "Sexuality and Discourse: Notes from a Chicana Survivor." In *Chicana Lesbians: The Girls Our Mothers Warned Us About*, ed. Carla Trujillo, 159–184. Berkeley: Third Woman Press, 1991.

Portillo-Trambley, Estela. *Rain of Scorpions and Other Writings*. Berkeley: Tonatiuh-Quinto Sol International, 1975.

Sánchez, Rosaura. "The History of Chicanas: Proposal for a Materialist Perspective." In *Between Borders: Essays on Mexican Chicana History*, ed. Adelaida R. Del Castillo, 1–29. Encino: Floricanto Press, 1990.

conflicts

Every section heading in *Feminisms* is arbitrary, in the sense that each essay in this volume could easily be placed under many—or even most—sections in the book. Of all the sections, "Conflicts" is the most arbitrary, because feminist criticism always gets produced in the context of conflict. Like all academic discourse, feminist criticism and theory is fundamentally argumentative: to publish an article, a critic must have an original point to make, and an original point, by definition, disputes or at least departs from an argument someone else has made. For all its radical resistance to the premises and conventions of mainstream academic work, feminist criticism still makes arguments. What makes feminist conflict distinct is that it always begins from a shared set of political goals. Roughly speaking, all feminists agree that women are and have been oppressed under the system of patriarchy, and that feminists need to act to overturn that oppression. There is no unanimity, however, about what such action should entail (see our section on "Practice" for more on this debate). This section includes essays that place the conflicts among feminists in the foreground of their arguments, implicitly italicizing the "s" in "feminisms."

At first, feminist criticism was chiefly in conflict with mainstream, masculinist critical practices and theory, and in many ways that conflict still continues. As feminist criticism developed in its own right during the 1970s and 1980s, internal methodological conflicts ensued as feminist academics sought to theorize their critical practice. Deep divisions arose, for instance, between those whose work emulated the psychoanalytically and linguistically inclined French feminism and those whose Anglo-American feminism engaged more directly with history and with social issues. (For comprehensive and influential summaries emanating from opposite sides of that debate, see Toril Moi's *Sexual/Textual Politics* [1985], speaking in favor of French feminism, and Janet Todd's *Feminist Literary History* [1988], arguing for the Anglo-American position.) That debate sometimes took the form of arguments over whether feminist criticism should be more "theoretical" or more "empirical." The identity politics of the late 1980s and early 1990s brought other differences among feminists to the fore: theorists argued that feminism now had a "mainstream" that was markedly white, middle-class, Western, and heterosexual, and that feminist criticism and theory had been participating in the marginalization of women of color, working-class women, Third World women, and lesbians. In the 1990s, few if any feminist critics would dispute that insight, but conflicts persist as theorists seek to grapple with differences among and between feminists.

Indeed, "difference" has always been a source of debate among feminist theorists. The first two essays in this section participate in a conflict over difference that arose in the early 1980s, with Annette Kolodny's influential call for a pluralist feminist criticism, "Dancing Through the Minefield" (in "Practice"). Kolodny's essay appeared at the moment when American feminist critics were moving away from androgyny (or the effacement of gender differentiation) as a standard for art and for scholarship, and were beginning to embrace "difference." That is, from the early part of the decade, American feminist theorists became increasingly convinced that gender, having a significant impact upon experience, must make important differences in the production and evaluation of literary texts. At issue among the writers who wrote in response to Kolodny's essay—such as Jane Marcus and Nina Baym—are such questions as: Does the difference of gender inhere in the body (an "essentialist" view), or is it culturally constructed? What do the signs of gender difference look like in literary texts? What difference does gender make when a critic undertakes to evaluate a work written by a woman, or one written by a man? Should feminist criticism adopt a "pluralist" theoretical stance? Does it need "theory" at all? Marcus's essay takes issue with Kolodny's answers to these questions, and Baym disputes Marcus's position.

In "Storming the Toolshed" (1982), Jane Marcus revives the battlefield metaphor Annette Kolodny invoked in "Dancing Through the Minefleld," but revises it, too. Marcus sees the pluralist "relaxation of . . . tensions" among feminists (and between feminists and the academy) as premature, arguing—in her memorable phrase—that "Dancing shoes will not do. We still need our heavy boots and mine detectors." Beginning by examining the role of literary theory in feminist critical practice, Marcus decries theoreticians' tendency to dismiss the contributions of feminist theorists to literary study. Marcus advocates a form of intellectual affirmative action, as she insists that "our [feminists'] historical losses at their [the male academic establishment's] hands are incalculable. . . . It is up to them to make reparations." She illustrates the radical potential of "lupine" criticism (in which feminist critics metaphorically double as flowers and as wolves) with reference to feminist work on Virginia Woolf, emphasizing especially the "collective and collaborative" studies that challenge conventional notions of individual achievement. She also gleefully recounts the tackling of "the two taboo subjects, Woolf's socialist politics and her love of women," thus helping to subvert the received idea of a ladylike, nonfeminist Woolf.

What separates Marcus most distinctly from Kolodny is less her critical program than the tone of her dismissal of pluralism as the model for feminist criticism: far from seeking to efface conflict, Marcus seems to revel in it. Evidently her tone struck Nina Baym, as we see in the last footnote of "The Madwoman and Her Languages: Why I Don't Do Feminist Literary Theory" (1984). Baym and Marcus take the same departure point: Baym begins by saying that "the central issue in academic literary feminism right now is theory itself," which does not diverge far from Marcus's statement that "the most serious issue" is "the division between theory and practice." But rather than endorsing theory as a "power tool" (Marcus's phrase) for feminism, Baym renews Kolodny's plea for pluralism, and asks feminists to return to the "empirically" based study which predated the theoretical revolution in feminist criticism. Baym confronts theoretically based feminist theses that she sees as counterproductive to feminism's goals; for example, she objects to the use Sandra M. Gilbert and Susan Gubar (cited approvingly by Kolodny) make of the "madwoman" as a figure for female authors, rejects the notion of a distinctly "female" language, and repudiates psychoanalytic assumptions she reads as misogynist.

Baym—whose groundbreaking work on nineteenth-century American women's novels has been central to many other feminists' projects—does not speak from an antifeminist, but rather an antitheory (and antitotalizing) position. Her position anticipates the late-1980s emphasis on the fact that not all women (nor even all feminists) are alike: as Baym puts it, "a difference more profound for feminism than the male-female difference emerges: the difference between woman and woman." The pluralism Baym advocates, however, is not the mode adopted in later feminist statements about differences among women. In those statements, more open conflict prevails.

The metaphor for conflict shifts from battlegrounds to domestic spaces in Biddy Martin and Chandra Talpade Mohanty's "Feminist Politics: What's Home Got to Do with It?" (1986). Martin and Mohanty enter the debate about "identity politics," the issue of whether one's experience and "positionality" (i.e., class, race, sexual orientation, nation, religion, etc.)—or one's home, so to speak—must limit one to writing from a specific perspective defined by those identity markers. Can a "white" woman write about "women of color"? Can a heterosexual woman write about lesbians? When a woman of color writes about her own experience, can she speak for other women of color, as well? If mainstream feminism has marginalized the perspectives and experiences of Third World women, is there anything in Western feminism that can be of use from those perspectives? Martin and Mohanty use the principles of deconstruction to show that maintaining such oppositions as white/color, West/East, heterosexual/lesbian only operates to perpetuate the power of the dominant term in each pair. Doing a close reading of an autobiographical essay by Minnie Bruce Pratt ("white, middle-class, Christian-raised, southern, and lesbian"), Martin and Mohanty argue that Pratt's text questions "the all-too-common conflation of experience, identity, and political perspective." By maintaining "complex positionalities" that avoid settling into a fixed identity, Pratt writes "an enactment of careful and constant differentiations which refuses the all-too-easy polemic that opposes victims to perpetrators." Martin and Mohanty see Pratt's writing as leading to "a conception of power that refuses totalizations, and can therefore account for the possibility of resistance." Implicitly disputing the charge that deconstruction is not a political practice, Martin and Mohanty see the prospect of reclaiming "home" from the radical Right as a concept newly useful to building feminist community.

Valerie Smith, too, addresses the relationship between deconstruction and identity politics, but from a more skeptical position. In "Black Feminist Theory and the Representation of the 'Other'" (1989), Smith suggests that deconstruction's incorporation into academic institutions may compromise its usefulness for oppositional critical practices. She begins her essay by alluding to an earlier conflict among feminists and male critics over the dangers of white men's appropriation of feminist criticism (see *Men in Feminism*, edited by Alice Jardine and Paul Smith in 1987), to show the parallel between that situation and what has happened to black women writers. Smith argues black male critics and white feminist critics alike use black women as the subject matter that can bring abstract deconstructionist theory back to the realm of history, experience, and the body. Smith sees this use of black women as the "other" of critical theory as replicating the age-old Western practice of conflating black women "with the body and therefore with animal passions and slave labor," which is, to say the least, "conceptually problematic."

As an alternative, Smith invokes a black feminist critical theory that recognizes that "the meaning of blackness in this country shapes profoundly the experience of gender, just as the conditions of womanhood affect ineluctably the experience of race," a theory that is always "holding in balance the three variables of race, gender, and class and destabilizing the centrality of any one." In this respect,

Smith's argument is less in conflict with Martin and Mohanty's than her critique of deconstruction might suggest. Smith offers a reading of *Sarah Phillips* (1984) by Andrea Lee, a fictional text about a black American middle-class woman who is simultaneously an insider and an outsider to the worlds she inhabits, to conclude provocatively that "the circumstances of race and gender alone protect no one from the seductions of reading her own experience as normative and fetishizing the experience of the other." In this way, Smith places herself both inside and outside the debate over identity politics.

Feminist theoretical arguments over positionality, experience, and identity often hinge on the concept of "essentialism," or the much-disputed idea that certain traits of women are essential to women's nature, ineluctable, eternal, and—by implication—unchangeable. In "Upping the Anti (sic) in Feminist Theory," (from Marianne Hirsch and Evelyn Fox Keller's important 1990 anthology, *Conflicts in Feminism*), Teresa de Lauretis shows that poststructuralist arguments seeking to purge "essence" from feminist theory tend to perpetuate the binary system of thought they purport to critique. De Lauretis demonstrates that poststructuralist theory would not be possible without the insights it inherits from the very thinkers its practitioners dismiss as "essentialist," and argues that feminism actually *has* an essence, an "essential difference" to be found in feminism's "political, personal, critical, and textual practices," its participation in social and cultural formations, and the conflicting views of itself that constitute the history of feminist theory. She envisions two distinct drives at work in feminism: "an erotic, narcissistic drive" and "an ethical drive," constantly in creative conflict with each other, especially in lesbian feminist theory where—as de Lauretis explains—the erotic and the ethical are often interchangeable. Like Martin and Mohanty and Smith, de Lauretis advocates blurring the boundaries between binary opposition, or—as she puts it—"upping the anti" by "analyzing the undecidability. . . of the alternatives" in such pairings as theory vs. practice, women's studies vs. feminist cultural theory, or feminist theory vs. feminist criticism in literary studies. Her final definition of feminist theory incorporates "its specific, emergent, and conflictual history," the differences and the conflicts among and within feminists, as central to the movement's identity.

—RRW

STORMING THE TOOLSHED

(1982)

I. FEMINIST SCHOLARS AND LITERARY THEORY

Sections II and III of this article reflect their occasions. "Lupine Criticism" was given as a talk at the Modern Language Association (MLA) meeting in San Francisco in 1979. Florence Howe chaired the session with panelists Mary Helen Washington, Sydney Janet Kaplan, Suzanne Juhasz, and Tillie Olsen.[1] There was a large and enthusiastic audience, and the session was remarkable historically for discussion of race, class, and sexual identity, particularly lesbianism, and for vocal criticism and participation from the audience. The sparse audience for feminist sessions the following year in Houston, the current debate in the National Women's Studies Association over the primacy of the issues of racism and lesbian identity,[2] and the concurrent minimization of differences in feminist literary criticism itself by Annette Kolodny and others in recent issues of *Feminist Studies*[3] make it imperative that we reexamine our history. It was, after all, a playful but serious prediction made in "Lupine Criticism" that aggressive, historical feminist scholarship on Virginia Woolf might cease if the practitioners became absorbed into the academy and stopped combining political activism and the position of "outsidership" with their scholarly work.

In "Dancing Through the Minefield," Kolodny's liberal relaxation of the tensions among us and the tensions between feminists and the academy reflects a similar relaxation on the part of historians and political activists. What this does is to isolate Marxist feminists and lesbians on the barricades while "good girl" feminists fold their tents and slip quietly into the establishment. There is a battlefield (race, class, and sexual identity) within each one of us, another battlefield where we wage these wars with our own feminist colleagues (as in *Signs*), and a third battlefield where we defend ourselves from male onslaughts both on our work and on the laws that govern our lives as women in society. It is far too early to tear down the barricades. Dancing shoes will not do. We still need our heavy boots and mine detectors.

The most serious issue facing feminist critics today is that which divides the profession as a whole, the division between theory and practice. Leaning on the Greeks, our culture still posits philosophy, music, and mathematics as the highest forms of intellectual endeavor. They have been the fields most zealously guarded against female incursion, the fields where it has been most difficult for women to gain training. The English composer Dame Ethel Smyth defended herself from criticism of her battles for status and position among women musicians: she could not withdraw from the world to compose, to act the artist who simply cultivates her own garden, she said, when someone had locked up all the tools.[4] Literary theory is a branch of philosophy. Its most vigorous practitioners in the United States have been male. It is no historical accident that the hegemony of the theoreticians and the valorization of theory itself parallels the rise of feminist criticism. While we have been doing literary housekeeping, they have been gazing at the stars. They refuse to bear the burden of the sins of their literary fathers or to make amends for centuries of critical abuse of women writers involving the loss, destruction, bowdlerization, or misevaluation of women's texts, diaries, letters, and biographies.

When feminist critics first forced open the toolshed, they polished and sharpened the rusty spades and hoes and rakes men long since had discarded. They learned history, textual criticism, biography, the recovery of manuscripts. They began to search for and reprint women's works and to study the image of woman in Western art. Many moved into linguistics to get at the origins of oppression in language, while others worked to find the writing of women of color.[5] We were all forced to become historians and biographers and to train ourselves in those disciplines. We devoured theories of female psychology, anthropology, and myth to broaden our grasp of the work of women artists. The more materialist and particular the labor of feminist critics became, the more abstract and antimaterialist became the work of the men (they left in Europe the Marxist origins of structuralism and deconstruction). The more we spoke in moral indignation and anger, the more Parnassian were the whispers of male theorists. If the last conference of the School of Criticism and Theory is any model to go by,[6] soon they will have retreated so far from life and literature that they will be analyzing the songs of birds in the garden of Paradise (Adamic only).

Geoffrey Hartman claims for the theorists that literary criticism is in the wilderness.[7] While one may grant that Hartman's manner is a distinct imitation of John the Baptist, one must point out that the theorists are not in the wilderness at all but in a labyrinthine garden with high hedges they have constructed themselves. The arrogance of the metaphor indicates the cause of their isolation. If there is one true word in literary criticism and they are the precursors of their master's voice, the profession is lost. But historians of our difficult era will have little doubt about the social origins of the idea of born-again literary critics. I am reminded of the words of the Victorian aesthetician, Vernon Lee, in a letter to Ethel Smyth. It was bad enough to be a voice crying in the wilderness, she said, but a female philosopher was a "vox clamans" in the closet.[8]

There are some feminist theorists of note, among whom one may cite especially the work of Gayatri Spivak in literature and Julia Lesage in film criticism.[9] Lesage and her colleagues on the film journal *Jump-Cut* have, in fact, made the most revolutionary breakthrough in feminist theory and practice by trying to effect a rapprochement between the left and lesbians. The lesbian-feminist special issue of *Jump-Cut* is a tour de force of brilliant and ground-breaking essays and includes an editorial in which the male editors attempt to deal with what we may call "reparations" for the long battles of the sexes. The writing and publication of these essays is a hopeful sign, but not a victory, until feminist critics who are neither left nor lesbian read and debate these issues and bring them into the classroom.

There were no feminist critics speaking at the first meeting of the School of Criticism and Theory at Northwestern University in the spring of 1981, though the intelligent response of Mary Douglas, the anthropologist, to one of the more reactionary papers, was the highlight of the conference.[10] Protest at the omission of feminists was met by the response that there *are* no feminist theorists, at least none whom the men find "interesting." If there is as yet no feminist critical theory that men find interesting, there is no reason to suppose that it is not at this very moment being written, nor is there any reason to suppose that men will ever be as interested as we are in developments in our own field. Recent critical books attacking the hegemony of the theorists ignore both feminists and Marxists or give them a light cuff, while the heavy blows are aimed at theorists of their own sex. We are excluded from their discourse (theorizing is a male activity); consequently no intellectual intercourse can take place. Even a Marxist critic like Frederic Jameson is loyal to the old boys.[11]

Just as Virginia Woolf predicted both the birth of Shakespeare's sister and our work for her arrival, so one may also predict the birth of the feminist critic of genius. She must reject with Virginia Woolf the patriarchal view of literature as a competition with prizes of "ornamental pots" from the headmaster. The feminist critic is always at odds with the headmaster. She is, as Adrienne Rich argues "disloyal" to civilization.[12] She must refuse the ornamental pot, even if it is very fashionable and made in France. She must break the measuring rod, even if it is finely calibrated in the literary laboratories at Yale. We shall have a theory of our own when our practice develops it. "Masterpieces are not single and solitary births," Woolf wrote in *A Room of One's Own*, "they are the outcome of many years of thinking in common, of thinking by the body of the people, so that the experience of the mass is behind the single voice." Woolf was discussing Shakespeare as the product of history. But her socialist analysis can be extended to criticism as well. By her analysis one can imagine that there were many little Geoffrey Hartman's before there was one big Geoffrey Hartman, as in literature there were many little Shakespeares before the master himself.[13]

We have already produced feminist critics to match their male counterparts: Mary Ellman, Kate Millett, Ellen Moers, Elaine Showalter, Sandra Gilbert and Susan Gubar can outdo Harold Bloom at his own game; Gayatri Spivak speaks as an equal among the French deconstructionists; Julia Lesage challenges film theory. Many lesser-known feminists have worked steadily for new readings and new values in their own fields. But even if we were to construct the feminist super-critic from the collective voice of all of them, it is doubtful that the self-appointed priesthood would find her analysis interesting. I suspect that this literary amazon is even now slouching toward Ephesus to be born—the critic who will deliver us from slavery to the canon, from racist, sexist, and classist misreadings. But one can be sure that, welcome as she will be among us, the chosen critics will see her as a false messiah.

I do not think we should surrender easily. It is they and their fathers who excluded and oppressed us and our mothers, they who decided to exclude women writers from what was taught, women students from who was taught. Our historical losses at their hands are incalculable. It is not up to us to beg them to find our work interesting. It is up to them to make reparations: to establish secure women's studies departments, black studies departments, chairs of feminist literary criticism and women's history, to read the work of women and black writers, and to teach it.

After this digression upon theory I would like to return to the subject of the rest of this article. If "Lupine Criticism" is an example of a battle within a small area of literary criticism, fought among one's peers, "One Cheer for Democracy, or Talking Back to Quentin Bell" is a direct confrontation with Virginia Woolf's nephew, official biographer, and owner of her literary estate. In his essay, "Bloomsbury and the Vulgar Passions," given on a lecture tour of the United States and published in *Critical Inquiry*, Bell once again mocks Virginia Woolf's *Three Guineas* for its feminism and pacifism.[14] He minimizes her contribution to political thought by comparing it unfavorably to a pamphlet by his father, Clive Bell, as well as E. M. Forster's "Two Cheers for Democracy" and *A Passage to India*. I admire Bell's *Bloomsbury*[15] and am grateful, as are other Woolf scholars, for the painstaking work of his biography and for the publication of the letters and diaries. Because we are dependent on the estate for permission to publish, it has been difficult for Woolf scholars to take issue with his analysis without jeopardizing their careers. The year 1982 is the centenary of Virginia Woolf's birth. In the thirties she predicted that in fifty years men would allow women writers free speech. Could she have imagined this deadlock in criticism, this "separate but equal" free speech as it now exists in literary criticism, where feminist critics are excluded from discourse with male theorists?[16] She suffered from these same exclusions herself, was chastised for her feminism all her life, and continues to be chastised after her death. She died, I believe, in an ethical torment over her pacifism in a terrible war. It seems only natural to take up her weapons. Our first target is the shed where the power tools of literary theory have been kept. There is no doubt that in the hands of feminist critics they will transform the study of literature.

II. LUPINE CRITICISM

It is amusing to imagine what Virginia Woolf would think of an MLA meeting. You know how she despised lectures and did not believe that literature should be taught to middle-class students. She herself only lectured to women and working-class people. She gave lectures to women students and fellow professional women, to the Workers' Education League and the Working Women's Cooperative Guild. She refused offers to lecture to men, to men's colleges and universities, and to male-dominated institutions. While she was in Italy, studying Mussolini's fascism firsthand, she refused, with a simple and defiant No, her government's offer of a Companion of Honour, wanting no companionship whatever with the concerns of the British Empire. She refused a degree from Manchester University, and, much to the horror of the editor of her letters, Nigel Nicolson, she even refused quite proudly to give the prestigious Clark Lectures at Cambridge, despite the fact that she was the first woman invited to do so. Her editor feels that this act "only weakened the cause of women in general" and confesses he cannot understand why the only prize she ever accepted was a woman's prize, the Femina Vie Heureuse prize for *To the Lighthouse*.[17]

We all know why she did it, and why, if she were here today, she would accept the Florence Howe Award for her essays on women writers and refuse any other honors. Lecturing, she wrote, "incites the most debased of human passions— vanity, ostentation, self-assertion, and the desire to convert." We confess all these sins and more; feminist literary criticism seems to demand them at the moment just for defense. "Why not create a new form of society founded on poverty and equality?" Woolf asked. "Why not bring together people so that they can talk, without mounting platforms or reading papers or wearing expensive clothes or eating expensive food? Would not such a society be worth, even as a form of education, all the papers on art and literature that have ever been read since the world began? Why not abolish prigs and prophets? Why not invent human intercourse?"[18]

In the last decade, the Commission on Women and the Women's Caucus of the MLA, with Florence Howe at the helm, and also a vast community of women scholars working together have undertaken the enormous task of revaluating women's work, uncovering forgotten lives and books, reprinting our own literature. Virginia Woolf is our model for this task. We—I say ostentatiously, self-assertively, with some vanity, and a veritable passion to make converts—in this very room are inventing "human intercourse."

Writers like Tillie Olsen and Adrienne Rich have inspired us, not only with their creative work but with their theoretical and historical essays. They continue the work in which Virginia Woolf as a feminist literary critic was engaged, a historical process she called "thinking back through our mothers."[19] Woolf would take a particular delight in what Mary Helen Washington and her colleagues are doing on black and Third World women writers. She would applaud with Suzanne Juhasz the women poets who tell the truth. Loving Katherine Mansfield as she did, and Elizabeth Robins, the forgotten feminist who influenced both Mansfield and Woolf herself, she would rub her hands with glee that Sydney Kaplan and her feminist colleagues are delivering Mansfield's ghost from the hands of the lugubrious Middleton Murry.

We in a new generation of feminist Virginia Woolf criticism have also had the advantage of collective and collaborative work, and we have sustained each other in many trials. Whenever two or three of us are gathered together sharing notes on manuscripts and letters, we feel what Virginia Woolf described in her meetings with her Greek teacher, Janet Case, and with Margaret Llewelyn Davies of the Working Women's Cooperative Guild; we are at "the heart of the women's republic."[20] It is an open secret that Virginia Woolf's literary estate is hostile to feminist critics. There are two taboo subjects: on one hand her lesbian identity, woman-centered life, and feminist work, and on the other, her socialist politics. If you wish to discover the truth regarding these issues, you will have a long, hard struggle. In that struggle you will find the sisterhood of feminist Woolf scholarship.

It all began with Ellen Hawkes's review, "The Virgin in the Bell Biography." She was duly denounced from the pulpit of the English Institute but, despite excommunication, has had a great influence. A group of feminist Woolf scholars protested her expulsion and organized a conference at Santa Cruz. Here Madeline Moore brought together many feminists—Sara Ruddick, Tillie Olsen, and Florence Howe among them. Madeline Moore published many of the papers in a 1977 special issue of *Women's Studies*.[21]

The MLA Woolf Seminar has been notably feminist in its papers during the last five years. At one meeting, for example, Margaret Comstock chaired a session on *Between the Acts* with papers by Judy Little and Diane Gillespie, later published in *Women and Literature*. Feminists, including Kate Ellis and Ellen Hawkes, spoke at the Princeton Woolf Conference organized by Joanna Lipking. And at the Bucknell Woolf Conference in 1977, Carolyn Heilbrun, Eve Merriam, and the late Ellen Moers spoke. (Here let me note that Ellen Moers's death diminishes us all; *Literary Women* has provided us with tools and structures for building feminist literary criticism.) These conferences and seminars cemented scholarly friendships and set new directions for Woolf studies.

The publication of Woolf's letters and diaries has greatly facilitated our work. Yet the manuscripts of the novels retain the utmost fascination. We organized a special issue of the *Bulletin of the New York Public Library* with papers from the MLA Woolf Seminar on *The Years*, including Grace Radin's rendering of "two enormous chunks" of material removed from the galleys just before it went to press, Sallie Sears's essay on sexuality, and Margaret Comstock's "The Loudspeaker and the Human Voice" on the politics of the novel. Woolf's "Professions for Women" turned out to be three times the length and feminist strength of the version published by Leonard Woolf in *Collected Essays*. It has been reprinted by the New York Public Library in Mitchell Leaska's edition of *The Pargiters*.[22]

The original speech "Professions for Women" was delivered in January 1931, to a group of professional women. Preceding Virginia Woolf on the platform was Dame Ethel Smyth, the great English lesbian-feminist composer. Virginia Woolf's pacifism always receded when she spoke as a feminist. Her violent feelings came pouring out in her description of Ethel Smyth: "She is of the race of the pioneers: She is among the ice-breakers, the window-smashers, the indomitable and irresistible armoured tanks who climbed the rough ground; went first; drew the enemy's fire and left a pathway for those who came after her. I never knew whether to be angry that such heroic pertinacity was called for, or glad that it had the chance of showing itself."[23]

In our field the ice breakers and window smashers have been Tillie Olsen, Adrienne Rich, Florence Howe, Ellen Moers, and Carolyn Heilbrun. Our work has been made possible because they drew the enemy's fire. Like Virginia Woolf, we acknowledge our debt, half in anger that such belligerence is necessary, half in gladness that they have fought so well. For the last five years much feminist work on Woolf has appeared in *Virginia Woolf Miscellany*, edited, among others, by the indomitable J. J. Wilson at Sonoma State University. The Fall 1979 issue of *Twentieth-Century Literature* contains splendid and important work by feminists: Ellen Hawkes's edition of Woolf's early utopian feminist fantasy, "Friendships Gallery," written for Violet Dickinson; Susan Squier and Louise De Salvo's edition of an early forty-four-page unpublished story about a woman historian; Madeline Moore's edition of the Orlando manuscripts; and Brenda Silver's edition of two very important late manuscripts called "Anon" and "The Reader."[24]

Doubtless I have left out much new work, but this list itself is an impressive example of the comradeship and collective effort of feminist Woolf scholarship. You will note that all this work is American. We have escaped the domination of the Leavises' point of view that still prevents many British readers from seeing Woolf as anything but "elitist" and "mad." The exception is Michele Barrett's edition of Woolf's *Women and Writing*.[25]

Quentin Bell has announced that the "bottom of the barrel" has been reached in Woolf manuscripts, but we are not finished yet. There is a great deal of literary housekeeping to be done. Virginia Woolf wrote to Ethel Smyth about her own struggle for recognition as a composer, "Somehow the big apples come to the top of the basket. But of course I realize that the musicians' apple lies longest at the bottom and has the hardest struggle to rise."[26] I find these "Granny Smyth" apples to be tart and tasty indeed and am editing Dame Ethel's letters to Virginia Woolf.

What feminist scholars have found in the apples at the bottom of the barrel is a taste of the two taboo subjects, Woolf's socialist politics and her love of women. When the fifth volume of her letters was published, reviewers rushed to reassure readers that Woolf did not really mean it when she wrote to Ethel Smyth, "Women alone stir my imagination."[27] Nigel Nicolson insisted to me that Woolf was only joking. While Quentin Bell is ready to admit privately that *Letter to a Young Poet* and "Thoughts on Peace in an Air Raid" are "more Marxist than the Marxists," his public lecture, "Bloomsbury and the Vulgar Passions," dismisses *Three Guineas* as silly and unimportant.[28]

Quentin Bell is not amused by feminist criticism of Virginia Woolf. He has invented a name for us. He calls us "lupines." There is a particular variety of flower, the lupine, that grows in the American West, covering the rocky slopes of the Big Horns, the Tetons, and the Wind River Mountains in July. It is electric blue, startlingly erect, and extremely hardy. Perhaps we feminist Woolf critics can survive the patronizing label of British cultural imperialism by appropriating it ourselves. During the struggle for woman suffrage, a patronizing journalist called the most militant of the activists "Suffragettes." After a few weeks of smoldering rage at the insult, the women simply pinned that badge to their own breasts and wore it proudly.

In *Three Guineas* Virginia Woolf suggests that women might wear a tuft of horsehair on the left shoulder to indicate motherhood, as a response to male military decorations. Lupine criticism is obviously here to stay. We might as well accept the label and wear it proudly. If the proliferation and hardiness of the flower is any indication of our tenacity, we have a great future. We have not yet ceased to be "prigs and prophetesses," but we have made a start at inventing human intercourse.

Yet achievement and even struggle in common do not come easily. The first of our two volumes of feminist criticism on Virginia Woolf was finished in 1977, but we were unable to find an American publisher. The essays have circulated among feminist critics and have been cited in books and articles in print for years. Because University of Nebraska Press bought the book from Macmillan/London, the price in America is very high.[29] These incontrovertible economic facts are not lost on young scholars. Virginia Woolf founded the Hogarth Press in order to publish what she wanted to write. Feminists often feel forced by economic realities to choose other methodologies and structures that will ensure sympathetic readings from university presses. We may be as middle class as Virginia Woolf, but few of us have the economic security her aunt Caroline Emelia Stephen's legacy gave her. The samizdat circulation among networks of feminist critics works only in a system where repression is equal. If all the members are unemployed or underemployed, unpublished or unrecognized, sisterhood flourishes, and sharing is a source of strength. When we all compete for one job or when one lupine grows bigger and bluer than her sisters with unnatural fertilizers from the establishment, the ranks thin out. Times are hard and getting harder.

Being an outsider is a lonely life. Virginia Woolf proposed a *Society of Outsiders*. Lupine criticism, I think, will only flourish in the collective and in the wild. In captivity, in the rarefied hothouse atmosphere of current academic criticism, it may wither and die. From my last climbing trip in the Wind Rivers, I brought back some wild lupines and carefully transplanted them. My mother warned me that Chicago clay would stifle them, and she was right. Garden lupines are very pretty, and doubtless our colleagues would find us less offensive in the cultivated state. The British label was meant as an insult, and it might be an adjective as well as a noun. If we are going to wear it, sister lupines, let us wear it with wild Woolfian abandon.

III. ONE CHEER FOR DEMOCRACY, OR TALKING BACK TO QUENTIN BELL

Quentin Bell, largely responsible for making the Bloomsbury bed, now refuses to lie in it. In his book on Bloomsbury and his biography of his aunt, he provided readers with the materials for what he now calls "false generalizations."[30] "Bloomsbury and the Vulgar Passions" is a deliberately mystifying title that does not clarify the politics of the period but muddies the waters even more.

Virginia Woolf's clear understanding of the role of the intellectual in relation to the revolution is evident in her title *Three Guineas*.[31] She wants women and the working classes to unite against the war, but she does not presume to speak for any but her own class and sex. In "The Leaning Tower" and *Letter to a Young Poet*[32] she insists on organization in one's own class and has faith that the working class can produce its own leaders. Her title, a deliberate play on Brecht's *Threepenny Opera*, exposes the economic origins of the social problems she discusses. Neither pence nor pounds can accurately describe the contributions expected of a woman in her position. Over the years American academics have shared her frustrating experience, signing petitions and writing checks to help in the civil rights movement and the movement to stop the war in Vietnam. Like her, they sought to relieve social ills by imagining free universities like the one Woolf describes in *Three Guineas*.[33] Current feminism grew out of women's effort to find a place in movements for social change which assumed that race and class and the present war were more important than sex grievances. Woolf was the first to identify the enemy openly as "patriarchy."

Why does Bell choose Keynes's elitist phrase for an essay calculated to reduce the political power of *Three Guineas* to an entirely personal cause? If *Three Guineas* is merely an aunt's elegy for a dead nephew, as Bell argues, is not such ferocious grief a "vulgar passion" too? The phrase is not Bell's; it is the phrase of a man he admires, Maynard Keynes. It is a Victorian upper-class phrase. Few members of Margaret Llewelyn Davies's Working Women's Cooperative Guild would know what it means.[34] The phrase itself is heavy with ambiguity, and it is used by Bell in both positive and negative ways. Curiously, it works to the disadvantage of Virginia Woolf either way. It is men like his father, Keynes, and Forster who remain intellectually above the vulgar passions when Bell considers it correct to be so, and men again who are responsive to the vulgar passions of a nation at war, when this is the attitude he admires.

There is a famous point in Bell's biography of Virginia Woolf when the reader, swept along by the swift flow of prose, brisk and cool like an English trout stream in spring, is suddenly thrown into white water. Bell bursts into capital letters. The reader is on the rocks. "But were we then to scuttle like frightened spinsters before the Fascist thugs? She belonged, inescapably, to the Victorian world of Empire, Class and Privilege. Her gift was for the pursuit of shadows, for the ghostly whispers of the mind and for Pythian incomprehensibility, when what was needed was the swift and lucid phrase that could reach the ears of unemployed working men or Trades Union officials."[35] To the generation of thirties intellectuals (John Lehmann was one, and Woolf wrote her scathing *Letter to a Young Poet* to him), Virginia Woolf was "a fragile middle-aged poetess, a sexless Sappho," and "a distressed gentlewoman caught in a tempest." Bell recalls his "despair" as he urged the Rodmell Labour Party to adopt a resolution supporting the United Front, when Virginia, who was the local party secretary, turned the debate from the question. He does not call her a skilled politician for manipulating the meeting, on pacifist principle, away from patriotic militarism. He says, indeed, that she was closer to the feeling of "the masses" than he was. "I wanted to talk politics, the masses wanted to talk about the vicar's wife."[36]

But, I venture, it was precisely her "swift and lucid phrases" that annoyed him, for she spoke to the Workers' Education Association, and she wrote in the *Daily Worker* of a different kind of united front: while the capitalist, imperialist patriarchs were waging their wars, workers should join women in an assault on culture. "Trespass," she urged them, on the sacred precincts of home front institutions while the warriors are in the field. She was arguing for total subversion of the world of empire, class, and privilege. And among the shadows she pursued most vigorously were upper-class, young, male "missionaries to the masses." Take off those "pro-proletarian spectacles," she urged the generation of Auden, Spender, Lehmann, and Bell; if you really want to make the revolution, you must empty your pockets of your fathers' money, you must convert the men of your *own* class.[37] Virginia Woolf took as hard a line on the role of the intellectual in the class struggle as did Lenin or Trotsky. Its ethical imperative is even improved by the addition of feminism to the socialist-pacifist position. Quentin Bell's objections are honest ones, and there were many who agreed with him. He is infuriated by her feminism and enraged by her pacifism, and he fights back like a man.

It is dirty fighting to be sure. She is dead and cannot respond like the "Lapland Witch" Gerald Brenan says she was.[38] E. M. Forster was a dirty fighter, too. He said in his Rede Lecture that Woolf was not a great writer because "she had no great cause at heart."[39] But we have already put *A Room of One's Own* and *Three*

Guineas on the shelf next to Milton, Wollstonecraft, Mill, and Swift, and where is Forster's "Two Cheers for Democracy"? It is an embarrassment. Forster said he would give up his country before he would give up his friend. But that was not at issue. Nobody was asking him to give up his friend. And *Three Guineas* has some antifascist feminist thuggery of its own. One thing it does not have is "Pythian incomprehensibility." It is a Cassandra-cry in the crowd of thirties' political pamphlets. No spinsterish whispers either. The loudspeaker blares for all to hear, a withering revolutionary feminist analysis of fascism. The Hitlers and Mussolinis have no monopoly on fascism, she says. The origin of fascism is the patriarchal family. And "the daughters of educated men" had better root it out of the hearts of their English brothers before the latter rush off to fight foreign fascism.

Men on the left were horrified. But the argument that elements of fascism lurk behind patriarchal power struggles is still too radical for people. It was the subject of Lina Wertmuller's shattering feminist film *Seven Beauties*, and all the Bettelheims came out with their battering rams and big guns to remind us of how long it will be before men will "tolerate free speech in women."[40]

During the period covered by the fifth volume of Woolf's letters (1932–35), the political and personal insults that she had received from men were creating the deep sense of grievance that finally burst out in *The Years* and *Three Guineas*.[41] *The Years* itself is the most brilliant indictment in modern literature of the world of empire, class, and privilege, of capitalism and patriarchy. Structurally it is exciting, too, in its portrait of the artist as charwoman of the world. *The Years* was to have been a new form of her opera for the oppressed, alternating chapters of fact and fiction. The documentaries have been reprinted in *The Pargiters*.[42] It is too bad that Leonard talked her out of it. He was fearful of mixing fact and fiction. Her fearlessness went into the writing of both books. But she was justifiably terrified of what the male critics would say.

It is doubtful that she would have predicted her nephew's continuing hostility to *Three Guineas*. I believe there is a direct line in English history from the Clapham Sect to Bloomsbury. The anonymous reviewer in the *Times Literary Supplement* who called Virginia Woolf "the best pamphleteer in England"[43] was (consciously or unconsciously) echoing the very words applied to the antislavery pamphlets of her great-grandfather, James Stephen. That Virginia Woolf should have added feminism to the Stephen family causes is the most natural development in the world.[44] Her pacifism was not a "temporary" phenomenon but a firmly held principle of a tripartite political philosophy. It was largely derived from the important and neglected influence of her Quaker aunt, Caroline Emelia Stephen, described by Quaker historians as almost single-handedly responsible for the revival of the practically moribund English Society of Friends in the late nineteenth century.[45] It is true, as Bell says, that she modified her position at the last, actually wanted to join the fire wardens, and appears to have been willing to defend her beleaguered country in "Thoughts on Peace in an Air Raid." I have described these changes of attitude elsewhere.[46]

Bell's essay is written in response to yet another season of bad press for Bloomsbury. Virginia Woolf wrote to him during an earlier one, stating "Bloomsbury is having a very bad press at the moment; so please take up your hammer and chisel and sculpt a great flaming Goddess to put them all to shame."[47] There was certainly a family precedent. When Fitzjames Stephen was

hounded out of office for prejudicing the jury in the Maybrick case after a lifetime of legal bullying and misogyny as the "Giant Grim," Leslie Stephen took
up his hammer and chisel and sculpted a genial friendly giant in his biography of
his brother. Virginia Stephen herself had participated in Maitland's biography of
her father, largely to offset the influence of her Aunt Caroline, who had mountains of evidence that the great man had a terrible temper.[48]

Did Bell perhaps agree with Mirsky's dismissal of Bloomsbury and Virginia
Woolf in *The Intelligentsia of Great Britain*,[49] the "bad press" referred to? He took
up his hammer and chisel but produced no "great flaming Goddess" but a "sexless Sappho," a "distressed gentlewoman caught in a tempest." I suspect in the
end we will all come to see Bell's "sexless Sappho" as a true portrait of the artist
who equated chastity with creativity. But she will not do as a portrait of the so-
cialist/pacifist/feminist, the "outsider" who "spat out" *Three Guineas* as an original contribution to an analysis of the origins of fascism in the patriarchal family.
If she began the book as an elegy for Bell's brother, Julian, there is nothing unusual to her method in that, for all her work is elegy. Even *A Room of One's Own*
is a female elegy written in a college courtyard for the female writers of the past.
The narrator has been denied access to the library which contains the manuscripts
of the two great male elegies in poetry and prose, Milton's *Lycidas* and Thackeray's *Henry Esmond*, and so she is driven to invent the female elegy. If grieving
for Julian Bell's death in Spain forced her to the conclusion that she must speak
directly to women of her class, to the mothers, sisters, and wives of the war makers, the public effect of a private sorrow is impressive.

But *Three Guineas* is a stubbornly feminist elegy, singing the sorrows of women
under patriarchy, relentlessly repeating itself as history has repeated itself, trying
to establish a feminist ethics. To my mind, and to the minds of other feminists,
Three Guineas is the pure historical product of the Clapham Sect reform move-
ment. It owes much to the "rational mysticism" of Caroline Emelia Stephen's
The Light Arising.[50] But if the historian can free himself of sex bias, he will see
Three Guineas in relation to Bertrand Russell's philosophy and to G. E. Moore's
Principia Ethica. In fact it might be seen as "Principia Ethica Femina," volume l.[51]

If Woolf later, in "Thoughts on Peace in an Air Raid," admitted woman's complicity in war and concluded that "we must compensate the man for his gun,"[52]
she did not suggest how. Bell thinks she has come close to the vulgar passions
(which are now positive) in this essay, and he is disposed to grant her some
credit.[53] I thought so too in 1976. But I am now disposed to think that "Thoughts
on Peace in an Air Raid" is just what the title suggests, a defensive position taken
under extreme pressure. The militant feminism of *Three Guineas*, its equally militant pacifism, socialism, and antifascism, are "saddening" and "exasperating" to
Bell. Many European and American feminist historians are studying the forms of
Italian and German fascism and their relation to the patriarchal family, marriage,
and the treatment of women and children, and they have found Woolf's pamphlet
a strikingly original and eerily correct analysis.[54] I believe Bell labors under the
misconception that feminism is not political—a major mistake—as well as under
minor misconceptions that pacificism in World War II was not a respectable political stance (it was certainly not popular) and that Virginia Woolf could not have
been much of a socialist because she did not work in Labour Party Committees
or associate with the working classes. Even when Bell imagines a committee

meeting he sees only Mr. A., Mr. B., Mr. C., Mr. D., and the chairman. I seem to recall that the committee meeting which caused his admirable prose style to flood the gates was chaired by his aunt, Mrs. W., and she prevented him from passing his resolution. It is a long time to hold a grudge.

It is a failure of the imagination to suppose that all pacifists were, like Clive Bell, ad hoc peaceniks for a particular war. Quakers, like Caroline Stephen and Violet Dickinson, Virginia's early mentors, were opposed to all wars.

It seems oddly un-English and more like an American pragmatist or utilitarian argument to judge the quality of a pamphlet by its contemporary effectiveness. James Stephen turned out antislavery pamphlets that failed to stop the slavers. But it was not until he had been dead many years that his son finally got an anti-slavery bill through Parliament. How much immediate effect did Mill's *Subjection of Women* have? Women did not get the vote until 1928, and the condition of women is still not by any means satisfactory. *Three Guineas* is still read (and this might be a better measure of "effectiveness") by those who hunger for its message, who feel as guilty as Woolf did about fighting for feminism when atrocities and wars demand one's attention. Seeking for the deepest cause of imperialist and capitalist war, she found it in male aggression. She was saddened, but urged women to stop encouraging aggression. I wish she had been more successful.

If effectiveness is the criterion of a pamphlet's success, is there any way of measuring the success of *Three Guineas* in keeping America out of the war when it was published in the *Atlantic* as "Women Must Weep or Unite against the War"? I suppose it is just as possible to imagine that her pamphlet had that power as to assert that Forster's *A Passage to India* had an immense influence in dissuading Britons from their imperialist passions.[55] I do not share Bell's enthusiasm for *A Passage to India*. It seems so pale and liberal compared to the radical antiimperialism and anticapitalism of *Mrs. Dalloway* or *The Years*. Virginia Woolf once described Mrs. Humphry Ward's novels as hanging in the lumber room of literature like the mantles of our aunts, covered with beads and bugles. Well, there is something about E. M. Forster's novels reminiscent of our unmarried uncles' silk pajamas, something elegant, but rather effete. They have not worn well. And Woolf's novels get harder and tougher year by year, ethically unyielding and morally challenging.

Any member of the Women's International League for Peace and Freedom or the Women's Cooperative Guild, as well as many left-wing feminists and many socialists, would have seen Virginia Woolf's ideology as more powerful than the liberalism of Keynes or Forster. For those readers, *Three Guineas* is not forced or unsatisfactory. It was not at the time, as Bell implies, nor is it now, a political ir-relevance.[56] It is hard to believe that the world is as neatly divided into hawks and doves as Bell would have us believe and that one changes feathers over every war. Some of us imagine Virginia Woolf as a great blue heron anyway, and she describes herself as a misfit, an outsider. As for her ability to feel the vulgar passions, to hear the demotic voice, let him read the song of the caretaker's children in *The Years*. It is the voice of the colonial chickens come home to roost. The full measure of *Three Guineas*'s effect is yet to be weighed, for it deals with older, more universal, and more deeply rooted social ills than the Spanish fascism that prompted it. Her intent reminds me of a surrealist poem by Laura Riding:

She opens the heads of her brothers
And lets out the aeroplanes
"Now," she says, "you will be able to think better."[57]

NOTES

1. Two of the papers delivered at that meeting have since been published: Mary Helen Washington, "New Lives and New Letters: Black Women Writers at the End of the Seventies," *College English* 43, no. 1 (January 1981): 1–11; and Florence Howe, "Those We Still Don't Read," *College English* 43, no. 1 (January 1981): 12–16.

2. See *Women's Studies Quarterly* 9, no. 3 (Fall 1981), particularly the reprint of speeches by Adrienne Rich, "Disobedience Is What the NWSA Is Potentially About," pp. 4–6; and Audre Lorde, "The Uses of Anger," pp. 7–10.

3. See Annette Kolodny, "Dancing Through the Minefield: Some Observations on the Theory, Practice, and Politics of a Feminist Literary Criticism," *Feminist Studies* 6, no. 1 (Spring 1980): 1–25; and Judith Gardiner's response, "Marching through Our Field," *Feminist Studies* 8, no. 3 (1982): 629–75. Gardiner distinguishes between liberal, radical, and socialist feminist critics. Gayatri Spivak's unpublished "A Response to Annette Kolodny" (Department of English, University of Texas at Austin, 1980) is an even stronger critique of Kolodny's position. She writes: "To embrace pluralism (as Kolodny recommends) is to espouse the politics of the masculinist establishment. Pluralism is the method employed by the *central* authorities to neutralize opposition by seeming to accept it. The gesture of pluralism on the part of the *marginal* can only mean capitulation to the center."

4. Dame Ethel Smyth's story of her struggle against the masculine establishment in music is told in *Female Pipings in Eden* (London: Peter Davies, 1934). A revival of Dame Ethel's work has begun: several papers were delivered at the First National Congress on Women and Music at New York University in March 1981; her memoirs have been reprinted, *Impressions That Remained* (New York: Da Capo Press, 1981), with a new introduction by Ronald Crichton; and Da Capo Press (1980) has also reprinted the score of her *Mass in D* for solo, chorus, and orchestra, with a new introduction by Jane Bernstein.

5. See Gloria T. Hull, Patricia Bell Scott, and Barbara Smith, eds., *But Some of Us Are Brave: Black Women's Studies* (Old Westbury, N.Y.: Feminist Press, 1981).

6. The conference, entitled "A Controversy of Critics," was sponsored by the School of Criticism and Theory at Northwestern University in May 1981.

7. Geoffrey Hartman, *Criticism in the Wilderness: The Study of Literature Today* (New Haven, Conn.: Yale University Press, 1980).

8. Quoted by Ethel Smyth in *Maurice Baring* (London: Heinemann, 1937), p. 206.

9. See Gayatri Spivak, "Feminism and Critical Theory," *Women's Studies International Quarterly* 1, no. 3 (1978): 241–46, and "Three Feminist Readings: McCullers, Drabble, and Habermas," *Union Seminary Quarterly Review* 35, no. 1–2 (Fall–Winter 1978–79): 15–38. The most important essays by Julia Lesage are "Subversive Fantasy in *Celine and Julie Go Boating*, " *Jump-Cut* 24–25 (March 1981): 36–43, which deals with the semiotics of body language and domestic space, "Dialectical, Revolutionary, Feminist," *Jump-Cut* 20 (May 1979): 20–23, and "Artful Racism, Artful Rape: D. W. Griffith's *Broken Blossoms*," *Jump-Cut* 26 (May 1981). See also the entire lesbian feminist special issue of *Jump-Cut* (24–25 [March 1981]), especially its bibliography, p. 21; Ruby Rich's analysis of the teacher in girls' schools playing the roles of "good cop" and "bad cop" in her study of *Mädchen in Uniform*, "From Repressive Tolerance to Erotic Liberation," pp. 44–50; and Bonnie Zimmerman's discussion of lesbian vampire films, "Daughters of Darkness: Lesbian Vampires," pp. 23–24.

10. Julia Lesage uses Mary Douglas's *Purity and Danger: An Analysis of Concepts of Pollution and Taboo* (London: Routledge & Kegan Paul, 1966) as a theoretical construct for the

analysis of *Celine and Julie Go Boating* (see n. 9 above): this theory was also very useful to Marina Warner in her analysis of female heroism in *Joan of Arc* (New York: Alfred A. Knopf, Inc., 1981).

11. See Gerald Graff's *Poetic Statement and Critical Dogma* (Evanston, Ill.: Northwestern University Press, 1970), and *Literature against Itself* (Chicago: University of Chicago Press, 1979); Frank Lentricchia's *After the New Criticism* (Chicago: University of Chicago Press, 1980); Fredric Jameson's *The Political Unconscious: Narrative as a Socially Symbolic Act* (Ithaca, N.Y.: Cornell University Press, 1981); and Terry Eagleton's "The Idealism of American Criticism," *New Left Review* 127 (May–June 1981): 53–65, which reviews Lentricchia and Jameson and surveys the field. Eagleton notes that these critics refuse to discuss gender and maintain sexist attitudes, but his own review does not mention the brilliant work done by feminist critics in the United States in the last decade, nor has Eagleton's work itself deviated from male discourse despite its Marxism. If Annette Kolodny's espousal of the pluralist position from the margin may be seen as a capitulation to a misogynist power structure, Jameson's Marxist pluralism, in its refusal to deal with gender, should show those tempted to follow Kolodny's lead that male bonding transcends theoretical enmities and is more primary among American critics than the issues that divide them intellectually.

12. Rich (n. 2 above), p. 5.

13. Virginia Woolf, *A Room of One's Own* (New York: Harcourt, Brace and World 1929: reprint ed. 1957), pp. 68–69, 110.

14. Quentin Bell, "Bloomsbury and the Vulgar Passions," *Critical Inquiry* 6, no. 2 (Winter 1979): 239–56.

15. Quentin Bell, *Bloomsbury* (London: Weidenfeld & Nicolson, 1968).

16. Recent contributions to feminist critical theory include: Myra Jehlen, "Archimedes and the Paradox of Feminist Criticism," *Signs: Journal of Women in Culture and Society* 6, no. 4 (Summer 1981): 575–601; and Nina Baym, "Melodramas of Beset Manhood: How Theories of American Fiction Exclude Women Authors," *American Quarterly* 33, no. 2 (Summer 1981): 123–39. In press is a special issue of *Critical Inquiry* (8, no. 2 [Winter 1981]) edited by Elizabeth Abel called "Writing and Sexual Difference," with essays by Elaine Showalter, Mary Jacobus, Margaret Homans, Susan Gubar, Nancy Vickers, Nina Auerbach, Annette Kolodny, Froma Zeitlin, Judith Gardiner, Catharine Stimpson, and Gayatri Spivak.

17. Nigel Nicolson's introduction to *The Letters of Virginia Woolf, 1932–1935*, vol. 5, *The Sickle Side of the Moon*, ed. Nigel Nicolson and Joanne Trautmann (New York: Harcourt Brace Jovanovich, 1979), pp. xi–xvii, is a sustained attack on Woolf's politics and feminism. Carolyn Heilbrun's feminist review of this volume appears in *Virginia Woolf Miscellany* 14 (Spring 1980): 4; and Nicolson's reply in *Virginia Woolf Miscellany* 16 (Spring 1981): 5. See also Jane Marcus, review of *Sickle Side of the Moon*, ed. Nicolson and Trautmann, *Chicago Tribune Book World* (November 4, 1979).

18. Virginia Woolf, "Why?" in *The Death of the Moth* (New York: Harcourt Brace, 1942), pp. 227–34.

19. Woolf, *A Room of One's Own*, p. 79. See also Jane Marcus, ed., *New Feminist Essays on Virginia Woolf* (London: Macmillan, 1981), pp. 1–30.

20. Virginia Woolf, *The Diary of Virginia Woolf*, ed. Anne Olivier Bell (New York: Harcourt Brace Jovanovich, 1977), p. 146.

21. Ellen Hawkes, "The Virgin in the Bell Biography," *Twentieth-Century Literature* 20 (April 1974): 96–113; and Hawkes, "A Form of One's Own," *Mosaic* 8, no. 1 (1974): 77–90.

22. See *Bulletin of the New York Public Library* 80, no. 2 (Winter 1977); and Virginia Woolf, *The Pargiters*, ed. Mitchell Leaska (New York: New York Public Library and Readex Books, 1977).

23. Woolf, *The Pargiters*, p. xxciii.

24. See *Twentieth-Century Literature* 25, no. 3–4 (Fall–Winter 1979). The collection was conceived and edited by Lucio Ruotolo at Stanford University.

25. Virginia Woolf, *Women and Writing*, ed. Michele Barrett (London: Women's Press, 1979), also published in 1980 by Harcourt Brace Jovanovich.

26. Virginia Woolf, *The Letters of Virginia Woolf, 1929–1931*, vol. 4, *A Reflection of the Other Person*, ed. Nigel Nicolson and Joanne Trautmann (New York: Harcourt Brace Jovanovich, 1978), p. 348.

27. Ibid., p. 203.

28. Bell, "Bloomsbury and the Vulgar Passions," pp. 239–56.

29. See *New Feminist Essays on Virginia Woolf*, ed. Jane Marcus (Lincoln: University of Nebraska Press, 1981). The second volume of *New Feminist Essays on Virginia Woolf*, ed. Jane Marcus (Lincoln: University of Nebraska Press, in press) will contain Martine Stemerick's "The Madonna's Clay Feet," part of a University of Texas Ph.D. dissertation based on unpublished manuscripts, including essays by Julia Stephen. Alice Fox, an Elizabethan scholar, has written an essay called "Virginia Liked Elizabeth." Also included are Beverly Schlack's "Fathers in General: The Patriarchy in Virgina Woolf's Fiction"; "1897: Virginia Woolf at Fifteen" by Louise DeSalvo; Evelyn Haller's "Isis Unveiled: Virginia Woolf's Use of Egyptian Myth"; and "Political Aesthetics: The Feminine Realism of Virginia Woolf and Dorothy Richardson" by Diane Gillespie. Ann McLaughlin contributes "An Uneasy Sisterhood: Woolf and Katherine Mansfield." Emily Jensen's lesbian reading of "Mrs. Dalloway's Respectable Suicide" is included, as is Louise DeSalvo's "Tinder and Flint," a study of Vita Sackville-West and Woolf, and Susan Squier's "A Track of One's Own." Sally Scars adds a close reading of *Between the Acts* in "Theater of War"; and the collection contains Carolyn Heilbrun's "Virginia Woolf in Her Fifties." Political scientist Naomi Black contributes "Virginia Woolf and the Women's Movement"; and I have reprinted "No More Horses: Virginia Woolf on Art and Propaganda" (from *Women's Studies* 4, no. 2–3 [1977]: 265–90) to give a perspective on Woolf's politics.

30. Bell, *Bloomsbury* (n. 15 above); Quentin Bell, *Virginia Woolf* 2 vols. (London: Hogarth Press, 1972); and Bell, "Bloomsbury and the Vulgar Passions" (n. 14 above).

31. Virginia Woolf, *Three Guineas* (London: Hogarth Press, 1939).

32. Virginia Woolf, "The Leaning Tower," in *The Moment and Other Essays* (New York: Harcourt Brace, 1948), pp. 128–54; and Woolf, *Letter to a Young Poet*, Letters Series no. 8 (London: Hogarth Press, 1939).

33. See Adrienne Rich, "Toward a Woman-centered University," in *On Lies, Secrets, and Silence: Selected Prose, 1966–1978* (New York: W. W. Norton & Co., 1979), pp. 125–55.

34. Virginia Woolf was a life-long member and shared its socialist, feminist, and pacifist politics. See Marcus, "No More Horses: Virginia Woolf on Art and Propaganda"; and Black, in Marcus, ed., *New Feminist Essays on Virginia Woolf*, vol. 2.

35. Bell, *Virginia Woolf*, 2: 186.

36. Ibid.

37. Woolf, "The Leaning Tower," p. 154.

38. Gerald Brenan, *Personal Record, 1920–1972* (London: Jonathan Cape, 1974).

39. E. M. Forster, *Virginia Woolf, the Rede Lecture, 1941* (Cambridge: Cambridge University Press, 1942).

40. See Bruno Bettelheim, "Surviving," in *Surviving and Other Essays* (New York: Alfred A. Knopf, Inc., 1979), pp. 275–314; see also pp. 20–23.

41. See Nicolson's attack on Woolf's politics in the introduction to *The Letters of Virginia Woolf, 1932–1935*, vol. 5, *The Sickle Side of the Moon* (n. 17 above), pp. xi–xvii.

42. Woolf, *The Pargiters*.

43. Virginia Woolf, *A Writer's Diary* (New York: Harcourt Brace Jovanovich, 1953), p. 234.

44. The Stephen family background is discussed in Stemerick (n. 29 above); and in Jane Marcus, "Niece of a Nun," in *Virginia Woolf: A Feminist Slant*, ed. Jane Marcus (Lincoln: University of Nebraska Press, 1983).

45. Catherine Smith discusses Caroline Stephen in her study of English women mys-

tics (Bucknell University, English Department, in preparation). See also Smith, "Jane Lead: The Feminist Mind and Art of a Seventeenth Century Protestant Mystic," in *Women of Spirit: Female Leadership in the Jewish and Christian Tradition*, ed. Rosemary Reuther and Eleanor McLaughlin (New York: Simon & Schuster, 1979), pp. 184–85. Robert Tod is preparing a biography for the English Society of Friends' Quaker biography series (Haverford College, in preparation); and see also Jane Marcus, "A Nun and Her Niece: Virginia Woolf, Caroline Stephen, and the Cloistered Imagination" (paper presented at the Virginia Woolf Society meeting at the Modern Language Association, New York, 1981).

46. Bell, "Bloomsbury." See also Marcus, "No More Horses: Virginia Woolf on Art and Propaganda" (n. 29 above).

47. Woolf, *Letters*, 5:383.

48. Woolf, *Letters*, 1: 148, 151–52, 165, 180.

49. Dmitry Mirsky, *The Intelligentsia of Great Britain*, trans. Alec Brown (New York: Conici, Friede, 1935).

50. Caroline Emelia Stephen, *The Light Arising: Thoughts on the Central Radiance* (Cambridge: W. Heffer & Sons, 1908).

51. Jaakko Hintinkka's "Virginia Woolf and Our Knowledge of the External World," *Journal of Aesthetics and Art Criticism* 38, no. 1 (Fall 1979): 5–14 is relevant here.

52. Virginia Woolf, "Thoughts on Peace in an Air Raid," in *The Death of the Moth* (New York: Harcourt Brace, 1942), pp. 243–48.

53. Bell, "Bloomsbury and the Vulgar Passions."

54. See Maria-Antonietta Macciocchi's translated work, "Female Sexuality in Fascist Ideology," *Feminist Review* 1 (1979): 59–82.

55. Bell, "Bloomsbury and the Vulgar Passions."

56. Ibid.

57. Laura Riding, "In the Beginning," *Collected Poetry of Laura Riding* (New York: Random House, 1938), p. 358.

THE MADWOMAN AND HER LANGUAGES

why i don't do feminist literary theory

(1 9 8 4)

Perhaps the central issue in academic literary feminism right now is theory itself. "Early" academic literary feminism—if one may use this word for an enterprise only launched in the early 1970s—developed along two clear paths. First, a pragmatic, empirical attempt to look at women—in society or in texts—as images in literature, as authors, as readers; second, a visionary attempt to describe women's writing in a reconstructed future, an attempt in which description often merged with exhortation. Theory developed later, mainly in response to what Elaine Showalter has described as an androcentric "critical community increasingly theoretical in its interests and indifferent to women's writing."[1] In other words, feminist theory addresses an audience of prestigious male academics and attempts to win its respect. It succeeds, so far as I can see, only when it ignores or dismisses the earlier paths of feminist literary study as "naive" and grounds its own theories in those currently in vogue with the men who make theory: deconstruction, for example, or Marxism. These grounding theories manifest more than mere indifference to women's writing; they are irretrievably misogynist. As a result of building on misogynist foundations, feminist theorists mainly excoriate their deviating sisters.

Feminism has always been bifurcated by contention between pluralists and legalists. Pluralists anticipate the unexpected, encourage diversity; legalists locate the correct position and marshal women within the ranks. As for recent literary theory, it is deeply legalistic and judgmental. Infractions—the wrong theory, theoretical errors, or insouciant disregard for theoretical implications—are crimes. Pluralists "dance"; theorists "storm" or "march."[2] Literary theories—in striking contrast to scientific theories—are designed to constrain what may allowably be said or discovered. Such totalizing by feminist theorists reproduces to *the letter* the appropriation of women's experience by men, substituting only the appropriation and naming of that experience by a subset of women: themselves.[3] Such structural repetition undermines the feminist project.

It is easier to totalize when one restricts application of theories to texts already sanctioned by the academy. These restrictions, however, elide such difficult matters as the relation of the canon to standards of "literariness,"[4] or of gender to genre. There is nothing natural or universal about "creative writing." Women or men in western society undertaking to produce what they hope will be viewed as "serious" writing do so in complicated, culturally mediated ways. "Seriousness" as a criterion of literary merit, for one obvious example, implies a profound Victorian patriarchal didacticism, and is often used to denigrate the popular women's genres. Still, no matter how our standards change in future, to name a work as "literary" will always endow it with a degree of artifice that must inevitably traverse and confuse any hypothesized necessary, immutable relation between "women writing" and "writing by women."

Present feminist theory encourages us, as a chief means of expanding the concept of the literary, to study private—hence presumably "natural"—writings of women. But even diaries and letters are written according to rules. And such "expansion" could well be understood rather as a contraction of the idea of writing, and an iteration of the stereotype of woman as a wholly private, purely expressive being. Such reinscription, indeed incarceration, of women in the private sphere seems to me an ominous countertrend in an era notable for dramatic entry of women into hitherto all-male preserves of public activity: not to mime men but to save our own lives *from* men. More specific to literature, the trend involves rendering invisible the public forms in which women have long written and continue to write so well. We neglect the writings—as writings—of (for example) Hannah Arendt, Margaret Mead, Suzanne Langer, and Rachel Carson. Indeed, we neglect all "non-imaginative" discourse: feature writing, journalism, scientific works both professional and popular, philosophical essays, legal briefs, advertising. At the root of the neglect, simply, is the desire to maintain "difference," for all current theory requires sexual difference as its ground. The title of a special issue of the androcentric journal *Critical Inquiry*, "Writing and Sexual Difference," made this assumption clear, and it appropriated the feminist label for theories that necessarily assumed differences fully known. Differences abound; but what they are, how they are constituted, what they entail, and whether they must be constant, seem to me above all questions that a feminist might ask, questions that are least adequately answered. Today's feminist literary theory makes asking an act of empirical anti-theory, and hence a heresy. It is finally more concerned to be theoretical than to be feminist. It speaks from the position of the *castrata*.

To accept woman as castrated is to evince a "hegemonic" mindset that recapitulates and hence capitulates to fear, dislike, and contempt of women. What will concern me in the rest of this essay are some foci of misogyny in present theory. I concentrate on four recurrent motifs, which I name: the madwoman; a female language; the father; the mother.

I. THE MADWOMAN

The name comes from Sandra M. Gilbert and Susan Gubar's impressive and influential study of nineteenth-century British women writers, *The Madwoman in the Attic*.[5] Their book applies traditional close-reading and image-study techniques to the texts of already-canonized nineteenth-century women writers, in search of a sign of the writers'—presumably shared—biographical situation as writers. It assumes, then, that a sign will be found, and finds it in the recurrent figure of the madwoman. Literary achievement for the nineteenth-century woman, they claim, was psychologically costly because it required defiance of the misogynist strictures and structures of Victorian patriarchy. Defiance had to be hidden; suppressed, it smoldered as a pure rage revealed in the furious madwoman who disrupts or ruptures so many women's texts. Gilbert and Gubar derived this theory of the woman writer from Harold Bloom's "anxiety of influence." That theory had created authorship as an exclusively male phenomenon, wherein would-be-powerful poet sons struggled to overthrow, while avowing loyalty to, already-powerful poet fathers. Possibly, its ulterior motive was to eliminate women from the canon; possibly, the hostile male tradition against which Gilbert and Gubar found their madwomen authors struggling in what they labelled an "anxiety of authorship" was, at least partly, hypostatized in the work they took as their starting point. Possibly, however, Bloom simply expressed traditional misogyny in contemporary terms.

Gilbert and Gubar modified Bloom in one important way. His approach was ahistorical, imposing a quasi-Freudian father and son conflict on literary history as a function of the ineluctable nature of the (male) poet's psyche. The "anxiety of authorship," however, is advanced as a historical concept, a fruitfully accurate description of the state of literature and attitudes toward it in a particular place at a particular time. But though advanced as a historical fact, the anxiety of authorship, except for Emily Dickinson, is demonstrated only by intra-textual evidence; thus *The Madwoman in the Attic* assumes the existence of the historical and literary situation which its textual readings require. Strikingly absent, too, from consideration of the historical moment in the analysis is the appearance among women of a realizable ambition to become professional writers. Traditionally hermeneutic, Gilbert and Gubar concentrate on a hidden message—female anxiety of authorship—while reading past the surface evidence that their studies provide for the arrival of the woman professional author.

The madwoman who names Gilbert and Gubar's book is the nonlingual Bertha Mason from *Jane Eyre*. Gilbert and Gubar read her as "Jane's truest and darkest double . . . the ferocious secret self Jane has been trying to repress" (360). Jane, then—though Gilbert and Gubar do not explicitly say this—must be a vision of woman as she might in future become, rather than any woman presently existing, since women presently existing contain the madwoman within their psyche. While seeing this figure as Jane's alter ego as well as Brontë's, Gilbert and Gubar find little redemptive about her, and considering the way she is described, this is no wonder. "In the deep shade, at the further end of the room, a figure ran backwards and forwards. What it was, whether beast or human being, one could not, at first sight, tell; it grovelled, seemingly, on all fours; it snatched and growled like some wild animal; but it was covered with clothing, and a quantity of dark, grizzled hair, wild as a mane, hid its head and face." Further on, Jane notes how "the clothed hyena rose up, and stood tall on its hind feet" (chapter 26).

I can't ignore the work Brontë has put into defining Bertha out of humanity. Not a scintilla of recognition of Bertha's likeness to herself disturbs Jane's consciousness, or fashions an ironic narrator discourse by which she might be corrected. The creature is wholly hateful, and no wonder: she has *stolen Jane's man.* Jane's rage against Rochester, one might say, is deflected to what a feminist might well see as an innocent victim. The woman rather than the man becomes her adversary; that woman's death is as necessary for Jane's liberation as is Rochester's blinding. How, then, do Gilbert and Gubar "read" a woman's death as a good thing for women? It seems to me that they have been so far convinced by Brontë's rhetoric as not to see Bertha as a woman. "She" is simply the figuration of anger, at once true and false—true to the situation of women in patriarchy, but since patriarchy is a false system, witness to its falseness. Her disappearance will simply mark the passing of a false order, not the passing of a female subject. Gilbert and Gubar are not, to be sure, entirely happy with the novel's denouement, suggesting that "Brontë was unable clearly to envision viable solutions to the problem of patriarchal oppression" (369), but they refer here to the unfortunate damage inflicted on Rochester. They do not doubt that Bertha's elimination from the fiction is a pure good.

II. A FEMALE LANGUAGE

Among Charlotte Brontë's outrages on her madwoman is the denial of ability to speak; Bertha will never get to tell her own story (Jean Rhys corrected this in *Wide Sargasso Sea*). But, simultaneously influential with Gilbert and Gubar's work, French feminist literary theory appears to accept the figure of the madwoman as redemptive. She is taken to be not what women have regrettably been made by a contemptuous and oppressive culture, but what women either essentially are, or have fortunately been allowed to remain, in a society that brackets but cannot obliterate the innate disruptive, revolutionary force of the female. Since society is bad, this force is good. The madwoman, articulating "otherness," becomes the subject. But, so long silent, what will she say, and how will she say it? A theory of uniquely female language emerges. Descriptions and prescriptions result from a common procedure: features of the dominant language, masculine because dominant, are identified; opposite features are advanced as appropriate for women.

Christiane Makward, one of the important translators of and commentators on French feminism, describes the female language: "open, nonlinear, unfinished, fluid, exploded, fragmented, polysemic, attempting to speak the body i.e., the unconscious, involving silence, incorporating the simultaneity of life as opposed to or clearly different from pre-conceived, oriented, masterly or 'didactic' languages."[6] The women usually associated with this idea are Hélène Cixous and Luce Irigaray, both trained as psychoanalysts by Jacques Lacan, their worldview marked with his patriarchism. While they sometimes attempt to write in the style they recommend, both agree that such a language has never existed before. It is not a language that socially marked "women" have used in the past because such socially marked women are not "true" women at all. A student of the nineteenth-century concept of true womanhood experiences an odd sense of time warp: application of the theory demonstrates, mainly, the absence of "woman" from "women's" writing. The theory is also applied by certain especially ingenious critics to discover the mandated language in canonical women's texts via deconstruction.[7] Deconstruction, however, is a procedure whose vocabulary, shared by nonfeminists and men, yields identical results no matter whose texts it analyzes.

More often the theory is an agenda for the way women might or should write in future; to me it seems a guarantee of continued oppression. The most militant theorists do not use the language they call for; the theory incorporates wholly traditional notions of the feminine. Domna C. Stanton, another sponsor of French feminist theory in this country, writes, "recurring identification of the female in *écriture féminine* with madness, antireason, primitive darkness, mystery" represents a "revalorization of traditional 'feminine' stereotypes."[8] Makward, again, writes that "the theory of femininity is dangerously close to repeating in 'deconstructive' language the traditional assumptions." It is an essentialist definition making women "incapable of speaking as a woman; therefore, the most female course of action is to observe an hour of silence, or to scream. . . . Women are resigning themselves to silence, and to nonspeech. The speech of the other will then swallow them up, will speak *for* them."[9]

Actually, "women" are not resigning themselves to silence and nonspeech; we cannot afford to, and as we enter the public arena in increasing numbers we are not silent, and we do not (publicly) scream. Wishing to speak *to effect*, we use rational sequential discourse and, evidently, we use it well. Have we, then, chosen to become *men*? Before assenting, consider that this open, nonlinear, exploded, fragmented, polysemic idea of our speech is congruent with the idea of the hopelessly irrational, disorganized, "weaker sex" desired by the masculine Other. The theory leads to a language that is intensely private, politically ineffectual, designed to fail. Women entering public life, whether as Supreme Court justices or organizers of tenants' unions, disprove the theory empirically, and, indeed, would follow it at their peril. They leave "advanced" theorists of women's literature far in the rear, expose their theory as an esoteric luxury. Of course, along with relegating "woman" to uselessness, the theory affirms belles-lettres as an elite pastime.

Feminists reacting to this theory maintain that nothing inherently bars us from the use of common speech, denying the argument that the "mother tongue" is really an alien, "father" tongue. In one essay, Hélène Cixous announces: "Too bad for [men] if they fall apart upon discovering that women aren't men, or that the mother doesn't have one. But isn't this fear convenient for them? Wouldn't the worst be, isn't the worst, in truth, that women aren't castrated?"[10] Cixous's identification of language with castration derives from the Lacanian reading of Freud's late version of the Oedipus complex, in which the threat of castration becomes the instrument of male socialization. Cixous's suggestion here is quite different from her assertions elsewhere that women really are castrated and hence, having nothing to lose, must remain unreconstructedly asocial.

In their recent essay "Sexual Linguistics,"[11] Gilbert and Gubar propose that twentieth-century women's writing has been shaped by our need to contend with the "intensified misogyny with which male writers greeted the entrance of women into the literary marketplace" (a belated greeting, by the way, since women have dominated the market since the mid-nineteenth century); this, along with men's anxiety over the loss of their own literary language, Latin, the father tongue (another tardy awareness, since men have used English as their primary literary language since the seventeenth century), forced women into fantasies of "alternative speech." Such fantasies have dominated women's writing since the turn of the century and consist in a subterranean celebration of the real state of affairs, which is that it is women, not men, who have the primary relation to language (the mother tongue). Thus, men and women's writing alike in this century represents sharply differentiated recognitions, however distorted, of the linguistic as well as biological primacy of the mother.

In this intriguing argument, it is now men not women who experience anxieties of authorship; women not men who own the language; nevertheless, Gilbert and Gubar can only see women's writings as compensatory and competitive fantasies. Men are ceded possession of the very language that is the woman's domain, women driven into a defensive posture. I would respond that if women are "really" primary in the essentialist way that Gilbert and Gubar describe them, then the historical phenomena described could not have happened; that it need not happen (history is always contingent, anyhow, not necessary); and finally, most crucially, that it did not happen so massively that we must identify the form of twentieth-century women's writing with it.

As alternative linguistic fantasists, women are not distinguishable from male modernists (of course their content is different, but their language is not); and modernism is only one kind of feminine practice in the twentieth century. The idea of an alternative language is as much an apotheosis of the modernist creed as a residue of exclusion from modernism. Emily Dickinson (no longer the cowering recluse of *The Madwoman in the Attic*) appears in "Sexual Linguistics" as the great celebrant of maternal witchcraft; but while granting that she may be the strongest womanist poet in English, we cannot deny that she has been perceived by many excellent critics as a precursor of modernism in her private, expressive, self-communing verse. Virginia Woolf and Gertrude Stein, other prime instances in the new Gilbert and Gubar argument, are also as modernist as they are feminist. We can view modernism, in short, as the creation as much of women as of men writers, a view which the gender-differentiating theory Gilbert and Gubar employ cannot encompass. My point would not be that there are no differences; but that when you start with a theory of difference, you can't see anything but. And when you start with a *misogynist* theory of difference, you are likely to force women into shapes that many may find unnatural or uncongenial. Such women also have voices. If they—we—are drowned out or denied, what has our theory accomplished except to divide woman from woman?

Another way of viewing modernism is not as something new in our century, but as the culmination of entrepreneurial, self-oriented individualism that, in the nineteenth century, was identified by many popular women writers as especially masculine, controlled by selfish and self-aggrandizing commercial motives, involving a will to power, a drive to omnipotence, and the like. Against such values, nineteenth-century women (at least in America) fashioned a "female" ethic—not of private, alternative musings, but of domestic responsibility and communal action apart from self. Nineteenth-century popular American women writers, including feminists, were vitally concerned to gain access to the public sphere in order to transform it by their social and domestic idealism; for this goal, none other than the language in use could possibly serve. Therefore, they availed themselves of it; nor did they have any doubt that it was "their" language as much as it was men's. Hence, we might identify a linguistic tradition of woman's writing precisely by its reappropriation of the mother tongue, its emergence from privatism with an implicit claim that this powerful language is ours as much as it is men's.

And yet again, Elizabeth Hampstead's excellent work *Read This Only to Your-*

self: The Private Writings of Midwestern Women,[12] shows that nineteenth-century working-class women, unaffected by pretensions to "literariness" and uninterested in public discourse, wrote letters and diaries in a way opposite to that enjoined by any theories of women's language that have subsequently emerged to locate and, I believe, enforce sexual difference.

III. THE FATHER

It becomes clear that the theory of women's language is closely tied to a theory of the feminine personality; and because Freud is the originator of modern psychological theorizing on the feminine, an encounter with Freud might seem unavoidable. Yet we live in an age in which Freud is much questioned. As science, of course, his theories have yet to win respectability. As cure, his methods do no better than chance. As a body of philosophical writings, his works are shot through with inconsistencies and vaguenesses. And from various sources within the profession he founded, there are now serious doubts expressed about his integrity. What cannot be doubted, however, is the profound misogyny that underlies his descriptions of and prescriptions for women.

Thus, one would think that he could have been ignored by feminists interested in a theoretical base for their own forays into a theory of women's writing. On the contrary, however, literary feminist theorists have elevated him (and Lacan, his up-to-date surrogate) and in so doing have probably given his ideas new currency and prestige. To my perception (and at the risk of undercutting my own position I have to say it) this attachment to Freud—assuming that it is not simply opportunistic—manifests precisely that masochism that Freud and his followers identified with the female. We are most "daddy's girl" when we seek—as Jane Gallop not long ago expressed it—to seduce him.[13] Our attempt to seduce him, or our compliance with his attempt to seduce us, guarantees his authority. If Freud is right, there is no feminism.

Observing the Lacanian basis of contemporary French feminist theory, Christiane Makward roots "the problem of the feminine" in psychoanalytic theory because "the vast majority of those critics and writers—female or male—which [sic] have attempted to rationalize their perception of the different in the relation of women to language have done so on the basis of neo-Freudian postulates."[14] The key phrase here is "perception of the different." The most important questions (to me) for research and analysis—what differences there "really" are, how they are constituted, and what they "signify," not to mention the problematic role of language in the very framing of the questions—are all bypassed by this axiomatic assumption of known, immutable difference. To the extent that any idea of a recuperated future, no matter how modest, is an inalienable part of the concept of "feminism," we have here a program that, despite its claims, must be named antifeminist.

The program is not unique to French feminists, with their particular historical relation to Lacan. In England, Juliet Mitchell has been a strong exponent of the need to retain Freud in a feminist vision of the female personality, and in this country the more recent work of Nancy Chodorow has had a striking impact on feminist literary criticism.[15] Chodorow argued that the questions "why do women want to be mothers?" and "why do they raise daughters who want to be mothers in turn?" could not be accounted for by any combination of biological marking and upbringing, but required an intrapsychic, specifically Freudian explanation. She proposed that girls failed to separate from their mothers because the mothers failed to separate from them with a resulting fluidity of boundary between self and others. In effect, Chodorow answered her questions by adducing the stereotyped notion of the female personality, which, to be sure, she rearticulated in somewhat more timely language; in so doing she gave that stereotype a new efficacy in the construction of a feminine reality. Despite the comments of feminist psychologists that at best Chodorow's was an untested hypothesis, this theory must have satisfied a need among literary feminist critics, for it has inspired numerous readings of women writers based on the assumption of their less organized, more connected and fluid personalities.

It is certainly no secret that the historical Freud was both misogynist and antifeminist. It is demonstrable, too, that the misogynist and antifeminist tendencies in Freud's writings became much more pronounced in his work after World War I, when he broke with many of his followers because of his new emphasis on the castration complex. The post–World War I malaise, exacerbated by the relatively rapid emancipation of women after 1920, manifested itself in his case by defection and dissent of his followers precisely on the question of the feminine; by the virtual disappearance of that kind of female patient who had made his reputation and on whom, therefore, he depended (the hysteric, who did indeed use "body language" as her means of speaking); and by the appearance of women psychoanalysts. One might say that the obedient daughter who could only speak with and through her body, and who was released into speech by Freud thus becoming his creation, gave way to or was supplanted by the rebellious daughter who dared to match him word for word. Her rebellion, of course, was no more than the representation of herself as an equal, rejecting his stewardship, his fatherhood. It is not really surprising that Freud reacted with a marked intensification of his ideas about female inferiority, but he might have done differently.

For example, the Oedipus complex (itself, now, an ever more problematic concept) shifted attention from the boy's loving attachment to his mother to his fearful relation with his father. The mother was altered from the subject of a compelling heterosexual love to the object of a same-sex rivalry. And the castration complex, introduced to explain how the Oedipus complex came to an end, made it impossible for girls, who cannot be castrated, to become adults.[16] "In the absence of fear of castration the chief motive is lacking which leads boys to surmount the Oedipus complex," Freud wrote in "Femininity" (1933). "Girls remain in it for an indeterminate length of time; they demolish it late and, even so, incompletely. In these circumstances the formation of the super-ego must suffer; it cannot attain the strength and independence which give it its cultural significance, and feminists are not pleased when we point out to them the effects of this factor upon the average feminine character."[17] Freud's gibe at the feminists makes his purpose clear; he catches feminists in the double bind, denying that they are women, and asserting that, as women, these feminists cannot be the rational beings they claim to be, capable of original thought. It was part of Freud's intellectual *machismo* to reserve original thought for the male; that is a reservation still immensely powerful in all academia.

Freud's late writing—"Some Psychical Consequences of the Anatomical Distinction between the Sexes" (1925), "Female Sexuality" (1931), and "Femininity" (an essay added to the *New Introductory Lectures* in 1933)—greatly exaggerated his never slight attention to the penis. Not having a penis is a *lack*, an objectively real *inferiority*, a castration *in fact*.[18] The little girl on first seeing a little boy's penis is instantly struck with her shame and inferiority while the boy regards the naked little girl with "horror at the mutilated creature or triumphant contempt for her."[19] Those without the penis can never be initiated into the culture's higher life, nor contribute to it. The aims of therapy are different according to the genital apparatus of the patient: those with a penis are helped to enter the world, those with a vagina are taught to "resign" themselves to marginality. Any woman's attempt to overcome feelings of inferiority vis-à-vis men is interpreted as the wish for a penis which, "unrealizable," is, or can be, the "beginning of a psychosis."[20] Of course this is all a fantasy; yet claiming that fantasy overrode the real world, Freud advanced this fantastic difference as the legitimizing basis of every sexist stereotype and proscription. This fantasy, or so it seems to me, is too patently useful, too crassly interested, and too culturally sophisticated, to qualify as an emanation from the Unconscious.

Lacan too—or perhaps, Lacan even more. At least Freud knew that his "laws" of human development were mostly broken; his livelihood depended on the broken law. Lacan's laws are unbreakable, and he is hence a far less "forgiving" father than Freud. With Lacan, we are always and forever outside. Lacan's deployment of the castration complex as the basis of the model for the symbolic order into which children—boys—are initiated, takes one particularly "sexist" element in Freud's rich system (which contained many ungendered insights) and makes it the whole story. Lacan claimed throughout his career that he had rescued Freud from a dated biologism by reformulating his theory as linguistics, but he resorted to biologism shamelessly when it suited him. Thus, in his 1972 seminar, produced in an ambience not unlike that faced by Freud in the 1920s—the growth of feminism, the arrival of female analysts as competition—he *pronounced* women into silence:

> There is no woman but excluded by the nature of things which is the nature of words, and it has to be said that if there is one thing about which women themselves are complaining at the moment, it's well and truly that—it's just that they don't know what they are saying, which is all the difference between them and me.[21]

Them and me: the difference (since women are clearly doing just what Lacan's theory says they can't do) is not how women act but what they essentially are and cannot help but be. Lacan's defenders, including Juliet Mitchell and Jacqueline Rose, have claimed that he was attempting, here and elsewhere in his attacks on the French feminists, to counter their return to an overt biologism and a worship of the Eternal Feminine. But I find linguistic essentialism no improvement on the biological. Lacan's ideas of women belong neither to his realms of the real nor the symbolic, but to his imaginary. Both Freud and Lacan make haste to correct the fantasies of *others* that their own prevail. Not truth, but power, is the issue.

IV. THE MOTHER

In attempting to save Freud for feminism (to save him more generally for today's world), many have turned to the concept of the pre-Oedipal mother and proposed her to balance the Oedipal father in the life-history of the child. But it seems to me that the pre-Oedipal mother plays, in such thinking, the role that patriarchs always allot to mothers: she shores up the father. Since the aim is to help out Freud rather than to help out women, such a result may have been inherent in the project.

The very term pre-Oedipal suggests the primacy of the Oedipal phase. Why not call the Oedipal phase the "post-Cerean"? Even more bizarre is the coinage "phallic mother," which suggests that the child responds to the pre-Oedipal mother only because she or he believes that the mother has a penis. The pre-Oedipal mother is rudely rejected when the child discovers the mother's appalling "lack," such rejection indicating that the attachment to the mother was based on fantasy, now to be rectified by the Oedipal phase. In a word, the child was never "really" attached to the mother, only fantasized such an attachment; the "real" attachment was always to the father.

The concept also affirms the mother's disappearance as agent and subject from the child's life early on—by age five if development is "normal." And, while allowing influence, it limits it to a global, nonverbal or preverbal, endlessly supportive, passively nurturing presence. Here is one source for the idea of the *adult* woman's language as unbounded, polysemous, and the like—a residual memory of our mother in the days before we understood her language, that is, in the days before we had a language of our own. Many feminists celebrate the mother's body fluids as her "language."

Of course we all know, in our rational moments, that the mother's influence lasts far beyond the age of five. But even if we were to grant its waning at that age, we surely know that the mother's role in the child's earliest life is not so simple as this pre-Oedipal model makes it out to be. (At least we who have been mothers know.) To take the matter of most concern for literary theory, we know that the mother is the language teacher, and begins her task before the child is even a year old; normal children in all cultures are thoroughly verbal though not yet fully syntactical by the age of three. And there is—*pace* Lacan—no sudden break, no startling initiation into the order dominated or constructed by language; language from the first is part of the child's relation to the mother. What purpose does the theory of an exclusively nonverbal stage serve? It minimizes the mother.

As the mother's influence on children of both sexes persists long beyond the age of five, so does that influence on a maturing child become yet more complex, albeit increasingly diluted, encompassing many activities that patriarchal rhetoric attributes to the father. Mothers make children into human and social beings through a continuous process in which instruction and nurturance are indistinguishable. No doubt, the social world into which our mothers initiated us, and into which we initiate our sons and daughters, is dominated by men and supported by a rationalizing symbol system; but it differs crucially from the patriarchal social world of Freud and Lacan, in that mothers are demonstrably unlike the mothers of their theories.

Pre-Oedipal, then, is an interested fantasy of the maternal. Its purpose—to contain and confine mothers and hence women within the field of the irrational—is evident; to espouse such a fantasy is to accede to a male appropriation of the mother and her language. Why do feminists do it? Perhaps it is no more than hegemonic fatigue. I offer two other possibilities: first, women feel the same fear and jealousy of the mother that appears in part to underlie Freud's writing (this is the thesis of Dorothy Dinnerstein's *The Mermaid and the Minotaur*);[22] second, a theory in which women have had nothing to do with the world is comforting and inspiring. To put this somewhat differently: the Freudian and the feminist agendas may coincide because feminists do not like their mothers, or because feminists prefer to endow women with a revolutionary power that we cannot have if we have been part of the system all along. To say this is not to blame the victim, but rather to question our ability to carry, after so many centuries of implication, any pure revitalizing force. Our powers are limited, and our agendas for change will have to take internal limitation into account.

These issues are sharply evident in recent feminist literary work on mothers and daughters. It provides testimony, often unwitting and in contradiction to its stated intentions, of the deep-seated hostility of daughters to mothers. (Mothers do not speak of daughters in this discourse.) Adrienne Rich's *Of Woman Born* excoriates the male establishment for forcing the *role* of motherhood on women while denying us the *experience* of it, but is strikingly cold when not silent on the writer's own mother. Nor does Rich's poetry speak to her mother, committed to women though it may be.[23] Even at the moment when the daughter-writer or daughter-feminist claims that she is seeking the mother in order to make strengthening contact she reveals that the mother she seeks is not *her* mother, but another mother, preferably an imaginary mother. Perhaps feminism has become confused with maturation.

In much criticism, it is the pre-Oedipal mother who is looked for, sought not to combat patriarchy, but to defend against the real mother. Here, for example, from *The Lost Tradition*, a collection of essays on the mother-daughter relation (all written from the standpoint of daughters): "confronting the Terrible Mother in order to move beyond the entanglements of the mother/daughter relationship . . . claiming her as metaphor for the sources of our own creative powers, women are creating new self-configurations in which the mother is no longer the necessary comfort but the seed of a new being, and in which we are no longer the protected child but the carriers of the new woman whose birth is our own."[24] We have made the mother our child, we are self-mothered, we move beyond the entanglements of our real mother by imprisoning her in metaphor. The Terrible Mother is called on to perform a matricide.

Karen Elias-Button also comments that the mothers portrayed in contemporary fiction by women "seem to have little existence apart from their children and dread their daughters' independence as if it means their own death."[25] If works with such images were written by men, no feminist would hesitate to label them projections: how like a male to imagine that his mother has no life except in him! "The most disturbing villain in recent women's fiction is not the selfish or oppressive male but instead the bad mother."[26] The author may "dispose of" fear of the mother "by rendering the mother so repulsive or ridiculous that the reader must reject her as her fictional daughter does. Another tactic is for the author to kill the mother in the course of the narrative."[27] The matricidal impulse could not be plainer. Moving into the past, we find that today's women writers join a long tradition. The mothers of fictional heroines in the period ending with Jane Austen "are usually bad and living, or good and dead."[28] "The women novelists of the period from Fanny Burney to Mrs. Gaskell and George Eliot create very few positive images of motherhood."[29] Real mothers—of Harriet Martineau, George Eliot, Emily Dickinson, Ellen Glasgow, Edith Wharton, Willa Cather—all are faulted by their daughters for failing them, and these daughters are taken at their word by today's feminist daughter-critic.

Think, now, for a moment, about Jane Eyre and Bertha Mason. Who, after all, might Bertha Mason be—she to whom Rochester is *already married*? *Jane Eyre* is replete with images of ferocious female power and Jane turns to Rochester, at first, as to a refuge. That refuge is sullied by the presence in the nest of another woman, who is made repulsive and ridiculous so that the reader must reject her; and is killed before the narrative is out, so that the daughter can replace her. Even Gilbert and Gubar perform an unconscious matricide when they define a literary tradition, "handed down not from one woman to another but from the stern literary 'fathers' of patriarchy to all their 'inferiorized' female descendents" (*Madwoman*, 50). Evidently by the time of the Brontës and George Eliot there were literary mothers available; either these nineteenth-century women rejected them as Jane rejected Bertha, or Gilbert and Gubar forgot about them as they were caught up in the challenge of producing a respectable (fathered rather than mothered) feminist literary theory.

A difference more profound for feminism than the male-female difference emerges: the difference between woman and woman. If the speaking woman sees other women as her mother, sees herself but not her mother as a woman, then she can see her mother (other women) only as men or monsters. There is no future for a commonality of women if we cannot traverse the generations. One sees only here and there signs of something different. Julia Kristeva says that we must challenge "the myth of the archaic mother"[30] in order for women to enter society as participant beings—but her language is aggressive toward the myth, not its patriarchal perpetrators; Dinnerstein writes that one must come to see the "first parent" as "no more and no less than a fellow creature."[31] Dinnerstein seems sentimental here, but her point is crucial. It goes beyond her own Freudian emphasis to imply that the family model of daddy, mommy, and me, is inimical to the human future. And, since the family triangle, and its inevitable oddly-named "romance," is the veritable nurturing ground of patriarchy, it "must" be abandoned before there can be a "true" feminist theory. It has probably never existed in reality; one can wonder what a theory deliberately developed from childhood fantasies describes other than childish fantasies, and how such a theory serves feminist intentions. Indeed, whether children "see" the world as Freudians say they do is something we will never know so long as Freudian scholars are the only ones to ask the question.

I am, evidently, a pluralist. Essays in feminist journals are permeated with musts and shoulds,[32] with homily and exhortation and a fractiousness that at most puts "sisterhood" under erasure and at least means that the totalizing assumptions of theory are fictions. In the late sixties, feminism was called "women's liberation." It seemed to promise us that we could, at last, try to be and do what we wanted; it proposed that women could help each other to become what they wanted. "Women's liberation" didn't suggest we all had to be one thing. To find oneself again a conscript, within a decade, is sad.

NOTES

1. Elaine Showalter, "Feminist Criticism in the Wilderness," *Critical Inquiry*, 8 (1981), 181.

2. I borrow these terms from Wendy Martin, *An American Triptych: Ann Bradstreet, Emily Dickinson, Adrienne Rich* (Chapel Hill: University of North Carolina Press, 1983), p. 229. These terms do not apply to theories as such, but to styles that appear to override theories.

3. These words were originally written before the appalling account of life in the French Mouvement Libération des Femmes—a feminist ideal for many literary theorists—appeared in *Signs*. See Dorothy Kaufmann-McCall, "Politics of Difference: The Women's Movement in France from May 1968 to Mitterand," *Signs*, 9 (1983), 282–93.

4. See Lillian S. Robinson, "Treason our Text: Feminist Challenges to the Literary Canon," *Tulsa Studies in Women's Literature*, 2 (1983), 83–98; see also this volume, pp. 115–128.

5. Sandra M. Gilbert and Susan Gubar, *The Madwoman in the Attic: The Woman Writer and the Nineteenth-Century Imagination* (New Haven: Yale University Press, 1979). Subsequent references are cited parenthetically in the text.

6. Christiane Makward, "To Be or Not to Be . . . a Feminist Speaker," in *The Future of Difference*, eds. Alice Jardine and Hester Eisenstein (Boston: C. K. Hall, 1980), p. 96.

7. Mary Jacobus, "The Questions of Language: Men or Maxims and *The Mill on the Floss*," *Critical Inquiry*, 8 (1981), 222.

8. Domna C. Stanton, "Language and Revolution: The Franco-American Disconnection," in *The Future of Difference*, p. 86.

9. Makward, p. 100.

10. Hélène Cixous, "The Laugh of the Medusa," *Signs*, 1 (1976), 885; see also this volume, pp. 347–362. As Diane Griffin Crowder, an expert on Cixous, has recently observed in a review in *Tulsa Studies*, "Cixous is not a feminist in any sense that the American movement would recognize." *Tulsa Studies in Women's Literature*, 4 (1985), 149. This being patently the case, the zeal of American literary feminists to put her at the apex of feminist theory is all the more puzzling.

11. Sandra M. Gilbert and Susan Gubar, "Sexual Linguistics," *New Literary History*, 16 (1985), 515–43.

12. Elizabeth Hampsten, *Read This Only to Yourself: The Private Writings of Midwestern Women* (Bloomington: Indiana University Press, 1982).

13. Jane Gallop, *The Daughter's Seduction: Feminism and Psychoanalysis* (Ithaca, N.Y.: Cornell University Press, 1982). A young literary-academic feminist of my acquaintance tells me that most feminists of her generation are feminists precisely because they recognize the abjectness of their attitudes toward men. That recognition has been the starting point for many of us; but a theory that valorizes or prescribes abjectness seems to me to confuse the starting point with the end.

14. Makward, p. 102.

15. Nancy Chodorow, *The Reproduction of Mothering* (Berkeley and Los Angeles: University of California Press, 1976). Another influential book of the same sort is Carol Gilligan, *In a Different Voice* (Cambridge, Mass.: Harvard University Press, 1982). Both of these works have had more impact on feminist literary studies than in their own social science fields, largely because the evidence on which their arguments are based are, by social science standards, deplorably weak.

16. The real Freudian scandal, however—one to shame a feminist advocate of a meeting of feminism and psychoanalysis—is the substitution of the Oedipus complex for the seduction theory on the grounds that it would be impossible for all those women (and men) to have been telling the truth when they testified to childhood sexual abuse. What we are learning of child abuse these days exposes this uncharacteristic eruption of "common sense" into Freud's discourse as a dreadful hypocrisy. And indeed, the logic of this replacement was always poor—much like saying that it would be impossible for all those cases of tuberculosis to have been caused by the same bacteria.

17. Sigmund Freud, "Femininity," in *Psychoanalysis and Feminism,* ed. Juliet Mitchell (New York: Pantheon, 1974), p. 88.

18. Sigmund Freud, "Analysis Terminable and Interminable," in *The Collected Writings of Sigmund Freud,* 5 (London: Hogarth Press, 1953–1974), p. 356.

19. Sigmund Freud, "Some Psychical Consequences of the Anatomical Distinction Between the Sexes," in *Psychoanalysis and Feminism,* p. 191. Note that for Freud there is only "the" distinction. I hope it is clear that my argument does not deny differences; I stress the plural. I believe that differences are multiple, variable, and largely unresearched and not understood; therefore any theory based on only one is pernicious.

20. Freud, "Analysis Terminable and Interminable," p. 357.

21. Quoted in Juliet Mitchell and Jacqueline Rose, eds., *Feminine Psychology: Jacques Lacan and the école freudienne* (New York: Norton, 1982), p. 144.

22. Dorothy Dinnerstein, *The Mermaid and the Minotaur: Sexual Arrangements and Human Malaise* (New York: Harper, 1976).

23. Adrienne Rich, *Of Woman Born* (New York: Norton, 1976).

24. Karen Elias-Button, "The Muse as Medusa," in *The Lost Tradition: Mothers and Daughters in Literature,* eds. Cathy N. Davidson and E. M. Broner (New York: Ungar, 1980), p. 205.

25. Elias-Button, p. 192.

26. Judith Kegan Gardiner, "On Female Identity and Writing By Women," *Critical Inquiry,* 8 (1981), 356.

27. Ibid.

28. Janet Todd, *Women's Friendship in Literature* (New York: Columbia University Press, 1980), p. 2.

29. Susan Peck MacDonald, "Jane Austen and the Tradition of the Absent Mother," in *The Lost Tradition,* p. 58.

30. Julia Kristeva, "Women's Time," *Signs,* 7 (1981), 29.

31. Dinnerstein, p. 164.

32. See Jane Marcus in her attack on pluralism, "Storming the Toolshed," *Signs,* 7 (1982), 622–40, especially p. 626: "she must . . . she must . . . she must." If that *she* is *me,* somebody (once again) is telling me what I "*must*" do to be a true woman, and that somebody is asserting (not incidentally) her own monopoly on truth as she does so. I've been here before.

BIDDY MARTIN AND
CHANDRA TALPADE MOHANTY

FEMINIST POLITICS: WHAT'S HOME GOT TO DO WITH IT?

(1986)

We began working on this project after visiting our respective "homes" in Lynchburg, Virginia and Bombay, India in the fall of 1984—visits fraught with conflict, loss, memories, and desires we both considered to be of central importance in thinking about our relationship to feminist politics. In spite of significant differences in our personal histories and academic backgrounds, and the displacements we both experience, the political and intellectual positions we share made it possible for us to work on, indeed to write, this essay together. Our separate readings of Minnie Bruce Pratt's autobiographical narrative entitled "Identity: Skin Blood Heart" became the occasion for thinking through and developing more precisely some of the ideas about feminist theory and politics that have occupied us. We are interested in the configuration of home, identity, and community; more specifically, in the power and appeal of "home" as a concept and a desire, its occurrence as metaphor in feminist writings, and its challenging presence in the rhetoric of the New Right.

Both leftists and feminists have realized the importance of not handing over notions of home and community to the Right. Far too often, however, both male leftists and feminists have responded to the appeal of a rhetoric of home and family by merely reproducing the most conventional articulations of those terms in their own writings. In her recent work, Zillah Eisenstein identifies instances of what she labels revisionism within liberal, radical, and socialist feminist writings: texts by women such as Betty Friedan, Andrea Dworkin, and Jean Bethke Elshtain, in which the pursuit of safe places and ever-narrower conceptions of community relies on unexamined notions of home, family, and nation, and severely limits the scope of the feminist inquiry and struggle.[1] The challenge, then, is to find ways of conceptualizing community differently without dismissing its appeal and importance.

It is significant that the notion of "home" has been taken up in a range of writings by women of color, who cannot easily assume "home" within feminist communities as they have been constituted.[2] Bernice Johnson Reagon's critique of white feminists' incorporation of "others" into their "homes" is a warning to all feminists that "we are going to have to break out of little barred rooms" and cease holding tenaciously to the invisible and only apparently self-evident boundaries around that which we define as our own, "if we are going to have anything to do with what makes it into the next century." Reagon does not deny the appeal and the importance of "home" but challenges us to stop confusing it with political coalition and suggests that it takes what she calls an old-age perspective to know when to engage and when to withdraw, when to break out and when to consolidate.[3]

For our discussion of the problematics of "home," we chose a text that demonstrates the importance of both narrative and historical specificity in the attempt to reconceptualize the relations between "home," "identity," and political change. The volume in which Pratt's essay appears, *Yours in Struggle: Three Feminist Perspectives on Anti-Semitism and Racism* (Brooklyn, N.Y.: Long Haul Press, 1984), is written by Elly Bulkin, Minnie Bruce Pratt, and Barbara Smith, each of whom ostensibly represents a different experience and identity and consequently a different (even if feminist) perspective on racism and anti-Semitism. What makes this text unusual, in spite of what its title may suggest, is its questioning of the all-too-common conflation of experience, identity, and political perspective.

What we have tried to draw out of this text is the way in which it unsettles not only any notion of feminism as an all-encompassing home but also the assumption that there are discrete, coherent, and absolutely separate identities—homes within feminism, so to speak—based on absolute divisions between various sexual, racial, or ethnic identities. What accounts for the unsettling of boundaries and identities, and the questioning of conventional notions of experience, is the task that the contributors have set for themselves: to address certain specific questions and so to situate themselves in relation to the tensions between feminism, racism, and anti-Semitism. The "unity" of the individual subject, as well as the unity of feminism, is situated and specified as the product of the interpretation of personal histories; personal histories that are themselves situated in relation to the development within feminism of particular questions and critiques.

Pratt's autobiographical narrative is the narrative of a woman who identifies herself as white, middle-class, Christian-raised, southern, and lesbian. She makes it very clear that unity through incorporation has too often been the white middle-class feminist's mode of adding on difference without leaving the comfort of home. What Pratt sets out to explore are the exclusions and repressions which support the seeming homogeneity, stability, and self-evidence of "white identity," which is derived from and dependent on the marginalization of differences within as well as "without."

Our decision to concentrate on Pratt's narrative has to do with our shared concern that critiques of what is increasingly identified as "white" or "Western" feminism unwittingly leave the terms of West/East, white/nonwhite polarities intact; they do so, paradoxically, by starting from the premise that Western feminist discourse is inadequate or irrelevant to women of color or Third World women. The implicit assumption here, which we wish to challenge, is that the terms of a totalizing feminist discourse *are adequate* to the task of articulating the situation of white women in the West. We would contest that assumption and argue that the reproduction of such polarities only serves to concede "feminism" to the "West" all over again. The potential consequence is the repeated failure to contest the feigned homogeneity of the West and what seems to be a discursive and political stability of the hierarchical West/East divide.

Pratt's essay enacts as much as it treats the contradictory relations between skin, blood, heart, and identity and between experience, identity, and community in ways that we would like to analyze and discuss in more detail. Like the essays that follow it, it is a form of writing that not only anticipates and integrates diverse audiences or readers but also positions the narrator as reader. The perspective is multiple and shifting, and the shifts in perspective are enabled by the attempts to define self, home, and community that are at the heart of Pratt's enterprise. The historical grounding of shifts and changes allows for an emphasis on the pleasures and terrors of interminable boundary confusions, but insists, at the same time, on our responsibility for remapping boundaries and renegotiating connections. These are partial in at least two senses of the word: politically partial, and without claim to wholeness or finality.

It is this insistence that distinguishes the work of a Reagon or a Pratt from the more abstract critiques of "feminism" and the charges of totalization that come from the ranks of antihumanist intellectuals. For without denying the importance of their vigilante attacks on humanist beliefs in "man" and Absolute Knowledge wherever they appear, it is equally important to point out the political limitations of an insistence on "indeterminacy" which implicitly, when not explicitly, denies the critic's own situatedness in the social, and in effect refuses to acknowledge the critic's own institutional home.

Pratt, on the contrary, succeeds in carefully taking apart the bases of her own privilege by resituating herself again and again in the social, by constantly referring to the materiality of the situation in which she finds herself. The form of the personal historical narrative forces her to re-anchor herself repeatedly in each of the positions from which she speaks, even as she works to expose the illusory coherence of those positions. For the subject of such a narrative, it is not possible to speak from, or on behalf of, an abstract indeterminacy. Certainly, Pratt's essay would be considered a "conventional" (and therefore suspect) narrative from the point of view of contemporary deconstructive methodologies, because of its collapsing of author and text, its unreflected authorial intentionality, and its claims to personal and political authenticity.

Basic to the (at least implicit) disavowal of conventionally realist and autobiographical narrative by deconstructionist critics is the assumption that difference can emerge only through self-referential language, i.e., through certain relatively specific formal operations present in the text or performed upon it. Our reading of Pratt's narrative contends that a so-called conventional narrative such as Pratt's is not only useful but essential in addressing the politically and theoretically urgent questions surrounding identity politics. Just as Pratt refuses the methodological imperative to distinguish between herself as actual biographical referent and her narrator, we have at points allowed ourselves to let our reading of the text speak for us.

It is noteworthy that some of the American feminist texts and arguments that have been set up as targets to be taken apart by deconstructive moves are texts and arguments that have been critiqued from within "American" feminist communities for their homogenizing, even colonialist gestures; they have been critiqued, in fact, by those most directly affected by the exclusions that have made possible certain radical and cultural feminist generalizations. Antihumanist attacks on "feminism" usually set up "American feminism" as a "straw man" and so contribute to the production—or, at the very least, the reproduction—of an image of "Western feminism" as conceptually and politically unified in its monolithically imperialist moves.

We do not wish to deny that too much of the conceptual and political work of "Western" feminists is encumbered by analytic strategies that do indeed homogenize the experiences and conditions of women across time and culture; nor do we wish to deny that "Western" feminists have often taken their own positions as referent, thereby participating in the colonialist moves characteristic of traditional humanist scholarship. However, such critiques run the risk of falling into culturalist arguments, and these tend to have the undesired effect of solidifying the identification of feminism with the West rather than challenging the hegemony of specific analytic and political positions. The refusal to engage in the kind of feminist analysis that is more differentiated, more finely articulated, and more attentive to the problems raised in poststructuralist theory makes "bad feminism" a foil supporting the privilege of the critics' "indeterminacy." Wary of the limitations of an antihumanism which refuses to rejoin the political, we purposely chose a text that speaks from within "Western feminist discourse" and attempts to expose the bases and supports of privilege even as it renegotiates political and personal alliances.[4]

One of the most striking aspects of "Identity: Skin Blood Heart" is the text's movement away from the purely personal, visceral experience of identity suggested by the title to a complicated working out of the relationship between home, identity, and community that calls into question the notion of a coherent, historically continuous, stable identity and works to expose the political stakes concealed in such equations. An effective way of analyzing Pratt's conceptualization of these relationships is to focus on the manner in which the narrative works by grounding itself in the geography, demography, and architecture of the communities that are her "homes"; these factors function as an organizing mode in the text, providing a specific concreteness and movement for the narrative.

Correspondingly, the narrative politicizes the geography, demography, and architecture of these communities—Pratt's homes at various times of her history—by discovering local histories of exploitation and struggle. These are histories quite unlike the ones she is familiar with, the ones with which she grew up. Pratt problematizes her ideas about herself by juxtaposing the assumed histories of her family and childhood, predicated on the invisibility of the histories of people unlike her, to the layers of exploitation and struggles of different groups of people for whom these geographical sites were also home.

Each of the three primary geographical locations—Alabama (the home of her childhood and college days), North Carolina (the place of her marriage and coming out as a lesbian), and Washington, D.C. (characterized by her acute awareness of racism, anti-Semitism, class, and global politics)—is constructed on the tension between two specific modalities: being home and not being home. "Being home" refers to the place where one lives within familiar, safe, protected boundaries; "not being home" is a matter of realizing that home was an illusion of coherence and safety based on the exclusion of specific histories of oppression and resistance, the repression of differences even within oneself. Because these locations acquire meaning and function as sites of personal and historical struggles, they work against the notion of an unproblematic geographic location of home in Pratt's narrative. Similarly, demographic information functions to ground and concretize race, class, and gender conflicts. Illusions of home are always undercut by the discovery of the hidden demographics of particular places, as demography also carries the weight of histories of struggle.

Pratt speaks of being "shaped" in relation to the buildings and streets in the town in which she lived. Architecture and the layouts of particular towns provide concrete, physical anchoring points in relation to which she both sees and does not see certain people and things in the buildings and on the streets. However, the very stability, familiarity, and security of these physical structures are undermined by the discovery that these buildings and streets witnessed and obscured particular race, class, and gender struggles. The realization that these "growing up places" are hometowns where Pratt's eye "has only let in what I have been taught to see" politicizes and undercuts any physical anchors she might use to construct a coherent notion of home or her identity in relation to it.

> Each of us carries around those growing up places, the institutions, a sort of backdrop, a stage set. So often we act out the present against the backdrop of the past, within a frame of perception that is so familiar, so safe that it is terrifying to risk changing it even when we know our perceptions are distorted, limited, constricted by that old view.

The traces of her past remain with her but must be challenged and reinterpreted. Pratt's own histories are in constant flux. There is no linear progression based on "that old view," no developmental notion of her own identity or self. There is instead a constant expansion of her "constricted eye," a necessary reevaluation and return to the past in order to move forward to the present. Geography, demography, and architecture, as well as the configuration of her relationships to particular people (her father, her lover, her workmate), serve to indicate the fundamentally relational nature of identity and the negations on which the assumption of a singular, fixed, and essential self is based. For the narrator, such negativity is represented by a rigid identity such as that of her father, which sustains its appearance of stability by defining itself in terms of what it is not: not black, not female, not Jewish, not Catholic, not poor, etc. The "self" in this narrative is not an essence or truth concealed by patriarchal layers of deceit and lying in wait of discovery, revelation, or birth.[5]

It is this very conception of self that Pratt likens to entrapment, constriction, a bounded fortress that must be transgressed, shattered, opened onto that world which has been made invisible and threatening by the security of home. While Pratt is aware that stable notions of self and identity are based on exclusion and secured by terror, she is also aware of the risk and terror inherent in breaking through the walls of home. The consciousness of these contradictions characterizes the narrative.

In order to indicate the fundamentally constructive, interpretive nature of Pratt's narrative, we have chosen to analyze the text following its own narrative organization in three different scenarios: scenarios that are characterized not by chronological development but by discontinuous moments of consciousness. The scenarios are constructed around moments in Pratt's own history which propel her in new directions through their fundamental instability and built-in contradictions.

Scenario 1

I live in a part of Washington, D.C. that white suburbanites called "the jungle" during the uprising of the '60s—perhaps still do, for all I know. When I walk the two-and-a-half blocks to H St. NE, to stop in at the bank, to leave my boots off at the shoe-repair-and-lock shop, I am most usually the only white person in sight. I've seen two other whites, women, in the year I've lived here. [This does not count white folks in cars, passing through. In official language, H St. NE, is known as "The H Street Corridor," as in something to be passed through quickly, going from your place, on the way to elsewhere.]

This paragraph of the text locates Minnie Bruce Pratt in a place that does not exist as a legitimate possibility for home on a white people's map of Washington, D.C. That place is H Street N.E., where Pratt lives, a section of town referred to as "the jungle" by white suburbanites in the sixties, also known as "the H Street Corridor as in something to be passed through quickly, going from your place to elsewhere" (p. 11). That, then, is *potentially* Pratt's home, the community in which she lives. But this "jungle," this corridor, is located at the edge of homes of white folk. It is a place outside the experience of white people, where Pratt must be the outsider because she is white. This "being on the edge" is what characterizes her "being in the world as it is," as opposed to remaining within safe bounded places with their illusion of acceptance. "I will try to be at the edge between my fear and outside, on the edge at my skin, listening, asking what new thing will I hear, will I see, will I let myself feel, beyond the fear," she writes. It is her situation on the edge that expresses the desire and the possibility of breaking through the narrow circle called home without pretense that she can or should "jump out of her skin" or deny her past.

The salience of demography, a white woman in a black neighborhood, afraid to be too familiar and neighborly with black people, is acutely felt. Pratt is comforted by the sounds of the voices of black people, for they make her "feel at home" and remind her of her father's southern voice, until she runs into Mr. Boone, the janitor with the downcast head and the "yes ma'ams," and Pratt responds in "the horrid cheerful accents of a white lady." The pain is not just the pain of rejection by this black man; it is the pain of acknowledging the history of the oppression and separation of different groups of people which shatters the protective boundaries of her self and renders her desire to speak with others problematic. The context of this personal interaction is set immediately in terms of geographical and political history.

Mr. Boone's place of origin (hometown) is evoked through the narration of the history of local resistance struggles in the region from which he comes.

He's a dark, red-brown man from the Yemessee in South Carolina—that swampy land of Indian resistance and armed communities of fugitive slaves, that marshy land at the headwaters of the Combahee, once site of enormous rice plantations and location of Harriet Tubman's successful military action that freed many slaves.

This history of resistance has the effect of disrupting forever all memories of a safe, familiar southern home. As a result of this interaction, Pratt now remembers that home was repressive space built on the surrendering of all responsibility. Pratt's self-reflection, brought on by a consciousness of difference, is nourished and expanded by thinking contextually of other histories and of her own responsibility and implication in them. What we find extraordinary about Pratt as narrator (and person) is her refusal to allow guilt to trap her within the boundaries of a coherent "white" identity. It is this very refusal that makes it possible for her to make the effort to educate herself about the histories of her own and other peoples—an education that indicates to her her own implication in those histories.

Pratt's approach achieves significance in the context of other white feminists' responses to the charge of racism in the women's movement. An all-too-common response has been self-paralyzing guilt and/or defensiveness; another has been the desire to be educated by women of color. The problem is exacerbated by the tendency on the part of some women of color to assume the position of ultimate critic or judge on the basis of the authenticity of their personal experience of oppression. An interesting example of the assignment of fixed positions—the educator/critic (woman of color) and the guilty and silent listener (white woman)—is a recent essay written collaboratively by Elizabeth Spelman and Maria Lugones. The dynamics set up would seem to exempt both parties from the responsibilities of working through the complex historical relations between and among structures of domination and oppression.

In this scenario, the street scene is particularly effective, both spatially and metaphorically. The street evokes a sense of constant movement, change, and temporality. For instance, Pratt can ask herself why the young black woman did not speak to her, why she herself could not speak to the professional white woman in the morning but does at night, why the woman does not respond—all in the space of one evening's walk down three blocks. The meetings on the street also allow for a focus on the racial and ethnic demography of the community as a way of localizing racial, sexual, and class tensions. Since her present location is nowhere (the space does not exist for white people), she constantly has to problematize and define herself anew in relation to people she meets in the street. There is an acute consciousness of being white, woman, lesbian, and Christian-raised, and of which of these aspects is salient in different "speakings."

> Instead, when I walk out in my neighborhood, each speaking to another person has become fraught for me, with the history of race and sex and class; as I walk I have a constant interior discussion with myself questioning how I acknowledge the presence of another, what I know or don't know about them, and what it means how they acknowledge me.

Thus, walking down the street and speaking to various people—a young white man, young black woman, young professional white woman, young black man, older white woman are all rendered acutely complex and contradictory in terms of actual speakings, imagined speakings, and actual and imagined motivations, responses, and implications—there is no possibility of a coherent self with a continuity of responses across these different "speaking-to's." History intervenes. For instance, a respectful answer from a young black man might well be "the response violently extorted by history." The voices, sounds, hearing, and sight in particular interactions or within "speaking to's" carry with them their own particular histories; this narrative mode breaks the boundaries of Pratt's experience of being protected, of being a majority.

Scenario 2

> Yet I was shaped by my relation to those buildings and to the people in the buildings, by ideas of who should be in the Board of Education, of who should be in the bank handling money, of who should have the guns and the keys to the jail, of who should be *in* the jail; and I was shaped by what I didn't see, or didn't notice, on those streets.

The second scenario is constructed in relation to her childhood home in Alabama and deals very centrally with her relation to her father. Again, she explores that relationship to her father in terms of the geography, demography, and architecture of the hometown; again she reconstructs it by uncovering knowledges, not only the knowledge of those Others who were made invisible to her as a child but also the suppressed knowledge of her own family background. The importance of her elaborating the relation to her father through spatial relations and historical knowledges lies in the contextualization of that relation, and the consequent avoidance of any purely psychological explanation. What is effected, then, is the unsettling of any self-evident relation between blood, skin, heart. And yet, here as elsewhere, the essential relation between blood, skin, heart, home, and identity is challenged without dismissing the power and appeal of those connections.

Pratt introduces her childhood home and her father in order to explain the source of her need to change "what she was born into," to explain what she, or any person who benefits from privileges of class and race, has to gain from change. This kind of self-reflexivity characterizes the entire narrative and takes the form of an attempt to avoid the roles and points of enunciation that she identifies as the legacy of her culture: the roles of judge, martyr, preacher, and peacemaker, and the typically white, Christian, middle-class, and liberal pretense of a concern for Others, an abstract moral or ethical concern for what is right. Her effort to explain her own need to change is elaborated through the memory of childhood scenes, full of strong and suggestive architectural/spatial metaphors which are juxtaposed with images suggesting alternative possibilities.

The effort to explain her motivation for change reminds her of her father. "When I try to think of this, I think of my father. . . . " Pratt recounts a scene from her childhood in which her father took her up the marble steps of the courthouse in the center of the town, the courthouse in which her grandfather had judged for forty years, to the clock tower in order to show her the town from the top and the center. But the father's desire to have her see as he saw, to position her in relation to her town and the world as he was positioned, failed. She was unable, as a small child, to make it to the top of the clock tower and could not see what she would have seen had she been her father or taken his place.

From her vantage point as an adult, she is now able to reconstruct and analyze what she would have seen and would not have seen from the center and the top of the town. She would have seen the Methodist church, the Health Department, for example, and she would not have seen the sawmill of Four Points where the white mill folks lived, or the houses of blacks in Veneer Mill quarters. She had not been able to take that height because she was not her father and could not become like him: she was a white girl, not a boy. This assertion of her difference from the father is undercut, however, in a reversal characteristic of the moves enacted throughout the essay, when she begins a new paragraph by acknowledging: "Yet I was shaped by my relation to those buildings and to the people in the buildings."

What she has gained by rejecting the father's position and vision, by acknowledging her difference from him, is represented as a way of looking, a capacity for seeing the world in overlapping circles, "like movement on the millpond after a fish has jumped, instead of the courthouse square with me at the middle, even if I am on the ground." The contrast between the vision that her father would have her learn and her own vision, her difference and "need," emerges as the contrast between images of constriction, of entrapment, or ever-narrowing circles with a bounded self at the center—the narrow steps to the roof of the courthouse, the clock tower with a walled ledge—and, on the other hand, the image of the millpond with its ever shifting centers. The apparently stable, centered position of the father is revealed to be profoundly unstable, based on exclusions, and characterized by terror.

Change, however, is not a simple escape from constraint to liberation. There is no shedding the literal fear and figurative law of the father, and no reaching a final realm of freedom. There is no new place, no new home. Since neither her view of history nor her construction of herself through it is linear, the past, home, and the father leave traces that are constantly reabsorbed into a shifting vision. She lives, after all, on the edge. Indeed, that early experience of separation and difference from the father is remembered not only in terms of the possibility of change but also in relation to the pain of loss, the loneliness of change, the undiminished desire for home, for familiarity, for some coexistence of familiarity and difference. The day she couldn't make it to the top of the tower "marks the last time I can remember us doing something together, just the two of us; thereafter, I knew on some level that my place was with women, not with him, not with men."

This statement would seem to make the divisions simple, would seem to provide an overriding explanation of her desire for change, for dealing with racism and anti-Semitism, would seem to make her one of a monolithic group of Others in relation to the white father. However, this division, too, is not allowed to remain stable and so to be seen as a simple determinant of identity.

Near the end of her narrative, Pratt recounts a dream in which her father entered her room carrying something like a heavy box, which he put down on her desk. After he left, she noticed that the floor of her room had become a field of dirt with rows of tiny green seed just sprouting. We quote from her narration of the dream, her ambivalence about her father's presence, and her interpretation of it:

> He was so tired; I flung my hands out angrily, told him to go, back to my mother; but crying, because my heart ached; he was my father and so tired. . . . The box was still there, with what I feared: my responsibility for what the men of my culture have done. . . . I was angry: why should I be left with this: I didn't want it: I'd done my best for years to reject it: I wanted no part of what was in it: the benefits of my privilege, the restrictions, the injustice, the pain, the broken urgings of the heart, the unknown horrors. And yet it is mine: I am my father's daughter in the present, living in a world he and my folks helped create. A month after I dreamed this he died; I honor the grief of his life by striving to change much of what he believed in: and my own grief by acknowledging that I saw him caught in the grip of racial, sexual, cultural fears that I still am trying to understand in myself.

Only one aspect of experience is given a unifying and originating function in the text: that is, her lesbianism and love for other women, which has motivated and continues to motivate her efforts to reconceptualize and re-create both her self and home. A careful reading of the narrative demonstrates the complexity of lesbianism, which is constructed as an effect, as well as a source, of her political and familial positions. Its significance, that is, is demonstrated in relation to other experiences rather than assumed as essential determinant.

What lesbianism becomes as the narrative unfolds is that which makes "home" impossible, which makes her self nonidentical, which makes her vulnerable, removing her from the protection afforded those women within privileged races and classes who do not transgress a limited sphere of movement. Quite literally, it is her involvement with another woman that separates the narrator not only from her husband but from her children, as well. It is that which threatens to separate her from her mother, and that which remains a silence between herself and her father. That silence is significant, since, as she points out—and this is a crucial point—her lesbianism is precisely what she can deny, and indeed must deny, in order to benefit fully from the privilege of being white and middle-class and Christian. She can deny it, but only at great expense to herself. Her lesbianism is what she experiences most immediately as the limitation imposed on her by the family, culture, race, and class that afforded her both privilege and comfort, at a price. Learning at what price privilege, comfort, home, and secure notions of self are purchased, the price to herself and ultimately to others is what makes lesbianism a political motivation as well as a personal experience.

It is significant that lesbianism is neither marginalized nor essentialized, but constructed at various levels of experience and abstraction. There are at least two ways in which lesbianism has been isolated in feminist discourse: the homophobic oversight and relegation of it to the margins, and the lesbian-feminist centering of it, which has had at times the paradoxical effect of removing lesbianism and sexuality from their embeddedness in social relations. In Pratt's narrative, lesbianism is that which exposes the extreme limits of what passes itself off as simply human, as universal, as unconstrained by identity, namely, the position of the white middle class. It is also a positive source of solidarity, community, and change. Change has to do with the transgression of boundaries, those boundaries so carefully, so tenaciously, so invisibly drawn around white identity.[6] Change has to do with the transgression of those boundaries.

The insight that white, Christian, middle-class identity, as well as comfort and home, is purchased at a high price is articulated very compellingly in relation to her father. It is significant that there is so much attention to her relation to her father, from whom she describes herself as having been estranged—significant and exemplary of what we think is so important about this narrative.[7] What gets articulated are the contradictions in that relation, her difference from the father, her rejection of his positions, and at the same time her connections to him, her love for him, the ways in which she is his daughter. The complexity of the father-daughter relationship and Pratt's acknowledgment of the differences within it—rather than simply between her self and her father—make it impossible to be satisfied with a notion of difference from the father, literal or figurative, which would (and in much feminist literature does) exempt the daughter from her implication in the structures of privilege/oppression, structures that operate in ways much more complex than the male/female split itself. The narrator expresses the pain, the confusion attendant upon this complexity.

The narrative recounts the use of threat and of protections to consolidate home, identity, community, and privilege, and in the process exposes the underside of the father's protection. Pratt recalls a memory of a night, during the height of the civil rights demonstrations in Alabama, when her father called her in to read her an article in which Martin Luther King, Jr. was accused of sexually abusing young teenaged girls. "I can only guess that he wanted me to feel that my danger, my physical, sexual danger, would be the result of the release of others from containment. I felt frightened and profoundly endangered, by King, by my father: I could not answer him. It was the first, the only time, I could not answer him. It was the first, the only time, he spoke of sex, in any way, to me."

What emerges is the consolidation of the white home in response to a threatening outside. The rhetorics of sexual victimization or vulnerability of white women is used to establish and enforce unity among whites and to create the myth of the black rapist.[8] Once again, her experience within the family is reinterpreted in relation to the history of race relations in an "outside" in which the family is implicated. What Pratt integrates in the text at such points is a wealth of historical information and analysis of the ideological and social/political operations beyond her "home." In addition to the historical information she unearths both about the atrocities committed in the name of protection, by the Ku Klux Klan and white society in general, and about the resistance to those forms of oppression, she points to the underside of the rhetoric of home, protection, and threatening Others that is currently promoted by Reagan and the New Right. "It is this threatening 'protection' that white Christian men in the U.S. are now offering."

When one conceives of power differently, in terms of its local, institutional, discursive formations, of its positivity, and in terms of the production rather than suppression of forces, then unity is exposed to be a potentially repressive fiction.[9] It is at the moment at which groups and individuals are conceived as agents, as social actors, as desiring subjects that unity, in the sense of coherent group identity, commonality, and shared experience, becomes difficult. Individuals do not fit neatly into unidimensional, self-identical categories. Hence the need for a new sense of political community which gives up the desire for the kind of home where the suppression of positive differences underwrites familial identity. Pratt's narrative makes it clear that connections have to be made at levels other than abstract political interests. And the ways in which intimacy and emotional solidarity figure in notions of political community avoid an all-too-common trivialization of the emotional, on the one hand, and romanticization of the political, on the other.

Scenario 3

> Every day I drove around the market house, carrying my two boys between home and grammar school and day care. To me it was an impediment to the flow of traffic, awkward, anachronistic. Sometimes in early spring light it seemed quaint. I had no knowledge and no feeling of the sweat and blood of people's lives that had been mortared into its bricks: nor of their independent joy apart from that place.

The third scenario involves her life in an eastern rural North Carolina town, to which she came in 1974 with her husband and two children. Once again Pratt characterizes her relation to the town, as well as to her husband and children, by means of demographic and architectural markers and metaphors that situate her at the periphery of this "place which is so much like home": a place in which everything would seem to revolve around a stable center, in this case the market house.

> I drove around the market house four times a day, traveling on the surface of my own life: circular, repetitive, like one of the games at the county fair. . . .

Once again she is invited to view her home town from the top and center, specifically from the point of view of the white "well-to-do folks," for whom the history of the market house consisted of the fruits, the vegetables, and the tobacco exchanged there. "But not slaves, they said." However, the black waiter serving the well-to-do in the private club overlooking the center of town contests this account, providing facts and dates of the slave trade in that town. This contradiction leaves a trace but does not become significant to her view of her life in that town, a town so much like the landscape of her childhood. It does not become significant, that is, until her own resistance to the limitations of home and family converges with her increasing knowledge of the resistance of other people; converges but is not conflated with those other struggles.

What Pratt uncovers of the town histories is multilayered and complex. She speaks of the relation of different groups of people to the town and their particular histories of resistance—the breaking up of Klan rallies by Lumbee Indians, the long tradition of black culture and resistance, Jewish traditions of resistance, anti-Vietnam protest, and lesbians' defiance of military codes—with no attempt to unify or equate the various struggles under a grand polemics of oppression. The coexistence of these histories gives the narrative its complex, rich texture. Both the town and her relation to it change as these histories of struggle are narrated. Indeed, there is an explicit structural connection between moments of fear and loss of former homes with the recognition of the importance of interpretation and struggle.

From our perspectives, the integrity of the narrative and the sense of self have to do with the refusal to make easy divisions and with the unrelenting exploration of the ways in which the desire for home, for security, for protection—and not only the desire for them, but the expectation of a right to these things—operates in Pratt's own conception of political work. She describes her involvement in political work as having begun when feminism swept through the North Carolina town in which she was living with her husband and her two sons in the 1970s, a period in her life when she felt threatened as a woman and was forced to see herself as part of a class of people; that she describes as anathema to the self-concept of middle-class white people, who would just like to "be," unconstrained by labels, by identities, by consignment to a group, and would prefer to ignore the fact that their existence and social place are anything other than self-evident, natural, human.

What differentiates her narration of her development from other feminist narratives of political awakening is its tentativeness, its consisting of fits and starts, and the absence of linear progress toward a visible end.[10] This narrator pursues the extent and the ways in which she carried her white, middle-class conceptions of home around with her, and the ways in which they informed her relation to politics. There is an irreconcilable tension between the search for a secure place from which to speak, within which to act, and the awareness of the price at which secure places are bought, the awareness of the exclusions, the denials, the blindnesses on which they are predicated.

The search for a secure place is articulated in its ambivalence and complexity through the ambiguous use of the words *place* and *space* in precisely the ways they have become commonplace within feminist discourse. The moments of terror when she is brought face to face with the fact that she is "homesick with nowhere to go," that she has no place, the "kind of vertigo" she feels upon learning of her own family's history of racism and slaveholding, the sensation of her body having no fixed place to be, are remembered concurrently with moments of hope, when "she thought she had the beginning of a place for myself."

What she tried to re-create as a feminist, a woman aware of her position vis-à-vis men as a group, is critiqued as a childish place:

> Raised to believe that I could be where I wanted and have what I wanted, as a grown woman I thought I could simply claim what I wanted, even the making of a new place to live with other women. I had no understanding of the limits that I lived within, nor of how much my memory and my experience of a safe space to be was based on places secured by omission, exclusions or violence, and on my submitting to the limits of that place.

The self-reflexiveness that characterizes the narrative becomes especially clear in her discussion of white feminists' efforts at outreach in her North Carolina community. She and her NOW fellow workers had gone forward "to a new place": "Now we were throwing back safety lines to other women, to pull them in as if they were drowning, to save them. . . . What I felt, deep down, was hope that they would join me in my place, which would be the way I wanted it. I didn't want to have to limit myself."

However, it is not only her increasing knowledge of her exclusion of Others from that place that initiates her rethinking. What is most compelling is her account of her realization that her work in NOW was also based on the exclusion of parts of herself, specifically her lesbianism.[11] Those moments when she would make it the basis of a sameness with other women, a sameness that would make a new place possible, are less convincing than the moments when that possibility too is undercut by her seeing the denials, the exclusions, and the violence that are the conditions of privilege and indeed of love in its Christian formulation. The relationship between love and the occlusion or appropriation of the Other finds expression in her description of her attempts to express her love for her Jewish lover in a poem filled with images from the Jewish tradition, a way of assuming, indeed insisting upon, their similarity by appropriating the other's culture.

The ways in which appropriation or stealth, in the colonial gesture, reproduces itself in the political positions of white feminists is formulated convincingly in a passage about what Pratt calls "cultural impersonation," a term that refers to the tendency among white women to respond with guilt and self-denial to the knowledge of racism and anti-Semitism, and to borrow or take on the identity of the Other in order to avoid not only guilt but pain and self-hatred.[12] It is Pratt's discussion of the negative effects, political and personal, of cultural impersonation that raises the crucial issue of what destructive forms a monolithic (and overly theoretical) critique of identity can take. The claim to a lack of identity or positionality is itself based on privilege, on a refusal to accept responsibility for one's implication in actual historical or social relations, on a denial that positionalities exist or that they matter, the denial of one's own personal history and the claim to a total separation from it. What Minnie Bruce Pratt refuses over and over is the facile equation of her own situation with that of other people.

> When, after Greensboro, I groped toward an understanding of injustice done to others, injustice done outside my narrow circle of being, and to folks not like me, I began to grasp, through my own experience, something of what that injustice might be. . . .
>
> But I did not feel that my new understanding simply moved me into a place where I joined others to struggle *with* them against common injustices. Because *I* was implicated in the doing of some of these injustices, and I held myself, and my people responsible.

The tension between the desire for home, for synchrony, for sameness, and the realization of the repressions and violence that make home, harmony, sameness imaginable, and that enforce it, is made clear in the movement of the narrative by very careful and effective reversals which do not erase the positive desire for unity, for Oneness, but destabilize and undercut it. The relation between what Teresa de Lauretis has called the negativity of theory and the positivity of politics is a tension enacted over and over again by this text.[13] The possibility of recreating herself and of creating new forms of community not based on "home" depends for Minnie Bruce Pratt upon work and upon knowledge, not only of the traditions and culture of Others but also of the positive forms of struggle within her own. It depends on acknowledging not only her ignorance and her prejudices but also her fears, above all the fear of loss that accompanies change.

The risk of rejection by one's own kind, by one's family, when one exceeds the limits laid out or the self-definition of the group, is not made easy; again, the emphasis on her profoundly ambivalent relationship to her father is crucial. When the alternatives would seem to be either the enclosing, encircling, constraining circle of home, or nowhere to go, the risk is enormous. The assumption of, or desire for, another safe place like "home" is challenged by the realization that "unity"—interpersonal as well as political—is itself necessarily fragmentary, itself that which is struggled for, chosen, and hence unstable by definition; it is not based on "sameness," and there is no perfect fit. But there is agency as opposed to passivity.

The fear of rejection by one's own kind refers not only to the family of origin but also to the potential loss of a second family, the women's community, with its implicit and often unconscious replication of the conditions of home.[14] When we justify the homogeneity of the women's community in which we move on the basis of the need for community, the need for home, what, Pratt asks, distinguishes our community from the justifications advanced by women who have joined the Klan for "family, community, and protection"? The relationship between the loss of community and the loss of self is crucial. To the extent that identity is collapsed with home and community and based on homogeneity and comfort, on skin, blood, and heart, the giving up of home will necessarily mean the giving up of self and vice versa.

> Then comes the fear of nowhere to go; no old home with family: no new one with women like ourselves: and no place to be expected with folks who have been systematically excluded by ours. And with our fear comes the doubt: Can I maintain my principles against my need for the love and presence of others like me? It is lonely to be separated from others because of injustice, but it is also lonely to break with our own in opposition to that injustice.

The essay ends with a tension between despair and optimism over political conditions and the possibilities for change. Pratt walks down Maryland Avenue in Washington, D.C.—the town that is now her "hometown"—protesting against U.S. invasions, Grenada, the marines in Lebanon, the war in Central America, the acquittals of the North Carolina Klan and Nazi perpetrators. The narrative has come full circle, and her consciousness of her "place" in this town—the Capital—encompasses both local and global politics, and her own implication in them. The essay ends with the following statement: "I continue the struggle with myself and the world I was born in."

Pratt's essay on feminism, racism, and anti-Semitism is not a litany of oppression but an elaboration, indeed an enactment, of careful and constant differentiations which refuses the all-too-easy polemic that opposes victims to perpetrators. The exposure of the arbitrariness and the instability of positions within systems of oppression evidences a conception of power that refuses totalizations, and can therefore account for the possibility of resistance. "The system" is revealed to be not one but multiple, overlapping, intersecting systems or relations that are historically constructed and re-created through everyday practices and interactions, and that implicate the individual in contradictory ways. All of that without denying the operations of actual power differences, overdetermined though they may be. Reconceptualizing power without giving up the possibility of conceiving power.

Community, then, is the product of work, of struggle; it is inherently unstable, contextual; it has to be constantly reevaluated in relation to critical political priorities; and it is the product of interpretation, interpretation based on an attention to history, to the concrete, to what Foucault has called subjugated knowledges.[15] There is also, however, a strong suggestion that community is related to experience, to history. For if identity and community are not the product of essential connections, neither are they merely the product of political urgency or necessity. For Pratt, they are a constant recontextualizing of the relationship between personal/group history and political priorities.

It is crucial, then, to avoid two traps, the purely experiential and the theoretical oversight of personal and collective histories. In Pratt's narrative, personal history acquires a materiality in the constant rewriting of herself in relation to shifting interpersonal and political contexts. This rewriting is an interpretive act which is itself embedded in social and political practice.

> In this city where I am no longer of the majority by color or culture, I tell myself every day: In this *world* you aren't the superior race or culture, and never were, whatever you were raised to think: and are you getting ready to be *in* this world?
>
> And I answer myself back: I'm trying to learn how to live, to have the speaking-to extend beyond the moment's word, to act so as to change the unjust circumstances that keep us from being able to speak to each other; I'm trying to get a little closer to the longed-for but unrealized world, where we each are able to live, but not by trying to make someone less than us, not by someone else's blood or pain: yes, that's what I'm trying to do with my living now.

We have used our reading of this text to open up the question of how political community might be reconceptualized within feminist practice. We do not intend to suggest that Pratt's essay, or any single autobiographical narrative, offers "an answer." Indeed, what this text has offered is a pretext for posing questions. The conflation of Pratt the person with the narrator and subject of this text has led us and our students to want to ask, for example, how such individual self-reflection and critical practice might translate into the building of political collectivity. And to consider more specifically, the possible political implications and effects of a white middle-class woman's "choice" to move to H St. NE. Certainly, we might usefully keep in mind that the approach to identity, to unity, and to political alliances in Pratt's text is itself grounded in and specific to her complex positionalities in a society divided very centrally by race, gender, class, ethnicity, and sexualities.

NOTES

1. Zillah Eisenstein, *Feminism and Sexual Equality* (New York: Monthly Review Press, 1984).

2. See, for example, Bernice Johnson Reagon, "Coalition Politics: Turning the Century" and Barbara Smith's introduction in *Home Girls: A Black Feminist Anthology* (New York: Kitchen Table Press, 1984), and Cherríe Moraga, *Loving in the War Years* (Boston: South End Press, 1984).

3. Of course, feminist intellectuals have read various antihumanist strategies as having made similar arguments about the turn of the last century and the future of this one. In her contribution to a *Yale French Studies* special issue on French feminism, Alice Jardine argues against an "American" feminist tendency to establish and maintain an illusory unity based on incorporation, a unity and centrism that relegate differences to the margins or out of sight. "Feminism," she writes, "must not open the door to modernity then close it behind itself." In her Foucauldian critique of American feminist/humanist empiricism, Peggy Kamuf warns against the assumption that she sees guiding much feminist thought, "an unshaken faith in the ultimate arrival at essential truth through the empirical method of accumulation of knowledge, knowledge about women" ("Replacing Feminist Criticism," *Diacritics*, Summer 1982, p. 45). She goes on to spell out the problem of humanism in a new guise:

> There is an implicit assumption in such programs that this knowledge about women can be produced in and of itself without seeking any support within those very structures of power which—or so it is implied—have prevented knowledge of the feminine in the past. Yet what is it about those structures which could have succeeded until now in excluding such knowledge if it is not a similar appeal to a "we" that has had a similar faith in its own eventual constitution as a delimited and totalizable object?

4. For incisive and insistent analyses of the uses and limitations of deconstructive and poststructuralist analytic strategies for feminist intellectual and political projects, see in particular the work of Teresa de Lauretis, *Alice Doesn't: Feminism, Semiotics, Cinema* (Bloomington: Indiana University Press, 1984), and Alice Jardine, *Gynesis: Configurations of Woman and Modernity* (Ithaca: Cornell University Press, 1985).

5. This notion of a female "true self" underlying a male-imposed "false consciousness" is evident in the work of cultural feminists such as Mary Daly, *Gyn/ecology: The Metaethics of Radical Feminism* (Boston: Beacon Press, 1978); Susan Brownmiller, *Against Our Will: Men, Women, and Rape* (New York: Simon and Schuster, 1975); and Susan Griffin, *Woman and Nature: The Roaring inside Her* (New York: Harper and Row, 1978) and *Pornography and Silence* (New York: Harper and Row, 1981).

6. For analyses and critiques of tendencies to romanticize lesbianism, see essays by Carole Vance, Alice Echols, and Gayle Rubin in *Pleasure* and *Danger*, ed. Carole S. Vance (Boston: Routledge and Kegan Paul, 1984), on the "cultural feminism" of such writers as Griffin, Rich, Daly, and Gearheart.

7. Feminist theorists such as Nancy Chodorow (*The Reproduction* of *Mothering: Psychoanalysis and the Sociology* of *Gender* [Berkeley: University of California Press, 1978]), Carol Gilligan (*In a Different Voice* [Boston: Harvard University Press, 1983]), and Adrienne Rich (*Of Woman Born* [New York: W. W. Norton, 1976]) have focused exclusively on the psychosocial configuration of mother/daughter relationships. Jessica Benjamin, in "A Desire of One's Own" (*Feminist Studies/Critical* Studies, ed. Teresa de Lauretis [Bloomington: Indiana University Press, 1986]), points to the problem of not theorizing "the father" in feminist psychoanalytic work, emphasizing the significance of the father in the construction of sexuality within the family.

8. See critiques of Brownmiller (1975) by Angela Davis (*Women, Race, and Class* [Boston: Doubleday, 1983]), bell hooks (*Ain't I a Woman: Black Women and Feminism* [Boston: South End Press, 1981]), and Jacquelyn Dowd Hall ("The Mind That Burns in Each Body: Women, Rape, and Racial Violence," in *Powers of Desire*, ed. Ann Snitow, Christine Stansell, and Sharon Thompson [New York: Monthly Review Press, 1983], pp. 328–49).

9. For a discussion of the relevance of Foucault's reconceptualization of power to feminist theorizing, see Biddy Martin, "Feminism, Criticism, and Foucault," *New German Critique*, no. 27 (1982), pp. 3–30.

10. One good example of the numerous narratives of political awakening in feminist

work is the transformation of the stripper in the film *Not A Love Story* (directed by Bonnie Klein, 1982) from exploited sex worker to enlightened feminist. Where this individual's linear and unproblematic development is taken to be emblematic of problems in and feminist solutions to pornography, the complexities of the issues involved are circumvented and class differences are erased.

11. For a historical account of the situation of lesbians and attitudes toward lesbianism in NOW, see Sidney Abbot and Barbara Love, *Sappho Was A Right On Woman: A Liberated View of Lesbianism* (New York: Stein and Day, 1972).

12. For writings that address the construction of colonial discourse, see Homi Bhabha, "The Other Question—the Stereotype and Colonial Discourse," *Screen* 24 (November–December 1983): 18–36; Frantz Fanon, *Black Skin White Masks* (London: Paladin, 1970); Albert Memmi, *The Colonizer and the Colonized* (Boston: Beacon Press, 1965); Chandra Talpade Mohanty, "Under Western Eyes: Feminist Scholarship and Colonial Discourses," forthcoming in *boundary 2* (1985); Edward Said, *Orientalism* (New York: Vintage, 1979); and Gayatri Chakravorty Spivak, "French Feminism in an International Frame," *Yale French Studies*, no. 62 (1981), pp. 154–84.

13. See especially the introduction in de Lauretis, *Alice Doesn't*, and Teresa de Lauretis, "Comparative Literature among the Disciplines: Politics" (unpublished manuscript).

14. For an excellent discussion of the effects of conscious and unconscious pursuits of safety, see Carole Vance's introduction to *Pleasure and Danger* in which she elaborates upon the obstacles to theorizing embedded in such pursuits.

15. Michel Foucault, *The History of Sexuality: Vol. 1* (New York: Vintage, 1980).

BLACK FEMINIST THEORY AND THE REPRESENTATION OF THE "OTHER"

(1989)

In her now classic review essay "Critical Cross-Dressing: Male Feminists and the Woman of the Year," Elaine Showalter considers the ways in which a number of prominent English and American male theorists—among them Wayne Booth, Robert Scholes, Jonathan Culler, and Terry Eagleton—have employed feminist criticism within their own critical positions. Although Showalter praises Culler's ability to read as a feminist and confront "what might be implied by reading as a man and questioning or [surrendering] paternal privileges," she suggests that often male theorists, specifically Eagleton, borrow the language of feminism to compete with women instead of examining "the masculinist bias of their own reading system."[1] This general direction by male theorists, she argues, resembles a parallel phenomenon in popular culture—the rise of the male heroine. Her discussion of *Tootsie* indicates that Dorothy Michaels, the woman character Dustin Hoffman impersonates in the movie, derives her power not in response to the oppression of women but from an instinctive male reaction to being treated like a woman. For a man to act/write like/as a woman is thus not necessarily a tribute to women, but more likely a suggestion that women must be taught by men how to assert themselves.

In her essay Showalter problematizes the function of feminist criticism in response to a growing tendency among Western white male theorists to incorporate feminism in their critical positions. Because the black feminist as writer of both critical and imaginative texts appears with increasing frequency in the work of male Afro-Americanists and Anglo-American feminists, I consider here the place of the black feminist in these apposite modes of inquiry. I begin by defining various stages of the black feminist enterprise within the context of changes in these other theoretical positions, and I suggest how the black feminist has been employed in relation to them. I then offer a reading of *Sarah Phillips* (1984) by Andrea Lee, a fictional text about an upper-middle-class young black woman that thematizes this issue of the status of the "other" in a text by and about someone simultaneously marginal and privileged.

It is not my intention to reclaim the black feminist project from those who are not black women; to do so would be to define the field too narrowly, emphasizing unduly the implications of a shared experience between "black women as critics and black women as writers who represent black women's reality."[2] Indeed, as the following remarks indicate, I understand the phrase *black feminist theory* to refer not only to theory written (or practiced) by black feminists, but also to a way of reading inscriptions of race (particularly but not exclusively blackness), gender (particularly but not exclusively womanhood), and class in modes of cultural expression. Rather, I examine black feminism in the context of these related theoretical positions in order to raise questions about the way the "other" is represented in oppositional discourse. This sort of question seems especially important now that modes of inquiry once considered radical are becoming increasingly institutionalized.

Feminist literary theory and Afro-Americanist literary theory have developed along parallel lines. Both arose out of reactive, polemical modes of criticism. Recognizing that the term *literature* as it was commonly understood in the academy referred to a body of texts written by and in the interest of a white male elite, feminist critics (mostly white) and Afro-Americanist critics (mostly male) undertook the archaeological work of locating and/or reinterpreting overlooked and misread women and black writers.

Black feminist criticism originated from a similar impulse. In reaction to critical acts of omission and condescension, the earliest practitioners identified ways in which white male, Anglo-American feminist, and male Afro-Americanist scholars and reviewers had ignored and condescended to the work of black women and undertook editorial projects to recover their writings. To mention but a few examples: Mary Helen Washington called attention to the ways in which the androcentric Afro-American literary tradition and establishment privileged the solitary, literate adventurers found in texts by male authors such as Frederick Douglass and Richard Wright and ignored the more muted achievements of the female protagonists featured in the work of women writers such as Harriet Jacobs, Zora Neale Hurston and Gwendolyn Brooks.[3] Barbara Smith notes the ways in which not only Elaine Showalter, Ellen Moers, and Patricia Meyer Spacks, but also Robert Bone and Darwin Turner dismiss the writings of black women. And Deborah E. McDowell cites the omissions of Spacks, Bone, David Littlejohn, and Robert Stepto.[4] The legacy of oversights and condescension occasioned a number of editorial projects that recovered black women's writings; these much-needed projects continue to be undertaken.[5]

From the reactive impulse of these first-stage archaeological projects developed work of greater theoretical sophistication. More recent studies are less concerned with oversights in the work of others, involved instead with constructing alternative literary histories and traditions and exploring changes in assumptions about the nature of critical activity as assumptions about the nature of literature are transformed. As the kinds of questions Anglo-American feminists and male Afro-Americanists pose became increasingly self-referential—for instance, revealing the critics' own complicities and conceptualizing the links between various instances of practical criticism—they have each been drawn inevitably toward a third oppositional discourse: the discourse of deconstruction.

It should not surprise us that a number of Anglo-American feminists and Afro-Americanists have found contemporary theory compatible with the goals of their broader critical enterprise. The techniques and assumptions of deconstructive criticism destabilize the narrative relations that enshrine configurations according to genre, gender, culture, or models of behavior and personality. However, the alliances between contemporary theory on the one hand, and Anglo-American feminists or Afro-Americanists on the other, have raised inevitable questions about the institutionalization of each of these putatively marginal modes of inquiry. Anglo-American feminists as well as male Afro-Americanists are being asked to consider the extent to which their own adherence to a deconstructive practice, which by now has been adopted into the academy, undermines the fundamental assumptions of their broader, more profoundly oppositional enterprise.

The question of the place of feminist critical practice in the institution, for instance, prompted the 1982 dialogue in *Diacritics* between Peggy Kamuf and Nancy K. Miller. Kamuf argues that as long as mainstream feminists install writing by and about women at the center of their modes of inquiry and attempt to locate knowledge about women within an institutionalized humanistic discourse, they sustain the very ways of knowing that have historically excluded women's work:

> If feminist theory lets itself be guided by questions such as what is women's language, literature, style or experience, from where does it get its faith in the form of these questions to get at truth, if not from the central store that supplies humanism with its faith in the universal truth of man?[6]

In turn, Miller addresses what she perceives to be Kamuf's overinvestment in deconstructive operations. Reasserting the significance of women as historical and material subjects, she suggests that the destabilization of all categories of identity, including the category "woman," may well serve the interests of a male hegemony whose own power is under siege. As she argues,

> What bothers me about the metalogically "correct" position is what I take to be its necessary implications for practice: that by glossing "woman" as an archaic signifier, it glosses over the *referential* suffering of women. . . . It may also be the case that having been killed off with "man," the author can now be rethought beyond traditional notions of biography, now that through feminist rewritings of literary history the security of a masculine identity, the hegemony of homogeneity, has been radically problematized.[7]

Some of the most provocative and progressive work in Anglo-American feminist theory seeks to mediate these two positions. In *Crossing the Double-Cross: The Practice of Feminist Criticism*, Elizabeth A. Meese explores the possibilities of an interactive relation between feminist literary criticism and deconstruction. She argues for and illustrates a mode of feminist inquiry that employs the power of deconstruction's critique of difference even as it seeks to challenge and politicize the enterprise of critical theory.[8] Likewise, Teresa de Lauretis situates her collection of essays entitled *Feminist Studies/Critical Studies* as a juncture in which "feminism is being both integrated and quietly suffocated within the institutions."[9] She urges a feminist model of identity that is "multiple, shifting, and often self-contradictory . . . an identity made up of heterogeneous and heteronomous representations of gender, race, and class, and often indeed across languages and cultures":[10]

> Here is where ... feminism differs from other contemporary modes of radi-
> cal, critical or creative thinking, such as postmodernism and philosophical an-
> tihumanism: feminism defines itself as a political instance, not merely a
> sexual politics but a politics of experience, of everyday life, which later then
> in turn enters the public sphere of expression and creative practice, displac-
> ing aesthetic hierarchies and generic categories, and which thus establishes
> the semiotic ground for a different production of reference and meaning.[11]

Recent work in Afro-American literary theory has occasioned a similar anxiety about institutionalization. Robert B. Stepto, Henry Louis Gates, and Houston A. Baker have been accused of dismantling the black subject when they bring contemporary theory to bear on their readings of black texts. In his 1984 study, *Blues, Ideology, and Afro-American Literature: A Vernacular Theory*, Baker himself argues that the presence of Afro-American critics in historically white academic institutions of higher learning has spawned a generation of scholars whose work is overly dependent on their white colleagues' assumptions and rhetoric.[12] To his mind, Stepto and Gates, two self-styled Reconstructionists, fall victim to this kind of co-optation in their early work. Both Stepto's "Teaching Afro-American Literature: Survey or Tradition: The Reconstruction of Instruction" and Gates's "Preface to Blackness: Text and Pretext" seek to explore the figurative power and complexity not only of Afro-American written art, but indeed of Afro-American cultural life more broadly defined.[13] Stepto's essay, like his book, *From Behind the Veil: A Study of Afro-American Narrative*, argues for the primacy of a pregeneric myth, the quest for freedom and literacy, in the Afro-American literary tradition.[14] But as Baker argues, Stepto's articulation of this myth underscores its apparent "agentlessness." According to Stepto, the pregeneric myth is simply "set in motion." Writes Baker, "the efficacy of motion suggested here seems to have no historically based community or agency or agencies for its origination or perpetuation."[15]

Gates's "Preface to Blackness" explores the extent to which social institutions and extraliterary considerations have intruded into the critical discourse about Afro-American literature. In order to reaffirm the textuality of instances of black written art, he argues for a semiotic understanding of literature as a system of signs that stand in an arbitrary relation to social reality. For Baker, such a theory of language, literature, and culture suggests that " 'literary' meanings are conceived in a nonsocial, noninstitutional manner by the 'point of consciousness' of a language and maintained and transmitted, without an agent, within a closed circle of 'intertextuality.' "[16] Baker's position indicates his concern that in their efforts to align the aims of Afro-American critical activity with the goals and assumptions of prevailing theoretical discourses, both Stepto and Gates extract black writers from their relationship to their audience and from the circumstances in which they wrote and were read.

Interestingly, Baker's critique of Stepto and Gates appears in revised form within the same work in which he develops his own considerations about ways in which contemporary theory may be used to explore the workings of the vernacular in black expressive culture. Whether he succeeds in his effort to adjust the terms of poststructuralist theory to accommodate the nuances of black vernacular culture remains debatable. For Joyce Ann Joyce, however, Gates, Stepto, and Baker have all adopted a critical "linguistic system" that reflects their connection to an elite academic community of theoreticians and denies the significance of race for critic and writer alike. The intensity of this debate among Afro-Americanists is underscored by the fact that Joyce's essay occasions strikingly acrimonious responses from both Gates and Baker.

At these analogous points of self-scrutiny, then, feminists and Afro-Americanists alike have considered the extent to which they may betray the origins of their respective modes of inquiry when they seek tn employ the discourse of contemporary theory. When Anglo-American feminists have argued for the inclusion of Anne Bradstreet or Kate Chopin within the literary canon, and when male Afro-Americanists have insisted on the significance of Charles Chesnutt or Jean Toomer, what they have argued is a recognition of the literary activity of those who have written despite political, cultural, economic, and social marginalization and oppression. They argue, in other words, that to exclude the work of blacks and women is to deny the historical existence of these "others" as producers of literature. If feminists and Afro-Americanists now relinquish too easily the material conditions of the lives of blacks and women, they may well relinquish the very grounds on which their respective disciplines were established.

These debates from within feminist and Afro-Americanist discourse coincided with black feminist charges that the cultural productions of black women were excluded from both modes of inquiry. Audre Lorde, bell hooks (Gloria Watkins), Angela Davis, Barbara Smith, Mary Helen Washington, and Deborah McDowell, to name but a few, have all argued that the experiences of women of color needed to be represented if these oppositional discourses were to remain radical. The eruptions of these critical voices into feminist and Afro-Americanist literary theory, like their self-contained critical and theoretical utterances, question the totalizing tendencies of mainstream as well as reactive critical practice and caution that the hope of oppositional discourse rests on its awareness of its own complicities.

These twin challenges have resulted in an impulse among Anglo-American feminists and Afro-Americanists to rematerialize the subject of their theoretical positions. Meese, as I suggested earlier, examines the contributions deconstructive method can make to feminist critical practice, but only insofar as feminist assumptions repoliticize her use of theory. De Lauretis affirms the basis of feminism in "a politics of everyday life." And similarly, in his more recent work, for instance "The Blackness of Blackness: A Critique of the Sign of the Signifying Monkey," Gates argues for a material basis of his theoretical explanations by translating them into the black idiom, renaming principles of criticism where appropriate, and naming indigenous principles of criticism.

The black woman as critic, and more broadly as the locus where gender-, class-, and race-based oppression intersect, is often invoked when Anglo-American feminists and male Afro-Americanists begin to rematerialize their discourse. This may be the case because the move away from historical specificity associated with deconstruction resembles all too closely the totalizing tendency commonly associated with androcentric criticism. In other words, when historical specificity is denied or remains implicit, all the women are presumed white, all the blacks male. The move to include black women as historial presences and as speaking subjects in critical discourse may well then be used as a defense against charges of racial hegemony on the part of white women and sexist hegemony on the part of black males.

Meese ensures that the discourse of feminism grounds her explorations into deconstructive practice by unifying her chapters around the problems of race, class, and sexual preference. She thus offers readings not only of works by Mary Wilkins Freeman, Marilynne Robinson, Tillie Olsen, and Virginia Woolf, but also of the fiction of Alice Walker and Zora Neale Hurston. The politics of de Lauretis's introduction are likewise undergirded in the material conditions of working women's lives. She buttresses, for instance, her observations about the conflicting claims of different feminisms with evidence drawn from a speech by the black feminist activist, writer, and attorney Flo Kennedy. And in her critique of the (white) feminist discourse in sexuality, she cites Hortense Spillers's work on the absence of feminist perspectives on black women's sexuality. Zora Neale Hurston, Phillis Wheatley, Alice Walker, and Rebecca Cox Jackson, the black Shaker visionary, ground Gates's essay "Writing 'Race' and the Difference It Makes," just as discussions of writings by Hurston and Linda Brent are central to Baker's consideration of the economics of a new American literary history.

That the black woman appears in all of these texts as a historicizing presence testifies to the power of the insistent voices of black feminist literary and cultural critics. Yet it is striking that at precisely the moment when Anglo-American feminists and male Afro-Americanists begin to reconsider the material ground of their enterprise, they demonstrate their return to earth, as it were, by invoking the specific experiences of black women and the writings of black women. This association of black women with reembodiment resembles rather closely the association, in classic Western philosophy and in nineteenth-century cultural constructions of womanhood, of women of color with the body and therefore with animal passions and slave labor. Although in these theoretical contexts the impulse to rehistoricize produces insightful readings and illuminating theories, and is politically progressive and long overdue, nevertheless the link between black women's experiences and "the material" seems conceptually problematic.

If *Tootsie* can help us understand the white male theorists' use of feminism, I suggest that Amy Jones's 1987 film *Maid to Order* might offer a perspective on the use of the black woman or the black feminist in Anglo-American feminist or Afro-Americanist discourse. *Maid to Order is* a comic fantasy about a spoiled, rich white young woman from Beverly Hills (played by Ally Sheedy) who is sent by her fairy godmother (played by Beverly D'Angelo) to work as a maid in the home of a ludicrously nouveau riche agent and his wife in Malibu. She shares responsibilities with two other maids—one black, played by Merry Clayton, and one Latina, played by Begona Plaza. From the experience of deprivation and from her friendship with the black maid, she learns the value of love and labor; she is transformed, in other words, into a better person.

With its subtle critique of the racist policies for hiring domestic help in Southern California, *Maid to Order* seems rather progressive for a popular fantasy film. Yet even within this context, the figure of the black woman is commodified in ways that are familiar from classic cinematic narratives. From movies such as John Stahl's 1934 version of *Imitation of Life* (or Douglas Sirk's 1959 remake) and Fred Zinnemann's 1952 *Member of the Wedding* to a contemporary film such as *Maid to*

Order, black women are employed, if not sacrificed, to humanize their white superordinates, to teach them something about the content of their own subject positions. When black women operate in oppositional discourse as a sign for the author's awareness of materialist concerns, then they seem to be fetishized in much the same way as they are in mass culture.

If Anglo-American feminists and male Afro-Americanists are currently in the process of rematerializing their theoretical discourse, black feminists might be said to be emerging into a theoretical phase. The early, archaeological work gave way among black feminists as well to a period in which they offered textual analyses of individual works or clusters of works. Recent, third-stage black feminist work is concerned much less with the silences in other critical traditions; rather, the writings of Susan Willis, Hazel V. Carby, Mary Helen Washington, Dianne F. Sadoff, Deborah E. McDowell, Hortense Spillers, and others have become increasingly self-conscious and self-reflexive, examining ways in which literary study—the ways in which, for instance, we understand the meaning of influence, the meaning of a tradition, the meaning of literary periods, the meaning of literature itself—changes once questions of race, class, and gender become central to the process of literary analysis. In this third stage, then, black feminist theorists might be said to challenge the conceptualizations of literary study and to concern themselves increasingly with the effect of race, class, and gender on the practice of literary criticism.

Black feminist literary theory proceeds from the assumption that black women experience a unique form of oppression in discursive and nondiscursive practices alike because they are victims at once of sexism, racism, and by extension classism. However, as Elizabeth V. Spelman and Barbara Smith demonstrate separately, one oversimplifies by saying merely that black women experience sexism and racism. "For to say merely *that*, suggests that black women experience one form of oppression, as blacks—the same thing black men experience—and that they experience another form of oppression, as women—the same thing white women experience."[17] Such a formulation erases the specificity of the black woman's experience, constituting her as the point of intersection between black men's and white women's experience.

As an alternative to this position, what Smith calls the additive analysis, black feminist theorists argue that the meaning of blackness in this country shapes profoundly the experience of gender, just as the conditions of womanhood affect ineluctably the experience of race. Precisely because the conditions of the black woman's oppression are thus specific and complex, black feminist literary theorists seek particularized methodologies that might reveal the ways in which that oppression is represented in literary texts. These methods are necessarily flexible, holding in balance the three variables of race, gender, and class and destabilizing the centrality of any one. More generally, they call into question a variety of standards of valuation that mainstream feminist and androcentric Afro-Americanist theory might naturalize.

Proceeding from a point related to but different from the centers of these other modes of inquiry, black feminist critics demonstrate that the meaning of political action, work, family, and sexuality, indeed any feature of the experience of culture, varies depending on the material circumstances that surround and define one's point of reference. And as gender and race taken separately determine the conditions not only of oppression but also of liberation, so too does the interplay between these categories give rise to its own conception of liberation.

I want to resist the temptation to define or overspecify the particular questions that a black feminist theoretical approach might pose of a text. But I would characterize black feminist literary theory more broadly by arguing that it seeks to explore representations of black women's lives through techniques of analysis which suspend the variables of race, class, and gender in mutually interrogative relation.

The fiction of tradition represents one theoretical conception to which a number of black feminist theorists return. In a persuasively argued recent essay, Deborah McDowell examines the relationship between novels of racial uplift in the 1920s and recent black fiction.[18] Although Hazel V. Carby asserts in her book, *Reconstructing Womanhood,* that she is not engaged in the process of constructing the contours of a black female literary tradition, yet she establishes a lineage of black women intellectuals engaged in the ideological debates of their time. Mary Helen Washington and Dianne Sadoff likewise consider how race, class, and gender affect, respectively, the meaning of literary influence and the politics of literary reception. I focus here for a moment on the ways in which Washington's "'Taming All That Anger Down': Rage and Silence in Gwendolyn Brooks's *Maud Martha*"[19] and Sadoff's "Black Matrilineage: The Case of Alice Walker and Zora Neale Hurston"[20] make use of these three variables in their reformulation of the fiction of literary tradition.

In this essay, as in much of her recent writing, Washington argues that the material circumstances of black women's lives require one to develop revisionist strategies for evaluating and reading their work. She demonstrates here that precisely because the early reviewers and critics failed to comprehend the significance of race and gender for both a black woman writer and a young black urban girl, they trivialized Brooks and her only novel, a text made up of vignettes which are themselves comprised of short, declarative sentences.

Contemporary reviewers likened Brooks's style "to the exquisite delicacy of a lyric poem," Washington writes. They gave it "the kind of ladylike treatment that assured its dismissal."[21] But by examining the subtext of color prejudice, racial self-hatred, sexual insecurity, and powerlessness that underlies virtually every chapter, Washington demonstrates that the structure and grammar of the novel enact not what one reviewer called the protagonist's "spunk," but rather her repressed anger. In her discussion of the historical conditions that circumscribe the lives of black women in the 1940s and 1950s, Washington suggests ways in which Maud's oppression recalls Brooks's own marginal position within the publishing industry. Brooks inscribes not only Maud Martha's frustration, then, but also her own.

Washington's discussion here considers as well Brooks's reluctance to represent black women as heroic figures as a further sign of her oppression by a racist and sexist literary establishment. She thus prompts not only new readings of the text, but also of the relation between author and character. Indeed, Washington's discussion, turning as it does on the representation of the circumstances of Maud's life, enables a redefinition of the way a range of texts in the Afro-American canon are read. In her words, "if Maud Martha is considered an integral part of the

Afro-American canon, we will have to revise our conception of power and power-lessness, of heroism, of symbolic landscapes and ritual grounds."[22]

In her article, Dianne Sadoff argues that black women writers share neither the anxiety of influence Harold Bloom attributes to male writers nor the primary anxiety of authority Sandra Gilbert and Susan Gubar attribute to white women writers. Rather, she demonstrates that "race and class oppression intensify the black woman writer's need to discover an untroubled matrilineal heritage. In celebrating her literary foremothers, the contemporary black woman writer covers over more profoundly than does the white writer her ambivalence about matrilineage, her own misreading of precursors, and her link to an oral as well as a written tradition."[23]

Sadoff's examination of the relationship between Zora Neale Hurston and Alice Walker reveals a compelling tension between the explicit subjects of each author's work and the subversive material that underlies those surfaces. An ancestor claimed as significant by most recent black women writers, Zora Neale Hurston misrepresents herself within her fiction, Sadoff argues. *Their Eyes Were Watching God* may announce itself, for instance, as a celebration of heterosexual love, but Hurston manipulates narrative strategies to ensure that the male is eliminated and the female liberated. Sadoff goes on to show that Walker affirms her tie to Hurston by inscribing a similar double agenda throughout her work, problematizing the status of heterosexual love in similar ways. Moreover, while her essays document her enthusiastic pursuit of Hurston as a literary foremother, her novels display a profound anxiety about biological motherhood. Sadoff's readings demonstrate, then, that the peril of uniqueness compels an intense need on the part of black women writers to identify a literary matrilineage even as their historical circumstances occasion their ambivalence about the fact and process of mothering.

These two essays thus show that the black feminist enterprise, at this stage necessarily materialist, calls for a reconception of the politics of literary reception, the meaning of literary influence, and the content of literary tradition.

At this point in its evolution, black feminist literary theory does not yet appear to replicate the totalizing tendency I attributed to Anglo-American feminism and male Afro-Americanism earlier. No doubt because it has remained marginal, what has been primarily a heterosexual, Afro-American-centered feminist discourse has been concerned with refining its own mode of inquiry, perhaps at the expense of annexing to itself the experiences of "others" such as lesbians and other women of color.

Fiction by black women has, however, achieved significant visibility operating simultaneously as a body of texts both marginal and mainstream. Andrea Lee's *Sarah Phillips* thematizes this very issue and suggests that the very activity of conceptualizing the self as insider may occasion a fetishization of the "other."

The stories that make up Andrea Lee's *Sarah Phillips* appeared separately in *The New Yorker* magazine before they were collected and published together in 1984. This fact about the publishing history alone suggests that in at least one way this is a text of privilege; the content of the stories themselves also foregrounds the issue of class position. Each story is a vignette taken from the life of the title character, the daughter of a prosperous Baptist minister and his schoolteacher wife. With the exception of the first, entitled "In France," the stories are arranged chronologically to sketch Sarah Phillips's girlhood and adolescence in private schools and progressive summer camps in and around Philadelphia, undergraduate years at Harvard, and obligatory expatriation to Europe after graduation.

In addition to their common subject, the majority of the stories share a common structure. Most of the stories establish a community of insiders, disparate voices brought into unison, poised in a continuous present. In each instance, the stasis achieved by the choice of verb tenses, imagery, and patterns of allusion is interrupted by the presence of an outsider, someone who is constituted as the "other" according to the characteristics and assumptions of the narrative community. In virtually every instance, the presence of this "other" serves to historicize a vignette that had existed for the narrator as a moment out of time. The stories thus enact a tension between the narrative of the community of privilege, posited as ahistorical, and a destabilizing eruption, posited as inescapably historical.

Contemporary reviews identified two problematic areas of the text—the significance of Sarah's class position and the ambiguous relation between narrator and protagonist. Mary Helen Washington places it in a tradition with William Wells Brown's *Clotel*, Frances E. W. Harper's *Iola Leroy*, and James Weldon Johnson's *Autobiography of an Ex-Colored Man*, all works about a privileged black narrator tenuously connected to his or her blackness who needs to escape the problematic meanings of that identity. Washington argues that in these other novels, in varying degrees the narrators recognize the complex interplay between issues of class and race. The narrator of *Sarah Phillips*, in contrast, participates in the character's capitulation to her own position. Washington writes: "By the fourth or fifth story, I felt that the privileged kid had become the privileged narrator, no longer willing to struggle over issues of race and class, unable to bear the 'alarming knowledge' that these issues must reveal."[24]

Sherley Anne Williams compares the text to Richard Wright's *Black Boy*, arguing that both works "literally and figuratively [renounce] oral culture and black traditions for personal autonomy." She remarks that *Sarah Phillips* holds up to mockery "not the pretensions of her upper middle class heroine, but the 'outworn rituals' of black community."[25]

Both reviews suggest a point of contrast between Lee on the one hand and other contemporary black women writers who construct fictional communities of privilege. Toni Morrison, like Paule Marshall, Gloria Naylor, and Ntozake Shange, to name but a few, occasionally centers her novels on middle-class black characters. But as Susan Willis has written, in Morrison's novels, black middle-class life is generally characterized by a measure of alienation from the cultural heritage of the black rural South. Her characters are saved from "the upper reaches of bourgeois reification" by "eruptions of 'funk'"—characters or experiences that invoke the characters' cultural past and repressed emotional lives.[26] The energy of the text is thus in every case with the characters who represent "funk": Sula, Pilate, Son, even Cholly Breedlove; Morrison consistently problematizes what it means to be black and privileged.

Lee's narrator, on the other hand, seems as alienated from outsiders as the protagonist does. The text is sufficiently invested in its own construction of what it means to be privileged that it marginalizes those different from the protagonist herself. Rather than disparage *Sarah Phillips* on the basis of its politics, however, I should like to consider ways in which the "other" is figured here. For it seems to me that like the examples drawn earlier from feminist and Afro-Americanist discourse, this text also equates that "other" with the historical or the material.

My argument focuses primarily on a story entitled "Gypsies," in which a family of itinerants disrupt the orderliness of Sarah's suburban girlhood and force at least a symbolic acknowledgment of her place in a broader historical reality. But I begin with a reading of "In France," the story with which the volume begins, for it establishes a perspective by means of which the other stories may be read.

"In France" violates the chronological arrangement of stories, since it recounts the most recent events in the protagonist's life. The story breaks the pattern of the other stories in the volume in yet another way, for it is the only one to situate Sarah as an alien in her environment. The reader learns at once that Sarah is an American in Paris, but her story is filtered through the account of another American living there, a girl named Kate who seems to be missing. Rumors circulate that Kate is being held hostage by her present lover and ex-boyfriend lover who were "collecting her allowance and had bought a luxurious Fiat—the same model the Pope drove—with the profits."[27]

As it is recounted here, Kate's story invokes an absent double, underscoring Sarah's isolation. Moreover, the rumor of her mistreatment at the hands of her male friends presages the abuse Sarah's lover Henri and his friends inflict on her later in the story. We learn that after the death of her father and her graduation from Harvard, Sarah "cast off kin and convention in a foreign tongue" (4) and went to study French in Switzerland. Upon meeting Henri she leaves school and moves into the Paris apartment he shares with his friends Alain and Roger. Together they spend their time in cafés, museums, their apartment, and on occasional weekend expeditions into the country. The story turns on one such trip to the island of Jersey, when ostensibly harmless banter among the four of them suddenly turns nasty.

In this exchange Henri verbally assaults Sarah with racial insults, saying:

> Did you ever wonder . . . why our beautiful Sarah is such a mixture of races? . . . It's a very American tale. This *Irlandaise* was part redskin, and not only that but part Jew as well—some Americans are part Jew, aren't they? And one day this *Irlandaise* was walking through the jungle near New Orleans, when she was raped by a jazz musician as big and black as King Kong, with sexual equipment to match. And from this agreeable encounter was born our little Sarah, *notre Negresse pasteurisée.* (11)

Sarah responds in two ways. In the shock of the moment she recognizes that she cannot ignore this parody of miscegenation. Her class position notwithstanding, she plays some role in the drama of race relations from which such stereotypes derive. Several hours later, the meaning of the insult strikes her again, this time in a dream—one that impels her to return home: "I awoke with a start from a horrid dream in which I was conducting a monotonous struggle with an old woman with a dreadful spidery strength in her arms; her skin was dark and leathery, and she smelled like one of the old Philadelphia churchwomen who used to babysit with me" (14).

The dream prompts her to reflect more calmly on the fact that she will never be able to escape the call of her personal history. She remarks:

> I had hoped to join the ranks of dreaming expatriates for whom Paris can become a self-sufficient universe, but my life there had been no more than a slight hysteria, filled with the experimental naughtiness of children reacting against their training. It was clear, much as I did not want to know it, that my days in France had a number, that for me the bright, frank, endlessly beckoning horizon of the runaway had been, at some point, transformed into a complicated return. (15)

The story thus suggests that the past is inescapable. It anticipates Sarah's return home even though that return remains undramatized. I would argue that the subsequent stories, all of which center on events from Sarah's earlier life, function symbolically as that return home. The recurrent patterns that run through these other vignettes recapitulate the tension within the first story between escape and return. They indicate that the past may elude integration into the present, but it can also never be avoided.

In "Gypsies," the narrator attributes to Franklin Place, the street on which Sarah grows up, the ubiquity of a symbol. The opening description works against historical or geographical specificity, and instead represents the neighborhood in terms of the icons of upper-middle-class suburban culture. That is to say, in the opening paragraph the narrator locates the street in her dreams and nightmares, in her patterns of associations, before she locates it in a Philadelphia suburb. In this description, the suburb is represented as an abstraction, the fulfillment of a fantasy, distinct from the conditions of the world outside its boundaries:

> Franklin Place, the street that ran like a vein through most of my dreams and nightmares, the stretch of territory I automatically envisioned when someone said "neighborhood," lay in a Philadelphia suburb. The town was green and pretty, but had the constrained, slightly unreal atmosphere of a colony or a foreign enclave, that was because the people who owned the rambling houses behind the shrubbery were black. For them—doctors, ministers, teachers who had grown up in Philadelphia row houses—the lawns and tree-lined streets represented the fulfillment of a fantasy long deferred, and acted as a barrier against the predictable cruelty of the world. (39)

If this opening paragraph bestows a quality of unreality on the landscape against which this and several of the other stories take place, subsequent paragraphs render the world beyond the neighborhood even more ephemeral. From the narrator's perspective, historical events and political struggle represent levels of experience with which one may engage, but only imaginatively, the songs of cicadas providing a musical transition from Franklin Place to the world of those less privileged. As the narrator remarks:

> For as long as I could remember, the civil rights movement had been unrolling like a dim frieze behind the small pleasures and defeats of my childhood; it seemed dull, a necessary burden on my conscience, like good grades or hungry people in India. My occasional hair-raising reveries of venturing into the netherworld of Mississippi or Alabama only added a voluptuous edge to

the pleasure of eating an ice-cream cone while seated on a shady curb of Franklin Place. (39–40)

The image of the civil rights movement as a frieze fixes and aestheticizes the process of historical change, as if the inertia of Sarah's life had afflicted the world beyond the parameters of her neighborhood.

The illusion of timelessness and unassailability is sustained additionally by the narrator's tendency to cast the particular in terms of the habitual or familiar through her use of the second-person pronoun and the English equivalent of the French imperfect tense. For even as she narrows the focus of the story to the time of her encounter with the Gypsies, the narrator describes that particular day in terms that homogenize or encompass, terms that, in other words, move away from particularity. Indeed, the impulse toward generalization and away from particularity is rendered nowhere more clearly than in the description of Sarah in which she is described as if she were a twin of her best friend Lyn Yancey.

On the day in question, a battered red pickup truck bearing its load of log furniture and a family of Gypsies disturbs the peace of Franklin Place, a neighborhood of sedans, station wagons, and sports cars. Neither black nor white, the Gypsies defy the categories available to Sarah and Lyn: the wife's breasts swaying back and forth in a way in which "the well-contained bosoms of [their] mothers never do" (43). Despite their marginal status, the Gypsies articulate the assumptions about race and class shared by the majority culture. "It's a real crime for colored to live like this," says the wife. "You are very lucky little girls, very lucky, do you understand? When my son was your age he never got to play like you girls" (43).

At dinner that evening, Sarah repeats for her family her conversation with the Gypsies. The exchange that ensues disrupts the veneer of family harmony, introducing social reality into the magic of the private sphere. Her father, ordinarily a man of great restraint, loses his sense of decorum. "Most of the world despises gypsies, but a gypsy can always look down on a Negro! Heck, that fellow was right to spit! You can dress it up with trees and big houses and people who don't stink too bad, but a nigger neighborhood is still a nigger neighborhood" (44).

Sarah and Lyn later meet at the swim club. The narrator's description of the pool at night betrays if not the young girls' yearnings, then her own nostalgia for the familiar tranquility. The language thus shifts dramatically from the father's clipped vernacular speech. Their rediscovered contentment lasts only until the return home, however, for on the street they confront the Gypsies again, an insistent presence that cannot be ignored. The final paragraph of the story suggests that the protagonist's life has been altered profoundly. The narrator remarks, "nothing looked different, yet everything was, and for the first time Franklin Place seemed genuinely connected to a world that was neither insulated nor serene. Throughout the rest of the summer, on the rare occasions when a truck appeared in our neighborhood, Lyn and I would dash to see it, our hearts pounding with perverse excitement and a fresh desire for knowledge" (46). This final formulation resonates with a certain falseness; the narrator allows Sarah and Lyn the freedom to be entertained by historical events, as if the dim frieze of the civil rights movement might somehow amuse or stimulate them. Indeed, throughout the collection, stories conclude with similar ambivalence; Lee leaves unresolved the issue as to whether the insiders' acknowledgment of the other is symbolic or transformative.

The story thus constitutes a community of insiders rendered ahistorical and homogeneous by the allusions, descriptions, and grammar of the narrator. The presence of someone from outside of that community reminds the residents of Franklin Place of the contingencies on which their apparently stable lives are founded. Simultaneously, the outsider reminds the privileged community of the circumstances of their history. The exchange destabilizes the narrator's ability to totalize the experience the story describes.

Lee's persistent interest in eruptions into communities of privilege causes these stories to be useful texts within which to observe the relation between the presence of the "other" in theoretical discourse. The black woman protagonist in these stories locates herself within, rather than outside of, the normative community, be it an integrated camp for middle-class children, her neighborhood, or her family. Her very presence within these exclusionary communities suggests that the circumstances of race and gender alone protect no one from the seductions of reading her own experience as normative and fetishizing the experience of the other.

This essay offers three perspectives on the contemporary black feminist enterprise. It shows how black feminism is invoked in mainstream feminist and Afro-Americanist discourse, it presents in broad outlines the space black feminist theory occupies independently, and it suggests how one contemporary black woman novelist thematizes the relationship between those who occupy privileged discursive spaces and the "other."

I have approached the subject from three perspectives in part because of my own evident suspicion of totalizing formulations. But my approach reflects as well the black feminist skepticism about the reification of boundaries that historically have excluded the writing of black women from serious consideration within the academic literary establishments. Since, to my mind, some of the most compelling and representative black feminist writing treads the boundary between anthropology and criticism, or between cultural theory and literary theory, it seems appropriate that a consideration of this critical perspective would approach it from a variety of points of view.

NOTES

1. Elaine Showalter, "Critical Cross-Dressing: Male Feminism and the Woman of the Year," in Alice Jardine and Paul Smith, eds., *Men in Feminism* (New York: Methuen, 1987), 127.

2. Hazel V. Carby, *Reconstructing Womanhood: The Emergence of the Afro-American Woman Novelist* (New York: Oxford University Press, 1987), 9.

3. Mary Helen Washington "Introduction," in Mary Helen Washington, ed., *Black-Eyed Susans: Classic Stories by and about Black Women* (Garden City, N.Y.: Anchor Books, 1975), x–xxxii.

4. See Barbara Smith, "Toward a Black Feminist Criticism," *Conditions Two* 1 (October 1977), and Deborah E. McDowell, "New Directions for Black Feminist Criticism," *Black American Literature Forum* 14. Both were reprinted in Elaine Showalter, ed., *The New Feminist Criticism: Essays on Women, Literature, and Theory* (New York: Pantheon, 1985), 168–185 and 186–199, respectively.

5. See, for instance, the reprint series that McDowell edits for Beacon Press and her Rutgers University Press reprint of Nella Larsen's *Quicksand* and *Passing*; Washington's three anthologies, *Black-Eyed Susans, Midnight Birds*, and *Invented Lives* and her Feminist Press edition of Paule Marshall's *Brown Girl, Brownstones*; Nellie McKay's edition of Louise Meriwether's *Daddy Was a Number Runner*; and Gloria T. Hull's edition of Alice Dunbar-Nelson's diary, *Give Us Each Day*, to name but a few. Black women are not exclusively responsible for these kinds of editorial projects. See also William Andrews, *Sisters of the Spirit: Three Black Women's Autobiographies of the Nineteenth Century*; Henry Louis Gates's edition of Harriet E. Wilson's *Our Nig* and his Oxford University Press reprint series; and Jean Fagan Yeilin's edition of Harriet Jacobs's *Incidents in the Life of a Slave Girl*.

6. Peggy Kamuf, "Replacing Feminist Criticism," *Diacritics* 12 (Summer 1982): 44.

7. Nancy K. Miller, "The Text's Heroine: A Feminist Critic and Her Fictions," *Diacritics* 12 (Summer 1982): 49–50.

8. Elizabeth A. Meese, *Crossing the Double-Cross: The Practice of Feminist Criticism* (Chapel Hill: University of North Carolina Press, 1986).

9. Teresa de Lauretis, "Feminist Studies/Critical Studies: Issues, Terms, and Contexts," in Teresa de Lauretis, ed., *Feminist Studies/Critical Studies* (Bloomington: Indiana University Press, 1986), 2.

10. Ibid., 9.

11. Ibid., 10.

12. Houston A. Baker, Jr., *Blues Ideology and Afro-American Literature* (Chicago: University of Chicago Press, 1984).

13. See Robert B. Stepto, "Teaching Afro-American Literature: Survey or Tradition: The Reconstruction of Instruction," and Henry Louis Gates, Jr., "Preface to Blackness: Text and Pretext," both in Dexter Fisher and Robert B. Stepto, eds., *Afro-American Literature: The Reconstruction of Instruction* (New York: Modern Language Association of America, 1979), 8–24 and 44–69, respectively.

14. Robert B, Stepto, *From Behind the Veil: A Study of Afro-American Narrative* (Urbana: University of Illinois Press, 1979).

15. Baker, *Blues*, 94.

16. Ibid., 101.

17. Elizabeth V. Spelman, "Theories of Race and Gender: The Erasure of Black Women," *Quest* 5 (1979): 42.

18. Deborah E. McDowell, "'The Changing Same': Generational Connections and Black Women Novelists," *New Literary History* 18 (Winter 1987).

19. Mary Helen Washington, "'Taming All That Anger Down': Rage and Silence in Gwendolyn Brooks's *Maud Martha*," in Henry Louis Gates, Jr., ed., *Black Literature and Literary Theory* (New York: Methuen, 1984), 249–262.

20. Dianne F. Sadoff, "Black Matrilineage: The Case of Alice Walker and Zora Neale Hurston," *Signs* 11 (Autumn 1985): 4–26.

21. Washington, "Taming," 249.

22. Ibid., 260.

23. Sadoff, "Black Matrilineage," 5.

24. Mary Helen Washington, "Young, Gifted and Black," *Women's Review of Books* 2 (March 1985): 3.

25. Sherley Anne Williams, "Roots of Privilege: New Black Fiction," *Ms.* 13 (June 1985): 71.

26. See Susan Willis, "Eruptions of Funk: Historicizing Toni Morrison," in *Specifying: Black Women Writing the American Experience* (Madison: University of Wisconsin Press, 1987), 83–109.

27. Andrea Lee, *Sarah Phillips* (New York: Penguin Books, 1984), 3. Subsequent references to this edition are noted in the text by page number.

TERESA DE LAURETIS

UPPING THE ANTI (SIC) IN FEMINIST THEORY

(1990)

I. ESSENTIALISM AND ANTI-ESSENTIALISM

Nowadays, the term *essentialism* covers a range of metacritical meanings and strategic uses that go the very short distance from convenient label to buzzword. Many who, like myself, have been involved with feminist critical theory for some time and who did use the term, initially, as a serious critical concept, have grown impatient with this word—essentialism—time and again repeated with its reductive ring, its self-righteous tone of superiority, its contempt for "them"—those guilty of it. Yet, few would deny that feminist theory is all about an essential difference, an irreducible difference, though not a difference between woman and man, nor a difference inherent in "woman's nature" (in woman as nature), but a difference in the feminist conception of woman, women, and the world.

Let us say, then, that there is an essential difference between a feminist and a non-feminist understanding of the subject and its relation to institutions; between feminist and non-feminist knowledges, discourses, and practices of cultural forms, social relations, and subjective processes; between a feminist and a non-feminist historical consciousness. That difference is essential in that it is constitutive of feminist thinking and thus of feminism: it is what makes the thinking feminist, and what constitutes certain ways of thinking, certain practices of writing, reading, imaging, relating, acting, etc., into the historically diverse and culturally heterogeneous social movement which, qualifiers and distinctions notwithstanding, we continue with good reasons to call feminism.[1] Another way to say this is that the essential difference of feminism lies in its historical specificity—the particular conditions of its emergence and development, which have shaped its object and field of analysis, its assumptions and forms of address; the constraints that have attended its conceptual and methodological struggles; the erotic component of its political self-awareness; the absolute novelty of its radical challenge to social life itself.

But even as the specific, essential difference of feminism may not be disputed, the question of the nature of its specificity or what is of the essence in feminist thought and self-representation has been an object of contention, an issue over which divisions, debates, and polarizations have occurred consistently, and without resolution, since the beginning of that self-conscious critical reflection that constitutes the theory of feminism. The currency of the term "essentialism" may be based on nothing more than its capacity to circumvent this very question—the nature of the specific difference of feminism—and thus to polarize feminist thought on what amounts to a red herring. I suggest that the current enterprise of "anti-essentialist" theorists engaged in typologizing, defining and branding various "feminisms" along an ascending scale of theoretico-political sophistication where "essentialism" weighs heavy at the lower end, may be seen in this perspective.[2]

Which is not to say that there should be no critique of feminist positions or no contest for the practical as well as the theoretical meanings of feminism, or even no appeal for hegemony by participants in a social movement which, after all potentially involves all women. My polemical point here is that either too much or too little is made of the "essentialism" imputed to most feminist positions (notably those labeled cultural, separatist or radical, but others as well, whether labeled or not), so that the term serves less the purposes of effective criticism in the ongoing elaboration of feminist theory than those of convenience, conceptual simplification or academic legitimation. Taking a more discerning look at the *essence* that is in question in both *essentialism* and *essential difference*, therefore, seems like a very good idea.

Among the several acceptations of "essence" (from which "essentialism" is apparently derived) in the OED, the most pertinent to the context of use that is in question here are the following:

> 1. Absolute being, substance in the metaphysical sense; the reality underlying phenomena.
> 2. That which constitutes the being of a thing; that "by which it is what it is." In two different applications (distinguished by Locke as *nominal essence* and *real essence* respectively):
>   a. of a conceptual entity: The totality of the properties, constituent elements, etc., without which it would cease to be the same thing; the indispensable and necessary attributes of a thing as opposed to those which it may have or not. . . .
>   b. of a real entity: Objective character, intrinsic nature as a "thing-in-itself"; "that internal constitution, on which all the sensible properties depend."

Examples of a., dated from 1600 to 1870, include Locke's statement in the *Essay on Human Understanding*: "The Essence of a Triangle, lies in a very little compass . . . three Lines meeting at three Angles, make up that Essence"; and all the examples given for b., from 1667 to 1856, are to the effect that the essence of a real entity, the "thing-in-itself," is either unknown or unknowable.

Which of these "essences" are imputed to feminist "essentialists" by their critics? If most feminists, however one may classify trends and positions—cultural, radical, liberal, socialist, poststructuralist, and so forth—agree that women are made, not born, that gender is not an innate feature (as sex may be) but a sociocultural construction (and precisely for that reason it is oppressive to women), that patriarchy is historical (especially so when it is believed to have superseded a previous matriarchal realm), then the "essence" of woman that is described in the writings of many so-called essentialists is not the *real essence*, in Locke's terms, but more likely a *nominal* one. It is a totality of qualities, properties, and attributes that such feminists define, envisage, or enact for themselves (and some in fact attempt to live out in "separatist" communities), and possibly also wish for other women. This is more a project, then, than a description of existent reality; it is an admittedly feminist project of "re-vision," where the specifications *feminist* and *re*-vision already signal its historical location, even as the (re)vision projects itself outward geographically and temporally (universally) to recover the past and to claim the future. This may be utopian, idealist, perhaps misguided or wishful thinking, it may be a project one does not want to be a part of, but it is not essentialist as is the belief in a God-given or otherwise immutable nature of woman.

In other words, barring the case in which woman's "essence" is taken as absolute being or substance in the traditional metaphysical sense (and this may actually be the case for a few, truly fundamentalist thinkers to whom the term *essentialist* would properly apply), for the great majority of feminists the "essence" of woman is more like the essence of the triangle than the essence of the thing-in-itself: it is the specific properties (e.g., a female-sexed body), qualities (a disposition to nurturance, a certain relation to the body, etc.), or necessary attributes (e.g., the experience of femaleness, of living in the world as female) that women have developed or have been bound to historically, in their differently patriarchal sociocultural contexts, which make them women, and not men. One may prefer one triangle, one definition of women and/or feminism, to another and, within her particular conditions and possibilities of existence, struggle to define the triangle she wants or wants to be—feminists do want differently. And in these very struggles, I suggest, consist the historical development and the specific difference of feminist theory, the essence of the triangle.

It would be difficult to explain, otherwise, why thinkers or writers with political and personal histories, projects, needs, and desires as different as those of white women and women of color, of lesbians and heterosexuals, of differently abled women, and of successive generations of women, would all claim feminism as a major—if not the only—ground of difference; why they would address both their critiques or accusations and their demands for recognition to other women, feminists in particular; why the emotional and political stakes in feminist theorizing should be so high, dialogue so charged, and confrontation so impassioned; why, indeed, the proliferation of typologies and the wide currency of "essentialism" on one hand, countered by the equally wide currency of the term *male theory* on the other.[3] It is one of the projects of this paper to up the *anti* in feminist theoretical debates, to shift the focus of the controversy from "feminist essentialism," as a category by which to classify feminists or feminisms, to the historical specificity, the essential difference of feminist theory itself. To this end I first turn to two essays which prompted my reflection on the uses of "essentialism" in current Anglo-American feminist critical writing, Chris Weedon's *Feminist Practice and Poststructuralist Theory*, published in London in 1987, and Linda Alcoff's "Cultural Feminism versus Post-Structuralism: The Identity Crisis in Feminist Theory," published in the Spring 1988 issue of *Signs*. Then I will go on to argue that the essential difference of feminist theory must be looked for in the form as well as the contents of its political, personal, critical, and textual practices, in the diverse oppositional stances feminism has taken vis-à-vis social and cultural formations, and in the resulting divisions, self-conscious reflection, and conceptual elaboration that constitute the effective history of feminism. And thus a division such as the one over the issue of "essentialism" only *seems to* be a purely "internal," intra-feminist one, a conflict within feminism. In fact, it is not.

The notion of an "essential womanhood, common to all women, suppressed or repressed by patriarchy" recurs in Weedon's book as the mark of "radical-feminist theory," whose cited representatives are Mary Daly, Susan Griffin, and Adrienne Rich. "Radical-feminist theory" is initially listed together with "socialist-feminist and psychoanalytic-feminist theories" as "various attempts to systematize individual insights about the oppression of women into relatively coherent theories of patriarchy," in spite of the author's statement, on the same page, that radical-feminist writers are hostile to theory because they see it as a form of male dominance which co-opts women and suppresses the feminine (p. 6). As one reads on, however, socialist feminism drops out altogether while psychoanalytic feminism is integrated into a new and more "politically" sophisticated discourse called "feminist poststructuralism." Thus, three-fourths of the way through the book, one finds this summary statement:

> For poststructuralist feminism, neither the liberal-feminist attempt to redefine the truth of women's nature within the terms of existing social relations and to establish women's full equality with men, nor the radical-feminist emphasis on fixed difference realized in a separatist context, is politically adequate. Poststructuralist feminism requires attention to historical specificity in the production, for women, of subject positions and modes of femininity and their place in the overall network of social power relations. In this the meaning of biological sexual difference is never finally fixed. . . . An understanding of how discourses of biological sexual difference are mobilized, in a particular society, at a particular moment, is the first stage in intervening in order to initiate change. (p. 135)

There is more than simple irony in the claim that this late-comer, poststructuralist feminism, dark horse and winner of the feminist theory contest, is the "first stage" of feminist intervention. How can Weedon, at one and the same time, so strongly insist on attention to historical specificity and social—not merely individual—change, and yet disregard the actual historical changes in Western culture brought about in part, at least, by the women's movement and at least in some measure by feminist critical writing over the past twenty years?

One could surmise that Weedon does not like the changes that have taken place (even as they allow the very writing and publication of her book), or does not consider them sufficient, though that would hardly be reason enough to disregard them so blatantly. A more subtle answer may lie in the apolegetic and militant project of her book, a defense of poststructuralism vis-à-vis both the academic establishment and the general educated reader, but with an eye to the women's studies corner of the publishing market; whence, one must infer, the lead position in the title of the other term of the couple, feminist practice. For, as the Preface states, "the aim of this book is to make poststructuralist theory accessible to readers to whom it is unfamiliar, to argue its political usefulness to feminism and to consider its implications for feminist critical practice" (p. vii).

Somehow, however, in the course of the book, the Preface's modest claim "to point to a possible direction for future feminist cultural criticism" (p. vii) is escalated into a peroration for the new and much improved feminist theory called feminist poststructuralism or, indifferently, poststructural feminism.

In the concluding chapter on "Feminist Critical Practice" (strangely in the singular, as if among so many feminisms and feminist theories, only one practice could properly be called both feminist and critical), the academic contenders are narrowed down to two. The first is the poststructural criticism produced by British feminists (two are mentioned, E. Ann Kaplan and Rosalind Coward) looking "at the mechanisms through which meaning is constructed" mainly in popular culture and visual representation; the second is "the other influential branch of feminist criticism [that] looks to fiction as an expression of an already constituted gendered experience" (p. 152). Reappearing here, the word *experience*, identified earlier on as the basis for radical-feminist politics ("many feminists assume that women's experience, unmediated by further theory, is the source of true knowledge," p. 8), links this second branch of feminist (literary) criticism to radical-feminist ideology. Its standard-bearers are Americans, Showalter's gynocritics and the "woman-centred criticism" of Gilbert and Gubar, whose reliance on the concept of authorship as a key to meaning and truth also links them with "liberal-humanist criticism" (pp. 154–55).

A particular subset of this—by now radical-liberal—feminist criticism "dedicated to constructing traditions" (p. 156) is the one concerned with "black and lesbian female experience"; here the problems and ideological traps appear most clearly, in Weedon's eyes, and are "most extreme in the case of lesbian writing and the construction of a lesbian aesthetic" (p. 158). The reference works for her analysis, rather surprisingly in view of the abundance of Black and lesbian feminist writings in the 1980s, are a couple of rather dated essays by Barbara Smith and Bonnie Zimmerman reprinted in a collection edited by Elaine Showalter and, in fact, misnamed *The New Feminist Criticism*.[4] But even more surprisingly—or not at all so, depending on one's degree of optimism—it is again poststructuralist criticism that, with the help of Derridean deconstruction, can set all of these writers straight, as it were, as to the real, socially constructed and discursively produced nature of gender, race, class, and sexuality—as well as authorship and experience! Too bad for us that no exemplary poststructuralist feminist works or critics are discussed in this context (Cixous, Kristeva, and Irigaray figure prominently, but as psychoanalytic feminists earlier in the book). Now, I should like to make it clear that I have no quarrel with poststructuralism as such, or with the fundamental importance for all critical thinking, feminist theory included, of many of the concepts admirably summarized by Weedon in passages such as the following:

> For a theoretical perspective to be politically useful to feminists, it should be able to recognize the importance of the *subjective* in constituting the meaning of women's lived reality. It should not deny subjective experience, since the ways in which people make sense of their lives is a necessary starting point for understanding how power relations structure society. Theory must be able to address women's experience by showing where it comes from and how it relates to material social practices and the power relations which structure them. . . . In this process subjectivity becomes available, offering the indi-

vidual both a perspective and a choice, and opening up the possibility of political change. (pp. 8–9)

But while I am in complete agreement that experience is a difficult, ambiguous
and often oversimplified term, and that feminist theory needs to elaborate further "the relationship between experience, social power and resistance" (p. 8), I
would insist that the notion of experience in relation both to social-material practices and to the formation and processes of subjectivity is a feminist concept, not
a poststructuralist one (this is an instance of that essential difference of feminism
which I want to reclaim from Weedon's all-encompassing "poststructuralism"),
and would be still unthinkable were it not for specifically feminist practices, political, critical, and textual: consciousness raising, the rereading and revision of
the canon, the critique of scientific discourses, and the imaging of new social
spaces and forms of community. In short, the very practices of those feminist critics Weedon allocates to the "essentialist" camp. I would also add that "a theory
of the relationship between experience, social power and resistance" is precisely
one possible definition of feminist, not of poststructuralist, theory, as Weedon
would have it, since the latter does not countenance the notion of experience
within its conceptual horizon or philosophical presuppositions; and that, moreover, these issues have been posed and argued by several non-denominational
feminist theories in the United States for quite some time: for example, in the
works of Biddy Martin, Nancy K. Miller, Tania Modleski, Mary Russo, Kaja
Silverman, as well as myself, and even more forcefully in the works of feminist
theorists and writers of color such as Gloria Anzaldúa, Audre Lorde, Chandra
Mohanty, Cherríe Moraga, and Barbara Smith.

So my quarrel with Weedon's book is about its reductive opposition—all the
more remarkable, coming from a proponent of deconstruction—of a *lumpen* feminist essentialism (radical-liberal-separatist and American) to a phantom feminist
poststructuralism (critical-socialist-psychoanalytic and Franco-British), and with
the by-products of such a *parti-pris*: the canonization of a few, (in)famous feminists as signposts of the convenient categories set up by the typology, the agonistic narrative structure of its account of "feminist theories," and finally its failure
to contribute to the elaboration of feminist critical thought, however useful the
book may be to its other intended readers, who can thus rest easy in the fantasy
that poststructuralism is the theory and feminism is just a practice.

The title of Alcoff's essay, "Cultural Feminism versus Post-Structuralism: The
Identity Crisis in Feminist Theory," bespeaks some of the same problems: a manner of thinking by mutually oppositional categories, an agonistic frame of argumentation, and a focus on division, a "crisis in feminist theory" that may be read
not only as a crisis *over* identity, a metacritical doubt and a dispute among feminists as to the notion of identity, but also as a crisis *of* identity, of self-definition,
implying a theoretical impasse for feminism as a whole. The essay, however, is
more discerning, goes much further than its title suggests, and even contradicts
it in the end, as the notion of identity, far from fixing the point of an impasse,
becomes an active shifter in the feminist discourse of woman.[5]

Taking as its starting point "the concept of woman," or rather, its redefinition
in feminist theory ("the dilemma facing feminist theorists today is that our very

self-definition is grounded in a concept that we must deconstruct and deessentialize in all of its aspects"), Alcoff finds two major categories of responses to the dilemma, or what I would call the paradox of woman (p. 406). Cultural feminists, she claims, "have not challenged the defining of woman but only that definition given by men" (p. 407), and have replaced it with what they believe a more accurate description and appraisal, "the concept of the essential female" (p. 408). On the other hand, the poststructuralist response has been to reject the possibility of defining woman altogether and to replace "the politics of gender or sexual difference . . . with a plurality of difference where gender loses its position of significance" (p. 407). A third category is suggested, but only indirectly, in Alcoff's unwillingness to include among cultural feminists certain writers of color such as Moraga and Lorde in spite of their emphasis on cultural identity, for in her view "their work has consistently rejected essentialist conceptions of gender" (p. 412). Why an emphasis on racial, ethnic, and/or sexual identity need not be seen as essentialist is discussed more fully later in the essay with regard to identity politics and in conjunction with a third trend in feminist theory which Alcoff sees as a new course for feminism, "a theory of the gendered subject that does not slide into essentialism" (p. 422).

Whereas the narrative structure underlying Weedon's account of feminist theories is that of a contest where one actor successively engages and defeats or conquers several rivals, Alcoff's develops as a dialectics. Both the culturalist and the poststructuralist positions display internal contradictions: for example, not all cultural feminists "give explicitly essentialist formulations of what it means to be a woman" (p. 411), and their emphasis on the affirmation of women's strength and positive cultural roles and attributes has done much to counter images of woman as victim or of woman as male when in a business suit; but insofar as it reinforces the essentialist explanations of those attributes that are part and parcel of the traditional notion of womanhood, cultural feminism may, and for some women does, foster another form of sexist oppression. Conversely, if the poststructuralist critique of the unified, authentic subject of humanism is more than compatible with the feminist project to "deconstruct and de-essentialize" woman (as Alcoff puts it, in clearly poststructuralist terms), its absolute rejection of gender and its negation of biological determinism in favor of a cultural-discursive determinism result, as concerns women, in a form of nominalism. If "woman" is a fiction, a locus of pure difference and resistance to logocentric power, and if there are no women as such, then the very issue of women's oppression would appear to be obsolete and feminism itself would have no reason to exist (which, it may be noted, is a corollary of poststructuralism and the stated position of those who call themselves "post-feminists"). "What can we demand in the name of women," Alcoff asks, "if 'women' do not exist and demands in their name simply reinforce the myth that they do?" (p. 420).

The way out—let me say, the sublation—of the contradictions in which are caught these two mainstream feminist views lies in "a theory of the subject that avoids both essentialism and nominalism" (p. 421), and Alcoff points to it in the work of a few theorists, "a few brave souls," whom she rejoins in developing her notion of "woman as positionality": "woman is a position from which a feminist politics can emerge rather than a set of attributes that are 'objectively identifiable'" (pp. 434–435). In becoming feminist, for instance, women take up a position, a point of perspective, from which to interpret or (re)construct values and meanings. That position is also a politically assumed identity, and one relative to their sociohistorical location, whereas essentialist definitions would have woman's identity or attributes independent of her external situation; however, the positions available to women in any sociohistorical location are neither arbitrary nor undecidable. Thus, Alcoff concludes,

> If we combine the concept of identity politics with a conception of the subject as positionality, we can conceive of the subject as nonessentialized and emergent from a historical experience and yet retain our political ability to take gender as an important point of departure. Thus we can say at one and the same time that gender is not natural, biological, universal, ahistorical, or essential and yet still claim that gender is relevant because we are taking gender as a position from which to act politically. (p. 433)

I am, of course, in agreement with her emphases on issues and arguments that have been central in my work, such as the necessity to theorize experience in relation to practices, the understanding of gendered subjectivity as "an emergent property of a historicized experience" (p. 431), and the notion that identity is an active construction and a discursively mediated political interpretation of one's history. What I must ask, and less as a criticism of Alcoff's essay than for the purposes of my argument here, is: why is it still necessary to set up two opposing categories, cultural feminism and poststructuralism, or essentialism and anti-essentialism, thesis and antithesis, when one has already achieved the vantage point of a theoretical position that overtakes them or sublates them?

Doesn't the insistence on the "essentialism" of cultural feminists reproduce and keep in the foreground an image of "dominant" feminism that is at least reductive, at best tautological or superseded, and at worst not in our interests? Doesn't it feed the pernicious opposition of low versus high theory, a low-grade type of critical thinking (feminism) that is contrasted with the high-test theoretical grade of a poststructuralism from which some feminists would have been smart enough to learn? As one feminist theorist who's been concurrently involved with feminism, women's studies, psychoanalytic theory, structuralism, and film theory from the beginning of my critical activity, I know that learning to be a feminist has grounded, or embodied, all of my learning and so en-gendered thinking and knowing itself. That engendered thinking and that embodied, situated knowledge (in Donna Haraway's phrase)[6] are the stuff of feminist theory, whether by "feminist theory" is meant one of a growing number of feminist critical discourses—on culture, science, subjectivity, writing, visual representation, social institutions, etc.—or more particularly, the critical elaboration of feminist thought itself and the ongoing (re)definition of its specific difference. In either case, feminist theory is not of a lower grade than that which some call "male theory," but different in kind; and it is its essential difference, the essence of that triangle, that concerns me here as a theorist of feminism.

Why then, I ask again, continue to constrain it in the terms of essentialism and anti-essentialism even as they no longer serve (but did they ever?) to formulate our questions? For example, in her discussion of cultural feminism, Alcoff accepts another critic's characterization despite some doubt that the latter "makes it appear too homogeneous and . . . the charge of essentialism is on shaky ground" (p. 411). Then she adds:

> In the absence of a clearly stated position on the ultimate source of gender difference, Echols *infers* from their emphasis on building a feminist free-space and woman-centered culture that cultural feminists hold some version of essentialism. I share Echols's *suspicion*. Certainly, *it is difficult to render the views of Rich and Daly into a coherent whole without supplying a missing premise* that there is an innate female essence. (p 412; emphasis added)

But why do it at all? What is the purpose, or the gain, of supplying a missing premise (innate female essence) in order to construct a coherent image of feminism which thus becomes available to charges (essentialism) based on the very premise that had to be supplied? What motivates such a project, the suspicion, and the inferences?

II. THEORIZING BEYOND RECONCILIATION

For a theorist of feminism, the answer to these questions should be looked for in the particular history of feminism, the debates, internal divisions, and polarizations that have resulted from its engagement with the various institutions, discourses, and practices that constitute the social, and from its self-conscious reflection on that engagement; that is to say, the divisions that have marked feminism as a result of the divisions (of gender, sex, race, class, ethnicity, sexuality, etc.) in the social itself, and the discursive boundaries and subjective limits that feminism has defined and redefined for itself contingently, historically in the process of its engagement with social and cultural formations. The answer should be looked for, in other words, in the form as well as the contents that are specific to feminist political practices and conceptual elaboration, in the paradoxes and contradictions that constitute the effective history, the essential difference, of feminist thought.

In one account that can be given of that history, feminist theory has developed a series of oppositional stances not only vis-à-vis the wider, "external" context (the social constraints, legislation, ideological apparati, dominant discourses and representations against which feminism has pitched its critique and its political strategies in particular historical locations), but also, concurrently and interrelatedly, in its own "internal," self-critical processes.[7] For instance, in the seventies, the debates on academic feminism vs. activism in the United States defined an opposition between theory and practice which led, on the one hand, to a polarization of positions either *for* theory or *against* theory in nearly all cultural practices and, on the other, to a consistent, if never fully successful, effort to overcome the opposition itself.[8] Subsequently, the internal division of the movement over the issue of separatism or "mainstreaming," both in the academy and in other institutional contexts, recast the practice/theory opposition in terms of lesbian vs. heterosexual identification, and of women's studies vs. feminist cultural theory among others. Here, too, the opposition led to both polarization (e.g., feminist criticism vs. feminist theory in literary studies) and efforts to overcome it by an expanded, extremely flexible, and ultimately unsatisfactory redefinition of the notion of "feminist theory" itself.

Another major division and the resulting crucial shift in feminist thought were prompted, at the turn of the decade into the eighties, by the wider dissemination of the writings of women of color and their critique of racism in the women's movement. The division over the issue of race vs. gender, and of the relative importance of each in defining the modes of women's oppression, resistance, and agency, also produced an opposition between a "white" or "Western feminism" and a "U.S. Third World feminism" articulated in several racial and ethnic hyphenations, or called by an altogether different name (e.g., black "womanism").[9] Because the oppositional stance of women of color was markedly, if not exclusively, addressed to white women in the context of feminism—that is to say, their critique addressed more directly white feminists than it did (white) patriarchal power structures, men of color, or even white women in general—once again that division on the issue of race vs. gender led to polarization as well as to concerted efforts to overcome it, at least internally to feminist theoretical and cultural practices. And once again those efforts met with mostly unsatisfactory or inadequate results, so that no actual resolution, no dialectic sublation has been achieved in this opposition either, as in the others. For even as the polarization may be muted or displaced by other issues that come to the fore, each of those oppositions remains present and active in feminist consciousness and, I want to argue, must so remain in a feminist theory of the female-sexed or female-embodied social subject that is based on its specific and emergent history.

Since the mid-eighties, the so-called feminist sex wars (Ruby Rich) have pitched "pro-sex" feminists vs. the anti-pornography movement in a conflict over representation that recast the sex/gender distinction into the form of a paradoxical opposition: sex and gender are either collapsed together, and rendered both analytically and politically indistinguishable (MacKinnon, Hartsock) or they are severed from each other and seen as endlessly recombinable in such figures of boundary crossing as transsexualism, transvestism, bisexualism, drag and impersonation (Butler), cyborgs (Haraway), etc. This last issue is especially central to the lesbian debate on sadomasochism (*Coming to Power, Against Sadomasochism*), which recasts the earlier division of lesbians between the women's liberation movement, with its more or less overt homophobia (Bearchell, Clark), and the gay liberation movement, with its more or less overt sexism (Frye), into the current opposition of radical S/M lesbianism to mainstream cultural lesbian feminism (Rubin, Califia), an opposition whose mechanical binarism is tersely expressed by the recent magazine title *On Our Backs* punning on the long-established feminist periodical *Off Our Backs*. And here may be also mentioned the opposition pro and against psychoanalysis (e.g., Rose and Wilson) which, ironically, has been almost completely disregarded in these sexuality debates, even as it determined the conceptual elaboration of sexual difference in the seventies and has since been fundamental to the feminist critique of representation in the media and the arts.[10]

This account of the history of feminism in relation to both "external" and "internal" events, discourses, and practices suggests that two concurrent drives, impulses or mechanisms, are at work in the production of its self-representation: *an erotic, narcissistic drive* that enhances images of feminism as difference, rebellion, daring, excess, subversion, disloyalty, agency, empowerment, pleasure and danger, and rejects all images of powerlessness, victimization, subjection, acquiescence, passivity, conformism, femininity; and *an ethical drive* that works toward community, accountability, entrustment, sisterhood, bonding, belonging to a common world of women or sharing what Adrienne Rich has poignantly called "the dream of a common language." Together, often in mutual contradiction, the erotic and ethical drives have fueled not only the various polarizations and the construction of oppositions but also the invention or conceptual imaging of a "continuum" of experience, a global feminism, a "house of difference," or a separate space where "safe words" can be trusted and "consent" be given uncoerced. And, as I suggest in my discussion of a recent text of Italian feminism by the Milan Women's Bookstore collective, an erotic and an ethical drive may be seen to underlie and sustain at once the possibility of, and the difficulties involved in, the project of articulating a female symbolic.[11] Are these two drives together, most often in mutual contradiction, what particularly distinguishes lesbian feminism, where the erotic is as necessary a condition as the ethical, if not more?

That the two drives often clash or bring about political stalemates and conceptual impasses is not surprising, for they have contradictory objects and aims, and are forced into open conflict in a culture where women are not supposed to be, know, or see themselves as subjects. And for this very reason perhaps, the two drives characterize the movement of feminism, and more emphatically lesbian feminism, its historically intrinsic, essential condition of contradiction, and the processes constitutive of feminist thought in its specificity. As I have written elsewhere, "the tension of a twofold pull in contrary directions—the critical negativity of its theory, and the affirmative positivity of its politics—is both the historical condition of existence of feminism and its theoretical condition of possibility."[12] That tension, as the condition of possibility and effective elaboration of feminist theory, is most productive in the kind of critical thinking that refuses to be pulled to either side of an opposition and seeks instead to deconstruct it, or better, to disengage it from the fixity of polarization in an "internal" feminist debate and to reconnect it to the "external" discursive and social context from which it finally cannot be severed except at the cost of repeatedly reducing a historical process, a movement, to an ideological stalemate. This may be the approach of those writers whom Alcoff would call "brave souls . . . attempting to map out a new course" (p. 407). But that course, I would argue, does not proceed in the manner of a dialectic, by resolving or reconciling the given terms of an opposition—say, essentialism/anti-essentialism or pro-sex/anti-pornography—whether the resolution is achieved discursively (for example, alleging a larger, tactical or political perspective on the issue) or by pointing to their actual sublation in existing material conditions (for example, adducing sociological data or statistical arguments). It proceeds, in my view, by what I call upping the "anti": by analyzing the undecidability, conceptual as well as pragmatic, of the alternative *as given*, such critical works release its terms from the fixity of meaning into which polarization has locked them, and reintroduce them into a larger contextual and conceptual frame of reference; the tension of positivity and negativity that marks feminist discourse in its engagement with the social can then displace the impasse of mere "internal" opposition to a more complex level of analysis.[13]

Seen in this larger, historical frame of reference, feminist theory is not merely a theory of gender oppression in culture, as both MacKinnon and Rubin maintain, from the respective poles of the sex/gender and pro-sex/anti-pornography debates, and as is too often reiterated in women's studies textbooks;[14] nor is it the essentialist theory of women's nature which Weedon opposes to an anti-essentialist, poststructuralist theory of culture. It is instead a developing theory of the female-sexed or female-embodied social subject, whose constitution and whose modes of social and subjective existence include most obviously sex and gender, but also race, class, and any other significant sociocultural divisions and representations; a developing theory of the female-embodied social subject that is based on its specific, emergent, and conflictual history.

NOTES

Another version of this essay was published in *Differences: A Journal of Feminist Cultural Studies* 1, no. 2 (Fall 1989) with the title "The Essence of the Triangle or, Taking the Risk of Essentialism Seriously: Feminist Theory in Italy, the U.S., and Britain." The essay was initially written for the issue of *Differences* devoted to "The Essential Difference: Another Look at Essentialism," but then rethought in the context of the project of this book, addressing the problem of "conflicts in feminism." The two versions have in common the arguments set out in Part I, but then, in Parts II and III, present two quite distinct accounts of what I call the effective history of feminist theory and its specific, essential difference as a developing theory of the female-sexed or female-embodied social subject: there, an account, one possible history of feminist theory in Italy, here one account of feminist theory in North America.

1. For two very different historical views of feminism, see Rosalind Delmar, "What Is Feminism?," in *What Is Feminism: A Re-Examination.*, ed. Juliet Mitchell and Ann Oakley (New York: Pantheon Books, 1986), pp. 8–33, and Karen Offen, "Defining Feminism: A Comparative Historical Approach," *Signs: Journal of Women In Culture and Society* 14, no. 1 (Autumn 1988): 119–57.

2. The typological project is central to, for example, Alice Echols, "The New Feminism of Yin and Yang," in *Powers of Desire: The Politics of Sexuality,* ed. Ann Snitow, Christine Stansell, and Sharon Thompson (New York: Monthly Review Press, 1983), 439–59, and "The Taming of the Id: Feminist Sexual Politics, 1968–83," in *Pleasure and Danger: Exploring Female Sexuality,* ed. Carole S. Vance (Boston: Routledge & Kegan Paul, 1984), 50–72; Hester Eisenstein, *Contemporary Feminist Thought* (Boston: G. K. Hall, 1983); Zillah Eisenstein, *The Radical Future of Liberal Feminism* (New York: Longman, 1981); Alison M. Jaggar and Paula S. Rothenberg, *Feminist Frameworks: Alternative Theoretical Accounts of the Relations Between Women and Men* (New York: McGraw-Hill, 1984); and more recently Chris Weedon, *Feminist Practice and Poststructuralist Theory* (Oxford: Basil Blackwell, 1987). In this proliferation of typologies, essentialism as the belief in "female nature" is associated with cultural feminism, "separatist" (read: lesbian) feminism, radical feminism (with qualifications), and occasionally liberal feminism, while socialist feminism and now poststructuralist or deconstructive feminism come out at the top of the scale. Third World feminism is also widely used as a term but seldom given official type status in the typologies. A notable exception is Jaggar and Rothenberg's anthology which, in its 1984 revised edition, adds the new category "Feminism and Women of Color" to the five categories of the 1978 edition of *Feminist Frameworks*: conservatism, liberalism, traditional Marxism, radical feminism, and socialist feminism. On their part, Black, Latina, Asian, and other U.S. Third World feminists have not participated in the making of such typologies, possibly because of their ongoing argument with and ambivalence toward the larger category of "white feminism."

And hence, perhaps, Jaggar and Rothenberg's respectful labeling of the new category "Feminism *and* Women of Color," suggesting a distance between the two terms and avoiding judgment on the latter.

3. María C. Lugones and Elizabeth V. Spelman, "Have We Got a Theory for You!: Feminist Theory, Cultural Imperialism and the Demand for 'the Woman's Voice,'" *Women's Studies International Forum* 6, no. 6 (1983): 573–81.

4. *The New Feminist Criticism: Essays on Women, Literature, and Theory*, ed. Elaine Showalter (New York: Pantheon Books, 1985) includes Barbara Smith, "Toward a Black Feminist Criticism," first published in 1977, and Bonnie Zimmerman, "What Has Never Been: An Overview of Lesbian Feminist Criticism," first published in 1981.

5. Since Alcoff refers extensively to my own work, this essay is in a sense a dialogue with her and with myself—that dialogue in feminist critical writing which often works as a variation of consciousness raising or better, its transformation into a significant form of feminist cultural practice, and one not always reducible to "academic" activity.

6. Donna Haraway, "Situated Knowledges: The Science Question in Feminism and the Privilege of Partial Perspective," *Feminist Studies* 14, no. 3 (Fall 1988): 575–99.

7. The quotation marks around "internal" and "external" are there to denaturalize any notion of boundary between feminism and what is thought of as its outside, its other, non-feminism. For, even as we must speak of divisions within feminism, of a feminist political thought, a feminist discourse, a feminist consciousness, etc., we nonetheless well know that no permanent or stable boundary insulates feminist discourse and practices from those which are not feminist. In fact, as Ernesto Laclau and Chantal Mouffe argue in *Hegemony and Socialist Strategy: Towards a Radical Democratic Politics* (London: Verso, 1985), "the irresoluble interiority/exteriority tension is the condition of any social practice. . . . It is in this terrain, where neither a total interiority nor a total exteriority is possible, that the social is constituted" (p. 111). In thinking through the relation of feminism to other social discourses and practices, I find very useful their notion of *articulation*. If we abandon the notion of "'*society*' as a sutured and self-defined totality," Laclau and Mouffe state, we may instead conceive of the social as a field of differences, where no single underlying principle fixes, and hence constitutes, the whole field of differences (p. 111); but the "impossibility of an ultimate fixity of meaning implies that there have to be partial fixations—otherwise, the very flow of differences would be impossible. Even in order to differ, to subvert meaning, there has to be *a* meaning." Thus they define a "practice of articulation" as "the construction of nodal points which partially fix meaning," an attempt to arrest the flow of differences, to construct a center (pp. 112–13). In this sense, the history of feminist theory would be the history of a series of practices of articulation.

8. I am indebted to Kirstie McClure for pointing out to me that the opposition between theory and practice is a long-standing element of the Western intellectual tradition well before Marxism. One of the classic modern efforts to overcome that opposition, and an equally unsuccessful effort, is Kant's essay "On the Common Saying: 'This May be True in Theory, but it does not Apply in Practice,'" in *Kant's Political Writings*, ed. Hans Reiss (Cambridge: Cambridge University Press, 1970), 61–92.

9. See, for example, Alice Walker, *In Search of Our Mothers' Gardens: Womanist Prose* (San Diego, CA: Harcourt Brace Jovanovich, 1983); bell hooks, *Feminist Theory: From Margin to Center* (Boston: South End Press, 1984); Audre Lorde, "An Open Letter to Mary Daly," in *Sister Outsider: Essays and Speeches* (Trumansburg, NY: The Crossing Press, 1984), 66–71; and especially Chela Sandoval's dissertation, "Oppositional Consciousness in the Postmodern World: U.S. Third World Feminism, Semiotics and New World Cinema," University of California, Santa Cruz, 1993.

10. See B. Ruby Rich, "Feminism and Sexuality in the 1980s," *Feminist Studies* 12, no. 3 (Fall 1988): 525–61; Catharine A. MacKinnon, *Feminism Unmodified: Discourses on Life and Law* (Cambridge: Harvard University Press, 1987); Nancy Hartsock, "The Feminist Stand-

point: Developing the Ground for a Specifically Feminist Historical Materialism," in *Discovering Reality*, ed. Sandra Harding and Merill B. Hintikka (Dordrecht, Netherlands: Reidel, 1983), 283–310; Judith Butler, "Gender Differences: Feminist Theory and Psychoanalytic Narrative," 1988 manuscript; Donna Haraway, "A Manifesto for Cyborgs: Science, Technology and Socialist Feminism in the 1980s," *Socialist Review* 80 (1985): 65–107; Samois, *Coming to Power: Writings and Graphics on Lesbian S/M* (Boston: Alyson Publications, 1982); *Against Sadomasochism: A Radical Feminist Analysis*, ed. Robin Ruth Linden, Darlene R. Pagano, Diana E. H. Russell, and Susan Leigh Star (East Palo Alto, CA: Frog in the Well Press, 1982); Chris Bearchell, "Why I am a gay liberationist: thoughts on sex, freedom, the family and the state," *Resources for Feminist Research / Documentation sur la Recherche Féministe [RFR/DRF]* 12, no. 1 (March/Mars 1983): 57–60; Wendy Clark, "The Dyke, the Feminist and the Devil," in *Sexuality: A Reader*, ed. Feminist Review (London: Virago, 1987), 201–15; Marilyn Frye, "Lesbian Feminism and the Gay Rights Movement: Another View of Male Supremacy, Another Separatism," in *The Politics of Reality: Essays in Feminist Theory* (Trumansburg, NY: The Crossing Press, 1983), 128–50; Pat Califia, "Introduction," in *Macho Sluts: Erotic Fiction* (Boston: Alyson Publications, 1988), 9–27; Gayle Rubin, "Thinking Sex: Notes for a Radical Theory of the Politics of Sexuality," in *Pleasure and Danger*, pp. 267–319; Jacqueline Rose, "Femininity and Its Discontents," *Feminist Review* 14 (Summer 1983): 5–21, a response to Elizabeth Wilson, "Psychoanalysis: Psychic Law and Order," *Feminist Review* 8 (Summer 1981).

11. Teresa de Lauretis, "The Essence of the Triangle or, Taking the Risk of Essentialism Seriously: Feminist Theory in Italy, the U.S., and Britain," *Differences: A Journal of Feminist Cultural Studies* 1, no. 2 (Summer 1989): 3–37. The text I discuss there is Libreria delle Donne di Milano, *Non credere di avere dei diritti: La generazione della libertà femminile nell'idea e nelle vicende di un gruppo di donne* ["Don't Think You Have Any Rights: The Engendering of Female Freedom in the Thought and Vicissitudes of a Women's Group"] (Turin: Rosenberg & Sellier, 1987). An English translation of this book is forthcoming by Indiana University Press with the title *Sexual Difference: A Theory of Social-Symbolic Practice* (1990).

12. Teresa de Lauretis, *Technologies of Gender: Essays on Theory, Film, and Fiction* (Bloomington: Indiana University Press, 1987), 26.

13. See, for example, Moira Gatens, "A Critique of the Sex/Gender Distinction," in *Beyond Marxism: Interventions After Marx*, ed. J. Allen and P. Patton (Sydney: Intervention Press, 1983), 143–60; B. Ruby Rich, "Anti-Porn: Soft Issue, Hard World," *The Village Voice*, July 20, 1982; Sue-Ellen Case, "Towards a Butch-Femme Aesthetic," *Discourse: Journal for Theoretical Studies in Media and Culture* 11, no. 1 (Fall–Winter 1988–89): 55–73; and Mariana Valverde, "Beyond Gender Dangers and Private Pleasures: Theory and Ethics in the Sex Debates," *Feminist Studies* 15, no. 2 (Summer 1989): 237–54.

14. For example, Jaggar and Rothenberg in *Feminist Frameworks*: "We believe that the feminist struggle must be guided by feminist theory, by a systematic analysis of the underlying nature and causes of women's oppression" (p. xii).

body

"**W**rite yourself. Your body must be heard." Since Hélène Cixous first issued this call in 1975, there have been continual attempts to sort out just what it means, what a discourse that "let the body be heard" would look like, and whether it is even possible. What would it mean for the body to have a language? What would the body say?

Of course, one could take these questions literally, but their real import is to raise the issue of sexual difference, to suggest that perhaps difference extends into the realm of language. Indeed, the essays here raise the possible existence of *l'écriture féminine*, "feminine writing," which is different from the kind of writing usually valued in Western culture, and which is specifically gendered. Although not restricted to writers who are biologically sexed female (Cixous offers Jean Genet as one of her examples), feminine writing nonetheless is seen here to vary along gender lines, to correspond to culturally determined gender codes: *his* language is rational, logical, hierarchical, and linear; *her* language is arational (if not irrational), contralogical (if not illogical), resistant to hierarchies, and circular.

At the heart of the movement that is called *l'écriture féminine* (founded by several women writers in France, including Cixous and Irigaray in the mid-1970s) is a refusal to accept the traditional Western separation of mind and body. As in so many other kinds of oppositional definitions, one term has historically been privileged at the expense of the other, and one has been linked with the male, one with the female (for an elaboration of the implications of these oppositions for feminism, see Shoshana Felman's essay in "Institutions"). Woman, linked with body rather than mind, was supposed to be antithetical to writing, an activity said to be restricted to the mental. The authors associated with *l'écriture féminine* have challenged these traditional notions in two ways: first, by celebrating woman's association with the body, thereby refusing the subordination of body to mind, and second, by refusing to accept the separation between the two. "Writing the body" or "letting the body be heard" are clearly attempts at refusing the sense of writing as a strictly mental thing.

The field that has, to date, most thoroughly explored the connections between mind, body, and language is psychoanalysis, so the writings of Sigmund Freud and French psychoanalyst Jacques Lacan serve as important subtexts to both Cixous's and Irigaray's essays (readers who are not familiar with Lacanian theory and terminology may want to read the introduction to "Desire" before reading the essays here). Questions of the relation between being biologically sexed female and culturally gendered feminine are central to all five of the essays. Unlike Freud, who saw female sexuality as a "dark continent" that had not yet been explored, these authors see female sexuality as something that is likely to be apparent in a woman's written text. Although the five would not necessarily agree with Freud's postulate that "biology is destiny," they do raise the possibility that biology makes itself heard in literary discourse.

Hélène Cixous's influential and often-cited essay, "The Laugh of the Medusa" (published in French in 1975; revised and translated into English 1976), is impossible to summarize, and for good reasons. Simultaneously, this essay *is about* and *is* "feminine writing." Here, Cixous both discusses and illustrates her theories of women's writing; it is not linear, logical, or progressive, which means it is not constrained by traditional (masculine? patriarchal?) notions of argumentation and development. The movement of the essay is more fluid than direct, more experiential than argumentative. Cixous aims for her reader to understand the nature of women's writing as much from the way in which she writes, as from what she writes about.

Cixous's essay is highly quotable and challenging. Her claim that women writers always retain a bit of the mother in them ("There is always within her at least a little of that good mother's milk. She writes in white ink.") provides a richness of evocation and metaphor that has spoken to a large number of feminist writers and critics. But such claims also remain troubling to feminists who have resisted a sense of being tied to the biological. Cixous's writing provides a central focus for questions of separatism, biological determinism, and bodily metaphors—how far should we take our insistence upon difference? "The Laugh of the Medusa," as its title might suggest, ultimately celebrates that which in women has been denigrated for centuries, and urges us to embrace "difference" and to use it.

In "This Sex Which Is Not One" (published in French 1977; translated into English 1985), Luce Irigaray carries on Cixous's celebration of the difference of the female body, and develops issues she raises in *Speculum of the Other Woman* (part of which is reprinted in this volume, in "Gaze"). Rejecting traditional psychoanalytic notions, which take male sexuality as the norm and model, Irigaray suggests that female sexuality is not marked by "lack" (the lack of a penis, of a singular sex organ), but by multiplicity and abundance. Working by analogy, then, Irigaray argues that femininity—and the language of femininity—is not singular (not "one") either, but multiple. Therefore, woman's pleasure in language, like her pleasure in sexuality, is not direct, linear or singular: "'She' sets off in all directions leaving 'him' unable to discern the coherence of any meaning." Being forced into masculine language, on the other hand, leaves woman always missing pieces of herself, makes her experience herself as fragmented. Irigaray suggests that the realization of this language would not result in women's "wholeness," if by that we mean "unicity" and singularity, nor in "ownership" (she finds property and ownership to be foreign to femininity), but that its realization would allow for woman's "nearness" to herself.

"This Sex Which Is Not One" closes with an analysis of the oppression of women, an oppression which Irigaray sees in terms set out by Marx and French anthropologist Claude Lévi-Strauss; women are turned into property, into objects of exchange between men, a transaction which denies their subjectivity and turns them into objects. Irigaray urges women to use their nearness to themselves to develop a closeness to each other, to work together to resist the oppression that denies them their pleasure and their language.

Ann Rosalind Jones summarizes and critiques the work of four French feminist writers (Julia Kristeva, Luce Irigaray, Hélène Cixous, and Monique Wittig) in "Writing the Body: Toward an Understanding of *L'Écriture féminine*" (1981). She explains at what points these writers differ from and agree with one another, noting that while Irigaray, Cixous, and Wittig envision a separate language for women, metaphorically based on women's physical experience of sexuality, Kristeva sees women's role in language primarily as providing oppositional force within traditional discourses. Jones offers several cautions about *l'écriture féminine*, though. She warns against the notion of an "essential" female sexuality, noting that all psychoanalytic models of sexuality (from which Irigaray and Cixous work) recognize sexuality as culturally constructed. To accept these cultural constructs as "natural," she argues, could be dangerous. She further cautions against the political effects of taking "women" as too generalized a category, since race, class, and national origin may account for more differences than would gender. Finally, Jones questions whether "writing from the body" is possible—given many women's difficulties with using language—or desirable—given the richness of our historical connections to cultural and linguistic traditions. Despite these reservations, Jones urges American feminists to take the critique offered by *l'écriture féminine* seriously, and to put its hopeful offer of real possibilities into play.

Both Cixous and Irigaray place their writing about the body within a discussion of economics—Irigaray to argue that women's bodies have been made objects of exchange, Cixous to suggest that women's bodies may offer a model for economics in which exchange is not operative. In "Mama's Baby, Papa's Maybe: An American Grammar Book" (1987), Hortense Spillers, like Irigaray, examines the relation between language, the body, and ownership, and like Cixous, examines the relation between language and maternity. Unlike Irigaray, though, Spillers grounds her analysis in a specific history of racialized and enslaved bodies that were literally owned and traded; unlike Cixous, she examines a maternity in which relations between mother and child are subjected to an accounting in which maternity equals the (re)production of more slave labor. Moving away from *l'écriture féminine*, and into a more material context, Spillers situates her discussion of "the body" within the history of dominance, specifically, a history of the "captive" body. Acknowledging the power and attraction of the poststructural impulse to metaphorize the body, Spillers nonetheless asks us to remember that "before the 'body' there is the 'flesh,' that zero degree of social conceptualization that does not escape concealment under the brush of discourse." She seeks to examine the intersection between myth-making, human biology, and the "project of culture," and points to the captive body as a site which "brings into focus a gathering of our social realities as well as a metaphor for value so thoroughly interwoven in their literal and figurative emphases that distinctions between them are virtually useless."

Spillers reads contemporary social theory of the African-American family in the context of a history of dominance, enslavement, and torture, a history in which families were violently sundered, paternity was often denied, and maternity was stripped away. When language and the dominant culture are understood to be ruled by the "Law of the Father," she asks, what happens to language and literature in a dominated culture in which fathers have been systematically dispossessed? (For an explanation of the term "Law of the Father," see the introduction to "Desire" in this volume.) Does one become subject to a "Law of the Mother"? What happens to naming, then, in a culture embedded in a literal history of stripping away "real names" and in which the figural relation between language and maternity/paternity is tainted by the violent sundering of families? Spillers argues that the loss of land, name, and parents becomes a "metaphor of displacement for other human and cultural features and relations," including the relation to gender, one's own body, and language.

In "'Women of Color' Writers and Feminist Theory" (1994), Margaret Homans looks at the role of "the body" in contemporary feminist criticism. In one way, Homans echoes Cixous's earlier questioning of the separation and hierarchizing of mind and body, though here Homans examines the way that bifurcation replicates itself in feminist theory itself. She begins with a narrative by Alice Walker and an observation by Barbara Christian that people of color theorize in forms that are different from traditional Western logic, and often unrecognizable as theory to white people. She then asks what theoretical work Walker's narrative might be doing. To answer this question, Homans must frame her question with debates about race and feminist theory, and about poststructuralism and feminist theory. Homans points out that white feminist theorists often see women of color as not doing "theory," but instead invoke them as examples or representatives of the experience of oppression. She points out that in the same way that the European tradition categorizes the black person as "body" so the white can represent "mind," white feminist theory too often employs the same binary thinking that separates "theory and examples, or mind and body, [so] the black woman equals the body or the example." Homans discusses a "cultural problematic" in some of the most influential texts of Donna Haraway, Judith Butler, and Diana Fuss, a problem she identifies as connected to "race relations in the academy . . . and . . . the uses of postmodernist theory for feminist political practice." Homans questions what it means to identify women of color with the body within a context in which theoretical abstraction *from* the body is valued, and asks, "What is the status of *any* body in that context?"

In raising these questions, Homans does not simply challenge white feminists' use of women of color writers (an activity in which, she acknowledges, she herself engages), but also interrogates the usefulness of a postmodern critique that would completely disembody identity. As a solution to the problem of a disembodied postmodernism, Homans returns to a narrative by Patricia Williams and the one by Alice Walker with which she began, to suggest that, like many of women of color writers, Williams and Walker represent their bodies by setting humanist and poststructuralist versions of identity into a constructive dialogue. In so doing, Homans argues, they simultaneously set out a way of theorizing that is neither disembodied nor so concrete it cannot function abstractly: "Walker and Williams both write of their selves as unstable constructions provisionally made up of different and continuously shifting elements and especially of different languages. At the same time, they keep in mind practical considerations about living and acting politically in the world." Homans argues then for an *embodied* feminist criticism that nevertheless understands the construction of identity, and the place of the body in culture.

—DPH

THE LAUGH OF THE MEDUSA

(1975)

I shall speak about women's writing: about *what it will do*. Woman must write her self: must write about women and bring women to writing, from which they have been driven away as violently as from their bodies—for the same reasons, by the same law, with the same fatal goal. Woman must put herself into the text—as into the world and into history—by her own movement.

The future must no longer be determined by the past. I do not deny that the effects of the past are still with us. But I refuse to strengthen them by repeating them, to confer upon them an irremovability the equivalent of destiny, to confuse the biological and the cultural. Anticipation is imperative.

Since these reflections are taking shape in an area just on the point of being discovered, they necessarily bear the mark of our time—a time during which the new breaks away from the old, and, more precisely, the (feminine) new from the old (*la nouvelle de l'ancien*). Thus, as there are no grounds for establishing a discourse, but rather an arid millennial ground to break, what I say has at least two sides and two aims: to break up, to destroy; and to foresee the unforeseeable, to project.

I write this as a woman, toward women. When I say "woman," I'm speaking of woman in her inevitable struggle against conventional man; and of a universal woman subject who must bring women to their senses and to their meaning in history. But first it must be said that in spite of the enormity of the repression that has kept them in the "dark"—that dark which people have been trying to make them accept as their attribute—there is, at this time, no general woman, no one typical woman. What they have *in common* I will say. But what strikes me is the infinite richness of their individual constitutions: you can't talk about *a* female sexuality, uniform, homogeneous, classifiable into codes—any more than you can talk about one unconscious resembling another. Women's imaginary is inexhaustible, like music, painting, writing: their stream of phantasms is incredible.

I have been amazed more than once by a description a woman gave me of a world all her own which she had been secretly haunting since early childhood. A world of searching, the elaboration of knowledge, on the basis of a systematic experimentation with the bodily functions, a passionate and precise interrogation of her erotogeneity. This practice, extraordinarily rich and inventive, in particular as concerns masturbation, is prolonged or accompanied by a production of forms, a veritable aesthetic activity, each stage of rapture inscribing a resonant vision, a composition, something beautiful. Beauty will no longer be forbidden.

I wished that that woman would write and proclaim this unique empire so that other women, other unacknowledged sovereigns, might exclaim: I, too, overflow; my desires have invented new desires, my body knows unheard-of songs. Time and again I, too, have felt so full of luminous torrents that I could burst—burst with forms much more beautiful than those which are put up in frames and sold for a stinking fortune. And I, too, said nothing, showed nothing; I didn't open my mouth, I didn't repaint my half of the world. I was ashamed. I was afraid, and I swallowed my shame and my fear. I said to myself: You are mad! What's the meaning of these waves, these floods, these outbursts? Where is the ebullient, infinite woman who, immersed as she was in her naïveté, kept in the dark about herself, led into self-disdain by the great arm of parental-conjugal phallocentrism, hasn't been ashamed of her strength? Who, surprised and horrified by the fantastic tumult of her drives (for she was made to believe that a well-adjusted normal woman has a . . . divine composure), hasn't accused herself of being a monster? Who, feeling a funny desire stirring inside her (to sing, to write, to dare to speak, in short, to bring out something new), hasn't thought she was sick? Well, her shameful sickness is that she resists death, that she makes trouble.

And why don't you write? Write! Writing is for you, you are for you; your body is yours, take it. I know why you haven't written. (And why I didn't write before the age of twenty-seven.) Because writing is at once too high, too great for you, it's reserved for the great—that is for "great men"; and it's "silly." Besides, you've written a little, but in secret. And it wasn't good, because it was in secret, and because you punished yourself for writing, because you didn't go all the way, or because you wrote, irresistibly, as when we would masturbate in secret, not to go further, but to attenuate the tension a bit, just enough to take the edge off. And then as soon as we come, we go and make ourselves feel guilty—so as to be forgiven; or to forget, to bury it until next time.

Write, let no one hold you back, let nothing stop you: not man; not the imbecilic capitalist machinery, in which publishing houses are the crafty, obsequious relayers of imperatives handed down by an economy that works against us and off our backs; and not *yourself*. Smug-faced readers, managing editors, and big bosses don't like the true texts of women—female-sexed texts. That kind scares them.

I write woman: woman must write woman. And man, man. So only an oblique consideration will be found here of man; it's up to him to say where his masculinity and femininity are at: this will concern us once men have opened their eyes and seen themselves clearly.[1]

Now women return from afar, from always: from "without," from the heath where witches are kept alive; from below, from beyond "culture"; from their childhood which men have been trying desperately to make them forget, condemning it to "eternal rest." The little girls and their "ill-mannered" bodies immured, well-preserved, intact unto themselves, in the mirror. Frigidified. But are they ever seething underneath! What an effort it takes—there's no end to it—for the sex cops to bar their threatening return. Such a display of forces on both sides that the struggle has for centuries been immobilized in the trembling equilibrium of a deadlock.

Here they are, returning, arriving over and again, because the unconscious is impregnable. They have wandered around in circles, confined to the narrow room in which they've been given a deadly brainwashing. You can incarcerate them, slow them down, get away with the old Apartheid routine, but for a time only. As soon as they begin to speak, at the same time as they're taught their name, they can be taught that their territory is black: because you are Africa, you are black. Your continent is dark. Dark is dangerous. You can't see anything in the dark, you're afraid. Don't move, you might fall. Most of all, don't go into the forest. And so we have internalized this horror of the dark.

Men have committed the greatest crime against women. Insidiously, violently, they have led them to hate women, to be their own enemies, to mobilize their immense strength against themselves, to be the executants of their virile needs. They have made for women an antinarcissism! A narcissism which loves itself only to be loved for what women haven't got! They have constructed the infamous logic of antilove.

We the precocious, we the repressed of culture, our lovely mouths gagged with pollen, our wind knocked out of us, we the labyrinths, the ladders, the trampled spaces, the bevies—we are black and we are beautiful.

We're stormy, and that which is ours breaks loose from us without our fearing any debilitation. Our glances, our smiles, are spent; laughs exude from all our mouths; our blood flows and we extend ourselves without ever reaching an end; we never hold back our thoughts, our signs, our writing; and we're not afraid of lacking.

What happiness for us who are omitted, brushed aside at the scene of inheritances; we inspire ourselves and we expire without running out of breath, we are everywhere!

From now on, who, if we say so, can say no to us? We've come back from always.

It is time to liberate the New Woman from the Old by coming to know her—by loving her for getting by, for getting beyond the Old without delay, by going out ahead of what the New Woman will be, as an arrow quits the bow with a movement that gathers and separates the vibrations musically, in order to be more than her self.

I say that we must, for, with a few rare exceptions, there has not yet been any writing that inscribes femininity; exceptions so rare, in fact, that, after plowing through literature across languages, cultures, and ages,[2] one can only be startled at this vain scouting mission. It is well known that the number of women writers (while having increased very slightly from the nineteenth century on) has always been ridiculously small. This is a useless and deceptive fact unless from their species of female writers we do not first deduct the immense majority whose workmanship is in no way different from male writing, and which either obscures women or reproduces the classic representations of women (as sensitive—intuitive—dreamy, etc.).[3]

Let me insert here a parenthetical remark. I mean it when I speak of male writing. I maintain unequivocally that there is such a thing as *marked* writing; that, until now, far more extensively and repressively than is ever suspected or admitted, writing has been run by a libidinal and cultural—hence political, typically masculine—economy; that this is a locus where the repression of women has been perpetuated, over and over, more or less consciously, and in a manner that's frightening since it's often hidden or adorned with the mystifying charms of fiction; that this locus has grossly exaggerated all the signs of sexual opposition (and not sexual difference), where woman has never *her* turn to speak—this being all the more serious and unpardonable in that writing is precisely *the very possibility of change*, the space that can serve as a springboard for subversive thought, the precursory movement of a transformation of social and cultural structures.

Nearly the entire history of writing is confounded with the history of reason, of which it is at once the effect, the support, and one of the privileged alibis. It has been one with the phallocentric tradition. It is indeed that same self-admiring, self-stimulating, self-congratulatory phallocentrism.

With some exceptions, for there have been failures—and if it weren't for them, I wouldn't be writing (I-woman, escapee)—in that enormous machine that has been operating and turning out its "truth" for centuries. There have been poets who would go to any lengths to slip something by at odds with tradition—men capable of loving love and hence capable of loving others and of wanting them, of imagining the woman who would hold out against oppression and constitute herself as a superb, equal, hence "impossible" subject, untenable in a real social framework. Such a woman the poet could desire only by breaking the codes that negate her. Her appearance would necessarily bring on, if not revolution—for the bastion was supposed to be immutable—at least harrowing explosions. At times it is in the fissure caused by an earthquake, through that radical mutation of things brought on by a material upheaval when every structure is for a moment thrown off balance and an ephemeral wildness sweeps order away, that the poet slips something by, for a brief span, of woman. Thus did Kliest expend himself in his yearning for the existence of sister-lovers, maternal daughters, mother-sisters, who never hung their heads in shame. Once the palace of magistrates is restored, it's time to pay: immediate bloody death to the uncontrollable elements.

But only the poets—not the novelists, allies of representationalism. Because poetry involves gaining strength through the unconscious and because the unconscious, that other limitless country, is the place where the repressed manage to survive: women, or as Hoffman would say, fairies.

She must write her self, because this is the invention of a *new insurgent* writing which, when the moment of her liberation has come, will allow her to carry out the indispensable ruptures and transformations in her history, first at two levels that cannot be separated.

a) Individually. By writing her self, woman will return to the body which has been more than confiscated from her, which has been turned into the uncanny stranger on display—the ailing or dead figure, which so often turns out to be the nasty companion, the cause and location of inhibitions. Censor the body and you censor breath and speech at the same time.

Write your self. Your body must be heard. Only then will the immense resources of the unconscious spring forth. Our naphtha will spread, throughout the world, without dollars—black or gold—nonassessed values that will change the rules of the old game.

To write. An act which will not only "realize" the decensored relation of woman to her sexuality, to her womanly being, giving her access to her native strength; it will give her back her goods, her pleasures, her organs, her immense bodily territories which have been kept under seal; it will tear her away from the superegoized structure in which she has always occupied the place reserved for the guilty (guilty of everything, guilty at every turn: for having desires, for not having any; for being frigid, for being "too hot"; for not being both at once; for being too motherly and not enough; for having children and for not having any; for nursing and for not nursing . . .)—tear her away by means of this research, this job of analysis and illumination, this emancipation of the marvelous text of her self that she must urgently learn to speak. A woman without a body, dumb, blind, can't possibly be a good fighter. She is reduced to being the servant of the militant male, his shadow. We must kill the false woman who is preventing the live one from breathing. Inscribe the breath of the whole woman.

b) An act that will also be marked by woman's *seizing* the occasion to *speak*, hence her shattering entry into history, which has always been based *on her suppression*. To write and thus to forge for herself the antilogos weapon. To become *at will* the taker and initiator, for her own right, in every symbolic system, in every political process.

It is time for women to start scoring their feats in written and oral language.

Every woman has known the torment of getting up to speak. Her heart racing, at times entirely lost for words, ground and language slipping away—that's how daring a feat, how great a transgression it is for a woman to speak—even just open her mouth—in public. A double distress, for even if she transgresses, her words fall almost always upon the deaf male ear, which hears in language only that which speaks in the masculine.

It is by writing, from and toward women, and by taking up the challenge of speech which has been governed by the phallus, that women will confirm women in a place other than that which is reserved in and by the symbolic, that is, in a place other than silence. Women should break out of the snare of silence. They shouldn't be conned into accepting a domain which is the margin or the harem.

Listen to a woman speak at a public gathering (if she hasn't painfully lost her wind). She doesn't "speak," she throws her trembling body forward; she lets go of herself, she flies; all of her passes into her voice, and it's with her body that she vitally supports the "logic" of her speech. Her flesh speaks true. She lays herself bare. In fact, she physically materializes what she's thinking; she signifies it with her body. In a certain way she *inscribes* what she's saying, because she doesn't deny her drives the intractable and impassioned part they have in speaking. Her speech, even when "theoretical" or political, is never simple or linear or "objectified," generalized: she draws her story into history.

There is not that scission, that division made by the common man between the logic of oral speech and the logic of the text, bound as he is by his antiquated relation—servile, calculating—to mastery. From which proceeds the niggardly lip service which engages only the tiniest part of the body, plus the mask.

In women's speech, as in their writing, that element which never stops resonating, which, once we've been permeated by it, profoundly and imperceptibly touched by it, retains the power of moving us—that element is the song: first music from the first voice of love which is alive in every woman. Why this privileged relationship with the voice? Because no woman stockpiles as many defenses for countering the drives as does a man. You don't build walls around yourself, you don't forgo pleasure as "wisely" as he. Even if phallic mystification has generally contaminated good relationships, a woman is never far from "mother" (I mean outside her role functions: the "mother" as nonname and as source of goods). There is always within her at least a little of that good mother's milk. She writes in white ink.

Woman for women.—There always remains in woman that force which produces/ is produced by the other—in particular, the other woman. *In* her, matrix, cradler; herself giver as her mother and child; she is her own sister-daughter. You might object, "What about she who is the hysterical offspring of a bad mother?" Everything will be changed once woman gives woman to the other woman. There is hidden and always ready in woman the source; the locus for the other. The mother, too, is a metaphor. It is necessary and sufficient that the best of herself be given to woman by another woman for her to be able to love herself and return in love the body that was "born" to her. Touch me, caress me, you the living no-name, give me my self as myself. The relation to the "mother," in terms of intense pleasure and violence, is curtailed no more than the relation to childhood (the child that she was, that she is, that she makes, remakes, undoes, there at the point where, the same, she mothers herself). Text: my body—shot through with streams of song; I don't mean the overbearing, clutchy "mother" but, rather, what touches you, the equivoice that affects you, fills your breast with an urge to come to language and launches your force; the rhythm that laughs you; the intimate recipient who makes all metaphors possible and desirable; body (body? bodies?), no more describable than god, the soul, or the Other; that part of you that leaves a space between yourself and urges you to inscribe in language your woman's style. In women there is always more or less of the mother who makes everything all right, who nourishes, and who stands up against separation; a force that will not be cut off but will knock the wind out of the codes. We will rethink womankind beginning with every form and every period of her body. The Americans remind us, "We are all Lesbians"; that is, don't denigrate woman, don't make of her what men have made of you.

Because the "economy" of her drives is prodigious, she cannot fail, in seizing the occasion to speak, to transform directly and indirectly *all* systems of exchange based on masculine thrift. Her libido will produce far more radical effects of political and social change than some might like to think.

Because she arrives, vibrant, over and again, we are at the beginning of a new history, or rather of a process of becoming in which several histories intersect with one another. As subject for history, woman always occurs simultaneously in several places. Woman un-thinks[4] the unifying, regulating history that homogenizes and channels forces, herding contradictions into a single battlefield. In woman, personal history blends together with the history of all women, as well as national and world history. As a militant, she is an integral part of all liberations. She must be farsighted, not limited to blow-by-blow interaction. She foresees that her liberation will do more than modify power relations or toss the ball over to the other camp; she will bring about a mutation in human relations, in thought, in all praxis: hers is not simply a class struggle, which she carries forward into a much vaster movement. Not that in order to be a woman-in-struggle(s) you have to leave the class struggle or repudiate it; but you have to split it open, spread it out, push it forward, fill it with the fundamental struggle so as to prevent the class struggle, or any other struggle for the liberation of a class of people, from operating as a form of repression, pretext for postponing the inevitable, the staggering alteration in power relations and in the production of individuals. This alteration is already upon us—in the United States, for example, where millions of night crawlers are in the process of undermining the family and disintegrating the whole of American sociality.

The new history is coming; it's not a dream, though it does extend beyond men's imagination, and for good reason. It's going to deprive them of their conceptual orthopedics, beginning with the destruction of their enticement machine.

It is impossible to *define* a feminine practice of writing, and this is an impossibility that will remain, for this practice can never be theorized, enclosed, coded—which doesn't mean that it doesn't exist. But it will always surpass the discourse that regulates the phallocentric system; it does and will take place in areas other than those subordinated to philosophico-theoretical domination. It will be conceived of only by subjects who are breakers of automatisms, by peripheral figures that no authority can ever subjugate.

Hence the necessity to affirm the flourishes of this writing, to give form to its movement, its near and distant byways. Bear in mind to begin with (1) that sexual opposition, which has always worked for man's profit to the point of reducing writing, too, to his laws, is only a historico-cultural limit. There is, there will be more and more rapidly pervasive now, a fiction that produces irreducible effects of femininity. (2) That it is through ignorance that most readers, critics, and writers of both sexes hesitate to admit or deny outright the possibility or the pertinence of a distinction between feminine and masculine writing. It will usually be said, thus disposing of sexual difference: either that all writing, to the extent that it materializes, is feminine; or, inversely—but it comes to the same thing—that the act of writing is equivalent to masculine masturbation (and so the woman who writes cuts herself out a paper penis); or that writing is bisexual, hence neuter, which again does away with differentiation. To admit that writing is precisely working (in) the in-between, inspecting the process of the same and of the other without which nothing can live, undoing the work of death—to admit this is first to want the two, as well as both, the ensemble of the one and the other, not fixed in sequences of struggle and expulsion or some other form of death but infinitely dynamized by an incessant process of exchange from one subject to another. A process of different subjects knowing one another and beginning one another anew only from the living boundaries of the other: a multiple and inexhaustible course with millions of encounters and transformations of the same into the other and into the in-between, from which woman takes her forms (and man, in his turn; but that's his other history).

In saying "bisexual, hence neuter," I am referring to the classic conception of bisexuality, which, squashed under the emblem of castration fear and along with the fantasy of a "total" being (though composed of two halves), would do away with the difference experienced as an operation incurring loss, as the mark of dreaded sectility.

To this self-effacing, merger-type bisexuality, which would conjure away castration (the writer who puts up his sign: "bisexual written here, come and see," when the odds are good that it's neither one nor the other), I oppose the *other bisexuality* on which every subject not enclosed in the false theater of phallocentric representationalism has founded his/her erotic universe. Bisexuality: that is, each one's location in self (*repérage en soi*) of the presence—variously manifest and insistent according to each person, male or female—of both sexes, nonexclusion either of the difference or of one sex, and, from this "self-permission," multiplication of the effects of the inscription of desire, over all parts of my body and the other body.

Now it happens that at present, for historico-cultural reasons, it is women who are opening up to and benefiting from this vatic bisexuality which doesn't annul differences but stirs them up, pursues them, increases their number. In a certain way, "woman is bisexual"; man—it's a secret to no one—being poised to keep glorious phallic monosexuality in view. By virtue of affirming the primacy of the phallus and of bringing it into play, phallocratic ideology has claimed more than one victim. As a woman, I've been clouded over by the great shadow of the scepter and been told: idolize it, that which you cannot brandish. But at the same time, man has been handed that grotesque and scarcely enviable destiny (just imagine) of being reduced to a single idol with clay balls. And consumed, as Freud and his followers note, by a fear of being a woman! For, if psychoanalysis was constituted from woman, to repress femininity (and not so successful a repression at that—men have made it clear), its account of masculine sexuality is now hardly refutable: as with all the "human" sciences, it reproduces the masculine view, of which it is one of the effects.

Here we encounter the inevitable man-with-rock, standing erect in his old Freudian realm, in the way that, to take the figure back to the point where linguistics is conceptualizing it "anew," Lacan preserves it in the sanctuary of the phallos (ϕ) "sheltered" from *castration's lack!* Their "symbolic" exists, it holds power—we, the sowers of disorder, know it only too well. But we are in no way obliged to deposit our lives in their banks of lack, to consider the constitution of the subject in terms of a drama manglingly restaged, to reinstate again and again the religion of the father. Because we don't want that. We don't fawn around the supreme hole. We have no womanly reason to pledge allegiance to the negative. The feminine (as the poets suspected) affirms: " . . . And yes," says Molly, carrying *Ulysses* off beyond any book and toward the new writing: "I said yes, I will Yes."

The Dark Continent is neither dark nor unexplorable.—It is still unexplored only because we've been made to believe that it was too dark to be explorable. And because they want to make us believe that what interests us is the white continent, with its monuments to Lack. And we believed. They riveted us between two horrifying myths: between the Medusa and the abyss. That would be enough to set half the world laughing, except that it's still going on. For the phallologocentric sublation[5] is with us, and it's militant, regenerating the old patterns, anchored in the dogma of castration. They haven't changed a thing: they've theorized their desire for reality! Let the priests tremble, we're going to show them our sexts!

Too bad for them if they fall apart upon discovering that women aren't men, or that the mother doesn't have one. But isn't this fear convenient for them? Wouldn't the worst be, isn't the worst, in truth, that women aren't castrated, that they have only to stop listening to the Sirens (for the Sirens were men) for history to change its meaning? You only have to look at the Medusa straight on to see her. And she's not deadly. She's beautiful and she's laughing.

Men say that there are two unrepresentable things: death and the feminine sex. That's because they need femininity to be associated with death; it's the jitters that give them a hard-on! for themselves! They need to be afraid of us. Look at the trembling Perseuses moving backward toward us, clad in apotropes. What lovely backs! Not another minute to lose. Let's get out of here.

Let's hurry: the continent is not impenetrably dark. I've been there often. I was overjoyed one day to run into Jean Genet. It was in *Pompes funèbres*.[6] He had come there led by his Jean. There are some men (all too few) who aren't afraid of femininity.

Almost everything is yet to be written by women about femininity: about their sexuality, that is, its infinite and mobile complexity, about their eroticization, sudden turn-ons of a certain miniscule-immense area of their bodies; not about destiny, but about the adventure of such and such a drive, about trips, crossings, trudges, abrupt and gradual awakenings, discoveries of a zone at one time timorous and soon to be forthright. A woman's body, with its thousand and one thresholds of ardor—once, by smashing yokes and censors, she lets it articulate the profusion of meanings that run through it in every direction—will make the old single-grooved mother tongue reverberate with more than one language.

We've been turned away from our bodies, shamefully taught to ignore them, to strike them with that stupid sexual modesty; we've been made victims of the old fool's game: each one will love the other sex. I'll give you your body and you'll give me mine. But who are the men who give women the body that women blindly yield to them? Why so few texts? Because so few women have as yet won back their body. Women must write through their bodies, they must invent the impregnable language that will wreck partitions, classes, and rhetorics, regulations and codes, they must submerge, cut through, get beyond the ultimate reserve-discourse, including the one that laughs at the very idea of pronouncing the word "silence," the one that, aiming for the impossible, stops short before the word "impossible" and writes it as "the end."

Such is the strength of women that, sweeping away syntax, breaking that famous thread (just a tiny little thread, they say) which acts for men as a surrogate umbilical cord, assuring them—otherwise they couldn't come—that the old lady is always right behind them, watching them make phallus, women will go right up to the impossible.

When the "repressed" of their culture and their society returns, it's an explosive, *utterly* destructive, staggering return, with a force never yet unleashed and equal to the most forbidding of suppressions. For when the Phallic period comes to an end, women will have been either annihilated or borne up to the highest and most violent incandescence. Muffled throughout their history, they have lived in dreams, in bodies (though muted), in silences, in aphonic revolts.

And with such force in their fragility; a fragility, a vulnerability, equal to their incomparable intensity. Fortunately, they haven't sublimated; they've saved their skin, their energy. They haven't worked at liquidating the impasse of lives without futures. They have furiously inhabited these sumptuous bodies: admirable hysterics who made Freud succumb to many voluptuous moments impossible to confess, bombarding his Mosaic statue with their carnal and passionate body words, haunting him with their inaudible and thundering denunciations, dazzling, more than naked underneath the seven veils of modesty. Those who, with a single word of the body, have inscribed the vertiginous immensity of a history which is sprung like an arrow from the whole history of men and from biblico-capitalist society, are the women, the supplicants of yesterday, who come as fore-bears of the new women, after whom no intersubjective relation will ever be the same. You, Dora, you the indomitable, the poetic body, you are the true "mistress" of the Signifier. Before long your efficacity will be seen at work when your speech is no longer suppressed, its point turned in against your breast, but written out over against the other.

In body.—More so than men who are coaxed toward social success, toward sublimation, women are body. More body, hence more writing. For a long time it has been in body that women have responded to persecution, to the familial-conjugal enterprise of domestication, to the repeated attempts at castrating them. Those who have turned their tongues 10,000 times seven times before not speaking are either dead from it or more familiar with their tongues and their mouths than anyone else. No, I-woman am going to blow up the Law: an explosion henceforth possible and ineluctable; let it be done, right now, *in* language.

Let us not be trapped by an analysis still encumbered with the old automatisms. It's not to be feared that language conceals an invincible adversary, because it's the language of men and their grammar. We mustn't leave them a single place that's any more theirs alone than we are.

If woman has always functioned "within" the discourse of man, a signifier that has always referred back to the opposite signifier which annihilates its specific energy and diminishes or stifles its very different sounds, it is time for her to dislocate this "within," to explode it, turn it around, and seize it; to make it hers, containing it, taking it in her own mouth, biting that tongue with her very own teeth to invent for herself a language to get inside of. And you'll see with what ease she will spring forth from that "within"—the "within" where once she so drowsily crouched—to overflow at the lips she will cover the foam.

Nor is the point to appropriate their instruments, their concepts, their places, or to begrudge them their position of mastery. Just because there's a risk of identification doesn't mean that we'll succumb. Let's leave it to the worriers, to masculine anxiety and its obsession with how to dominate the way things work— knowing "how it works" in order to "make it work." For us the point is not to take possession in order to internalize or manipulate, but rather to dash through and to "fly."[7]

Flying is woman's gesture—flying in language and making it fly. We have all learned the art of flying and its numerous techniques; for centuries we've been able to possess anything only by flying; we've lived in flight, stealing away, finding, when desired, narrow passageways, hidden crossovers. It's no accident that *voler* has a double meaning, that it plays on each of them and thus throws off the agents of sense. It's no accident: women take after birds and robbers just as robbers take after women and birds. They (*illes*)[8] go by, fly the coop, take pleasure in jumbling the order of space, in disorienting it, in changing around the furniture, dislocating things and values, breaking them all up, emptying structures, and turning propriety upside down.

What woman hasn't flown/stolen? Who hasn't felt, dreamt, performed the gesture that jams sociality? Who hasn't crumbled, held up to ridicule, the bar of separation? Who hasn't inscribed with her body the differential, punctured the system of couples and opposition? Who, by some act of transgression, hasn't overthrown successiveness, connection, the wall of circumfusion?

A feminine text cannot fail to be more than subversive. It is volcanic; as it is written it brings about an upheaval of the old property crust, carrier of masculine investments; there's no other way. There's no room for her if she's not a he. If she's a her-she, it's in order to smash everything, to shatter the framework of institutions, to blow up the law, to break up the "truth" with laughter.

For once she blazes *her* trail in the symbolic, she cannot fail to make of it the chaosmos of the "personal"—in her pronouns, her nouns, and her clique of referents. And for good reason. There will have been the long history of gynocide. This is known by the colonized peoples of yesterday, the workers, the nations, the species off whose backs the history of men has made its gold; those who have known the ignominy of persecution derive from it an obstinate future desire for grandeur; those who are locked up know better than their jailers the taste of free air. Thanks to their history, women today know (how to do and want) what men will be able to conceive of only much later. I say woman overturns the "personal," for if, by means of laws, lies, blackmail, and marriage, her right to herself has been extorted at the same time as her name, she has been able, through the very movement of mortal alienation, to see more closely the inanity of "propriety," the reductive stinginess of the masculine-conjugal subjective economy, which she doubly resists. On the one hand she has constituted herself necessarily as that "person" capable of losing a part of herself without losing her integrity. But secretly, silently, deep down inside, she grows and multiplies, for, on the other hand, she knows far more about living and about the relation between the economy of the drives and the management of the ego than any man. Unlike man, who holds so dearly to his title and his titles, his pouches of value, his cap, crown, and everything connected with his head, woman couldn't care less about the fear of decapitation (or castration), adventuring, without the masculine temerity, into anonymity, which she can merge with, without annihilating herself: because she's a giver.

I shall have a great deal to say about the whole deceptive problematic of the gift. Woman is obviously not that woman Nietzsche dreamed of who gives only in order to.[9] Who could ever think of the gift as a gift-that-takes? Who else but man, precisely the one who would like to take everything?

If there is a "propriety of woman," it is paradoxically her capacity to depropriate unselfishly, body without end, without appendage, without principle "parts." If she is a whole, it's a whole composed of parts that are wholes, not simple partial objects but a moving, limitlessly changing ensemble, a cosmos tirelessly traversed by Eros, an immense astral space not organized around any one sun that's any more of a star than the others.

This doesn't mean that she's an undifferentiated magma, but that she doesn't lord it over her body or her desire. Though masculine sexuality gravitates around the penis, engendering that centralized body (in political anatomy) under the dictatorship of its parts, woman does not bring about the same regionalization which serves the couple head/genitals and which is inscribed only within boundaries. Her libido is cosmic, just as her unconscious is worldwide. Her writing can only keep going, without ever inscribing or discerning contours, daring to make these vertiginous crossings of the other(s) ephemeral and passionate sojourns in him, her, them, whom she inhabits long enough to look at from the point closest to their unconscious from the moment they awaken, to love them at the point closest to their drives; and then further, impregnated through and through with these brief, identificatory embraces, she goes and passes into infinity. She alone dares and wishes to know from within, where she, the outcast, has never ceased to hear the resonance of fore-language. She lets the other language speak—the language of 1,000 tongues which knows neither enclosure nor death. To life she refuses nothing. Her language does not contain, it carries; it does not hold back, it makes possible. When id is ambiguously uttered—the wonder of being several—she doesn't defend herself against these unknown women whom she's surprised at becoming, but derives pleasure from this gift of alterability. I am spacious, singing flesh, on which is grafted no one knows which I, more or less human, but alive because of transformation.

Write! and your self-seeking text will know itself better than flesh and blood, rising, insurrectionary dough kneading itself, with sonorous, perfumed ingredients, a lively combination of flying colors, leaves, and rivers plunging into the sea we feed. "Ah, there's her sea," he will say as he holds out to me a basin full of water from the little phallic mother from whom he's inseparable. But look, our seas are what we make of them, full of fish or not, opaque or transparent, red or black, high or smooth, narrow or bankless; and we are ourselves sea, sand, coral, seaweed, beaches, tides, swimmers, children, waves. . . . More or less wavily sea, earth, sky—what matter would rebuff us? We know how to speak them all.

Heterogeneous, yes. For her joyous benefits she is erogenous; she is the erotogeneity of the heterogeneous: airborne swimmer, in flight, she does not cling to herself; she is dispersible, prodigious, stunning, desirous and capable of others, of the other woman that she will be, of the other woman she isn't, of him, of you.

Woman, be unafraid of any other place, of any same, or any other. My eyes, my tongue, my ears, my nose, my skin, my mouth, my body-for-(the)-other—not that I long for it in order to fill up a hole, to provide against some defect of mine, or because, as fate would have it, I'm spurred on by feminine "jealousy"; not because I've been dragged into the whole chain of substitutions that brings that which is substituted back to its ultimate object. That sort of thing you would expect to come straight out of "Tom Thumb," out of the *Penisneid* whispered to us by old grandmother ogresses, servants to their father-sons. If they believe, in order to muster up some self-importance, if they really need to believe that we're dying of desire, that we are this hole fringed with desire for their penis—that's their immemorial business. Undeniably (we verify it at our own expenses—but also to our amusement), it's their business to let us know they're getting a hard-on, so that we'll assure them (we the maternal mistresses of their little pocket signifier) that they still can, that it's still there—that men structure themselves only by being fitted with a feather. In the child it's not the penis that the woman desires, it's not that famous bit of skin around which every man gravitates. Pregnancy cannot be traced back, except within the historical limits of the ancients, to some form of fate, to those mechanical substitutions brought about by the unconscious of some eternal "jealous woman"; not to penis envies; and not to narcissism or to some sort of homosexuality linked to the ever-present mother! Begetting a child doesn't mean that the woman or the man must fall ineluctably into patterns or must recharge the circuit of reproduction. If there's a risk there's not an inevitable trap: may women be spared the pressure, under the guise of consciousness-raising, of a supplement of interdictions. Either you want a kid or you don't—*that's your business.* Let nobody threaten you; in satisfying your desire, let not the fear of becoming the accomplice to a sociality succeed the old-time fear of being "taken." And man, are you still going to bank on everyone's blindness and passivity, afraid lest the child make a father and, consequently, that in having a kid the woman land herself more than one bad deal by engendering all at once child—mother—father—family? No; it's up to you to break the old circuits. It will be up to man and woman to render obsolete the former relationship and all its consequences, to consider the launching of a brand-new subject, alive, with defamilialization. Let us demater-paternalize rather than deny woman, in an effort to avoid the cooptation of procreation, a thrilling era of the body. Let us defetishize. Let's get away from the dialectic which has it that the only good father is a dead one, or that the child is the death of his parents. The child is the other, but the other without violence, bypassing loss, struggle. We're fed up with the reuniting of bonds forever to be severed, with the litany of castration that's handed down and genealogized. We won't advance backward anymore; we're not going to repress something so simple as the desire for life. Oral drive, anal drive, vocal drive—all these drives are our strengths, and among them is the gestation drive—just like the desire to write: a desire to live self from within, a desire for the swollen belly, for language, for blood. We are not going to refuse, if it should happen to strike our fancy, the unsurpassed pleasures of pregnancy which have actually been always exaggerated or conjured away—or cursed—in the classic texts. For if there's one thing that's been repressed, here's just the place to find it: in the taboo of the pregnant woman. This says a lot about the power she seems invested with at the time, because it has always been suspected, that, when pregnant, the woman not only doubles her market value, but—what's more important—takes on intrinsic value as a woman in her own eyes and, undeniably, acquires body and sex.

There are thousands of ways of living one's pregnancy; to have or not to have with that still invisible other a relationship of another intensity. And if you don't have that particular yearning, it doesn't mean that you're in any way lacking. Each body distributes in its own special way, without model or norm, the nonfinite and changing totality of its desires. Decide for yourself on your position in the arena of contradictions, where pleasure and reality embrace. Bring the other to life. Women know how to live detachment; giving birth is neither losing nor increasing. It's adding to life an other. Am I dreaming? Am I misrecognizing? You, the defenders of "theory," the sacrosanct yes-men of Concept, enthroners of the phallus (but not the penis):

Once more you'll say that all this smacks of "idealism," or what's worse, you'll splutter that I'm a "mystic."

And what about the libido? Haven't I read the "Signification of the Phallus"? And what about separation, what about that bit of self for which, to be born, you undergo an ablation—an ablation, so they say, to be forever commemorated by your desire?

Besides, isn't it evident that the penis gets around in my texts, that I give it a place and appeal? Of course I do. I want all. I want all of me with all of him. Why should I deprive myself of a part of us? I want all of us. Woman, of course, has a desire for a "loving desire" and not a jealous one. But not because she is gelded; not because she's deprived and needs to be filled out, like some wounded person who wants to console herself or seek vengeance. I don't want a penis to decorate my body with. But I do desire the other for the other, whole and entire, male or female; because living means wanting everything that is, everything that lives, and wanting it alive. Castration? Let others toy with it. What's a desire originating from a lack? A pretty meager desire.

The woman who still allows herself to be threatened by the big dick, who's still impressed by the commotion of the phallic stance, who still leads a loyal master to the beat of the drum: that's the woman of yesterday. They still exist, easy and numerous victims of the oldest of farces: either they're cast in the original silent versions in which, as titanesses lying under the mountains they make with their quivering, they never see erected that theoretic monument to the golden phallus looming, in the old manner, over their bodies. Or, coming today out of their *infans* period and into the second, "enlightened" version of their virtuous debasement, they see themselves suddenly assaulted by the builders of the analytic empire and, as soon as they've begun to formulate the new desire, naked, nameless, so happy at making an appearance, they're taken in their bath by the new old men, and then, whoops! Luring them with flashy signifiers, the demon of interpretation—oblique, decked out in modernity—sells them the same old handcuffs, baubles, and chains. Which castration do you prefer? Whose degrading do you like better, the father's or the mother's? Oh, what pwetty eyes, you pwetty little girl. Here, buy my glasses and you'll see the Truth-Me-Myself tell you everything you should know. Put them on your nose and take a fetishist's look (you are me, the other analyst—that's what I'm telling you) at your body and the body of the other. You see? No? Wait, you'll have everything explained to you, and you'll know at last which sort of neurosis you're related to. Hold still, we're going to do your portrait, so that you can begin looking like it right away.

Yes, the naïves to the first and second degree are still legion. If the New Women, arriving now, dare to create outside the theoretical, they're called in by the cops of the signifier, fingerprinted, remonstrated, and brought into the line of order that they are supposed to know; assigned by force of trickery to a precise place in the chain that's always formed for the benefit of a privileged signifier. We are pieced back to the string which leads back, if not to the Name-of-the-Father, then, for a new twist, to the place of the phallic-mother.

Beware, my friend, of the signifier that would take you back to the authority of a signified! Beware of diagnosis that would reduce your generative powers.

"Common" nouns are also proper nouns that disparage your singularity by classifying it into species. Break out of the circles; don't remain within the psychoanalytic closure. Take a look around, then cut through!

And if we are legion, it's because the war of liberation has only made as yet a tiny breakthrough. But women are thronging to it. I've seen them, those who will be neither dupe nor domestic, those who will not fear the risk of being a woman; will not fear any risk, any desire, any space still unexplored in themselves, among themselves and others or anywhere else. They do not fetishize, they do not deny, they do not hate. They observe, they approach, they try to see the other woman, the child, the lover—not to strengthen their own narcissism or verify the solidity or weakness of the master, but to make love better, to invent.

Other love.—In the beginning are our differences. The new love dares for the other, wants the other, makes dizzying, precipitous flights between knowledge and invention. The woman arriving over and over again does not stand still; she's everywhere, she exchanges, she is the desire-that-gives. (Not enclosed in the paradox of the gift that takes nor under the illusion of unitary fusion. We're past that.) She comes in, comes-in-between herself me and you, between the other me where one is always infinitely more than one and more than me, without the fear of ever reaching a limit; she thrills in our becoming. And we'll keep on becoming! She cuts through defensive loves, motherages, and devourations: beyond selfish narcissism, in the moving, open, transitional space, she runs her risks. Beyond the struggle-to-the-death that's been removed to the bed, beyond the love-battle that claims to represent exchange, she scorns at an Eros dynamic that would be fed by hatred. Hatred: a heritage, again, a reminder, a duping subservience to the phallus. To love, to watch-think-seek the other in the other, to despecularize, to unhoard. Does this seem difficult? It's not impossible, and this is what nourishes life—a love that has no commerce with the apprehensive desire that provides against the lack and stultifies the strange; a love that rejoices in the exchange that multiplies. Wherever history still unfolds as the history of death, she does not tread. Opposition, hierarchizing exchange, the struggle for mastery which can end only in at least one death (one master—one slave, or two nonmasters ≠ two dead)—all that comes from a period in time governed by phallocentric values. The fact that this period extends into the present doesn't prevent woman from starting the history of life somewhere else. Elsewhere, she gives. She doesn't "know" what she's giving, she doesn't measure it; she gives, though, neither a counterfeit impression nor something she hasn't got. She gives more, with no assurance that she'll get back even some unexpected profit from what she puts out. She gives that there may be life, thought, transformation. This is an "economy" that can no longer be put in economic terms. Wherever she loves, all the old concepts of management are left behind. At the end of a more or less conscious computation, she finds not her sum but her differences. I am for you what you want me to be at the moment you look at me in a way you've never seen me before: at every instant. When I write, it's everything that we don't know we can be that is written out of me, without exclusions, without stipulation, and everything we will be calls us to the unflagging, intoxicating, unappeasable search for love. In one another we will never be lacking.

Translated by Keith Cohen and Paula Cohen

NOTES

1. Men still have everything to say about their sexuality, and everything to write. For what they have said so far, for the most part, stems from the opposition activity/passivity from the power relation between a fantasized obligatory virility meant to invade, to colonize, and the consequential phantasm of woman as a "dark continent" to penetrate and to "pacify." (We know what "pacify" means in terms of scotomizing the other and misrecognizing the self.) Conquering her, they've made haste to depart from her borders, to get out of sight, out of body. The way man has of getting out of himself and into her whom he takes not for the other but for his own, deprives him, he knows, of his own bodily territory. One can understand how man, confusing himself with his penis and rushing in for the attack, might feel resentment and fear of being "taken" by the woman, of being lost in her, absorbed or alone.

2. I am speaking here only of the place "reserved" for women by the Western world.

3. Which works, then, might be called feminine? I'll just point out some examples: one would have to give them full readings to bring out what is pervasively feminine in their significance. Which I shall do elsewhere. In France (have you noted our infinite poverty in this field?—the Anglo-Saxon countries have shown resources of distinctly greater consequence), leafing through what's come out of the twentieth century—and it's not much—the only inscriptions of femininity that I have seen were by Colette, Marguerite Duras, . . . and Jean Genet.

4. *Dé-pense*, a neologism formed on the verb *penser*, hence "unthinks," but also "spends" (from *depenser*).—Tr.

5. Standard English term for the Hegelian *Aufhebung*, the French *la relève*.

6. Jean Genet, *Pompes funèbres* (Paris, 1948), p. 185 [privately published].

7. Also, "to steal." Both meanings of the verb *voler* are played on, as the text itself explains in the following paragraph.—Tr.

8. *Illes* is a fusion of the masculine pronoun *ils*, which refers back to birds and robbers, with the feminine pronoun *elles*, which refers to women.—Tr.

9. Reread Derrida's text, "Le style de la femme," in *Nietzsche aujourd'hui* (Union Générale d'Editions, Coll. 10/18), where the philosopher can be seen operating an *Aufhebung* of all philosophy in its systematic reducing of woman to the place of seduction: she appears as the one who is taken for; the bait in person, all veils unfurled, the one who doesn't give but who gives only in order to (take).

THIS SEX WHICH IS NOT ONE

(1977)

Female sexuality has always been conceptualized on the basis of masculine parameters. Thus the opposition between "masculine" clitoral activity and "feminine" vaginal passivity, an opposition which Freud—and many others—saw as stages, or alternatives in the development of a sexually "normal" woman, seems rather too clearly required by the practice of male sexuality. For the clitoris is conceived as a little penis pleasant to masturbate so long as castration anxiety does not exist (for the boy child), and the vagina is valued for the "lodging" it offers the male organ when the forbidden hand has to find a replacement for pleasure-giving.

In these terms, woman's erogenous zones never amount to anything but a clitoris-sex that is not comparable to the noble phallic organ, or a hole-envelope that serves to sheathe and massage the penis in intercourse: a non-sex, or a masculine organ turned back upon itself, self-embracing.

About woman and her pleasure, this view of the sexual relation has nothing to say. Her lot is that of "lack," "atrophy" (of the sexual organ), and "penis envy," the penis being the only sexual organ of recognized value. Thus she attempts by every means available to appropriate that organ for herself: through her somewhat servile love of the father-husband capable of giving her one, through her desire for a child-penis, preferably a boy, through access to the cultural values still reserved by right to males alone and therefore always masculine, and so on. Woman lives her own desire only as the expectation that she may at least come to possess an equivalent of the male organ.

Yet all this appears quite foreign to her own pleasure, unless it remains within the dominant phallic economy. Thus, for example, woman's autoeroticism is very different from man's. In order to touch himself, man needs an instrument: his hand, a woman's body, language. . . . And this self-caressing requires at least a minimum of activity. As for woman, she touches herself in and of herself without any need for mediation, and before there is any way to distinguish activity from passivity. Woman "touches herself" all the time, and moreover no one can forbid her to do so, for her genitals are formed of two lips in continuous contact. Thus, with herself, she is already two—but not divisible into one(s)—that caress each other.

This autoeroticism is disrupted by a violent break-in: the brutal separation of the two lips by a violating penis, an intrusion that distracts and deflects the woman from this "self-caressing" she needs if she is not to incur the disappearance of her own pleasure in sexual relations. If the vagina is to serve *also*, but *not only*, to take over the little boy's hand in order to assure an articulation between auto-eroticism and heteroeroticism in intercourse (the encounter with the totally other always signifying death), how, in the classic representation of sexuality, can the perpetuation of autoeroticism for woman be managed? Will woman not be left with the impossible alternative between a defensive virginity, fiercely turned in upon itself, and a body open to penetration that no longer knows, in this "hole" that constitutes its sex, the pleasure of its own touch? The more or less exclusive—and highly anxious—attention paid to erection in Western sexuality proves to what extent the imaginary that governs it is foreign to the feminine. For the most part, this sexuality offers nothing but imperatives dictated by male rivalry: the "strongest" being the one who has the best "hard-on," the longest, the biggest, the stiffest penis, or even the one who "pees the farthest" (as in little boys' contests). Or else one finds imperatives dictated by the enactment of sadomasochistic fantasies, these in turn governed by man's relation to his mother: the desire to force entry, to penetrate, to appropriate for himself the mystery of this womb where he has been conceived, the secret of his begetting, of his "origin." Desire/need, also to make blood flow again in order to revive a very old relationship—intrauterine, to be sure, but also prehistoric—to the maternal.

Woman, in this sexual imaginary, is only a more or less obliging prop for the enactment of man's fantasies. That she may find pleasure there in that role, by proxy, is possible, even certain. But such pleasure is above all a masochistic prostitution of her body to a desire that is not her own, and it leaves her in a familiar state of dependency upon man. Not knowing what she wants, ready for anything, even asking for more, so long as he will "take" her as his "object" when he seeks his own pleasure. Thus she will not say what she herself wants; moreover, she does not know, or no longer knows, what she wants. As Freud admits, the beginnings of the sexual life of a girl child are so "obscure," so "faded with time," that one would have to dig down very deep indeed to discover beneath the traces of this civilization, of this history, the vestiges of a more archaic civilization that might give some clue to woman's sexuality. That extremely ancient civilization would undoubtedly have a different alphabet, a different language. . . . Woman's desire would not be expected to speak the same language as man's; woman's desire has doubtless been submerged by the logic that has dominated the West since the time of the Greeks.

Within this logic, the predominance of the visual, and of the discrimination and individualization of form, is particularly foreign to female eroticism. Woman takes pleasure more from touching than from looking, and her entry into a dominant scopic economy signifies, again, her consignment to passivity: she is to be the beautiful object of contemplation. While her body finds itself thus eroticized, and called to a double movement of exhibition and of chaste retreat in order to stimulate the drives of the "subject," her sexual organ represents *the horror of nothing to see*. A defect in this systematics of representation and desire. A "hole" in its scoptophilic lens. It is already evident in Greek statuary that this nothing-to-see has to be excluded, rejected, from such a scene of representation. Woman's genitals are simply absent, masked, sewn back up inside their "crack."

This organ which has nothing to show for itself also lacks a form of its own. And if woman takes pleasure precisely from this incompleteness of form which allows her organ to touch itself over and over again, indefinitely, by itself, that pleasure is denied by a civilization that privileges phallomorphism. The value granted to the only definable form excludes the one that is in play in female autoeroticism. The *one* of form, of the individual, of the (male) sexual organ, of the proper name, of the proper meaning . . . supplants, while separating and dividing, that contact of *at least two* (lips) which keeps woman in touch with herself, but without any possibility of distinguishing what is touching from what is touched.

Whence the mystery that woman represents in a culture claiming to count everything, to number everything by units, to inventory everything as individualities. *She is neither one nor two.* Rigorously speaking, she cannot be identified either as one person, or as two. She resists all adequate definition. Further, she has no "proper" name. And her sexual organ, which is not *one* organ, is counted as *none.* The negative, the underside, the reverse of the only visible and morphologically designatable organ (even in the passage from erection to detumescence does pose some problems): the penis.

But the "thickness" of that "form," the layering of its volume, its expansions and contractions and even the spacing of the moments in which it produces itself as form—all this the feminine keeps secret. Without knowing it. And if woman is asked to sustain, to revive, man's desire, the request neglects to spell out what it implies as to the value of her own desire. A desire of which she is not aware, moreover, at least not explicitly. But one whose force and continuity are capable of nurturing repeatedly and at length all the masquerades of "femininity" that are expected from her.

It is true that she still has the child, in relation to whom her appetite for touch, for contact, has free rein, unless it is already lost, alienated by the taboo against touching of a highly obsessive civilization. Otherwise her pleasure will find, in the child, compensations for and diversion from the frustrations that she too often encounters in sexual relations per se. Thus maternity fills the gaps in a repressed female sexuality. Perhaps man and woman no longer caress each other except through that mediation between them that the child—preferably a boy— represents? Man, identified with his son, rediscovers the pleasure of maternal fondling; woman touches herself again by caressing that part of her body: her baby-penis-clitoris.

What this entails for the amorous trio is well known. But the Oedipal interdiction seems to be a somewhat categorical and factitious law—although it does provide the means for perpetuating the authoritarian discourse of fathers—when it is promulgated in a culture in which sexual relations are impracticable because man's desire and woman's are strangers to each other. And in which the two desires have to try to meet through indirect means, whether the archaic one of a sense-relation to the mother's body, or the present one of active or passive extension of the law of the father. These are regressive emotional behaviors, exchanges of words too detached from the sexual arena not to constitute an exile with respect to it: "mother" and "father" dominate the interactions of the couple, but as social roles. The division of labor prevents them from making love. They produce or reproduce. Without quite knowing how to use their leisure. Such little as they have, such little indeed as they wish to have. For what are they to do with leisure? What substitute for amorous resource are they to invent? Still . . .

Perhaps it is time to return to that repressed entity, the female imaginary. So woman does not have a sex organ? She has at least two of them, but they are not identifiable as ones. Indeed, she has many more. Her sexuality, always at least double, goes even further: it is *plural*. Is this the way culture is seeking to characterize itself now? Is this the way texts write themselves/are written now? Without quite knowing what censorship they are evading? Indeed, woman's pleasure does not have to choose between clitoral activity and vaginal passivity, for example. The pleasure of the vaginal caress does not have to be substituted for that of the clitoral caress. They each contribute, irreplaceably, to woman's pleasure. Among other caresses. . . . Fondling the breasts, touching the vulva, spreading lips, stroking the posterior wall of the vagina, brushing against the mouth of the uterus, and so on. To evoke only a few of the most specifically female pleasures. Pleasures which are somewhat misunderstood in sexual difference as it is imagined—or not imagined, the other sex being only the indispensable complement to the only sex.

But *woman has sex organs more or less everywhere*. She finds pleasure almost anywhere. Even if we refrain from invoking the hystericization of her entire body, the geography of her pleasure is far more diversified, more multiple in its differences, more complex, more subtle, than is commonly imagined—in an imaginary rather too narrowly focused on sameness.

"She" is indefinitely other in herself. This is doubtless why she is said to be whimsical, incomprehensible, agitated, capricious . . . not to mention her language, in which "she" sets off in all directions leaving "him" unable to discern the coherence of any meaning. Hers are contradictory words, somewhat mad from the standpoint of reason, inaudible for whoever listens to them with readymade grids, with a fully elaborated code in hand. For in what she says, too, at least when she dares, woman is constantly touching herself. She steps ever so slightly aside from herself with a murmur, an exclamation, a whisper, a sentence left unfinished. . . . When she returns, it is to set off again from elsewhere. From another point of pleasure, or of pain. One would have to listen with another ear, as if hearing an *"other meaning" always in the process of weaving itself, of embracing itself with words, but also of getting rid of words in order not to become fixed, congealed in them*. For if "she" says something, it is not, it is already no longer, identical with what she means. What she says is never identical with anything, moreover; rather, it is contiguous. *It touches (upon)*. And when it strays too far from that proximity, she breaks off and starts over at "zero": her body-sex.

It is useless, then, to trap women in the exact definition of what they mean, to make them repeat (themselves) so that it will be clear; they are already elsewhere in that discursive machinery where you expected to surprise them. They have returned within themselves. Which must not be understood in the same way as within yourself. They do not have the interiority that you have, the one you per-haps suppose they have. Within themselves means *within the intimacy of that si-lent, multiple, diffuse touch*. And if you ask them insistently what they are thinking about, they only reply: Nothing. Everything.

Thus what they desire is precisely nothing, and at the same time everything. Always something more and something else besides that *one*—sexual organ, for example—that you give them, attribute to them. Their desire is often interpreted, and feared, as a sort of insatiable hunger, a voracity that will swallow you whole. Whereas it really involves a different economy more than anything else, one that upsets the linearity of a project, undermines the goal-object of desire, diffuses the polarization toward a single pleasure, disconcerts fidelity to a single dis-course. . . .

Must this multiplicity of female desire and female language be understood as shards, scattered remnants of a violated sexuality? A sexuality denied? The ques-tion has no simple answer. The rejection, the exclusion of a female imaginary certainly puts woman in the position of experiencing herself only fragmentarily, in the little-structured margins of a dominant ideology, as waste, or excess, what is left of a mirror invested by the (masculine) "subject" to reflect himself, to copy himself. Moreover, the role of "femininity" is prescribed by this masculine specula(riza)tion and corresponds scarcely at all to woman's desire, which may be recovered only in secret, in hiding, with anxiety and guilt.

But if the female imaginary were to deploy itself, if it could bring itself into play otherwise than as scraps, uncollected debris, would it represent itself, even so, in the form of *one* universe? Would it even be volume instead of surface? No. Not unless it were understood, yet again, as a privileging of the maternal over the feminine. Of a phallic maternal, at that. Closed in upon the jealous posses-sion of its valued product. Rivaling man in his esteem for productive excess. In such a race for power, woman loses the uniqueness of her pleasure. By closing herself off as volume, she renounces the pleasure that she gets from the *nonsuture of her lips*: she is undoubtedly a mother, but a virgin mother; the role was assigned to her by mythologies long ago. Granting her a certain social power to the extent that she is reduced, with her own complicity, to sexual impotence.

(Re-)discovering herself, for a woman, thus could only signify the possibility of sacrificing no one of her pleasures to another, of identifying herself with none of them in particular, *of never being simply one*. A sort of expanding universe to which no limits could be fixed and which would not be incoherence nonetheless—nor that polymorphous perversion of the child in which the erogenous zones would lie waiting to be regrouped under the primacy of the phallus.

Woman always remains several, but she is kept from dispersion because the other is already within her and is autoerotically familiar to her. Which is not to say that she appropriates the other for herself, that she reduces it to her own prop-erty. Ownership and property are doubtless quite foreign to the feminine. At least sexually. But not *nearness*. Nearness so pronounced that it makes all discrimination of identity, and thus all forms of property, impossible. Woman derives pleasure from what is *so near that she cannot have it, nor have herself*. She herself enters into a ceaseless exchange of herself with the other without any possibility of identifying either. This puts into question all prevailing economies: their calculations are ir-remediably stymied by woman's pleasure, as it increases indefinitely from its pas-sage in and through the other.

However, in order for woman to reach the place where she takes pleasure as a woman, a long detour by way of the analysis of the various systems of oppression brought to bear upon her is assuredly necessary. And claiming to fall back on the single solution of pleasure risks making her miss the process of going back through a social practice that *her* enjoyment requires.

For woman is traditionally a use-value for man, an exchange value among men; in other words, a commodity. As such, she remains the guardian of material sub-stance, whose price will be established, in terms of the standard of their work and of their need/desire, by "subjects": workers, merchants, consumers. Women are marked phallically by their fathers, husbands, procurers. And this branding de-termines their value in sexual commerce. Woman is never anything but the lo-cus of a more or less competitive exchange between two men, including the competition for the possession of mother earth.

How can this object of transaction claim a right to pleasure without removing her/itself from established commerce? With respect to other merchandise in the marketplace, how could this commodity maintain a relationship other than one of aggressive jealousy? How could material substance enjoy her/itself without pro-voking the consumer's anxiety over the disappearance of his nurturing ground? How could that exchange—which can in no way be defined in terms "proper" to woman's desire—appear as anything but a pure mirage, more foolishness, all too readily obscured by a more sensible discourse and by a system of apparently more tangible values?

A woman's development, however radical it may seek to be, would thus not suf-fice to liberate woman's desire. And to date no political theory or political prac-tice has resolved, or sufficiently taken into consideration this historical problem, even though Marxism has proclaimed its importance. But women do not consti-tute, strictly speaking, a class, and their dispersion among several classes makes their political struggle complex, their demands sometimes contradictory.

There remains, however, the condition of underdevelopment arising from women's submission by and to a culture that oppresses them, uses them, makes of them a medium of exchange, with very little profit to them. Except in the quasi-monopolies of masochistic pleasure, the domestic labor force, and repro-duction. The power of slaves? Which are not negligible powers, moreover. For where pleasure is concerned, the master is not necessarily well served. Thus to reverse the relation, especially in the economy of sexuality, does not seem a de-sirable objective.

But if women are to preserve and expand their autoeroticism, their homosexu-ality, might not the renunciation of heterosexual pleasure correspond once again to the disconnection from power that is traditionally theirs? Would it not involve a new prison, a new cloister, built of their own accord? For women to undertake tactical strikes, to keep themselves apart from men long enough to learn to de-fend their desire, especially through speech, to discover the love of other women while sheltered from men's imperious choices that put them in the position of rival commodities, to forge for themselves a social status that compels recognition, to earn their living in order to escape from the condition of prostitute . . . these are certainly indispensable stages in the escape from their proletarization on the exchange market. But if their aim were simply to reverse the order of things, even supposing this to be possible, history would repeat itself in the long run, would revert to sameness: to phallocratism. It would leave room neither for women's sexuality, nor for women's imaginary, nor for women's language to take (their) place.

NOTE

This text was originally published as "Ce Sexe qui n'en est pas un," in *Cahiers du Grif*, no. 5. English translation: "This Sex Which Is Not One," trans. Claudia Reeder, in *New French Feminisms*, ed. Elaine Marks and Isabelle de Courtivron (New York, 1981), pp. 99–106.

WRITING THE BODY:

toward an understanding of l'écriture féminine

(1981)

France is today the scene of feminisms. The Mouvement de Libération des Femmes (MLF) grows every year, but so do the factions within it: feminist journals carry on bitter debates, a group of women writers boycotts a feminist publishing house, French women at conferences in the United States contradict each other's positions at top volume (Monique Wittig to Hélène Cixous: "Ceci est un scandale!"). But in the realm of theory, the French share a deep critique of the modes through which the West has claimed to discern evidence—or reality—and a suspicion concerning efforts to change the position of women that fail to address the forces in the body, in the unconscious, in the basic structures of culture that are invisible to the empirical eye. Briefly, French feminists in general believe that Western thought has been based on a systematic repression of women's experience. Thus their assertion of a bedrock female nature makes sense as a point from which to deconstruct language, philosophy, psychoanalysis, the social practices, and direction of patriarchal culture as we live in and resist it.

This position, the turn to *féminité* as a challenge to male-centered thinking, has stirred up curiosity and set off resonances among American feminists, who are increasingly open to theory, to philosophical, psychoanalytic, and Marxist critiques of masculinist ways of seeing the world. (Speakers at recent U.S. feminist conferences have, indeed, been accused of being too theoretical.) And it seems to me that it is precisely through theory that some of the positions of the French feminists need to be questioned—as they have been in France since the beginnings of the MLF. My intention, then, is to pose some questions about theoretical consistency and (yes, they can't be repressed!) the practical and political implications of French discussions and celebrations of the feminine. For if one posits that female subjectivity is derived from women's physiology and bodily instincts as they affect sexual experience and the unconscious, both theoretical and practical problems can and do arise.

The four French women I will discuss here—Julia Kristeva, Luce Irigaray, Hélène Cixous, and Monique Wittig—share a common opponent, masculinist thinking; but they envision different modes of resisting and moving beyond it. Their common ground is an analysis of Western culture as fundamentally oppressive, as phallogocentric. "I am the unified, self-controlled center of the universe," man (white, European, and ruling class) has claimed. "The rest of the world, which I define as the Other, has meaning only in relation to me, as man/father, possessor of the phallus."[1] This claim to centrality has been supported not only by religion and philosophy, but also by language. To speak and especially to write from such a position is to appropriate the world, to dominate it through verbal mastery. Symbolic discourse (language, in various contexts) is another means through which man objectifies the world, reduces it to his terms, speaks in place of everything and everyone else—including women.

How, then, are the institutions and signifying practices (speech, writing, images, myths, and rituals) of such a culture to be resisted? These French women agree that resistance does take place in the form of *jouissance*, that is, in the direct reexperience of the physical pleasures of infancy and of later sexuality, repressed but not obliterated by the Law of the Father.[2] Kristeva stops here; but Irigaray and Cixous go on to emphasize that women, historically limited to being sexual objects for men (virgins or prostitutes, wives or mothers), have been prevented from expressing their sexuality in itself or for themselves. If they can do this, and if they can speak about it in the new languages it calls for, they will establish a point of view (a site of *différence*) from which phallogocentric concepts and controls can be seen through and taken apart, not only in theory, but also in practice. Like Cixous, Wittig has produced a number of *textes féminins*, but she insists that the theory and practice of *féminité* must be focused on women among themselves, rather than on their divergence from men or from men's views of them. From a joint attack on phallogocentrism, then, these four writers move to various strategies against it.

Julia Kristeva, a founding member of the semiotic-Marxist journal *Tel Quel*, and the writer of several books on avant-garde writers, language, and philosophy, finds in psychoanalysis the concept of the bodily drives that survive cultural pressures toward sublimation and surface in what she calls "semiotic discourse": the gestural, rhythmic, preferential language of such writers as Joyce, Mallarmé, and Artaud.[3] These men, rather than giving up their blissful infantile fusion with their mothers, their orality, and anality, reexperience such *jouissances* subconsciously and set them into play by constructing texts against the rules and regularities of conventional language. How do women fit into this scheme of semiotic liberation? Indirectly, as mothers, because they are the first love objects from which the child is typically separated and turned away in the course of his initiation into society. In fact, Kristeva sees semiotic discourse as an incestuous challenge to the symbolic order, asserting as it does the writer's return to the pleasures of his preverbal identification with his mother and his refusal to identify with his father and the logic of paternal discourse. Women, for Kristeva, also speak and write as "hysterics," as outsiders to male-dominated discourse, for two reasons: the predominance in them of drives related to anality and childbirth, and their marginal position vis-à-vis masculine culture. Their semiotic style is likely to involve repetitive, spasmodic separations from the dominating discourse, which, more often, they are forced to imitate.[4]

Kristeva doubts, however, whether women should aim to work out alternative discourses. She sees certain liberatory potentials in their marginal position, which is (admirably) unlikely to produce a fixed, authority-claiming subject/speaker or language: "In social, sexual and symbolic experiences, being a woman has always provided a means to another end, to becoming something else: a subject-in-the-making, a subject on trial." Rather than formulating a new discourse, women should persist in challenging the discourses that stand: "If women have a role to play, . . . it is only in assuming a *negative* function: reject everything finite, definite, structured, loaded with meaning, in the existing state of society. Such an attitude places women on the side of the explosion of social codes: with revolutionary movements."[5] In fact, "woman" to Kristeva represents not so much a sex as an attitude, any resistance to conventional culture and language; men, too, have access to the *jouissance* that opposes phallogocentrism:

> A feminist practice can only be . . . at odds with what already exists so that we may say "that's not it" and "that's still not it." By "woman" I mean that which cannot be represented, what is not said, what remains above and beyond nomenclatures and ideologies. There are certain "men" who are familiar with this phenomenon.[6]

For Luce Irigaray, on the contrary, women have a specificity that distinguishes them sharply from men. A psychoanalyst and former member of l'École freudienne at the University of Paris (Vincennes), she was fired from her teaching position in the fall of 1974, three weeks after the publication of her study of the phallocentric bias in Freud. *Speculum de l'autre femme* is this study, a profound and wittily sarcastic demonstration of the ways in which Plato and Freud define woman: as irrational and invisible, as imperfect (castrated) man. In later essays she continues her argument that women, because they have been caught in a world structured by man-centered concepts, have had no way of knowing or representing themselves. But she offers as the starting point for a female self-consciousness the facts of women's bodies and women's sexual pleasure, precisely because they have been so absent or so misrepresented in male discourse. Women, she says, experience a diffuse sexuality arising, for example, from the "two lips" of the vulva, and a multiplicity of libidinal energies that cannot be expressed or understood within the identity-claiming assumptions of phallocentric discourse ("I am a unified, coherent being, and what is significant in the world reflects my male image").[7] Irigaray argues further that female sexuality explains women's problematic relationship to (masculine) logic and language:

> . . . *woman has sex organs just about everywhere.* She experiences pleasure almost everywhere. . . . The geography of her pleasure is much more diversified, more multiple in its differences, more complex, more subtle, than is imagined—in an imaginary [system] centered a bit too much on one and the same.
>
> "She" is infinitely other in herself. That is undoubtedly the reason she is called temperamental, incomprehensible, perturbed, capricious—not to mention her language in which "she" goes off in all directions and in which "he" is unable to discern the coherence of any meaning. Contradictory words seem a little crazy to the logic of reason, and inaudible for him who listens with ready-made grids, a code prepared in advance. In her statements—at least when she dares to speak out—woman retouches herself constantly.[8]

Irigaray concedes that women's discovery of their autoeroticism will not, by itself, arrive automatically or enable them to transform the existing order: "For a woman to arrive at the point where she can enjoy her pleasure as a woman, a long detour by the analysis of the various systems that oppress her is certainly necessary."[9] Irigaray herself writes essays using Marxist categories to analyze men's use and exchange of women, and in others she uses female physiology as a source of critical metaphors and counterconcepts (against physics, pornography, Nietzsche's misogyny, myth),[10] rather than literally. Yet her focus on the physical bases for the difference between male and physical sexuality remains the same: women must recognize and assert their *jouissance* if they are to subvert phallocentric oppression at its deepest levels.

Since 1975, when she founded women's studies at Vincennes, Hélène Cixous has been a spokeswoman for the group Psychanalyse et Politique and a prolific writer of texts for their publishing house, des femmes. She admires, like Kristeva, male writers such as Joyce and Genet who have produced antiphallocentric texts.[11] But she is convinced that women's unconscious is totally different from men's, and that it is their psychosexual specificity that will empower women to overthrow masculinist ideologies and to create new female discourses. Of her own writing she says, "Je suis là où ça parle" ("I am there where the it/id/the female unconscious speaks.").[12] She has produced a series of analyses of women's suffering under the laws of male sexuality (the first-person narrative *Angst*, the play *Portrait de Dora*, the libretto for the opera *Le Nom d'Oedipe*) and a growing collection of demonstrations of what id-liberated female discourse might be: *La, Ananké,* and *Illa*. In her recent *Vivre l'orange* (des femmes, 1979), she celebrates the Brazilian writer Clarice Lispector for what she sees as a peculiarly female attentiveness to objects, the ability to perceive and represent them in a nurturing rather than dominating way. She believes that this empathetic attentiveness and the literary modes to which it gives rise, arise from libidinal rather than social-cultural sources: the "typically feminine gesture, not culturally but libidinally, [is] to produce in order to bring about life, pleasure, not in order to accumulate."[13]

Cixous criticizes psychoanalysis for its "thesis of a 'natural' anatomical determination of sexual difference-opposition," focusing on physical drives rather than body parts for her definition of male-female contrasts: "It is at the level of sexual pleasure in my opinion that the difference makes itself most clearly apparent in as far as woman's libidinal economy is neither identifiable by a man nor referable to the masculine economy."[14] In her manifesto for *l'écriture féminine*, "The Laugh of the Medusa" (1975), her comparisons and lyricism suggest that she admires in women a sexuality that is remarkably constant and almost mystically superior to the phallic single-mindedness it transcends:

> Though masculine sexuality gravitates around the penis, engendering that centralized body (in political anatomy) under the dictatorship of its parts, woman does not bring about the same regionalization which serves the couple head/genitals and which is inscribed only within boundaries. Her libido is cosmic, just as her unconscious is worldwide.

She goes on immediately, in terms close to Irigaray's, to link women's diffuse sexuality to women's language—written language, in this case:

> Her writing can only keep going, without ever inscribing or discerning contours. . . . She lets the other language speak—the language of 1,000

> tongues which knows neither enclosure nor death. . . . Her language does not contain, it carries; it does not hold back, it makes possible.[15]

The passage ends with her invocation of other bodily drives (*pulsions* in French) in a continuum with women's self-expression:

> Oral drive, anal drive, vocal drive—all these drives are our strengths, and among them is the gestation drive—just like the desire to write: a desire to live self from within, a desire for the swollen belly, for language, for blood.

In her theoretical and imaginative writing alike (*La Jeune Née*, 1975, typically combines the two) Cixous insists on the primacy of multiple, specifically female libidinal impulses, in women's unconscious and in the writing of the liberatory female discourses of the future.

What Kristeva, Irigaray, and Cixous do in common, then, is to oppose women's bodily experience (or, in Kristeva's case, women's bodily effect as mothers) to the phallic/symbolic patterns embedded in Western thought. Although Kristeva does not privilege women as the only possessors of prephallocentric discourse, Irigaray and Cixous go further: if women are to discover and express who they are, to bring to the surface what masculine history has repressed in them, they must begin with their sexuality. And their sexuality begins with their bodies, with their genital and libidinal difference from men.

For various reasons, this is a powerful argument. We have seen versions of it in the radical feminism of the United States, too. In the French context, it offers an island of hope in the void left by the deconstruction of humanism, which has been revealed as an ideologically suspect invention by men. If men are responsible for the reigning binary system of meaning—identity/other, man/nature, reason/chaos, man/woman—women, relegated to the negative and passive pole of this hierarchy, are not implicated in the creation of its myths. (Certainly, they are no longer impressed by them!) And the immediacy with which the body, the id, *jouissance*, are supposedly experienced promises a clarity of perception and a vitality that can bring down mountains of phallocentric delusion. Finally, to the extent that the female body is seen as a direct source of female writing, a powerful alternative discourse seems possible: to write from the body is to recreate the world.

But *féminité* and *écriture féminine* are problematic as well as powerful concepts. They have been criticized as idealist and essentialist, bound up in the very system they claim to undermine; they have been attacked as theoretically fuzzy and as fatal to constructive political action.[16] I think all these objections are worth making. What's more, they must be made if American women are to sift out and use the positive elements in French thinking about *féminité*.

First off, the basic theoretical question: can the body be a source of self-knowledge? Does female sexuality exist prior to or in spite of social experience? Do women in fact experience their bodies purely or essentially, outside the damaging acculturation so sharply analyzed by women in France and elsewhere? The answer is no, even in terms of the psychoanalytic theory on which many elements in the concept of *féminité* depend. Feminists rereading Freud and Jacques Lacan, and feminists doing new research on the construction of sexuality all agree that sexuality is not an innate quality in women or in men, it is developed through the individual's encounters with the nuclear family and with the symbolic systems set in motion by the mother-father pair as the parents themselves carry out socially imposed roles toward the child. Freud, Juliet Mitchell has shown, describes the process through which girls in our society shift their first love for their mothers to a compensatory love for their fathers and develop a sense of their own anatomy as less valued socially than that of boys.[17] Nancy Chodorow has documented and theorized the difficulty of this shift and used it to account for the complex affective needs of girls and women.[18] To the analysis of the process through which sexual identity is formed Lacan adds the role of the father as bearer of language and culture; he identifies the symbolic value attributed to the phallus as the basis for contrasts and contrasting values that the child incorporates as she attempts to make sense of and fit herself into the phallocentric world. So if early gender identity comes into being in response to patriarchal structures— as, for example, Chodorow, Lacan, and Dorothy Dinnerstein argue[19]—and if even the unconscious is sexed in accordance with the nuclear family, then there seems to be no essential stratum of sexuality unsaturated with social arrangements and symbolic systems. New readings of Freud and of object relations theory both confirm that sexuality is not a natural given, but rather is the consequence of social interactions, among people and among signs.

Theoretical work and practical evidence strongly suggest that sexual identity ("I am a woman, I experience my body as sexual in this way") never takes shape in isolation or in a simply physical context. The child becomes male or female in response to the females and males she encounters in her family and to the male and female images she constructs according to her experience—especially her loss of direct access to either parent.[20] The desires of the child and of the adult who grows out of the child finally result not from the isolated erotic sensitivies of the child's body; these sensitivies are interpreted through the meanings the child attaches to her body through early experience in a sexed world. To take from psychoanalysis the concepts of drive and libido without talking about what happens later to the child's systems of self-perception is to drop out the deepest level at which phallocentric society asserts its power: the sexed family as it imprints itself on the child's sense of herself as a sexed being.

Psychoanalytic theory is not feminist dogma, and feminists have also analyzed the sexist ideologies that confront women past the age of childhood in the family. Not surprisingly, these ideologies make their way into many women's day-to-day experience of their bodies, even in situations that we have designed to be free of male domination. For instance, liberatory practices such as masturbation, lesbianism, and woman-centered medicine coexist with thoroughly phallocentric habits of thought and feeling; they are not liberatory simply because they aspire to be. Some women discover, for example, that their masturbation is accompanied by puzzlingly unenlightened fantasies; contrary to the claims of *féminité*, women's autoeroticism, at least in these decades, is shot through with images from a phallically dominated world. Similarly, many lesbians recognize their need to resist roles of domination and submission that bear a grim, even parodic resemblance to heterosexual relationships. Women giving birth may wonder whether the optimistic, even heroic terminology of natural childbirth is not related to the suspect ideal of "taking it like a man." Even in the self-help clinics set up to spare women the sexist bias of the male gynecological establishment, a phallocentric *magasin des images* may prevail. A counselor at such a clinic, showing a friend of mine her cervix for the first time in a mirror, made a remark (unintentionally; that's the point) that struck us both as far less liberating than it was intended to be: "Big, isn't it? Doesn't it look powerful? As good as a penis any day." All in all, at this point in history, most of us perceive our bodies through a jumpy, contradictory mesh of hoary sexual symbolization and political counter-response. It is possible to argue that the French feminists make of the female body too unproblematic pleasurable and totalized an entity.

Certainly, women's physiology has important meanings for women in various cultures, and it is essential for us to express those meanings rather than to submit to male definitions—that is, appropriations—of our sexuality. But the female body hardly seems the best site to launch an attack on the forces that have alienated us from what our sexuality might become. For if we argue for an innate, precultural femininity, where does that position (though in *content* it obviously diverges from masculinist dogma) leave us in relation to earlier theories about women's "nature"? I myself feel highly flattered by Cixous's praise for the nurturant perceptions of women, but when she speaks of a drive toward gestation, I begin to hear echoes of the coercive glorification of motherhood that has plagued women for centuries. If we define female subjectivity through universal biological/libidinal given, what happens to the project of changing the world in feminist directions? Further, is women's sexuality so monolithic that a notion of a shared, typical femininity does justice to it? What about variations in class, in race, and in culture among women? What about changes over time in *one* woman's sexuality (with men, with women, by herself)? How can one libidinal voice—or the two vulval lips so startlingly presented by Irigaray—speak for all women?

The psychoanalytic critique *of féminité* as a concept that overlooks important psychosocial realities is not the only critique that can be brought against positions like Irigaray's and Cixous's. Other French women have made a strong, materialist attack on what they call *néo-féminité*, objecting to it as an ideal bound up through symmetrical opposition in the very ideological system feminists want to destroy. (*Questions féministes*, the journal founded in 1977 with Simone de Beauvoir as titular editor, is a central source for this kind of thinking in France.) Materialist feminists such as Christine Delphy and Colette Guillaumin are suspicious of the logic through which *féminité* defines men as phallic—solipsistic, aggressive, excessively rational—and then praises women, who, by nature of their contrasting sexuality, are other-oriented, empathetic, multiimaginative. Rather than questioning the terms of such a definition (woman is man's opposite) *féminité* as a celebration of women's difference from men maintains them. It reverses the values assigned to each side of the polarity, but it still leaves man as the determining referent, not departing from the opposition male/female, but participating in it.

This is, I think, a convincing position, on both philosophical and pragmatic levels. What we need to do is to move outside that male-centered, binary logic altogether. We need to ask not how Woman is different from Man (though the question of how women differ from what men *think* they are is important). We need to know how women have come to be who they are through history, which is the history of their oppression by men and male-designed institutions. Only through an analysis of the power relationships between men and women, and practices based on that analysis, will we put an end to our oppression—and only then will we discover what women are or can be. More strategically, we need to know whether the assertion of a shared female nature made by *féminité* can help us in feminist action toward a variety of goals: the possibility of working, or working in marginal or newly defined ways, or of not working in the public world at all; the freedom for a diversity of sexual practices; the right to motherhood, childlessness, or some as yet untheorized participation in reproduction; the affirmation of historically conditioned female values (nurturance, communal rather than individualistic ambitions, insistence on improving the quality of private life); *and* the exploration of new ones. If we concentrate our energies on opposing a counterview of Woman to the view held by men in the past and the present, what happens to our ability to support the multiplicity of women and the various life possibilities they are fighting for in the future?

In a critique of *féminité* as praise of women's difference from men, the name of Monique Wittig must be mentioned. Active in the early seventies in the Féministes révolutionnaires and a contributor from the beginning to *Questions féministes*, Wittig has written four quite different books, which are nonetheless related through her focus on women among themselves: the schoolgirls of *L'Opoponax*, the tribal sisterhood of *Les Guérrillères*, the passionate couple of *Le Corps lesbien*, the users of the postphallocentric vocabulary laid out in *Brouillon pour un dictionnaire des amantes*. Wittig writes her novels, her monologues, and histories to explore what social relationships among women-identified women are or might be.[21] She rewrites traditional culture in mocking takeovers: one entry in *Brouillon pour un dictionnaire* is "Ainsi parlait Frederika, conte pour enfants" ("Thus Spake Frederika, children's story"), surely one of the least reverent allusions to Friedrich Nietzsche to come out of French critiques of culture. She also invents new settings, such as the ceremonies and festivals of *Les Guérrillères* and *Le Corps lesbien*, and new modes, such as the feminized epic of *Les Guérrillères* and the lyric dialogue of *Le Corps lesbien*, to represent what a female/female life— separatist but not isolationist—might be.

As Wittig's talks at recent conferences in the United States show, she is suspicious both of the oppositional thinking that defines woman in terms of man and of the mythical/idealist strain in certain formulations of *féminité*.[22] In her argument for a more politically centered understanding of women at the Second Sex Conference in New York (September 1979), she used a Marxist vocabulary which may be more familiar to U.S. feminists than the philosophical and psychoanalytic frameworks in which Irigaray and Cixous work:

> It remains . . . for us to define our oppression in materialist terms, to say that women are a class, which is to say that the category "woman," as well as "man," is a political and economic category, not an eternal one. . . . Our first task . . . is thoroughly to dissociate "women" (the class within which we fight) and "woman," the myth. For "woman" does not exist for us; it is only an imaginary formation, while "women" is the product of a social relationship.[23]

Colette Guillaumin, arguing along similar lines in *Questions féministes*, points out that the psychic characteristics praised by advocates of *féminité* have in fact been determined by the familial and economic roles imposed on women by men.

There is nothing liberatory, she insists, in women's claiming as virtues qualities that men have always found convenient. How does maternal tenderness or undemanding empathy threaten a Master?[24] The liberating stance is, rather, the determination to analyze and put an end to the patriarchal structures that have produced those qualities without reference to the needs to women.

I have another political objection to the concept of *féminité* as a bundle of Everywoman's psychosexual characteristics: it flattens out the lived differences among women. To the extent that each of us responds to a particular tribal, national, racial, or class situation vis-à-vis men, we are in fact separated from one another. As the painful and counterproductive splits along class and racial lines in the American women's movement have shown, we need to understand and respect the diversity in our concrete social situations. A monolithic vision of shared female sexuality, rather than defeating phallocentrism as doctrine and practice, is more likely to blind us to our varied and immediate needs and to the specific struggles we must coordinate in order to meet them. What is the meaning of "two lips" to heterosexual women who want men to recognize their clitoral pleasure—or to African or Middle Eastern women who, as a result of pharaonic clitoridectomies, have neither lips nor clitoris through which to *jouir*? Does a celebration of the Maternal versus the Patriarchal make the same kind of sense, or any sense, to white, middle-class women who are fighting to maintain the right to abortion, to black and Third World women resisting enforced sterilization, to women in subsistence-farming economies where the livelihood of the family depends on the work of every child who is born and survives? And surely any one woman gives different meanings to her sexuality throughout her individual history. Freedom from sexual expectations and activity may well be what girls in the Western world most need because they are typically sexualized all too soon by the media, advertising, peer pressures, and child pornography; women of various ages undergo radical changes in sexual identity and response as they enter relationships with men, with women, or choose celibacy and friendship as alternatives. And it is hard to see how the situations of old women, consigned to sexual inactivity because of their age or, if they are widowed, to unpaid work in others' families or to isolated poverty, can be understood or changed through a concept of *jouissance*. I wonder again whether one libidinal voice, however nonphallocentrically defined, can speak to the economic and cultural problems of all women.

Hence, I would argue that we need the theoretical depth and polemical energy of *féminité* as an alternative idea. But a historically responsive and powerful unity among women will come from our ongoing, shared practice, our experience in and against the material world. As a lens and a partial strategy, *féminité* and *écriture féminine* are vital. Certainly, women need to shake off the mistaken and contemptuous attitudes toward their sexuality that permeate Western (and other) cultures and languages at their deepest levels, and working out self-representations that challenge phallocentric discourses is an important part of that ideological struggle. Women have already begun to transform not only the subject matter, but also the ways of producing meaning in poetry, fiction, film, and visual arts. (Indeed, feminist research suggests that the French may have been too hasty in their claim that women are only now beginning to challenge the symbolic order.) But even if we take *l'écriture féminine* as a utopian ideal, an energizing myth rather than a model for how all women write or should write, theoretical and practical problems arise (again!) from an ideal defined in this way. Can the body be the source of a new discourse? Is it possible, assuming an unmediated and *jouissant* (or, more likely, a positively reconstructed) sense of one's body, to move from that state of unconscious excitation directly to a written female text?

Madeleine Gagnon says yes, in *La Venue à l'écriture*, written with Cixous in 1977. Her view is that women, free from the self-limiting economy of male libido ("I will come once and once only, through one organ alone; once it's up and over, that's it; so I must beware, save up, avoid premature overflow"), have a greater spontaneity and abundance in body and language both.

> We have never been masters of others or of ourselves. We don't have to con-
> front ourselves in order to free ourselves. We don't have to keep watch on
> ourselves, or to set up some other erected self in order to understand our-
> selves. All we have to do is let the body flow, from the inside; all we have to
> do is erase . . . whatever may hinder or harm the new forms of writing; we re-
> tain whatever fits, whatever suits us. Whereas man confronts himself con-
> stantly. He pits himself against and stumbles over his erected self.[25]

But psychoanalytic theory and social experience both suggest that the leap from body to language is especially difficult for women.[26] Lacanian theory holds that a girl's introduction into language (the symbolic order represented by the father and built on phallic/nonphallic oppositions) is complex, because she cannot iden-tify directly with the positive poles of that order. And in many preliterate and postliterate cultures, taboos against female speech are enforced: injunctions to si-lence, mockery of women's chatter or "women's books" abound. The turn tak-ing in early consciousness-raising groups in the United States was meant precisely to overcome the verbal hesitancy induced in women by a society in which men have had the first and the last word. Moreover, for women with jobs, husbands or lovers, children, activist political commitments, finding the time and justifica-tion to write at all presents an enormous practical and ideological problem.[27] We are more likely to write, and to read each other's writing, if we begin by working against the concrete difficulties and the prejudices surrounding women's writing than if we simplify and idealize the process by locating writing as a spontaneous outpouring from the body.

Calls for a verbal return to nature seem especially surprising coming from women who are otherwise (and rightly!) suspicious of language as penetrated by phallocentric dogma. True, conventional narrative techniques, as well as gram-mar and syntax, imply the unified viewpoint and mastery of outer reality that men have claimed for themselves. But literary modes and language itself cannot be the only targets for transformation; the *context* for women's discourses needs to be thought through and broadened out. A woman may experience *jouissance* in a private relationship to her own body, but she writes for others. Who writes? Who reads? Who makes women's texts available to women? What do women want to read about other women's experience? To take a stance as a woman poet or nov-elist is to enter into a role crisscrossed with questions of authority, of audience, of the modes of publication and distribution. I believe that we are more indebted to the "body" of earlier women writers and to feminist publishers and booksellers than to any woman writer's libidinal/body flow. The novelist Christiane Rochefort sums up with amusing directness the conflicting public forces and voices that create the dilemma of the French woman who wants to write:

> Well. So here you are now, sitting at your writing table, alone, not allowing anybody anymore to interfere. Are you free?
>
> First, after this long quest, you are swimming in a terrible soup of values— for, to be safe, you had to refuse the so-called female values, which are not female but a social scheme, and to identify with male values, which are not male but an appropriation by men—or an attribution to men—of all human values, mixed up with the anti-values of domination-violence-oppression and the like. In this mixture, where is your real identity?
>
> Second, you are supposed to write in certain forms, preferably: I mean you feel that in certain forms you are not too much seen as a usurper. Novels. Minor poetry, in which case you will be stigmatized in French by the name of "poetesse" not everybody can afford it. . . .
>
> You are supposed, too, to write about certain things: house, children, love. Until recently there was in France a so-called *littérature féminine*.
>
> Maybe you don't want to write *about*, but to write, period. And of course, you don't want to obey this social order. So, you tend to react against it. It is not easy to be genuine.[28]

Whatever the difficulties, women are inventing new kinds of writing. But as Irigaray's erudition and plays with the speaking voice show (as do Cixous's mischievous puns and citations of languages from Greek though German to Portuguese, and Wittig's fantastic neologisms and revision of conventional genres), they are doing so deliberately, on a level of feminist theory and literary self-consciousness that goes far beyond the body and the unconscious. That is also how they need to be read. It takes a thorough-going familiarity with *male* figure-heads of Western culture to recognize the intertextual games played by all these writers; their work shows that a resistance to culture is always built, at first, of bits and pieces of that culture, however they are disassembled, criticized, and transcended. Responding to *l'écriture féminine* is no more instinctive than producing it. Women's writing will be more accessible to writers and readers alike if we recognize it as a conscious response to socioliterary realities, rather than accept it as an overflow of one woman's unmediated communication with her body. Eventually, certainly, the practice of women writers will transform what we can see and understand in a literary text; but even a woman setting out to write about her body will do so against and through her socioliterary mothers, midwives, and sisters. We need to recognize, too, that there is nothing universal about French versions of *écriture féminine*. The speaking, singing, tale telling, and writing of women in cultures besides that of the Ile de France need to be looked at and understood in their social context if we are to fill in an adequate and genuinely empowering picture of women's creativity.

But I risk, after all this, overstating the case against *féminité* and *l'écriture féminine*, and that would mean a real loss. American feminists can appropriate two important elements, at least, from the French position: the critique of phallocentrism in all the material and ideological forms it has taken, and the call for new representations of women's consciousness. It is not enough to uncover old heroines or to imagine new ones. Like the French, we need to examine the words, the syntax, the genres, the archaic and elitist attitudes toward language and representation that have limited women's self-knowledge and expression during the long centuries of patriarchy. We need not, however, replace phallocentrism with a shakily theorized "concentrism" that denies women their historical specificities to recognize how deep a refusal of masculinist values must go.[29] If we remember that what women really share is an oppression on all levels, although it affects us each in different ways—if we can translate *féminité* into a concerted attack not only on language, but also directly upon the sociosexual arrangements that keep us from our own potentials and from each other—then we are on our way to becoming "les jeunes nées" envisioned by French feminisms at their best.

NOTES

1. For a summary of the intellectual background of French feminism, see Elaine Marks, "Women and Literature in France," *Signs* 3, no. 4 (Summer 1978): 832–42. Phallogocentrism at work is powerfully analyzed by Shoshana Felman in her study of the characters and critics of a short story by Balzac, "Women and Madness: the Critical Phallacy," *Diacritics* 5, no. 4 (Winter 1975): 2–10, and in this volume.

2. *Jouissance* is a word rich in connotations, "Pleasure" is the simplest translation. The noun comes from the verb *jouir*, meaning to enjoy, to revel in without fear of the cost; also, to have an orgasm. See Stephen Heath's Translator's Note in Roland Barthes's *Image-Music-Text* (New York: Hill and Wang, 1978), p. 9. A note to Introduction 3 in *New French Feminisms: An Anthology*, ed. Elaine Marks and Isabelle de Courtivron (Amherst: University of Massachusetts Press, 1980), explains feminist connotations of *jouissance* as follows:

> This pleasure, when attributed to a woman, is considered to be of a different order from the pleasure that is represented within the male libidinal economy often described in terms of the capitalist gain and profit motive. Women's *jouissance* carries with it the notion of fluidity, diffusion, duration. It is a kind of potlatch in the world of orgasms, a giving, expending, dispensing of pleasure without concern about ends or closure. [p. 36, n. 8]

The Law of the Father is Lacan's formulation for language as the medium through which human beings are placed in culture, a medium represented and enforced by the figure of the father in the family. See Anika Lemaire, *Jacques Lacan*, trans. David Macey (London: Routledge and Kegan Paul, 1977), especially Part 7, "The Role of the Oedipus in accession to the symbolic."

3. Julia Kristeva's books include *Semiotike: Recherches pour une semanalyse* (Paris: Tel Quel, 1969); *Le Texte du roman* (The Hague: Mouton, 1970); *Des Chinoises* (Paris: des femmes, 1974); *La Révolution du langage poétique* (Paris: Seuil, 1974); *Polylogue* (Paris: Seuil, 1977); and *Pouvoirs de l'horreur: essai sur l'abjection* (Paris: Seuil, 1980). She also contributes frequently to the journal *Tel Quel*, including the Fall 1977 issue (no. 74) on women and women's writing. For her criticism of certain notions of *féminité*, see her interview with Françoise van Rossum-Guyon, "A Partier de *Polylogue*," in *Revue des sciences humaines* 168, no. 4 (December 1977): 495–501.

4. Kristeva, "Le Sujet en procès," in *Polylogue*, p. 77. See, in the same volume, her discussion of maternity as an experience that breaks down the categories of masculinist thought, in "Maternité selon Giovanni Bellini," pp. 409–38. She expands her argument about the meanings of maternity for women's creativity, in "Un nouveau type d'intellectuel: le dissident" and "Héréthique de l'amour," *Tel Quel*, no. 74 (Fall 1977): 3–8, 30–49. For an explanation of her theory of the semiotic and of Irigaray's concepts of *l'écriture*

féminine, see Josette Féral, "Antigone, or the Irony of the Tribe," *Diacritics* 8, no. 2 (Fall 1978): 2–14.

5. "Oscillation du 'pouvoir' au 'refus,'" an interview by Xavière Gauthier in *Tel Quel*, no. 58 (Summer 1974), translated in *New French Feminisms*, pp. 166–67. This collection of translated excerpts from French feminist writers is likely to be very useful to English-language readers.

6. Kristeva, "La femme, ce n'est jamais ça," an interview in *Tel Quel*, no. 59 (Fall 1974), translated in *New French Feminisms*, pp. 134–38. Kristeva has written mainly about male writers, but see her comments on some typically feminine themes in a dozen recent French women writers in "Oscillation," *Tel Quel*, no. 48 (Summer 1974): 100–102. She comments on certain elements of women's style in her interview with van Rossum-Guyon (see n.3), although she derives them from social rather than libidinal sources.

7. Luce Irigaray, an interview, "Women's Exile," in *Ideology & Consciousness*, no. 1 (1977): 62–67, translated and introduced by Diana Adlam and Couze Venn.

8. Irigaray, "Ce Sexe qui n'en est pas un," in *Ce Sexe qui n'en est pas un* (Paris: Minuit, 1977), translated in *New French Feminisms*, p. 103, and in this volume. Irigaray's books since *Ce Sexe* are *Et l'une ne bouge sans l'autre* (Paris: Minuit, 1979) and *Amante marine* (Paris: Minuit, 1980). Her first book was a clinical study, *Le Langage des déments* (The Hague: Mouton, 1973).

9. *New French Feminisms*, p. 105.

10. Irigaray discusses the historical position of women in Marxist terms in "Le Marché aux femmes," in *Ce Sexe*. Her responses to Nietzsche are in *Amante marine*.

11. Hélène Cixous's studies of male writers include her doctoral thesis, *L'Exil de Joyce ou l'art du remplacement* (Paris: Grasset, 1968); *Prénoms de personne (sur Hoffman, Kleist, Poe, Joyce)* (Paris: Seuil, 1974); and introductions to James Joyce and Lewis Carroll for Aubier. Since 1975, all her books have been published by des femmes.

12. Cixous, "Entretien avec Françoise van Rossum-Guyon," *RSH* 168 (December 1977): 488. "Ça parle" is a Lacanian formula, but elsewhere (in her fiction/essay *Partie* [Paris: des femmes, 1976], for example) she mocks what she sees as the Father/phallus obsession of recent psychoanalysis.

13. Cixous, "Entretien," p. 487; and *Vivre l'orange* [includes an English version by Cixous with Ann Liddle and Sarah Cornell] (Paris: des femmes, 1980), pp. 9, 105–107.

14. Cixous, "Sorties," in *La Jeune née* (Paris: Bibliotheque 10/18, 1975).

15. *New French Feminisms*, pp. 259–60.

16. The opening manifesto of *Questions féministes* is a long and persuasive critique of *néo-féminité*, translated in *New French Feminisms* as "Variations on Common Themes," pp. 212–30. See also the appraisal by Beverly Brown and Parveen Adama, "The Feminine Body and Feminist Politics," *m/f* 3 (1979): 33–37.

17. Juliet Mitchell, *Psychoanalysis and Feminism* (New York: Vintage, 1975). See especially "The Holy Family, Part 4: The Different Self, the Phallus and the Father," pp. 382–98.

18. Nancy Chodorow, *The Reproduction of Mothering* (Berkeley: University of California Press, 1978).

19. Dorothy Dinnerstein, *The Mermaid and the Minotaur: Sexual Arrangements and Human Malaise* (New York: Harper and Row, 1977).

20. Jacqueline Rose, in an article on Freud's analysis of the hysteric Dora, emphasizes that the male/female roles internalized by the child enter the unconscious at such a deep level that they govern the production of dreams. Dora, who desires a woman, represents herself as a man—a striking example of the socialized image of desire, "'Dora'—Fragment of an Analysis," *m/f* [1979]: 5–21.

21. Wittig's books have all been translated into English: *L'Opopanax* by Helen Weaver (Plainfield, Vt.: Daugter's Press Reprint, 1976); *Les Guérillères* by David Le Vay (New York:

Avon, 1973); *The Lesbian Body* by David Le Vay (New York: Avon, 1976); *Lesbian Peoples: Material for a Dictionary* (with substantial revisions) by Wittig and Sande Zeig (New York: Avon, 1979).

22. Wittig, "The Straight Mind," speech given at the Feminist as Scholar Conference in May 1979 at Barnard College, New York, N.Y.

23. Wittig, "One Is Not Born a Woman," text of the speech given at the City University of New York Graduate Center, September 1979.

24. Colette Guillaumin, "Question de différence," *Questions féministes* 6 (September 1979): 3–21. Guillaumin points out that the claim to "difference" comes from other oppressed groups as well (Third World and U.S. blacks, for example), who have not yet succeeded in putting their desire for political self-determination into effect. To assert their difference against the ruling class strengthens their group solidarity, but at the expense of an analysis of the political sources of that difference.

25. Madeleine Gagnon, "Corps I," *New French Feminisms*, p. 180. See Changal Chawaf for a similar statement, in "La Chair linguistique," *New French Feminisms*, pp. 177–78.

26. Cora Kaplan combines psychoanalytic and anthropological accounts of women's hesitations to speak, in "Language and Gender," *Papers on Patriarchy* (Brighton, England: Women's Publishing Collective, 1976). Similarly, Sandra M. Gilbert and Susan Gubar demonstrate how socially derived ambivalence toward the role of writer has acted upon women's writing in English, in *The Madwoman in the Attic: The Woman Writer and the Nineteenth-Century Literary Imagination* (New Haven: Yale University Press, 1979).

27. See Tillie Olsen's *Silences* (New York: Delacorte, 1979) for a discussion of the practical demands and self-doubts that have hindered women's writing, especially "The Writer-Woman: One out of Twelve," pp. 177–258.

28. Christiane Rochefort, "Are Women Writers Still Monsters?" a speech given at the University of Wisconsin, Madison, Wis., February 1975, translated in *New French Feminisms*, pp. 185–86.

29. "Concentrism" is Elaine Showalter's term, used in a speech, "Feminist Literary Theory and Other Impossibilities," given at the Smith College Conference on Feminist Literary Criticism, Northampton, Mass., October 25, 1980.

MAMA'S BABY, PAPA'S MAYBE

an american grammar book

(1987)

〜〜〜〜〜〜〜〜〜〜〜〜〜〜〜〜〜〜〜〜〜〜〜〜〜〜〜〜〜〜

I

Let's face it. I am a marked woman, but not everybody knows my name. "Peaches" and "Brown Sugar," "Sapphire" and "Earth Mother," "Aunty," "Granny," God's "Holy Fool," a "Miss Ebony First," or "Black Woman at the Podium": I describe a locus of confounded identities, a meeting ground of investments and privations in the national treasury of rhetorical wealth. My country needs me, and if I were not here, I would have to be invented.

W. E. B. DuBois predicted as early as 1903 that the twentieth century would be the century of the "color line." We could add to this spatiotemporal configuration another thematic of analogously terrible weight: if the "black woman" can be seen as a particular figuration of the split subject that psychoanalytic theory posits, then this century marks the site of "its" profoundest revelation. The problem before us is deceptively simple: the terms enclosed in quotation marks in the preceding paragraph isolate overdetermined nominative properties. Embedded in bizarre axiological ground, they demonstrate a sort of telegraphic coding; they are markers so loaded with mythical prepossession that there is no easy way for the agents buried beneath them to come clean. In that regard, the names by which I am called in the public place render an example of signifying property *plus*. In order for me to speak a truer word concerning myself, I must strip down through layers of attenuated meanings, made an excess in time, over time, assigned by a particular historical order, and there await whatever marvels of my own inventiveness. The personal pronouns are offered in the service of a collective function.

In certain human societies, a child's identity is determined through the line of the Mother, but the United States, from at least one author's point of view, is not one of them: "In essence, the Negro community has been forced into a matriarchal structure which, because it is so far out of line with the *rest of American society*, seriously retards the progress of the group as a whole, and imposes a crushing burden on the Negro male, and in consequence, on a great many Negro women as well" [Moynihan 75; emphasis mine].

The notorious bastard, from Vico's banished Roman mothers of such sons, to Caliban, to Heathcliff, and Joe Christmas, has no official female equivalent. Because the traditional rites and laws of inheritance rarely pertain to the female child, bastard status signals to those who need to know which son of the Father's is the legitimate heir and which one the impostor. For that reason, property seems wholly the business of the male. The "she" cannot, therefore, qualify for bastard, or "natural son" status, and that she cannot provides further insight into the coils and recoils of patriarchal wealth and fortune. According to Daniel Patrick Moynihan's celebrated "Report" of the late sixties, the "Negro Family" has no Father to speak of—his Name, his Law, his Symbolic function mark the impressive missing agencies in the essential life of the black community, the "Report" maintains, and it is, surprisingly, the fault of the Daughter, or the female line. The stunning reversal of the castration thematic, displacing the Name and the Law of the Father to the Territory of the Mother and Daughter, becomes an aspect of the African-American female's misnaming. We attempt to undo this misnaming in order to reclaim the relationship between Fathers and Daughters within this social matrix for a quite different structure of cultural fictions. For Daughters and Fathers are here made to manifest the very same *rhetorical* symptoms of absence and denial, to embody the double and contrastive agencies of a *prescribed* internecine degradation. "Sapphire" enacts her "Old Man" in drag, just as her "Old Man" becomes "Sapphire" in outrageous caricature.

In other words, in the historic outline of dominance, the respective subject-positions of "female" and "male" adhere to no symbolic integrity. At a time when current critical discourses appear to compel us more and more decidedly toward gender "undecidability," it would appear reactionary, if not dumb, to insist on the integrity of female/male gender. But undressing these conflations of meaning, as they appear under the rule of dominance, would restore, as figurative possibility, not only Power to the Female (for Maternity), but also Power to the Male (for Paternity). We would gain, in short, the *potential* for gender differentiation as it might express itself along a range of stress points, including human biology in its intersection with the project of culture.

Though among the most readily available "whipping boys" of fairly recent public discourse concerning African-Americans and national policy, the "Moynihan Report" is by no means unprecedented in its conclusions; it belongs, rather, to a class of symbolic paradigms that 1) inscribe "ethnicity" as a scene of negation and 2) confirm the human body as a metonymic figure for an entire repertoire of human and social arrangements. In that regard, the "Report" pursues a behavioral rule of public documentary. Under the Moynihan rule, "ethnicity" itself identifies a total objectification of human and cultural motives—the "white" family, by implication, and the "Negro Family," by outright assertion, in a constant opposition of binary meanings. Apparently spontaneous, these "actants" are *wholly* generated, with neither past nor future, as tribal currents moving out of time. Moynihan's "families" are pure present and always tense. "Ethnicity" in this case freezes in meaning, takes on constancy, assumes the look and the affects of the Eternal. We could say, then, that in its powerful stillness, "ethnicity," from the point of view of the "Report," embodies nothing more than a mode of memorial time, as Roland Barthes outlines the dynamics of myth [see "Myth Today" 109–59; esp. 122–23]. As a signifier that has no movement in the field of signification, the use of "ethnicity" for the living becomes purely appreciative, although one would be unwise not to concede its dangerous and fatal effects.

"Ethnicity" perceived as mythical time enables a writer to perform a variety of conceptual moves all at once. Under its hegemony, the human body becomes a defenseless target for rape and veneration, and the body, in its material and abstract phase, a resource for metaphor. For example, Moynihan's "tangle of pathology" provides the descriptive strategy for the work's fourth chapter, which suggests that "underachievement" in black males of the lower classes is primarily the fault of black females, who achieve out of all proportion both to their numbers in the community and to the paradigmatic example before the nation: "Ours is a society which presumes male leadership in private and public affairs. . . . A subculture, such as that of the Negro American, in which this is not the pattern, is placed at a distinct disadvantage" [75]. Between charts and diagrams, we are asked to consider the impact of qualitative measure on the black male's performance on standardized examinations, matriculation in schools of higher and professional training, etc. Even though Moynihan sounds a critique on his own argument here, he quickly withdraws from its possibilities, suggesting that black males should reign because that is the way the majority culture carries things out: "It is clearly a disadvantage for a minority group to be operating under one principle, while the great majority of the population . . . is operating on another" [75]. Those persons living according to the perceived "matriarchal" pattern are, therefore, caught in a state of social "pathology."

Even though Daughters have their own agenda with reference to this order of Fathers (imagining for the moment that Moynihan's fiction—and others like it— does not represent an adequate one and that there *is*, once we dis-cover him, a Father here), my contention that these social and cultural subjects make doubles, unstable in their respective identities, in effect transports us to a common historical ground, the socio-political order of the New World. That order, with its human sequence written in blood, *represents* for its African and indigenous peoples a scene of *actual* mutilation, dismemberment, and exile. First of all, their New-World, diasporic plight marked a *theft of the body*—a willful and violent (and unimaginable from this distance) severing of the captive body from its motive will, its active desire. Under these conditions, we lose at least *gender* difference *in the outcome*, and the female body and the male body become a territory of cultural and political maneuver, not at all gender-related, gender-specific. But this body, at least from the point of view of the captive community, focuses a private and particular space, at which point of convergence biological, sexual, social, cultural, linguistic, ritualistic, and psychological fortunes join. This profound intimacy of interlocking detail is disrupted, however, by externally imposed meanings and uses: 1) the captive body becomes the source of an irresistible, destructive sensuality; 2) at the same time—in stunning contradiction—the captive body reduces to a thing, becoming *being for* the captor; 3) in this absence *from* a subject position, the captured sexualities provide a physical and biological expression of "otherness"; 4) as a category of "otherness," the captive body translates into a potential for pornotroping and embodies sheer physical powerlessness that slides into a more general "powerlessness," resonating through various centers of human and social meaning.

But I would make a distinction in this case between "body" and "flesh" and impose that distinction as the central one between captive and liberated subject-positions. In that sense, before the "body" there is the "flesh," that zero degree of social conceptualization that does not escape concealment under the brush of discourse, or the reflexes of iconography. Even though the European hegemonies stole bodies—some of them female—out of West African communities in concert with the African "middleman," we regard this human and social irreparability as high crimes against the *flesh*, as the person of African females and African males registered the wounding. If we think of the "flesh" as a primary narrative, then we mean its seared, divided, ripped-apartness, riveted to the ship's hole, fallen, or "escaped" overboard.

One of the most poignant aspects of William Goodell's contemporaneous study of the North American slave codes gives precise expression to the tortures and instruments of captivity. Reporting an instance of Jonathan Edward's observations on the tortures of enslavement, Goodell narrates: "The smack of the whip is all day long in the ears of those who are on the plantation, or in the vicinity; and it is used with such dexterity and severity as not only to lacerate the skin but to tear out small portions of the flesh at almost every stake" [22]. The anatomical specifications of rupture, of altered human tissue, take on the objective description of laboratory prose—eyes beaten out, arms, backs, skulls branded, a left jaw, a right ankle, punctured; teeth missing, as the calculated work of iron, whips, chains, knives, the canine patrol, the bullet.

These undecipherable markings on the captive body render a kind of hieroglyphics of the flesh whose severe disjunctures come to be hidden to the cultural seeing by skin color. We might well ask if this phenomenon of marking and branding actually "transfers" from one generation to another, finding its various *symbolic substitutions* in an efficacy of meanings that repeat the initiating moments? As Elaine Scarry describes the mechanisms of torture [Scarry 27–59], these lacerations, woundings, fissures, tears, scars, openings, ruptures, lesions, rendings, punctures of the flesh create the distance between what I would designate a cultural *vestibularity* and the *culture*, whose state apparatus, including judges, attorneys, "owners," "soul drivers," "overseers," and "men of God," apparently colludes with a protocol of "search and destroy." This body whose flesh carries the female and the male to the frontiers of survival bears in person the marks of a cultural text whose inside has been turned outside.

The flesh is the concentration of "ethnicity" that contemporary critical discourses neither acknowledge nor discourse away. It is this "flesh and blood" entity, in the vestibule for "pre-view" of a colonized North America, that is essentially ejected from "The Female Body in Western Culture" [see Suleiman, ed.], but it makes good theory, or commemorative "herstory" to want to "forget," or to have failed to realize, that the African female subject, under these historic conditions, is not only the target of rape—in one sense, an interiorized violation of body and mind—but also the topic of specifically *externalized* acts of torture and prostration that we imagine as the peculiar province of *male* brutality and torture inflected by other males. A female body strung from a tree limb, or bleeding from the breast on any given day of field work because the "overseer," standing the length of a whip, has popped her flesh open, adds a lexical and living dimension to the narratives of women in culture and society [Davis 9]. This materialized scene of unprotected female flesh—of female flesh "ungendered"— offers a praxis and a theory, a text for living and for dying, and a method for reading both through their diverse mediations.

Among the myriad uses to which the enslaved community was put, Goodell identifies its value for medical research: "Assortments of diseased, *damaged,* and disabled Negroes, deemed incurable and otherwise worthless are *bought up,* it seems (by medical institutions, to be experimented and operated upon for purposes of 'medical education' and the interest of medical science" [86–87; Goodell's emphasis]. From the *Charleston Mercury* for October 12, 1838, Goodell notes this advertisement:

> 'To planters and others.—Wanted, fifty Negroes, any person, having sick Negroes, considered incurable by their respective physicians, and wishing to dispose of them, Dr. S. will *pay cash* for Negroes affected with scrofula, or king's evil, confirmed hypochondriasm, apoplexy, diseases of the liver, kidneys, spleen, stomach and intestines, bladder and its appendages, diarrhea, dysentery, etc. The *highest cash price will be paid,* on application as above.' at No. 110 Church Street, Charleston. [87; Goodell's emphasis]

This profitable "atomizing" of the captive body provides another angle on the divided flesh: we lose any hint or suggestion of a dimension of ethics, of relatedness between human personality and its anatomical features, between one human personality and another, between human personality and cultural institutions. To that extent, the procedures adopted for the captive flesh demarcate a total objectification, as the entire captive community becomes a living laboratory.

The captive body, then, brings into focus a gathering of social realities as well as a metaphor for value so thoroughly interwoven in their literal and figurative emphases that distinctions between them are virtually useless. Even though the captive flesh/body has been "liberated," and no one need pretend that even the quotation marks do not *matter,* dominant symbolic activity, the ruling episteme that releases the dynamics of naming and valuation, remains grounded in the originating metaphors of captivity and mutilation so that it is as if neither time nor history, nor historiography and its topics, show movement, as the human subject is "murdered" over and over again by the passions of a bloodless and anonymous archaism, showing itself in endless disguise. Faulkner's young Chick Mallison in *The Mansion* calls "it" other names—"the ancient subterrene atavistic fear—" [227]. And I would call it the Great Long National Shame. But people do not talk like that anymore—it is "embarrassing," just as the retrieval of mutilated female bodies will likely be "backward" for some people. Neither the shameface of the embarrassed, nor the not-looking-back of the self-assured is of much interest to us, and will not help at all if rigor is our dream. We might concede, at the very least, that sticks and bricks *might* break our bones, but words will most certainly *kill* us.

The symbolic order that I wish to trace I this writing, calling it an "American grammar," begins at the "beginning," which is really a rupture and a radically different kind of cultural continuation. The massive demographic shifts, the violent formation of a modern African consciousness, that take place on the subsaharan Continent during the initiative strikes which open the Atlantic Slave Trade in the fifteenth century of our Christ, interrupted hundreds of years of black African culture. We write and think, then, about an outcome of aspects of

African-American life in the United States under the pressure of those events. I might as well add that the familiarity of this narrative does nothing to appease the hunger of recorded memory, nor does the persistence of the repeated rob these well-known, oft-told events of their power, even now, to startle, in a very real sense, every writing as revision makes the "discovery" all over again.

2

The narratives by African peoples and their descendants, though not as numerous from those early centuries of the "execrable trade" as the researcher would wish, suggest, in their rare occurrence, that the visual shock waves touched off when African and European "met" reverberated on both sides of the encounter. The narrative of the "Life of Olaudah Equiano, or Gustavus Vassa, the African, Written by Himself," first published in London in 1789, makes it quite clear that the first Europeans Equiano observed on what is now Nigerian soil were as unreal for him as he and others must have been for the European captors. The cruelty of "these white men with horrible looks, red faces, and long hair," of these "spirits," as the narrator would have it, occupies several pages of Equiano's attention, alongside a firsthand account of Nigerian interior life [27 ff.]. We are justified in regarding the outcome of Equiano's experience in the same light as he himself might have—as a "fall," as a veritable descent into the loss of communicative force.

If, as Todorov points out, the Mayan and Aztec peoples "lost control of communication" [61] in light of Spanish intervention, we could observe, similarly, that Vassa falls among men whose language is not only strange to him, but whose habits and practices strike him as "astonishing":

> [The sea, the slave ship] filled me with astonishment, which was soon converted to terror, when I was carried on board. I was immediately handled, and tossed up to see if I was sound, by some of the crew; and I was now persuaded that I had gotten into a world of bad spirits, and that they were going to kill me. Their complexions, too, differing so much from ours, their long hair, and the language they spoke (which was different from any I had very heard), united to confirm me in this belief. [Equiano 27]

The captivating party does not only "earn" the right to dispose of the captive body as it sees fit, but gains, consequently, the right to name and "name" it: Equiano, for instance, identifies at least three different names that he is given in numerous passages between his Benin homeland and the Virginia colony, the latter and England—"Michael," "Jacob," "Gustavus Vassa" [35; 36].

The nicknames by which African-American women have been called, or regarded, or imagined on the New World scene—the opening lines of this essay provide examples—demonstrate the powers of distortion that the dominant community seizes as its unlawful prerogative. Moynihan's "Negro Family," then, borrows its narrative energies from the grid of associations, from the semantic and iconic folds buried deep in the collective past, that come to surround and signify the captive person. Though there is no absolute point of chronological initiation, we might repeat certain familiar impression points that lend shape to the business of dehumanized naming. Expecting to find direct and amplified reference to African women during the opening years of the Trade, the observer is disappointed time and again that this cultural subject is concealed beneath the mighty debris of the itemized account, between the lines of the massive logs of commercial enterprise that overrun the sense of clarity we believed we had gained concerning this collective humiliation. Elizabeth Donnan's enormous, four-volume documentation becomes a case in point.

Turning directly to this source, we discover what we had not expected to find— that this aspect of the search is rendered problematic and that observations of a field of manners and its related sociometries are an outgrowth of the industry of the "exterior other" [Todorov 3], called "anthropology" later on. The European males who laded and captained these galleys and who policed and corralled these human beings, in hundreds of vessels from Liverpool to Elmina, to Jamaica; from the Cayenne Islands, to the ports at Charleston and Salem, and for three centuries of human life, were not curious about this "cargo" that bled, packed like so many live sardines among the immovable objects. Such inveterate obscene blindness might be denied, point blank, as a possibility for anyone, except that we know it happened.

Donnan's first volume covers three centuries of European "discovery" and "conquest," beginning 50 years before pious Cristobal, Christum Ferens, the bearer of Christ, laid claim to what he thought was the "Indies." From Gomes Eannes de Azurara's "Chronicle of the Discovery and Conquest of Guinea, 1441–1448" [Donnan 1:18–41], we learn that the Portuguese probably gain the dubious distinction of having introduced black Africans to the European market of servitude. We are also reminded that "Geography" is not a divine gift. Quite to the contrary, its boundaries were shifted during the European "Age of Conquest" in giddy desperation, according to the dictates of conquering armies, the edicts of prelates, the peculiar myopia of the medieval Christian mind. Looking for the "Nile River," for example, according to the fifteenth-century Portuguese notion, is someone's joke. For all that the pre-Columbian "explorers" knew about the science of navigation and geography, we are surprised that more parties of them did not end up "discovering" Europe. Perhaps, from a certain angle, that is precisely all that they found—an alternative reading of ego. The Portuguese, having little idea where the Nile ran, at least understood right away that there were men and women darker-skinned than themselves, but they were not specifically knowledgeable, or ingenious, about the various families and groupings represented by them. De Azurara records encounters with "Moors," "Mooresses," "Mulattoes," and people "black as Ethiops" [1:28], but it seems that the "Land of Guinea," or of "Black Men," or of "The Negroes" [1:35] was located anywhere southeast of Cape Verde, the Canaries, and the River Senegal, looking at an eighteenth-century European version of the subsaharan Continent along the West African coast [1:frontispiece].

Three genetic distinctions are available to the Portuguese eye, all along the riffs of melanin in the skin: in a field of captives, some of the observed are "white enough, fair to look upon, and well-proportioned." Others are less "white like mulattoes," and still others "black as Ethiops, and so ugly, both in features and in body, as almost to appear (to those who saw them) the images of a lower hemisphere" [1:28]. By implication, this "third man," standing for the most aberrant phenotype to the observing eye, embodies the linguistic community most unknown to the European. Arabic translators among the Europeans could at least "talk" to the "Moors" and instruct them to ransom themselves, or else. . . .

Typically, there is in this grammar of description the perspective of "declension," not of simultaneity, and its point of initiation is solipsistic—it begins with a narrative self, in an apparent unity of feeling, and unlike Equiano, who also saw "ugly" when he looked out, this collective self uncovers the means by which to subjugate the "foreign code of conscience," whose most easily remarkable and irremediable difference is perceived in skin color. By the time of De Azurara's mid-fifteenth-century narrative and a century and a half before Shakespeare's "old black ram" of an Othello "tups" that "white ewe" of a Desdemona, the magic of skin color is already installed as a decisive factor in human dealings.

In De Azurara's narrative, we observe males looking at other males, as "female" is subsumed here under the general category of estrangement. Few places in these excerpts carve out a distinct female space, though there are moments of portrayal that perceive female captives in the implications of socio-cultural function. When the field of captives (referred to above) is divided among the spoilers, no heed is paid to relations, as fathers are separated from sons, husbands from wives, brothers from sisters and brothers, mothers from children—male and female. It seems clear that the political program of European Christianity promotes this hierarchical view among *males*, although it remains puzzling to us exactly how this version of Christianity transforms the "pagan" also into the "ugly." It appears that human beings came up with degrees of "fair" and then the "hideous," in its overtones of bestiality, as the opposite of "fair," all by themselves without stage direction, even though there is the curious and blazing exception of Nietzsche's Socrates, who was Athens's ugliest and wisest and best citizen. The intimate choreography that the Portuguese narrator sets going between the "faithless" and the "ugly" transforms a partnership of dancers into a single figure. Once the "faithless," indiscriminate of the three stops of Portuguese skin color, are transported to Europe, they become an *altered* human factor:

> And so their lot was now quite contrary to what it had been, since before they had lived in perdition of soul and body; of their souls, in that they were yet pagans, without the clearness and the light of the Holy Faith; and of their bodies, in that they lived like beasts, without any custom of reasonable beings—for they had no knowledge of bread and wine, and they were without covering of clothes, or the lodgment of houses; and worse than all, through the great ignorance that was in them, in that they had no understanding of good, but only knew how to live in bestial sloth. [1:30]

The altered human factor renders an alterity of European ego, an invention, or "discovery" as decisive in the full range of its social implications as the birth of a newborn. According to the semantic alignments of the excerpted passage, personhood, for this European observer, locates an immediately outward and superficial determination, gauged by quite arbitrarily opposed and specular categories: that these "pagans" did not have "bread" and "wine" did not mean that they were feastless, as Equiano observes about the Benin diet, c. 1745, in the province of Essaka:

> Our manner of living is entirely plain; for as yet the natives are unacquainted
> with those refinements in cookery which debauch the taste; bullocks, goats,
> and poultry supply the greatest part of their food. (These constitute likewise
> the principal wealth of the country, as the chief articles of commerce.) The
> flesh is usually stewed in a pan; to make it savory we sometimes use pepper,
> and other spices, and we have salt made of wood ashes. Our vegetables are
> mostly plaintains, eadas, yams, beans and Indian corn. The head of the fam-
> ily usually eats alone; his wives and slaves have also their separate
> tables. . . . [Equiano 8]

Just as fufu serves the Ghanaian diet today as a starch-and-bread-substitute, palm
wine (an item by the same name in the eighteenth-century palate of the Benin
community) need not be Heitz Cellars Martha's Vineyard and vice-versa in order
for a guest, say, to imagine that she has enjoyed. That African housing arrangements of the fifteenth century did not resemble those familiar to De Azurara's
narrator need not have meant that the African communities he encountered were
without dwellings. Again, Equiano's narrative suggests that by the middle of the
eighteenth century, at least, African living patterns were not only quite distinct
in their sociometrical implications, but that also their architectonics accurately reflected the climate and availability of resources in the local circumstance: "These
houses never exceed one story in height; they are always built of wood, or stakes
driven into the ground, crossed with wattles, and neatly plastered within and
without" [9]. Hierarchical impulse in *both* De Azurara's and Equiano's narratives
translates all *perceived* difference as a fundamental degradation *or* transcendence,
but at least in Equiano's case, cultural practices are not observed in any intimate
connection with skin color. For all intents and purposes, the politics of melanin,
not isolated in its strange powers from the imperatives of a mercantile and competitive economics of European nation-states, will make of "transcendence" and
"degradation" the basis of a historic violence that will rewrite the histories of
modern Europe and black Africa. These mutually exclusive nominative elements
come to rest on the same governing semantics . . . the ahistorical, or symptoms of
the "sacred."

By August 1518, the Spanish king, Francisco de Los Covos, under the aegis of
a powerful negation, could order "4000 negro slaves both male and female, provided they be Christians" to be taken to the Caribbean, "the islands and the
mainland of the ocean sea already discovered or to be discovered" [Donnan 1:42].
Though the notorious "Middle Passage" appears to the investigator as a vast
background without boundaries in time and space, we see it related in Donnan's
accounts to the opening up of the entire Western hemisphere for the specific purposes of enslavement and colonization. De Azurara's narrative belongs, then, to
a discourse of appropriation whose strategies will prove fatal to communities
along the coastline of West Africa, stretching, according to Olaudah Equiano,
"3400 miles, from Senegal to Angola, and [will include] a variety of kingdoms"
[Equiano 5].

The conditions of the "Middle Passage" are among the most incredible narratives available to the student, as it remains not easily imaginable. Late in the
chronicles of the Atlantic Slave Trade, Britain's Parliament entertained discussions concerning possible "regulations" for slave vessels. A Captain Perry visited
the Liverpool port, and among the ships that he inspected was "The Brookes,"

probably the most well-known image of the slave galley with its representative *personae* etched into the drawing like so many cartoon figures. Elizabeth Donnan's second volume carries the "Brookes Plan," along with an elaborate delineation of its dimensions from the investigative reporting of Perry himself: "Let it now be supposed . . . further, that every man slave is to be allowed six feet by one foot four inches for room, every woman five feet ten by one foot four, every boy five feet by one foot two, and every girl four feet six by one foot . . . " [2:592, n]. The owner of "The Brookes," James Jones, had recommended that "five females be reckoned as four males, and three boys or girls as equal to two grown persons" [2:592].

These sealed inequalities complement the commanding terms of the dehumanizing, ungendering, and defacing project of African persons that De Azurara's narrator might have recognized. It has been pointed out to me that these measurements do reveal the application of the gender rule to the material conditions of passage, but I would suggest that "gendering" takes place within the confines of the domestic, an essential metaphor that then spreads its tentacles for male and female subject over a wider ground of human and social purposes. Domesticity appears to gain its power by way of a common origin of cultural fictions that are grounded in the specificity of proper names, more exactly, a patronymic, which, in turn, situates those persons it "covers" in a particular place. Contrarily, the cargo of a ship might not be regarded as elements of the domestic, even though the vessel that carries it is sometimes romantically (ironically?) personified as "she." The human cargo of a slave vessel—in the fundamental effacement and remission of African family and proper names—offers a *counter*-narrative to notions of the domestic.

Those African persons in "Middle Passage" were literally suspended in the "oceanic," if we think of the latter in its Freudian orientation as an analogy for undifferentiated identity: removed from the indigenous land and culture, and not-yet "American" either, these captive persons, without names that their captors would recognize, were in movement across the Atlantic, but they were also *no-where* at all. Inasmuch as, on any given day, we might imagine the captive personality did not know where s/he was, we could say that they were the culturally "unmade," thrown in the midst of a figurative darkness that "exposed" their destinies to an unknown course. Often enough for the captains of these galleys, navigational science of the day was not sufficient to guarantee the intended destination. We might say that the slave ship, its crew, and its human-as-cargo stand for a wild and unclaimed richness of *possibility* that is not interrupted, not "counted"/"accounted," or differentiated, until its movement gains the land thousands of miles away from the point of departure. Under these conditions, one is neither female, nor male, as both subjects are taken into "account" as *quantities*. The female in "Middle Passage," as the apparently smaller physical mass, occupies "less room" in a directly translatable money economy. But she is, nevertheless, quantifiable by the same rules of accounting as her male counterpart.

It is not only difficult for the student to find "female" in "Middle Passage," but also, as Herbert S. Klein observes, "African women did not enter the Atlantic slave trade in anything like the numbers of African men. At all ages, men outnumbered women on the slave ships bound for America from Africa" [Klein 29]. Though this observation does not change the reality of African women's captivity and servitude in New World communities, it does provide a perspective from which to contemplate the *internal* African slave trade, which, according to Africanists, remained a predominantly *female* market. Klein nevertheless affirms that those females forced into the trade were segregated "from men for policing purposes" ["African Women" 35]. He claims that both "were allotted the same space between decks . . . and both were fed the same food" [35]. It is not altogether clear from Klein's observations *for whom* the "police" kept vigil. It is certainly known from evidence presented in Donnan's third volume ("New England and the Middle Colonies") that insurrection was both frequent and feared in passage, and we have not yet found a great deal of evidence to support a thesis that female captives participated in insurrectionary activity [see White 63–64]. Because it was the rule, however—not the exception—that the African female, in both indigenous African cultures and in what becomes her "home," performed tasks of hard physical labor—so much so that the quintessential "slave" is *not* a male, but a female—we wonder at the seeming docility of the subject, granting her a "feminization" that enslavement kept at bay. Indeed, across the spate of discourse that I examined for this writing, the acts of enslavement and responses to it comprise a more or less agonistic engagement of confrontational hostilities among males. The visual and historical evidence betrays the dominant discourse on the matter as incomplete, but *counter*-evidence is inadequate as well: the sexual violation of captive females and their own express rage against their oppressors did not constitute events that captains and their crews rushed to record in letters to their sponsoring companies, or sons on board in letters home to their New England mamas.

One suspects that there are several ways to snare a mockingbird, so that insurrection might have been involved, from time to time, rather more subtle means than mutiny on the *Felicity*, for instance. At any rate, we get very little notion in the written record of the life of women, children, and infants in "Middle Passage," and no idea of the fate of the pregnant female captive and the unborn, which startling thematic bell hooks addresses in the opening chapter of her pathfinding work [see hooks 15–49]. From hooks's lead, however, we might guess that the "reproduction of mothering" in this historic instance carries few of the benefits of a *patriarchalized* female gender, which, from one point of view, is the *only* female gender there is.

The relative silence of the record on this point constitutes a portion of the disquieting lacunae that feminist investigation seeks to fill. Such silence is the nickname of distortion, of the unknown human factor that a revised public discourse would both undo *and* reveal. This cultural subject is inscribed historically as anonymity/anomie in various public documents of European-American mal(e)venture, from Portuguese De Azurara in the middle of the fifteenth century, to South Carolina's Henry Laurens in the eighteenth.

What confuses and enriches the picture is precisely the sameness of anonymous portrayal that adheres tenaciously across the division of gender. In the vertical columns of accounts and ledgers that comprise Donnan's work, the terms "Negroes" and "Slaves" denote a common status. For instance, entries in one account, from September 1700 through September 1702, are specifically descriptive of the names of the ships and the private traders in Barbados who will receive the stipulated goods, but "No. Negroes" and "Sum sold for per head" are so exactly arithmetical that it is as if these additions and multiplications belong to the other side of an equation [Donnan 2:25]. One is struck by the detail and precision that characterize these accounts, as a narrative, or story, is always implied by a man or woman's name: "Wm. Webster," "John Dunn," "Thos. Brownbill," "Robt. Knowles." But the "other" side of the page, as it were, equally precise, throws no *fac*e in view. It seems that nothing breaks the uniformity in this guise. If in no other way, the destruction of the African name, of kin, of linguistic, and ritual connections is so obvious in the vital stats sheet that we tend to overlook it. Quite naturally, the trader is not interested, in an *semantic* sense, in this "baggage" that he must deliver, but that he is not is all the more reason to search out the metaphorical implications of *naming* as one of the key sources of a bitter Americanizing for African persons.

The loss of the indigenous name/land provides a metaphor of displacement for other human and cultural features and relations, including the displacement of the genitalia, the female's and the male's desire that engenders the future. The fact that the enslaved person's access to the issue of his/her own body is not entirely clear in this historic period throws in crisis all aspects of the blood relations, as captors apparently felt no obligation to acknowledge them. Actually trying to understand how the confusions of consanguinity worked becomes the project, because the outcome goes far to explain the rule of gender and its application to the African female in captivity.

3

Even though the essays in Claire C. Robertson's and Martin A. Klein's *Women and Slavery in Africa* have specifically to do with aspects of the internal African slave trade, some of their observations shed light on the captivities of the Diaspora. At least these observations have the benefit of altering the kind of questions we might ask of these silent chapters. For example, Robertson's essay, which opens the volume, discusses the term "slavery" in a wide variety of relationships. The enslaved person as *property* identifies the most familiar element of a most startling proposition. But to overlap *kinlessness* on the requirements of property might enlarge our view of the conditions of enslavement. Looking specifically at documents from the West African societies of Songhay and Dahomey, Claude Meillassoux elaborates several features of the property/kinless constellation that are highly suggestive for our own quite different purposes.

Meillassoux argues that "slavery creates an economic and social agent whose virtue lies in being outside the kinship system" ["Female Slavery," Robertson and Klein 50]. Because the Atlantic trade involved heterogeneous social and ethnic formations in an explicit power relationship, we certainly cannot mean "kinship system" in precisely the same way that Meillassoux observes at work within the intricate calculus of descent among West African societies. However, the idea becomes useful as a point of contemplation when we try to sharpen our own sense of the African female's reproductive uses within the diasporic enterprise of enslavement and the genetic reproduction of the enslaved. In effect, under conditions of captivity, the offspring of the female does not "belong" to the Mother, nor is s/he "related" to the "owner," though the latter "possesses" it, and in the

African-American instance, often fathered it, *and*, as often, without whatever benefit of patrimony. In the social outline that Meillassoux is pursuing, the offspring of the enslaved, "being unrelated both to their begetters and to their owners . . . , find themselves in the situation of being orphans" [50].

In the context of the United States, we could not say that the enslaved offspring was "orphaned," but the child does become, under the press of a patronymic, patrifocal, patrilineal, and patriarchal order, the man/woman on the boundary, whose human and familial status, by the very nature of the case, had yet to be defined. I would call this enforced state of breach another instance of vestibular cultural formation where "kinship" loses meaning, *since it can be invaded at any given and arbitrary moment by the property relations*. I certainly do not mean to say that African peoples in the New World did not maintain the powerful ties of sympathy that bind blood-relations in a network of feeling, of continuity. It is precisely *that* relationship—not customarily recognized by the code of slavery—that historians have long identified as the inviolable "Black Family" and further suggest that this structure remains one of the supreme social achievements of African-Americans under conditions of enslavement [see John Blassingame 79 ff.].

Indeed, the *revised* "Black Family" of enslavement has engendered an older tradition of historiographical and sociological writings than we usually think. Ironically enough, E. Franklin Frazier's *Negro Family in the United States* likely provides the closest *contemporary* narrative of conceptualization for the "Moynihan Report." Originally published in 1939, Frazier's work underwent two redactions in 1948 and 1966. Even though Frazier's outlook on this familial configuration remains basically sanguine, I would support Angela Davis's skeptical reading of Frazier's "Black Matriarchate" [Davis 14]. "*Except where the master's will was concerned*," Frazier contends, this matriarchal figure "developed a spirit of independence and a keen sense of her personal rights" [1966: 47; emphasis mine]. The "exception" in this instance tends to be overwhelming, as the African-American female's "dominance" and "strength" come to be interpreted by later generations, both black and white, oddly enough as a "pathology," as an instrument of castration. Frazier's larger point, we might suppose, is that African-Americans developed such resourcefulness under conditions of captivity that "family" must be conceded as one of their redoubtable social attainments. This line of interpretation is pursued by Blassingame and Eugene Genovese [*Roll, Jordan, Roll* 70–75], among other U.S. historians, and indeed assumes a centrality of focus in our own thinking about the impact and outcome of captivity.

It seems clear, however, that "Family," as we practice and understand it "in the West"—the *vertical* transfer of a bloodline, of a patronymic, of titles and entitlements, of real estate and the prerogatives of "cold cash," from *fathers* to *sons* and in the supposedly free exchange of affectional ties between a male and a female of *his* choice—becomes the mythically revered privilege of a free and freed community. In that sense, African peoples in the historic Diaspora had nothing to prove, *if* the point had been that they were not capable of "family" (read "civilization"), since it is stunningly evident, in Equiano's narrative, for instance, that Africans were not only capable of the concept and the practice of "family," including "slaves," but in modes of elaboration and naming that were at lest as complex as those of the "nuclear family" "in the West."

Whether or not we decide that the support systems that African-Americans derived under conditions of captivity should be called "family," or something else, strikes me as supremely impertinent. The point remains that captive persons were *forced* into patterns of *dispersal*, beginning with the Trade itself, into the *horizontal* relatedness of language groups, discourse formations, bloodlines, names, and properties by the legal arrangements of enslavement. It is true that the most "well-meaning" of "masters" (and there must have been *some*) *could not*, *did not* alter the *ideological* and hegemonic mandates of dominance. It must be conceded that African-Americans, under the press of a hostile and compulsory patriarchal order, bound and determined to destroy them, or to preserve them only in the service and at the behest of the "master" class, exercised a degrees of courage and will to survive that startles the imagination even now. Although it makes good revisionist history to read this tale *liberally*, it is probably truer than we know at this distance (and truer than contemporary social practice in the community would suggest on occasion) that the captive person developed, time and time again, certain ethical and sentimental features that tied her and him, *across* the landscape to others, often sold from hand to hand, of the same and different blood in a common fabric of memory and inspiration.

We might choose to call this connectedness "family," or "support structure," but that is a rather different case from the moves of a dominant symbolic order, pledged to maintain the supremacy of race. It is that order that forces "family" to modify itself when it does not mean family of the "master," or dominant enclave. It is this rhetorical and symbolic move that declares primacy over any other human and social claim, and in that political order of things, "kin," just as gender formation, has no decisive legal or social efficacy.

We return frequently to Frederick Douglass's careful elaborations of the arrangements of captivity, and we are astonished each reading by two dispersed, yet poignantly related, familial enactments that suggest a connection between "kinship" and "property." Douglass tells us early in the opening chapter of the 1845 *Narrative* that he was separated in infancy from his mother: "For what this separation is [sic] done, I do not know, unless it be to hinder the development of the child's affection toward its mother, and to blunt and destroy the natural affection of the mother for the child. This is the inevitable result" [22].

Perhaps one of the assertions that Meillassoux advances concerning indigenous African formations of enslavement might be turned as a question against the perspective of Douglass's witness: is the genetic reproduction of the slave and the recognition of the rights of the slave to his or her offspring a check on the *profitability* of slavery? And how so, if so? We see vaguely the route to framing a response, especially to the question's second half and perhaps to the first: the enslaved must not be permitted to perceive that he or she has any human rights that matter. Certainly if "kinship" were possible, the property relations would be undermined, since the offspring would then "belong" to a mother and a father. In the system that Douglass articulates, genetic reproduction becomes, then, not an elaboration of the life-principle in its cultural overlap, but an extension of the boundaries of proliferating properties. Meillassoux goes so far as to argue that "slavery exists where the slave class is reproduced through institutional apparatus: war and market" [50]. Since, in the United States, the market of slavery identified the chief institutional means for maintaining a class of enforced servile labor, it seems that the biological reproduction of the enslaved was not alone sufficient to reenforce the *estate* of slavery. If, as Meillassoux contends, "femininity loses its sacredness in slavery" [64], then so does "motherhood" as female blood-rite/right. To that extent, the captive female body locates precisely a moment of converging political and social vectors that mark the flesh as a prime commodity of exchange. While this proposition is open to further exploration, suffice it to say now that this open exchange of female bodies in the raw offers a kind of Ur-text to the dynamics and signification and representation that the gendered female would unravel.

For Douglass, the loss of his mother eventuates in alienation from his brother and sister who live in the same house with him: "The early separation of us from our mother had well nigh blotted the fact of our relationship from our memories" [45]. What could this mean? The *physical* proximity of the siblings survives the mother's death. They grasp their connection in the physical sense, but Douglass appears to mean a *psychological* bonding whose success mandates the *mother's* presence. Could we say, then, that the *feeling* of kinship is *not* inevitable? That it describes a relationship that appears "natural," but must be "cultivated" under actual material conditions? If the child's humanity is mirrored initially in the eyes of its mother, or the maternal function, then we might be able to guess that the social subject grasps the whole dynamic of resemblance and kinship by way of the same source.

There is an amazing thematic synonymity on this point between aspects of Douglass's *Narrative* and Malcolm El-Hajj Malik El Shabazz's *Autobiography of Malcolm X* [21 ff.]. Through the loss of the mother, in the latter contemporary instance, to the institution of "insanity" and the state—a full century after Douglass's writing and under social conditions that might be designated a post-emancipation neo-enslavement—Malcolm and his siblings, robbed of their activist father in a kkk-like ambush, are not only widely dispersed across a makeshift social terrain, but also show symptoms of estrangement and "disremembering" that require many years to heal, and even then, only by way of Malcolm's prison ordeal turned, eventually, into a redemptive occurrence.

The destructive loss of the natural mother, whose biological/genetic relationship to the child remains unique and unambiguous, opens the enslaved young to social ambiguity and chaos: the ambiguity of his/her fatherhood and to a structure of other relational elements, now threatened, that would declare the young's connection to a genetic and historic future by way of his own siblings. That the father in Douglass's case was most likely the "master," not by any means special to Douglass, involves a hideous paradox. Fatherhood, at best a supreme cultural courtesy, attenuates here on the one hand into a monstrous accumulation of power on the other. One has been "made" and "bought" by disparate currencies, linking back to a common origin of exchange and domination. The denied genetic link becomes the chief strategy of an undenied ownership, as if the interrogation into the father's identity—the blank space where his proper name will fit—were answered by the fact, *de jure* of a material possession. "And this is done," Douglass asserts, "too obviously to administer to the [master's] own lusts, and make a gratification of their wicked desires profitable as well as pleasurable" [23].

Whether or not the captive female and/or her sexual oppressor derived "pleasure" from their seductions and couplings is not a question we can politely ask. Whether or not "pleasure" is possible at all under conditions that I would aver as non-freedom for both or either of the parties has not been settled. Indeed, we could go so far as to entertain the very real possibility that "sexuality," as a term of implied relationship and desire, is dubiously appropriate, manageable, or accurate to any of the familial arrangements under a system of enslavement, from the master's family to the captive enclave. Under this arrangements, the customary lexis of sexuality, including "reproduction," "motherhood," "pleasure," and "desire" are thrown into unrelieved crisis.

If the testimony of Linda Brent/Harriet Jacobs is to be believed, the official mistresses of slavery's "masters" constitute a privileged class of the tormented, if such contradiction can be entertained [Brent 29–35]. Linda Brent/Harriet Jacobs recounts in the course of her narrative scenes from a "psychodrama," opposing herself and "Mrs. Flint," in what we have come to consider the classic alignment between captive woman and free. Suspecting that her husband, Dr. Flint, has sexual designs on the young Linda (and the doctor is nearly humorously incompetent at it, according to the story line), Mrs. Flint assumes the role of a perambulatory nightmare who visits the captive woman in the spirit of a veiled seduction. Mrs. Flint imitates the incubus who "rides" its victim in order to exact confession, expiation, and anything else that the immaterial power might want. (Gayle Jones's *Corregidora* [1975] weaves a contemporary fictional situation around the historic motif of entangled female sexualities.) This narrative scene from Brent's work, dictated to Lydia Maria Child, provides an instance of a repeated sequence, purportedly based on "real" life. But the scene in question appears to so commingle its signals with the fictive, with casebook narrative from psychoanalysis, that we are certain that the narrator has her hands on an explosive moment of New-World/U.S. history that feminist investigation is beginning to unravel. The narrator recalls:

> Sometimes I woke up, and found her bending over me. At other times she whispered in my ear, as though it were her husband who was speaking to me, and listened to hear what I would answer. If she startled me, on such occasion, she would slide stealthily away; and the next morning she would tell me I had been talking in my sleep, and ask who I was talking to. At last, I began to be fearful for my life. . . . [Brent 33]

The "jealous mistress" here (but "jealous" for whom?) forms an analogy with the "master" to the extent that male dominative modes give the male the material means to fully act out what the female might only *wish*. The mistress in the case of Brent's narrative becomes a metaphor for *his* madness that arises in the ecstasy of unchecked power. Mrs. Flint enacts a male alibi and prosthetic motion that is mobilized *at night*, at the material place of the dream work. In both male and female instances, the subject attempts to *inculcate* his or her will into the vulnerable, supine body. Though this is barely hinted on the surface of the text, we might say that Brent, between the lines of her narrative, demarcates a sexuality that is neuter-bound, inasmuch as it represents an open vulnerability to a gigantic sexualized repertoire that may be alternately expressed as male/female. Since the gendered female *exists for* the male, we might suggest that the ungendered female—in an amazing stroke of pansexual potential—might be invaded/raided by another *woman* or man.

If *Incidents in the Life of a Slave Girl* were a novel, and not the memoirs of an escaped female captive, then we might say that "Mrs. Flint" is also the narrator's projection, her creation, so that for all her pious and correct umbrage toward the outrage of her captivity, some aspect of Linda Brent is released in a manifold repetition crisis that the doctor's wife comes to stand in for. In the case of both an imagined fiction and the narrative we have from Brent/Jacobs/Child, published only four years before the official proclamations of Freedom, we could say that African-American women's community and Anglo-American women's community, under certain shared cultural conditions, were the twin actants on a common psychic landscape, were subject to the same fabric of dread and humiliation. Neither could claim her body and its various productions—for quite different reasons, albeit—as her own, and in the case of the doctor's wife, *she* appears not to have wanted *her* body at all, but to desire to enter someone else's, specifically, Linda Brent's, in an apparently classic instance of sexual "jealousy" and appropriation. In fact, from one point of view, we cannot unravel one female's narrative from the other's, cannot decipher one without tripping over the other. In that sense, these "threads cable-strong" of an incestuous, interracial genealogy uncover slavery in the United States as one of the richest displays of the psychoanalytic dimensions of culture before the science of European psychoanalysis takes hold.

4

But just as we duly regard similarities between life conditions of American women—captive and free—we must observe those undeniable contrasts and differences so decisive that the African-American female's historic claim to the territory of womanhood and "femininity" still tends to rest too solidly on the subtle and shifting calibrations of a liberal ideology. Valerie Smith's reading of the tale of Linda Brent as a tale of "garreting" enables our notion that female gender for captive women's community is the tale writ between the lines and in the not-quite spaces of an American domesticity. It is this tale that we try to make clearer, or, keeping with the metaphor, "bring on line."

If the point is that the historic conditions of African-American women might be read as an unprecedented occasion in the national context, then gender and the arrangements of gender are both crucial and evasive. Holding, however, to a specialized reading of female gender as an *outcome* of a certain political, sociocultural empowerment within the context of the United States, we would regard dispossession as the *loss* of gender, or one of the chief elements in an altered reading of gender: "Women are considered of no value, *unless* they continually increase their owner's stock. They were put on par with animals" [Brent 49; emphasis mine]. Linda Brent's witness appears to contradict the point I would make, but I am suggesting that even though the enslaved female reproduced other enslaved persons, we do not read "birth" in this instance as a reproduction of mothering precisely because the female, like the male, has been robbed of the parental right, the parental function. One treads dangerous ground in suggesting an equation between female gender and mothering; in fact, feminist inquiry/praxis and the actual day-to-day living of numberless American women—black and white—have gone far to break the enthrallment of a female subject-position to the theoretical and actual situation of maternity. Our task here would be lightened considerably if we could simply slide over the powerful "No," the significant *exception*. In the historic formation to which I point, however, motherhood and female gendering/ungendering appear so intimately aligned that they seem to speak the same language. At least it is plausible to say that motherhood, while it does not exhaust the problematics of female gender, offers one prominent line of approach to it. I would go farther: Because African-American women experienced uncertainty regarding their infants' lives in the historic situation, gendering, in its coeval reference to African-American women, *insinuates* an implicit and unresolved puzzle both within current feminist discourse and within those discursive communities that investigate the entire problematics of culture. Are we mistaken to suspect that history—at least in this instance—repeats itself yet again?

Every feature of social and human differentiation disappears in public discourses regarding the African-American person, as we encounter, in the juridical codes of slavery, personality reified. William Goodell's study not only demonstrates the rhetorical and moral passions of the abolitionist project, but also lends insight into the corpus of law that underwrites enslavement. If "slave" is perceived as the essence of stillness (an early version of "ethnicity"), or of an undynamic human state, fixed in time and space, then the law articulates this impossibility as its inherent feature: "Slaves shall be deemed, sold, taken, reputed and adjudged in law to be *chattels personal*, in the hands of their owners and possessors, and their executors, administrators, and assigns, to all intents, constructions, and purposes whatsoever" [23; Goodell emphasis].

Even though we tend to parody and simplify matters to behave as if the various civil codes of the slave-holding United States were monolithically informed, unified, and executed in their application, or that the "code" itself is spontaneously generated in an undivided historic moment, we read it nevertheless as exactly this: the *peak points*, the salient and characteristic features of a human and social procedure that evolves over a natural historical sequence and represents, consequently, the narrative *shorthand* of a transaction that is riddled, *in practice*, with contradictions, accident, and surprise. We could suppose that the legal encodations of enslavement stand for the statistically average case, that the legal code provides the *topics* of a project increasingly threatened and self-conscious. It is, perhaps, not by chance that the laws regarding slavery appear to crystallize in the precise moment when agitation against the arrangement becomes articulate in certain European and New-World communities. In that regard, the slave codes that Goodell describes are themselves an instance of the counter and isolated text that seeks to silence the contradictions and antitheses engendered by it. For example, aspects of Article 461 of the South Carolina Civil Code call attention to just the sort of uneasy oxymoronic character that the "peculiar institution" attempts to sustain in transforming *personality* into *property*.

1) The "slave" is movable by nature, but "immovable by the operation of law" [Goodell 24]. As I read this, law itself is compelled to a point of saturation, or a reverse zero degree, beyond which it cannot move in the behalf of the enslaved *or* the free. We recall, too, that the "master," under these perversions of judicial power, is impelled to *treat* the enslaved as property, and not as person. These laws stand for the kind of social formulation that armed forces will help excise from a

living context in the campaigns of civil war. They also embody the untenable human relationship that Henry David Thoreau believed occasioned acts of "civil disobedience," the moral philosophy to which Martin Luther King, Jr. would subscribe in the latter half of the twentieth century.

2) Slaves shall be *reputed* and *considered* real estate, "subject to be mortgaged, according to the rules prescribed by law" [Goodell 24]. I emphasize "reputed" and "considered" as predicate adjectives that invite attention because they denote a *contrivance*, not an intransitive "is," or the transfer of nominative property from one syntactic point to another by way of a weakened copulative. The status of the "reputed" can change, as it will significantly before the nineteenth century closes. The mood here—the "shall be"—is pointedly subjunctive, or the situation devoutly to be wished. The slave-holding class is forced, in time, to think and do something else in the narrative of violence that enslavement itself has been preparing for a couple of centuries.

Louisiana's and South Carolina's written codes offer a paradigm for praxis in those instances where a *written* text is missing. In that case, the "chattel principle has . . . been affirmed and maintained by the courts, and involved in legislative acts" [Goodell 25]. In Maryland, a legislative enactment of 1798 shows so forceful a synonymity of motives between branches of comparable governance that a line between "judicial" and "legislative" functions is useless to draw: "In case the personal property of a ward shall consist of specific articles, such as slaves, working beasts, animals of any kind, stock, furniture, plates, books, and so forth, the Court if it shall deem it advantageous to the ward, may at any time, pass an order for the sale thereof" [56]. This inanimate and corporate ownership—the voting district of a ward—is here spoken for, or might be, as a single slave-holding male in determinations concerning property.

The eye pauses, however, not so much at the provisions of this enactment as at the details of its delineation. Everywhere in the descriptive document, we are stunned by the simultaneity of disparate items in a grammatical series: "Slave" appears in the same context with beasts of burden, *all* and *any* animal(s), various livestock, and a virtually endless profusion of domestic content from the culinary item to the book. Unlike the taxonomy of Borges's "Certain Chinese encyclopedia," whose contemplation opens Foucault's *Order of Things*, these items from a certain American encyclopedia do not sustain discrete and localized "powers of contagion," nor has the ground of their concatenation been desiccated beneath them. That imposed uniformity comprises the shock, that somehow this mix of named things, live and inanimate, collapsed by contiguity to the same text of "realism," carries a disturbingly prominent item of misplacement. To that extent, the project of liberation for African-Americans has found urgency in two passionate motivations that are twinned—1) to break apart, to rupture violently the laws of American behavior that make such syntax possible; 2) to introduce a new *semantic* field/fold more appropriate to his/her own historic movement. I regard this twin compulsion as distinct, though related, moments of the very same narrative process that might appear as a concentration or a dispersal. The narratives of Linda Brent, Frederick Douglass, and Malcolm El-Hajj Malik El Shabazz (aspects of which are examined in this essay) each represent both narrative ambitions as they occur under the auspices of "author."

Relatedly, we might interpret the whole career of African-Americans, a decisive factor in national political life since the mid-seventeenth century, in light of the *intervening, intruding* tale, or the tale—like Brent's "garret" space—"between the lines," which are already inscribed, as a *metaphor* of social and cultural management. According to this reading, gender, or sex-role assignation, or the clear differentiation of sexual stuff, sustained elsewhere in the culture, does not emerge for the African-American female in this historic instance, except indirectly, except as a way to reenforce through the process of birthing, "the reproduction of the relations of production" that involves "the reproduction of the values and behavior patterns necessary to maintain the system of hierarchy in its various aspects of gender, class, and race or ethnicity" [Margaret Strobel, "Slavery and Reproductive Labor in Mombasa," Robertson and Klein 121]. Following Strobel's lead, I would suggest that the foregoing identifies one of the three categories of reproductive labor that African-American females carry out under the regime of captivity. But his replication of ideology is never simple in the case of female subject-positions, and it appears to acquire a thickened layer of motives in the case of African-American females.

If we can account for an originary narrative and judicial principle that might have engendered a "Moynihan Report," many years into the twentieth century, we cannot do much better than look at Goodell's reading of the *partus sequitur ventrem*: the condition of the slave mother is "forever entailed on all her remotest posterity." This maxim of civil law, in Goodell's view, the "genuine and degrading principle of slavery, inasmuch as it places the slave upon a level with brute animals, prevails universally in the slave-holding states" [Goodell 27]. But what is the "condition" of the mother? Is it the "condition" of enslavement the writer means, or does he mean the "mark" and the "knowledge" of the *mother* upon the child that here translates into the culturally forbidden and impure? In an elision of terms, "mother" and "enslavement" are indistinct categories of the illegitimate inasmuch as each of these synonymous elements defines, in effect, a cultural situation that is *father-lacking*. Goodell, who does not only report this maxim of law as an aspect of his own factuality, but also regards it, as does Douglass, as a fundamental degradation, supposes descent and identity through the female line as comparable to a brute animality. Knowing already that there are human communities that align social reproductive procedure according to the line of the mother, and Goodell himself might have known it some years later, we can only conclude that the provisions of patriarchy, here exacerbated by the preponderant powers of an enslaving class, declare Mother Right, by definition, a negating feature of human community.

Even though we are not even talking about any of the matriarchal features of social production/reproduction—matrifocality, matrilinearity, matriarchy—when we speak of the enslaved person, we perceive that the dominant culture, in a fatal misunderstanding, assigns a matriarchist value where it does not belong; actually *misnames* the power of the female regarding the enslaved community. Such naming is false because the female could not, in fact, claim her child, and false, once again, because "motherhood" is not perceived in the prevailing social climate as a legitimate procedure of cultural inheritance.

The African-American male has been touched, therefore, by the *mother, handed* by her in ways that he cannot escape, and in ways that the white American male is allowed to temporize by a fatherly reprieve. This human and historic development—the text that has been inscribed on the benighted heart of the continent—takes us to the center of an inexorable difference in the depths of American women's community: the African-American woman, the mother, the daughter, becomes historically the powerful and shadowy evocation of a cultural synthesis long evaporated—the law of the Mother—only and precisely because legal enslavement removed the African-American male not so much from sight as from *mimetic* view as a partner in the prevailing social fiction of the Father's name, the Father's law.

Therefore, the female, in this order of things, breaks in upon the imagination with a forcefulness that marks both a denial and an "illegitimacy." Because of this peculiar American denial, the black American male embodies the *only* American community of males which has had the specific occasion to learn *who* the female is within itself, the infant child who bears the life against the could-be fateful gamble, against the odds of pulverization and murder, including her own. It is the heritage of the *mother* that the African-American male must regain as an aspect of his own personhood—the power of "yes" to the "female" within.

This different cultural text actually reconfigures, in historically ordained discourse, certain *representational* potentialities for African-Americans: 1) motherhood as female blood-rite is outraged, is denied, at the *very same time* that it becomes the founding term of a human and social enactment; 2) a dual fatherhood is set in motion, comprised of the African father's *banished* name and body and the captor father's mocking presence. In this play of paradox, only the female stands *in the flesh*, both mother and mother-dispossessed. This problematizing of gender places her, in my view, *out* of the traditional symbolics of female gender, and it is our task to make a place for this different social subject. In doing so, we are less interested in joining the ranks of gendered femaleness than gaining the *insurgent* ground as female social subject. Actually *claiming* the monstrosity (of a female with the potential to "name"), which her culture imposes in blindness, "Sapphire" might rewrite after all a radically different text for a female empowerment.

WORKS CITED

Barthes, Roland. *Mythologies*. Trans. Annette Lavers. New York: Hill and Wang, 1972.

Blassingame, John. *The Slave Community: Plantation Life in the Antebellum South*. New York: Oxford UP, 1972.

Brent Linda, *Incidents in the Life of a Slave Girl*. Ed. L. Maria Child. Introduced by Walter Teller. Rpt. New York: Harvest/HBJ Books, 1973.

Davis, Angela Y. *Women, Race, and Class*. New York: Random House, 1981.

De Azurara, Gomes Eannes. *The Chronicle of the Discovery and Conquest of Guinea*. Trans. C. Raymond Beazley and Edgar Prestage. London: Hakluyt Society, 1896, 1897, in Elizabeth Donnan, *Documents Illustrative of the History of the Slave Trade to America*. Washington, D.C.: Carnegie Institution of Washington, 1932, 1:18–41.

Donnan, Elizabeth. *Documents Illustrative of the History of the Slave Trade to America*; 4 vols. Washington, D.C.: The Carnegie Institute of Washington, 1932.

Douglass, Frederick. *Narrative of the Life of Frederick Douglass An American Slave, Written by Himself*. Rpt. New York: Signet Books, 1968.

El Shabazz, Malcolm El-Hajj Malik. *Autobiography of Malcolm X*. With Alex Haley. Introduced by M. S. Handler. New York: Grove Press, 1966.

Equiano, Olaudah. "The Life of Olaudah Equiano, or Gustavus Vassa, The African, Written by Himself," in *Great Slave Narratives*. Introduced and selected by Arna Bontemps. Boston: Beacon Press, 1969. 1–192.

Faulkner, William. *The Mansion*. New York: Vintage Books, 1965.

Frazier, E. Franklin. *The Negro Family in the United States*. Rev. with forward by Nathan Glazer. Chicago: The U of Chicago P, 1966.

Genovese, Eugene. *Roll, Jordan, Roll: The World the Slaves Made*. New York: Pantheon Books, 1974.

Goodell, William. *The American Slave Code in Theory and Practice Shown By Its Statues, Judicial Decisions, and Illustrative Facts*; 3rd ed. New York: American and Foreign Anti-Slavery Society, 1853.

hooks, bell. *Ain't I a Woman: Black Women and Feminism*. Boston: South End Press, 1981.

Klein, Herbert S. "African Women in the Atlantic Slave Trade." Robertson and Klein 29–39.

Meillassoux, Claude. "Female Slavery." Robertson and Klein 49–67.

Moynihan, Daniel P. "The Moynihan Report" [*The Negro Family: The Case for National Action*. Washington, D.C.: U.S. Department of Labor, 1965]. *The Moynihan Report and the Politics of Controversy: A Transaction Social Science and Public Policy Report*. Ed. Lee Rainwater and William L. Yancey. Cambridge: MIT Press, 1967. 47–94.

Robertson, Claire C., and Martin A. Klein, eds. *Woman and Slavery in Africa*. Madison: U of Wisconsin P, 1983.

Scarry, Elaine. *The Body in Pain: The Making and Unmaking of the World*. New York: Oxford UP, 1985.

Smith, Valerie. "Loopholes of Retreat: Architecture and Ideology in Harriet Jacobs's *Incidents in the Life of a Slave Girl*." Paper presented at the 1985 American Studies Association Meeting, San Diego. Cited in Henry Louis Gates, Jr. "What's Love Got to Do With It?" *New Literary History* 18.2 (Winter 1987): 360.

Strobel, Margaret. "Slavery and Reproductive Labor in Mombasa." Robertson and Klein 111–30.

Suleiman, Susan Rubin, ed. *The Female Body in Western Culture*. Cambridge: Harvard UP, 1986.

Todorov, Tzvetan. *The Conquest of America: The Question of the Other*. Trans. Richard Howard. New York: Harper Colophon Books, 1984.

White, Deborah Grey. *Ar'n't I A Woman? Female Slaves in the Plantation South*. New York: Norton, 1985.

"WOMEN OF COLOR" WRITERS AND FEMINIST THEORY

(1994)

Alice Walker's 1983 volume *In Search of Our Mothers' Gardens* ends with the auto-biographical narrative/essay, "Beauty: When the Other Dancer Is the Self." Haunted in adulthood by self-doubt because of an eye blinded and scarred in childhood by a brother's BB-gun shot, Walker narrates in this essay the story of her healing, first surgical, then, in time, psychological. The essay ends in this way: looking steadily into her eyes one day at naptime, and recalling a televised image of the earth from outer space, Walker's three-year-old daughter says to her, "Mommy, there's a *world* in your eye." Rushing to a mirror while her daughter naps, Walker confirms the insight her daughter has given her: that her blemished eye is indeed lovable and integral to her identity or, as she puts it, "deeply suitable to my personality, and even characteristic of me." She notes that her two eyes operate independently of each other, the blind eye drifting in fatigue or boredom, or "bearing witness" in excitement. The final paragraph recounts a dream Walker has that night. She is dancing, "happier than I've ever been in my life." She is joined by another joyous dancer, and "we dance and kiss and hold each other through the night." This other dancer, the essay concludes, is "beautiful, whole and free. And she is also me."[1]

Barbara Christian writes in her 1987 essay "The Race for Theory," "people of color have always theorized—but in forms quite different from the Western form of abstract logic. . . . our theorizing . . . is often in narrative forms, in the stories we create, in riddles and proverbs . . . since dynamic rather than fixed ideas seem more to our liking. . . . My folk [she says punningly] have always been a race for theory."[2] If Christian is right, Walker's moving narrative is also doing the work of theory, and I believe it is. What *is*, then, the theoretical work that a scene like Walker's is doing? Before attempting to answer that question, I would like to frame it in the context of debates about black and white feminisms and poststructuralist theory, debates that might either authorize my endorsement of Christian's claim or invalidate it, or do both in different ways.

Toni Morrison has recently been writing about the cultural work whites have required of blacks in this country, long after the end of slavery. In *Playing in the Dark*, her 1992 essays on the ways in which whiteness has been constructed in and as American literature by means of the repression of what she calls the "Africanist presence," she argues that the "Africanist character" has been used as "surrogate and enabler," "the vehicle by which the American self knows itself as not enslaved, but free; not repulsive, but desirable; not helpless, but licensed and powerful."[3] More recently and specifically, she has focused her anger on the requirement that black persons signify the body so that mind can be white. Writing about Clarence Thomas in her Introduction to the essays she collected on the Hill/Thomas controversy, she calls attention to the *New York Times*'s "curious spotlight on his body"—mention of his accomplishments as a weight lifter—in their initial story, before Hill's allegations became public.[4] Morrison writes: "a reference to a black person's body is de rigueur in white discourse. Like the unswerving focus on the female body (whether the woman is a judge, an actress, a scholar, or a waitress), the black man's body is voluptuously dwelled upon in biographies about them, journalism on them, remarks about them. 'I wanted to find out,' said Senator Pete Domenici, 'as best I could what his life—from outhouse to the White House . . . has been like'" (xiv). Although Morrison also discusses the equally overdetermined construction of Anita Hill as a black woman as "contradiction itself, irrationality in the flesh" (xvi), it is odd that when she writes about the requirement that certain groups serve as white culture's body she uses the timeworn analogy between black men and all women, for she of all people is attuned to the specificity of black women's subjection to this cultural work. And indeed some of the essays she collected make exactly this point about Hill even if Morrison herself does not.[5]

Setting aside the specifics of the Hill/Thomas controversy, it is possible that, even more than black men or than all women taken together, black women have been required to do the cultural work of embodying the body for white culture. Or so Valerie Smith had been arguing long before October 1991. In her 1989 essay "Black Feminist Theory and the Representation of the 'Other'" Smith calls attention to what she finds a disturbing trend: the use of black women writers by white feminists (as well as black men) to represent the ground of experience, or as Smith puts it, "to rematerialize the subject of their theoretical positions."[6] Smith writes:

> That the black woman appears in all of these texts as a historicizing presence testifies to the power of the insistent voices of black feminist literary and cultural critics. Yet it is striking that at precisely the moment when Anglo-American feminists and male Afro-Americanists begin to reconsider the material ground of their enterprise, they demonstrate their return to earth, as it were, by invoking the specific experiences of black women and the writings of black women. This association of black women with reembodiment resembles rather closely the association, in classic Western philosophy and in nineteenth-century cultural constructions of womanhood, of women of color with the body and therefore with animal passions and slave labor. (45)

Smith is referring here to writing by Elizabeth Meese and Teresa de Lauretis. Meese, Smith points out, illustrates her argument for a politicized deconstructive practice with readings of Walker and Hurston, and de Lauretis uses Flo Kennedy and Hortense Spillers to argue for grounding feminism in "'a politics of everyday life'" (44–45). But Meese and de Lauretis are not alone in performing this kind of gesture. And this is why I would be hesitant to say right away what theoretical work I think Walker's essay is doing: you would have to think that I am doing just what bothers Smith—using a black woman writer as an example of white feminist theory.

Toril Moi, to choose an example more safely remote than myself, in 1985 notoriously and bluntly asserted a position that could hardly be articulated now: "Some feminists might wonder why I have said nothing about black or lesbian (or black-lesbian) feminist criticism in America in this survey. The answer is simple: this book purports to deal with the theoretical aspects of feminist criticism. So far, lesbian and/or black feminist criticism have presented exactly the same *methodological* and *theoretical* problems as the rest of Anglo-American feminist criticism."[7] If it is the same theory, one wonders on reading this passage, why not use some black or lesbian writers to evoke it? Part of what is shocking about this statement is Moi's assumption that without offering readings of work by women of color she can nonetheless expect us to believe her that none of it would alter her definition of feminist theory. Her theory, while purporting to be race-neutral, derives only from white writers and excludes whatever women of color might have to say that differs from the white model. But my point in quoting this embarrassing passage is to call attention to its assumption that whites provide the theory whereas black women could only provide more examples. Moi's failure to invoke the writings of black women is thus of a piece with Meese's and de Lauretis's flawed invocations of them, in Valerie Smith's view: in each case, in a world view that binarizes into theory and examples, or mind and body, the black woman equals the body or the example.[8]

At this point I want to discuss the ways in which three more white women theorists, whose writings are currently of much greater importance to feminism than are Moi's, construct African American women, and in some cases Chicana women, as grounds of embodiment in the context of theoretical abstractions.[9] I want to emphasize that my reason for discussing these theorists—Donna Haraway, Judith Butler, and Diana Fuss—is their inescapable importance for anyone thinking about feminist theory today. What I want to uncover is a cultural problematic in some of their most influential writings, a problematic that does not lessen the very great value of their work but that none of them has fully articulated herself. (My critique applies only to the texts I will discuss here, and is not intended to be generalized to more recent writing; Butler's new book reached me too late to be considered here.[10]) The problem I see here could be viewed both as a problem of race relations in the academy and as part of the widespread debate over the uses of postmodernist theory for feminist political practice.[11] What does it mean to identify "women of color" with the body in a postmodern context; and what is the status of *any* body in that context?

In her pathbreaking essay "A Manifesto for Cyborgs," which appeared in the same year as Moi's *Sexual/Textual Politics* (1985), Donna Haraway uses some African American and Chicana writers, together with the generic grouping "women of color," to render concrete her extremely and deliberately abstruse account of the cyborg. One of her reiterated points about the cyborg as a model for feminism is its praiseworthy demystification of biological origins. Because it has none, no mother specifically, the cyborg would prevent feminists from romanticizing nature or the notion of woman's essence. Because "it skips the step of original unity," it teaches us to avoid the illusions perpetrated by both liberal and essentialist feminisms, illusions that would reinstall feminism in the patriarchal myth of bounded identity.[12] Haraway underscores the cyborgs' unnaturalness when she describes them as "floating signifiers" (*MC* 71) or as "ether, quintessence" (*MC* 70). The cyborg is, if not precisely disembodied, all surface, no depth—ironic, related to others by affinity, not blood; as abstract as a microelectronic signal.[13]

Near the start of her manifesto, Haraway cites a claim made by Chicana writer (and her student at the time) Chela Sandoval, that "women of color" negate the possibility of an essential identity of "woman" and thus that women of color are paradigmatically postmodern because cyborgian: "no 'she', no singularity, but a sea of differences among U.S. women who have affirmed their historical identity as U.S. women of color" (*MC* 73). "Women of color," like cyborgs, unite through affinity rather than through blood, because their blood identity is, happily, impossible to establish.[14] Toward the end of the essay—and it is generally at the ends of white women's essays or chapters that black and other "of color" women writers turn up—Cherríe Moraga and Audre Lorde, along with some women science fiction writers including Octavia Butler, are invoked as rather different paradigms of cyborg identity. Here Haraway fleshes out her claim that "women of color" are cyborgs by offering brief accounts of Audre Lorde's figure of the "Sister Outsider" and of Cherríe Moraga's book *Loving in the War Years*. "Sister Outsider" is a cyborg because she sounds like the "offshore women" who do the labor of the integrated circuit, like the young Korean women Haraway has discussed earlier. Never mind that, in the context in which Lorde invented this figure in *Zami*, "Sister Outsider" refers specifically and concretely to the ambiguous position of the black lesbian in the 1950s Greenwich white gay-girl scene: here she floats offshore in the ether of microelectronic signaling.

Haraway celebrates Moraga for the linguistic dislocations of her bilingual book—written in Spanish and English, it cannot be tied down to one linguistic identity—and for her reclaiming of the story of La Malinche, the cyborg equivalent to Eve, the anti-mother-figure who originates not through legitimate birth but through cross-cultural betrayal and bastardy. Haraway writes: "Moraga's writing, her superb literacy, is presented in her poetry as the same kind of violation as Malinche's mastery of the conqueror's language—a violation, an illegitimate production, that allows survival" (*MC* 94). Her "superb literacy"? Haraway intends a compliment to Moraga's mastery of languages through her violation of their boundaries, but I cannot get away from the condescension of the phrase, however ironic. Moreover, the word "literacy," alluding to the remarkableness of Moraga's being literate at all under conditions of racism and poverty, calls to mind the legally enforced illiteracy of African Americans under slavery. The cyborg, according to Julia Erhardt, frighteningly resembles the African American slave as depicted in Hortense Spillers's "Mama's Baby, Papa's Maybe"—deprived of a maternal origin through the enforced separation of parents from children, a hybrid (part animal, part machine), a bastard. Is slavery what Haraway celebrates when she celebrates the cyborg?[15] I do not want to diminish the historical specificity of slavery by generalizing it, but certainly there is an uncomfortable similarity between what Valerie Smith objects to in white feminists and Haraway's rhetorical practice. As Erhardt writes, "Haraway's move of employing [what Spillers calls] 'the body of the black woman in her material and abstract phase as a resource of metaphor' [see *MB* 66] is precisely the practice of rhetorical domination Spillers denounces in her piece" (*AI* 5). Haraway's women of color work for her—they do the work of her theory,

Haraway does much the same thing with Sojourner Truth in a more recent essay, in which she makes Sojourner Truth into the successor to Jesus Christ, the "figure" of the "suffering servant" as trickster, who represents universal "humanity."[16] Haraway is aware of just the dangers I am pointing to now, insisting that her use of Sojourner Truth "resist[s] representation, resist[s] literal figuration" (86). Instead, Truth can be seen to "refigure a nongeneric, nonoriginal humanity after the breakup of the discourses of Eurocentric humanism" (96) because of Haraway's attention to the particularity of her situation as a northern former slave and speaker of Afro-Dutch English. But it would seem impossible for Haraway to use her as a figure of Trinh Minh-ha's "inappropriate/d other" without appropriating her and the referential spectacle of her body in just the way that Erhardt's critique of the cyborg as slave would predict. Contrast Alice Walker's brief essay "A Name Is Sometimes an Ancestor Saying Hi, I'm with You," in which she claims, simply, to *be* Sojourner Truth: "She smiles within my smile. That irrepressible great heart rises in my chest. Every experience that roused her passion against injustice in her lifetime shines from my eyes."[17] Like Haraway, Walker connects Sojourner Truth with Jesus Christ, but she understands Christ's and Truth's representational status differently from Haraway: "the transformation required of us is not simply to be 'like' Christ, but to *be* Christ" (*AN* 98). Whereas Haraway delicately eschews "literal figuration," Walker openly embraces a literal and bodily identification that, if it is appropriative (and I would not deny that the essay is arrogant), is at least based on "this name Sojourner Truth and I share" (she has pointed out that a Sojourner is a Walker and that Alice means truth) and thus on a personal identification rather than on generalizations about Truth's representative qualities, however evasive and tricksterlike Truth (and "the truth of representation") has become.

Valerie Smith's argument both applies and applies differently, then, to what Haraway and some other white poststructuralist feminists are doing with certain African American and Chicana women writers and with the category "women of color." Haraway would seem to be using Lorde and Moraga to lend concreteness to her anti-essential argument, but what she is really doing is using them as an alibi for dematerializing the female body. The text of Moraga's *Loving in the War Years* does not quite bear out Haraway's emphasis on the cyborg aspects of Moraga's self-representation and of La Malinche's heritage. For one thing, skin color—a physical fact—matters a great deal. Moraga dwells on her love for her mother's darkness and explores the complexity of living a Chicana life with a white skin. Moraga sees race as having been both a cyborgian choice for her (because, with a white father, she can pass) and also not a choice: she refers again and again to "the women of my race."[18] Secondly, she romanticizes the physicality of her mother's body (*L* 94) and she links her lesbianism directly to her love for her mother, her darkness, and her smell. In Moraga's cyborgian, lesbian critique of the family, she nonetheless holds on to the value of blood bonds, especially the blood tie to the mother, precisely that which Haraway's cyborg rejects. Moraga writes of "finding familia among friends where blood ties are formed through suffering and celebration shared" (*L* 111). The notion of forming blood ties makes Moraga inhabit ambiguously both a cyborgian ideology and an older, more romantic one. Similarly ambiguous is her memorable chapter title, "From a Long Line of Vendidas" (or sexual sellouts): this long line is both cultural—her descent, as a traitor to Chicano ideas about women's subservience, from La Malinche—and, at the same time, biological: her descent from her mother, who, because she married a white man and bore racial bastards, was, like La Malinche, a *vendida*. When Haraway makes Moraga into a co-celebrant of the tradition of La Malinche and defines that tradition entirely through its postmodern antinaturalness, she overlooks Moraga's insistence on biological inheritance and her persistent, somatic nostalgias for her own blood mother's body.

Thinking about Haraway's use of Moraga, I was also reminded of Gloria Anzaldúa, whose autobiographical and multilingual *Borderlands/ La Frontera* constructs a subject that tropes itself simultaneously through conventions of identity—words like *inner life, the self, deep core, integrity*—and as a shifting borderland, simultaneously geographic, linguistic, cultural, racial, and sexual, never stably occupied by one culture or another but by many, where home is "this thin edge of / barbwire."[19] In her important early essay, "Speaking in Tongues," Anzaldúa encompasses what to white feminist theory might appear a paradox: "The act of writing is the act of making soul, alchemy. It is the quest for the self, for the center of the self, which we women of color have come to think as 'other.'"[20] Anzaldúa here equates *making* soul—constructing an identity—with *discovering* the self, an act that would seem to presume the prior existence of what is, in the first sentence, in the process of being made. Clearly, finding that that preexistent self is other—a situation a cyborg might enjoy—is represented here as a rift to be healed, not celebrated.

So Haraway has it both ways: perhaps because Moraga really does celebrate bodily identity, she grounds Haraway's argument by providing an example, and therefore, as in Valerie Smith's critique, she works for the white woman to represent reembodiment. But the argument she is serving is, self-contradictorily, an argument against embodiment—against biological definitions of woman and against nostalgia for biological origins, an argument that forgets the very body that allows Moraga to work as an example in the first place. Haraway's brief for postmodernism leads her to highlight only the cyborg aspects of Moraga's text and to downplay her ambivalence.

Virtually the same pattern as in Haraway appears in Judith Butler's use of a black woman—in this case not a writer but a singer—in her 1989 essay "Gendering the Body: Beauvoir's Philosophical Contribution," in the Introduction to her 1990 book *Gender Trouble*, and again in her 1991 essay "Imitation and Gender Insubordination."[21] I will focus here on *Gender Trouble*, the most widely influential of these three texts. Butler argues (with great philosophical rigor) that there is no such thing as essential or even stable identity, that all identities are constructs or effects of discourses, rather than, as common sense is thought to tell us, that identity is the origin and cause of everything else. She is skeptical of the value to feminism even of strategic essentialism and identity politics, because she believes they are founded on the dangerous illusion of stable identity. Butler has been the subject of the same kind of controversy within feminism that has surrounded Haraway: while her deconstruction of identity unquestionably holds out emancipatory promises, some feminists worry about both the status of the body in her theory ("is there a body in this text?" queries Susan Bordo [*UW* 38]) and its political utility. Time and again, discussions of postmodern feminist politics founder on the question of how to act politically without using totalizing categories such as "women."

Just as Haraway initially and briefly uses Chela Sandoval to make the analogy between cyborgs and "women of color" that she will concretize later on, Butler implicitly invokes the generic category of women of color briefly at the beginning of *Gender Trouble* as part of what authorizes her critique of identity. In her Introduction, she offers this rationale for putting her poststructuralist understanding of identity at the center of feminist theory: "it may be time to entertain a radical critique that seeks to free feminist theory from the necessity of having to construct a single or abiding ground which is invariably contested by those identity positions or anti-identity positions that it invariably excludes. Do the exclusionary practices that ground feminist theory in a notion of 'women' as subject paradoxically undercut feminist goals to extend its claims to 'representation'?" (*GT* 5). That is, Butler argues, "identity" is a category that imposes a false and coercive unity, just as white, middle-class, Western feminism itself has been accused of imposing one interpretive grid on the multiplicity of female lives by privileging the category "woman" over those of race, ethnicity, class, nationality, age, and so on. Identity, like some kinds of white feminism, must be done away with because of what it excludes. Historically it was from "women of color"— chiefly African Americans—that these accusations against white, middle-class feminism initially and most effectively came, and thus Butler, although without referring to anyone in particular, uses a generic allusion to this group (while, like Haraway, seeking precisely not to totalize it as a group) to justify her anti-identity poststructuralism.

She makes it clear that this point refers to the general category of women of color, in her 1992 essay "Contingent Foundations," when she defends postmodern feminism in this way: "There is the refrain that, just now, when women are beginning to assume the place of subjects, postmodern positions come along to announce that the subject is dead. ... Some see this as a conspiracy against women and other disenfranchised groups who are now only beginning to speak on their own behalf. But what precisely is meant by this, and how do we account for the very strong criticisms of the subject as an instrument of Western imperialist hegemony theorized by Gloria Anzaldúa, Gayatri Spivak, and various theorists of postcoloniality?"[22] Butler would seem to be characterizing my own criticism, in her reference to this anti-postmodern "refrain," and refuting it. But as I suggested in discussing Haraway, this use of Anzaldúa to justify an anti-identity position, fleeting as it is—Butler supplies a footnote to Anzaldúa's entire book, not to any particular passage—does not do justice to Anzaldúa's careful positioning on both sides of the debate. Nor does the use of Anzaldúa, Spivak, and "various theorists of postcoloniality," to stand for grievances that have come largely from African American women, do justice to the specificity of any of these positions. And to turn Anzaldúa into a one-dimensional figure for anything at all is to do precisely what I have been arguing feminist theorists should be wary of doing.

Toward the end of the Introduction to *Gender Trouble*, Butler cites the example of Aretha Franklin singing "You Make Me Feel Like a Natural Woman" (*GT* 22) in support of her anti-identity position. In a footnote Butler explains how: "'Like a natural woman' is a phrase that suggests that 'naturalness' is only accomplished through analogy or metaphor. In other words, 'You make me feel like a metaphor of the natural,' and without 'you', some denaturalized ground would be revealed" (*GT* 154–55). And then Butler compares what she calls "Aretha's claim" to Beauvoir's claim that "one is not born, but rather becomes a woman."[23] Or as Butler clarifies the point in "Imitation and Gender Insubordination," "[a]lthough Aretha appears to be all too glad to have her naturalness confirmed, she also seems fully and paradoxically mindful that that confirmation is never guaranteed, that the effect of naturalness is only achieved as a consequence of that moment of heterosexual recognition. After all, Aretha sings, you make me feel *like* a natural woman, suggesting that this is a kind of metaphorical substitution, an act of imposture, a kind of sublime and momentary participation in an ontological illusion produced by the mundane operation of heterosexual drag" (*IGI* 27–28). There are very few examples of anything in *Gender Trouble*, in "Gendering the Body," or in "Imitation and Gender Insubordination." Although Butler uses Aretha Franklin as an example of her poststructuralist critique of identity, her very uniqueness as an example and the fact that Butler uses her three times (and does not come up with other examples for the same point) suggest that she is also an example of exemplariness itself. And it matters that we are more likely to conjure up a physical image of the singer performing in her body than we are to conjure up similar images of the white European writers whose theories Franklin exemplifies—Lacan or Beauvoir, even Wittig or Foucault.

Thus, like Haraway, Butler uses a "woman of color" as a form of embodiment—an example, a body—who nonetheless justifies a critique of bodily or biologically based theories of gender, a critique of identity even more severe than Haraway's. This is not to say that I necessarily disagree with Butler's reading of the song. But like Butler's allusion to Anzaldúa, it goes by too fast, for all the times it is repeated. Lines from the body of the song would suggest that the singer is less clearly on the poststructuralist side of the identity debate than Butler wants her to be. "When my soul was in the lost and found / You came along to claim it"[24] suggests, like the passage from Anzaldúa about both questing for and making the soul, that the soul (the natural woman?) already exists even if it is now alienated from its owner. The line Butler cites in support of her anti-identity position is the song's refrain, and that is exactly the term she uses to denote and disparage the pro-identity position in the passage quoted above from "Contingent Foundations." Reading these essays together, with the 1992 essay (which does not use Aretha Franklin but does use the word *refrain*) seen as a gloss upon the texts from 1989, 1990, and 1991 (the ones that do use Aretha Franklin), one could conclude that Butler's 1992 text, in its choice of the word *refrain*, knows that Franklin's refrain coincides with a pro-identity position (the naive feminists' refrain) as much as it does with her own anti-identity position. It is also worth mentioning that Franklin sings not her own words but those of Carole King (born Carol Klein, in Brooklyn), another way perhaps in which a black woman enacts or embodies a white woman's words, and a situation that calls to mind the political context of Aretha Franklin's success; through the 1960s, African Americans were allowed to succeed only in those arenas—such as sports, music, and dance—that whites could imagine as being reducible to bodily performance. I like Aretha Franklin's singing, but it makes me think too unhappily about the ways black women have always done this country's work of embodiment to feel happy about Butler's use of her.

There is something odd about both Haraway's and Butler's invoking African American, Chicana, and other "women of color" to justify the use of post-modernist or poststructuralist theory in feminism given that many black women critics, like Barbara Christian and Joyce Ann Joyce, have recently argued exactly the opposite: the elitist irrelevance of theory to black women's lives. Christian's "The Race for Theory" attacks theory, or what she calls the New Philosophy, as hegemonic, an instrument for egoistic career advancement, disembodied, and replicating the mind/body split exclusively in favor of abstraction. She writes that feminist theorists fail to "take into account the complexity of life—that women are of many races and ethnic backgrounds [and classes] with different histories and cultures. . . . Seldom do they note these distinctions, because if they did they could not articulate a theory" (*RT* 233). Presupposing that theory depends on cat-egorical distinctions and cannot deal with concrete particulars, and preferring the concrete to the abstract, Christian could in a sense be said to share Toril Moi's view that feminist theory and black women's writing have little to do with each other.

In some ways Christian's position resembles that taken by a larger group of black feminists. The writers with whom Christian speaks in concert have tended to claim experience rather than its supposed opposite, abstract categories, as the ground from which any criticism and theory should be generated. Early in the history of black feminism, its defining practitioners—such as Mary Helen Wash-ington, Deborah McDowell, and Barbara Smith—embraced what we would now term essentialism and posited that the function of black feminist criticism was to establish a correct representation of black women and that such criticism could only be practiced by women who were themselves black, Similarly, from the same period, the Combahee River Collective's "Black Feminist Statement" has been construed by most readers as defining "identity politics" to mean that you act according to who you are and that identity precedes culture and politics.[25] More recently, in the same year that Christian's essay came out, Joyce Ann Joyce pub-lished a highly controversial attack on the use of white European theory (chiefly deconstruction) by black theorists such as Henry Louis Gates, Jr. and Houston Baker, an attack that, like Christian's, seeks to recall black theory to its experien-tial and sensual roots.[26] Patricia Hill Collins, publishing in *Signs* in 1989, wrote that "living life as an African American woman is a necessary prerequisite for pro-ducing black feminist thought."[27] In 1990, bell hooks reported a "resistance on the part of most black folks to hearing about real connection between postmodernism and black experience" (*Y* 25).

Although a number of black feminists have also been writing in eurocentric theoretical modes, and hooks discusses this "resistance" in order to "interrogate" it, in 1989 it was still possible for Diana Fuss (in her book *Essentially Speaking*) to point out, and to call "disturbing," the "relative absence of Afro-American *femi-nist* poststructuralism. With the exception of the recent work of Hazel Carby and Hortense Spillers, black feminist critics have been reluctant to renounce essen-tialist critical positions and humanist literary practices."[28] She asks why so many women of color "resist" joining "the race for theory" and thus risk being accused of conservatism, as Joyce is by Baker (*ES* 95). She proposes that the answer lies in "political necessity," in the strategic use of essentialism for the aims of political solidarity within an embattled group (*ES* 95).

It is disturbing (to use Fuss's word) to think about how closely this apologetic, conciliatory account resembles Toril Moi's blunt statement about the lack of theoretical innovation in black women critics. In thinking she needs to apologize at all, and in focusing on what black feminists don't do, Fuss is listening as inattentively as Moi is to what African American feminists are saying. Even though one aim of her book is to defamiliarize poststructuralism and to encourage tolerance for apparently essentialist positions, here her standards for what constitutes the category of the disturbing do not derive from the group of which she speaks but rather from a standpoint where poststructuralism is intrinsically good. Fuss's chapter on race is unique in her feminist book in focusing almost exclusively on men: all the blacks are men, to borrow that unhappily still appropriate phrase, just as in the other chapters nearly all the women are white.

But the important point for my argument is that Fuss, like Butler and Haraway, closes her text with black women who are simultaneously identified with the body, retrograde notions of identity, and essentialism—doing the work of embodiment—and used to justify poststructuralism; or rather, what she sees as the majority of untheoretical black women are used for the one purpose, while Spillers and Carby are singled out for praise as endorsing poststructuralism, just as Aretha Franklin, Anzaldúa, and Moraga are by Butler and Haraway. But as in the case of Moraga, a closer reading of the writers being deployed here suggests that the picture is more complex. Yes, Spillers and Carby are associated with "theory," but neither of them celebrates disembodiment as wholeheartedly as the whites I have been discussing. There are specific historical reasons why bodily definitions of the human should appeal to some black feminists at just the moment when they are anathema to white poststructuralists.

Spillers's essay "Mama's Baby, Papa's Maybe" after all argues for reclaiming gender identities violently expropriated by slavery, specifically that of the black mother, quantified, commodified, unsexed by the slave trade. To quote again from Erhardt's paper, arguing that the cyborg sounds ominously like the black slave, "For Haraway a genderless cyborg world represents a world without end; for Spillers, a culture inhabited by hermaphrodite bestial bastard hybrids (in this case, one which was historically realized) represents the end of the world" (*AI* 4). With a logic that recalls Nancy K. Miller's "[o]nly those who have it can play with not having it,"[29] Spillers writes at the start of her essay:

> At a time when current critical discourses appear to compel us more and more decidedly toward gender "undecidability," it would appear reactionary, if not dumb, to insist on the integrity of female/male gender. But undressing these conflations of meaning, as they appear under the rule of dominance, would restore, as figurative possibility, not only Power to the Female (for Maternity), but also Power to the Male (for Paternity). We would gain, in short, the *potential* for gender differentiation as it might express itself along a range of stress points, including human biology in its intersection with the project of culture. (*MB* 66)

While Spillers is often careful to define gender as a social category, she also has a lot to say about the flesh: "only the female stands *in the flesh*, both mother and mother-dispossessed" (*MB* 80), she writes in the last paragraph of the essay.

In a related fashion, Hazel Carby, in the important statement on black feminist theory that introduces her book *Reconstructing Womanhood*, denounces reliance on the category of "experience" as "essentialist and ahistorical" because "experience" assumes that the infinitude of human experiences can be totalized.[30] But she also recuperates much that has traditionally made part of the category of experience by defining her approach as "materialist," an analysis of the impact of the concrete material conditions of production on the works of black women writers. Had Fuss been able to take into consideration bell hooks's 1990 essay "Postmodern Blackness," that essay's critiques of those in the black community who disdain theory and postmodernism would have supported my point about Carby and Spillers. Arguing against those who would retain the category of (black) identity as essence, she nonetheless insists on the compatibility of the postmodern critique of identity and the retention of "the authority of experience" (*Y* 29) as a useful political category: the postmodern "critique allows us to affirm multiple black identities, varied black experience" (*Y* 28).[31]

What I am suggesting, then, to summarize, is that Valerie Smith's critique of the use of black women writers by white feminists, valid though it is, needs to be inflected by two additional considerations. First—and for specific historical reasons, not naïveté—at least some black feminist critics are using black women writers in something like the way that Valerie Smith says whites are using them. Writers like Christian and Collins use black women to represent experience, sensuality, emotion, matter, practice as opposed to theory, and survival. When Smith turns from white to black feminisms, she discusses the ways in which Carby, Spillers, and others focus on the specific "material circumstances" of black women. Although her point is to differentiate between the "totalizing" use to which white feminists put black women to represent embodiment and the specificity of Carby et al.'s attention to particular material experiences, I would argue that this shift amounts to a change of emphasis rather than an absolute difference. But in any case, whether or not white and black feminisms are using black women in the same way, there is an overriding difference: because of the history of slavery, whether an African American woman works for herself or for a white woman is freighted with political and cultural meanings.

As a way of dramatizing the ambiguity that can arise from this situation, let me return briefly to Aretha Franklin. Some pages back I argued that Franklin's singing of "Natural Woman" may not be so deconstructive as Butler claims and, at the same time, that Butler relies on Franklin's "naturalness," her status as a visualizable popular icon, to make an antinatural point. (This could also serve as a summary of my argument about Moraga's and Haraway's use of her.) The relation between these potentially contradictory arguments might be clarified by saying that while I would defend Franklin's partisanship for the naturalness of womanhood—as I would defend those black feminist critics who, for whatever reasons, continue to construct the body and/or black female identity as natural—I would object to a white philosopher's making use of this very gesture.[32] A recent news item about Franklin in *Newsweek* features a photograph of her over the caption "Whole Lot of Shaking Going On."[33] The three-sentence report concerns Franklin's bravura singing at a concert, but the news is her body: "During a vigorous rendition of 'This Old Heart of Mine,' Aretha came dangerously close to overflowing her low-cut beaded bustier—and proving that she is every ounce a Natural Woman" (49). This news item demonstrates at once, and contradictorily, the unlikeliness that "ordinary" readers would hear Franklin's line as Butler does—of course most listeners hear only her valorization of the natural—and the distastefulness (to say the least) of having her "naturalness" displayed, photographically and textually, as a joke for a white audience. Her performances of "Natural Woman" may articulate as much enthusiasm for the natural as *Newsweek*'s report attributes to her, but the report does so from a point of view that is not Franklin's own and thus constitutes a use of her body that offends because it is not her own.

The second consideration with which we would need to inflect Smith's critique is this: when at least some prominent white feminist poststructuralist theorists—Fuss, Butler, and Haraway—use black or, in the case of Moraga and Anzaldúa, Chicana women, they do so not simply to make them do the work of embodiment or identification but also to make their embodiment at the same time an alibi for poststructuralist disembodiment or the deconstructing of identity. (It is not just that Butler uses Franklin, but that she uses her in this particular way.) This second usage of "women of color" would seem opposite to, and therefore the antidote to, the usage decried in Smith's critique, and attractive on those grounds; but it is problematic because the usage decried by Smith is authorized by some "women of color" themselves and also because the political utility of arguments that dissociate feminism from the body has yet to be decided. It is problematic also because the status of a figure of embodiment in an argument against embodied identity must finally be that of excluded other: even though these figures are enlisted in the cause of poststructuralism, they must finally be left out of it. They define it by their difference from it. The woman of color as deployed by Haraway et al. is still a figure, a figure for something—a bounded identity—serving a larger cause. And enlisting black women as figureheads for poststructuralism does not yet make a convincing case for its utility for women of color. That is, there certainly are poststructuralist black feminisms, but we would not know that from the texts I have discussed.

Let me stop focusing on the white theorists, for whose self-contradictory arguments the embodied black woman tends to become part of the machinery for validating disembodiment, to say something about the uses to which black women have been putting figures of their own embodiment. I would like to return to Christian's claim that her folk theorize in narrative forms and to turn specifically to a narrative essay by Patricia Williams together with the autobiographical story by Alice Walker with which I began. Continuing the line of argument I began with my brief discussions of Moraga and Anzaldúa, I wish to suggest that when Williams and Walker image their own bodies, they set up a constructive dialogue between poststructuralist and humanist views of identity rather than either reducing the black woman's body to sheer ground or matter or, to the contrary, using that body to validate disembodiment. I realize that in turning to black women's narrativized self-embodiments, I am open to the accusation that I am using women of color in just the ways I have been objecting to, as "examples" following a discussion of "theory." But I would justify this practice in two ways. First, not to give African American women writers' theories the same kind of close scrutiny I have just given to white feminists would leave me open to the opposite danger, the one that befell Toril Moi. Second, because I will be talking about figures that these authors have already encapsulated and embodied as figures, my practice follows and is authorized by theirs. Thus they are working—doing cultural and psychological work—for themselves at least as much as for me.[34] Perhaps it could even be said that I am working for them.

The link that Erhardt demonstrates between the cyborg and Spillers's enslaved women can help us see that Patricia Williams's self-presentation includes many of the cyborg's hallmarks too. Spillers opens her essay by describing herself as a hybrid and a construct: listing the names a black woman academic can be called, from "Brown Sugar" to "Black Woman at the Podium," Spillers writes: "I describe a locus of confounded identities, a meeting ground of investments and privations in the national treasury of rhetorical wealth. My country needs me, and if I were not here, I would have to be invented" (*MB* 65). Very similarly, Patricia Williams opens "Owning the Self in a Disowned World" with what she calls her "disintegration into senselessness," which is making her crazy and giving her a headache.[35] She describes herself as caught between conflicting expectations or, as Spillers puts it, "confounded identities" (*MB* 65). She reflects on Derek Bell's "Chronicle of the Twenty-Seventh Year Syndrome," the disease afflicting only young black professional women: "if they are not married to, or have not yet received a marriage proposal from, a black man by their twenty-seventh year, they fall into a deep coma from which they awaken only after several weeks, physically intact but having lost all their professional skills" (191). This leads Williams to tell the story of Judge Maxine Thomas, who suffered a terminal nervous breakdown in her chambers and whose life was dissected in the media according to conflicting demands: "A woman who was too individualistic. . . . A woman who couldn't think for herself. . . . A woman who had the perfect marriage. . . . A woman who had no marriage at all" (193). A woman who was too professional, too unfeeling; a woman who wasn't professional enough, too emotional. Reflecting on her own and her mother's morning rituals of self-construction—clothes, makeup, jewelry—Williams herself feels "very close to being Maxine. When I am fully dressed, my face is hung with contradictions" (196). The fine line between herself and Maxine Thomas is that "I try not to wear all my contradictions at the same time. I pick and choose among them; like jewelry" (196). Maxine Thomas "split at the seams," but Williams will not, quite yet anyway.

At the close of the essay, Williams presents a figure that may recall Butler's use of Aretha Franklin. Here, it is a dream of Williams herself. In the dream, there are two of her: one self who is "creeping" around the back wall of an amphitheater, the other who is on stage, magnificently performing. She is wearing outrageously feminine hair and clothing from her unprofessional youth (a beehive and a sequined, low-cut red dress). Here are the final two paragraphs of the essay:

> The me-that-is-on-stage *is* laughing loudly and long. She is extremely vivacious, the center of attention. She is, just as I have always dreamed of being, fascinating: showy yet deeply intelligent. She is not beautiful in any traditional sense, as I am not in real life—her mouth and teeth are very large, her nose very long, like a claymation model of myself—but her features are riveting. And she is radiantly, splendidly good-natured. She is lovely in the oddest possible combination of ways. I sit down in the small circle of friends-

around-myself, to watch myself, this sparkling homely woman, dressed like a moment lost in time. I hear myself speaking: *Voices that in the chasm speak from the slow eloquent fact of the chasm. They speak and speak, like flowing water.*

From this dream, into a complicated world, a propagation of me's awakens, strong, single-hearted, and completely refreshed. (201)

This dream seems to cure the headache with which Williams begins the essay. Donna Haraway ends her manifesto, "I would rather be a cyborg than a goddess" (*MC* 101); but both Williams and Spillers already know what it is to be a cyborg, better than Haraway—by her own admission—can ever do, and they know that being a cyborg gives them a headache. Even Barbara Christian, for all her alleged "resistance" to theory (Fuss's term), sometimes feels like a cyborg too, and she doesn't like it either, it makes her tired: "I, for one, am tired of being asked to produce a black feminist literary theory as if I were a mechanical man" (*RT* 227). How does the dream relieve Williams of the headache, the fatigue, of being a cyborg?

The dream both celebrates a post-Lacanian, cyborgian, split subjectivity and perceives that split as something painful, in need of healing. For example, there are two Williamses but they collaborate to make possible the pleasure of voyeurism. The self in the sequined dress may represent the stressful requirement for black professional women to be "feminine," but this performer's intelligence integrates the professional and the woman, for her charm is characterized by "the oddest possible combination." Her "femininity" is both a costume—heterosexual drag—and her deep identity. The dream produces "a propagation of me's," but somehow they are, collectively, "single-hearted" too. Williams wants to have it both ways—to be whole and split, to be single and multiple, to have a self and to deconstruct the notion of self, to be practical and theoretical—and this dream represents that wish in a way that Williams seems to find satisfying. It does not just embody a theory: it does for her the work of a cure.

Williams's dream-figure is both like and unlike Butler's Aretha Franklin, whose words suggest both the desire to be a natural woman and the greater recognition that there is no such thing. Both dream-women link embodiment and identity on the one hand to the denaturalizing of identity on the other. But the difference is that while Butler explicitly—even, we might say, coercively—turns that ambiguity toward justification of her denaturalizing project and privileges the poststructuralist reading of Aretha Franklin's song over the natural gender one, Williams leaves the two possibilities open, and lets her sequined self work for the better health and pleasure of her own body: her "me's" awake "refreshed." Williams's dream-figure may constitute a recognition that cyborg identity is unavoidable for a professional black woman, but it makes that recognition in the form that, as we have seen, identifies the black woman with her body: an example at the end of an essay. Williams celebrates embodiment as the only salve for a self wounded by the demands of life as a cyborg. And so I might legitimate my own turning to Williams as an example by her own celebratory practice of doing so—but only because I am using her as a figure for her own effective and pragmatic ambivalence (perhaps, one might say, her strategic ambivalence), not, as Haraway or Butler might, as a figure for a philosophically pure but deconcretized position.

The same point might also justify my returning now to the Alice Walker essay with which I began. As you will remember, Walker, like Williams, ends with a celebratory dream of herself as two selves, a dream that resolves an anxiety, in this case about her appearance and by extension about her value in the world. Walker's account of her dream involves and ends by emphasizing the same ambiguity as Williams's, between split and whole, between a Lacanian-poststructuralist cyborg self and a liberal humanist self. Walker becomes two dancers, but they kiss and hold each other. There are two dancers, but the other dancer is "whole. . . . And she is also me." Possibly there is a third, since the fear of blindness has been safely projected onto Stevie Wonder, to whose music she dances. Like Williams's "propagation of me's," Walker devises a collective self that is both one and many. As in Williams's essay, this doubled, divided dream-self answers the emotionally and politically strategic need to say "I" without falling into the trap of reduplicating an invidious humanism or the phallocentric oneness of form. If Walker, like Williams, has suffered from having a divided self—as figured synecdochally by her having two eyes (I's) that operate independently of each other—then she can also turn that division to her advantage in avoiding an imprisoning self-identity.

Walker and Williams both write of their selves as unstable constructions provisionally made up of different and continuously shifting elements and especially of different languages. At the same time, they keep in mind practical considerations about living and acting politically in this world. As for hooks writing on postmodernism, it is crucial to them that a deconstructive understanding of the self not militate against political activism, as it is often thought to do. Walker's split or fragmented self is a touchstone of Lacanian psychology and therefore of poststructuralism, but she does not derive it from that source. It is a *world* that her eye resembles, the body understood as politicized even in that intensely personal and physical moment in her daughter's bedroom: the eye or I is founded not on the notion of a core self but rather on the global village (a concept that is central to the "Manifesto for Cyborgs," although in the affectively different form of the international integrated circuit).

Living by the Word, Walker's more recent essay collection, extends this notion of the multiple self and extends this representation of it too as historicized and politicized, its origins traceable to non-Western cultures rather than to Western theory. The doubled self that ends the first essay collection reappears at the start of the next one in a brief journal entry about a dream of a woman with two heads who dispenses advice: "what I realized in the dream is that two-headedness was at one time an actual physical condition and that two-headed people were considered wise. . . . [T]wo-headed people, like blacks, lesbians, Indians, 'witches,' have been suppressed, and, in their case, suppressed out of existence. . . . For surely two-headed people have existed. And it is only among blacks (to my knowledge) that a trace of their existence is left in the language. Rootworkers, healers, wise people with 'second sight' are called 'two-headed' people."[36] Perhaps a two-headed woman could have done something for Patricia Williams's headache. This distinctively non-Western wise woman—who exists simultaneously as a real referential being and as a cyborgian effect of language—grounds Walker's experiments with nonunitary selves in the politics of postcolonial culture and aligns that experimentation not with the white middle-class domain of pure, theoretical poststructuralist psychoanalysis but with the historical fact of Walker's varied ancestry instead. As in Moraga's "From a Long Line of Vendidas," blood ancestry matters along with cyborgian affinity. The identity "black" in Walker's case means being descended not only from African slaves but from a Cherokee great-great-grandmother and also from a white slave owner and rapist, all of whom, later in the volume, she animates as living voices in her head, experienced somatically as well as psychically, competing noisily to be heard by her. Walker's ancestors politicize the female body and construct its identity pragmatically as a contentious argument, not a stable and timeless unity, and always as a body. Walker, we might say, has a headache, too, to go along with her eye-strain— the headache of slavery's cyborg "confounded identities"—and she cures it by listening to all the voices in her head and then channeling them into aesthetic wholes signed with the unmistakable signature of Alice Walker. For the other distinctive feature of the journal entry about the two-headed woman is its insistence on Walker's name as an identity and as a form of concerted action. The entry ends:

> When I asked her what I/we could/should do, she took up her walking stick and walked expressively and purposefully across the room. Dipping a bit from side to side.
> She said: Live by the Word and keep walking. (2)

NOTES

1. Alice Walker, "Beauty: When the Other Dancer is the Self," in her *In Search of Our Mothers' Gardens: Womanist Prose* (San Diego, 1983), p. 393.

2. Barbara Christian, "The Race for Theory" (1987), rpt. in *Gender and Theory: Dialogues in Feminist Criticism*, ed. Linda Kaufmann (Oxford, 1989), p. 226; hereafter cited in text as *RT.*

3. Toni Morrison, *Playing in the Dark: Whiteness and the Literary Imagination* (Cambridge, Mass., 1992), pp. 51–52.

4. Toni Morrison, Introduction, *Race-ing Justice, En-Gendering Power: Essays on Anita Hill, Clarence Thomas, and the Construction of Social Reality*, ed. Toni Morrison (Cambridge, Mass., 1992), p. xiii, hereafter cited in text.

5. Kimberlé Crenshaw points out that Hill was appropriated by white feminists to tell a story about sexual harassment that did not take into account black women's historical experience of their bodies' legal expropriation under slavery, a story that—because it seemed to be a white woman's story—allowed Thomas to cast himself as "the victim of racial discrimination with Hill as the perpetrator" ("Whose Story Is It, Anyway? Feminist and Antiracist Appropriations of Anita Hill," in *Race-ing Justice, En-Gendering Power,* p. 415).

6. Valerie Smith, "Black Feminist Theory and the Representation of the 'Other,'" in *Changing Our Own Words: Essays on Criticism, Theory, and Writing by Black Women*, ed. Cheryl A. Wall (New Brunswick, N.J., 1989), p. 44; see also this volume, pp. 311–325. Hereafter cited in text.

7. Toril Moi, *Sexual/Textual Politics: Feminist Literary Theory* (London, 1985), p. 86.

8. It is for this reason that I use the terms *black* and *white* in this paper, despite the danger that such usage perpetuates the very phenomenon of racism: these terms name a his-

torical reality. On the political need for these terms in continuing to recognize racism, see bell hooks, *Yearning: Race, Gender, and Cultural Politics* (Boston, 1990), p. 52; hereafter cited in text as *Y*.

9. My project thus parallels Elizabeth Abel's recent critique of white feminists who write on African American writers (Barbara Johnson and myself), although the nature and direction of her critique differs from mine. See Elizabeth Abel, "Black Writing, White Reading: Race and the Politics of Feminist Interpretation," *Critical Inquiry*, 19 (1993), 470–98; see also this volume, pp. 827–852.

10. Judith Butler, *Bodies that Matter: On the Discursive Limits of "Sex"* (New York, 1993).

11. Although Haraway certainly identifies herself with postmodern theory, while Butler and Fuss more distinctly align themselves with deconstructive poststructuralism (which overlaps with but is not coextensive with postmodern theory), I allude here to the sort of questions asked again and again in such a volume as *Feminism/Postmodernism*, ed. Linda Nicholson (New York, 1990)—questions in regard to which the kind of poststructuralism practiced by Butler and Fuss could certainly be subsumed within postmodern theory

12. Donna Haraway, "A Manifesto for Cyborgs: Science, Technology, and Socialist Feminism in the 1990s," *Socialist Review*, 15, no. 80 (Mar.–Apr. 1985), 67; hereafter cited in text as *MC*.

13. It is still a matter of contention among feminist intellectuals what the political utility of such a concept is, or what it might constitute as a practice involving actual female bodies. While Haraway's postmodern project has for good reason galvanized the feminist community, some have expressed measured skepticism. Susan Squier, writing about Haraway's enthusiasm for postmodern fragmentation in another context, comments that while "cyborgization . . . may *metaphorically* embody the emancipatory possibility of escaping the unitary, gendered and bounded construction of the human subject, on the level of scientific and medical practice such concepts continue the narrative of sadism and masculine usurpation of female procreative power that Haraway has previously documented." Susan Squier, rev. of *Gender and Genius* by Christine Battersby and *Primitive Visions* by Donna Haraway, *The Minnesota Review*, ns 37 (Spring 1992), 155. Susan Bordo puts her worry more succinctly: "the postmodern body is no body at all." Susan Bordo *Unbearable Weight: Feminism, Western Culture, and The Body* (Berkeley, 1993), p. 229, hereafter cited in text as *UW*.

14. As Bordo points out (*UW*, p. 229), "women of color" is a problematic term because it totalizes exactly the individuals who are being used to demonstrate the failure of totalization. By initially using quotation marks, Haraway acknowledges this problem, but after a first usage she drops them. I thank Diana Paulin (in conversation at the University of Washington, Seattle) for pointing out, in response to an earlier version of this paper that my own use of the term "women of color" unintentionally replicated the usage I criticize in Haraway and others. I have since tried to defamiliarize this term by using quotation marks when referring to others' use of it or to substitute more specific referents.

15. See Julia Erhardt, "Am I (Black or) Blue?: A Critique of Cyborg Feminism," unpublished paper, Yale University, 1992, hereafter cited in text as *AI*; Hortense Spillers "Mama's Baby, Papa's Maybe: An American Grammar Book," *Diacritics*, 17, no. 2 (Summer 1987), 65–81; see also this volume, pp. 384–405. Hereafter cited in text as *MB*.

16. See Donna Haraway, "Ecce Homo, Ain't (Ar'n't) I a Woman, and Inappropriate/d Others: The Human in a Post-Humanist Landscape," in *Feminists Theorize the Political*, ed. Judith Butler and Joan W. Scott (New York, 1992), pp. 86–100, hereafter cited in text. Haraway's title refers to Trinh T. Minh-ha's "She, The Inappropriate/d Other," *Discourse* 8 (1986–87) (cited in Haraway, p. 91).

17. Alice Walker, "A Name Is Sometimes an Ancestor Saying Hi, I'm with you," in *Living By the Word: Selected Writings 1973–1987* (San Diego, 1988), p. 98; hereafter cited in text as *AN*.

18. Cherríe Moraga, *Loving in the War Years* (Boston, 1983), p. 140; hereafter cited in text as *L*.

19. Gloria Anzaldúa, *Borderlands/La Frontera: The New Mestiza* (San Francisco, 1987), p. 3.

20. Gloria Anzaldúa, "Speaking in Tongues: A Letter to Third World Women Writers," in *This Bridge Called My Back: Writings by Radical Women of Color,* ed. Cherríe Moraga and Gloria Anzaldúa (Watertown, Mass., 1981), p. 169.

21. Judith Butler, "Gendering the Body: Beauvoir's Philosophical Contribution," in *Women, Knowledge, and Reality: Explorations in Feminist Philosophy,* ed. Ann Garry and Marilyn Pearsall (Boston, 1989), pp. 253–62; *Gender Trouble: Feminism and the Subversion of Identity* (New York, 1990), hereafter cited as *GT*; and "Imitation and Gender Insubordination," in *Inside/Out: Lesbian Theories, Gay Theories,* ed. Diana Fuss (New York, 1991), hereafter cited as *IGI*.

22. Judith Butler, "Contingent Foundations: Feminism and the Question of 'Postmodernism,'" in *Feminists Theorize the Political,* p. 14.

23. Simone de Beauvoir, *The Second Sex,* tr. H. M. Parshley (New York, 1974), p. 30, qtd. in *GT,* p. 155; see also Butler, "Gendering the Body," p. 254.

24. Aretha Franklin, "(You Make Me Feel Like) A Natural Woman," by Goffin, Wexler, and King (Screen Gems-EMI Music, BMI), on *The Best of Aretha Franklin,* Atlantic, CS 81280-4-Y, 1984.

25. Combahee River Collective, "Black Feminist Statement," in *This Bridge Called My Back,* pp. 210–18.

26. Joyce Ann Joyce, "The Black Canon: Reconstructing Black American Literary Criticism" and "'Who the Cap Fit': Unconsciousness and Unconscionableness in the Criticism of Houston A. Baker, Jr. and Henry Louis Gates, Jr.," in *New Literary History,* 18 (1987), 335–44 and 371–84.

27. Patricia Hill Collins, "The Social Construction of Black Feminist Thought," *Signs,* 14 (1989), 745–73.

28. Diana Fuss, *Essentially Speaking: Feminism, Nature, and Difference* (New York, 1989), pp. 94–95; hereafter cited in text as *ES*.

29. Nancy K. Miller, "The Text's Heroine: A Feminist Critic and Her Fictions," *Diacritics,* 12, no. 2 (Summer 1982), 53.

30. Hazel V. Carby, *Reconstructing Womanhood: The Emergence of the Afro-American Woman Novelist* (New York, 1987), p. 16.

31. Susan Bordo argues on the basis of her reading of Audre Lorde and Luce Irigaray for an "embodied postmodernism," one that acknowledges not an essence of the body or identity but the "historically located body" (*UW,* pp. 40–41), so that, with bell hooks, it would still be possible to speak of "black identity" and "experiences" as historically constituted. I would identify my own position with this one.

32. See Jay Clayton's discussion of the difference made by the pragmatic situation of a writer: no matter how sensitive or imaginative, "a work by a white writer cannot function in the same way as a work by a black. . . . To speak from a position of marginality is to engage listeners in a different social relation from that of the dominant culture." Jay Clayton, "The Narrative Turn in Recent Minority Fiction," *American Literary History,* 2 (1989), 389.

33. Jean Seligman with Jennifer Boeth, "Whole Lot of Shaking Going On," *Newsweek,* 10 May 1993, p. 49; hereafter cited in text.

34. In accord with Donna Haraway's notion of "situated knowledges" (see her *Simians, Cyborgs, and Women: The Reinvention of Nature* [New York, 1991], pp. 183–201), I recognize that my reading of Walker and Williams is symptomatic of my critical positioning as a feminist scholar, raised on deconstruction but deeply invested in the practical politics of feminism and women's studies, and also as a women's studies teacher often assailed from both sides, by students who find poststructuralist feminism hopelessly arid and alien to their

experience and by other, equally impassioned students who find identity-based feminisms hopelessly naive.

35. Patricia J. Williams, "Owning the Self in a Disowned World," in her *The Alchemy of Race and Rights* (Cambridge, Mass., 1991), p. 183; hereafter cited in text.

36. Alice Walker, "Journal (April 17th, 1984)," in *Living by the Word*, pp. 1–2; hereafter cited in text.

gaze

"The gaze" is an abstraction theorists use to describe the act of looking, or, more specifically, the representation of that act. In *Ways of Seeing* (1972), art historian John Berger explains the close connection in Western culture between women and the gaze. "A woman must continually watch herself. She is almost continually accompanied by her own image of herself. Whilst she is walking across a room or whilst she is weeping at the death of her father, she can scarcely avoid envisaging herself walking or weeping. From earliest childhood she has been taught and persuaded to survey herself continually." That surveillance, Berger insists, is intrinsic to relations between the sexes: "Men look at women. Women watch themselves being looked at. This determines not only most relations between men and women but also the relation of women to themselves. The surveyor of woman in herself is male: the surveyed female." The theory of the gaze asks what is at stake for women in this process of being looked at: Can a woman be represented without being objectified? Can a woman be the bearer of the gaze, instead of or in addition to its object? Can the concept of the gaze operate outside the heterosexual economy of men's looks at women?

The theory of the gaze began as the study of the objectification of women in visual texts, and—as Berger's explanation implies—it originally operated within a specifically heterocentric framework. This section begins with Luce Irigaray's feminist investigation of the role played by the gaze in Sigmund Freud's theory of human sexual development, and moves on to a foundational text in feminist film theory that makes critical use of psychoanalysis, Laura Mulvey's essay on the gaze in classic Hollywood film. We then offer two examples of how the theory of the gaze has come to be useful in the criticism of literary texts, and (in the case of Elizabeth Meese's essay) has undergone revision to accommodate a lesbian-centered perspective.

Berger says of the woman who watches herself being watched that "She turns herself into an object—and most particularly an object of vision: a sight." As Luce Irigaray's "Another 'Cause'—Castration" (French edition 1974; English translation, 1985) argues, this objectification of women operates throughout Freudian and Lacanian psychoanalysis. (For an explanation of the basic principles of Lacan, see the introduction to "Desire" in this volume; that section also contains an essay by Jane Gallop that critiques and complicates "Another 'Cause'.") This selection is part of a longer essay, "The Blind Spot of an Old Dream of Symmetry," from *Speculum of the Other Woman*, and is Irigaray's interrogation of Freud's essay "On Femininity" (in *New Introductory Lectures*), probably the most influential essay ever written on female sexuality. Irigaray begins by questioning several concepts central to Freud's theory of penis envy: She asks why the little girl should necessarily recognize the penis as a valuable, enviable organ at all; why she should experience a sense of "lack" of sexual organs when she clearly has not only one but several; and, finally, how it benefits Freud to believe that he has the thing that women envy. Working from these contradictions in Freud's essay, Irigaray shows that woman functions for Freud as a mirror that reflects back what the man wants to see.

The whole issue of visibility becomes central to Irigaray's questioning here. As Jane Gallop (in "Desire") and Laura Mulvey explain, the field of vision has a central place in Lacanian psychoanalytic thought. Lacan describes the original experience of the split in the subject as an experience before a mirror, and has described "the gaze" as itself a source of pleasure (see Mulvey's essay here and Lacan's *Four Fundamental Concepts of Psychoanalysis* for a fully elaborated theory of the gaze). For Irigaray, the privilege accorded to visibility in Freud's thought—the male sex organ is more highly valued than the female because it can be seen, and therefore desired—results in a fundamental misrepresentation, or nonrepresentation, of woman's desire.

Irigaray understands Freud's insistence on visibility as an issue of power, as he assigns himself the role of seeing the woman's supposed lack. As Irigaray says, "the gaze has always been involved": she suggests that what is really at stake for Freud is the possibility that women and girls envy not the penis, but "the omnipotence of gazing, knowing . . . the eye-penis . . . the phallic gaze." Irigaray's essay—characteristically written in the playful, associative prose style that has come to be associated with *l'écriture féminine*—suggests the ludicrousness of the "penis envy alleged against women," which is, after all, just "a remedy for man's fear of losing one. If *she* envies it, then *he* must have it. If *she* envies what *he* has, then it must be valuable." What "*he* has," Irigaray implies, is the prerogative of directing the knowing gaze at the woman, who always remains an object, never a subject, in Freudian discourse.

In "Visual Pleasure and Narrative Cinema" (1975), Laura Mulvey, an avant-garde filmmaker herself, turns her attention toward the representation of women as *objects* of the gaze, hence objects of desire in traditional Hollywood films. How do we get pleasure from cinema? Is that pleasure oppressive to women? Mulvey argues that the classic narrative film of the thirties and forties exploits women by using male desire to code the erotic into the dominant patriarchal order. In these films, the camera is used to display women as the objects of fetishistic or voyeuristic gazes (sexually "abnormal" ways of looking), which make them concurrently alluring and threatening. To allay that threat—which Mulvey links, through the use of psychoanalytic theory, to the castration complex—traditional cinema uses three techniques: women are punished at the end of films, their bodies are fragmented by camera shots, or they are made into sexual icons. Mulvey urges new techniques of filmmaking that will end this oppressive use of women as nothing more than objects of desire and that will make film viewing a more self-conscious, and egalitarian, experience. More recent work in media studies (such as the essays in *The Female Gaze: Women as Viewers of Popular Culture*, edited by Lorraine Gamman and Margaret Marshment [1989] and Mulvey's own revisiting of her original essay [1988]) has experimented with the idea that the cinematic gaze need not always carry masculine connotations.

In the late 1980s, feminist literary critics began borrowing the concept of the gaze from the visual arts, using it as a gender-inflected term for discussing narrative point of view. Beth Newman, in "'The Situation of the Looker-On': Gender, Narration, and Gaze in *Wuthering Heights*" (1990), employs a psychoanalytically informed feminist narratology to analyze the workings of the gaze in Emily Brontë's novel. Newman appropriates a central question of feminist film theory—"Is the gaze male?"—and applies it to the characters and the narrative structure of *Wuthering Heights*. By identifying scenes in which a male character looks at a female character who responds by looking back, Newman shows that Brontë's text suggests that the male gazer is not always all-powerful. As Newman explains (through a revisionist reading of Lacan), "The gaze can serve to destabilize the viewer as well as to confer mastery, especially if the gazer is caught looking by another subject who sees the gaze and perceives it as an expression of desire."

Newman argues for a feminist subversion of the power structure implicit in the gaze: "*Wuthering Heights* suggests that the gaze (and therefore the novel, which reproduces that gaze), however coercive, is never a locus of complete control—that the gaze even opens a space for resisting that control." Newman sees Brontë as envisioning the possibility of disrupting the politics of the gaze: she says Brontë imagines "not a simple inversion in which the woman is permitted to turn the tables with an appropriating look back but a destruction of the hierarchical positioning of male and female that the gendered gaze entails." Through detailed analysis of the interactions of characters and the structure of the narrative frame, Newman demonstrates that Brontë's experiments with the gaze hold powerful potential for a "feminist poetics of the novel."

Though it does not engage directly in the psychoanalytic discussion of the gaze, Elizabeth Meese's essay "When Virginia Looked at Vita, What Did She See; or, Lesbian: Feminist: Woman—What's the Difference?" (1992) is an experiment in what happens when heterocentric assumptions about the gaze get set aside. Like Irigaray, Meese writes in a style that stretches the boundaries of academic convention, in this case, interpolating personal letters to her lover with analyses of theory and of Virginia Woolf's texts to and about Vita Sackville-West, including her novel *Orlando*; like Newman, she focuses her investigation of desire and looking not upon male-authored texts, but on the practice of women writers: in this case, Woolf and Meese herself. Unlike any of the other theorists in this section, Meese does not look at a gaze exchanged between men and women, but focuses exclusively on lesbians looking at one another.

Meese's answer to her title's question is that when Virginia looks at Vita, she "sees first and foremost, a lesbian, and invests in Vita, through the character of Orlando, the history of women 'like' her—five hundred years of lesbianism." Meese draws upon Lacan as well as other theorists in her reading of the workings of desire in Woolf's novel, pointing to the gaps in the narration left by the "Biographer" who tells Orlando's fantastic four-century-long life story. Speaking from the position of lesbian reader, Meese asks, "How do I see what Virginia sees? How do I see her seeing Vita?" Her answer is that "'the Biographer' tells me how to imagine Virginia looking at Vita, a gap and an overflow. And my lover and I (re)enact the scene." In such moments of Meese's essay—here, a segue into a letter addressed to that lover—the interconnections among the gazes inside and outside of texts come into the foreground. Meese is tracing out a web of gazes exchanged among author and author's beloved, biographer and biographer's subject, narrator and character, character and character, reader and character, reader and reader's beloved. In this altered model of the gaze, its monolithic oppression of woman by man is effectively deconstructed through the multiplicity of looks that play into the writing (and reading) of lesbian texts.

—RRW & DPH

ANOTHER "CAUSE"—CASTRATION

(1974)

AS MIGHT BE EXPECTED

The little girl's hostility toward her mother finds other justifications. Such as: the impossibility of satisfying the child's sexual desires; the mother inciting the child to masturbate and then forbidding it to do so; the fact that the bond to the mother is supposedly destined to disappear as a result of its primitive character, since early object cathexes are always highly ambivalent; "it is the special nature of the mother-child relation that leads, with equal inevitability, to the destruction of the child's love; for even the mildest upbringing cannot avoid using compulsion and introducing restrictions, and any such intervention in the child's liberty must provoke as a reaction an inclination to rebelliousness and aggressiveness." But "all these factors . . . are, after all, also in operation in the relation of the *boy* [Freud's italics] to his mother and are yet unable to alienate him from the maternal object." So some specific factor must intervene in the mother-daughter relation and in the development of that relation which would explain "the termination of the attachment of girls to their mother" (p. 124).

> I *believe* we have found this specific factor, and indeed *where we expected to find it*, even though in a surprising form. *Where we expected to find it*, I say, for it lies in the castration complex. After all, the *anatomical* distinction [between the sexes] *must* express itself in *psychical* consequences. *It was, however, a surprise to learn from analyses that girls hold their mother responsible* for their lack of a penis and do not forgive her for their being thus put at a disadvantage. (p. 124)

One might cite or even recite Freud at length, the Freud of "female sexuality" at least, on the basis of these "I believes," these "where we expected to find its," these "castration complexes"; and also relate them to his failure to be "surprised" at the "psychical consequences" of an "anatomical distinction," or to his rather univocal appeal to anatomy to explain a psychical economy—which would supposedly know no other mimesis than that of "nature" according to this interpretation?—and to all those expressions of surprise which, perhaps, mask the upsurge of an *unheimlich* that is much more uncanny, blinding. . . .

THE GAZE, ALWAYS AT STAKE

So the little girl does not forgive her mother for not giving her a penis. At the *"sight* of the genitals of the other sex," girls *"notice the* [sexual?] *difference* and, it must be admitted, its significance too. They feel seriously *wronged*, often declare that they want to *'have something like it too'* . . . and fall victim to *'envy for the penis'*, which will leave ineradicable traces on their development and the formation of their character" (p. 125).

The dramatization is quite good, and one can imagine, or dream up, recognition scenes along these lines in the consulting room of psychoanalyst Freud. By rights, though, the question should still be raised of the respective relationships between the gaze and sexual difference, since, he tells us, you have to see it to believe it. And therefore, one must lose sight of something to see it anew? Admittedly. But all the same. . . . Unless all the potency, and the difference (?) were displaced into the gaze(s)? So Freud will see, without being seen? Without being seen seeing? Without even being questioned about the potency of his gaze? Which leads to envy of the omnipotence of gazing, knowing? About sex/about the penis. To envy and jealousy of the eye-penis, of the phallic gaze? He will be able to see that I don't have one, will realize it in the twinkling of an eye. I shall not see if he has one. More than me? But he will inform me of it. Displaced castration? *The gaze is at stake from the outset.* Don't forget, in fact, what "castration," or the knowledge of castration, owes to the gaze, at least for Freud. The gaze has always been involved.

Now the little girl, the woman, supposedly has *nothing* you can see. She exposes, exhibits the possibility of a *nothing to see.* Or at any rate she shows nothing that is penis-shaped or could substitute for a penis. This is the odd, the uncanny thing, as far as the eye can see, this nothing around which lingers in horror, now and forever, an overcathexis of the eye, of appropriation by the gaze, and of the *phallomorphic* sexual metaphors, its reassuring accomplices.[1]

This nothing, which actually cannot well be mastered in the twinkling of an eye, might equally well have acted as an inducement to perform castration upon an age-old oculocentrism. It might have been interpreted as the intervention of a difference, of a deferent, as a challenge to an imaginary whose functions are often improperly regulated in terms of sight. Or yet again as the "symptom," the "signifier," of the possibility of an *other* libidinal economy, of a heterogeneity unknown in the practice of and discourse about the (designated) libido. Now the "castration complex" in becoming a woman will merely close off, repress? or censure? such possible interpretations. Woman's castration is defined as her having nothing you can see, as her *having* nothing. In her having nothing penile, in seeing that she has No Thing. Nothing *like* man. That is to say, *no sex/organ* that can be seen in a *form* capable of founding its reality, reproducing its truth. *Nothing to be seen is equivalent to having no thing. No being and no truth.*[2] The contract, the collusion, between *one* sex/organ and the victory won by visual dominance therefore leaves woman with her sexual void, with an "actual castration" carried out in actual fact. She has the option of a "neutral" libido or of sustaining herself by "penis envy."

ANATOMY IS "DESTINY"

This "neuter" is hard for Freud to account for in his theory of the difference of the sexes, as we can see from his repeated admissions that the subject of woman's sexuality is still very "obscure." As for what he will have to say about it, what has become "apparent" to him about it, female sexuality can be graphed along the axes of visibility of (so-called) masculine sexuality. For such a demonstration to hold up, the little girl must immediately become a little boy. In the beginning . . . the little girl was (only) a little boy. In other words THERE NEVER IS (OR WILL BE) A LITTLE GIRL. All that remains is to assign her sexual function to this "little boy" with no penis, or at least no penis of any recognized value. Inevitably, the trial of "castration" must be undergone. This "little boy," who was, in all innocence and ignorance of sexual difference, *phallic*, notices how ridiculous "his" sex organ looks. "He" *sees* the disadvantage for which "he" is *anatomically destined*: "he" has only a tiny little sex organ, no sex organ at all, really, an almost invisible sex organ. The almost imperceptible clitoris. The humiliation of being so badly equipped, of cutting such a poor figure, in *comparison* with the penis, with *the* sex organ can only lead to a desire to "have something like it too," and Freud claims that this desire will form the basis for "normal womanhood." In the course of the girl's discovery of her castration, her dominant feelings are of envy, jealousy, and hatred toward the mother—or in fact any woman—who has no penis and could not give one. She desires to be a man or at any rate "like" a man since she cannot actually become one.[3] The little girl does not submit to the "facts" easily, she keeps waiting for "it to grow," and "believes in that possibility for improbably long years." Which means that no attempt will be made by the little girl—nor by the mother? nor by the woman?—to find symbols for the state of "this nothing to be seen," to defend its goals, or to lay claim to its rewards. *Here again no economy would be possible whereby sexual reality can be represented by/for woman.* She remains forsaken and abandoned in her lack, default, absence, envy, etc. and is led to submit, to follow the dictates issued univocally by the sexual desire, discourse, and law of man. Of the father, in the first instance.

WHAT THE FATHER'S DISCOURSE COVERS UP

So, borrowing Freud's own terms, let us question him for example, about his relationship to the parental function. That is, to the exercise of the law—notably the psychoanalytic law—of castration. Why this fear, horror, phobia . . . felt when there is nothing to be seen, why does having nothing that can be seen threaten *his* libidinal economy? And remember in this regard that in the castration scenario Freud has just outlined, it is the boy who looks and is horrified first, and that the little girl merely doubles and confirms by reduplication what he is supposed to have seen. Or not seen. "In [boys] the castration complex arises after they have learnt from *the sight of the female genitals* that the organ which they value so highly need not necessarily accompany the body. At this the boy calls to mind the threats he brought on himself by his doings with that organ, he begins to give credence to them and falls under the influence of *fear of castration*, [Freud's italics] which will be the most powerful motive force in his subsequent development" (p. 125). After which, Freud goes on: "The castration complex of girls is *also* started by the *sight* of the genitals of the other sex. Etc."

Here again the little girl will have to act *like* the little boy, feel the same urge to see, look in the same way, and her resentment at not having a penis must follow and corroborate the horrified astonishment the little boy feels when faced with the strangeness of the nonidentical, the nonidentifiable. The "reality" of the girl's castration could be summed up as follows: you men can see nothing, can know nothing of this; can neither discover nor recognize yourselves in this. All that remains, therefore, is for me, for her (or them), to accept this fact. As a biological fact! The girl thus "enters" into the castration complex in the same way as the boy, like a boy. She "comes out" of it feminized by a decision, which she is duty bound to ratify, that there cannot be a nothing to be seen. The idea that a "nothing to be seen," a something not subject to the rule of visibility or of specula(riza)tion, might yet have some reality, would indeed be intolerable to man. It would serve to threaten the theory and practice of the representation by which he aims to sublimate, or avoid the ban on, masturbation. Auto-erotism has been permitted, authorized, encouraged insofar as it is deferred, exhibited in sublated ways. All this is endangered (caught in the act, one might say) by a *nothing*—that is, a nothing the same, identical, identifiable. By a fault, a flaw, a lack, an absence, outside the system of representations and auto-representations. Which are man's. By a *hole* in men's signifying economy. A nothing that might cause the ultimate destruction, the splintering, the break in their systems of "presence," of "re-presentation" and "representation." A nothing threatening the process of production, reproduction, mastery, and profitability, of meaning, dominated by the phallus—that *master signifier* whose law of functioning erases, rejects, denies the surging up, the resurgence, the recall of a *heterogeneity* capable of reworking the principle of its authority. That authority is minted in concepts, representations, and formalizations of language which prescribe, even today, the prevailing theory and practice of "castration." And what weak instruments these are, products of the very system they pretend to challenge. Such collusion with phallocentrism serves only to confirm its power.

THE NEGATIVE IN PHALLOCENTRIC DIALECTIC

Thus the matter before us leads us to ask ourselves, and to ask them:
(1) Does the little girl, the woman, really have "penis envy" in the sense Freud gives to that expression; that is, of wanting "to have something like it too"? This assumption, in fact, governs everything said now and later about female sexuality. For this "envy" programs all of woman's instinctual economy, even, though she does not realize it, *before* the discovery of her castration, at the point when, supposedly, she only was, and wanted to be, a boy.

(2) What is the relationship of that "envy" to man's "desire"? In other words, is it possible that the phobia aroused in man, and notably in Freud, by the uncanny strangeness of the "nothing to be seen" cannot tolerate *her* not having this "envy"? *Her* having other desires, of a different nature from *his* representation of

the sexual and from his representations of sexual desire. From his projected, re-flected *auto-representations*, shall we say? If woman had desires other than "penis envy," this would call into question the unity, the uniqueness, the simplicity of the mirror charged with sending man's image back to him—albeit inverted. Call into question its flatness. The specularization, and speculation, of the purpose of (*his*) desire could no longer be two-dimensional. Or again: the "penis envy" at-tributed to woman soothes the anguish man feels, Freud feels, about the coher-ence of his narcissistic construction and reassures him against what he calls castration anxiety. For if his desire can be signified only as "penis envy," it is a good thing that he has it (one). And that what he has should represent the only goods acceptable for sexual trading.

(3) Why does the term "envy" occur to Freud? Why does Freud choose it? Envy, jealousy, greed are all correlated to lack, default, absence. All these terms describe female sexuality as merely the *other side* or even the *wrong side* of a male sexualism. It could be admitted that the little girl accords a special status to the penis as the instrument of her sexual pleasure and that she displays a centrifugal-centripetal tropism for it. But "penis envy," in the Freudian and indeed psycho-analytic sense, means nothing less than that the little girl, the woman, must despise *her own* pleasure in order to procure a—doubtless ambiguous—remedy for man's castration anxiety. The possibility of losing his penis, of having it cut off, would find a real basis in the *biological* fact of woman's castration. The fear of not having it, of losing it, would be re-presented in the anatomical amputation of woman, in her resentment at lacking a sex organ and in her correlative "envious" urge to gain possession of it. The castration anxiety of not having it, or losing it, would thus be supported by the representation of the female sex, whereas *the de-sire to have it* would confirm man in the assurance that he has it, still, while re-minding him at the same time—in one of the essential rules of the game—that he risks having her take it away from him. The fact remains that "penis envy" must above all be interpreted as a symptomatic index—laid down as a law of the economy of woman's sexuality—of the pregnancy of the desire for the same, whose guarantee, and transcendental signifier or signified, will be the phallus. The Phallus. If it were not so, why not *also* analyze the "envy" for the vagina? Or the uterus? Or the vulva? Etc. The "desire" felt by each pole of sexual differ-ence "to have something like it too"? The resentment at being faulty, lacking, with respect to a heterogene, to an other? The "disadvantage" mother nature puts you to by providing only *one* sex organ? All of this would require, entail, demand an other sex, a different sex—a sex that shared in the same while remaining different[4]—for sexual pleasure to be possible. But finally, in Freud, sexual plea-sure boils down to being plus or minus one sex organ: the penis. And sexual "oth-erness" comes down to "not having it." Thus, woman's lack of penis and her envy of the penis *ensure the function of the negative*, serve as representatives of the nega-tive, in what could be called a *phallocentric*—or phallotropic—dialectic.[5] And if "sexual function" demands that the little boy should turn away from his—real—mother whom convention forbids he should get with child, if what is indicated by the "castration complex" forces him to "sublimate" his instincts toward his mother, let us say that, as far as he is concerned, man will *lose nothing* thereby,

and that the loss will amount only to a risk, a fear, a "fantasy" of loss. And that the *nothing* of sex, the *not* of sex, will be borne by woman.

But, ipso facto, "castration" cannot be what makes the relation between the sexes practicable or assures the possibility for both repetition and "displacement" of the relation *between two sexes*. It must serve as a reminder of the negative which is attributed to woman, to the female sex—in *reality* too, for more verisimilitude—an attribution that would guarantee its "sublation"[6] in the sublimation of the penis. With sex and sexualness being sublated into representations, ideas, laws, dominated by the Phallus. The relationship to the negative, for man, will always have been imaginary—imagined, imaginable—, hence the impetus it gives to fictive, mythic, or ideal productions that are only afterward defined as laws assuring the permanence and circularity of this system. The legislation reestablishes, then, the castration complex, notably of woman, which will serve, along with other edicts, to transform into a historical program the fables relating to men's sexual practices.

(4) As for woman, one may wonder why she submits so readily to this make-believe, why she "mimics" so perfectly as to forget she is acting out man's contraphobic projects, projections, and productions of her desire. Specifically, why does she accept that her desire only amounts to "penis envy"? What fault, deficiency, theft, rape, rejection, repression, censorship, of representations of her sexuality bring about such a subjection to man's desire-discourse-law about her sex? Such an atrophy of her libido? Which will never be admissible, envisionable, except insofar as it props up male desire. For the "penis envy" alleged against woman is—let us repeat—a remedy for man's fear of losing one. If *she* envies it, then *he* must have it. If *she* envies what *he* has, then it must be valuable. The only thing valuable enough to be envied? The very standard of all value. Woman's fetishization of the male organ must indeed be an indispensable support of its price on the sexual market.

IS WORKING OUT THE DEATH DRIVES LIMITED TO MEN ONLY?

So let us speculate that things happen this way because, in psychoanalytic parlance, *the death drives can be worked out only by man*,[7] never, under any circumstances, by woman. She merely "services" the work of the death instincts. Of man.

Thus, by suppressing her drives, by pacifying and making them passive, she will function as pledge and reward for the "total reduction of tension." By the "free flow of energy" in coitus, she will function as a promise of the libido's evanescence, just as in her role as "wife" she will be assigned to maintain coital homeostasis, "constancy." To guarantee that the drives are "bound" in/by marriage. She will also be the place referred to as "maternal" where the automatism of repetition, the reestablishment of an earlier economy, the infinite regression of pleasure, can occur. Back to the sleep of Lethe, to lethargy. Except that she is charged at the same time with preserving, regenerating, and rejuvenating the organism, notably through sexual reproduction. She is wholly devoted to giving life, then, source and re-source of life. To being still the restoring, nourishing mother who prolongs the work of death by sustaining it; death makes a detour through the revitalizing female-maternal.

You will have realized that the "sexual function" also requires aggressiveness from the male, and that this authorizes an economy of death drives whereby the "subject" disengages and protects himself by diverting his energies to the "object." And, by maintaining the subject-object polarity in sexual activity, woman will provide man with an outlet for that "primary masochism" which is dangerous and even life-threatening for the "psychic" as well as the "organic" self. Now, Freud states that this "primary" or "erogenous" masochism will be reserved to woman and that both her "constitution" and "social rules" will forbid her any sadistic way to work out these masochistic death drives. She can only "turn them around" or "turn them inward." The sadism of the anal-sadistic stage is also transformed, at a secondary level, into masochism: activity is turned into passivity, sadism is "turned back" from the "object" onto the "subject." Secondary masochism added to primary masochism—this is apparently the "destiny" of the death drives in woman, and they survive only because of their unalterably sexuate nature, through the erotization of this "masochism."

But further, in order to trans-form his death drives and the whole instinctual dualism, in order to use his life to ward off death for as long as it takes to choose a death, man will have to work on building up his ego. On raising his own tomb, if you like. The new detour along the road to death, through/for the construction of narcissistic monuments, involves pulling the libido back from the object onto the self and desexualizing it so it can carry out more sublimated activities. Now, if this ego is to be valuable, some "mirror"[8] is needed to reassure it and re-insure it of its value. Woman will be the foundation for this specular duplication, giving man back "his" image and repeating it as the "same." If an *other* image, an *other* mirror were to intervene, this inevitably would entail the risk of mortal crisis. Woman will therefore be this sameness—or at least its mirror image—and, in her role of mother, she will facilitate the repetition of the same, in contempt for her difference. Her own sexual difference. Moreover, through her "penis envy," she will supply anything that might be lacking in this specula(riza)tion. Calling back, now and forever, that *remainder* that melts into the depths of the mirror, that sexual energy necessary to carry out the work. The work of death.

So "woman" can function as place—evanescent beyond, point of discharge—as well as time—eternal return, temporal detour—for the sublimation and, if possible, mastery of the work of death. She will also be the representative-representation (*Vorstellung-Repräsentanz*), in other words, of the death drives that cannot (or theoretically could not) be perceived without horror, that the eye (of) consciousness refuses to recognize. In a protective misprision that cannot be put aside without the failure of a certain gaze: which is the whole point of castration. Up to this point, *the main concepts of psychoanalysis, its theory, will have taken no account of woman's desire,* not even of "her" castration. For their ways are too narrowly derived from the history and the historicization of (so-called) male sexuality. From that process by which consciousness comes into being and woman remains the place for the inscription of repressions. All of which demands that, without knowing it, she should provide a basis for such fantasies as the amputation of her sex organ, and that the "anatomy" of her body should put up the security for reality. She provides irrefutable, because natural, proof that this is not a matter of the silent action of the death drives. She will therefore be despoiled, without recourse, of all valid, valuable images of her sex/organs, her body. She is condemned to "psychosis," or at best "hysteria," for lack—censorship? foreclusion? repression?—of a valid signifier for her "first" desire and for her sex/organs.

This doesn't mean that the question of castration isn't raised for woman but rather that it refers back in reality to the father's castration, including the father of psychoanalysis—to his fear, his refusal, his rejection, of an *other* sex. For if to castrate woman is to inscribe her in the law of the same desire, *of the desire for the same*, what exactly is "castration"? And what is the relationship of the agent of castration to the concept and its practice?

NOTES

1. Cf. the relationship Freud establishes between castration anxiety, the fear of losing one's sight, and the fear of one's father's death (in "The Uncanny," *SE*, XVII: 219–52). Or again this: "It often happens that neurotic men declare that they feel there is something uncanny about the female genital organs. This *unheimlich* place, however, is the entrance to the former *Heim* (home) of all human beings, to the place where each one of us lived once upon a time and in the beginning. . . . In this case, too, then, the *unheimlich* is what was once *heimisch*, familiar; the prefix 'un' is the token of repression" ("The Uncanny," p. 245). For the moment let us concentrate on the strange disquiet felt about the female genitals. The woman-mother would be *unheimlich* not only by reason of a repression of a primitive relationship to the maternal but also because her sex/organs are strange, yet close; while "heimisch" as a mother, woman would remain "un" as a woman. Since woman's sexuality is no doubt the most basic form of the *unheimlich*.

2. This echoes Leibniz's question in *Principles of Nature and of Grace Founded on Reason*: "Why is there something rather than nothing?" Or again: "That which is truly not *one* entity, is not truly one *entity* either": Leibniz, letter to Arnauld, April 30, 1687. (Leibniz, *Philosophical Writings*, ed. G. H. R. Parkinson, trans. Mary Morris and G. H. R. Parkinson [London: Dent, 1934 and 1973], pp. 199 and 67.)

3. In other words, the "fact of castration" will leave woman with only one option—the semblance, the mummery of femininity, which will always already have been to "act like" the value recognized by/for the male. The fact that certain men want to "act like" women thus raises the question whether they thereby take back for themselves that "femininity" which was assigned to woman as an inferior copy of their relation to the origin.

4. Of course this will initially imply bisexuality, but here it would evoke instead the "brilliance" of the mirror which explodes into sexual pleasure, like and unlike according to each sex.

5. This might be understood as a tautology, unless the word "a" is re-marked. In other words, if dialectic has *the* one, *the* same as the horizon of its process, then it is necessarily phallocentric.

6. Translation of *Aufhebung*.

7. For the following section, the reader should refer to *Beyond the Pleasure Principle*, "Instincts and their Vicissitudes," *SE*, XIV, and "The Economic Problem of Masochism," *SE*, XIX.

8. A certain flat mirror would thus serve to desexualize drives and thereby work out funeral monuments for the "subject's" ego.

VISUAL PLEASURE AND NARRATIVE CINEMA

(1975)

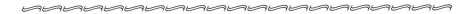

I INTRODUCTION

(a) A Political Use of Psychoanalysis

This paper intends to use psychoanalysis to discover where and how the fascination of film is reinforced by pre-existing patterns of fascination already at work within the individual subject and the social formations that have moulded him. It takes as its starting-point the way film reflects, reveals and even plays on the straight, socially established interpretation of sexual difference which controls images, erotic ways of looking and spectacle. It is helpful to understand what the cinema has been, how its magic has worked in the past, while attempting a theory and a practice which will challenge this cinema of the past. Psychoanalytic theory is thus appropriated here as a political weapon, demonstrating the way the unconscious of patriarchal society has structured film form.

The paradox of phallocentrism in all its manifestations is that it depends on the image of the castrated woman to give order and meaning to its world. An idea of woman stands as linchpin to the system: it is her lack that produces the phallus as a symbolic presence, it is her desire to make good the lack that the phallus signifies. Recent writing in *Screen* about psychoanalysis and the cinema has not sufficiently brought out the importance of the representation of the female form in a symbolic order in which, in the last resort, it speaks castration and nothing else. To summarise briefly: the function of woman in forming the patriarchal unconscious is twofold: she firstly symbolises the castration threat by her real lack of a penis and secondly thereby raises her child into the symbolic. Once this has been achieved, her meaning in the process is at an end. It does not last into the world of law and language except as a memory, which oscillates between memory of maternal plentitude and memory of lack. Both are posited on nature (or on anatomy in Freud's famous phrase). Woman's desire is subjugated to her image as bearer of the bleeding wound; she can exist only in relation to castration and cannot transcend it. She turns her child into the signifier of her own desire to possess a penis (the condition, she imagines, of entry into the symbolic). Either she must gracefully give way to the word, the name of the father and the law, or else struggle to keep her child down with her in the half-light of the imaginary. Woman then stands in patriarchal culture as a signifier for the male other, bound by a symbolic order in which man can live out his fantasies and obsessions through linguistic command by imposing them on the silent image of woman still tied to her place as bearer, not maker, of meaning.

There is an obvious interest in this analysis for feminists, a beauty in its exact rendering of the frustration experienced under the phallocentric order. It gets us nearer to the roots of our oppression, it brings closer an articulation of the problem, it faces us with the ultimate challenge: how to fight the unconscious structured like a language (formed critically at the moment of arrival of language) while still caught within the language of the patriarchy? There is no way in which we can produce an alternative out of the blue, but we can begin to make a break by examining patriarchy with the tools it provides, of which psychoanalysis is not the only but an important one. We are still separated by a great gap from important issues for the female unconscious which are scarcely relevant to phallocentric theory: the sexing of the female infant and her relationship to the symbolic, the sexually mature woman as non-mother, maternity outside the signification of the phallus, the vagina. But, at this point, psychoanalytic theory as it now stands can at least advance our understanding of the *status quo*, of the patriarchal order in which we are caught.

(b) Destruction of Pleasure as a Radical Weapon

As an advanced representation system, the cinema poses questions about the ways the unconscious (formed by the dominant order) structures ways of seeing and pleasure in looking. Cinema has changed over the last few decades. It is no longer the monolithic system based on large capital investment exemplified at its best by Hollywood in the 1930s, 1940s and 1950s. Technological advances (16mm and so on) have changed the economic conditions of cinematic production, which can now be artisanal as well as capitalist. Thus it has been possible for an alternative cinema to develop. However self-conscious and ironic Hollywood managed to be, it always restricted itself to a formal *mise en scène* reflecting the dominant ideological concept of the cinema. The alternative cinema provides a space for the birth of a cinema which is radical in both a political and an aesthetic sense and challenges the basic assumptions of the mainstream film. This is not to reject the latter moralistically, but to highlight the ways in which its formal preoccupations reflect the psychical obsessions of the society which produced it and, further, to stress that the alternative cinema must start specifically by reacting against these obsessions and assumptions. A politically and aesthetically avant-garde cinema is now possible, but it can still only exist as a counterpoint.

The magic of the Hollywood style at its best (and of all the cinema which fell within its sphere of influence) arose, not exclusively, but in one important aspect, from its skilled and satisfying manipulation of visual pleasure. Unchallenged, mainstream film coded the erotic into the language of the dominant patriarchal order. In the highly developed Hollywood cinema it was only through these codes that the alienated subject, torn in his imaginary memory by a sense of loss, by the terror of potential lack in fantasy, came near to finding a glimpse of satisfaction: through its formal beauty and its play on his own formative obsessions. This article will discuss the interweaving of that erotic pleasure in film, its meaning and, in particular, the central place of the image of woman. It is said that analysing pleasure, or beauty, destroys it. That is the intention of this article. The satisfaction and reinforcement of the ego that represent the high point of film history hitherto must be attacked. Not in favour of a reconstructed new pleasure, which cannot exist in the abstract, nor of intellectualised unpleasure, but to make way for a total negation of the ease and plenitude of the narrative fiction film. The alternative is the thrill that comes from leaving the past behind without simply rejecting it, transcending outworn or oppressive forms, and daring to break with normal pleasurable expectations in order to conceive a new language of desire.

II PLEASURE IN LOOKING/FASCINATION WITH THE HUMAN FORM

A   The cinema offers a number of possible pleasures. One is scopophilia (pleasure in looking). There are circumstances in which looking itself is a source of pleasure, just as, in the reverse formation, there is pleasure in being looked at. Originally, in his *Three Essays on Sexuality*, Freud isolated scopophilia as one of the component instincts of sexuality which exist as drives quite independently of the erotogenic zones. At this point he associated scopophilia with taking other people as objects, subjecting them to a controlling and curious gaze. His particular examples centre on the voyeuristic activities of children, their desire to see and make sure of the private and forbidden (curiosity about other people's genital and bodily functions, about the presence or absence of the penis and, retrospectively, about the primal scene). In this analysis scopophilia is essentially active. (Later, in 'Instincts and Their Vicissitudes,' Freud developed his theory of scopophilia further, attaching it initially to pregenital auto-eroticism, after which, by analogy, the pleasure of the look is transferred to others. There is a close working here of the relationship between the active instinct and its further development in a narcissistic form.) Although the instinct is modified by other factors, in particular the constitution of the ego, it continues to exist as the erotic basis for pleasure in looking at another person as object. At the extreme, it can become fixated into a perversion, producing obsessive voyeurs and Peeping Toms whose only sexual satisfaction can come from watching, in an active controlling sense, an objectified other.

At first glance, the cinema would seem to be remote from the undercover world of the surreptitious observation of an unknowing and unwilling victim. What is seen on the screen is so manifestly shown. But the mass of mainstream film, and the conventions within which it has consciously evolved, portray a hermetically sealed world which unwinds magically, indifferent to the presence of the audience, producing for them a sense of separation and playing on their voyeuristic fantasy. Moreover the extreme contrast between the darkness in the auditorium (which also isolates the spectators from one another) and the brilliance of the shifting patterns of light and shade on the screen helps to promote the illusion of voyeuristic separation. Although the film is really being shown, is there to be seen, conditions of screening and narrative conventions give the spectator an illusion of looking in on a private world. Among other things, the position of the spectators in the cinema is blatantly one of repression of their exhibitionism and projection of the repressed desire onto the performer.

B   The cinema satisfies a primordial wish for pleasurable looking, but it also goes further, developing scopophilia in its narcissistic aspect. The conventions of mainstream film focus attention on the human form. Scale, space, stories are all anthropomorphic. Here, curiosity and the wish to look intermingle with a fascination with likeness and recognition: the human face, the human body, the relationship between the human form and its surroundings, the visible presence of the person in the world. Jacques Lacan has described how the moment when a child recognises its own image in the mirror is crucial for the constitution of the ego. Several aspects of this analysis are relevant here. The mirror phase occurs at a time when children's physical ambitions outstrip their motor capacity, with the result that their recognition of themselves is joyous in that they imagine their mirror image to be more complete, more perfect than they experience in their own body. Recognition is thus overlaid with misrecognition: the image recognised is conceived as the reflected body of the self, but its misrecognition as superior projects this body outside itself as an ideal ego, the alienated subject which, reintrojected as an ego ideal, prepares the way for identification with others in the future. This mirror moment predates language for the child.

Important for this article is the fact that it is an image that constitutes the matrix of the imaginary, of recognition/misrecognition and identification, and hence of the first articulation of the I, of subjectivity. This is a moment when an older fascination with looking (at the mother's face, for an obvious example) collides with the initial inklings of self-awareness. Hence it is the birth of the long love affair/despair between image and self-image which has found such intensity of expression in film and such joyous recognition in the cinema audience. Quite apart from the extraneous similarities between screen and mirror (the framing of the human form in its surroundings, for instance), the cinema has structures of fascination strong enough to allow temporary loss of ego while simultaneously reinforcing it. The sense of forgetting the world as the ego has come to perceive it (I forgot who I am and where I was) is nostalgically reminiscent of that presubjective moment of image recognition. While at the same time, the cinema has distinguished itself in the production of ego ideals, through the star system for instance. Stars provide a focus or centre both to screen space and screen story where they act out a complex process of likeness and difference (the glamorous impersonates the ordinary).

C   Sections A and B have set out two contradictory aspects of the pleasurable structures of looking in the conventional cinematic situation. The first, scopophilic, arises from pleasure in using another person as an object of sexual stimulation through sight. The second, developed through narcissism and the constitution of the ego, comes from identification with the image seen. Thus, in film terms, one implies a separation of the erotic identity of the subject from the object on the screen (active scopophilia), the other demands identification of the ego with the object on the screen through the spectator's fascination with and recognition of his like. The first is a function of the sexual instincts, the second of ego libido. This dichotomy was crucial for Freud. Although he saw the two as interacting and overlaying each other, the tension between instinctual drives and self-preservation polarises in terms of pleasure. But both are formative structures, mechanisms without intrinsic meaning. In themselves they have no signification, unless attached to an idealisation. Both pursue aims in indifference to perceptual reality, and motivate eroticised phantasmagoria that affect the subject's perception of the world to make a mockery of empirical objectivity.

During its history, the cinema seems to have evolved a particular illusion of reality in which this contradiction between libido and ego has found a beautifully complementary fantasy world. In *reality* the fantasy world of the screen is subject to the law which produces it. Sexual instincts and identification processes have a meaning within the symbolic order which articulates desire. Desire, born with language, allows the possibility of transcending the instinctual and the imaginary, but its point of reference continually returns to the traumatic moment of its birth: the castration complex. Hence the look, pleasurable in form, can be threatening in content, and it is woman as representation/image that crystallises this paradox.

III WOMAN AS IMAGE, MAN AS BEARER OF THE LOOK

A   In a world ordered by sexual imbalance, pleasure in looking has been split between active/male and passive/female. The determining male gaze projects its fantasy onto the female figure, which is styled accordingly. In their traditional exhibitionist role women are simultaneously looked at and displayed, with their appearance coded for strong visual and erotic impact so that they can be said to connote *to-be-looked-at-ness*. Woman displayed as sexual object is the *leitmotif* of erotic spectacle: from pin-ups to strip-tease, from Ziegfeld to Busby Berkeley, she holds the look, and plays to and signifies male desire. Mainstream film neatly combines spectacle and narrative. (Note, however, how in the musical song-and-dance numbers interrupt the flow of the diegesis.) The presence of woman is an indispensable element of spectacle in normal narrative film, yet her visual presence tends to work against the development of a story-line, to freeze the flow of action in moments of erotic contemplation. This alien presence then has to be integrated into cohesion with the narrative. As Budd Boetticher has put it:

> What counts is what the heroine provokes, or rather what she represents. She is the one, or rather the love or fear she inspires in the hero, or else the concern he feels for her, who makes him act the way he does. In herself the woman has not the slightest importance.

(A recent tendency in narrative film has been to dispense with this problem altogether; hence the development of what Molly Haskell has called the 'buddy movie,' in which the active homosexual eroticism of the central male figures can carry the story without distraction.) Traditionally, the woman displayed has functioned on two levels: as erotic object for the characters within the screen story, and as erotic object for the spectator within the auditorium, with a shifting tension between the looks on either side of the screen. For instance, the device of the show-girl allows the two looks to be unified technically without any apparent break in the diegesis. A woman performs within the narrative; the gaze of the spectator and that of the male characters in the film are neatly combined without breaking narrative verisimilitude. For a moment the sexual impact of the performing woman takes the film into a no man's land outside its own time and space. Thus Marilyn Monroe's first appearance in *The River of No Return* and Lauren Bacall's songs in *To Have and Have Not*. Similarly, conventional close-ups of legs (Dietrich, for instance) or a face (Garbo) integrate into the narrative a different mode of eroticism. One part of a fragmented body destroys the Renaissance space, the illusion of depth demanded by the narrative; it gives flatness, the quality of a cut-out or icon, rather than verisimilitude, to the screen.

B   An active/passive heterosexual division of labour has similarly controlled narrative structure. According to the principles of the ruling ideology and the psychical structures that back it up, the male figure cannot bear the burden of sexual objectification. Man is reluctant to gaze at his exhibitionist like. Hence the split between spectacle and narrative supports the man's role as the active one of advancing the story, making things happen. The man controls the film fantasy and also emerges as the representative of power in a further sense: as the bearer of the look of the spectator, transferring it behind the screen to neutralise the extradiegetic tendencies represented by woman as spectacle. This is made possible through the processes set in motion by structuring the film around a main controlling figure with whom the spectator can identify. As the spectator identifies with the main male protagonist, he projects his look onto that of his like, his screen surrogate, so that the power of the male protagonist as he controls events coincides with the active power of the erotic look, both giving a satisfying sense of omnipotence. A male movie star's glamorous characteristics are thus not those of the erotic object of the gaze, but those of the more perfect, more complete, more powerful ideal ego conceived in the original moment of recognition in front of the mirror. The character in the story can make things happen and control events better than the subject/spectator, just as the image in the mirror was more in control of motor co-ordination.

   In contrast to woman as icon, the active male figure (the ego ideal of the identification process) demands a three-dimensional space corresponding to that of the mirror recognition, in which the alienated subject internalised his own representation of his imaginary existence. He is a figure in a landscape. Here the function of film is to reproduce as accurately as possible the so-called natural conditions of human perception. Camera technology (as exemplified by deep focus in particular) and camera movements (determined by the action of the protagonist), combined with invisible editing (demanded by realism), all tend to blur the limits of screen space. The male protagonist is free to command the stage, a stage of spatial illusion in which he articulates the look and creates the action. (There are films with a woman as main protagonist, of course. To analyse this phenomenon seriously here would take me too far afield. Pam Cook and Claire Johnston's study of *The Revolt of Mamie Stover* in Phil Hardy [ed.], *Raoul Walsh* [Edinburgh, 1974], shows in a striking case how the strength of this female protagonist is more apparent than real.)

C1   Sections III A and B have set out a tension between a mode of representation of woman in film and conventions surrounding the diegesis. Each is associated with a look: that of the spectator in direct scopophilic contact with the female form displayed for his enjoyment (connoting male fantasy) and that of the spectator fascinated with the image of his like set in an illusion of natural space, and through him gaining control and possession of the woman within the diegesis. (This tension and the shift from one pole to the other can structure a single text. Thus both in *Only Angels Have Wings* and in *To Have and Have Not*, the film opens with the woman as object of the combined gaze of spectator and all the male protagonists in the film. She is isolated, glamorous, on display, sexualised. But as the narrative progresses she falls in love with the main male protagonist and becomes his property, losing her outward glamorous characteristics, her generalised sexuality, her show-girl connotations; her eroticism is subjected to the male star alone. By means of identification with him, through participation in his power, the spectator can indirectly possess her too.)

But in psychoanalytic terms, the female figure poses a deeper problem. She also connotes something that the look continually circles around but disavows: her lack of a penis, implying a threat of castration and hence unpleasure. Ultimately, the meaning of woman is sexual difference, the visually ascertainable absence of the penis, the material evidence on which is based the castration complex essential for the organisation of entrance to the symbolic order and the law of the father. Thus the woman as icon, displayed for the gaze and enjoyment of men, the active controllers of the look, always threatens to evoke the anxiety it originally signified. The male unconscious has two avenues of escape from this castration anxiety: preoccupation with the re-enactment of the original trauma (investigating the woman, demystifying her mystery), counterbalanced by the devaluation, punishment or saving of the guilty object (an avenue typified by the concerns of the *film noir*); or else complete disavowal of castration by the substitution of a fetish object or turning the represented figure itself into a fetish so that it becomes reassuring rather than dangerous (hence overvaluation, the cult of the female star).

This second avenue, fetishistic scopophilia, builds up the physical beauty of the object, transforming it into something satisfying in itself. The first avenue, voyeurism, on the contrary, has associations with sadism: pleasure lies in ascertaining guilt (immediately associated with castration), asserting control and subjugating the guilty person through punishment or forgiveness. This sadistic side fits in well with narrative. Sadism demands a story, depends on making something happen, forcing a change in another person, a battle of will and strength, victory/defeat, all occurring in a linear time with a beginning and an end. Fetishistic scopophilia, on the other hand, can exist outside linear time as the erotic instinct is focused on the look alone. These contradictions and ambiguities can be illustrated more simply by using works by Hitchcock and Sternberg, both of whom take the look almost as the content or subject matter of many of their films. Hitchcock is the more complex, as he uses both mechanisms. Sternberg's work, on the other hand, provides many pure examples of fetishistic scopophilia.

C2   Sternberg once said he would welcome his films being projected upside-down so that story and character involvement would not interfere with the spectator's undiluted appreciation of the screen image. This statement is revealing but ingenuous: ingenuous in that his films do demand that the figure of the woman (Dietrich, in the cycle of films with her, as the ultimate example) should be identifiable; but revealing in that it emphasises the fact that for him the pictorial space enclosed by the frame is paramount, rather than narrative or identification processes. While Hitchcock goes into the investigative side of voyeurism, Sternberg produces the ultimate fetish, taking it to the point where the powerful look of the male protagonist (characteristic of traditional narrative film) is broken in favour of the image in direct erotic rapport with the spectator. The beauty of the woman as object and the screen space coalesce; she is no longer the bearer of guilt but a perfect product, whose body, stylised and fragmented by close-ups, is the content of the film and the direct recipient of the spectator's look.

Sternberg plays down the illusion of screen depth; his screen tends to be one-dimensional, as light and shade, lace, steam, foliage, net, streamers and so on reduce the visual field. There is little or no mediation of the look through the eyes of the main male protagonist. On the contrary, shadowy presences like La Bessière in *Morocco* act as surrogates for the director, detached as they are from audience identification. Despite Sternberg's insistence that his stories are irrelevant, it is significant that they are concerned with situation, not suspense, and cyclical rather than linear time, while plot complications revolve around misunderstanding rather than conflict. The most important absence is that of the controlling male gaze within the screen scene. The high point of emotional drama in the most typical Dietrich films, her supreme moments of erotic meaning, take place in the absence of the man she loves in the fiction. There are other witnesses, other spectators watching her on the screen, their gaze is one with, not standing in for, that of the audience. At the end of *Morocco*, Tom Brown has already disappeared into the desert when Amy Jolly kicks off her gold sandals and walks after him. At the end of *Dishonoured*, Kranau is indifferent to the fate of Magda. In both cases, the erotic impact, sanctified by death, is displayed as a spectacle for the audience. The male hero misunderstands and, above all, does not see.

In Hitchcock, by contrast, the male hero does see precisely what the audience sees. However, although fascination with an image through scopophilic eroticism can be the subject of the film, it is the role of the hero to portray the contradictions and tensions experienced by the spectator. In *Vertigo* in particular, but also in *Marnie* and *Rear Window*, the look is central to the plot, oscillating between voyeurism and fetishistic fascination. Hitchcock has never concealed his interest in voyeurism, cinematic and non-cinematic. His heroes are exemplary of the symbolic order and the law—a policeman (*Vertigo*), a dominant male possessing money and power (*Marnie*)—but their erotic drives lead them into compromised situations. The power to subject another person to the will sadistically or to the gaze voyeuristically is turned onto the woman as the object of both. Power is backed by a certainty of legal right and the established guilt of the woman (evoking castration, psychoanalytically speaking). True perversion is barely concealed under a shallow mask of ideological correctness—the man is on the right side of the law, the woman on the wrong. Hitchcock's skillful use of identification processes and liberal use of subjective camera from the point of view of the male protagonist draw the spectators deeply into his position, making them share his uneasy gaze.

The spectator is absorbed into a voyeuristic situation within the screen scene and diegesis, which parodies his own in the cinema.

In an analysis of *Rear Window*, Douchet takes the film as a metaphor for the cinema. Jeffries is the audience, the events in the apartment block opposite correspond to the screen. As he watches, an erotic dimension is added to his look, a central image to the drama. His girlfriend Lisa had been of little sexual interest to him, more or less a drag, so long as she remained on the spectator side. When she crosses the barrier between his room and the block opposite, their relationship is reborn erotically. He does not merely watch her through his lens, as a distant meaningful image, he also sees her as a guilty intruder exposed by a dangerous man threatening her with punishment, and thus finally giving him the opportunity to save her. Lisa's exhibitionism has already been established by her obsessive interest in dress and style, in being a passive image of visual perfection; Jeffries's voyeurism and activity have also been established through his work as a photojournalist, a maker of stories and captor of images. However, his enforced inactivity, binding him to his seat as a spectator, puts him squarely in the fantasy position of the cinema audience.

In *Vertigo*, subjective camera predominates. Apart from one flashback from Judy's point of view, the narrative is woven around what Scottie sees or fails to see. The audience follows the growth of his erotic obsession and subsequent despair precisely from his point of view. Scottie's voyeurism is blatant: he falls in love with a woman he follows and spies on without speaking to. Its sadistic side is equally blatant: he has chosen (and freely chosen, for he had been a successful lawyer) to be a policeman, with all the attendant possibilities of pursuit and investigation. As a result, he follows, watches and falls in love with a perfect image of female beauty and mystery. Once he actually confronts her, his erotic drive is to break her down and force her *to tell* by persistent cross-questioning.

In the second part of the film, he re-enacts his obsessive involvement with the image he loved to watch secretly. He reconstructs Judy as Madeleine, forces her to conform in every detail to the actual physical appearance of his fetish. Her exhibitionism, her masochism, make her an ideal passive counterpart to Scottie's active sadistic voyeurism. She knows her part is to perform, and only by playing it through and then replaying it can she keep Scottie's erotic interest. But in the repetition he does break her down and succeeds in exposing her guilt. His curiosity wins through; she is punished.

Thus, in *Vertigo*, erotic involvement with the look boomerangs: the spectator's own fascination is revealed as illicit voyeurism as the narrative content enacts the processes and pleasures that he is himself exercising and enjoying. The Hitchcock hero here is firmly placed within the symbolic order, in narrative terms. He has all the attributes of the patriarchal superego. Hence the spectator, lulled into a false sense of security by the apparent legality of his surrogate, sees through his look and finds himself exposed as complicit, caught in the moral ambiguity of looking. Far from being simply an aside on the perversion of the police, *Vertigo* focuses on the implications of the active/looking, passive/looked-at split in terms of sexual difference and the power of the male symbolic encapsulated in the hero. Marnie, too, performs for Mark Rutland's gaze and masquerades as the perfect to-be-looked-at image. He, too, is on the side of the law until, drawn in by obsession with her guilt, her secret, he longs to see her in the act of committing a crime, make her confess and thus save her. So he, too, becomes complicit as he acts out the implications of his power. He controls money and words; he can have his cake and eat it.

IV SUMMARY

The psychoanalytic background that has been discussed in this article is relevant to the pleasure and unpleasure offered by traditional narrative film. The scopophilic instinct (pleasure in looking at another person as an erotic object) and, in contradistinction, ego libido (forming identification processes) act as formations, mechanisms, which mould this cinema's formal attributes. The actual image of woman as (passive) raw material for the (active) gaze of man takes the argument a step further into the content and structure of representation, adding a further layer of ideological significance demanded by the patriarchal order in its favourite cinematic form—illusionistic narrative film. The argument must return again to the psychoanalytic background: women in representation can signify castration, and activate voyeuristic or fetishistic mechanisms to circumvent this threat. Although none of these interacting layers is intrinsic to film, it is only in the film form that they can reach a perfect and beautiful contradiction, thanks to the possibility in the cinema of shifting the emphasis of the look. The place of the look defines cinema, the possibility of varying it and exposing it. This is what makes cinema quite different in its voyeuristic potential from, say, strip-tease, theatre, shows and so on. Going far beyond highlighting a woman's to-be-looked-at-ness, cinema builds the way she is to be looked at into the spectacle itself. Playing on the tension between film as controlling the dimension of time (editing, narrative) and film as controlling the dimension of space (changes in distance, editing), cinematic codes create a gaze, a world and an object, thereby producing an illusion cut to the measure of desire. It is these cinematic codes and their relationship to formative external structures that must be broken down before mainstream film and the pleasure it provides can be challenged.

To begin with (as an ending), the voyeuristic-scopophilic look that is a crucial part of traditional filmic pleasure can itself be broken down. There are three different looks associated with cinema: that of the camera as it records the pro-filmic event, that of the audience as it watches the final product, and that of the characters at each other within the screen illusion. The conventions of narrative film deny the first two and subordinate them to the third, the conscious aim being always to eliminate intrusive camera presence and prevent a distancing awareness in the audience. Without these two absences (the material existence of the recording process, the critical reading of the spectator), fictional drama cannot achieve reality, obviousness and truth. Nevertheless, as this article has argued, the structure of looking in narrative fiction film contains a contradiction in its own premises: the female image as a castration threat constantly endangers the unity of the diegesis and bursts through the world of illusion as an intrusive, static, one-dimensional fetish. Thus the two looks materially present in time and space are obsessively subordinated to the neurotic needs of the male ego. The camera becomes the mechanism for producing an illusion of Renaissance space, flowing movements compatible with the human eye, an ideology of representation that revolves around the perception of the subject; the camera's look is disavowed in order to create a convincing world in which the spectator's surrogate can perform with verisimilitude. Simultaneously, the look of the audience is denied an intrinsic force: as soon as fetishistic representation of the female image threatens to break the spell of illusion, and the erotic image on the screen appears directly (without mediation) to the spectator, the fact of fetishisation, concealing as it does castration fear, freezes the look, fixates the spectator and prevents him from achieving any distance from the image in front of him.

This complex interaction of looks is specific to film. The first blow against the monolithic accumulation of traditional film conventions (already undertaken by radical film-makers) is to free the look of the camera into its materiality in time and space and the look of the audience into dialectics and passionate detachment. There is no doubt that this destroys the satisfaction, pleasure and privilege of the 'invisible guest,' and highlights the way film has depended on voyeuristic active/passive mechanisms. Women, whose image has continually been stolen and used for this end, cannot view the decline of the traditional film form with anything much more than sentimental regret.

"THE SITUATION OF THE LOOKER-ON"

gender, narration, and gaze
in wuthering heights

(1 9 9 0)

> [T]he phenomena that compose the fictive universe are never pre-
> sented to us "in themselves" but from a certain perspective a certain
> point of view, etc. This visual vocabulary is metaphorical or rather syn-
> ecdochic: "vision" here replaces total perception; but it is a convenient
> metaphor for many of the characteristics of "real" vision all have
> equivalents in the phenomenon of fiction.
>
> TZVETAN TODOROV

> The gaze is not necessarily male (literally) but to own and activate
> the gaze given our language and the structure of the unconscious is
> to be in the "masculine" position.
>
> E. ANN KAPLAN

Visual metaphors have so thoroughly pervaded our theoretical vocabulary for the
novel that they have come to seem natural and inevitable. Even the presumably
value-free language of structuralist narratology has been unable to purge them;
Genette's important reformulation of the Anglo-American concept "point of
view," for example, turns on the distinction between a narrator who "speaks" and
a "focalizor" who "sees."[1] Such terms implicitly invoke a gaze: a look that the
subject(s) whose perceptions organize the story direct at the characters and acts
represented. As my second epigraph suggests, this gaze in turn raises issues important for feminist criticism, especially for the kind that draws on psychoanalysis for a theory of gender difference. Given the significance of the gaze and other
visual phenomena in feminist theory, we might pose an alternative question to
Genette's "Who speaks?" and "Who sees?" We might ask, Why "sees"? Since
novels are verbal structures rather than visual ones, why has our vocabulary for
discussing their techniques and effects relied on visual metaphors? Are these visual metaphors meaningful in any way for feminist literary criticism? And does
this orientation tell us anything about the novel as a genre?

    The questions arise in part because point of view (however we choose to revise
the concept) is neither an inescapable category of narrative nor even a constant
concern for theories of the novel that emphasize form. As an analytical concept,
it is virtually irrelevant to the study of tales in an oral tradition; as an aspect of
narrative, it does not seem to be a factor in prenovelistic scripted narrative texts,

including those with embedding and multiple narrators (e.g., *A Thousand and One Nights*).[2] Visual metaphors and the study of the phenomena generally termed point of view are relatively recent occurrences in the discourse on the novel, beginning with Henry James and reaching critical mass (as one might say) in the 1960s and after. Theoretical and critical discourse on the novel is considerably older—Clara Reeve and Sir Walter Scott come to mind as prominent examples. If we think of James's writing on the novel as a watershed in the theory of the genre, the reason may be that his criticism was the first to pay explicit attention to the kinds of formal issues we have come to associate with the novel ever since, which are perhaps most lucidly expressed in visual metaphors. Yet other approaches are conceivable. For example, Bakhtin's efforts to define the generic specificity of the novel proceed without recourse to these metaphors, relying instead on a set of terms (perhaps no less metaphorical) referring to languages and voice.

I want to consider the relation between novelistic narrative and visual acts and metaphors through a reading of Emily Brontë's *Wuthering Heights*, a novel in which narration is both foregrounded and linked repeatedly and emphatically to visual phenomena—in fact, to a gaze. The place of the visual in *Wuthering Heights* is in some ways curious. Presented as a series of diary entries recording an orally told tale that is itself full of references to folk ballads and other vestiges of a moribund oral tradition, Brontë's novel would seem more obviously to raise questions about "orality" (in Walter Ong's sense of the term), or about audience and the spoken word, than to unravel the relation between seeing and telling, between narration and the gaze.[3] Yet this relation seems to me not only a central thematic concern of the novel but also the structuring principle. Emily Brontë would seem not only to have anticipated the post-Jamesian preoccupation with visual terminology but even to have teased out some of that terminology's implications for a feminist poetics of the novel.

I

> Flirting is mostly just looking.
>
> HELEN GURLEY BROWN

In the early paragraphs of his diary Lockwood recounts a recent flirtation in which a woman's look filled him with fear. The next few pages of the diary parodically rewrite this scene twice, underscoring its importance:

> While enjoying a month of fine weather at the seacoast, I was thrown into the company of a most fascinating creature, a real goddess in my eyes, as long as she took no notice of me. I "never told my love" vocally; still, if looks have language, the merest idiot might have guessed I was over head and ears: she understood me at last and looked a return—the sweetest of all imaginable looks. And what did I do? I confess it with shame—shrunk icily into myself, like a snail; at every glance retired colder and farther; till, finally, the poor innocent was led to doubt her own senses, and, overwhelmed with confusion at her supposed mistake, persuaded her mama to decamp. (15)

"If looks have language": Lockwood's look, articulating the desire he does not tell "vocally," suggests that looking is both a mode of telling and a source of pleasure. Like many real-life voyeurs, however, Lockwood cannot enjoy looking once his look is detected. This limitation is important, as the word he uses to invoke the charms of his "creature" or "goddess" suggests. *Fascinating*, derived from *fascinum*, "witchcraft," resonates with the now obsolete meaning of *fascinate*—"to bewitch," which itself survives in a still current definition: "to transfix and hold spellbound by an irresistible power." Lockwood's account of his abortive flirtation intimates a psychic structure whereby a woman who "looks a return" at a man threatens to immobilize him, to deprive him of his self-command, to render him stock-still—practically to paralyze him. We have not far to travel from Lockwood's "fascinating creature" to Freud's "Medusa's Head," the direct sight of which evokes the terror of castration in the male spectator, a terror that turns him to stone.[4]

Freud's reading of Medusa locates the spectator's horror in a response to the sight of the female genitals, not to the return of a woman's look; but details associated with Medusa suggest that her gaze may be an even more significant aspect of the horror she provokes. Following H. J. Rose's account of Medusa in *The Handbook of Greek Mythology*, Teresa de Lauretis observes, "Medusa's power to cast the spell which in many cultures is actually called 'the evil eye,' is directly represented in her horribly 'staring eyes,' which are a constant feature of her figurative and literary representations; while the serpents in their hair . . . are a variable attribute of all three Gorgons" (110). In many cultures the power of the evil eye is warded off with a representation of an eye that stares back, performing the same apotropaic function of "intimidating the Evil Spirit" that Freud attributes to the genitals of both sexes. Perhaps the sight that makes the Medusa threatening to the male spectator may be understood as the sight of someone else's look— the knowledge that the other sees and therefore resists being reduced to an appropriable object. That is, Medusa defies the male gaze as Western culture has constructed it: as the privilege of a male subject, a means of relegating women (or "Woman") to the status of object (of representation, discourse, desire, etc.). Such defiance is surely unsettling, disturbing the pleasure the male subject takes in gazing and the hierarchical relations by which he asserts his dominance. No wonder, then, that Lockwood retires farther "at every glance," shrinking into himself "like a snail."

Jacques Lacan's seminars on the gaze may illuminate the connections between the returning female gaze and castration anxiety, which seem knotted together not only in Lockwood's response to his "goddess" but also, as I argue below, in the way most of the significant male characters in Brontë's novel respond to a woman's returning gaze. Lacan asserts that the scopic drive is the drive "that most completely eludes the term castration" (78). Yet he also claims that "the gaze is presented to us only in the form of a strange contingency, symbolic of what we find on the horizon, as the thrust of our experience, namely, the lack that constitutes castration anxiety" (72–73). Stephen Heath, in a reading of these seminars, puts the two remarks together to explain the ambivalent function of the look in castration anxiety: "The scopic drive may elude the term of castration but the look returns the other, castration, the other—evil—eye." In other words (according to the outlines of Heath's reading of Lacan), the subject's pleasure in looking (without being seen) may defer his necessary confrontation with the "fact" of castration, because such undisturbed looking returns the subject to the sense of completeness associated with the scopophilic pleasures of the mirror stage. But the returning look "from the place of the other" disrupts that sense of wholeness (Heath 88). Heath calls attention to the implicit gendering of the gaze in Lacan's discourse, where, he observes, the woman is absent as the subject of the look except when she "sees herself seeing herself" (i.e., sees herself as the object of a gaze). The returned, disturbing look that brings castration back into the picture, Heath notes, is thus a woman's: "What then of the look for the woman, of woman subjects in seeing? The reply given by psychoanalysis is from the phallus. If the woman looks, the spectacle provokes, castration is in the air, the Medusa's head is not far off; thus, she must not look, is absorbed herself on the side of the seen" (92).

What goes wrong with Lockwood's flirtation, we can now see, is that his "fascinating creature," not content to be "absorbed . . . on the side of the seen," instead "looks a return." The next few lines in Lockwood's diary return to Yorkshire and the narrative present, gloss the story of this seaside flirtation by rewriting it as a grotesque parody, and suggest more clearly a relation between a gazing female "creature" and castration anxiety. Alone in the sitting room of Wuthering Heights with a litter of vigilant dogs, Lockwood tries to pet the "canine mother," but his attentions are rebuffed: "My caress provoked a long, guttural gnarl" (15–16). Lockwood fears (the gloss suggests) that his "real goddess" might have proved a bitch goddess, reciprocating his attentions as the four-footed bitch at the Heights does—with the threat of bodily mutilation. Other details in this scene underscore Lockwood's fear of the returning female gaze. Partially reassured by his immobility ("I sat still"), as the male subject in "Medusa's Head" is ambivalently reassured by his stiffening,[5] he requites the dogs' stares with mocking looks—at which the canine mother attacks, provoking him to fend her off with a poker. Like Freud's (male) spectator, Lockwood defends against a threatened castration with an act of phallic assertion, a defense that foregrounds the psychosexual dynamics of the gaze for the male subject. Within these dynamics, to be the object of the gaze—to be spectacle instead of spectator—is to lose one's position of mastery and control—in short, to be emasculated.

The second parodic rewriting of the scene of flirtation involves Lockwood's first encounter with Catherine Heathcliff.[6] Though she is often regarded as a saccharine imitation of her mother (e.g., by Gilbert and Gubar), the gaze provides a context for reading Catherine as more subversive than readers of the novel have been willing to grant. Lockwood's first encounter with her emphasizes her defiance of the male gaze. Upon seeing her, he appropriates her as an object of visual pleasure, remarking with approval her "admirable form" and "exquisite little face" (19), but he expresses ambivalence about her eyes: "had they been agreeable in expression, they would have been irresistible" (19). He is ambivalent because Catherine is doubly a "looker"—both an attractive woman (the modern colloquial sense of the word) and someone who looks back. Spectator as well as spectacle, she disturbs Lockwood's pleasure in gazing: "She never opened her mouth. I stared—she stared also. At any rate, she kept her eyes on me, in a cool, regardless manner, exceedingly embarrassing and disagreeable" (18). Catherine's "regardless" look (an intriguing oxymoron), a look that does not look, is a variant of the "sweetest of all imaginable looks" that has already routed Lockwood. Whereas the earlier look makes him an object for another subject, Catherine's refuses even that much; it returns only the failure of his gaze to obtain the recognition that it has ambivalently solicited. In each case, the woman's look is represented as provoking, withering, annihilating.

Catherine's impudently assertive look makes her a monstrous woman to almost every male character in the novel—a "little witch," as Lockwood puts it (23). Her impudence seems a tactic chosen deliberately to provoke, the most effective means at her disposal to taunt those whose captive and unwilling inmate she has become. Shortly after vanquishing Lockwood with her "regardless look," she fends off Joseph (the pharisaical servant) with the evil eye: "Go, I'm looking at you!" (23). Much later, Joseph appeals to the power of her gaze to explain the influence she comes to exercise over Hareton, equating her assertive look with a transgression of her feminine role: "It's yon flaysome, graceless quean, ut's witched ahr lad, wi' her bold een, un' her forrard ways . . . " (251). Even Heathcliff finds the power of her gaze preternaturally disconcerting: "What fiend possesses you to stare back at me, continually, with those infernal eyes? Down with them! and don't remind me of your existence again" (251). Her look marks her as sexually loose, with the "forrard ways" of a "quean" (Joseph's word) or a "slut" (Heathcliff's [252]). Through Catherine, the text parodically inscribes the dynamics involved in the gaze and articulates the psychological fact that when a woman looks back she asserts her "existence" as a subject, her place outside the position of object to which the male gaze relegates her and by which it defines her as "woman." The novel even confronts these dynamics straightforwardly, having Catherine explicitly deny to Heathcliff that he has anything to fear from her gaze: "I'll not take my eyes from your face, till you look back at me! No, don't turn away! *do* look! You'll see nothing to provoke you" (219).

By parodying and challenging what Mary Ann Doane calls "the sexual politics of looking" (86), the text even raises a question that feminist theory has been asking: Is the gaze male? That is, is it possible to elude the patriarchal "regime of the specular" (N. K. Miller 175)? If so, Catherine's look of "mock malignity," itself an act of resistance, changes nothing. A gaze that escaped patriarchal specular relations would not simply reverse the positions of male and female, as Catherine's malign look pretends to do, but would eliminate the hierarchy altogether. Catherine's situation underscores the difficulty of doing that. In assuming the role of spectator, she seeks a "masculine" position that because she is a woman, redefines her as a "monster" or "witch." Even as a spectator, then, Catherine is locked into exaggerating the role of the woman whose gaze is dangerous to men, engaging in a kind of female impersonation or masquerade, an imitation of femininity as a construct. Such a masquerade can register a protest against the gender conventions it mimics, but there is no clear evidence that it can dismantle them.[7]

II

> The frame . . . marks the possibility of accession to the object by the gaze as a readable object.
>
> LOUIS MARIN[8]

I have been considering the meaning of the gaze for what is signified in *Wuthering Heights*. But the novel also ties the gaze inextricably to the signifier, the process of narration producing the signified, the theme and "content." It does so in three ways: through its extradiegetic frame (Lockwood's diary entry), the many metadiegetic embeddings within Nelly's narrative that call our attention back to the dynamics of framing, and the constitutive features of Nelly's narrative itself.[9] The correlation of gazing and narrating affirmed by the novel's signifying process may seem merely metaphorical, a kind of poetic license; after all, it is not really necessary to see in order to narrate. Indeed, through Lockwood, *Wuthering Heights* does explore narration as a metaphorical seeing, a fetishized substitute for a more direct gaze at an object that is simultaneously feared and desired. Yet, at the same time, Nelly's narrative and the several narratives within it link narration and the visual in a very literal seeing.

The many embeddings in Brontë's novel have often been examined for reliability, irony, and perspective—in short, for "point of view." Gilbert and Gubar, for example, discuss the narrative layers as "a Romantic storytelling method that emphasizes the ironic disjunctions between different perspectives on the same events" (249), and McCarthy, Shunami, and other commentators make similar assumptions.[10] But this explanation does not adequately account for the persistence of embedding in the novel. To begin with, Lockwood's diary does not cast doubt on what Nelly says; instead, it corroborates her story, with one crucial exception: his attitude toward Catherine, a difference eliminated by the end of the novel. More noticeable are the similarities between Nelly's and Lockwood's attitudes toward the story, especially their shared estrangement from the passion it recounts. Moreover, if we question Nelly's objectivity (as of course we should), our suspicions are grounded on her own admissions of bias (especially against Cathy); the incorporated narratives of Heathcliff, Isabella, and Zillah offer no significant alternatives to Nelly's version. They sometimes express less indulgence toward characters for whom Nelly feels affection, but such differences do little to undermine her credibility or to ironize her perspective.[11] Rather, these narratives keep the story going when the demands of the plot require Nelly to be absent. She splices them into her own narration, permitting them to pick up where her direct observation necessarily leaves off. That is, the other narrators *speak* because Nelly requires them to *see* for her. Their function is to link narration to vision, telling to seeing.

The relation between Nelly's story and Lockwood's enframing diary, too, can be articulated in visual terms, though differently. The framing story that considered thematically explores the sexual politics of gazing serves in narratorial terms to situate Nelly's story, which is for Lockwood preeminently the story of Catherine: "and—that pretty girl-widow, I should like to know her history" (36). The visual significance of the connection between the two narratives emerges here, in Lockwood's defensive and compensatory interest in knowing Catherine's "history." He hopes that this knowledge will at once satisfy his desire for Catherine and cure him of it by teaching him to guard himself against the power of her gaze: "I'll extract wholesome medicine from Mrs. Dean's bitter herbs; and firstly, let me beware of the fascination that lurks in Catherine Heathcliff's brilliant eyes" (130). Having looked Catherine in the eye only to be stared down, he now seeks to look again, as it were, through Nelly's eyes—that is, by hearing and appropriating Nelly's story. Lockwood's scopic drive is thus what links the frame of *Wuthering Heights* to the narrative it introduces. Hearing a story about the object of his desire becomes a means of satisfying his desire to gaze at her, becomes a substitute, a metaphor, for the pleasure of looking.

This function of listening as a metaphor for looking is made explicit late in the novel when Nelly reveals that during most of her narration Lockwood has been gazing at Catherine's portrait: "You're too young to rest always contented, living by yourself; and I some way fancy no one could see Catherine Linton, and not love her. You smile; but why do you look so lively and interested, when I talk about her? and why have you asked me to hang her picture over your fireplace? and why—" (204–05). Looking at Catherine through the double mediation of a portrait and a narrative—two representations of his object—Lockwood, a latter-day Perseus, has found himself a shield. The complexities of embedding in this passage suggest, moreover, that just as listening functions for Lockwood as a substitute for gazing, so too does his own narrative act. The return to the frame, effected through Nelly's direct address to Lockwood, signals Lockwood's presence in the text as narrator—a presence marked by the quotation marks enclosing the passage in the text (though these may be editorial emendations)[12] and by the attribution tags in the next few lines of text that set off Nelly's narrative as discourse Lockwood quotes. (These diacritical marks are omitted once we return to Nelly's narrative itself.) That is, the text presents Lockwood as narrator at the very moment it represents him as a spectator gazing at Catherine's portrait. The conjunction of gazing and telling here suggests an analogy between the two activities.

Lockwood's position as narrator is expressed in his own phrase "the situation of the looker-on" (58). The words occur in a curious passage in which Lockwood offers Nelly a motive for his interest in her story:

> I perceive that people in these regions acquire over people in towns the value that a spider in a dungeon does over a spider in a cottage, to their various occupants; and yet the deepened attraction is not entirely owing to the situation of the looker-on. They *do* live more in earnest, more in themselves, and less in surface change, and frivolous external things. . . . (58)

The metaphor works against its own characterization of life in the provinces, and the structure of the novel calls into question the implied characterization of Lockwood himself. The inclusion of a spider in this scenario, by invoking a figure for storytelling much older than visual ones (i.e., weaving), suggests that provincial life is not lived with the unmediated intensity Lockwood imagines; the mediating function of narrative is part of the very activity he observes. *Wuthering Heights* exposes as a fantasy his suggestion that provincial people live "more in themselves" because they are indifferent to the objectifying tendencies of the gaze; as I argue below, the novel implicates provincial domestic life during the last quarter of the eighteenth century in a patriarchal specular economy. Moreover, Lockwood places the scene in a dungeon—not a Foucauldian or Benthamite panopticon but an old-fashioned prison in which the gazer is less free than the objects of the gaze. That is, he depicts "the situation of the looker-on" as one of harmless passivity. But the novel equivocates about this claim as well, suggesting that his voyeuristic role arrogates power to itself, a power that takes the form of the ability to narrate, to appropriate another's story—not just Nelly's story but Catherine's. The role of onlooker, the conventional position of the masculine spectator with respect to the feminine spectacle, is in this novel precisely the situation of the narrator—specifically, of the narrator as voyeur defending himself against the threat of the feminine by objectifying a woman, by telling her story, writing it down in his diary, and seeking in this oblique way to make it—and her—his own.

But the gaze can serve to destabilize the viewer as well as to confer mastery, especially if the gazer is caught looking by another subject who sees the gaze and perceives it as an expression of desire. For Lockwood, the presumably mastering situation of the looker-on is rendered precarious because Nelly Dean, another vigilant watcher, remarks his pleasure in looking. Lockwood's supine passivity (he is bedridden during most of her narrative) suggests that he is in the "feminine" position with respect to Nelly's controlling gaze, but it also highlights another difference between his seeing and Nelly's. Whereas looking is an erotic experience for Lockwood, Nelly's gaze is less libidinous. Her exclusion from the erotic exchanges that structure the kinship relations in the novel puts her in a position to oversee these relations, to exercise a limited control over them. The oldest woman in two motherless households, she acts more as guardian than as housekeeper. In her role as "patriarchy's paradigmatic housekeeper," in Gilbert and Gubar's memorable phrase (291), and as bearer of the shield that shows Catherine's reflected image to Lockwood, Nelly watches on behalf of men while seeking to remain outside the circuit of desire. So long as she succeeds in banishing her own desire from the consciousness of the other players, she is an excellent spy, an effective policing agent for the families who employ her, as James Kavanagh has pointed out (94). As a character in her own narration, Nelly keeps one eye always at the keyhole; her main task, quite literally, is to supervise. As a *narrator* she never completely abandons this task, carefully overseeing Lockwood's looking on.

She does her police work so effectively that hardly anyone ever suspects it. Joseph best articulates the general underestimation of Nelly's gaze: "*shoo* cannot stale t'sowl uh nob'dy! Shoo wer niver soa handsome, bud whet a body mud look at her 'baht [i.e., without] winking" (251). Since Nelly is not herself an object of visual pleasure, her look falls into a blind spot in the male gaze. Significantly, the character most aware of Nelly's gaze (though only when it is too late) is Cathy, who suffers most from Nelly's habits of supervision—especially since they are tied to Nelly's propensity to play the stool pigeon, to see and tell, and to exercise an often decisive influence over Cathy's fate. For example, the violent scene that destroys Cathy's health and her marriage erupts after one of Nelly's narrative interventions. When Edgar asks about Cathy's whereabouts, Nelly not only answers the question but seasons her answer with a spicy story:

"Yes, she's in the kitchen, sir," I answered. "She's sadly put out by Mr. Heathcliff's behaviour; and, indeed, I do think it's time to arrange his visits on another footing. There's harm in being too soft, and now it's come to this—" And I related the scene in the court, and, as near as I dared, the whole subsequent dispute. (98)

She prefaces her story with some words of advice to the master of the house, urging him to exercise his authority over both Cathy and Isabella, whose wayward desires threaten that authority. (At issue in the "scene in the court" and "the whole subsequent dispute" is Isabella's attraction to Heathcliff.) Nelly's telling is enabled by her habit of looking, which here authorizes a threefold telling: she narrates, informs on, and advises all at once. Looking as telling, then, works in the service of regulating the family—or, precisely, of regulating the erotic relations of its members—to preserve order for the male head of the house.

But in this instance Nelly's practice of seeing and telling, far from maintaining family order, is disruptive. It incites Edgar to strike Heathcliff, and this violence provokes the fit from whose effects Cathy never fully recovers. Here and elsewhere, the acts of narration that Nelly's gaze makes possible produce consequences she can neither predict nor control. When Cathy first goes into her fit, Nelly makes light of Edgar's terror with another story: "I told him how she had resolved, previous to his coming, on exhibiting a fit of frenzy. I incautiously gave the account out loud" (102). Nelly's story unleashes monstrous energies in Cathy, who "start[s] up—her hair flying over her shoulders, her eyes flashing, the muscles of her neck and arms standing out preternaturally." Cathy has twice been transformed into a Medusa figure: first, by Nelly's tale-telling within the story, which incites Cathy to rage, and again in the narration as discourse, where Nelly represents Cathy to Lockwood as a monster with wild hair and flashing eyes.[13] Too late, Edgar recognizes that Nelly's habit of seeing and telling has become the bane of his marriage: "The next time you bring a tale to me, you shall quit my service, Ellen Dean," he warns her. Nelly's response almost explicitly relates tale-telling, a gaze, and family discipline. "I didn't know that, to humor [Cathy], I should wink at Mr. Heathcliff," she complains. "Next time you may gather intelligence for yourself!" (110).

But Nelly again brings him tales when young Catherine reaches sexual maturity and begins her correspondence with Linton Heathcliff; and Edgar, far from firing Nelly, depends on her to supervise his daughter's activities. Once more, Nelly's supervision proves ineffective: instead of keeping her ward away from sickly Linton, Nelly's actions further the events that bring Catherine and her property into his possession. *Wuthering Heights* suggests strongly that the male-headed bourgeois family is unthinkable without surveillance to keep the sexuality of its subordinate members in line and its property in the right hands. But the novel also reveals that such surveillance can destroy the relations it is installed to maintain and that the controlling gaze can never be *wholly* in control. *Wuthering Heights*, then, through its representations *of* the gaze and its own organization *as* a network of gazes, offers a context in which to understand how narration, seeing, and knowing are connected in the evolution and permutations of the techniques that we now call point of view, from Richardson's voyeuristic epistolary fictions to the varieties of first-person and "omniscient" storytelling we associate with the novel.[14] This context consists of the parallel "rises" of the novel and the bourgeois family, with its tension between unprecedented possibilities for privacy and ever greater intrusions into that privacy in the interests of regulating sexual behavior. *Wuthering Heights* provides a way of reading the history of the novel and the development of point of view in conjunction with the emergence of the bourgeois family and the *gendered* gaze in which each member is constituted as a subject.[15] The fictive gaze that structures novelistic narration may thus be an expression of the gaze that structures the bourgeois family itself, and perhaps—since discourse is productive as well as expressive—has even worked to produce that gaze or to solidify the power relations the gaze produces as one of its effects. But *Wuthering Heights* suggests that the gaze (and therefore the novel, which reproduces that gaze), however coercive, is never a locus of complete control—that the gaze even opens a space for resisting that control.

III

Contemporary readings of *Wuthering Heights* typically object to the novel's ending, which acquiesces in the bourgeois family (complete with domestic angel and male patriarch) that the first part of the novel stringently criticizes.[16] I agree with the general tendency of such readings: the movement of the plot and the reduction in tonal intensity seem symptomatic of Brontë's inability to conceive of a family that would neither subjugate women nor defuse, repress, or otherwise domesticate desire; and in this she seems little different from her sister Charlotte or from such middle-class nineteenth-century critics of gender relations and the family as John Stuart Mill (in *The Subjection of Women*) or—mutatis mutandis—from most of us. Nevertheless, her critique of specular relations keeps the novel from simply capitulating to the ideology of the patriarchal family and sacrificing the subversive energies and critical edge of volume 1 to the demands of closure.

The courtship of Catherine and Hareton at the end, read in the light of the gaze, tells the utopian story of a subtle but essential transformation of the structures the novel faults. To be sure, the transformation envisaged has limits. It involves the domestication (and figurative castration) of a potent male figure (Hareton), not the release of the woman from the domestic sphere. Catherine's efforts to claim kin with a reluctant Hareton even suggest—despite the commanding imperatives in which she voices her claim—the persistence of the repressive familial structures underwriting domesticity: "You're my cousin, you shall own me," she puns, insidiously, though unwittingly (247). But at the same time the novel revises domestic relations to suggest mutuality, not the unequal power relations of male dominance. It does so by means of the gaze.

Until Catherine intervenes, Hareton is awkward and inarticulate, almost without language—incapable of combining looking and speaking in socially meaningful ways. These activities, which are crucial to narrative as *Wuthering Heights* represents it, may be said to constitute subjectivity itself, their meaningful conjunction defining what we recognize as human. Heathcliff has carefully cultivated Hareton's degradation by cutting the boy off from the specular relations in which subjectivity is constituted. Thus Heathcliff offers the following parody of paternal advice before he sends Hareton off to "entertain" Catherine: "And behave like a gentleman, mind! Don't use any bad words; and don't stare, when the young lady is not looking at you, and be ready to hide your face when she is; and, when you speak, say your words slowly . . . " (177). Such advice about how to act around girls reduces almost to absurdity the specular economy the novel explores. Heathcliff is teaching Hareton to fear the female gaze and to associate it with imposed muteness. "I've tied his tongue," Heathcliff boasts to Nelly. "He'll not venture a single syllable! . . . " (177). Boorish Hareton resembles fastidious Lockwood in this respect.

Eventually Catherine seeks to "civilize" Hareton by getting him to speak to her and return her gaze. "I can't tell what to do to make you talk to me," she complains (247); but he remains on the defensive, "his gaze fixed on the ground" (248). She finally softens his "obdurate perversity" with a kiss. To Nelly's silent reproach, Catherine offers this excuse: "Well! what should I have done, Ellen? He wouldn't shake hands, and he wouldn't look" (248).

Significantly, at this crucial moment Nelly's narrative momentarily runs aground: "Whether the kiss convinced Hareton, I cannot tell," she remarks, adding, "he was very careful, for some minutes, that his face should not be seen; and when he did raise it, he was sadly puzzled where to turn his eyes" (248). Hareton's puzzlement is understandable (wherever he looks, a pair of eyes is poised to read the desire in his own), but what precisely makes Nelly here unable to tell? Only once before has insufficient knowledge disabled her narrative, producing the three-year gap in volume 1 between Heathcliff's disappearance and his return. Is there a small but significant gap here? Has Nelly been "winking"? "I overheard no further distinguishable talk," she continues, "but, *on looking round again*, I perceived two such radiant countenances bent over the page of the accepted book, that I did not doubt the treaty had been ratified on both sides" (249; my emphasis). Nelly does not tell how Hareton finally solves the problem of "where to turn his eyes," but later descriptions of the two as lovers imply that Catherine has succeeded in making him look. Yet the momentous occasion of an exchange of gazes that does not annihilate the male gazer is nowhere represented as an event in Nelly's story. The reader who nevertheless infers it must locate it in a moment when Nelly relaxes the vigilance that enables her to tell.

Her narrative about the family's behavior at breakfast the morning after suggests that an unrepresented scene of reciprocal gazing must be inferred:

> He dared not speak to her, there; he dared hardly look, and yet she went on teasing . . . at last, Hareton uttered a smothered laugh.
>
> Mr. Heathcliff started; his eye rapidly surveyed our faces. Catherine met it with her accustomed look of nervousness, and yet defiance, which he abhorred.
>
> "It is well you are out of my reach"; he exclaimed. "What fiend possesses you to stare back at me, continually, with those infernal eyes? Down with them! and don't remind me of your existence again. I thought I had cured you of laughing!"
>
> "It was me," muttered Hareton. (250–51)

Some earlier exchange of gazes seems implicit in his "dar[ing] hardly look" at Catherine "there," before his mentor, who continues to attribute "infernal" powers to the woman's gaze. Hareton, in contrast, experiences not the destructive powers Heathcliff, Joseph, and Lockwood all fear from the woman who "look[s] a return," not terror and annihilation, not castration, but joy. The inarticulate curses with which he formerly approximated human speech give way here to something quite different: to laughter. Hélène Cixous has written that the Medusa who has terrorized the male subject, looked at "straight on," is actually "beautiful . . . and . . . laughing" (255). Brontë has uncannily anticipated Cixous's analysis of the masculine fear of the woman's gaze in suggesting that Hareton, alone among the male characters in the novel, is able to laugh back.[17] Still, if this laughter in response to Catherine's flirtatious "teasing" is a sign of a reciprocal gaze that neither appropriates nor annihilates, if Hareton's gaze is something other than the male gaze that figures in the novel, what is this gaze like? We cannot know because it cannot be represented, since representation is always already dominated by masculine power structures (including specular ones). It therefore must escape Nelly's narratorial gaze.

What Brontë imagines, then, is a defusing of the gaze: not a simple inversion in which the woman is permitted to turn the tables with an appropriating look back but a destruction of the hierarchical positioning of male and female that the gendered gaze entails. The difference between this gaze and the hierarchically gendered one is registered in a relation of sameness, the resemblance between Catherine's and Hareton's eyes. Nelly observes to Lockwood, "Perhaps you have never remarked that their eyes are precisely similar, and they are those of Catherine Earnshaw" (254). The equivocation in Nelly's "precisely similar"—the two pairs of eyes are not exactly identical but, rather, precisely almost alike—places the emphasis less on their resemblance than on the original that both sets of eyes reflect: the eyes of Cathy Earnshaw. That is, Hareton gazes as though through a woman's eyes; transferred to Hareton, these become the sign of the difference of his gaze from the usual male gaze in the novel. A female gaze, then, in a male character? Not quite; instead, a gaze that is strictly neither male nor female, thereby escaping the differential relations that express themselves in the hierarchical terms *active/passive, subject/object.*

Nelly's account of finding Heathcliff dead offers an alternative reading of the consequences of the woman's returning gaze, partially restoring the one rejected in the story of Hareton and Catherine—but with a difference. When Nelly discovers Heathcliff "dead and stark" on what had been Cathy's bed, she recalls, "His eyes met mine so keen and fierce, I started; and then he seemed to smile" (264). Heathcliff goes to his grave with his eyes fixed in a gaze so intense that it makes his death mask an affront. "I tried to close his eyes—to extinguish, if possible, that frightful, life-like gaze of exultation. They would not shut" (264). The dead, like women, must not seem to look back, lest they take us with them, make us one of them—a belief that perhaps elucidates the problem of the woman's returning gaze by suggesting a dangerous identification with the other or a recognition of the other's claims.[18] But Heathcliff's gaze looks not to any earthly being that could return it but to the dead—to the ghost of Cathy Earnshaw, whose gaze he has long solicited and whose spectral presence he believes he has discerned in his last days. The death Nelly sees is thus an erotic consummation: at once an intense gaze, a stiffening (he was "perfectly still" and "stark"), and a smile. The language of this scene suggests that Heathcliff too has perhaps looked Medusa in the eye at last, to experience, like Hareton, not horror but joy. But his joy arises in a satisfaction so intense that it is annihilating. Longing to be reunited with that other who was a part of himself, he yearns to complete himself, to restore a primary loss for which the gaze of another (generally the mother) functions as a part object, Lacan's *objet petit a*, something the subject construes as a piece of what has been lost from the self (Silverman 156). Thus Heathcliff experiences his longed-for vision as a triumph, not a defeat, though self-completion here is synonymous with death. Through Heathcliff, then, *Wuthering Heights* suggests that the woman's gaze as an object of male perception is simultaneously feared and desired, desired because it offers the possibility of lost wholeness, feared because it insists that the subject is not whole, that wholeness has indeed been lost.

IV

In concluding, I return to the original question: What is at stake in the visual metaphors that pervade our vocabularies for analyzing the novel? I have been arguing that they are an index of the psychosexual relations that constitute the bourgeois family, a set of relations that the novel both represents and (re)produces. It might seem logical for a feminist, then, to contend that novelistic narration as practiced in the eighteenth and nineteenth centuries is inherently antifeminist, inherently gynophobic, because its visual underpinnings duplicate the structures of gazing that work most obviously at the expense of women. Such an argument would extend to fiction what Laura Mulvey, in "Visual Pleasure and Narrative Cinema," claims for film and would lead to the same renunciation of classical novelistic representation that some feminist critics and filmmakers have articulated for classical cinematic representation.[19] In this context the sexual politics of Virginia Woolf's important technical innovation become clear: her use of free indirect discourse in *Mrs. Dalloway* and *To the Lighthouse* disperses the narratorial look, distributing it across multiple focalizors and permitting no gaze any undue power. (Woolf's technical tour de force is articulated in Lily Briscoe's claim that "[f]ifty pairs of eyes were not enough to get around that one woman [Mrs. Ramsay]" [294]). Ironically, though, Woolf was perfecting this technique in the late 1920s, just as film was poised to supersede the novel as the dominant form of mass-cultural narrative.

Despite the fetishizing and appropriating tendencies of novelistic narrative, I do not claim such a pernicious role for the novel. Discourses and representations are not likely to function as monolithic, total systems in which a single aspect (however powerful) cancels all internal resistance to or questioning of the status quo. In *Wuthering Heights*, certainly, the power of the gazes that enable both Nelly's and Lockwood's storytelling is itself contested. Brontë punishes Lockwood's fetishizing gaze with frustrated desire and thwarts the project of Nelly's narrative, which is to make Lockwood marry Catherine. Moreover, some things escape even Nelly's vigilant gaze, disabling her ability to tell—in particular, the moment (a crucial one, for my reading of the novel) when Hareton's and Catherine's gazes meet and overturn the structures of gazing that the novel has parodied and criticized.[20] Nor is Nelly's gaze all that is being undermined here; by imagining something still unrepresentable, the novel adumbrates the limits of representation itself. Whether the narrator functions as voyeur or as supervisor, then, "the situation of the looker-on" is unstable. For all the power Lockwood's and Nelly's gazes arrogate, they end in impotence. Thus, although *Wuthering Heights* ends in cozy domesticity, the gaps in its enunciation express a feminist resistance to the patriarchal order in which its story partially acquiesces: for the narrative undercuts the conditions of its own telling even while implicating them in a specular economy that fetishizes and appropriates women.

NOTES

1. Genette's term is actually *focalization* (189–94), which expresses a relation between the narrator's knowledge (of events, etc.) and the characters' perceptions as presented by the narrator. Genette chooses this abstract word "[t]o avoid the too specifically visual connotations of the terms *vision, field*, and *point of view*" (189), but the visual connotations remain. Though not found in Genette, the term *focalizor* (Genette's "Who sees?") is used by Bal to locate a particular subject of vision (102–06).

2. Martin observes that "[f]eatures such as point of view . . . —so important to the literary critic—scarcely exist in the oral tale" (21). In fact, even in certain kinds of novels, the embedding of one narrative act within another does not necessarily produce the complexities of alternative points of view that twentieth-century readers are likely to look for. See Newman.

3. Macovski comes close to examining the oral dimension of narration in *Wuthering Heights* but emphasizes "interpretative rhetoric and the epistemological chasm between listeners and narrators" rather than storytelling as oral performance. The scarcity of critical comment on gazing is surprising, since this motif is also persistent in the novel. I have seen it noted only once, by Nancy Armstrong (*Desire* 196–97). One reason may be that it is developed in the parts of the novel that readers (academic and Hollywood) have found less inspiring than the story of Cathy and Heathcliff. The motif's absence from *their* story registers a relationship that does not yet recognize a split between gazing subject and object—a relationship reflected in Cathy's famous declaration "I am Heathcliff" and Heathcliff's reciprocal assertions.

4. "The terror of Medusa is . . . a terror of castration linked to the sight of something" (Freud 273), namely, the female genitals, which confirm the existence of human beings supposedly "castrated." Presumably this interpretation is one pretext for Lacan's association of the gaze with castration anxiety. Also relevant here is Lacan's linking of the gaze with the "evil eye" and witchcraft (115–19).

5. Freud explains the spectator's turning to stone on seeing Medusa as a "consolation": "the stiffening reassures him of the fact" that "he is still in possession of a penis" (273).

6. Hereafter I refer to Catherine Earnshaw (the first Catherine) as Cathy and to her daughter as Catherine.

7. Gilbert and Gubar dismiss Catherine as a "profoundly dutiful" daughter who is "merely impersonating a witch"; a *real* witch, they argue, would "threaten culture," while "Cathy II's vocation is to serve it" (299–300). Although I agree that Catherine is not out to destroy "culture"—a project that would justify masculine fears of the woman as dangerous and thus in need of suppression and constant surveillance—I would argue that she seeks to undermine the specular economy of patriarchal culture, to resist the way that economy seeks to deny women the status of subject. Impersonation would be one way of offering such resistance. Still, the subversive and liberatory possibilities of such a parodic masquerade seem at best ambivalent. Doane, following the argument of Michèle Montrelay's "Inquiry into Femininity," contends that "[t]his kind of masquerade, an excess of femininity, . . . as Montrelay explains, is necessarily regarded by men as evil incar-

nate: 'It is this evil which scandalises whenever woman plays out her sex in order to evade the word and the law. Each time she subverts a law or a word which relies on the predominantly masculine structure of the look'" (82). But Russo points out that such masquerading remains suspect as a feminist strategy for a number of reasons, including the historical and anthropological association of parodic images of woman with violence against women and with misogynistic responses like fear, loathing, and ridicule.

8. Translated and quoted from *Détruire la peinture* in Mary Ann Caws's *Reading Frames* (13).

9. Although Genette himself acknowledges the confusion inherent in this use of the prefix *meta*, I have adopted his terminology as the most readily available (228–32).

10. I find more persuasive (but not exhaustive) two differently nuanced readings of the framing device as the destabilizing of identity and authority. Bersani, for example explains that the frame serves to disperse a structured narratorial or authorial identity (229); and Yaeger describes it as a means of avoiding a single point of identification or transference that would suppress the subversiveness of the text as a *"process . . . that remains involved in social struggle"* (200).

11. The most compelling account of the way Nelly's storytelling promotes a particular set of interests that undermine her objectivity is offered by James Kavanagh. His Marxist-Lacanian reading of Nelly's narratorial role differs from the more usual "unreliable narrator" arguments by placing the emphasis less on her individual needs and desires and questions of self-interest than on her role in the family, as mediator between individual desire and social and cultural law (see esp. 44–53 and 94–96).

12. No manuscript of the novel survives. The punctuation of this passage in the Norton edition follows that of the first edition.

13. During her ensuing delirium Cathy fails to recognize her face in the mirror. What happens, we may ask, when Medusa looks in the mirror? Cathy's failure to recognize herself overturns the misrecognition of Lacan's mirror stage, suggesting not the illusory control and wholeness provided by the mirror image but the lack of such self-mastery. Other Victorian novels have analogous scenes of women (or girls) contemplating reflections of lack rather than of wholeness: for example, little Jane Eyre in the red room and, later, looking in the mirror to see Bertha Mason's grotesque image; young Maggie Tulliver after cutting her hair; Esther Summerson regarding her disfigured face in the glass.

Another way of regarding this scene would be to observe that Cathy, unlike Lacan's narcissistically self-observing woman, cannot "see herself seeing herself"; with Edgar keeping his distance and Heathcliff banished, she cannot see herself as the object of any gaze (even her own). This exacts a price: seeing herself unseen, she loses her sense of self and identity. (She is only just beginning to realize that she has been the object of Nelly's gaze which does not take her as an object of desire.) Later, as I argue below, Hareton achieves subjectivity by engaging in specularity, by acknowledging himself as both subject and object of a gaze.

14. Both D. A. Miller and Mark Seltzer, invoking the work of Michel Foucault, have explored the relation between surveillance and narration in nineteenth-century fiction. Miller emphasizes the novel's ruse of seeming to carve out a domestic space free of surveillance, the better to produce subjects who internalize the effects of supervision (thereby exempting themselves from the direct institutional intervention represented by the police the courts, and so on).

My reading of *Wuthering Heights* is partly enabled by their readings of nineteenth-century fiction. Nevertheless, I differ from them in regarding the control exercised by the machinery of surveillance (including the novel as a "technology" that reproduces these mechanisms) as limited instead of total. This different conclusion may well reflect our different emphases. Because I am concerned directly and especially with feminist psychoanalytic approaches to gender, I have explored the machinery of surveillance within the family, which (in Miller's reading) the nineteenth-century novel falsely represents as outside that machinery. Moreover, the gaze that interests me is gendered and intersubjective (involving specific gendered subjects) rather than institutional (like Foucault's panoptic gaze, where the individual bearer of the gaze is faceless and therefore dispensable). When the gaze is related to individual psychosexual subjects (or to the family as a confederation of such subjects), personal, libidinal desires (as opposed to larger social or institutional ones) may unsettle the social imperatives that certain family members represent. This does not mean, however, that social imperatives can be overcome, except locally.

For a more extended discussion of the different "gazes" in contemporary theory, see Copjec. She argues that Lacan's gaze, unlike Foucault's (or even the Lacan-inspired gaze invoked in film theory), allows for the possibility of resistance. That resistance arises in desire—both the subject's desire (which resists the discourses and apparatuses that construct the subject) and the other's (which disrupts power by unsettling the other's power to control it).

15. That the rise of the novel is related to the rise of the middle class has long been a commonplace. While Ian Watt and, more recently, Michael McKeon have offered socioeconomic and ideological reasons for this conjunction, Nancy Armstrong's *Desire and Domestic Fiction* relates the novel's emergence specifically to changes in familial and gender arrangements as the middle class achieved its dominance. In particular, she argues that the rise of the novel must be related to "the rise of the domestic woman," the middle- to upper-class woman constructed by eighteenth-century conduct books as holding sway over the domestic sphere.

For Armstrong, one important index of the shift from the aristocratic ideal of the family (represented in its corrupt form by *Pamela*'s Mr. B) to the domestic middle-class paradigm (represented by Pamela herself) is "a shift in the direction and dynamics of gazing" from "voyeurism to supervision," which is for her also a shifting of "the power of the gaze from the male to the female" (124, 278n42). That is, Armstrong too sees the nineteenth-century bourgeois family as in some way constructed of individuals assigned various gender positions within a "dynamics of gazing." But her analysis differs from my own. The "shift" she articulates would involve a purging of the psychosexual from the dynamics of both the family and the gaze—a purging that seems extremely unlikely within a set of family relations that were becoming, in Lawrence Stone's words, "increasingly 'a stifling fortress of emotional bonding,' [in which] relations between parents and children grew more intrusive" and "[s]upervision . . . more intense and oppressive" (669). *Wuthering Heights* suggests, I think, that there was no such "shift," that both gazes coexisted, and that supervision, even when conducted by a woman (e.g., Nelly), aimed at serving the paterfamilias (e.g., Edgar Linton) or at gratifying voyeuristic desire (e.g., Lockwood's).

16. This critique has been articulated, in somewhat different terms, by Armstrong ("Emily Brontë"), Bersani, Gilbert and Gubar, and Kavanagh.

17. Since I have already acknowledged a figurative castration for Hareton, I should point out that *Wuthering Heights* makes this the condition for a mutual gaze, not its consequence. The wound (an accidental gunshot to the arm), self-inflicted and temporary, is not wrought by Catherine's "bold een"; rather, those eyes draw Hareton into a relationship of reciprocal and productive desire. For a reading of the importance of laughter as part of the disruptive, emancipatory energies of *Wuthering Heights*, see Yaeger.

18. "It is generally considered to be a bad omen if, when a corpse is being prepared for burial, the eyes are found to be still open. The dead man is looking for someone to accompany him into the grave" (Radford and Radford 73).

19. Since publishing her ground-breaking essay, Mulvey has reevaluated that position both by considering the ways in which Hollywood films manifesting a masculine libidinal economy nevertheless allow the woman spectator to identify with the "never fully repressed" active functioning of the libido ("Afterthoughts" 13) and by exploring the way

melodrama solicits the identification of the woman spectator and offers the pleasures attendant on that identification.

20. Such a renarrativization, in which the climactic scene occurs offstage, as it were, betrays my desire to read a particular kind of story—a desire that Doane, in her interpretation of a 1948 photograph titled "Un regard oblique," identifies as "the analyst's own perpetual desire to find a not-seen that might break the hold of representation" (86). My reading of *Wuthering Heights* betrays, rather, my desire to find a not-represented that breaks the hold of seeing—or, precisely, of the gaze, and not only of the gaze in (or out of) the novel but also of the gaze as a structuring principle of narrative.

WORKS CITED

Armstrong, Nancy. *Desire and Domestic Fiction: A Political History of the Novel.* New York: Oxford UP, 1987.

———. "Emily Brontë in and out of Her Time." *Genre* 15 (1982): 243–64.

Bakhtin, M. M. *The Dialogic Imagination.* Trans. Caryl Emerson and Michael Holquist. Austin: U of Texas P, 1981.

Bal, Mieke. *Narratology: Introduction to the Study of Narrative.* Trans. Christine van Boheemen. Toronto: U of Toronto P, 1985.

Bersani, Leo. *A Future for Astyanax: Character and Desire in Literature.* Boston: Little, 1976.

Brontë, Emily. *Wuthering Heights.* 1847. New York: Norton,

Brown, Helen Gurley. *Sex and the Single Girl.* New York: Pocket, 1962.

Caws, Mary Ann. *Reading Frames in Modern Fiction.* Princeton: Princeton UP, 1985.

Cixous, Hélène. "The Laugh of the Medusa." Trans. Keith Cohen and Paula Cohen. *Signs* 1 (1976): 875–94. Rpt. in *New French Feminisms.* Ed. Elaine Marks and Isabelle de Courtivron. Amherst: U of Massachusetts P, 1980. 245–64; see also this volume pp. 347–362.

Copjec, Joan. "The Delirium of Clinical Perfection." *Oxford Literary Review* 8 (1986): 57–65.

de Lauretis, Teresa. *Alice Doesn't: Feminism Semiotics Cinema.* Bloomington: Indiana UP, 1984.

Doane, Mary Ann. "Film and the Masquerade: Theorising the Female Spectator." *Screen* 23.3–4 (1982): 74–87.

Freud, Sigmund. "Medusa's Head." 1940. *The Complete Psychological Works of Sigmund Freud.* Ed. and trans. James Strachey. Vol. 18. London: Hogarth, 1955. 273–74. 24 vols. 1953–74.

Genette, Gérard. *Narrative Discourse: An Essay in Method.* Trans. Jane E. Lewin. Ithaca: Cornell UP, 1980.

Gilbert, Sandra, and Susan Gubar. *The Madwoman in the Attic: The Woman Writer and the Nineteenth-Century Literary Imagination.* New Haven: Yale UP, 1979

Heath. Stephen. "Difference." *Screen* 19.3 (1978): 51–112.

Kaplan, E. Ann. *Women and Film: Both Sides of the Camera.* New York: Methuen, 1983.

Kavanagh, James. *Emily Brontë.* London: Methuen, 1985.

Lacan, Jacques. "Of the Gaze as *Objet Petit a.*" 1973. *The Four Fundamental Concepts of Psychoanalysis.* Ed. Jacques-Alain Miller. Trans. Alan Sheridan. New York: Norton, 1981. 57–119.

Macovski, Michael S. "*Wuthering Heights* and the Rhetoric of Interpretation." *ELH* 54 (1987): 363–84.

Martin, Wallace. *Recent Theories of Narrative.* Ithaca: Cornell UP, 1986.

McCarthy, Terence. "The Incompetent Narrators of *Wuthering Heights.*" *Modern Language Quarterly* 42 (1981): 48–64.

McKeon, Michael. *The Origins of the English Novel 1600–1740.* Baltimore: Johns Hopkins UP, 1987.

Miller, D. A. *The Novel and the Police.* Berkeley: U of California P, 1988.

Miller, Nancy K. *Subject to Change: Reading Feminist Writing.* New York: Columbia UP, 1988.

Montrelay, Michèle "Inquiry into Femininity." Trans. Parveen Adams. *French Feminist Thought: A Reader.* Ed. Toril Moi. Oxford: Blackwell, 1987. 227–49.

Mulvey, Laura. "Afterthoughts . . . Inspired by *Duel in the Sun.*" *Framework* 15–17 (1981): 12–25.

———. "Visual Pleasure and Narrative Cinema." *Screen* 16.3 (1975): 6–18.

Newman, Beth. "Narratives of Seduction and the Seductions of Narrative: The Frame Structure of Mary Shelley's *Frankenstein.*" *ELH* 53 (1986): 141–63.

Ong, Walter. *Orality and Literacy: The Technologizing of the Word.* London: Methuen, 1982.

Radford, E., and M. A. Radford, eds. *The Encyclopedia of Superstition.* 1947. Rev. Christina Hole Chester Springs: Dufour, 1961.

Russo, Mary. "Female Grotesques: Carnival and Theory." *Feminist Studies / Critical Studies.* Ed. Teresa de Lauretis. Bloomington: Indiana UP, 1986. 213–29.

Seltzer, Mark. *Henry James and the Art of Power.* Ithaca: Cornell UP, 1984.

Shunami, Gideon. "The Unreliable Narrator in *Wuthering Heights.*" *Nineteenth Century Fiction* 27 (1973): 449–68.

Silverman, Kaja. *The Subject of Semiotics.* New York: Oxford UP, 1983.

Stone, Lawrence. *The Family, Sex and Marriage in England 1500–1800.* New York: Harper, 1977.

Todorov, Tzvetan. *Introduction* to *Poetics.* Trans. Richard Howard. Minneapolis: U of Minnesota P, 1981.

Watt, Ian. *The Rise of the Novel: Studies in Defoe, Richardson and Fielding.* Berkeley: U of California P, 1957

Woolf, Virginia. *To the Lighthouse.* New York: Harcourt, 1927.

Yaeger, Patricia. *Honey-Mad Women: Emancipatory Strategies in Women's Writing.* New York: Columbia UP, 1988.

WHEN VIRGINIA LOOKED AT VITA, WHAT DID SHE SEE; OR, LESBIAN : FEMINIST : WOMAN— WHAT'S THE DIFFER(E/A)NCE?

(1 9 9 2)

> I am reduced to a thing that wants Virginia.
> —VITA SACKVILLE-WEST,
> *LETTERS OF VITA SACKVILLE-WEST TO VIRGINIA WOOLF*

> I lie in bed making up stories about you.
> —VIRGINIA WOOLF TO VITA SACKVILLE-WEST

> "I don't know if love's a feeling. Sometimes I think it's a matter of seeing. Seeing you.
> —MARGUERITE DURAS, *EMILY L.*

"Lesbian" and "Woman" interest me most when "Feminism" occupies the site of the conjunction, the colon as copula that seeks to balance the terms, to strike relationships between them which do not necessarily exist. I always write about the lesbian : woman as though she were a feminist, as if she (all three of us) occupied the same body. This improper speaking disturbs me as a way of defining the "lesbian" (body), as flesh or word. I suspect that impropriety marks every instance of speaking or writing about the lesbian, just as it does *the* body, *the* woman. In regard to this problematic of sexual identity and definition, Stephen Heath observes:

> We exist as individuals in relation to and in the relations of language, the systems of meaning and representation in which, precisely, we find ourselves— try to imagine the question of who you are and any answer outside of language, outside of those systems. Sexual relations are relations through language, not to a given other sex; the body is not a direct immediacy, it is tressed, marked out, intrinsically involved with meanings. Of course, we can shake our heads, appeal to the fact that *we know* the direct experience of the body, two bodies in love, making love. Yet "direct experience," "the body" and so on are themselves specific constructions, specific notions; the appeal to which is never natural but always part of a particular system. (154)

What does this mean when applied to my lover's body? That I will never have "it," never write "it," approximating my lover's beauty only imperfectly in letters.

But one thing I know: *we are dangerous*. Imperfections in the letter demand caution. The slip and slide of the signifying chain requires the lover's vigilance just as compellingly as her mouth and hands attend to her beloved when she makes love to her.

Letters are ill-suited to the body, to the "natural." As the Biographer in *Orlando* explains, taking the teenage writer's text as a subject:

> He [Orlando] was describing, as all young poets are for ever describing, nature, and in order to match the shade of green precisely he looked (and here he showed more audacity than most) at the thing itself, which happened to be a laurel bush growing beneath the window. After that, of course, he could write no more. Green in nature is one thing, green in literature another. Nature and letters seem to have a natural antipathy; bring them together and they tear each other to pieces. (17)

In the postmodern, anti-romantic frame, the "liter-al" and the "letteral" (differ(e/a)nce) are at war with one another. The belief in language's capacity to stand in for its subject, or to render the object a subject, is shattered but not forgotten; the operation of "meaning" is what is.

With respect to knowing and speaking the body, Rodolphe Gasché comments, "Of the body—the body proper—we can speak only improperly. So it will not only be necessary to talk about it in metaphors, but also to develop the discourse of the body, by a process of substitution, as a chain of figures amongst others. Wishing to speak *of* the body, we can therefore only speak of quite other things, to the point where we might ask ourselves if the body does not consist precisely in those other things, in that grouping of initially heterogeneous elements. In which case the body would be dependent on a certain confusion, because it is always more or less than a body properly speaking" (3). There is no properly spoken body, no body properly speaking, it being always "more" or "less." We speak it improperly as an always imperfect translation, a bad match of flesh and word, but also as a violation of the law, its spirit if not its letter, identity and language.

The body is a "sum(mary)" of the words accumulated to articulate it, more or less; Gasché continues, "the sum of the body is the result of a selection, of an elimination (subtraction) of many things. The only things selected to go into the sum(ma) are of the sort that can be summarised in one's own sum" (11). But according to some (sum), this body is never a sum, never whole, always a hole; or, any/every textual body is an imperfect body. In this sense, the lesbian (like the feminist, the woman, and the text) has an improper body that fails according to language's phallic measure. By all rights (writes), man's textual, that is, his "liter-al" body is similarly deficient or inadequate, but the (w)hole of woman's body is doubly marked.[1]

"Difference"/"Differance"—e/a—what's the differ(e/a)nce? A letter here, a letter there. When a woman chooses not to measure up, she can be a lesbian, and sometimes a feminist (if she thinks of it in particular socio-cultural terms). She posts a letter, "L," to those who care to read it. Every lesbian: woman might be one.

Dear L—

Although these words appear and will reappear, remember that they were written in your name, just as Virginia and Vita wrote to one another.

Dear V—

Do you believe that desire is more interesting than consummation? And so we must become experts of deferral. Deferral—was it you or I who determined that?

V.

An agony inhabits deferred desire, the pain and excitement of letters writing tracks never finished word upon word: Can there be a meaning without consummation? But what ambiguity is there in the way my tongue traces ever so slowly gently the tip just meeting the surface of you fold by fold around whorl to whorl I follow the subtle turns of your ear wanting to take it all in at once seeking the dark of your certain desiring places enigmas just at the point where inner and outer meet, writing my way down your body letter after letter one formless ecstatic sound following another toward places we have not met before, that I only imagine we will discover, there first and there again. We wait always for the next time which will be the first time. Still, because not still at all, I know you understand just how these words feel on/in your body.

Love
L

How to know you is the mystery I engage as your lover. It is installed at the heart of the lover's task, never finished, compelling vision and voice, moving tongue and hands.

> *"But could I ever know her?"*
> —VIRGINIA ON VITA

Virginia Woolf's *Orlando: A Biography* (1928) has been called "the longest and most charming love letter in literature" (Nicolson 202). I like that. The lesbian love letter is a genre that I am inventing as I write.[2] Woolf dedicates her hook "To V. Sackville-West." Her "dedication" to Vita precedes the text, an exergue, a going forth that suggests something before the letter of the text, that presents itself as an answer to Vita's letters, especially *Seducers in Ecuador* (1924), a study in the curiosity of vision, love letters, property and tradition, dedicated to Virginia four years earlier. It is another letter in the series of letters that constitutes their relationship, their "*epistolarium* of love" (Leaska, *Letters of VS-W* 27).[3] Something re-presents itself in these exchanges, where Michael Leaska's "virgin, shy, schoolgirlish" (really) Virginia so seductively engages Vita, "a grenadier, hard, handsome, manly" (Glendinning 128). An affection that the text as gift stands (in) for. Like true gifts, the text is something uncalled for, unexpected. A surprise of love. Love: a gift of what one does not have. (Vita to Virginia: "I wish, in a way, that we could put the clock back a year. I should like to startle you again— even though I didn't know then that you were startled" [*Letters* 151]. Or, as Virginia describes their sexual intimacy, "The night you were snared, that winter, at Long Barn [18 December 1925]" [*Letters* 301].) Through the agency of the letter,

Virginia : Vita constitutes herself as subject, and startles her lover by desire's request that the lover make the asker a subject, not an object: "I try to invent you for myself, but find I really have only 2 twigs and 3 straws to do it with. I can get the sensation of seeing you—hair, lips, colour, height, even, now and then, the eyes and hands, but I find you going off, to walk in the garden, to play tennis, to dig, to sit smoking and talking, and then I can't invent a thing you say" (*Letters* 3:204–205). In other words, they take each other and themselves, through the lover/other, as subjects of desire, but also as objects, the beloved of the speaker/lover. As Brossard puts it, "a lesbian is . . . the centre of a captivating *image* which any woman can claim for herself" (*Aerial* 121). Through the letter, Woolf stakes out her claim.

Orlando begins with the qualified certainty of Orlando's sex as male: "He—for there could be no doubt of his sex, though the fashion of the time did something to disguise it—was in the act of slicing at the head of a Moor which swung from the rafters" (13). But "his" clothing poses an element of confusion, making it impossible to read sex "literally," as an indicator of sexual position. Woolf's narrator-Biographer, however, chooses to read from another position, the "unscientific" one of "riot and confusion of the passions and emotions" (16) where, for the speaker and the character, the sex and "nature" of others is not quite clear: "Ransack the language as he might, words failed him. . . . For in all she [Sasha, his beloved] said, however open she seemed and voluptuous, there was something hidden; in all she did, however daring, there was something concealed" (47). The implication of the concealed emerges as the shadowy other employed to produce the one.

In a sense, critical interest in androgyny in Woolf's work prepares us for and distracts us from (as it disguises) her lesbian interests—a diversionary tactic she deploys. Rachel Blau DuPlessis describes Woolf's circumstances as follows: "Orlando is released into a space not only beyond narrative conventions but also beyond sexual norms. Lesbianism is the unspoken contraband desire that marriage liberates and that itself frees writing. The love of women appears with some circumspection, intermingled with the androgynous, ambisexual marriage and the doubled gender identities of Orlando" (*Writing* 63). Makiko Minow-Pinkney, Maria DiBattista and Francette Pacteau also shed light on the question. Minow-Pinkney regards the sex change in *Orlando* as a fantasy concerning "the transgression of boundaries as a play with the limit, as a play of difference" (122) enacting "alteration not resolution" or a Hegelian synthesis of the either/or to the static reification of "both" (131). Orlando swings from pole to pole "as if she belonged to neither [sex]; and indeed, for the time being she seemed to vacillate; she was man; she was woman; she knew the secrets, shared the weaknesses of each. It was a most bewildering and whirligig state of mind to be in" (158). The differences between the sexes elude specification in "pure" (as opposed to relational) terms, a phenomenon Woolf's text enacts as it moves through epochs and sexes: "It is a matter of where the dividing line is, and its location varies historically and socially. Any definition only has meaning in relation to a specific socio-historical context, since there is no innate bond between signifier and signified" (130). As such, then, the transgressions androgyny enacts, Minow-Pinkney maintains, "can only be presented in metonymical displacements, a sliding of one form into another" (131). These slips and slides, the hide-and-seek of how sexual identity can be represented, remain in motion, but the slide of "one form into another" depends upon preexisting types.

DiBattista views androgyny similarly, as "a double triumph. It overwhelms those stubborn, basically artificial divisions between men and women and thus discovers the basis of a legitimate social order governed by the law of equal association. And it also liberates the mind of women from the most enduring form of cultural and biological tyranny—the tyranny of sex!" (19). Androgyny is a way out of the either/or trap through the substitution of a both/and relationship. Arguing along similar lines, DuPlessis sees the "Orlando figure" as "both A and not-A, a logical contradiction, but a narratable prototype of constant heterogeneity" (*Writing* 63). According to DiBattista, the ruse of the "objective biographer" permits Woolf to "hide . . . the radical subjectivity and indeterminism that invariably attends the treatment of sex in social and political life and in fiction itself. Sex is not a fact, but a space in the psychic life, a hole or lapsus in identity onto which are projected the imagoes, archetypes, or stereotypes comprehended in terms male and female" (118). Pacteau presents a more complex, labile view of androgyny. It is and is not, because it vexes representation: "Androgyny can be said to belong to the domain of the imaginary, where desire is unobstructed; gender identity to that of the symbolic, the Law" (63). In other words, she calls the "some thing" that exceeds the law "androgyny."

Probably there are some limits and circumstances that desire does not know or recognize. It eludes apprehension, only finding itself, and that, sometimes obscurely, in the lover. How, then can I know her, or even recognize who she is in me?

> Dear L,
>
> I have many pictures of you in various poses and moods, some when you don't know I am watching. I like those best, except when you are here and really looking at me instead of the lens. Now I look at pictures.
>
> I have been waiting for your call, a reward for waiting. Just a sound is worth my attention. Such a small thing. But then we both know how it makes all the difference, begins to spin out the matrix of difference and meaning we live in. I am always so intent on hearing your voice, more lovely than Satie, etching tracks on the surface of memory like the tips of my fingers trying to memorize the smooth skin on your hand, your arms and back, to remember precisely the viscosity of fluid you when we make love. Fine calibrations of measure and degree, surface and interior distance. Ways of trying to know you/me/what it is we see in one another.
>
> Love,
> L

Starting again. The lesbian question is this: when Virginia looks at Vita, what does she see? What happens when a woman thinks of woman "in what is called 'that way'" (Vita, in Nicolson 29)? It is the question Rachel Bowlby as a feminist reader of Woolf fails to ask. Or that Michael Leaska answers in too literal and limited a way: "In the early months Virginia saw Vita as supple, savage, and patrician. To Vita, Virginia was the 'gentle genius'—lovely, idolized, and remote" (Leaska, *Letters* 11). This answer begs the question, saying nothing about attraction and affection between women, about lesbian relationship. Is the question—

what does one "see" in the other—too personal, too speculative (from the Latin *specere*, to look at)? Another improper embodiment for the serious critical inquirer who would prefer not to look?

This is the difference between Bowlby, the feminist critic, who can write a chapter about *Orlando* without mentioning the word *lesbian*, and me. Or Nigel Nicolson who avoids the word in his affectionate "liberal"-minded description of *Orlando*: "The effect of Vita on Virginia is all contained in *Orlando*, the longest and most charming love letter in literature, in which she explores Vita, weaves her in and out of the centuries, tosses her from one sex to the other, plays with her, dresses her in furs, lace and emeralds, teases her, flirts with her, drops a veil of mist around her, and ends by photographing her in the mud at Long Barn, with dogs, awaiting Virginia's arrival next day" (218). I say it matters when a critic avoids (a form of suppression) the word *lesbian*; as long as the word matters, makes a social, political or artistic difference, it matters when *lesbian* is not spoken.

These critics also differ substantially from the more probing and explicit treatment of lesbianism Sherron Knopp offers in her essay, " 'If I Saw You Would You Kiss Me?': Sapphism and the Subversiveness of Virginia Woolf's *Orlando*"—an exploration in which Knopp, while refusing, unlike Blanche Wiesen Cook, to specify her relationship to their relationship, installs the lesbian subject at the center of her argument, as she claims, "Yet the extent to which Vita and Virginia did love each other—profoundly and, in every sense of the words, erotically and sexually (the frequency or infrequency with which they went to bed is irrelevant)—is something that continues to be resisted, denied, ignored, qualified out of significance, or simply unrecognized, even by the feminist revolution that enshrined Virginia as its saint" (24). The lesbian critic, "reading as a lesbian critic," reading "in *that* way," searches for something else and finds it, there in the sometimes silent language of the look between those two women, the space between words, the awesome passion of their engagement, even when they are (only) writing. Asking this improper question marks the lesbian scene or angle of vision, brings it into being. Virginia chooses to look, and sees. (Virginia to Vita: "and Vita is a dear old rough coated sheep dog: or alternatively, hung with grapes, pink with pearls, lustrous, candle lit"; *Letters* 79). This lesbian gaze is incompatible with Trautmann's desexualizing view of Virginia and Vita as cloistered nuns, a figure that is meant (before such explosive works as *The Three Marias* and *Lesbian Nuns: Breaking Silence*) to undercut the sensuality and eroticism of their lives and texts: "Part of both women's solitude, as discussed before, was an almost fierce sexlessness, or more accurately, a narcissistic sexuality, a state for contemplating themselves and their own feminine sensibilities, which at these times substituted in intensity for the erotic. In this solitude no man could get at them for a while. Both Vita and Virginia had this and other qualities of the cloistered nun" (32). The critical assortment of faulty or incomplete deductions and simple analogies produces the barren, imprisoned reading its figures lead us to make, as it runs counter to the playful eroticism in the desiring regard of one woman for another that marks these modern love letters as lesbian.

When Virginia looked at Vita, did she see Orlando/*Orlando*? What did she want? In 1928 she wrote to Vita, demanding her love through the imperative "first" choice:

Love Virginia (imperative)
Love Virginia (absolute)
Love? Virginia? (interrogative)
Mine was the 1st.
                    (*Letters* 3:446)

Did she discover, in this looking, a projection of indirection and inflection, a go-ing and a return, or, in other words (her—Virginia's/Vita's?), "style"? In the pro-cess of writing *Orlando*, Virginia writes to Vita: "Shall I come Saturday for the night?—seems the only chance. Let me know. . . . Should you say, if I rang you up to ask, that you were fond of me? If I saw you would you kiss me? If I were in bed would you—I'm rather excited about Orlando tonight: have been lying by the fire and making up the last chapter" (*Letters* 246). Orlando/Vita (who signs her name so, and to whom Virginia addresses other "love" letters), and *Orlando*, that novel inventing and commemorating Vita, excite Virginia. Are they sepa-rable? What's the differ(e/a)nce: Vita and Orlando, "Orlando" and Orlando or *Or-lando*? As she completes her novel, Virginia is not certain: "The question now is, will my feelings for you be changed? I've lived in you all these months—coming out, what are you really like? Do you exist? Have I made you up?" (*Letters* 264).

Orlando/*Orlando* performs a trajectory of desire as it constructs and propels it-self toward its desiderata, or as DeSalvo puts it, *Orlando* is "a book in which [Vir-ginia] would possess Vita utterly" (204). But as Orlando's biographer notes, the meditation on love, that "first question," yields an unending metaphorics rather than the certainty of conclusion: "And as the first question had not been settled—What is love?—back it would come at the least provocation or none, and hustle Books or Metaphors or What one lives for into the margins, there to wait till they saw their chance to rush into the field again" (100). Line by line, desire marks out a future, or as the Biographer tells us three times on a page, "Life and a lover" (185). Concerning this mysterious trajectory, Lacan writes, "What counts is not that the other sees where I am, but that [s]he sees where I am going, that is to say, quite precisely, that [s]he sees where I am not. In every analysis of the intersubjective relation, what is essential is not what is there, what is seen. What structures it is what is not there" (*Seminar I* 224). This is true and not true, isn't it? Perhaps true only to the extent that we *are* interested in the "intersubjective relation" as Virginia pursues the volcanic Vesuvius, Vita (Glendinning 124). We want to see what she sees, to know how she wants to be seen. We also want to see what she cannot see, the "what is not there" of desire as she writes it.

Dear "Orlando"—
    I reread all your letters today for signs of how, then, you knew that I would later stand in front of you showing my passion, that I will later still, though you already know it and knew it then, make love to you in words and ways you will forget only with great difficulty and after a long time. What wisdom is it that lets you write a future for me—seeing me where I was not yet, as I look at you now—that even I had not read for me and was powerless to in-vent. This must be the way that desire through its persistent longing makes what we will become for one another, as in the deferred space of love, a fu-ture consummation first imagines and then writes itself as it waits for us to take ourselves down full length, length to length, our bodies finally side by

side one on the other and again, searching for the points, compelling the intersection where two no longer feel like two, subject and object indistinct, as with my eyes closed I cannot tell my pleasure from yours, and begin to feel that certain ecstasy we are learning to become in one another.

Love,
V.

Pacteau argues that "Fantasy, rooted in the absence of an object, is contingent upon a distance; that between viewer and viewed, where the unconscious comes to rest, along which look and psyche travel" (77–78). The complex intersection of observer and observed—in an intricate fabric of desire, in an erotics of en-gaze-ment—recalls Barthes's exploration of the ecstasy of the gaze, as the object pierces the subject in an ecstatic confusion of activity and passivity. Jane Gallop explains, "Ecstasy etymologically derives from the Greek *ekstasis*, from *ex-*, 'out,' plus *histanai*, 'to place.' Thus, it means something like 'placed out.' Ecstasy is when you are no longer within your own frame: some sort of going outside takes place" (15). Barthes calls this excessive ecstatic pleasure *jouissance*; Orlando / the Biographer / Virginia sums it up in "Ecstasy! . . . Ecstasy!" (287); "Laughter, Laughter!" (271); "Life, Life, Life!" (270)—the Latin translation of which, Leaska points out, becomes "Vita, Vita, Vita!" (46), the lover's signature.

> *"I try to invent you for myself."*
> —VIRGINIA ON VITA

"For myself." "You" for "me." That there is an "I" and a "you," has great import. As Peggy Kamuf explains, "If there is to be a coming together in a convention of meaning, 'I' and 'you' cannot be subsumed into only an 'I.' By itself, in other words, 'I' makes no sense. There is no meaning, no contract without the more-than-one of an 'I/you' articulated by their difference" (53). Vita writes from Teheran that she wants a picture of Virginia and asks if her own has turned up: "It is a torment not being able to visualize when one wants to. I can visualize you as a matter of fact surprisingly well,—but always as you stood on your doorstep that last evening, when the lamps were lit and the trees misty, and I drove away" (*Letters* 112). Virginia saw in Vita the spec(tac)ular image of herself, of Virginia the lesbian lover. She invents the lesbian woman who loves women, who might love her, whom she might love. Through speculation, surmise and even imagination, Woolf, like Orlando's biographer, attempts "to elucidate a secret that has puzzled historians for a hundred years": to fill in the "hole in the manuscript [record of Orlando's life] big enough to put your finger through" (119). She invents herself as she writes the other, or as Linda Kauffman puts it in her probing work on epistolarity and desire, "Since every letter to the beloved is also a self-address, . . . the heroine's project—aided by her reading and her writing—also involves self-creation, self-invention" (25). Through the Biographer and Vita, Woolf constructs herself as a lesbian of letters at the same time that she gives us the lesbian in letters. But who *is* "she"?

Dear V—
You invite perceptual study:

Parallax, n. [Gr. *parallaxis*, from *parallas sein*, to vary, to decline or wander; *para*, beyond, and *allassein*, to change.]

PARALLAX
P, star; R, point on earth's surface; A,
center of the earth; angle RPA, parallax

1. the apparent change in the position of an object resulting from the change in the direction or position from which it is viewed.
2. the amount or angular degree of such change; specifically, in astronomy, the apparent difference in the position of a heavenly body with reference to some point on the surface of the earth and some other point, as the center of the earth (*diurnal*, of *geocentric*, *parallax*) *or* a point on the sun (*annual*, or *heliocentric*, *parallax*): the parallax of an object may be used in determining its distance from the observer.

—*Webster's New World Dictionary*

What is the parallax of you, the graceful angle we compose of you me surface and center, seen in this way, a bright star that suddenly changes direction in the night sky, a new sun I gradually alter myself to see. Was it you who moved or I, standing now in a shy ecstasy (mine and yours) at the door as you come up the walk, your head turned eyes slightly angled toward me waiting through the distance between years the night the morning hours slowly assembling themselves with diurnal regularity toward such an orderly vision, like the way my words ultimately compose themselves on the page, toward the feel of you.

Love,
L

The parallax distance is a function of the view, the coursing of desire, the elaboration of fantasy. Pacteau explains the figure of the androgyne in similar terms: "The androgyne dwells in a distance. The androgynous figure has to do with *seduction*, that which comes before undressing, seeing, touching. It can only exist in the shadow area of an image; once unveiled, once we throw a light on it, it becomes a woman or man, and I (myself) resume my position on the side of the female. The perfect symmetry of the figure of the androgyne positions the viewer at the convergence of the feminine and the masculine where 's/he' oscillates. The androgyne is excessive in its transgression of the boundaries of gender identity; however, this threat of superabundance, of overflowing, is safely contained within the frame of the feminine and the masculine" (78–79). The androgyne, as a gap, an excess, resembles the lesbian, but without community, without the socio-politics of identity and the history of movement and struggle, and is still caught within the oppositional categories of gender. The androgyne, as such, then, is the "first figure," but s/he is a figure in motion, the "origin" that never was, a potential only to be re-figured or given over to the either/or. The androgyne, as/when represented, according to Pacteau, shows (up) "as an attempt to objectify desire, to reduce into one *still* image a process, is in itself contrary to the dynamics of the fantasy that produces it. . . . Representation of the androgynous 'in between' is an impossibility. Perhaps it is because of the image's overwhelming concern with the 'body' as the site of all truth. The 'body' as an entity, as an end in itself, cannot contain the excess of the androgynous fantasy" (81).

Letters, like all texts, but love letters in particular as a signed pledge from me to you, leave "the door open for all sorts of improprieties and expropriations" (Kamuf 25); as Kamuf explains, there "is no guarantee that [s/]he [the signer] feels what [s/]he expresses or expresses what [s/]he feels" (25). (Vita to Virginia: "Do you ever mean what you say, or say what you mean? or do you just enjoy baffling the people who try to creep a little nearer?" *Letters* 52) What ever does the letter—L, for example—mean?

In/through Orlando/*Orlando*, Virginia becomes (most like) Vita; she imagines her (as) lover, her love affair. When she began the book, she wrote to Vita, "Yesterday morning I was in despair. . . . I couldn't screw a word from me; and at last dropped my head in my hands: dipped my pen in the ink, and wrote these words, as if automatically, on a clean sheet: Orlando: A Biography. No sooner had I done this than my body was flooded with rapture and my brain with ideas. I wrote rapidly till 12. . . . But listen; suppose Orlando turns out to be Vita; and its *[sic]* all about you and the lusts of your flesh and the lure of your mind (heart you have none, who go gallivanting down the lanes with [Mary] Campbell) . . . Shall you mind? Say yes, or No: . . . " (*Letters* 237). On these grounds, Françoise Defromont argues that *Orlando* is a public exposé of Vita's affections and infidelities, and Virginia's jealousy, which she displaces in/through writing (185). Similarly, Knopp describes the novel as both "public proclamation" and private exploration: "Far from being a way to create distance in the relationship, *Orlando* was a way to heighten intimacy—not a substitute for physical lovemaking but an extension of it" (27). A love affair of the letter (when I inscribe the words on the paper, I get excited).

We could say that Virginia saw herself and not herself, herself as she wished to be-come (that is, a woman like the Vita she saw), herself as she wished vita to see her (a woman Vita could love), and Vita as Virginia wished her to be, the one who puts Virginia on the "first rung of her ladder." Virginia sees, first and foremost, a lesbian, and invests in Vita, through the character of Orlando, the history of women "like" her—500 years of lesbianism, or 400 years of English tradition—one of Woolf's most striking realizations, and the very awareness that produces (itself) in the curious construction of Orlando, larger than life, longer than life, all of life.

Vita responds to the experience of *Orlando* by remarking that it gives a new meaning to narcissism: "you have invented a new form of Narcissism,—I confess,—I am in love with Orlando—this is a complication I had not foreseen" (*Letters* 289). Virginia/ Orlando/ Vita. Desire, according to Lacan, is always triangulated, but I see Virginia/Vita–Orlando/Virginia/Vita—Virginia/Leonard; Vita—Virginia/Violet/Rosamund—Harold. Father : mother/ lover/ daughter.

Vita's image returns (her) to herself. But it is Virginia's narcissism as well—an auto-erotic gesture (loving one's self enough to create a lover), a self-engendering move (becoming lesbian, beloved and beloved), a creation of one's (and one's self as) lover and love object,[4] a brilliant circuitry. A "writer's holiday," "an escapade" (*WD* 117–18, 124), Orlando/*Orlando* is a love affair.

> Dear V—
>
> My lover is a writer. She makes secret turns of phrase and tongue as she inscribes me, (re)writing my love for her. How her text makes me trace my passion on her body, how she (trans)forms me into her perfect lover she will not explain. Is it the writer who (be)comes the lover, or the other way around? I cannot say. She will not tell me. Sometimes she says that I am the one making (up) this intimate story, the title of which is "L," the subtitle and author for the moment unknown—inconnu, secret, clandestine, but very very beautiful.
>
> Love,
> L

"intimate letters"
—VIRGINIA TO VITA (*Letters* 3:117)

In writing *Orlando*, Virginia Woolf set out to make an intimate story very public, or perhaps it was to make a public story very intimately her own. She wrote in her diary on October 22, 1927: "I am writing *Orlando* half in a mock style very clear and plain, so that people will understand every word. But the balance between truth & fantasy must be careful" (*Diary* 3:162). As Defromont contends in *Virginia Woolf, Vers la maison de lumière*, Woolf's texts explore the relation between life, writing and libidinal energy, "between talent and femininity, emotion and art" (171). *Flush*, the biography of Elizabeth Barrett Browning's spaniel, most pointedly displays this investigation (61–62). Woolf struggles between the poles of intellect and instinct, the differ(e/a)nce constitutive of *jouissance* in both instances (137).

In *Signature Pieces*, Kamuf suggests a way of describing the relationship between Virginia and her lover Vita and the text or letter/character of Orlando, or *Orlando*. Kamuf writes provocatively that the signature is "an always divisible limit within the difference between writer and work, 'life' and 'letters.' Signature articulates the one with the other, the one *in* the other: it both divides and joins. It is this double-jointedness of signatures that will be lost to any discourse that continues to posit an essential exteriority of subjects to the texts they sign" (viii). Thus the problematic of lesbian : writing is inscribed in what Defromont describes as the "or/and, *Or/l/and/*o)" (209), the passage from one sex to the other, one writing function to the next. *Orlando* is (a) play on words, on/in the letter. The signature "is the mark of an articulation at the border between life and letters, body and language. An articulation both joins and divides; it joins and divides identity with/from difference. A difference from itself, within itself, articulates the signature on the text it signs" (Kamuf 39–40). It joins and divides "the historically singular subject to which it refers (or seems to refer) and the formal generality of language" (Kamuf 41).

Desire writes the absence in/of its heart, a lack, as Lacan puts it, "beyond anything which can represent it. It is only ever represented as a reflection on a veil" (*Seminar II* 223), the shadowy hand on a fine sheet of paper or the faint tracks on the sheets after rising, inscribing the love letter. Will I be able to read it? The

Biographer cautions us that "the most poetic is precisely that which cannot be written down. For which reasons we leave a great blank here, which must be taken to indicate that the space is filled to repletion" (253). How do I see what Virginia sees? How do I see her seeing Vita? In a sense, "the Biographer" tells me how to imagine Virginia looking at Vita, a gap and an overflow. And my lover and I (re)enact the scene/seen.

> Dear L—
>
> It is you startled I see in the near distance eyes opened and my fluid love for you begins to move, the shudders of desire rush over me, lap on lap. Orlando sees the woman s/he loves and thinks of names—melon, pineapple, olive tree, emerald, the clear-eyed fox startled as it crosses the snow (37). These names the senses supply to construct their desire in the lover, to approximate "the green flame [that] seems hidden in the emerald, or the sun prisoned in a hill" (47).
>
> What names do I have for that desiring lover whose dark eyes are haunted with me, who is startled by the love we make together, whose surprise takes me by surprise, leads me to invent something more. Leads me to recall that other time at Long Barn where one woman startled another in love, and then to plot a narrative in which we all invent our parts. Invention—the events, the feelings, the names for the words that fail to speak what is hidden, concealed in the ways we move in one another, how much we want it in the space of deferral, whether we are together or apart.
>
> This letter locates us side by side, puts us here in the same place, even though I know you are away, that I must wait for your return as I construct my desire in memory of your body. It must be the lover's work to write love letters, character after character, arranging the white spaces and the dark shapes, forms of silence and sound, presence and absence, hour after hour, with the same careful attention she pays to her lover's body, as she waits for her to come back so she can put this letter aside and lead her to the bedroom, take off her clothes, arrange her gently but ever so quickly on the bed and continue together with a violent tenderness to compose their love in gestures and sounds that have no easy names, shapes that come to us from a place beyond meaning, or memory.
>
> Love,
> L

Like Woolf, who first places Chloe and Olivia in the laboratory, and then sees their differences (from one another, two women who are not waiting for men but for each other, an economy of difference not lack, not sameness; and their sufficiency, not waiting for a man to fulfill them, to fill them up, to plug up the w/hole so the body can be summed up).[5] She sees their secret, hers and mine, or at least the possibility of a future for them. In Vita, she sees herself loving Vita (her); she sees lesbian : woman. Her lesbian feminist readers see it too, and some feminist readers can learn to recognize the figure as well. Virginia writes to Vita about a woman who sent her a letter: "A woman writes that she has to stop and kiss the page when she reads O.—Your race I imagine. The percentage of Lesbians is rising in the States, all because of you" (*Letters* 318). More writing : more lesbians.

Dear Vita and Virginia,

How can I read your letters without, above all, wanting to write? Years of correspondence, circulating affection and longing make me desire more letters. I don't want them to end or to stop, so I continue (y)our correspondence.

Dear V, Your sheepdog puts her muzzle on her paws and waits at the door. Will you pet her when you arrive? Will you remember the feel of her fur and discover new ways to startle her? Love, V.

Dear V and V, I feel empty when I write one without the other. Even the letter V—one side an obverse mirroring of the other, only connected at that precise swelling point. There must be a name for this effect—V. In any case, it reads like a lesbian effect; a lesbian can claim it as her own. (Y)ours is, after all, "a captivating image."

VVVVVVVVVVVVVVVVVV

Taking flight,
Love,
L

NOTES

1. In "The Match in the Crocus," Judith Roof observes that "the representation of the lesbian is an open site for the play of sexual difference in its relationship to the perception and representation of sexuality. Conscious of a kind of phallic preeminence, women writers are faced with the difficulty of representing perceptions unaccounted for in a phallic economy in terms of that economy" (109).

2. In this essay I advance no claims to offering a "new interpretation" of *Orlando* or of the relationship between Woolf and Sackville-West; rather, I am seeking a different expression of critical perspective and meaning. This essay departs from previous criticism because of my insistence on reading the lesbian text of Woolf and Sackville-West in terms of the lesbian text of my own experience, in terms, that is, of my own lesbian : desire and the lesbian love letter.

I am, of course, indebted to previous scholarship on Woolf and desire; it makes this writing possible. The following works have been particularly useful to me: Louise DeSalvo, "Lighting the Cave: The Relationship between Vita Sackville-West and Virginia Woolf"; Sonya Rudikoff, "How Many Lovers Had Virginia Woolf?" *Hudson Review* 32, 4 (Winter 1979): 54–66; Joanne Trautmann, *The Jessamy Brides* (University Park: Pennsylvania State University Press, 1973), and especially Sherron E. Knopp, "'If I Saw You Would You Kiss Me?': Sapphism and the Subversiveness of Virginia Woolf's *Orlando*," *PMLA* 103 (1988): 24–34. Finally, critics considering Virginia Woolf owe much to Jane Marcus's pioneering and persistent work, as do students of desire to Linda Kauffman's *Discourses of Desire*.

3. For discussions of Woolf's "letters," see Leaska's introduction to *The Letters of Vita Sackville-West to Virginia Woolf* and Catharine Stimpson's "The Female Sociograph: The Theater of Virginia Woolf's Letters. "

4. See Jacqueline Rose, *Sexuality and the Field of Vision*, pp. 167–83, on the question of narcissism.

5. In chapters seven and eight (pp. 138–87) of *Virginia Woolf and the Languages of Patriarchy*, Jane Marcus traces the repressed lesbian narrative of Woolf's relation to other lesbian writers who were her contemporaries, and offers an insightful analysis of lesbian interests in Woolf's texts, particularly in *A Room of One's Own*. See Marcus's observations (pp. 152, 169) concerning lesbian coding in the Chloe and Olivia passage.

WORKS CITED

Brossard, Nicole. *The Aerial Letter.* Trans. Marlene Wildeman. Toronto: Women's Press, 1988.

Cook, Blanche Wiesen. " 'Women alone stir my imagination': Lesbianism and Cultural Tradition." *Signs* 4 (1979): 718–39.

Defromont, Françoise. *Virginia Woolf: Vers la maison de lumière.* Paris: Editions des femmes, 1985.

DeSalvo, Louise. "Lighting the Cave: The Relationship between Vita Sackville-West and Virginia Woolf." *Signs* 8, 2 (Winter 1982): 195–214.

DiBattista, Maria. *Virginia Woolf's Major Novels: The Fables of Anon.* New Haven: Yale University Press, 1980.

DuPlessis, Rachel Blau. *Writing beyond the Ending: Narrative Strategies of Twentieth-Century Women Writers.* Bloomington: Indiana University Press, 1985.

Gallop, Jane. *Thinking Through the Body.* New York: Columbia University Press, 1988.

Gasché, Rodolphe. *"Ecce Homo* or the Written Body." *Oxford Literary Review* 7 *(*1985): 3–24.

Glendinning, Victoria. *Vita: A Life of V. Sackville-West.* New York: Knopf, 1983.

Heath, Stephen. *The Sexual Fix.* London and Basingstoke, U.K.: Macmillan Press Ltd., 1982.

Kamuf, Peggy. *Signature Pieces: On the Institution of Authorship.* Ithaca, N.Y., and London: Cornell University Press, 1988.

Kauffman, Linda S. *Discourses of Desire: Gender, Genre, and Epistolary Fiction.* Ithaca, N.Y., and London: Cornell University Press, 1986.

Knopp, Sherron E. " 'If I Saw You Would You Kiss Me?': Sapphism and the Subversiveness of Virginia Woolf's *Orlando." PMLA* 103 (1988): 24–34.

Lacan, Jacques. *The Seminar of Jacques Lacan.* Ed. Jacques Alain Miller. Book I: *Freud's Papers on Technique, 1953–1954.* Trans. John Forrester. New York and London: W. W. Norton, 1988.

———. *The Seminar of Jacques Lacan.* Book II: *The Ego in Freud's Theory and in the Technique of Psychoanalysis, 1954–1955.* Trans. Sylvana Tomaselli. New York and London: W. W. Norton, 1988.

Leaska, Mitchell A. "Introduction." In *The Letters of Vita Sackville-West to Virginia Woolf.* Ed. Louise DeSalvo and Mitchell A. Leaska, 11–46. New York: William Morrow, 1985.

Marcus, Jane. *Virginia Woolf and the Languages of Patriarchy.* Bloomington and Indianapolis: Indiana University Press, 1987.

Minow-Pinkney, Makiko. *Virginia Woolf and the Problem of the Subject.* Brighton, U.K.: Harvester Press, 1987.

Nicolson, Nigel. *Portrait of a Marriage.* New York: Athenaeum, 1973.

Pacteau, Francette. "The Impossible Referent: Representations of the Androgyne." In *Formations of Fantasy.* Ed. by Victor Burgin, James Donald and Cora Kaplan, 62–84. London and New York: Methuen, 1986.

Roof, Judith. "The Match in the Crocus: Representations of Lesbian Sexuality." In *Discontented Discourses: Feminism/Textual Intervention/Psychoanalysis.* Ed. Marleen S. Barr and Richard Feldstein, 100–16. Urbana and Chicago: University of Illinois Press, 1989.

Rose, Jacqueline. *Sexuality in the Field of Vision.* London: Verso, 1986.

Sackville-West, Vita. *The Letters of Vita Sackville-West to Virginia Woolf.* Ed. Louise DeSalvo and Mitchell A. Leaska. New York: William Morrow, 1985.

———. *Seducers in Ecuador and The Heir.* London Virago Press, 1987.

Stimpson, Catharine R. "The Female Sociograph: The Theater of Virginia Woolf's Letters." In *The Female Autograph.* Ed. Domna C. Stanton and Jeanine Parisier Plottel, 193–203. New York: New York Literary Forum, 1984.

Trautmann, Joanne. *The Jessamy Brides: The Friendship of Virginia Woolf and V. Sackville-West*. University Park: Pennsylvania State University Press, 1973.

Woolf, Virginia. *The Diary of Virginia Woolf*, vol. 3, *1925–1930*. Ed. Anne Olivier Bell and Andrew McNeillie. New York: Harcourt Brace Jovanovich, 1980.

———. *Flush: A Biography*. New York: Harcourt, Brace and World, 1933.

———. *The Letters of Virginia Woolf*, vol. 3, *1923–1928*. Ed. Nigel Nicolson and Joanne Trautmann. New York and London: Harcourt Brace Jovanovich, 1977.

———. *Orlando: A Biography*. Harcourt Brace Jovanovich, 1956.

———. *A Writer's Diary* [*WD*]. Ed. Leonard Woolf. New York: Harcourt Brace Jovanovich, 1953.

desire

In a late essay, Sigmund Freud asked his now famous question: "What does the woman [the little girl] want?" The essays in this section take up that question of wanting—of desire—from a number of different points of view, asking not only what the woman wants, but what is wanted of/from her. Freud's own answer, that the little girl wanted a penis, has been heatedly debated ever since (as is evident from the essays in "Body" and "Gaze," sections of *Feminisms* that probably should be read in conjunction with this one). The essayists here return to that debate to explore whether or not female desire must always be subordinate to male desire.

The term "desire" is dense with intertextual connections. It is usually understood here as it was used by the French psychoanalyst and rereader of Freud, Jacques Lacan. According to Lacan, each person encounters a deep split when s/he begins to use language; his own contention that we "enter language" suggests his sense of the exteriority of linguistic experience. He argued that language is a force that utterly changes the being who uses it and that creates and structures the unconscious. Because language is always metaphorical (it always *stands for* something else and can never *be* that thing), there is always a gap between expressing a wish and receiving its answer, since language can never fully express exactly what we want. That gap is desire. For Lacan, our desire is always for *jouissance*, a term that refers both to orgasm and to a state of blissful, ecstatic union that would complete us, would heal the "split" that occurred when we entered language. This desire is unrealizable. Its impossibility does not, however, keep us from continually seeking its fulfillment.

"Desire" becomes an issue for feminists because of the precarious relation women have to it in this system. "The Woman" is understood, by Lacan, to be desirable to man because of the (false) beliefs that she will be able to complete him, that she is his Other (all that he is not), and that union with her is a union with all he is not. Lacan's famous assertion, "Woman does not exist," does not refer to real women, but to this imaginary woman who could complete man. Desire is also important to women because of how their own desires are defined—and thereby limited—within psychoanalytic discourse; as Luce Irigaray warns (in her essay in "Gaze"), such restrictions within the realm of discourse may well limit the possibilities open to women in the world of lived experience.

The symbol most central to desire, for Lacan, is the phallus. Although it bears a connection to the physical penis, Lacan argued (in the essay "The Signification of the Phallus" in *Écrits*) that it did not represent the physical organ itself, but came, metaphorically, to stand for all that was desirable. The origin of this signification is, for Lacan as it was for Freud, the castration complex; the male fears the loss of the penis, the female feels the anxiety of never having had one, and therefore the penis comes to represent that which is desirable. But Lacan insists that its symbolic force always exceeds its reference to the physical organ. Not surprisingly, though, this is one point that has troubled feminist writers deeply; the line separating phallus and penis is very fine. Lacan's "phallocentric" (i.e., centered on the phallus) reliance on a male metaphor irrevocably marks his work as male-dominated and male-privileging, and therefore raises serious questions for its applicability to feminist thought.

Feminists have nonetheless used psychoanalysis in their critique of gender, despite misgivings about its phallocentrism. Psychoanalysis provides a framework for understanding how gender is defined, how it comes into being. Further, one of Freud's chief contributions, as Dianne Hunter points out in "Hysteria, Psychoanalysis and Feminism: The Case of Anna O.," was the idea of listening to what hysterical women had to say; for literary critics, the model of listening to (or reading) previously uninterpretable texts is a powerful one. Finally, feminists have recognized that psychoanalysis has been (with Marxism) a discourse that has shaped the twentieth century. To ignore it, to refuse to participate in it and change it, would be to be concede this important ground to other, and often hostile, forces. (See Cora Kaplan's "Pandora's Box: Subjectivity, Class and Sexuality in Socialist Feminist Criticism" in "Class," and Mary Jacobus's "Reading Woman (Reading)" in "Men," for further arguments in favor of including psychoanalysis in feminism.)

Two other Lacanian terms will be useful in reading the following essays: "the symbolic" and "the imaginary." For Lacan, language exists in "the order of the symbolic," because language symbolizes things in the world. "The symbolic" refers to the connection between signifier (a word) and signified (what it stands for), which is always arbitrarily established; we could just as easily call a dog "un chien" since there is no essential connection between the four-footed furry creature and the word "dog." The system in which these symbols work is always outside the subject who uses it, and that subject is never in control of the system. Lacan calls this arbitrary system the "Law of the Father," because of its structural similarity to the establishment of paternity and its chronological connection to the Oedipal complex. "The imaginary," on the other hand, is the realm of the image. Unlike symbols, whose connection to what they signify is arbitrary, images have a visual relation to the signified. The imaginary is typified, for Lacan, in the relation of the subject to his/her mirror image: that image both is and is not the subject. Whereas the symbolic is triadic—signifier, signified, and signifying system—the imaginary is dyadic—image and signified.

Desire has become an issue for literary critics because it exists within the field of language; as Lacan understood it, desire was the motivation for all language. As one of the most intense involvements with language, literature can be understood as a playing out of desire. Desire is its origin and root. The essays here explore the ways literature can be shaped by and can be a vehicle for desire. The writers here are concerned with how desire shapes some issues that are crucial to feminist criticism: Are desire and its forms specific to each gender? Does desire shape our understanding of sameness and difference? As the readings that follow show, the central questions about desire for literary critics in the 1980s and 1990s have moved beyond a strictly Lacanian formulation to encompass questions of social and political power: How is desire related to political power? How is sexual/political desire expressed in literary representations?

Part explanation, part analysis and part interrogation, Jane Gallop's "The Father's Seduction" (1982) uses Irigaray's analytic technique to read Irigaray's "Blind Spot in an Old Dream of Symmetry" (a section of which, "Another 'Cause'—Castration" is reprinted in "Gaze"). Gallop points to contradictions in Irigaray's essay, and pursues issues of the writer's own desires as apparent in her text. In particular, Gallop examines Irigaray's own position as an analyst: If Freud is the "father" of psychoanalysis, is Irigaray the (hysterical?) daughter? And if she is, how does her desire (as daughter) for the father mark her text? Questions of sameness and difference, of symmetry and asymmetry, are at issue here: Irigaray uses Freud's technique to analyze Freud; Gallop uses Irigaray's technique to analyze Irigaray; and throughout, the question of the analyst's desire remains problematic.

If, as Irigaray argues elsewhere in *Speculum of the Other Woman,* any theory is always masculine, where does that leave Irigaray's own theorizing? Gallop explores the difficulties Irigaray faces in trying to represent female desire without recourse to a patriarchal system of representation, that is, without recourse to the "Law of the Father." Irigaray's project is to raise the possibility of a sexuality— and a system of representation—not governed by the phallus, not guided by the principle of sameness, "univocity" and one-ness. But, Gallop asks, how can Irigaray offer a *different* version of femininity without being seduced by the *same*? If she solves the problem, and offers an answer, she risks coming to completion and closure—the mark of phallic "unicity." To avoid this problematic closure, Irigaray offers only questions—but how does one offer new options with only questions? Gallop marks these attempts to avoid authority, to avoid the artificial precision of phallocentrism, but points to the occasion when even Irigaray insists on precision—her statement that she doesn't advocate a daughter's having sex with her father—as evidence of the difficulty of escaping the "Law of the Father" and of Irigaray's own desire for/seduction by the father.

Eve Kosofsky Sedgwick marks a move toward combining psychoanalytic and socialist theories in the discussion of desire; as Julia Kristeva does in "Women's Time" (reprinted here in "History"), Sedgwick explores the connection between desire and the political. In the Introduction and first chapter ("Gender Asymmetry and Erotic Triangles") of *Between Men: English Literature and Male Homosocial Desire* (1985), Sedgwick traces the links between male homosocial desire (which she carefully delineates as not homosexual, but homophobic) and patriarchal culture. Here she sets out the theoretical groundwork on which the rest of her book is built, questioning how far the connections between radical feminism, which sees gender as *the* fundamental issue, and Marxist theory, which sees power relations and economics as fundamental, can be drawn.

Sedgwick concludes that one can trace the relations of sexual desire and political power through an examination of the "exchange of women"—a theory that women are used to cement relations between men, an idea that has been developed and refined both by Freud and by anthropologists Claude Lévi-Strauss and Gayle Rubin, and applied to women's psychic lives by Irigaray (see her essay "This Sex Which Is Not One" in "Body"). Warning that sexual desire and political power cannot be simply equated, Sedgwick seeks to examine the historical relation between the two through representations, questioning "what *counts* as sexual, and questioning as well the effect that the sexual has on political power.

Where Sedgwick is concerned with the way that relations "between men" work to oppress women by representing women as significant only insofar as they make possible bonds between men, Terry Castle, in "Sylvia Townsend Warner and the Counterplot of Lesbian Fiction" (1993), examines fiction in which relations between women are central. In this chapter from her book *The Apparitional Lesbian,* Castle revises Sedgwick's paradigm in order to theorize a way of defining "lesbian fiction," and to theorize the question of how desire between women can be imagined and represented. Sedgwick argues that canonical fiction of the eighteenth and nineteenth centuries is structured by a paradigm of love triangles, in which two men organize homosocial bonds with each other through a woman. Castle asks what happens when this triangle is undone, when the single female in the figure is connected to another female, that is, when female-female bonding enters the picture. Castle argues that "within this new *female* homosocial structure, the possibility of male bonding is radically suppressed: for the male term is now isolated just as the female term was in the male homosocial structure." Furthermore, she argues, this female homosocial desire is as dynamic as male desire, and, in its most radical form, becomes lesbian desire.

Castle then turns to a novel which she argues is paradigmatic of this new lesbian desire, Sylvia Townsend Warner's 1936 novel, *Summer Will Show*. In her analysis of this historical fiction—in which a man's wife and his mistress not only meet, but discard him and fall in love with each other—Castle shows how Townsend Warner explicitly revises several canonical nineteenth-century novels to revise the plot of male homosocial desire, so that male bonding is suppressed and female bonding is allowed to "take." Castle argues that Townsend Warner's novel provides a paradigm for defining lesbian fiction; it is, she argues, fiction that is noncanonical, that satirizes or parodies canonical fiction in order to "decanoniz[e], so to speak, the canonical structure of desire itself. Insofar as it documents a world in which men are 'between women' rather than vice versa, it is an insult to the conventional geometries of fictional eros."

In the review with which we conclude this section, "Male Heroes and Female Sex Objects: Sexism in Spike Lee's *Malcolm X*" (1993), bell hooks examines the ways that desire shapes the politics of black filmmaking. hooks surveys Lee's career, pointing out that in his desire for a bigger audience, he has succumbed more and more to a patriarchal image of relations between the sexes, and marginalized any representation of black women as full characters. In representing black men's desires for white women as nothing but sexual (in both *Jungle Fever* and *Malcolm X*), and in never representing relationships between black and white women (and only rarely representing relationships between black women), Lee projects an image of black womanhood as undesirable, because domineering, and of white womanhood as desirable, because innocent. hooks shows the way that the male homosocial bonding that Sedgwick identifies as typical of eighteenth- and nineteenth-century male European fiction continues to shape—misshape, actually—late-twentieth-century black cinema and points to its political effect: "Scenes of black male homosocial bonding in the prison context reaffirm the patriarchal assumption that it is only the actions of black men that matter. This creates a version of black political struggle where the actions of dedicated, powerful, black female activists are systematically devalued and erased." Like each of the other writers in this section, hooks explores the relationship between desire and gender oppression; like the others, she examines how desire is played out in representations.

—DPH

THE FATHER'S SEDUCTION

(1982)

The first third of Luce Irigaray's *Speculum de l'autre femme* is called 'The Blind Spot of an Old Dream of Symmetry.' It is a close reading of 'Femininity,' one of Freud's *New Introductory Lectures on Psycho-Analysis* (1933). This encounter between Irigaray's feminist critique and Freud's final text on woman is an important training ground for a new kind of battle, a feminine seduction/disarming/ unsettling of the positions of phallocratic ideology. Irigaray's tactic is a kind of reading: close reading, which separates the text into fragments of varying size, quotes it and then comments with various questions and associations. She never sums up the meaning of Freud's text, nor binds all her commentaries, questions, associations into a unified representation, a coherent interpretation. Her commentaries are full of loose ends and unanswered questions. As a result, the reader does not so easily lose sight of the incoherency and inconsistency of the text.

That could be seen as a victory for feminism. The Man's order is disturbed by the woman with the impertinent questions and the incisive comments. But as with all seductions, the question of complicity poses itself. The dichotomy active/passive is always equivocal in seduction, that is what distinguishes it from rape. So Freud might have been encouraging Irigaray all along, 'asking for it.' 'By exhibiting this "symptom," this crisis-point in metaphysics where the sexual "in-difference" which assured metaphysics its coherence and "closure" finally exposes itself, Freud proposes it to analysis: his text asking to be heard, to be read' (*Speculum*, p. 29).

Freud might have seduced Irigaray. It might be psychoanalysis that has won over feminism. The very strategy of reading with which Irigaray works Freud over is presented by Freud himself earlier in these *New Introductory Lectures* where he writes, 'we ask the dreamer, too, to free himself from the impression of the manifest dream, to divert his attention from the dream as a whole on to the separate portions of its content and to report to us in succession everything that occurs to him in relation to each of these portions—what associations present themselves to him if he focuses on each of them separately.'[1]

Freud's text asks for analysis. Not just any analysis, but the peculiar technique developed in psychoanalysis for dealing with dreams and other 'symptoms.' Freud proposed the model of the rebus for understanding dreams. According to the dictionary, a rebus is 'a riddle composed of words or syllables depicted by symbols or pictures that suggest the sound of the words or syllables they represent.' As a total picture, a unified representation, the rebus makes no sense. It is only by separating the picture into its elements, dealing with them one at a time, making all possible associations, that one can get anywhere. So psychoanalysis in its technique if not its theory offers an alternative to coherent, unified representation.

The rebus-text shatters the manifest unity so as to produce a wealth of associations which must necessarily be reduced if the goal of interpretation is to reach a final, definitive meaning, the 'latent dream-thoughts.' The unconscious is reappropriated to the model of consciousness—a circumscription analogous to the reappropriation of otherness, femininity to sameness, masculinity. Whereas Freud proposes the rebus as merely a path to the 'latent thoughts,' Irigaray radicalizes Freud's rebus. Irigaray's dream-analysis ('The Blind Spot of an Old *Dream* of Symmetry') does not offer a final latent thought, but merely presents the abundance of associations, not editing those that 'lead nowhere.'

Yet Irigaray's encounter with Freud is not a psychoanalysis. Freud is not there to associate. Irigaray both asks questions (the analyst's role) and supplies associations (the dreamer's role). And since many questions go unanswered they appear directed to the reader, who thus becomes the dreamer. She does not aim to decipher Freud's peculiar psyche, but rather to unravel 'an old dream,' everyone's dream, even Irigaray's dream. The dream is everyone's inasmuch as everyone is within 'the metaphysical closure,' inasmuch as any reader is a 'subject,' which is to say has been philosophically reduced to a unified, stable, sexually indifferent subject, trapped in the old dream of symmetry.

('Symmetry' from the Greek *summetros*—'of like measure'; from *sun*—'like, same,' and *metron*—'measure.' Symmetry is appropriating two things to like measure, measure by the same standard: for example the feminine judged by masculine standards. Judged by masculine measures, woman is inadequate, castrated.)

On the first page of *Speculum*, Irigaray interrupts Freud's text with the attributive indicator: 'he says, they [masculine plural] say.' She repeatedly does that, attributing Freud's words to both a masculine singular and a masculine plural subject pronoun. The old dream belongs to any subject, to anyone speaking and therefore in the position of subject. 'Every theory of the "subject" [Every theory about the subject as well as every theory produced by a subject] will always have been appropriate(d) to the "masculine"' (*Speculum*, p. 165). The neutral 'subject' is actually a desexualized, sublimated guise for the masculine sexed being. Woman can be subject by fitting male standards which are not appropriate to, cannot measure any specificity of femininity, any difference. Sexual indifference is not lack of sexuality, but lack of any different sexuality, the old dream of symmetry, the other, woman, circumscribed into woman as man's complementary other, his appropriate opposite sex.

But what of '*the blind spot* of an old dream of symmetry'? What is the blind spot? What cannot be seen, what is excluded from the light? According to Freud, the sight of woman's genitalia horrifies the young boy because he sees an absence. Mark that he does not see what is there, he sees the absence of a phallus. Nothing to see, nothing that looks like a phallus, nothing of like measure (*summetros*), no coherent visual representation in a familiar form. Nothing to see becomes nothing of worth. The privilege of sight over other senses, oculocentrism, supports and unifies phallocentric, sexual theory (theory—from the Greek *theoria*, from *theoros*, 'spectator,' from *thea*, 'a viewing'). *Speculum* (from *specere*, 'to look at') makes repeated reference to the oculocentrism of theory. 'Every theory of the "subject" will always have been appropriate(d) to the "masculine."' Every *theoria*, every viewing of the subject will have always been according to phallomorphic standards. Hence there is no valid representation of woman; but only a lack.

The female sex organs are the blind spot. Freud's theory must occult female sexuality, in order to manifest symmetry. But a blind spot can also be thought as the locus of greatest resistance in a dream, the least easily interpretable point and thus the most tantalizing. To call a text a dream in a Freudian context is not like calling it an illusion. To point to the blind spot of a dream is *not a moral condemnation*. For it to be a moral condemnation, it would be grounded in an ethic of absolute *luc*idity and en*light*enment. The etymology of such words implies the morality of oculocentrism. Dreams are the 'royal road to the unconscious' and ask for reading destructive of unified 'phallomorphic' representation, the very reading Irigaray gives. The locus of greatest resistance, 'the blind spot' is the heart of the dream, the crisis-point crying, begging for analysis.

Blind also like Oedipus is blinded. Freud is assimilated by Irigaray to Oedipus. Freud, man, is never really out of the Oedipus complex, never resolves his Oedipal phase. According to Freud, the end of the Oedipus complex marks the end of the boy's phallic phase. The phallic phase is characterized by the opposition phallic/castrated. In that phase there is no representation of an other sex—the vagina, for example, is 'unknown.' Supposedly, the difference between the phallic phase and adult sexuality is that the dichotomy phallic/castrated gives way to the opposition masculine/feminine. But if, as Irigaray finds in her reading of Freud, the boy, the man, never resolves his Oedipal complex, then he never leaves the phallic phase, and the opposition masculine/feminine merely masks the opposition phallic/castrated. 'A boy's mother is the first object of his love, and she remains so too during the formation of his Oedipus complex and, *in essence, all through his life*' (*NIL*, p. 118, my italics). Woman's destiny is to become her husband's mother: 'A marriage is not made secure until the wife has succeeded in making her husband her child as well and in acting as a mother to him' (*NIL*, pp. 133–4). The blind spot is the price of man's inability to escape his Oedipal destiny. Theory cannot see woman, but can only represent, represent, make present again endlessly, 'all through his life,' Mother, the masculine subject's *own* original complementary other.

Oedipus/Freud is an old riddle-solver. Oedipus solved the riddle of the sphinx; Freud learned to read the rebus of dreams. In the Freud text that Irigaray analyzes there is another riddle at stake: 'Throughout history people have knocked their heads against the riddle of the nature of femininity.' Yet Irigaray never quotes or comments on this sentence. It occurs on the second page of 'Femininity' and is followed by four lines of poetry—the only poetry in this text. Irigaray only begins her reading of 'Femininity' after the poetry, in fact immediately after the poetry, thus ignoring the first two pages of text. Reading *Speculum*, one would never notice she does not begin at the beginning, for the paragraph she does start with 'makes sense' as an opening for Freud's lecture.

What are we to make of this exclusion of a large section of the text? Although here and there a few words or even a short sentence are omitted from Irigaray's reinscription of Freud, this is the only exclusion of such major proportion. Perhaps we must read this as another blind spot of an old dream of symmetry.

The section omitted is introductory and diverse, speaking of many things and not just on the topic of femininity. So one of the effects of Irigaray's omission is to give a more consistent, more unified representation of the text. In the same way, omitting the poetry homogenizes the discourse. The heterogeneous must be ignored by phallocentrism. Irigaray's forgetting renders Freud's text more phallocentric. Perhaps, then, the 'forgetting' is a tactical decision. Does she choose to ignore the materiality of the text in order to delineate and condemn the 'phallocentric theory'? She does not consistently use this tactic. At other moments in *Speculum* she emphasizes the crisis-points of confusion and contradiction, signalling the workings of the unconscious and the 'feminine' in Freud's text. Is it the inconsistency of her strategy, the lack of unity to her reading, that makes it most effective as an unsettling of phallocentric discourse?

Whatever the foundation for it, her omission, like Freud's 'blind spot,' has the effect of begging for analysis, implicating her reader in the kind of reading she is doing. In this addendum to Irigaray's dream-work, this investigation of her 'blind spot,' I would like to spend some time on the lines of poetry, as the least homogenized part of Freud's discourse, most resistant to an economy of the same. In this I am following the lead of another feminist, Lacanian reader, Shoshana Felman, who has written: '*Literature . . . is the unconscious of psychoanalysis*; . . . the unthought out shadow in psychoanalytic *theory* is precisely its own involvement with literature; . . . literature *in* psychoanalysis functions precisely as its "*unthought*": as the condition of possibility *and* the self-subversive *blind spot* of psychoanalytic *thought*.'[2] Felman's terms are resonant with those at play in Irigaray. The 'shadow in *theory*' calls to the oculocentric etymology of theory, and the appearance of the 'blind spot,' also in that visual register, implicates this quotation in our present investigation. 'Literature' in Felman's discussion plays the same role (support and blind spot) in relation to psychoanalytic theory as 'the feminine' in Irigaray's reading. It might be appropriate to look at the effect of this poetry on Freud's 'Femininity.'

Freud has just said: 'Throughout history people have knocked their heads against the riddle of the nature of femininity' and then he quotes: 'Heads in hieroglyphic bonnets/ Heads in turbans and black birettas/ Heads in wigs and thousand other/ Wretched, sweating heads of humans.' A puzzling inclusion, in many ways. Why quote poetry about heads instead of about woman? The poem has the effect of emphasizing the marginal word 'heads,' which is used in Freud's sentence in a figurative sense and ought to efface itself. Yet the poetry, repeating the word four times, makes 'heads' the dominant word in the sentence. The 'riddle of femininity' is eclipsed by an obsession with heads.

Irigaray suggests (*Speculum*, p. 39) that in Freud's theory the materiality of sex is obliterated by 'the Idea of sex' (she capitalizes to recall Plato and metaphysics). In other words, the riddle of sex, of sexual difference, the puzzling otherness there in its unresolved materiality is occulted, leaving in its place metaphysics, the Idea, in other words, 'heads . . . heads . . . heads.'

The enigmatic 'hieroglyphic bonnet' suggests Egypt and in this riddle context reminds us of the riddle of the Sphinx. We think of Oedipus and the way solving riddles leads to blindness. A 'solved' riddle is the reduction of heterogeneous material to logic, to the homogeneity of logical thought, which produces a blind spot, the inability to see the otherness that gets lost in the reduction. Only the unsolved riddle, the process of riddle-work before its final completion, is a confrontation with otherness.

Hieroglyphs themselves are a sort of riddle. Indeed, like a rebus, they present pictures which as a whole are not unified, and can only be read if one distinguishes the elements. 'Hieroglyphic' has the figurative sense of 'having a hidden meaning' and also 'hard to read, undecipherable.' As if the mysterious 'hieroglyphic bonnet' were itself a hieroglyph, this reader cannot determine if it is undecipherable or has a hidden meaning she cannot uncover. Such is also the puzzle of this entire poetic interruption. Why did Freud put it here? Why did Irigaray forget it?

The four lines are from Heinrich Heine's *Nordsee* (North Sea), from a section of the poem entitled 'Fragen' (Questions). As an intrusion into Freud's lecture the poem indeed poses many questions: Why a poem about heads? Why a poem here and nowhere else? What is a hieroglyphic bonnet? Perhaps this hieroglyphic intrusion is not unlike Irigaray's interruptions. She often inserts a parenthetic question mark into Freud's or her own text, not altering the statement, but merely calling it into question. Much of her commentary consists in merely asking questions. And the largest section of her next book *Ce Sexe qui n'en est pas un* is, like Heine's poem, entitled 'Questions.'[3] Of course, unlike Irigaray's questions, Heine's are well buried. Freud's text only attributes the lines to *Nordsee*, not mentioning the title 'Fragen.' (Although it appears in a footnote to the English translation, the title 'Fragen' is in neither the German nor the French versions.) And there are no questions in the four lines of poetry quoted. Simply the reader's question: Why are these lines here?

None the less, might not Irigaray's impertinent questions already be implicit in the disruption to Freud's lecture, the interruption of his discourse, the distraction from his main point, wrought by Heine's poetry, Heine's 'Fragen'? After all, it can be construed to make her point about the sublimation of sex into 'heads.' Does she forget the poem so as to forget her already inscribed place in Freud's text? her own complicity in the dream symmetry she decries? Is she not reducing Freud to a single discourse, thus making his text more phallic, more centred? Perhaps any text can be read as either body (site of contradictory drives and heterogeneous matter) or Law? The exclusion of the Heine poem serves to place Freud more firmly on the side of the Law, which enables Irigaray to be more firm, more certain of her position against him. To be against the Law is to be outside the Law. But to be against a body is a more ambiguous, unsettling position.

In Heine's 'Questions' a youth asks the sea to answer 'life's hidden riddle, the riddle primeval and painful.' He asks specifically: 'Tell me, what signifies man? From whence doth he come? And where doth he go?' There is no answer, only the murmuring of the sea. The poem then ends with the line: 'And a fool is awaiting the answer.'[4]

At the beginning of the section called 'Questions' in *Ce Sexe*, Irigaray writes: 'Since the writing and publication of *Speculum*, many questions have been asked. And this book is, in a way, a collection of questions. It does not "really" answer them. It pursues their questioning. It continues to interrogate' (p. 119). The fool waits for an answer. Irigaray is not interested in the answer. She pursues a cease-less questioning which has not time and is not foolish enough to wait for an answer.

The first part of Irigaray's 'Questions' takes place in a philosophy seminar, where, in response to *Speculum*, she has been invited as 'authority on women,' for the students to ask her questions. The situation is somewhat analogous to that of 'Femininity,' in which Freud is lecturing on women, professing about women, allowing the audience to learn from his expertise. Tied up in this dialectic of questions and answers is the problematic of 'authority on women.' To have a theory of woman is already to reduce the plurality of woman to the coherent and thus phallocentric representations of theory. Irigaray, as professor of woman, is in the role of 'subject of theory,' subject theorizing, a role appropriate to the masculine. She is in Freud's role, dreaming his dream. How can she avoid it without simply giving up speaking, leaving authority to men and phallocentrism?

She begins the transcribed seminar with this introduction: 'There are questions that I don't really see how I could answer. In any case "simply"' (*Ce Sexe*, p. 120). She can respond to a question, give associations, keep talking, hopefully continue to interrogate. But she 'doesn't see,' has a blind spot which she exposes: her in-ability to give a 'simple' answer, a unified, definitive answer, the kind valorized by an ideology of well-framed representation. She is inadequate to a phallo-morphic answer. The phallus is singular ('simple'), represents a unified self, as opposed to the indefinite plurality of female genitalia (clitoris, vagina, lips—how many?, cervix, breasts—Irigaray is fond of making the list, which never has quite the same elements, never is 'simply' finished).

'In other words,' she continues, 'I don't know how to conduct here some *renversement* [overthrow/reversal] of the pedagogic relation in which, holding a truth about woman, a theory of woman, I could answer your questions: answer for woman in front of you.' The pedagogic relation expects her as 'authority' to have a 'truth,' a 'theory' which would allow her to 'simply' answer. She would then 'answer for woman,' speak for her not as her. Woman would be the subject-matter, the material of her discourse. She would trade woman, just as women have always been 'merchandise' in a commerce between men. Woman is passed from the hands of the father to the husband, from the pimp to the john, from the pro-fessor to the student who asks questions about the riddle of femininity.

There is a certain pederasty implicit in pedagogy. A greater man penetrates a lesser man with his knowledge. The *homo*sexuality means that both are measur-able by the same standards, by which measure one is greater than the other. Irigaray uncovers a sublimated male homosexuality structuring all our institutions: pedagogy, marriage, commerce, even Freud's theory of so-called heterosexuality. Those structures necessarily exclude women, but are unquestioned because sublimated—raised from suspect homosexuality to secure homology, to the sexu-ally indifferent *logos*, science, logic.

But what of Irigaray's phrase: 'I don't know how to conduct here some *renversement* of the pedagogic relation'? Again she is admitting, from the position of supposed knowledge, her inadequacy—'I don't know.' That already is a rever-sal of the pedagogic relation. The teacher 'knows,' the student does not. But what Irigaray does not know is how to reverse the relation, how to get out of the posi-tion of authority. Her lack of knowledge is specifically her inability to speak her lack of knowledge, her inability to make a non-phallic representation. Of course there is also the sense that a woman in the role of authority is already a reversal. But she cannot carry off that reversal, cannot profess about women, cannot 'simply' theorize. 'Renversement' means both 'reversal' and 'overthrow.' The pedagogic relation ought to be overthrown, but this subversion tends to be a reversal, which would bring us back to the same. If men and women, teachers and students switched places, there would still be an economy of symmetry, in which the knowledge of the one, the theory of the one, was the gauge for measuring the worth of the other, still no dialogue between two different sexes, knowledges, only a homologue with one side lacking what the other has.

'I will thus not bring definitions into a questioned discourse.' She does not know what to do to bring about an upset of the pedagogic, pederastic relation, but she can decide what not to do. She refuses definitions, definiteness which fixes plurality into unified representations. She will not bring definitions from outside into a 'questioned discourse.' The process of questioning is a specific dialectic shattering stable assumptions and producing contextual associations. To bring in ready-made definitions as answer to questions is not really to allow one's discourse or authority to be called into question. Such prepared answers are not part of a specific dialogue, but simply immutable truth that is unaffected by dialogue. That sort of relation—the mocked-up, artificial, Socratic dialogue of pedagogy with the 'answer' prior to and independent of the question and the questioning—denies any possibility of an unsettling contact with the questioner's otherness, one that might affect definition. Good pedagogic definition remains aloof from the situation, free from the desires of student and teacher, free from desire, sexually indifferent. Irigaray's uncertain, indeterminate attempt to respond to questions without giving definitive answers thus attempts really to engage the questions, to dialogue with something *hetero* (other) rather than being trapped in the *homo* (same).

Compare Irigaray's seminar to Freud's situation in the 'lecture' on femininity. First, there is the difference between lecture and seminar, the seminar supposedly implying a plurality of contribution, whereas the lecture divides into speaker presumed to have knowledge and listeners presumed to learn—to be lacking in knowledge.[5] But as Irigaray reminds us in the first footnote of *Speculum*, 'Femininity' is a fictive lecture. In the preface to the *New Introductory Lectures*, Freud writes: 'These new lectures . . . have never been delivered. . . . If, therefore, I once more take my place in the lecture room, it is only by an artifice of the imagination; it may help me not to forget to bear the reader in mind as I enter more deeply into my subject.'

As he 'enters more deeply into his subject,' in this case as he 'enters more deeply' into woman, he needs an 'artifice of the imagination,' a fantasy that he is really communicating not just trapped in his own sameness. Freud fantasizes the lecture hall so as to conjure up the comforting pederastic relation as he penetrates into femininity. Whereas Irigaray will not give answers, and publishes the questions posed by others, Freud, with the exception of the Heine fragment and its hidden questions, writes from an imaginary dialogue in which otherness is simply a fantasy, an artificial projection. Such is, according to Irigaray, the so-called heterosexual encounter: man's relation is only to his imaginary other; femininity is no more encountered as otherness and difference than in Freud's audience.

Irigaray takes Freud's fictive lecture and forces it into a dialogic context. She becomes the reader, not Freud's imagined reader, but an impertinent questioner. Although Freud begins his lecture 'Ladies and Gentlemen,' a few pages later (right after the Heine poem and its shift of emphasis from woman to man), he says: 'Nor will you have escaped worrying over this problem, because *you* are men; as for the *women among you* this will not apply, *they* are themselves this riddle' (my italics). When he explicitly addresses the audience as sexed beings, he reserves the second person pronoun for men, and refers to women with the third person pronoun. Freud talks *to* men *about* women. I have provided my own translation because Strachey's translation (*NIL*, p. 113) covers over this telling inequity in Freud's text, using the second person pronoun for both sexes. Irigaray's 'impertinence' is her assumption of the place of Freud's interlocutor, an exclusively male position. As a woman, this lecture does not speak to her, only about her. But she speaks up, responds, breaking the homosexual symmetry.

Irigaray impertinently asks a few questions, as if the student, the women, the reader were not merely a lack waiting to be filled with Freud's knowledge, but a real interlocutor, a second viewpoint. And in her questions a certain desire comes through, not a desire for a 'simple answer,' but for an encounter, a hetero-sexual dialogue. Not in the customary way we think heterosexual—the dream of symmetry, two opposite sexes complementing each other. In that dream the woman/student/reader ends up functioning as mirror, giving back a coherent, framed representation to the appropriately masculine subject. There is no real sexuality of the *heteros*. 'Will there ever be any relation between the sexes?'—asks Irigaray (*Speculum*, p. 33).

Irigaray's reading of Freud seeks that 'relation between the sexes.' Her aggression is not merely some man-hating, penis-envying urge to destroy the phallocentric oppressor. She lays fiery siege to the Phallus, out of a yearning to get beyond its prohibitiveness and touch some masculine body. It is the rule of the Phallus as standard for any sexuality which denigrates women, and makes any relation between the sexes impossible, any relation between two modalities of desire, between two desires unthinkable. The rule of the Phallus is the reign of the One, of Unicity. In the 'phallic phase,' according to Freud, 'only one kind of genital organ comes into account—the male.'[6] Freud, man, is arrested in the phallic phase, caught in the reign of the One, obsessively trying to tame otherness in a mirror-image of sameness.

In the transcribed seminar, Irigaray says: 'What I desire and what I am waiting for, is what men will do and say if their sexuality gets loose from the empire of phallocratism' (*Ce Sexe*, pp. 133–4). The masculine exists no more than does the feminine. The specificity of both is suppressed by the reign of the Idea, the Phallus. Freud is not without a certain awareness of this. Something like the trace of a non-phallic masculinity can be read in a footnote that appears a few sentences after his statement about 'one kind of genital organ': 'It is remarkable, by the way, what a small degree of interest the other part of the male genitals, the little sac with its contents, arouses in the child. From all one hears in analyses one could not guess that the male genitals consist of anything more than the penis.' 'By the way,' in a remark marginal to the central thrust of his argument can be found that which must be left aside by phallocentrism. Yet it is precisely because of the anatomical discrepancies in 'all one hears in analysis' that analysis can be the place where the untenable reductions that constitute the reign of the phallus are most noticeable.

The difference, of course, between the phallic suppression of masculinity and the phallic suppression of femininity is that the phallic represents (even if inaccurately) the masculine and not the feminine. By giving up their bodies, men gain power—the power to theorize, to represent themselves, to exchange women, to reproduce themselves and mark their offspring with their name. All these activities ignore bodily pleasure in pursuit of representation, reproduction, production. 'In this "phallocratic" power, man is not without loss: notably in regard to the enjoyment of his body' (*Ce Sexe*, p. 140).

Irigaray's reading of Freud's theory continually discovers an ignoring of pleasure. The theory of sexuality is a theory of the sexual function (ultimately the reproductive function) and questions of pleasure are excluded, because they have no place in an economy of production. Commenting on Freud's discussion of breast-feeding, Irigaray remarks: 'Every consideration of pleasure in nursing appears here to be excluded, unrecognized, prohibited. That, certainly, would introduce some nuances in such statements' (*Speculum*, p. 13). A consideration of pleasure would introduce a few nuances into the theory ('nuance,' from *nue*, cloud). A consideration of pleasure might cloud the theory, cloud the view, reduce its ability to penetrate with clarity, to appropriate. The distinction of active and passive roles becomes more ambiguous when it is a question of pleasure. And it is the distinction active/passive which is in question in Freud's discussion of nursing.

Freud writes: 'A mother is active in every sense towards the child; the act of nursing itself may equally be described as the mother suckling the baby or as her being sucked by it' (*NIL*, p. 115). The sentence seems contradictory. If a mother is so clearly 'active in every sense,' why is the only example chosen so easily interpretable as either active or passive? The difficulty is symptomatic of one of the most insistent problems for Freud—the relation of the dichotomies active/passive and masculine/feminine. According to Freud, the opposition active/passive characterizes the anal phase, whereas masculine/feminine is the logic of adult sexuality. In this discussion of the mother Freud is trying to show how improper it is to identify feminine with passive, masculine with active, since a mother is clearly feminine and clearly active. Again and again in different books and articles over a span of twenty years,[7] Freud will try to differentiate and articulate the anal dichotomy and the adult sexual opposition. Without much success.

In 'Femininity' Freud refers to the confusion of these two oppositions as 'the error of superimposition.' The footnote to the English translation indicates that such an error consists in 'mistaking two different things for a single one' (*NIL*, p. 115). Thus 'the error of superimposition' is emblematic of what Irigaray finds as the general 'error' of Freud's sexual theory—mistaking two different sexes for a single one.

In the French translation of the text,[8] 'Überdeckungsfehler' ('the error of superimposition') becomes 'l'erreur de raisonnement analogique,' 'the error of analogical reasoning.' The specific superimposition in this text is both analogical and anal-logical. Anal logic organizes everything according to the opposition active/passive. The phrase 'analogical reasoning' ties the whole problematic of defining sexual difference in a non-anal logic to another persistent embarrassment. For Freud, analogy is dangerously seductive. In 1905 he writes: 'Shall we not *yield to the temptation* to construct [the formation of a joke] on the analogy of the formation of a dream?' In 1937: 'I have not been able to *resist the seduction* of an analogy.'[9] Is not the guilty compulsion to analogy symptomatic of Freud's inability to escape anal logic?

Irigaray suggests that Freud's model of sexuality has a strong anal erotic bias. The faeces become other products (a baby, a penis, a representation, a theory)[10] but the emphasis is on the product. Why else would the ambiguous nursing (describable in either active or passive terms) be so clearly an 'activity'? Indeed breast-feeding constitutes the model of the Freudian oral phase, which is defined as prior to the opposition active/passive. Freud's anal logic thus even intrudes into the very stage defined as pre-anal. In this case, the inconsistency cannot be explained as a legacy in a later stage from the earlier anal period. We are faced with the anal fixation of the theory itself.

An accusation of contradiction could be levelled at this point. Earlier in the present text Freud has been deemed 'arrested in the phallic phase.' Now he is judged 'arrested' in the anal phase. It is not a question of resolving this contradiction, of fixing the diagnosis of Freud's personal pathology. Freud himself acknowleged that the stages of development are not clearly separate and distinct. The attempt to isolate each stage could be considered an effect to reduce sexuality to only one modality at any given moment, symptomatic of the rule of the One.

The investment in unicity, in one sexuality, shows itself in Freud's description of the little girl 'in the phallic phase.' (Of course, the very assimilation of the girl into a *phallic* phase is already a sign of 'an error of superimposition,' analogical reasoning.) Freud insists that, in the phallic phase, little girls only get pleasure from their clitoris and are unfamiliar with the rest of their genitalia. (Remember the phallic phase is characterized as recognizing only one kind of sexual organ.) Yet others have found girls at this stage aware of vaginal sensations, and Freud dismisses this peremptorily as well as somewhat contradictorily: 'It is true that there are a few isolated reports of early vaginal sensations as well, but it could not be easy to distinguish these from sensations in the anus or vestibulum; *in any case they cannot play a great part.* We are *entitled to keep our view* that in the phallic phase of girls the clitoris is the leading erotogenic zone' (*NIL*, p. 118, italics mine). Why 'can they not play a great part'? Because then 'we' would not be 'entitled to keep our *view*,' keep our *theoria*. Entitled by what or whom? The blind spot is obvious; what must be protected is 'our view,' appropriate to the masculine.

Freud insists on reducing the little girl's genitalia to her clitoris because that organ fits 'our view,' is phallomorphic, can be measured by the same standard (*summetros*). 'We are now obliged to recognize that the little girl is a little man' (*NIL*, p. 118), declares Freud, making the phallocentric pederastic economy clear. The girl is assimilated to a male model, male history and, 'naturally,' found lacking. The condition of that assimilation is the reduction of any possible complexity, plural sexuality, to the one, the simple, in this case to the phallomorphic clitoris.

Once reduced to phallomorphic measures, woman is defined as 'really castrated,' by Freud/man. As such she is the guarantee against man's castration anxiety. She has no desires that don't complement his, so she can mirror him, provide him with a representation of himself which calms his fears and phobias about (his own potential) otherness and difference, about some 'other view' which might not support his narcissistic overinvestment in his penis. 'As for woman, *on peut se demander* [one could wonder, ask oneself] why she submits so easily . . . to the counter-phobic projects, projections, productions of man relative to his desire' (*Speculum*, p. 61).

The expression for wondering, for speculation, which Irigaray uses above, is the reflexive verb 'se demander,' literally 'to ask oneself.' Most of the 'impertinent questions' in *Speculum* seem to be addressed to Freud, or men, or the reader. But this question of woman's easy submission she must ask herself. And the answer is not so obvious. A little later, she attempts to continue this line of questioning: 'And why does she lend herself to it so easily? Because she's suggestible? Hysterical? But one can catch sight of the vicious circle' (*Speculum*, p. 69). This question of the complicity, the suggestibility of the hysteric who 'finally says in analysis [what is not] foreign to what she is expected to say there' (*Speculum*, p. 64) leads us to the contemplation of another vicious circle—the (hysterical) daughter's relationship to the father (of psychoanalysis).

The daughter's desire for her father is desperate: 'the only redemption of her value as a girl would be to seduce the father, to draw from him the mark if not the admission of some interest' (*Speculum*, p. 106). If the phallus is the standard of value, then the Father, possessor of the phallus, must desire the daughter in order to give her value. But the Father is a man (a little boy in the anal, the phallic phase) and cannot afford to desire otherness, an other sex, because that opens up his castration anxiety. The father's refusal to seduce the daughter, to be seduced by her (seduction wreaking havoc with anal logic and its active/passive distribution), gains him another kind of seduction (this one more one-sided, more like violation), a veiled seduction in the form of the law. The daughter submits to the father's rule, which prohibits the father's desire, the father's penis, out of the desire to seduce the father by doing his bidding and thus pleasing him.

That is the vicious circle. The daughter desires a heterosexual encounter with the father, and is rebuffed by the rule of the homo-logical, raising the homo over the hetero, the logical over the sexual, decreeing neither the hetero nor the sexual worthy of the father. Irigaray would like really to respond to Freud, provoke him into a real dialogue. But the only way to seduce the father, to avoid scaring him away, is to please him, and to please him one must submit to his law which proscribes any sexual relation.

Patriarchal law, the law of the father, decrees that the 'product' of sexual union, the child, shall belong exclusively to the father, be marked with his name. Also that the womb which bears that child should be a passive receptacle with no claims on the product, the womb 'itself possessed as a means of (re)production' (*Speculum*, p. 16). Irigaray understands woman's exclusion from production via a reading of Marx and Engels which she brings in as a long association near the end of her reading of Freud's dream. That exclusion of the woman is inscribed in her relation to the father. Any feminist upheaval, which would change woman's definition, identity, name as well as the foundations of her economic status, must undo the vicious circle by which the desire for the father's desire (for his penis) causes her to submit to the father's law, which denies his desire/penis, but operates in its place, and according to Irigaray, even procures for him a surplus of pleasure.

The question of why woman complies must be asked. To ask that question is to ask what woman must not do anymore, what feminist strategy ought to be. Only a fool would wait for an answer, deferring the struggle against phallocentrism until a definitive explanation were found. In lieu of that 'answer,' I would like slowly to trace a reading of a section of *Speculum* which concerns the father and the daughter, in this case specifically the father of psychoanalysis and his hysterics, but also the father of psychoanalytic theory and his daughter Irigaray.

Irigaray reads in Freud an account of an episode from the beginnings of psychoanalysis which *'caused [him] many distressing hours'* (Irigaray's italics)" 'In the period in which the main interest was directed to discovering infantile sexual traumas, almost all my woman patients told me that they had been seduced by their father. I was driven to recognize in the end, that these reports were untrue and so came to understand that hysterical symptoms are derived from phantasies and not from real occurrences' (*NIL*, p. 120; *Speculum*, p. 40). Irigaray suggests that the reader 'imagine that x, of the masculine gender, of a ripe age, uses the following language, how would you interpret it: "it caused me many distressing hours," "almost all *my* woman patients told *me* that they had been seduced by *their father.*"' Irigaray invites her reader to interpret Freud. She does not offer a definitive reading, closing the text, making it her property, but only notes those phrases which seem interpretable, drawing the rebus but not giving the solution, so as to induce her reader to play analyst.

'And let us leave the interpretation to the discretion of each analyst, be she/he improvised for the occasion. It would even be desirable if she/he were, otherwise he/she would risk having already been seduced, whatever her/his sex, or her/his gender, by the *father* of psychoanalysis' (pp. 40–1, Irigaray's italics). The reader is considered an analyst and capable of his/her own interpretation. But Irigaray recognizes that 'the analyst' in question may not 'really' be a psychoanalyst, but rather be the recipient of a sort of battlefield promotion, prepared only by the experience of reading Freud with Irigaray. *Speculum* becomes a 'training analysis,' the reading of it preparing the reader to make her/his own interpretations. And the analyst trained by *Speculum* is likely to be a better analyst of Freud than a proper psychoanalyst, for any analyst—male or female, masculine or feminine, *Irigaray herself*—is likely to have been seduced by Freud, seduced by his theory.

There is a contrast here between two different kinds of analyst. The one privileged by Irigaray is an amateur, a 'wild analyst,'[11] not 'entitled' to analyze, but simply a reader, who can catch symptoms and make her/his own interpretations. The other sort of analyst is a professional, which is to say has investments in analysis as an identity and an economically productive system, and a transference onto Freud, that is, a belief in Freud's knowledge. The analyst is likely to 'see' according to Freud's theory, having been seduced into sharing 'our view,' giving a predictable 'Freudian' interpretation, one that always hears according to the same standards, returning every text to pre-existent Freudian models, 'bringing definitions into a discourse from outside.' Irigaray as an analyst is perhaps not as likely to give an attentive, specific interpretation as is her reader. So that, once again, as in the *Ce Sexe* seminar, she proceeds to some sort of overthrow of a certain hierarchy between theoretical writer as distributor of knowledge and reader as passive, lacking consumer.

But certain questions pose themselves to this reader at this point. Can Irigaray really overthrow the pedagogic relation, or is this merely a ruse to flatter the reader into less resistance, a ploy to seduce her reader? For she *does* go on to interpret, simply having deferred it for a few sentences. As in an artificial, Socratic (pederastic) dialogue, if she asks the reader to think for him/her self, that reader will produce an answer which the teacher expected all along, the right answer. Like Freud in the *New Introductory Lectures*, Irigaray is fantasizing a reader, one who would make the same associations as she does, one created in her own image.

It is thus interesting that at this point Irigaray is reasoning by analogy—Freud : hysteric :: father : daughter :: Freud : any other psychoanalyst. Analogy, as Irigaray has said, is one of the 'eternal operations' which support the defining of difference in function of the a priori of the same' (*Speculum*, p. 28). The analogy of analyst to father is the analytic analogy *par excellence*, the fact of transference. Transference is the repetition of infantile prototype relations, of unconscious desires in the analytic relation. Without transference, psychoanalysis is simply literary criticism, by an unimplicated, discriminating reader, lacking either affect or effect.

The example of *the* analytic analogy suggests a way of overturning the phallocentric effects of analogy. Analogy cannot simply be avoided, it is radically tempting. Transference occurs everywhere, not just in psychoanalysis but in any relation where the other is 'presumed to know,' relations to teachers, loved ones, doctors. But psychoanalysis provides the opportunity to analyze the transference, take cognizance of it as such and work it through. Likewise Irigaray's use of analogy in a context where analogy has been analyzed provides a way of making the economic function of analogy evident. The phallocentric effect of analogy would be explicit, and thus less powerful.

Her use of analogy as well as her projection of a reader in her own image, a narcissistic mirror, means she has acceded to a certain economy of the homo . . . and the auto . . . , the economy which men have and women are excluded from. Of course, the 'answer' is not to set up another homosexual economy, but that may be necessary as one step to some hetero-sexuality. 'Of course, it is not a question, in the final analysis, of demanding the *same* attributions. Still it is necessary that women arrive at the same so that consideration be made, be imposed of the differences that they would elicit there' (*Speculum*, pp. 148–9). Women need to reach the 'same': that is, be 'like men,' able to represent themselves. But they also need to reach 'the same,' 'the homo': their own homosexual economy, a female homosexuality that ratifies and glorifies female standards. The two 'sames' are inextricably linked. Female homosexuality, when raised to an ideology, tends to be either masculine (women that are 'like men') or essentialistic (based on some ascertainable female identity). The latter is as phallic as the former for it reduces heterogeneity to a unified, rigid representation. But without a female homosexual economy, a female narcissistic ego, a way to represent herself, a woman in a heterosexual encounter will always be engulfed by the male homosexual economy, will not be able to represent her difference. Woman must demand 'the same,' 'the homo' and then not settle for it, not fall into the trap of thinking a female 'homo' is necessarily any closer to a representation of otherness, an opening for the other.

Yet having posed these questions of Irigaray's own imaginary economy, I might also say she was right about her reader. Her fantasized reader would be the impertinent questioner she is. I am asking Irigaray Irigarayan questions, reopening the interrogation when Luce becomes too tight, when she seems to settle on an answer. I have been seduced into a transference onto her, into following her suggestion, into saying 'what is not foreign to what I am expected to say,' into playing 'wild analysis.'

'This seduction,' she continues, 'is covered of course, in practice or theory, by a normative statement, by a *law*, which denies it.' A new element is introduced by Irigaray and emphasized: the law. This term, foreign to the Freud passage she is reading, not suggested by him, is Irigaray's own association, her remaining in excess of the Freudian seduction. 'Law' is a political term, refers to patriarchy, the law of the father, and here will refer to Freud's legislative control of his theory, his normative prescriptions.

Her text continues with another sentence from Freud: 'It was only later that I was able to recognize in the phantasy of being seduced by the father *the expression of the typical Oedipus complex* in women' (*NIL*, p. 120; *Speculum*, p. 41, Irigaray's italics). The seduction by the father is not only a mere fantasy, but is the manifestation of a typical complex, one that is supposed to be universal, and therefore a law of Freudian theory. Given Irigaray's introduction to this passage, we read that the Oedipus complex, the incest taboo, the law forbidding intercourse between father and daughter, covers over a seduction, masks it so it goes unrecognized. Also covered over is a seduction in the theory, whereby psychoanalysts through their transference onto Freud (their unfulfillable desire for his love and approval) accept his immutable theoretical laws.

'It would be too risky, it seems, to admit that the father could be a seducer, and even eventually that he desires to have a daughter *in order* to seduce her. That he wishes to become an analyst in order to exercise by hypnosis, suggestion, transference, interpretation bearing on the sexual economy, on the proscribed, prohibited sexual representations, a *lasting seduction upon the hysteric*' (Irigaray's italics) (p. 41). Freud as a father must deny the possibility of being seductive. Patriarchy is grounded in the uprightness of the father. If he were devious and unreliable, he could not have the power to legislate. The law is supposed to be just—that is, impartial, indifferent, free from desire.

'It is necessary to endure the law which exculpates the operation. But, of course, if under cover of the law the seduction can now be practised at leisure, it appears just as urgent to interrogate *the seductive function of the law itself*' (Irigaray's italics) (p. 41). For example, the law which prohibits sexual intercourse between analyst and patient actually makes the seduction last forever. The sexually actualized seduction would be complicitous, nuanced, impossible to delineate into active and passive roles, into the anal logic so necessary for a traditional distribution of wealth and power. But the 'lasting seduction' of the law is never consummated and as such maintains the power of the prohibited analyst. The seduction which the daughter desires would give her contact with the father as masculine sexed body. The seduction which the father of psychoanalysis exercises refuses her his body, his penis, and asks her to embrace his law, his indifference, his phallic uprightness.

Psychoanalysis works because of the tranference, which is to say because the hysteric transfers her desire to seduce her father, to be seduced by him, onto her analyst. But since the fantasy of seducing the father is produced in analysis, it is produced for the analyst. In order to please him, in order to seduce him, in order to give him what he wants. The installation of the law in psychoanalysis, the prohibition of the analyst's penis by the Doctor in a position to validate the hysteric, to announce her as healthy, sets up the desperate situation outlined by Irigaray: 'the only redemption of her value as a girl would be to seduce the father' (*Speculum*, p. 106).

'Thus is it not simply true, nor on the other hand completely false, to claim that the little girl fantasizes being seduced by her father, because it is just as pertinent to admit that *the father seduces his daughter* but that, refusing to recognize and realize his desire—not always it is true—'*he legislates to defend himself from it*' (*Speculum*, p. 41, Irigaray's italics). The father's law is a counterphobic mechanism. He must protect himself from his desire for the daughter. His desire for the feminine threatens his narcissistic overvaluation of his penis. It is so necessary to deny his attraction for the little girl that Freud denies her existence: 'We must admit that the little girl is a little man.' If the father were to desire his daughter he could no longer exchange her, no longer possess her in the economy by which true, masterful possession is the right to exchange. If you cannot give something up for something of like value, if you consider it nonsubstitutable, then you do not possess it any more than it possesses you. So the father must not desire the daughter for that threatens to remove him from the homosexual commerce in which women are exchanged between men, in the service of power relations and community for the men.

Also: if the father desires his daughter as daughter he will be outside his Oedipal desire for his mother, which is to say also beyond 'the phallic phase.' So the law of the father protects him and patriarchy from the potential havoc of the daughter's desirability. Were she recognized as desirable in her specificity as daughter, not as son ('little man') nor as mother, there would be a second sexual economy besides the one between 'phallic little boy' and 'phallic mother.' An economy in which the stake might not be a reflection of the phallus, the phallus's desire for itself.

'In place of the desire for the sexed body of the father there thus comes *to be proposed, to be imposed, his law*, that is to say an institutionalizing and institutionalized discourse. In part, defensive (Think of those "distressing hours." . . .)' (pp. 41–2, Irigaray's italics). The father gives his daughter his law and protects himself from her desire for his body, protects himself from his body. For it is only the law—and not the body—which constitutes him as patriarch. Paternity is corporeally uncertain, without evidence. But patriarchy compensates for that with the law which marks each child with the father's name as his exclusive property.

'That is not to say that the father *should* make love with his daughter—from time to time it is better to state things precisely—but that it would be good to call into question this mantle of the law with which he drapes his desire, and his sex (organ)' (p. 42, Irigaray's italics). The strategic difference between a prescriptive 'should' and a suggestive 'it would be good' is emphasized by this sentence. But suggestion may have always been a more devious, more powerful mode of prescription.

'It would be good' to question the law's appearance of indifference, as Irigaray questions it, and find the phallic stake behind it. 'It would be good' to lift 'the mantle of the law' so that the father's desire and his penis are exposed. But that does not mean the 'answer' is for the father to make love to his daughter. Irigaray, above all, avoids giving an answer, a prescription such as 'the father *should* make love with his daughter.' Not that he might not, not that it might not be a way to lift the law and expose the sexed body. The 'should' is underlined, because that is what Irigaray will not say. She will not lay down a law about how to lift the law.

If she did lay down such a law—'the father should make love with his daughter'—it would, like all laws, mask and support a desire. The negated appearance of this law suggests the mechanism Freud called *Verneinung*—'Procedure whereby the subject, while formulating one of his wishes, thoughts or feelings which has been repressed hitherto, contrives, by disowning it, to continue to defend himself against it.'[12] What surfaces that Irigaray needs to disown is her desire to impose the law upon the father, her desire for a simple reversal rather than an overthrow of patriarchy.

This sentence is marked as symptomatic, asking for analysis, by the parenthetical remark, 'from time to time it is better to state things precisely.' 'From time to time' pretends this is a random moment; it just happens to fall at this moment that she will be precise. But this is the only such remark in all of her reading of Freud; this is the point where she is most afraid of a misunderstanding. Her desire to be precise is in direct contradiction to something she says later in *Speculum* about feminist strategies of language: 'No clear nor univocal statement can, in fact, dissolve this mortgage, this obstacle, all of them being caught, trapped, in the same reign of credit. It is as yet better to speak only through equivocations, allusions, innuendos, parables. . . . Even if you are asked for some *précisions* [precise details]' (*Speculum*, p. 178). All clear statements are trapped in the same economy of values, in which clarity (oculocentrism) and univocity (the One) reign. Precision must be avoided, if the economy of the One is to be unsettled. Equivocations, allusions, etc. are all flirtatious; they induce the interlocutor to listen, to encounter, to interpret, but defer the moment of assimilation back into a familiar model. Even if someone asks for *précisions*, even if that someone is oneself, it is better for women to avoid stating things precisely.

Yet on one point Luce Irigaray tightens up, prefers to be precise, to return to an economy of clarity and univocity. The locus of her conservatism, her caution, her need to defend herself, is the question of making love with the father. It is terrifying to lift the mantle of the law and encounter the father's desire. What if in making love the father still remained the law, and the daughter were just passive, denied? The father's law has so restructured the daughter and her desires that it is hard, well nigh impossible, to differentiate the Father (that is to say, the Law) from the male sexed body. What if making love with the father were merely a ruse to get the impertinent daughter to give up her resistance to the law?

Irigaray clutches for something stable, something precise, because she too is a 'subject,' with a stake in identity. And the law of the father gives her an identity, even if it is not her own, even if it blots out her feminine specificity. To give it up is not a 'simple' matter. It must be done over and over.

Later she will say of her method in *Speculum*, 'what was left for me to do was to *have an orgy with the philosophers*' (*Ce Sexe*, p. 147, Irigaray's italics). Intercourse with the philosophers, the father of psychoanalysis included, is her method of insinuation into their system, of inducing them to reveal the phallocentrism, the desire cloaked in their sexual indifference. Perhaps these are merely two different moments in her inconsistency: a brave, new, loose moment—'have an orgy with the philosophers'—and a defensive, cautious moment—refusal to make love with the father.

But perhaps these are not merely two moments. The two situations are *analogous, but not the same*. Some terms may be more frightening, more sensitive than others. 'Father' may be more threatening than 'philosophers.' She writes in *Ce Sexe*: 'As far as the family is concerned, *my answer will be simple* and clear: the family has always been the privileged locus of the exploitation of women. Thus, as far as familialism is concerned, there is no ambiguity!' (pp. 139–40, my italics). Yet earlier in the same text she says she cannot give a 'simple answer.' Also: 'faire l'amour' (make love) may be more threatening than 'faire la noce' (have an orgy). Maybe what frightens her is not seduction of the father or by the father but 'making love.' 'Love' has always been sublimated, idealized desire, away from the bodily specificity and towards dreams of complementarity, and the union of opposites, difference resolved into the One. 'Love' is entangled with the question of woman's complicity; it may be the bribe which has persuaded her to agree to her own exclusion. It may be historically necessary to be momentarily blind to father-love; it may be politically effective to defend—tightly, unlucidly—against its inducements, in order for a 'relation between the sexes,' in order to rediscover some feminine desire, some desire for a masculine body that does not respect the Father's law.

NOTES

1. Sigmund Freud, *New Introductory Lectures on Psycho-Analysis, Standard Edition*, vol. XXII, pp. 10–11. Hereafter referred to as *NIL*.

2. Shoshana Felman. 'To Open the Question,' *Literature and Psychoanalysis: The Question of Reading: Otherwise, Yale French Studies*, 55–6 (1977) p. 10. All italics Felman's except 'blind spot.'

3. Luce Irigaray, *Ce Sexe qui n'en est pas un* (Éditions de Minuit, 1477). In this context of questions it is interesting to notice Felman's titles: 'The Question of Reading,' 'To Open the Question.'

4. *The Poems of Heine, Complete*, trans. Edgar Alfred Bowring (G. Bell and Sons, 1916) p. 260.

5. Is then the ironic lesson of Jacques Lacan's 'Seminars,' which are enormous lectures, in which he functions as the only and ultimate 'subject presumed to know,' that a seminar is always merely a disguised lecture, that one does not know how to overthrow the pedagogic relation?

6. Freud, 'The Infantile Genital Organization,' *Standard Edition*, vol. XIX, p. 142.

7. The most glaring of these symptomatic attempts to disengage the anal definitions

from the genital can be found in a 1915 footnote to the third of Freud's *Three Essays on the Theory of Sexuality*; a footnote to Chapter 4 of *Civilization and its Discontents* (1930); and here in 'Femininity' (1933).

8. *Nouvelles Conférences sur la psychanalyse* (Gallimard, Collection Idées). This is the edition Irigaray uses.

9. The first quotation is from *Jokes and their Relation to the Unconscious*, the second from 'Constructions in Analysis.' The italics in both are mine.

10. Freud provides the model for metaphorization of faeces in 'On Transformations of Instinct as Exemplified in Anal Erotism' (1917), *Standard Edition*, vol. XVII.

11. The term is Freud's from his article on '"Wild" Psychoanalysis,' *Standard Edition*, vol. XI.

12. J. Laplanche and J. B. Pontalis, *The Language of Psycho-analysis*, p. 201.

WORKS CITED

Felman, Shoshana, 'To Open the Question,' *Yale French Studies* 55–6 (1978/79).

Freud, Sigmund, *Civilization and its Discontents, The Standard Edition of the Complete Psychological Works* (Hogarth Press, 1953–74) vol. XXI.

———, 'Constructions in Analysis,' *Standard Edition*, vol. XXIII.

———, 'Female Sexuality,' *Standard Edition*, vol. XXI.

———, 'The Infantile Genital Organization,' *Standard Edition*, vol. XIX.

———, 'Jokes and Their Relation to the Unconscious,' *Standard Edition*, vol. VIII.

———, *New Introductory Lectures on Psycho-Analysis, Standard Edition*, vol. XXII.

———, 'On Transformations of Instinct as Exemplified in Anal Erotism,' *Standard Edition*, vol. XVII.

———, '"Wild" Psychoanalysis,' *Standard Edition*, vol. XI.

Heine, Heinrich, *The Poems, Complete*, trans. Edgar Alfred Bowring (G. Bell and Sons, 1916).

Irigaray, Luce, *Ce Sexe qui n'en est pas un* (Éditions de Minuit, 1977).

———, *Speculum de l'autre femme* (Éditions de Minuit, 1974).

Lacan, Jacques, 'A la mémoire d'Ernest Jones: Sur sa théorie du symbolisme,' *Écrits* (Éditions du Seuil, 1966).

———, 'The Agency of the Letter in the Unconscious,' *Écrits: A Selection*, trans. Alan Sheridan (Tavistock and Norton, 1977).

———, 'La Chose freudienne,' *Écrits*.

———, 'The Freudian Thing,' *Écrits: A Selection*.

———, *The Four Fundamental Concepts of Psycho-Analysis*, trans. Alan Sheridan (Hogarth and Norton, 1976).

———, 'The Insistence of the Letter in the Unconscious,' trans. Jan Miel, *Structuralism* (Anchor Books, 1970).

———, 'L' Instance de la lettre dans l' inconscient,' *Écrits*.

———, 'Intervention sur le transfert,' *Écrits*.

———, 'Kant avec Sade,' *Écrits*.

———, 'The Mirror Stage,' *Écrits: A Selection*.

———, 'Position de l'inconscient,' *Écrits*.

———, 'Propos directifs pour un congrès sur la sexualité féminine,' *Écrits*.

INTRODUCTION FROM *BETWEEN MEN*

(1985)

I. HOMOSOCIAL DESIRE

The subject of this book is a relatively short, recent, and accessible passage of English culture, chiefly as embodied in the mid-eighteenth- to mid-nineteenth-century novel. The attraction of the period to theorists of many disciplines is obvious: condensed, self-reflective, and widely influential change in economic, ideological, and gender arrangements. I will be arguing that concomitant changes in the structure of the continuum of male "homosocial desire" were tightly, often causally bound up with the other more visible changes; that the emerging pattern of male friendship, mentorship, entitlement, rivalry, and hetero- and homosexuality was in an intimate and shifting relation to class; and that no element of that pattern can be understood outside of its relation to women and the gender system as a whole.

"Male homosocial desire": the phrase in the title of this study is intended to mark both discriminations and paradoxes. "Homosocial desire," to begin with, is a kind of oxymoron. "Homosocial" is a word occasionally used in history and the social sciences, where it describes social bonds between persons of the same sex; it is a neologism, obviously formed by analogy with "homosexual," and just as obviously meant to be distinguished from "homosexual." In fact, it is applied to such activities as "male bonding," which may, as in our society, be characterized by intense homophobia, fear and hatred of homosexuality.[1] To draw the "homosocial" back into the orbit of "desire," of the potentially erotic, then, is to hypothesize the potential unbrokenness of a continuum between homosocial and homosexual—a continuum whose visibility, for men, in our society, is radically disrupted. It will become clear, in the course of my argument, that my hypothesis of the unbrokenness of this continuum is not a *genetic* one—I do not mean to discuss genital homosexual desire as "at the root of" other forms of male homosociality—but rather a strategy for making generalizations about, and marking historical differences in, the *structure* of men's relations with other men. "Male homosocial desire" is the name this book will give to the entire continuum.

I have chosen the word "desire" rather than "love" to mark the erotic emphasis because, in literary critical and related discourse, "love" is more easily used to name a particular emotion, and "desire" to name a structure; in this study, a series of arguments about the structural permutations of social impulses fuels the critical dialectic. For the most part, I will be using "desire" in a way analogous to the psychoanalytic use of "libido"—not for a particular affective state or emotion, but for the affective or social force, the glue, even when its manifestation is hostility or hatred or something less emotively charged, that shapes an important relationship. How far this force is properly sexual (what, historically, it means for something to be "sexual") will be an active question.

The title is specific about *male* homosocial desire partly in order to acknowledge from the beginning (and stress the seriousness of) a limitation of my subject; but there is a more positive and substantial reason, as well. It is one of the main projects of this study to explore the ways in which the shapes of sexuality, and what *counts* as sexuality, both depend on and affect historical power relationships.[2] A corollary is that in a society where men and women differ in their access to power, there will be important gender differences, as well, in the structure and constitution of sexuality.

For instance, the diacritical opposition between the "homosocial" and the "homosexual" seems to be much less thorough and dichotomous for women, in our society, than for men. At this particular historical moment, an intelligible continuum of aims, emotions, and valuations links lesbianism with the other forms of women's attention to women: the bond of mother and daughter, for instance, the bond of sister and sister, women's friendship, "networking," and the active struggles of feminism.[3] The continuum is crisscrossed with deep discontinuities—with much homophobia, with conflicts of race and class—but its intelligibility seems now a matter of simple common sense. However agonistic the politics, however conflicted the feelings, it seems at this moment to make an obvious kind of sense to say that women in our society who love women, women who teach, study, nurture, suckle, write about, march for, vote for, give jobs to, or otherwise promote the interests of other women, are pursuing congruent and closely related activities. Thus the adjective "homosocial" as applied to women's bonds (by, for example, historian Carroll Smith-Rosenberg)[4] need not be pointedly dichotomized as against "homosexual"; it can intelligibly denominate the entire continuum.

The apparent simplicity—the unity—of the continuum between "women loving women" and "women promoting the interests of women," extending over the erotic, social, familial, economic, and political realms, would not be so striking if it were not in strong contrast to the arrangement among males. When Ronald Reagan and Jesse Helms get down to serious logrolling on "family policy," they are men promoting men's interests. (In fact, they embody Heidi Hartmann's definition of patriarchy: "relations between men, which have a material base, and which, though hierarchical, establish or create interdependence and solidarity among men that enable them to dominate women.")[5] Is their bond in any way congruent with the bond of a loving gay male couple? Reagan and Helms would say no—disgustedly. Most gay couples would say no—disgustedly. But why not? Doesn't the continuum between "men-loving-men" and "men-promoting-the-interests-of-men" have the same intuitive force that it has for women?

Quite the contrary: much of the most useful recent writing about patriarchal structures suggests that "obligatory heterosexuality" is built into male-dominated kinship systems, or that homophobia is a *necessary* consequence of such patriarchal institutions as heterosexual marriage.[6] Clearly, however convenient it might be to group together all the bonds that link males to males, and by which males enhance the status of males—usefully symmetrical as it would be, that grouping meets with a prohibitive structural obstacle. From the vantage point of our own society, at any rate, it has apparently been impossible to imagine a form of patriarchy that was not homophobic. Gayle Rubin writes, for instance, "The suppression of the homosexual component of human sexuality, and by corollary, the oppression of homosexuals, is . . . a product of the same system whose rules and relations oppress women."[7]

The historical manifestations of this patriarchal oppression of homosexuals have been savage and nearly endless. Louis Crompton makes a detailed case for describing the history as genocidal.[8] Our own society is brutally homophobic; and the homophobia directed against both males and females is not arbitrary or gratuitous, but tightly knit into the texture of family, gender, age, class, and race relations. Our society could not cease to be homophobic and have its economic and political structures remain unchanged.

Nevertheless, it has yet to be demonstrated that, because most patriarchies structurally include homophobia, therefore patriarchy structurally *requires* homophobia. K. J. Dover's recent study, *Greek Homosexuality*, seems to give a strong counter-example in classical Greece. Male homosexuality, according to Dover's evidence, was a widespread, licit, and very influential part of the culture. Highly structured along lines of class, and within the citizen class along lines of age, the pursuit of the adolescent boy by the older man was described by stereotypes that we associate with romantic heterosexual love (conquest, surrender, the "cruel fair," the absence of desire in the love object), with the passive part going to the boy. At the same time, however, because the boy was destined in turn to grow into manhood, the assignment of roles was not permanent.[9] Thus the love relationship, while temporarily oppressive to the object, had a strongly educational function; Dover quotes Pausanias in Plato's *Symposium* as saying "that it would be right for him [the boy] to perform any service for one who improves him in mind and character."[10] Along with its erotic component, then, this was a bond of mentorship; the boys were apprentices in the ways and virtues of Athenian citizenship, whose privileges they inherited. These privileges included the power to command the labor of slaves of both sexes, and of women of any class including their own. "Women and slaves belonged and lived together," Hannah Arendt writes. The system of sharp class and gender subordination was a necessary part of what the male culture valued most in itself: "Contempt for laboring originally [arose] out of a passionate striving for freedom from necessity and a no less passionate impatience with every effort that left no trace, no monument, no great work worthy to remembrance";[11] so the contemptible labor was left to women and slaves.

The example of the Greeks demonstrates, I think, that while heterosexuality is necessary for the maintenance of any patriarchy, homophobia, against males at any rate, is not. In fact, for the Greeks, the continuum between "men loving men" and "men promoting the interests of men" appears to have been quite seamless. It is as if, in our terms, there were no perceived discontinuity between the male bonds at the Continental Baths and the male bonds at the Bohemian Grove[12] or in the boardroom or Senate cloakroom.

It is clear, then, that there is an asymmetry in our present society between, on the one hand, the relatively continuous relation of female homosocial and homosexual bonds, and, on the other hand, the radically discontinuous relation of male homosocial and homosexual bonds. The example of the Greeks (and of other, tribal cultures, such as the New Guinea "Sambia" studies by G. H. Herdt) shows, in addition, that the structure of homosocial continuums is culturally contingent, not an innate feature of either "maleness" or "femaleness." Indeed, closely tied though it obviously is to questions of male vs. female power, the explanation will require a more exact mode of historical categorization than "patriarchy," as well, since patriarchal power structures (in Hartmann's sense) characterize both Athenian and American societies. Nevertheless, we may take as an explicit axiom that the historically differential shapes of male and female homosociality—much as they themselves may vary over time—will always be articulations and mechanisms of the enduring inequality of power between women and men.

Why should the different shapes of the homosocial continuum be an interesting question? Why should it be a *literary* question? Its importance for the practical politics of the gay movement as a minority rights movement is already obvious from the recent history of strategic and philosophical differences between lesbians and gay men. In addition, it is theoretically interesting partly as a way of approaching a larger question of "sexual politics": What does it mean—what difference does it make—when a social or political relationship is sexualized? If the relation of homosocial to homosexual bonds is so shifty, then what theoretical framework do we have for drawing any links between sexual and power relationships?

II. SEXUAL POLITICS AND SEXUAL MEANING

This question, in a variety of forms, is being posed importantly by and for the different gender-politics movements right now. Feminist along with gay male theorists, for instance, are disagreeing actively about how direct the relation is between power domination and sexual sadomasochism. Start with two arresting images: the naked, beefy motorcyclist on the front cover, or the shockingly battered nude male corpse on the back cover, of the recent so-called "Polysexuality" issue of *Semiotext(e)* (4, no. 1 [1981])—which, for all the women in it, ought to have been called the semisexuality issue of *Polytext*. It seemed to be a purpose of that issue to insist, and possibly not only for reasons of radical-chic titillation, that the violence imaged in sadomasochism is not mainly theatrical, but is fully continuous with violence in the real world. Women Against Pornography and the framers of the 1980 NOW Resolution on Lesbian and Gay Rights share the same view, but without the celebratory glamor: to them too it seems intuitively clear that to sexualize violence or an image of violence is simply to extend, unchanged, its reach and force.[13] But, as other feminist writers have reminded us another view is possible. For example: is a woman's masochistic sexual fantasy really only an internalization and endorsement, if not a cause, of her more general powerlessness and sense of worthlessness? Or may not the sexual drama stand in some more oblique, or even oppositional, relation to her political experience of oppression?[14]

The debate in the gay male community and elsewhere over "man-boy love" asks a cognate question: can an adult's sexual relationship with a child be simply a continuous part of a more general relationship of education and nurturance? Or must the inclusion of sex qualitatively alter the relationship, for instance in the direction of exploitiveness? In this case, the same NOW communiqué that had assumed an unbroken continuity between sexualized violence and real, social violence, came to the opposite conclusion on pedophilia: that the injection of the sexual charge *would* alter (would corrupt) the very substance of the relationship. Thus, in moving from the question of sadomasochism to the question of pedophilia, the "permissive" argument and the "puritanical" argument have essentially exchanged their assumptions about how the sexual relates to the social.

So the answer to the question "what difference does the inclusion of sex make" to a social or political relationship, is—it varies: just as, for different groups in different political circumstances, homosexual activity can be either supportive of or oppositional to homosocial bonding. From this and the other examples I have mentioned, it is clear that there is not some ahistorical *Stoff* of sexuality, some sexual charge that can be simply added to a social relationship to "sexualize" it in a constant and predictable direction, or that splits off from it unchanged. Nor does it make sense to *assume* that the sexualized form epitomizes or simply condenses a broader relationship. (As, for instance, Kathleeen Barry, in *Female Sexual Slavery*, places the Marquis de Sade at the very center of all forms of female oppression, including traditional genital mutilation, incest, and the economic as well as the sexual exploitation of prostitutes.)

Instead, an examination of the relation of sexual desire to political power must move along two axes. First, of course, it needs to make use of whatever forms of analysis are most potent for describing historically variable power asymmetries, such as those of class and race, as well as gender. But in conjunction with that, an analysis of representation itself is necessary. Only the model of representation will let us do justice to the (broad but not infinite or random) range of ways in which sexuality functions as a signifier for power relations. The importance of the rhetorical model in this case is not to make the problems of sexuality or of violence or oppression sound less immediate and urgent; it is to help us analyze and use the really very disparate intuitions of political immediacy that come to us from the sexual realm.

For instance, a dazzling recent article by Catharine MacKinnon, attempting to go carefully over and clear out the grounds of disagreement between different streams of feminist thought, arrives at the following summary of the centrality of sexuality per se for every issue of gender:

> Each element of the female *gender* stereotype is revealed as, in fact, *sexual*. Vulnerability means the appearance/reality of easy sexual access; passivity means receptivity and disabled resistance . . . ; softness means pregnability by something hard. . . . Woman's infantilization evokes pedophilia; fixation on dismembered body parts . . . evokes fetishism; idolization of vapidity, necrophilia. Narcissism insures that woman identifies with that image of herself

that man holds up. . . . Masochism means that pleasure in violation becomes her sensuality.

And MacKinnon sums up this part of her argument: "Socially, femaleness means femininity, which means attractiveness to men, which means sexual attractiveness, which means sexual availability on male terms."[15]

There's a whole lot of "mean"-ing going on. MacKinnon manages to make every manifestation of sexuality mean the same thing, by making every instance of "meaning" mean something different. A trait can "mean" as an element in a semiotic system such as fashion ("softness means pregnability"); or anaclitically, it can "mean" its complementary opposite ("Woman's infantilization evokes pedophilia"); or across time, it can "mean" the consequence that it enforces ("Narcissism insures that woman identifies. . . . Masochism means that pleasure in violation becomes her sensuality"). MacKinnon concludes, "What defines woman as such is what turns men on." But what defines "defines"? That every node of sexual experience is in *some* signifying relation to the whole fabric of gender oppression, and vice versa, is true and important, but insufficiently exact to be of analytic use on specific political issues. The danger lies, of course, in the illusion that we do know from such a totalistic analysis where to look for our sexuality and how to protect it from expropriation when we find it.

On the other hand, one value of MacKinnon's piece was as a contribution to the increasing deftness with which, over the last twenty years, the question has been posed, "Who or what is the subject of the sexuality we (as women) enact?" It has been posed in terms more or less antic or frontal, phallic or gyno-, angry or frantic—in short, perhaps, Anglic or Franco-. But in different terms it is this same question that has animated the complaint of the American "sex object" of the 1960s, the claim since the 70s for "women's control of our own bodies," and the recently imported "critique of the subject" as it was used by French feminists.

Let me take an example from the great ideological blockbuster of white bourgeois feminism, its apotheosis, the fictional work that has most resonantly thematized for successive generations of American women the constraints of the "feminine" role, the obstacles to and the ravenous urgency of female ambition, the importance of the economic motive, the compulsiveness and destructiveness of romantic love, and (what MacKinnon would underline) the centrality and the total alienation of female sexuality. Of course, I am referring to *Gone With the Wind*. As MacKinnon's paradigm would predict, in the life of Scarlett O'Hara, it is expressly clear that to be born female is to be defined entirely in relation to the role of "lady," a role that does take its shape and meaning from a sexuality of which she is not the subject but the object. For Scarlett, to survive as a woman does mean learning to see sexuality, male power domination, and her traditional gender role as all meaning the same dangerous thing. To absent herself silently from each of them alike, and learn to manipulate them from behind this screen as objects or pure signifiers, as men do, is the numbing but effective lesson of her life.

However, it is *only* a white bourgeois feminism that this view apotheosizes. As in one of those trick rooms where water appears to run uphill and little children look taller than their parents, it is only when viewed from one fixed vantage in any society that sexuality, gender roles, and power domination can seem to line up in this perfect chain of echoic meaning. From an even slightly more ec-centric or disempowered perspective, the *dis*placements and *dis*continuities of the signifying chain come to seem increasingly definitive. For instance, if it is true in this novel that all the women characters exist in some meaning-ful relation to the role of "lady," the signifying relation grows more tortuous—though at the same time, in the novel's white bourgeois view, more totally determining—as the women's social and racial distance from that role grows. Melanie is a woman as she is a lady; Scarlett is a woman as she is required to be and pretends to be a lady; but Belle Watling, the Atlanta prostitute, is a woman not in relation to her own role of "lady," which is exiguous, but only negatively, in a compensatory and at the same time parodic relation to Melanie's and Scarlett's. And as for Mammy, her mind and life, in this view, are *totally* in thrall to the ideal of the "lady," but in a relation that excludes herself entirely: she is the template, the support, the enforcement, of Scarlett's "lady" role, to the degree that her personal femaleness loses any meaning whatever that is not in relation to Scarlett's role. Whose mother is Mammy?

At the precise intersection of domination and sexuality is the issue of rape. *Gone With the Wind*—both book and movie—leaves in the memory a most graphic image of rape:

> As the negro came running to the buggy, his black face twisted in a leering grin, she fired point-blank at him. . . . The negro was beside her, so close that she could smell the rank odor of him as he tried to drag her over the buggy side. With her own free hand she fought madly, clawing at his face, and then she felt his big hand at her throat and, with a ripping noise, her basque was torn open from breast to waist. Then the black hand fumbled between her breasts, and terror and revulsion such as she had never known came over her and she screamed like an insane woman.[16]

In the wake of this attack, the entire machinery by which "rape" is signified in this culture rolls into action. Scarlett's menfolk and their friends in the Ku Klux Klan set out after dark to kill the assailants and "wipe out that whole Shantytown settlement," with the predictable carnage on both sides. The question of how much Scarlett is to blame for the deaths of the white men is widely mooted, with Belle Watling speaking for the "lady" role—"She caused it all, prancin' bout Atlanta by herself, enticin' niggers and trash"—and Rhett Butler, as so often, speaking from the central vision of the novel's bourgeois feminism, assuring her that her desperate sense of guilt is purely superstitious (chs. 46, 47). In preparation for this central incident, the novel had even raised the issue of the legal treatment of rape victims (ch. 42). And the effect of that earlier case, the classic effect of rape, had already been to abridge Scarlett's own mobility and, hence, personal and economic power: it was to expedite her business that she had needed to ride by Shantytown in the first place.

The attack on Scarlett, in short, fully means rape, both *to her* and to all the forces in her culture that produce and circulate powerful meanings. It makes no difference at all that one constituent element of rape is missing; but the missing constituent is simply sex. The attack on Scarlett had been for money; the black hands had fumbled between the white breasts because the man had been told that was where she kept her money; Scarlett knew that; there is no mention of any other motive; but it does not matter in the least, the absent sexuality leaves no gap in the character's, the novel's, or the society's discourse of rape.

Nevertheless, *Gone With the Wind* is not a novel that omits enforced sexuality. We are shown one actual rape in fairly graphic detail; but when it is white hands that scrabble on white skin, its ideological name is "blissful marriage." "[Rhett] had humbled her, used her brutally through a wild mad night and she had gloried in it" (ch. 54). The sexual predations of white men on Black women are also a presence in the novel, but the issue of force vs. content is never raised there; the white male alienation of a Black woman's sexuality is shaped differently from the alienation of the white woman's, to the degree that rape ceases to be a meaningful term at all. And if forcible sex ever did occur between a Black male and female character in this world, the sexual event itself would have no signifying power, since Black sexuality "means" here only as a grammatic transformation of a sentence whose true implicit subject and object are white.

We have in this protofeminist novel, then, in this ideological microcosm, a symbolic economy in which both the meaning of rape and rape itself are insistently circulated. Because of the racial fracture of the society, however, *rape and its meaning circulate in precisely opposite directions*. It is an extreme case; the racial fracture is, in America, more sharply dichotomized than others except perhaps for gender. Still, other symbolic fractures such as class (and by fractures I mean the lines along which the quantitative differentials of power may in a given society be read as qualitative differentials with some other name) are abundant and actively disruptive in every social constitution. The signifying relation of sex to power, of sexual alienation to political oppression, is not the most stable, but precisely the most volatile of social nodes, under this pressure.

Thus, it is of serious political importance that our tools for examining the signifying relation be subtle and discriminate ones, and that our literary knowledge of the most crabbed or oblique paths of meaning not be oversimplified in the face of panic-inducing images of real violence, especially the violence of, around, and to sexuality. To assume that sex signifies power in a flat, unvarying relation of metaphor or synecdoche will always entail a blindness, not to the rhetorical and pyrotechnic, but to such historical categories as class and race. Before we can fully achieve and use our intuitive grasp of the leverage that sexual relations seem to offer on the relations of oppression, we need more—more different, more complicated, more diachronically apt, more off-centered—more daring and prehensile applications of our present understanding of what it may mean for one thing to signify another.

III. SEX OR HISTORY?

It will be clear by this point that the centrality of sexual questions in this study is important to its methodological ambitions, as well. I am going to be recurring to the subject of sex as an especially charged leverage-point, or point for the exchange of meanings, *between* gender and class (and in many societies, race), the sets of categories by which we ordinarily try to describe the divisions of human labor. And methodologically, I want to situate these readings as a contribution to a dialectic within femininst theory between more and less historicizing views of the oppression of women.

In a rough way, we can label the extremes on this theoretical spectrum "Marxist feminism" for the most historicizing analysis, "radical feminism" for the least. Of course, "radical feminism" is so called not because it occupies the farthest "left" space on a conventional political map, but because it takes gender itself, gender alone, to be the most radical division of human experience, and a relatively unchanging one.

For the purposes of the present argument, in addition, and for reasons that I will explain more fully later, I am going to be assimilating "French" feminism—deconstructive and/or Lacanian-oriented feminism—to the radical-feminist end of this spectrum. "French" and "radical" feminism differ on very many very important issues, such as how much respect they give to the brute fact that everyone gets categorized as either female or male; but they are alike in seeing all human culture, language, and life as structured in the first place—structured radically, transhistorically, and essentially *similarly*, however coarsely or finely—by a drama of gender difference. (Chapter 1 discusses more fully the particular terms by which this structuralist motive will be represented in the present study.) French-feminist and radical-feminist prose tend to share the same vatic, and perhaps imperialistic, uses of the present tense. In a sense, the polemical energy behind my arguments will be a desire, through the rhetorically volatile subject of sex, to recruit the representational finesse of deconstructive feminism in the service of a more historically discriminate mode of analysis.

The choice of sexuality as a thematic emphasis of this study makes salient and problematical a division of thematic emphasis between Marxist-feminist and radical-feminist theory as they are now practiced. Specifically, Marxist feminism, the study of the deep interconnections between on the one hand historical and economic change, and on the other hand the vicissitudes of gender division, has typically proceeded in the absence of a theory of sexuality and without much interest in the meaning or experience of sexuality. Or more accurately, it has held implicitly to a view of female sexuality as something that is essentially of a piece with reproduction, and hence appropriately studied with the tools of demography; or else essentially of a piece with a simple, prescriptive hegemonic ideology, and hence appropriately studied through intellectual or legal history. Where important advances have been made by Marxist-feminist-oriented research into sexuality, it has been in areas that were already explicitly distinguished as deviant by the society's legal discourse: signally, homosexuality for men and prostitution for women. Marxist feminism has been of little help in unpacking the historical meanings of women's experience of heterosexuality, or even, until it becomes legally and medically visible in this century, of lesbianism.[17]

Radical feminism, on the other hand, in the many different forms I am classing under that head, has been relatively successful in placing sexuality in a prominent and interrogative position, one that often allows scope for the decentered and the contradictory. Kathleen Barry's *Female Sexual Slavery*, Susan Griffin's *Pornography and Silence*, Gilbert and Gubar's *The Madwoman in the Attic*, Jane Gallop's *The Daughter's Seduction*, and Andrea Dworkin's *Pornography: Men Possessing Women* make up an exceedingly heterogeneous group of texts in many respects—in style, in urgency, in explicit feminist identification, in French or American affiliation, in "brow"-elevation level. They have in common, however, a view that sexuality is centrally problematical in the formation of women's experience. And in more or less sophisticated formulations, the subject as well as the ultimate object of female heterosexuality within what is called patriarchal culture are seen as male. Whether in literal interpersonal terms or in internalized psychological and linguistic terms, this approach privileges sexuality and often sees it within the context of the structure that Lévi-Strauss analyzes as "the male traffic in women."

This family of approaches has, however, shared with other forms of structuralism a difficulty in dealing with the diachronic. It is the essence of structures viewed as such to reproduce themselves; and historical change from this point of view appears as something outside of structure and threatening—or worse, *not* threatening—to it, rather than in a formative and dialectical relation with it. History tends thus to be either invisible or viewed in an impoverishingly glaring and contrastive light.[18] Implicitly or explicitly, radical feminism tends to deny that the meaning of gender or sexuality has ever significantly changed; and more damagingly, it can make future change appear impossible, or necessarily apocalyptic, even though desirable. Alternatively, it can radically oversimplify the prerequisites for significant change. In addition, history even in the residual, synchronic form of class or racial difference and conflict becomes invisible or excessively coarsened and dichotomized in the universalizing structuralist view.

As feminist readers, then, we seem poised for the moment between reading sex and reading history, at a choice that appears (though, it must be, wrongly) to be between the synchronic and the diachronic. We know that it must be wrongly viewed in this way, not only because in the abstract the synchronic and the diachronic must ultimately be considered in relation to one another, but because specifically in the disciplines we are considering they are so mutually inscribed: the narrative of Marxist history is so graphic, and the schematics of structuralist sexuality so narrative.

I will be trying in this study to activate and use some of the potential congruences of the two approaches. Part of the underpinning of this attempt will be a continuing meditation of ways in which the category *ideology* can be used as part of an analysis of *sexuality*. The two categories seem comparable in several important ways: each mediates between the material and the representational, for instance; ideology, like sexuality as we have discussed it, *both* epitomizes *and* itself influences broader social relations of power; and each, I shall be arguing, mediates similarly between diachronic, narrative structures of social experience and synchronic, graphic ones. If commonsense suggests that we can roughly group historicizing, "Marxist" feminism with the diachronic and the narrative, and "radical," structuralist, deconstructive, and "French" feminisms with the synchronic and the graphic, then the methodological promise of these two mediating categories will be understandable.

In *The German Ideology*, Marx suggests that the function of ideology is to conceal contradictions in the status quo by, for instance, recasting them into a diachronic narrative of origins. Corresponding to that function, one important structure of ideology is an idealizing appeal to the outdated values of an earlier system, in defense of a later system that in practice undermines the material basis of those values.[19]

For instance, Juliet Mitchell analyzes the importance of the family in ideologically justifying the shift to capitalism, in these terms:

> The peasant masses of feudal society had individual private property; their ideal was simply more of it. Capitalist society seemed to offer more because it stressed the *idea* of individual private property in a new context (or in a context of new ideas). Thus it offered individualism (an old value) plus the apparently new means for its greater realization—freedom and equality (values that are conspicuously absent from feudalism). However, the only place where this ideal could be given an apparently concrete base was in the maintenance of an old institution: the family. Thus the family changed from being the economic basis of individual private property under feudalism to being the focal point of the *idea* of individual private property under a system that banished such an economic form from its central mode of production—capitalism.... The working class work socially in production for the private property of a few capitalists *in the hope of* individual private property for themselves and their families.[20]

The phrase "A man's home is his castle" offers a nicely condensed example of ideological construction in this sense. It reaches *back* to an emptied-out image of mastery and integration under feudalism in order to propel the male wageworker *forward* to further feats of alienated labor, in the service of a now atomized and embattled, but all the more intensively idealized home. The man who has this home is a different person from the lord who has a castle; and the forms of property implied in the two possessives (his [mortgaged] home/his [inherited] castle) are not only different but, as Mitchell points out, mutually contradictory. The contradiction is assuaged and filled in by transferring the lord's political and economic control over the *environs* of his castle to an image of the father's personal control over the *inmates* of his house. The ideological formulation thus permits a criss-crossing of agency, temporality, and space. It is important that ideology in this sense, even when its form is flatly declarative ("A man's home is his castle"), is always at least implicitly narrative, and that, in order for the reweaving of ideology to be truly invisible, the narrative is necessarily chiasmic in structure: that is, that the subject of the beginning of the narrative is different from the subject at the end, and that the two subjects cross each other in a rhetorical figure that conceals their discontinuity.

It is also important that the sutures of contradiction in these ideological narratives become most visible under the disassembling eye of an alternative narrative, ideological as that narrative may itself be. In addition, the diachronic opening-out of contradictions within the status quo, even when the project of that diachronic recasting is to conceal those very contradictions, can have just the opposite effect of making them newly visible, offering a new leverage for critique. For these reasons, distinguishing between the construction and the critique of ideological narrative is not always even a theoretical possibility, even with relatively flat texts; with the fat rich texts that we are taking for examples in this project, no such attempt will be made.

Sexuality, like ideology, depends on the mutual redefinition and occlusion of synchronic and diachronic formulations. The developmental fact that, as Freud among others has shown, even the naming of sexuality as such is always retroactive in relation to most of the sensations and emotions that constitute it,[21] is *historically* important. What *counts* as the sexual is, as we shall see, variable and itself political. The exact, contingent space of indeterminacy—the place of shifting over time—of the mutual boundaries between the political and the sexual is, in fact, the most fertile space of ideological formation. This is true because ideological formation, like sexuality, depends on retroactive change in the naming or labelling of the subject.[22]

The two sides, the political and the erotic, necessarily obscure and misrepresent each other—but in ways that offer important and shifting affordances to all parties in historical gender and class struggle.

IV. WHAT THIS BOOK DOES

The difficult but potentially productive tension between historical and structuralist forms of feminism, in the theoretical grounding of this book, is echoed by a tension in the book between historical and more properly literary organization, methodologies, and emphases. Necessarily because of my particular aptitudes and training, if for no better reason, the historical argument almost throughout is embodied in and guided by the readings of the literary texts. For better and for worse, the large historical narrative has an off-centering effect on the discrete readings, as the introversive techniques of literary analysis have in turn on the historical argument. The resulting structure represents a continuing negotiation between the book's historicizing and dehistoricizing motives. The two ways in which I have described to myself the purpose of this book express a similar tension: first, to make it easier for readers to focus intelligently on male homosocial bonds throughout the heterosexual European erotic ethos; but secondly, to use the subject of sexuality to show the usefulness of certain Marxist-feminist historical categories for literary criticism, where they have so far had relatively little impact.

Chapter 1 of the book, "Gender Asymmetry and Erotic Triangles," locates the book's focus on male homosocial desire within the structural context of triangular, heterosexual desire. René Girard, Freud, and Lévi-Strauss, especially as he is interpreted by Gayle Rubin, offer the basic paradigm of "male traffic in women" that will underlie the entire book. In the next three chapters a historically deracinated reading of Shakespeare's Sonnets, a partially historical reading of Wycherley's *The Country Wife,* and a reading of Sterne's *A Sentimental Journey* in relation to the inextricable gender, class, and national anxieties of mid-eighteenth-century English men both establish some persistent paradigms for discussion, and begin to locate them specifically in the terms of modern England.

Chapters 5 and 6, on homophobia and the Romantic Gothic, discuss the paranoid Gothic tradition in the novel as an exploration of the changing meaning and importance of homophobia in England during and after the eighteenth century. A reading of James Hogg's *Confessions of a Justified Sinner* treats homophobia not most immediately as an oppression of homosexual men, but as a tool for manipulating the entire spectrum of male bonds, and hence the gender system as a whole.

Chapters 7 and 8 focus on more "mainstream," public Victorian ideological fictions, and on the fate of the women who are caught up in male homosocial exchange. This section treats three Victorian texts, historical or mock-historical, that claim to offer accounts of changes in women's relation to male bonds: Tennyson's *The Princess*, Thackeray's *Henry Esmond*, and Eliot's *Adam Bede*; it approaches most explicitly the different explanatory claims of structuralist and historical approaches to sex and gender.

Chapters 9 and 10, on Dickens' Victorian Gothic, show how Dickens's last two novels delineate the interactions of homophobia with nineteenth-century class and racial as well as gender division.

Finally, a Coda, "Toward the Twentieth Century: English Readers of Whitman," uses an account of some influential English (mis-)understandings of Whitman's poetry, to sketch in the links between mid-Victorian English sexual politics and the familiar modern Anglo-American landscape of male homosexuality, heterosexuality, and homophobia as (we think) we know them.

The choices I have made of texts through which to embody the argument of the book are specifically *not* meant to begin to delineate a separate male-homosocial literary canon. In fact, it will be essential to my argument to claim that the European canon as it exists is already such a canon, and most so when it is most heterosexual. In this sense, it would perhaps be easiest to describe this book (as will be done more explicitly in chapter 1) as a recasting of, and a refocusing on, René Girard's triangular schematization of the existing European canon in *Deceit, Desire, and the Novel*. In fact, I have simply chosen texts at pleasure from within or alongside the English canon that represented particularly interesting interpretive problems, or particularly symptomatic historical and ideological nodes, for understanding the politics of male homosociality.

I hope it is obvious by this point that I mean to situate this book in a dialectically usable, rather than an authoritative, relation to the rapidly developing discourse of feminist theory. Of course, the readings and interpretations are as careful in their own terms as I have known how to make them; but at the same time I am aware of having privileged certain arresting (and hence achronic) or potentially generalizable formulations, in the hope of making interpretations like these dialectically available to readers of other texts, as well. The formal models I have had in mind for this book are two very different books, Girard's *Deceit, Desire, and the Novel* and Dorothy Dinnerstein's *The Mermaid and the Minotaur*: not in this instance because of an agreement with the substance of their arguments, but because each in a relatively short study with an apparently idiosyncratic focus nevertheless conveys a complex of ideas forcefully enough—even, repetitiously enough—to make it a usable part of any reader's repertoire of approaches to her or his personal experience and future reading. *From* that position in the repertoire each can be—must be—criticized and changed. To take such a position has been my ambition for this book. Among the directions of critique and alteration that seem to me most called for, but which I have been unable so far to incorporate properly in the argument itself, are the following:

First, the violence done by my historicizing narrative to the literary readings proper shows perhaps most glaringly in the overriding of distinctions and structural considerations of genre. And in general, the number and the *different*ness of the many different mechanisms of mediation between history and text—mechanisms with names like, for instance, "literary convention," "literary history"—need to be reasserted in newly applicable formulations.

At the same time, the violences done to a historical argument by embodying it in a series of readings of works of literature are probably even more numerous and damaging. Aside from issues of ideological condensation and displacement that will be discussed in chapters 7 and 8, the form of violence most obvious to me is simply the limitation of my argument to the "book-writing classes"—a group that is distinctive in more than merely socioeconomic terms, but importantly in those terms as well.

Next, the isolation, not to mention the absolute subordination, of women, in the structural paradigm on which this study is based (see chapter 1 for more on this) is a distortion that necessarily fails to do justice to women's own powers, bonds, and struggles.[23] The absence of lesbianism from the book was an early and, I think, necessary decision, since my argument is structured around the distinctive relation of the male homosocial spectrum to the transmission of unequally distributed power. Nevertheless, the exclusively heterosexual perspective of the book's attention to women is seriously impoverishing in itself, and also an index of the larger distortion. The reading of *Henry Esmond* is the only one that explicitly considers the bond of woman with woman in the context of male homosocial exchange, but much better analyses are needed of the relations between female-homosocial and male-homosocial structures.

The book's almost exclusive focus on male authors is, I think, similarly justified for this early stage of this particular inquiry; but it has a similar effect of impoverishing our sense of women's own cultural resources of resistance, adaptation, revision, and survival. My reluctance to distinguish between "ideologizing" and "de-ideologizing" narratives may have had, paradoxically, a similar effect of presenting the "canonical" cultural discourse in an excessively protean and inescapable (*because* internally contradictory) form. In addition, the relation between the traffic-in-women paradigm used here and hypotheses, such as Dinnerstein's, Chodorow's, and Kristeva's in *Powers of Horror*, of a primary fear in men and women of the maternal power of women, is yet to be analyzed.

Again, the lack of entirely usable paradigms, at this early moment in feminist theory, for the complicated relations among violence, sexual violence, and the sadomasochistic sexualization of violence,[24] has led me in this book to a perhaps inappropriately gentle emphasis on modes of gender oppression that could be (more or less metaphorically) described in economic terms.

At the same time, the erotic and individualistic bias of literature itself, and the relative ease—not to mention the genuine pleasure—of using feminist theoretical paradigms to write about eros and sex, have led to a relative deemphasis of the many, crucially important male homosocial bonds that are less glamorous to talk about—such as the institutional, bureaucratic, and military.

Finally, and I think most importantly, the focus of this study on specifically English social structures, combined with the hegemonic claim for "universality" that has historically been implicit in the entire discourse of European social and psychological analysis, leave the relation of my discussion to non-European cultures and people entirely unspecified, and at present, perhaps, to some extent unspecifiable. A running subtext of comparisons between English sexual ideology and some ideologies of American racism is not a token attempt to conceal that gap in the book's coverage, but an attempt to make clear to other American readers some of the points of reference in white America that I have used in thinking about English ideology. Perhaps what one can most appropriately ask of readers who find this book's formulations useful is simply to remember that, important as it is that they be criticized at every step of even European applications, any attempt to treat them as cross-cultural or (far more) as universal ought to involve the most searching and particular analysis.

As a woman and a feminist writing (in part) about male homosexuality, I feel I must be especially explicit about the political groundings, assumptions, and ambitions of this study in that regard, as well. My intention throughout has been to conduct an antihomophobic as well as feminist inquiry. However, most of the (little) published analysis up to now of the relation between women and male homosexuality has been at a lower level of sophistication and care than either feminist or gay male analysis separately. In the absence of workable formulations about the male homosocial spectrum, this literature has, with only a few recent exceptions,[25] subscribed to one of two assumptions: either that gay men and all women share a "natural," transhistorical alliance and an essential identity of interests (e.g., in breaking down gender stereotypes);[26] or else that male homosexuality is an epitome, a personification, an effect, or perhaps a primary cause of woman-hating.[27] I do not believe either of these assumptions to be true. Especially because this study discusses a continuum, a potential structural congruence, and a (shifting) relation of meaning between male homosexual relationships and the male patriarchal relations by which women are oppressed, it is important to emphasize that I am not assuming or arguing either that patriarchal power is primarily or necessarily homosexual (as distinct from homosocial), or that male homosexual desire has a primary or necessary relationship to misogyny. Either of those arguments would be homophobic and, I believe, inaccurate. I will, however, be arguing that homophobia directed by men against men is misogynistic, and perhaps transhistorically so. (By "misogynistic" I mean not only that it is oppressive of the so-called feminine in men, but that it is oppressive of women.) The greatest potential for misinterpretation lies here. Because "homosexuality" and "homophobia" are, in any of their avatars, historical constructions, because they are likely to concern themselves intensely with each other and to assume interlocking or mirroring shapes, because the theater of their struggle is likely to be intrapsychic or intra-institutional as well as public, it is not always easy (sometimes barely possible) to distinguish them from each other. Thus, for instance, Freud's study of Dr. Schreber shows clearly that *the repression of homosexual desire* in a man who by any commonsense standard was heterosexual, occasioned paranoid psychosis; the psychoanalytic use that has been made of this perception, however, has been, not against *homophobia* and its schizogenic force, but against *homosexuality*—against homosexuals—on account of an association between "homosexuality" and mental illness.[28] Similar confusions have marked discussions of the relation between "homosexuality" and fascism. As the historically constructed nature of "homosexuality" as an institution becomes more fully understood, it should become possible to understand these distinctions in a more exact and less prejudicious theoretical context.

Thus, profound and intuitable as the bonds between feminism and antihomophobia often are in our society, the two forces are not the same. As the alliance between them is not automatic or transhistorical, it will be most fruitful if it is analytic and unpresuming. To shed light on the grounds and implications of that alliance, as well as, through these issues, on formative literary texts, is an aim of the readings that follow.

NOTES

1. The notion of "homophobia" is itself fraught with difficulties. To begin with, the word is etymologically nonsensical. A more serious problem is that the linking of fear and hatred in the "-phobia" suffix, and in the word's usage, does tend to prejudge the question of the cause of homosexual oppression: it is attributed to fear, as opposed to (for example) a desire for power, privilege, or material goods. An alternative term that is more suggestive of collective, structurally inscribed, perhaps materially based oppression is "heterosexism." This study will, however, continue to use "homophobia," for three reasons. First, it will be an important concern here to question, rather than to reinforce, the presumptively symmetrical opposition between homo- and heterosexuality, which seems to be implicit in the term "heterosexism." Second, the etiology of individual people's attitudes toward male homosexuality will not be a focus of discussion. And third, the ideological and thematic treatments of male homosexuality to be discussed from the late eighteenth century onward do combine fear and hatred in a way that is appropriately called phobic. For a good summary of social science research on the concept of homophobia, see Morin and Garfinkle, "Male Homophobia."

2. For a good survey of the background to this assertion, see Weeks, *Sex,* pp. 1–18.

3. Adrienne Rich describes these bonds as forming a "lesbian continuum," in her essay, "Compulsory Heterosexuality and Lesbian Existence," in Stimpson and Person, *Women,* pp. 62–91, especially pp. 79–82.

4. "The Female World of Love and Ritual," in Cott and Pleck, *Heritage,* pp. 311–42; usage appears on, e.g., pp. 316, 317.

5. "The Unhappy Marriage of Marxism and Feminism: Towards a More Progressive Union," in Sargent, *Women and Revolution,* pp. 1–41; quotation is from p. 14.

6. See, for example, Rubin, "Traffic," pp. 182–83.

7. Rubin, "Traffic," p. 180.

8. Crompton, "Gay Genocide"; but see chapter 5 for a discussion of the limitations of "genocide" as an understanding of the fate of homosexual men.

9. On this, see Miller, *New Psychology,* ch. 1.

10. Dover, *Greek Homosexuality,* p. 91.

11. Arendt, *Human Condition, p.* 83, quoted in Rich, *On Lies,* p. 206.

12. On the Bohemian Grove, an all-male summer camp for American ruling-class men, see Domhoff, *Bohemian Grove;* and a more vivid, although homophobic, account, van der Zee, *Men's Party.*

13. The NOW resolution, for instance, explicitly defines sadomasochism, pornography, and "pederasty" (meaning pedophilia) as issues of "exploitation and violence," *as opposed to* "affectional/sexual preference/orientation." Quoted in *Heresies 12,* vol. 3, no 4 (1981), p. 92.

14. For explorations of these viewpoints, see *Heresies, ibid.*; Snitow et al., *Powers*; and Samois, *Coming*.

15. MacKinnon, "Feminism," pp. 530–31.

16. Mitchell, *Gone*, p. 780. Further citations will be incorporated within the text and designated by chapter number.

17. For a discussion of these limitations, see Vicinus, "Sexuality." The variety of useful work that is possible within these boundaries is exemplified by the essays in Newton et al., *Sex and Class*.

18. On this, see McKeon, "Marxism."

19. Juliet Mitchell discusses this aspect of *The German Ideology* in *Women's Estate*, pp. 152–58.

20. Mitchell, *Woman's Estate*, p. 154.

21. The best and clearest discussion of this aspect of Freud is Laplanche, *Life and Death*, especially pp. 25–47.

22. On this, see ch. 8 of *Between Men*.

23. For an especially useful discussion of the absence of women from the work of Girard, see Moi, "Missing Mother."

24. On this see (in addition to Snitow et al., *Powers*) Breines and Gordon, "Family Violence."

25. The following books are, to a greater or lesser extent, among the exceptions: Fernbach, *Spiral Path*; Mieli, *Homosexuality*; Rowbotham and Weeks, *Socialism*; Dworkin, *Pornography*.

26. The most influential recent statement of this position is Heilbrun, *Androgyny*.

27. See Irigaray, "Goods"; and Frye, *Politics*, pp. 128–51. Jane Marcus's work on Virginia Woolf makes use of Maria-Antonietta Macciocchi's homophobic formulation, "the Nazi community is made by homosexual brothers who exclude the woman and valorize the mother." Marcus says, "The Cambridge Apostles' notions of fraternity surely appeared to Woolf analogous to certain fascist notions of fraternity." Macciocchi's formulation is quoted in Jane Caplan, "Introduction to Female Sexuality in Fascist Ideology," *Feminist Review* 1 (1979), p. 62. Marcus's essay is "Liberty, Sorority, Misogyny," in Heilbrun and Higonnet, *Representation*, pp. 60–97; quotation is from p. 67.

28. On this see Hocquenghem, *Homosexual Desire*, pp. 42–67.

GENDER ASYMMETRY AND EROTIC TRIANGLES

(1 9 8 5)

The graphic schema on which I am going to be drawing most heavily in the readings that follow is the triangle. The triangle is useful as a figure by which the "commonsense" of our intellectual tradition schematizes erotic relations, and because it allows us to condense into a juxtaposition with that folk-perception several somewhat different streams of recent thought.

René Girard's early book, *Deceit, Desire, and the Novel,* was itself something of a schematization of the folk-wisdom of erotic triangles. Through readings of major European fictions, Girard traced a calculus of power that was structured by the relation of rivalry between the two active members of an erotic triangle. What is most interesting for our purposes in his study is its insistence that, in any erotic rivalry, the bond that links the two rivals is as intense and potent as the bond that links either of the rivals to the beloved: that the bonds of "rivalry" and "love," differently as they are experienced, are equally powerful and in many senses equivalent. For instance, Girard finds many examples in which the choice of the beloved is determined in the first place, not by the qualities of the beloved, but by the beloved's already being the choice of the person who has been chosen as a rival. In fact, Girard seems to see the bond between rivals in an erotic triangle as being even stronger, more heavily determinant of actions and choices, than anything in the bond between either of the lovers and the beloved. And within the male-centered novelistic tradition of European high culture, the triangles Girard traces are most often those in which two males are rivals for a female; it is the bond between males that he most assiduously uncovers.

The index to Girard's book gives only two citations for "homosexuality" per se, and it is one of the strengths of his formulation not to depend on how homosexuality as an entity was perceived or experienced—indeed, on what was or was not considered sexual—at any given historical moment. As a matter of fact, the symmetry of his formulation always depends on *suppressing* the subjective, historically determined account of which feelings are or are not part of the body of "sexuality." The transhistorical clarity gained by this organizing move naturally has a cost, however. Psychoanalysis, the recent work of Foucault, and feminist historical scholarship all suggest that the place of drawing the boundary between the sexual and the not-sexual, like the place of drawing the boundary between the realms of the two genders, is variable, but is *not* arbitrary. That is (as the example of *Gone With the Wind* suggests), the placement of the boundaries in a particular society affects not merely the definitions of those terms themselves—sexual/nonsexual, masculine/feminine—but also the apportionment of forms of power that are not obviously sexual. These include control over the means of production and reproduction of goods, persons, and meanings. So that Girard's account, which thinks it is describing a dialectic of power abstracted from either the male/female or the sexual/nonsexual dichotomies, is leaving out of consideration categories that in fact preside over the distribution of power in every known society. And because the distribution of power according to these dichotomies is not and possibly cannot be symmetrical, the hidden symmetries that Girard's triangle helps us discover will always in turn discover hidden obliquities. At the same time, even to bear in mind the lurking possibility of the Girardian symmetry is to be possessed of a graphic tool for historical measure. It will make it easier for us to perceive and discuss the mutual inscription in these texts of male homosocial and heterosocial desire, and the resistances to them.

Girard's argument is of course heavily dependent, not only on a brilliant intuition for taking seriously the received wisdom of sexual folklore, but also on a schematization from Freud: the Oedipal triangle, the situation of the young child that is attempting to situate itself with respect to a powerful father and a beloved mother. Freud's discussions of the etiology of "homosexuality" (which current research seems to be rendering questionable as a set of generalizations about personal histories of "homosexuals")[1] suggest homo- and heterosexual outcomes in adults to be the result of a complicated play of desire for and identification with the parent of each gender: the child routes its desire/identification through the mother to arrive at a role like the father's, or vice versa. Richard Klein summarizes this argument as follows:

> In the normal development of the little boy's progress towards heterosexuality, he must pass, as Freud says with increasing insistence in late essays like "Terminable and Interminable Analysis," through the stage of the "positive' Oedipus, a homoerotic identification with his father, a position of effeminized subordination to the father, as a condition of finding a model for his own heterosexual role. Conversely, in this theory, the development of the male homosexual requires the postulation of the father's absence or distance and an abnormally strong identification by the child with the mother, in which the child takes the place of the father. There results from this scheme a surprising neutralization of polarities: heterosexuality in the male . . . presupposes a homosexual neutralization phase as the condition of its normal possibility: homosexuality, obversely, requires that the child experience a powerful heterosexual identification.[2]

I have mentioned that Girard's reading presents itself as one whose symmetry is undisturbed by such differences as gender; although the triangles that most shape his view tend, in the European tradition, to involve bonds of "rivalry" between males "over" a woman, in his view *any* relation of rivalry is structured by the same play of emulation and identification, whether the entities occupying the corners of the triangle be heroes, heroines, gods, books, or whatever. In describing the Oedipal drama, Freud notoriously tended to place a male in the generic position of "child" and treat the case of the female as being more or less the same, "mutatis mutandis"; at any rate, as Freud is interpreted by conventional American psychoanalysis, the enormous difference in the degree and kind of female and male power enters psychoanalytic view, when at all, as a result rather than as an active determinant of familial and intrapsychic structures of development. Thus, both Girard and Freud (or at least the Freud of this interpretive tradition) treat the erotic triangle as symmetrical—in the sense that its structure would be relatively unaffected by the power difference that would be introduced by a change in the gender of one of the participants.

In addition, the asymmetry I spoke of in section 1 of the Introduction—the radically disrupted continuum, in our society, between sexual and nonsexual male bonds, as against the relatively smooth and palpable continuum of female homosocial desire—might be expected to alter the structure of erotic triangles in ways that depended on gender, and for which neither Freud nor Girard would offer an account. Both Freud and Girard, in other words, treat erotic triangles under the Platonic light that perceives no discontinuity in the homosocial continuum—none, at any rate, that makes much difference—even in modern Western society. There is a kind of bravery about the proceeding of each in this respect, but a historical blindness, as well.

Recent readings and reinterpretations of Freud have gone much farther in taking into account the asymmetries of gender. In France, recent psychoanalytic discourse impelled by Jacques Lacan identifies power, language, and the Law itself with the phallus and the "name of the father." It goes without saying that such a discourse has the potential for setting in motion both feminist and virulently misogynistic analyses; it does, at any rate, offer tools, though not (so far) historically sensitive ones, for describing the mechanisms of patriarchal power in terms that are at once intrapsychic (Oedipal conflict) and public (language and the Law). Moreover, by distinguishing (however incompletely) the phallus, the locus of power, from the actual anatomical penis,[3] Lacan's account creates a space in which anatomic sex and cultural gender may be distinguished from one another and in which the different paths of *men's* relations to male power might be explored (e.g. in terms of class). In addition, it suggests ways of talking about the relation between the individual male and the cultural institutions of masculine domination that fall usefully under the rubric of representation.

A further contribution of Lacanian psychoanalysis that will be important for our investigation is the subtlety with which it articulates the slippery relation—already adumbrated in Freud—between desire and identification. The schematic elegance with which Richard Klein, in the passage I have quoted, is able to summarize the feminizing potential of desire for a woman and the masculine potential of subordination to a man, owes at least something to a Lacanian grinding of the lenses through which Freud is being viewed. In Lacan and those who have learned from him, an elaborate meditation on introjection and incorporation forms the link between the apparently dissimilar processes of desire and identification.

Recent American feminist work by Dorothy Dinnerstein and Nancy Chodorow also revises Freud in the direction of greater attention to gender/power difference. Coppélia Kahn summarizes the common theme of their argument (which she applies to Shakespeare) as follows:

Most children, male or female, in Shakespeare's time, Freud's, or ours, are not only borne but raised by women. And thus arises a crucial difference between the girl's developing sense of identity and the boy's. For though she follows the same sequence of symbiotic union, separation and individuation, identification, and object love as the boy, her femininity arises in relation to a person of the *same* sex, while his masculinity arises in relation to a person of the *opposite* sex. Her femininity is reinforced by her original symbiotic union with her mother and by the identification with her that must precede identity, while his masculinity is threatened by the same union and the same identification. While the boy's sense of *self* begins in union with the feminine, his sense of *masculinity* arises against it.[4]

It should be clear, then, from what has gone before, on the one hand that there are many and thorough asymmetries between the sexual continuums of women and men, between female and male sexuality and homosociality, and most pointedly between homosocial and heterosocial object choices for males; and on the other hand that the status of women and the whole question of arrangements between genders, is deeply and inescapably inscribed in the structure even of relationships that seem to exclude women—even in male homosocial/homosexual relationships. Heidi Hartmann's definition of patriarchy in terms of "relationships between men" (see introduction 1), in making the power relationships between men and women appear to be dependent on the power relationships between men and men, suggests that large-scale social structures are congruent with the male–male–female erotic triangles described most forcefully by Girard and articulated most thoughtfully by others. We can go further than that, to say that in any male-dominated society, there is a special relationship between male homosocial (*including* homosexual) desire and the structures for maintaining and transmitting patriarchal power: a relationship founded on an inherent and potentially active structural congruence. For historical reasons, this special relationship may take the form of ideological homophobia, ideological homosexuality, or some highly conflicted but intensively structured combination of the two. (Lesbianism also must always be in a special relation to patriarchy, but on different [sometimes opposite] grounds and working through different mechanisms.)

Perhaps the most powerful recent argument through (and against) a traditional discipline that bears on these issues has occurred within anthropology. Based on readings and critiques of Lévi-Strauss and Engels, in addition to Freud and Lacan, Gayle Rubin has argued in an influential essay that patriarchal heterosexuality can best be discussed in terms of one or another form of the traffic in women: it is the use of women as exchangeable, perhaps symbolic, property for the primary purpose of cementing the bonds of men with men. For example, Lévi-Strauss writes, "The total relationship of exchange which constitutes marriage is not established between a man and a woman, but between two groups of men, and the woman figures only as one of the objects in the exchange, not as one of the partners."[5] Thus, like Freud's "heterosexual" in Richard Klein's account, Lévi-Strauss's normative man uses a woman as a "conduit of a relationship" in which the true *partner* is a man.[6] Rejecting Lévi-Strauss's celebratory treatment of this relegation of women, Rubin offers, instead, an array of tools for specifying and analyzing it.

Luce Irigaray has used the Lévi-Straussian description of the traffic in women to make a resounding though expensive leap of register in her discussion of the relation of heterosexual to male homosocial bonds. In the reflections translated into English as "When the Goods Get Together," she concludes: "[Male] homosexuality is the law that regulates the sociocultural order. Heterosexuality amounts to the assignment of roles in the economy."[7] To begin to describe this relation as having the asymmetry of (to put it roughly) *parole* to *langue* is wonderfully pregnant; if her use of it here is not a historically responsive one, still it has potential for increasing our ability to register historical difference.

The expensiveness of Irigaray's vision of male homosexuality is, oddly, in a sacrifice of sex itself: the male "homosexuality" discussed here turns out to represent anything but actual sex between men, which—although it is also, importantly, called "homosexuality"—has something like the same invariable, tabooed status for her larger, "real" "homosexuality" that incest has in principle for Lévi-Straussian kinship in general. Even Irigaray's supple machinery of meaning has the effect of transfixing, then sublimating, the quicksilver of sex itself.

The loss of the diachronic in a formulation like Irigaray's is, again, most significant, as well. Recent anthropology, as well as historical work by Foucault, Sheila Rowbotham, Jeffrey Weeks, Alan Bray, K. J. Dover, John Boswell, David Fernbach, and others, suggests that among the things that have changed radically in Western culture over the centuries, and vary across cultures, about men's genital activity with men are its frequency, its exclusivity, its class associations, its relation to the dominant culture, its ethical status, the degree to which it is seen as defining nongenital aspects of the lives of those who practice it, and, perhaps most radically, its association with femininity or masculinity in societies where gender is a profound determinant of power. The virility of the homosexual orientation of male desire seemed as self-evident to the ancient Spartans, and perhaps to Whitman, as its effeminacy seems in contemporary popular culture. The importance of women (not merely of "the feminine," but of actual women as well) in the etiology and the continuing experience of male homosexuality seems to be historically volatile (across time, across class) to a similar degree. Its changes are inextricable from the changing shapes of the institutions by which gender and class inequality are structured.

Thus, Lacan, Chodorow and Dinnerstein, Rubin, Irigaray, and others, making critiques from within their multiple traditions, offer analytical tools for treating the erotic triangle not as an ahistorical, Platonic form, a deadly symmetry from which the historical accidents of gender, language, class, and power detract, but as a sensitive register precisely for delineating relationships of power and meaning, and for making graphically intelligible the play of desire and identification by which individuals negotiate with their societies for empowerment.

NOTES

1. On this, see Bell et al., *Sexual Preferences*.
2. Review of *Homosexualities*, p. 1077.
3. On this see Gallop, *Daughter's Seduction*, pp. 15–32.
4. Kahn, *Man's Estate*, pp. 9–10.
5. *The Elementary Structures of Kinship* (Boston: Beacon, 1969), p. 115; quoted in Rubin, "Traffic," p. 174.

6. Rubin, *ibid.*
7. Irigaray, "Goods," pp. 107–10.

WORKS CITED

Arendt, Hannah. *The Human Condition*. Chicago: University of Chicago Press, 1958.

Barry, Kathleen. *Female Sexual Slavery*. New York: Prentice-Hall, 1979.

Bell, Alan P., Martin S. Weinberg, and Sue Kiefer Hammersmith. *Sexual Preference: Its Development in Men and Women*. Bloomington: Indiana University Press, 1981.

Bray, Alan. *Homosexuality in Renaissance England*. London: Gay Men's Press, 1982.

Breines, Wini, and Linda Gordon. "The New Scholarship on Family Violence." *Signs* 8, no. 3 (Spring 1983), pp. 490–531.

Chodorow, Nancy. "Mothering, Male Dominance, and Capitalism." In *Capitalist Patriarchy and the Case for Socialist Feminism*. Ed. Zillah Eisenstein. New York: Monthly Review Press, 1979, pp. 83–106.

———. *The Reproduction of Mothering: Psychoanalysis and the Sociology of Gender*. Berkeley: University of California Press, 1978.

Cott, Nancy F., and Elizabeth H. Pleck, eds. *A Heritage of Her Own: Toward a New Social History of American Women*. New York: Simon and Schuster, 1979.

Crompton, Louis. "Gay Genocide: From Leviticus to Hitler." In *The Gay Academic*. Ed. Louie Crew. Palm Springs, Calif.: ETC Publications, 1978, pp. 67–91.

Dickens, Charles. *David Copperfield*. Ed. Trevor Blount. Harmondsworth, Sussex: Penguin, 1966.

———. *The Mystery of Edwin Drood*. Ed. Margaret Cardwell. Oxford: Oxford University Press, 1972.

———. *Our Mutual Friend*. Ed. Stephen Gill. Harmondsworth: Penguin, 1971.

Dinnerstein, Dorothy. *The Mermaid and the Minotaur: Sexual Arrangements and Human Malaise*. New York: Harper & Row–Colophon, 1976.

Domhoff, G. William. *The Bohemian Grove and Other Retreats: A Study in Ruling-Class Cohesiveness*. New York: Harper & Row, 1974.

Dover, K. J. *Greek Homosexuality*. New York: Random House–Vintage, 1980.

Dworkin, Andrea. *Pornography: Men Possessing Women*. New York: G. P. Putnam's Sons–Perigee Books, 1981.

Eliot, George. *Adam Bede*. Illustrated Cabinet Edition. 2 vols. Boston: Dana Estes, n.d.

Fernbach, David. *The Spiral Path: A Gay Contribution to Human Survival*. Alyson Press, 1981.

Foucault, Michel. *The History of Sexuality: Volume 1. An Introduction*. Tr. Robert Hurley. New York: Pantheon, 1978.

Frye, Marilyn. *The Politics of Reality: Essays in Feminist Theory*. Trumansburg, N.Y.: The Crossing Press, 1983.

Gallop, Jane. *The Daughter's Seduction: Feminism and Psychoanalysis*. Ithaca: Cornell University Press, 1982.

Gilbert, Sandra, and Susan Gubar, *The Madwoman in the Attic: The Woman Writer and the Nineteenth-Century Literary Imagination*. New Haven: Yale University Press, 1979.

Girard, René. *Deceit, Desire, and the Novel: Self and Other in Literary Structure*. Tr. Yvonne Freccero. Baltimore: Johns Hopkins University Press, 1972.

Griffin, Susan. *Pornography and Silence: Cultures Revenge Against Nature*. New York: Harper & Row, 1981.

Heilbrun, Carolyn G. *Toward a Recognition of Androgyny*. New York: Harper & Row–Colophon, 1973.

Heilbrun, Carolyn G., and Margaret Higonnet, eds. *The Representation of Women in Fiction:*

Selected Papers from the English Institute, 1981. New series, no. 7. Baltimore: Johns Hopkins University Press, 1978.

Herdt, G. H. *Guardians of the Flutes: Idioms of Masculinity: A Study of Ritualized Homosexual Behavior.* New York: McGraw-Hill, 1981.

Hocquenghem, Guy. *Homosexual Desire.* Tr. Daniella Dangoor. London: Allison & Busby, 1978.

Hogg, James. *The Private Memoirs and Confessions of a Justified Sinner.* New York: Norton, 1970.

Irigaray, Luce. "When the Good Get Together." In *New French Feminisms.* Ed. Elaine Marks and Isabelle de Courtivron. New York: Schocken, 1981, pp. 107–11.

Kahn, Coppélia. *Man's Estate: Masculine Identity in Shakespeare.* Berkeley: University of California Press, 1981.

Klein, Richard. Review of *Homosexualities in French Literature. MLN* 95, no. 4 (May 1980), pp. 1070–80.

Kristeva, Julia. *Powers of Horror: An Essay on Abjection.* Tr. S. Roudiez. New York: Columbia University Press, 1982.

Laplanche, Jean. *Life and Death in Psychoanalysis.* Tr. Jeffrey Mehlman. Baltimore: Johns Hopkins University Press, 1976.

Lévi-Strauss, Claude. *The Elementary Structures of Kinship.* Boston: Beacon Press, 1969.

MacKinnon, Catharine A. "Feminism, Marxism, Method, and the State: An Agenda for Theory." *Signs* 7, no. 3 (Spring 1982), pp. 515–44.

McKeon, Michael. "The 'Marxism' of Claude Lévi-Strauss." *Dialectical Anthropology* 6 (1981), pp. 123–50.

Mieli, Mario. *Homosexuality and Liberation: Elements of a Gay Critique.* London: Gay Men's Press, 1977.

Miller, Jean Baker. *Psychology of Women.* Boston: Beacon Press, 1976.

Mitchell, Juliet. *Women's Estate.* New York: Random House–Vintage, 1973.

Mitchell, Margaret. *Gone With the Wind.* New York: Avon, 1973.

Moi, Toril. "The Missing Mother: The Oedipal Rivalries of René Girard." *Diacritics* 12, no. 2 (Summer 1982), pp. 21–31.

Morin, Stephen M., and Ellen M. Garfinkle. "Male Homophobia." In *Gayspeak: Gay Male and Lesbian Communication.* Ed. James W. Chesebro. New York: Pilgrim Press, 1981, pp. 117–29.

Rowbotham, Sheila, and Jeffrey Weeks. *Socialism and the New Life: The Personal and Sexual Politics of Edward Carpenter and Havelock Ellis.* London: Pluto Press, 1977.

Rubin, Gayle. "The Traffic in Women: Notes Toward a Political Economy of Sex." In *Toward an Anthropology of Women.* Ed. Rayna Reiter. New York: Monthly Review Press, 1975, pp. 157–210.

Samois, ed. *Coming to Power: Writing and Graphics on Lesbian S/M.* Boston: Alyson, 1982.

Sargent, Lydia, ed. *Women and Revolution: A Discussion of the Unhappy Marriage of Marxism and Feminism.* Boston: South End Press, 1981.

Snitow, Ann, Christine Stansell, and Sharon Thompson, eds. *Powers of Desire: The Politics of Sexuality.* New York: Monthly Review Press–New Feminist Library, 1983.

Sterne, Laurence. *A Sentimental Journey Through France and Italy.* Ed. Graham Petrie. Hammondsworth: Penguin, 1967.

Stimpson, Catharine R., and Ethel Spector Person, eds. *Women: Sex and Sexuality.* Chicago: University of Chicago Press, 1980.

Tennyson, Alfred, Lord. *The Princess: A Medley.* In *The Poems of Tennyson.* Ed. Christopher Ricks. London: Longmans, 1969, pp. 743–844.

Thackeray, William Makepeace. *The History of Henry Esmond, Esq. Written By Himself.* Biographical Edition. New York: Harper, 1903.

van der Zee, John. *The Greatest Men's Party on Earth: Inside the Bohemian Grove.* New York: Harcourt Brace Jovanovich, 1974.

Vicinus, Martha. "Sexuality and Power: A Review of Current Work in the History of Sexuality." *Feminist Studies* 8, no. I (Spring 1982), pp. 133–56.

Weeks, Jeffrey. *Coming Out: Homosexual Politics in Britain from the Nineteenth Century to the Present.* London: Quartet Books, 1977.

———. *Sex, Politics, and Society: The Regulation of Sexuality Since 1800.* London: Longman, 1981.

Wycherley, William. *The Country Wife.* Ed. Thomas H. Fujimura. Regents Restoration Drama Series. Lincoln, Neb.: University of Nebraska Press, 1965.

TERRY CASTLE

SYLVIA TOWNSEND WARNER AND THE COUNTERPLOT OF LESBIAN FICTION

(1993)

What is a lesbian fiction? According to what we might call the "Queen Victoria Principle" of cultural analysis, no such entity, of course, should even exist. The reader will recollect the instance of regal *faiblesse* I mentioned in my introduction: how when Queen Victoria was asked by her ministers in 1885 whether the recently legislated Criminal Law Amendment Act outlawing homosexual acts between men should be made to apply to women as well, she is supposed to have expressed disbelief that such acts between women were physically possible. Desire between men was conceivable, indeed could be pictured vividly enough to require policing. Desire between women was not.[1] The love of woman for woman, along with whatever "indecency" it might entail, simply could not be represented. According to this primal (il)logic, it would follow, therefore, that "lesbian fiction" is also inconceivable: a non-concept, a nothingness, a gap in the meaning of things—anything but a story there to be read.

We pride ourselves nowadays on have made some intellectual advances on the Victorian position. We know that lesbian fiction, like lesbianism itself, exists; we may even be able to name a few celebrated (or reviled) lesbian novels—*The Well of Loneliness, Nightwood, Orlando, The Desert of the Heart, The Female Man*, and so on. And yet, on what theoretical basis do we make such denominations? What characteristics inform our definition of "lesbian fiction" itself? Is a "lesbian novel" simply any narrative depicting sexual relations between women? If this were the case, then any number of works by male writers, including Diderot's *La Religieuse*, for example, or some of the other pornographic or semipornographic texts of male voyeurism, would fall under the rubric of lesbian fiction. Yet this does not feel exactly right. Would a lesbian novel be a novel, then, written by a lesbian? This can't be the case, or certain of Willa Cather's novels, say, or Marguerite Yourcenar's, would have to be classed as lesbian novels, when it is not clear that they really are. "A novel written by a lesbian depicting sexual relations between women" might come closer, but relies too heavily on the opacities of biography and eros, and lacks a certain psychic and political specificity.

The concept of "lesbian fiction," one has to conclude, remains somewhat undertheorized. It remains undertheorized, paradoxically, even in those places where one might expect to see it brought under the most intense scrutiny—in critical studies specifically dealing with the subject of homosexual desire in fiction. To date, the most provocative and influential study on this theme has undoubtedly been Eve Kosofsky Sedgwick's *Between Men: English Literature and Male Homosocial Desire* (1985). This brilliant meditation on "homosexuality" in literature, which Sedgwick wrote, as she recounts in her introduction, out of a specifically "antihomophobic and feminist" position, can justly be said to have galvanized the world of gay literary studies, at least as far as that world is presently constituted in the United States.[2]

And yet how is the question of lesbian fiction handled in this book? The answer, simply, is not at all. To be fair to Sedgwick, she is aware of the omission and candidly acknowledges it in her introduction. "The absence of lesbianism from the book," she writes, "was an early and, I think, necessary decision, since my argument is structured around the distinctive relation of the male homosocial spectrum to the transmission of unequally distributed power relations."[3] In other words, the very terms of Sedgwick's argument do not allow for any consideration of lesbian desire or its representation. But how can this be so?

Put in the most basic form, Sedgwick's thesis (which will already be familiar to many readers) is that English literature, at least since the late seventeenth century, has been structured by what she calls the "erotic triangle" of male homosocial desire. Drawing on the work of René Girard, Claude Lévi-Strauss, and especially Gayle Rubin, whose classic feminist essay, "The Traffic in Women," underpins much of the thinking here, Sedgwick argues that just as patriarchal culture has traditionally been organized around a ritualized "traffic" in women—the legal, economic, religious, and sexual exchange of women between men (as in the cherished institutions of heterosexual love and marriage)—so the fictions produced within patriarchal culture have tended to mimic, or represent, the same triangular structure. English literature is "homosocial," according to Sedgwick, to the extent that its hidden subject has always been male bonding—the bonding mediated "between" two men through, around, or over, the body and soul of a woman. In fiction as in life, the "normative man," she writes, uses a woman "as a 'conduit of a relationship' in which the true *partner* is a man" (26).

In a series of bravura readings, Sedgwick traces the persistence of the male-female-male "homosocial paradigm" in English writing from Shakespeare and Wycherley through the novels of Sterne, Hogg, Thackeray, Eliot, and Dickens. What she discovers along the way is that homosociality also has its discontents. These arise, not unexpectedly, from the ambiguous relationship between homo*sociality* and homo*sexuality*. The system of male domination, according to Sedgwick, depends on the maintenance of highly charged attachments between men. "It is crucial to every aspect of social structure within the exchange-of-women framework," she writes, "that heavily freighted bonds between men exist, as the backbone of social form or forms" (86). At the same time, she points out, when these male–male attachments become *too* freighted—that is, explicitly sexual—the result is an ideological contradiction of potentially crippling magnitude. If a man can become "like" a women in the act of homosexual intercourse, what is to distinguish such a man from any woman? By doing away with the "female middle term" and blurring the putative difference between "male" and "female," the overt eroticization of male bonds undermines the very conceptual distinction on which modern patriarchy is founded.

How then to separate "functional" male bonds—those that bolster the structure of male domination—from those that weaken it? In Sedgwick's insinuating re-reading of patriarchal cultural history, literature itself has been a primary means of resolving, or of attempting to resolve, this potentially disruptive ideological problem. Its solution has been to emphasize, with an almost paranoiac insistence, the necessity of triangulation itself—of preserving the male-female-male "erotic paradigm" precisely as a way of fending off the destabilizing threat of male homosexuality. The plots of classic English and American fiction, according to Sedgwick, are blatantly, often violently, homophobic: in Hogg's *Confessions of a Justified Sinner* or Dickens's *Our Mutual Friend*—to take two of her more memorable examples—the homoerotic desire of man for man is shown to lead, as if by Gothic compulsion, to morbidity, persecution, mania, and murder. By activating what she calls the standard plot mechanisms of "homosexual panic," these novels, along with many others, reveal themselves as none too subtly disguised briefs on behalf of the mediated eros of male homosocial desire. The triangular male-female-male figure returns at the conclusion of each story—triumphantly reinstalled—as a sign both of normative (namely, heterosexual) male bonding and of a remobilization of patriarchal control.

The obsession with vindicating male homosociality at the expense of male homosexuality has not been confined, writes Sedgwick, to the works of the English literary tradition. Indeed, in the most ambitious formulation of her argument, she asserts that the entire European literary canon since the Renaissance might be considered a massively elaborated (and ultimately coercive) statement on male bonding. What makes a literary work "canonical," in her view, is precisely in fact the degree of its absorption in the issue of male homosociality. She makes this provocative claim in a crucial passage—once again from the introduction—in which she explains the somewhat idiosyncratic assortment of texts to which individual chapters of *Between Men* are dedicated:

> The choices I have made of texts through which to embody the argument of the book are specifically *not* meant to begin to delineate a separate male-homosocial literary canon. In fact, it will be essential to my argument to claim that the European canon as it exists is already such a canon, and most so when it is most heterosexual. . . . I have simply chosen texts at pleasure from within or alongside the English canon that represented particularly interesting interpretive problems, or particularly symptomatic historical and ideological modes, for understanding the politics of male homosociality. (17)

Literature canonizes the subject of male homosociality; in return, it would seem, the subject of male homosociality canonizes the work of literature.

Within such a totalizing scheme, with its insistent focus on relations "between men," what place might there be for relations between women? Sedgwick is aware, or at least half-aware, that her theory in some ways fails "to do justice to women's own powers, bonds, and struggles" (18). She freely acknowledges that her reluctance to distinguish between what she calls "ideologizing" and "de-ideologizing" narratives may have led her to present "the 'canonical' cultural discourse in an excessively protean and inescapable . . . form." Yet at the same time she makes it clear that she can offer little in the way of comment on "women's own cultural resources of resistance, adaptation, revision, and survival." She is content to send out a somewhat perfunctory appeal to her readers for "better analyses of the relations between female-homosocial and male-homosocial structures" (18).

If the subject of female bonding sets up a kind of intellectual or emotional "blockage" in Sedgwick's argument, the specialized form of female bonding represented by lesbianism seems to provoke in her, interestingly enough, even deeper resistance. In the one or two somewhat strained paragraphs of *Between Men* that Sedgwick *does* devote to women's bonds, she more or less summarily dismisses *lesbianism* as a useful category of analysis. In contrast to the spectacularly polarized arrangement she finds in the realm of male desire, she can see no real cultural or ideological distinction, in the case of women, between homosociality and homosexuality:

> The diacritical opposition between the "homosocial" and the "homosexual" seems to be much less thorough and dichotomous for women, in our society, than for men. At this particular historical moment, an intelligible continuum of aims, emotions, and valuations links lesbianism with the other forms of women's attention to women: the bond of mother and daughter, for instance, the bond of sister and sister, women's friendship, "networking," and the active struggles of feminism. The continuum is crisscrossed with deep discontinuities—with much homophobia, with conflicts of race and class— but its intelligibility seems now a matter of simple common sense. However agonistic the politics, however conflicted the feelings, it seems at this moment to make an obvious kind of sense to say that women in our society who love women, women who teach, study, nurture, suckle, write about, march for, vote for, give jobs to, or otherwise promote the interests of other women, are pursuing congruent and closely related activities. (2–3)

Lesbians, defined here, with telling vagueness, only as "women who love women," are really no different, Sedgwick seems to imply, from "women promoting the interests of other women." Their way of bonding is so "congruent" with that of other women, it turns out, that one need no longer call it homosexual. "The adjective 'homosocial' as applied to women's bonds," she concludes, "*need not be pointedly dichotomized as against 'homosexual'; it can intelligibly denominate the entire continuum*" (3; my emphasis). By a disarming sleight of phrase, an entire category of women—lesbians—is lost to view.

In the face of these rhetorically tortured and—for Sedgwick—uncharacteristically sentimental passages, one's immediate impulse may be to remark, somewhat uncharitably, that she has not "gotten the point," so to speak, of pointedly dichotomizing lesbian from straight existence. What may appear "intelligible" or "simple common sense" to a nonlesbian critic will hardly seem quite so simple to any female reader who has ever attempted to walk down a city street holding hands with, let alone kissing or embracing, another woman. The homosexual panic elicited by women publicly signaling their sexual interest in another continues, alas, even "at this particular historical moment," to be just as virulent as that inspired by male homosexuality, if not more so.[4] To obscure the fact that lesbians are women who have sex with each other—and that this is not exactly the same, in the eyes of society, as voting for women or giving them jobs—is, in essence, not to acknowledge the separate peril and pleasure of lesbian existence.

Are we then simply to blame Sedgwick for succumbing, albeit belatedly, to the

Queen Victoria Principle? I think not—for what I am calling, perhaps too tendentiously, the "blockage" in her theory, is intimately related, paradoxically, to its strength. It is precisely because Sedgwick has recognized so clearly the canonical power of *male-male* desire—and has described so well its shaping role in the plots of eighteenth- and nineteenth-century English and American literature—that she does not "get the point" of *female-female* desire. For to do so would mean undoing, if only imaginatively, the very structure she is elsewhere at such pains to elaborate: the figure of the male homosocial triangle itself.

To theorize about female-female desire, I would like to suggest, is precisely to envision the taking apart of this supposedly intractable patriarchal structure. Female bonding, at least hypothetically, destabilizes the "canonical" triangular arrangement of male desire, is an affront to it, and ultimately—in the radical form of lesbian bonding—displaces it entirely. Even Sedgwick's own geometrical model intimates as much. As the figure below suggests, the male-female-male erotic triangle remains stable only as long as its single female term is unrelated to any other female term. Once two female terms are conjoined in space, however, an alternative structure comes into being, a female-male-female triangle, in which one of the male terms from the original triangle now occupies the "in between" or subjugated position of the mediator.

Within this new *female* homosocial structure, the possibility of male bonding is radically suppressed: for the male term is now isolated, just as the female term was in the male homosocial structure.

 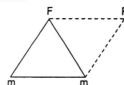

But one can go still further. In the original male-female-male configuration, we may recollect, the relationship between the dominant male terms was not static. Indeed, this was the inherent problem in the structure from the patriarchal perspective: that the two male terms might hook up directly, so to speak, replacing the heterosexual with an explicitly homosexual dyad. Yet exactly the same dynamism is characteristic of the female homosocial triangle. In the most radical transformation of female bonding—i.e., from homosocial to *lesbian* bonding—the two female terms indeed merge and the male term drops out. At this point, it is safe to say, not only is male bonding suppressed, it has become impossible—there being no male terms left to bond.

A pleasing elaboration of the Sedgwickian model, perhaps—but does it have any literary applications? If we restrict ourselves, as Sedgwick herself does, to the canon of eighteenth- and nineteenth-century English and American fiction, the answer would have to be no, or not really. Indeed, one might easily argue that just as the major works of realistic fiction from this period constitute a brief against male homosexuality (Sedgwick's point), so they also constitute, even more blatantly, a brief against female homosociality. Even in works in which female homosocial bonds are depicted, these bonds are inevitably shown giving way to the power of male homosocial triangulation. In Charlotte Brontë's *Shirley*, for example, a novel that explicitly thematizes the conflict between male and female bonding, the original female homosocial bond between Shirley Keeldar and Caroline Helstone (a bond triangulated through the character of the mill owner Robert Moore) is replaced at the end of the novel by not just one, but two interlocking male homosocial triangles, symbolized in the marriages of Robert with Caroline and of Robert's brother Louis with Shirley. True, *Shirley* represents an unusually tormented and ambivalent version of the male homosocial plot: but even Brontë, like other Victorian novelists, gives way in the end to the force of fictional and ideological convention.[5]

But what if we turn our attention to twentieth-century writing? Are there any contemporary novels that undo the seemingly compulsory plot of male homosocial desire? It will come as no surprise that I am about to invoke such a work, and that I propose to denominate it, without further ado, an exemplary "lesbian fiction." The work I have in mind is Sylvia Townsend Warner's 1936 *Summer Will Show*, a historical fiction set in rural Dorset and Paris during the revolution of 1848. What makes this novel paradigmatically "lesbian," in my view, is not simply that it depicts a sexual relationship between two women, but that it so clearly, indeed almost schematically, figures this relationship as a breakup of the supposedly "canonical" male-female-male erotic triangle. As I shall try to demonstrate in what follows, it is exactly this kind of subverted triangulation, or erotic "counterplotting," that is in fact characteristic of lesbian novels in general.

Summer Will Show is not, I realize, a well-known piece of fiction—indeed quite the opposite. Even among Townsend Warner devotees it is still a relatively unfamiliar work, despite a Virago reprint in 1987. Townsend Warner's earlier novel *Lolly Willowes* (1926) remains generally better known; later works, such as the novel *The Corner That Held Them* (1948), the biography of T.H. White (1967), and the short story collection *Kingdoms of Elfin* (1977) have attracted more critical attention.* What notice *Summer Will Show* has received has tended to be condescending in nature: because Townsend Warner wrote the novel during the period of her most passionate involvement with the British Communist party and intended it in part as an allegory of the Spanish Civil War, it has often been dismissed as a "Marxist novel" or leftist period piece. While not entirely an *un*read work of modern English fiction, *Summer Will Show* is at the very least an *under*read one.

Yet some of the resistance the work has met with must also have to do, one suspects, with its love story, which challenges so spectacularly the rigidly heterosexual conventions of classic English and American fiction. This story begins de-

---

*Townsend Warner's brilliant and varied writings, many of which touch on the theme of homosexuality, have been sorely neglected since her death in 1978—not least by gay and lesbian readers and critics. Her most enthusiastic admirer, somewhat unexpectedly, remains George Steiner, who in the pages of the *Times Literary Supplement* (December 2–8, 1988), pronounced *The Corner That Held Them* a "masterpiece" of modern English fiction. Claire Harman's biography, *Sylvia Townsend Warner*, will no doubt help to rectify this curious situation, as should Wendy Mulford's *This Narrow Place*, a superb study of the relationship between Townsend Warner and the poet Valentine Ackland, her lover of thirty years. Also of great interest is Townsend Warner's correspondence, edited by William Maxwell. Besides displaying Townsend Warner's matchless wit and unfailingly elegant style, the letters also demonstrate that she was capable of imagining Queen Victoria's sex life, even if Queen Victoria could not have imagined hers (see letter to Llewelyn Powys, December 7, 1933).

ceptively simply, in a seemingly recognizable literary landscape: that of nine-teenth-century fiction itself. The tall, fair-haired heroine, Sophia Willoughby, is the only daughter of wealthy landed gentry in Dorset, the heiress of Blandamer House (in which she resides), and the wife of a feckless husband, Frederick, who, after marrying her for her money and fathering her two small children, has aban-doned her and taken a mistress in Paris. At the start of the novel, Sophia is walk-ing with her children, a boy and a girl, on a hot summer's day to the limekiln on the estate, in the hope that by subjecting them to a traditional remedy—limekiln fumes—she can cure them of the whooping cough they have both contracted.

Already in these opening pages, given over to Sophia's reveries on the way to the limekiln, we have a sense of her proud, powerful, yet troubled nature: like another Gwendolen Harleth or even a new Emma Bovary, she broods over her unhappy marriage and yearns ambiguously for "something decisive," a new kind of fulfillment, some "moment when she should exercise her authority" (11).[6] While devoted to her children, she also feels constricted by them and infuriated at her husband for leaving them entirely to her care. As for Frederick himself, she harbours no lingering romantic illusions there, only "icy disdain," mixed with a sense of sexual grievance. It is not so much that she is jealous—their marriage had been devoid of passion—but that she resents his freedom and his predict-ably chosen "bohemian" mistress:

> For even to Dorset the name of Minna Lemuel had made its way. Had the husband of Mrs. Willoughby chosen no other end than to be scandalous, he could not have chosen better. A byword, half actress, half strumpet; a Jewess; a nonsensical creature bedizened with airs of prophecy, who trailed across Europe with a tag-rag of poets, revolutionaries, musicians and circus-riders snuffing at her heels, like an escaped bitch with a procession of mongrels af-ter her; and ugly; and old, as old as Frederick or older—this was the woman whom Frederick had elected to fall in love with, joining the tag-rag proces-sion, and not even king in that outrageous court, not even able to dismiss the mongrels, and take the creature into keeping. (31)

At the same time, however, Sophia feels an odd gratitude to the other woman: thanks to Minna, Sophia reminds herself, she is "a mother, and a landowner; but fortunately, she need no longer be counted among the wives" (20).

All this is to change as a result of the limekiln visit itself. With Sophia looking on, the limekiln keeper—a silent, frightening-looking man with sores on his arms—suspends each of the children over the kiln. Though terrified, they inhale the fumes and Sophia takes them home. In the next few weeks, her attention is distracted by the arrival of her nephew Caspar, the illegitimate mulatto child of an uncle in the West Indies. At her uncle's request, she takes Caspar to Cornwall to place him in a boarding school. Returning home, she finds her own children mortally ill: the limekiln keeper was in fact carrying smallpox and has infected both children. Sophia delays writing to her husband to inform him; yet Frederick comes anyway, having been recalled by a letter written by the doctor who is at-tending the children.

At once Sophia senses a subtle change in her husband, a mystifying new re-finement, which she attributes—balefully, yet also with growing curiosity—to the influence of his unseen mistress. Listening to him repeat the words *"Ma fleur"* over his dying daughter's sickbed, it seems to Sophia as if a stranger were speaking through him: someone possessed of "a deep sophistication in sorrow." The intrusive cadence, she reminds herself angrily, must be copied from "that Minna's Jewish contralto." Yet afterward, when both of the children are dead and Frederick has gone back to Paris, Sophia finds herself haunted by a memory of the voice—one that seems, "according to her mood, an enigma, a nettle-sting, a caress" (83).

With the death of Sophia's children, the crucial action of the novel commences. Distraught, grief-stricken, yet also peculiarly obsessed with her husband's other life, Sophia decided to seek him out in Paris, for the purpose (she tells herself) of forcing him to give her more children. Yet, as if driven by more mysterious urgings, she finds herself, on the very evening of her arrival, at the apartment on the Rue de la Carabine where Minna holds her salon. Entering the apartment unobserved, Sophia joins the crowd of guests (including Frederick himself) who are listening to their hostess tell a story.

The story, which is presented as an embedded narrative, is a hypnotic account of Minna's childhood in Eastern Europe—of the pogrom in which her parents were killed, of her own escape from the murderers, and of her eventual rescue by a vagrant musician. The experience of persecution has made her an artist, a storyteller, a romantic visionary, and a political revolutionary. As Sophia listens, seemingly mesmerized by the Jewish woman's charismatic "siren voice," she forgets entirely about Frederick and the putative reason she has come. Suddenly the tale is interrupted—barricades are being put up outside in the streets; the first skirmishes of what will become the February Revolution are about to begin. Minna's listeners, mainly artists and intellectuals who support the revolt, depart, along with Frederick, who has not yet seen his wife. And Sophia, still as if under a spell, finds herself alone in the room with Minna.

She is utterly, heart-stoppingly, captivated. Not by Minna's beauty—for Frederick's mistress is a small, dark, and sallow woman, with "a slowly flickering glance" and "large supple hands" that seem to "caress themselves together in the very gesture of her thought" (127). Yet something in this very look, "sombre and attentive," alive with tenderness and recognition, ineluctably draws Sophia to her. ("I cannot understand," Sophia finds herself thinking, "what Frederick could see in you. But *I* can see a great deal" [154].) Minna in turn seems equally delighted with her lover's wife. Together they look out on the barricades: Frederick is below and now sees Sophia; he is piqued when she refuses his offer of a cab. Minna also ignores him, so he leaves. Minna then confides in Sophia her hopes for the success of the insurrection. Sophia, entranced yet also exhausted, falls asleep on Minna's sofa. When she awakens the next day, her hostess is sitting beside her. Inspired by the strange "ardour" of the Jewish woman's attention, the normally reticent Sophia suddenly finds herself overcome by an urge to recount the story of *her* own life. As if freed from an invisible bondage, she finds herself talking for hours. When Frederick returns that afternoon, he is momentarily "felled" to discover his wife and mistress "seated together on the pink sofa, knit into this fathomless intimacy, and turning from it to entertain him with an identical patient politeness." For "neither woman, absorbed in this extraordinary colloquy, had expressed by word or sign the slightest consciousness that there was anything unusual about it" (157).

Nor, might it be said, does Townsend Warner. The attraction between Sophia and Minna is treated, if anything, as a perfectly natural elaboration of the wife-mistress situation. The two women, it is true, separate for several weeks, in part because Sophia is afraid of the depth—and complication—of her new attachment. While the political turmoil in the city grows, she stays with her wealthy, superannuated French aunt, Léocadie, who tries to reconcile her with Frederick. Yet she is drawn back into Minna's orbit soon enough, when she hears that Minna has given away almost all of her money to the striking workers and is destitute. Outraged with Frederick for "casting off" his mistress (which is how Sophia describes the situation to herself), she determines to fulfill his "obligations" herself. She returns to the now-shabby apartment on the Rue de la Carabine, and finding Minna weak with cold and hunger, decides to stay and care for her. As her absorption in the other woman grows—and is reciprocated—Sophia gradually feels her old identity, that of the heiress of Blandamer, slipping away. As if "by some extraordinary enchantment," she is inexorably caught up in Minna's world and in the revolutionary activity in which Minna is involved.

Meanwhile Frederick, incensed by the alliance between his wife and his (now) ex-mistress, cuts off Sophia's allowance in order to force her to return to him. Yet his machinations serve only to intensify—indeed to eroticize—the intimacy between the two women. When Sophia tells her friend that Frederick has told the bank not to honor her signature "as he is entitled to do being my husband," they suddenly comprehend their desire for what it is:

> "You will stay? You must, if only to gall him."
> "I don't think that much of a reason."
> "But you will stay?"
> "I will stay if you wish it."
> It seemed to her that the words fell cold and glum as ice-pellets. Only beneath the crust of thought did her being assent as by right to that flush of pleasure, that triumphant cry.
> "But of course," said Minna a few hours later, thoughtfully licking the last oyster shell, "we must be practical." (274)

Townsend Warner, to be sure, renders the scene of their passionate coming together elliptically—with only a cry (and an oyster) to suggest the moment of consummation—yet the meaning is clear: Sophia has severed all ties with the past—with her husband, her class, and with sexual convention itself.[7]

In the final section of the novel, spring gives way to summer; the popular insurrection, dormant for several months, flares once again. Inspired by her newfound love for Minna, Sophia throws herself into political activity, becoming a courier for a group of communists who are collecting weapons in preparation for open civil war. Her last contact with her husband comes about when her nephew Caspar suddenly turns up in Paris, alienated and sullen, having run away from the school in Cornwall: Sophia is forced to ask Frederick for money to pay for the youth's schooling in Paris. Without her knowledge, Frederick, who now cynically supports the government, instead buys Caspar a place in the Gardes Mobiles, the force opposing the now-imminent June rebellion.

Returning from one of her courier missions, Sophia finds that street fighting has begun in the neighborhood around the Rue de la Carabine. Minna is already on the barricades. Together they join in the battle, loading and reloading the workers' rifles. The Gardes Mobiles launch an attack on the barricade and Sophia, to her surprise, recognizes Caspar in their midst. He plunges a bayonet into Minna, who falls, apparently mortally wounded. Sophia shoots Caspar in retaliation, but is herself captured and taken away with some other prisoners to be executed, only to be freed the next day because she is a woman. She searches frantically for Minna but cannot discover if she is alive or dead. The revolt has been put down and the workers' hopes seemingly destroyed. Returning to Minna's apartment, yet still harboring a hope that her lover will return, Sophia opens one of the pamphlets that she had been delivering the previous day. It is Marx's *Communist Manifesto*. As she settles down to read—exhausted but also arrested by its powerful opening words—the novel comes ambiguously to an end.

I will return to this somewhat curious denouement in a moment: I would like to draw attention first to the more obviously revisionist aspects of Townsend Warner's narrative. For *Summer Will Show*—as I hope even my highly compressed account of its characters and incidents will have indicated—is a work obsessed with "revising" on a number of counts. In the most literal sense the novel is a kind of revisionist fantasia: in recounting the story of her pseudo-Victorian heroine, Sophia Willoughby, Townsend Warner constantly pastiches—yet also rewrites—Victorian fiction itself. The opening scene at the limekiln, for example, both recalls and traduces the episode in *Great Expectations* in which Pip is dangled over a limekiln by the infamous Orlick: the "great expectations" here belong, ironically, to the observer, Sophia herself. The early episodes involving the mulatto Caspar and the uncle in the West Indies likewise rework and subvert elements from *Wuthering Heights* and *Jane Eyre*. After Sophia's arrival in Paris, a curiously erotic scene in which Minna shows her her duelling pistols (154–6) is an almost direct parody of a similar moment in *Shirley*: Minna's guns are about to be given up to the striking workers of Paris: the guns that Caroline Helstone shows to Shirley Keeldar are their protection *against* the striking workers of Briarfield. Minna herself is a kind of revolutionary variant on a George Eliot heroine. Her Jewishness and political radicalism bring to mind characters and situations from *Daniel Deronda* and *Felix Holt*; her appearance—and passionate intelligence—may be modeled on Eliot's own. Yet she is far more deviant than any Eliot heroine is ever allowed to be. Tellingly, her very name appears to originate in the famous passage in *The Mill on the Floss* in which Maggie Tulliver declares her wish to "avenge" all the unfortunate dark-haired heroines of English literature—"Rebecca, and Flora MacIvor, and Minna, and all the rest of the dark unhappy ones."[8] Maggie's Minna is the hapless heroine of Sir Walter Scott's *The Pirate* abandoned by her lover on a frigid Scottish beach. By contrast, Townsend Warner's Minna—with her freedom from convention, her sexual charisma, and survivor's instinct—is at once a satirical rewrite of the first Minna and a more resilient version of Maggie herself.

But it is not only English fiction that Townsend Warner is rewriting in *Summer Will Show*. In a somewhat tongue-in-cheek note composed in the 1960s, she revealed that in order to write the book she "re-read Berlioz's *Mémoires*, and with an effort put the French novelists out of my mind."[9] Berlioz is certainly there, but so too are the French novelists. The scenes at Minna's Parisian salon have the flavour of Staël and Hugo as well as of Stendhal and Balzac; Sophia's right-wing aunt, Léocadie, along with her egregious confessor Père Hyacinthe, are straight out of *La Comédie humaine*. But it is Flaubert, obviously, and *his* novel of 1848, that Townsend Warner is most deeply conscious of displacing. Anyone who doubts the subterranean importance of *L'Éducation sentimentale* to *Summer Will Show* need only consider the name Frédéric—or Frederick—and the parodistic relationship that exists between Flaubert's antihero, Frédéric Moreau, and Townsend Warner's comic villain, Frederick Willoughby.*

To invoke Flaubert's masterpiece, however, is also to return—with a vengeance— to the Sedgwickian issue of erotic triangulation. For what is *L'Éducation senti- mentale* if not a classic work, in Sedgwick's terms, of male homosocial bonding? Flaubert's Frédéric, we recall, acts out his emotional obsession with his friend Arnoux by falling in love first with Arnoux's wife, then with his mistress. Townsend Warner's Frederick, by contrast, not only has no male friend, his wife and his mistress fall in love with each other. In the very act of revising Flaubert— of substituting her own profoundly "anticanonical" fiction in place of his own— Townsend Warner also revises the plot of male homosocial desire. Indeed, all of her revisionist gestures can, I think, be linked with this same imaginative im- pulse: the desire to plot *against* the seemingly indestructible heterosexual narra- tive of classic European fiction.

This work of counterplotting can best be figured, as I suggested at the outset, as a kind of dismantling and displacement of the male homosocial triangle itself. Granted, at the beginning of *Summer Will Show*, the hoary Sedgwickian structure still seems firmly in place. Sophia is more or less mired in the "in between" po- sition that patriarchal society demands of her. As the only heiress of Blandamer, "the point advancing on the future, as it were, of that magnificent triangle in which Mr. and Mrs. Aspen of Blandamer House, Dorset, England, made up the other two apices" (3), she has functioned, we are led to deduce, as the social me- diator between her own father, who has been forced to give her up in marriage in order to perpetuate the Aspen family line, and Frederick, the son-in-law, who has enriched himself by allying himself with the Aspen patrimony.

Yet instabilities in this classic male-female-male triad soon become apparent. The deaths of Sophia's children are the first sign of a generalized weakening of male homosocial bonds; these deaths, we realize, are not just a transforming loss for Sophia, but for Frederick also, who loses, through them, his only remaining biological and symbolic connection to Sophia's dead father, his partner in the novel's original homosocial triangle. Significantly, perhaps, it is the son who is the first of the children to die: in a way that prefigures the symbolic action of the novel as a whole, the patrilineal triangle of father-mother-son here disappears, leaving only a female-male-female triangle, composed of Sophia, Frederick, and their daughter. Even at this early stage, one might argue, Townsend Warner rep-

---

*Frederick Willoughby is condemned by his name on two counts of course: if his first name recalls the stooge of Flaubert's *L'Éducation sentimentale*, his last he shares with the unprin- cipled villain of Austen's *Sense and Sensibility*. In Austen's novel, we recall, the more hap- less of the two heroines is abandoned by (John) Willoughby in favour of a rich heiress. To the extent that (Frederick) Willoughby—now married to his rich heiress—is himself aban- doned by wife and mistress both, one might consider Townsend Warner's novel a displaced sequel to Austen's: a kind of comic postlude, or "revenge of Marianne Dashwood."

resents the female-dominant triangle as "stronger," or in some sense more durable, than the male-dominant one.

Yet other episodes in the first part of the novel suggest a disintegration of male homosocial structures. When Sophia delays writing to Frederick during the children's illness, her doctor, thinking the absence of her husband a scandal, writes to him without her knowledge. The letter is intercepted by the doctor's young wife, who brings it to Sophia and offers to destroy it. "Why should all this be done behind your back?" exclaims the outraged Mrs. Hervey, "what right have they to interfere, to discuss and plot, and settle what they think best to be done? As if, whatever happened, you could not stand alone, and judge for yourself! As if you needed a man!" (72). Admittedly, Sophia decided in the end to let the letter be sent, but the intimation here of an almost conspiratorial bonding between the two women—against *both* of their husbands—directly foreshadows the more powerful bonding of Sophia with Minna. And as will be true later, a strong current of erotic feeling runs between the two women. "She might be in love with me," Sophia thinks after Mrs. Hervey "awkwardly" embraces her during one of their first meetings. Now, as she looks at the letter "lying so calmly" on Mrs. Hervey's lap, it suddenly seems only a pretext: "some other motive, violent and unexperienced as the emotions of youth, trembled undeclared between them." Later, they walk hand in hand in a thunderstorm, and Sophia briefly entertains a fancy of going on a European tour with Mrs. Hervey—"large-eyed and delighted and clutching a box of watercolour paints"—at her side (78).

With the love affair between Sophia and Minna, one might say that the male homosocial triad reaches its point of maximum destabilization and collapses altogether. In its place appears a new configuration, the triad of *female* homosocial desire. For Frederick, obviously, is now forced into the position of the subject term, the one "in between," the odd one out—the one, indeed, who can be patronized. Sophia and Minna do just this during their first supper together, following the memorable colloquy on the pink sofa. Sophia takes it upon herself to order wine, a discreetly masculine gesture that inspires Minna to remark, "How much I like being with English people! They manage everything so quietly and so well." Sophia, catching her drift, instantly rejoins, "And am I as good as Frederick?" "You are much better," Minna replies. After a short meditation on Frederick's shortcomings, the two women subside into complacent amity. "Poor Frederick!" says one. "Poor Frederick!" says the other (161–62).

We might call this the comedy of female-female desire: as two women come together, the man who has brought them together seems oddly reduced, transformed into a figure of fun. Later he will drop out of sight altogether—which is another way of saying that in every lesbian relationship there is a man who has been sacrificed. Townsend Warner will call attention to this "disappearing man" phenomenon at numerous points, sometimes in a powerfully literal way. When Sophia returns, for example, to the Rue de la Carabine to help the poverty-stricken Minna, only to find her lying chilled and unconscious on the floor, she immediately lies down to warm her, in "a desperate calculated caress." Yet this first, soon-to-be eroticized act of lying down with Minna also triggers a reverie—on the strangeness of the season that has brought them together, on the vast distance each has traversed to arrive at this moment, and on the man "between them" who is, of course, not there:

> It was spring, she remembered. In another month the irises would be com-
> ing into flower. But now it was April, the cheat month, when the deadliest
> frosts might fall, when snow might cover the earth, lying hard and authentic
> on the English acres as it lay over the wastes of Lithuania. There, in one di-
> rection, was Blandamer, familiar as a bed; and there, in another was Lithuania,
> the unknown, where a Jewish child had watched the cranes fly over, and had
> stood beside the breaking river. And here, in Paris lay Sophia Willoughby, ly-
> ing on the floor in the draughty passage-way between bedroom and dress-
> ing-closet, her body pressed against the body of her husband's mistress. (251)

The intimacy, here and later, is precisely the intimacy enjoined by the breakup
of monolithic structures, indeed, by the breakup of triangulation itself. For what
Sophia and Minna discover, even as they muse over "poor Frederick," is that they
need him no longer: in the draughty passageway leading to a bedroom, the very
shape of desire is "pressed" out of shape, becoming dyadic, impassioned,
lesbian.[10]

What is particularly satisfying about Townsend Warner's plotting here is that it
illustrates so neatly—indeed so trigonometrically—what we might take to be the
underlying principle of lesbian narrative itself: namely, that for female bonding
to "take," as it were, to metamorphose into explicit sexual desire, male bonding
must be suppressed. (Male homo*social* bonding, that is; for lesbian characters in
novels can, and do, quite easily coexist with male homo*sexual* characters, as Djuna
Barnes's *Nightwood*, or even *Orlando* in its final pages, might suggest).[11] Townsend
Warner's Frederick has no boyhood friend, no father, no father-in-law, no son, no
gang, *no novelist on his side* to help him retriangulate his relationship with his
wife—or for that matter, with his mistress either. To put it axiomatically: in the
absence of male homosocial desire, lesbian desire emerges.

Can such a principle help us to theorize in more general ways about lesbian
fiction? Obviously, I think it can. It allows us to identify first of all two basic mimetic contexts in which, in realistic writing, plots of lesbian desire are most likely
to flourish: the world of schooling and adolescence (the world of premarital relations) and the world of divorce, widowhood, and separation (the world of
postmarital relations). In each of these mimetic contexts, male erotic triangulation is either conspicuously absent or under assault. In the classically gynocentric
setting of the girls' school, for example, male characters are generally isolated or
missing altogether: hence the powerfully female homosocial/homosexual plots of
Colette's *Claudine à l'école*, Clemence Dane's *Regiment of Women*, Dorothy
Strachey's *Olivia*, Antonia White's *Frost in May*, Christa Winsloe's *The Child
Manuela* (on which the film *Mädchen in Uniform* is based), Lillian Hellman's *The
Children's Hour*, Muriel Spark's *The Prime of Miss Jean Brodie*, Catharine Stimpson's
Class Notes or more recently, Jeanette Winterson's *Oranges Are Not the Only Fruit*,
in which the juvenile heroine woos her first love while attending a female Bible
study group.

Yet the figure of male homosociality is even more pitilessly compromised in
novels of postmarital experience. In the novel of adolescence, it is true, male
homosocial desire often reasserts itself, belatedly, at the end of the fiction: the
central lesbian bond may be undermined or broken up, usually by having one of
the principals die (as in *The Child Manuela* or *The Children's Hour*), get married (as
in *Oranges Are Not the Only Fruit*), or reconcile herself in some other way with the

erotic and social world of men (as in *Claudine à l'école* or *The Prime of Miss Jean Brodie*). We might call this "dysphoric" lesbian counterplotting. To the extent that it depicts female homosexual desire as a finite phenomenon—a temporary phase in a larger pattern of heterosexual *Bildung*—the lesbian novel of adolescence is almost always dysphoric in tendency.[12]

In post-marital lesbian fiction, however, male homosocial bonds are generally presented—from the outset—as debilitated to the point of unrecuperability. Typically in such novels, it is the very failure of the heroine's marriage or heterosexual love affair that functions as the pretext for her conversion to homosexual desire. This conversion is radical and irreversible: once she discovers (usually ecstatically) her passion for women, there is no going back. We might call this "euphoric" lesbian counterplotting: it is an essentially comic, even utopian plot plan. A new world is imagined in which male bonding has no place. Classic lesbian novels following the euphoric pattern include Jane Bowles's *Two Serious Ladies*, Jane Rule's *The Desert of the Heart*, and Patricia Highsmith's *The Price of Salt*, as well as numerous pulp romances of recent vintage, such as Ann Bannon's *Journey to a Woman* and Katharine V. Forrest's *An Emergence of Green*. In that it too begins with a failed marriage (that of Robin Vote and Felix Volkbein), even such a baroquely troubled work as *Nightwood*, paradoxically, might be considered euphoric in this respect: though its depiction of lesbian love is often malign, the novel takes for granted a world in which female erotic bonds predominate—so much so that the very possibility of male homosociality seems negated from the start.*

With its insouciant, sometimes coruscating satire on male bonding, *Summer Will Show* typifies the postmarital or conversion fiction: its energies are primarily comic and visionary. It is a novel of liberation. As Minna says to Sophia at one point: "You have run away. . . . You'll never go back now, you know. I've encouraged a quantity of people to run away, but I have never seen any one so decisively escaped as you" (217). Yet is this the whole story? Given that the novel concludes with Minna herself apparently slain on the barricades, a victim of Caspar (who in turn is the pawn of Frederic), how complete, finally, is what I am calling, perhaps too exuberantly, its "undoing" of the classic male homosocial plot?

That the ending of *Summer Will Show* poses a problem cannot be denied: Wendy Mulford, one of Townsend Warner's most astute critics, calls it an

---

*The reader may object, rightly, that the most famous lesbian novel of all, Radclyffe Hall's *The Well of Loneliness*, does not seem to fall clearly into either the euphoric or the dysphoric category. It may well be that we need to devise a new category—that of "lesbian epic"— to contain Hall's manic-depressive extravaganza. True, in that it manages to work unhappy variations on both the premarital and the postmarital plot types (Stephen's first love, Angela, is a married woman who refuses to leave her husband; her second, Mary, leaves Stephen in order to marry a male friend). *The Well of Loneliness* often leans in a dysphoric direction. Yet the introduction midway through the novel of the Natalie Barney character, Valérie Seymour, and Hall's tentative limnings of a larger lesbian society in Paris, also seem to promise an end to Stephen's intolerable "loneliness"—if only in some as yet ill-defined, unknown future. With its multiplying characters and subplots, constant shifts in setting and mood and powerfully "ongoing" narrative structure, *The Well* seems more a kind of Homeric or Tennysonian quest-fiction—a lesbian *Odyssey*—than a novel in the ordinary sense.

unconvincing "botch"—though not, interestingly, for any purely narratological reason. For Mulford, Minna's bayoneting by Caspar is symptomatic of Townsend Warner's own emotional confusion in the 1930s, over whether to devote herself to her writing or to revolutionary (specifically Marxist) political struggle. To the extent that Minna, the storytelling romantic, represents the potentially anarchical freedom of the artist, she has to be "sacrificed," Mulford argues, in order to "free the dedicated revolutionary" in Sophia, who functions here as a stand-in for the novelist herself. At the same time, Mulford conjectures, "[Townsend Warner's] unconscious was unable to consent to such a move"—hence the novel's descent into bathos and melodrama at this point.[13]

Yet Mulford already oversimplifies, I think, in assuming without question that Minna is dead. Granted, Minna seems to be dead (during the onslaught on the barricade Sophia sees Caspar's bayonet "jerk" into Minna's breast), yet, in a curious turnabout in the novel's final pages, Townsend Warner goes out of her way—seemingly gratuitously—to hint that she may in fact still be alive. Although unsuccessful, Sophia's attempts to locate Minna's body raise the possibility that her lover has survived: a witness to the scene on the barricades, Madam Guy, concedes that Minna was indeed alive when she was dragged away by soldiers; her daughter confirms it (397–98). Later visits to "all the places where enquiries may be made" turn up nothing, but the man who accompanies Sophia reminds her that the officials in charge may be misleading her on purpose—the implication being that her friend may in fact be held prisoner somewhere (399). The ambiguity is hardly resolved even at the last. When Sophia returns to Minna's apartment and takes up the *Communist Manifesto*, her peculiarly composed attitude seems as much one of waiting as of tragic desolation: far from being traumatized by seeing "the wine that Minna had left for her" or Minna's slippers on the floor, she merely sits down to read, as though Minna were at any moment about to return. The utopian tract she peruses in turn hints symbolically at the thematics of return: if we take seriously the analogy that Townsend Warner has made throughout the novel between her heroine's political and sexual transformation, the inspiriting presence of the *Manifesto* here, with its promise of revolutionary hope resurrected, may also portend another kind of resurrection—that of Minna herself.

The novelist here seems to test how much implausibility we are willing to accept—for according to even the loosest standard of probability (such as might hold, say, in Victorian fiction) the possibility that Minna should survive her bayoneting by Caspar, an event which itself already strains credibility, must appear fanciful in the extreme. Yet it cannot be denied that Townsend Warner herself seems drawn back to the idea—almost, one feels, because it *is* incredible. Having offered us a plausible (or semiplausible) ending, she now hints, seemingly capriciously, at a far more unlikely plot turn, as if perversely determined to revert to the most fantastical kind of closure imaginable.

Without attempting to diminish any of the ambiguity here, I think Warner's restaging of her conclusion—this apparent inability to let go of the possibility of euphoric resolution however improbable such a resolution must seem—can tell us something useful, once again, about lesbian fiction. By its very nature lesbian fiction has—and can only have—a profound attenuated relationship with what we think of, stereotypically, as narrative verisimilitude, plausibility, or "truth to life." Precisely because it is motivated by a yearning for that which is, in a cultural sense, implausible—the subversion of male homosocial desire—lesbian fiction characteristically exhibits, even as it masquerades as "realistic" in surface detail, a strongly fantastical, allegorical, or utopian tendency. The more insistently it gravitates toward euphoric resolution, moreover, the most implausible—in every way—it may seem.

The problem with Townsend Warner's novel—if in fact it is a problem—is not so much that it forfeits plausibility at the end but that it forfeits it from the start. There is nothing remotely believable about Sophia Willoughby's transformation from "heiress of Blandamer" into lover of her husband's mistress and communist revolutionary, if by "believability" we mean conformity with the established mimetic conventions of canonical English and American fiction. The novelist herself seems aware of this, and without ever entirely abandoning the framing pretense of historicity (the references to real people and events, the "Berliozian" local color), often hints at the artificial, "as if" or hypothetical nature of the world her characters inhabit. Metaphorically speaking, everything in the novel has a slightly suspect, theatrical, even phantasmagorical air. Revolutionary Paris resembles a stage set: the rebels near Minna's house are arrayed like "comic opera bandits" (177), a bloody skirmish in the streets is a "clinching raree-show" (171). Trying to convince her to return to her husband, Sophia's aunt Léocadie becomes a "ballerina," with Frederick "the suave athletic partner, respectfully leading her round by one leg as she quivered on the tip-toe of the other" (203). Elsewhere Frederick is a "tenor" plotting with the "basso" Père Hyacinthe (192). The captivating Minna, in turn, is a "gifted tragedy actress" (217), a "play-acting Shylock" (212), or someone "in a charade" (268). Sometimes Minna leaves the human realm altogether, metamorphosing into something from a fairy tale or myth—a "Medusa," a "herb-wife," a "siren," a "sorceress"—or a creature out of beast fable or Grandville cartoon. She is a "macaw," Sophia thinks, a "parrot," "some purple-plumaged bird of prey, her hooked nose impending," or perhaps the "sleekest" of cats (326). Her passion for Minna, Sophia concludes, is like the poet's —"of a birth as rare / As 'tis of object strange and high . . . begotten by despair / Upon impossibility" (289).

These built-in intimations of artifice and romance, of delight and high fakery, present on almost every page of *Summer Will Show*, work against the superficial historicism of the narrative, pushing it inexorably towards the fantastic. Of course a hankering after the fantastic is present elsewhere in Townsend Warner's writing: *Lolly Willowes*, we recall, begins as a seemingly straightforward tale about a spinster in an ordinary English village, but swerves abruptly into the marvellous when the spinster joins a coven of witches led by the Devil. Indeed the development of Townsend Warner's writing career as a whole suggests a progressive shifting away from realism toward the explicitly antimimetic modes of allegory and fable: in her last published stories, collected in *Kingdoms of Elfin*, she dispensed with human subjects entirely, choosing to commemorate instead the delicate passions of a race of elves.

Yet the fantastical element in *Summer Will Show*, is not, I think, simply a matter of authorial idiosyncrasy. Other lesbian novels display the same oscillation between realistic and fabulous modes. One need only think again of *Orlando* or *Nightwood*, or, indeed, of Joanna Russ's *The Female Man*, Elizabeth Jolley's *Miss*

Peabody's Inheritance, Lois Gould's *A Sea-Change*, Sarah Schulman's *After Delores*,
Margaret Erhart's *Unusual Company*, Michelle Cliff's *No Telephone to Heaven*, or any
of Jeanette Winterson's recent novels, to see how symptomatically lesbian fiction
resists any simple recuperation as "realistic." Even as it gestures back at a supposedly familiar world of human experience, it almost invariably stylizes and es-
tranges it—by presenting it parodistically, euphuistically, or in some other
rhetorically heightened, distorted, fragmented, or phantasmagoric way. In the
most extreme manifestation of this tendency, the pretence of mimesis collapses
completely. In Monique Wittig's *Les Guérillères* or Sally Gearheart's *The Wanderground*, for example, two explicitly utopian lesbian novels, the fictional world itself is fantastically transfigured, becoming a kind of sublime Amazonian dream
space: the marvellous inversion, in short, of that real world—"between men"—
the rest of us inhabit.[14]

What then *is* a lesbian fiction? Taking Sylvia Townsend Warner's *Summer Will
Show* as our paradigm, we can now begin to answer the question with which we
started. Such a fiction will be, both in the ordinary and in a more elaborated sense,
noncanonical. Like Townsend Warner's novel itself, the typical lesbian fiction is
likely to be an underread, even unknown, text—and certainly an underappreci-
ated one. It is likely to stand in a satirical, inverted, or parodic relationship to
more famous novels of the past—which is to say that it will exhibit an ambition
to displace the so-called canonical works that have preceded it. In the case of
Summer Will Show, Townsend Warner's numerous literary parodies—of Flaubert,
Eliot, Brontë, Dickens, and the rest—suggest a wish to displace, in particular, the
supreme texts of nineteenth-century realism, as if to infiltrate her own fiction
among them as a kind of subversive, inflammatory, pseudo-canonical substitute.

But, most important, by plotting against what Eve Sedgwick has called the
"plot of male homosociality," the archetypal lesbian fiction decanonizes, so to
speak, the canonical structure of desire itself. Insofar as it documents a world in
which men are "between women" rather than vice versa, it is an insult to the
conventional geometries of fictional eros. It dismantles the real, as it were, in a
search for the not-yet-real, something unpredicted and unpredictable. It is an assault on the banal: a retriangulating of triangles. As a consequence, it often looks
odd, fantastical, implausible, "not there"—utopian in aspiration if not design. It
is, in a word, imaginative. This is why, perhaps, like lesbian desire itself, it is still
difficult for us to acknowledge—even when (Queen Victoria notwithstanding) it
is so palpably, so plainly, there.

NOTES

1. To judge by how frequently it is repeated, the story of Queen Victoria's pronounce-
ment has taken on, alas, the status of cultural myth—the "truth" of which is that lesbians
don't really exist. Whenever it is retold—even seemingly jokingly, by antihomophobic historians and critics—it almost always prefigures the erasure of lesbianism from the discourse
that is to follow, usually through some equation of homosexuality with male homosexuality only. For an example of this phenomenon, see Richard Ellmann's *Oscar Wilde*, p. 409n.,
in which lesbianism—and Queen Victoria's views thereupon—are mentioned in a footnote,
then never referred to again.

2. Theoretical writing on lesbian fiction has been sparse until very recently. Jane Rule's

somewhat impressionistic *Lesbian Images* avoided theoretical speculation altogether; Catharine Stimpson's "Zero Degree Deviancy: The Lesbian Novel in English," while ahead of its time, focused only on a few fairly well-known books (*The Well of Loneliness, Nightwood*, Rita Mae Brown's *Rubyfruit Jungle*. With the recent burgeoning of interest in lesbian and gay writing, however, some interesting new studies have begun to appear. Bonnie Zimmerman's *The Safe Sea of Women: Lesbian Fiction, 1969–1988*—on structural and thematic patterns found in post-Stonewall lesbian fiction—is one such study; Judith Roof's *A Lure of Knowledge: Lesbian Sexuality and Theory*—on the "symptomatic configurations" of lesbian desire in modern culture—is another. Both Zimmerman and Roof offer close readings of several works, as do Elaine Hobby and Chris White in *What Lesbians Do in Books.* Valuable shorter studies have recently appeared in various edited collections: see, for example, essays by Valerie Miner, Lee Lynch, Diane A. Bogus, Elizabeth Meese, Marilyn R. Farwell, Judith Fetterley, Jane Marcus, and Shari Benstock in *Lesbian Texts and Contexts: Radical Revisions*; by Judith Mayne and Michèle Aina Barale in *Inside/Out: Lesbian Theories, Gay Theories*; by Sherron E. Knopp and Clare Whatling in *Sexual Sameness: Textual Differences in Lesbian and Gay Writing*; and by Katie King, Sally Munt, Hilary Hinds, and others in *New Lesbian Criticism: Literary and Cultural Readings.* The most useful bibliographic studies of lesbian fiction remain Jeannette Foster's classic *Sex Variant Women in Literature* and Barbara Grier's supplement to Foster, *The Lesbian in Literature.*

3. Sedgwick, *Between Men.* Page numbers of citations are noted in parentheses. Since the publication of *Between Men*, it is true, Sedgwick has begun to explore the subject of lesbianism (and of lesbian authorship) more fruitfully, notably in relation to what she calls "the epistemology of the closet"—the peculiar way in which the reality of homosexuality is at once affirmed and denied, elaborated and masked, in modern cultural discourse. Two of her recent essays are especially relevant here: "Privilege of Unknowing" (on Diderot's *La Religieuse*) and "Across Gender, Across Sexuality: Willa Cather and Others." Even in these seemingly more encompassing pieces, however, Sedgwick's unwillingness to separate herself from the spectacle of male bonding is still in evidence. In the Diderot essay, Sedgwick chooses a work that can be labeled *lesbian* only problematically, if at all: as Sedgwick herself says at one point, "because of the mid-eighteenth-century origin of the novella and because of its conventual venue, the question of lesbian sexual desire—*is* what is happening sexual desire, and will it be recognized and named as such?—looks, there, less like the question of the The Lesbian than the question of sexuality *tout court*." This may be true, but Sedgwick's immediate and seemingly reflexive transformation of the "lesbian sexual desire" she admits to seeing in *La Religieuse* into a figure for "sexuality *tout court*"—the site at which the "privilege of unknowing" is manifest—might also be taken as a symptom of a certain "unknowingness" regarding lesbianism itself: whatever *it* (lesbianism) is, Sedgwick implies, it is not worth bothering about in and of itself; it is simply a metaphor for other things that can't be talked about, such as (no surprise here) *male* homosexuality. Having disposed, at least theoretically, of any lesbian element in *La Religieuse,* Sedgwick then proceeds to slot the novel comfortably back into the framework of male homosocial desire. Citing approvingly Jay Caplan's observation that "this novel has the form of a message addressed by one father to another about their symbolic (and hence, absent) daughter," Sedgwick concludes that *La Religieuse* displays the "distinctively patriarchal triangular structure" of mail homosocial bonding (119)—thus foreclosing any more complex reading of its erotic relations. Tellingly, Sedgwick wonders at one point whether her own resistance to lesbian desire may perhaps have limited her understanding of the novel, but decides that this can't be so: "it would not be enough," she assures her reader, "to say that it is my fear of my own sexual desire for Suzanne [Diderot's heroine] that makes me propulsively individuate her as an 'other' in my reading of this book" (120). In the Cather piece, Sedgwick's resistance to lesbianism manifests itself less openly but is still palpable: she is interested in Cather, whom she refers to as "the mannish lesbian

author," primarily to the extent that Cather exemplifies a "move toward a minority gay identity whose more effectual cleavage, whose more determining separatism, would be that of homo/hetero*sexual* choice rather than those of male/female *gender*" (65–66). In choosing in the story "Paul's Case" to depict a young homosexual man sympathetically, argues Sedgwick, Cather at once performed an act of symbolic contrition for writing a hostile editorial in her youth about Oscar Wilde ("cleansing," in Sedgwick's lurid phrasing, "her own sexual body of the carrion stench of Wilde's victimization") and provided a wholesome model of "cross-gender liminality." That Sedgwick prefers such "liminality" to what she disdainfully labels "gender separatism" (of which lesbian separatism is a subcategory) is obvious: Cather is praised, because like "James, Proust, Yourcenar, Compton-Burnett, Renault" and others she is part of the "rich tradition of cross-gender inventions of homosexuality of the past century" (66). Sedgwick concludes with a swooning paean to Cather's *The Professor's House*, that "gorgeous homosocial romance of two men on a mesa in New Mexico" (68). Lesbian authors, it seems, are valuable here exactly to the extent that they are able to imagine and represent—what else?—male homosocial bonding. Thus the elevation of Cather, Yourcenar, Compton-Burnett, and Renault (significant choices all) to an all-new lesbian pantheon: of lesbians who enjoy writing about male-male eros, triangulated or otherwise, more than its female equivalent. What is missing here is any room for the lesbian writer who *doesn't* choose to celebrate men's "gorgeous homosocial romances"—for whom indeed such romances are anathema, precisely because they get in the way, so damagingly, of women's homosocial romances.

4. Witness one of the findings of a survey conducted by lesbian sex therapist Joanne Loulan among 1,566 lesbians between 1985 and 1987. While 80 percent of all lesbians surveyed reported that they liked to hold hands with their partners, only 17 percent said they felt able to hold hands in public. This "poignant" finding, writes Loulan, is "a statement about the oppression of lesbians in our culture. Heterosexuals assume they have the right to hold hands with their partner in public; most lesbians do not." See Loulan, *Lesbian Passion*, p. 205.

5. The "interlocking male homosocial triangles" at the end of *Shirley* can be visualized as follows:

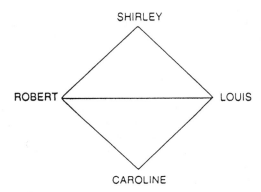

Here the line linking Robert and Louis separates Caroline and Shirley. One can imagine, of course, some hypothetical renewal of erotic bonding between the two women that would recross, so to speak, the line of male bonding; but one would be on the way then to writing a lesbian "postmarital" sequel to Brontë's novel.

6. Townsend Warner, *Summer Will Show* (Virago, 1987). All page numbers noted parenthetically refer to this edition.

7. Since I wrote these words in 1989, two scholars have taken issue—on rather different grounds—with my "decisive" sexualization of the Sophia/Minna relationship. In "Celi-

bate Sisters-in-Revolution: Towards Reading Sylvia Townsend Warner," Robert L. Caserio argues that Townsend Warner intended Sophia and Minna to be seen as chaste "sisters in revolution," akin to the celibate feminists Rhoda Nunn and Mary Barfoot in George Gissing's *The Odd Women* (1893) and Sophia and Constance Baines in Arnold Bennett's *Old Wives' Tale* (1908). And in "Ideology, *Écriture*, 1848: Sylvia Townsend Warner Unwrites Flaubert," Sandy Petrey suggests that the "oyster" passage I cite as a sign of erotic communion is at the very least cryptic and "equivocal" about what is going on between Sophia and Minna, and should be regarded instead as an instance of Townsend Warner's predilection for ambiguity and "semiotic flux." While intrigued by these criticisms, I remain convinced that Townsend Warner intended the "oyster" episode and following ellipsis to signify the sexual consummation of Sophia's and Minna's relationship. I am left unpersuaded in the end by Caserio's somewhat prim literary historical interpretation: given Townsend Warner's subversive comic outlook and her own exuberantly physical relationship with Valentine Ackland, I think it makes more sense to read *Summer Will Show* as a joyful send-up of the whole pious "celibate sisterhood" tradition. (Wrote Townsend Warner after her first lovemaking with Ackland: "I had not believed it possible to give such pleasure, and to satisfy such a variety of moods, to feel so demanded and so secure, to be loved by anyone so beautiful and to see that beauty enhanced by loving me. The nights were so ample that there was even time to fall asleep in them." [See Harman, *Sylvia Townsend Warner*, p. 108.]) If any couple served as an immediate "model" for Sophia and Minna, it was not, I propose, the chaste Rhoda Nunn and Mary Barfoot, or the sisterly Sophia and Constance Baines, but the decidedly sexy and unsisterly Sylvia Townsend Warner and Valentine Ackland.

As for Petrey's rather more philosophically oriented claims about "semiotic flux," I can respond best by pointing up a hidden paradox in his argument. It may well be, as Petrey suggests, that we need not assume in the case of the oyster passage a "crippling Puritanical blindness in the reviewers who do not seem to have understood the two women's flushes of pleasure and triumphant cries the way we do." The oyster in the scene, after all, as he points out, may be just an oyster. Yet I find it significant that no sense of such "semiotic flux" impairs Petrey's conviction that Minna and *Frederick* have been lovers. He takes it for granted that the heterosexual pair have at one time or another had sexual intercourse, though strictly speaking, the text provides no more "proof" of this than it does for my (admittedly brazen) reading of the scene between Sophia and Minna. (One could conceivably argue that the whole purported liaison between Minna and Frederick is merely Sophia's paranoid fantasy.) Typically, it is lesbian lovemaking that evokes the hermeneutic doubt (is it there?) while ambiguities connected with heterosexual lovemaking go unmentioned.

8. George Eliot, *The Mill on the Floss*, book 5, chapter 4.

9. Townsend Warner, *Letters*, p. 40. Townsend Warner seems to have had Berlioz in mind—and his despairing comment on the hardships suffered by artists and musicians during the 1848 revolution—when she created the character of Guitermann, the impoverished Jewish musician befriended by Sophia late in the novel. See *The Memoirs of Hector Berlioz*, pp. 44–45.

10. A very similar plot twist occurs, interestingly, in a novel that Townsend Warner certainly knew—and paid homage to in *Summer Will Show*—Colette's *La Seconde*, first published in 1929 and translated into English (as *The Other One*) in 1931. In Colette's novel as in Townsend Warner's, a wife and mistress discover to their mutual delight that they vastly prefer each other's company to that of the man they are supposedly competing for. Colette, it is true, does not eroticize the relationship between her two women characters as explicitly as Townsend Warner does, but her depiction of their alliance (scandalous to the husband) is exhilarating none the less. The Colettian "wife-husband-other woman" configuration turns up again in Townsend Warner's writing, in the slyly comic short story

"An Act of Reparation." Here a divorced woman named Lois accidentally meets the young, somewhat befuddled new wife of her former husband while out shopping. After the young woman confesses her anxiety about cooking, Lois goes home with her and shows her how to make oxtail stew. The husband, returning home, smugly concludes that Lois is trying to win him back by showing off her superior culinary skills; but Lois herself knows she is merely performing an "act of reparation" to the young wife, whom she now pities, with unexpected tenderness, for being stuck with the boorish ex-husband.

11. That overtly lesbian and gay male characters often end up inhabiting the same fictional space makes a kind of theoretical and well as mimetic sense: if the imperative toward heterosexual bonding in a fictional work is weak enough to allow one kind of homosexual bonding, chances are it will also allow the others. Two lesbian novels lending support to this idea are May Sarton's *Mrs. Stevens Hears the Mermaids Singing* and Jane Rule's *Memory Board*, both of which include important male homosexual characters.

12. I borrow the euphoric/dysphoric distinction from Nancy K. Miller, who in *The Heroine's Text* uses the terms to refer to the two kinds of narrative "destiny" stereotypically available to the heroines of eighteenth- and nineteenth-century fiction. A euphoric plot, Miller argues, ends with the heroine's marriage, a dysphoric plot with her death or alienation from society. That the terms undergo a dramatic reversal in meaning when applied to lesbian fiction should be obvious: from a lesbian viewpoint, marriage can only by dysphoric in its implications; even death or alienation—if only in a metaphoric sense—may seem preferable.

13. Mulford, *This Narrow Place*, pp. 121–22.

14. That lesbian novelists have been drawn to science fiction should come as no surprise; to the degree that science fiction itself is a form of utopian fantasy, one that posits a fictional world radically different from our own, it lends itself admirable to the representation of alternative sexual structures.

WORKS CITED

Bannon, Ann. *Journey to a Woman*. New York: Arno, 1975.

Barale, Michèle Aina. "Below the Belt: (Un)Covering *The Well of Loneliness*." In Diana Fuss, ed., *Inside/Out: Lesbian Theories, Gay Theories*, pp. 235–58. New York: Routledge, 1991.

Barnes, Djuna. *Nightwood*. New York: New Directions, 1946.

Benstock, Shari. "Expatriate Sapphic Modernism: Entering Literary History." In Karla Jay and Joanne Glasgow, eds., *Lesbian Texts and Contexts: Radical Revisions*, pp. 183–203. New York: New York University Press, 1990.

Berlioz, Hector. *The Memoirs of Hector Berlioz*. Trans. David Cairns. London: Victor Gollancz, 1969.

Bogus, Diane A. "The 'Queen B' Figure in Black Literature." In Karla Jay and Joanne Glasgow, eds., *Lesbian Texts and Contexts: Radical Revisions*, pp. 275–90. New York: New York University Press, 1990.

Bowles, Jane. *Two Serious Ladies*. In *My Sister's Hand and Mine: The Collected Works of Jane Bowles*. New York: Ecco, 1978.

Bristow, Joseph, ed. *Sexual Sameness: Textual Difference in Lesbian and Gay Writing*. New York and London: Routledge, 1992.

Brontë, Charlotte. *Shirley*. Oxford: Oxford University Press, 1981.

Cliff, Michelle. *No Telephone to Heaven*. New York: Dutton, 1987.

Colette, Sidonie Gabrielle. *Claudine à l'école*. Paris: A. Michel, 1978.

Diderot, Denis. *The Nun*. Trans. Leonard Tancock. Harmondsworth, Middlesex: Penguin, 1974.

Ellmann, Richard. *Oscar Wilde*. New York: Vintage, 1988.

Erhart, Margaret. *Unusual Company*. New York: New American Library, 1987.

Farwell, Marilyn R. "Heterosexual Plots and Lesbian Subtexts: Toward a Theory of Lesbian Narrative Space." In Karla Jay and Joanne Glasgow, eds., *Lesbian Texts and Contexts: Radical Revisions*, pp. 91–103. New York: New York University Press, 1990.

Fetterley, Judith. "*My Antonía*, Jim Burden and the Dilemma of the Lesbian Writer." In Karla Jay and Joanne Glasgow, eds., *Lesbian Texts and Contexts: Radical Revisions*, pp. 145–63. New York: New York University Press, 1990.

Flaubert, Gustave. *The Sentimental Education*. Trans. Perdita Burlingame. New York: New American Library, 1972.

Forrest, Katherine V. *An Emergence of Green*. Tallahassee, Fla.: Naiad, 1987.

Foster, Jeannette. *Sex Variant Women in Literature*. 3d ed. Tallahassee, Fla.: Naiad, 1985.

Fuss, Diana, ed. *Inside/Out: Lesbian Theories, Gay Theories*. New York and London: Routledge, 1991.

Gearhart, Sally Miller. *The Wanderground*. Boston: Alyson, 1984.

Gould, Lois. A *Sea-Change*. New York: Simon and Schuster, 1976.

Grier, Barbara, ed. *The Lesbian in Literature*. 3d ed. Tallahassee, Fla.: Naiad, 1981.

Hall, Radclyffe. *The Well of Loneliness*. New York: Anchor, 1990.

Harman, Claire. *Sylvia Townsend Warner: A Biography*. London: Chatto and Windus, 1989.

Hellman, Lillian. *The Children's Hour*. New York: Knopf, 1934.

Highsmith, Patricia [Claire Morgan]. *The Price of Salt*. Rev. ed. Tallahassee, Fla.: Naiad, 1984.

Hinds, Hillary. "*Oranges are not the Only Fruit*: Reaching Audiences Other Lesbian Texts Cannot Reach." In Sally Munt, ed., *New Lesbian Criticism: Literary and Cultural Readings*, pp. 153–72. New York: Columbia University Press, 1992.

Hobby, Elaine, and Chris White, eds. *What Lesbians Do in Books*. London: Women's Press, 1991.

Jay, Karla, and Joanne Glasgow, eds. *Lesbian Texts and Contexts: Radical Revisions*. New York: New York University Press, 1990.

Jolley, Elizabeth. *Miss Peabody's Inheritance*. Harmondsworth, Middlesex: Penguin, 1984.

King, Katie. "Audre Lord's Lacquered Layerings: The Lesbian Bar as a Site of Literary Production." In Sally Munt, ed., *New Lesbian Criticism: Literary and Cultural Readings*, pp. 75–94. New York: Columbia University Press, 1992.

Knopp, Sherron E. "'If I saw you would you kiss me?': Sapphism and the Subversiveness of Virginia Woolf's *Orlando*." In Joseph Bristow, ed., *Sexual Sameness: Textual Differences in Lesbian and Gay Writing*, pp. 111–27. New York and London: Routledge, 1992.

Loulan, Joanne. *Lesbian Passion: Loving Ourselves and Each Other*. San Francisco: Spinsters/Aunt Lute, 1987.

Lynch, Lee. "Cruising the Libraries." In Karla Jay and Joanne Glasgow, eds., *Lesbian Texts and Contexts: Radical Revisions*, pp. 39–48. New York; New York University Press, 1990.

Marcus, Jane. "Sapphistory: The Woolf and the Well." In Karla Jay and Joanne Glasgow, eds. *Lesbian Texts and Contexts: Radical Revisions*, pp. 164–80. New York; New York University Press, 1990.

Maxwell, William, ed. *Selected Letters of Sylvia Townsend Warner*. London: Chatto and Windus, 1982.

Mayne, Judith. "A Parallax View of Lesbian Authorship." In Diane Fuss, ed., *Inside/Out: Lesbian Theories, Gay Theories*, pp. 173–84. New York: Routledge, 1991.

Meese, Elizabeth. "Theorizing Lesbian: Writing—A love Letter." in Karla Jay and Joanne Glasgow, eds., *Lesbian Texts and Contexts: Radical Revisions*, pp. 70–88. New York: New York University Press, 1990.

Miller, Nancy K. *The Heroine's Text: Readings in the French and English Novel, 1722–1792*. New York: Columbia University Press, 1980.

Miner, Valerie. "An Imaginative Collectivity of Writers and Readers." In Karla Jay and Joanne Glasgow, eds., *Lesbian Texts and Contexts: Radical Revisions*, pp. 13–27. New York: New York University Press, 1990.

Mulford, Wendy. *This Narrow Place—Sylvia Townsend Warner and Valentine Ackland: Life, Letters, and Politics, 1930–1961*. London: Pandora, 1988.

Munt Sally, ed. *New Lesbian Criticism: Literary and Cultural Readings*. New York: Columbia University Press, 1992.

Petrey, Sandy. "Ideology, *Écriture*, 1848: Sylvia Townsend Warner Unwrites Flaubert." *RSSI: Recherches sémiotiques, Semiotic Inquiry* (1991) 11:159–80.

Roof, Judith. *A Lure of Knowledge: Lesbian Sexuality and Theory*. New York: Columbia University Press, 1991.

Rubin, Gayle. "The Traffic in Women: Notes on the 'Political Economy' of Sex." In Rayna R. Reiter, ed., *Toward an Anthropology of Women*, pp. 157–210. New York: Monthly Review Press, 1975.

Rule, Jane. *The Desert of the Heart*. Tallahassee, Fla.: Naiad, 1985.

———. *Lesbian Images*. New York: Doubleday, 1975.

———. *Memory Board*. Tallahassee, Fla.: Naiad, 1987.

Russ, Joanna. *The Female Man*. New York: Bantam, 1975.

Sarton, May. *Mrs. Stevens Hears the Mermaids Singing*. New York: Norton, 1975.

Schulman, Sarah. *After Delores*. New York: Dutton, 1988.

Sedgwick, Eve Kosofsky. "Across Gender, Across Sexuality: Willa Cather and Others." *SAQ: South Atlantic Quarterly* (1989) 88:53–72.

———. *Between Men: English Literature and Male Homosocial Desire*. New York: Columbia University Press, 1985.

———. "Privilege of Unknowing." *Genders* (Spring 1988) 1:102–24.

Spark, Muriel. *The Prime of Miss Jean Brodie*. New York: New American Library, 1984.

Stimpson, Catharine. *Class Notes*. New York: Avon, 1979.

———. "Zero Degree Deviancy: The Lesbian Novel in English." *Critical Inquiry* (1981) 8:363–80.

Strachey, Dorothy ["Olivia"]. *Olivia*. London: Virago, 1987.

Warner, Sylvia Townsend. *The Corner That Held Them*. London: Chatto and Windus, 1948.

———. *Kingdom of Elfin*. London: Chatto and Windus, 1977.

———. *Lolly Willowes*. London: Chatto and Windus, 1926.

———. *Selected Letters of Sylvia Townsend Warner*. Ed. William Maxwell. London: Chatto and Windus, 1982.

———. *Summer Will Show*. London: Virago, 1987.

Whatling, Claire. "Reading Awry: Joan Nestle and the Recontextualization of Heterosexuality." In Joseph Bristow, ed., *Sexual Sameness: Textual Differences in Lesbian and Gay Writing*, pp. 210–26. New York and London: Routledge, 1992.

White, Antonia. *Frost in May*. London: Virago, 1980.

Winsloe, Christa. *The Child Manuela*. Trans. Agnes Neill Scott. New York: Farrar and Rinehart, 1933.

Winterson, Jeanette. *Oranges are not the Only Fruit*. London: Pandora, 1985.

Wittig, Monique. *Les Guérillères*. Trans. David Le Vay. Boston: Beacon, 1985.

Woolf, Virginia. *Orlando: A Biography*. New York: Harcourt Brace Jovanovich, 1956.

Zimmerman, Bonnie. *The Safe Sea of Women: Lesbian Fiction 1969–1988*. Boston: Beacon, 1990.

MALE HEROES AND FEMALE SEX OBJECTS
sexism in spike lee's malcolm x
(1993)

In all Spike Lee's films, he is at his creative best in scenes highlighting black males. Portraying black masculinity through a spectrum of complex and diverse portraits, he does not allow audiences to hold a stereotypical image. For that reason alone, I imagined *Malcolm X* would be a major work, one of his best films. At last, I thought, Spike's finally going to just do it—make a film that will allow him to focus almost exclusively on black men, since women were always at the periphery of Malcolm's life. Thinking that the film would not focus centrally on females, I was relieved. Like many females in Lee's audience, I have found his representation of women in general, and black women in particular, to be consistently stereotypical and one-dimensional.

Ironically, Nola Darling in *She's Gotta Have It* remains one of Lee's most compelling representations of black womanhood. Though a failed portrait of a liberated woman, Darling is infinitely more complex than any of the women who follow her in Lee's work. *She's Gotta Have It* showed an awareness on Lee's part that there has indeed been a Women's Liberation movement that converged with the so-called 'sexual revolution.' Nola Darling was not obsessed with conventional heterosexist politics. Throughout much of the film she seemed to be trying to forge a sexual practice that would meet her needs. This film shows that Lee is capable of thinking critically about representations of black women, even though he ends the film by placing Nola Darling in a misogynist, sexist framework that ultimately punishes her for daring to oppose sexist norms of female sexual behavior. Rape is the punishment that puts her back in her place. And it is this scene in the film that ruptures what began as a transgressive narrative and makes it humdrum, commonplace.

Just as Lee abandons Nola Darling, undermining the one representation of black womanhood that breaks new cinematic ground, from that moment on he apparently abandoned all desire to give viewing audiences new and different representations of black females. Lee's desire to reach a larger, mainstream audience may account for the shift in perspective. Once he moved out of the world of independent filmmaking into mainstream cinema, he was seeking to acquire an audience not necessarily interested in challenging, unfamiliar representations. No matter how daring his films, how transgressive their subject matter, to have a predictable success he provided viewers with stock images. Uncompromising in his commitment to create images of black males that challenge shallow perceptions and bring the issue of racism to the screen, he conforms to the status quo when it comes to images of females. Sexism is the familiar construction that links his films to all the other Hollywood dramas folks see. Just when the viewer might possibly be alienated by the radical take on issues in a Spike Lee film, some basic sexist nonsense will appear on the screen to entertain, to provide comic relief, to comfort audiences by letting them know that the normal way of doing things is not being fully challenged.

Certainly the female role that most conformed to this pattern was the character of Tina played by Rosie Perez in *Do the Right Thing*. She is the nagging, bitchified, seductive female who is great to bone (not to be taken seriously, mind you). No matter how bitchified she is, in the final analysis her man, played by Spike, has her under control. This same misogynist message is played out all the more graphically in *School Daze* where the collective humiliation of black females enhances black male bonding. Yet it is *Mo' Better Blues* that sets paradigms for black gender relations. Black females are neatly divided into two categories—ho' or mammy/madonna. The ho' is out for what she can get, using her pussy to seduce, conquer, and exploit the male. The mammy/madonna nurtures, forgives, provides unconditional love. Black men, mired in sexism and misogyny, tolerate the strong, 'bitchified,' tell-it-like-it-is black woman but also seek to escape her. In *Mo' Better Blues* the black woman who gets her man in the end does so by surrendering her will to challenge and confront. She simply understands and accepts. It's a bleak picture. In the final analysis, mo' better is mo' bitter.

Jungle Fever plays out the same tired patterns, only the principal black woman character, Drew (Lonette McKee), is a combination of bitch/ho' and mammy/madonna. The film begins with scenes of lovemaking, where she is busy pleasuring her man. We see her later in the film cooking and cleaning. Even her job is mainly about looking good. Her most bitchified, 'intense' read of Flipper (Wesley Snipes) occurs when he comes to her workplace. As with all of Spike Lee's representations of black heterosexuality, men and women never really communicate. Portrayals of white female characters are equally stereotypical. They are sex objects, spoils in the war between white males and black males over which group will dominate the planet.

In *Jungle Fever* white and black women never meet, they exist in a world apart. This media construction is a fiction which belies the reality that the vast majority of working black women encounter white women daily on the job, encounters that are charged with tension, power struggles fueled by racism and sexism. These aspects of white and black female interactions are only hinted at in *Jungle Fever* in the one improvised scene where black women gather to discuss Drew's situation and their collective obsession with getting and keeping a man.

Within the cultural marketplace, *Jungle Fever* courted viewers by claiming to address the taboo subject of interracial sex and desire, highlighting black male interactions with white females. Despite the shallowness of the film, this focus drew crowds. Overall, however, the film had nothing new or revelatory to share about race, gender, or desire. No doubt the crowd-drawing appeal of such material accounts for the fact that Spike Lee's cinematic reconstruction of Malcolm X's life begins with a sorry remake of *Jungle Fever*. Anyone who has studied Malcolm X's life and work knows that no one has considered his involvement with white women as the high point of his career as small time pimp and hustler. Yet it is this involvement that most captures Spike's imagination, so much so that almost half of the film focuses on Malcolm's relationship with a white woman named Sophia.

The young Malcolm X was sexist and misogynist, and, in fact, made a point of treating women badly. Yet Lee ignores the sexism that shaped and determined Malcolm's attitude towards women and makes it appear that his lust for Sophia is solely a response to racism, that having the white man's woman is a way to rebel and assert power. Like the younger Malcolm, the real-life Sophia was a hustler, not the portrait of an innocent little girl trapped in a woman's body which Lee gives viewers. It was disturbing to see Lee's version of Malcolm's life begin with and focus centrally on his lust for white female bodies, but it was even more disturbing that this relationship was portrayed as yet another example of 'jungle fever.' Spike Lee refuses to allow for the possibility that there could be meaningful affectional ties between a black man and a white woman which transcend the sexual. The film does not show that Malcolm maintained contact with Sophia long after their sexual relationship ended. In Lee's version, relationships between black men and white women never transcend the sexual. Indeed, in Lee's cinematic world, every relationship between a black man and a woman, whether white or black, is mediated by his constant sexualization of the female.

Fictively re-creating the relationship between Malcolm X and Betty Shabazz provided an opportunity tor Spike Lee to bring to Hollywood cinema a different representation of black womanhood and black heterosexuality. Lee did not rise to the challenge. All his films show darker skinned men choosing lighter skinned black female partners. Malcolm X should have been different. By his choice as a fair-skinned black male of a darker skinned partner, Malcolm was disrupting black politics of desire which reflected internalized racism. Rather than honoring through his representations the significance of this choice, Lee reinscribes the same color caste conventions he exploits in all his films. Though a madonna figure in *Malcolm X*, Shabazz is portrayed as an advocate of 'women's rights' challenging Malcolm's sexism and misogyny. This portrait falsely constructs an image of black womanhood that would not have been acceptable for female initiates in the Nation of Islam, who were taught not to be manipulative or seductive, to be obedient to male authority. Lee's fictive Shabazz seduces and traps. She 'reads' her man in the bitchified manner that is Lee's trademark representation of heterosexual black coupling. Even though the real-life Shabazz shared with her that she did not argue with Malcolm, no doubt because she was conforming to the Nation of Islam codes of behavior which were informed by sexist notions of appropriate female behavior, Lee's film portrays them as fighting. Indeed, the most intense scene in the film is their near violent argument. As with all good nanny/madonna figures, the fictional Shabazz fights with her man because she has his best interests at heart. This image is consistent with the way Spike Lee's films depict black marriage; couples are either fucking or fighting. Like other female characters in *Malcolm X*, Shabazz must be molded and shaped by Lee so that her character mirrors prevailing stereotypes. Lee's film conforms to racist/sexist iconography that depicts white women as innocent and therefore desirable and black woman as controlling-domineering therefore undesirable. Had Lee chosen to represent Shabazz as submissive, his film would have challenged Hollywood's stereotypical portrayal of black women as always domineering—or as always sexual.

One of the most serious gaps in Lee's fictive portrayal of Malcolm's life is the fictive erasure of Malcolm's half sister (whom he referred to as his sister), Ella Little. She is not present in the film and their relationship is never discussed by other characters. A major influence in Malcolm's life, Ella, along with their brother, Reginald, converted him to Islam, helped educate him for critical consciousness. By not portraying Ella or referring to her influence, Spike creates a fictive world of black heterosexuality in which all interaction between black women and men is overdetermined by sexuality, always negotiated by lust and desire. Conveniently, this allows the film to reinscribe and perpetually affirm male domination of females, making it appear natural.

By not portraying Ella, Lee is able to create a film that does not break with Hollywood conventions and stereotypes. In Hollywood films the super-masculine hero is most often portrayed as a loner, an outlaw, a cultural orphan estranged from family and society. To have shown the bonds between Ella and Malcolm which were sustained throughout his life, Lee would have needed both to break with Hollywood representations of the male hero as well as provide an image of black womanhood never before imagined on the Hollywood screen. The character of Ella would have been a powerful, politically conscious black woman who could not be portrayed as a sex object. Lee's portraits of black women in *Malcolm X* mirror the usual stereotypes found in films by white directors. Ella was radical in her thinking about blackness, more of a leader than a follower. To represent her fictively, Lee would have had to disrupt the fiction that politics is a male realm, that the fight to end racism is really a struggle between white and black men.

It reveals much about the nature of sexism and misogyny that the erased, symbolically murdered figure of Ella is replaced by a fictional, older black male character, Baines, who initiates Malcolm into the political realm. The invention of this make-believe character allows Lee to fictively create a hierarchical world of male power that conforms to popular black nationalist, sexist insistence that males are best taught by males. Scenes of black male homosocial bonding in the prison context reaffirm the patriarchal assumption that it is only the actions of men that matter. This creates a version of black political struggle where the action of dedicated, powerful, black female activists are systematically devalued and erased. By writing Ella out of Malcolm's history, Spike Lee continues Hollywood's devaluation of black womanhood.

reading

In literary terms, "reading" can mean two distinct things; the first meaning centers on texts, the second on receivers of texts. First, "a reading" is an interpretation, one critic's version of what a piece of writing has to say. "A feminist reading," in this usage, would be an interpretation of a text assuming gender's centrality to what the text means. In "a feminist reading" of a text, gender can come into play as something represented in the text (as in "images-of-woman" criticism); as something shaping the experience, and therefore, the writing, of the author (as in gynocriticism); or as a significant influence in the life—and, therefore, the interior experience—of the particular reader who is trying to understand what the text says.

"Reading," in its second literary sense, refers directly to that interior experience of readers, understood as an activity or a process. Rarely do theorists or critics make empirical studies of what actual readers do when they peruse books, although a few do apply psychoanalytic or ethnographic principles to their observations of real readers reading. More often, reader-response theorists hypothesize a universalized abstraction called "the reader," and they describe what "he" feels, thinks, or does when confronted with a given text. For such critics, "reading" is something conceptual, based—one assumes—on their own personal experiences with texts. In the theoretical work of such reader-response specialists as Peter Brooks, Norman Holland, David Bleich, and Wolfgang Iser, gender seldom surfaces as a potential influence upon "the reader's" experience. "Feminist reading," then, would be the reception and processing of texts by a reader who is conceived of not only as possibly female, but also as conscious of the tradition of women's oppression in patriarchal culture. The feminist reader—whether in fact male or female—is committed to breaking the pattern of that oppression by calling attention to the ways some texts can perpetuate it. The essays in this section focus on "reading" in this second, active (and activist) sense.

Judith Fetterley's *The Resisting Reader* (1978) is one of the first attempts to conceptualize feminist reading, a process that Fetterley says occurs when a female reader confronts an androcentric (male-centered) or even a misogynist (anti-woman) text. Explaining that "great" American literature treats male experience as universal, Fetterley argues in her "Introduction: On the Politics of Literature" that reading the American canon requires one to "identify as male," to sympathize with masculine heroes whose troubles are overtly or covertly associated with the women in their stories. This has led, Fetterley says, to the "immasculation" of the woman reader, who must identify "against herself" as she reads, thus becoming a "divided self." The "resisting reader" would work to "exorcise" the male-imposed part of that self, to be conscious of the way American classics exclude and alienate her. Fetterley's book fills out the readings of novels she sketches in the introductory chapter reprinted here.

In a project that resists theorizing about readers in general to concentrate instead on a flesh-and-blood community of readers in the American Midwest, Janice Radway's chapter "The Readers and their Romances" from *Reading the Romance* (1984) takes us into an empirical study of how some real women say they actually read. Working from interviews, conversations, and questionnaires inquiring into the reading practice of a group of suburban white women in the pseudonymous "Smithton," Radway takes an anthropological approach to try to explain how and why the women love to read commercially produced romances. She provides statistics to support her descriptions of the kinds of setting, action, characters, and closure that appeal most strongly to her sample group. Following the principles of anthropologist Clifford Geertz and psychoanalyst Nancy Chodorow, Radway also speculates about the basic needs these women seem to satisfy with their romance reading. Although she is careful in the beginning of her chapter to limit her generalizations to the race and class, the regional and educational background of "the Smithton women," her project raises broader questions about the "therapeutic value" of romance reading for women living in "a culture that creates needs in [them] that it cannot fulfill." In Radway's work, "reading" is more than a process: it is a way of life, a means of coping with the troublesome gender politics of ordinary middle-class experience.

Patrocinio P. Schweickart, in her 1986 essay, "Reading Ourselves: Toward a Feminist Theory of Reading," revisits reader-response theory for a specifically polemical purpose: "to *change the world.*" Arguing that reader-centered criticism must attend to "difference" if it is to be taken seriously, Schweickart begins by supplying three parables of reading, leading to a fourth. Schweickart retells Wayne Booth's story of his life as a reader, in which he compares himself to Malcolm X and suppresses crucial differences arising from racial experience; she juxtaposes Booth's story with Malcolm X's own version of how he became a reader, a story that—Schweickart asserts—speaks only for and to men, suppressing the differences gender can make. Schweickart answers the two men's stories with two versions of feminist reading. The first—a woman's angry encounter with texts written by misogynist men—is from Virginia Woolf's *A Room of One's Own*; the second—a woman's confrontation of Emily Dickinson's poems, texts by another woman whose interior experience is nevertheless pointedly *not* identical to the female reader's own—is from Adrienne Rich's "Vesuvius at Home."

Schweickart's essay points out that *how* feminists read depends on *what* they read (that is, whether the literary text was written from a male or a female perspective). Schweickart tackles questions that had been raised by Jonathan Culler in "Reading as a Woman" (1982), about whether being a woman is a biological or a cultural matter, and whether reading from a feminine point of view is possible for a man. To address those questions, Schweickart appeals to female psychology: she cites the suggestion of feminist psychoanalysts that women's identities (their "ego boundaries") are less strictly delineated than those of men. In the end, Schweickart sees reading theory as a potentially powerful tool for "building and maintaining connections among women."

Wai-Chee Dimock looks to reader-centered theory as a means of building and maintaining connections between two kinds of literary criticism that often came into conflict during the 1980s: feminism and new historicism. In "Feminism, New Historicism, and the Reader," Dimock analyzes the "ideal reader" of Charlotte Perkins Gilman's "The Yellow Wallpaper" to show that the text was aimed at an audience that, in Gilman's day, did not yet exist: a reader "created in the image of professionalism at its most idealized, endowed with the sacred attributes of specialized knowledge and interpretive competence," a reader who is—in spite of being "professionalized" through the text's address—female. Dimock points to "this gap—in the non-identity between the ideal reader invoked by the story and the actual women reading it" as the space in which Gilman's story does its "cultural work," as new historicists would call it. She sketches out the strife between new historicist and feminist criticism, and cautions against oversimplifying the difference between the two approaches. Dimock's essay tries to destabilize that difference, as well as the difference between male and female readers, resisting essentialism in her concept of the relation between gender and reading. Dimock uses the figure of the reader to illuminate the inevitable interconnection between gender and history; her example of "The Yellow Wallpaper" shows that neither feminist nor historicist claims about the text's significance make sense in isolation from each other. Here as in Fetterley's, Radway's, and Schweickart's essays, the reader becomes the bearer of meaning.

—RRW

INTRODUCTION

on the politics of literature

(1978)

I

Literature is political. It is painful to have to insist on this fact, but the necessity of such insistence indicates the dimensions of the problem. John Keats once objected to poetry "that has a palpable design upon us." The major works of American fiction constitute a series of designs on the female reader, all the more potent in their effect because they are "impalpable." One of the main things that keep the design of our literature unavailable to the consciousness of the woman reader, and hence impalpable, is the very posture of the apolitical, the pretense that literature speaks universal truths through forms from which all the merely personal, the purely subjective, has been burned away or at least transformed through the medium of art into the representative. When only one reality is encouraged, legitimized, and transmitted and when that limited vision endlessly insists on its comprehensiveness, then we have the conditions necessary for that confusion of consciousness in which impalpability flourishes. It is the purpose of this book to give voice to a different reality and different vision, to bring a different subjectivity to bear on the old "universality." To examine American fictions in light of how attitudes toward women shape their form and content is to make available to consciousness that which has been largely left unconscious and thus to change our understanding of these fictions, our relation to them, and their effect on us. It is to make palpable their designs.

American literature is male. To read the canon of what is currently considered classic American literature is perforce to identify as male. Though exceptions to this generalization can be found here and there—a Dickinson poem, a Wharton novel—these exceptions usually function to obscure the argument and confuse the issue: American literature is male. Our literature neither leaves women alone nor allows them to participate. It insists on its universality at the same time that it defines that universality in specifically male terms. "Rip Van Winkle" is paradigmatic of this phenomenon. While the desire to avoid work, escape authority, and sleep through the major decisions of one's life is obviously applicable to both men and women, in Irving's story this "universal" desire is made specifically male. Work, authority, and decision making are symbolized by Dame Van Winkle, and the longing for flight is defined against her. She is what one must escape from, and the "one" is necessarily male. In Mailer's *An American Dream*, the fantasy of eliminating all one's ills through the ritual of scapegoating is equally male: the sacrificial scapegoat is the woman/wife and the cleansed survivor is the husband/male. In such fictions the female reader is co-opted into participation in an experience from which she is explicitly excluded; she is asked to identify with a selfhood that defines itself in opposition to her; she is required to identify against herself.

The woman reader's relation to American literature is made even more problematic by the fact that our literature is frequently dedicated to defining what is peculiarly American about experience and identity. Given the pervasive male bias of this literature, it is not surprising that in it the experience of being American is equated with the experience of being male. In Fitzgerald's *The Great Gatsby*, the background for the experience of disillusionment and betrayal revealed in the novel is the discovery of America, and Daisy's failure of Gatsby is symbolic of the failure of America to live up to the expectations in the imagination of the men who "discovered" it. America is female; to be American is male; and the quintessential American experience is betrayal by woman. Henry James certainly defined our literature, if not our culture, when he picked the situation of women as the subject of *The Bostonians*, his very American tale.

Power is the issue in the politics of literature, as it is in the politics of anything else. To be excluded from a literature that claims to define one's identity is to experience a peculiar form of powerlessness—not simply the powerlessness which derives from not seeing one's experience articulated, clarified, and legitimized in art, but more significantly the powerlessness which results from the endless division of self against self, the consequence of the invocation to identify as male while being reminded that to be male—to be universal, to be American—is to be *not female*. Not only does powerlessness characterize woman's experience of reading, it also describes the content of what is read. Each of the works chosen for this study presents a version and an enactment of the drama of men's power over women. The final irony, and indignity of the woman reader's relation to American literature, then, is that she is required to dissociate herself from the very experience the literature engenders. Powerlessness is the subject and powerlessness the experience, and the design insists that Rip Van Winkle/Frederic Henry/Nick Carraway/Stephen Rojack speak for us all.

The drama of power in our literature is often disguised. In "Rip Van Winkle," Rip poses as powerless, the henpecked husband cowering before his termagant Dame. Yet, when Rip returns from the mountains, armed by the drama of female deposition witnessed there, to discover that his wife is dead and he is free to enjoy what he has always wanted, the "Shucks, M'am, I don't mean no harm" posture dissolves. In Sherwood Anderson's "I Want to Know Why," the issue of power is refracted through the trauma of a young boy's discovery of what it means to be male in a culture that gives white men power over women, horses, and niggers. More sympathetic and honest than "Rip," Anderson's story nevertheless exposes both the imaginative limits of our literature and the reasons for those limits. Storytelling and art can do no more than lament the inevitable—boys must grow up to be men; it can provide no alternative vision of being male. Bathed in nostalgia, "I Want to Know Why" is infused with the perspective it abhors, because finally to disavow that perspective would be to relinquish power.

The lament is self-indulgent; it offers the luxury of feeling bad without the responsibility of change. And it is completely male-centered, registering the tragedy of sexism through its cost to men. At the end we cry for the boy and not for the whores he will eventually make use of.

In Hawthorne's "The Birthmark," the subject of power is more explicit. The fact of men's power over women and the full implications of that fact are the crux of the story. Aylmer is free to experiment on Georgiana, to the point of death, because she is both woman and wife. Hawthorne indicates the attractiveness of the power that marriage puts in the hands of men through his description of Aylmer's reluctance to leave his laboratory and through his portrayal of Aylmer's inherent discomfort with women and sex. And why does Aylmer want this power badly enough to overcome his initial reluctance and resistance? Hitherto Aylmer has failed in all his efforts to achieve a power equal to that of "Mother" nature. Georgiana provides an opportunity for him to outdo nature by remaking her creation. And if he fails, he still will have won because he will have destroyed the earthly embodiment and representative of his adversary. Hawthorne intends his character to be seen as duplicitous, and he maneuvers Aylmer through the poses of lover, husband, and scientist to show us how Aylmer attempts to gain power and to use that power to salve his sense of inadequacy. But even so, Hawthorne, like Anderson, is unwilling to do more with the sickness than call it sick. He obscures the issue of sexual politics behind a haze of "universals" and clothes the murder of wife by husband in the language of idealism.

Though the grotesque may serve Faulkner as a disguise in the same way that the ideal serves Hawthorne, "A Rose for Emily" goes farther than "The Birthmark" in making the power of men over women an overt subject. Emily's life is shaped by her father's absolute control over her; her murder of Homer Barron is *re*action, not action. Though Emily exercises the power the myths of sexism make available to her, that power is minimal; her retaliation is no alternative to the patriarchy which oppresses her. Yet Faulkner, like Anderson and Hawthorne, ultimately protects himself and short-circuits the implications of his analysis, not simply through the use of the grotesque, which makes Emily eccentric rather than central, but also through his choice of her victim. In having Emily murder Homer Barron, a northern day-laborer, rather than Judge Stevens, the southern patriarch, Faulkner indicates how far he is willing to go in imagining even the minimal reversal of power involved in retaliation. The elimination of Homer Barron is no real threat to the system Judge Stevens represents. Indeed, a few day-laborers may have to be sacrificed here and there to keep that system going.

In *A Farewell to Arms*, the issue of power is thoroughly obscured by the mythology, language, and structure of romantic love and by the invocation of an abstract, though spiteful, "they" whose goal it is to break the good, the beautiful, and the brave. Yet the brave who is broken is Catherine; at the end of the novel Catherine is dead, Frederic is alive, and the resemblance to "Rip Van Winkle" and "The Birthmark" is unmistakable. Though the scene in the hospital is reminiscent of Aylmer's last visit to Georgiana in her chambers, Hemingway, unlike Hawthorne, separates his protagonist from the source of his heroine's death, locating the agency of Catherine's demise not simply in "them" but in her biology. Frederic survives several years of war, massive injuries, the dangers of a desperate retreat, and the threat of execution by his own army; Catherine dies in her first pregnancy. Clearly, biology is destiny. Yet, Catherine is as much a scapegoat as Dame Van Winkle, Georgiana, Daisy Fay, and Deborah Rojack. For Frederic to survive, free of the intolerable burdens of marriage, family, and fatherhood, yet with his vision of himself as the heroic victim of cosmic antagonism intact, Catherine must die. Frederic's necessities determine Catherine's fate. He is, indeed, the agent of her death.

In its passionate attraction to the phenomenon of wealth, *The Great Gatsby* reveals its author's consuming interest in the issue of power. In the quintessentially male drama of poor boy's becoming rich boy, ownership of women is invoked as the index of power: he who possesses Daisy Fay is the most powerful boy. But when the rich boy, fearing finally for his territory, repossesses the girl and, by asking "Who is he," strips the poor boy of his presumed power, the resultant animus is directed not against the rich boy but against the girl, whose rejection of him exposes the poor boy's powerlessness. The struggle for power between men is deflected into safer and more certain channels, and the consequence is the familiar demonstration of male power over women. This demonstration, however, is not simply the result of a greater safety in directing anger at women than at men. It derives as well from the fact that even the poorest male gains something from a system in which all women are at some level his subjects. Rather than attack the men who represent and manifest that system, he identifies with them and acquires his sense of power through superiority to women. It is not surprising, therefore, that the drama of *The Great Gatsby* involves an attack on Daisy, whose systematic reduction from the glamorous object of Gatsby's romantic longings to the casual killer of Myrtle Wilson provides an accurate measure of the power available to the most "powerless" male.

By his choice of scene, context, and situation, Henry James in *The Bostonians* directly confronts the hostile nature of the relations between men and women and sees in that war the defining characteristics of American culture. His honesty provides the opportunity for a clarification rather than a confusion of consciousness and offers a welcome relief from the deceptions of other writers. Yet the drama, while correctly labeled, is still the same. *The Bostonians* is an unrelenting demonstration of the extent, and an incisive analysis of the sources, of the power of men as a class over women as a class. Yet, though James laments women's oppression, and laments it because of its effects *on women*, he nevertheless sees it as inevitable. *The Bostonians* represents a kind of end point in the literary exploration of sex/class power; it would be impossible to see more clearly and feel more deeply and still remain convinced that patriarchy is inevitable. Indeed, there is revolution latent in James's novel, and, while he would be the last to endorse it, being far more interested in articulating and romanticizing the tragic elements in women's powerlessness, *The Bostonians* provides the material for that analysis of American social reality which is the beginning of change.

Norman Mailer's *An American Dream* represents another kind of end point. Mailer is thoroughly enthralled by the possibility of power that sexism makes available to men, absolutely convinced that he is in danger of losing it, and completely dedicated to maintaining it, at whatever cost. It is impossible to imagine a more frenzied commitment to the maintenance of male power than Mailer's. In *An American Dream* all content has been reduced to the enactment of men's power over women, and to the development and legitimization of that act Mailer brings every strategy he can muster, not the least of which is an extended elaboration of the mythology of female power. In Mailer's work the effort to obscure the issue, disguise reality, and confuse consciousness is so frantic that the antitheses he provides to protect his thesis become in fact his message and his confusions shed a lurid illumination. If *The Bostonians* induces one to rearrange James's conceptual framework and so to make evitable his inevitable, *An American Dream* induces a desire to eliminate Mailer's conceptual framework altogether and start over. Beyond his frenzy is only utter nausea and weariness of spirit and a profound willingness to give up an exhausted, sick, and sickening struggle. In Mailer, the drama of power comes full circle; at once the most sexist writer, he is also the most freeing, and out of him it may be possible to create anew.

II

But what have I to say of *Sexual Politics* itself? Millett has undertaken a task which I find particularly worthwhile: the consideration of certain events or works of literature from an unexpected, even startling point of view. Millett never suggests that hers is a sufficient analysis of any of the works she discusses. Her aim is to wrench the reader from the vantage point he has long occupied, and force him to look at life and letters from a new coign. Hers is not meant to be the last word on any writer, but a wholly new word, little heard before and strange. For the first time we have been asked to look at literature as women; we, men, women and Ph.D.s, have always read it as men. Who cannot point to a certain overemphasis in the way Millett reads Lawrence or Stalin or Euripides? What matter? We are rooted in our vantage points and require transplanting which, always dangerous, involves violence and the possibility of death.

—Carolyn Heilbrun[1]

The method that is required is not one of correlation but of *liberation*. Even the term "method" must be reinterpreted and in fact wrenched out of its usual semantic field, for the emerging creativity in women is by no means a merely cerebral process. In order to understand the implications of this process it is necessary to grasp the fundamental fact that women have had the power of *naming* stolen from us. We have not been free to use our own power to name ourselves, the world, or God. The old naming was not the product of dialogue—a fact inadvertently admitted in the Genesis story of Adam's naming the animals and the woman. Women are now realizing that the universal imposing of names by men has been false because partial. That is, inadequate words have been taken as adequate.

—Mary Daly[2]

Re-vision—the act of looking back, of seeing with fresh eyes, of entering an old text from a new critical direction—is for us more than a chapter in cultural history: it is an act of survival. Until we can understand the assumptions in which we are drenched we cannot know ourselves. And this drive to self-knowledge, for woman, is more than a search for identity: it is part of her refusal of the self-destructiveness of male-dominated society. A radical critique of literature, feminist in its impulse, would take the work first of all as a clue to how we live, how we have been living, how we have been led to imagine ourselves, how our language has trapped as well as liberated us; and how we can begin to see—and therefore live—afresh.

—Adrienne Rich[3]

A culture which does not allow itself to look clearly at the obvious through the universal accessibility of art is a culture of tragic delusion, hardly viable.

—Cynthia Ozick[4]

When a system of power is thoroughly in command, it has scarcely need to speak itself aloud; when its workings are exposed and questioned, it becomes not only subject to discussion, but even to change.

—Kate Millett[5]

Consciousness is power. To create a new understanding of our literature is to make possible a new effect of that literature on us. And to make possible a new effect is in turn to provide the conditions for changing the culture that the literature reflects. To expose and question that complex of ideas and mythologies about women and men which exist in our society and are confirmed in our literature is to make the system of power embodied in the literature open not only to discussion but even to change. Such questioning and exposure can, of course, be carried on only by a consciousness radically different from the one that informs the literature. Such a closed system cannot be opened up from within but only from without. It must be entered into from a point of view which questions its values and assumptions and which has its investment in making available to consciousness precisely that which the literature wishes to keep hidden. Feminist criticism provides that point of view and embodies that consciousness.

In "A Woman's Map of Lyric Poetry," Elizabeth Hampsten, after quoting in full Thomas Campion's "My Sweetest Lesbia," asks, "And Lesbia, what's in it for her?"[6] The answer to this question is the subject of Hampsten's essay and the answer is, of course, nothing. But implicit in her question is another answer—a great deal, for someone. As Lillian Robinson reminds us, "and, always, *cui bono*—who profits?"[7] The questions of who profits, and how, are crucial because the attempt to answer them leads directly to an understanding of the function of literary sexual politics. Function is often best known by effect. Though one of the most persistent of literary stereotypes is the castrating bitch, the cultural reality is not the emasculation of men by women but the *immasculation* of women by men. As readers and teachers and scholars, women are taught to think as men, to identify with a male point of view, and to accept as normal and legitimate a male system of values, one of whose central principles is misogyny.

One of the earliest statements of the phenomenon of immasculation, serving indeed as a position paper, is Elaine Showalter's "Women and the Literary Curriculum." In the opening part of her article, Showalter imaginatively re-creates the literary curriculum the average young woman entering college confronts:

In her freshman year she would probably study literature and composition, and the texts in her course would be selected for their timeliness, or their relevance, or their power to involve the reader, rather than for their absolute standing in the literary canon. Thus she might be assigned any one of the texts which have recently been advertised for Freshman English: an anthology of essays, perhaps such as *The Responsible Man*, "for the student who wants

> literature relevant to the world in which he lives," or *Conditions of Men, or Man in Crisis: Perspectives on The Individual and His World*, or again, *Representative Men: Cult Heroes of Our Time*, in which thirty-three men represent such categories of heroism as the writer, the poet, the dramatist, the artist, and the guru, and the only two women included are the Actress Elizabeth Taylor and The Existential Heroine Jacqueline Onassis. . . . By the end of her freshman year, a woman student would have learned something about intellectual neutrality; she would be learning, in fact, how to think like a man.[8]

Showalter's analysis of the process of immasculation raises a central question: "What are the effects of this long apprenticeship in negative capability on the self-image and the self-confidence of women students?" And the answer is self-hatred and self-doubt: "Women are estranged from their own experience and unable to perceive its shape and authenticity. . . . they are expected to identify as readers with a masculine experience and perspective, which is presented as the human one. . . . Since they have no faith in the validity of their own perceptions and experiences, rarely seeing them confirmed in literature, or accepted in criticism, can we wonder that women students are so often timid, cautious, and insecure when we exhort them to 'think for themselves.'?"[9]

The experience of immasculation is also the focus of Lee Edwards's article, "Women, Energy, and *Middlemarch*." Summarizing her experience, Edwards concludes:

> Thus, like most women, I have gone through my entire education—as both student and teacher—as a schizophrenic, and I do not use this term lightly, for madness is the bizarre but logical conclusion of our education. Imagining myself male, I attempted to create myself male. Although I knew the case was otherwise, it seemed I could do nothing to make this other critically real.

Edwards extends her analysis by linking this condition to the effects of the stereotypical presentation of women in literature:

> I said simply, and for the most part silently that, since neither those women nor any women whose acquaintances I had made in fiction had much to do with the life I led or wanted to lead, I was not female. Alien from the women I saw most frequently imagined, I mentally arranged them in rows labelled respectively insipid heroines, sexy survivors, and demonic destroyers. As organizer I stood somewhere else, alone perhaps, but hopefully above them.[10]

Intellectually male, sexually female, one is in effect no one, nowhere, immasculated.

Clearly, then, the first act of the feminist critic must be to become a resisting rather than an assenting reader and, by this refusal to assent, to begin the process of exorcizing the male mind that has been implanted in us. The consequence of this exorcism is the capacity for what Adrienne Rich describes as re-vision—"the act of looking back, of seeing with fresh eyes, of entering an old text from a new critical direction." And the consequence, in turn, of this re-vision is that books will no longer be read as they have been read and thus will lose their power to bind us unknowingly to their designs. While women obviously cannot rewrite literary works so that they become ours by virtue of reflecting our reality, we can accurately name the reality they do reflect and so change literary criticism from a closed conversation to an active dialogue.

In making available to women this power of naming reality, feminist criticism is revolutionary. The significance of such power is evident if one considers the strength of the taboos against it:

> I permit no woman to teach . . . she is to keep silent.
>
> —St. Paul

> By Talmudic law a man could divorce a wife whose voice could be heard next door. From there to Shakespeare: "Her voice was ever soft, / Gentle, and low—an excellent thing in woman." And to Yeats: "The women that I picked spoke sweet and low / And yet gave tongue." And to Samuel Beckett, guessing at the last torture, The Worst: "a woman's voice perhaps, I hadn't thought of that, they might engage a soprano."
>
> —Mary Ellmann[11]

> The experience of the class in which I voiced my discontent still haunts my nightmares. Until my face froze and my brain congealed, I was called prude and, worse yet, insensitive, since I willfully misread the play in the interest of proving a point false both to the work and in itself.
>
> —Lee Edwards[12]

The experience Edwards describes of attempting to communicate her reading of the character of Shakespeare's Cleopatra is a common memory for most of us who have become feminist critics. Many of us never spoke; those of us who did speak were usually quickly silenced. The need to keep certain things from being thought and said reveals to us their importance. Feminist criticism represents the discovery/recovery of a voice, a unique and uniquely powerful voice capable of canceling out those other voices, so movingly described in Sylvia Plath's *The Bell Jar,* which spoke about us and to us and at us but never for us.

III

The eight works analyzed in this book were chosen for their individual significance, their representative value, and their collective potential. They are interconnected in the ways that they comment on and illuminate each other, and they form a dramatic whole whose meaning transcends the mere sum of the parts. These eight are meant to stand for a much larger body of literature; their individual and collective designs can be found elsewhere repeatedly.

The four short stories form a unit, as do the four novels. These units are subdivided into pairs. "Rip Van Winkle" and "I Want to Know Why" are companion pieces whose focus is the fear of and resistance to growing up. The value of Anderson's story lies mainly in the light it sheds on Irving's, making explicit the fear of sexuality only implied in "Rip" and focusing attention on the strategy of deflecting hostility away from men and onto women. "The Birthmark" and "A Rose for Emily" are richly related studies of the consequences of growing up and, by implication, of the reasons for the resistance to it. In both stories sexual desire leads to death. More significantly, they are brilliant companion analyses of that sex/class hostility that is the essence of patriarchal culture and that underlies the adult identity Anderson's boy recoils from assuming. "The Birthmark" is the story of how to murder your wife and get away with it; "A Rose for Emily" is the story of how the system which allows you to murder your wife makes it possible for your wife to murder you.

Both *A Farewell to Arms* and *The Great Gatsby* are love stories; together they demonstrate the multiple uses of the mythology of romantic love in the maintenance of male power. In addition they elaborate on the function of scapegoating evident in "Rip Van Winkle" and "The Birthmark." In its more obvious connection of the themes of love and power *The Great Gatsby* brings closer to consciousness the hostility which *A Farewell to Arms* seeks to disguise and bury. *The Bostonians* and *An American Dream* form the most unlikely and perhaps the most fascinating of the pairs. In both, the obfuscation of romantic love has been cleared away and the issue of power directly joined. James's novel describes a social reality—male power, female powerlessness—which Mailer's denies by creating a social mythology—female power, male powerlessness—that inverts that reality. Yet finally, the intention of Mailer's mythology is to maintain the reality it denies. *The Bostonians* forces the strategies of *An American Dream* into the open by its massive documentation of women's oppression, and *An American Dream* provides the political answer to *The Bostonians*'s inevitability by its massive, though unintended, demonstration of the fact that women's oppression grows not out of biology but out of men's need to oppress.

The sequence of both the stories and the novels is generated by a scale of increasing complexity, increasing consciousness, and increasing "feminist" sympathy and insight. Thus, the movement of the stories is from the black and white of "Rip Van Winkle," with its postulation of good guy and villain and its formulation in terms of innocent fable, to the complexity of "A Rose for Emily," whose action forces sexual violence into consciousness and demands understanding for the erstwhile villain. The movement of the novels is similar. *A Farewell to Arms* is as simplistic and disguised and hostile as "Rip Van Winkle"; indeed, the two have many affinities, not the least of which is the similarity of their sleep-centered protagonists who believe that women are a bad dream that will go away if you just stay in bed long enough. The sympathy and complexity of consciousness in *The Bostonians* is even larger than that in "A Rose for Emily," and is exceeded only by the imagination of *An American Dream*, which is "feminist" not by design but by default. Yet the decision to end with *An American Dream* comes not simply from its position on the incremental scale. *An American Dream* is "Rip Van Winkle" one hundred and fifty years later, intensified to be sure, but *exactly the same story*. Thus, the complete trajectory of the immasculating imagination of American literature is described by the movement from "Rip Van Winkle" to *An American Dream*, and that movement is finally circular. This juxtaposition of beginning and end provides the sharpest possible exposure of that circular quality in the design of our literature, apparent in the movements within and between works, which defines its imaginative limits. Like the race horse so loved by Anderson's boy, the imagination which informs our "classic" American literature runs endlessly round a single track, unable because unwilling to get out of the race.

NOTES

1. Carolyn Heilbrun, "Millett's Sexual Politics: A Year Later," *Aphra* 2 (Summer 1971), 39.

2. Mary Daly, *Beyond God the Father: Toward a Philosophy of Women's Liberation* (Boston: Beacon, 1973), p. 8.

3. Adrienne Rich, "When We Dead Awaken: Writing as Re-Vision," *College English* 34 (1972), 18.

4. Cynthia Ozick, "Women and Creativity: The Demise of the Dancing Dog," *Motive* 29 (1969); reprinted in *Woman in Sexist Society*, eds. Vivian Gornick and Barbara Moran (New York: Signet–New American Library, 1972), p. 450.

5. Kate Millett, *Sexual Politics* (Garden City: Doubleday, 1970), p. 58.

6. *College English* 34 (1973), 1075.

7. "Dwelling in Decencies: Radical Criticism and the Feminist Perspective," *College English* 32 (1971), 887; reprinted in *Sex, Class, and Culture* (Bloomington: Indiana University Press, 1978), p. 16.

8. *College English* 32 (1971), 855.

9. Ibid., 856–57.

10. *Massachusetts Review* 13 (1972), 226, 227.

11. *Thinking About Women* (New York: Harcourt Brace Jovanovich, 1968), pp. 149–50.

12. Edwards, p. 230.

THE READERS AND THEIR ROMANCES

(1984)

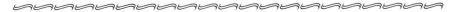

Surrounded by corn and hay fields, the midwestern community of Smithton, with its meticulously tended subdivisions of single-family homes, is nearly two thousand miles from the glass-and-steel office towers of New York City where most of the American publishing industry is housed. Despite the distance separating the two communities, many of the books readied for publication in New York by young women with master's degrees in literature are eagerly read in Smithton family rooms by women who find quiet moments to read in days devoted almost wholly to the care of others. Although Smithton's women are not pleased by every romance prepared for them by New York editors, with Dorothy Evans's help they have learned to circumvent the industry's still inexact understanding of what women want from romance fiction. They have managed to do so by learning to decode the iconography of romantic cover art and the jargon of back-cover blurbs and by repeatedly selecting works by authors who have pleased them in the past.

In fact, it is precisely because a fundamental lack of trust initially characterized the relationship between Smithton's romance readers and the New York publishers that Dorothy Evans was able to amass this loyal following of customers. Her willingness to give advice so endeared her to women bewildered by the increasing romance output of the New York houses in the 1970s that they returned again and again to her checkout counter to consult her about the "best buys" of the month. When she began writing her review newsletter for bookstores and editors, she did so because she felt other readers might find her "expert" advice useful in trying to select romance fiction. She was so successful at developing a national reputation that New York editors began to send her galley proofs of their latest titles to guarantee their books a review in her newsletter. She now also obligingly reads manuscripts for several well-known authors who have begun to seek her advice and support. Although her status in the industry does not necessarily guarantee the representivity of her opinions or those of her customers, it does suggest that some writers and editors believe that she is not only closely attuned to the romance audience's desires and needs but is especially able to articulate them. It should not be surprising to note, therefore, that she proved a willing, careful, and consistently perceptive informant.

I first wrote to Dot in December 1979 to ask whether she would be willing to talk about romances and her evaluative criteria. I asked further if she thought some of her customers might discuss their reading with someone who was interested in what they liked and why. In an open and enthusiastic reply, she said she would be glad to host a series of interviews and meetings in her home during her summer vacation. At first taken aback by such generosity, I soon learned that Dot's unconscious magnanimity is a product of a genuine interest in people. When I could not secure a hotel room for the first night of my planned visit to Smithton, she insisted that I stay with her. I would be able to recognize her at the airport, she assured me, because she would be wearing a lavender pants suit.

The trepidation I felt upon embarking for Smithton slowly dissipated on the drive from the airport as Dot talked freely and fluently about the romances that were clearly an important part of her life. When she explained the schedule of discussions and interviews she had established for the next week, it seemed clear that my time in Smithton would prove enjoyable and busy as well as productive. My concern about whether I could persuade Dot's customers to elaborate honestly about their motives for reading was unwarranted, for after an initial period of mutually felt awkwardness, we conversed frankly and with enthusiasm. Dot helped immensely, for when she introduced me to her customers, she announced, "Jan is just people!" Although it became clear that the women were not accustomed to examining their activity in any detail, they conscientiously tried to put their perceptions and judgments into words to help me understand why they find romance fiction enjoyable and useful.

During the first week I conducted two four-hour discussion sessions with a total of sixteen of Dot's most regular customers. After she informed them of my interest, they had all volunteered to participate. About six more wanted to attend but were away on family vacations. These first discussions were open-ended sessions characterized by general questions posed to the group at large. In the beginning, timidity seemed to hamper the responses as each reader took turns answering each question. When everyone relaxed, however, the conversation flowed more naturally as the participants disagreed among themselves, contradicted one another, and delightedly discovered that they still agreed about many things. Both sessions were tape-recorded. I also conducted individual taped interviews with five of Dot's most articulate and enthusiastic romance readers. In addition, I talked informally to Dot alone for hours at odd times during the day and interviewed her more formally on five separate occasions. Along with twenty-five others approached by Dot herself at the bookstore, these sixteen all filled out a pilot questionnaire designed before I had departed from Philadelphia.

Upon returning from my visit to Smithton, I read as many of the specific titles mentioned during the discussions and interviews that I could acquire, transcribed the tapes, and expanded a field-work journal I had kept while away. In reviewing all of the information and evaluations I had been given, it became clear that I had neither anticipated all of the potentially meaningful questions that might be asked; nor had I always included the best potential answers for the directed-response questions. Accordingly, I redesigned the entire questionnaire and mailed fifty copies to Dot in mid-autumn of 1980. I asked her to give the questionnaire to her "regular" customers (those whom she recognized and had advised more than once about romance purchases) and to give no additional directions other than those on the questionnaire and in an attached explanatory letter. She returned forty-two completed questionnaires to me in early February 1981, during my second sojourn in Smithton.

At that time, I stayed with Dot and her family for a week, watched her daily routine, and talked with her constantly. I also spent three full days at the bookstore observing her interactions with her customers and conversing informally with them myself. I reinterviewed the same five readers during this period, checked points about which I was uneasy, and tested the hypotheses I had formulated already. I also talked at length with Maureen, one of Dot's most forthright readers, who had recently begun writing her own romances.

It is clear that the Smithton group cannot be thought of as a scientifically designed random sample. The conclusions drawn from the study, therefore, should be extrapolated only with great caution to apply to other romance readers. In fact, this study's propositions ought to be considered hypotheses that now must be tested systematically by looking at a much broader and unrelated group of romance readers. Despite the obvious limitations of the group, however, I decided initially to conduct the study for two reasons.

The first had to do with Dot's indisputable success and developing reputation on the national romance scene. The second was that the group was already self-selected and stably constituted. Dot's regular customers had continued to return to her for advice *because* they believed her perceptions accorded reasonably well with theirs. They had all learned to trust her judgment and to rely on her for assistance in choosing a varied array of romance reading material. They found this congenial because it freed all of them from the need to rely solely on a single "line" of books like the Harlequins, that had recently begun to offend and irritate them. It also enabled them to take back some measure of control from the publishers by selectively choosing only those books they had reason to suspect would satisfy their desires and needs. Although there are important variations in taste and habit within the Smithton group, all of the women agree that their preferences are adequately codified by Dorothy Evans.

The nature of the group's operation suggests that it is unsatisfactory for an analyst to select a sample of romances currently issued by American publishers, draw conclusions about the meaning of the form by analyzing the plots of the books in the sample, and then make general statements about the cultural significance of the "romance." Despite the industry's growing reliance on the techniques of semiprogrammed issue to reduce the disjunction between readers' desires and publishers' commodities, the production system is still characterized by a fundamental distance between the originators, producers, and consumers of the fantasies embodied in those romances. Consequently, it must be kept in mind that the people who read romance novels are *not* attending to stories they themselves have created to interpret their own experiences. Because the shift to professional production has reduced self-storytelling substantially, there is no sure way to know whether the narratives consumed by an anonymous public are in any way congruent with those they would have created for themselves and their peers had they not been able to buy them.

Although repeated purchase and consumption of a professionally produced and mass-marketed commodity hints that some kind of audience satisfaction has been achieved, this is not a guarantee that each individual text's interpretation of experience is endorsed by all buyers. In fact, what the Smithton group makes clear is that its members continue to possess very particular tastes in romance fiction that are not adequately addressed by publishers. However, because these corporations have designed their products to appeal to a huge audience by meeting the few preferences that all individuals within the group have in common, they have successfully managed to create texts that are minimally acceptable to Dot and her readers. Moreover, because the Smithton women feel an admittedly intense need to indulge in the romantic fantasy and, for the most part, cannot fulfill that need with their own imaginative activity, they often buy and read books they do not really like or fully endorse. As one reader explained, "Sometimes even a bad book is better than nothing." The act of purchase, then, does not always signify approval of the product selected; with a mass-production system it can just as easily testify to the existence of an ongoing, still only partially met, need.

Precisely because romance publishers have not engineered a perfect fit between the product they offer and all of their readers' desires, the Smithton women have discovered that their tastes are better served when the exchange process is mediated by a trusted selector who assembles a more suitable body of texts from which they can safely make their choices. This particular reliance on a mediator to guide the process of selection suggests that to understand what the romance means, it is first essential to characterize the different groups that find it meaningful and then to determine what each group identifies as its "romance" before attempting any assessment of the significance of the form. Despite the overtly formulaic appearance of the category, there are important differences among novels *for those who read them* that prompt individual decisions to reject or to read. We must begin to recognize this fact of selection within the mass-production process, make some effort to comprehend the principles governing such selection, and describe the content that gives rise to those principles.[1] The Smithton women comprise only one small, relatively homogeneous group that happens to read romances in a determinate way. While their preferences may be representative of those held by women similar to them in demographic characteristics and daily routine, it is not fair to assume that they use romance fiction in the same way as do women of different background, education, and social circumstance. Conclusions about the romance's meaning for highly educated women who work in male-dominated professions, for instance, must await further study.

The reading habits and preferences of the Smithton women are complexly tied to their daily routines, which are themselves a function of education, social role, and class position. Most Smithton readers are married mothers of children, living in single-family homes in a sprawling suburb of a central midwestern state's second largest city (population 850,000 in 1970).[2] Its surrounding cornfields notwithstanding, Smithton itself is an urbanized area. Its 1970 population, which was close to 112,000 inhabitants, represented a 70 percent increase over that recorded by the 1960 census. The community is essentially a "bedroom" community in that roughly 90 percent of those employed in 1970 worked outside Smithton itself. Although this has changed slightly in recent years with the building of the mall in which Dot herself works, the city is still largely residential and dominated by single-family homes, which account for 90 to 95 percent of the housing stock.

Dot and her family live on the fringe of one of Smithton's new housing developments in a large, split-level home. When I last visited Smithton, Dot, her husband, Dan, her eldest daughter, Kit, and her mother were living in the house, which is decorated with Dot's needlework and crafts, projects she enjoyed when her children were young. Dot's other two children, Dawn, who is nineteen and married, and Joe, who is twenty-one, do not live with the family. Dot herself was forty-eight years old at the time of the study. Dan, a journeyman plumber, seems both bemused by Dot's complete absorption in romances and proud of her success at the bookstore. Although he occasionally reads thrillers and some nonfiction, he spends his leisure time with fellow union members or working about the house.

Although she is now a self-confident and capable woman, Dot believes she was once very different. She claims that she has changed substantially in recent years, a change she attributes to her reading and her work with people in the bookstore. When asked how she first began reading romances, she responded that it was really at her doctor's instigation. Although he did not suggest reading specifically, he advised her about fifteen years ago that she needed to find an enjoyable leisure activity to which she could devote at least an hour a day. He was concerned about her physical and mental exhaustion, apparently brought on by her conscientious and diligent efforts to care for her husband, three small children, and her home. When he asked her what she did for herself all day and she could list *only* the tasks she performed for others, he insisted that she learn to spend some time on herself if she did not want to land in a hospital. Remembering that she loved to read as a child, she decided to try again. Thus began her interest in romance fiction. Dot read many kinds of books at first, but she soon began to concentrate on romances for reasons she cannot now explain. Her reading became so chronic that when she discovered that she could not rely on a single shop to provide all of the latest releases by her favorite authors, she found in necessary to check four different bookstores to get all of the romances she wanted. Most of her customers commented that before they discovered Dot they did the same thing. Some still attend garage sales and flea markets religiously to find out-of-print books by authors whose more recent works they have enjoyed.

Dot would have continued as one of the legion of "silent" readers had not one of her daughters encouraged her to look for a job in a bookstore to make use of her developing expertise. Although hesitant about moving out into the public world, she eventually mustered the courage to try, soon finding employment at the chain outlet where she still works. She discovered that she thoroughly enjoyed the contact with other "readers," and, as she developed more confidence, she began to make suggestions and selections for uncertain buyers. In the first edition of her newsletter, she explained the subsequent events that led to the creation of her romance review:

> Soon it became apparent that the women who were regular customers were searching me out for my opinions on their selections. Also, the Area Supervisor of our store had noticed a sharply marked increase in sales of the general category of romances. . . . So the interviews and articles in . . . periodicals began and brought more attention to my so-called expertise.
>
> The idea for a newsletter and rating of new releases every month . . . belongs to my daughter, who felt we could make this available to a much larger group of women readers. As most of them know the prices of books

are rising and the covers are not always a good indicator of the content of the book.[3]

With the help of her daughter, Kit, she planned, executed, and wrote the first edition of "Dorothy's Diary of Romance Reading," in April 1980. Despite reservations about taking up the role of critical mediator, she explained in her inaugural editorial that she was persuaded to such an authoritarian act by the intensity of her customers' needs and by the inability of the production system to meet them. "I know many women," she commented, "who need to read as an escape as I have over the years and I believe this is good therapy and much cheaper than tranquilizers, alcohol or addictive TV serials which most of my readers say bores them." She added that she intended to separate "the best or better books from the less well written, so as to save the reader money and time." "However," she concluded, "I would never want to take from the ladies the right to choose their own reading materials, only to suggest from my own experience."[4]

Still conscious of the hierarchy implicit in the critic-consumer relationship, Dot continues to be careful about offering evaluative suggestions at the store. Her first question to a woman who solicits her advice is calculated to determine the kinds of romances the reader has enjoyed in the past. "If they are in my category," she explained in one of our interviews, "I start saying, 'OK, what was the last good book you read?' And then if they tell me that, I usually can go from there." Her services, like semi-programmed publication techniques, are designed to gauge already formulated but not fully expressed reader preferences, which she subsequently attempts to satisfy by selecting the proper material from a much larger corpus of published works. Dot can be more successful than distant publishing firms attempting the same service through market research because she personalizes selection at the moment of purchase in a way that the absent publishers cannot.

Dot's unusual success is a function of her participant's understanding of the different kinds of romances, acquired as the consequence of her voracious reading, and of her insistence on the individuality of her readers and their preferences. This is especially evident at the stage in her advising process when she finally displays a selection of books for her customers. "Sometimes," she laments, "I have people who say, 'Well, which one do *you* say is the best of these three?'" Her response indicates the depth of her respect for the singularity of readers and romances despite the fact that those readers are usually thought of as category readers and the romances considered formulaic performances:

> I will say, "They are not alike, they are not written by the same author, they are totally and completely different settings and I cannot say you will like this one better than this one because they are totally and completely different books." [But they always continue with] "Which one did you like best?" And I'll say, "Don't try to pin me down like that because it's not right." I won't go any further. They have to choose from there because otherwise you're getting sheep. See, I like it when some of my women say, "Hey, I didn't care for that book." And I say, "Hey, how come?"[5]

Because Dot is ever mindful of her readers' dissatisfaction with some of the material flowing from the New York publishers and simultaneously aware of their desire to maintain and satisfy their own personal tastes, she has created a role for herself by facilitating a commercial exchange that benefits the reader as much as it does the producer. At the same time, Dot continues to perpetuate generic distinctions within a category that the publishers themselves are trying to rationalize and standardize. Hers is a strategy which, if not consciously calculated to empower readers with a selective ability, at least tends to operate in that way. By carefully identifying a book's particular historical setting, by relating the amount of sexually explicit description it contains, by describing its use of violence and cruelty, and by remarking about its portrayal of the heroine/hero relationship, she alerts the reader to the book's treatment of the essential features that nearly all of her customers focus on in determining the quality of a romance.

In addition to recognizing individual tastes and respecting personal preferences, Dot also performs another essential function for her regular customers. Although I suspect she was not always as effective at this as she is now, she capably defends her readers' preferences for romance fiction *to themselves*. One would think this unnecessary because so many of her customers come to her expressly seeking romances, but Dot finds that many of her women feel guilty about spending money on books that are regularly ridiculed by the media, their husbands, and their children. Dot encourages her customers to feel proud of their regular reading and provides them with a model of indignant response that they can draw upon when challenged by men who claim superior taste. By questioning them rhetorically about whether their romance reading is any different from their husbands' endless attention to televised sports, she demonstrates an effective rejoinder that can be used in the battle to defend the leisure pursuit they enjoy so much but which the larger culture condemns as frivolous and vaguely, if not explicitly, pornographic.

Dot's vociferous defense of her customers' right to please themselves in any way that does not harm others is an expression of her deeply held belief that women are too often the object of others' criticism and the butt of unjustified ridicule. Although she is not a feminist as most would understand that term, she is perfectly aware that women have been dismissed by men for centuries, and she can and does converse eloquently on the subject. During my second stay in Smithton, she admitted to me that she understands very well why women have pushed for liberal abortion laws and remarked that even though her devoutly held religious convictions would prevent her from seeking one herself, she believes all women should have the right to *choose* motherhood and to control their own bodies. She also feels women should have the right to work and certainly should be paid equally with men. Many of our conversations were punctuated by her expressions of anger and resentment at the way women are constantly "put down" as childish, ignorant, and incapable of anything but housework or watching soap operas.

At first glance, Dot's incipient feminism seems deeply at odds with her interest in a literary form whose ultimate message, one astute observer has noted, is that "pleasure for women is men."[6] The traditionalism of romance fiction will not be denied here, but it is essential to point out that Dot and many of the writers and readers of romances interpret these stories as chronicles of female triumph. Although the particular way they do so will be explored later, suffice it to say here that Dot believes a good romance focuses on an intelligent and able heroine who finds a man who recognizes her special qualities and is capable of loving and caring for her as she wants to be loved. Thus Dot understands such an ending to say that female independence and marriage are compatible rather than mutually exclusive. The romances she most values and recommends for her readers are those with "strong," "fiery" heroines who are capable of "defying the hero," softening him, and showing him the value of loving and caring for another.

It is essential to introduce this here in order to take account adequately of Dot's personal influence on her customers and on their preferences in romance fiction. Because she is an exceptionally strong woman convinced of her sex's capabilities, when she expresses her opinions about a woman's right to pleasure, Dot not only supports her customers but confers legitimacy on the preoccupation they share with her. I suspect that in providing this much-needed reinforcement Dot also exerts an important influence on them that must be taken into account. She encourages her customers to think well of themselves not only by demonstrating her interest in them and in their desires but also by presenting them with books whose heroines seem out of the ordinary. Therefore, while the members of the Smithton group share attitudes about good and bad romances that are similar to Dot's, it is impossible to say whether these opinions were formed by Dot or whether she is simply their most articulate advocate. Nonetheless, it must be emphasized that this group finds it possible to select and construct romances in such a way that their stories are experienced as a reversal of the oppression and emotional abandonment suffered by women in real life. For Dot and her customers, romances provide a utopian vision in which female individuality and a sense of self are shown to be compatible with nurturance and care by another.

All of the Smithton readers who answered the questionnaire were female. Dot reported that although she suspects some of the men who buy romances "for their wives" are in fact buying them for themselves, all of the people she regularly advises are women. While the few houses that have conducted market-research surveys will not give out exact figures, officials at Harlequin, Silhouette, and Fawcett have all indicated separately that the majority of romance readers are married women between the ages of twenty-five and fifty. Fred Kerner, Harlequin's vice-president for publishing, for instance, recently reported to Barbara Brotman, of the *Chicago Tribune*, that "Harlequin readers are overwhelmingly women of whom 49 percent work at least part-time. They range in age from twenty-four to forty-nine, have average family incomes of $15,000–20,000, and have high school diplomas but haven't completed college."[7] Harlequin will reveal little else about its audience, but a company executive did tell Margaret Jensen that the Harlequin reading population matches the profile of the "North American English-speaking female population" in age, family income, employment status, and geographical location.[8] For example, he said that 22 percent of the female population and Harlequin readers are between the ages of twenty-five and thirty-four. Carol Reo, publicity director for Silhouette Romances, has also revealed that the romance audience is almost entirely female, but indicates that 65 percent of Silhouette's potential market is under the age of forty and that 45 percent attended college.[9] If these sketchy details are accurate, the Smithton readers may be more representative of the Silhouette audience than they are of Harlequin's.[10] Unfortunately, the lack of detailed information about the total American audience for Harlequins as well as for other kinds of romances makes it exceedingly difficult to judge the representivity of the Smithton group. Still, it appears evident that the Smithton readers are somewhat younger than either Jensen's Harlequin readers or the Mills and Boon audience.

The age differential may account for the fact that neither Dot nor many of her customers are Harlequin fans. Although Dot reviews Harlequins and slightly more than half of her customers (twenty-four) reported reading them, a full eighteen indicated that they *never* read a Harlequin romance. Moreover, only ten of Dot's customers indicated that Harlequins are among the kinds of romances they *most* like to read. The overwhelming preference of the group was for historicals, cited by twenty (48 percent) as their favorite subgenre within the romance category.[11] Because historicals typically include more explicit sex than the Harlequins and also tend to portray more independent and defiant heroines, we might expect that this particular subgenre would draw younger readers who are less offended by changing standards of gender behavior. This would seem to be corroborated by the fact that only two of the women who listed Harlequins as a favorite also listed historicals.

In addition, the Smithton group also seemed to like contemporary mystery romances and contemporary romances, which were cited by another twelve as being among their favorites. Silhouettes are contemporary romances and, like the historicals, are less conventional than the Harlequins. Not only is their sexual description more explicit but it is not unusual for them to include heroines with careers who expect to keep their jobs after marriage. The similarity between Smithton's tastes and the content of the Silhouettes may thus explain why both audiences are younger than that for the relatively staid Harlequins.

Despite the discrepancies in the various reports, romance reading apparently correlates strongly with the years of young adulthood and early middle age. This is further borne out in the present study by the Smithton women's responses to a question about when they first began to read romances. Although fifteen (36 percent) of the women reported that they began in adolescence between the ages of ten and nineteen, sixteen (38 percent) indicated that they picked up the habit between the ages of twenty and twenty-nine. Another ten (24 percent) adopted romance reading after age thirty.[12]

Thirty-two women (76 percent) in the Smithton group were married at the time of the survey, a proportion that compares almost exactly with the 75 percent of married women included in Jensen's group.[13] An additional three (7 percent) of the Smithton women were single, while five (12 percent) were either widowed, separated, or divorced and not remarried.

Moreover, most of the women in the Smithton group were mothers with children *under* age eighteen (70 percent). Indeed, within the group, only five (12 percent) reported having no children at all. Nine (21 percent) of the Smithton women reported only one child, twelve (29 percent) claimed two children, eleven (27 percent) had three children, and three (7 percent) had four children. Interestingly enough, only five (12 percent) reported children under the age of five, while twenty-four of the women indicated that they had at least one child under age eighteen. Eleven (27 percent), however, reported that all of their children were over age eighteen. Fifteen (36 percent) reported children between ten and eighteen, and another fifteen (36 percent) had at least one child over age eighteen. The relatively advanced age of the Smithton readers' children is not surprising if one takes into account the age distribution of the women themselves and the fact that the mean age at first marriage within the group was 19.9 years.

Once again, the limited size of the sample and the lack of corroborating data from other sources suggest caution in the formation of hypotheses. Nonetheless, it appears that within the Smithton group romance reading correlates with motherhood and the care of children *other* than infants and toddlers.[14] This seems logical because the fact of the older children's attendance at school would allow the women greater time to read even as the children themselves continued to make heavy emotional demands on them for nurturance, advice, and attentive care. It will be seen later that it is precisely this emotional drain caused by a woman's duty to nurture and care for her children and husband that is addressed directly by romance reading at least within the minds of the women themselves.

Given the fact that fifteen (36 percent) of the Smithton readers reported children age ten and under, it should not be surprising to note that sixteen of the women (38 percent) reported that in the preceding week they were keeping house and/or caring for children on a full-time basis. Another nine (21 percent) were working part-time, while still another nine (21 percent) were holding down full-time jobs. In addition, two women failed to respond, two stated that they were retired, one listed herself as a student, and three indicated that they were currently unemployed and looking for work. These statistics seem to parallel those of the Mills and Boon study which found that 33 percent of the sample were represented by full-time housewives, while another 30 percent included housewives with full- or part-time jobs. Both studies suggest that romance reading is very often squeezed into busy daily schedules.

Although Fred Kerner's comment about the average $15,000–$20,000 income of the Harlequin audience is not very illuminating, neither is it at odds with the details reported by Dot's customers. Although four (10 percent) did not answer the question, eighteen (43 percent) in the group indicated a family income of somewhere between $15,000 and $24,999. Another fourteen (33 percent) claimed a joint income of $25,000 to $49,999, while four (10 percent) listed family earnings of over $50,000. The greater affluence of the Smithton group is probably accounted for by the fact that Dot's bookstore is located in one of the twelve most affluent counties in a state with 115. The median family income in Smithton, as reported by the 1970 United States census, was almost $11,000, which compares with the state median income of just slightly less than $9,000.

Before turning to the group's reading history and patterns, it should be noted that exactly half of the Smithton readers indicated that they had earned a high school diploma. Ten (24 percent) of the women reported completing less than three years of college; eight (19 percent) claimed at least a college degree or better. Only one person in the group indicated that she had not finished high school, while two failed to answer the question. Once again, as the Smithton readers appear to be more affluent than Harlequin readers, so also do they seem better educated; the Harlequin corporation claims that its readers are educated below even the statistical norm for the North American female population.

One final detail about the personal history of the Smithton women ought to be mentioned here: attendance at religious services was relatively high among Dot's customers. Although eight (19 percent) of the women indicated that they had not been to a service in the last two years, fifteen (36 percent) reported attendance "once a week or more," while another eight (19 percent) indicated attendance "once or a few times a month." Another nine (21 percent) admitted going to services a few times a year, while two (5 percent) did not answer the question. The women reported membership in a wide variety of denominations. Eight (19 percent) of the women indicated that they were Methodists and eight (19 percent) checked "Christian but non-denominational." The next two groups most heavily represented in the sample were Catholics and Baptists, each with five (12 percent) of the Smithton women.

When the reading *histories* of these women are examined, it becomes clear that, for many of them, romance reading is simply a variation in a pattern of leisure activity they began early in life. Indeed, twenty-two of Dot's customers reported that they first began to read for pleasure before age ten. Another twelve (27 percent) adopted the habit between the ages of eleven and twenty. Only seven (17 percent) of the Smithton women indicated that they began pleasure reading after their teen years. These results parallel earlier findings about the adoption of the book habit. Phillip Ennis found in 1965, for instance, that of the 49 percent of the American population who were "current readers," 34 percent consisted of those who started reading early in life and 15 percent consisted of those who began reading at an advanced age.[15]

When *current* reading habits are examined, however, it becomes clear that the women think that it is the romances that are especially necessary to their daily routine. Their intense reliance on these books suggests strongly that they help to fulfill deeply felt psychological needs. Indeed, one of the most striking findings to come out of the Smithton study was that thirty-seven (88 percent) of Dot's readers indicated that they read religiously every day. Only five of her regular customers claimed to read more sporadically. Twenty-two of the women, in fact, reported reading more than sixteen hours per week, and another ten (24 percent) claimed to read between eleven and fifteen hours weekly.[16] When asked to describe their typical reading pattern once they have begun a new romance, eleven (26 percent) selected the statement, "I won't put it down until I've finished it unless it's absolutely necessary." Thirty more indicated reading "as much of it as I can until I'm interrupted or have something else to do." None of Dot's customers reported a systematic reading pattern of "a few pages a day until done," and only one admitted that she reads solely when she is in the mood. These figures suggest that the Smithton women become intensely involved in the stories they are reading and that once immersed in the romantic fantasy, Dot's customers do not like to return to reality without experiencing the resolution of the narrative.

This need to see the story and the emotions aroused by it resolved is so intense that many of the Smithton women have worked out an ingenious strategy to insure a regular and predictable arrival at the anticipated narrative conclusion. Although they categorize romances in several ways, one of the most basic distinctions they make is that between "quick reads" and "fat books." Quick reads contain less than two hundred pages and require no more than two hours of reading time. Harlequins, Silhouettes, and most Regencies are considered quick reads for occasions when they know they will not be able to "make it through" a big book. If, for example, a woman has just finished one romance but still "is not ready to quit," as one of my informants put it, she will "grab a thin one" she knows she can finish before going to sleep. Fat books, on the other hand, tend to be saved for weekends or long evenings that promise to be uninterrupted, once again because the women dislike having to leave a story before it is concluded. This kind of uninterrupted reading is very highly valued within the Smithton group because it is associated with the pleasure of spending time alone.[17] Although a detailed exploration of the importance of this narrative and emotional resolution must be delayed until chapter 4, where the structure of the romance story and its developing effect on the reader will be considered in detail, let it be said here that the Smithton readers' strategies for avoiding disruption or discontinuity in the story betoken a profound need to arrive at the *ending* of the tale and thus to achieve or acquire the emotional gratification they already can anticipate.

The remarkable extent of their familiarity with the genre is attested to by the number of romances these women read each week. Despite the fact that twenty-six (62 percent) of Dot's customers claimed to read somewhere between one and four books *other* than romances every week, more than a third (fifteen) reported reading from five to nine romances weekly. An additional twenty-two (55 percent) completed between one and four romances every week, while four women indicated that they consume anywhere from fifteen to twenty-five romances during that same period of time. This latter figure strikes me as somewhat implausible because it implies a reading rate of one hundred romances a month. I think this is unlikely given the fact that far fewer romances were issued monthly by publishers at the time of the study. Of course, the women could be reading old romances, but the figure still seems exaggerated. Nonetheless, it is evident that Dot's customers read extraordinary amounts of romance fiction.

Although their chronic reading of these books might sound unusual or idiosyncratic, the Yankelovich findings about romance reading, as noted before, indicate that romance readers are generally heavy consumers. Most, however, are probably not as obsessed as the Smithton readers seem to be. Unfortunately, the Yankelovich discovery that the average romance reader had read nine romances in the last six months does not tell us what proportion of the group read an even larger number of novels. Although 40 percent of the heavy readers (those who had read more than twenty-five books in the last six months) reported having read a romance, thus suggesting the possibility of a correlation between high levels of consumption and romance reading, the study gives no indication of how many of the romance readers actually read anywhere near the number the Smithton women report, which ranges from twenty-four to more than six hundred romances every six months.[18] I think it is safe to say that the Smithton group's reliance on romances is not strictly comparable to that of the occasional reader. Rather, Dot's customers are women who spend a significant portion of every day participating vicariously in a fantasy world that they willingly admit bears little resemblance to the one they actually inhabit. Clearly, the experience must provide some form of required pleasure and reconstitution because it seems unlikely that so much time and money would be spent on an activity that functioned merely to fill otherwise unoccupied time.

The women confirmed this in their answers to a directed-response question about their reasons for reading romance fiction. When asked to rank order the three most important motives for romance reading out of a list of eight, nineteen

(45 percent) of the women listed "simple relaxation" as the first choice. Another eight (19 percent) of the readers reported that they read romances "because reading is just for me; it is my time." Still another six (14 percent) said they read "to learn about faraway places and time"; while five (12 percent) insisted that their primary reason is "to escape my daily problems." When these first choices are added to the second and third most important reasons for reading, the totals are distributed as in Table 1:

TABLE 1

Question: Which of the Following Best Describes Why You Read Romances?

a. To escape my daily problems	13
b. To learn about faraway places and times	19
c. For simple relaxation	33
d. Because I wish I had a romance like the heroine's	5
e. Because reading is just for me; it is my time	28
f. Because I like to read about the strong, virile heroes	4
g. Because reading is at least better than other forms of escape	5
h. Because romantic stories are never sad or depressing	10

On the basis of these schematic answers alone I think it logical to conclude that romance reading is valued by the Smithton women because the experience itself is *different* from ordinary experience. Not only is it a relaxing release from the tension produced by daily problems and responsibilities, but it creates a time or space within which a woman can be entirely on her own, preoccupied with her personal needs, desires, and pleasure. It is also a means of transportation or escape to the exotic or, again, to that which is different.

It is important to point out here that the responses to the second questionnaire are different in important ways from the answers I received from the women in the face-to-face interviews and in the first survey. At the time of my initial visit in June 1980, our conversations about their reasons for romance reading were dominated by the words "escape" and "education." Similarly, when asked by the first questionnaire to describe briefly what romances do "better" than other books available today, of the thirty-one answering the undirected question, fourteen of the first respondents *volunteered* that they like romance fiction because it allows them to "escape." It should be noted that "relaxation" was given only once as an answer, while no woman mentioned the idea of personal space.

Both answers *c* and *e* on the second form were given initially in the course of the interviews by two unusually articulate readers who elaborated more fully than most of the women on the meaning of the word "escape." They considered these two answers synonymous with it, but they also seemed to prefer the alternate responses because they did not so clearly imply a desire to avoid duties and responsibilities in the "real" world. Although most of the other women settled for the word "escape" on the first questionnaire, they also liked their sister readers' terms better. Once these were introduced in the group interviews, the other women agreed that romance reading functions best as relaxation and as a time for self-indulgence. Because the switch seemed to hint at feelings of guilt, I decided to add the more acceptable choices to the second survey. Although both answers *c* and *e* also imply movement away from something distasteful in the real present to a somehow more satisfying universe, a feature that appears to testify to romance reading's principal function as a therapeutic release and as a provider of vicarious pleasure, the fact of the women's preference for these two terms over their first spontaneous response suggests again that the women harbor complex feelings about the worth and propriety of romance reading.[19]

The women provided additional proof of their reliance on romance reading as a kind of tranquilizer or restorative agent in their responses to questions about preferred reading times and the habit of rereading favorite romances. When asked to choose from among seven statements the one that best described their reading pattern, twenty-four (57 percent) eschewed specification of a particular time of day in order to select the more general assertion, "It's hard to say when I do most of my reading, since I read every chance I get." Another fourteen claimed to read mostly in the evenings, usually because days were occupied with employment outside the home. In the case of either pattern, however, romances are not picked up idly as an old magazine might be merely to fill otherwise unoccupied time. Rather, romance reading is considered so enjoyable and beneficial by the women that they deliberately work it into busy schedules as often and as consistently as they can.

Rereading is not only a widely practiced habit among the Smithton women but tends to occur most frequently during times of stress or depression. Three-fourths of Dot's customers reported that they reread favorite books either "sometimes" (twenty-one) or "often" (eleven). They do so, they explained in the interviews, when they feel sad or unhappy because they know exactly how the chosen book will affect their state of mind. Peter Mann similarly discovered that 46 percent of his Mills and Boon readers claimed to reread "very often," while another 38 percent reported repeat reading "now and then."[20] Unfortunately, he has provided no further information about why or when the women do so. Although it is possible that they may reread in order to savor the details of particular plots, it is clear that for the most part the Smithton women do not. For them, rereading is an activity engaged in expressly to lift the spirits. The following comment from one of the first questionnaires illustrates nicely the kind of correlation the Smithton women see between their daily needs and the effects of romance reading: "Romances are not depressing and very seldom leave you feeling sad inside. When I read for enjoyment I want to be entertained and feel lifted out of my daily routine. And romances are the best type of reading for this effect. Romances also revive my usually optimistic outlook which often is very strained in day-to-day living." Although all of Dot's customers know well that most romances end happily, when their own needs seem unusually pressing they often refuse even the relatively safe gamble of beginning a new romance. Instead, they turn to a romance they have completed previously because they already know how its final resolution will affect them. Romance reading, it would seem, can be valued as much for the sameness of the response it evokes as for the variety of the adventures it promises.[21]

Interestingly enough, the Smithton readers hold contradictory opinions about the repetitious or formulaic quality of the fiction they read. On the one hand, they are reluctant to admit that the characters appearing in romances are similar.

As Dot's daughter, Kit, explained when asked to describe a typical heroine in the historical romance, "there isn't a typical one, they all have to be different or you'd be reading the same thing over and over." Her sentiments were echoed frequently by her mother's customers, all of whom claim to value the variety and diversity of romance fiction.

On the other hand, these same women exhibit fairly rigid expectations about what is permissible in a romantic tale and express disappointment and outrage when those conventions are violated. In my first interview with Dot, she discussed a particular author who had submitted a historical novel to her publisher. Although the author explained repeatedly that the book was not a romance, the publisher insisted on packaging it with a standard romance cover in the hope of attracting the huge romance market. The author knew this would anger the audience and, as Dot remarked, "she was not surprised when she got irate letters." Clearly, romances may not deviate too significantly if regular readers are to be pleased. They expect and, indeed, rely upon certain events, characters, and progressions to provide the desired experience.

Dot herself often finds it necessary but difficult to overcome her customers' fixed expectations when she discovers a romance she thinks they will enjoy even though it fails to follow the usual pattern. In the case of *The Fulfillment*, for example, which Dot loved and wanted to share with her women, she worked out an entire speech to get them to buy the book and read it through. The following is a verbatim transcription of her re-creation of that speech: "Now this is a good book—but please don't think that it is the run of the mill. It isn't. At one point in this book, you're gonna want to put it down—and you're gonna say, 'Dot didn't tell me this'—and I said, 'Don't put it down. You keep reading.' Every one of them came back and said, 'You were right. I thought why did she give me this book?' They said, 'I kept reading like you said and it was great.'" The problem with this particular book was the fact that the hero died three-quarters of the way through the tale. However, because the author had worked out an unusually complex plot involving the heroine simultaneously with another equally attractive man in an acceptable way, the women did not find her sudden remarriage distasteful. Without Dot's skillful encouragement, however, most of the women would never have read the book past the hero's death.

Dot also tries to circumvent set expectations in her newsletter. She occasionally tells booksellers and readers about books classified by their publishers as something other than a romance. Erroneous categorization occurs, she believes, because the publishers really do not understand what a romance is and thus pay too much attention to meaningless, superficial details that lead to mistaken identifications. Because Jacqueline Marten's *Visions of the Damned* suffered this fate, Dot attempted to alert her readers to the problem classification. Her way of doing so provides an essential clue to the proper identification of a romance, which the women rely on despite their claim that all romantic novels are different. Of Marten's story, she wrote, "This book, because of cover and title, was classed as an occult. What a mistake! *Visions* is one of the best love stories I've read of late. Get it and read it. I loved it."[22] Although *Visions of the Damned* concerns itself with extrasensory perception and reincarnation, Dot believes that the book's proper plot structure is what makes it a romance. It is not the mere use of the romantic subject matter that qualifies Marten's books as a romance, she explained, but rather its manner of developing the loving relationship. As Dot remarked in a later interview, "Not all love stories are romances." Some are simply novels about love.

If the Smithton readers' stipulations are taken seriously, a romance is, first and foremost, a story about a woman. That woman, however, may not figure in a larger plot simply as the hero's prize, as Jenny Cavileri does, for instance in Erich Segal's *Love Story*, which the Smithton readers claim is not a romance. To qualify as a romance, the story must chronicle not merely the events of a courtship but *what it feels like* to be the *object* of one. Dot's customers insist that this need not be accomplished by telling the story solely from the heroine's point of view, although it is usually managed in this way. Although five of the women refuse to read first-person narratives because they want to be privy to the hero's thoughts and another ten indicate that they prefer to see both points of view, twenty-three of Dot's regular customers indicate that they have no preference about the identity of the narrator. However, all of the women I spoke to, regardless of their taste in narratives, admitted that they want to identify with the heroine as she attempts to comprehend, anticipate, and deal with the ambiguous attentions of a man who inevitably cannot understand her feelings at all. The point of the experience is the sense of exquisite tension, anticipation, and excitement created within the reader as she imagines the possible resolutions and consequences for a woman of an encounter with a member of the opposite sex and then observes that once again the heroine in question has avoided the ever-present potential for disaster because the hero has fallen helplessly in love with her.

In all their comments about the nature of the romance, the Smithton women placed heavy emphasis on the importance of *development* in the romance's portrayal of love. The following two definitions were echoed again and again in other remarks:

> Generally there are two people who come together for one reason or another, *grow to love each other* and *work together solving problems* along the way—united for a purpose. They are light easy reading and always have a happy ending which makes one feel more light-hearted.
>
> I think [a romance] is a man and woman meeting, the growing awareness, the culmination of the love—*whether it's going to jell or if it's going to fall apart*—but they [the heroine and the hero] have recognized that they have fallen in love [emphasis added].

The women usually articulated this insistence on process and development during discussions about the genre's characteristic preoccupation with what is typically termed "a love-hate relationship." Because the middle of every romantic narrative must create some form of conflict to keep the romantic pair apart until the proper moment, many authors settle for misunderstanding or distrust as the cause of the intermediary delay of the couple's happy union. Hero and heroine are shown to despise each other overtly, even though they are "in love," primarily because each is jealous or suspicious of the other's motives and consequently fails to trust the other. Despite the frequency with which this pattern of conflict is suddenly explained away by the couple's mutual recognition that only misunderstanding is thwarting their relationship, the Smithton women are not convinced when a hero decides within two pages of the novel's conclusion that he has been mistaken about the heroine and that his apparent hatred is actually affection. Dot's customers dislike such "about faces"; they prefer to see a hero and heroine gradually overcome distrust and suspicion and grow to love each other.

TABLE 2

Question: What Are the Three Most Important Ingredients in a Romance?

Response	First Most Important Feature	Second Most Important Feature	Third Most Important Feature	Total Who Checked Response In One of Top Three Positions
a. A happy ending	22	4	6	32
b. Lots of scenes with explicit sexual description	0	0	0	0
c. Lots of details about faraway places and times	0	1	2	3
d. A long conflict between hero and heroine	2	1	1	4
e. Punishment of the villain	0	2	3	5
f. A slowly but consistently developing love between hero and heroine	8	9	6	23
g. A setting in a particular historical period	3	4	3	10
h. Lots of love scenes with some explicit sexual description	3	7	3	13
i. Lots of love scenes without explicit sexual description	0	3	1	4
j. Some detail about heroine and hero after they've gotten together	1	7	14	22
k. A very particular kind of hero and heroine	3	4	3	10

Although this depiction of love as a gradual process cannot be considered the defining feature of the genre for all of the Smithton women, slightly more than half (twenty-three) believe it one of the "three most important ingredients" in the narrative. As might have been predicted, when responding to a request to rank order narrative features with respect to their importance to the genre, Dot's customers generally agreed that a happy ending is indispensable. Twenty-two of the women selected this as the essential ingredient in romance fiction out of a list of eleven choices, while a total of thirty-two listed it in first, second, or third place. The runner-up in the "most important" category, however, was "a slowly but consistently developing love between hero and heroine," placed by twenty-three of the women in first, second, or third place. Considered almost equally important by Dot's customers was the romance's inclusion of "some detail about the heroine and the hero after they have finally gotten together."[23] Twenty-two of the women thought this one of the three most important ingredients in the genre. Table 2 summarizes the ranking responses of the Smithton women.

The obvious importance of the happy ending lends credence to the suggestion that romances are valued most for their ability to raise the spirits of the reader. They manage to do so, the rankings imply, by involving that reader vicariously in the gradual evolution of a loving relationship whose culmination she is later permitted to enjoy in the best romances through a description of the heroine's and hero's life together after their necessary union. When combined with the relative unimportance of detailed reports about sexual encounters, it seems clear that the Smithton readers are interested in the verbal working out of a romance, that is, in the reinterpretation of misunderstood actions and in declarations of mutual love rather than in the portrayal of sexual contact through visual imagery.

Beatrice Faust has recently argued in *Women, Sex, and Pornography* that female sexuality is "tactile, verbal, intimate, nurturant, process-oriented and somewhat inclined to monogomy," traits she attributes to biological predisposition and social reinforcement through culture.[24] Although there are important problems with Faust's reliance on biology to account for female preferences in sexual encounters as well as with her assertion that such tastes characterize all women, her parallel claim that women are not excited by the kinds of visual displays and explicit description of physical contact that characterize male pornography is at least true of the Smithton readers. Dot and her customers are more interested in the affective responses of hero and heroine to each other than in a detailed account of their physical contact. Interestingly enough, the Smithton women also explained that they do not like explicit description because they prefer to imagine the scene in detail by themselves. Their wish to participate in the gradual growth of love and trust and to witness the way in which the heroine is eventually cared for by a man who also confesses that he "needs" her suggests that the Smithton women do indeed want to see a woman attended to sexually in a tender, nurturant, and emotionally open way. It should be added that these preferences also hint at the existence of an equally powerful wish to see a man dependent upon a woman.

Although Dot's customers will not discuss in any detail whether they themselves are sexually excited by the escalation of sexual tension in a romance, they willingly acknowledge that what they enjoy most about romance reading is the opportunity to project themselves into the story, to become the heroine, and thus to share her surprise and slowly awakening pleasure at being so closely watched by someone who finds her valuable and worthy of love. They have elaborated this preference into a carefully articulated distinction between good and bad romances, which differ principally in the way they portray the hero's treatment of the heroine.

A substantial amount of popular and even scholarly writing about mass-produced entertainment makes the often correct assumption that such fare is cynically engineered to appeal to the tastes of the largest possible audience in the interest of maximum profit.[25] However, a certain portion of it is still written by sincere, well-meaning people who are themselves consumers of the form they work in and indeed proponents of the values it embodies. Despite publishers' efforts at rationalization of romance production through the use of carefully calculated "tip sheets to writers," the genre is not yet entirely written by men and women who do it only to make money. Although many of the most successful authors in the field are professional writers, a significant number of them are "amateurs" drawn to the genre by a desire to write the kind of material they love to read. More often than not, it is the work of *these* women that the Smithton readers like best.

In a letter to the readers of Dot's newsletter, for instance, LaVyrle Spencer has explained that her first book "was written because of one very special lady, Kathleen Woodiwiss," whose book, *The Flame and the Flower,* "possessed me to the point where I found I, too, wanted to write a book that would make ladies' hearts throb with anticipation." She continued, "I even got to the point where I told myself I wanted to do it for her, Kathleen, to give her a joyful reading experience like she'd given me."[26] *The Fulfillment* resulted from this inspiration.

Jude Deveraux, another successful author, also commented in Dot's newsletter on Woodiwiss's role in her decision to become a writer. She so enjoyed *The Flame and the Flower* that she dashed out to buy two more romances to re-create the pleasure Woodiwiss's book had provided. "I planned to stay up all night and read them," she explained to Dot's subscribers, but "by ten o'clock I was so disgusted I threw the books across the room. They were nothing but rape sagas." She gave up, turned off the light, and thought, "If I read the perfect romance, what would the plot be?" Deveraux spent the night creating dialogue in her head and when she arose the next morning, she began writing. The book that resulted, *The Enchanted Land,* with its independent heroine and thoughtful hero, was mentioned often by Dot's customers as one of their favorites.[27]

Even the incredibly prolific and very professional Janet Dailey confesses that she too began the career that has made her a millionaire, by some observers' reckoning, because she wanted to write the kinds of books she most enjoyed reading.[28] Convinced by her husband to go ahead and try, she set out to write a romance. Since that day in 1968, millions of readers have informally acknowledged through their repeat purchases of her books that she understands very well what her readers want.

Given the fact that many romance writers were romance readers before they set pen to paper, it seems logical to expect that their views of the romance might parallel those held by their readers. Of course, this is not universally the case because many romances are considered failures by readers. Some otherwise popular books do not please the entire audience, thus bearing witness to the possibility of a discrepancy between writers' and readers' definitions and conceptions. Rosemary Rogers, for example, is universally detested by the Smithton readers who consider her books "trashy," "filthy," and "perverted." Her views of the romance are at least not representative of this group of regular readers.

Despite exceptions like these, it is striking to note that there is a distinct similarity between the Smithton conception of the romance and that implied in comments about the form by writers who are themselves enthusiastic readers. In an article on "Writing the Gothic Novel," for instance, Phyllis Whitney has cautioned aspiring writers, "no feeling, no story—and that's a rule!"[29] She explains that even though explicit sexual description must never appear in a gothic, this prohibition does not mean sexual feeling should not figure in the stories. In fact, she goes on to say, anticipation and excitement *must* "smolder" beneath the surface in scenes that are "underplayed, suggested rather than stated." That way, Whitney elaborates, "the reader's imagination will work for you."[30] She understands that women like the Smithton readers project themselves into the story by identifying with the heroine as she responds to the hero with all of her "strongly passionate nature." Whitney also knows that those women wish to be shown repeatedly that men can attend to a woman in the manner she most desires. To clarify her point she explains finally that "in the true love scenes, there is always an underlying tenderness that, for a woman, can be an exciting factor in sex—James Bond to the contrary."[31] Like Beatrice Faust and the Smithton women, Phyllis Whitney seems to believe that "women want to love and be made love to as they love babies—that is, in a nurturant fashion."[32] Whitney closes with perhaps her most central piece of advice: "I doubt that you can write Gothic novels unless you like reading them. . . . While I am in the process of writing, I am submerged in my heroine and her problems—and having a wonderful time. Me and all those dark-browed heroes! I'm sure this is the first necessary ingredient, though I'm mentioning it last."[33]

Her attitude has been echoed by Jeanne Glass, an editor at Pyramid Publications, a house that attempts to specialize in the kinds of romances that Smithton readers like. She has written that the sex in romances must be "sensual, romantic, breathy—enough to make the pulse race, but not rough-guy, explicit, constantly brutal." She adds that the predominant flavor must be an "understanding of female *emotions*: hesitancy, doubt, anger, confusion, loss of control, exhilaration, etc."[34]

These comments suggest that some romance writers agree with the Smithton group that a romance is a love story whose gradually evolving course must be experienced from the heroine's point of view. These writers understand that the goal and raison d'être of the genre is its actual, though perhaps temporary, effect on readers like the Smithton women. While explicit description of sexual encounters may be included in some of the genre's variations, the writers agree with their readers that the emphasis in the encounters must be on the love that is being conveyed through sexual contact and not on its physical details.

If readers' and writers' interpretations of their own experiences are taken into account, then, the romance cannot be dismissed as a mere pretense for masturbatory titillation. The reading experience is valued for the way it makes the reader feel, but the feeling it creates is interpreted by the women themselves as a general sense of emotional well-being and visceral contentment. Such a feeling is brought on by the opportunity to participate vicariously in a relationship characterized by *mutual* love and by the hero's quite unusual ability to express his devotion gently and with concern for his heroine's pleasure. The question that needs to be asked, therefore, is *why* the readers find it essential and beneficial to seek out this particular kind of vicarious experience. That can perhaps best be answered by comparing good and bad romances. In explaining what they do when they have determined a particular text's quality, the Smithton women provide clues to both the *deprivation* that prompts their activity and the *fears* that are assuaged and managed in the reading experience.

The reactions of the Smithton women to books they are not enjoying are indicative of the intensity of their need to avoid offensive material and the feelings it typically evokes. Indeed, twenty-three (55 percent) reported that when they find themselves in the middle of a bad book, they put it down immediately and refuse to finish it. Some even make the symbolic gesture of discarding the book in the garbage, particularly if it has offended them seriously. This was the universal fate suffered by Lolah Burford's *Alyx* (1977), a book cited repeatedly as a perfect example of the pornographic trash distributed by publishers under the guise of the romance.

Another nine (21 percent) of the women indicated that although they do not read the rest of the book, they at least skip to the ending "to see how it came out." In responding to the question about why she must read the ending of a book even in the face of evidence that the book is insulting, Maureen explained that to cease following a story in the middle is to remain suspended in the heroine's nightmare while she *is* the heroine. Her comments were corroborated by every other woman I spoke to who engaged in this kind of behavior. In elaborating upon the problem, Maureen also mentioned the kind of books that most upset her:

> MAUREEN: A lot of your thicker books—it's rape—sometimes gang rape. I could not handle that in my own life. And since I'm living as the heroine, I cannot handle it in a book. And I hate myself for reading them. But if I start it, I have to get myself out of there, so I have to read my way out.
>
> INTERVIEWER: So you must finish a book?
>
> MAUREEN :   Yes, I have to finish it. Even if it's only skimming, one word per page—or sometimes I just read the ending. I have to finish it. But it leaves a bad taste in my mouth forever.

Because nearly all romances end in the union of the two principal characters, regardless of the level of violence inflicted on the heroine during the course of the story, by reading that "happy" conclusion Maureen at least formally assures herself that all works out for the heroine as it should. She cannot simply dismiss the story as a badly managed fiction precisely because she becomes so involved in the tale that she lives it emotionally as her own. She and other readers like her feel it necessary to continue the imaginative pretense just long enough to share the heroine's achievement of mutual love that is the goal of all romance-reading experiences.

This need to read one's way out of a bad situation and to resolve or contain all of the unpleasant feelings aroused by it is so strong in some of the Smithton readers that they read the whole book even when they hate it. In fact, ten (24 percent) of Dot's customers indicated that they *always* finish a book no matter what its quality. Nevertheless, this habit does not testify to a wish or even a need to see women abused. Rather, it is the mark of the intensity with which they desire to be told that an ideal love is possible *even in the worst of circumstances* and that a woman can be nurtured and cared for even by a man who appears gruff and indifferent.

It is necessary to raise this issue of the romance readers' attitude toward the violence that undeniably exists in some romances because several commentators, including Ann Douglas, have recently suggested that women enjoy the experience of reading about others of their sex who are mistreated by men. In "Soft-Porn Culture," Douglas asserts that "the women who couldn't thrill to male nudity in *Playgirl* are *enjoying* the titillation of seeing themselves, not necessarily as they are, but as some men would like to see them: illogical, innocent, *magnetized by male sexuality and brutality*."[35] Although it is hard to disagree with her point about traditional male sexuality, which is still treated as compelling, especially in the Harlequins about which Douglas writes, there is good reason to believe that male brutality is a concern in recent romances, not because women are magnetized or drawn to it, but because they find it increasingly prevalent and horribly frightening.

Clifford Geertz maintains that all art forms, like the Balinese cockfight, render "ordinary everyday experience comprehensible by presenting it in terms of acts and objects which have had their practical consequences removed and been reduced . . . to a level of sheer appearance, where the meaning can be more powerfully articulated and more exactly perceived."[36] If Geertz is correct, then it seems likely that the romance's preoccupation with male brutality is an attempt to understand the meaning of an event that has become almost unavoidable in the real world. The romance may express misogynistic attitudes not because women share them but because they increasingly need to know how to deal with them.

The romance also seems to be exploring the consequences of attempts to counter the increased threat of violence with some sort of defiance. While the final effect of such a display may be, as Douglas claims, the formulation of the message—"don't travel alone"; "men can't stand it"; "men won't let you get away with it"[37]—the motive behind the message is less one of total assent than one of resignation born of fear about what might happen if the message was ignored. Romantic violence may also be the product of a continuing inability to imagine any situation in which a woman might acquire and use resources that would enable her to withstand male opposition and coercion.

When the Smithton readers' specific dislikes are examined in conjunction with their preferences in romance fiction, an especially clear view of the genre's function as an artistic "display" of contemporary cultural habits develops. In particular, when the events and features that the readers *most* detest are taken as indicators of their fears, it becomes possible to isolate the crucial characteristics and consequences of gender relations that prove most troubling to the Smithton women. In chapter 4, through an examination of "the ideal romance," I shall demonstrate that the same awful possibilities of violence that dominate bad romances are always evoked as potential threats to female integrity even in good romances, simply because women are trying to *explain* this situation to themselves. Because the explanation finally advanced in the good romance remains a highly conservative one of traditional categories and definitions, when events that occur in reality are displayed in the text, they are always reinterpreted as mere threats. However, in those romances where the potential consequences of male–female relations are too convincingly imagined or permitted to control the tenor of the book by obscuring the developing love story, the art form's role as *safe* display is violated. In that case, the story treads too closely to the terrible real in ordinary existence that it is trying to explain. Then, the romance's role as conservator of the social structure and its legitimizing ideology is unmasked because the contradictions the form usually papers over and minimizes so skillfully render the romantic resolution untenable even for the women who are usually most convinced by it.

Dot first acquainted me with the features of such a "bad" romance during our initial interview when she informed me that her customers can tell the difference between romances written by women and those written by men. She agrees with their dismissal of male-authored romances, she explained, because very few men are "perceptive" or "sensitive" and because most cannot imagine the kind of "gentleness" that is essential to the good romance. When asked to elaborate on the distinction between a good romance and a bad one, she replied that the latter was "kinky, you know, filled with sado-masochism, cruelty, and all sorts of things." She concluded decisively, "I detest that!"

Her readers apparently do too for in response to a question requesting them to select the three things that "should never appear in a romance" from a list of eleven choices, rape was listed by eleven of the women as the most objectionable feature, while a sad ending was selected by an additional ten. The rest of the group divided almost evenly over explicit sex, physical torture of the heroine or hero, and bed-hopping. Despite the apparent range of dislikes, when their rankings are summarized, clear objections emerge. The women generally agree that bed-hopping or promiscuous sex, a sad ending, rape, physical torture, and weak heroes have no place in the romance. Their choices here are entirely consistent with their belief in the therapeutic value of romance reading. The sad ending logically ranks high on their list of objections because its presence would negate the romance's difference and distance from day-to-day existence, dominated as it so often is by small failures, minor catastrophies, and ongoing disappointments. In addition, without its happy ending, the romance could not hold out the utopian promise that male–female relations can be managed successfully.

I suspect bed-hopping is so objectionable in a romance because the genre is exploring the possibilities and consequences for women of the American middle class of adopting what has been dubbed "the new morality." Most students of the romance have observed that after the 1972 appearance of Woodiwiss's unusually explicit *The Flame and the Flower,* romance authors were free to treat their heroines as sexual creatures capable of arousal and carnal desire. Indeed, the extraordinary popularity of Woodiwiss's novel and its rapid imitation by others seem to suggest that large numbers of American women had been affected by feminism and the sexual revolution of the 1960s. The strong reader distaste for bed-hopping or promiscuous sex suggests, however, that this change in sexual mores was and still is tolerable only within very strict limits. Hence, the "good" romance continues to maintain that a woman acknowledge and realize her feelings *only* within traditional, monogamous marriage. When another text portrays a heroine who is neither harmed nor disturbed by her ability to have sex with several men, I suspect it is classified as "bad" because it makes explicit the threatening implications of an unleashed feminine sexuality capable of satisfying itself outside the structures of patriarchal domination that are still perpetuated most effectively through marriage.[38] Such a portrayal also strays too close to the suggestion that men do not care for women as individuals but, as the saying goes, are interested only in one thing.

In fact, the Smithton women revealed that they suspected as much when they voiced their anger about male promiscuity and repeatedly complained about romances that advance the double standard. "We do not want to be told," one of Dot's customers explained, "that if you love a man you'll forgive him." Neither do they wish to adopt male standards; Dot and her customers would prefer that men learn to adhere to theirs. The Smithton women overwhelmingly believe that sex is a wonderful form of intimate communication that should be explored only by two people who care for each other deeply and intend to formalize their relationship through the contract of marriage. For them, the romance is neither a recommendation for female revolt nor a strictly conservative refusal to acknowledge any change. It is, rather, a cognitive exploration of the possibility of adopting and managing some attitude changes about feminine sexuality by making room for them within traditional institutions and structures that they understand to be protective of a woman's interests.

Rape and physical torture of the heroine and the hero are obviously objectionable because the readers are seeking an opportunity to be shown a happier, more trouble-free version of existence. Such features are probably also distasteful, however, because the romance, which is never simply a love story, is also an exploration of the meaning of patriarchy for women. As a result, it is concerned with the fact that men possess and regularly exercise power over them in all sorts of circumstances. By picturing the heroine in relative positions of weakness, romances are not necessarily endorsing her situation, but examining an all-too-common state of affairs in order to display possible strategies for coping with it. When a romance presents the story of a woman who is misunderstood by the hero, mistreated and manhandled as a consequence of his misreading, and then suddenly loved, protected, and cared for by him because he recognizes that he mistook the meaning of her behavior, the novel is informing its readers that the minor acts of violence they must contend with in their own lives can be similarly reinterpreted as the result of misunderstandings or of jealousy born of "true love." The readers are therefore assured that those acts do not warrant substantial changes or traumatic upheaval in a familiar way of life.[39]

Woodiwiss's handling of what one reader called "a little forceful persuasion" is acceptable to the Smithton women because they are fully convinced by her attempt to show that the hero's sexual sway over the heroine is always the product of his passion and her irresistibility. Indeed, one publishing house understands this quite well, for in its directions to potential writers it states that rape is not recommended but that one will be allowed under specific conditions if the author feels it is necessary to make a point.[40] Should that rape occur "between the heroine and the hero," the directions specify, it must "never be initiated with the violent motivation that exists in reality" because "a woman's fantasy is to lose control" with someone who really cares for her. "A true rape" can be included only if "it moves the story forward" and if it happens to someone other than the heroine.

Vicious or "true" rape upsets the tenuous balance for most of the Smithton readers because they feel they would not be able to forgive or explain away an overtly malicious act. They cannot understand how a heroine finds it within herself to ignore such an event, forgive the man who violated her, and then grow to love him. As Ann, one of Dot's most outspoken customers, put it, "I get tired of it if they [the heroes] keep grabbing and using sex as a weapon for domination because they want to win a struggle of the wills. I'm tending to get quite a few of these in Harlequins and I think they're terrible." Her comment prompted excited discussion among those in the interview group who had read the recent Harlequins. All of the women agreed that they found Harlequin's new, more explicit preoccupation with male violence nauseating, and several even admitted that they stopped buying them to avoid being subjected to this form of male power. The following explanation of several Harlequin plots was given by another of Dot's customers:

> Four of the eight in the last shipment—they're married and separated four to eight years and all of a sudden *he* decides that they should have stayed together and *he* punishes her. They're gonna get together and live happily ever after, after *he* punishes her! Right!

> That sounds terrible.

> Well, they are. He tricks her into coming back or meeting with him or whatever and he has some sort of powerhold over her either emotionally or physically—either he'll take her child away or ruin her father. He's determined to win her back. She's good enough to have him now.[41]

This reader's scorn for a typical pattern of explanation in romance fiction makes it clear that there are limits to what can be justified by evoking the irrationality of passionate love. Although opinions about acceptability probably vary tremendously within the entire romance audience, Dot's readers at least seem to agree about the conditions that must be met. Violence is acceptable to them only if it is described sparingly, if it is controlled carefully, or if it is *clearly* traceable to the passion or jealousy of the hero. On the other hand, if it is represented as brutal and vicious, if it is extensively detailed and carried out by many men, or if it is depicted as the product of an obvious desire for power, these same women find that violence offensive and objectionable. This curious and artificial distinction that they draw between "forceful persuasion" and "true rape" is a function of the very pressing need to know how to deal with the realities of male power and force in day-to-day existence.

I suspect their willingness to see male force interpreted as passion is also the product of a wish to be seen as so desirable to the "right" man that he will not take "no" for an answer. Because he finds her irresistible, the heroine need not take any responsibility for her own sexual feelings. She avoids the difficulty of choosing whether to act on them or not. Although female sexuality is thus approvingly incorporated into the romantic fantasy, the individual ultimately held responsible for it is not the woman herself, but once again, a man.

If the qualities of a bad romance reveal the fears and concerns that are troubling to the women who read them, the characteristics they identify with good romances point to the existence of important needs and desires that are met and fulfilled by the perfect romantic fantasy. According to Dot and her customers, the relative excellence of a romance is a function of its treatment of three different

TABLE 3

Question: Which of the Following Do You Feel Should Never Be Included in a Romance?

Response	First Most Objectionable	Second Most Objectionable	Third Most Objectionable	Total
a. Rape	11	6	2	19
b. Explicit sex	6	2	1	9
c. Sad ending	10	4	6	20
d. Physical torture	5	6	7	18
e. An ordinary heroine	1	1	1	3
f. Bed-hopping	4	12	6	22
g. Premarital sex	0	0	1	1
h. A cruel hero	1	5	6	12
i. A weak hero	4	5	7	16
j. A hero stronger than the heroine	0	0	0	0
k. A heroine stronger than the hero	0	1	3	4

aspects of the story. These include the personality of the heroine, the character of the hero, and the particular manner in which the hero pursues and wins the affections of the heroine. If these individuals and relationships are not presented properly, not even ingenious plotting will rescue the novel from "the garbage dump."

On first discussing romances with the Smithton readers, I was struck by the fact that individual books were inevitably registered in their memories as the stories of particular *women*. When specific titles were volunteered to illustrate a point, they were always linked with a capsule plot summary beginning with a statement about the heroine and continuing with the principal events of what was, to the speaker, her tale. Because of her perceived centrality in the romance and because of their admitted tendency to project themselves into the heroine's being, the Smithton readers hold particularly exacting expectations about the qualities the heroine should have and the kinds of behavior she should exhibit.

So consistent are their feelings about heroines, in fact, that no discrepancy appears between their orally reported preferences and those acknowledged on the anonymous questionnaires. Dot's customers inevitably responded to my query about the characteristics of a good heroine with the statement that she must have three traits: intelligence, a sense of humor, and independence. On the questionnaire, nineteen (45 percent) of the women selected intelligence from a list of nine other possibilities as the characteristic they *most* liked to see in a heroine, while nine (21 percent) picked a sense of humor. The only other traits to score significantly were femininity and independence. When the group's rankings are totaled, intelligence joins independence and a sense of humor as the three traits that score significantly higher than all of the others. It seems especially important to note that three-fourths of the group selected intelligence (79 percent) and a sense of humor (74 percent) at least once, whereas independence was chosen by almost half (48 percent) of the Smithton women. Femininity, with its connotation of demure deference, was, however, still a choice of fourteen of the Smithton readers.

It may seem curious to insist here on the importance of the heroine's intelligence and independence to the Smithton women when so many "objective" students of the genre have commented on her typical passivity and quivering helplessness.[42] This harsh analytical judgment, however, is often founded on an assessment of the heroine's ultimate success in solving a mystery, making her desires known, or in refusing to be cowed by the hero. The *results* of her actions, in short, are always measured on a scale whose highest value is accorded the autonomous woman capable of accomplishing productive work in a nondomestic sphere. While the romantic heroine understandably compares badly with this ideal woman, it is important to note that neither Dot nor her readers find such an ideal attractive, nor do they scrutinize and evaluate the heroine's success in effecting change or in getting others to do what she wants in order to assess her character. The heroine's personality is, instead, inevitably and securely established for them at the beginning of the tale through a series of simple observations about her abilities, talents, and career choice. Because the Smithton women accept those assertions at face value, they search no further for incidents that might comment on or revise her early portrayal. Not only do they believe in the heroine's honest desire to take care of herself, but they also believe in the mimetic accuracy of the extenuating circumstances that always intervene to thwart her intended actions. The Smithton women are, in sum, significantly more inclined than their feminist critics to recognize the inevitability and reality of male power and the force of social convention to circumscribe a woman's ability to act in her own interests. It must also be said that they are comfortable with the belief that a woman should be willing to sacrifice extreme self-interest for a longterm relationship where mutually agreed-upon goals take precedence over selfish desire.

The point I want to make here is that when analysis proceeds from within the belief system actually brought to bear upon a text by its readers, the analytical interpretation of the meaning of a character's behavior is more likely to coincide with that meaning as it is constructed and understood by the readers themselves. Thus the account offered to explain the desire to experience this particular fantasy is also more likely to approximate the motives that actually initiate the readers' decision to pick up a romance. While the romantic heroine may appear foolish, dependent, and even pathetic to a woman who has already accepted as given the equality of male and female abilities, she appears courageous, and even valiant, to another still unsure that such equality is a fact or that she herself might want to assent to it.

The Smithton women seem to be struggling simultaneously with the promise and threat of the women's movement as well as with their culture's now doubled capacity to belittle the intelligence and activities of "the ordinary housewife." Therefore, while they are still very conservative and likely to admit the rightness of traditional relations between men and women, at the same time they are angered by men who continue to make light of "woman's work" as well as by "women's libbers" whom they accuse of dismissing mothers and housewives as ignorant, inactive, and unimportant. Their desire to believe that the romantic heroine is as intelligent and independent as she is asserted to be even though she is also shown to be vulnerable and most interested in being loved is born of their apparently unconscious desire to realize some of the benefits of feminism within traditional institutions and relationships—hence, the high value attached to the simple *assertion* of the heroine's special abilities. With a few simple statements rather than with truly threatening action on the part of the heroine, the romance author demonstrates for the typical reader the compatibility of a changed sense of the female self and an unchanged social arrangement. In the utopia of romance fiction, "independence" and a secure individual "identity" are never compromised by the paternalistic care and protection of the male.

Although chapter 4 will explore the particular strategies employed by Smithton's favorite romance authors to avoid the real contradictions between dependency and self-definition, I would like to quote here from a lengthy and exuberant discussion carried on in one of the interviews when I asked Dot, her daughter, Kit, and Ann to describe the "ideal" romantic heroine. Rather than list a series of abstract traits as others generally did, these women launched into a fifteen-minute, communally produced plot summary of Elsie Lee's *The Diplomatic Lover* (1971). The delight with which they described the heroine and what they perceived to be her constant control of her situation is as good an example as any of the desire they share with feminists to believe in the female sex's strength and capabilities and in themselves as well. When I asked them why they liked the book so much after they told me they had xeroxed the text for their own use (the book is now out of print), the extended reply began in the following way:

DOT: It's just classic.

ANN: She *decides* that she wants to lose her virginity and picks *him*.

KIT: Well, he's really nice looking; he's a movie star and he's . . .

DOT: Well, the thing is, actually, because she is in a modern workaday world. She's in Washington, D.C., in the diplomatic corps.

KIT: And *she* makes the decision, you know. And she's the only one [in the diplomatic community] who's a virgin and her name is Nanny.

ANN: Yes.

DOT: And they call her Nanny-No-No because she's always saying no, no, no!

ANN: She knows, she's read all the textbooks; but she's just never found anyone that set her blood to boiling.

DOT: And she's known him for years.

ANN: But he walks into the room at this one party and all of a sudden . . .

KIT: She makes the decision! It's her birthday.

ANN: She mentally licks her chops.

KIT: She's twenty-three. She decides, "Well, this is it!"

ANN: Yes.

DOT: But you know it's not distasteful. There's nothing . . . it was unusual.

KIT: It was very intimate.

DOT: It's not bold.[43]

In the midst of recounting the rest of the tale, they proudly exclaimed that Nanny "spoke six languages," was "a really good artist," and "did not want to marry him even though she was pregnant" because she believed he was an "elegant tom-cat" and would not be faithful to her. These untraditional skills and unconventional attitudes are obviously not seen as fulfilling or quite proper by Lee herself because they are legitimated and rendered acceptable at the novel's conclusion when the hero convinces Nanny of his love, refuses to live without her, and promises to take care of her in the future. Here is the group's recitation of this moment:

> DOT: He starts stalking her and this is visually . . .
> KIT: It's hysterical.
> DOT: You can see it.
> KIT: She's backin' off.
> DOT: She's trying to get to the stairway to get to her room.
> KIT: And make a mad dash.
> ANN: She's what they call a "petite pocket Venus type."
> DOT: Yes, and he's stalking her and she's backing away and saying, "No, I won't marry you!"
> ANN: "I ain't going!"
> KIT: "No, just forget that!"
> DOT: "No, I don't need you!"
> ANN: "And he says I'll camp on your doorstep; I'll picket; unfair to, you know . . . "

As in all romances, female defiance is finally rendered ineffectual and childlike as well as unnecessary by Lee's conclusion. Nonetheless, if we are to understand the full meaning of the story for these women, it is essential to recognize that their temporary reveling in her intelligence, independence, self-sufficiency, and initiative is as important to their experiencing of the book as the fact of her final capture by a man who admits that he needs her. Indeed, after recounting the resolution of this tale, Dot, Kit, and Ann relived again her "seduction of him" by marveling over the moment "when she asks him, and he's drinking and he about chokes to death!"

In novels like *The Diplomatic Lover,* which the Smithton women like best, the happy ending restores the status quo in gender relations when the hero enfolds the heroine protectively in his arms. That ending, however, can also be interpreted as an occasion for the vicarious enjoyment of a woman's ultimate triumph. Dot's readers so interpret it because the heroine, they claim, maintains her integrity on her own terms by exacting a formal commitment from the hero and simultaneously provides for her own future in the only way acceptable to her culture.

The Smithton readers' interest in a strong but still traditional heroine is complemented by their desire to see that woman loved by a very special kind of hero. As noted earlier, these women will read many romances they do not especially like, even when the hero mistreats the heroine, because the experience of the happy ending is more important to them than anything else and because it successfully explains away many individual incidents they do not condone. Nevertheless, they prefer to see the heroine desired, needed, and loved by a man who is strong and masculine, but equally capable of unusual tenderness, gentleness, and concern for her pleasure. In fact, when asked to rank ten male personality traits as to desirability, not one of the Smithton readers listed independence in first, second, or third place. Although this might be explained by suggesting that the women felt no need to single this characteristic out because they assumed that men are, by nature, independent, their interview comments suggest otherwise. Throughout their discussions of particular books, they repeatedly insisted that what they remembered and liked most about favorite novels was the skill with which the author described the hero's recognition of his own deep feelings for the heroine and his realization that he could not live without her. While the women want to feel that the heroine will be protected by the hero, they also seem to want to see her dependency balanced by its opposite, that is, by the hero's dependence on her. In this context, the Smithton women's constant emphasis on the importance of mutuality in love makes enormous sense.

I do not want to suggest here that male protectiveness and strength are not important elements in the romantic fantasy; they are. Remember, sixteen (38 percent) of the women indicated that they think a weak hero is one of the three most objectionable features in a romance. In addition, almost 25 percent of Dot's customers agreed that out of nine traits strength is the third most important in a hero. Still, neither strength nor protectiveness is considered as important as intelligence, gentleness, and an ability to laugh at life, all of which were placed significantly more often by the readers in one of the three top positions on the questionnaire. However, because Dot and her customers rarely initiated discussion of the romantic hero and just as seldom volunteered opinions about specific male characters, it has been difficult to develop a complex picture of their ideal or of the motivation prompting its formation. Even when their responses are displayed in a graph, certain mysteries persist.

The principal difficulty involves the marked preference for an "intelligent" hero. Although it is hard to say why intelligence was ranked so high by the Smithton women, it is possible that the choice is consistent with the high value they place on books, learning, and education and their own upward mobility as well as being a way of reaffirming male excellence and agentivity without also automatically implying female inferiority. The word did appear in discussions of the ideal hero, but the women offered little that would explain its prominence in their questionnaire responses. A few oral comments seemed to hint at the existence of an expectation that an "intelligent" man would be more likely to appreciate and encourage the extraordinary abilities of the ideal heroine, but this link was not volunteered consistently enough to warrant its formulation as the motive behind the fantasy. Equally hard to explain is the emphasis on a sense of humor, although I suspect the interest in this trait masks a desire to see a hero who is up to a "verbal duel" with the heroine. Not only does this create the air of "lightness" so important to the Smithton women, but it also helps to show off the heroine's tart-tongued facility to advantage.

This vagueness about the actual content of the hero's personality persisted throughout many commentaries that tended to center instead on his ability to establish the proper relationship with the heroine. The Smithton women are less interested in the particularities of their heroes as individuals than in the roles the most desirable among them perform. Gentleness and tenderness figure often in their accounts of favorite novels not so much as character traits exhibited by particular men but as the distinguishing feature of the attention accorded the heroine by all good heroes in the outstanding novels. The focus never shifts for these readers away from the woman at the center of the romance. Moreover, men are rarely valued for their intrinsic characteristics but become remarkable by virtue of the special position they occupy vis-à-vis the heroine. The romantic fantasy is therefore not a fantasy about discovering a uniquely interesting life partner, but a ritual wish to be cared for, loved, and validated in a particular way.

TABLE 4

Question: What Qualities Do You Like to See in a Hero?

Response	Most Important	Second Most Important	Third Most Important	Total
a. Intelligence	14	11	5	30
b. Tenderness	11	8	7	26
c. Protectiveness	3	4	7	14
d. Strength	3	3	9	15
e. Bravery	1	4	2	7
f. Sense of humor	8	5	6	19
g. Independence	0	0	0	0
h. Attractiveness	2	5	3	10
i. A good body	0	2	2	4
j. Other	0	0	0	0
Blank		1	1	

In distinguishing the ideal romance from Rosemary Rogers's "perversions," one of the five customers I interviewed at length wondered whether her editor had been male because, she reasoned, "it's a man's type book." When pressed to elaborate, she retorted, "because a man likes the sex in it, you know, Matt Helm and all that type." The distinction she sees here between sex and romance was continually employed by the Smithton women to differentiate pornography, which they associate with men, from their own interest in "insightful love," which they wish men could manage. As Joy said of the recent Harlequins, "all they worry about is sex—that's the first thing on their minds. They don't worry about anything else." She continued, "they don't need that; they need humor and love and caring." Similarly, in one of our final discussions, Dot also elaborated on the differences between pornography and romance and between men and women and, in doing so, identified in a wistful tone the particular characteristic she and her customers believe all men should possess:

> I've always thought that women are more insightful into men's psyches than men are into women's. Well, men just don't take the time. They just don't. And it's always been interesting to me that psychiatrists are probably... 85 to 90 percent of the psychiatrists in this country are men and I'm sure they know the book. I'm sure they know the textbook. But as far as insightful, I think that is one of the most rare commodities that there is ... is an insightful man. . . . I don't think men look deep. I think they take even a man at face value. Whatever they see—that's what the man is.

What the Smithton women are looking for in their search for the perfect ro-

mantic fantasy is a man who is capable of the same attentive observation and intuitive "understanding" that they believe women regularly accord to men. We
will see in chapter 4, in a more thorough examination of the Smithton group's
favorite romances, that the fantasy generating the ideal romantic story thus fulfills two deeply felt needs that have been activated in women by early object-
relations and cultural conditioning in patriarchal society. On the one hand, the
story permits the reader to identify with the heroine at the moment of her greatest success, that is, when she secures the attention and recognition of her culture's
most powerful and essential representative, a man. The happy ending is, at this
level, a sign of a woman's attainment of legitimacy and personhood in a culture
that locates both for her in the roles of lover, wife, and mother.

On the other hand, by emphasizing the intensity of the hero's uninterrupted
gaze and the tenderness of his caress at the moment he encompasses his beloved
in his still always "masculine" arms, the fantasy also evokes the memory of a period in the reader's life when she was the center of a profoundly nurturant
individual's attention. Because this imaginative emotional regression is often denied women in ordinary existence because men have been prompted by the
culture's asymmetrical conditioning to deny their own capacities for gentle
nurturance, it becomes necessary to fulfill this never-ending need in other areas.
Nancy Chodorow has suggested, in *The Reproduction of Mothering*, that one way
for women to provide this essential sustenance for themselves is through the
mothering of others. By taking care of a child in this intense emotional way and
by identifying with her child, Chodorow reasons, a woman is able to nurture herself, albeit vicariously. However, Chodorow does not comment at any length
about whether this vicarious care and attention prove a perfectly adequate substitute. The ideal romance, at least as it is conceived by the Smithton women,
argues effectively that it is not. Its stress on the emotional bonding between hero
and heroine suggests that women still desire to be loved, cared for, and understood by an adult who is singularly capable of self-abnegating preoccupation with
a loved one's needs.

In the next chapter we will discover that it is the constant impulse and duty to
mother others that is responsible for the sense of depletion that apparently sends
some women to romance fiction. By immersing themselves in the romantic fantasy, women vicariously fulfill their needs for nurturance by identifying with a
heroine whose principal accomplishment, if it can even be called that, is her success at drawing the hero's attention to herself, at establishing herself as the object of his concern and the recipient of his care. Because the reader experiences
that care vicariously, her need is assuaged only as long as she can displace it onto
a fictional character. When that character's story is completed, when the book
must be closed, the reader is forced to return to herself and to her real situation.
Although she may feel temporarily revived, she has done nothing to alter her relations with others. More often than not, those relations remain unchanged and
in returning to them a woman is once again expected and willing to employ her
emotional resources for the care of others. If she is then not herself reconstituted
by another, romance reading may suggest itself again as a reasonable compensatory solution. Therefore, the romance's short-lived therapeutic value, which is
made both possible and necessary by a culture that creates needs in women that
it cannot fulfill, is finally the cause of its repetitive consumption.

NOTES

1. In the course of completing this study of the Smithton readers, I have learned of at least five other such groups functioning throughout the country. Most seem to be informal networks of neighbors or co-workers who exchange romances and information about these books on a regular basis. I have also been told of a group similar to Dot's clustered about a Texas bookseller and have received information about the California-based "Friends of the English Regency," which also publishes a review newsletter and holds an annual Regency "Assemblee" at which it confers the "Georgette" award on favorite Regency romances. There is no way to tell how common this "reading club" phenomenon is, but it is worth investigating. If these clubs are widely relied upon to mediate the mass-production publishing process by individualizing selection, then a good deal of speculation about the meaning of mass-produced literature based on the "mass man" [sic] hypothesis will have to be reviewed and possibly rewritten.

2. These and all other figures about Smithton were taken from the *Census of the Population, 1970*. I have rounded off the numbers slightly to disguise the identity of Smithton.

3. Evans, "Dorothy's Diary," April 1980, pp. 1–2.

4. Ibid., p. 2.

5. All spoken quotations have been taken directly from taped interviews. Nearly all of the comments were transcribed verbatim, although in a few cases repeated false starts were excised and marked with ellipses. Pauses in a speaker's commentary have been marked with dashes. I have paragraphed lengthy speeches only when the informant clearly seemed to conclude one topic or train of thought in order to open another deliberately. Lack of paragraphing, then, indicates that the speaker's comments continued apace without significant rest or pause.

6. Snitow, "Mass Market Romance," p. 150.

7. Brotman, "Ah, Romance!," p. Bl.

8. Jensen, "Women and Romantic Fiction," p. 289.

9. Quoted in Brotman, "Ah, Romance!," p. Bl.

10. See also Mann, *A New Survey*, passim.

11. Readers were instructed to identify the particular kind of romance they liked to "read the most" from a list of ten subgenres. The titles had been given to me by Dot during a lengthy discussion about the different kinds of romances. Although I expected the women to check only one subgenre, almost all of them checked several as their favorites. The categories and totals follow: gothics, 6; contemporary mystery romances, 5; historicals, 20; contemporary romances, 7; Harlequins, 10; Regencies, 4; family sagas, 1; plantation series, 3; spy thrillers, 0; transcendental romances, 0; other, 2.

12. It should be pointed out, however, that these findings could also indicate that romances were not heavily advertised or distributed when the majority of women in this sample were teenagers. Thus, the fact that so many have picked up the romance habit may be as much a function of the recent growth of the industry as of any particular need or predisposition on the part of women at a particular stage in their life cycle. Still, as I will make clear in this and subsequent chapters, romances do address needs associated with the role of mothering for *this* particular group of readers.

13. Jensen, "Women and Romantic Fiction," pp. 290–91.

14. Jensen also reports that all of the married women in her sample have children and that three quarters have children still living at home (ibid., p. 291).

15. Cited in Yankelovich, Skelly, and White, *The 1978 Consumer Research Study on Reading*, p. 325.

16. This compares with the eight-hour weekly average claimed by book readers who read fiction for leisure as reported in Yankelovich, Skelly, and White, ibid., p. 126.

17. Although the Smithton women also commented, as did Jensen's informants, on the ease with which "light reading" like Harlequins and Silhouettes can be picked up and put down when other demands intervene, all of Dot's customers with whom I spoke expressed a preference for finishing a romance in one sitting. Jensen does not say whether her readers would have preferred to read in this way, although she does comment rather extensively on the fact that it is the material circumstances of their jobs as housewives and mothers that most often necessitate what she calls "snatch" reading. She refers to an alternate pattern of reading several books, one after the other, as the "binge." This is not exactly equivalent to the Smithton readers' practice with fat books, but some of them did mention engaging in such behavior as a special treat to themselves. See Jensen, "Women and Romantic Fiction," pp. 300–301 and 312–14.

18. Yankelovich, Skelly, and White, *The 1978 Consumer Research Study on Reading*, pp. 141, 144.

19. The Smithton readers' patterns of explanation and justification will be explored in greater detail in chapter 3.

20. Mann, A *New Survey*, p. 17.

21. For further discussion of this curious failure to trust that a new romance will end happily despite extensive prior acquaintance with the genre, see chapter 6 of *Reading the Romance*.

22. Evans, "Dorothy's Diary," April 1980, p. 1.

23. I included this choice on the final questionnaire because in many of the interviews the women had expressed a distaste for romances that end abruptly with the declaration of love between the principal characters.

24. Faust, *Women, Sex, and Pornography*, p. 67.

25. Richard Hoggart is one of the few who disagrees with this argument. See his comments in *The Uses of Literacy*, pp. 171–75. Jensen has also acknowledged that many Harlequin authors "apparently share the backgrounds, attitudes, and fantasies of their women readers" ("Women and Romantic Fiction," pp. 118–19).

26. Quoted in Evans, "Dorothy's Diary," May 1980, p. 2.

27. Quoted in Evans, "Dorothy's Diary," Newsletter 4, 1980, p. 2. (This issue is not dated by month.)

28. Berman, "They Call Us Illegitimate," p. 38.

29. Whitney, "Writing the Gothic Novel," p. 10.

30. Ibid.

31. Ibid., p. 11.

32. Faust, *Women, Sex, and Pornography*, p. 63.

33. Whitney, "Writing the Gothic Novel," p. 43.

34. Quoted by Glass, "Editor's Report," p. 33.

35. Douglas, "Soft-Porn Culture," p. 28 (italics added).

36. Geertz, "Deep Play," p. 443.

37. Douglas, "Soft-Porn Culture," p. 25.

38. On the connection between patriarchy and marriage, see Hartmann, "The Family as Locus of Gender, Class, and Political Struggle," especially pp. 366–76.

39. None of the Smithton women commented on whether they had ever been hit, pushed around, or forced to have sexual relations against their will, although several did tell me that they know this goes on because it happens to their friends. In summarizing current studies on wife abuse, Rohrbaugh has commented in *Women: Psychology's Puzzle* that "many researchers in this field agree with Judge Stewart Oneglia's estimate that '50 percent of all marriages involve some degree of physical abuse of the woman'" (p. 350). Rohrbaugh also points out that "studies that define wife abuse as anything from an occasional hard slap to repeated, severe beating suggest that there are 26 million to 30 million abused wives in the United States today" (p. 350). If these figures are accurate, it seems

clear that a good many romance readers may very well need to be given a model "explanation" for this sort of behavior.

40. I would like to thank Star Helmer for giving me a copy of Gallen Books' "tipsheet" for contemporary romances.

41. The italics have been added here to indicate where Ann placed special emphasis and changed her intonation during her remarks. In each case, the emphasis conveyed both sarcasm and utter disbelief. Two of the most difficult tasks in using ethnographic material are those of interpreting meanings clearly implied by a speaker but not actually said and adequately conveying them in written prose.

42. See, especially, Modleski, "The Disappearing Act," pp. 444–48.

43. Again, the italics have been added here to indicate where special emphasis was conveyed through intonation. In each case, the emphasis was meant to underscore the distance between this heroine's behavior and that usually expected of women.

WORKS CITED

Berman, Phyllis. "They Call Us Illegitimate." *Forbes* 6 (March 1978): 37–38.

Brotman, Barbara. "Ah, Romance! Harlequin Has an Affair for Its Readers." *Chicago Tribune*, 2 June 1980, p. Bl.

Douglas, Ann. "Soft-Porn Culture." *New Republic*, 30 August 1980, pp. 25–29.

Evans, Dorothy. "Dorothy's Diary of Romance Reading." April 1980–September 1981. Mimeographed newsletters.

Faust, Beatrice. *Women, Sex, and Pornography: A Controversial and Unique Study.* New York: Macmillan Publishing Co., 1980.

Geertz, Clifford. "Deep Play: Notes on the Balinese Cockfight." In *The Interpretation of Cultures*, pp. 412–53. New York: Basic Books, 1973.

Glass, Jeanne. "Editor's Report." *Writer* 90 (April 1977): 33.

Hartmann, Heidi I. "The Family as the Locus of Gender, Class, and Political Struggle: The Example of Housework." *Signs* 6 (Spring 1981): 366–94.

Hoggart, Richard. *The Uses of Literacy: Changing Patterns in English Mass Culture.* Fair Lawn, N.J.: Essential Books, 1957.

Jensen, Margaret. "Women and Romantic Fiction: A Case Study of Harlequin Enterprises, Romances, and Readers." Ph.D. dissertation, McMaster University, 1980.

Mann, Peter H. A *New Survey: The Facts about Romantic Fiction.* London: Mills and Boon, 1974.

Modleski, Tania. "The Disappearing Act: A Study of Harlequin Romances." *Signs* 5 (Spring 1980): 435–48.

Rohrbaugh, Joanna Bunker. *Women: Psychology's Puzzle.* New York: Basic Books, 1979.

Snitow, Ann Barr. "Mass Market Romance: Pornography for Women Is Different." *Radical History Review* 20 (Spring/Summer 1979): 141–61.

Whitney, Phyllis. "Writing the Gothic Novel." *Writer* 80 (February 1967): 9–13, 42–43.

Yankelovich, Skelly, and White. *The 1978 Consumer Research Study on Reading and Book Purchasing* Prepared for the Book Industry Study Group. Darien, Conn.: The Group, 1978.

PATROCINIO P. SCHWEICKART

READING OURSELVES
toward a feminist theory of reading
(1986)

THREE STORIES OF READING

A. Wayne Booth begins his presidential address to the 1982 MLA Convention by considering and rejecting several plausible myths that might enable us "to dramatize not just our inescapable plurality but the validity of our sense that [as teachers and scholars of literature and composition] we belong together, somehow working on common ground." At last he settles on one story that is "perhaps close enough to our shared experience to justify the telling."[1]

Once upon a time there was a boy who fell in love with books. When he was very young he heard over and over the legend of his great-grandfather, a hardworking weaver who so desired knowledge that he figured out a way of working the loom with one hand, his legs, and his feet, leaving the other hand free to hold a book, and worked so steadily in that crooked position that he became permanently crippled. The boy heard other stories about the importance of reading. Salvation, he came to believe, was to be found in books. When he was six years old, he read *The Wizard of Oz*—his first *real* book—and was rewarded by his Great-Aunt Manda with a dollar.

When the boy grew up, he decided to become a teacher of "litcomp." His initiation into the profession was rigorous, and there were moments when he nearly gave up. But gradually, "there emerged from the trudging a new and surprising love, a love that with all my previous reading I had not dreamed of: the love of skill, of craft, of getting clear in my mind and then in my writing what a great writer had got right in his work" (Booth, p. 315). Eventually, the boy, now grown, got his doctorate, and after teaching for thirteen years in small colleges, he returned to his graduate institution to become one of its eminent professors.

Booth caps his narration by quoting from *The Autobiography of Malcolm X*. It was in prison that Malcolm learned to read:

> For the first time I could pick up a book and now begin to understand what the book was saying. Anyone who has read a great deal can imagine the new world that opened. Let me tell you something: from then until I left that prison, in every free moment I had, if I was not reading in the library, I was

> reading on my bunk. . . . [M]onths passed without my even thinking about
> being imprisoned. In fact, up to then, I never had been so truly free in my
> life. (As quoted by Booth, p. 317)

"Perhaps," says Booth, "when you think back now on my family's story about Great-grandfather Booth, you will understand why reading about Malcolm X's awakening speaks to the question of where I got my 'insane love' [for books]" (p. 317).

B. When I read the Malcolm X passage quoted in Booth's address, the ellipsis roused my curiosity. What, exactly, I wondered, had been deleted? What in the original exceeded the requirements of a Presidential Address to the MLA? Checking, I found the complete sentence to read: "Between Mr. Muhammad's teachings, my correspondence, my visitors—usually Ella and Reginald—and my reading, months passed without my even thinking about being imprisoned."[2] Clearly, the first phrase is the dissonant one. The reference to the leader of the notorious Black Muslims suggests a story of reading very different from Booth's. Here is how Malcolm X tells it. While serving time in the Norfolk Prison Colony, he hit on the idea of teaching himself to read by copying the dictionary.

> In my slow, painstaking, ragged handwriting, I copied into my tablet every
> thing on that first page, down to the punctuation marks. . . . Then, aloud, to
> myself, I read back everything I'd written on the tablet. . . . I woke up the
> next morning thinking about these words—immensely proud to realize that
> not only had I written so much at one time, but I'd written words that I never
> knew were in the world. . . . That was the way I started copying what even-
> tually became the entire dictionary. (p. 172)

After copying the dictionary, Malcolm X began reading the books in the prison library. "No university would ask any student to devour literature as I did when this new world opened to me, of being able to read and *understand*" (p. 173). Reading had changed the course of his life. Years later, he would reflect on how "the ability to read awoke inside me some long dormant craving to be mentally alive" (p. 179).

What did he read? What did he understand? He read Gregor Mendel's *Findings in Genetics* and it helped him to understand "that if you started with a black man, a white man could be produced; but starting with a white man, you never could produce a black man—because the white chromosome is recessive. And since no one disputes that there was but one Original Man, the conclusion is clear" (p. 175). He read histories, books by Will Durant and Arnold Toynbee, by W. E. B. Du Bois and Carter G. Woodson, and he saw how "the glorious history of the black man" had been "bleached" out of the history books written by white men.

> [His] eyes opened gradually, then wider and wider, to how the world's white
> men had indeed acted like devils, pillaging and raping and bleeding and
> draining the whole world's non-white people. . . . I will never forget how
> shocked I was when I began reading about slavery's total horror. . . . The
> world's most monstrous crime, the sin and the blood on the white man's
> hands, are almost impossible to believe. (p. 175)

He read philosophy—the works of Schopenhauer, Kant, Nietzsche, and Spinoza—and he concluded that the "whole stream of Western Philosophy was now wound up in a cul-de-sac" as a result of the white man's "elaborate, neurotic necessity to hide the black man's true role in history" (p. 180). Malcolm X read voraciously, and book after book confirmed the truth of Elijah Muhammad's teachings. "It's a crime, the lie that has been told to generations of black men and white both. . . . Innocent black children growing up, living out their lives, dying of old age—and all of their lives ashamed of being black. But the truth is pouring out of the bag now" (p. 181).

Wayne Booth's story leads to the Crystal Ballroom of the Biltmore Hotel in Los Angeles, where we attend the protagonist as he delivers his Presidential Address to the members of the Modern Language Association. Malcolm X's love of books took him in a different direction, to the stage of the Audubon Ballroom in Harlem, where, as he was about to address a mass meeting of the Organization of Afro-American Unity, he was murdered.

C. As we have seen, an ellipsis links Wayne Booth's story of reading to Malcolm X's. Another ellipsis, this time not graphically marked, signals the existence of a third story. Malcolm X's startling reading of Mendel's genetics overlooks the most rudimentary fact of human reproduction: whether you start with a black man or a white man, without a woman, you get *nothing*. An excerpt from Virginia Woolf's *A Room of One's Own* restores this deleted perspective.[3]

The heroine, call her Mary, says Woolf, goes to the British Museum in search of information about women. There she discovers to her chagrin that woman is, "perhaps, the most discussed animal in the universe?"

> Why does Samuel Butler say, "Wise men never say what they think of women"? Wise men never say anything else apparently. . . . Are they capable of education? Napoleon thought them incapable. Dr. Johnson thought the opposite. Have they souls or have they not souls? Some savages say they have none. Others, on the contrary, say women are half divine and worship them on that account. Some sages hold that they are shallower in the brain; others that they are deeper in consciousness. Goethe honoured them; Mussolini despises them. Wherever one looked men thought about women and thought differently. (pp. 29–30)

Distressed and confused, Mary notices that she has unconsciously drawn a picture in her notebook, the face and figure of Professor von X. engaged in writing his monumental work, *The Mental, Moral, and Physical Inferiority of the Female Sex.* "His expression suggested that he was labouring under some emotion that made him jab his pen on the paper as if he were killing some noxious insect as he wrote, but even when he had killed it that did not satisfy him; he must go on killing it. . . . A very elementary exercise in psychology . . . showed me . . . that the sketch had been made in anger" (pp. 31–32).

Nothing remarkable in that, she reflects, given the provocation. But "How explain the anger of the professor? . . . For when it came to analysing the impression left by these books, . . . there was [an] element which was often present and could not be immediately identified. Anger, I called it. . . . To judge from its effects, it was anger disguised and complex, not anger simple and open" (p. 32).

Disappointed with essayists and professors, Mary turns to historians. But apparently women played no significant role in history. What little information Mary finds is disturbing: "Wife-beating, I read, was a recognized right of a man, and was practiced without shame by high as well as low" (p. 44). Oddly enough, literature presents a contradictory picture.

> If women had no existence save in fiction written by men, we would imagine her to be a person of utmost importance; very various; heroic and mean; splendid and sordid; infinitely beautiful and hideous in the extreme; as great as a man, some think even greater. But this is women in fiction. In fact, as Professor Trevelyan points out, she was locked up, beaten and flung about the room. (p. 45)

At last, Mary can draw but one conclusion from her reading. Male professors, male historians, and male poets cannot be relied on for the truth about women. Woman herself must undertake the study of woman. Of course, to do so, she must secure enough money to live on and a room of her own.

Booth's story, we recall, is told within the framework of a professional ritual. It is intended to remind us of "the loves and fears that inform our daily work" and of "what we do when we are at our best," to show, if not a unity, then enough of a "center" "to shame us whenever we violate it." The principal motif of the myth is the hero's insane love for books, and the way this develops with education and maturity into "critical understanding," which Booth defines as that synthesis of thought and passion which should replace, "on the one hand, sentimental and uncritical identifications that leave minds undisturbed, and on the other, hypercritical negations that freeze or alienate" (pp. 317–18). Booth is confident that the experience celebrated by the myth is archetypal. "Whatever our terms for it, whatever our theories about how it happens or why it fails to happen more often, can we reasonably doubt the importance of the moment, at any level of study, when any of us—you, me, Malcolm X, my great-grandfather—succeeds in entering other minds, or 'taking them in,' as nourishment for our own?" (p. 318).

Now, while it is certainly true that something one might call "critical understanding" informs the stories told by Malcolm X and Virginia Woolf, these authors fill this term with thoughts and passions that one would never suspect from Booth's definition. From the standpoint of the second and third stories of reading, Booth's story is utopian. The powers and resources of his hero are equal to the challenges he encounters. At each stage he finds suitable mentors. He is assured by the people around him, by the books he reads, by the entire culture, that he is right for the part. His talents and accomplishments are acknowledged and justly rewarded. In short, from the perspective of Malcolm X's and Woolf's stories, Booth's hero is fantastically privileged.

Utopian has a second meaning, one that is by no means pejorative, and Booth's story is utopian in this sense as well. In overlooking the realities highlighted by the stories of Malcolm X and Virginia Woolf, Booth's story anticipates what might be possible, what "critical understanding" might mean for *everyone*, if only we could overcome the pervasive systemic injustices of our time.

READER-RESPONSE THEORY AND FEMINIST CRITICISM

Reader-response criticism, as currently constituted, is utopian in the same two senses. The different accounts of the reading experience that have been put forth overlook the issues of race, class, and sex, and give no hint of the conflicts, sufferings, and passions that attend these realities. The relative tranquility of the tone of these theories testifies to the privileged position of the theorists. Perhaps, someday, when privileges have withered away or at least become more equitably distributed, some of these theories will ring true. Surely we ought to be able to talk about reading without worrying about injustice. But for now, reader-response criticism must confront the disturbing implications of our historical reality. Paradoxically, utopian theories that elide these realities betray the utopian impulses that inform them.

To put the matter plainly, reader-response criticism needs feminist criticism. The two have yet to engage each other in a sustained and serious way, but if the promise of the former is to be fulfilled, such an encounter must soon occur. Interestingly, the obvious question of the significance of gender has already been explicitly raised, and—this testifies to the increasing impact of feminist criticism as well as to the direct ideological bearing of the issue of gender on reader-response criticism—not by a feminist critic, but by Jonathan Culler, a leading theorist of reading: "If the experience of literature depends upon the qualities of a reading self, one can ask what difference it would make to the experience of literature and thus to the meaning of literature if this self were, for example, female rather than male. If the meaning of a work is the experience of a reader, what difference does it make if the reader is a woman?"[4]

Until very recently this question has not occurred to reader-response critics. They have been preoccupied with other issues. Culler's survey of the field is instructive here, for it enables us to anticipate the direction reader-response theory might take when it is shaken from its slumber by feminist criticism. According to Culler, the different models (or "stories") of reading that have been proposed are all organized around three problems. The first is the issue of control: Does the text control the reader, or vice versa? For David Bleich, Norman Holland, and Stanley Fish, the reader holds controlling interest. Readers read the poems they have made. Bleich asserts this point most strongly: the constraints imposed by the words on the page are "trivial," since their meaning can always be altered by "subjective action." To claim that the text supports this or that reading is only to "moralistically claim . . . that one's own objection is more authoritative than someone else's."[5]

At the other pole are Michael Riffaterre, Georges Poulet, and Wolfgang Iser, who acknowledge the creative role of the reader, but ultimately take the text to be the dominant force. To read, from this point of view, is to create the text according to *its* own promptings. As Poulet puts it, a text, when invested with a reader's subjectivity, becomes a "subjectified object," a "second self" that depends on the reader, but is not, strictly speaking, identical with him. Thus, reading "is a way of giving way not only to a host of alien words, images and ideas, but also to the very alien principle which utters and shelters them. . . . I am on loan to another, and this other thinks, feels, suffers and acts within me."[6] Culler argues persuasively that, regardless of their ostensible theoretical commitments, the prevailing stories of reading generally vacillate between these reader-dominant and text-dominant poles. In fact, those who stress the subjectivity of the reader as against the objectivity of the text ultimately portray the text as determining the responses of the reader. "The more active, projective, or creative the reader is, the more she is manipulated by the sentence or by the author" (p. 71).

The second question prominent in theories of reading is closely related to the first. Reading always involves a subject and an object, a reader and a text. But what constitutes the objectivity of the text? What is "in" the text? What is supplied by the reader? Again, the answers have been equivocal. On the face of it, the situation seems to call for a dualistic theory that credits the contributions of both text and reader. However, Culler argues, a dualistic theory eventually gives way to a monistic theory, in which one or the other pole supplies everything. One might say, for instance, that Iser's theory ultimately implies the determinacy of the text and the authority of the author: "The author guarantees the unity of the work, requires the reader's creative participation, and through his text, prestructures the shape of the aesthetic object to be produced by the reader."[7] At the same time, one can also argue that the "gaps" that structure the reader's response are not built into the text, but appear (or not) as a result of the particular interpretive strategy employed by the reader. Thus, "there is no distinction between what the text gives and what the reader supplies; he supplies *everything*."[8] Depending on which aspects of the theory one takes seriously, Iser's theory collapses either into a monism of the text or a monism of the reader.

The third problem identified by Culler concerns the ending of the story. Most of the time stories of reading end happily. "Readers may be manipulated and misled, but when they finish the book their experience turns into knowledge . . . as though finishing the book took them outside the experience of reading and gave them mastery of it" (p. 79). However, some critics—Harold Bloom, Paul de Man, and Culler himself—find these optimistic endings questionable, and prefer instead stories that stress the impossibility of reading. If, as de Man says, rhetoric puts "an insurmountable obstacle in the way of any reading or understanding," then the reader "may be placed in impossible situations where there is no happy issue, but only the possibility of playing out the roles dramatized in the text" (Culler, p. 81).

Such have been the predominant preoccupations of reader-response criticism during the past decade and a half. Before indicating how feminist critics could affect the conversation, let me consider an objection. A recent and influential essay by Elaine Showalter suggests that we should not enter the conversation at all. She observes that during its early phases, the principal mode of feminist criticism was "feminist critique," which was counter-ideological in intent and concerned with the feminist as *reader*. Happily, we have outgrown this necessary but theoretically unpromising approach. Today, the dominant mode of feminist criticism is "gynocritics," the study of woman as *writer*, of the "history, styles, themes, genres, and structures of writing by women; the psychodynamics of female creativity; the trajectory of the individual or collective female career; and the evolution and laws of a female literary tradition." The shift from "feminist critique" to "gynocritics"—from emphasis on woman as reader to emphasis on woman as writer—has put us in the position of developing a feminist criticism that is "genuinely woman-centered, independent, and intellectually coherent."

> To see women's writing as our primary subject forces us to make the leap to a new conceptual vantage point and to redefine the nature of the theoretical problem before us. It is no longer the ideological dilemma of reconciling revisionary pluralisms but the essential question of difference. How can we constitute women as a distinct literary group? What is the *difference* of women's writing?[9]

But why should the activity of the woman writer be more conducive to theory than the activity of the woman reader is? If it is possible to formulate a basic conceptual framework for disclosing the "difference" of women's writing, surely it is no less possible to do so for women's reading. The same difference, be it linguistic, biological, psychological, or cultural, should apply in either case. In addition, what Showalter calls "gynocritics" is in fact constituted by feminist *criticism*—that is, *readings*—of female texts. Thus, the relevant distinction is not between woman as reader and woman as writer, but between feminist readings of male texts and feminist readings of female texts, and there is no reason why the former could not be as theoretically coherent (or irreducibly pluralistic) as the latter.

On the other hand, there are good reasons for feminist criticism to engage reader-response criticism. Both dispute the fetishized art object, the "Verbal Icon," of New Criticism, and both seek to dispel the objectivist illusion that buttresses the authority of the dominant critical tradition. Feminist criticism can have considerable impact on reader-response criticism, since, as Culler has noticed, it is but a small step from the thesis that the reader is an active producer of meaning to the recognition that there are many different kinds of readers, and that women—because of their numbers if because of nothing else—constitute an essential class. Reader-response critics cannot take refuge in the objectivity of the text, or even in the idea that a gender-neutral criticism is possible. Today they can continue to ignore the implications of feminist criticism only at the cost of incoherence or intellectual dishonesty.

It is equally true that feminist critics need to question their allegiance to text and author-centered paradigms of criticism. Feminist criticism, we should remember, is a mode of *praxis*. The point is not merely to interpret literature in various ways; the point is to *change the world*. We cannot afford to ignore the activity of reading, for it is here that literature is realized as *praxis*. Literature acts on the world by acting on its readers.

To return to our earlier question: What will happen to reader-response criticism if feminists enter the conversation? It is useful to recall the contrast between Booth's story and those of Malcolm X and Virginia Woolf. Like Booth's story, the "stories of reading" that currently make up reader-response theory are mythically abstract, and appear, from a different vantage point, to be by and about readers who are fantastically privileged. Booth's story had a happy ending; Malcolm's and Mary's did not. For Mary, reading meant encountering a tissue of lies and silences; for Malcolm it meant the verification of Elijah Muhammad's shocking doctrines.

Two factors—gender and politics—which are suppressed in the dominant models of reading gain prominence with the advent of a feminist perspective. The feminist story will have *at least* two chapters: one concerned with feminist readings of male texts, and another with feminist readings of female texts. In addition, in this story, gender will have a prominent role as the locus of political struggle. The story will speak of the difference between men and women, of the way the experience and perspective of women have been systematically and fallaciously assimilated into the generic masculine, and of the need to correct this error. Finally, it will identify literature—the activities of reading and writing—as an important arena of political struggle, a crucial component of the project of interpreting the world in order to change it.

Feminist criticism does not approach reader-response criticism without preconceptions. Actually, feminist criticism has always included substantial reader-centered interests. In the next two sections of this paper, I will review these interests, first with respect to male texts, then with respect to female texts. In the process, I will uncover some of the issues that might be addressed and clarified by a feminist theory of reading.

THE FEMALE READER AND THE LITERARY CANON

Although reader-response critics propose different and often conflicting models, by and large the emphasis is on features of the process of reading that do not vary with the nature of the reading material. The feminist entry into the conversation brings the nature of the text back into the foreground. For feminists, the question of *how* we read is inextricably linked with the question of *what* we read. More specifically, the feminist inquiry into the activity of reading begins with the realization that the literary canon is androcentric, and that this has a profoundly damaging effect on women readers. The documentation of this realization was one of the earliest tasks undertaken by feminist critics. Elaine Showalter's 1971 critique of the literary curriculum is exemplary of this work.

> [In her freshman year a female student] . . . might be assigned an anthology of essays, perhaps such as *The Responsible Man*, . . . or *Conditions of Man*, or *Man in Crisis*, or again, *Representative Man: Cult Heroes of Our Time*, in which thirty-three men represent such categories of heroism as the writer, the poet, the dramatist, the artist, and the guru, and the only two women included are the actress Elizabeth Taylor, and the existential Heroine Jacqueline Onassis.
>
> Perhaps the student would read a collection of stories like *The Young Man in American Literature: The Initiation Theme*, or sociological literature like *The Black Man and the Promise of America*. In a more orthodox literary program she might study eternally relevant classics, such as *Oedipus*; as a professor remarked in a recent issue of *College English*, all of us want to kill our fathers and marry our mothers. And whatever else she might read, she would inevitably arrive at the favorite book of all Freshman English courses, the classic of adolescent rebellion, *The Portrait of the Artist as a Young Man*.
>
> By the end of her freshman year, a woman student would have learned something about intellectual neutrality; she would be learning, in fact, how to think like a man. And so she would go on, increasingly with male professors to guide her.[10]

The more personal accounts of other critics reinforce Showalter's critique.

> The first result of my reading was a feeling that male characters were at the very least more interesting than women to the authors who invented them. Thus if, reading their books as it seemed their authors intended them, I naively identified with a character, I repeatedly chose men; I would rather have been Hamlet than Ophelia, Tom Jones instead of Sophia Western, and, perhaps, despite Dostoevsky's intention, Raskolnikov not Sonia.
>
> More peculiar perhaps, but sadly unsurprising, were the assessments I accepted about fictional women. For example, I quickly learned that power was unfeminine and powerful women were, quite literally, monstrous. . . . Bitches all, they must be eliminated, reformed, or at the very least, condemned. . . . Those rare women who are shown in fiction as both powerful and, in some sense, admirable are such because their power is based, if not on beauty, then at least on sexuality.[11]

For a woman, then, books do not necessarily spell salvation. In fact, a literary education may very well cause her grave psychic damage: schizophrenia "is the bizarre but logical conclusion of our education. Imagining myself male, I attempted to create myself male. Although I knew the case was otherwise, it seemed I could do nothing to make this other critically real."[12]

To put the matter theoretically, androcentric literature structures the reading experience differently depending on the gender of the reader. For the male reader, the text serves as the meeting ground of the personal and the universal. Whether or not the text approximates the particularities of his own experience, he is invited to validate the equation of maleness with humanity. The male reader feels his affinity with the universal, with the paradigmatic human being, precisely because he is male. Consider the famous scene of Stephen's epiphany in *The Portrait of the Artist as a Young Man*.

> A girl stood before him in midstream, alone and still, gazing out to sea. She seemed like one whom magic had changed into the likeness of a strange and beautiful seabird. Her long slender bare legs were delicate as a crane's and pure save where an emerald trail of seaweed had fashioned itself as a sign upon the flesh. Her thighs, fuller and softhued as ivory, were bared almost to the hips, where the white fringes of her drawers were like feathering of soft white down. Her slateblue skirts were kilted boldly about her waist and dovetailed behind her. Her bosom was a bird's, soft and slight, slight and soft, as the breast of some dark plumaged dove. But her long fair hair was girlish: and touched with the wonder of mortal beauty, her face.[13]

A man reading this passage is invited to identify with Stephen, to feel "the riot in his blood," and, thus, to ratify the alleged universality of the experience. Whether or not the sight of a girl on the beach has ever provoked similar emotions in him, the male reader is invited to feel his *difference* (concretely, *from the girl*) and to equate that with the universal. Relevant here is Lévi-Strauss's theory that woman functions as currency exchanged between men. The woman in the text converts the text into a woman, and the circulation of this text/woman becomes the central ritual that establishes the bond between the author and his male readers.[14]

The same text affects a woman reader differently. Judith Fetterley gives the most explicit theory to date about the dynamics of the woman reader's encounter with androcentric literature. According to Fetterley, notwithstanding the prevalence of the castrating bitch stereotype, "the cultural reality is not the emasculation of men by women, but the *immasculation* of women by men. As readers and teachers and scholars, women are taught to think as men, to identify with a male point of view, and to accept as normal and legitimate a male system of values, one of whose central principles is misogyny."[15]

The process of immasculation does not impart virile power to the woman reader. On the contrary, it doubles her oppression. She suffers "not simply the powerlessness which derives from not seeing one's experience articulated, clarified, and legitimized in art, but more significantly, the powerlessness which results from the endless division of self against self, the consequence of the invocation to identify as male while being reminded that to be male—to be universal— . . . is to be *not female*."[16]

A woman reading Joyce's novel of artistic awakening, and in particular the passage quoted above, will, like her male counterpart, be invited to identify with Stephen and therefore to ratify the equation of maleness with the universal. Androcentric literature is all the more efficient as an instrument of sexual politics because it does not allow the woman reader to seek refuge in her difference. Instead, it draws her into a process that uses her against herself. It solicits her complicity in the elevation of male difference into universality and, accordingly, the denigration of female difference into otherness without reciprocity. To be sure, misogyny is abundant in the literary canon.[17] It is important, however, that Fetterley's argument can stand on a weaker premise. Androcentricity is a sufficient condition for the process of immasculation.

Feminist critics of male texts, from Kate Millett to Judith Fetterley, have worked under the sign of the "Resisting Reader." Their goal is to disrupt the process of immasculation by exposing it to consciousness, by disclosing the androcentricity of what has customarily passed for the universal. However, feminist criticism written under the aegis of the resisting reader leaves certain questions unanswered, questions that are becoming ripe for feminist analysis: Where does the text get its power to draw us into its designs? Why do some (not all) demonstrably sexist texts remain appealing even after they have been subjected to thorough feminist critique? The usual answer—that the power of male texts is the power of the false consciousness into which women as well as men have been socialized—oversimplifies the problem and prevents us from comprehending both the force of literature and the complexity of our responses to it.

Fredric Jameson advances a thesis that seems to me to be a good starting point for the feminist reconsideration of male texts: "The effectively ideological is also at the same time necessarily utopian."[18] This thesis implies that the male text draws its power over the female reader from authentic desires, which it rouses and then harnesses to the process of immasculation.

A concrete example is in order. Consider Lawrence's *Women in Love,* and for the sake of simplicity, concentrate on Birkin and Ursula. Simone de Beauvoir and Kate Millett have convinced me that this novel is sexist. Why does it remain appealing to me? Jameson's thesis prompts me to answer this question by examining how the text plays not only on my false consciousness but also on my authentic liberatory aspirations—that is to say, on the very impulses that drew me to the feminist movement.

The trick of role reversal comes in handy here. If we reverse the roles of Birkin and Ursula, the ideological components (or at least the most egregious of these, e.g., the analogy between women and horses) stand out as absurdities. Now, if we delete these absurd components while keeping the roles reversed, we have left the story of a woman struggling to combine her passionate desire for autonomous conscious being with an equally passionate desire for love and for other human bonds. This residual story is not far from one we would welcome as expressive of a feminist sensibility. Interestingly enough, it also intimates a novel Lawrence might have written, namely, the proper sequel to *The Rainbow*.

My affective response to the novel Lawrence did write is bifurcated. On the one hand, because I am a woman, I am implicated in the representation of Ursula and in the destiny Lawrence has prepared for her: man is the son of god, but woman is the daughter of man. Her vocation is to witness his transcendence in rapt silence. On the other hand, Fetterley is correct that I am also induced to identify with Birkin, and in so doing, I am drawn into complicity with the reduction of Ursula, and therefore of myself, to the role of the other.

However, the process of immasculation is more complicated than Fetterley allows. When I identify with Birkin, I unconsciously perform the two-stage rereading described above. I reverse the roles of Birkin and Ursula and I suppress the obviously ideological components that in the process show up as absurdities. The identification with Birkin is emotionally effective because, stripped of its patriarchal trappings, Birkin's struggle and his utopian vision conform to my own. To the extent that I perform this feminist rereading *unconsciously*, I am captivated by the text. The stronger my desire for autonomous selfhood and for love, the stronger my identification with Birkin, and the more intense the experience of bifurcation characteristic of the process of immasculation.

The full argument is beyond the scope of this essay. My point is that *certain* (not all) male texts merit a dual hermeneutic: a negative hermeneutic that discloses their complicity with patriarchal ideology, and a positive hermeneutic that recuperates the utopian moment—the authentic kernel—from which they draw a significant portion of their emotional power.[19]

READING WOMEN'S WRITING

Showalter is correct that feminist criticism has shifted emphasis in recent years from "critique" (primarily) of male texts to "gynocritics," or the study of women's writing. Of course, it is worth remembering that the latter has always been on the feminist agenda. *Sexual Politics*, for example, contains not only the critique of Lawrence, Miller, and Mailer that won Millett such notoriety, but also her memorable rereading of *Villette*.[20] It is equally true that interest in women's writing has not entirely supplanted the critical study of patriarchal texts. In a sense "critique" has provided the bridge from the study of male texts to the study of female texts. As feminist criticism shifted from the first to the second, "feminist critique" turned its attention from androcentric texts per se to the androcentric critical strategies that pushed women's writing to the margins of the literary canon. The earliest examples of this genre (for instance, Showalter's "The Double Critical Standard," and Carol Ohmann's "Emily Brontë in the Hands of Male Critics") were concerned primarily with describing and documenting the prejudice against women writers that clouded the judgment of well-placed readers, that is, reviewers and critics.[21] Today we have more sophisticated and more comprehensive analyses of the androcentric critical tradition.

One of the most cogent of these is Nina Baym's analysis of American literature.[22] Baym observes that, as late as 1977, the American canon of major writers did not include a single woman novelist. And yet, in terms of numbers and commercial success, women novelists have probably dominated American literature since the middle of the nineteenth century. How to explain this anomaly?

One explanation is simple bias of the sort documented by Showalter, Ohmann, and others. A second is that women writers lived and worked under social conditions that were not particularly conducive to the production of "excellent" literature: "There tended to be a sort of immediacy in the ambitions of literary women leading them to professionalism rather than artistry, by choice as well as by social pressure and opportunity."[23] Baym adduces a third, more subtle, and perhaps more important reason. There are, she argues, "gender-related restrictions that do not arise out of the cultural realities contemporary with the writing woman, but out of later critical theories . . . which impose their concerns anachronistically, after the fact, on an earlier period."[24] If one reads the critics most instrumental in forming the current theories about American literature (Matthiessen, Chase, Feidelson, Trilling, etc.), one finds that the theoretical model for the canonical American novel is the "melodrama of beset manhood." To accept this model is also to accept as a consequence the exclusion from the canon of "melodramas of beset womanhood," as well as virtually all fiction centering on the experience of women.[25]

The deep symbiotic relationship between the androcentric canon and androcentric modes of reading is well summarized by Kolodny.

> *Insofar as we are taught to read, what we engage are not texts, but paradigms.* . . . Insofar as literature is itself a social institution, so, too, reading is a highly socialized—or learned—activity. . . . We read well, and with pleasure, what we already know how to read; and what we know how to read is to a large extent dependent on what we have already read [works from which we have developed our expectations and learned our interpretative strategies]. What we then choose to read—and, by extension, teach and thereby "canonize"—usually follows upon our previous reading.[26]

We are caught, in other words, in a rather vicious circle. An androcentric canon generates androcentric interpretive strategies, which in turn favor the canonization of androcentric texts and the marginalization of gynocentric ones. To break this cycle, feminist critics must fight on two fronts: for the revision of the canon to include a significant body of works by women, and for the development of the reading strategies consonant with the concerns, experiences, and formal devices that constitute these texts. Of course, to succeed, we also need a community of women readers who are qualified by experience, commitment, and training, and who will enlist the personal and institutional resources at their disposal in the struggle.[27]

The critique of androcentric reading strategies is essential, for it opens up some ideological space for the recuperation of women's writing. Turning now to this project, we observe, first, that a large volume of work has been done, and, second, that this endeavor is coming to look even more complicated and more diverse than the criticism of male texts. Certainly, it is impossible in the space of a few pages to do justice to the wide range of concerns, strategies, and positions associated with feminist readings of female texts. Nevertheless, certain things can be said. For the remainder of this section, I focus on an exemplary essay: "Vesuvius at Home: The Power of Emily Dickinson," by Adrienne Rich.[28] My commentary anticipates the articulation of a paradigm that illuminates certain features of feminist readings of women's writing.

I am principally interested in the rhetoric of Rich's essay, for it represents an implicit commentary on the process of reading women's writing. Feminist readings of male texts are, as we have seen, primarily resisting. The reader assumes an adversarial or at least a detached attitude toward the material at hand. In the opening pages of her essay, Rich introduces three metaphors that proclaim a very different attitude toward her subject.

> The methods, the exclusions, of Emily Dickinson's existence could not have been my own; yet more and more, as a woman poet finding my own methods, I have come to understand her necessities, could have served as witness in her defense. (p. 158)

> I am traveling at the speed of time, along the Massachusetts Turnpike. . . . "Home is not where the heart is," she wrote in a letter, "but the house and adjacent buildings." . . . I am traveling at the speed of time, in the direction of the house and buildings. . . . For years, I have been not so much envisioning Emily Dickinson as trying to visit, to enter her mind through her poems and letters, and through my own intimations of what it could have meant to be one of the two mid-nineteenth-century American geniuses, and a woman, living in Amherst, Massachusetts. (pp. 158–59)

> For months, for most of my life, I have been hovering like an insect against the screens of an existence which inhabited Amherst, Massachusetts between 1830 and 1886 (p. 158) . . . Here [in Dickinson's bedroom] I become again, an insect, vibrating at the frames of windows, clinging to the panes of glass, trying to connect. (p. 161)

A commentary on the process of reading is carried on silently and unobtrusively through the use of these metaphors. The first is a judicial metaphor: the feminist reader speaks as a witness in defense of the woman writer. Here we see clearly that gender is crucial. The feminist reader takes the part of the woman writer against patriarchal misreadings that trivialize or distort her work.[29] The second metaphor refers to a principal tenet of feminist criticism: a literary work cannot be understood apart from the social, historical, and cultural context within which it was written. As if to acquiesce to the condition Dickinson had imposed on her friends, Rich travels through space and time to visit the poet on her own *premises*. She goes to Amherst, to the house where Dickinson lived. She rings the bell, she goes in, then upstairs, then into the bedroom that had been "freedom" for the poet. Her destination, ultimately, is Dickinson's mind. But it is not enough to read the poet's poems and letters. To reach her heart and mind, one must take a detour through "the house and adjacent buildings."

Why did Dickinson go into seclusion? Why did she write poems she would not publish? What mean these poems about queens, volcanoes, deserts, eternity, passion, suicide, wild beasts, rape, power, madness, the daemon, the grave? For Rich, these are related questions. The revisionary re-reading of Dickinson's work is of a piece with the revisionary re-reading of her life. "I have a notion genius knows itself; that Dickinson chose her seclusion, knowing what she needed. . . . She carefully selected her society and controlled the disposal of her time. . . . Given her vocation, she was neither eccentric nor quaint; she was determined to survive, to use her powers, to practice necessary economies" (p. 160).

> To write [the poetry that she needed to write] she had to enter chambers of the self in which
>
> > Ourself, concealed—
> > Should startle most—
>
> and to relinquish control there, to take those risks, she had to create a relationship to the outer world where she could feel in control. (p. 175)

The metaphor of visiting points to another feature of feminist readings of women's writing, namely, the tendency to construe the text not as an object, but as the manifestation of the subjectivity of the absent author—the "voice" of another woman. Rich is not content to revel in the textuality of Dickinson's poems and letters. For her, these are doorways to the "mind" of a "woman of genius." Rich deploys her imagination and her considerable rhetorical skill to evoke "the figure of powerful will" who lives at the heart of the text. To read Dickinson, then, is to try to visit with her, to hear her voice, to make her live *in* oneself, and to feel her impressive "personal dimensions."[30]

At the same time, Rich is keenly aware that visiting with Dickinson is *only* a metaphor for reading her poetry, and an inaccurate one at that. She signals this awareness with the third metaphor. It is no longer possible to visit with Dickinson; one can only enter her mind through her poems and letters as one can enter her house—through the back door out of which her coffin was carried. In reading, one encounters only a text, the trail of an absent author. Upstairs, at last, in the very room where Dickinson exercised her astonishing craft, Rich finds herself again "an insect, vibrating at the frames of windows, clinging to panes of glass, trying to connect." But though "the scent is very powerful," Dickinson herself is absent.

Perhaps the most obvious rhetorical device employed by Rich in this essay, more obvious even than her striking metaphors, is her use of the personal voice. Her approach to Dickinson is self-consciously and unabashedly subjective. She clearly describes her point of view—what she saw as she drove across the Connecticut Valley toward Amherst (ARCO stations, McDonald's, shopping plazas, as well as "light-green spring softening the hills, dogwood and wild fruit trees blossoming in the hollows"), and what she thought about (the history of the valley, "scene of Indian uprisings, religious revivals, spiritual confrontations, the blazing-up of the lunatic fringe of the Puritan coal," and her memories of college weekends in Amherst). Some elements of her perspective—ARCO and McDonald's—would have been alien to Dickinson; others—the sight of dogwood and wild fruit trees in the spring, and most of all, the experience of being a woman poet in a patriarchal culture—would establish their affinity.

Rich's metaphors together with her use of the personal voice indicate some key issues underlying feminist readings of female texts. On the one hand, reading is necessarily subjective. On the other hand, it must not be wholly so. One must respect the autonomy of the text. The reader is a visitor and, as such, must observe the necessary courtesies. She must avoid unwarranted intrusions—she must be careful not to appropriate what belongs to her host, not to impose herself on the other woman. Furthermore, reading is at once an intersubjective encounter and something less than that. In reading Dickinson, Rich seeks to enter her mind, to feel her presence. But the text is a screen, an inanimate object. Its subjectivity is only a projection of the subjectivity of the reader.

Rich suggests the central motivation, the regulative ideal, that shapes the feminist reader's approach to these issues. If feminist readings of male texts are motivated by the need to disrupt the process of immasculation, feminist readings of female texts are motivated by the need "to connect," to recuperate, or to formulate—they come to the same thing—the context, the tradition, that would link women writers to one another, to women readers and critics, and to the larger community of women. Of course, the recuperation of such a context is a necessary basis for the nonrepressive integration of women's point of view and culture into the study of a Humanities that is worthy of its name.[31]

FEMINIST MODELS OF READING: A SUMMARY

As I noted in the second section, mainstream reader-response theory is preoccupied with two closely related questions: (1) Does the text manipulate the reader, or does the reader manipulate the text to produce the meaning that suits her own interests? and (2) What is "in" the text? How can we distinguish what it supplies from what the reader supplies? Both of these questions refer to the subject–object relation that is established between reader and text during the process of reading. A feminist theory of reading also elaborates this relationship, but for feminists, gender—the gender inscribed in the text as well as the gender of the reader—is crucial. Hence, the feminist story has two chapters, one concerned with male texts and the other with female texts.

The focus of the first chapter is the experience of the woman reader. What do male texts *do* to her? The feminist story takes the subject–object relation of reading through three moments. The phrasing of the basic question signals the first moment. Control is conferred on the text: the woman reader is immasculated by the text. The feminist story fits well at this point in Iser's framework. Feminists insist that the androcentricity of the text and its damaging effects on women readers are not figments of their imagination. These are implicit in the "schematized aspects" of the text. The second movement, which is similarly consonant with the plot of Iser's story, involves the recognition of the crucial role played by the subjectivity of the woman reader. Without her, the text is *nothing*. The process of immasculation is latent in the text, but it finds its actualization only through the reader's activity. In effect, the woman reader is the agent of her own immasculation.[32]

Here we seem to have a corroboration of Culler's contention that dualistic models of reading inevitably disintegrate into one of two monisms. Either the text (and, by implication, the author) or the woman reader is responsible for the process of immasculation. The third moment of the subject–object relation—ushered in by the transfiguration of the heroine into a feminist—breaks through this dilemma. The woman reader, now a feminist, embarks on a critical analysis of the reading process, and she realizes that the text has power to structure her experience. Without androcentric texts she will not suffer immasculation. However, her recognition of the power of the text is matched by her awareness of her essential role in the process of reading. Without her, the text is nothing—it is inert and harmless. The advent of feminist consciousness and the accompanying commitment to emancipatory *praxis* reconstitutes the subject–object relationship within a dialectical rather than a dualistic framework, thus averting the impasse described by Culler between the "dualism of narrative" and the "monism of theory." In the feminist story, the breakdown of Iser's dualism does not indicate a mistake or an irreducible impasse, but the necessity of *choosing* between two modes of reading. The reader can submit to the power of the text, or she can take control of the reading experience. The recognition of the existence of a choice suddenly makes visible the normative dimension of the feminist story: She *should* choose the second alternative.

But what does it mean for a reader to take control of the reading experience? First of all, she must do so without forgetting the androcentricity of the text or its power to structure her experience. In addition, the reader taking control of the text is not, as in Iser's model, simply a matter of selecting among the concretizations allowed by the text. Recall that a crucial feature of the process of immasculation is the woman reader's bifurcated response. She reads the text both as a man and as a woman. But in either case, the result is the same: she confirms her position as other. Taking control of the reading experience means reading the text as it was *not* meant to be read, in fact, reading it against itself. Specifically, one must identify the nature of the choices proffered by the text and, equally important, what the text precludes—namely, the possibility of reading as a woman *without* putting one's self in the position of the other, of reading so as to affirm womanhood as another, equally valid, paradigm of human existence.

All this is easier said than done. It is important to realize that reading a male text, no matter how virulently misogynous, could do little damage if it were an isolated event. The problem is that within patriarchal culture, the experience of immasculation is paradigmatic of women's encounters with the dominant literary and critical traditions. A feminist cannot simply refuse to read patriarchal texts, for they are everywhere, and they condition her participation in the literary and critical enterprise. In fact, by the time she becomes a feminist critic, a woman has already read numerous male texts—in particular, the most authoritative texts of the literary and critical canons. She has introjected not only androcentric texts, but also androcentric reading strategies and values. By the time she becomes a feminist, the bifurcated response characteristic of immasculation has become second nature to her. The feminist story stresses that patriarchal constructs have objective as well as subjective reality; they are inside and outside the text, inside and outside the reader.

The pervasiveness of androcentricity drives feminist theory beyond the individualistic models of Iser and of most reader-response critics. The feminist reader agrees with Stanley Fish that the production of the meaning of a text is mediated by the interpretive community in which the activity of reading is situated: the meaning of the text depends on the interpretive strategy one applies to it, and the choice of strategy is regulated (explicitly or implicitly) by the canons of acceptability that govern the interpretive community.[33] However, unlike Fish, the feminist reader is also aware that the ruling interpretive communities are androcentric, and that this androcentricity is deeply etched in the strategies and modes of thought that have been introjected by all readers, women as well as men.

Because patriarchal constructs have psychological correlates, taking control of the reading process means taking control of one's reactions and inclinations. Thus, a feminist reading—actually a re-reading—is a kind of therapeutic analysis. The reader recalls and examines how she would "naturally" read a male text in order to understand and therefore undermine the subjective predispositions that had rendered her vulnerable to its designs. Beyond this, the pervasiveness of immasculation necessitates a collective remedy. The feminist reader hopes that other women will recognize themselves in her story, and join her in her struggle to transform the culture.[34]

"Feminism affirms women's point of view by revealing, criticizing and examining its impossibility."[35] Had we nothing but male texts, this sentence from Catharine MacKinnon's brilliant essay on jurisprudence could serve as the definition of the project of the feminist reader. The significant body of literature written by women presents feminist critics with another, more heartwarming, task: that of recovering, articulating, and elaborating positive expressions of women's point of view, of celebrating the survival of this point of view in spite of the formidable forces that have been ranged against it.

The shift to women's writing brings with it a shift in emphasis from the negative hermeneutic of ideological unmasking to a positive hermeneutic whose aim is the recovery and cultivation of women's culture. As Showalter has noted, feminist criticism of women's writing proposes to articulate woman's difference: What does it mean for a woman to express herself in writing? How does a woman write as a woman? It is a central contention of this essay that feminist criticism should also inquire into the correlative process of *reading*: What does it mean for a woman to read without condemning herself to the position of other? What does it mean for a woman, reading as a woman, to read literature written by a woman writing as a woman?[36]

The Adrienne Rich essay discussed in the preceding section illustrates a contrast between feminist readings of male texts and feminist readings of female texts. In the former, the object of the critique, whether it is regarded as an enemy or as symptom of a malignant condition, is the text itself, *not* the reputation or the character of the author.[37] This impersonal approach contrasts sharply with the strong personal interest in Dickinson exhibited by Rich. Furthermore, it is not merely a question of friendliness toward the text. Rich's reading aims beyond "the unfolding of the text as a living event," the goal of aesthetic reading set by

Iser. Much of the rhetorical energy of Rich's essay is directed toward evoking the personality of Dickinson, toward making *her* live as the substantial, palpable presence animating her works.

Unlike the first chapter of the feminist story of reading, which is centered around a single heroine—the woman reader battling her way out of a maze of patriarchal constructs—the second chapter features two protagonists—the woman reader and the woman writer—in the context of two settings. The first setting is judicial: one woman is standing witness in defense of the other; the second is dialogic: the two women are engaged in intimate conversation. The judicial setting points to the larger political and cultural dimension of the project of the feminist reader. Feminist critics may say with Harold Bloom that reading always involves the "art of defensive warfare."[38] What they mean by this, however, would not be Bloom's individualistic, agonistic encounter between "strong poet" and "strong reader," but something more akin to "class struggle." Whether concerned with male or female texts, feminist criticism is situated in the larger struggle against patriarchy.

The importance of this battle cannot be overestimated. However, feminist readings of women's writing opens up space for another, equally important, critical project, namely, the articulation of a model of reading that is centered on a female paradigm. While it is still too early to present a full-blown theory, the dialogic aspect of the relationship between the feminist reader and the woman writer suggests the direction that such a theory might take. As in all stories of reading, the drama revolves around the subject–object relationship between text and reader. The feminist story—exemplified by the Adrienne Rich essay discussed earlier—features an intersubjective construction of this relationship. The reader encounters not simply a text, but a "subjectified object": the "heart and mind" of another woman. She comes into close contact with an interiority—a power, a creativity, a suffering, a vision—that is *not* identical with her own. The feminist interest in construing readings as an intersubjective encounter suggests an affinity with Poulet's (rather than Iser's) theory, and, as in Poulet's model, the subject of the literary work is its author, *not* the reader: "A book is not only a book; it is a means by which an author actually preserves [her] ideas, [her] feelings, [her] modes of dreaming and living. It is a means of saving [her] identity from death. . . . To understand a literary work, then, is to let the individual who wrote it reveal [herself] to us *in* us."[39]

For all this initial agreement, however, the dialogic relationship the feminist reader establishes with the female subjectivity brought to life in the process of reading is finally at odds with Poulet's model. For the interiorized author is "alien" to Poulet's reader. When he reads, he delivers himself "bound hand and foot, to the omnipotence of fiction." He becomes the "prey" of what he reads. "There is no escaping this takeover." His consciousness is "invaded," "annexed," "usurped." He is "dispossessed" of his rightful place on the "center stage" of his own mind. In the final analysis, the process of reading leaves room for only one subjectivity. The work becomes "a sort of human being" at "the expense of the reader whose life it suspends."[40] It is significant that the metaphors of mastery and submission, of violation and control, so prominent in Poulet's essay, are entirely absent in Rich's essay of Dickinson. In the paradigm of reading implicit in her essay, the dialectic of control (which shapes feminist readings of male texts) gives way to the dialectic of communication. For Rich, reading is a matter of "trying to connect" with the existence behind the text.

The dialectic also has three moments. The first involves the recognition that genuine intersubjective communication demands the duality of reader and author (the subject of the work). Because reading removes the barrier between subject and object, the division takes place *within* the reader. Reading induces a doubling of the reader's subjectivity, so that one can be placed at the disposal of the text while the other remains with the reader. Now, this doubling presents a problem, for in fact there is only one subject present—the reader. The text—the words on the page—has been written by the writer, but meaning is always a matter of interpretation. The subjectivity roused to life by reading, while it may be attributed to the author, is nevertheless not a separate subjectivity but a projection of the subjectivity of the reader. How can the duality of subjects be maintained in the absence of the author? In an actual conversation, the presence of another person preserves the duality. Because each party must assimilate and interpret the utterances of the other, we still have the introjection of the subject–object division, as well as the possibility of hearing only what one wants to hear. But in a real conversation, the other person can interrupt, object to an erroneous interpretation, provide further explanations, change her mind, change the topic, or cut off conversation altogether. In reading, there are no comparable safeguards against the appropriation of the text by the reader. This is the second moment of the dialectic—the recognition that reading is necessarily subjective. The need to keep it from being *totally* subjective ushers in the third moment of the dialectic.

In the feminist story, the key to the problem is the awareness of the double context of reading and writing. Rich's essay is wonderfully illustrative. To avoid imposing an alien perspective on Dickinson's poetry, Rich informs her reading with the knowledge of the circumstances in which Dickinson lived and worked. She repeatedly reminds herself and her readers that Dickinson must be read in light of her own premises, that the "exclusions" and "necessities" she endured, and, therefore, her choices, were conditioned by her own world. At the same time, Rich's sensitivity to the context of writing is matched by her sensitivity to the context of reading. She makes it clear throughout the essay that her reading of Dickinson is necessarily shaped by her experience and interests as a feminist poet living in the twentieth-century United States. The reader also has her own premises. To forget these is to run the risk of imposing them surreptitiously on the author.

To recapitulate, the first moment of the dialectic of reading is marked by the recognition of the necessary duality of subjects; the second, by the realization that this duality is threatened by the author's absence. In the third moment, the duality of subjects is referred to the duality of contexts. Reading becomes a mediation between author and reader, between the context of writings and the context of reading.

Although feminists have always believed that objectivity is an illusion, Rich's essay is the only one, as far as I know, to exhibit through its rhetoric the necessary subjectivity of reading coupled with the equally necessary commitment to reading the text as it was meant to be read.[41] The third moment of the dialectic is apparent in Rich's weaving—not blending—of the context of writing and the context of reading, the perspective of the author and that of the reader. The central rhetorical device effecting this mediation is her use of the personal voice. As in most critical essays, Rich alternates quotes from the texts in question with her own commentary, but her use of the personal voice makes a difference. In her hands, this rhetorical strategy serves two purposes. First, it serves as a reminder that her interpretation is informed by her own perspective. Second, it signifies her tactful approach to Dickinson; the personal voice serves as a gesture warding off any inclination to appropriate the authority of the text as a warrant for the validity of the interpretation. Because the interpretation is presented as an *interpretation*, its claim to validity rests on the cogency of the supporting arguments, *not* on the authorization of the text.

Rich accomplishes even more than this. She reaches out to Dickinson not by identifying with her, but by establishing their affinity. Both are American, both are women poets in a patriarchal culture. By playing this affinity against the differences, she produces a context that incorporates both reader and writer. In turn, this common ground becomes the basis for drawing the connections that, in her view, constitute the proper goal of reading.

One might ask: Is there something distinctively female (rather than "merely feminist") in this dialogic model? While it is difficult to specify what "distinctively female" might mean, there are currently very interesting speculations about differences in the way males and females conceive of themselves and of their relations with others. The works of Jean Baker Miller, Nancy Chodorow, and Carol Gilligan suggest that men define themselves through individuation and separation from others, while women have more flexible ego boundaries and define and experience themselves in terms of their affiliations and relationships with others.[42] Men value autonomy, and they think of their interactions with others principally in terms of procedures for arbitrating conflicts between individual rights. Women, on the other hand, value relationships, and they are most concerned in their dealings with others to negotiate between opposing needs so that the relationship can be maintained. This difference is consistent with the difference between mainstream models of reading and the dialogic model I am proposing for feminist readings of women's writing. Mainstream reader-response theories are preoccupied with issues of control and partition—how to distinguish the contribution of the author/text from the contribution of the reader. In the dialectic of communication informing the relationship between the feminist reader and the female author/text, the central issue is not of control or partition, but of managing the contradictory implications of the desire for relationship (one must maintain a minimal distance from the other) and the desire for intimacy, up to and including a symbiotic merger with the other. The problematic is defined by the drive "to connect," rather than that which is implicit in the mainstream preoccupation with partition and control—namely, the drive to get it right. It could also be argued that Poulet's model represents reading as an intimate, intersubjective encounter. However, it is significant that in his model, the prospect of close rapport with another provokes both excitement and anxiety. Intimacy, while desired, is also viewed as a threat to one's integrity. For Rich, on the other hand, the prospect of merging with another is problematical, but not threatening.

Let me end with a word about endings. Dialectical stories look forward to optimistic endings. Mine is no exception. In the first chapter the woman reader becomes a feminist, and in the end she succeeds in extricating herself from the androcentric logic of the literary and critical canons. In the second chapter the feminist reader succeeds in effecting a mediation between her perspective and that of the writer. These "victories" are part of the project of producing women's culture and literary tradition, which in turn is part of the project of overcoming patriarchy. It is in the nature of people working for revolutionary change to be optimistic about the prospect of redirecting the future.

Culler observes that optimistic endings have been challenged (successfully, he thinks) by deconstruction, a method radically at odds with the dialectic. It is worth noting that there is a deconstructive moment in Rich's reading of Dickinson. Recall her third metaphor: the reader is an insect "vibrating the frames of windows, clinging to the panes of glass, trying to connect." The suggestion of futility is unmistakable. At best, Rich's interpretation of Dickinson might be considered as a "strong misreading" whose value is in its capacity to provoke other misreadings.

We might say this—but must we? To answer this question, we must ask another: What is at stake in the proposition that reading is impossible? For one thing, if reading is impossible, then there is no way of deciding the validity of an interpretation—the very notion of validity becomes problematical. Certainly it is useful to be reminded that the validity of an interpretation cannot be decided by appealing to what the author "intended," to what is "in" the text, or to what is "in" the experience of the reader. However, there is another approach to the problem of validation, one that is consonant with the dialogic model of reading described above. We can think of validity not as a property inherent in an interpretation, but rather as a *claim* implicit in the *act* of propounding an interpretation. An interpretation, then, is not valid or invalid in itself. Its validity is contingent on the agreement of others. In this view, Rich's interpretation of Dickinson, which is frankly acknowledged as conditioned by her own experience as a twentieth-century feminist poet, is not necessarily a misreading. In advancing her interpretation, Rich implicitly claims its validity. That is to say, to read a text and then to write about it is to seek to connect not only with the author of the original text, but also with a community of readers. To the extent that she succeeds and to the extent that the community is potentially all-embracing, her interpretation has that degree of validity.[43]

Feminist reading and writing alike are grounded in the interest of producing a community of feminist readers and writers, and in the hope that ultimately this community will expand to include everyone. Of course, this project may fail. The feminist story may yet end with the recognition of the impossibility of reading. But this remains to be seen. At this stage I think it behooves us to *choose* the dialectical over the deconstructive plot. It is dangerous for feminists to be overly enamored with the theme of impossibility. Instead, we should strive to redeem the claim that it is possible for a woman, reading as a woman, to read literature written by women, for this is essential if we are to make the literary enterprise into a means for building and maintaining connections among women.

NOTES

I would like to acknowledge my debt to David Schweickart for the substantial editorial work he did on this chapter.

1. Wayne Booth, Presidential Address, "Arts and Scandals 1982," *PMLA* 98 (1983): 313. Subsequent references to this essay are cited parenthetically in the text.

2. *The Autobiography of Malcolm X*, written with Alex Haley (New York: Grover Press, 1964), p. 173. (Subsequent references are cited parenthetically in the text.)

3. Virginia Woolf, *A Room of One's Own* (New York: Harcourt Brace Jovanovich, 1981). (Subsequent references are cited parenthetically in the text.)

4. Jonathan D. Culler, *On Deconstruction: Theory and Criticism after Structuralism* (Ithaca: Cornell University Press, 1982), p. 42. (Subsequent references are cited parenthetically in the text.) Wayne Booth's essay "Freedom of Interpretation: Bakhtin and the Challenge of Feminist Criticism," *Critical Inquiry* 9 (1982): 45–76, is another good omen of the impact of feminist thought on literary criticism.

5. David Bleich, *Subjective Criticism* (Baltimore: Johns Hopkins University Press, 1978), p. 112.

6. Georges Poulet, "Criticism and the Experience of Interiority," trans. Catherine and Richard Macksey, in *Reader-Response Criticism: From Formalism to Structuralism*, ed. Jane Tompkins (Baltimore: Johns Hopkins University Press, 1980), p. 43. Poulet's theory is not among those discussed by Culler. However, since he will be useful to us later, I mention him here.

7. This argument was advanced by Samuel Weber in "The Struggle for Control: Wolfgang Iser's Third Dimension," cited by Culler in *On Deconstruction*, p. 75.

8. Stanley E. Fish, "Why No One's Afraid of Wolfgang Iser," *Diacritics* 11 (1981): 7. Quoted by Culler in *On Deconstruction*, p. 75.

9. Elaine Showalter, "Feminist Criticism in the Wilderness," *Critical Inquiry* 8 (1981): 182–85. Showalter argues that if we see feminist critique (focused on the reader) as our primary critical project, we must be content with the "playful pluralism" proposed by Annette Kolodny: first because no single conceptual model can comprehend so eclectic and wide-ranging an enterprise, and second because "in the free play of the interpretive field, feminist critique can only compete with alternative readings, all of which have the built-in obsolescence of Buicks, cast away as newer readings take their place" (p. 182). Although Showalter does not support Wimsatt and Beardsley's proscription of the "affective fallacy," she nevertheless subscribes to the logic of their argument. Kolodny's "playful pluralism" is more benign than Wimsatt and Beardsley's dreaded "relativism," but no less fatal, in Showalter's view, to theoretical coherence.

10. Elaine Showalter, "Women and the Literary Curriculum," *College English* 32 (1971): 855. For an excellent example of recent work following in the spirit of Showalter's critique, see Paul Lauter, *Reconstructing American Literature* (Old Westbury, N.Y.: Feminist Press, 1983).

11. Lee Edwards, "Women, Energy, and *Middlemarch*," *Massachusetts Review* 13 (1972): 226.

12. Ibid.

13. James Joyce, *The Portrait of the Artist as a Young Man* (London: Jonathan Cape, 1916), p. 195.

14. See also Florence Howe's analysis of the same passage, "Feminism and Literature," in *Images of Women in Fiction: Feminist Perspectives*, ed. Susan Koppelman Cornillon (Bowling Green, Ohio: Bowling Green State University Press, 1972), pp. 262–63.

15. Judith Fetterley, *The Resisting Reader: A Feminist Approach to American Fiction* (Bloomington: Indiana University Press, 1978), p. xx. Although Fetterley's remarks refer specifically to American literature, they apply generally to the entire traditional canon.

16. Fetterley, *Resisting Reader,* p. xiii.

17. See Katharine M. Rogers, *The Troublesome Helpmate: A History of Misogyny in Literature* (Seattle: University of Washington Press, 1966).

18. Fredric Jameson, *The Political Unconscious: Narrative as a Socially Symbolic Act* (Ithaca: Cornell University Press, 1981), p. 286.

19. In *Woman and the Demon: The Life of a Victorian Myth* (Cambridge: Harvard University Press, 1982), Nina Auerbach employs a similar—though not identical—positive hermeneutic. She reviews the myths and images of women (as angels, demons, victims, whores, etc.) that feminist critics have "gleefully" unmasked as reflections and instruments of sexist ideology, and discovers in them an "unexpectedly empowering" mythos. Auerbach argues that the "most powerful, if least acknowledged creation [of the Victorian cultural imagination] is an explosively mobile, magic woman, who breaks the boundaries of family within which her society restricts her. The triumph of this overweening creature is a celebration of the corporate imagination that believed in her" (p. 1). See also idem, "Magi and Maidens: The Romance of the Victorian Freud," *Critical Inquiry* 8 (1981): 281–300. The tension between the positive and negative feminists hermeneutics is perhaps most apparent when one is dealing with the "classics." See, for example, Carol Thomas Neely, "Feminist Modes of Shakespeare Criticism: Compensatory, Justificatory, Transformational," *Women's Studies* 9 (1981): 3–15.

20. Kate Millett, *Sexual Politics* (New York: Avon Books, 1970).

21. Elaine Showalter, "The Double Critical Standard and the Feminine Novel," chap. 3 in *A Literature of Their Own: British Women Novelists from Brontë to Lessing* (Princeton: Princeton University Press, 1977), pp. 73–99; Carol Ohmann, "Emily Brontë in the Hands of Male Critics," *College English* 32 (1971): 906–13.

22. Nina Baym, "Melodramas of Beset Manhood: How Theories of American Fiction Exclude Women Authors," *American Quarterly* 33 (1981): 123–39.

23. Ibid., p. 125.

24. Ibid., p. 130. One of the founding works of American literature is "The Legend of Sleepy Hollow," about which Leslie Fiedler writes: "It is fitting that our first successful homegrown legend would memorialize, however playfully, the flight of the dreamer from the shrew" (*Love and Death in the American Novel* [New York: Criterion, 1960], p. xx).

25. Nina Baym's *Woman's Fiction: A Guide to Novels by and about Women in America, 1820–70* (Ithaca: Cornell University Press, 1978) provides a good survey of what has been excluded from the canon.

26. Annette Kolodny, "Dancing Through the Minefield: Some Observations on the Theory, Practice, and Politics of a Feminist Literary Criticism," *Feminist Studies* 6 (1980): 10–12. Kolodny elaborates the same theme in "A Map for Rereading: Or, Gender and the Interpretation of Literary Texts," *New Literary History 11* (1980): 451–67.

27. For an excellent account of the way in which the feminist "interpretive community" has changed literary and critical conventions, see Jean E. Kennard, "Convention Coverage, or How to Read Your Own Life," *New Literary History* 8 (1981): 69–88. The programs of the MLA Convention during the last twenty-five years offer more concrete evidence of the changes in the literary and critical canons, and of the ideological and political struggles effecting these changes.

28. In Adrienne Rich, *On Lies, Secrets, and Silence: Selected Prose, 1966–1978* (New York: W. W. Norton, 1979). (Subsequent references are cited parenthetically in the text.)

29. Susan Glaspell's story "A Jury of Her Peers" revolves around a variation of this judicial metaphor. The parable of reading implicit in this story has not been lost on feminist critics. Annette Kolodny, for example, discusses how it "explores the necessary gender marking which *must* constitute any definition of 'peers' in the complex process of unraveling truth or meaning." Although the story does not exclude male readers, it alerts us to the fact that "symbolic representations depend on a fund of shared recognitions and po-

tential references," and in general, "female meaning" is inaccessible to "male inter-pretation." "However inadvertently, [the male reader] is a *different kind of* reader and, . . . where women are concerned, he is often an inadequate reader" ("Map for Rereading," pp. 460–63).

30. There is a strong counter-tendency, inspired by French poststructuralism, which privileges the appreciation of textuality over the imaginative recovery of the woman writer as subject of the work. See, for example, Mary Jacobus, "Is There a Woman in This Text?" *New Literary History* 14 (1982): 117–41, especially the concluding paragraph. The last sentence of the essay underscores the controversy: "Perhaps the question that feminist critics should be asking is not 'Is there a woman in this text?' but rather: 'Is there a text in this woman?'"

31. I must stress that although Rich's essay presents a significant paradigm of feminist readings of women's writing, it is not the only such paradigm. An alternative is proposed by Caren Greenberg, "Reading Reading: Echo's Abduction of Language," in *Women and Language in Literature and Society*, ed. Sally McConnell-Ginet, Ruth Borker, and Nelly Furman (New York: Praeger, 1980), pp. 304–9.

Furthermore, there are many important issues that have been left out of my discussion. For example:

a. The relationship of her career as reader to the artistic development of the woman writer. In *The Madwoman in the Attic* (New Haven: Yale University Press, 1980) Sandra Gilbert and Susan Gubar show that women writers had to struggle to overcome the "anxiety of authorship" which they contracted from the "sentences" of their predecessors, male as well as female. They also argue that the relationship women writers form with their female predecessors does not fit the model of oedipal combat proposed by Bloom. Rich's attitude toward Dickinson (as someone who "has been there," as a "foremother" to be recovered) corroborates Gilbert and Gubar's claim.

b. The relationship between women writers and their readers. We need actual reception studies as well as studies of the way women writers conceived of their readers and the way they inscribed them in their texts.

c. The relationship between the positive and the negative hermeneutic in feminist readings of women's writing. Rich's reading of Dickinson emphasizes the positive hermeneutic. One might ask, however, if this approach is applicable to *all* women's writing. Specifically, is this appropriate to the popular fiction written by women, e.g., Harlequin Romances? To what extent is women's writing itself a bearer of patriarchal ideology? Janice Radway addresses these issues in "Utopian Impulse in Popular Literature: Gothic Romances and 'Feminist Protest,'" *American Quarterly* 33 (1981): 140–62, and "Women Read the Romance: The Interaction of Text and Context," *Feminist Studies* 9 (1983): 53–78. See also Tania Modleski, *Loving with a Vengeance: Mass-Produced Fantasies for Women* (New York: Methuen, 1982).

32. Iser writes:

> Text and reader no longer confront each other as object and subject, but instead the "division" takes place within the reader [herself]. . . . As we read, there occurs an artificial division of our personality, because we take as a theme for ourselves something we are not. Thus, in reading there are two levels—the alien "me" and the real, virtual "me"—which are never completely cut off from each other. Indeed, we can only make someone else's thoughts into an absorbing theme for ourselves provided the virtual background of our personality can adapt to it. ("The Reading Process: A Phenomenological Approach," in Tompkins, *Reader-Response Criticism*, p. 67)

Add the stipulation that the alien "me" is a male who has appointed the universal into his maleness, and we have the process of immasculation described in the third section.

33. Stanley E. Fish, *Is There a Text in This Class? The Authority of Interpretive Communities* (Cambridge: Harvard University Press, 1980), especially pt. 2.

34. Although the woman reader is the "star" of the feminist story of reading, this does not mean that men are excluded from the audience. On the contrary, it is hoped that on hearing the feminist story they will be encouraged to revise their own stories to reflect the fact that they, too, are gendered beings, and that, ultimately, they will take control of their inclination to appropriate the universal at the expense of women.

35. Catharine A. MacKinnon, "Feminism, Marxism, Method, and the State: Toward Feminist Jurisprudence," *Signs* 8 (1981): 637.

36. There is lively debate among feminists about whether it is better to emphasize the essential similarity of women and men, or their difference. There is much to be said intellectually and politically for both sides. However, in one sense, the argument centers on a false issue. It assumes that concern about women's "difference" is incompatible with concern about the essential humanity shared by the sexes. Surely, "difference" may be interpreted to refer to what is distinctive in women's lives and works, *including* what makes them essentially human; unless, of course, we remain captivated by the notion that the standard model for humanity is male.

37. Although opponents of feminist criticism often find it convenient to characterize such works as a personal attack on authors, for feminist critics themselves, the primary consideration is the function of the text as a carrier of patriarchal ideology, and its effect as such especially (but not exclusively) on women readers. The personal culpability of the author is a relatively minor issue.

38. Harold Bloom, *Kabbalah and Criticism* (New York: Seabury, 1975), p. 126.

39. Poulet, "Criticism and the Experience of Interiority," p. 46.

40. Ibid., p. 47. As Culler has pointed out, the theme of control is prominent in mainstream reader-response criticism. Poulet's story is no exception. The issue of control is important in another way. Behind the question of whether the text controls the reader or vice versa is the question of how to regulate literary criticism. If the text is controlling, then there is no problem. The text itself will regulate the process of reading. But if the text is not necessarily controlling, then, how do we constrain the activities of readers and critics? How can we rule out "off-the-wall" interpretations? Fish's answer is of interest to feminist critics. The constraints, he says, are exercised not by the text, but by the institutions within which literary criticism is situated. It is but a small step from this idea to the realization of the necessarily political character of literature and criticism.

41. The use of the personal conversational tone has been regarded as a hallmark of feminist criticism. However, as Jean E. Kennard has pointed out ("Personally Speaking: Feminist Critics and the Community of Readers," *College English* 43 [1981]: 140–45), this theoretical commitment is not apparent in the overwhelming majority of feminist critical essays. Kennard found only five articles in which the critic "overtly locates herself on the page." (To the five she found, I would add three works cited in this essay: "Women, Energy, and *Middlemarch*," by Lee Edwards; "Feminism and Literature," by Florence Howe; and "Vesuvius at Home," by Adrienne Rich.) Kennard observes further that, even in the handful of essays she found, the personal tone is confined to a few introductory paragraphs. She asks: "If feminist criticism has on the whole remained faithful to familiar methods and tone, why have the few articles with an overt personal voice loomed so large in our minds?" Kennard suggests that these personal introductions are invitations "to share a critical response which depends upon unstated, shared beliefs and, to a large extent, experience; that of being a female educated in a male tradition in which she is no longer comfortable." Thus, these introductory paragraphs do not indicate a "transformed critical methodology; they are devices for transforming the reader. I read the later portions of these essays— and by extension other feminist criticism—in a different way because I have been invited to participate in the underground. . . . I am part of a community of feminist readers" (pp. 143–44).

I would offer another explanation, one that is not necessarily inconsistent with

Kennard's. I think the use of a personal and conversational tone represents an overt gesture indicating the dialogic mode of discourse as the "regulative ideal" for all feminist discourse. The few essays—indeed, the few introductory paragraphs—that assert this regulative ideal are memorable because they strike a chord in a significant segment of the community of feminist critics. To the extent that we have been touched or transformed by this idea, it will be implicit in the way we read the works of others, in particular, the works of other women. Although the ideal must be overtly affirmed periodically, it is not necessary to do so in all of our essays. It remains potent as long as it is assumed by a significant portion of the community. I would argue with Kennard's distinction between indicators of a transformed critical methodology and devices for transforming the reader. To the extent that critical methodology is a function of the conventions implicitly or explicitly operating in an interpretive community—that is, of the way members of the community conceive of their work and of the way they read each other—devices for transforming readers are also devices for transforming critical methodology.

42. Jean Baker Miller, *Toward a New Psychology of Women* (Boston: Beacon Press, 1976); and Nancy Chodorow, *The Reproduction of Mothering: Psychoanalysis and the Sociology of Gender* (Berkeley and Los Angeles: University of California Press, 1978); and Carol Gilligan, *In a Different Voice: Psychological Theory and Women's Development* (Cambridge: Harvard University Press, 1982).

43. I am using here Jürgen Habermas's definition of truth or validity as a claim (implicit in the act of making assertions) that is redeemable through discourse—specifically, through the domination-free discourse of an "ideal speech situation." For Habermas, consensus attained through a domination-free discourse is the warrant for truth. See "Wahrheitstheorien," in *Wirklichkeit und Reflexion: Walter Schulz zum 60. Geburtstag* (Pfullingen: Nesge, 1973), pp. 211–65. I am indebted to Alan Soble's unpublished translation of this essay.

FEMINISM, NEW HISTORICISM, AND THE READER

(1991)

The relation between feminist criticism and New Historicism is a peculiar one, exciting considerable interest and curiosity (not to say unease) and, especially in English Renaissance studies, occasioning some unusually acrimonious polemics. The acrimony has to do, at least in part, with the marginal status accorded by one to the other: figuring in each other's discourse at best as a point of departure and at worst as an *overlooked* point of departure. New Historicists and feminists seem to talk at cross purposes, keeping their mutual distance, relegating each other to a kind of non-presence.[1] If the feminist chronicling of women's oppression and celebration of women's difference have appeared misguided to many New Historicists, the New Historicist universalization of power and blurring of genders have struck many feminists as nothing short of reactionary.[2]

In this essay I want to rethink the relation between feminist criticism and New Historicism, using that *relation*, in turn, as a leverage point, an artificially concocted but no less serviceable juncture from which and against which both critical enterprises might be evaluated, held up for mutual reflection, and perhaps for mutual realignment. Eventually I want to challenge not only their supposed disagreement but also their presumed distinction, to show that the discrete identity imputed to each in fact impoverishes both. Still, it is useful, at the outset, to rehearse those presumed distinctions and supposed disagreements, if only to bring into focus some of the tacit premises that have given rise to so much hostility and mistrust. I begin, then, with an imaginary confrontation between New Historicism and feminist criticism, dressed up momentarily as parties at war, and, for dramatic effect, I stage the battle over the body of that most familiar and cherished of figures: the figure of the reader.

Or perhaps I should say, familiar and cherished by one side. For feminist critics as different as Nina Baym and Annette Kolodny, Margaret Homans and Louise Rosenblatt, Janice Radway and Cathy N. Davidson, the figure of the reader has served as a crucial organizing center: a site of contestation, a site of celebration, and a site from which to construct an alternative canon.[3] This is not true of New Historicists, who, preoccupied as they are with the sociocultural field at the text's moment of production (rather than its moment of reception), have been much less concerned with the reader either as a figure of the past or as a figure of the present moment.[4] Partly to redress the imbalance, and partly to manufacture an occasion for war, I begin with a more or less caricatured appearance of the reader in a more or less caricatured New Historicist exercise, one designed to be uncongenial to feminists.

My starting point, however, is neither a feminist text nor a New Historicist one, but an important (and eminently nonpartisan) essay by Steven Marcus called "Reading the Illegible." Marcus uses the paradigm of reading to describe a cultural phenomenon generated by the complexity of modern life, which "not perceived as a coherent system of signs," demands to be read—to be organized and interpreted—into some semblance of clarity and order.[5] In the specific example Marcus analyzes, the subject for reading happens to be the urban landscape, but, beyond that, he seems also to be giving us a definition of reading in the broadest sense of the word, taking it beyond the generic boundaries of the literary text, and using it to include a wide range of activities, activities that have to do with the interpretation of signs, the adjudication of meanings, and the construction of reality. Understood in this nongeneric sense, reading might be said to be a phenomenon peculiar to modernity. Unlike the medieval preoccupation with exegesis and the Puritan preoccupation with typology, reading in its modern guise is not centered on or authorized by one particular text, least of all the Bible. Modern society is a society of interpretation, interpretation at once deregulated and *de rigueur*,[6] for in this world, a world increasingly acted upon by forces unknown and unseen, and increasingly removed from our immediate comprehension, all of us, whether or not we accept the label, have to become readers of sorts. Indeed, from the mid-nineteenth century onward, reading might be said to be one of the most commonplace cultural activities, an activity dictated by the mysteries of modern life, by the gap, at once titillating and worrisome, between immediate experience and apprehended meaning, between what we see and what we think it signifies.[7]

Still, if all of us are readers, and if reading is what we do every minute of our lives, the phenomenon cannot be very interesting. What makes it interesting, a subject worthy of historical analysis, is its emergence, in its modern, nongeneric form, as a field that sustains and indeed requires special knowledge, a field where the recession of meaning goes hand in hand with the concentration of expertise, and where standards of competence are erected over and against an illiteracy that is, paradoxically, the rule rather than the exception. The rise of the medical profession is a dramatic case in point. As we learn from Paul Starr's magisterial study, *The Social Transformation of American Medicine*, the spectacular ascent of physicians both in social status and in economic power had everything to do with their ability to institute a new set of reading conventions, conventions that established not only their own expertise, but also the lack of it in those they served. From being a more or less marginal, more or less disreputable group up to the mid-nineteenth century, medical practitioners effectively solidified their identity—by regulating certification and licensing and by building an elaborate system of specialized knowledge, technical procedures, and rules of behavior—so that, by the second half of the nineteenth century, the profession had come to occupy a central place in American society, and their success was reflected, according to Starr, not only in their authority over the "construction of reality," the "interpretation of experience," and the "meaning of things," but also in the medical illiteracy of those they served, ordinary people who were incapable of reading their own symptoms and who had to defer to the judgment of these more qualified, or at least more certified, experts.[8]

The American Medical Association was not alone in its triumph. The same half-century also saw the rise of other professional groups, most notably the American Bar Association, as well as other organizations less powerful and less prosperous, such as the American Historical Association, the American Economic Association, and, of course, the MLA.[9] As the names of these august institutions suggest, the rise of professional communities has everything to do with the redistribution of social authority. And, whether we call such authority "professional sovereignty" (as Paul Starr does) or "professional jurisdiction" (as Andrew Abbott does),[10] it would seem to be predicated on a set of reading conventions, on the authority of expert readers, and conversely, on the dependency of the illiterate. Indeed the rise of professionalism—a phenomenon that has fascinated sociologists from Émile Durkheim to Talcott Parsons to Daniel Bell[11]—might also be described as the rise of a new way of reading, with a new way of organizing knowledge and a new way of structuring authority.

Given the centrality of reading in a culture of professionalism, one obvious way to historicize the literary reader is to ask whether this figure inhabits a structure of authority comparable to that inhabited by its nonfictive counterparts, by the professionals who also happen to be expert readers. Along those lines, a New Historicist might be tempted to pursue a set of interrelated questions: In a culture more generally governed by the ideal of interpretive competence, what sort of *literary* reading conventions might we expect to find? If interpretation is itself a valuable social asset, an asset whose usefulness extends far beyond the domain of the literary, how might it in turn shape the literary domain? Do reading conventions in texts generate structures of authority in the same way that reading conventions in the social realm do? And are we prepared to argue that such structures are historically specific, that there might be a textual structure that would answer to the structure of authority underwritten by professionalism?

Charlotte Perkins Gilman's "The Yellow Wallpaper," a story that has inspired numerous feminist readings,[12] turns out, from this perspective, also to be an ideal text for an imaginary New Historicist exercise, ideal not only because this is a story told by a mad narrator and therefore one that foregrounds the question of interpretive authority, and not only because there is actually a doctor in the story, but also because, by a happy coincidence, Gilman herself happened to be a paragon of professionalism in the late nineteenth century. For about thirteen years of her life, from 1887 to 1900, between the time she left her first husband and the time she married her second, Gilman supported herself in California, making a living as an editor of magazines (the *Impress* and the *Forerunner*), a veteran on the lecture circuit, and a respected authority on the economics of housework.[13] Between 1898 and 1904 she published four books on the subject, including *Women and Economics* (1898), *Concerning Children* (1900), *The Home: Its Work and Influence* (1903), and *Human Work* (1904). In the tradition of the scientific homemaking movement (a movement begun by Catharine Beecher in the 1840s and reaching its zenith in the early twentieth century), Gilman believes that housework should be professionalized, arguing that this would secure not only gender equality for women, but, just as important, managerial efficiency for the home.[14] Her lifelong interest in architectural design reflects the same faith in professionalism.[15] For her, ideal apartment houses should provide "trained professional service" for "professional women with families"; they should have no kitchens, so that cooking would be done not by women but by professional cooks; and they should provide supervised cleaning by "efficient workers" hired by "the manager of the establishment," as well as day-care administered by "well-trained professional nurses."[16] Indeed, for her, the goals of feminism can be achieved only through the agency of professionalism, only by bringing specialized knowledge, rational authority, and administrative expertise to the home.

In itself, Gilman's commitment to professionalism is hardly remarkable. What is remarkable, however, is the apparent discrepancy between *Women and Economics* (1898) and "The Yellow Wallpaper" (1892), written just six years before. In this story about mental collapse, a story that ends with the narrator crawling on all fours, where is the redeeming hand of professionalism? And, when we witness the terrible mistakes of the husband (who, of course, is a doctor), and when we see what befalls him at the end, are we not supposed to lose faith in the very ground of professional authority?

These questions, perplexing as they might seem, are actually not impossible to answer, especially if we are willing to entertain the possibility that the husband might not be the only model of professional authority, and that another, more commendable figure might be lurking behind the scene. In any case, it is surely significant that the husband is not just a doctor but an emphatically bad one. This means, of course, that he is a bad reader, who, when confronted with a set of symptoms, repeatedly fails to come up with the right interpretation. As his wife becomes crazier and crazier, he becomes more and more optimistic in his diagnosis. Indeed he tells her: "But you really are better, dear, whether you can see it or not. I am a doctor, dear, and I know." And he adds, "Can you not trust me as a physician when I tell you so?"[17]

Over and over again, the husband urges his wife to trust the soundness of his judgment by reminding her that as a doctor he has an interpretive authority over her life. But the point, of course, is that he really has no such authority, because, being a bad reader, he should never have been a doctor in the first place.[18] What makes him a villain of sorts, then, is not so much that he is a cruel husband as that he is an incompetent doctor. But if he is giving professionalism a bad name here, there is no reason why that bad name should be the last word on the subject. Indeed, the very fact that he is such a noticeably unworthy specimen should alert us to the possibility that there might be a worthier example somewhere else, a professional who not only occupies a position of authority, but actually has a legitimate claim to it.

Where might such an alternative position be found, what would be its structure of authority, and who would be the privileged figure within that structure? If we look for it merely within the actualized fictional world of "The Yellow Wallpaper," only within that immanent structure where every available position is occupied by a particular character, we are bound to be disappointed, I think, because neither the mad narrator, nor the husband the doctor, nor the sister-in-law can claim to be a figure of authority. However, if we were to think of "The Yellow Wallpaper" as a compositional structure—as a structure generated by a mode of rhetorical address—we might indeed argue for an alternative position, a position that is invisible, unembodied, and yet existing as an object of inference or perhaps even as a structural predicate. Such a position, we might further argue, can indeed function as a virtual repository where the absent attributes of professionalism—rational authority, expert knowledge, and interpretive competence—can be securely lodged.

As must be obvious by now, such a virtual position can be occupied only by one figure. In the absence of any competent reader inside the story, it is the outside reader—or, I should say, the implied reader—who is called upon to occupy the position of interpretive authority, functioning both as the text's ideal recipient and its necessary coordinate. As my vocabulary suggests, what is being invoked here is the model of reading associated with Wolfgang Iser, invoked in order to provide a supplement to the more familiar model of positionality, and to suggest an opening, a point of exit from the closed system of the text. Such a procedure, of course, runs the risk of conjuring up an idealized reader. Even more dangerously, at least to my mind, it also runs the opposite risk, that is, of turning the reader into a strictly textual phenomenon, strictly immanent within the text and ontologically dependent upon its functions, and so returning once again to a textual system of absolute closure.[19]

To reduce such risks, it is helpful to supplement Iser, in turn, with Tony Bennett's concept of the "reading formation." By this Bennett means a set of determinations which "mediate the relation between text and context, connecting the two and providing the mechanisms . . . , [the] intertexual and discursive relations which produce readers for texts and texts for readers."[20] Bennett's concept is especially important here, because, in speaking of reading as a "formation," a reciprocal process by which readers and texts are mutually produced and mutually productive, he also restores a dialectical agency to the reading process, claiming for it a larger operating field as well as a larger instrumental effect.

This emphasis—on the dialectical agency of reading, on the interplay between production and reception—seems to be crucial in any attempt to historicize the reader. It is also crucial, I think, to any historical criticism (including New Historicism, though not confined to it) that, for various political or philosophical reasons, might wish not to reduce subject-positions merely to structural effects, merely to something that is given or entailed. Unlike Iser's model, which remains hostage to a system of textual immanence, Bennett's model is structurally contingent but not necessarily structurally determinate. It constitutes the reader not only as a figure of structural dictate but also as a figure of structural potential.

Of course, in "The Yellow Wallpaper" the subject-position we are trying to imagine happens not at all to be a critical position but rather an authoritative one, which, as we have seen, none of the characters can occupy. But, as we have also seen, there is nonetheless a virtual position, commanded by a virtual figure. After all, quite aside from the meager cast of three characters, isn't someone else there as well, invisible to the others, but necessary to the unfolding of the text, someone who can do what the others seem incapable of doing for themselves, that is, interpret their story for them? When we come to the end of the story, when the husband is lying on the floor and the wife is crawling around, isn't someone else still sitting, still sane and still rational, whose sanity and rationality are the very credentials by which she can diagnose the ailments of these characters? Against the pathetic benightedness of all the characters in the story—who can hardly tell what is delusion or hallucination from what is "real"—isn't someone else always there with open eyes, always granted a clear knowledge, both of the "reality" of the wife's madness and of the "reality" of the marital situation? And against the husband's less than professional expertise, isn't someone else always make a competent judgment or, should we say, a competent reading?

The position of authority in "The Yellow Wallpaper" is occupied by the reader, and, we might add, not just any reader but a reader with a specific and historically recognizable profile, created in the image of professionalism at its most idealized, endowed with the sacred attributes of specialized knowledge and interpretive competence. To return, then, to my initial question about whether or not there might be a textual structure that would answer to the structure of authority underwritten by professionalism, the answer would seem to be yes. Indeed, one is almost obligated here to argue that, in the literary domain, what is professionalized is not just the careers of authors, but, less tangible though no less significantly, the literary form itself, which, in the case of "The Yellow Wallpaper," comprises a network of knowledge between author and reader, a network maintained largely at the expense of the characters in the story. Along those lines, one would have to argue that the literary domain is not really distinct from the social domain, that by a homologous process professionalism would seem also to have inscribed a differential structure here, a structure of authority and dependency. Within the text, the characters are "professionalized," in the sense that they are organized into fields of subjectivities, which is also to say, fields of knowledge. They become subjects for us to know. And, presiding over the text, administering to its interpretation, is the reader, professionalized in the more familiar sense of the word, in the sense that she is assigned a privileged position, a position of readerly expertise and readerly knowledge.

Here, then, is the New Historicist reading, much simplified, to be sure, but still recognizable as such in its Foucauldian grid of power, knowledge, and subjectivity, and in its view of subjectivity as the determinate effect of discursive formations whose structural totality generates, saturates, and circumscribes all individual practices.[21] Such a reading would have argued that "The Yellow Wallpaper" is a text embedded in and structured by the culture of professionalism, a text in which the unequal distribution of knowledge and the unequal distribution of authority are reproduced in its very literary form. Along those lines, such an argument would also have theorized about the homologous genesis of social and literary forms, about the power relations inscribed in such forms, and about the permeable boundary, or perhaps even the lack of boundary, between the literary and the social.

This is an argument I did make when I taught the book, but it is also an argument I now want to resist making.[22] Or rather, it is an argument I want both to make and to unmake, both to set forth and to destabilize. And one way to destabilize that argument, I think, is to consider the gender of the reader. I have been referring to the reader as a "she"; this is not so much a polemical posture on my part as a deferential gesture to Gilman, because this is the pronoun she herself would have used.

In a little essay called "Why I Wrote 'The Yellow Wallpaper,'" Gilman explained why she had to write the book. She herself, she said, had been subjected to the "rest cure" administered by Dr. S. Weir Mitchell, the same treatment the narrator was subject to, and it had left her "so near the borderline of utter mental ruin that I could see over." What saved her, and what restored to her "some mea-sure of power," was her decision to defy the doctor and to go back to work— "work, the normal life of every human being; work, in which is joy and growth and service, without which one is a pauper and a parasite." And it was in the spirit of work that she wrote "The Yellow Wallpaper." She wrote it, she said, "to save people from being driven crazy, and it worked."[23] In a later essay, she also ex-plained for whose benefit all this work was being done: "One girl reads this, and takes fire! Her life is changed. She becomes a power—a mover of others—I write for her."[24]

What difference does it make to specify a "she" here, or, to put the question more generally, what difference does it make to introduce the category of gender into the paradigm of reading? A big difference, I think. Because if we are going to acknowledge that the implied reader in "The Yellow Wallpaper" is not just a professional but also a woman, we will also have to ask whether such a conjunc-tion was actually in place when the story was being written, whether gender and occupational identity did indeed coincide and coalesce at that particular histori-cal moment. Once we put the question that way, it becomes clear that there is in fact an interesting mismatch between the two defining attributes of the implied reader. At the turn of the century, the professional who was also a woman was a rare breed indeed. Professionalism was something denied to women and some-thing they were trying to attain. No women practiced law before the 1870s, and as late as 1873, the Supreme Court still upheld a decision by the Illinois Supreme Court to refuse Myra Bradwell admission to the Illinois bar solely on the grounds that she was woman.[25] Meanwhile, women made up no more than 2.8 percent of the medical profession in 1880, and even by 1900 the figure was a mere 5.6 per-cent.[26] The reader in "The Yellow Wallpaper" who is both a woman and a pro-fessional is very much an ideal reader, not only in the sense that she is the right reader, but also in the sense that she is not quite real yet, not quite there in the flesh.

It is in this gap—in the non-identity between the ideal reader invoked by the story and the actual women reading it—that we can speak of the dialectical agency of the text, or, to use a more familiar phrase, of its cultural work. For, given such a gap, a gap between the putative and the actual, doesn't the story have its work cut out? Isn't that gap both the space within which the story labors, and the space that it labors to narrow and eventually to eliminate? As Gilman's own re-peated celebration of "work" suggests, the idea is hardly foreign to her. "The Yellow Wallpaper," then, is not just the product of a culture of professionalism, not just an inert index; it is also a transformative agency, with the power to pro-duce effects of its own. It has that power because, within a gendered paradigm, the structure of professional authority it ostensibly relies upon is actually some-thing it is in the process of bringing into being. Its supposed ground turns out to be its desired consequence. A feminist reading of the story would focus on the reader, not as a site of homologous formation, not as the locus from which we can see a line of continuity between the text and the culture of professionalism, but as a figure constituted by a deliberate and enabling gap, a gap that, even as it shadows forth the temporal distance between what the female reader is and what she might become, also restores to the text the possibility of agency in the world.

I have dramatized the disagreement between a New Historicist and a feminist reading not to show that one is victorious over the other but to make a different—and somewhat paradoxical—point, namely, that the two readings are in fact not at odds, that, in some sense, they are not even adjacent, since the two phenomena that they describe turn out to be nonadjacent in the first place. This nonadjacency comes about because, even granting the primacy of a culture of professionalism, we must still point to a temporal discrepancy—a noncoincidence between what Raymond Williams calls the dominant, the residual, and the emergent—within that historical formation.[27] To the extent that "The Yellow Wallpaper" is conditioned by history, this "history" must itself be seen not as a field of synchronized unity but as a field of uneven development. The professionalism that prevails in one instance as a dominant standard can figure in another instance only as an emerging potential.[28] Given this structure of delays and relays—this nonadjacency between the established and the deferred—professionalism and feminism might be said to be in contact only through the mediated space of a temporal lag.

Even if we are to focus on a figure that seems common to both—the figure of the reader—we are still bound to encounter not a unified entity but a sedimented construct, a figure traversed by time and dispersed in time, making its staggered appearances in a variety of stages, in its residual, established, and emergent forms, and through its inflections by class, gender, and race.[29] There are readers and readers, it would seem, and, when we meditate on their points of divergence as well as their points of coincidence, when we think about their uneven genesis, conflicting identities, and different modes of reception, "history" itself will have to be reconceived as something less than homogeneous, something less than synchronized.

This, at least to my mind, is one way to understand that well-known phrase "the textuality of history."[30] By this phrase we usually refer to the idea that the past is transmitted by texts, that it can never be recovered or apprehended as a lived totality. Here I want to use the phrase in a somewhat different sense, focusing not on the process of textual transmission but on the dynamics of historical development, on its sedimented, non-uniform, and therefore untotalizable *texture*. History itself has a texture, I argue, because at any given moment there is a precarious conjunction of the "has been" and the "not yet," the "already" and the "probably," a conjunction brought into play by the very passage of time, by the uneven velocities and shifting densities of social change. To historicize a text, then, is also to recover those uneven velocities and shifting densities, to deconstruct its spatial unity into a virtual (and uncharted) sequence, a momentary conjunction of temporal traces, with no particular center of gravity and no particular teleology. Any reading that tries to lock the text into a single posture—to impute to it a center and teleology—can do so only through an act of historical repression, only by turning a temporal relation of multiple sedimentation into a spatial relation of either opposition or containment.[31]

But—and this is a "but" that needs to be rendered in large print—if we are indeed committed to the idea of multiple sedimentation, as a practical program rather than a polemical statement, what we must then proceed to challenge, it would seem, is not just the model of containment associated with New Historicism but also the model of opposition associated with feminism. After all, it is not just New Historicism that threatens to lock the text into a single posture.

Feminism (or, I should say, a certain brand of feminism, what its critics call essentialist feminism) threatens to do much the same thing, though obviously from the other direction. In celebrating gender as the ground of difference and in identifying the female as the positive term within this topography of difference, feminism also comes dangerously close to reifying gender into a binary opposition, and reifying opposition itself into a unitary term.

The shortcomings of essentialist feminism have been pointed out, most emphatically by Toril Moi, and they are indeed such as to deserve emphasis.[32] Still, the phrase "essentialist feminism" might be guilty of doing some essentializing of its own, since the so-called essentialist feminists are by no means as rigid or ossified as their critics would like to make out.[33] What concerns me, then, is not the merit or shortcoming of individual practitioners so much as the general term "feminism" itself, and it is this that I want to interrogate and unsettle. I want to bring a kind of heuristic weight to bear on the meaning of this word, to test its contents and its contours, and to ask to what extent a "feminist" project can be understood as a self-sufficient and autonomous enterprise.

Indeed, playing the devil's advocate now, I want to deconstruct the neat opposition I have so far relied upon—the opposition between New Historicism and feminist criticism—and, with that in mind, I return to the second reading with the question, What is so "feminist" about it? Such a question, I hope, is not without its shock effect. Most people, it is safe to say, will immediately label the second reading "feminist," not only because it has vindicated both Gilman and "The Yellow Wallpaper" but also because, in singling out the female reader as the text's privileged reader and in locating the text's agency in the trajectory of that figure, it has claimed for gender a centrally determinative (and indeed centrally redemptive) status. In all these respects, it is identifiably feminist, tracing its genealogy most directly to Annette Kolodny's essay "A Map for Rereading: Gender and the Interpretation of Literary Texts," an essay instrumental in forging a new critical paradigm, the paradigm of gender and reading. Within this paradigm, the relation between two terms once considered separate—gender and reading—is now understood to be neither fortuitous nor incidental but primary and constitutive. Gender, that is to say, enters into the reading process not as an external or even secondary consideration, but as an organizing principle, as the perceptual coordinates by which details are selected and meaning imposed, in short, as the cognitive ground shaping an entire field of vision.

Kolodny's essay has inspired and informed an entire generation of feminist critics. And yet, to those of us sensitized to the danger of essentialism, the essay also comes very close to embodying just those dangers. In introducing the category of gender into the reading process, Kolodny not only dismantles an older model, one that universalizes reading, but also puts a new one in its place, one that foregrounds gender differential and proceeds, on that basis, to separate reading into two distinct and distinctive modes, using gender, of course, as the line of division. What she emphasizes, accordingly, is the mutual illegibility between genders, and, more particularly, the illegibility of a female text to male readers. Summing up "The Yellow Wallpaper" and "A Jury of Her Peers" (a story by Susan Keating Glaspell), Kolodny suggests that while neither story "necessarily excludes the male as reader—indeed, both in a way are directed specifically at educating him to become a better reader—they do nonetheless insist that, however inadvertently, he is a *different kind* of reader and that, where women are concerned, he is often an inadequate reader."[34]

"A different kind of reader": the phrase is resounding but also problematic, because, in positing gender simply as a category of *difference*—simply as the ground of distinction between two discrete terms—Kolodny has put herself on the edge (and, some would say, over the edge) of a binary opposition, opposing male to female, and, in so doing, constituting each of them into a stable and unified identity. Gender, in short, operates as a principle of reification here, and it is within the reified landscape that Kolodny can speak of "male texts" and "female meaning" as if they were discrete and substantive terms.

All the same, it is a mistake simply to find fault with Kolodny or to critique her on absolute grounds. Rather, her critical practice must itself be contextualized, must be seen, that is, against the background of its inception, in 1980, when feminist theory was just beginning to emerge as a newly articulated and not fully legitimized form of discourse, one that had to struggle not just for visibility but also for a kind of internal coherence. If Kolodny's differential map of gender came close to being a binary opposition, and if her appeal to female unity came close to reifying female identity, those dangers were nonetheless necessary, and perhaps even beneficial, in an emerging discourse that was still struggling to be heard, still struggling to claim for itself a recognizable voice and a recognizable profile. Within this context, the traditional feminist appeal to "female experience" or to "the women's tradition" bespeaks not a theoretical naivete but a tactical wisdom.[35] By the same token, however, it is also understandable why a new generation of feminists writing today should feel the urgent need *not* to think about gender simply as a category of identity (which is also to say, not to think about gender simply as a category of difference): why Eve Sedgwick, for instance, would want to invoke the notion of the "continuum" in order to describe the mobile distribution of sexual identities and the asymmetrical structuring of gender relations; why Alice Jardine would choose to analyze "woman" as signifying effect rather than as originary subject; why Judith Butler would argue for a feminism that deconstructs the very concept of "identity" itself; and why Mary Poovey would seize upon the idea of "uneven development" to emphasize the unstable ideological work of gender, its nonuniform institutional articulations, and hence its inability, at any given moment, to achieve anything like a totalization of the social field.[36]

I hope that by now I have contextualized my own reading of "The Yellow Wallpaper" as well. Indebted to the paradigm of gender and reading but mindful of its potentially reifying hazards, I have tried not to posit a binary opposition between male and female reader, not to homogenize difference within the field of gender.[37] Instead I have tried to mobilize and multiply the grounds of difference, to analyze it as a relational and sequential rather than substantive phenomenon, and hence not a phenomenon that can be imputed to any single generative site or fixated along any single line of demarcation. What I have come up with, then, is a figure of internal difference,[38] who in this case happens to be the female reader, a figure not quite professionalized yet, not quite what she is supposed to be, and mobilized, therefore, by the very force of incipience, by the discrepancy which both constitutes and destabilizes her temporal being. Suspended between the dominant and the dormant, lagging behind the male reader but not willing to remain there for good, such an emerging figure also collapses the binary oppo-sition between genders into a complexly imbricated and complexly sequential play of identity and difference.

And yet, to what extent is this female reader a *feminist* construct? It is a figure that pleases feminists, to be sure, one that is heartwarming and edifying to con-jure up. Still, if this figure embodies an internal gap, as I have tried to argue, a gap that redeems both the text and the author, this redeeming feature is none-theless not the effect of gender organization but the effect of temporal discrep-ancy. In other words, what makes the female reader the locus of "not yet"—what suspends her between the "not" and the "yet" and preserves her as an indeter-minate and therefore untotalized quantum—is not the agency of gender but the agency of history. Or, to be more precise, we might say that the agency of gender is itself historical, because it is history—understood as the medium of sequence, succession, and sedimentation—that produces the space between the "not" and the "yet," within which gender can operate as a principle of difference.

To put it this way is also to see how symbiotic "gender" and "history" are and how unfruitful it is to oppose a feminist reading to a historicist reading. Indeed, in order not to reify gender into an unvarying category of difference and in order not to limit difference to an unvarying site of production, a feminist reading must also be a historical reading. It must try, that is, not just to describe or taxonomize difference but also to trace its shifting contexts, modalities, and operative axes. It must study the changing pattern, throughout history, of what functions as dif-ference and what counts as difference. In short, what I am emphasizing here is the grounding of gender in time, a grounding that is simultaneously its unset-tling. Gender is most useful as an analytic category when it is seen as a temporal (and temporary) construct, when it is understood to be constituted in time and constrained by time, propelled by temporal necessity and subject to temporal reconfiguration.

Does that mean, then, that gender is completely subsumed by history and that a feminist reading is really no more than a historicist reading? This is a formula-tion I want to resist as well. If the relation between feminism and historicism is not one of categoric opposition, neither is it one of categoric subordination. For just as a vigorous historicizing of gender reorients the entire concept, so a vigor-ous engendering of history transforms the very meaning of what it is to be his-torical. Gender, that is, is to be understood not as an incidental addition to a stable historical field but as a principle productive of uneven textures, productive of the discrepancy between the dominant and the emergent, inflecting and disturbing the very shape of historical time, challenging not only normative temporality but also its spatial disposition of margins and limits. Since I have labored thus far to show that history is crucial as a category of gender studies, I want to turn my at-tention now to the other side of the argument—which also happens to echo the title of an important essay by Joan Wallach Scott—namely, that gender is equally crucial as a category of historical analysis.[39]

It is helpful here, in fact, to return to the New Historicist reading offered ear-lier in the essay, the reading that was inspected, found wanting, and set aside. What is it that makes that reading so unsatisfactory? The problem, I submit, is not that it is too historical but that it is not historical enough. Indeed, the charge of essentialism, so often leveled at feminism, can be directed against this reading as well, against its tendency to reify power relations within the literary *form* itself, as if power could inhere in a form and be ontological to that form, independent of the shifting contexts in which it figures, the varying uses to which it is put, and the changing audiences it speaks to and for. This essentializing tendency in New Historicism reinstates the very timelessness which it sets out to critique. The text, that is, is imaged here as an atemporal circulatory medium, ceaselessly negotiating with its synchronic social forms but otherwise untempered by diachronic inflections, untempered by the destabilizing effects of the passage of time.

The absence of the diachronic in New Historicism is regrettable but also forgivable, since a truly historical understanding—one based not on the knowledge of particular events but on the ability to generalize about continuity and change, to discern the shape of temporal movement and the facilitating conditions for that shape—is a gift rare not only among critics but (if I might say so) among historians as well. But it is precisely here, against this incapacity or impasse, that gender can intervene as a category of historical analysis, as a conceptual vehicle that urges upon us a version of the diachronic, more local and more modest, perhaps, but no less vital. For if gender is indeed to be understood as a principle of unevenness, as a fault line along which normative temporality is broken up, decentered, and dispersed into various stages of the residual, the dominant, and the emergent, any historical inquiry that takes gender as its analytic coordinate will also come to grips with that fractured temporality, which is to say it will be diachronic, the diachronicity here being generated not so much by the subject itself as by the analytic frame, which breaks up the seeming unity of time into its multiple sediments and infinite relays. In the case of "The Yellow Wallpaper," it is the gendered reader, understood both as a historical figure and as a historied figure, that provides the point of entry for this radically destabilized sense of time. But, speaking more generally, we might also say that gender, as a principle of unevenness, will be important for any attempt to conceptualize history, not as a homologous or synchronized formation but as field of endless mutations and permutations, a field where the temporal nonidentity between cause and effect and the structural nonidentity between system and subject quite literally open up a space for alternatives, however visionary and unsustained. History, thus engendered and thus decentered, is anything but a totalizing category. In fact, it is not even over and done with, but a realm of unexhausted and inexhaustible possibility.

NOTES

1. This is a crude generalization, needless to say, but, at least to my mind, it described the work of leading New Historicists such as Stephen Greenblatt and Walter Benn Michaels and the work of leading feminists such as Sandra Gilbert and Susan Gubar. Also needless to say, there are important exceptions here. For New Historicist work in American Studies that addresses gender, see Richard Brodhead, "Sparing the Rod: Discipline and Fiction in Antebellum America," *Representations*, 21 (1988), 67–96; Gillian Brown, "The Empire of Agoraphobia," *Representations*, 20 (1987), 134–57; T. Walter Herbert, "Nathaniel Hawthorne, Una Hawthorne, and *The Scarlet Letter*: Interactive Selfhoods and the Cultural

Construction of Gender," *PMLA*, 103 (1988), 285–97; Myra Jehlen, "The Ties that Bind: Race and Sex in *Pudd'nhead Wilson*," *American Literary History*, 2 (1990), 39–55; David Leverenz, *Manhood and the American Renaissance* (Ithaca: Cornell Univ. Press, 1989).

2. For an implicit New Historicist critique of feminists, see Walter Benn Michaels, *The Gold Standard and the Logic of Naturalism* (Berkeley: Univ. of California Press, 1987), pp. 3–28, 217–44. For a more explicit critique, see Jonathan Goldberg, "Shakespearean Inscriptions: The Voicing of Power," in *Shakespeare and the Question of Theory*, ed. Patricia Parker and Geoffrey Hartman (New York: Methuen, 1985), pp. 116–37. For feminist critiques of New Historicists, see Lynda E. Boose, "The Family in Shakespeare Studies; or—Studies in the Family of Shakespeareans; or—The Politics of Politics," *Renaissance Quarterly*, 40 (1987), 707–42, especially 727–42; Marguerite Waller, "Academic Tootsie: The Denial of Difference and the Difference it Makes," *Diacritics*, 17 (1987), 2–20; Judith Lowder Newton, "History as Usual? Feminism and the 'New Historicism,'" in *The New Historicism*, ed. H. Aram Veeser (New York: Routledge, 1989), pp. 152–67.

3. Nina Baym, "Melodramas of Beset Manhood: How Theories of American Fiction Exclude Women Authors," *American Quarterly*, 33 (1981), 123–39; Annette Kolodny, "A Map for Rereading: Or, Gender and the Interpretation of Literary Texts," *New Literacy History*, 11 (1980), 451–67, reprinted in *The New Feminist Criticism*, ed. Elaine Showalter (New York: Pantheon, 1985), pp. 46–62, and Kolodny, "Dancing Through the Minefield: Some Observations on the Theory, Practice, and Politics of a Feminist Literary Criticism," *Feminist Studies*, 6 (1980), 1–25; Margaret Homans, "Eliot, Wordsworth, and the Scenes of the Sister's Instruction," *Critical Inquiry*, 8 (1981), 223–41; Louise Rosenblatt, *The Reader, The Text, the Poem: The Transactional Theory of the Literary Work* (Carbondale: Southern Illinois Univ. Press, 1978); Janice Radway, *Reading the Romance: Women, Patriarchy, and Popular Literature* (Chapel Hill: Univ. of North Carolina Press, 1984); Cathy N. Davidson, *Revolution and the Word* (New York: Oxford Univ. Press, 1986). See also a useful collection, *Gender and Reading*, ed. Elizabeth Flynn and Patrocinio P. Schweickart (Baltimore: Johns Hopkins Univ. Press, 1986).

4. On this point, see Brook Thomas, *The New Historicism and Other Old-Fashioned Topics* (Princeton: Princeton Univ. Press, 1991). Significantly, this is *not* true of feminist New Historicists, who have been very attentive indeed to the figure of the reader. See, for example, Nancy Armstrong, *Desire and Domestic Fiction* (New York: Oxford Univ. Press, 1987); Cathy N. Davidson, *Revolution and the Word*; Jane Tompkins, *Sensational Designs: The Cultural Work of American Fiction* (New York: Oxford Univ. Press, 1985).

5. Steven Marcus, "Reading the Illegible," in *The Victorian City: Images and Realities*, 2 vols., ed. H. J. Dyos and Michael Wolff (London: Routledge & Kegan Paul, 1973), I, 257–76.

6. See Sacvan Bercovitch, *The Office of "The Scarlet Letter"* (Baltimore: Johns Hopkins Univ. Press, 1991).

7. Most American historians have pointed to the second half of the nineteenth century as a cultural divide, when modern habits of perception and interpretation came into being. See, for instance, Thomas Haskell, *The Emergence of Professional Social Science* (Urbana: Univ. of Illinois Press, 1977); John Higham, "The Reorientation of American Culture in the 1890s," in his *Writing American History: Essays on Modern Scholarship* (Bloomington: Indiana Press, 1970), pp. 73–102; Samuel P. Hays, *The Response to Industrialism: 1885–1914* (Chicago: Univ. of Chicago Press, 1957); Robert Wiebe, *The Search for Order, 1877–1920* (New York: Hill and Wang, 1967).

8. Paul Starr, *The Social Transformation of American Medicine* (New York: Basic Books, 1982). See especially pp. 3–29, on "the social origins of professional sovereignty." Quotations from pp. 13, 19, 13. For related argument, see Eliot Freidson, *Profession of Medicine: A Study of the Sociology of Applied Knowledge* (New York: Dodd, Mead, 1970), and Freidson, *Professional Dominance: The Social Structure of Medical Care* (New York: Atherton, 1970).

9. The American Bar Association was founded in 1878, the MLA in 1883, the AHA in 1884, and the AEA in 1885. For the rise of professionalism, see Burton J. Bledstein, *The Culture of Professionalism: The Middle Class and the Formation of Higher Education in America* (New York: Norton, 1976); Anton-Hermann Chroust, *The Rise of the Legal Profession in America* (Norman: Univ. of Oklahoma Press, 1965); Mary Furner, *Advocacy and Objectivity: A Crisis in the Professionalization of American Social Science, 1865–1905* (Lexington: Univ. of Kentucky Press, 1975); Thomas Haskell, *The Emergency of Professional Social Science*; Magali Sarfatti Larson, *The Rise of Professionalism* (Berkeley: Univ. of California Press, 1977). See also a valuable collection, *The Authority of Experts*, ed. Thomas Haskell (Bloomington: Indiana Univ. Press, 1984).

10. Andrew Abbott, *The System of Professions* (Chicago: Univ. of Chicago Press, 1988).

11. Émile Durkheim, *Professional Ethics and Civic Morals*, trans. Cornelia Brookfield (Glencoe, Ill.: Free Press, 1958); this highly favorable account of professionalism was first delivered as lectures at Bordeaux in the 1890s. In *The Acquisitive Society* (1922), R. H. Tawney also praises the professions as a fortress of disinterestedness in a rapacious society. The first critical view of professionalism was Talcott Parsons' seminal essay "The Professions and Social Structure" (1939), collected in *Essays in Sociological Theory* (Glencoe, Ill.: Free Press, 1954), pp. 34–49. For recent accounts of professionalism, see Daniel Bell, *The Coming of Post-Industrial Society* (New York: Basic Books, 1973); Alvin Gouldner, *The Future of Intellectuals and the Rise of the New Class* (New York: Seabury, 1979); Ivan Illich, *Disabling Professions* (London: M. Bovars, 1977).

12. See Sandra Gilbert and Susan Gubar, *The Madwoman in the Attic: The Woman Writer and the Nineteenth-Century Literary Imagination* (New Haven: Yale Univ. Press, 1979), pp. 89–92; Annette Kolodny, "A Map for Rereading"; Jean Kennard, "Convention Coverage, or How to Read Your Own Life," *New Literary History*, 13 (1981), 69–88; Paula Treichler, "Escaping the Sentence," *Tulsa Studies in Women's Literature*, 3 (1984), 61–77; Judith Fetterley, "Reading about Reading," in *Gender and Reading*, pp. 147–64. For critiques of this feminist orthodoxy, see Janice Haney-Peritz, "Monumental Feminism and Literature's Ancestral House," *Women's Studies*, 12 (1986), 113–28; and Mary Jacobus, "An Unnecessary Maze of Sign-Reading," in her *Reading Woman: Essays in Feminist Criticism* (New York: Columbia Univ. Press, 1986), p. 299–48.

13. See, for example, Polly Wynn Allen, *Building Domestic Liberty: Charlotte Perkins Gilman's Architectural Feminism* (Amherst: Univ. of Massachusetts Press, 1988); Mary A. Hill, *Charlotte Perkins Gilman: The Making of a Radical Feminist, 1860–1896* (Philadelphia: Temple Univ. Press, 1980).

14. For an account of the scientific homemaking profession, see Julie Matthaei, *An Economic History of Women in America: Women's Work, the Sexual Division of Labor, and the Development of Capitalism* (New York: Schocken, 1982), pp. 157–67.

15. See Dolores Hayden, *The Grand Domestic Revolution: A History of Feminist Designs for American Homes, Neighborhoods, and Cities* (Cambridge: MIT Press, 1981).

16. Charlotte Perkins Gilman, *Women and Economics* (Boston: Small, Maynard, 1898), pp. 241–42.

17. Charlotte Perkins Gilman, "The Yellow Wallpaper," *The New England Magazine*, May 1892. Quotation from reprint (Old Westbury, NY: Feminist Press, 1973), 23–24.

18. A diagnosis is usually taken to be more scientific or more objective than a reading. Here, however, I emphasize the degree to which it is governed by interpretive conventions.

19. See Wolfgang Iser, *The Implied Reader* (Baltimore: Johns Hopkins Univ. Press, 1974), and *The Act of Reading* (Baltimore: Johns Hopkins Univ. Press, 1978). My critique of Iser parallels Robert Holub, *Reception Theory* (London: Methuen, 1984). For a different critique (challenging Iser's distinction between the determinate and indeterminate), see Stanley Fish, "Why No One is Afraid of Wolfgang Iser," *Diacritics*, 11 (March 1981), 2–13.

20. Tony Bennett, "Texts in History: The Determinations of Readings and Their Texts," in *Post-Structuralism and the Question of History*, ed. Derek Attridge, Geoff Bennington, and Robert Young (New York: Cambridge Univ. Press, 1987), pp. 63–81; quotation from p. 74. For a helpful discussion of Iser and Bennett in the context of Bakhtin, see David Shepherd, "Bakhtin and the Reader," in *Bakhtin and Cultural Theory*, ed. Ken Hirschkop and David Shepherd (Manchester: Manchester Univ. Press, 1989), pp. 91–108.

21. This is, of course, the paradigm in *Discipline and Punish*, trans. Alan Sheridan (New York: Pantheon, 1979). For critiques of the structural determinism in Foucault and in New Historicism, see Frank Lentricchia, "Foucault's Legacy: A New Historicism?" in *Ariel and the Police* (Madison: Univ. of Wisconsin Press, 1988), pp. 86–102; Louis Montrose, "Texts and Histories," in *Redrawing the Boundaries of Literary Studies in English*, ed. Giles Gunn and Stephen Greenblatt (New York: MLA, 1991); Carolyn Porter, "Are We Being Historical Yet?" *South Atlantic Quarterly*, 87 (1988), 743–86; Edward Said, *The World, the Text, and the Critic* (Cambridge; Harvard Univ. Press, 1983).

22. Here I thank my students at Rutgers for their spirited (and skeptical) response to my New Historicist reading.

23. Charlotte Perkins Gilman, "Why I Wrote 'The Yellow Wallpaper,'" *Forerunner*, October 1913, reprinted in *The Charlotte Perkins Gilman Reader*, ed. Ann J. Lane (New York: Pantheon, 1980), p. 20.

24. Charlotte Perkins Gilman, "Thoughts and Figgerings," December 1926, quoted in Allen, *Building Domestic Liberty*, p. 145.

25. *Bradwell v. Illinois*, 83 U.S. 130. See Lawrence Friedman, *A History of American Law* (New York: Simon and Schuster, 1985), p. 639; Nadine Taub and Elizabeth M. Schneider, "Perspectives on Women's Subordination and the Role of Law," in *The Politics of Law*, ed. David Kairys (New York: Pantheon, 1982), p. 125.

26. Starr, *Social Transformation of American Medicine*, p. 117.

27. Raymond Williams, *Marxism and Literature* (Oxford: Oxford Univ. Press, 1977), pp. 121–27.

28. For a suggestive account of the genesis of agency through the noncoherence of discursive formations, see Anthony Appiah, "Tolerable Falsehoods; Agency and the Interests of Theory," in *Consequences of Theory: Selected Papers from the English Institute, 1987–88*, ed. Jonathan Arac and Barbara Johnson (Baltimore: Johns Hopkins Univ. Press, 1991), pp. 63–90.

29. There is no occasion to discuss race in this paper, but for a stimulating analysis, see Susan S. Lanser, "Feminist Criticism, 'The Yellow Wallpaper,' and the Politics of Color in America," *Feminist Studies*, 15 (1989), 415–41.

30. The well-known formulation, in its entirety, is "the historicity of texts and the textuality of history." See Louis Montrose, "Renaissance Literary Studies and the Subject of History," *English Literary Renaissance*, 16 (1986), 5–12.

31. The "containment" position is more forcefully articulated by Stephen Greenblatt. See his "Invisible Bullets: Renaissance Authority and Its Subversion," in *Political Shakespeare*, ed. Jonathan Dollimore and Alan Sinfield (Ithaca, 1985), pp. 18–47. For a critique of Greenblatt, see Donald Pease, "Toward a Sociology of Literary Knowledge: Greenblatt, Colonialism, and the New Historicism," in *The Consequences of Theory*, pp. 108–53.

32. Toril Moi, *Sexual/Textual Politics* (London: Methuen, 1985). For related discussions, see Diana Fuss, *Essentially Speaking* (New York: Routledge, 1989). See also *Differences*, I (Summer, 1989), a special issue entitled "The Essential Difference: Another Look at Essentialism."

33. See, for example, the considerable difference between Elaine Showalter's earlier book, *A Literature of Their Own* (Princeton: Princeton Univ. Press, 1977) and her more recent work, *The Female Malady* (New York: Pantheon, 1985), or between her "Feminist Criti-

cism in the Wilderness," *Critical Inquiry*, 8 (1981), 179–206, and her "Critical Cross-Dressing: Male Feminists and the Woman of the Year," *Raritan*, 3 (1983), 130–49.

34. Annette Kolodny, "A Map for Rereading," 57. Italics in original text.

35. For a persuasive defense of essentialist feminism on the ground of tactical necessity, see Paul Smith, *Discerning the Subject* (Minneapolis: Univ. of Minnesota Press, 1988), pp. 132–51. In a different context, Gayatri Spivak has also argued for a *strategic* alliance with essentialism in order to recover the subjectivity written out of conventional historiography. See her "Subaltern Studies: Deconstructing Historiography," in *In Other Worlds* (New York: Methuen, 1988), pp. 197–221, especially pp. 206–07.

36. Eve Kosofsky Sedgwick, *Between Men: English Literature and Male Homosocial Desire* (New York: Columbia Univ. Press, 1985); Alice Jardine, *Gynesis: Configurations of Woman and Modernity* (Ithaca: Cornell Univ. Press, 1985); Judith Butler, *Gender Trouble: Feminism and the Subversion of Identity* (New York: Routledge, 1990); Mary Poovey, *Uneven Developments: The Ideological Work of Gender in Mid-Victorian England* (Chicago: Univ. of Chicago Press, 1988).

37. For an interesting critique of *l'écriture féminine* as the metaphorization of difference and the linking of metaphoricity to binarism, see Domna C. Stanton, "Difference on Trial," in *The Poetics of Gender*, ed. Nancy K. Miller (New York: Columbia Univ. Press, 1986), pp. 157–82.

38. The figure of "internal difference" is of course a central poststructuralist postulate. For a feminist deployment of this figure (emphasizing class, but addressing the same problems of binarism), see Jane Gallop, "Annie Leclerc Writing a Letter, with Vermeer," in *The Poetics of Gender*, pp. 137–56.

39. Joan Wallach Scott, "Gender: A Useful Category of Historical Analysis," *American Historical Review*, 81 (1986), 1053–75. See also Joan Kelly, "The Social Relations of the Sexes," in her *Women, History, and Theory* (Chicago: Univ. of Chicago Press, 1984), pp. 1–18.

discourse

T hrough the 1980s, feminism and literary theory seemed constantly to be arguing, continually returning to that exasperated question: "Can we talk?" Some feminists—having worked through such poststructuralist critical approaches as deconstruction, psychoanalysis, narratology, and dialogics—have ended up repudiating "theory" as a patriarchal device wielded for dominance of the literary field (see, for example, Nina Baym's "The Madwoman and Her Languages" in "Conflicts" and Jane Tompkins's "Me and My Shadow" in "Autobiography"). Barbara Christian—in her influential essay "The Race for Theory"—spoke in 1987 for many when she wrote, "I, for one, am tired of being asked to produce a black feminist literary theory as if I were a mechanical man. . . . For I feel that the new emphasis on literary critical theory is as hegemonic as the world which it attacks."

For many other feminists, however, mainstream literary theories hold the promise of precise vocabularies, widely circulated premises, and analytic methods that can lend form to feminist observations and can enable feminist critics to engage in conversation with a critical community that does not necessarily take feminist values for granted. As each of the entries in this section illustrates, the (usually) male originators of poststructuralist theory seldom attend to gender in their formulations of such concepts as text, voice, reader, genre, or discourse. The task for these five feminists—among many others, including Rachel Blau DuPlessis, Rita Felski, Marjorie Garber, Marianne Hirsch, Alice Jardine, Nancy K. Miller, Naomi Schor, and Patricia Yeager, to mention a few who are not represented in this volume—has been to insert gender into the models proposed by androcentric theorists and to ask what impact consideration of "femininity" or "the female" might have on the ways theories can inform the process of reading.

We call this section "Discourse," partly because an original meaning of that word was "to talk". One might interpret the section's heading in that sense, as a conversation among theoretical communities, but "discourse" has come to mean something else in current critical vocabularies. Broadly speaking, "discourse" refers to a particular use of language in a given time and place: novels, television commercials, or political speeches are not themselves "discourses," in this usage, but rather instances of discourse, of ways language gets used on given topics in a particular culture and society. Each of the five essays here uses "discourse" to mean something slightly different (and Susan Stanford Friedman's piece uses it in at least two different senses); each usage carries assumptions that are linked to the literary theory the writer has chosen to employ and revise. These five ways of talking about discourse are by no means comprehensive, but they suggest both the variety and the unity among feminisms' dialogues with literary theory.

Catherine Belsey's "Constructing the Subject: Deconstructing the Text" (1985) may be one of the more difficult selections in *Feminisms* for readers uninitiated into literary theory to grasp, but such readers might consider tackling it first and last, as an introduction to and summary of the recent interplay of feminisms and literary theory. Belsey's focus is "literary discourse," and her project is to survey the major assumptions that have dominated critical thinking about what to do with literature in a poststructuralist era. Belsey carefully weaves together the primary concern of feminism—to change the world by eliminating the subjugation of women—with the positions of theorists whose approaches seem, on the face of it, to be apolitical, or else to make class struggle, rather than gender inequities, their highest priority. Establishing definitions for such crucial concepts as "subject," "identity," "discourse," and "ideology," Belsey shows how those terms cross boundaries between the linguistically based theories of Benveniste and de Saussure, the psychoanalysis of Lacan, the Marxism of Althusser and Macherey, and the semiotic cultural critique of Barthes.

For Belsey, the method of analyzing literary discourse that draws upon the most fruitful accumulation of these concepts is deconstruction, an approach she finds particularly helpful to the feminist who wishes to challenge the subject position constructed for readers within "classic realism." Belsey asserts that critics who follow deconstruction's invitation to "find the multiplicity and diversity of . . . possible meanings" rather than the unity of a text will find it "implicitly criticizes its own ideology; it contains within itself the critique of its own values." Placing an overlay of gender on that deconstructive tenet, Belsey looks at some Sherlock Holmes stories to demonstrate that the shadowy, silent, mysterious and magical presence of sexualized women in those stories undercuts the narratives' overt endorsements of logic, positivism, and science. Deconstruction, then, is one way to uncover the operations of gender in literary discourse.

In Susan S. Lanser's "Toward a Feminist Narratology" (1986, a version of the introduction to her 1992 book, *Fictions of Authority*), "discourse" takes on a more specific meaning, borrowed from such structuralist narratologists as Gérard Genette, Seymour Chatman, and Mieke Bal. Here, narrative texts are broken down into two components: "story," or "what happens" in a narrative, and "discourse," or how "what happens" gets rendered in language. The study of narrative discourse seeks to describe and classify the various possible ways that stories can be told, with attention to such matters as voice, perspective, temporal organization, and repetition. Observing that feminists typically shun narratology and that narratologists draw almost exclusively on male-written texts to illustrate their models, Lanser suggests that narratives written or spoken by women cannot always be adequately described within narrative theory's androcentric models. In raising this issue, Lanser seeks to extend the purposes of narratology beyond their traditional boundaries: she is interested in feminist narratology's potential for helping to interpret texts, to describe gendered differences in writing, and to be more explicit than structuralism has typically been about its ideological positioning as a critical practice.

To illustrate this suggestion, Lanser analyzes a text that stretches traditional definitions of narrative, a letter ostensibly written by a woman, which has at least three entirely different meanings, depending on the perspective of its reader. Lanser shows that the "public" or "private" nature of a narrative utterance has an important effect on the way a reader receives it. As she points out, the "public/private" opposition has played a significant role in the tradition of women's writing, which has, in Western culture, so often taken the form of letters. By thinking about the perspectives from which a narrative can be read and interpreted, Lanser extends narratology's reference beyond the limits of the text, into the "rhetorical circumstance" producing it. In this way, feminist narratology can introduce the concerns of the world of lived experience into structuralist-inspired literary theory and—in so doing—address feminist critiques of the "disembodied" nature of so much of theory.

More straightforwardly than the other contributors to this section, Barbara Johnson (In "Apostrophe, Animation, and Abortion," 1986) equates "discourse" with "rhetoric" and asks what its relation to the body and the "real world" might be: as she so powerfully inquires, "Is there any *inherent* connection between figurative language and questions of life and death?" The question of life and death here is about abortion; the discourse under scrutiny is the poetic figure of apostrophe, or the address to an absent entity that paradoxically both animates and silences the addressee. To bring abortion and apostrophe together is to raise the issue of "discursive positions," or the place from which you speak (for example, as the no-longer-pregnant woman? as the aborted fetus?) in a poem. Johnson looks at poems about abortion, pregnancy, childbirth, and the death of children written in various periods by men and by women, and observes that a difficulty for poets seems to be "the attempt to achieve a full elaboration of any discursive position other than that of child." Johnson's deconstruction of apostrophe in those poems points to the "undecidability" of matters of life and death in poetic discourse, and, in bringing this up, she alludes to the controversy over poststructuralism's reputation for uselessness in the face of politics. As Johnson argues, though (and Belsey, for one, would probably agree), undecidability is not an apolitical condition, but rather is what brings politics into being, what gives them birth.

In Dale Bauer's book, *Feminist Dialogics: A Theory of Failed Community* (1988), discourse and politics come together in another form. Bauer draws upon the work of Mikhail M. Bakhtin, the Russian theorist of the novel who combined the concerns of formalist discourse analysis with attention to sociology, ideology, and politics. One of Bakhtin's most influential ideas is that literary discourse in novels never proceeds from a single voice, but is always "polyvocal," "dialogic" in the sense that it is implicitly taking part in a dialogue. *Every* utterance, in this view, contains in it the traces of other articulated positions, which it answers, affirms, revises, or contradicts. On a more literal level, too, novels are "dialogic" in that they contain representations of narrators and characters who say things that diverge from one another's stated positions, and from the author's own. A novel is like a playing field or—as Bauer would have it—a battleground where discourses representing the interests of different groups struggle for dominance.

Bakhtin thinks primarily in terms of class struggle, but Bauer transfers his theory to the realm of gender. Her study of novels by Nathaniel Hawthorne, Henry James, Edith Wharton, and Kate Chopin looks at the voice of the heroine of nineteenth-century American literature who plays the Bakhtinian "fool," misreading and incomprehending, hence subverting, the dominant discourses in the text. According to Bauer, even a heroine's silence—not unusual in the selected corpus—takes on meaning from the perspective of feminist dialogics, through the effort of the feminist reader who tries to read the heroine's voice "back into" the text that excludes it. Bauer scrutinizes the struggle for power and authority in the "battle of languages" that emerges among competing voices in fiction. To take one of Bauer's examples, Hawthorne's *The Blithedale Romance* offers the voices of "the pragmatist, the social reformer, the artist, the feminist," and the discourse of each is continually in dialogic engagement with the others. To be sure, dialogue—talk, conversation, speech addressed to another—is at the center of each of these feminist analyses of discourse, and—as Bauer so accurately points out—power and authority are what is always at stake in theory and criticism of literature, as they are in literary discourse itself.

Susan Stanford Friedman's "When a 'Long' Poem Is a 'Big' Poem: Self-Authorizing Strategies in Women's Twentieth-Century 'Long Poems'" (1990) looks closely at the workings of power in the discourse of literary criticism. Through the example of a recently codified genre, the "long poem" usually written by men, Friedman shows how generic categories can either exclude women poets or, alternatively, be appropriated by women writers, poets, and critics alike. "Discourse" appears in two guises in Friedman's piece, one referring to criticism and the other to poetic writing. First, she speaks of the discourse of genre theory and the part it plays in maintaining "the authority of the dominant cultural discourses" that designate men's "long poems" as "big," "important," "potent," works asking crucial "quest-ions" (here Friedman puns on that quintessentially masculine theme, the quest) about implicitly masculine concerns. Then Friedman shows how twentieth-century women poets writing long poems have challenged those assumptions by introducing four new modes of poetic discourse into the genre.

One such mode is the "discourse of the satiric Other," an "aggressive and confrontational" style not often found in women's literature but exemplified by Mina Loy's mock-heroic epic *Anglo-Mongrels and the Rose*. A second mode is a new "discourse of history," a "(her)story in which the inside is the outside and the outside is the inside," where traditional distinctions between public and private, personal and political break down in long poems like Alicia Ostriker's *The Mother/Child Papers*. The third strategy, a term borrowed from Adrienne Rich, is the "discourse of re-vision," "in which the outsider immerses herself in the discourse of the inside in order to transform it," as does Judy Grahn in *The Queen of Wands*. The fourth mode is the "discourse of linguistic experimentalism," associated with *l'écriture féminine* and found in Betsy Warland's *serpent (w)rite*. Friedman stresses that these four categories, like all generic designations, are never mutually exclusive, and that all four strategies may coexist in any long poem written by a woman. Her intention is not to impose a potentially hierarchical system of categorization upon women's long poems, but rather to insist that the discourses of those poems, like the discourse of the literary criticism that comments upon them, are necessarily gendered.

—RRW

CATHERINE BELSEY

CONSTRUCTING THE SUBJECT

deconstructing the text

(1985)

THE SUBJECT IN IDEOLOGY

One of the central issues for feminism is the cultural construction of subjectivity. It seems imperative to many feminists to find ways of explaining why women have not simply united to overthrow patriarchy. Why, since all women experience the effects of patriarchal practices, are not all women feminists? And why do those of us who think of ourselves as feminists find ourselves inadvertently colluding, at least from time to time, with the patriarchal values and assumptions prevalent in our society? Since the late seventeenth century feminists have seen subjectivity as itself subject to convention, education, and culture in its broadest sense. Now feminist criticism has allowed that fiction too plays a part in the process of constructing subjectivity. But how?

In his influential essay 'Ideology and Ideological State Apparatuses,' Louis Althusser includes literature among the ideological apparatuses which contribute to the process of *reproducing* the *relations of production*, the social relationships which are the necessary condition for the existence and perpetuation of the capitalist mode of production. He does not here develop the argument concerning literature, but in the context both of his concept of ideology and also of the work of Roland Barthes on literature and Jacques Lacan on psychoanalysis it is possible to construct an account of some of the implications for feminist theory and practice of Althusser's position. The argument is not only that literature represents the myths and imaginary versions of real social relationships which constitute ideology, but also that classic realist fiction, the dominant literary form of the nineteenth century and arguably of the twentieth, 'interpellates' the reader, addresses itself to him or her directly, offering the reader as the position from which the text is most 'obviously' intelligible, the position of the *subject in (and of) ideology*.

According to Althusser's reading (re-reading) of Marx, ideology is not simply a set of illusions, as *The German Ideology* seems to argue, but a system of representations (discourses, images, myths) concerning the real relations in which people live. But what is represented in ideology is 'not the system of the real relations which govern the existence of individuals, but the imaginary relation of those individuals to the real relations in which they live' (Althusser 1971, p. 155). In other words, ideology is both a real and an imaginary relation to the world—real in that it is the way in which people really live their relationship to the social relations which govern their conditions of existence, but imaginary in that it discourages a full understanding of these conditions of existence and the ways in which people are socially constituted within them. It is not, therefore, to be thought of as a system of ideas in people's heads, nor as the expression at a higher level of real material relationships, but as the necessary condition of action within the social formation. Althusser talks of ideology as a 'material practice' in this sense: it exists in the behaviour of people acting according to their beliefs (ibid., pp. 155–9).

As the necessary condition of action, ideology exists in commonplaces and truisms as well as in philosophical and religious systems. It is apparent in all that is 'obvious' to us, in 'obviousnesses which we cannot *fail to recognise* and before which we have the inevitable and natural reaction of crying out (aloud or in the "still, small voice of conscience"): "That's obvious! That's right! That's true!"' (ibid., p. 161). If it is true, however, it is not the whole truth. It is a set of omissions, gaps rather than lies, smoothing over contradictions, appearing to provide answers to questions which in reality it evades, and masquerading as coherence in the interests of the social relations generated by and necessary to the reproduction of the existing mode of production.

It is important to stress, of course, that ideology is in no sense a set of deliberate distortions foisted upon a helpless working class by a corrupt and cynical bourgeoisie (or upon victimized women by violent and power hungry men). If there are groups of sinister men in shirt-sleeves purveying illusions to the public these are not the real makers of ideology. Ideology has no creators in that sense, since it exists necessarily. But according to Althusser ideological practices are supported and reproduced in the institutions of our society which he calls Ideological State Apparatuses (ISAs). The phrase distinguishes from the Repressive State Apparatus which works by force (the police, the penal system, the army) those institutions whose existence helps to guarantee consent to the existing mode of production. The central ISA in contemporary capitalism is the educational system, which prepares children to act consistently with the values of society by inculcating in them the dominant versions of appropriate behaviour as well as history, social studies and, of course, literature. Among the allies of the educational ISA are the family, the law, the media and the arts, all helping to represent and reproduce the myths and beliefs necessary to enable people to work within the existing social formation.

The destination of all ideology is the subject (the individual in society) and it is the role of ideology to *construct people as subjects*:

> I say: the category of the subject is constitutive of all ideology, but at the same time and immediately I add that *the category of the subject is only constitutive of all ideology in so far as all ideology has the function (which defines it) of 'constituting' concrete individuals as subjects.* (ibid., p. 160)

Within the existing ideology it appears 'obvious' that people are autonomous individuals, possessed of subjectivity or consciousness which is the source of their beliefs and actions. That people are unique, distinguishable, irreplaceable identities is 'the elementary ideological effect' (ibid., p. 161).

The obviousness of subjectivity has been challenged by the linguistic theory which has developed on the basis of the work of Saussure. As Emile Benveniste argues, it is language which provides the possibility of subjectivity because it is language which enables the speaker to posit himself or herself as 'I,' as the subject of a sentence. It is in language that people constitute themselves as subjects. Consciousness of self is possible only through contrast, differentiation: 'I' cannot be conceived without the conception 'non-I,' 'you,' and dialogue, the fundamental condition of language, implies a reversible polarity between 'I' and 'you.' 'Language is possible only because each speaker sets himself up as a *subject* by referring to himself as *I* in his discourse' (Benveniste 1971, p. 225). But if language is a system of differences with no positive terms, 'I' designates only the subject of a specific utterance. 'And so it is literally true that the basis of subjectivity is in the exercise of language. If one really thinks about it, one will see that there is no other objective testimony to the identity of the subject except that which he himself thus gives about himself' (ibid., p. 226).

Within ideology, of course, it seems 'obvious' that the individual speaker is the origin of the meaning of his or her utterance. Post-Saussurean linguistics, however, implies a more complex relationship between the individual and meaning, since it is language itself which, by differentiating between concepts, offers the possibility of meaning. In reality, it is only by adopting the position of the subject within language that the individual is able to produce meaning. As Derrida puts it,

> What was it that Saussure in particular reminded us of? That 'language [which consists only of differences] is not a function of the speaking subject.' This implies that the subject (self-identical or even conscious of self-identity, self-conscious) is inscribed in the language, that he is a 'function' of the language. He becomes a *speaking* subject only by conforming his speech . . . to the system of linguistic prescriptions taken as the system of differences. (Derrida 1973, pp. 145–6)

Derrida goes on to raise the question whether, even if we accept that it is only the signifying system which makes possible the speaking subject, the signifying subject, we cannot none the less conceive of a non-speaking, non-signifying subjectivity, 'a silent and intuitive consciousness' (ibid., p. 146). The problem here, he concludes, is to define consciousness-in-itself as distinct from consciousness of something, and ultimately as distinct from consciousness of self. If consciousness is finally consciousness of self, this in turn implies that consciousness depends on differentiation, and specifically on Benveniste's differentiation between 'I' and 'you,' a process made possible by language.

The implications of this concept of the primacy of language over subjectivity have been developed by Jacques Lacan's reading of Freud. Lacan's theory of the subject as constructed in language confirms the *decentering* of the individual consciousness so that it can no longer be seen as the origin of meaning, knowledge and action. Instead, Lacan proposes that the infant is initially an 'hommelette'—'a little man and also like a broken egg spreading without hindrance in all directions' (Coward and Ellis 1977, p. 101). The child has no sense of identity, no way of conceiving of itself as a unity, distinct from what is 'other,' exterior to it. During the 'mirror-phase' of its development, however, it 'recognizes' itself in the mirror as a unit distinct from the outside world. This 'recognition' is an identifcation with an 'imaginary' (because imaged) unitary and autonomous self. But it is only with its entry into language that the child becomes a full subject. If it is to participate in the society into which it is born, to be able to act deliberately within the social formation, the child must enter into the symbolic order, the set of signifying systems of culture of which the supreme example is language. The child who refuses to learn the language is 'sick,' unable to become a full member of the family and of society.

In order to speak the child is compelled to differentiate; to speak of itself it has to distinguish 'I' from 'you.' In order to formulate its needs the child learns to identify with the first person singular pronoun, and this identification constitutes the basis of subjectivity. Subsequently it learns to recognize itself in a series of subject-positions ('he' or 'she,' 'boy' or 'girl,' and so on) which are the positions from which discourse is intelligible to itself and others. 'Identity,' subjectivity, is thus a matrix of subject-positions, which may be inconsistent or even in contradiction with one another.

Subjectivity, then, is linguistically and discursively constructed and displaced across the range of discourses in which the concrete individual participates. It follows from Saussure's theory of language as a system of differences that the world is intelligible only in discourse: there is no unmediated experience, no access to the raw reality of self and others. Thus:

> As well as being a system of signs related among themselves, language incarnates meaning in the form of the series of positions it offers for the subject from which to grasp itself and its relations with the real. (Nowell-Smith 1976, p. 26)

The subject is constructed in language and in discourse and, since the symbolic order in its discursive use is closely related to ideology, in ideology. It is in this sense that ideology has the effect, as Althusser argues, of constituting individuals as subjects, and it is also in this sense that their subjectivity appears 'obvious.' Ideology suppresses the role of language in the construction of the subject. As a result, people 'recognize' (misrecognize) themselves in the ways in which ideology 'interpellates' them, or in other words, addresses them as subjects, calls them by their names and in turn 'recognizes' their autonomy. As a result, they 'work by themselves' (Althusser 1971, p. 169), they 'willingly' adopt the subject-positions necessary to their participation in the social formation. In capitalism they 'freely' exchange their labour-power for wages, and they 'voluntarily' purchase the commodities produced. In patriarchal society women 'choose' to do the housework, to make sacrifices for their children, not to become engineers. And it is here that we see the full force of Althusser's use of the term 'subject,' originally borrowed, as he says, from law. The subject is not only a grammatical subject, 'a centre of initiatives, author of and responsible for its actions,' but also a *subjected being* who submits to the authority of the social formation represented in ideology as the Absolute Subject (God, the king, the boss, Man, conscience): 'the individual is *interpellated as a (free) subject in order that he shall submit freely to the commandments of the Subject, i.e. in order that he shall (freely) accept his subjection*' (ibid., p. 169).

Ideology interpellates concrete individuals as subjects, and bourgeois ideology in particular emphasizes the fixed identity of the individual. 'I'm just *like* that'— cowardly, perhaps, or aggressive, generous or impulsive. Astrology is only an extreme form of the determinism which attributes to us given essences which cannot change. Popular psychology and popular sociology make individual behaviour a product of these essences. And underlying them all, ultimately unalterable, is 'human nature.' In these circumstances, how is it possible to suppose that, even if we could break in theoretical terms with the concepts of the ruling ideology, we are ourselves capable of change, and therefore capable both of acting to change the social formation and of transforming ourselves to constitute a new kind of society? A possible answer can be found in Lacan's theory of the precariousness of conscious subjectivity, which in turn depends on the Lacanian conception of the unconscious.

In Lacan's theory the individual is not in reality the harmonious and coherent totality of ideological misrecognition. The mirror-phase, in which the infant perceives itself as other, an image, exterior to is own perceiving self, necessitates a splitting between the *I* which is perceived and the *I* which does the perceiving. The entry into language necessitates a secondary division which reinforces the first, a split between the *I* of discourse, the subject of the utterance, and the *I* who speaks, the subject of the enunciation. There is thus a contradiction between the conscious self, the self which appears in its own discourse, and the self which is only partly represented there, the self which speaks. The unconscious comes into being in the gap which is formed by this division. The unconscious is constructed in the moment of entry into the symbolic order, simultaneously with the construction of the subject. The repository of repressed and pre-linguistic signifiers, the unconscious is a constant source of potential disruption of the symbolic order. To summarize very briefly what in Lacan is a complex and elusive theory, entry into the symbolic order liberates the child into the possibility of social relationship; it also reduces its helplessness to the extent that it is now able to articulate its needs in the form of demands. But at the same time a division within the self is constructed. In offering the child the possibility of formulating its desires the symbolic order also betrays them, since it cannot by definition formulate those elements of desire which remain unconscious. Demand is always only a metonymy of desire (Lemaire 1977, p. 64). The subject is thus the site of contradiction, and is consequently perpetually in the process of construction, thrown into crisis by alterations in language and in the social formation, capable of change. And in the fact that the subject is a *process* lies the possibility of transformation.

In addition, the displacement of subjectivity across a range of discourses implies a range of positions from which the subject grasps itself and its relations with the real, and these positions may be incompatible or contradictory. It is these incompatibilities and contradictions within what is taken for granted that exert a pressure on concrete individuals to seek new, non-contradictory subject-positions. Women as a group in our society are both produced and inhibited by contradictory discourses. Very broadly, we participate both in the liberal—humanist discourse of freedom, self-determination and rationality and at the same time in the specifically feminine discourse offered by society of submission, relative inadequacy and irrational intuition. The attempt to locate a single and coherent subject-position within these contradictory discourses, and in consequence to find a non-contradictory pattern of behaviour, can create intolerable pressures. One way of responding to this situation is to retreat from the contradictions and from discourse itself, to become 'sick'—more women than men are treated for mental illness. Another is to seek a resolution of the contradictions in the discourses of feminism. That the position of women in society has changed so slowly, in spite of such a radical instability in it, may be partly explained in terms of the relative exclusion of women from the discourse of liberal humanism. This relative exclusion, supported in the predominantly masculine institutions of our society, is implicit, for example, in the use of masculine terms as generic ('rational man,' etc.).

Women are not an isolated case. The class structure also produces contradictory subject-positions which precipitate changes in social relations not only between whole classes but between concrete individuals within those classes. Even at the conscious level, although this fact may itself be unconscious, the individual subject is not a unity, and in this lies the possibility of deliberate change.

This does not imply the reinstatement of individual subjects as the agents of change and changing knowledge. On the contrary, it insists on the concept of a dialectical relationship between concrete individuals and the language in which their subjectivity is constructed. In consequence, it also supports the concept of subjectivity as in process.

It is because subjectivity is perpetually in process that literary texts can have an important function. No one, I think, would suggest that literature alone could precipitate a crisis in the social formation. None the less, if we accept Lacan's analysis of the importance of language in the construction of the subject it becomes apparent that literature as one of the most persuasive uses of language may have an important influence on the ways in which people grasp themselves and their relation to the real relations in which they live. The interpellation of the reader in the literary text could be argued to have a role in reinforcing the concepts of the world and of subjectivity which ensure that people 'work by themselves' in the social formation. On the other hand, certain critical modes could be seen to challenge these concepts, and to call in question the particular complex of imaginary relations between individuals and the real conditions of their existence which helps to reproduce the present relations of class, race and gender.

THE SUBJECT AND THE TEXT

Althusser analyzes the interpellation of the subject in the context of ideology in general; Benveniste in discussing the relationship between language and subjectivity is concerned with language in general. None the less, it readily becomes apparent that capitalism in particular needs subjects who work by themselves, who freely exchange their labour-power for wages. It is in the epoch of capitalism that ideology emphasizes the value of individual freedom, freedom of conscience and, of course, consumer choice in all the multiplicity of its forms. The ideology of liberal humanism assumes a world of non-contradictory (and therefore fundamentally unalterable) individuals whose unfettered consciousness is the origin of meaning, knowledge and action. It is in the interest of this ideology above all to suppress the role of language in the construction of the subject, and its own role in the interpellation of the subject, and to present the individual as a free, unified, autonomous subjectivity. Classic realism, still the dominant popular mode in literature, film and television drama, roughly coincides chronologically with the epoch of industrial capitalism. It performs, I wish to suggest, the work of ideology, not only in its representation of a world of consistent subjects who are the origin of meaning, knowledge and action, but also in offering the reader, as the position from which the text is most readily intelligible, the position of subject as the origin both of understanding and of action in accordance with that understanding.

It is readily apparent that Romantic and post-Romantic poetry, from Wordsworth through the Victorian period at least to Eliot and Yeats, takes subjectivity as its central theme. The developing self of the poet, his consciousness of himself as poet, his struggle against the constraints of an outer reality, constitute the preoccupations of *The Prelude, In Memoriam* or *Meditations in Time of Civil War.* The 'I' of these poems is a kind of super-subject, experiencing life at a higher level of intensity than ordinary people and absorbed in a world of selfhood which the phenomenal world, perceived as external and antithetical, either nourishes or constrains. This transcendence of the subject in poetry is not presented as unproblematic, but it is entirely overt in the poetry of this period. The 'I' of the poem directly addresses an individual reader who is invited to respond equally directly to this interpellation.

Fiction, however, in this same period, frequently appears to deal rather in social relationships, the interaction between the individual and society, to the increasing exclusion of the subjectivity of the author. Direct intrusion by the author comes to seem an impropriety; impersonal narration, 'showing' (the truth) rather than 'telling' it, is a requirement of prose fiction by the end of the nineteenth century. In drama too the author is apparently absent from the self-contained fictional world on the stage. Even the text effaces its own existence as text: unlike poetry, which clearly announces itself as formal, if only in terms of the shape of the text on the page, the novel seems merely to transcribe a series of events, to report on a palpable world, however fictional. Classic realist drama displays transparently and from the outside how people speak and behave.

Nevertheless, as we know while we read or watch, the author is present as a shadowy authority and as source of the fiction, and the author's presence is substantiated by the name on the cover or the programme: 'a novel by Thomas Hardy,' 'a new play by Ibsen.' And at the same time, as I shall suggest in this section, the *form* of the classic realist text acts in conjunction with the expressive theory and with ideology by interpellating the reader as subject. The reader is invited to perceive and judge the 'truth' of the text, the coherent, non-contradictory interpretation of the world as it is perceived by an author whose autonomy is the source and evidence of the truth of the interpretation. This model of inter-subjective communication, of shared understanding of a text which re-presents the world, is the guarantee not only of the truth of the text but of the reader's existence as an autonomous and knowing subject in a world of knowing subjects. In this way classic realism constitutes an ideological practice in addressing itself to readers as subjects, interpellating them in order that they freely accept their subjectivity and their subjection.

It is important to reiterate, of course, that this process is not inevitable, in the sense that texts do not determine like fate the ways in which they *must* be read. I am concerned at this stage primarily with ways in which they are conventionally read: conventionally, since language is conventional, and since modes of writing as well as ways of reading are conventional, but conventionally also in that new conventions of reading are available. In this sense meaning is never a fixed essence inherent in the text but is always constructed by the reader, the result of a 'circulation' between social formation, reader and text (Heath 1977–8, p. 74). In the same way, 'inscribed subject positions are never hermetically sealed into a text, but are always positions in ideologies' (Willemen 1978, p. 63). To argue that classic realism interpellates subjects in certain ways is not to propose that this process is ineluctable; on the contrary it is a matter of choice. But the choice is ideological: certain ranges of meaning (there is always room for debate) are 'obvious' within the currently dominant ideology, and certain subject-positions are equally 'obviously' the positions from which these meanings are apparent.

Classic realism is characterized by 'illusionism,' narrative which leads to 'closure,' and a 'hierarchy of discourses' which establishes the 'truth' of the story. 'Illusionism' is, I hope, self-explanatory. The other two defining characteristics of classic realism need some discussion. Narrative tends to follow certain recurrent patterns. Classic realist narrative, as Barthes demonstrates in *S/Z*, turns on the creation of enigma through the precipitation of disorder which throws into disarray the conventional cultural and signifying systems. Among the commonest sources of disorder at the level of plot in classic realism are murder, war, a journey or love. But the story moves inevitably towards closure which is also disclosure, the dissolution of enigma through the re-establishment of order, recognizable as a reinstatement or a development of the order which is understood to have preceded the events of the story itself.

The moment of closure is the point at which the events of the story become fully intelligible to the reader. The most obvious instance is the detective story where, in the final pages, the murderer is revealed and the motive made plain. But a high degree of intelligibility is sustained throughout the narrative as a result of the hierarchy of discourses in the text. The hierarchy works above all by means of a privileged discourse which places as subordinate all the discourses that are literally or figuratively between inverted commas.

By these means classic realism offers the reader a position of knowingness which is also a position of identification with the narrative voice. To the extent that the story first constructs, and then depends for its intelligibility, on a set of assumptions shared between narrator and reader, it confirms both the transcendent knowingness of the reader-as-subject and the 'obviousness' of the shared truths in question,

DECONSTRUCTING THE TEXT

Ideology, masquerading as coherence and plenitude, is in reality inconsistent, limited, contradictory, and the realist text as a crystallization of ideology participates in this incompleteness even while it diverts attention from the fact in the apparent plenitude of narrative closure. The object of deconstructing the text is to examine *the process of its production*—not the private experience of the individual author, but the mode of production, the materials and their arrangement in the work. The aim is to locate the point of contradiction within the text, the point at which it transgresses the limits within which it is constructed, breaks free of the constraints imposed by its own realist form. Composed of contradictions, the text is no longer restricted to a single, harmonious and authoritative reading. Instead it becomes *plural*, open to rereading, no longer an object for passive consumption but an object of work by the reader to produce meaning.

It is the work of Derrida which has been most influential in promoting deconstruction as a critical strategy. Refusing to identify meaning with authorial intention or with the theme of the work, deconstruction tends to locate meaning in areas which traditional criticism has seen as marginal—in the metaphors, the set of oppositions or the hierarchies of terms which provide the framework of the text. The procedure, very broadly, is to identify in the text the contrary meanings which are the inevitable condition of its existence as a signifying practice, locating the trace of otherness which undermines the overt project.

Derrida, however, says little specifically about literary criticism or about the question of meaning in fiction. Nor is his work directly political. In order to produce a politics of reading we need to draw in addition on the work of Roland Barthes and Pierre Macherey. In *S/Z*, first published in 1970 (English translation 1975), Barthes deconstructs (without using the word) a short story by Balzac. *Sarrasine* is a classic realist text concerning a castrato singer and a fortune. The narrative turns on a series of enigmas (What is the source of the fortune? Who is the little old man? Who is La Zambinella? What is the connection between all three?). Even in summarizing the story in this way it is necessary to 'lie': there are not 'three' but two, since the little old 'man' is 'La' Zambinella. Barthes breaks the text into fragments of varying lengths for analysis, and adds a number of 'divagations,' pieces of more generalized commentary and exploration, to show *Sarrasine* as a 'limit-text,' a text which uses the modes of classic realism in ways which constitute a series of 'transgressions' of classic realism itself. The sense of plenitude, of a full understanding of a coherent text which is the normal result of reading the realist narrative, cannot here be achieved. It is not only that castration cannot be named in a text of this period. The text is compelled to transgress the conventional antithesis between the genders whenever it uses a pronoun to speak of the castrato. The story concerns the scandal of castration and the death of desire which follows its revelation; it concerns the scandalous origin of wealth; and it demonstrates the collapse of language, of antithesis (difference) as a source of meaning, which is involved in the discourse of these scandals.

Each of these elements of the text provides a point of entry into it, none privileged, and these approaches constitute the degree of polyphony, the 'parsimonious plural' of the readable (*lisible*) text. The classic realist text moves inevitably and irreversibly to an end, to the conclusion of an ordered series of events, to the disclosure of what has been concealed. But even in the realist text certain modes of signification within the discourse—the symbolic, the codes of reference and the *semes*—evade the constraints of the narrative sequence. To the extent that these are 'reversible,' free-floating and of indeterminate authority, the text is plural. In the writable (*scriptible*), wholly plural text all statements are of indeterminate origin, no single discourse is privileged, and no consistent and coherent plot constrains the free play of the discourses. The totally writable, plural text does not exist. At the opposite extreme, the readable text is barely plural. The readable text is merchandize to be consumed, while the plural text requires the production of meanings through the identification of its polyphony. Deconstruction in order to reconstruct the text as a newly intelligible, plural object is the work of criticism.

Barthes's own mode of writing demonstrates his contempt for the readable: *S/Z* is itself a polyphonic critical text. It is impossible to summarize adequately, to reduce to systematic accessibility, and it is noticeable that the book contains no summarizing conclusion. Like *Sarrasine*, *S/Z* offers a number of points of entry, critical discourses which generate trains of thought in the reader, but it would be contrary to Barthes's own (anarchist) argument to order all these into a single, coherent methodology, to constitute a new unitary way of reading, however comprehensive, and so to become the (authoritative) author of a new critical orthodoxy. As a result, the experience of reading *S/Z* is at once frustrating and exhilarating. Though it offers a model in one sense—it implies a new kind of critical practice—it would almost certainly not be possible (or useful) to attempt a wholesale imitation of its critical method(s).

It seems clear that one of the most influential precursors of *S/Z*, though Barthes does not allude to it, was Pierre Macherey's (Marxist) *A Theory of Literary Production*, first published in 1966 (English translation 1978). Despite real and important differences between them, there are similarities worth noting. For instance, Macherey anticipates Barthes in demonstrating that contradiction is a condition of narrative. The classic realist text is constructed on the basis of enigma. Information is initially withheld on condition of a 'promise' to the reader that it will finally be revealed. The discourse of this 'truth' brings the story to an end. The movement of narrative is thus both towards discourse—the end of the story—and towards concealment—prolonging itself by delaying the end of the story through a series of 'reticences,' as Barthes calls them, snares for the reader, partial answers to the questions raised, equivocations (Macherey 1978, pp. 28–9; Barthes 1975, pp. 75–6). Further, narrative involves the reader in an experience of the inevitable in the form of the unforeseen (Macherey 1978, p. 43). The hero encounters an obstacle: will he attempt to overcome it or abandon the quest? The answer is already determined, though the reader, who has only to turn the page to discover it, experiences the moment as one of choice for the hero. In fact, of course, if the narrative is to continue the hero must go on (Barthes 1975, p. 135). Thus the author's autonomy is to some degree illusory. In one sense the author determines the nature of the story: he or she decides what happens. In another sense, however, this decision is itself determined by the constraints of the narrative (Macherey 1978, p. 48), or by what Barthes calls the 'interest' (in both the psychological and the economic senses) of the story (Barthes 1975, p. 135).

The formal constraints imposed by literary form on the project of the work in the process of literary production constitute the structural principle of Macherey's analysis. It is a mistake to reduce the text to the product of a single cause, authorial determination *or* the mechanics of the narrative. On the contrary, the literary work 'is composed from a real diversity of elements which give it substance' (Macherey 1978, p. 49). There may be a direct contradiction between the project and the formal constraints, and in the transgression thus created it is possible to locate an important object of the critical quest.

Fiction for Macherey (he deals mainly with classic realist narrative) is intimately related to ideology, but the two are not identical. Literature is a specific and irreducible form of discourse, but the language which constitutes the raw material of the text is the language of ideology. It is thus an inadequate language, incomplete, partial, incapable of concealing the real contradictions it is its purpose to efface. This language, normally in flux, is arrested, 'congealed' by the literary text.

The realist text is a determinate representation, an intelligible structure which claims to convey intelligible relationships between its elements. In its attempt to create a coherent and internally consistent fictive world the text, in spite of itself, exposes incoherences, omissions, absences and transgressions which in turn reveal the inability of the language of ideology to create coherence. This becomes apparent because the contradiction between the diverse elements drawn from different discourses, the ideological project and the literary form, creates an absence at the centre of the work. The text is divided, split as the Lacanian subject is split, and Macherey compares the 'lack' in the consciousness of the work, its silence, what it cannot say, with the unconscious which Freud explored (ibid., p. 85).

The unconscious of the work (*not*, it must be insisted, of the author) is constructed in the moment of its entry into literary form, in the gap between the ideological project and the specifically literary form. Thus the text is no more a transcendent unity than the human subject. The texts of Jules Verne, for instance, whose work Macherey analyses in some detail, indicate that 'if Jules Verne chose to be the spokesman of a certain ideological condition, he could not choose to be what he in fact became' (ibid., p. 94). What Macherey reveals in Verne's *The Secret of the Island* is an unpredicted and contradictory element, disrupting the colonialist ideology which informs the conscious project of the work. Within the narrative, which concerns the willing surrender of nature to improvement by a team of civilized and civilizing colonizers, there *insists* an older and contrary myth which the consciousness of the text rejects. Unexplained events imply another mysterious presence on what is apparently a desert island. Captain Nemo's secret presence, and his influence on the fate of the castaways from a subterranean cave, is the source of the series of enigmas and the final disclosure which constitute the narrative. But his existence in the text has no part in the overt ideological project. On the contrary, it represents the return of the repressed in the form of a re-enacting of the myth of Robinson Crusoe. This myth evokes both a literary ancestor—Defoe's story—on which all subsequent castaway stories are to some degree conditional, and an ancestral relationship to nature—the creation of an economy by Crusoe's solitary struggle to appropriate and transform the island—on which subsequent bourgeois society is also conditional. The Robinson Crusoe story, the antithesis of the conscious project of the narrative, is also the condition of its existence. It returns, as the repressed experience returns to the consciousness of the patient in dreams and slips of the tongue and in doing so it unconsciously draws attention to an origin and a history from which both desert island stories and triumphant bourgeois ideology are unable to cut themselves off, and with which they must settle their account. *The Secret of the Island* thus reveals, through the discord within it between the conscious project and the insistence of the disruptive unconscious, the *limits* of the coherence of nineteenth-century ideology.

The object of the critic, then, is to seek not the unity of the work, but the multiplicity and diversity of its possible meanings, its incompleteness, the omissions which it displays but cannot describe, and above all its contradictions. In its absences, and in the collisions between its divergent meanings, the text implicitly criticizes its own ideology; it contains within itself the critique of its own values, in the sense that it is available for a new process of production of meaning by the reader, and in this process it can provide a knowledge of the limits of ideological representation.

Macherey's way of reading is precisely contrary to traditional Anglo-American critical practice, where the quest is for the unity of the work, its coherence, a way of repairing any deficiencies in consistency by reference to the author's philosophy or the contemporary world picture. In thus smoothing out contradiction, closing the text, criticism becomes the accomplice of ideology. Having created a canon of acceptable texts, criticism then provides them with acceptable interpretations, thus effectively censoring any elements in them which come into collision with the dominant ideology. To deconstruct the text, on the other hand, is to open it, to release the possible positions of its intelligibility, including those which reveal the partiality (in both senses) of the ideology inscribed in the text.

THE CASE OF SHERLOCK HOLMES

In locating the transitions and uncertainties of the text it is important to remember, Macherey insists, sustaining the parallel with psychoanalysis, that the problem of the work is not the same as its *consciousness* of a problem (Macherey 1978, p. 93). In 'Charles Augustus Milverton,' one of the short stories from *The Return of Sherlock Holmes*, Conan Doyle presents the reader with an ethical problem. Milverton is a blackmailer; blackmail is a crime not easily brought to justice since the victims are inevitably unwilling to make the matter public; the text therefore proposes for the reader's consideration that in such a case illegal action may be ethical. Holmes plans to burgle Milverton's house to recover the letters which are at stake, and both Watson and the text appear to conclude, after due consideration, that the action is morally justifiable. The structure of the narrative is symmetrical: one victim initiates the plot, another concludes it. While Holmes and Watson hide in Milverton's study a woman shoots him, protesting that he has ruined her life. Inspector Lestrade asks Holmes to help catch the murderer. Holmes replies that certain crimes justify private revenge, that his sympathies are with the criminal and that he will not handle the case. The reader is left to ponder the ethical implications of his position.

Meanwhile, on the fringes of the text, another narrative is sketched. It too contains problems but these are not foregrounded. Holmes's client is the Lady Eva Blackwell, a beautiful debutante who is to be married to the Earl of Dovercourt. Milverton has secured letters she has written 'to an impecunious young squire in the country.' Lady Eva does not appear in the narrative in person. The content of the letters is not specified, but they are 'imprudent, Watson, nothing worse.'

Milverton describes them as 'sprightly.' Holmes's sympathies, and ours, are with the Lady Eva. None the less we, and Holmes, accept without question on the one hand that the marriage with the Earl of Dovercourt is a desirable one and on the other that were he to see the letters he would certainly break off the match. The text's elusiveness on the content of the letters, and the absence of the Lady Eva herself, deflects the reader's attention from the potentially contradictory ideology of marriage which the narrative takes for granted.

This second narrative is also symmetrical. The murderer too is a woman with a past. She is not identified. Milverton has sent her letters to her husband who in consequence 'broke his gallant heart and died.' Again the text is unable to be precise about the content of the letters since to do so would be to risk losing the sympathy of the reader for either the woman or her husband.

In the mean time Holmes has become engaged. By offering to marry Milverton's housemaid he has secured information about the layout of the house he is to burgle. Watson remonstrates about the subsequent fate of the girl, but Holmes replies:

> 'You can't help it, my dear Watson. You must play your cards as best you can when such a stake is on the table. However, I rejoice to say that I have a hated rival who will certainly cut me out the instant that my back is turned. What a splendid night it is.'

The housemaid is not further discussed in the story.

The sexuality of these three shadowy women motivates the narrative and yet is barely present in it. The disclosure which ends the story is thus scarcely a disclosure at all. Symbolically Holmes has burnt the letters, records of women's sexuality. Watson's opening paragraph constitutes an apology for the 'reticence' of the narrative; 'with *due suppression* the story may be told'; 'The reader will excuse me if I conceal the date *or any other fact*' (my italics).

The project of the Sherlock Holmes stories is to dispel magic and mystery, to make everything explicit, accountable, subject to scientific analysis. The phrase most familiar to all readers—'Elementary, my dear Watson'—is in fact a misquotation, but its familiarity is no accident since it precisely captures the central concern of the stories. Holmes and Watson are both men of science. Holmes, the 'genius,' is a scientific conjuror who insists on disclosing how the trick is done. The stories begin in enigma, mystery, the impossible, and conclude with an explanation which makes it clear that logical deduction and scientific method render all mysteries accountable to reason:

> I am afraid that my explanation may disillusionize you, but it has always been my habit to hide none of my methods, either from my friend Watson or from anyone who might take an intelligent interest in them. ('The Reigate Squires,' *The Memoirs of Sherlock Holmes*)

The stories are a plea for science not only in the spheres conventionally associated with detection (footprints, traces of hair or cloth, cigarette ends), where they have been deservedly influential on forensic practice, but in all areas. They reflect the widespread optimism characteristic of their period concerning the comprehensive power of positivist science. Holmes's ability to deduce Watson's train of thought, for instance, is repeatedly displayed, and it owes nothing to the supernatural. Once explained, the reasoning process always appears 'absurdly simple,' open to the commonest of common sense.

The project of the stories themselves, enigma followed by disclosure, echoes precisely the structure of the classic realist text. The narrator himself draws attention to the parallel between them:

> 'Excellent!' I cried.
> 'Elementary,' said he. 'It is one of those instances where the reasoner can produce an effect which seems remarkable to his neighbour because the latter has missed the one little point which is the basis of the deduction. The same may be said, my dear fellow, for the effect of some of these little sketches of yours, which is entirely meretricious, depending as it does upon your retaining in your hands some factors in the problem which are never imparted to the reader. Now, at present I am in the position of these same readers, for I hold in this hand several threads of one of the strangest cases which ever perplexed a man's brain, and yet I lack the one or two which are needful to complete my theory. But I'll have them, Watson, I'll have them!' ('The Crooked Man,' *Memoirs*)

(The passage is quoted by Macherey [1978, p. 35] in his discussion of the characteristic structure of narrative.)

The project also requires the maximum degree of 'realism'—verisimilitude, plausibility. In the interest of science no hint of the fantastic or the implausible is permitted to remain once the disclosure is complete. This is why even their own existence as writing is so frequently discussed within the texts. The stories are alluded to as Watson's 'little sketches,' his 'memoirs.' They resemble fictions because of Watson's unscientific weakness for story-telling:

> 'I must admit, Watson, that you have some power of selection which atones for much which I deplore in your narratives. Your fatal habit of looking at everything from the point of view of a story instead of as a scientific exercise has ruined what might have been an instructive and even classical series of demonstrations.' ('The Abbey Grange,' *The Return of Sherlock Holmes*)

In other words, the fiction itself accounts even for its own fictionality, and the text thus appears wholly transparent. The success with which the Sherlock Holmes stories achieve an illusion of reality is repeatedly demonstrated. In their Foreword to *The Sherlock Holmes Companion* (1962) Michael and Mollie Hardwick comment on their own recurrent illusion 'that we were dealing with a figure of real life rather than of fiction. How vital Holmes appears, compared with many people of one's own acquaintance.'

De Waal's bibliography of Sherlock Holmes lists twenty-five 'Sherlockian' periodicals apparently largely devoted to conjectures, based on the 'evidence' of the stories, concerning matters only hinted at in the texts—Holmes's education, his income and his romantic and sexual adventures. According to *The Times* in December 1967, letters to Sherlock Holmes were then still commonly addressed to 221B Baker Street, many of them asking for the detective's help.

None the less these stories, whose overt project is total explicitness, total veri-similitude in the interests of a plea for scientificity, are haunted by shadowy, mysterious and often silent women. Their silence repeatedly conceals their sexuality, investing it with a dark and magical quality which is beyond the reach of scientific knowledge. In 'The Greek Interpreter' (*Memoirs*) Sophie Kratides has run away with a man. Though she is the pivot of the plot she appears only briefly: 'I could not see her clearly enough to know more than that she was tall and graceful, with black hair, and clad in some sort of loose white gown.' Connotatively the white gown marks her as still virginal and her flight as the result of romance rather than desire. At the same time the dim light surrounds her with shadow, the unknown. 'The Crooked Man' concerns Mrs. Barclay, whose husband is found dead on the day of her meeting with her lover of many years before. Mrs. Barclay is now insensible, 'temporarily insane' since the night of the murder and therefore unable to speak. In 'The Dancing Men' (*Return*) Mrs. Elsie Cubitt, once engaged to a criminal, longs to speak but cannot bring herself to break her silence. By the time Holmes arrives she is unconscious, and she remains so for the rest of the story. Ironically the narrative concerns the breaking of the code which enables her former lover to communicate with her. Elsie's only contribution to the correspondence is the word, 'never.' The precise nature of their relationship is left mysterious, constructed of contrary suggestions. Holmes says she feared and hated him; the lover claims, 'She had been engaged to me, and she would have married me, I believe, if I had taken over another profession.' When her husband moves to shoot the man whose coded messages are the source of a 'terror' which is 'wearing her away,' Elsie restrains him with compulsive strength. On the question of her motives the text is characteristically elusive. Her husband recounts the story:

> 'I was angry with my wife that night for having held me back when I might have caught the skulking rascal. She said that she feared that I might come to harm. For an instant it had crossed my mind that what she really feared was that *he* might come to harm, for I could not doubt that she knew who this man was and what he meant by those strange signals. But there is a tone in my wife's voice, Mr. Holmes, and a look in her eyes which forbid doubt, and I am sure that it was indeed my own safety that was in her mind.'

After her husband's death Elsie remains a widow, faithful to his memory and devoting her life to the care of the poor, apparently expiating something unspecified, perhaps an act or a state of feeling, remote or recent.

'The Dancing Men' is 'about' Holmes's method of breaking the cipher. Its project is to dispel any magic from the deciphering process. Elsie's silence is in the interest of the story since she knows the code. But she also 'knows' her feelings towards her former lover. Contained in the completed and fully disclosed story of the decipherment is another uncompleted and undisclosed narrative which is more than merely peripheral to the text as a whole. Elsie's past is central and causal. As a result, the text with its project of dispelling mystery is haunted by the mysterious state of mind of a woman who is unable to speak.

The classic realist text had not yet developed a way of signifying women's sexuality except in a metaphoric or symbolic mode whose presence disrupts the realist surface. Joyce and Lawrence were beginning to experiment at this time with modes of sexual signification but in order to do so they largely abandoned the codes of realism. So much is readily apparent. What is more significant, however, is that the presentation of so many women in the Sherlock Holmes stories as shadowy, mysterious and magical figures precisely contradicts the project of explicitness, transgresses the values of the texts, and in doing so throws into relief the poverty of the contemporary concept of science. These stories, pleas for a total explicitness about the world, are unable to explain an area which none the less they cannot ignore. The version of science which the texts present would constitute a clear challenge to ideology: the interpretation of all areas of life, physical, social and psychological, is to be subject to rational scrutiny and the requirements of coherent theorization. Confronted, however, by an area in which ideology itself is uncertain, the Sherlock Holmes stories display the limits of their own project and are compelled to manifest the inadequacy of a bourgeois scientificity which, working within the constraints of ideology, is thus unable to challenge it.

Perhaps the most interesting case, since it introduces an additional area of shadow, is 'The Second Stain' (*Return*), which concerns two letters. Lady Hilda Trelawney Hope does speak. She has written before her marriage 'an indiscreet letter . . . a foolish letter, a letter of an impulsive, loving girl.' Had her husband read the letter his confidence in her would have been for ever destroyed. Her husband is none the less presented as entirely sympathetic, and here again we encounter the familiar contradiction between a husband's supposed reaction, accepted as just, and the reaction offered to the reader by the text. In return for her original letter Lady Hilda gives her blackmailer a letter from 'a certain foreign potentate' stolen from the dispatch box of her husband, the European Secretary of State. This political letter is symbolically parallel to the first sexual one. Its contents are equally elusive but it too is 'indiscreet,' 'hot-headed'; certain phrases in it are 'provocative.' Its publication would produce 'a most dangerous state of feeling' in the nation. Lady Hilda's innocent folly is the cause of the theft: she knows nothing of politics and was not in a position to understand the consequences of her action. Holmes ensures the restoration of the political letter and both secrets are preserved.

Here the text is symmetrically elusive concerning both sexuality and politics. Watson, as is so often the case where these areas are concerned, begins the story by apologizing for his own reticence and vagueness. In the political instance what becomes clear as a result of the uncertainty of the text is the contradictory nature of the requirements of verisimilitude in fiction. The potentate's identity and the nature of his indiscretion cannot be named without involving on the part of the reader either disbelief (the introduction of a patently fictional country would be dangerous to the project of verisimilitude) or belief (dangerous to the text's status as fiction, entertainment; also quite possibly politically dangerous). The scientific project of the texts require that they deal in 'facts,' but their nature as fiction forbids the introduction of facts.

The classic realist text instills itself in the space between fact and illusion through the presentation of a simulated reality which is plausible but *not real*. In this lies its power as myth. It is because fiction does not normally deal with 'politics' directly, except in the form of history or satire, that it is ostensibly innocent and therefore ideologically effective. But in its evasion of the real also lies its weakness as 'realism.' Through their transgression of their own values of explicitness and verisimilitude, the Sherlock Holmes stories contain within themselves an implicit critique of their limited nature as characteristic examples of classic realism. They thus offer the reader through the process of deconstruction a form of knowledge, not about 'life' or 'the world,' but about the nature of fiction itself.

Thus, in adopting the form of classic realism, the only appropriate literary mode, positivism is compelled to display its own limitations. Offered as science, it reveals itself to a deconstructive reading as ideology at the very moment that classic realism, offered as verisimilitude, reveals itself as fiction. In claiming to make explicit and *understandable* what appears mysterious, these texts offer evidence of the tendency of positivism to push to the margins of experience whatever it cannot explain or understand. In the Sherlock Holmes stories classic realism ironically tells a truth, though not the truth about the world which is the project of classic realism. The truth the stories tell is the truth about ideology, the truth which ideology represses, its own existence as ideology itself.

WORKS CITED

Althusser, Louis (1971) *Lenin and Philosophy and Other Essays,* tr. Ben Brewster (London: New Left Books).

Barthes, Roland (1975) *S/Z,* tr. Richard Miller (London: Cape).

Benveniste, Emile (1971) *Problems in General Linguistics* (Miami: University of Miami Press).

Conan Doyle, Arthur (1950) *The Memoirs of Sherlock Holmes* (Harmondsworth: Penguin).

Conan Doyle, Arthur (1976) *The Return of Sherlock Holmes* (London: Pan).

Coward, Rosalind and John Ellis (1977) *Language and Materialism* (London: Routledge & Kegan Paul).

Derrida, Jacques (1973) *Speech and Phenomena,* tr. David B. Allison (Evanston, Ill.: Northwestern University Press).

De Waal, Ronald (1972) *The World Bibliography of Sherlock Holmes* (Greenwich, Conn.: New York Graphic Society).

Hardwick, Michael and Mollie (1972) *The Sherlock Holmes Companion* (London: John Murray).

Heath, Stephen (1977–8) "Notes of Suture," *Screen* 18:4, pp. 48–76.

Lemaire, Anika (1977) *Jacques Lacan,* tr. David Macey (London: Routledge & Kegan Paul).

Macherey, Pierre (1978) *A Theory of Literary Production,* tr. Geoffrey Wall (London: Routledge & Kegan Paul).

Nowell-Smith, Geoffrey (1976) 'A Note on History Discourse,' *Edinburgh 76 Magazine* 1, pp. 26–32.

Saussure, Ferdinand de (1974) *Course in General Linguistics,* tr. Wade Baskin (London: Fontana).

Willemen, Paul (1978) 'Notes on Subjectivity—On Reading "Subjectivity Under Siege,"' *Screen* 19:1, pp. 41–69.

TOWARD A FEMINIST NARRATOLOGY

(1986)

> What you choose and reject theoretically, then, depends upon what
> you are practically trying to do. This has always been the case with
> literary criticism: it is simply that it is often very reluctant to realize
> the fact. In any academic study we select the objects and methods of
> procedure which we believe the most important, and our assessment
> of their importance is governed by frames of interest deeply rooted
> in our practical forms of social life. Radical critics are no different in
> this respect: it is just that they have a set of social priorities with which
> most people at present tend to disagree. This is why they are com-
> monly dismissed as "ideological," because "ideology" is always a way
> of describing other people's interests rather than one's own.
>
> TERRY EAGLETON (211)

Feminist criticism, like narratology and all good theories perhaps, is an optimistic enterprise, eager to account for the whole of its relevant universe. For nearly
two decades it has not only offered new ways of seeing a vast range of texts by
both women and men, in virtually every genre and language; it has also scrutinized the assumptions, theories, and methods of literary scholarship, from biography and history to deconstruction and psychoanalysis, from archetypal criticism
to reader response. Yet in the sometimes sharp debates both within feminist criticism (especially between "American" and "French" approaches[1]) and between
feminism and other critical modes, structuralist-formalist methods have been virtually untouched. In consequence, narratology has had little impact on feminist
scholarship, and feminist insights about narrative have been similarly overlooked
by narratology. The title of this essay may therefore seem startling, as if I am trying to force an intersection of two lines drawn on different planes: the one scientific, descriptive, and non-ideological, the other impressionistic, evaluative, and
political (a false opposition that I hope my opening epigraph helps to dissolve).

   Although feminism and narratology cannot really be said to have a history, there
have been a few gestures of synthesis. While narratological studies are absent
from nearly all of the otherwise eclectic and wide-ranging collections of feminist
approaches to literature, the excellent volume *Women and Language in Literature
and Society* (1980) does incorporate essays of structuralist bent.[2] The only direct

efforts to link feminism and narratology of which I am aware are Mária Minich Brewer's critique of narratology in "A Loosening of Tongues," Mieke Bal's application of it in "Sexuality, Symbiosis and Binarism" and the recent *Femmes imaginaires*,[3] my own attempt to forge a feminist poetics of point of view in *The Narrative Act*, and the very recent essay of Robyn Warhol.[4] Even feminist critics who acknowledge considerable debt to their formalist or structuralist training have sharply criticized its limitations. Naomi Schor vows that she could not practice feminist criticism at all in the "subtle oppression exercised [in American departments of French] by structuralism at its least self-critical and doctrinaire" (ix); Josephine Donovan, speaking from an Anglo-American perspective, rejects "the dissection of literature as if it were an aesthetic machine made up of paradoxes, images, symbols, etc., as so many nuts and bolts easily disintegrated from the whole" ("Women's Poetics" 108).[5] It would be safe, I think, to say that no contemporary theory, whether Anglo-American or continental, has exerted so little influence on feminist criticism or been so summarily dismissed as formalist-structuralist narratology.

In part, of course, this coolness toward narratology—both the practice and the word[6]—is characteristic of the profession as a whole. At the end of her excellent book on narrative poetics, Shlomith Rimmon-Kennan feels compelled to ask whether she has written "an introduction . . . or an obituary" to the field (130). Terry Eagleton uses even stronger death imagery when he likens structuralism to "killing a person in order to examine more conveniently the circulation of the blood" (109). To psychoanalytic critics like Peter Brooks, a formalist narratology, however valuable, cannot grasp "our experience of reading narrative as a dynamic operation" (316).[7] And there is perhaps no surer barometer of professional sentiment than David Lodge's brilliant satire, *Small World*, in which Morris Zapp says of a Sorbonne narratologist, "'Hasn't his moment passed? I mean, ten years ago everybody was into that stuff, actants and functions and mythemes and all that jazz. But now . . . '" (134). Those Anglo-American scholars who were never comfortable with structuralism in general or narratology in particular have probably been relieved at its decline, while most critics grounded in Continental thinking have moved on to post-structuralist theories that offer an exhilarating openness against which narratology may seem mechanical, empirical, hardly conducive to the *plaisir du texte*.

Given a literary climate at best indifferent to narratology, my desire to explore the compatibility of feminism and narratology is also a way to think about what narratology can and cannot do, what place it might have in the contemporary critical environment of American departments of literature, and how it might enrich the hermeneutical enterprise for critics who are not themselves theorists of narrative. My immediate task, however, will be more circumscribed: to ask whether feminist criticism, and particularly the study of narratives by women, might benefit from the methods and insights of narratology and whether narratology, in turn, might be altered by the understandings of feminist criticism and the experience of women's texts. It is in the frank desire to say yes to both these questions that this essay has been conceived. It is in the supposition that the readers of this journal are more involved with narratology than with feminism that my emphasis will be on the second question rather than the first.

There are compelling reasons why feminism (or any explicitly political criticism) and narratology (or any largely formal poetics) might seem incompatible. The technical, often neologistic, vocabulary of narratology has alienated critics of many persuasions and may seem particularly counterproductive to critics with political concerns. Feminists also tend to be distrustful of categories and oppositions, of "a conceptual universe organized into the neat paradigms of binary logic" (Schor ix)[8]—a distrust which explains part of the attraction of feminist theory to Derridean deconstruction. But there are (at least) three more crucial issues about which feminism and narratology might differ: the role of gender in the construction of narrative theory, the status of narrative as mimesis or semiosis, and the importance of context for determining meaning in narrative.

The most obvious question feminism would ask of narratology is simply this: upon what body of texts, upon what understandings of the narrative and referential universe, have the insights of narratology been based? It is readily apparent that virtually no work in the field of narratology has taken gender into account, either in designating a canon or in formulating questions and hypotheses. This means, first of all, that the narratives which have provided the foundation for narratology have been either men's texts or texts treated as men's texts. Genette's formulation of a "Discours du récit" on the basis of Proust's *A la Recherche du temps perdu*, Propp's androcentric morphology of a certain kind of folktale, Greimas on Maupassant, Iser on male novelists from Bunyan to Beckett, Barthes on Balzac, Todorov on the *Decameron*—these are but evident examples of the ways in which the masculine text stands for the universal text. In the structuralist quest for "invariant elements among superficial differences" (Lévi-Strauss 8), for (so-called) universals rather than particulars, narratology has avoided questions of gender almost entirely. This is particularly problematic for those feminist critics—in this country, the majority—whose main interest is the "difference or specificity of women's writing" (Showalter, "Women's Time" 38). The recognition of this specificity has led not only to the rereading of individual texts but to the rewriting of literary history; I am suggesting that it also lead to a rewriting of narratology that takes into account the contributions of women as both producers and interpreters of texts.[9]

This challenge does not deny the enormous value of a body of brilliant narrative theory for the study of women's works; indeed, it has been applied fruitfully to such writers as Colette (Bar, "The Narrating and the Focalizing") and Eliot (Costello) and is crucial to my own studies of narrative voice in women's texts. It does mean that until women's writings, questions of gender, and feminist points of view are considered, it will be impossible even to know the deficiencies of narratology. It seems to me likely that the most abstract and grammatical concepts (say, theories of time) will prove to be adequate. On the other hand, as I will argue later in this essay, theories of plot and story may need to change substantially. And I would predict that the major impact of feminism on narratology will be to raise new questions, to add to the narratological distinctions that already exist, as I will be suggesting below in my discussions of narrative level, context, and voice.

A narratology for feminist criticism would also have to reconcile the primarily semiotic approach of narratology with the primarily mimetic orientation of most (Anglo-American) feminist thinking about narrative. This difference reminds us that "literature is at the juncture of two systems"; one can speak about it as

a representation of life
an account of reality
a mimetic document

and as

a non-referential linguistic system
an enunciation supposing a narrator and a listener
primarily a linguistic construct.
(Furman 64–65)

Traditionally, structuralist narratology has suppressed the representational aspects of fiction and emphasized the semiotic, while feminist criticism has done the opposite. Feminist critics tend to be more concerned with characters than with any other aspect of narrative and to speak of characters largely as if they were persons. Most narratologists, in contrast, treat characters, if at all, as "patterns of recurrence, motifs which are continually recontextualized in other motifs"; as such, they "lose their privilege, their central status, and their definition" (Weinsheimer 195). This conception could seem to threaten one of feminist criticism's deepest premises: that narrative texts, and particularly texts in the novelistic tradition, are profoundly (if never simply) referential—and influential—in their representations of gender relations. The challenge to both feminism and narratology is to recognize the dual nature of narrative, to find categories and terms that are abstract and semiotic enough to be useful, but concrete and mimetic enough to seem relevant for critics whose theories root literature in "the real conditions of our lives" (Newton 125).

The tendency to pure semiosis is both cause and effect of a more general tendency in narratology to isolate texts from the context of their production and reception and hence from what "political" critics think of as literature's ground of being—the "real world." This is partly a result of narratology's desire for a precise, scientific description of discourse, for many of the questions concerning the relationship of literature to the "real world"—questions of why, so what, to what effect—are admittedly speculative. Thus "when narratology does attempt to account for the contextual, it does so in terms of narrative conventions and codes. Yet their capacity to account for social, historical, or contextual differences always remains limited by the original formalist closure within which such codes and conventions are defined" (Brewer 1143). This is why early in the history of formalism, critics like Medvedev and Bakhtin called for a "sociological poetics" that would be dialectically theoretical and historical: "Poetics provides literary history with direction in the specification of the research material and the basic definitions of its forms and types. Literary history amends the definitions of poetics, making them more flexible, dynamic, and adequate to the diversity of the historical material" (30). My insistence on writing women's texts into the historical canon of narratology has precisely this aim of making it more adequate to the diversity of narrative.

Finally, feminist criticism would argue that narratology itself is ideological, indeed in an important sense fictional. One need not agree wholeheartedly with Stanley Fish that "formal units are always a function of the interpretive model one brings to bear (they are not 'in the text')" (13), to recognize that no interpretive system is definitive or inevitable. But as Fish also reminds us, every theory must believe itself the best theory possible (361). Formalist-structuralist narratology may "know" that its categories are not immanent, but it proceeds as if there were "a stable and immediately knowable text, directly available to classificatory operations that are themselves neutral and innocent of interpretive bias" (Chambers 18–19). Feminist criticism has simply not had this luxury: in its critique of masculine bias, it has of necessity taken the view that theory sometimes says more about the reader than about the text.

A narratology for feminist criticism would begin, then, with the recognition that revision of a theory's premises and practices is legitimate and desirable. It would probably be cautious in its construction of systems and favor flexible categories over fixed sets. It would scrutinize its norms to be sure of what they are normative. It would be willing to look afresh at the question of gender and to reform its theories on the basis of women's texts, as Robyn Warhol's essay on the "engaging narrator," just published in *PMLA*, begins to do. In both its concepts and its terminology, it would reflect the mimetic as well as the semiotic experience that is the reading of literature, and it would study narrative in relation to a referential context that is simultaneously linguistic, literary, historical, biographical, social, and political. Granted, narratology might have to be willing to cede some precision and simplicity for the sake of relevance and accessibility, to develop terminology less confusing, say, than a series like analepsis, prolepsis, paralepsis, and metalepsis. The valuable and impressive work that has been done in the field would be opened to a critique and supplement in which feminist questions were understood to contribute to a richer, more useful, and more complete narratology. For as I have been trying to suggest, a narratology that cannot adequately account for women's narratives is an inadequate narratology for men's texts as well.

A re-formed narratology should be of particular interest to feminist critics because fiction is the dominant genre in the study of women and literature. The necessarily semiotic nature of even a revised narratology will help to balance feminist criticism's necessarily mimetic commitments. The comprehensiveness and care with which narratology makes distinctions can provide invaluable methods for textual analysis. As Mieke Bal argues, "The use of formally adequate and precise tools is not interesting in itself, but it can clarify other, very relevant issues and provides insights which otherwise remain vague" ("Sexuality" 121). Narratology and feminist criticism might profitably join forces, for example, to explore the teleological aspects of narrative, which have concerned narratologists like Ann Jefferson and Marianna Torgovnick and feminist critics like Rachel Blau DuPlessis. I can imagine a rich dialogue between Armine Mortimer Kotin's and Nancy K. Miller's analyses of the plot of *La Princesse de Clèves*. And a major benefit of narratology is that it offers a relatively independent (pre-textual) framework for studying groups of texts. It could, for example, provide a particularly valuable foundation for exploring one of the most complex and troubling questions for feminist criticism: whether there is indeed a "woman's writing" and/or a female tradition, whether men and women do write differently. For given the volatile nature of the question, the precision and abstraction of narratological systems offers the safety for investigation that more impressionistic theories of difference do not. This kind of research would demonstrate the particular responsiveness of narratology to certain problems for which other theories have not been adequate and hence illustrate its unique value for feminist scholarship.

I would like to begin the movement toward a feminist narratology by identifying some of the questions a feminist reading might raise for narratology. I will emphasize here not so much the fruitful applications which narratology could currently offer but the questions that it does not yet seem to have addressed. I have chosen, instead of a typical piece of fiction, a far more anomalous work because it presents many complexities in a short space of text and allows me to examine several aspects of women's writing and writing in general. The text is a letter, allegedly written by a young bride whose husband censored her correspondence. It appeared in *Atkinson's Casket* in April 1832, sandwiched between a discussion of angels and directions for "calisthenic exercises."[10] No indication is given of the letter's source, authenticity, or authorship. I am assuming, but cannot be certain, that it is apocryphal; I make no assumptions about the author's sex. Here is the text as it appears in the *Casket*:

Female Ingenuity

Secret Correspondence.—A young Lady, newly married, being obliged to show her husband, all the letters she wrote, sent the following to an intimate friend.

I cannot be satisfied, my Dearest Friend!
blest as I am in the matrimonial state.
unless I pour into your friendly bosom,
which has ever been in unison with mine,
the various deep sensations which swell
with the liveliest emotions of pleasure
my almost bursting heart. I tell you my dear
husband is one of the most amiable of men,
I have been married seven weeks, and
have never found the least reason to
repent the day that joined us, my husband is
in person and manners far from resembling
ugly, crass, old, disagreeable, and jealous
monsters, who think by confining to secure;
a wife, it is his maxim to treat as a
bosom-friend and confidant, and not as a
plaything or menial slave, the woman
chosen to be his companion. Neither party
he says ought to obey implicitly;—
but each yield to the other by turns—
An ancient maiden aunt, near seventy,
a cheerful, venerable, and pleasant old lady,
lives in the house with us—she is the delight of both young and old—she is civil to all the neighborhood round,
generous and charitable to the poor—
I know my husband loves nothing more
than he does me; he flatters me more
than the glass, and his intoxication

(for so I must call the excess of his love)
often makes me blush for the unworthiness
of its object, and I wish I could be more deserving
of the man whose name I bear. To
say all in one word, my dear, and to
crown the whole, my former gallant lover
is now my indulgent husband, my fondness
is returned, and I might have had
a Prince, without the felicity I find with
him. Adieu! May you be as blest as I am unable to wish that I could be more
happy.
N. B.—The key to the above letter, is to read the first and then every alternate line.

For purposes of easy reference, I reproduce below the decoded subtext that this
reading of alternate lines will yield:

I cannot be satisfied, my Dearest Friend!
unless I pour into your friendly bosom,
the various deep sensations which swell
my almost bursting heart. I tell you my dear
I have been married seven weeks, and
repent the day that joined us, my husband is
ugly, crass, old, disagreeable, and jealous[;]
a wife, it is his maxim to treat as a
plaything or menial slave, the woman
he says ought to obey implicitly;
An ancient maiden aunt, near seventy,
lives in the house with us—she is the devil to all the neighborhood round.
I know my husband loves nothing more
than the glass, and his intoxication
often makes me blush for the unworthiness
of the man whose name I bear. To
crown the whole, my former gallant lover
is returned, and I might have had
him. Adieu! May you be as blest as I am unhappy.

Written for two readers (the prying husband and the intimate friend) this letter
is in an unusually obvious sense a double construction, a blatant specimen of writing over and under censorship. The surface text and subtext are strikingly different both in story and narration, and a narrative theory adequate for describing
the whole will have to account for both and for the narrative frame that binds
them. In particular, such a text raises for discussion questions about narrative
voice, narrative situation, and plot.

Perhaps the most obvious difference between the letters, apart from their contrasting stories, is the difference between the two voices. Some linguists have argued that there is a "woman's language" or a discourse of the powerless:[11] speech
that is "polite, emotional, enthusiastic, gossipy, talkative, uncertain, dull, and

chatty" in contrast to men's speech or powerful speech, which is "capable, direct, rational, illustrating a sense of humor, unfeeling, strong (in tone and word choice) and blunt" (Kramarae 58). The two letters illustrate many of the differences between these two modes of speech. The surface text is virtually a sampler of "women's language": its self-effacing narrator praises the "more deserving" husband and blushes for her own "unworthiness"; her "liveliest emotions" generate a discourse of repetition, hyperbole, convolution, and grammatical anomaly. It is the voice of one who clearly can*not* "say all in one word," who can assert herself only in empty phrases and a syntax of negativity. The voice of the subtext is, by contrast, strikingly simple and direct, in the kind of language that commands (an all-too-ready) authority.[12] This second narrator shows herself angry, strong, decisive, sure of her judgments, acutely aware of her husband's deficiencies and of her own lost opportunities. Her speech acts—"I repent," "I know," "she is the devil," "I am unhappy"—are acts of conviction; such a voice requires enormous confidence and would probably be accorded an immediate credibility. Beneath the "feminine" voice of self-effacement and emotionality, then, lies the "masculine" voice of authority that the writer cannot inscribe openly. The subtext also exposes the surface text, and hence the surface voice, as a subterfuge, revealing the "feminine style" to be a caricature donned to mask a surer voice in the process of communicating to a woman under the watchful eyes of a man. But this also means that the powerless form called "women's language" is revealed as a potentially subversive—hence powerful—tool.

In *The Narrative Act* I called for a poetics that would go beyond formal classifications in order to describe the subtle but crucial differences between voices like these. For in structural terms the two voices are similar: both are first-person/protagonist (autodiegetic) narrators (though they are addressing different narratees). Most of the qualities that distinguish the two voices have yet to be codified by narratology. One might ask, for example, what kinds of illocutionary acts the narrator undertakes and whether she undertakes them in a discourse of "presence" or "absence," if we take "absence" to encompass such practices as "irony, ellipsis, euphemism, litotes, periphrasis, reticence, pretermission, digression, and so forth" (Hamon 99). This question, in turn, might lead to a (much-needed) theory that would define and describe *tone* in narrative. Tone might be conceived at least in part as a function of the relationship between the deep and superficial structures of an illocutionary act (e.g., the relationship between an act of judgment and the language in which the judgment is expressed).

This double text recalls an even sharper lesson about narrative voice, the lesson formulated by Bakhtin: that in narrative there is no single voice, that in far subtler situations than this one, voice impinges upon voice, yielding a structure in which discourses of and for the other constitute the discourses of self; that, to go as far as Wayne Booth does, "We are constituted in polyphony" (51). The blatant heteroglossia of this letter—and I shall suggest below that it is even more layered than at first appears—is but a sharper version of the polyphony of all voice and, certainly in visible ways, of the female voices in many women's narratives. For the condition of being woman in a male-dominant society may well necessitate the double voice, whether as conscious subterfuge or as tragic dispossession of the self. Thus in a text like Charlotte Perkins Gilman's "The Yellow Wallpaper," the narrator speaks her desires underneath a discourse constructed for her by her husband, John; in Susan Glaspell's "A Jury of Her Peers" two women protect a third from a conviction for murder by communicating in "women's language" under the watchful but unseeing eyes of the Law; in novel after novel Jane Austen constitutes a narrative voice that cannot be pinned down, that can be read according to one's own desires; a novel like Marge Piercy's *Small Changes* builds a double structure through which both its author and its protagonist work out the necessity of living in a world of double discourse (Hansen). A narratology adequate to women's texts (and hence to all texts, though polyphony is more pronounced and more consequential in women's narratives and in the narratives of other dominated peoples) would have to acknowledge and account for this polyphony of voice, identifying and disentangling its strands, as recent studies by Graciela Reyes and Michael O'Neal begin to do.

If we return with this understanding of voice to the double-text letter, it is easy to identify those verbal features that distinguish one from the other by examining the forms of "excess" that were pared away in the decoding process. The first and less significant is a combination of repetition and hyperbole that serves as "filler," yielding phrases like "which has ever been in unison with mine" and "with the liveliest emotions of pleasure." The second is more important, for it creates the syntactic hinge that binds and finally transforms the whole: a series of negations that the subtext will reverse:

> I . . . have *never* found the least reason to repent
> my husband is . . . *far from* resembling . . . monsters
> a wife, it is his maxim to treat . . . *not* as a plaything
> *Neither* party, he says ought to obey implicitly
> I am *unable* to wish that I could be more happy—

This negativity is more than the link between two texts; it is the means by which the two letters finally yield a third: a story, a third voice, a third audience. For the negativity makes of the surface text not one narrator's simple proclamation of happiness but the indictment of an entire social system. What indeed, does the surface paint but the very portrait of marriage that it claims to erase? Each negative statement suggests departure from a social norm, a norm in which brides repent their marriages, husbands are monstrous, women are treated as playthings or slaves, and women's desires are unthinkable. In other words, the surface text, by saying what one particular marriage is not, shows the terrible contours of what its narrator expected marriage to be. While the subtext condemns one man and laments one woman's fate, the surface letter condemns an entire society, presenting as typical the conditions which the subtext implies to be individual. The subtext, then, becomes an instance of the surface text rather than its antithesis; the two versions reveal not opposing but related truths. It is fitting, then, that they meet at their point of dissatisfaction, at the single line—the first—that does not change: "I cannot be satisfied, my dearest Friend!"

In the light of this reading, women's language becomes not simply a vehicle for constructing a more legitimate (masculine, powerful) voice but the voice through which the more global judgment of patriarchal practices is exercised. This text differs from the "palimpsestic" discourse feminist criticism frequently describes in which "surface designs" act simply as a cover to "conceal or obscure deeper, less accessible (and less socially acceptable) levels of meaning" (Gilbert and Gubar 73). Here the "surface design" turns out to be a more damning discourse than the text it purports to protect. The text designed for the husband conceals an undertext (the text designed for the confidante), but the undertext, in turn, creates a new reading of the surface text and hence a third text designed, I would argue, for yet another addressee. This third text is the one constituted by the *public* "display-text"[13] that is the letter *as it appeared* in *Atkinson's Casket*. Its addressee is the *literary* reader; she is neither the duped male nor the sister-confidante but the unidentified public narratee of either sex who can see beyond the immediate context of the writer's epistolary circumstance to read the negative discourse as covert cultural analysis. Thus the literary context of this text provides a third and entirely different reading from the readings yielded to the private audiences of husband and friend. At the same time, it is *the knowledge of* the other two texts, the access to the private texts, that opens the third reading, in a version, perhaps, of what Genette calls *hypertextualité* (*Palimpsestes* 11).

The fact that this letter has several narratees suggests the importance of recognizing the narrative levels a text may contain. Gérard Genette has made an extremely important contribution to narratology in distinguishing the multiple diegetic levels possible in a single text because one narrative may enclose or generate another (Genette, *Narrative Discourse* 227–37; *Nouveau Discours* 55–64). Genette speaks of the outermost level as the *extradiegetic*, of a narrative incorporated within this one as *intradiegetic*, and of a third narrative level as *metadiegetic*. Extradiegetic narrators, says Genette, are usually "author-narrators"—Jane Eyre, George Eliot's "third person" voice—and "as such they occupy the same narrative level as their public—that is, as you and me" (*Narrative Discourse* 229). But as Genette also makes clear, there is no *necessary* connection between extradiegetic narration and a public audience; letter-writers and diarists (Pamela, Werther) may also be extradiegetic narrators. Intradiegetic (and metadiegetic) narrators—Rochester when he is telling Jane Eyre the story of Bertha Mason, the characters in *Middlemarch*—are conventionally able to address only narratees inscribed *within* the text. In *Frankenstein* Walton's letters to his sister constitute an extradiegetic narrative; Frankenstein's story, told to Walton, is intradiegetic, and the monster's history, narrated to Frankenstein and enclosed within the tale he tells Walton, is metadiegetic. Genette's notion of levels provides a precise way of speaking about such embedded narratives and identifying their narratees—and for describing transgressions across narrative levels (called metalepses) like those Diderot's narrator commits in *Jacques le fataliste*.

But Genette himself recognizes that narrative level has been made too much of, and that indeed it does not take us very far. In the *Nouveau Discours* he makes clear just how relative the distinction of levels is by generating an imaginary scene in which three men sit down, one offers to tell the others a story which he warns will be long, and the storyteller begins, "'For a long time I used to go to bed early...'" (64). With a frame of only a sentence, says Genette, the entirety of Proust's *A la Recherche* suddenly becomes an intradiegetic narration. If we look at the letter in terms of Genette's levels, we could identify as either an extradiegetic narrator or simply as an editor the voice that presents the letter as a specimen of "Female Ingenuity" and explains both its context and its secret code to the readers of *Atkinson's Casket*.[14] The diegetic level of the letter is then contingent on this initial decision. And both the surface letter and the subtext, being interlinear, exist on the same level, in an unusual case of double diegesis. Genette's notion of levels does not allow us to say much about the narrative situation of this letter because it applies only to internal relations among parts of a text. It does not describe any individual narrative act *per se,* and it closes off the text from considerations external and contextual.

To provide a more complete analysis of narrative level, I would propose as a complement to Genette's system a distinction between public and private narration. By public narration I mean simply narration (implicitly or explicitly) addressed to a narratee who is external (that is, heterodiegetic)[15] to the textual world and who can be equated with a public readership; private narration, in contrast, is addressed to an explicitly designated narratee who exists only within the textual world. Public narration evokes a direct relationship between the reader and the narratee and clearly approximates most closely the nonfictional author–reader relationship, while in private narration the reader's access is indirect, as it were "through" the figure of a textual persona. Such a distinction, combined with Genette's notions of both level and person, would yield the typology shown on the facing page.

I propose this notion of public and private narrative levels as an additional category particularly relevant to the study of women's texts. For women writers, as feminist criticism has long noted, the distinction between private and public contexts is a crucial and a complicated one. Traditionally speaking, the sanctions against women's writing have taken the form not of prohibitions to write at all but of prohibitions to write for a public audience. As Virginia Woolf comments, "Letters did not count": letters were private and did not disturb a male discursive hegemony. Dale Spender takes the distinctions even further, arguing that the notions of public and private concern not only the general context of textual production but its gender context as well: that is, writing publicly becomes synonymous with writing for and to men. Spender comments:

> The dichotomy of male/female, public/private is maintained by permitting women to write . . . for themselves (for example, diaries) and for each other in the form of letters, "accomplished" pieces, moral treatises, articles of interest for other women—particularly in the domestic area—and even novels for women. . . . There is no contradiction in patriarchal order while women write for women and therefore remain within the limits of the private sphere; the contradiction arises only when women write for men. (192)

The bride's letter both illustrates Spender's formulation and expands it in important ways. The only public level of narration here is the narration that presents the letter in the *Casket* as the "display" of a correspondence. In relation to this level, the letter itself is a private text, designed for a private readership. Yet the surface letter is intended by its narrator to be an eminently *public* text in relation to the subtext, which is the private text she urgently hopes will *not* be available to the "public" who is her husband. In terms of the I-narrator's intentions, the "public" text is indeed designed for the man, the private (indeed secret) text for the female friend. One must already, then, redefine the simple distinction of public and private to create a category in which a narration is private but is designed to be read as well by someone other than its officially designated narratee;[16] I will call this a semi-private narrative act. To the extent that the surface letter is in some sense public, it dramatizes the way in which women's public discourse may be contaminated by internal or external censorship. This, in turn, helps to explain why historically women writers have chosen, more frequently than men, private forms of narration—the letter, the diary, the memoir addressed to a single individual—rather than forms that require them to address a public readership, and why public and private narratives by women employ different narrative strategies.[17] The concept could also be applied fruitfully to texts in which the narrative level is unclear, as in Gilman's "The Yellow Wallpaper" and Craik's *A Life for a Life*, which seem to implicate a public narratee while purporting to write a private diary.

LEVEL	PERSON	PUBLIC	PRIVATE
extradiegetic	heterodiegetic (third-person)	narration of *Emma* or *Middlemarch*	moments of "metalepse" in *Jacques le fataliste* when narrator consorts with his characters
	homodiegetic (first-person)	Jane Eyre's narration	letters of Walton or Werther
intradiegetic or metadiegetic	heterodiegetic (third-person)	?	tales of the *Heptameron* or *Scheherezade*
	homodiegetic (first-person)	the "found" memoir of Lionel Verney in Mary Shelley's *The Last Man* or Pirandello's *Six Characters*	narratives of Frankenstein and the Monster

The application of the distinction public/private to literary texts requires us to think in more complex ways about the dichotomy of gender that Spender attaches to private and public discourse. Here again the letter is illustrative. For if my analysis is persuasive in suggesting the existence of a third text available only to one who has read both the second and the first, and read in the light of a particular understanding both of women and of textuality, then the public text—that is, the one which is directed by the extradiegetic narrator or editor to "anyone"—is also the most hidden text, the hardest to see, for nothing really points to its existence except itself, and it requires a reader who brings to it particular kinds of knowledge. Since it is at the public level of narration that the ideal reading becomes possible, the letter *presented as a display text* also *escapes* the gender associations of the original structure of the intradiegetic narrative (in which it seems that public = male and private = female), suggesting a kind of paradigm for reading "as a woman" that encompasses but is not determined by the question of sex. Equally, when women write novels that use private narrative forms, they are nonetheless writing for a public, and a public that cannot entirely be dichotomized in gender terms. How individual writers negotiate this complex context of gender and public-ity constitutes another important area to investigate.

The difference between Genette's formulation of narrative levels and my own illustrates, I hope, the difference between purely formal and contextual approaches to meaning in narrative. Just as speech act theory understood that the minimal unit of discourse was not the sentence but the *production* of the sentence in a specific context, so the kind of narratology I am proposing would understand that the minimal narrative is the narrative as produced. In the case of the letter that appears in the *Casket*, questions of context are closely related to interpretive possibilities. For depending on whether one sees the letter as a historical document or as a text written deliberately for display—and whether, if "display text," an imitation or a parody—different readings of the letter emerge. If the text is an authentic document, a letter actually written by an unhappy wife that somehow came into the hands of the *Casket*, then the text might become important historical evidence of the ways in which women's writing is conditioned by censorship. If the text were constructed as imitation, it stands as evidence of the *perception*, if not the historical fact, of censorship. But the letter may well have been intended as a parody of the "female style." Indeed, the history of this style, and its connection to the epistolary, provides the context for an interesting possibility. Historically, the letter has such overdetermined associations with women that what became thought of as the "female style," a style acclaimed for its artlessness, its sense of immediacy and lack of forethought, was a style tied to the epistolary mode (Donovan, "The Silence is Broken" 212–14). If the letter is in fact a "display text," it may well be a display of "female ingenuity" not only in the obvious sense of a clever composition that finds a "woman's way" around censorship, but in the service of a broader and literary design: to make mockery of the assumptions about women's "artless" epistolary style, to reveal woman as man's equal in intellectual capacity. For "ingenuity," the *OED* tells us, means not only the (oxymoronic) union of straightforward openness with the genius for skillful, inventive design but also the quality or condition of being a free-born man. And if the letter was written by its own editor, it also provided a convenient and safe vehicle for criticizing male dominance, since an editor need take no responsibility for a private "found" text.

The rhetorical complexity of the letter reminds us that narrative meaning is also a function of narrative circumstance. Narratology has not yet provided satisfying language through which to make distinctions of rhetorical context;[18] feminist criticism, in its concern with questions of authenticity and authorship, might find it difficult even to talk about a text this uncertain in origin. A feminist narratology might acknowledge the existence of multiple texts, each constructed by a (potential) rhetorical circumstance. To the extent that such questions determine the very *meaning* of narrative, they are questions for narratology.

The final element of my discussion of difference between the bride's two letters—the question of story or plot—I will treat only sketchily here, for it lies out-side my area of expertise. In traditional terms, the surface text—the one written for the husband—can barely be said to have a plot, and one might of course ar-gue that it is not a narrative at all. There is not a singular verb tense in the text; every independent predication is cast in the stative or iterative mode. All the ac-tion that the text implies, hence all there is of story, precedes the narrative mo-ment; by the time of the writing all conflict—the gap between expectations and reality—has already been resolved (and not by the protagonist's actions at all). Notions of both plot and character are strained by such a structure in which the *actant* is really a recipient, in which nothing whatever is predicted of which the fulfillment would constitute plot as it is narratologically defined. And although one could also see this stasis as the basis for a plot left to the reader's imagina-tion, to the extent that plot is a function of modalized predication and hence of desire (Costello, Brooks), the surface text refuses even the possibility of plot: "I am *unable to wish* that I could be more happy."

Thus the first text creates stasis of both event and character, an idyll of har-mony in which the "indulgent husband," as "bosom friend," is a synthesis of the confidante with her "friendly bosom" and the "gallant lover": all characters but the protagonist coalesce into one idealized whole. But the subtext does offer the elements of a possible plot. Here we have a full-blown triangle—husband, lover, wife—in which the necessity for a confidante becomes logical. The plot of this subtext is actually highly conventional: drunken husband, sinister maiden aunt,[19] gallant suitor in the wings. But here too the expectations for story, though more fully roused, are shunted aside. While there is one singular event—"my former gallant lover is returned"—the narrator says, "I *might have* had him," suggesting that there is no real possibility of change.

Can one speak narratologically of plot or even story in these two letters, or is one condemned simply to negative definitions—plotlessness, or story without plot? Narratology is rich in its efforts to pin down the nature of plot. The formu-lations of Propp, Bremond, Todorov, Costello, Pavel, Prince, all offer useful ways to talk about large numbers of texts, perhaps of most (premodernist) texts. But in the case of the letter, each schema fails. Although the subtext is a catalogue of acts of villainy, for example, one cannot say of it as Propp says of his folktales that "each new act of villainy, each new lack creates a new move" (92). In his canon movement is possible; here it is not.[20] The units of anticipation and ful-fillment or problem and solution that structure plot according to narrative theo-rists of plot assume that textual actions are based on the (intentional) deeds of protagonists; they assume a power, a possibility, that may be inconsistent with what women have experienced both historically and textually, and perhaps in-consistent even with women's desires. A radical critique like Mária Brewer's sug-gest that plot has been understood as a "discourse of male desire recounting itself through the narrative of adventure, project, enterprise, and conquest," the "dis-course of desire as separation and mastery" (1151, 1153).

If standard narratological notions of plot do not adequately describe (some) women's texts, then what is needed is a radical revision in theories of plot. For one thing, as Katherine Rabuzzi notes (in Donovan, "Jewett's Critical Theory" 218), "'by and large, most women have known a nonstoried existence.'" Women's experience, says Donovan, often seems, when held against the masculine plot, "static, and in a mode of waiting. It is not progressive, or oriented toward events happening sequentially or climactically, as in the traditional masculine story plot" (218–19). This letter, or a novel like Sarah Orne Jewett's *The Country of the Pointed Firs*, can thus only be defined as a "plotless text." (Donovan, "Women's Poetics," 106). Similarly, some of Grace Paley's finest stories (for example, "Friends" and "Rushy and Edie" in the most recent collection, *Later the Same Day*), which a traditional narratology would describe as "plotless," are constituted by plots of women's attempts to "make sense" of their world.[21] A contemporary popular novel like Meg Wolitzer's *Hidden Pictures*, which sets up negative possibilities that neither occur nor are noted *not* to occur, when measured against plot theories becomes a "flawed" story making worrisome predictions that it does not fulfill. Yet one could also see this plot as a structure of anxiety and (gradual) relief that corresponds to real-world experiences of women in the difficult circumstances of this novel's protagonists, a lesbian couple raising a son in suburbia. If again and again scholars of women's writing must speak in terms of the "plot*less*" (*usually* in quotation marks, suggesting their dissatisfaction with the term), then perhaps something is wrong with the notions of plot that have followed from Propp's morphology. Perhaps narratology has been mistaken in trying to arrive at a single definition and description of plot. We will learn more about women's narratives—and about scores of twentieth-century texts—if we make ourselves find language for describing their plots in positive rather than negative terms.

There is another level of plot, too, that the bride's letter urges us to think about. There is, in fact, one sequence of anticipation and fulfillment that this text does fully constitute, and it occurs in the act of writing. In the case of both letters, whether the narrator's life is happy or miserable, what she "cannot be satisfied" without is, simply, *the telling*—narrative itself. The act of writing becomes the fulfillment of desire, telling becomes the single predicated act, as if to tell were in itself to resolve, to provide closure. *Récit* and *histoire*, rather than being separate elements, converge, so that telling becomes integral to the working out of story. Communication, understanding, being understood, becomes not only the objective of the narration but the act that can transform (some aspect of) the narrated world. In a universe where waiting, inaction, reception, predominate, and action is only minimally possible, the narrative act itself becomes the source of possibility.

What happens in the letter, then, is that the wish for the other's happiness substitutes for the possibility of change in one's own life; the writer's experience serves as a (positive or negative) stimulus to the reader's own story. The confidante thus becomes an active participant not simply in narration, but in plot itself; the wish for the narratee's happiness transfers the imperatives of plot, so that the possibilities of change and fulfillment are given over to the narratee. The letter thus suggests a plot behind women's "plotless" narrative, the subversive plot of sharing an experience so that the listener's life may complete the speaker's tale. I would be eager for narratology to talk about such a crossing of the plot of narration with the story plot.

My analysis of this coded letter suggests in sketchy ways aspects of narrative that a revised poetics might scrutinize and codify. A comprehensive theory of voice would develop a framework for describing the elements that constitute polyphony and would formulate a linguistically based theory of narrative tone. Attention to the rhetorical context of narrative—its generic status and the public or private level of the narration—would be understood as important determinants of narrative meaning. And theories of plot and story would be reexamined to find alternatives to the notion of plot as active acquisition or solution and to incorporate the plot that may be generated by the relationship between narrator and narratee. Once it is clear that some (women's) texts cannot be adequately described by traditional, formalist narratology, we begin to see that other texts—postmodernist texts, texts by writers of Asia and Africa, perhaps—may be similarly unaccounted for. It is only, I believe, such an expansive narratology that can begin to fulfill the wish Gerald Prince expresses at the end (164) of his *Narratology*: that "ultimately, narratology can help us understand what human beings are."

NOTES

I am grateful to Michael Ragussis, Leona Fisher, Caren Kaplan, and Harold Mosher for invaluable criticism of this essay in successive manuscript stages.

1. A simple distinction between so-called "American" and "French" feminisms is impossible. By "French" feminism is usually meant feminism conceived within the theoretical premises of poststructuralism and hence heavily indebted to the writings of Derrida, Foucault, Lacan, Kristeva, Cixous, and Irigaray. "American" feminism tends to be conceived within the political imperatives of the American women's liberation movement and the historical experience of women in general and women writers in particular. Both modes are practiced in the United States, and the two have become increasingly intertwined. Nonetheless, the debates go on. For further discussion of the differences see, for example, the introduction and bibliography and the essay by Ann Jones in Showalter, *The New Feminist Criticism*; for an example of the new synthesis, see Meese.

2. See especially Furman 45–54.

3. A piece of Bal's book on the Hebrew Bible is available to English-language readers as "Sexuality, Sin and Sorrow."

4. It is revealing that the single sentence in my book most cited by reviewers is the statement that "my training is deeply formalist, and my perspective as deeply feminist"; clearly many scholars consider feminism and narratology an odd pair.

5. I find it ironic that Donovan's rejection of formalist "dissection" is justified by finding it incompatible with what Evelyn Beck and I have called a "women's epistemology" (Lapser and Beck 86).

6. Particularly in the wake of the new psychoanalytic narrative theories the term *narratology* has fallen into disuse, perhaps perceived as too narrowly structuralist. Critics disagree about the differences between *narratology* and *narrative poetics*; see, for example, Rimmon-Kenan's attempt to distinguish the two in *Narrative Fiction* (133 n.1). By *narratology* I mean simply that branch of poetics concerned with defining and describing all aspects of narrative.

I have chosen throughout this essay to use the word *narratology* rather than *narrative poetics* partly to foreground the dissonance between narratology and feminism and partly to identify more precisely the formalist/structuralist practices that I am discussing here. I will, however, be calling in this essay for a study of narrative that is finally less formalist than *narratology* generally connotes. For that reason, and since I am also suggesting a less alienating terminology for the study of narrative, I can also see the advantages of *narrative poetics*, and I would not hesitate to make the change.

7. While there is a reader-oriented narratology that emphasizes the process of text production, Rimmon-Kenan is right to imply that "the more far-reaching 'revisionism' of some reader-oriented studies . . . is often at odds with the very project of narrative poetics" (118).

8. Oppositional thinking has, of course, been sharply disadvantageous to women, as to other dominated groups. Binary pairs of the variety P/not-P are precisely the structures that create hierarchy (as in nonwhite, illiterate, un-American). Categories and classifications, while sometimes also used by feminists, are ripe for Procrustean distortions, for premature closures, for stifling rigidities.

9. In *The Narrative Act* I have in fact worked with women's texts as well as with men's, and I have also included the narrative theories of neglected women like Vernon Lee and Käte Friedemann. But I did not really undertake the radical reevaluation I am now calling for, one which would mean *beginning* with women's writings (both narrative and theoretical) in order not to remarginalize the marginal, in compensation for a training that has been so strongly biased in favor of male discourse.

10. I discovered this letter quite accidentally. While browsing through the stacks of the University of Wisconsin-Madison library several years ago, I came across an odd compendium titled *The Genteel Female*, edited by Clifton Furness. Its endpapers consist of the page from *Atkinson's Casket* which contains the letter.

11. There are three controversies embedded in this topic: whether there is in fact a "women's language," whether it is exclusive to women, and whether it is a negative characteristic. In 1975 Robin Lakoff suggested that women use language forms that differ from men's, and that this language reinforces the social and political powerlessness of women. Other critics have argued that "women's language" is a fiction constructed upon sex stereotypes and that women do not actually speak differently from men. Still others agree that there is difference but rather than seeing the difference as negative, they consider "women's language" better oriented to concern for others and to the careful contextualizing of one's beliefs (rather than the "masculine" assertion of universals). For a sense of this controversy see Spender 32–51. A related question is whether it is more accurate to speak of "women's language" or of "powerless language." On the basis of empirical study in a courtroom context, O'Barr and Atkins found far more credibility accorded to female witnesses speaking in the "powerful style" than to those speaking in the "powerless style."

12. Richard Sennett believes that simple, direct discourse in the active voice bespeaks a confidence that frequently inspires a too-easy and hence dangerous obeisance. See *Authority*, chapter 5.

13. Mary Louise Pratt uses the term to designate a text or speech act whose relevance lies in its tellability, and which is thus detachable from its immediate circumstances of production. Literary texts and jokes are examples. See Pratt 136–48.

14. I thank Harold Mosher for the suggestion that this figure is not actually a narrator at all but merely an editor. I had been considering this voice to be similar to the one that introduces, say, the governess's narrative in *The Turn of the Screw*. The problem, I believe, lies at least in part with Genette's own system, which does not distinguish an editor from an extradiegetic narrator. Such a narrator, after all, may appear only briefly to introduce a major intradiegetic narrative and may do so in the guise of an editor.

15. I am suggesting that not only narrators but also narratees can be heterodiegetic or homodiegetic—that is, within or outside the fictional world—and that a homodiegetic narrator can address a heterodiegetic narratee (although it would constitute a narrative transgression for a heterodiegetic narrator to address a homodiegetic narratee). I have decided not to use these terms, however, in order to avoid confusion with heterodiegetic and homodiegetic narrators and because of my commitment to simplify narrative terminology.

16. This is somewhat different from the case of a letter that is intercepted by a character for whom it was not destined, as happens frequently, say, in *Clarissa*. The difference is

that in this case the narrator *knows* her text will be intercepted and has structured the surface narrative accordingly.

17. The differences between private and public narration in narratives by women are a major focus of the book I am now completing on women writers and narrative voice.

18. As Susan Léger has pointed out to me, a book like Ross Chambers's *Story and Situation* is a healthy exception to this norm.

19. I am aware that my analysis of the letters has omitted any discussion of the maiden aunt and that her "maidenness" makes her a particularly interesting figure in the context of the portraits of marriage in these letters.

20. One could argue that the presence of a lover in the subtext keeps eternally open the possibility of action, even if that action seems to be thwarted by the given text. Such a possibility testifies to the power of the desire for plot.

21. For the example of these Paley stories I am indebted to Alan Wilde, whose book, *Middle Ground: Studies in Contemporary American Fiction* (Philadelphia: University of Pennsylvania Press, 1987), includes a chapter on her work.

WORKS CITED

Bakhtin, M. M. "Discourse in the Novel." *The Dialogic Imagination*. Trans. Caryl Emerson and Michael Holquist. Austin: U of Texas P, 1981. 259–422.

Bal, Mieke. *Femmes imaginaires: l'ancien testament au risque d'une narratologie critique*. Paris: Nizet; Montreal: HMH, 1986.

———. "The Narrating and the Focalizing: A Theory of the Agents in Narrative." *Style* 17 (1983):234–69.

———. "Sexuality, Semiosis and Binarism: A Narratological Comment on Bergen and Arthur." *Arethasa* 16.1–2 (1983):117–35.

———. "Sexuality, Sin, and Sorrow: The Emergence of Female Character (A Reading of Genesis 1–3)." *The Female Body in Western Culture*. Ed. Susan Rubin Suleiman. Cambridge: Harvard UP, 1986. 317–38.

Booth, Wayne C. "Freedom of Interpretation: Bakhtin and the Challenge of Feminine Criticism." *Critical Inquiry* 9 (1982):45–76.

Bremond, Claude. *Logique du récit*. Paris: Seuil, 1973.

Brewer, Mária Minich. "A Loosening of Tongues: From Narrative Economy to Women Writing." *MLN* 99 (1984):1141–61.

Brooks, Peter. "Narrative Desire." *Style* 18 (1984):312–27.

———. *Reading for the Plot*. New York: Knopf, 1984.

Chambers, Ross. *Story and Situation: Narrative Seduction and the Power of Fiction*. Minneapolis: U of Minnesota P, 1984.

Costello, Edward. "Modality and Narration: A Linguistic Theory of Plotting." Diss. Wisconsin, 1975.

Donovan, Josephine. "Sarah Orne Jewett's Critical Theory: Notes Toward a Feminine Literary Mode." *Critical Essays on Sarah Orne Jewett*. Ed. Gwen L. Nagel. Boston: Hall, 1984.

———. "The Silence is Broken." *Women and Language in Literature and Society*. Ed. Sally McConnel-Ginet et al. New York: Praeger, 1980. 205–18.

———. "Toward a Women's Poetics." *Tulsa Studies in Women's Literatare*. 3.1–2 (1984):99–110.

DuPlessis, Rachel Blau. *Writing Beyond the Ending: Narrative Strategies of Twentieth-Century Women Writers*. Bloomington: Indiana UP, 1985.

Eagleton, Terry. *Literary Theory: An Introduction*. Minneapolis: U of Minnesota P, 1983.

"Female Ingenuity." *Atkinson's Casket or Gems of Literature, Wit and Sentiment*. No. 4, Philadelphia, April 1832:186.

Fish, Stanley. *Is There a Text in this Class? The Authority of Interpretive Communities*. Boston: Harvard UP, 1980.

Furman, Nelly. "The politics of language: beyond the gender principle?" *Making a Difference: Feminist Literary Criticism*. Ed. Gayle Greene and Coppélia Kahn. London: Methuen, 1985. 59–79.

———. "Textual Feminism." *Women and Language in Literature and Society*. Ed. Sally McConnell-Ginet et al. New York: Praeger, 1980. 45–54.

Furness, Clifton, ed. *The Genteel Female*. New York: Knopf, 1931.

Genette, Gérard. *Narrative Discourse: An Essay in Method*. Trans. Jane E. Lewin. Ithaca: Cornell UP, 1980. Trans. of "Discours du récit." *Figures III*. Paris: Seuil, 1972.

———. *Nouveau Discours du récit*. Paris: Seuil, 1983.

———. *Palimpsestes: la littérature au second degré*. Paris: Seuil, 1982.

Gilbert, Sandra, and Susan Gubar. *The Madwoman in the Attic: The Woman Writer and the Nineteenth-Century Literary Imagination*. New Haven: Yale UP, 1979.

Hamon, Philip. "Text and Ideology: For a Poetics of the Norm." *Style* 17 (1983):95–119.

Hansen, Elaine Tuttle. "The Double Narrative Structure of *Small Changes*." *Contemporary American Women Writers: Narrative Strategies*. Ed. Catherine Rainwater and William J. Scheick. Lexington: UP of Kentucky, 1985.

Jefferson, Ann. "*Mise en abyme* and the Prophetic in Narrative." *Style* 17 (1983):196–208.

Kotin, Armine Mortimer. "Narrative Closure and the Paradigm of Self-Knowledge in *La Princesse de Clèves*." *Style* 17, (1983):181–95.

Kramarae, Cheris. "Proprietors of Language." *Women and Language in Literature and Society*. Ed. Sally McConnel-Ginet et al. New York: Praeger, 1980. 58–68.

Lakoff, Robin. *Language and Woman's Place*. New York: Harper and Row. 1975.

Lanser, Susan Sniader. *The Narrative Act: Point of View in Prose Fiction*. Princeton: Princeton UP, 1981.

Lanser, Susan Sniader, and Evelyn Torton Beck. "(Why) Are There No Great Women Critics?—And What Difference Does It Make?" *The Prism of Sex: Essays in the Sociology of Knowledge*. Ed. Julia Sherman and Evelyn T. Beck. Madison: U of Wisconsin P, 1979. 79–91.

Lévi-Strauss, Claude. *Myth and Meaning*. New York: Schocken, 1978.

Lodge, David. *Small World*. New York: Macmillan, 1984.

McConnell-Ginet, Sally, Ruth Borker, and Nelly Furman, eds. *Women and Language in Literature and Society*. New York: Praeger, 1980.

Medvedev, P. N., and M. M. Bakhtin. *The Formal Method in Literary Scholarship: A Critical Introduction to Sociological Poetics*. Trans. Albert J. Wehrle. Baltimore: Johns Hopkins UP, 1978.

Meese, Elizabeth A. *Crossing the Double-Cross: The Practice of Feminist Criticism*. Chapel Hill: U of North Carolina P, 1986.

Miller, Nancy K. "Emphasis Added: Plots and Plausibilities in Women's Fiction." *The New Feminist Criticism: Essays on Women, Literature, and Theory*. Ed. Elaine Showalter. New York: Pantheon, 1985. 339–60.

Newton, Judith. "Making—and Remaking—History: Another Look at 'Patriarchy.'" *Tulsa Studies in Women's Literature* 3.1–2 (1984): 125–41.

O'Barr, William M., and Bowman K. Atkins. "'Women's Language' or 'Powerless Language'?" *Women and Language in Literature and Society*. Ed. Sally McConnell-Ginet et al. New York: Praeger, 1980. 93–110.

O'Neal, Michael. "Point of View and Narrative Technique in the Fiction of Edith Wharton." *Style* 17 (1983):270–89.

Pavel, Thomas G. *The Poetics of Plot: The Case of English Renaissance Drama.* Minneapolis: U of Minnesota P, 1985.

Pratt, Mary Louise. *Toward a Speech Act Theory of Literary Discourse.* Bloomington: Indiana UP, 1977.

Prince, Gerald. *Narratology: The Form and Function of Narrative.* Berlin: Mouton, 1982.

Propp, Vladimir. *Morphology of the Folktale.* Ed. Louis A. Wagner. 2nd ed. Austin: U of Texas P, 1968.

Reyes, Graciela. *Polifonía textual: La citación en el relato literario.* Madrid: Gredos, 1984.

Rimmon-Kennan, Shlomith. *Narrative Fiction: Contemporary Poetics.* London: Methuen, 1983.

Schor, Naomi. *Breaking the Chain: Women, Theory, and French Realist Fiction.* New York: Columbia UP, 1985.

Sennett, Richard. *Authority.* New York: Knopf, 1980.

Showalter, Elaine, ed. *The New Feminist Criticism: Essays on Women, Literature, and Theory.* New York: Pantheon, 1985.

———. "Women's Time, Women's Space; Writing the History of Feminism Criticism." *Tulsa Studies in Women's Literature* 3:1–2 (1984):29–43.

Spender, Dale. *Man Made Language.* London: Routledge and Kegan Paul, 1980.

Torgovnick, Marianna. *Closure in the Novel.* Princeton: Princeton UP, 1981.

Warhol, Robyn R. "Toward a Theory of the Engaging Narrator: Earnest Interventions in Gaskell, Stowe, and Eliot." *PMLA* 101 (1986):811–18.

Weinsheimer, Joel. "Theory of Character: *Emma.*" *Poetics Today* 1:1–2 (1979):185–211.

BARBARA JOHNSON

APOSTROPHE, ANIMATION, AND ABORTION

(1 9 8 6)

> The abortion issue is as alive and controversial in the body politic as it is in the academy and the courtroom.
> JAY L. GARFIELD, *ABORTION: MORAL AND LEGAL PERSPECTIVES*

Although rhetoric can be defined as something politicians often accuse each other of using, the political dimensions of the scholarly study of rhetoric have gone largely unexplored by literary critics. What, indeed, could seem more dry and apolitical than a rhetorical treatise? What could seem farther away from budgets and guerrilla warfare than a discussion of anaphora, antithesis, prolepsis, and preterition? Yet the notorious CIA manual[1] on psychological operations in guerrilla warfare ends with just such a rhetorical treatise: an appendix on techniques of oratory which lists definitions and examples for these and many other rhetorical figures. The manual is designed to set up a Machiavellian campaign of propaganda, indoctrination, and infiltration in Nicaragua, underwritten by the visible display and selective use of weapons. Shoot softly, it implies, and carry a big schtick. If rhetoric is defined as language that says one thing and means another, then the manual is in effect attempting to maximize the collusion between deviousness in language and accuracy in violence, again and again implying that targets are most effectively hit when most indirectly aimed at. Rhetoric, clearly, has everything to do with covert operations. But are the politics of violence already encoded in rhetorical figures as such? In other words, can the very essence of a political issue—an issue like, say, abortion—hinge on the structure of a figure? Is there any *inherent* connection between figurative language and questions of life and death, of who will wield and who will receive violence in a given human society?

As a way of approaching this question, I will begin in a more traditional way by discussing a rhetorical device that has come to seem almost synonymous with the lyric voice: the figure of apostrophe. In an essay in *The Pursuit of Signs*, Jonathan Culler indeed sees apostrophe as an embarrassingly explicit emblem of procedures inherent, but usually better hidden, in lyric poetry as such.[2] Apostrophe in the sense in which I will be using it involves the direct address of an absent, dead, or inanimate being by a first-person speaker: "O wild West Wind, thou breath of Autumn's being. . . . " Apostrophe is thus both direct and indirect: based etymologically on the notion of turning aside, of digressing from straight speech, it manipulates the I/Thou structure of *direct* address in an indirect, fictionalized way. The absent, dead, or inanimate entity addressed is thereby made present, animate, and anthropomorphic. Apostrophe is a form of ventriloquism through which the speaker throws voice, life, and human form into the addressee, turning its silence into mute responsiveness.

Baudelaire's poem "Moesta et Errabunda,"[3] whose Latin title means "sad and vagabond," raises questions of rhetorical animation through several different grades of apostrophe. Inanimate objects like trains and ships or abstract entities like perfumed paradises find themselves called upon to attend to the needs of a plaintive and restless lyric speaker. Even the poem's title poses questions of life and death in linguistic terms: the fact that Baudelaire here temporarily resuscitates a dead language prefigures the poem's attempts to function as a finder of lost loves. But in the opening lines of the poem, the direct-address structure seems straightforwardly *un*figurative: "Tell me, Agatha." This could be called a minimally fictionalized apostrophe, although that is of course its fiction. Nothing at first indicates that Agatha is any more dead, absent, or inanimate than the poet himself.

The poem's opening makes explicit the relation between direct address and the desire for the *other's* voice: "Tell me—*you* talk." But something strange soon happens to the face-to-face humanness of this conversation. What Agatha is supposed to talk about starts a process of dismemberment that might have something to do with a kind of reverse anthropomorphism: "Does your heart sometimes take flight?" Instead of conferring a human shape, this question starts to undo one. Then, too, why the name Agatha? Baudelaire scholars have searched in vain for a biographical referent, never identifying one, but always presuming that one exists. In the Pléiade edition of Baudelaire's complete works, a footnote sends the reader to the only other place in Baudelaire's oeuvre where the name Agathe appears—a page in his *Carnets* where he is listing debts and appointments. This would seem to indicate that Agathe was indeed a real person. What do we know about her? A footnote to the *Carnets* tells us she was probably a prostitute. Why? See the poem "Moesta et Errabunda." This is a particularly stark example of the inevitable circularity of biographical criticism.

If Agathe is finally only a proper name written on two different pages in Baudelaire, then the name itself must have a function as a name. The name is a homonym for the word "agate," a semiprecious stone. Is Agathe really a stone? Does the poem express the Orphic hope of getting a stone to talk?

In a poem about wandering, taking flight, getting away from "here," it is surprising to find that, structurally, each stanza acts out not a departure but a return to its starting point, a repetition of its first line. The poem's structure is at odds with its *apparent* theme. But we soon see that the object of the voyage is precisely to return—to return to a prior state, planted in the first stanza as virginity, in the second as motherhood (through the image of the nurse and the pun on *mer/mère*) and finally as childhood love and furtive pleasure. The voyage outward in space is a figure for the voyage backward in time. The poem's structure of address backs up, too, most explicitly in the third stanza. The cry apostrophizing train and ship to carry the speaker off leads to a seeming reprise of the opening line, but by this point the inanimate has entirely taken over: instead of addressing

Agatha directly, the poem asks whether Agatha's heart ever speaks the line the poet himself has spoken four lines earlier. Agatha herself now drops out of the poem, and direct address is temporarily lost, too, in the grammar of the sentence *("Est-il vrai que . . . ")*. The poem seems to empty itself of all its human characters and voices, acting out a *loss* of animation—which is in fact its subject: the loss of childhood aliveness brought about by the passage of time. The poem thus enacts in its own temporality the loss of animation it situates in the temporality of the speaker's life.

At this point it launches into a new apostrophe, a new direct address to an abstract, lost state: "How far away you are, sweet paradise." The poem reanimates, addresses an image of fullness and wholeness and perfect correspondence ("what we love is worthy of our loves"). This height of liveliness, however, culminates strangely in an image of death. The heart that formerly kept trying to fly away now drowns in the moment of reaching its destination ["Où dans la volupté pure le coeur se noie!"]. There may be something to gain, therefore, by deferring arrival, as the poem next seems to do by interrupting itself before grammatically completing the fifth stanza. The poem again ceases to employ direct address and ends by asking two drawn-out, self-interrupting questions. Is that paradise now farther away than India or China? Can one call it back and animate it with a silvery voice? This last question—"Peut-on le rappeler avec des cris plaintifs/ Et l'animer encore d'une voix argentine?"—is a perfect description of apostrophe itself: a trope which, by means of the silvery voice of rhetoric, calls up and animates the absent, the lost, and the dead. Apostrophe itself, then, has become not just the poem's mode but also the poem's theme. In other words, what the poem ends up wanting to know is not how far away childhood is, but whether its own rhetorical strategies can be effective. The final question becomes: can this gap be bridged; can this loss be healed, through language alone?

Shelley's "Ode to the West Wind," which is perhaps the ultimate apostrophic poem, makes even more explicit the relation between apostrophe and animation. Shelley spends the first three stanzas demonstrating that the west wind is a figure for the power to animate: it is described as the breath of being, moving everywhere, blowing movement and energy through the world, waking it from its summer dream, parting the waters of the Atlantic, uncontrollable. Yet the wind animates by bringing death, winter, destruction. How do the rhetorical strategies of the poem carry out this program of animation through the giving of death?

The apostrophe structure is immediately foregrounded by the interjections, four times spelled "O" and four times spelled "oh." One of the bridges this poem attempts to build is the bridge between the "O" of the pure vocative, Jakobson's conative function, or the pure presencing of the second person, and the "oh" of pure subjectivity, Jakobson's emotive function, or the pure presencing of the first person.

The first three stanzas are grammatical amplifications of the sentence "O thou, hear, oh, hear!" All the vivid imagery, all the picture painting, come in clauses subordinate to this obsessive direct address. But the poet addresses, gives animation, gives the capacity of responsiveness, to the wind, not in order to make it speak but in order to make it listen to him—in order to make it listen to him doing nothing but address *it*. It takes him three long stanzas to break out of this intense near-tautology. As the fourth stanza begins, the "I" starts to inscribe itself grammatically (but not thematically) where the "thou" has been. A power struggle starts up for control over the poem's grammar, a struggle which mirrors the rivalry named in such lines as: "If I were now what I was then, I would ne'er have *striven as thus with thee* in prayer in my sore need." This rivalry is expressed as a comparison: "less free than thou," but then: "One *too like* thee." What does it mean to be "too like"? Time has created a loss of similarity, a loss of animation that has made the sense of similarity even more hyperbolic. In other words, the poet, in becoming less than—less like the wind—somehow becomes more like the wind in his rebellion against the loss of likeness.

In the final stanza the speaker both inscribes and reverses the structure of apostrophe. In saying "be thou me," he is attempting to restore metaphorical exchange and equality. If apostrophe is the giving of voice, the throwing of voice, the giving of animation, then a poet using it is always in a sense saying to the addressee, "Be thou me." But this implies that a poet has animation to give. And *that* is what this poem is saying is not, or is no longer, the case. Shelley's speaker's own sense of animation is precisely what is in doubt, so that he is in effect saying to the wind, "I will animate you so that you will animate, or reanimate, me." "Make me thy lyre. . . . "

Yet the wind, which is to give animation, is also a giver of death. The opposition between life and death has to undergo another reversal, another transvaluation. If death could somehow become a positive force for animation, then the poet would thereby create hope for his own "dead thoughts." The animator that will blow his words around the world will also instate the power of their deadness, their deadness as power, the place of maximum potential for renewal. This is the burden of the final rhetorical question. Does death necessarily entail rebirth? If winter comes, can spring be far behind? The poem is attempting to appropriate the authority of natural logic—in which spring always does follow winter—in order to clinch the authority of cyclic reversibility for its own prophetic powers. Yet because this clincher is expressed in the form of a rhetorical question, it expresses natural certainty by means of a linguistic device that mimics *no* natural structure and has no stable one-to-one correspondence with a meaning. The rhetorical question, in a sense, leaves the poem in a state of suspended animation. But that, according to the poem, is the state of maximum potential.

Both the Baudelaire and the Shelley, then, end with a rhetorical question that both raises and begs the question of rhetoric. It is as though the apostrophe is ultimately directed toward the reader, to whom the poem is addressing Mayor Koch's question: "How'm I doing?" What is at stake in both poems is, as we have seen, the fate of a lost child—the speaker's own former self—and the possibility of a new birth or a reanimation. In the poems that I will discuss next, these structures of apostrophe, animation, and lost life will take on a very different cast through the foregrounding of the question of motherhood and the premise that the life that is lost may be someone else's.

In Gwendolyn Brooks's poem "The Mother," the structures of address are shifting and complex. In the first line ("Abortions will not let you forget"), there is a "you" but there is no "I." Instead, the subject of the sentence is the word "abortions," which thus assumes a position of grammatical control over the poem. As entities that disallow forgetting, the abortions are not only controlling but animate and anthropomorphic, capable of treating persons as objects. While

Baudelaire and Shelley addressed the anthropomorphized other in order to re-possess their lost selves, Brooks is representing the self as eternally addressed and possessed by the lost, anthropomorphized other. Yet the self that is possessed here is itself already a "you," not an "I." The "you" in the opening lines can be seen as an "I" that has become alienated, distanced from itself, and combined with a generalized other, which includes and feminizes the reader of the poem. The grammatical I/Thou starting point of traditional apostrophe has been re-placed by a structure in which the speaker is simultaneously eclipsed, alienated, and confused with the addressee. It is already clear that something has happened to the possibility of establishing a clear-cut distinction in this poem between sub-ject and object, agent and victim.

The second section of the poem opens with a change in the structure of ad-dress. "I" takes up the positional place of "abortions," and there is temporarily no second person. The first sentence narrates: "I have heard in the voices of the wind the voices of my dim killed children." What is interesting about this line is that the speaker situates the children's voices firmly in a traditional romantic lo-cus of lyric apostrophe—the voices of the wind, Shelley's "West Wind," say, or Wordsworth's "gentle breeze."[4] Gwendolyn Brooks, in other words, is here ex-plicitly rewriting the male lyric tradition, textually placing aborted children in the spot formerly occupied by all the dead, inanimate, or absent entities previously addressed by the lyric. And the question of animation and anthropomorphism is thereby given a new and disturbing twist. For if apostrophe is said to involve language's capacity to give life and human form to something dead or inanimate, what happens when those questions are literalized? What happens when the lyric speaker assumes responsibility for producing the death in the first place, but without being sure of the precise degree of human animation that existed in the entity killed? What is the debate over abortion about, indeed, if not the question of when, precisely, a being assumes a human form?

It is not until line 14 that Brooks's speaker actually addresses the dim killed children. And she does so not directly, but in the form of a self-quotation: "I have said." This embedding of the apostrophe appears to serve two functions here, just as it did in Baudelaire: a self-distancing function, and a foregrounding of the question of the adequacy of language. But whereas in Baudelaire the distance between the speaker and the lost childhood is what is being lamented, and a res-toration of vividness and contact is what is desired, in Brooks the vividness of the contact is precisely the source of the pain. While Baudelaire suffers from the dimming of memory, Brooks suffers from an inability to forget. And while Baudelaire's speaker actively seeks a fusion between present self and lost child, Brooks's speaker is attempting to fight her way out of a state of confusion be-tween self and other. This confusion is indicated by the shifts in the poem's struc-tures of address. It is never clear whether the speaker sees herself as an "I" or a "you," an addressor or an addressee. The voices in the wind are not created *by* the lyric apostrophe; they rather initiate the need for one. The initiative of speech seems always to lie in the other. The poem continues to struggle to clarify the relation between "I" and "you," but in the end it only succeeds in expressing the inability of its language to do so. By not closing the quotation in its final line, the poem, which began by confusing the reader with the aborter, ends by im-plicitly including the reader among those aborted—and loved. The poem can no more distinguish between "I" and "you" than it can come up with a proper definition of life. For all the Yeatsian tripartite aphorisms about life as what is past or passing or to come, Brooks substitutes the impossible middle ground between "You were born, you had body, you died" and "It is just that you never giggled or planned or cried."

In line 28, the poem explicitly asks, "Oh, what shall I say, how is the truth to be said?" Surrounding this question are attempts to make impossible distinctions: got/did not get, deliberate/not deliberate, dead/never made. The uncertainty of the speaker's control as a subject mirrors the uncertainty of the children's status as an object. It is interesting that the status of the human subject here hinges on the word "deliberate." The association of deliberateness with human agency has a long (and very American) history. It is deliberateness, for instance, that underlies that epic of separation and self-reliant autonomy, Thoreau's *Walden*. "I went to the woods," writes Thoreau, "because I wished to live deliberately, to front only the essential facts of life" [66]. Clearly, for Thoreau, pregnancy was not an essential fact of life. Yet for him as well as for every human being that has yet existed, someone else's pregnancy is the very *first* fact of life. How might the plot of human subjectivity be reconceived (so to speak) if pregnancy rather than autonomy is what raises the question of deliberateness?

Much recent feminist work has been devoted to the task of rethinking the relations between subjectivity, autonomy, interconnectedness, responsibility, and gender. Carol Gilligan's book *In a Different Voice* (and this focus on "voice" is not irrelevant here) studies gender differences in patterns of ethical thinking. The central ethical question analyzed by Gilligan is precisely the decision whether to have, or not to have, an abortion. The first time I read the book, this struck me as strange. Why, I wondered, would an investigation of gender *differences* focus on one of the questions about which an even-handed comparison of the male and the female points of view is impossible? Yet this, clearly, turns out to be the point: there is difference *because* it is not always possible to make symmetrical oppositions. As long as there is symmetry, one is not dealing with difference but rather with versions of the same. Gilligan's difference arises out of the impossibility of maintaining a rigorously logical binary model for ethical choices. Female logic, as she defines it, is a way of rethinking the logic of choice in a situation in which none of the choices are good. "Believe that even in my deliberateness I was not deliberate": believe that the agent is not entirely autonomous, believe that I can be subject and object of violence at the same time, believe that I have not chosen the conditions under which I must choose. As Gilligan writes of the abortion decision, "the occurrence of the dilemma itself precludes nonviolent resolution" [94]. The choice is not between violence and nonviolence, but between simple violence to a fetus and complex, less determinate violence to an involuntary mother and/or an unwanted child.

Readers of Brooks's poem have often read it as an argument against abortion. And it is certainly clear that the poem is not saying that abortion is a good thing. But to see it as making a simple case for the embryo's right to life is to assume that a woman who has chosen abortion does not have the right to mourn. It is to assume that no case *for* abortion can take the woman's feelings of guilt and loss into consideration, that to take those feelings into account is to deny the right to choose the act that produced them. Yet the poem makes no such claim: it attempts the impossible task of humanizing both the mother and the aborted children while presenting the inadequacy of language to resolve the dilemma without violence.

What I would like to emphasize is the way in which the poem suggests that the arguments for and against abortion are structured through and through by the rhetorical limits and possibilities of something akin to apostrophe. The fact that apostrophe allows one to animate the inanimate, the dead, or the absent implies that whenever a being is apostrophized, it is thereby automatically animated, anthropomorphized, "person-ified." (By the same token, the rhetoric of calling makes it difficult to tell the difference between the animate and the inanimate, as anyone with a telephone answering machine can attest.) Because of the ineradicable tendency of language to animate whatever it addresses, rhetoric itself can always have already answered "yes" to the question of whether a fetus is a human being. It is no accident that the anti-abortion film most often shown in the United States should be entitled *The Silent Scream*. By activating the imagination to believe in the anthropomorphized embryo's mute responsiveness in exactly the same way that apostrophe does, the film (which is of course itself a highly rhetorical entity) is playing on rhetorical possibilities that are inherent in all linguistically based modes of representation.

Yet the function of apostrophe in the Brooks poem is far from simple. If the fact that the speaker addresses the children at all makes them human, then she must pronounce herself guilty of murder—but only if she discontinues her apostrophe. As long as she addresses the children, she can keep them alive, can keep from finishing with the act of killing them. The speaker's attempt to absolve herself of guilt depends on never forgetting, never breaking the ventriloquism of an apostrophe through which she cannot define her identity otherwise than as the mother eaten alive by the children she has never fed. Who, in the final analysis, exists by addressing whom? The children are a rhetorical extension of the mother, but she, as the poem's title indicates, has no existence apart from her relation to them. It begins to be clear that the speaker has written herself into a poem she cannot get out of without violence. The violence she commits in the end is to her own language: as the poem ends, the vocabulary shrinks away, words are repeated, nothing but "all" rhymes with "all." The speaker has written herself into silence. Yet hers is not the only silence in the poem: earlier she had said, "You will never . . . silence or buy with a sweet." If sweets are for silencing, then by beginning her apostrophe, "Sweets, if I sinned . . . " the speaker is already saying that the poem, which exists to memorialize those whose lack of life makes them eternally alive, is also attempting to silence once and for all the voices of the children in the wind. It becomes impossible to tell whether language is what gives life or what kills.

> Women have said again and again "This body is *my* body!" and they have
> reason to feel angry, reason to feel that it has been like shouting into the wind.
> —Judith Jarvis Thomson, "A Defense of Abortion"

It is interesting to note the ways in which legal and moral discussions of abortion tend to employ the same terms as those we have been using to describe the figure of apostrophe. "These disciplines [philosophy, theology, and civil and canon law] variously approached the question in terms of the point at which the embryo or fetus became 'formed' or recognizably human, or in terms of when a 'person' came into being, that is, infused with a 'soul' or 'animated'" [Blackmun, *Roe vs. Wade, Abortion: Moral and Legal Perspectives,* Garfield and Hennessey, Eds. 15]. The issue of "fetal personhood" [Garfield and Hennessey 55] is of course a way of bringing to a state of explicit uncertainty the fundamental difficulty of defining personhood in general [cf. Luker 6]. Even if the question of defining the nature of "persons" is restricted to the question of understanding what is meant by the word "person" in the United States Constitution (since the Bill of Rights guarantees the rights only of "persons"), there is not at present, and probably will never be, a stable legal definition. Existing discussions of the legality and morality of abortion almost invariably confront, leave unresolved, and detour around the question of the nature and boundaries of human life. As Justice Blackmun puts it in *Roe vs. Wade*: "We need not resolve the difficult question of when life begins. When those trained in the respective disciplines of medicine, philosophy, and theology are unable to arrive at any consensus, the judiciary, at this point in the development of man's knowledge, is not in a position to speculate as to the answer" [27]. In the case of *Roe vs. Wade*, the legality of abortion is derived from the pregnant couple's right to privacy—an argument which, as Catharine MacKinnon argues in *Roe vs. Wade:* A Study in Male Ideology" [Garfield and Hennessey 45–54], is itself problematic for women, since by protecting "privacy" the courts also protect the injustices of patriarchal sexual arrangements. When the issue is an unwanted pregnancy, some sort of privacy has already, in a sense, been invaded. In order for the personal to avoid being reduced once again to the non-political, privacy, like deliberateness, needs to be rethought in terms of sexual politics. Yet even the attempt to re-gender the issues surrounding abortion is not simple. As Kristin Luker convincingly demonstrates, the debate turns around the claims not only of woman vs. fetus or of woman vs. patriarchal state, but also of woman vs. woman:

> Pro-choice and pro-life activists live in different worlds, and the scope of their lives, as both adults and children, fortifies them in their belief that their views on abortion are the more correct, more moral, and more reasonable. When added to this is the fact that should "the other side" win, one group of women will see the very real devaluation of their lives and life resources, it is not surprising that the abortion debate has generated so much heat and so little light. [Luker 215]
>
> . . . .
>
> Are pro-life activists, as they claim, actually reaching their cherished goal of "educating the public to the humanity of the unborn child?" As we begin to seek an answer, we should recall that motherhood is a topic about which people have very complicated feelings, and because abortion has become the battleground for different definitions of motherhood, neither the pro-life nor the pro-choice movement has ever been "representative" of how most Americans feel about abortion. More to the point, all our data suggest that *neither of these groups will ever be able to be representative.* [224, emphasis in original]

It is often said, in literary-theoretical circles, that to focus on undecidability is to be apolitical. Everything I have read about the abortion controversy in its present form in the United States leads me to suspect that, on the contrary, the undecidable *is* the political. There is politics precisely because there is undecidability.

And there is also poetry. There are striking and suggestive parallels between the "different voices" involved in the abortion debate and the shifting address-structures of poems like Gwendolyn Brooks's "The Mother." A glance at several other poems suggests that there tends indeed to be an overdetermined relation between the theme of abortion and the problematization of structures of address. In Anne Sexton's "The Abortion," six 3-line stanzas narrate, in the first person, a trip to Pennsylvania where the "I" has obtained an abortion. Three times the poem is interrupted by the italicized lines:

> *Somebody who should have been born*
> *is gone.*

Like a voice-over narrator taking superegoistic control of the moral bottom line, this refrain (or "burden," to use the archaic term for both "refrain" and "child in the womb") puts the first-person narrator's authority in question without necessarily constituting the voice of a separate entity. Then, in the seventh and final stanza, the poem extends and intensifies this split:

> Yes, woman, such logic will lead
> to loss without death. Or say what you meant,
> you coward . . . this baby that I bleed.

Self-accusing, self-interrupting, the narrating "I" turns on herself (or is it someone else?) as "you," as "woman." The poem's speaker becomes as split as the two senses of the word "bleed." Once again, "saying what one means" can only be done by ellipsis, violence, illogic, transgression, silence. The question of who is addressing whom is once again unresolved.

As we have seen, the question of "when life begins" is complicated partly because of the way in which language blurs the boundary between life and death. In "Menstruation at Forty," Sexton sees menstruation itself as the loss of a child ("two days gone in blood")—a child that exists because it can be called:

> I was thinking of a son. . . .
> You! . . .
> Will you be the David or the Susan?
>   . . .
> David! Susan! David! David!
>   . . .
> my carrot, my cabbage,
> I would have possessed you before all women,
> calling your name,
> calling you mine.

The political consequences and complexities of addressing—of "calling"—are made even more explicit in a poem by Lucille Clifton entitled "The Lost Baby Poem." By choosing the word "dropped" ("i dropped your almost body down"), Clifton renders it unclear whether the child has been lost through abortion or through miscarriage. What is clear, however, is that that loss is both mourned and rationalized. The rationalization occurs through the description of a life of hardship, flight, and loss: the image of a child born into winter, slipping like ice into the hands of strangers in Canada, conflates the scene of Eliza's escape in *Uncle Tom's Cabin* with the exile of draft resisters during the Vietnam War. The guilt and mourning occur in the form of an imperative in which the notion of "stranger" returns in the following lines:

> if i am ever less than a mountain
> for your definite brothers and sisters. . . .
> . . . let black men call me stranger
> always   for your never named sake.

The act of "calling" here correlates a lack of name with a loss of membership. For the sake of the one that cannot be called, the speaker invites an apostrophe that would expel *her* into otherness. The consequences of the death of a child ramify beyond the mother-child dyad to encompass the fate of an entire community. The world that has created conditions under which the loss of a baby becomes desirable must be resisted, not joined. For a black woman, the loss of a baby can always be perceived as a complicity with genocide. The black mother sees her own choice as one of being either a stranger or a rock. The humanization of the lost baby addressed by the poem is thus carried out at the cost of dehumanizing, even of rendering inanimate, the calling mother.

Yet each of these poems exists, finally, *because* a child does not.[5] In Adrienne Rich's poem "To a Poet," the rivalry between poems and children is made quite explicit. The "you" in the poem is again aborted, but here it is the mother herself who could be called "dim and killed" by the fact not of abortion but of the institution of motherhood. And again, the structures of address are complex and unstable. The deadness of the "you" cannot be named: not suicide, not murder. The question of the life or death of the addressee is raised in an interesting way through Rich's rewriting of Keats's sonnet on his mortality. While Keats writes, "When I have fears that *I* will cease to be" ["When I Have Fears"], Rich writes "and I have fears that *you* will cease to be." If poetry is at stake in both intimations of mortality, what is the significance of this shift from "I" to "you"? On the one hand, the very existence of the Keats poem indicates that the pen has succeeded in gleaning something before the brain has ceased to be. No such grammatical guarantee exists for the "you." Death in the Keats poem is as much a source as it is a threat to writing. Hence, death, for Keats, could be called the mother of poetry while motherhood, for Rich, is precisely the death of poetry. The Western myth of the conjunction of word and flesh implied by the word "incarnate" is undone by images of language floating and vanishing in the toilet bowl of real-flesh needs. The word is not made flesh; rather, flesh unmakes the mother-poet's word. The difficulty of retrieving the "you" as poet is enacted by the structures of address in the following lines:

> I write this   not for you
> who fight to write your own
> words fighting up the falls
> but for another woman   dumb

In saying "I write this not for you," it is almost as though Rich is excluding as addressee anyone who could conceivably be reading this poem. The poem is setting aside both the "I" and the "you"—the pronouns Benveniste associates with personhood—and reaches instead toward a "she," which belongs in the category of "non-person." The poem is thus attempting the impossible task of directly addressing not a second person but a third person—a person who, if she is reading the poem, cannot be the reader the poem has in mind. The poem is trying to include what is by its own grammar excluded from it—to animate through language the non-person, the "other woman." Therefore, this poem, too, is bursting the limits of its own language, inscribing a logic that it itself reveals to be impossible—but necessary. Even the divorce between writing and childbearing is less absolute than it appears: in comparing the writing of words to the spawning of fish, Rich's poem reveals itself to be trapped between the inability to combine and the inability to separate the woman's various roles.

In each of these poems, then, a kind of competition is implicitly instated between the bearing of children and the writing of poems. Something unsettling has happened to the analogy often drawn by male poets between artistic creation and procreation. For it is not true that literature contains no examples of male pregnancy. Sir Philip Sidney, in the first sonnet from "Astrophel and Stella," describes himself as "great with child to speak," but the poem is ultimately produced at the expense of no literalized child. Sidney's labor pains are smoothed away by a midwifely apostrophe ("'Fool,' said my Muse to me, 'look in thy heart, and write!'") [*The Norton Anthology of Poetry* 1:12–14], and by a sort of poetic Caesarian section, out springs the poem we have, in fact, already finished reading. Mallarmé, in "Don du poème," describes himself as an enemy father seeking nourishment for his monstrous poetic child from the woman within apostrophe-shot who is busy nursing a literalized daughter. But since the woman presumably has two breasts, there seems to be enough to go around. As Shakespeare assures the fair young man, "But were some child of yours alive that time,/ You should live twice in it and in my rhyme" [*Sonnets* 17:13–14]. Apollinaire, in his play *Les Mamelles de Tirésias*, depicts woman as a de-maternalized neo-Malthusian leaving the task of childbearing to a surrealistically fertile husband. But again, nothing more disturbing than Tiresian cross-dressing seems to occur. Children are alive and well, and far more numerous than ever. Indeed, in one of the dedicatory poems, Apollinaire indicates that his drama represents a return to health from the literary reign of the *poète maudit*:

> La féconde raison a jailli de ma fable,
> Plus de femme stérile et non plus d'avortons . . .
>
> [Fertile reason springs out of my fable,
> No more sterile women, no aborted children]

This dig at Baudelaire, among others, reminds us that in the opening poem to *Les Fleurs du mal* ("Bénédiction"), Baudelaire represents the poet himself as an abortion manqué, cursed by the poisonous words of a rejecting mother. The question of the unnatural seems more closely allied with the bad mother than with the pregnant father.

Even in the seemingly more obvious parallel provided by poems written to dead children by male poets, it is not really surprising to find that the substitution of poem for child lacks the sinister undertones and disturbed address exhibited by the abortion poems we have been discussing. Ben Jonson, in "On My First Son," calls his dead child "his best piece of poetry," while Mallarmé, in an only semi-guilty *Aufhebung,* transfuses the dead Anatole to the level of an idea. More recently, Jon Silkin has written movingly of the death of a handicapped child ("something like a person") as a change of silence, not a splitting of voice. And Michael Harper, in "Nightmare Begins Responsibility," stresses the powerlessness and distrust of a black father leaving his dying son to the care of a "white-doctor-who-breathed-for-him-all-night." But again, whatever the complexity of the voices in that poem, the speaker does not split self-accusingly or infra-symbiotically in the ways we have noted in the abortion/motherhood poems. While one could undoubtedly find counter-examples on both sides, it is not surprising that the substitution of art for children should not be inherently transgressive for the male poet. Men have in a sense always had no choice but to substitute something for the literal process of birth. That, at least, is the belief that has long been encoded into male poetic conventions. It is as though male writing were by nature procreative, while female writing is somehow by nature infanticidal.

It is, of course, as problematic as it is tempting to draw general conclusions about differences between male and female writing on the basis of these somewhat random examples. Yet it is clear that a great many poetic effects may be colored according to *expectations* articulated through the gender of the poetic speaker. Whether or not men and women would "naturally" write differently about dead children, there is something about the connection between motherhood and death that refuses to remain comfortably and conventionally figurative. When a woman speaks about the death of children in any sense other than that of pure loss, a powerful taboo is being violated. The indistinguishability of miscarriage and abortion in the Clifton poem indeed points to the notion that *any* death of a child is perceived as a crime committed by the mother, something a mother ought by definition to be able to prevent. That these questions should be so inextricably connected to the figure of apostrophe, however, deserves further comment. For there may be a deeper link between motherhood and apostrophe than we have hitherto suspected.

The verbal development of the infant, according to Lacan, begins as a demand addressed to the mother, out of which the entire verbal universe is spun. Yet the mother addressed is somehow a personification, not a person—a personification of presence or absence, of Otherness itself.

> Demand in itself bears on something other than the satisfactions it calls for. It is demand of a presence or of an absence—which is what is manifested in the primordial relation to the mother, pregnant with that Other to be situated *within* the needs that it can satisfy. Insofar as [man's] needs are subjected to demand, they return to him alienated. This is not the effect of his real dependence . . . , but rather the turning into signifying form as such, from the fact that it is from the locus of the Other that its message is emitted. [*Ecrits* 286]

If demand is the originary vocative, which assures life even as it inaugurates alienation, then it is not surprising that questions of animation inhere in the rhetorical figure of apostrophe. The reversal of apostrophe we noted in the Shelley poem ("animate me") would be no reversal at all, but a reinstatement of the primal apostrophe in which, despite Lacan's disclaimer, there is precisely a link between demand and animation, between apostrophe and life-and-death dependency.[6] If apostrophe is structured like demand, and if demand articulates the primal relation to the mother as a relation to the Other, then lyric poetry itself—summed up in the figure of apostrophe—comes to look like the fantastically intricate history of endless elaborations and displacements of the single cry, "Mama!" The question these poems are asking, then, is what happens when the poet is speaking as a mother—a mother whose cry arises out of—and is addressed to—a dead child?

It is no wonder that the distinction between addressor and addressee should become so problematic in poems about abortion. It is also no wonder that the debate about abortion should refuse to settle into a single voice. Whether or not one has ever been a mother, everyone participating in the debate has once been a child. Rhetorical, psychoanalytical, and political structures are profoundly implicated in one another. The difficulty in all three would seem to reside in the attempt to achieve a full elaboration of any discursive position other than that of child.

NOTES

1. I would like to thank Tom Keenan of Yale University for bringing this text to my attention. The present essay has in fact benefited greatly from the suggestions of others, among whom I would like particularly to thank Marge Garber, Rachel Jacoff, Carolyn Williams, Helen Vendler, Steven Melville, Ted Morris, Stamos Metzidakis, Steven Ungar, and Richard Yarborough.

2. Cf. also Paul de Man, in "Lyrical Voice in Contemporary Theory": "Now it is certainly beyond question that the figure of address is recurrent in lyric poetry, to the point of constituting the generic definition of, at the very least, the ode (which can, in turn, be seen as paradigmatic for poetry in general)" [61].

3. For complete texts of the poems under discussion, see the appendix to this article in its original form, in *Diacritics* vol. 5, No. 4 (1975):29–47.

4. It is interesting to note that the "gentle breeze," apostrophized as "Messenger" and "Friend" in the 1805–6 *Prelude* (Book 1, line 5), is, significantly, not directly addressed in the 1850 version. One might ask whether this change stands as a sign of the much-discussed waning of Wordsworth's poetic inspiration, or whether it is, rather, one of a number of strictly rhetorical shifts that *give the impression* of a wane, just as the shift in Gwendolyn Brooks's poetry from her early impersonal poetic narratives to her more recent direct-address poems gives the impression of a politicization.

5. For additional poems dealing with the loss of babies, see the anthology *The Limits of Miracles* collected by Marion Deutsche Cohen. Sharon Dunn, editor of the *Agni Review*, told me recently that she has in fact noticed that such poems have begun to form almost a new genre.

6. An interesting example of a poem in which an apostrophe confers upon the total Other the authority to animate the self is Randall Jarrell's "A Sick Child," which ends: "All that I've never thought of—think of me!"

WORKS CITED

Allison et al., Eds. *The Norton Anthology of Poetry*. New York: W. W. Norton, 1975.

Apollinaire, Guillaume. *Les Mamelles de Tirésias. L'Enchanteur pourrissant*. Paris: Gallimard, 1972.

Baudelaire, Charles. *Oeuvres complètes*. Paris: Pléiade, 1976.

Brooks, Gwendolyn. "The Mother." *Selected Poems*. New York: Harper & Row, 1963.

Clifton, Lucille. "The Lost Baby Poem." *Good News About the Earth*. New York: Random House, 1972.

Cohen, Marion Deutsche, Ed. *The Limits of Miracles*. South Hadley, Eng.: Bergin & Garvey, 1985.

Culler, Jonathan. *The Pursuit of Signs*. Ithaca: Cornell UP, 1981.

de Man, Paul. "Lyrical Voice in Contemporary Theory." *Lyric Poetry: Beyond New Criticism*. Ed. Hosek and Parker. Ithaca: Cornell UP, 1985.

Gilligan, Carol. *In a Different Voice*. Cambridge, MA: Harvard UP, 1982.

Harper, Michael. *Nightmare Begins Responsibility*. Urbana: U of Illinois P, 1975.

Jarrell, Randall. "A Sick Child." *The Voice that is Great within Us*. Ed. Hayden Caruth. New York: Bantam, 1970.

Jonson, Ben. "On My First Son." *The Norton Anthology of Poetry*. Ed. Allison et al. New York: W. W. Norton, 1975.

Keats, John. "When I Have Fears." *The Norton Anthology of Poetry*. Ed. Allison et al. New York: W. W. Norton, 1975.

Lacan, Jacques. *Ecrits*. Trans. Sheridan. New York: W. W. Norton, 1977.

Luker, Kristin. *Abortion and the Politics of Motherhood*. Berkeley: U of California P, 1984.

Mallarmé, Stéphane. *Oeuvres complètes*. Paris: Pléiade, 1961.

———. *Pour un Tombeau d'Anatole*. Ed. Richard. Paris: Seuil, 1961.

Rich, Adrienne. "To a Poet." *The Dream of a Common Language*. New York: W. W. Norton, 1978.

Sexton, Anne. "The Abortion." *The Complete Poems*. Boston: Houghton Mifflin, 1981.

Shakespeare, William. *Sonnets*. Ed. Booth. New Haven: Yale UP, 1977.

Shelley, Percy Bysshe. "Ode to the West Wind." *The Norton Anthology of Poetry*. Ed. Allison et al. New York: W. W. Norton, 1975.

Sidney, Sir Philip. "Astrophel and Stella." *The Norton Anthology of Poetry*. Ed. Allison et al. New York: W. W. Norton, 1975.

Thomson, Judith Jarvis. "A Defense of Abortion." *Rights, Restitution, Risk*. Ed. William Parent. Cambridge, MA: Harvard UP, 1986.

Thoreau, Henry David. *Walden*. New York: Signet, 1960.

Wordsworth, William. *The Prelude*. Ed. de Selincourt. London: Oxford UP, 1959.

GENDER IN BAKHTIN'S CARNIVAL

(1988)

For Bakhtin, language bequeaths us many social voices, and these voices construct both selves and characters-as-selves. The explicit and implicit interplay of these voices reveals the way a specific historical and cultural context fashions the self. The cultural context also operates in a similar way to fashion the self according to gender differences. With Bakhtin's method, we can work toward a sociological and ideological stylistics of the novel. To add gender considerations, as I want to do here, is to refashion Bakhtin's sociological stylistics into a feminist dialogics.

The main charge against postmodern criticism, as Craig Owens reports it in "The Discourse of Others: Feminists and Postmodernism," is that it is essentially reluctant to engage the "insistent feminist voice": " . . . if one of the most salient aspects of our postmodern culture is the presence of an insistent feminist voice (and I use the terms *presence* and *voice* advisedly), theories of postmodernism have tended either to neglect or to repress that voice. The absence of discussions of sexual difference in writings about postmodernism, as well as the fact that few women have engaged in the modernism/postmodernism debate, suggest that postmodernism may be another masculine invention engineered to exclude women."[1] Thus, Owens attacks decontextualized literary criticism as a no-woman's-land (with exceptions like Gertrude Stein). Feminists, too, have been wont until recently to separate themselves from postmodernism—to read themselves *out* rather than *in* critical dialogue: Myra Jehlen writes in "Archimedes and the Paradox of Feminist Criticism" that feminists have been "too successful in constructing an alternate footing," and Teresa de Lauretis echoes this complaint when she notes that "the contradiction of feminist theory itself [is that it is] at once excluded from discourse and imprisoned within it."[2]

My project is to determine a viable intersection between feminism—my own feminist voice—and modern/postmodern criticism, particularly through Bakhtin. There is no zone which gender does not enter and dispute the territory. Owens questions the primacy of the visual, the same attack French feminists like Luce Irigaray make on all languages of "truth"; Owens claims that what the postmodern critics can't *see* is the feminist *voice*, with Wayne Booth a curious exception.[3] My aim is to show that the feminist voice (rather than the male gaze) can construct and dismantle the exclusive community and patriarchal critical discourse. With voice (and not with the gaze), these heroines can engage in the battle Bakhtin suggests is the basis for community. The opposition between the surveillant gaze and the disruptive (excessive or insistent) voice constitutes the structure of these ambivalent texts. My project in rereading these novels is not to look for a world elsewhere beyond patriarchal language, but to locate in language gendered voices.

Bakhtin opens the way for a feminist dialogic approach to texts by overstepping the "authority" of the text and emphasizing (in "Discourse in Life and Discourse in Art") the triangular relation between reader, text, author. The feminist struggle is not one between a conscious "awakened" or natural voice *and* the voice of patriarchy "out there." Rather, precisely because we all internalize the authoritative voice of patriarchy, we must struggle to refashion inherited social discourses into words which rearticulate intentions (here feminist ones) other than normaltive or disciplinary ones. One of Bakhtin's most crucial statements about reading and the listener's role comes toward the end of "Discourse in Life":

> This constant *coparticipant* [the listener's inherited social and ideological voices] in all our conscious acts determines not only the content of consciousness but also—and this is the main point for us—the very *selection* of the content, the selection of what precisely we become conscious of, and thus determines also those *evaluations* which permeate consciousness and which psychology usually calls the "emotional tone" of consciousness. It is precisely from this constant participant in all our conscious acts that the listener who determines artistic form is engendered.[4]

What the listener selects from the work of art—from the author's and characters' voices in the text—produces the critical orientation, the emotional tone. Power circulates through this participation. But what is more important is that this selection process always involved in reading/listening to the text "engenders" us. The act of reading is one of the modes by which we acquire our social—indeed, gendered—orientations to or identification with the world, as a form of cultural contact. By reading as a feminist—attuned to the exclusions and inclusions of interpretive communities—we foreground the sexual differences involved in our readings of the world, of all social signs. If, in fact, "One never reads except by identification" as Catherine Clément and Hélène Cixous debate in "Exchange," then this identification engenders (reinforces gender difference) at the same time that the act of reading reveals gender.[5]

I am not out to reduce the feminist ambivalence toward language or toward male codes in general, but to thematize that ambivalence. As Laura Mulvey argues about "visual pleasure," woman

> stands in patriarchal culture as signifier for the male other, bound by a symbolic order in which man can live out his fantasies and obsessions through linguistic command, by imposing them on the silent image of woman still tied to her place as bearer of meaning, not maker of meaning.[6]

In the texts that I will examine, the women refuse to be silent bearers of meaning, but have not yet been accepted as makers of meaning. When women step out of their traditional function as sign; when they refuse the imposition of the gaze; when they exchange their sign-status for that of manipulator of signs, they do so through dialogic polemics. And, at that moment of refusal, they become threatening to the disciplinary culture which appears naturalized. This refusal initiates the battle among voices. In these novels, there are no interpretive communities willing to listen to women's alien and threatening discourse.

Out of this contradiction in modes of reading the world, I want to propose a model for reading based on a feminist dialogics, on the translation of the gaze (of the community, of reading) into hearing dialogized voices. My effort, then, is to read the woman's voice—excluded or silenced by dominant linguistic or narrative strategies—back *into* the dialogue in order to reconstruct the process by which she was read out in the first place.[7] The women in these novels refuse to participate in a language which would erase their difference. Rather, by unsettling or displacing the dominant discourse, they reveal the vincibility of the One/Same. The ambivalence toward interpretive community arises from an aggressivity which is often masked by an alteration between a speaking and silenced female subject. Freud argues in *Civilization and Its Discontents* that ambivalence is accompanied by guilt (perhaps making women into Catherine Clément's "guilty ones").[8] Although inclusion in the community might mask this guilt, it would occur at the expense of a defiant voice.

Therefore, to end these novels with suicide or sacrifice is *not* to put an end to the dialogue about sexual difference as the plot traces out that trajectory. In three cases, the novels end ambivalently, with what Margaret Higonnet might call "speaking suicides."[9] If Bakhtin has it right, however, the dialogue never ends. Literary suicide and sacrifice are metaphors for a refusal to be conscripted; suicide forces the internal dialogue into the open, raising questions about sexual difference rather than closing them. Voice can be reconceived as a means of power and activity because it engages dialogue, opening up discourse as fluid. To open another's discourse is to make it vulnerable to change, to exposure, to the carnival. The feminine voices in these novels draw out the others' codes by which their authority is formulated. These resisting voices violate the codes, and with those linguistic impulses, their unconscious wills come into view. The contradiction between these wills and the disciplined wills of the community inform the events of the novel. The characters evade the prison house of language (or struggle against such imprisoning) for what Holquist and Clark term an ecosystem of language.[10] According to Bakhtin in *Problems of Dostoevsky's Poetics* (1929), " . . . the boundaries of the individual will can be in principle exceeded. One could put it this way: the artistic will of polyphony is a will to combine many wills, a will to the event."[11] Thus, the conflicting voices produce the event which draws the reader (as one who identifies) in as one of the many wills called into question by the novel. Identity, then, is always tested and altered. The alienating processes of the interpretive community are revealed through our own (often) alienated feminist identificatory reading. A feminist dialogics is a paradigm which acknowledges individual acts of reading as an experience of otherness and challenges the cultural powers which often force us to contain or restrict the otherness of textual voices.

My first reaction to Bakhtin was to become seduced by his theory of dialogism, since it seemed to offer a utopian ground for all voices to flourish; at least all voices could aspire to internal polemic or dialogism. Yet Bakhtin's blind spot is the battle. He does not work out the contradiction between the promise of utopia or community and the battle which always is waged for control. Within Bakhtin's metaphor of the struggle is a privileging of competition and ascendancy, as well as a privileging of the internally persuasive over the authoritative (even though this is the ground upon which Vološinov attacks Freud), of victors over victims in the battle. While Bakhtin privileges an overthrow of the traditional hierarchy, he also suggests a way to make discourse one's own before it expropriates the self speaking it. On the contrary, in Lacan's scheme, the experience of loss accompanies the acquisition of language.[12] But in Bakhtin's, the loss is a failure to have acquired enough social languages to engage in internal polemic—a battle with the reigning ideology of the culture. Bakhtin's will to dialogism is an empowering model, for it shows how to undermine powerful (authoritative) discourses at the site of the carnivalized body, the self which masquerades in authoritative life.

I want to turn the tables and investigate, instead, the external polemics—the means by which these heroines force the polemic to be a communal property rather than an internal one. The notion of internal polemics is a dangerous one for feminism in that it seems to argue for nonspeech or silence. However, language acquisition—the orchestration of many social languages—becomes cultural capital, a way to work within the dominant, prevailing values by subverting them consciously, by seeing through them and articulating that unveiling.

Because all language is "inherited" and because it is all socially and ideologically charged, the conflict of voices in a novel can reveal power structures and potential resistances to those structures. The dialogue begins when one speaker attempts to insert his or her utterance into a social situation; that is, inserts a voice, of whatever character, into the conversation that marks social relations. And, the listeners' role is to respond with their own perspective on the world. In "Discourse in Life and Discourse in Art," Vološinov/Bakhtin claims that style reveals the inner speech of the author, "which does not lend itself to control" and which is "a product of his entire social life" (Vološinov 114). In addition, style reveals the gap between social authority or what the author says—what is controlled—and the excess—the cultural unconscious—which isn't. As such, style suggests the gap between the inner life of the author, the orchestration of the characters' voice (the "second voice" of the novel), and the listener—"the constant participant in a person's inner and outer speech" (Vološinov 114). This listener, then, articulates the gap between internally persuasive speech and the authoritative discourses with which inner speech may come into conflict. With Bakhtin's dialogics, critics can theorize the process by which alien or rival social languages are excluded and silenced. The novels I examine show the process by which historically divergent voices are made uniform or made to appear uniform, a process which leads to a central, dominant ideological stance—to closure. In this way, the author orchestrates his or her themes, through the interrelation of voices, their contradictions, their juxtapositions, their exclusions.[13]

Characters represent social, ideological, and stratified voices, voices which are not univocally the author's but which compete with and foreground the prevailing codes in the society which the author opens up as topics of discourse. These voices, that is, represent thematized views of a social phenomenon—the dynamic languages from different contexts refashioned, brought into play, and dialogized in the novels. As they are structured in the work, these voices objectify and subvert the systematic power of language. The "feminine" in the novels, I would argue in Luce Irigaray's terms, emerges in a "disruptive excess"; this excess is a language—we might call it the voice of gender—which moves beyond the atomic self or body into the larger discursive corpus and which cannot entirely be accounted for in Bakhtin's dialogic model, thereby making useful a theory of feminist dialogics.[14]

Each character's voice within the dialogized novel represents ways of seeing the world; that voice competes for ascendancy to power or, at least, an intense relationship on the threshold where boundaries between the languages of self and other break down. In "Discourse in the Novel" (1934–35), Bakhtin explains novelization as a dialogizing force: "The novel orchestrates all its themes, the totality of the world of objects and ideas depicted and expressed in it, by means of the social diversity of speech types . . . and by the differing individual voices that flourish under such conditions. Authorial speech, the speeches of narrators, inserted genres, the speech of characters are merely those fundamental compositional unities with whose help heteroglossia . . . can enter the novel; each of them permits a multiplicity of social voices and a wide variety of their links and interrelationships (always more or less dialogized)" (DI 263). As Bakhtin demonstrates in *Problems of Dostoevsky's Poetics*, the author's voice blends with, contradicts, disappears, and reemerges throughout the novel, thereby creating in the characters fully articulated and "autonomous" voices with their "own individual word." Language, then, is no longer merely a carrier of theme, but is a theme itself. By noting the voices "that flourish under such conditions," we can grasp the hierarchy of social speech types—indeed, of social stratification—within the communities represented by fiction (DI 263). Thus, by experiencing the otherness in the text, we can grasp the powers which either restrict or subvert that otherness.

The dialogue leads to contradiction, constituting the battle Bakhtin figures as the locus of the utterance: "Within the arena of almost every utterance an intense interaction and struggle between one's own and another's word is being waged, a process in which they oppose or dialogically interanimate each other" (DI 354).[15] This internal clash of competing voices creates the split between the authoritative and the internally persuasive, between the desire to conform and the desire to resist (for Bakhtin, the centrifugal and centripetal forces of language). This dialogue cannot be reduced to a "final" meaning or intention. In fact, in the following readings of four American fictions, this dispossession of the atomic individual—the self—leads to an ideological conflict and contradiction which, as I argue, animates the dialogue. Bakhtin describes the discourse of the speaking character as an *ideologeme*: "It is precisely as ideologemes that discourse becomes the object of representation in the novel, and it is for the same reason novels are never in danger of becoming mere aimless verbal play . . . [or] susceptible to aestheticism as such, to a purely formalistic playing about with words" (DI 333). These ideologemes are arranged to demonstrate the social conflicts among ways of seeing the world. Although these novels begin with an orchestration of voices, a disciplinary action against the defiant voice occurs as a seemingly necessary outcome of plot—a silencing of the other.

Bakhtin's question is not "what is an author?" but "where is an author?" Once an author "transcribes" language in a novel, the order of the languages becomes a dialogic one, one "which orchestrates the intentional theme of the author" (DI 299). Significantly, society therefore speaks through the authors' (and characters') languages even as they speak. The author "ventriloquating" these voices does not represent his or her own voice; rather, the style—the author's choices and exclusions—articulates the play of gendered voices.

That is, in a feminist dialogics, these textual voices are sexually differentiated in an economy of otherness. If we conceive of the novel as a univocal or mono-logic presentation of the author's perspective or consciousness, a novel such as Hawthorne's *The Blithedale Romance* merely becomes propaganda for the argument against utopian social experiments or against Zenobia's liberating discourse. Yet, given the competing voices of the pragmatist, the social reformer, the artist, the feminist, we can analyze the novel in order to suggest how structural hierarchies—based on gender, class, power in general—are formulated in a battle of lan-guages.[16] The dialogic structure, then, would reveal the place of the reader's voice within the structure of the novel, for our critical voices, too, respond to the dia-logue in the novel. And in this response we are engendered, marked by the read-ings we construct.[17] We acquire "ourselves" by engaging in our own dialogue with others, and especially with texts that challenge our beliefs. In the act of reading, we divest ourselves of the illusion of monologic selfhood. Finally, we align our-selves with the symbolic order of our own world and test this order against the texts that have already been "spoken." We discover our own multiple identities (multivocality) against the grain of dominant ideology which fixes us as unitary subjects. Carroll Smith-Rosenberg writes that "'Language,' like class, is never static."[18] History keeps consciousness in flux; identity and gender, then, are polyvocal, often contradictory, always multiple.

Feminist criticism, in its earliest phase, addresses and redresses the exclusion, the silence, of the female voice. However, even as a "silenced" zone, the female voice competes and contests for authority. Bakhtin reminds us that "the novel always includes in itself the activity of coming to know another's word, a coming to knowledge whose process is represented in the novel" (DI 353). Coming to know another's words is the first step toward asserting self-consciousness in an interpretive community. Moreover, the operation of self-consciousness acts as a disruptive power of traditional codes:

> Self-consciousness, as the artistic dominant in the construction of the hero's image, is by itself sufficient to break down the monologic unity of an artistic world—but only on condition that the hero, as self-consciousness, is really represented and not merely expressed, that is, does not fuse with the author, does not become the mouthpiece for his voice. . . . If the umbilical cord unit-ing the hero to his creator is not cut, then what we have is not a work of art but a personal document. (PDP 51)

The metaphor of authoring as a female act—of giving birth and cutting the um-bilical cord—is telling and imperative for my revision of Bakhtin: if inscription into language is inherited, the identification Bakhtin makes between mothering/ authoring shows that inscription into the symbolic need not always be co-opted or repressive. In fact, the transition for both mother and child requires the let-ting go between mother-child and author-text (as Dickinson has it, too, in "After

Great Pain"). This letting-go encourages dialogism since the child/text speaks for itself and with others, just as the author/mother moves on to another production. To read Bakhtin as a feminist is to see the dialogic structure as an intermediate (or ambivalent) space between the imaginary (the creation of art) and the symbolic (the text)—a spatial rather than a symbolic representation.[19] The reader or listener, in this scheme, is between the two stages, an ambivalent space which privileges neither the imaginary nor the symbolic. It is the space of sexual play, of engendering. Hawthorne, James, Wharton, and Chopin do "cut the umbilical cord" of their creations, allowing their characters to reveal themselves in language. The dialogized novel, then, undermines an ideological unity (be it patriarchal or feminist, liberal or conservative) that the monologic novel erases in favor of ideological closure.

Although the novels of this study end, interestingly, with typically romantic resolutions, the dialogues remain unresolved, always a ground of competition. While the plot resolutions give closure to the novels, the dialogue resists that closure. This dialogue is "forever dying, living, being born," so we see the end as a moment rather than as a "final word" (DI 365). "What is realized in the novel is the process of coming to know one's own language as it is perceived in someone else's language, coming to know one's own belief system in someone else's system" (DI 365). I want to rephrase this notion for my own feminist intentions: this coming to know the other is at the heart of the feminist act of reading the novel, just as it is at the heart of the characters' coming to know themselves as other in a world where patriarchal language aspires to monologism. Gabriele Schwab asks the question this way in "Reader-Response and the Aesthetic Experience of Otherness": "How . . . can we, after the deconstructionist challenge, argue for a recognition of otherness in the act of reading—which also implies the recognition of textual constraints for interpretation—without denying that misreadings, creative as well as uncreative ones, are engendered by the semantic and structural instabilities of language itself?" The other of and within literature—or misreadings thematized to represent the other—can affect and change language itself.[20] For instance, feminists read phallocentric discourse as the other, reading themselves as signs in the margins and the "unsaids" of the text, or "overreading" their own intentions into the text. The women readers in the text assert their otherness not by surrendering, but by forcing their language into the context/contest of the dominant languages. That is, not by erasing but by highlighting their otherness can they do battle with patriarchal codes.

With this imperative in mind, I want to appropriate Bakhtin's explanation of one important stage which is crucial to my study of Hawthorne, James, Wharton, and Chopin. I refer here to the "other" as gendered rather than the "other" as counter-cultural. Bakhtin claims that the image of the Fool carries over into the modern novel from its earlier forms—in the picaresque adventure novel, for one. It is not that fools appear as characters, but that their characteristics of simplicity and naïveté inform the modern novel:

> Even if the image of the fool (and the image of the rogue as well) loses its fundamental organizing role in the subsequent development of novelistic prose, nevertheless the very aspect of *not grasping* the conventions of society (the degree of society's conventionality), not understanding lofty pathos—

charged labels, things and events—such incomprehension remains almost everywhere an essential ingredient of prose style. Either the prose writer represents the world through the words of a *narrator* who does not understand this world, does not acknowledge its poetic, scholarly or otherwise lofty and significant labels; or else the prose writer introduces a *character* who does not understand; or, finally, the direct style of the author himself involves a deliberate (polemical) failure to understand the habitual ways of conceiving the world. (DI 402)

This failure to understand is represented in each of the novels I consider, for the women's misreading of the social conventions results in a dialogue about those very interpretive norms. Zenobia's and Coverdale's, Maggie's, Lily's, and Edna's incomprehensions force them into a dialogic confrontation with the other voices, the other ideologemes represented in the novels. In fact, this failure shapes the styles of these novels. And in this resulting dialogue, the women's own ideologemes are made clear in the process of articulating their values to others and assimilating others' values to their own emerging ones. As women in patriarchal communities, they are essentially other to the norms of their community. As fool—a type I read as a resisting reader *within* the text—these women provide the means of unmasking dominant codes. Mary Russo refers to these women as Female Grotesques in her essay of the same name; they are "repressed and undeveloped."[21] Stupidity (a form of resistance) forces the unspoken repressions into the open, thus making them vulnerable to interpretation, contradiction, and dialogue.

Historically, the fool has not been a woman and has not exercised the freedom of, say, Lear's fool. But the freedom of Shakespeare's fool is that of wisdom and wit; the freedom of Bakhtin's fool is that of incomprehension. All the more important, then, is this variation on a literary topos: the play of speech which is traditionally allowed the male fool is denied these uncomprehending women. Nevertheless, these characters refuse to let their voices be inhabited by the discourse which reduces all bodies to the same voice. Umberto Eco explains the situation of the "comic" or misreading fool as follows: the character is not "at fault. Maybe the frame is wrong."[22] The role of the reader, that is, is to question and restructure the "cultural and intertextual frames" in which the character operates and is made foolish.

Bakhtin explains that "Stupidity (incomprehension) in the novel is always polemical: it interacts dialogically with an intelligence (a lofty pseudo intelligence) with which it polemicizes and whose mask it tears away" (DI 403). In other words, "naive" characters resist understanding the world according to dominant conventions, resist abstract categories of language, and also refuse to (or cannot) accept whole-heartedly the ideology of the other; their naïveté remains and because of this ignorance, not despite it, a struggle emerges. "For this reason stupidity (incomprehension) in the novel is always implicated in language, in the word: at its heart always lies a polemical failure to understand someone else's discourse, someone else's pathos-charged lie that has appropriated the world and aspires to conceptualize it, a polemical failure to understand generally accepted, canonized, inveterately false languages with their lofty labels for things and events. . . . " (DI 403). This polemical misunderstanding or misreading is not a question of what the characters will or will not accept; as fools, most often their polemics is an intentional narrative strategy and crucial to the revealing (and, indeed, unmasking) of dialogue in the novel.

For example, a "multitude of different novelistic-dialogic situations" exist between the heroine fools and others who are fixed in the dominant discourse: between, for example, Zenobia and Hollingsworth (the reformer), Zenobia and Coverdale (the poet-romancer), Maggie and the Jewish shopkeeper (the semiotician), Lily and the hat-makers (the coopted laborers), Edna and Adèle (the perfect mother-woman): all of these situations reveal the ideological structures of language, of institutional controls and discipline. The "fool" serves to defamiliarize the conventions which have been accepted as "natural," as myth:

> Regarding fools or regarding the world through the eyes of a fool, the novelist's eye is taught a sort of prose vision, the vision of a world confused by conventions of pathos and by falsity. A failure to understand languages that are otherwise generally accepted and that have the appearance of being universal teaches the novelist how to perceive them physically as *objects*, to see their relativity, to externalize them, to feel out their boundaries, that is, it teaches him how to expose and structure images of social languages. (DI 404)

"Confused" is the focal term: we are meant to be unsettled by these dialogues between fools and accepted languages, just as we are meant to be unsettled by feminist criticism which seeks to shake up the critical communities which do not acknowledge the excluded margins. What Bakhtin might teach us, then, is to conceive of the discourses within the novel as objects, as ideologemes which require interpretation and revision and which involve us in what Gabriele Schwab calls the "vertiginous undertow" of language.[23] In fact, such a "prose wisdom" allows us to see that no language is universal. Bakhtin calls this study of stupidity and incomprehension "a basic (and extremely interesting) problem in the history of the novel" (DI 404): that problem of misreading is the core of my study of Hawthorne, James, Wharton, and Chopin.

Finally, women "on the threshold" of a social or cultural crisis become powerful in the marginal realm which constitutes the carnival world. By "carnivalization," I mean here, as Bakhtin has it, the "transposition of carnival into the language of literature" which serves to make every voice in the communal performance heard and unrestricted by official or authoritative speech (PDP 122). The fool is able to assert her defiant voice through carnival, the masquerade, the parody of the "official" lives she leads. Bakhtin's carnival hero seeks to resist the essentializing framework "of *other people's* words about [them] that might finalize and deaden [them]" (PDP 59). The carnival is the realm of desire unmasked, taken out of the law of culture, and involved in an economy of difference. While the authoritative discourse demands conformity, the carnivalized discourse renders invalid any codes, conventions, or laws which govern or reduce the individual to an object of control. Contrary to Irigaray, I argue that the carnival (or masquerade) need not reinvest women in the specular economy or in masculine desire, but can take them out of it.[24] This is neither to condemn as Irigaray does nor to celebrate as Bakhtin does the intermediate space; I want to question its informing ambivalence. The carnival reveals the characters as subjects of their own discourse rather than objects of an official line or finalizing word. Because carnival potentially involves everyone, it sets the scene for dialogue, for communal heteroglossia:

> The laws, prohibitions, and restrictions that determine the structure and or-
> der of ordinary life, that is noncarnival, life are suspended during carnival:
> what is suspended first of all is hierarchical structure and all the forms of ter-
> ror, reverence, piety, and etiquette connected with it—that is, everything re-
> sulting from socio-hierarchical inequality or any other form of inequality
> among people (including age). All *distance* between people is suspended, and
> a special carnival category goes into effect: *free and familiar contact among
> people*. (PDP 122–23)

Carnival suspends discipline—the terror, reverence, piety, and etiquette which contribute to the maintenance of the social order. The carnival participants over-throw the hierarchical conventions which exclude them and work out a new mode of relation, one dialogic in nature. Therefore, they resist noncarnival life within community by reinventing relations in the carnival. These Bakhtinian fools re-sist convention, using the threat of the inconclusive, open-ended possibilities of dialogue to retain subversive force in the social arena. As Bakhtin explains, the carnival, however, cannot last. It is functional, a means of resisting conventions and revising them, without destroying them completely.[25]

I want to end with a claim from Adrienne Rich: "All silence has a meaning."[26] Through Bakhtin's principle of the dialogization of the novel, we can interpret the silenced or suicidal voice of female characters compelling a dialogue with those others who would prefer to think they do not exist. Annette Kolodny writes that we read "not texts but paradigms," not "reality" but instead ways of seeing and making meaning in the world.[27] As old conventions and ways of reading prove untenable, new interpretive communities emerge and transform our liter-ary history and allow for revised interpretations of experience. We cannot think of going beyond these communities, I would agree with Bakhtin, except through subverting them and the opposition between freedom and utopia. Such has been the revolution in the leftist, structuralist poetics and politics of the sixties and seventies, in current versions of reader-response criticism, and now in a feminist dialogics. Like Maggie in James's novel who reads the golden bowl, readers take up the symbolic object—the text—and make sense of it in the context of spe-cific historical, cultural, and social events. We learn to exercise our conventions on the text, but not to find a meaning hidden there. The act of reading, then, as cultural strategy is the first step toward revisioning and rearticulating voice (the "private property" of our internally persuasive language) and our place in the so-cial dialogue. Reading is not "free," but an activity determined by the text and by the ideological discourses one brings to bear on the text. We cannot posit our own readings as acts of disengagement or as acts of critical neutrality; rather, the acts of reading prove to engender us, reinforcing sexual difference. Interpreta-tion is an act that is always interanimated with *other* critical discourses and *other* ideologies, including those of sexual difference.

NOTES

1. Craig Owens, "The Discourse of Others: Feminists and Postmodernism," in *The Anti-Aesthetic*, ed. Hal Foster (Port Townsend, Washington: Bay Press, 1983), p. 61. The debate about what whether the "gaze" is male is informed by Mary Ann Doane's and E. Ann Kaplan's theorizing of the female gaze. Kaplan's essay—"Is the gaze male?" in *Women and Film* (New York: Methuen Press, 1983)—is interesting to me because she claims that feminist film critics "have (rightly) been wary of admitting the degree to which the pleasure [of looking] comes from identification with objectification" (p. 33). The problem of identificatory readings is beyond the scope of my study, but a crucial topic for the discussion of a specific female pleasure.

2. Myra Jehlen, "Archimedes and the Paradox of Literary Criticism," in *The Signs Reader* (Chicago: University of Chicago Press, 1982), p. 71. See also Teresa de Lauretis's *Alice Doesn't*, p. 7.

3. Wayne C. Booth, "Freedom of Interpretation: Bakhtin and the Challenge of Feminist Criticism," in *Critical Inquiry* 9, 1 (September 1982): 45–76. Although Booth takes sides against Bakhtin's reading of Rabelais in order to support his own feminist perspective, he ignores, I think, the potential in Bakhtin's theory for revisioning the silenced voices of women in the dialogue/discourse of social power.

Wayne Booth seems to be the target of the hour for feminist critics, despite his own recent turn to an "ethics of reading" which takes feminist concerns into account. In "Rereading as a Woman: The Body in Practice" (in *The Female Body in Western Culture* [Cambridge: Harvard University Press, 1986]), Nancy K. Miller accuses Booth of reiterating the old joke that "feminists have no sense of humor" (p. 354).

Patrocinio Schweickart also begins her dialogue with postmodernism in "Reading Ourselves: A Feminist Theory of Reading" (in *Gender and Reading: Essays on Readers, Texts, and Contexts* [Baltimore: Johns Hopkins University Press, 1986]) by responding to Wayne Booth's story of reading, a "utopian" fiction in which gender or class or race doesn't matter. In Booth's vision, reading delivers the utopian: "Booth's story [of his own love of reading] anticipates what might be possible, what 'critical understanding' might mean for *everyone*, if only we could overcome the pervasive systemic injustices of our time" (p. 35). Instead of this utopian vision, Schweickart calls for a feminist theory of reading: "While it is still too early to present a full-blown theory, the dialogic aspect of the relationship between the feminist reader and the woman writer suggests the direction that such a theory might take" (p. 52). It is not clear whether she means this "dialogic aspect" in Bakhtin's sense, but this essay will explore what a "feminist dialogism" might mean.

4. V. N. Vološinov, "Discourse in Life and Discourse in Art," in *Freudianism: A Marxist Critique*, trans. I. R. Titunik (New York: Academic Press, 1976), p. 115.

5. Hélène Cixous and Catherine Clément, *The Newly Born Woman*, trans. Betsy Wing (Minneapolis: University of Minnesota Press, 1986), p. 148.

6. Laura Mulvey, "Visual Pleasure and Narrative Cinema," in *Screen* 16, 3 (Autumn 1975): 7.

7. See Nancy Miller's "Arachnologies," in *The Poetics of Gender* (New York: Columbia University Press, 1986), especially page 292, note 27.

8. Catherine Clément formulates the subversiveness of guilt in her essay which is part of *The Newly Born Woman*.

9. Margaret Higonnet explains "suicide as interpretation" in "Speaking Silences: Women's Suicide" (in *The Female Body in Western Culture*). Women's consciousnesses are not finalized by suicide; as Higonnet argues, suicide is a narrative strategy; the death must be addressed by the other characters: "To take one's life is to force others to read one's death. . . . The act is a self-barred signature; its destructive narcissism seems to some par-

ticularly feminine" (pp. 68–69). Not for Higonnet, and I would argue, not for Bakhtin: the suicidal signature is a decision not to let others finalize or deaden one's character by monologism. In Bakhtin's vision, suicide forces the others to enter into a dialogic relation with the one to whom such a relation was denied in life. Higonnet claims, "Language becomes action; action becomes and yet requires language."

10. Michael Holquist and Katerina Clark, *Mikhail Bakhtin* (Cambridge: Belknap Press, 1984), p. 227.

11. Mikhail Bakhtin, *Problems of Dostoevsky's Poetics*, ed. and trans. Caryl Emerson (Minneapolis: University of Minnesota Press, 1984), p. 21. All further references will be made parenthetically throughout the chapters (PDP).

12. In *Figuring Lacan: Criticism and the Cultural Unconscious* (Lincoln: University of Nebraska Press, 1987), Juliet Flower MacCannell argues for Lacan's usefulness for a feminist subversion of language: "The feminist reaction to Lacan has been highly productive. In a mode quite different from the Oedipal rivalry generally assumed to be crucial to cultural creation, Lacan's reading by feminism has unleashed not a series of works designed to dethrone, decentre or deny Lacan but works dedicated to reformulating the imagery, the vocabulary and the network of associations attached to the figure of the woman" (p. 3). Desire and language, for Lacan, is associated with alienation. I see Bakhtin's sociolinguistics as a way to overcome this alienation effect.

13. See Marcelle Marini's "Feminism and Literary Criticism: Reflections on the Disciplinary Approach," in *Women in Culture and Politics: A Century of Change*. Marini points out that this dialogic model lands us "somewhere between the real and the utopic, without ever managing to take shape to the point of becoming society's image for an entire community." Such a context would overstep the "question of *one* feminine language and *one* masculine language; rather, in the end, of a plurality of languages, without definite ownership, in which flexible identities would be in a constant state of becoming. . . . " (p. 154).

14. Luce Irigaray, *This Sex Which Is Not One*, p. 78. Terry Castle's essay on carnivalization in the eighteenth-century novel opens up this topic of disruption for my reading of the carnival and the nineteenth-century didactic purpose. See "The Carnivalization of Eighteenth-Century English Narrative" in *PMLA* 99, 5 (October 1984): 903–916.

15. See Michael Holquist's "Answering as Authoring," in *Critical Inquiry* 10, 2 (December 1983): 307–319. Holquist's claims are important to my own argument: "Human being is acted out in a *logosphere*, a space where meaning occurs as a function of the constant struggle between centrifugal forces that seek to keep things apart and in motion, that increase difference and tend toward the extreme of life and consciousness, and centripetal forces that strive to make things cohere, to stay in place, and which tend toward the extreme of death and brute matter. . . . These forces contend with each other at all levels of existence: in the physical universe, the cells of the body, the processes of mind, as well as in the ideologies of social organization. The constant dialogue between—and among—these partners in the activity of being finds its most comprehensive model in the activity of communication" (p. 309).

16. Lacan writes in "The Mirror Stage," trans. Alan Sheridan (*Ecrits* [New York: W. W. Norton, 1977]) that we need to distrust the altruistic versions of the self: " . . . we place no trust in altruistic feeling, we who lay bare the aggressivity that underlies the activity of the philanthropist, the idealist, the pedagogue, and even the reformer" (p. 7). Without a claim to appropriate Lacanian psychoanalysis as my own method, I do want to suggest that this unmasking of altruism is part of the project of the readings which follow.

17. For a discussion of the dangers of this marking, see Monique Wittig's "The Mark of Gender," in *The Poetics of Gender*, pp. 63–73.

18. Carroll Smith-Rosenberg, "Writing History: Language, Class, and Gender," in *Feminist Studies/Critical Studies*, ed. Teresa de Lauretis (Bloomington: Indiana University Press, 1986), p. 36.

19. See Gabriele Schwab's "The Genesis of the Subject, Imaginary Functions, and Poetic Language," in *New Literary History* 15 (Spring 1984): 453–474. Schwab argues that the imaginary does not lose its importance at the genesis of the subject, but remains influential in the subject's development: "However both anticipation and elimination are also decided by the internalized image of the Other, and thus we always come back to the imaginary." See also Jessica Benjamin's "A Desire of One's Own" in *Feminist Studies/Critical Studies* for her fine discussion of the distinction between spatial and symbolic constitutive models of women's desire, especially page 95.

20. Gabriele Schwab, "Reader-Response and the Aesthetic Experience of Otherness," in *Stanford Literature Review* (Spring 1986), p. 112. See Nancy Miller's formulation of "overreading" in "Arachnologies," in *The Poetics of Gender*: "What I want to propose instead as a counterweight to this story of the deconstructed subject, restless with what he already knows, is a poetics of the *underread and* a practice of 'overreading.' The aim of this practice is double. It aims first to unsettle the interpretive model which thinks that it knows when it is rereading, and what is in the library, confronting its claims with Kolodny's counterclaim that 'what we engage are not texts but paradigms' (8)" (p. 274).

21. Mary Russo, "Female Grotesques," in *Feminist Studies/Critical Studies*, p. 219.

22. Umberto Eco, "The frames of comic 'freedom'" in *Carnival!*, p. 8. Eco's distinction between "comic" and "humor" is one I employ throughout my readings of the Bakhtinian fool: "Humor does not pretend, like carnival, to lead us beyond our own limits. . . . It is never off limits, it undermines limits from inside. . . . Humor does not promise us liberation: on the contrary, it warns us about the impossibility of global liberation, reminding us of the presence of a law that we no longer have reason to obey. In doing so it undermines the law. It makes us feel the uneasiness of living under a law—any law" (p. 8). In this revision of Bakhtin's carnival, Eco demonstrates his hesitancy to adopt carnival as a realm of "*actual* liberation" (p. 3), as I do. What he does claim, and what I would emphasize, is that the comic works on the basis of a rule or law unspoken, but already understood. Humor "casts in doubt other cultural codes. If there is a possibility of transgression, it lies in humor rather than in comic." Michael Andre Bernstein's "When the Carnival Turns Bitter" in *Bakhtin* works through the function of the "wise fool" upon which I draw my own distinction: "Even in English Renaissance drama where the 'wise fool' attached to a court enjoys the liberty to speak freely to his master on a permanent, if precarious, basis, the audience learns very quickly when the fool's words contain a truth which the master ignores only at his own peril and when the quips are merely witty repartee. Lear's fool, for example, seeks, too often in vain, to instruct his vain king" (pp. 106–107).

23. Schwab, "Reader-Response," p. 124.

24. Luce Irigaray, p. 133.

25. See Mary Ann Doane's "Film and the Masquerade: Theorising the Female Spectator," in *Screen* 23, 3–4 (1982): 74–87. Doane's comments on the masquerade are crucial: "To masquerade is to manufacture a lack in the form of a certain distance between oneself and one's image" (p. 82). That is, Doane suggests that the masquerader is in control, since "masquerade is anti-hysterical for it works to effect a separation between the cause of desire and oneself." I would say that the anti-hysterical effects a distance, but not a separation, between the subject and desire. See Mary Russo's essay for a defense of Irigaray, p. 223.

26. Adrienne Rich, "Disloyal to Civilization," in *On Lies, Secrets, and Silence* (New York: W. W. Norton & Company, 1979), p. 308.

27. Annette Kolodny, "Dancing Through the Minefield: Some Observations on Theory, Practice and Politics of a Feminist Literary Criticism," in *Feminist Studies* 6, 1 (Spring 1980): 8.

WHEN A "LONG" POEM IS A "BIG" POEM

self-authorizing strategies in women's twentieth-century "long poems"

(1990)

I want to initiate an excursion into and around the "long poem" by twentieth-century American women poets with a perverse attack on its generic name—"long poem"—not that I will propose a new term, which would undoubtedly vanish as soon as it appeared because the patronymic "long poem" is "au courant." It has (is) "currency" for a new generic category—new, that is, in critical discourse, not new, of course, in poetic praxis, where "long poems" go back several thousand years under a variety of names.[1] But I do want to explore my dis-ease with the term as an entrée into some generalizations about women's status as outsiders in relation to the genre and the self-authorizing strategies in which they have engaged to penetrate and transform its boundaries.

The name "long poem" is deceptively simple and descriptive—neutral, unweighted, un-overdetermined, as if it had achieved a value-free, scientific objectivity or that utopian ideal of what Roland Barthes calls the "innocence" of "writing degree zero" (*Writing* 75). It is also a useful term that appears to define itself. Its virtue lies in its breadth, an inclusiveness that incorporates all poetry that is "long." "What is a 'long poem?'" a student might ask. "Why, silly-billy," we can answer from our Olympian Heights, "a 'long poem' is a poem that is long." "Do you mean narrative poetry?" the student might persist in asking. "No," we can answer in pluralist righteousness, "it can be narrative or lyric or even prose or any combination thereof, just so long as it's 'long.'" "How long is 'long'? Fifty pages? A volume?" the student, who is by now getting obnoxious, might continue. "Is a 'sequence' too short for a 'long poem'? Is an epic too long to be a 'long poem'?" "No, no, no," say we in final exasperation, "can't you see the beauty of our term??? The 'long poem' is simply *anything* that is *long*. It is the great umbrella for everything that is not *short*."

What bothers me is that in its seeming inclusive neutrality, the term may obscure the exclusionary politics inherent in genre categories—especially in the binary "long" and "short" implied in the single category "long poem." In "The Law of Genre," Jacques Derrida offers fair warning. Genre appears to be a *description* of literary types, a taxonomy that borrows from the biological system of classifying species. But *description*, he argues, always implies *prescription*. Like any category, genre likes repetition, not anomaly. "Thus, as soon as genre announces itself," he writes, "one must respect a norm, one must not cross a line of demarcation, one must not risk impurity, anomaly, or monstrosity" (57). Literary taxonomy implicitly prescribes a *law* against "mixing," against the pollution of cross-species or cross-sex miscegenation. As Celeste Schenck writes in her feminist deconstruction of genre, "genre is more usefully conceived . . . as an overdetermined locus of political contention than a transcendental criterion or ideal type. . . . Moreover, beneath the western will-to-taxonomize lies not only a defensive history of exclusions constituting a political ideology, but also a fetishization of aesthetic purity . . . which has distinctly gendered overtones" (2–3).

And yet, the implicit power and authority of genre is such that we can scarcely read a literary text without some conscious or subliminal set of expectations based on the genre to which the text signals its membership. As Julia Kristeva argues, texts exist within a grid of generic intertexts that shape how we read (36–37).[2] No matter how unique, a literary text announces its place within a generic category through the use or abuse of the conventions that readers have come to associate with that genre. Even a text that radically departs from those conventions gains its special effect from the absence of what we expect to be present. Even a generic hybrid gains its status as anomaly through the tension created by a "mixing" of preexisting "unmixed" genres. These conventions—as well as departures from them—have a politics tied to their manifestation in the socio-political domain of history. As Sandra Gilbert and Susan Gubar have led the way in showing, feminist criticism has often demonstrated the gender inflections in the politics of genre—how women's "anxiety of authorship" played itself out in relationship to genre; how the most prestigious genres (like poetry, drama, and epic) erected threatening boundaries against women; how marginal or new genres (like letters, the novel, the gothic) invited women's participation; how genres heavily coded by their masculinist tradition (like the epic, the love lyric, the epithalamion, the elegy) required a fundamental re-vision to function as women's discourses.[3]

The descriptive simplicity of the term "long poem"—with its implicit ideology of pure form and value-free aesthetics—represses awareness of this gender-inflected politics with a displacement that substitutes the description "long" for the prescription "big."[4] A "long poem" is a "big poem," that is, a poem that situates itself within a long tradition of poems that ask very big questions in a very long way—historical, metaphysical, religious, and aesthetic questions. As a "big" poem, a "long" poem has volume—it is a many sided figure that swells up to take space. As a long sequence, it also takes up time—literally, lots of time to read. In this horizontal-vertical discourse, vast space and cosmic time are the narrative coordinates within which lyric moments occur, the coordinates as well of reality, of history. Big long poems go far, tunnel deep, and fly high. They have scope. They are "potent, important."[5]

This geometry of forms—long poems, big poems—may itself be a displacement for a geography of forms—the territorial imperative of literary history to map literary *landscapes*, canonize *centers*, chart pathways to *horizons*, define *margins*, patronize the *borderline*, and dismiss what is *beyond the pale*—to exercise, in short, the tyranny of categorical *boundaries*, to declare what is inside, what is outside, *us* and *them*.

As poems on the greatest historical-metaphysical-religious-aesthetic questions, big-long-important poems have assumed the authority of the dominant cultural discourses—even when they speak from a position of alienation, like Ezra Pound in *The Cantos* or William Carlos Williams in *Paterson*. The generic grid within which these and other big long poems are read has been established preeminently by the epic, which has a very big-long history of importance in western culture. The epic has been the preeminent poetic genre of the public sphere from which women have been excluded. As a narrative of brave men's deeds, the epic often centers on the "destiny" or "formation of a race or nation" (Benet 317). It reflects a comprehensive sweep of history, a cosmic universality of theme, and an elevated discourse of public ceremony. In Pound's words, the epic is "the speech of a nation through the mouth of one man" (*Literary Essays* 19); it is "a poem containing history" (*Spirit of Romance* 216). To which we might add—philosophy, religion, and aesthetics.[6] These genre codes for the epic intersect with societal gender codes to identify the epic as a preeminently masculine discourse. The "law of genre" prescribed in the practice of the epic is fundamentally phallic.[7] Within the dominant discourses of Western culture, women have never been allowed the authority to pronounce on history, philosophy, religion and aesthetics. The epic has consequently been the quintessential male territory whose boundaries enforce women's status as outsiders on the landscape of poetry.

I am well aware of the considerable debate on whether the term "epic" can be applied to any "long poems" after the advent of Romanticism.[8] No longer in a detached, omniscient third person, no longer structured primarily by narrative, Wordsworth's *The Prelude* and Whitman's *Song of Myself* introduced the poet's subjectivity as a major focus into the epic. In fragmenting that unitary self and intensifying the lyric as the principle of structure, modernist poets of the "long poem" further dissolved the authority of the epic bard to be what Thomas Maresca calls "the formulator and preserver of civilization's highest knowledge and belief" (70–71). But these departures from epic convention gain their particular power from being read within the epic grid. The "song of myself" in the "personal epics" of the nineteenth and twentieth centuries is elevated by its epic resonance into a song of the times, of a people. The anti-heroes in the anti-epics of the modernist and postmodernist poets acquire their ironic nexus of inflation/deflation in reaction to the heroes and epics of the premodernist "long poems." As re-scriptions of epic conventions, modern "long poems" depend for their ultimate effect on our awareness of the epic norms they undo and redo. Rooted in epic tradition, the twentieth-century "long poem" is an overdetermined discourse whose size, scope, and authority to define history, metaphysics, religion and aesthetics still erects a wall to keep women outside.

I am arguing therefore that the term "long poem" represses those aspects of the genre that have made it an uninviting form for women writers. Before we can study either the absence or presence of women's writing within this genre, we need to bring to consciousness this "political unconscious." Prior to the twentieth century, few women crossed the boundaries into the domain of the epic, the "long poem." We know the name—Corinna—but little more than the name of a Greek woman who wrote epics in the classical period.[9] Of the few women who wrote "long poems" in English before the twentieth century, not many have survived in critical memory. Mary Tighe's name is known, perhaps because her *Psyche, or the Legend of Love* influenced Keats. Elizabeth Barrett Browning wrote quite a number of "long poems," most importantly *Aurora Leigh*, whose epic poetics she defensively justified within the text itself.[10] George Eliot's *The Spanish Gypsy* narrates the dissolution of a romance and the regeneration of a "nation" of outsiders. Frances Watkins Harper's *Moses: A Story of the Nile* displaces her commitment to black emancipation onto the narrative of Jewish exodus. But as a matrix of historical and literary forces swelled ranks of women writing to a critical mass in this century, more and more women have been writing big-long-important poems exploring vast, cosmic questions of history, metaphysics, religion, and aesthetics. Gertrude Stein, Mina Loy, and H.D. were the first modern writers in English to cross this generic Rubicon, but since 1960, scores of women's "long poems" have appeared—as different in form and tradition as Ntozake Shange's blues-epic-drama *For colored girls who have considered suicide/when the rainbow is enuf*, Judy Grahn's projected four-volume Tarot tapestry *The Chronicle of Queens*, and Susan Howe's linguistic saga of Swift's Stella and Lear's Cordelia in *The Liberties* in her volume *Defenestration of Prague*.

As different as these twentieth-century women's "long poems" are, they share an uneasy position within the generic grid and exhibit a common need to feminize the phallic codes of the genre. One sign of this common dis-ease is the self-conscious intensity of their reflexive textuality. That is, these poems often signal their status as texts, specifically their status as big-long poems whose gender-inflections make them somehow different from the dominant examples of the genre. Susan Howe's description of Emily Dickinson's tough-minded intertextuality serves aptly for the women poets writing "long poems": "Forcing, abbreviating, pushing, padding, subtracting, riddling, interrogating, re-writing, she pulled text from text" (*My Emily Dickinson* 29). Certainly male poets have also pushed and pulled the texts of their male precursors, as Harold Bloom and others have argued. But in the psychopolitical "family" history of literary tradition, sons—not daughters—replace fathers. Aware of their absence within the tradition, women poets of the "long poem" often defensively and defiantly assert their presence. They engage in a feminization of the form—refusing the victim status of woman's objectification in men's texts and making themselves agents in the form's evolution, subjects in its creation.

To feminize the genre, women poets have practiced at least four strategies, each one of which deconstructs the opposition of inside/outside that Derrida identifies with the phallogocentrism of "the law of genre."[11] All four, in other words, dismantle the boundaries so as to position themselves *as women* writing inside a tradition in which women have been outsiders. Grahn characterizes this move as "looking at the outside from the inside and at the inside from the outside" (*Highest Apple* 67), while Barbara Christian relates it more specifically to the doubled consciousness of Afro-American women writers, who "are so often . . . perceived as being on the outside of so many realms, even as we are solidly on the inside" ("From the Inside Out"). Not specific to the "long poem," these "inside-outside" strategies take form in women's writing in a variety of genres. But their effect in the women's "long poem" is a distinct demasculinization of the genre that signals an oppositional writing and reading process. The first strategy is the creation of the discourse of the satiric Other, the outsider who ironically deflates the insider. The second is reclamation of the public domain from which women have been largely excluded through a discourse of history—a (her)story in which the inside is the outside and the outside is the inside. The third is the construction of the discourse of re-vision, in Adrienne Rich's sense of the term, in which the outsider immerses herself in the discourse of the inside in order to transform it. And the fourth is the invention of a discourse of linguistic experimentalism, a gynopoetic of the outside that establishes a new inside by turning the inside, inside out. I will illustrate these four strategies with brief discussions of four exemplary texts: Mina Loy's *Anglo-Mongrels and the Rose*, written in the 1920s; Alicia Ostriker's *The Mother/Child Papers*, which came out in 1980; Judy Grahn's *The Queen of Wands*, published in 1982 as the first volume of *The Chronicle of Queens*; and Betsy Warland's *serpent (w)rite*, which appeared in 1987.

The discourse of the satiric Other evokes Virginia Woolf's proverbial "Society of Outsiders" who refuse to join the mad crowd dancing round the mulberry bush of money and war in *Three Guineas*. Like the lecturer in *A Room of One's Own* who is ultimately grateful that she has been shut out of the men's colleges and dining halls and libraries, the satiric Other revels in her status as outsider, using her wit as a sword that pierces the balloon of the poem's self-important form as a big-long-poem. This means, of course, a comedic mockery of what she cannot possess, a carnivalesque disruption of the authority that the form of the poem itself evokes.

Mina Loy's mock-heroic epic *Anglo-Mongrels and the Rose* demonstrates this ironic stance of the outsider in its autobiographical narrative of the poet's development. Acquiring what Jonathan Williams calls "legendary status" among modern writers, *Anglo-Mongrels* appeared only partially, in fragments, and out of chronological order in the avant-garde press from 1923 to 1925. Jerome Rothenberg managed to assemble most of it for his 1974 poetry anthology, enough to call it "one of the lost master poems of the 20th century" (xxvi). In *The Last Lunar Baedeker*, the most complete edition of Loy's poetry to date, the 70-page text appears in probably complete form, along with Williams' assertion that it is "the missing link in the yet unwritten history of the long poem" (xxvi). This piece-meal publishing history itself represents women's simultaneous absence and presence within the generic tradition and introduces the epic's theme of women's diaspora within the male domain. Loy further acted out this exile in her wanderings. Born in Britain, she moved to New York, became an American citizen, and spent much of her life traveling.

Mocking the *künstlerroman* tradition of which it is a part, *Anglo-Mongrels* narrates the *bildung* of Ova, the daughter of the Jewish tailor Exodus and the English Gentile Ada. The mock-epic begins by reviewing the poet's lineage, her patrilineal and matrilineal legacy in a section called "Exodus." Her father's "exodus" from bondage in Hungary brings him to the promised land of England. But there his freedom is another kind of slavery, a perpetual exile of never belonging, permanent psychic diaspora. With the satiric playfulness that characterizes the text, Loy dubs him the "wondering Jew" (117). In an attempt to belong, the "alien" Exodus marries Ada, an English "Rose" whose sexuality has been repressed into "the ap parent impecca bility/ of the English"—chaste and without sin (129). Ova's birth evokes the scene of Sleeping Beauty's christening, but the godmother's gift of a "Jewish brain" could be the Black Fairy's curse or a good fairy's compensatory promise—we don't know (132). Ova, "this composite/ Anglo-Israelite," is a "Mongrel" Rose, no Sleeping Beauty and never at home with her father's God or her mother's "Gentle Jesus" (132, 148). While Esau Penfold, the boy who will one day be Ova's husband, is petted and praised, little Ova is pushed aside and told to "hush." Loy calls her "the mongrel-girl/ of Noman's Land" (143).

Neither Exodus nor Ada can nourish their girl-egg. Her father deceives her with a worthless gift of money, then expels her from the house. Between her mother and her Nurse, Ova is "jostled/ between revolving/ armoured towers/ . . . / of these/ two women's netherbodies" (139). Ova's awakening is all her own. In the section called "Ova Begins to Take Notice," the toddler becomes aware of the wonder of light, color, sound and words—a scene that mockingly echoes the opening pages of Joyce's *Portrait of the Artist as a Young Man*. The word she hears is not Stephen's nourishing "moocow," but "iarrhea"—diarrhea, the refuse and excrement that disgusts, that must be expelled, that nonetheless contains the mystery of incarnation in the mock-heroics of the epic:

> Sometimes a new word comes to her
> she looks before her
> and watches
> for its materialization
> "iarrhea"
>
> . . . .
>
> And in her ear
> a half inaudible   an
> iridescent hush
> forms "iarrhea"
>
> "It is
> quite green" She hears
>
> The cerebral
> mush convolving in her skull
> an obsessional
> colour-fetish
>
> veers
> to the souvenir
> of the delirious ball
> . . . .
> And instantly
> this fragmentary
> simultaneity
> of ideas
>
> embodies
>   the word (139–41)

Ova's awakening as a child through the agency of refuse and its representation prefigures her teenage revelation in a section called "Jews and Ragamuffins of Kilburn." Walking through the ghetto of outcasts with her disapproving nurse, Ova feels at home for the first time. This is, in fact, her legacy from her father, the one that means the most to her development as an artist. Structured like an egg, the mock-epic ends with a section on her father called "The Social Status of Exodus," in which the despised Jew collapses into the category of the despised woman. Like her father, the "mongrel-girl of Noman's Land" is exiled. But as an artist, she exiles herself from bourgeois "impecca   bility"; and as a woman, her body is the sign of her difference.[12]

Perhaps because satire is a particularly aggressive and confrontational discourse, or perhaps because the satiric lance turns ultimately against the poet herself, not many women writing "long poems" have engaged in this strategy. Anne Sexton, whose bitingly ironic slang is a trademark of her poetic voice, is an exception. Her volume *Transformations* retells the narratives of *Grimm's Fairy Tales* in the ironic voice of the excluded witch, who is faithful to the given plots, but utterly irreverent in her tone. Alicia Ostriker's 1971 volume *Once More in Darkness* plays ironically off the epic hero's classic *agon* by juxtaposing irreverent and contemporary colloquialisms alongside lyric enhancements of pregnancy and birth. More recently, Judy Grahn's *Edward the Dyke* quickly gained the status of an underground classic in its mock-heroic tale of a lesbian and her analyst, a grand adventure in the spiritual journey of analysis. *The Queen of Swords,* the second volume of Grahn's *The Chronicle of Queens,* returns to this satiric mode in configuring the descent of Innana to the underworld as a drama in a lesbian bar.

The second strategy, already implicit in Loy's mock epic of the "wondering Jew," is the (re)constitution of a discourse of history. Conventionally understood, "history" is the diachronic narration of events and forces at work in the public sphere, precisely the domain from which women have been overwhelmingly excluded, precisely the arena upon which the epic has been predominantly centered. To reclaim "history," women poets have re-defined it by breaking down the barriers between the "public" and the "private," the "political" and the "personal"—they have historicized the personal and personalized the historical. Like Woolf in *Three Guineas,* some women have shown that "the home"—the institutions of family and sexuality—is no haven in a heartless world, but is rather a contested terrain whose patterns replicate the larger structures of society. What is outside is inside; what is inside is outside—the personal is political in a dynamic whereby no realm is privileged as most important, whereby no site is immune from "history." Invisible in or objectified by conventional "histories," women poets have devised a discourse of (her)story in which they (re)make "history"—both in the acting and in the telling. Poems that exhibit this strategy in various ways include Adrienne Rich's *Sources,* Shirley Kaufman's *Claims: A Poem,* Irene Klepfisz's *Keeper of Accounts,* Sharon Doubiago's *Hard Country,* Gwendolyn Brooks's *In the Mecca,* Rosellen Brown's *Cora Fry,* Ruth Whitman's *Tansen Donner: a woman's journey,* Rita Dove's *Thomas and Beulah,* Kathleen Spivak's *The Jane Poems,* and Ostriker's *The Mother/Child Papers.*[13]

Ostriker's *The Mother/Child Papers* is a sequence of discrete lyrics that taken together narrate an epic of motherhood during the 1970s—from the pregnancy and birth of Gabriel in the early seventies, through the period of infancy and dependency with the son and two older daughters, and on to the years of letting go by the end of the decade. Inseparable from this "personal" narration, however, is the "public" story of the Vietnam War, the invasion of Cambodia, the murders at Kent State, the students' protests, the evacuation of Phnom Penh, the rise of feminism. The volume's title—*The Mother/Child Papers*—signals its historical

moment by echoing *The Pentagon Papers.* This resonance conflates the domain of
the state and the scene of the mother to suggest that the text's "history" is a
"leak" that violates the law of the public sphere. Formal aspects of the volume
extend the politics of its title. Sharp juxtapositions of "public" and "private" histories, interpenetration of spheres, and alternation of lyric and prosaic discourses
inscribe the poet's deconstruction as the binary upon which "history" has been
conventionally founded.

The volume opens with a documentary account in prose charting the birth of
the poet's son in the countdown of days leading up to and following the National
Guard's murder of four students at Kent State. The form combines the factual
document with the private journal, concluding the account of the alienating birth
with the question: "What does this have to do with Cambodia?" (6) By implication the poet establishes an analogue of violence between the state in Southeast
Asia, the Guard at Kent State, and the doctor who hates women. Having reflected, then deconstructed the binary of "public" and "private" in documentary
form, the poet repeats the process in lyric form. Liminal, inarticulate speech
weaves a cocoon around a more formal elegy that conflates a biblical epic of birth
and death:

<pre>
              was dreaming   be
    water   was   multiply
       dreaming   water   inherit
              in   earth
</pre>

The Guards kneeled, they raised their weapons, they fired
into the crowd to protect the peace. There was a sharp orange-red
explosion, diminished by the great warm daylight, a match scratching, a
whine, a tender thud, then the sweet tunnel, then nothing.
Then the tunnel again, the immense difficulty, pressure, then the head
finally is liberated, then they pull the body out.

<pre>
       was dreaming
       water was
                         falling and
                         rising all
                            along could
                            not see then
                            a barrier a
                            color red then
                               cold and
                            very afraid
                         (9–11)
</pre>

Against the power of the state that turns sons into cannon fodder, that murders and maims, Ostriker sets up the mother—"the power of a woman/ close to a
child, riding our tides/ into the sand dunes of the public sphere" (44). A mother,
a woman who births, has "an opportunity for supreme pleasure and heroism"—
in "the final stage of labor," she needs "no drugs because she becomes a goddess" (4–5). Our "first images/ of deity come" from "this power" of a mother (44).
But in this re-definition of the epic hero-as-mother, Ostriker writes against the
conventional valorization of the all-(for)giving Mother of the oedipal son's fantasy by recording in both documentary and lyric form the intensities of a mother's
erotic love and hate for her child. On the one hand, she feels:

but a baby
    any baby
your baby is
      the
most perfect human thing you can ever touch
translucent
and I want you to think about   touching
and the pleasure of   touching
and being touched by this most perfect thing
    this pear tree blossom
   this mouth these leafy hands these genitals
    like petals
  a warm scalp resting against your cheek
    fruit's warmth
    beginning—(43)

But on the other hand, she can feel trapped:

Hour after beastly hour.
        I swear I try.
You claw my skin, my nipple.
        Am witch. Am dry.
Cannot endure an existence
       chained to your cry.
Incubus.   Leech.   Scream.
    You confine me.Die. (22)

Reversing the narrative pattern of the traditional epic hero, Ostriker's mother must work through her ambivalence not to unite with the beloved, but to accept a separation. She must release her children into the world which might well make them victims. Her son might go to war. Her daughters face a domain in which their gifts might be invisible. This letting go, however, sets her free to (pro)create once again. Egg-shaped like Loy's *Anglo-Mongrel,* Ostriker's volume ends with another history of birth, of a woman—a poet?—who

crouches over a stool
    in a green room
  she is in labor, she is giving birth
  comfortable, she rides with this work
for hours, for days
    for the duration of this
    dream
    (62)

Ostriker's revisionist "history" of the 1970s that asserts the centrality of women's (pro)creation suggests the next feminizing strategy—creation of a discourse of revision. Rich's hyphenated spelling of the word "revision" in her classic 1971 essay "When We Dead Awaken: Writing as Re-Vision" articulates a stance toward the dominant discourses of culture and the forgotten or mis-read voices of women that characterizes many women writing "long poems" before and after the term gained currency. By "re-vision," Rich means "the act of looking back, of seeing with fresh eyes, of entering an old text from a new critical direction." This understanding of "the assumptions in which we are drenched" is "for us more than a chapter in cultural history: it is an act of survival" (35). H.D. pioneered this strategy for the feminization of culture in twentieth-century poetry—first in her short gyno-mythic poems in the twenties, then in her great revisionist epics in the forties and fifties, *Triology* and *Helen in Egypt*, and finally in their continuation in a series of "long poems," *Winter Love, Sagesse, Vale Ave*, and *Hermetic Definition*.[14] For H.D., there is a story within a story, the buried voices and visions of women that can be sought and brought to the surface in the very form that repressed them— for example, Homer's *Iliad* can be re-told from Helen's perspective in a way that utterly reverses the tradition it evokes. She uses her position as outsider to tunnel deep inside to find what has been repressed in the phallogocentric discourses of patriarchal culture.

Judy Grahn self-consciously situates her projected quartet *The Chronicle of Queens* in the revisionist tradition H.D. charted—both as a re-vision of the male epic, and a working class re-vision of H.D.'s work, which seems to presume a classical education.[15] In *The Queen of Wands*, Grahn lays out the plan for the whole. A forgotten Babylonian lament for the theft of the queen goddess serves as her buried Ur-text, whose trace the poet uncovers in the shards of the past and in the contemporary world around her: "this theme of a queen who has been stolen, of cities and temples ravaged by soldiers, of people cudgeled in their streets, of lamentation for a female power gone" (xii). Resonating with and revising modern poems like *The Waste Land*, Grahn's *Chronicle* connects the mythic past to the present moment of history by exploring the roots of sterility and the possibility of regeneration. Taking the great "webster" or spinning Spider Goddess of American Indians as her Muse, the poet sets out to re-weave the scattered strands of the story into a textual tapestry that will restore the queen and the female power she represents to the lands laid waste by the sterile "Foe" (xii–xiii).

Entitled "Gods and Heroes," Part I of the three-part *Queen of Wands* re-tells and revises the Homeric Helen of Troy, the woman who has remained "veiled" from us by past phallocentric tellings of her story. Unveiled by the poet's lyric meditations, Helen is El-Anna, the Egg of Being, "a poet,/ a singer and a weaver," the stolen queen who was deceived, "the Mother of my people" (27). Part II, entitled "Magicians," connects the Greek Helen with other stolen queens, magicians like the "good weef" or "word-wyfe," the Scandinavian Frigga, and most importantly the defiled and exploited sex goddesses of Hollywood, like Marilyn Monroe, to whom *The Queen of Wands* is dedicated. Used and abused, abandoned when their beauty is gone, the movie stars are the Helens, the stolen queens, of contemporary mass culture. It was her mysterious meeting with an old "crone," one of these desecrated stars, that confirmed the poet's sense of creative destiny, narrated in the lyric "In the tower of the crone," itself a re-vision of the fairy tale "Sleeping Beauty."

Part III, "Soldiers, Workers, and Gods," narrates in a succession of lyric moments the multiple forms of the stolen queen and announces her return in a rhythmic riddle that borrows its form from the folk tradition:

> The egg is always being made
> and making,

> always getting laid
> and laying;
> thread is being spun
> and spinning,
> truth is being found
> and finding,
> being all unsnarled
> and snarling,
> and the Grand Grand
> Mother is returning (78)

This lullaby-litany that repeats itself for several more stanzas prefigures the poet's recovery of her power in the (her)stories of common women. "Helen," the Spider says, you were always with us: "Helen you always were/ the factory/ Helen you always were producer" (80). Now, the poet can see and hear the lost queen in the voices of Hannah, the garment worker caught in the flames of the Triangle Fire; Nelda, the black slave whose descendants are "dreaming" a "dance of fire" (85); Nancy, the mother of soldier sons who die in war; and Annie Lee, a secretary whose lipstick tube is her wand, who hears "the singing/ of the loom" and sees "the strings of light/ like fingers and/ the fingers like a web, dancing" (91).[16]

Re-vision of patriarchal myths and texts concentrates specifically on phallic discourse in the fourth strategy that women have used to feminize the genre—the creation of a linguistically experimental gynopoetic. Feeling exiled from language itself, some women writers of the "long poem" have tunneled deep inside male discourse—inside the words, syntax, punctuation, rhythm, lineation, and spacing of poetic language—to deconstruct and erase its phallogocentrism. With Emily Dickinson standing behind her, Gertrude Stein is the major twentieth-century pioneer of this strategy, particularly in her prose-poems *Tender Buttons* and *Patriarchal Poetry* and lengthy cantos, *Stanzas in Meditation*. Her linguistic experiments in *Tender Buttons*, for example, destroy the conventions of representational reference and domesticate the "long poem" by focusing on the objects in a house, preeminently female space.[17] As Grahn writes about her, "Stein opened up language itself, the very bricks of it, the very of of it, the it of it, the the the of of" (*Highest Apple* 64). Contemporary "language-oriented" poets like Susan Howe, Rachel Blau DuPlessis, Daphne Marlatt, Kathleen Fraser, Beverly Dahlen, Frances Jaffer, and Betsy Warland continue Stein's project, sometimes in short lyrics, but often in volume-length "long poems."[18] Some black women poets, for whom the dominant poetic discourse is not only phallic, but also white, disrupt the conventional linguistic flow of the "long poem" with the rhythms and syntax of Black English—like Ntozake Shange in *For colored girls*—or with the colloquialisms, informal speech patterns, and violation of visual conventions used to situate poetic discourse in everyday, "common" life—like Toi Derricotte in *Natural Birth*, Pat Parker in "Goat Child" and "Womanslaughter" (*Movement* 19–30, 141–57), and Sherley Anne Williams in *Some One Sweet Angel Chile*.[19]

This strategy of linguistic experimentation finds its most intense form among those poets whose disruptions attempt to write the female body—to construct a gynopoetic discourse variously named "l'écriture féminine" by Hélène Cixous, "parler femme" by Luce Irigaray, "gynogrammar" by Betsy Warland, and "mother-tongue" by Daphne Marlatt, or more generally, the female "erotic" by

Audre Lorde. As Cixous' "The Laugh of the Medusa" suggests, this gynopoetic involves exploring the shape women's (pro)creativity and eroticism might give to a new poetic discourse.[20] Warland's *serpent (w)rite (a reader's gloss)* writes the female body as an epic whose *agon*—scene of action and struggle—is language itself. Warland engages in a process of "inspiralling" meditations on the problem of language for women, particularly as it is inscribed in the myth of creation in Genesis and acted out in the current scientific/linguistic battles over women's *wombs* and men's *bombs*. Warland's "gloss" on phallogocentric discourse both thematizes the issue of language and experiments with a form that has what she calls the "scent" of a woman's "sentence," the "fluency" of a woman's "fluids," the "inspiralling" of a woman's inner chambers.

Serpent (w)rite has eight unpaginated sections called "turns," which are introduced by a repeated graphic—a spiral like the whorl of a shell resting on wavy lines that are both serpent and sea. Each "turn" circles around the same questions, but also moves further into the labyrinthian spiral to provide a sense of narrative. "Turn one" initiates the quest in a moment of lesbian lovemaking that evokes Irigaray's punning conflation of mouth-lips and vaginal-lips in "When Our Lips Speak Together":

> we lose ourselves in each other
> smell
> a e i o u
> e
> i
> o
> u
> last lest list lost lust
> lest
> list
> lost
> lust
> your smell in / *lists* me
> . . . .
> we are 'lov / hers' of lost
> this the lost manuscript ("turn one")

Lost in each other, lost in the erotic vowels of the alphabet, the poet realizes that she is lost as well in the words men have written about women: "'hold your tongue woman.'" "Lost in thought," the poet begins her "inspiralling" meditations on the origins and meaning of language for women. Words are like odors. They can be "read" in the absence of their makers: "eyes smell word sprayed on page" and "smell signal scent / ence" ("turn one"). Her text is a patchwork of quotations that she glosses by reading its "scent / ence"—its smell, its judgment. Thinking about Adam's power to name, she despairs of women's "ventriloquism," their verbal and erotic "lip service" to men:

> Adam's words name
>
> Eve's words repeat

(lip service)
she took the words right out of His mouth

this is how we acquired language ("turn one")

But "inspiralling inclination" leads to a "gynogrammar spiraling" that holds out the possibility of women's speech. "All we can do is write our way home," the poet says in "turn four." This involves on the one hand being lost in complete silence—as when a whole page contains only these marks. "   (?)   " or "an open mouth   (   ) ." And on the other hand, it involves forging a speech spun out of women's bodies. "Begin it here/ in our bodies where word begins":

w(o)rd begins with
(o)pen m(o)uth with
w(o)man m(o)ther   ("turn four")

This language is a kind of "ssss-lang" based in the "fluency" of women's "scent / ence." Its mode of representation is more oral and visual than symbolic—thereby resonating with Lacanian feminism which sees the phallus as the "transcendental signifier" in the realm of the Symbolic. Like so much of Stein's experimental writing, sound instead of a symbolic equation of signifier and signified makes meaning—as in the pun: "phallus? Fell us?" ("turn three"). Visualization also constructs meaning—as in the word "scent / ence"; in the use of parentheses and hyphens—as in the title word "(w)rite"; in the presence or absence of punctuation or capitalization; in the explorations and juxtapositions of space. Words, syntax, and proverbial cliches are repeated and etymologically dismantled for their repressed politics, in much the same way Mary Daly does in *Gyn/ Ecology*. *Serpent (w)rite* ends with a quotation from Maria Sabina that sums up the poem's main point about women's enslavement in and liberation through language: "with my hands I catch word after word that holds us captive set us free wordsmells wombwords wordprints we track endlessly" ("turn eight"). Women's poetry can be a (w)rite—writing as ritual that undoes and redoes the myths and texts of patriarchy. Like the serpent in Genesis, *serpent (w)rite* offers forbidden knowledge from the tree of life. But this knowledge makes possible the survival of the human race, not its death.

In conclusion, the epic tradition that has established the major grid markers through which we read contemporary "long poems" has been thoroughly overdetermined as a masculine discourse of important quest-ions. Women writing within this tradition often engage in self-authorizing strategies that feminize the genre in one form or another so that the big quest-ions that women ask can be set to the "big" format of the "long" poem. The four self-authorizing strategies I have identified—the ironist, historicist, re-visionist, and experimentalist—all create a female space inside a genre that has left women outside. I don't propose these as exclusive strategies; nor do they have fixed boundaries. Rather, they have between them the "edgeless boundaries" that Derrida posits for things that are both "inside" and "outside." They are emphatically not useful categories for the classification of poems—a given text is likely to participate in more than one. Moreover, each of the strategies depends on the presence of the other inside itself in order to forward its play with the genre as an outsider. Loy's satire of British "apparent impeccability" and paean to "iarrhea" experiment with word, sound, and visualization just as Warland does in *serpent (w)rite*. Ostriker's juxtaposition of the "factual" documentary and the near-inarticulate lyric also disrupts conventional poetics. Grahn's rhythmic lullaby and etymological spinnings similarly undo and redo masculine poetic discourse. Conversely, Warland's text is a "re-vision" of Genesis whose patchwork of quotations from the male and female descendants of Adam and Eve recapitulates the Biblical patterns the poet deconstructs. With its interwoven strands of scientific and sacred texts, it also re-visions "history" into (her) story. I have proposed these strategies, then, as a way into the labyrinth that perhaps also includes the strategy of writing very big poems inside very little ones: the volcanic compression of very big questions into a very tight space—poems that are very big, but not long, like Emily Dickinson's oeuvre, which took shape within the little tradition of handmade books and gift-poems and ultimately became a massive body of irreducibly cosmic scope.

NOTES

1. A shorter version of this essay was presented at a session on the Long Poem chaired by James Justus at the Modern Language Association meeting in December 1987. I am indebted to him for suggesting that I write this essay and to Nellie McKay, Lynn Keller, Jay Clayton, and Norman Weinstein for references and to Alicia Ostriker and Rachel Blau DuPlessis for their challenges to my resistance to the category "long poem."

2. For some discussions of the generic category and debates about terminology, see for example, Keller; Rosenthal and Gail, "The Modern Sequence" and *The Modern Poetic Sequence*; Dembo; Riddell; Bernstein; and Miller. The current edition of the *Princeton Encyclopedia of Poetry and Poetics* does not contain an entry for the "long poem"; but the next edition will most likely have such an entry.

3. See also Culler's discussion of Kristeva and generic expectations in *Structuralist Poetics* (139–40, 145) and his contrasting analysis of Bloomian vs. Barthesian methodologies for intertextual reading in *The Pursuit of Signs* (100–18).

4. See for example, Gilbert and Gubar; Schenck; Friedman; Homans.

5. For a different view of the significance of length for the "long poem," see Li, who argues that the defining *length* of a "long poem" is not "volume," but "a quality of discourse"(4).

6. I am echoing H.D.'s "The Master" in *Collected Poems* (460).

7. For current definitions of the epic, see Yu, Preminger, Maresca, Bernstein, Friedman.

8. See Derrida's conflation of *genre* and *gender* in "The Law of Genre." See also Friedman for an extended discussion of the gender inflections of epic genre codes.

9. See for example, Rosenthal and Gall; Riddell; Keller; Bernstein; Miller; Li; Friedman.

10. See Bowra's discussion of Corinna's *Daughters of Asopus* in *Heroic Poetry* (549–50, 553) and New *Chapters*, ed. Powell (21–30).

11. See Barrett Browning's *The Battle of Marathon, An Essay on Mind, Prometheus Bound, The Seraphim,* and *The Drama of Exile* in *The Poetical Works*. For a discussion of *Aurora Leigh* as epic, see Friedman. According to Mary Loeffelholz (in conversation), a number of other nineteenth-century women poets wrote epics, a corpus of forgotten material that she is currently researching.

12. See Derrida's "The Law of Genre"; see also his *Of Grammatology* (27–73). Feminists have also transformed the opposition "inside/outside." See for example, Judy Grahn

in *The Highest Apple*, where she identifies women as both "outsiders" and "insiders" (62–72, 82).

13. Loy's stance as Outsider was so deeply felt that *Anglo-Mongrels* proved to be more of an end point than a beginning of her poetic development. She published occasional poems after Robert McAlmon printed some 58 pages of her mock-epic in 1925, but her creative efforts went increasingly into the visual arts. In the 1940s and 1950s, she lived mostly in New York's Bowery, at home with the winos and "bums" who provided the inspiration for a series of collages. To a large extent, she exiled herself from the world of the literati, indeed from literary discourse itself. For critical discussion of her work, see Burke.

14. Given this significance of "history" in the cultural definition and evolution of Judaism, it is more than coincidental that many of the poets using this strategy are Jewish. Some—like Rich, Kaufman, and Klepfisz—specifically use this re-constituted historical discourse to explore the meaning of their Jewish legacy. Levertov's long sequence about the death of her sister Olga (*To Stay Alive*) and Plath's *Three Women: A Poem for Three Voices* about pregnant women (*Collected Poems* 176–86) are somewhat more "personal," but their implicit redefinition of women's "personal" struggle as heroic also participates in this "historical" strategy. See also the statements on the cover of Doubiago's *Hard Country* by Carolyn Forché and Meridel Le Sueur, who writes: "Doubiago fearlessly enters the labyrinth of our history, our search and danger as woman as human as deep American wanderer. . . . It is a long saga, a woman's history and the history of us all."

15. For a discussion of H.D. as epic poet, see Friedman.

16. See Grahn, *The Highest Apple* (especially 49–57, 102–10, 135). Grahn further discussed her relationship with H.D.'s poetry in her talk at the Dual Centennial Colloquium on Emily Dickinson and H.D. at San Jose State University, October 1986. With the use of footnotes (another echo of *The Waste Land* but for a different purpose) and careful incorporation of explanation into the text of her poem, Grahn attempts to demystify mythology so that it is accessible to those without an extensive education. H.D. actually uses this technique of incorporated explanation quite extensively For Grahn's other articulations of "re-vision," see her *She Who* and *A Woman Is Talking To Death* in *The Work of a Common Woman* (75–132) and *The Queen of Swords*.

17. For other poets who use the discourse of re-vision in "long poems," see especially Bundenz, Clifton, DiPrima, Howe, DuPlessis, Lawrence, Morgan, Rich (*Twenty-One Love Poems*), Sexton (*Transformations*).

18. For discussion of Stein's experimentation in the context of phallogocentrism, see DeKoven. For a discussion that links Stein's form in *Tender Buttons* to the politics of genre, see Monroe. For discussion of *Stanzas in Meditation*, see Weinstein (82–99).

19. The term "language-oriented" is Rachel Blau DuPlessis' designation for contemporary women poets who share a linguistic experimentalism with the "L=A=N=G=U=A=G=E" poets, but who differ from that "school" in their "attitude toward referentiality and meaning" (Letter to author, 5 January 1988). DuPlessis' new volume, *Tabula Rosa*, contains a series of lyrics joined in a "long poem" in process, entitled *History of Poetry*. In addition to the volumes of these poets, see especially two journals devoted to women's linguistically experimental writing: the West Coast journal *HOW(ever)* and the Canadian journal *(f)Lip*.

20. Without using the term, Grahn's introduction to Parker's *Movement in Black* identifies "Goat Child" and "Womanslaughter" as "long poems," in spite of their relatively short length. She writes, "*Goat Child* was the first deliberately autobiographical poem by a woman that I had ever heard, although there was no reason (try sexism) why a woman's entire life couldn't be the storyline of a poem, a modern epic. . . . *Womanslaughter*. . . . is a major work, a major documentary poem and a feminist statement of commitment for women to defend other women from violent attack" (14). See also Brooks' *In the Mecca*.

21. For "long poems" that inscribe the epic of pregnancy, childbirth, and lactation with

experimental disruptions of poetic discourse see Ostriker's *The Mother/Child Papers* and Derricotte's *Natural Birth*. See also Clifton's Kali sequence in *Ordinary Woman* and Mary sequence in *Two-headed woman*; Plath, *Three Voices*; Grahn, *She Who* in *The Work of a Common Woman* (75–110).

WORKS CITED

Barthes, Roland. *Writing Degree Zero* (1953). Trans. Annette Lavers and Colin Smith. New York: Hill and Wang, 1968.

Benet, William Rose. *The Reader's Encyclopedia*. New York: Thomas Y Crowell, 1965.

Bernstein, Michael Andre. *The Tale of the Tribe: Ezra Pound and the Modern Verse Epic*. Princeton: Princeton UP, 1980.

Bowra, C. M. *Heroic Poetry*. London: Macmillan, 1952.

Brooks, Gwendolyn. *In the Mecca*. New York: Harper & Row, 1968.

Brown, Rosellen. *Cora Fry*. New York: Norton, 1977.

Browning, Elizabeth Barrett. *Aurora Leigh: A Poem* (1857). Chicago: Academy Chicago Ltd., 1979.

———. *The Poetical Works*. Boston: Houghton Mifflin, 1974.

Bundenz, Julia. *From the Gardens of Flora Baum*. Middletown: Wesleyan UP, 1984.

Burke, Carolyn. "Mina Loy." *Dictionary of Literary Biography: Volume IV: American Writers in Paris 1920–1939*, ed. Karen Lane Rood. Detroit: Gale Research, 1980. 259–60.

Christian, Barbara T. "From the Inside Out: Afro-American Women's Literary Tradition and the State." Center for Humanistic Studies Occasional Paper, Number 19. Minneapolis: U of Minnesota P, 1987.

Cixous, Hélène. "The Laugh of the Medusa" (1974). In *New French Feminisms: An Anthology*, eds. Elaine Marks and Isabelle de Courtivron. Amherst: U of Massachusetts P, 1980. 245–64.

Clifton, Lucille. *An Ordinary Woman*. New York: Random House, 1974.

———. *Two-headed woman*. Amherst: U of Massachusetts P, 1980.

Culler, Jonathan. *The Pursuit of Signs: Semiotics, Literature, Deconstruction*. Ithaca: Cornell UP, 1981.

———. *Structuralist Poetics: Structuralism Linguistics and the Study of Literature*. Ithaca: Cornell UP, 1975.

DeKoven, Marianne. *A Different Language: Gertrude Stein's Experimental Writing*. Madison: U of Wisconsin P, 1983.

Dembo, L. S. *Conceptions of Reality in Modern American Poetry*. Berkeley: U of California P, 1965.

Derricotte, Toi. *Natural Birth*. Trumansburg, NY: The Crossing Press, 1983.

Derrida, Jacques. *Of Grammatology*, trans. Gayatri Chakravorty Spivak. Baltimore: Johns Hopkins UP, 1976.

———. "The Law of Genre." *Critical Inquiry* 7 (Autumn 1980): 55–79.

DiPrima, Diane. *Loba*. Berkeley: Wingbow Press, 1978.

Dove, Rita. *Thomas and Beulah*. Pittsburgh: Carnegie-Mellon, 1986.

Doubiago, Sharon. *Hard Country*. Minneapolis: West End Press, 1982.

DuPlessis, Rachel Blau. *Tabula Rosa*. Elmwood, CT: Potes & Poets Press, 1987.

———. *Wells*. New York: Montemora, 1980.

Eliot, George. *The Spanish Gypsy*. In *Poems*. London: Hawarden Press, 1899. I, 1–245; II, 1–54.

(f.)Lip. 2544 West 54th Avenue, Vancouver, BC, Canada. V6K 1S9.

Friedman, Susan Stanford. "Gender and Genre Anxiety: Elizabeth Barrett Browning and H.D. as Epic Poets." *Tulsa Studies in Women's Literature* 5 (Fall 1986): 203–28.

Gilbert, Sandra M. and Susan Gubar. *The Madwoman in the Attic: The Woman Writer and the Nineteenth-Century Literary Imagination*. New Haven: Yale UP, 1979.

Grahn, Judy. *The Highest Apple: Sappho and the Lesbian Poetic Tradition*. San Francisco: Spinsters Ink, 1985.

———. *The Queen of Wands*. Trumansburg, NY: The Crossing Press, 1982.

———. *The Queen of Swords*. Boston: Beacon Press, 1987.

———. *The Work of a Common Woman: The Collected Poetry, 1964–1977*. Trumansburg, NY: The Crossing Press, 1978.

Harper, Frances Watkins. *Moses: A Story of the Nile*. Philadelphia: Merrihew, 1869.

H.D. (Hilda Doolittle). *Collected Poems, 1912–1944*, ed. Louis L. Martz. New York: New Directions, 1983.

———. *Helen in Egypt* (1961). New York: New Directions, 1974.

———. *Hermetic Definition*. New York: New Directions, 1972.

———. *Sagesse*. In *Hermetic Definition*. New York: New Directions, 1972.

———. *Triology* (1944–1946). New York: New Directions, 1973.

———. *Vale Ave. New Directions in Prose and Poetry 44*, ed. James Laughlin. New York: New Directions, 1982.

———. *Winter* Love. In *Hermetic Definition*. New York: New Directions, 1972.

Homans, Margaret. "'Syllables of Velvet': Dickinson, Rossetti, and the Rhetorics of Sexuality." *Feminist Studies* 11 (Fall 1985): 569–93.

Howe, Susan. *Defenestration of Prague*. New York: Kultur Foundation, 1983.

———. *My Emily Dickinson*. Berkeley: North Atlantic Books, 1985.

———. *Pythagorean Silence*. New York: Montemora, 1982.

HOW(ever). 871 Corbett Avenue, San Francisco, CA 94131.

Irigaray, Luce. "When Our Lips Speak Together." In *This Sex Which Is Not One*, trans. Catherine Porter. Ithaca: Cornell UP, 1985.

Kaufman, Shirley. *Claims: A Poem*. New York: The Sheep Meadow Press, 1984.

Keller, Lynn. "Poems Containing History: Problems of Definition of the Long Poem." Paper delivered at MLA, December 1987.

Kelpfisz, Irene. *Keeper of Accounts*. Watertown, MA: Persephone Press, 1982.

Kristeva, Julia. *Desire in Language: A Semiotic Approach to Literature and Art*. Trans. Leon S. Roudiez. New York: Columbia UP, 1980.

Lawrence, Karen. *The Inanna Poems*. Edmonton, Alberta: Longspoon Press, 1980.

Levertov, Denise. "Staying Alive." In *To Stay Alive*. New York: New Directions, 1971. 21–85.

Li, Victor P. H. "The Vanity of Length: The long poem as problem in Pound's *Cantos* and Williams' *Paterson*." *Genre* 19 (Spring 1986): 3–20.

Lorde, Audre. "Uses of the Erotic: The Erotic as Power." In *Sister Outsider: Essays & Speeches*. Trumansburg, NY: The Crossing Press, 1984. 53–59.

Loy, Mina. *The Last Lunar Baedeker*, ed. Roger L. Conover. Highlands, NC: The Jargon Society, 1982.

Maresca, Thomas. *Epic to Novel*. Columbus: Ohio State UP, 1979.

Marlatt, Daphne. *Touch to My Tongue*. Alberta: Longspoon Press, 1984.

Miller, James E., Jr. *The American Quest for a Supreme Fiction: Whitman's Legacy in the Personal Epic*. U of Chicago P, 1979.

Monroe, Jonathan. *A Poverty of Objects: The Prose Poem and the Politics of Genre*. Ithaca: Cornell UP, 1987.

Morgan, Robin. *Lady of the Beasts*. New York: Random House, 1976.

Ostriker, Alicia Suskin. *The Mother/Child Papers*. Santa Monica, CA: Momentum Press, 1980.

———. *Once More Out of Darkness*. New York: 1971.

Parker, Pat. *Movement in Black: The Collected Poetry, 1961–1978*. Trumansburg, NY: The Crossing Press, 1983.

Plath, Sylvia. *The Collected Poems*, ed. Ted Hughes. New York: Harper & Row, 1981.

Pound, Ezra. *Literary Essays*, ed. T. S. Eliot. New York: New Directions, 1975.

———. *Spirit of Romance* (1910). New York: New Directions, 1968.

Powell, J. V. *New Chapters in the History of Greek Literature*. London: Oxford UP, 1933.

Preminger, Alex, ed. *Princeton Encyclopedia of Poetry and Poetics*. Princeton: Princeton UP, 1974.

Rich, Adrienne. *Sources*. Woodside, CA: Hyeck Press, 1983.

———. *Twenty-One Love Poems*. In *The Dream of a Common Language*. New York: Norton, 1978. 25–38.

———. "When We Dead Awaken: Writing as Re-Vision." In *On Lies, Secrets and Silence*. New York: Norton, 1979. 33–50.

Riddell, Joseph N. "A Somewhat Polemical Introduction: The Elliptical Poem." *Genre* 11 (Winter 1978): 459–77.

Rosenthal, M. L. and Sally M. Gall. *The Modern Poetic Sequence: The Genesis of Modern Poetry*. New York: Oxford UP, 1983.

———. "The Modern Sequence and Its Precursors." *Contemporary Literature* 22 (Summer 1981): 308–325.

Schenck, Celeste M. "All of a Piece: Women's Poetry and Autobiography." Paper delivered at MLA, December 1986.

———. "Feminism and Deconstruction: Re-Constructing the Elegy." *Tulsa Studies in Women's Literature* 5 (Spring 1986): 13–28.

———. "Songs (From) the Bride: Feminism, Psychoanalysis, Genre." *Literature and Psychology* 23 (1987): 109–119.

Sexton, Anne. *Transformations*. Boston: Houghton Mifflin, 1971.

Shange, Ntozake. *For colored girls who have considered suicide/when the rainbow is enuf*. New York: Bantam, 1976.

Spivak, Kathleen. *The Jane Poems*. New York: Doubleday, 1974.

Stein, Gertrude. *Patriarchal Poetry*. In *The Yale Gertrude Stein*, ed. Richard Kostelanetz. New Haven: Yale UP, 1980. 106–146.

———. *Stanzas in Meditation*. Excerpted in *The Yale Gertrude Stein*, ed. Richard Kostelanetz. New Haven: Yale UP, 1980. 316–464.

———. *Tender Buttons* (1914). In *The Selected Writings of Gertrude Stein*, ed. Carl Van Vechten. New York: Vintage, 1962. 459–510.

Tighe, Mary. *Psyche, or the Legend of Love* (1805). New York: Garland Press, 1978.

Warland, Betsy. *serpent (w)rite*. Toronto: The Coach House Press, 1987.

Weinstein, Norman. *Gertrude Stein and the Literature of the Modern Consciousness*. New York: Frederick Ungar, 1970.

Whitman, Ruth. *Tamsen Donner: a woman's journey*. Cambridge: Alice James Books, 1977.

Williams, Sherley Anne. *Some One Sweet Angel Chile*. New York: William Morrow, 1982.

Woolf, Virginia. A *Room of One's Own* (1929). New York: Harcourt Brace and Jovanovich, 1957.

———. *Three Guineas* (1938). New York: Harcourt Brace and World.

Yu, Anthony C., ed. *Parnassus Revisited: Modern Critical Essays on the Epic Tradition*. Chicago: American Library Association, 1973.

ethnicity

"From margin to center": bell hooks's famous phrase seems comfortably enough to describe the movement of Women's Studies as a whole. Feminism has, after all, worked to pull women's voices, experiences, and concerns out of the periphery of official culture, and has insisted upon placing gender-related issues squarely in the middle of all academic fields of inquiry. If women have traditionally occupied the margins, though, women of color have been doubly marginalized. And such women, whose sexual orientation, class, or nationality differentiate them even further from the heterosexual, middle-class, North American "norm," have—until recently—been pushed so far into the margin as to have been almost imperceptible to the mainstream academic eye. The essays in this section (like many others throughout this volume) are working to redress the marginalization of women of color in mainstream feminisms, as well as in the culture at large.

Like "gender," the terms "ethnicity" and "race" are usually used within feminist theory to refer to cultural constructions, not biological conditions. "Ethnicity," as we are using it here, refers to a person's cultural orientation as it has been shaped by the traditions and experiences associated with that person's race, which is itself not a matter of biology, but another arbitrarily defined category within culture and society. Just as the usage of "gender" has, until recently, implied a focus on women while masculinity remained the invisible norm, the usage of "race" has connoted a focus on people of color, as if persons in the white mainstream had no race. "Ethnicity" is perhaps a more neutral term, in that many Caucasians identify with distinct ethnic groups (Irish-, Italian-, or French Canadian-Americans, for instance). In calling this section "Ethnicity," we do not mean to downplay the significance of race for the Native American, Chicana, African-American, Asian-American, and Caucasian critics represented here; we made this difficult decision in order to underline the emphasis in these essays upon cultural heritages rather than "blood." In these critics' work, a focus on ethnicity requires adjustments in the information and the perspective that a reader brings to the experience of reading. From their points of view, what you know (or, more importantly, don't know) about a literary work's extraliterary context will determine your appreciation of it, and what you have experienced (directly or imaginatively) will shape the perspective you take in evaluating or understanding it.

Experience, therefore, has played a crucial role in feminist criticism that places race and ethnicity at the center. In Paula Gunn Allen's "Kochinnenako in Academe: Three Approaches to Understanding a Keres Indian Tale" (1986), the experience in question is that of Native American tribal traditions. Allen reproduces an English-language version of an oral tale about a female character, translated in the early twentieth century by a white man. Allen subjects this Keres tale to three readings, showing how profoundly one's expectations and information will affect one's reading of a text from outside the mainstream culture. First, subtly applying the tools of structuralist narrative theory, Allen shows how the translator's unself-conscious allegiance to Western patriarchal story lines has caused him to distort the content and form of the tale. From a tribal perspective, she explains, the English rendition is nonsense, as it dismantles the ritual nature of the original to force it into a linear tale of conflict and resolution. Next, Allen considers what an Anglo-American feminist might say about the translated tale, observing that such a reader would have good reason to jump to false conclusions about the oppression of women in the culture supposedly represented by the story. Then Allen proposes a "feminist-tribal interpretation," bringing together her knowledge of the Keres "perception, aesthetics, and social system" with her awareness of what gender signifies in Keres culture.

The "feminist-tribal" perspective allows Allen to reveal "how the interpolations of patriarchal thinking distort all the relationships in the story and, by extension, how such impositions of patriarchy on gynocracy disorder harmonious social and spiritual relationships." As this last remark indicates, Allen is interested in the effect stories have on the world of lived experience; she asserts that the Westernization of Native American tales is partly responsible for the problematic relations between the sexes in tribes today. Like Barbara Smith's essay in this section, Allen's literary criticism is a form of activism, a way of bringing structuralist-inspired abstractions to life.

"Nothing happens in the 'real' world unless it first happens in the images in our heads," asserts Gloria Anzaldúa in "La conciencia de la mestiza: Towards a New Consciousness" (1987). This enormously influential essay is one of the few in *Feminisms* that is not, strictly speaking, a piece of "literary theory or criticism," but Anzaldúa's project of remaking North American culture by transforming those "images in our heads" closely parallels that of the literary critics represented in this section. Anzaldúa sketches out the consciousness of the *"mestiza,"* the Chicana living in the borderlands that link the southwestern United States with Mexico, the product of "racial, ideological, cultural and biological cross-pollination." For Anzaldúa, the space that exists between and within opposing worlds is a creative space, where *la mestiza* can revel in the strength and the ambiguities that result from the "struggle of flesh, [the] struggle of borders," the "cultural collision" she embodies.

Anzaldúa's argument invokes principles of deconstruction, as she advocates "a tolerance for contradictions, a tolerance for ambiguity," as well as "the breaking down of paradigms" that perpetuate oppression. She emphasizes the multiple possibilities that arise from being both inside and outside of cultures simultaneously. For example, "as a lesbian I have no race, my own people disclaim me; but I am all races because there is the queer of me in all races." Anzaldúa explores the relations between Anglo culture and the culture of the borderlands, arguing that the struggle for recovery in Chicano and Chicana culture must be specifically feminist in that it must end the destructive patterns set by Anglo-influenced gender roles. Her essay ends with some very beautiful autobiographical writing describing the relationship between her own family and the borderland itself. True to her argument for living on the border, Anzaldúa's essay blurs the boundaries between academic and personal writing, between scholarship and experience, and between theory and activism.

Amy Ling's "I'm Here: An Asian-American Woman's Response" (1987) seeks to place ethnically focused criticism in the context of feminist literary theory. This piece (like the Jane Tompkins essay in "Autobiography") is an answer to Ellen Messer-Davidow's essay in *New Literary History*, "The Philosophical Bases of Feminist Literary Criticisms." The plural form of Messer-Davidow's title, and the presence of no fewer than seven responses in that issue of the journal, indicate the growing awareness in the late 1980s of the multiplicity of perspectives that can shape feminist efforts. Indeed, Messer-Davidow's term "perspectivism" works well for Ling, who brings it up from the position of a critic working on Chinese-American women's literature written in English, her previously all-but-invisible field of study. Ling's response applies basic feminist principles about literary value and critical practices (like those represented here in "Canon" and "Practice") to explain what it means for her to do ethnically centered criticism of women's writing.

Ling points out that while all minorities are marginalized, some groups are treated as more peripheral to the mainstream than others. While she acknowledges that "we cannot all be remembered all the time," she expresses the (possibly "utopian") wish that "the result of . . . attention were that everyone would be not merely more tolerant of each other's perspectives but actively interested." Toward sparking that interest, Ling briefly describes the turn-of-the-century novels of "the Eaton sisters, the first writers of Asian ancestry to publish in the United States," and—like all the critics in this section—she emphasizes the importance of understanding something about the Eaton sisters' historical context for an appreciation of their texts.

To establish historical context for the texts she studies, Barbara Smith's "The Truth that Never Hurts: Black Lesbians in Fiction in the 1980s" (1990) moves freely among academic observations, personal anecdotes, and cultural analysis. Smith is one of the few authors in *Feminisms* explicitly to address activism, an issue far more central to academic feminisms than its representation in this volume would suggest. As Smith explains, the experience of activism affects not only the information a feminist critic brings to her work, but all her perceptions. In this project, Smith brings to bear what she knows about homophobia (as a scholar, as an activist, and as a black lesbian) upon her examination of the way African-American lesbians have been portrayed in the fiction of the 1980s. Taking Gloria Naylor's *The Women of Brewster Place*, Alice Walker's *The Color Purple*, and Audre Lord's *Zami: A New Spelling of My Name* as her examples, Smith analyzes each in terms of its "verisimilitude" (or believability on the level of such formal elements as plot, setting, and characterization) and its "authenticity" (or its plausibility and desirability as a statement of what the experience of black lesbians is like). Smith finds Naylor's portrayal of a black lesbian couple a "nightmare," strong in verisimilitude but—from the perspective of a black lesbian reader especially—lacking authenticity; she calls Walker's buoyant story of love between women an "idyll," a "fable," brimming with authenticity, but short on verisimilitude. For Smith, Lorde's autobiographical *Zami* splits the difference, providing "a vision of possibilities for Black Lesbians surviving whole, despite all."

In "Feminist and Ethnic Literary Theories in Asian-American Literature" (1993), Shirley Geok-lin Lim does not introduce any text by an Asian-American woman that embodies a similar wholeness. Her essay problematizes the concepts of experience and identity, on both pragmatic and theoretical grounds. To speak of "Asian-American" experience is pragmatically difficult because of the diversity of cultures represented within the phrase (Chinese-, Japanese-, Korean-, Filipino-, Southeast-Asian-, and Indian-American, to put the categories most broadly). Lim's theoretical survey of the emerging field of Asian-American literature foregrounds the inevitable struggles between ethnicity and feminism for women writers whose Asian Americanness allies them (ambivalently) with traditions that Western feminists would perceive as patriarchal. Lim's essay very clearly traces out the friction between women's studies and ethnic studies, both in terms of white feminists' neglect of women of color and in terms of Asian-American men's having overlooked women writers as they constructed their own canon through the 1970s. Her critique of white feminists remains for the most part implicit, while her reprimands to the male editors of Asian-American literary anthologies are spirited and detailed.

Lim turns to anthologies of Asian-American women's writing for definitions of Asian-American identity that can accommodate feminine and feminist values. Lim's close readings of two full-length texts by Asian-American women, however, "provide a caution against too easily assuming the merger of ethnic and feminist identities," as the texts tend to move from a critique of gender roles within Asian-American communities to a critique of racism in American culture, without harmonizing the two. Even Asian-American women poets who assert more obviously feminist identities by "writing the body" in a form Lim identifies as *l'écriture féminine* do not bridge the gap, because they ground their writing in a Western form of discourse. Still, Lim points to their work as a positive reminder "of how ethnic and gender identities are continuously negotiated in tension against each other, the very act . . . of writing composed of strategies of identity that challenge each other in a dialogical mode within the texts themselves."

If Lim finds dialogue about gender and ethnicity within the literary texts of Asian-American women, Elizabeth Abel looks for "possibilities of dialogue across as well as about racial boundaries." Writing from a white feminist perspective about the same women's studies/ethnic studies conflicts of interest that Lim points to, Abel does not spare white feminists from a detailed scrutiny as Lim does. Instead, Abel undertakes the "task of white self-criticism." Abel frames her theoretical argument with an account of two feminist readers—herself and black critic Lula Fragd—coming to very different conclusions about the racial identity of the two main characters in Toni Morrison's story "Recitatif." As Abel shows in fascinating detail, Morrison's text mentions that one character is black and the other white, but it obscures the possibility of determining which is which by representing racial difference in relative, not absolute terms. By offering explanations based in ethnic experience and racialized assumptions about such matters as clothing, musical taste, eating, and body size, Abel shows why she and Fragd come to opposite conclusions about the characters' races. Complicating the issue even more is Morrison's explanation that class is as significant a difference between the characters as is race, and that their relative class status defies racial stereotyping. While Abel does not try to reach a definitive conclusion about the characters' race, she succeeds in contributing "to a project many black feminists endorse: the racialization of whiteness." Her observations about her own assumptions become a step toward theorizing whiteness as ethnicity, rather than allowing it to remain in the invisible background against which "other" races are perceived.

Abel's essay also demonstrates, however, that there is no monolithic "white feminist" approach. She conducts three case studies of white feminists' readings of black culture, looking in detail at Barbara Johnson's deconstruction of Zora Neale Hurston (another example of Johnson's work appears in "Discourse"); Margaret Homans's psychoanalytic interpretations of Alice Walker and Toni Morrison (Homans's essay in "Practice" challenges Abel's reading); and Susan Willis's materialist feminist (or cultural studies–inspired) essay, "I Shop Therefore I Am" (reprinted in "Class"). Abel finds the deconstructionist model of race too figurative and the psychoanalytic model too literal; materialist feminism—the mode Abel identifies as most often practiced by black feminist critics themselves—strikes Abel as the most politically efficacious of the approaches she surveys. Abel's essay highlights the self-consciousness and anxiety, as well as the institutional power and assumed authority, of white feminists whose work carries them across racial borderlands. As Abel remarks in a moment of understatement, "Race enters complexly into feminist reading." Her reading of white feminist readings positions itself as a next step in the dialogue being opened here by Allen, Anzaldúa, Smith, and Lim. The conversation is by no means over.

—RRW

KOCHINNENAKO IN ACADEME

*three approaches to interpreting
a keres indian tale*

(1986)

I became engaged in studying feminist thought and theory at the same time I was first studying and teaching American Indian literature in the early seventies. Over the ensuing fifteen years, my own particular stance toward both feminist and American Indian life and thought have unfolded along intertwining lines. I have always included feminist content and perspectives in my teaching of American Indian subjects, though at first the mating was uneasy at best. My determination that both areas were mutually interdependent and mutually significant to a balanced pedagogy of American Indian studies led me to grow into an approach to both that is best described as tribal-feminism or feminist-tribalism. Both terms are applicable: if I am dealing with feminism, I approach it from a strong tribal posture, and when I am dealing with American Indian literature, history, culture, or philosophy I approach them from a strongly feminist one.

A feminist approach to the study and teaching of American Indian life and thought is essential because the area has been dominated by paternalistic, male-dominant modes of consciousness since the first writings about American Indians in the fifteenth century. This male bias has seriously skewed our understanding of tribal life and philosophy, distorting it in ways that are sometimes obvious but are most often invisible.

Often what appears to be a misinterpretation caused by racial differences is a distortion based on sexual politics. When the patriarchal paradigm that characterizes Western thinking is applied to gynecentric tribal modes, it transforms the ideas, significances, and raw data into something not only unrecognizable to the tribes, but also entirely incongruent with the significance of their philosophies and theories. We know that materials and interpretations amassed by the white intellectual establishment are in error, but we have not pinpointed the source of that error. It has been my belief that its major source has been male bias, and that feminist theory, when judiciously applied to the field, makes the error correctable, freeing the data for re-interpretation that is at least congruent with a tribal preceptual mode even while it is not identical to it.

To demonstrate the interconnections between tribal and feminist approaches as I use them in my work, I have developed an analysis of a traditional "Yellow Woman" story of the Laguna-Acoma Keres, as re-cast by my mother's great uncle, John M. Gunn, in his book *Schat Chen*.[1] My analysis utilizes three possible approaches and demonstrates the relationship of context to meaning, illuminating three consciousness styles, and providing students with a traditionally tribal and non-racist, feminist understanding of traditional and contemporary American Indian life.

SOME THEORETICAL CONSIDERATIONS

Analyzing tribal cultural systems from a mainstream feminist point of view allows a certain otherwise overlooked insight into the complex interplay of factors that have led to the systematic loosening of tribal ties, the disruption of tribal cohesion and complexity, and the growing disequilibrium of cultures that were anciently based on a belief in balance and relationship and the centrality of women, particularly elder women, as basic to harmonious, evenhanded ordering of human society. A feminist approach reveals not only the exploitation and oppression of the tribes by whites and white government, but it also reveals areas of oppression within the tribes, and the sources and nature of that oppression. To a large extent, such an analysis can provide strategies for ameliorating the effects of patriarchal colonialism, enabling many of the tribes to reclaim their ancient gynarchical, egalitarian, and sacred traditions. (In a system where all persons in power are called mother chief and where the supreme deity is female, and where social organization is matrilocal, matrifocal, and matrilineal, gynarchy is happening. However, it does not imply domination of men by women as patriarchy implies domination by males of all aspects of a society.)

At the present time, American Indians in general are not comfortable with feminist analysis or action within the reservation or urban Indian enclaves. Many Indian women are uncomfortable with feminism because they perceive it (correctly) as white-dominated. They (no so correctly) believe it is concerned with issues that have little bearing on their own lives. They are also uncomfortable with it because they have been reared in an anglophobic world, one that views white society with fear and hostility; but because the fear of and bitterness toward whites and their consequent unwillingness to examine the dynamics of white socialization, American Indian women often overlook the central areas of damage done to tribal tradition by white Christian and secular patriarchal dominance.

Militant and "progressive" American Indian men are even more likely to quarrel with feminism; they have benefited in certain ways from white male-centeredness, and while those benefits are of real danger to the tribes, the rewards are compelling.

It is within the context of growing violence against women, and the concomitant lowering of our status among Native Americans that I teach and write. Certainly I could not locate the mechanisms of colonization that have led to the virulent rise of woman-hating among American Indian men (and, to a certain extent, among many of the women)[2] without a secure and determined feminism. Just as certainly, feminist theory applied to my literary studies clarifies a number of issues for me, including the patriarchal bias that has been systematically imposed on traditional literary materials and the mechanism by which that bias has affected contemporary American Indian life, thought, and culture.

The oral tradition is more than the repository of a people's culture. It is the source of their identity as a people and as individuals within their tradition. When that wellspring of identity is tampered with, the sense of self is also tampered with; and when that tampering includes the sexist and classist assumptions of the white world within the body of the tradition, serious consequences necessarily ensue.

The oral tradition is a living body. It is in continuous flux, which enables it to accommodate itself to the real circumstances of the people's lives. That is its strength, but it is also its weakness, for when a people finds itself living within a racist, classist, and sexist reality, the oral tradition will reflect those values and will thus shape the people's consciousness to include racism, classism, and sexism, and they will incorporate that change, hardly noticing the shift. If the oral tradition is altered in certain subtle, fundamental ways, if elements alien to it are introduced so that its internal coherence is disturbed, it becomes the major instrument of colonization and oppression.

Such alterations have occurred in the past and are still occurring. Those who translate or "render" narratives make certain crucial changes, many of which are unconscious. The cultural bias of the translator will inevitably shape his or her perception of the materials being translated, often in ways that are not particularly noticeable to those so formed. In short, it's hard to see the forest when you're a tree. To a great extent, these changes are a result of the vast difference in languages; certain ideas and concepts that are implicit in the structure of an Indian language are not possible in English. Language embodies the unspoken assumptions and orientations of the culture it belongs to. So while the problem is one of translation, it is not simply one of word equivalences. The differences are perceptual and contextual as much as verbal or verbalizable.

Sometimes the shifts are contextual; indeed what usually goes on is that both the context and content are shifted, sometimes subtly, sometimes blatantly. The net effect is that the whole axis of the culture is shifted. When shifts of language and context are coupled with the almost infinite changes occasioned by christianization, secularization, economic dislocation from subsistence to industrial modes, destruction of the wilderness, and associated damage to the biota, much that is changed goes unnoticed or unremarked by the people being changed. This is not to suggest that Native Americans are unaware of the enormity of the change they have been forced to undergo by the several centuries of white presence in their midst, but it is to say that much of that change is at deep and subtle levels that are not easily noted or resisted.

John Gunn got the story I am using here from a Keres-speaking informant and did the translating himself. The story, which he titles "Sh-ah-cock and Miochin or the Battle of the Seasons," is in reality a ritual, here cast in a narrative form. The ritual brings about the change of season and of moiety among the Keres. Gunn doesn't mention this, perhaps because he was interested in stories and not in religion, or perhaps because his informant didn't mention the connection to him.

What is interesting about his rendering is the interpolation of European, classist, conflict-centered patriarchal assumptions which are used as plotting devices. These interpolations have the effect of dislocating the significance of the tale, and of subtly altering the ideational context of woman-centered, largely pacifistic people whose ritual story this is. I have developed three critiques of the tale as it appears in his book, using feminist and tribal understandings to discuss the various meanings of the story when it is read from three difference perspectives.

In the first reading, I apply tribal understanding to the story. In the second, I apply the sort of feminist perspective I applied to traditional stories, historical events, traditional culture, and contemporary literature when I began developing a feminist perspective. The third reading applies what I am calling a "feminist-tribal perspective." Each of these analyses is somewhat less detailed than it might be; but as I am interested in detailing modes of perception, and their impact on our understanding of cultural artifacts (and by extension our understanding people who come from different cultural contexts than our own), rather than critiquing a story, they are adequate.

YELLOW WOMAN STORIES

The Keres of Laguna and Acoma Pueblos in New Mexico have stories that are called "Yellow Woman" stories. The themes and to a large extent the motifs of these stories are always female-centered, and they are always told from Yellow Woman's point of view. Virtually any story that has a female protagonist can be a Yellow Woman story as long as its purpose is to clarify aspects of women's lives in general. Some older recorded versions of Yellow Woman tales (as in Gunn) make her the daughter of the *hocheni*. Gunn translates this to "ruler." But Keres notions of the *hocheni*'s function and position as *cacique* or "mother chief" differ greatly from Anglo-European ideas of rulership.

However, for Gunn to render *hocheni* as "ruler" is congruent with the European folk tale tradition, and his use of the term may have been one used by Gunn's informants, who were often Carlisle or Menaul Indian school educated, in an attempt to find an equivalent term signifying the deep respect and reverence the *hocheni tyi'a'muni* is granted and a term that Gunn could comprehend. Or he might have selected the term because he was writing a book for an anonymous Keres audience, one which included himself. As he spoke Laguna Keres, I think he was doing the translations himself, and his renderings of words (and contexts) were likely influenced by the way Lagunas themselves rendered local terms into English, but I doubt that he was conscious of the extent to which his renderings reflected European traditions and simultaneously distorted Laguna-Acoma ones.

Gunn was deeply aware of the importance and intelligence of the Keresan tradition, but he was also unable to grant it independent existence. His major impulse was to link the Western Keres with the Sumerians, in some strange way, in order to demonstrate the justice of his assessment of their intelligence.[3]

However it may be, Kochinnenako, Yellow Woman, is in some sense a name that means Woman-Woman because among the Keres, yellow is the color for women (as pink and red are among Anglo-European Americans), and it is the color ascribed to the northwest. Keres women paint their faces yellow on certain ceremonial occasions, and are so painted at death so that the guardian at the gate of the spirit world, Naiya Iyatiku (Mother Corn Woman), will recognize that the newly arrived person is a woman. It is also the name of a particular Iriaku, corn mother (sacred corn-ear bundle), and Yellow Woman stories, in their original form, detail rituals in which the Iriaku figures prominently.

Yellow Woman stories are about all sorts of things—abduction, meeting with happy powerful spirits, birth of twins, getting power from the spirit worlds and returning it to the people, refusing to marry, weaving, grinding corn, getting water, outsmarting witches, eluding or escaping malintentioned spirits, and more. Yellow Woman's sisters are often in the stories (Blue, White, and Red Corn), as is Grandmother Spider and her helper Spider Boy, the Sun God or one of his aspects, Yellow Woman's twin sons, witches, magicians, gamblers, and mothers-in-law.

Many Yellow Woman tales highlight her alienation from the people—she lives with her grandmother at the edge of the village, for example, or she is in some way atypical, maybe a woman who refuses to marry, one who is known for some particular special talent, or one who is very quick-witted and resourceful. In many ways Kochinnenako is a role-model, though she models some behaviors that are not likely to occur in the lives of many who hear the stories about her. She is, one might say, the Spirit of Woman.

The stories do not necessarily imply that difference is punishable; on the contrary, it is often her very difference that makes her special adventures possible, and these adventures often have happy outcomes for Kochinnenako and for her people. This is of significance among a people who value conformity and propriety above almost anything. It suggests that the behavior of women, at least at certain times or under certain circumstances, must be improper or non-conformist for the great good of the whole. Not that all the stories are graced with a happy ending. Some come to a tragic conclusion, and sometimes this conclusion is the result of someone's inability to follow the rules or perform a ritual in the proper way.

Other Kochinnenako stories are about her centrality to the harmony, balance, and prosperity of the group. "Sh-ah-cock and Miochin" is one of these. John Gunn prefaces the narrative with the comment that while this story is about a battle, war stories are rarely told by the Keres as they are not "a warlike people" and "very rarely refer to their exploits in war."

SH-AH-COCK AND MIOCHIN OR THE BATTLE OF THE SEASONS

In the Kush-kut-ret-u-nah-tit (white village of the north) was once a ruler by the name of Hut-cha-mun Ki-uk (the broken prayer stick), one of whose daughters, Ko-chin-ne-na-ko, became the bride of Sh-ah-cock (the spirit of winter), a person of very violent temper. He always manifested his presence by blizzards of snow or sleet or by freezing cold, and on account of his alliance with the ruler's daughter, he was most of the time in the vicinity of Kush-kutret, and as their manifestations continued from month to month and year to year, the people of Kush-kutret found that their crops would not mature, and finally they were compelled to subsist on leaves of the cactus.

On one occasion Ko-chin-ne-na-ko had wandered a long way from home in search of the cactus and had gathered quite a bundle and was preparing to carry home by singeing of the thorns, when on looking up she found herself confronted by a very bold but handsome young man. His attire attracted her gaze at once. He wore a shirt of yellow woven from silks of the corn, a melt made from the broad green blades of the same plant, a tall pointed hat made from the same kind of material and from the top of which waved a yellow corn tassel. He wore green leggings woven from kow-e-nuh, the green stringy moss that forms in springs and ponds. His moccasins were beautifully embroidered with flowers and butterflies. In his hand he carried a ear of green corn.

His whole appearance proclaimed him a stranger and as Ko-chin-ne-na-ko gazed in wonder, he spoke to her in a very pleasing voice asking her what she was doing. She told him that on account of the cold and drought, the people of Kush-kutret were forced to eat the leaves of the cactus to keep from starving.

"Here," said the young man, handing her the ear of green corn. "Eat this and I will go and bring more that you may take home with you."

He left her and soon disappeared going towards the south. In a short time he returned bringing with him a big load of green corn. Ko-chin-ne-na-ko asked him where he had gathered the corn and if it grew near by. "No," he replied, "it is from my home far away in the south, where the corn grows and the flowers bloom all the year round. Would you not like to accompany me back to my country?" Ko-chin-ne-na-ko replied that his home just be very beautiful, but that she could not go with him because she was the wife of Sh-ah-cock. And then she told him of her alliance with the Spirit of Winter, and admitted that her husband was very cold and disagreeable and that she did not love him. The strange young man urged her to go with him to the warm land of the south, saying that he did not fear Sh-ah-cock. But Ko-chin-ne-na-ko would not consent. So the stranger directed her to return to her home with the corn he had brought and cautioned her not to throw any of the husks out of the door. Upon leaving he said to her, "You must meet me at this place tomorrow. I will bring more corn for you."

Ko-chin-ne-na-ko had not proceeded far on her homeward way ere she met her sisters who, having become uneasy because of her long absence, had come in search of her. They were greatly surprised at seeing her with an armful of corn instead of cactus. Ko-chin-ne-na-ko told them the whole story of how she had obtained it, and thereby only added wonderment to their surprise. They helped her to carry the corn home; and there she had again to tell her story to her father and mother.

When she had described the stranger even from his peaked hat to his butterfly moccasins, and had told them that she was to meet him again the day following, Hutchamum Kiuk, the father, exclaimed:

"It is Mi-o-chin!"

"It is Mi-o-chin! It is Mi-o-chin!" echoed the mother. "Tomorrow you must bring him home with you."

The next day Ko-chin-ne-na-ko went again to the spot where she had met Mi-o-chin, for it was indeed Mi-o-chin, the Spirit of Summer. He was already there, awaiting her coming. With him he had brought a huge bundle of corn.

Ko-chin-ne-na-ko pressed upon him the invitation of her parents to accompany her home, so together they carried the corn to Kush Kut-ret. When it had been distributed there was sufficient to feed all the people of the city. Amid great rejoicing and thanksgiving, Mi-o-chin was welcomed at the Hotchin's (ruler's) house.

In the evening, as was his custom, Sh-ah-cock, the Spirit of Winter, returned to his home. He came in a blinding storm of snow and hail and sleet, for he was in a boisterous mood. On approaching the city, he felt within his very bones that Mi-o-chin was there, so he called in a loud and blustering voice:

"Ha! Mi-o-chin, are you here?"

For answer, Mi-o-chin advanced to meet him.

Then Sh-ah-cock, beholding him, called again,

"Ha! Mi-o-chin, I will destroy you."

"Ha! Sh-ah-cock, I will destroy you," replied Mi-o-chin, still advancing.

Sh-ah-cock paused, irresolute. He was covered from head to foot with frost (skah). Icycles [sic] (ya-et-tu-ne) draped him round. The fierce, cold wind proceeded from his nostrils.

As Mi-o-chin drew near, the wintry wind changed to a warm summer breeze. The frost and icycles melted and displayed beneath them, the dry, bleached bulrushes (ska-ra ska-ru-ka) in which Sh-ah-cock was clad.

Seeing that he was doomed to defeat, Sh-ah-cock cried out:

"I will not fight you now, for we cannot try our powers. We will make ready, and in four days from this time, we will meet here and fight for supremacy. The victor shall claim Ko-chin-ne-na-ko for his wife."

With this, Sh-ah-cock withdrew in a rage. The wind again roared and shook the very houses; but the people were warm within them, for Mi-o-chin was with them.

The next day Mi-o-chin left Kush Kut-ret for his home in the south. Arriving there, he began to make his preparations to meet Sh-ah-cock in battle.

First he sent an eagle as a messenger to his friend, Ya-chun-ne-ne-moot (kind of shaley rock that becomes very hot in the fire), who lived in the west, requesting him to come and help to battle with Sh-ah-cock. Then he called together the birds and the four legged animals—all those that live in sunny climes. For his advance guard and shield he selected the bat (pickikke), as its tough skin would best resist the sleet and hail that Sh-ah-cock would hurl at him.

Meantime Sh-ah-cock had gone to his home in the north to make his preparations for battle. To his aid he called all the winter birds and all of the four legged animals of the wintry climates. For his advance guard and shield he selected the Shro-ak-ah (a magpie).

When these formidable forces had been mustered by the rivals, they advanced, Mi-o-chin from the south and Sh-ah-cock from the north, in battle array.

Ya-chun-ne-ne-moot kindled his fires and piled great heaps of resinous fuel upon them until volumes of steam and smoke ascended, forming enormous clouds that hurried forth toward Kush Kut-ret and the battle ground. Upon these clouds rode Mi-o-chin, the Spirit of Summer, and his vast army. All the animals of the army, encountering the smoke from Ya-chun-ne-ne-moot's fires, were colored by the smoke so that, from that day, the animals from the south have been black or brown in color.

Sh-ah-cock and his army came out of the north in a howling blizzard and borne forward on black storm clouds driven by a freezing wintry wind. As he came on, the lakes and rivers over which he passed were frozen and the air was filled with blinding sleet.

When the combatants drew near to Kush Kut-ret, they advanced with fearful rapidity. Their arrival upon the field was marked by fierce and terrific strife.

Flashes of lightning darted from Mi-o-chin's clouds. Striking the animals of Sh-ah-cock, they singed the hair upon them, and turned it white, so that, from that day, the animals from the north have worn a covering of white or have white markings upon them.

From the south, the black clouds still rolled upward, the thunder spoke again and again. Clouds of smoke and vapor rushed onward, melting the snow and ice weapons of Sh-ah-cock and compelling him, at length, to retire from the field. Mi-o-chin, assured of victory, pursued him. To save himself from total defeat and destruction, Sh-ah-cock called for an armistice.

This being granted on the part of Mi-o-chin, the rivals met at Kush Kut-ret to arrange the terms of the treaty. Sh-ah-cock acknowledged himself defeated. He consented to give up Ko-chin-ne-na-ko to Mi-o-chin. This concession was received with rejoicing by Ko-chin-ne-na-ko and all the people of Kush Kut-ret.

It was then agreed between the late combatants that, for all time thereafter, Mi-o-chin was to rule at Kush Kut-ret during one-half of the year, and Sh-ah-cock was to rule during the remaining half, and that neither should molest the other.[4]

Or so John Gunn tells the tale, which I have quoted in its entirety because the way it is told lends itself to three kinds of analysis, that of an Indian literary commentator, that of a feminist, and that of an Indian feminist (or a feminist Indian).

John Gunn's version has a formal plot structure that makes the account seem to be a narrative. But had he translated it directly from the Keres, even in "narrative" form, as in a story-telling session, its ritual nature would have been more clearly in evidence.

How the account might go, if it were done that way, I can only surmise, based on renderings of Keres rituals in narrative forms I am acquainted with. But it would have sounded more like the following than like Gunn's rendition of it:

Long ago. Eh. There in the North. Yellow Woman. Up northward she went. Then she picked burrs and cactus. Then here went Summer. From the south he came. Above there he arrived. Thus spoke Summer. "Are you here? How is it going?" said Summer. "Did you come here?" Thus said Yellow Woman. Then answered Yellow Woman. "I pick these poor things because I am hungry." "Why do you not eat corn and melons?" asked Summer. Then he gave her some corn and melons. "Take it!" Then thus spoke Yellow Woman, "It is good. Let us go. To my house I take you." "Is not your husband there?" "No. He went hunting deer. Today at night he will come back."

Then in the north they arrived. In the west they went down. Arrived then they in the east. "Are you here?" Remembering Prayer Sticks said. "Yes," Summer said. "How is it going?" Summer said. Then he said, "Your daughter Yellow Woman, she brought me here." "Eh. That is good." Thus spoke Remembering Prayer Sticks. . . .

The story would continue, with many of the elements contained in Gunn's version, but organized along the axis of directions, movements of the participants, their maternal relationships to each other (daughter, mother, mother chief, etc.), and events sketched in only as they pertained to directions and the division of the year into its ritual/ceremonial segments, one of which belongs to the Kurena (summer supernaturals or powers who are connected to the Summer people or clans and the other which belongs to the Kashare, perhaps in conjunction with the Kopishtaya, the Spirits).

Summer, Mi-o-chin, is the Shiwana who lives on the south mountain, and Sh-ah-cock is the Shiwana who lives on the north mountain.[5] It is interesting to note that the Kurena wear three eagle feathers and *ctc'otika'* feathers (white striped) on their heads, bells, and woman's dress, and carry a reed flute, which, perhaps, is connected with Iyatiku's sister, Istoakoa, Reed Woman.

A KERES INTERPRETATION

When a traditional Keres reads this tale, she listens with certain information about her people in mind: she knows, for example, that *Hutchamun Kiuk* (properly it means "Remembering Prayer Sticks" through Gunn translates this as "Broken Prayer Sticks"),[6] refers to the ritual (sacred) identity of the *cacique* and that the story is a narrative version of a ceremony related to the planting of corn. She knows that Lagunas and Acomas don't have rulers in the Anglo-European sense of monarchs, lords, and such (though they do, in recent times have elected governors, but that's another matter), and that a person's social status is determined by her mother's clan and position in it, rather by her relationship to the *cacique* as his daughter. (Actually, in various accounts, the *cacique* refers to Yellow Woman as his mother, so the designation of her as his daughter is troublesome unless one is aware that relationships in the context of their ritual significance are being delineated here.)

In any case, our hypothetical Keresan reader also knows that the story is about a ritual that take place every year, and that the battle imagery refers to events that take place during the ritual; she is also aware that Kochinnenako's will, as expressed in her attraction to Miochin, is a central element of the ritual. She knows further that the ritual is partly about the coming of summer and partly about the ritual relationship and exchange of primacy between the two divisions of the tribe, and that the ritual described in the narrative is enacted by men, dressed as Miochin and Sh-ah-cock, and that Yellow Woman in her Corn Mother aspect is the center of this and other sacred rites of the Kurena, though in this ritual she may also be danced by a Kurena mask dancer. (Gunn include a drawing of this figure, made by a Laguna, and titled "Ko-chin-ne-na-ko—In the Mask Dances").

The various birds and animals along the forces such as warm air, fire, heat, sleet, and ice will be represented in the ritual; Hutchamun Kiuk is the timekeeper or officer who keeps track of the ritual calendar (which is intrinsically related to the equinoxes), and as such has a central role in the ritual. The presence of Kochinnenako and Hutchamun Kiuk, and the *Shiwana* Miochin and Sh-ah-cock means something sacred is going on for the Keres.

The ritual transfers focus of power or ritual axis, so to speak, held in turn by two moieties who constitution reflects the earth's bilateral division between summer and winter, from the winter to the summer people. Each moiety's right to power is confirmed by and reflective of the seasons, as it is reflected and support by the equinoxes. It is accomplished through the Iyani, ritual empowerment, of female Power, embodied in Kochinnenako as mask dancer or Iriaku. Without her empowering mediatorship among the south and north *Shiwana*, the *cacique*, and the village, the season and the moiety cannot change, and balance cannot be maintained.

It is understood that unchanging supremacy of one moiety/season over the other is unnatural and therefore undesirable because unilateral dominance of one aspect of existence and of society over another is not reflected or supported by reality at meteorological or spiritual levels. Whilst Sh-ah-cock, who after all is the Winter Spirit (Winter Cloud), *Shiwana* (one of several categories of supernaturals) is cold and connected to sleet, snow, ice, and hunger, not because he is a source of unmitigated evil (or of evil at all, for that matter).

Half of the people (not numerically but mystically, so to speak) are Winter, and in that sense are Sh-ah-cock; and while this portion of the gestalt that is the people may seem unlovely when their time is up, that same half is lovely indeed in the proper season. Similarly, Miochin will also age—that is, pass his time, and will then give way for his "rival"—which is also his complement—in turn. Thus harmony is preserved for the village, and thus each portion of the community takes responsibility for the prosperity and well-being of the people.

A Keres is of course aware that balance and harmony are two primary assumptions held by Keres society, and will not approach the narrative wondering whether the handsome Miochin will win the hand of the unhappy wife and triumph over the enemy, thereby heroically saving the people from disaster. The triumph of handsome youth over ugly age, or of virile liberality over withered tyranny doesn't make sense in a Keresan context because such a view contradicts central Keres values.

A traditional Keres, at least, is satisfied by the story because it reaffirms a Keres sense of rightness, of propriety. It is a tale that describes ritual events, and the Keres reader can visualize the ritual itself when reading Gunn's story. Such a reader is likely to be puzzled by the references to rulers and by the tone of heroic romance, but will be reasonably satisfied by the account because in spite of its Westernized changes, it still ends happily with the orderly transfer of focality between the moieties and seasons that has been accomplished in all its seasonal splendor as winter in New Mexico blusters and sleets its way north, and summer sings and warms its way home. In the end, the primary Keresan values of harmony, balance, and the centrality of woman in their maintenance have been validated, and the fundamental Keres principal of proper order is celebrated and affirmed once again.

A MODERN FEMINIST INTERPRETATION

A non-Keres feminist, reading this tale, is likely to suppose that this narrative is about the importance of men and the use of a passive female figure as a pawn in their bid for power.[7] And, given the way Gunn renders the story, she would have good reason to make such an inference. As Gunn recounts it, the story opens in classic patriarchal style and implies certain patriarchal complications: that Kochinnenako has married a man who is violent and destructive. She is the ruler's daughter, which might suggest that the traditional Keres are concerned with the abuses of power of the wealthy. This in turn suggests that the traditional Keres social system, like the traditional Anglo-Europeans ones, suffered from oppressive class structures in which the rich and powerful bring misery to the people, who, in the tale, are reduced to bare subsistence seemingly as a result of her unfortunate alliance. A reader making the usual assumptions Western readers make when enjoying folk tales will think she is reading a sort of Robin Hood story, replete with a lovely maid Marian, an evil Sheriff, and a green-clad agent of social justice with the Indian name *Miochin*.

Given the usual assumptions that underly European folk tales, given the Western romantic view of the Indian that is generally America's only view, and given the usual anti-patriarchal bias that characterizes feminist analysis, a feminist reader might assume that Kochinnenako has been compelled to make an unhappy match by her father the ruler who must be gaining some power from the alliance. Besides, his name is given as "Broken Prayer Stick," which might be taken to mean that he is an unholy man, remiss in his religious duties and weak in spiritual accomplishment.

Nor does Gunn's tale clarify these issues. Instead it proceeds in a way best calculated to confirm a feminist's interpretation of the tale as only another example of the low status women in tribal cultures hold. (Certainly an inordinate amount of effort on the part of students and recorders of traditional American Indian life has gone into creating the impression that the white woman's lot was glorious when and if compared to that of the savage squaw!) In accordance with his most sacred of American myths, Gunn makes it clear that Kochinnenako is not happy in her marriage; she thinks Sh-ah-cock is "cold and disagreeable, and she cannot love him." Certainly, contemporary American women will read that to mean that Sh-ah-cock is an emotionally uncaring, perhaps cruel husband, and that Kochinnenako is forced by her position in life to accept a life bereft of warmth and love. Our feminist reader might imagine that Kochinnenako, like many women, has been socialized into submission. So obedient is she, it seems, so lacking in spirit and independence, that she doesn't seize her chance to escape a bad situation, preferring instead to remain obedient to the patriarchal institution of marriage. As it turns out (in Gunn's tale), Yellow Woman is delivered from the clutches of her violent and unwanted mate by a timely intervention of a much more pleasant man, our hero.

A radical feminist is likely to read the story for its content vis-à-vis racism and resistance to oppression. From a radical perspective, it is politically significant that Sh-ah-cock is white. That is, winter is white. Snow is white. Blizzards are white. Clearly, while the story does not give much support to concepts of a people's struggles, it could be construed to mean that the oppressor is designated white in the story because the Keres are engaged in serious combat with white colonial power, and given the significance of storytelling in tribal culture, are chronicling that struggle in this tale. Read this way, it would seem to acknowledge the right and duty of the people in overthrowing the hated white dictator who, by this account, possesses the power of life and death over them.

Briefly, in this context, the story can be read as a tale about the nature of white oppression of Indian people, and Kochinnenako then becomes something of a revolutionary fighter through her collusion with the rebel Miochin in the overthrow of the tyrant Sh-ah-cock. In this reading, the tale becomes a cry for liberation and a direct command to women to aid in the people's struggle to overthrow the colonial powers that drain them of life and strength, deprive them of their rightful prosperity, and threaten them with extinction. An activist teacher could use this tale to instruct women in their obligation to the revolutionary struggle; the daughter, her sisters, and the mother are, after all, implicated in the attempt to bring peace and prosperity to the people; indeed, they are central to it, and such a teacher could, by so using the story, appear to be incorporating culturally diverse materials in the classroom while at the same time exploiting the romantic and moral appeal Native Americans often have for other Americans.

When read as a battle narrative, the story as Gunn renders it makes clear that the superiority of Miochin rests as much in his commitment to the welfare of the people as in his military prowess, and that because his attempt to free the people is backed up by their active invitation to him to come and liberate them, he is successful. Because of his success he is entitled to the hand of the ruler's daughter, Kochinnenako, one of the traditional Old World spoils of victory. Similarly, Sh-ah-cock is defeated not only because he is violent and oppressive, but also because the people, like Kochinnenako, find that they cannot love him.

A radical lesbian separatist might find herself uncomfortable with the story even though it is so clearly correct in identifying the enemy as white and violent, though, because the overthrow of the tyrant is placed squarely in the hands of another male figure, Miochin. This rescue is likely to be viewed with a jaundiced eye by many feminists (though more romantic women might be satisfied with it, since it's a story about an Indian woman of long ago), as Kochinnenako has to await the coming of a handsome stranger for her salvation, and her fate is decided by her father and the more salutory suitor Miochin. No one asks Kochinnenako what she wants to do; the reader is informed that her marriage is not to her liking when she admits to Miochin that she is unhappy in her marriage. Nevertheless, Kochinnenako acts like any passive, dependent woman who is exploited by the males in her life, who get what they want, regardless of her own needs or desires.

Some readers (like me) might find themselves hoping that Miochin is really female, disguised by males as one of them in order to buttress their position of relative power. After all, this figure is dressed in yellow and green, colors associated with corn, a plant always associated with Woman. Kochinnenako and her sisters are all Corn Women; her mother is, presumably, the head of the Corn Clan; and the Earth Mother of the Keres, Iyatiku, is Corn Woman herself. Alas, I haven't yet found evidence to support such a wishful notion, except to note that the mask dancer who impersonates Kochinnenako is male, dressed female, which is sort of the obverse side of the wish.

AN INDIAN-FEMINIST INTERPRETATION

The feminist interpretation I have sketched—which is a fair representation of an early reading of my own from what I took to be a feminist perspective—proceeds from two unspoken assumptions. These assumptions are that women are essentially powerless and that conflict is basic to human experience. The first is a fundamental feminist position, while the second is basic to Anglo-European thought; neither, however, is characteristic of Keres thought. To a modern feminist, marriage is an institution developed to establish and maintain male supremacy, and as the "ruler's" daughter, whom Kochinnenako marries determines which male will hold power over the people and who will inherit the throne.[8]

When Western assumptions are applied to tribal narratives, they become mildly confusing and moderately annoying from any perspective.[9] Western assumptions about the nature of human society (and thus of literature) when contextualizing a tribal story or ritual must necessarily leave certain elements unclear. For if the battle between Summer Spirit and Winter Spirit is about the triumph of warmth, generosity, and kindness over coldness, miserliness, and cruelty, supremacy of the good over the bad, why does the hero grant his protagonist rights over the village and Kochinnenako for half of each year?

The contexts of Anglo-European and Keres Indian life differ so greatly in virtually every assumption about the nature of reality, society, ethics, female roles, and the sacred importance of seasonal change, that simply telling a Keres tale with a Euro-American narrative context creates a dizzying series of false impressions and unanswerable (perhaps even unposable) questions.

For instance, marriage among traditional Keres is not particularly related to marriage among Anglo-European Americans. Paternity is not an issue among traditional Keres people; a child belongs to its mother's clan—not in the sense that she or he is owned by the clan, but in the sense of belonging within it.

This is one example of the great difference between patriarchal and traditional (that is, before Anglo colonization of family systems) Keres cultures. Another equally basic difference is the attitude toward conflict; the Keres can best be described as conflict-phobic, while Anglo and Euro-American culture is conflict-centered. These attitudes inform every aspect of both cultures and make them different in fundamental ways. So while the orderly and proper annual transference of power from Winter to Summer people through the agency of the Keres' central female figure is the major theme of the narrative from a Keres perspective, the triumph of good over evil becomes its major theme when it is retold by a white man.

Essentially what is happening is that Summer (a mask dancer dressed as Miochin) asks Kochinnenako permission, in a ritual manner, to enter the village. She (a mask dancer dressed as Yellow Woman or Iriaku—Yellow Corn) follows a specified ritual order of responses and events that enable Summer to enter. Some of these are acts she must perform and words she must say, and others are prohibitions. One of the latter is that she must not "throw any of the husks out of the door," a command that establishes both the identity of Miochin and constitutes his declaration of his ritual intention and his ritual relationship to her. It is also a directive to the people on the proper way to handle the corn.

Agency is Kochinnenako's ritual role here, and it is through her ritual agency that the orderly, harmonious transfer of primacy between the Summer and Winter people is accomplished. This transfer of course takes place at the time of the year that winter goes north and summer comes to the pueblo from the south, the time when the sun moves north, along the line the sun makes along the edge of the sun's house as ascertained by the Hotchin who is the calendar keeper and the official who determines the proper solar and astronomical times for various ceremonies. Thus, in the proper time, Kochinnenako empowers Summer to enter the village. Kochinnenako's careful observance of the ritual requirements of the situation, joined with the proper conduct of her sisters, her mother, the priests (symbolized by the title *Hutchamun Kiuk*, whom Gunn identifies as the ruler and Yellow Woman's father though he could as properly—more properly, actually— be called her mother), the animals and birds, the weather and the people at last bring summer to the village, ending the winter and the famine that accompanies winter's end.

A feminist who is conscious of tribal thought and practice will know that the real story of Sh-ah-cock and Miochin underscores the central role that woman plays in the orderly life of the people. Reading Gunn's version, she will be aware of the vast gulf between the Lagunas and John Gunn in their understanding of the role of women in a traditional gynecentric society such as that of the Western Keres. Knowing that the central role of woman is harmonizing spiritual relationships between the people and the rest of the universe, and empowering ritual activities, she will be able to read the story for its Western colonial content, aware that Gunn's version reveals more about American consciousness when it meets with tribal thought than it does about the tribe. When the story is analyzed from within the context to which it rightly belongs, its feminist content becomes clear, as do the various purposes to which a tribal story can be put by industrialized patriarchal people.

If she is familiar with the ritual color-code of this particular group of Native Americans, she will know that white is the color of Shipapu, the place where the four rivers of life come together and where our Mother Iyatiku lives. Thus she will know that it is appropriate that the Spirit of Woman's Power/Being (Yellow Woman) be "married" (that is, ritually connected in energy-transferring gestalts) first with Winter who is the power signified by the color white that informs clouds, the Mountain Tse-pina, Shipapu, originating Power, Koshare, and that half of the year; then with Summer whose color powers are yellow and green that inform Kurena, sunrise, growing and ripening time of Mother Earth, and whose direction is south and southeast and that portion of the year.

She will know that the story is about how the Mother Corn who is Iyatiku's "daughter"—that is, her essence in one of its aspects—comes to live as Remembering Prayer Stick's daughter first with the Winter people and then with the Summer people, and so on.

The net effect of Gunn's rendition of the story is the unhappy wedding of the woman-centered tradition of the western Keres to patriarchal Anglo-European tradition, and thus the dislocation of the central position of Keres women by their assumption under the rules of men. When one understands that the *Hotchin* is the person who tells the time and prays for all the people, even the white people, and that the *Hutchamun Kiuk* is the ruler only in the sense that the Constitution of the United States is the ruler of the citizens and government of the United States, the Keres organization of men, women, spirit folk, equinoxes, seasons, and clouds into a balanced and integral dynamic will be seen reflected in the narrative. Knowing this, she will also be able to see how the interpolations of patriarchal thinking distort all the relationships in the story, and, by extension, how such impositions of patriarchy upon gynocracy work to disorder harmonious social and spiritual relationships.

A careful tribal-feminist analysis of Gunn's rendition of a story that would be better titled "The Transfer of *Iyani* (ritual power, sacred power) from Winter to

Summer" will provide a tribally conscious feminist with an interesting example of how colonization works (and it does so, I am sure, innocent of its effect) to misinform both the colonized and the colonizer about the victim of colonization.

She will be able to note the process by which the victim of the translation process, the Keres woman who reads the tale, is misinformed because she reads Gunn's book, and even though she knows that something odd is happening in this tale, she is not likely to apply sophisticated feminist analysis to the rendition; in the absence of real knowledge of the process of story-changing, she is all too likely to find bits of the Gunn tale sticking in her mind and subtly altering her perception of herself, her role in her society, and her relationship to the larger world.

The hazard to male Keres readers is, of course, equally great. They are likely to imagine that the proper relationship of women to men is that of subservience. And it is in the service of this shockingly unconventional modern interpretation, brought on as much by reading Gunn as by other, perhaps more obvious mechanisms, that the relationships between men and women are so severely disordered at Laguna that wife-abuse, rape, and battery of women there has reached frightening levels in recent years.

POLITICAL IMPLICATIONS OF NARRATIVE STRUCTURE

The changes Gunn has made in the narrative are not only changes in content. They are structural as well. One of the more useful social functions of traditional tribal literature is its tendency to distribute value evenly among the various elements in the piece, providing a model or pattern for egalitarian structuring of things other than literary documents. However, egalitarian structures in both literature and society are not easily "read" by hierarchically included Westerners.

Still, the tendency to equal distribution of value among all elements in a field, whether the field is social, spiritual, or aesthetic (and the distinction is moot when tribal materials are under discussion) is an integral part of tribal consciousness, and is reflected in tribal social and aesthetic systems all over the Americas. In this structural framework, no single element is foregrounded leaving the others to supply "background." Thus, properly speaking, there are no heroes, no villains, no chorus, no "setting" (as inert ground against which dramas are played out). There are no minor characters, really, and what happens is that foreground slips along from one focal point to another until all the pertinent elements in the ritual conversation have had their say. Because of this tribal habit of mind toward equilibrium of all factors in a situation, "chiefs" for example, were largely created by whites, as was/is the supposedly lower status of women (derogatorily called squaws by whites, although the word was used to designate women of high status among Algonkians who lived on the Northern Atlantic coast and could be translated to something like queen[10]).

In tribal literatures, the timing of the foregrounding of various elements is dependent on the purpose the narrative is intended to serve. Tribal art functions something like a forest in which all elements coexist and where each is integral to the being of the others. Depending on the season, the interplay of various life-forms, the state of the overall biosphere and psychosphere, and the entity's reason for being there, certain plants will leap into focus on certain occasions. For example, when tribal women on the eastern seaboard were gathering sassafras, what they noticed, what stood out sharply in their attention, were the sassafras plants. But when they were out to get maple sugar, maples became foregrounded. But the foregrounding of sassafras or maple in no way lessens the value of the other plants or other features of the forest. When a woman goes after maple syrup, she is aware of the other plant forms that are also present.

In the same way, a story that is intended to convey the importance of the grandmother spirits will focus on grandmothers in their interaction with grandchildren and will convey little information about uncles. In traditional tales, a number of points will be made, and a number of elements will be present, all of which will bear some relationship to the subject of the story; within the time the storyteller has allotted to the story, and depending on the interests and needs of her audience at the time of the storytelling, each of these elements will receive its proper due.

Traditional American Indian stories work like a dynamic among clusters of loosely interconnected circles. The focus of the action shifts from one character to another as the story unfolds. There is no "point of view" as the term is generally understood unless the action itself, the story's purpose, can be termed "point of view." But as the old tales get translated and "rendered" in English, the Western notion of proper fictional form takes over the tribal narrative. Soon there appear to be heroes, point of view, conflict, crisis and resolution, and as Western tastes in story-crafting are imposed over the narrative structure of the ritual story, a Western story with Indian characters is produced. Mournfully, the new form often becomes confused with archaic form by the very people who tradition has been re-formed.

The "battle" between Summer and Winter is an accurate description of seasonal change in central New Mexico during the spring. This comes through in the Gunn rendition, but because the story is focused on conflict rather than on balance, the meteorological facts and their intrinsic relationship to human ritual are obscured. Only a non-Indian mind, accustomed to interpreting events in terms of battle, struggle, and opposition, would assume the process of transfer had to occur through a battle replete with protagonist, antagonist, a cast of thousands, and a pretty girl as the prize. For who but an industrialized patriarch would think that winter can be vanquished? As though the right brain could overcome the left? Winter and summer enjoy a relationship based on complementariness, mutuality, and this is the moral significance of the tale.

TRIBAL NARRATIVES AND WOMEN'S LIVES

Reading American Indian traditional songs and stories is not an easy task. Adequate comprehension requires that the reader be aware that Indians never think like whites and that any typeset version of traditional materials is distortive.

In many ways, literary conventions, as well as the conventions of literacy, militate against an understanding of traditional tribal materials. Western technological-industrialized minds cannot adequately interpret tribal materials because they are generally trained to perceive their entire world in ways which are alien to tribal understandings.

This problem is not exclusive to tribal literature. It is one that all ethnic writers who write out of a tribal or folk tradition must face, and one which is also shared by women writers who, after all, inhabit a separate folk tradition. Women's culture bears marked resemblance to tribal culture. The perceptual modes that women, even those of us who are literate, industrialized, and reared within masculinist academic traditions habitually engage in, are more resemblant of open-field perception than of foreground-background perceptions.

Women's traditional occupations, their arts and crafts, and their literature and philosophies are more often circular than linear, more synchronistic than chronological, and more dependent upon harmonious relationships of all elements within a field of perception than Western culture in general is thought to be. Indeed, the patchwork quilt is the best material example I can think of to describe the plot and process of a traditional tribal narrative, and quilting is a non-Indian woman's art, one that Indian women have taken to avidly and which they display in their ceremonies, rituals, and social gatherings, as well as in their homes.

It is the nature of woman's existence to be and to create background. This fact, viewed with unhappiness by many feminists, can be seen in a tribal way as being of ultimate importance. Certainly no art object is bereft of background. Certainly the quality of one's background will largely determine the quality of one's life and, therefore, the quality of one's performance in any given sphere of activity.

Westerners have for a long time discounted the importance of background. The earth herself, which is our most inclusive background, is dealt with summarily as a source of food, metals, water, and investment yield, while the fact that she is the fundamental agent of all planetary life is blithely ignored. Similarly women's activities—cooking, planting, harvesting, preservation, storage, home-building, decorating, maintaining, doctoring, nursing, soothing, and healing, which, along with the bearing, nurturing, and rearing of children are ignored as blithely—with consequences that are likely to be as disastrous to the sum and quality of planetary life in the end. An anti-background bias is bound to have social costs that have so far remained unexplored, but elite attitudes toward workers, non-white races, and women are all part of the price we pay for indulging in over-valuing the foreground.

In the Western mind, shadows are something that highlight the foreground. Contrast this with the tribal view that the mutual relationships among shadows and light in all their varying degrees of intensity create a living web of definition and depth, and significance arises from their interplay. Traditional and contemporary tribal arts and crafts testify powerfully to the importance of the perception of equalized balance of all elements in a field in tribal perception, aesthetics, and social systems.

Traditional peoples perceive their world in a unified-field fashion that is far from the single-focus perception that generally characterizes Western masculinist monotheistic modes of perception. Because of this, their cultures are consistently misperceived and misrepresented by folklorists, ethnographers, artists, writers, and social workers. A number of scholars have, in recent times, addressed themselves to this issue, but they have had little success because the demands of type are, after all, linear and fixed, while the requirements of tribal literature are spherical and moving. The one is unidimensional, monolithic, and chronological while the other is multidimensional and a-chronistic.

How one teaches or writes about the one in terms of the other is problematic. This paper itself is a pale representation of a tribal understanding of the Kochinnenako tale. As I reread what I have written, I am acutely aware that much of what I have said is likely to be understood in ways I did not intend; and I am also aware of how much I did not say that probably needed to be said if the real story of the transfer of responsibility from one segment of the tribe to the other is to be made clear.

In the end, the tale I have analyzed is not about Kochinnenako or Sh-ah-cock and Miochin. It is about the change of seasons, and it is about the centrality of woman as agent and empowerer of that change. It is about how a people engage themselves as a people within the spiritual cosmos of their lives and in an ordered and proper way that bestows the dignity of each upon all with careful respect, folkish humor, and ceremonial delight. It is about how everyone is part of the background that shapes the meaning and value of each one's life. It is about propriety, mutuality, and the dynamics of socio-environmental change.

NOTES

1. John M. Gunn, *Schat-Chen: History, Traditions and Narratives of the Queres Indians of Laguna and Acoma*. Albuquerque, New Mexico: Albright and Anderson, 1917. (Reprinted, New York: AMS, 1980.) Gunn, my mother's great uncle, lived among the Lagunas all of his adult life. He spoke Laguna (Keres) and gathered information in somewhat informal ways while sitting in the sun visiting with older people. He married Meta Atseye, my grandmother, years after her husband (John Gunn's brother) died, and may have taken much of his information from her stories or explanations of Laguna ceremonial events. She had a way of "translating" terms and concepts from Keres into English and from a Laguna conceptual framework into an American one—as she understood it. For example, she used to refer to the Navajo people as "gypsies," probably because they traveled in covered wagons.

2. An unpublished manuscript in my possession written by John Gunn after *Schat-Chen* is devoted to his researches and speculations into this idea.

3. Gunn, *Schat-Chen*, pp. 217–22.

4. Woman-hating among American Indian women often shows up in a displaced form where it is expressed as publically destructive actions against white women (or others who are not "Indian enough") who write or speak about Indian subjects, particularly about women's spirituality.

5. In his *Keresan Texts* (Vol. VIII, Part I, Publications of the American Ethnological Society, New York: The American Ethnological Society, 1928), Franz Boas writes "The second and the fourth of the shiwana appear in the tale of summer and winter. . . . Summer wears a shirt of buckskin with squash ornaments, shoes like moss to which parrot feathers are tied. His face is painted with red mica and flowers are tied on to it. . . . Winter wears a shirt of icicles and his shoes are like ice. His shirt is shiny and to its end are tied turkey feathers and eagle feathers." p. 284.

6. Boas, p. 288. Boas says he made the same mistake at first, having misheard the word they used.

7. When my sister, Carol Lee Sanchez, spoke to her university Woman's Studies class about the position of centrality women hold in our Keres tradition, one young woman, a self-identified radical feminist, was outraged. She insisted that Ms. Sanchez, and other Laguna women, had been "brainwashed" into believing that we had power over our lives. After all, she knew that no women anywhere have ever had that kind of power; her feminist studies had made that "fact" quite plain to her. The kind of cultural chauvinism that has been promulgated by well-intentioned but culturally entranced feminists can lead to serious misunderstandings such as this one, and in the process become a new racism based on what becomes the feminist canon. Not that feminists can be faulted entirely on this . . . they are, after all, reflecting the research and interpretation done in a patriarchal context, by male-biased researchers and scholars, most of whom would avidly support the young radical feminist's strenuous position. It's too bad, though, that feminists fall into the patriarchal trap.

8. For a detailed exposition of what this dynamic consists of, see Adrienne Rich, "Compulsive Heterosexuality and Lesbian Existence," *Signs: Journal of Women in Culture and Society*, Vol. 4, No. 4 (Summer 1980). Rpt. as a pamphlet with an updated foreword (Denver: Antelope Publications, 1982), 1612 St. Paul, Denver, Colorado 80206.

9. Elaine Jahner, a specialist in Lakota language and oral literature, has suggested to me that the Western obsession with Western plot in narrative structure led early informant George Sword to construct narratives in the Western fashion and tell them as Lakota traditional stories. Research has shown that Sword's stories are not recognized as Lakota traditional stories by Lakotas themselves; but the tribal narratives that are so recognized are loosely structured and do not exhibit the reliance on central theme or character that is so dear to the hearts of Western collectors. As time has gone by, the Sword stories have become a sort of model for later Lakota storytellers who, out of a desire to convey the tribal tales to Western collectors, have changed the old structures to ones more pleasing to American and European ears.

Education in Western schools, exposure to mass media, and the need to function in a white-dominated world have subtly, but perhaps permanently, altered the narrative structures of the old tales and with them the tribal conceptual modes of tribespeople. The shift has been away from associative, synchronistic, event-centered narrative and thought to a linear, foreground-centered one. Concurrently, tribal social organization and interpersonal relations have taken a turn toward authoritarian, patriarchal, linear, and misogynist modes— hence the rise of violence against women, an unthinkable event in older, more circular and tribal times.

10. For a detailed analysis of the term and the deliberate misinformation regarding the status of women in those cultures Anglo colonizers were earliest in contact with, see Robert Steven Grumet's article, "Skunksquaws, Shamans and Tradeswomen: Middle Atlantic Coastal Algonkian Women During the 17th and 18th Centuries," in *Women and Colonization: Anthropological Perspectives*, Mona Etienne and Eleanor Leacock, eds. (New York: Praeger Special Studies, J. F. Bergine Publishers, 1980), pp. 46–53. According to Grumet the English equivalence-term for Skunksquaw was "Queen" or even "Empress."

LA CONCIENCIA DE LA MESTIZA

towards a new consciousness

(1987)

> *Por la mujer de mi raza*
> *hablará el espíritu.*

José Vasconcelos, Mexican philosopher, envisaged *una raza mestiza, una mezcla de razas afines, una raza de color—la primera raza sínetesis del globo*. He called it a cosmic race, *la raza cósmica*, a fifth race embracing the four major races of the world.[1] Opposite to the theory of the pure Aryan, and to the policy of racial purity that white America practices, his theory is one of inclusivity. At the confluence of two or more genetic streams, with chromosomes constantly "crossing over," this mixture of races, rather than resulting in an inferior being, provides hybrid progeny, a mutable, more malleable species with a rich gene pool. From this racial, ideological, cultural and biological cross-pollination, an "alien" consciousness is presently in the making—a new *mestiza* consciousness, *una conciencia de mujer*. It is a consciousness of the Borderlands.

> *Una lucha de fronteras* / A Struggle of Borders
> Because I, a *mestiza*,
> continually walk out of one culture
> and into another, because I am in all cultures at the same time,
> *alma entre dos mundos, tres, cuatro,*
> *me zumba la cabeza con lo contradictorio.*
> *Estoy norteada por todas las voces que me hablan*
> *simultáneamente.*

The ambivalence from the clash of voices results in mental and emotional states of perplexity. Internal strife results in insecurity and indecisiveness. The *mestiza*'s dual or multiple personality is plagued by psychic restlessness.

In a constant state of mental nepantilism, an Aztec word meaning torn between ways, *la mestiza* is a product of the transfer of the cultural and spiritual values of one group to another. Being tricultural, monolingual, bilingual, or multilingual, speaking a patois, and in a state of perpetual transition, the *mestiza* faces the dilemma of the mixed breed: which collectivity does the daughter of a dark-skinned mother listen to?

El choque de un alma atrapado entre el mundo del espíritu y el mundo de la técnica a vecas la deja entullada. Cradled in one culture, sandwiched between two cultures, straddling all three cultures and their value systems, *la mestiza* undergoes a struggle of flesh, a struggle of borders, an inner war. Like all people, we perceive the version of reality that our culture communicates. Like others having or living in more than one culture, we get multiple, often opposing messages. The coming together of two self-consistent but habitually incompatible frames of reference[2] causes *un choque,* a cultural collision.

Within us and within *la cultura chicana,* commonly held beliefs of the white culture attack commonly held beliefs of the Mexican culture, and both attack commonly held beliefs of the indigenous culture. Subconsciously, we see an attack on ourselves and on our beliefs as a threat and we attempt to block it with a counter-stance.

But it is not enough to stand on the opposite riverbank, shouting questions, challenging patriarchal, white conventions. A counter-stance locks one into a duel of oppressor and oppressed; locked in mortal combat, like the cop and the criminal, both are reduced to a common denominator of violence. The counter-stance refutes the dominant culture's views and beliefs, and, for this, it is proudly defiant. All reaction is limited by, and dependent on, what it is reacting against. Because the counter-stance stems from a problem with authority—outer as well as inner—it's a step toward liberation from cultural domination. But it is not a way of life. At some point, on our way to a new consciousness, we will have to leave the opposite bank, the split between the two mortal combatants somehow healed so that we are on both shores at once and, at once, see through serpent and eagle eyes. Or perhaps we will decide to disengage from the dominant culture, write it off altogether as a lost cause, and cross the border into a wholly new and separate territory. Or we might go another route. The possibilities are numerous once we decide to act and not react.

A TOLERANCE FOR AMBIGUITY

These numerous possibilities leave *la mestiza* floundering in uncharted seas. In perceiving conflicting information and points of view, she is subjected to a swamping of her psychological borders. She has discovered that she can't hold concepts or ideas in rigid boundaries. The borders and walls that are supposed to keep the undesirable ideas out are entrenched habits and patterns of behavior; these habits and patterns are the enemy within. Rigidity means death. Only by remaining flexible is she able to stretch the psyche horizontally and vertically. *La mestiza* constantly has to shift out of habitual formations; from convergent thinking, analytical reasoning that tends to use rationality to move toward a single goal (a Western mode), to divergent thinking,[3] characterized by movement away from set patterns and goals and toward a more whole perspective, one that includes rather than excludes.

The new *mestiza* copes by developing a tolerance for contradictions, a tolerance for ambiguity. She learns to be an Indian in Mexican culture, to be Mexican from an Anglo point of view. She learns to juggle cultures. She has a plural personality, she operates in a pluralistic mode—nothing is thrust out, the good the bad and the ugly, nothing rejected, nothing abandoned. Not only does she sustain contradictions, she turns the ambivalence into something else.

She can be jarred out of ambivalence by an intense, and often painful, emotional event that inverts or resolves the ambivalence. I'm not sure exactly how. The work takes place underground—subconsciously. It is work that the soul performs. That focal point or fulcrum, that juncture where the *mestiza* stands, is where phenomena tend to collide. It is where the possibility of uniting all that is separate occurs. This assembly is not one where severed or separated pieces merely come together. Nor is it a balancing of opposing powers. In attempting to work out a synthesis, the self has added a third element which is greater than the sum of its severed parts. That third element is a new consciousness—a *mestiza* consciousness—and though it is a source of intense pain, its energy comes from continual creative motion that keeps breaking down the unitary aspect of each new paradigm.

En unas pocas centurias, the future will belong to the *mestiza*. Because the future depends on the breaking down of paradigms, it depends on the straddling of two or more cultures. By creating a new mythos—that is, a change in the way we perceive reality, the way we see ourselves, and the ways we behave—*la mestiza* creates a new consciousness.

The work of *mestiza* consciousness is to break down the subject-object duality that keeps her a prisoner and to show in the flesh and through the images in her work how duality is transcended. The answer to the problem between the white race and the colored, between males and females, lies in healing the split that originates in the very foundation of our lives, our culture, our languages, our thoughts. A massive uprooting of dualistic thinking in the individual and collective consciousness is the beginning of a long struggle, but one that could, in our best hopes, bring us to the end of rape, of violence, of war.

> *La encrucijada* / The Crossroads
> A chicken is being sacrificed
> at a crossroads, a simple mound of earth
> a mud shrine for *Eshu*,
> *Yoruba* god of indeterminacy,
> who blesses her choice of path.
> She begins her journey.

Su cuerpo es una bocacalle. La mestiza has gone from being the sacrificial goat to becoming the officiating priestess at the crossroads.

As a *mestiza* I have no country, my homeland cast me out; yet all countries are mine because I am every woman's sister or potential lover. (As a lesbian I have no race, my own people disclaim me; but I am all races because there is the queer of me in all races.) I am cultureless because, as a feminist, I challenge the collective cultural/religious male-derived beliefs of Indo-Hispanics and Anglos; yet I am cultured because I am participating in the creation of yet another culture, a new story to explain the world and our participation in it, a new value system with images and symbols that connect us to each other and to the planet. *Soy un amasamiento,* I am an act of kneading, of uniting and joining that not only has produced both a creature of darkness and a creature of light, but also a creature that questions the definitions of light and dark and gives them new meanings.

We are the people who leap in the dark, we are the people on the knees of the gods. In our very flesh, (r)evolution works out the clash of cultures. It makes us crazy constantly, but if the center holds, we've made some kind of evolutionary step forward. *Nuestra alma el trabajo,* the opus, the great alchemical work; spiritual *mestizaje,* a "morphogenesis,"[4] an inevitable unfolding. We have become the quickening serpent movement.

Indigenous like corn, like corn, the *mestiza* is a product of crossbreeding, designed for preservation under a variety of conditions. Like an ear of corn—a female seed-bearing organ—the *mestiza* is tenacious, tightly wrapped in the husks of her culture. Like kernels she clings to the cob; with thick stalks and strong brace roots, she holds tight to the earth—she will survive the crossroads.

Lavando y remojando el maíz en agua del cal, despojando el pellejo. Moliendo, mixteando, amasando, haciendo tortillas de masa.[5] She steeps the corn in lime, it swells, softens. With stone roller on *metate,* she grinds the corn, then grinds again. She kneads and moulds the dough, pats the round balls into *tortillas.*

> We are the porous rock in the stone *metate*
> squatting on the ground.
> We are the rolling pin, *el maíz y agua,*
> *la masa harina. Somos el amasijo.*
> *Somos lo molido en el metate.*
> We are the *comal* sizzling hot,
> the hot *tortilla,* the hungry mouth.
> We are the coarse rock.
> We are the grinding motion,
> the mixed potion, *somos el molcajete.*
> We are the pestle, *the comino, ajo, pimienta,*
> We are the *chile colorado,*
> the green shoot that cracks the rock.
> We will abide.

El camino de la mestiza / The Mestiza Way

Caught between the sudden contraction, the breath sucked in and the endless space, the brown woman stands still, looks at the sky. She decides to go down, digging her way along the roots of trees. Sifting through the bones, she shakes them to see if there is any marrow in them. Then, touching the dirt to her forehead, to her tongue, she takes a few bones, leaves the rest in their burial place.

She goes through her backpack, keeps her journal and address book, throws away the muni-BART metromaps. The coins are heavy and they go next, then the greenbacks flutter through the air. She keeps her knife, can opener and eyebrow pencil. She puts bones, pieces of bark, *hierbas,* eagle feather, snakeskin, tape recorder, the rattle and drum in her pack and she sets out to become the complete *tolteca.*[6]

Her first step is to take inventory. *Despojando, desgranando, quitando paja.* Just what did she inherit from her ancestors? This weight on her back—which is the baggage from the Indian mother, which the baggage from the Spanish father, which the baggage from the Anglo?

Pero es difícil differentiating between *lo heredado, lo adquirido, lo impuesto.* She puts history through a sieve, winnows out the lies, looks at the forces that we as a race, as women, have been a part of. *Luego bota lo que no vale, los desmientos, los desencuentos, el embrutecimiento. Aguarda el juicio, hondo y enraízado, de la gente antigua.* This step is a conscious rupture with all oppressive traditions of all cultures and religions. She communicates that rupture, documents the struggle. She reinterprets history and, using new symbols, she shapes new myths. She adopts new perspectives toward the dark-skinned, women and queers. She strengthens her tolerance (and intolerance) for ambiguity. She is willing to share, to make herself vulnerable to foreign ways of seeing and thinking. She surrenders all notions of safety, of the familiar. Deconstruct, construct. She becomes a *nahual*, able to transform herself into a tree, a coyote, into another person. She learns to transform the small "I" into the total Self. *Se hace moldeadora de su alma. Según la concepción que tiene de sí misma, así será.*

Que no se nos olvide los hombres

"Tú no sirves pa' nada—
you're good for nothing.
Eres pura vieja."

"You're nothing but a woman" means you are defective. Its opposite is to be *un macho*. The modern meaning of the word "machismo," as well as the concept, is actually an Anglo invention. For men like my father, being "macho" meant being strong enough to protect and support my mother and us, yet being able to show love. Today's macho has doubts about his ability to feed and protect his family. His "machismo" is an adaptation to oppression and poverty and low self-esteem. It is the result of hierarchical male dominance. The Anglo, feeling inadequate and inferior and powerless, displaces or transfers these feelings to the Chicano by shaming him. In the Gringo world, the Chicano suffers from excessive humility and self-effacement, shame of self and self-deprecation. Around Latinos he suffers from a sense of language inadequacy and its accompanying discomfort; with Native Americans he suffers from a racial amnesia that ignores our common blood, and from guilt because the Spanish part of him took their land and oppressed them. He has an excessive compensatory hubris when around Mexicans from the other side. It overlays a deep sense of racial shame.

The loss of a sense of dignity and respect in the macho breeds a false machismo that leads him to put down women and even to brutalize them. Coexisting with his sexist behavior is a love for the mother which takes precedence over that of all others. Devoted son, macho pig. To wash down the shame of his acts, of his very being, and to handle the brute in the mirror, he takes to the bottle, the snort, the needle, and the fist.

Though we "understand" the root causes of male hatred and fear, and the subsequent wounding of women, we do not excuse, we do not condone, and we will no longer put up with it. From the men of our race, we demand the admission/acknowledgment/disclosure/testimony that they wound us, violate us, are afraid of us and of our power. We need them to say they will begin to eliminate their hurtful put-down ways. But more than the words, we demand acts. We say to them: We will develop equal power with you and those who have shamed us.

It is imperative that *mestizas* support each other in changing the sexist elements in the Mexican-Indian culture. As long as woman is put down, the Indian and the Black in all of us is put down. The struggle of the *mestiza* is above all a feminist one. As long as *los hombres* think they have to *chingar mujeres* and each other to be men, as long as men are taught that they are superior and therefore culturally favored over *la mujer*, as long as to be a *vieja* is a thing of derision, there can be no real healing of our psyches. We're halfway there—we have such love of the Mother, the good mother. The first step is to unlearn the *puta/virgen* dichotomy and to see *Coatapopeuh-Coatlicue* in the Mother, *Guadalupe*.

Tenderness, a sign of vulnerability, is so feared that it is showered on women with verbal abuse and blows. Men, even more than women, are fettered to gender roles. Women at least have had the guts to break out of bondage. Only gay men have had the courage to expose themselves to the woman inside them and to challenge the current masculinity. I've encountered a few scattered and isolated gentle straight men, the beginnings of a new breed, but they are confused, and entangled with sexist behaviors that they have not been able to eradicate. We need a new masculinity and the new man needs a movement.

Lumping the males who deviate from the general norm with man, the oppressor, is a gross injustice. *Asombra pensar que nos hemos quedado en ese pozo oscuro donde el mundo encierra a las lesbianas. Asombra pensar que hemos, como femenistas y lesbianas, cerrado nuestros corazónes a los hombres, a nuestros hermanos los jotos, desheredados y marginales como nosotros.* Being the supreme crossers of cultures, homosexuals have strong bonds with the queer white, Black, Asian, Native American, Latino, and with the queer in Italy, Australia and the rest of the planet. We come from all colors, all classes, all races, all time periods. Our role is to link people with each other—the Blacks with Jews with Indians with Asians with whites with extraterrestrials. It is to transfer ideas and information from one culture to another. Colored homosexuals have more knowledge of other cultures; have always been at the forefront (although sometimes in the closet) of all liberation struggles in this country; have suffered more injustices and have survived them despite all odds. Chicanos need to acknowledge the political and artistic contributions of their queer. People, listen to what your *jotería* is saying.

The *mestizo* and the queer exist at this time and point on the evolutionary continuum for a purpose. We are a blending that proves that all blood is intricately woven together, and that we are spawned out of similar souls.

Somos una gente

Hay tantísimas fronteras
que dividen a la gente,
pero por cada frontera
existe también un puente.
                    —Gina Valdés[7]

Divided Loyalties. Many women and men of color do not want to have any dealings with white people. It takes too much time and energy to explain to the downwardly mobile, white middle-class women that it's okay for us to want to own "possessions," never having had any nice furniture on our dirt floors or "luxuries" like washing machines. Many feel that whites should help their own people rid themselves of race hatred and fear first. I, for one, choose to use some of my energy to serve as mediator. I think we need to allow whites to be our allies. Through our literature, art, *corridos,* and folktales we must share our history with them so when they set up committees to help Big Mountain Navajos or the Chicano farmworkers or *los Nicaragüenses* they won't turn people away because of their racial fears and ignorances. They will come to see that they are not helping us but following our lead.

Individually, but also as a racial entity, we need to voice our needs. We need to say to white society: We need you to accept the fact that Chicanos are different, to acknowledge your rejection and negation of us. We need you to own the fact that you looked upon us as less than human, that you stole our lands, our personhood, our self-respect. We need you to make public restitution: to say that, to compensate for your own sense of defectiveness, you strive for power over us, you erase our history and our experience because it makes you feel guilty—you'd rather forget your brutish acts. To say you've split yourself from minority groups, that you disown us, that your dual consciousness splits off parts of yourself, transferring the "negative" parts onto us. (Where there is persecution of minorities, there is shadow projection. Where there is violence and war, there is repression of shadow.) To say that you are afraid of us, that to put distance between us, you wear the mask of contempt. Admit that Mexico is your double, that she exists in the shadow of this country, that we are irrevocably tied to her. Gringo, accept the doppelgänger in your psyche. By taking back your collective shadow the intra-cultural split will heal. And finally, tell us what you need from us.

BY YOUR TRUE FACES WE WILL KNOW YOU

I am visible—see this Indian face—yet I am invisible. I both blind them with my beak nose and am their blind spot. But I exist, we exist. They'd like to think I have melted in the pot. But I haven't, we haven't.

The dominant white culture is killing us slowly with its ignorance. By taking away our self-determination, it has made us weak and empty. As a people we have resisted and we have taken expedient positions, but we have never been allowed to develop unencumbered—we have never been allowed to be fully ourselves. The whites in power want us people of color to barricade ourselves behind our separate tribal walls so they can pick us off one at a time with their hidden weapons; so they can whitewash and distort history. Ignorance splits people, creates prejudices. A misinformed people is a subjugated people.

Before the Chicano and the undocumented worker and the Mexican from the other side can come together, before the Chicano can have unity with Native Americans and other groups, we need to know the history of their struggle and they need to know ours. Our mothers, our sisters and brothers, the guys who hang out on street corners, the children in the playgrounds, each of us must know our Indian lineage, our afro-*mestisaje*, our history of resistance.

To the immigrant *mexicano* and the recent arrivals we must teach our history. The 80 million *mexicanos* and the Latinos from Central and South America must know of our struggles. Each one of us must know basic facts about Nicaragua, Chile, and the rest of Latin America. The Latinoist movement (Chicanos, Puerto Ricans, Cubans, and other Spanish-speaking people working together to combat racial discrimination in the marketplace) is good but it is not enough. Other than a common culture we will have nothing to hold us together. We need to meet on a broader communal ground.

The struggle is inner: Chicano, *indio*, American Indian, *mojado*, *mexicano*, immigrant Latino, Anglo in power, working-class Anglo, Black, Asian—our psyches resemble the bordertowns and are populated by the same people. The struggle has always been inner, and is played out in the outer terrains. Awareness of our situation must come before inner changes, which in turn come before changes in society. Nothing happens in the "real" world unless it first happens in the images in our heads.

El día de la Chicana

I will not be shamed again
Nor will I shame myself.

I am possessed by a vision: that we Chicanas and Chicanos have taken back or uncovered our true faces, our dignity and self-respect. It's a validation vision.

Seeing the Chicana anew in light of her history. I seek an exoneration, a seeing through the fictions of white supremacy, a seeing of ourselves in our true guises and not as the false racial personality that has been given to us and that we have given to ourselves. I seek our woman's face, our true features, the positive and the negative seen clearly, free of the tainted biases of male dominance. I seek new images of identity, new beliefs about ourselves, our humanity and worth no longer in question.

Estamos viviendo en la noche de la Raza, un tiempo cuando el trabajo se hace a lo quieto, en el oscuro. El día cuando aceptamos tal y como somos y para en donde vamos y porque—ese día será el día de la Raza. Yo tengo el conpromiso de expresar mi visión, mi sensibilidad, mi percepción de la revalidación de la gente mexicana, su mérito, estimación, honra, aprecio, y validez.

On December 2nd when my sun goes into my first house, I celebrate *el día de la Chicana y el Chicano.* On that day I clean my altars, light my *Coatalopeuh* candle, burn sage and copal, take *el baño para espantar basura*, sweep my house. On that day I bare my soul, make myself vulnerable to friends and family by expressing my feelings. On that day I affirm who we are.

On that day I look inside our conflicts and our basic introverted racial temperament. I identify our needs, voice them. I acknowledge that the self and the race have been wounded. I recognize the need to take care of our personhood, of our racial self. On that day I gather the splintered and disowned parts of *la gente mexicana* and hold them in my arms. *Todas las partes de nosotros valen.*

On that day I say, "Yes, all you people wound us when you reject us. Rejection strips us of self-worth; our vulnerability exposes us to shame. It is our innate identity you find wanting. We are ashamed that we need your good opinion, that we need your acceptance. We can no longer camouflage our needs, can no longer let defenses and fences sprout around us. We can no longer withdraw. To rage and look upon you with contempt is to rage and be contemptuous of ourselves. We can no longer blame you, nor disown the white parts, the male parts, the pathological parts, the queer parts, the vulnerable parts. Here we are weaponless with open arms, with only our magic. Let's try it our way, the *mestiza* way, the Chicana way, the woman way.

On that day, I search for our essential dignity as a people, a people with a sense of purpose—to belong and contribute to something greater than our *pueblo.* On that day I seek to recover and reshape my spiritual identity. *¡Anímate! Raza, a celebrar el día de la Chicana.*

El retorno

All movements are accomplished in six stages,
and the seventh brings return.
—I Ching

*Tanto tiempo sin verta casa mía,
mi cuna, mi hondo nido de la huerta.*
—"*Soledad*"[8]

I stand at the river, watch the curving, twisting serpent, a serpent nailed to the fence where the mouth of the Rio Grande empties into the Gulf.

I have come back. *Tanto dolor me costó el alejamiento.* I shade my eyes and look up. The bone beak of a hawk slowly circling over me, checking me out as potential carrion. In its wake a little bird flickering its wings, swimming sporadically like a fish. In the distance the expressway and the slough of traffic like an irritated sow. The sudden pull in my gut, *la tierra, los aguaceros.* My land, *el viento soplando la arena, el lagartijo debajo de un nopalito. Me acuerdo como era antes. Una región desértica de vasta llanuras, costeras de baja altura, de escasa lluvia, de chaparrales formados por mesquites y huizaches.* If I look real hard I can almost see the Spanish fathers who were called "the cavalry of Christ" enter this valley riding their burros, see the clash of cultures commence.

Tierra natal. This is home, the small towns in the Valley, *los pueblitos* with chicken pens and goats picketed to mesquite shrubs. *En las colonias* on the other side of the tracks, junk cars line the front yards of hot pink and lavender-trimmed houses—Chicano architecture we call it, self-consciously. I have missed the TV shows where hosts speak in half and half, and where awards are given in the category of Tex-Mex music. I have missed the Mexican cemeteries blooming with artificial flowers, the fields of aloe vera and red pepper, rows of sugar cane, of corn hanging on the stalks, the cloud of *polvareda* in the dirt roads behind a speeding pickup truck, *el sabor de tamales de rez y venado.* I have missed *la yegua colorada* gnawing the wooden gate of her stall, the smell of horse flesh from Carito's corrals. *He hecho menos las noches calientes sin aire, noches de linternas y lechuzas* making holes in the night.

I still feel the old despair when I look at the unpainted, dilapidated, scrap lumber houses consisting mostly of corrugated aluminum. Some of the poorest people in the U.S. live in the Lower Rio Grande Valley, an arid and semi-arid land of irrigated farming, intense sunlight and heat, citrus groves next to chaparral and cactus. I walk through the elementary school I attended so long ago, which remained segregated until recently. I remember how the white teachers used to punish us for being Mexican.

How I love this tragic valley of South Texas, as Ricardo Sánchez calls it; this borderland between the Nueces and the Rio Grande. This land has survived possession and ill-use by five countries: Spain, Mexico, the Republic of Texas, the U.S., the Confederacy, and the U.S. again. It has survived Anglo-Mexican blood feuds, lynchings, burnings, rapes, pillage.

Today I see the valley still struggling to survive. Whether it does or not, it will never be as I remember it. The borderlands depression that was set off by the 1982 peso devaluation in Mexico resulted in the closure of hundreds of valley businesses. Many people lost their homes, cars, land. Prior to 1982, U.S. store owners thrived on retail sales to Mexicans who came across the border for groceries and clothes and appliances. While goods on the U.S. side have become 10, 100, 1,000 times more expensive for Mexican buyers, goods on the Mexican side have become 10, 100, 1,000 times cheaper for Americans. Because the valley is heavily dependent on agriculture and Mexican retail trade, it has the highest unemployment rates along the entire border region; it is the valley that has been hardest hit.[9]

"It's been a bad year for corn," my brother, Nune, says. As he talks, I remember my father scanning the sky for a rain that would end the drought, looking up into the sky, day after day, while the corn withered on its stalk. My father has been dead for 29 years, having worked himself to death. The life span of a Mexican farm laborer is 56—he lived to be 38. It shocks me that I am older than he. I, too, search the sky for rain. Like the ancients, I worship the rain god and the maize goddess, but unlike my father I have recovered their names. Now for rain (irrigation) one offers not a sacrifice of blood, but of money.

"Farming is in a bad way," my brother says. "Two to three thousand small and big farmers went bankrupt in this country last year. Six years ago the price of corn was $8.00 per hundred pounds," he goes on. "This year it is $3.90 per hundred pounds." And, I think to myself, after taking inflation into account, not planting anything puts you ahead.

I walk out to the back yard, stare at *los rosales de mamá.* She wants me to help her prune the rose bushes, dig out the carpet grass that is choking them. *Mamagrande Ramona también tenía rosales.* Here every Mexican grows flowers. If they don't have a piece of dirt, they use car tires, jars, cans, shoe boxes. Roses are the Mexican's favorite flower. I think, how symbolic—thorns and all.

Yes, the Chicano and Chicana have always taken care of growing things and the land. Again I see the four of us kids getting off the school bus, changing into our work clothes, walking into the field with Papí and Mamí, all six of us bending to the ground. Below our feet, under the earth lie the watermelon seeds. We cover them with paper plates, putting *terremotes* on top of the plates to keep them from being blown away by the wind. The paper plates keep the freeze away. Next day or the next, we remove the plates, bare the tiny green shoots to the elements. They survive and grow, give fruit hundreds of times the size of the seed. We water them and hoe them. We harvest them. The vines dry, rot, are plowed under. Growth, death, decay, birth. The soil prepared again and again, impregnated, worked on. A constant changing of forms, *renacimientos de la tierra madre*.

> This land was Mexican
> once was Indian always
> and is.
> And will be again.

NOTES

1. José Vasconcelos, *La Raza Cósmica: Misión de la Raza Ibero-Americana* (México: Aguilar S.A. de Ediciones, 1961).

2. Arthur Koestler termed this "bisociation." Albert Rothenberg, *The Creative Process in Art, Science, and Other Fields* (Chicago: University of Chicago Press, 1979), p. 12.

3. In part, I derive my definitions for "convergent" and "divergent" thinking from Rothenberg, pp. 12–13.

4. To borrow chemist Ilya Prigogine's theory of "dissipative structures." Prigogine discovered that substances interact, not in predictable ways as it was taught in science, but in different and fluctuating ways to produce new and more complex structures, a kind of birth he called "morphogenesis," which created unpredictable innovations. Harold Gilliam, "Searching for a New World View," *This World* (January 1981), p. 23.

5. *Tortillas de masa harina*: corn tortillas are of two types, the smooth uniform ones made in a tortilla press and usually bought at a tortilla factory or supermarket, and *gorditas*, made by mixing masa with lard or shortening or butter (my mother sometimes puts in bits of bacon or *chicharrones*).

6. Gina Valdés, *Puentes y Fronteras: Coplas Chicanas* (Los Angeles, Calif.: Castle Lithograph, 1982), p. 2.

7. Richard Wilhelm, *The I Ching or Book of Changes*, trans. Cary F. Baynes (Princeton, N.J.: Princeton University Press, 1950), p. 98.

8. "*Soledad*" is sung by the group Haciendo Punto en Otro Son.

9. Out of the twenty-two border counties in the four border states, Hidalgo County (named for Father Hidalgo, who was shot in 1810 after instigating Mexico's revolt against Spanish rule under the banner of *la Virgen de Guadalupe*) is the most poverty-stricken county in the nation as well as the largest home base (along with Imperial in California) for migrant farm-workers. It was here that I was born and raised. I am amazed that both it and I have survived.

I'M HERE

an asian american woman's response

(1 9 8 7)

As one who has been working intensively and almost exclusively in the most basic and practical aspect of feminist scholarship, namely the unearthing and reclaiming of forgotten women writers, I initially felt flattered (They want to know what I think!), then somewhat peeved (They only want to know what I think because they want a token Chinese), and finally sobered (Well, and what *do* I think?) to be invited to comment on Ellen Messer-Davidow's theoretical essay "The Philosophical Bases of Feminist Literary Criticisms." First, I'm grateful to be nudged in this way to lift my head from the part of the garden in which I have been so intently digging—namely, searching for women of Chinese ancestry who have written in English and published in the United States—to see what my sister scholars are doing. I see that they are well aware of and have been debating extensively the same problems I have been struggling with, specifically, the dilemmas between politics and aesthetics, between self as central and self as other, between empowering one's self and one's people by retrieving one's past while negotiating with the powerful, and often hostile, outside forces that control our very survival. Or, put another way, how can I write about books that are important to me personally, as a Chinese American woman, and yet maintain a position in a traditional department of English that considers my writers not only third rate but third world and therefore extraneous to the discipline?

It may be true that *"negritude* has analogues with women's aesthetic practices," as Rachel DuPlessis writes in "For the Etruscans,"[1] following a tradition dating back to the mid-nineteenth century when white feminists saw a parallel between their own social situation and that of the black slaves. But white feminists do not have the hurdle of race or nationality between them and acceptance. Granted the hurdle of gender is still in many places very high; nonetheless, the writers white feminists are reclaiming will never be dismissed as "third world." As black women have already pointed out, white women are the grandmothers, mothers, wives, and sisters of white men; thus it would seem natural that granting equality and recognition to their own women would be the first, and a much easier, step for white men than to give respectful attention to descendants of former slaves, prostitutes, and aliens. This, at least, is the perspective from outside the outside. Which is not to say that white feminists do not also perceive themselves as outsiders, and, as such, empathetic allies in the struggle. It is a reminder that, like the descending levels of Dante's *Inferno*, there are many layers of "outside."

As one who has experienced great opposition to the work she is doing—with colleagues making such remarks as "You're a trailblazer, but you're blazing a trail to a place no one wants to go to"—I give a resounding cheer to Messer-Davidow's "perspectivism": "a feminist philosophy that counters objectivism, which privileges objects, and subjectivism, which privileges subjects. Perspectivism would bring together in processes of knowing the personal and cultural, subjective and objective, replacing dichotomies with a systemic understanding of how and what we see. It would explain how we affiliate culturally, acquire a self-centered perspective, experience the perspective of others, and deploy multiple perspectives in inquiry. It would show that perspectivity arises from and defines knowers qualified (in both senses of the word) by their experiences, self-reflection, and contingent standpoints." The open-mindedness of this feminist theory stands in direct contrast to the closed comments of masculinists who dismiss as "trivial" and "insignificant" anything that falls outside their purview. I applaud the philosophical basis that would not only validate the stance I have taken but would require all scholars to be aware of their own perspectives, that would make perspective central and basic to all inquiry instead of seemingly peripheral and irrelevant.

If "perspectivism" were the accepted way and everyone were aware of "agency" and "stance," her own and others', the alienation I initially experienced would be eliminated. For example, when I, a Chinese American woman trained in the traditional classics of Western European and American literature—the "malestream"—first read Maxine Hong Kingston, my overwhelming reaction was discomfort and embarrassment. My self-alienation had been so complete that I experienced my first reading of another Chinese American woman's book as "foreign" and "other" before I relaxed into the realization that I was actually and finally at home as I had been with no other writers I had previously read. My reaction was akin to the child Janie Crawford's experience of not recognizing herself in the photograph in *Their Eyes Were Watching God*. But my later embracing women writers of Chinese ancestry as my central area of research was "to jettison myself off the world," as far as the majority of my male colleagues was concerned. My insistence on the validity of my perspective caused them to wonder about their own, led them to question whether instead of representing a "universal" perspective, they, too, were representing only one perspective: WASP male, Jewish male, black male. This was a disquieting thought; they had grudgingly made room for black and women writers because women are, after all, half the human race, and blacks, well, we do owe them something, don't we? However, the proliferation of perspectives had to be stopped somewhere, for "After all," as one colleague logically explained, "we don't have any Chinese students here, so we don't need a Chinese expert." (When I asked how many sixteenth-century Englishmen we had here, he didn't wish to pursue that line of reasoning.) My perspective challenged the official (white male) canon, and was seen as another threat to the very foundations upon which they had structured their world. I was refusing to believe that only what I had been taught was Good Literature and that everything else—forgotten and ignored—was third rate and deserved to be forgotten and ignored. My stance was a refusal to be "the good little girl," a rejection of what has been called "cultural colonization."[2]

Perspectivism would validate, respect, and encourage every perspective so that WASP males, Jewish males, black males, and white females would need to stretch themselves out of their own skins to understand Maxine Hong Kingston, Lin Taiyi, or Han Suyin, as I have always had to stretch outside of myself to understand James Fenimore Cooper, Bernard Malamud, and Richard Wright. This is what I have always believed reading literature is really all about—getting inside other people's skins and experiencing their lives, regardless of the color of their skin, time period, gender, sexual preference, class, or ethnic background. And yet, at times, it seems a utopian notion.

So I am pleased to be asked to represent Asian American scholars, or more specifically Chinese American women, in this forum. I realize that any forum, even as it includes certain voices, must, of necessity, exclude others. After recently reading Helen Barolini's introduction to an anthology of writings by Italian American women,[3] an introduction that resonates in me in many ways—for Italian American women have suffered similar oppression from the men of their own culture, a similar sense of alienation from the dominant Anglo-American traditions, and the same affinity with black women writers that Chinese American women feel—I fear that the Italian American woman's perspective may have been overlooked, again. It is my guess that, for the present, the more visible minorities have been given the spotlight. As different perspectives develop, not all can be given equal time and space in every forum simply because of physical limitations, but this does not mean we should not encourage their development.

In fact, paradoxically, the more we hear about the experiences of each particular group, the more we learn how much we share as a community of women and how often our commonalities cross cultural and racial barriers. Reading Barolini, like reading Alice Walker's "In Search of Our Mothers' Gardens" and *The Color Purple*, Audre Lorde's poems and essays, and Virginia Woolf's *A Room of One's Own* is like finding sisters I didn't know I had. How can it be that so many different Others have had experiences and feelings so similar to mine?

And yet, despite our alliance in Outsiderhood, we all must function within the present system while we work for change, and I am a bit uncomfortable about rejecting all male theories simply because they were created by men, as Messer-Davidow seems prone to do. I fear she dismisses too lightly those who would borrow the "useful elements" of the "smorgasbord" of "traditional schools." I have two comments to make on this question. The first is to remind us of the Piaget model of the acquisition of knowledge: "one observes that the subject [in this case, an infant] looks neither at what is too familiar, because he is in a way surfeited with it, nor at what is too new because this does not correspond to anything in his schemata."[4] In other words, we learn by hooking small bits of moderately new knowledge onto old knowledge already in place in our heads. If something new is so radically different that it cannot be hooked onto what is already there, then it remains unattached or unlearned. Thus, if we as feminists can appropriate something useful for our purposes from what is already in the common storehouse, we make our new ideas more accessible to others who are not as far along as we. For example, traditionalists find the idea that women writers of Chinese ancestry are a part of American literature so peculiar that they cannot hear about them unless I link my writers to ones they are familiar with: Chuang Hua's fractured narrative in *Crossings* is akin to Faulkner's *The Sound and the Fury* and parts of Flaubert's *Madame Bovary*; Lin Taiyi's *Dawn Over Chungking* has the poignant power of Anne Frank's diary and her *War Tide* is a tour de force by a seventeen-year-old. In other words, progress is made through little steps, not giant leaps.

Secondly, I find W. E. B. Du Bois's notion of "double consciousness," from *The Souls of Black Folk*, useful in my study of Chinese American women. In fact, Du Bois's elaboration of this double consciousness is applicable to all women: "this sense of always looking at one's self through the eyes of others."[5] John Berger in *Ways of Seeing* noted the same visual and psychological phenomenon: "Men look at women. Women watch themselves being looked at."[6] Elaine Showalter, in "Toward a Feminist Poetics," explains the theoretical impasse in feminist criticism in similar language: "It comes from our own divided consciousness, the split in each of us. We are both the daughters of the male tradition . . . and sisters in a new women's movement."[7] Carol Gilligan notes in *In a Different Voice*: "The difficulty women experience in finding or speaking publicly in their own voices emerges repeatedly in the form of qualification and self-doubt, but also in intimations of a divided judgment, a public assessment and private assessment which are fundamentally at odds."[8] Mikhail Bakhtin's "dialogic imagination" is another useful tool because he too is conscious of "otherness," as experienced aurally, in the many voices in dialogue within one's head.[9] Rachel DuPlessis's essay "For the Etruscans" and Maxine Hong Kingston's *The Woman Warrior* and *China Men* are collages exhibiting the many voices in their heads. Must these theories of double consciousness and dialogic imagination be rejected simply because they were created by men? Though Messer-Davidow is generally against borrowing from male-created systems, she does modify her verb with an adverb: "feminist literary critics who borrow uncritically borrow troubles mainly because our two endeavors are fundamentally incompatible."

In this context, I am reminded of a memorable line by Audre Lorde: "The master's tools will never dismantle the master's house."[10] Much as I enjoy the ring of this line, however, and admire the fierce independence behind it, I find myself finally doubting its veracity. After all, a claw-foot hammer, even if it was made by a man, can both drive nails in and pry them out, depending on your purpose and which side of the head you are using. Tools possess neither memory nor loyalty; they are as effective as the hands wielding them. And, furthermore, why shouldn't women use tools? Annette Kolodny earlier had written, rightly, I believe, "that the many tools needed for our analysis will necessarily be largely inherited and only partly of our own making."[11] Malestream literary critics themselves have been borrowing liberally the tools of anthropology and linguistics. On the other hand, if Lorde was referring to the impossibility of the established system's ability to police itself, then I would, from experience, agree with her.

Messer-Davidow has done a fine intellectual analysis of the problem of women literary scholars in a man's world, and she is bold in arguing for independence, but what about the practical ramifications of secession? I find disquieting her assertion that "the subject of feminist literary criticisms appears to be not literature but the feminist study of ideas about sex and gender that people express in literary and critical media." Trained in literature and hanging on by the skin of my teeth to an English department, I am reluctant to agree that my primary subject is "not literature." I might be in fashion, since, as Elaine Showalter rightly analyzes the present situation in literary criticism, "literary science, in its manic generation of difficult terminology, . . . creates an elite corps of specialists who spend more and more time mastering the theory, less and less time reading the books" (140). However, if I were to agree with Messer-Davidow on this point, I would seem to be siding with a powerful colleague who published an article a number of years ago in which he stated that women's studies has no place in an English department.

If I am a feminist critic, my primary identification is still "literary critic," while "feminist" is the adjective modifying the kind of criticism I do, just as Chinese Americans are primarily Americans with a veneer of Chinese. However, Messer-Davidow is asking us all to be feminists first and then whatever else we are second. Thus we should by her view rightly be called "historical feminists," "literary critical feminists," "scientific feminists," "philosophical feminists," and so on. My proper place would perhaps then be in a women's studies department, but I know only of women's studies programs with part-time faculty borrowed from regular departments. Thus we face a "catch-22" (another borrowing from a male): only if a person is acceptable to a bona fide department will she be able to teach in women's studies, but the bona fide department wants nothing to do with women's studies. What now?

Perhaps what we ought to do is break out of the rigid (male-created) categories and boundaries that separate us. One of the most exciting aspects of Messer-Davidow's article is her pointing out that feminists in many different disciplines are a community all working on the same subject—ideas of sex and gender—though manifested in different "media." The work of feminists in other disciplines— for example, Carol Gilligan in psychology or Alison Jaggar in philosophy— enriches our work in literature and vice versa. Furthermore, in setting forth to discover what women of Chinese ancestry have written and published in the United States, if I find that these women have written what traditional department colleagues would not consider "fine literature," then I must, like Jane Tompkins, redefine "literature" to be broader than the "stylistic intricacy, psychological subtlety, [and] epistemological complexity" that is the current measure of a "good" book, and examine instead "how and why it worked for its readers, in its time."[12] In other words, I do not categorize a writer or her book as "good" or "bad" in the abstract but try to answer the questions: Good for what? For whom? Under what kind of circumstances? And I maintain that I am still studying literature, the written voice of a specific group of people at a specific time.

Take, for example, the Eaton sisters, the first writers of Asian ancestry to publish in the United States. Without knowing the political, social, and immigration history of the turn of the century, there would be no way of understanding why the elder sister, Edith Eaton (1867–1914), used the pseudonym Sui Sin Far (Cantonese for narcissus) and the younger, Winnifred Eaton (1877?–1954), published novels under the Japanese-sounding name Onoto Watanna. We need to be aware of the fact that the Chinese, imported here by the thousands to build the railroads in the late 1860s, were feared and hated as an economic threat while the Japanese, having won a war against China in 1895 and against Russia in 1905, were highly regarded. We must know that Edith felt a sympathy for her Chinese mother and, identifying with her mother's people, resented the injustices they suffered and fought for their rights in articles and stories. Winnifred, seeing her sister go the Chinese route and realizing that Caucasians could not distinguish between Chinese and Japanese, opted to be the favored "Oriental." Without this background information, we would not be aware that Edith's stories are filled with Chinese Americans in situations that emphasize their humanity and lovability because she was intent on opposing the prejudice that Chinese were "heathen" and "unassimilable." Without Edith's work for contrast, we would be less aware that Winnifred's novels, set in Japan and relating stories of romance between charming Japanese or Japanese Eurasian girls and Anglo men, reflected the taste of the day, exploiting stereotypes of the childlike female and the fatherly, powerful male. Not surprisingly, in view of the climate in which they wrote and the directions each chose, Edith produced only one volume of short stories and died relatively young while Winnifred published nearly twenty books and reached the twin pinnacles of popular recognition: Broadway and Hollywood.[13] Were we to use only the formal criteria that Tompkins iterated as the conventional critical standards of our day—"stylistic intricacy, psychological subtlety, epistemological complexity"—the work of the Eaton sisters would not measure up. But why must these be the only measure of the worth of a text? These measures would not reveal the richness of their personal histories or the significance of Edith's work in giving voice to a voiceless people, and of Winnifred's work in revealing the contortions that the prejudices of the day exacted of a woman who wanted to survive. Furthermore, we are anachronistically applying the standards of 1980 to work written in 1880, and many of the writers now considered part of the traditional "canon" would not measure up either.

Messer-Davidow asserts that the ambivalent position that feminist literary critics find themselves in "concerns the way we traditionally structure knowledge" and thus a "way of reconstituting knowledge that evolves from feminist perspectives" is essential. This she ably sets out to do; dissecting the act of criticism into its component parts and offering "perspectivism" as a solution. Her analysis is most impressive, but, being of a practical mind, I find that my problem is not so much one of structuring knowledge as it is my powerlessness versus their power. "Give me one good reason why I should read your writers, other than guilt," a former chairman said to me. How do I answer him? Because they're wonderful writers? Because you'll learn something? The question itself indicates that he is already firmly entrenched in the assumption that these writers are not important to him, except for his guilt in dismissing them unread. If his mind is closed, I can say nothing that will convince him to open it, just as, for example, if someone dislikes tofu, no amount of praise from a tofu-lover can persuade him that tofu is delicious. Perhaps the value of Messer-Davidow's essay may be that this former chair may eventually be persuaded by its theoretical analysis and its abstract language to admit the validity of a variety of perspectives. She at least employs the "discourse" so respected in academia. (Curiously, though she argues for perspectivism, Messer-Davidow reveals little of her own "agency" and "stance," other than her feminism.)

As a Chinese American woman literary scholar, I feel myself at times in the lonely position that Helen Barolini expresses in *The Dream Book* and that Barbara Smith writes of in "Toward a Black Feminist Criticism." We seem to be the only persons in the world asking the questions: "Where are the writers that are like us?" "Where are our models?" We hope we will not be the only ones to care about the answers. More often than not, we find our particular perspectives ignored. Barolini's introduction contains a myriad of grievances; I have similar complaints. Since the very nature of pioneering research means that no help can be had from those who went before us. I was excited when I received a review copy of Patricia K. Addis's *Through a Woman's I: An Annotated Bibliography of American Women's Autobiographical Writings, 1946–1976,* thinking I had found a research tool at long last. Great was my distress and indignation when I discovered that the "Index of Narratives by Subject Matter" lists "American Indian Woman's Experience" and "Black Woman's Experience" but has no comparable category "Asian American Woman's Experience." And yet Addis's bibliography includes at least five books by Asian American women, including one I had not previously known. Had the indexer realized that "Asian American Woman" is a legitimate category, s/he would have saved me much time and effort. Needless to say, "Italian American Woman's Experience" was also not listed, and in the "Index of Authors by Profession or Salient Characteristic," "Lesbian" is not a category though "Transsexual" is, with one listing under it: "Jorgensen, Christine."[14] This just demonstrates what I've written above—we cannot all be remembered all the time. Even Messer-Davidow herself forgets me. She gives "Hispanic" and "Native American" women the honor of being individually named, but Asian American women, once again, are relegated to the categories of "Third World" and "other."

On the other hand—in DuPlessis's "both/and" fashion (276)—I also feel the excitement of participating in a revolution. The old guard is being shaken, if it has not yet been overthrown. The work I am doing is part of what Adrienne Rich earlier called "re-vision" or "the act of looking back, of seeing with fresh eyes, of entering an old text from a new critical direction,"[15] and also of discovering a female tradition that had been ignored. The feminist perspective that Judith Fetterley applied to her readings of male "classics" in *The Resisting Reader,* for example, was refreshing and exhilarating. The contextual approach and clear-sightedness of Jane Tompkins in *Sensational Designs* is beautiful and breathtaking. The reclamation of forgotten authors by Elaine Showalter, Dale Spender, Catharine Stimpson, Elaine Hedges, Barbara Christian, Mary Helen Washington, Deborah McDowell—all contribute to the feminist rewriting of literary history. Our movement has gained in numbers and in momentum. We may each be working in separate corners of the garden, but we are all working in the same garden. Feminist scholars in different disciplines are all exploring "a common subject, as it is expressed in the particular media they treat," as Messer-Davidow puts it. Our discoveries are answering my father, who once said to me: "What have women ever done in the world? The best in any field—even the 'women's' fields of fashion, cooking, and decorating—have always been men."

The fact that *New Literary History* is highlighting Messer-Davidow's essay and asking for our responses is a recognition of the significance of our work. It would be ideal if the result of this attention were that everyone would be not merely more tolerant of each other's perspectives but actively interested, for only as all the diverse peoples that are Americans find their own voices and sing their individual and communal songs, can we enjoy the full richness and depth in this chorus that is America. Mitsuye Yamada's poem "Mirror, Mirror" expresses it succinctly and well:

> People keep asking me where I come from
>   says my son.
> Trouble is I'm american on the inside
>   and oriental on the outside
>
> No Doug
> Turn that outside in
> THIS is what American looks like.[16]

I may not be able to persuade anyone to like tofu or Asian American writers, but I can tell them, as we're all telling them, we're here.

NOTES

1. Rachel Blau DuPlessis, "For the Etruscans," in *The New Feminist Criticism: Essays on Women, Literature, and Theory,* ed. Elaine Showalter (New York, 1985), p. 285; hereafter cited in text.

2. See, among others, Leslie Marmon Silko's excellent essay on cultural colonization entitled "Language and Literature from a Pueblo Indian Perspective," in *English Literature: Opening Up the Canon,* ed. Leslie A. Fiedler and Houston A. Baker, Jr. (Baltimore, 1981), pp. 54–72.

3. *The Dream Book, An Anthology of Writings by Italian-American Women,* ed. Helen Barolini (New York, 1985), p. 9.

4. Jean Piaget, *The Origins of Intelligence in Children,* tr. Margaret Cook (New York, 1952), p. 68.

5. W. E. Burghardt Du Bois, *The Souls of Black Folk* (New York, 1961), p. 3.

6. John Berger, *Ways of Seeing* (Norwich, England, 1972), p. 47.

7. Elaine Showalter, "Toward a Feminist Poetics," in *The New Feminist Criticism,* ed. Showalter, p. 141; hereafter cited in text.

8. Carol Gilligan, *In a Different Voice: Psychological Theory and Women's Development* (Cambridge, Mass., 1982), p. 16.

9. Mikhail Bakhtin, *The Dialogic Imagination: Four Essays,* ed. Michael Holquist, tr. Caryl Emerson and Michael Holquist (Austin, 1981).

10. Audre Lorde, "The Master's Tools Will Never Dismantle the Master's House," in *Sister Outsider* (Trumansburg, N.Y., 1984), pp. 110–13.

11. Annette Kolodny, "Dancing Through the Minefield," in *The New Feminist Criticism,* ed. Showalter, p. 161.

12. Jane Tompkins, "Sentimental Power: Uncle Tom's Cabin and the Politics of Literary History," in *The New Feminist Criticism,* ed. Showalter, pp. 84, 85.

13. For further information about the Eaton sisters, see my essays "Edith Eaton: Pioneer Chinamerican Writer and Feminist," *American Literary Realism,* 16, No. 2 (1983), 287–98 and "Winnifred Eaton: Ethnic Chamelion," *MELUS,* 11, No. 3 (1984), 5–15.

14. Patricia K. Addis, *Through A Woman's I: An Annotated Bibliography of American Women's Autobiographical Writings, 1946–1976* (Metuchen, N.J., 1983), p. 565.

15. Adrienne Rich, "When We Dead Awaken: Writing as Re-Vision," *College English,* 34 (October 1972), 18.

16. Mitsuye Yamada, *Camp Notes* (San Lorenzo, Cal., 1976), n. pag.; this is the final poem in the chapbook.

BARBARA SMITH

THE TRUTH THAT NEVER HURTS

black lesbians in fiction in the 1980s

(1 9 9 0)

In 1977, when I wrote *Toward a Black Feminist Criticism,* I wanted to accomplish several goals. The first was simply to point out that Black women writers existed, a fact generally ignored by white male, Black male, and white female readers, teachers, and critics. Another desire was to encourage Black feminist criticism of these writers' work, that is, analyses that acknowledged the reality of sexual oppression in the lives of Black women. Probably most urgently, I wanted to illuminate the existence of Black Lesbian writers and to show how homophobia insured that we were even more likely to be ignored or attacked than Black women writers generally.

In 1985, Black women writers' situation is considerably different than it was in 1977. Relatively speaking, Black women's literature is much more recognized, even at times by the white, male literary establishment. There are a growing number of Black women critics who rely upon various Black feminist critical approaches to studying the literature. There has been a marked increase in the number of Black women who are willing to acknowledge that they are feminists, including some who write literary criticism. Not surprisingly, Black feminist activism and organizing have greatly expanded, a precondition which I cited in 1977 for the growth of Black feminist criticism. More writing by Black Lesbians is available, and there has even been some positive response to this writing from non-Lesbian Black readers and critics. The general conditions under which Black women critics and writers work have improved. The personal isolation we face and the ignorance and hostility with which our work is met have diminished in some quarters but have by no means disappeared.

One of the most positive changes is that a body of consciously Black feminist writing and writing by other feminists of color actually exists. The publication of a number of anthologies has greatly increased the breadth of writing available by feminists of color. These include *Conditions: Five, The Black Women's Issue* (1979); *This Bridge Called My Back: Writings by Radical Women of Color* (1981); *All the Women Are White, All the Blacks Are Men, But Some of Us Are Brave: Black Women's Studies* (1982); *A Gathering of Spirit: North American Indian Women's Issue* (1983); *Cuentos: Stories by Latinas* (1983); *Home Girls: A Black Feminist Anthology* (1983); *Bearing Witness/Sobreviviendo: An Anthology of Native American/Latina Art and Literature* (1984); and *Gathering Ground: New Writing and Art by Northwest Women of Color* (1984). First books by individual authors have also appeared, such as *Claiming an Identity They Taught Me to Despise* (1980) and *Abeng* (1984) by Michelle Cliff; *Narratives: Poems in the Tradition of Black Women* (1982) by Cheryl Clarke; *For Nights Like This One* (1983) by Becky Birtha; *Loving in the War Years: Lo Que Nunsa Paso por Sus Labios* (1983) by Cherríe Moraga; *The Words of a Woman Who Breathes Fire* (1983) by Kitty Tsui; and *Mohawk Trail* (1985) by Beth Brant (Degonwadonti). Scholarly works provide extremely useful analytical frameworks, for example, *Common Differences: Conflicts in Black and White Feminist Perspectives* by Gloria I. Joseph and Jill Lewis (1981); *Black Women Writers at Work* edited by Claudia Tate (1983); *When and Where I Enter: The Impact of Black Women on Race and Sex in America* by Paula Giddings (1984); and *Black Feminist Criticism: Perspectives on Black Women Writers* by Barbara Christian (1985).

Significantly, however, "small" or independent, primarily women's presses published all but the last four titles cited and almost all the authors and editors of these alternative press books (although not all of the contributors to their anthologies) are Lesbians. In his essay "The Sexual Mountain and Black Women Writers," critic Calvin Hernton writes:

> The declared and lesbian black feminist writers are pioneering a black feminist criticism. This is not to take away from other writers. All are blazing new trails. But especially the declared feminists and lesbian feminists—Barbara Smith, Ann Shockley, Cheryl Clarke, Wilmette Brown, and the rest—are at the forefront of the critics, scholars, intellectuals, and ideologues of our time.[1]

Yet Hernton points out that these writers are "subpopular," published as they are by nonmainstream presses. In contrast, non-Lesbian Black women writers have been published by trade publishers and are able to reach, as Hernton explains, a "wider popular audience."

In her excellent essay, "No More Buried Lives: The Theme of Lesbianism" on Audre Lorde's *Zami*, Gloria Naylor's *The Women of Brewster Place*, Ntozake Shange's *Sassafras, Cypress and Indigo*, and Alice Walker's *The Color Purple*, critic Barbara Christian makes a similar observation. She writes:

> Lesbian life, characters, language, values are *at present* and *to some extent* becoming respectable in American literature, partly because of the pressure of women-centered communities, partly because publishers are intensely aware of marketing trends. . . . I say, *to some extent*, because despite the fact that Walker received the Pulitzer for *The Color Purple* and Naylor the American Book Award for *The Women of Brewster Place*, I doubt if *Home Girls*, an anthology of black feminist and lesbian writing that was published by Kitchen Table Press, would have been published by a mainstream publishing company.[2]

Significantly, Christian says that "Lesbian life, characters, language, values" are receiving qualified attention and respectability, but Lesbian writers themselves are not. No doubt, this is why she suspects that no trade publisher would publish *Home Girls*, which contains work by women who write openly as Lesbians, and which defines Lesbianism politically as well as literally.

The fact that there is such a clear-cut difference in publishing options for Black Lesbian writers (who are published solely by independent presses) and for non-Lesbian and closeted Black women writers (who have access to both trade and alternative publishers) indicates what has *not* changed since 1977. It also introduces the focus of this essay.[3] I am concerned with exploring the treatment of Black Lesbian writing and Black Lesbian themes in the context of Black feminist writing and criticism.

Today, not only are more works by and about Black women available, but a body of specifically Black feminist writing exists. Although both the general category of Black women's literature and the specific category of Black feminist literature can be appropriately analyzed from a Black feminist critical perspective, explicitly Black feminist literature has a unique set of characteristics and emphases which distinguishes it from other work. Black feminist writing provides an incisive critical perspective on sexual political issues that affect Black women— for example, the issue of sexual violence. It generally depicts the significance of Black women's relationships with each other as a primary source of support. Black feminist writing may also be classified as such because the author identifies herself as a feminist and has a demonstrated commitment to women's issues and related political concerns. An openness in discussing Lesbian subject matter is perhaps the most obvious earmark of Black feminist writing and not because feminism and Lesbianism are interchangeable, which of course they are not.

For historical, political, and ideological reasons, a writer's consciousness about Lesbianism bears a direct relationship to her consciousness about feminism. It was in the context of the second wave of the contemporary feminist movement, influenced by the simultaneous development of an autonomous gay liberation movement, that the political content of Lesbianism and Lesbian oppression began to be analyzed and defined. The women's liberation movement was the political setting in which anti-Lesbian attitudes and actions were initially challenged in the late 1960s and early 1970s and where, at least in theory, but more often in fact, homophobia was designated unacceptable, at least in the movement's more progressive sectors.

Barbara Christian also makes the connection between feminist consciousness and a willingness to address Lesbian themes in literature. She writes:

> Some of the important contributions that the emergence of the lesbian theme has made to Afro-American Women's literature are: the breaking of stereotypes so that black lesbians are clearly seen as *women*, the exposure of homophobia in the black community, and an exploration of how that homophobia is related to the struggle of all women to be all that they can be—in other words to feminism.
>
> That is not to say that Afro-American women's literature has not always included a feminist perspective. The literature of the seventies, for example, certainly explored the relationship between sexism and racism and has been at the forefront of the development of feminist ideas. One natural outcome of this exploration is the lesbian theme, for society's attack on lesbians is the cutting edge of the anti-feminist definition of women.[4]

Black feminist writers, whether Lesbian or non-Lesbian, have been aware of and influenced by the movement's exploring, struggling over, and organizing around Lesbian identity and issues. They would be much more likely to take Black Lesbian experiences seriously and to explore Black Lesbian themes in their writing, in contrast with authors who either have not been involved in the women's movement or who are antifeminist. For example, in her very positive review of *Conditions: Five, The Black Women's Issue,* originally published in *Ms.* magazine in 1980, Alice Walker writes:

> Like black men and women who refused to be the exceptional "pet" Negro for whites, and who instead said they were "niggers" too (the original "crime" of "niggers" and lesbians is that they prefer themselves), perhaps black women writers and nonwriters should say simply, whenever black lesbians are being put down, held up, messed over, and generally told their lives should not be encouraged. *We are all lesbians.* For surely it is better to be thought a lesbian, and to say and write your life exactly as you experience it, than to be a token "pet" black woman for those whose contempt for our autonomous existence makes them a menace to human life.[5]

Walker's support of her Lesbian sisters in real life is not unrelated to her ability to write fiction about Black women who are lovers, as in *The Color Purple.* Her feminist consciousness undoubtedly influenced the positiveness of her portrayal. In contrast, an author like Gayl Jones, who has not been associated with or seemingly influenced by the feminist movement, has portrayed Lesbians quite negatively.[6]

Just as surely as a Black woman writer's relationship to feminism affects the themes she might choose to write about, a Black woman critic's relationship to feminism determines the kind of criticism she is willing and able to do. The fact that critics are usually also academics, however, has often affected Black women critics' approach to feminist issues. If a Black woman scholar's only connection to women's issues is via women's studies, as presented by white women academics, most of whom are not activists, her access to movement analyses and practice will be limited or nonexistent. I believe that the most accurate and developed theory, including literary theory, comes from practice, from the experience of activism. This relationship between theory and practice is crucial when inherently political subject matter, such as the condition of women as depicted in a writer's work, is being discussed. I do not believe it is possible to arrive at fully developed and useful Black feminist criticism by merely reading about feminism. Of course every Black woman has her own experiences of sexual political dynamics and oppression to draw upon, and referring to these experiences should be an important resource in shaping her analyses of a literary work. However, studying feminist texts and drawing only upon one's *individual* experiences of sexism are insufficient.

I remember the point in my own experience when I no longer was involved on a regular basis in organizations such as the Boston Committee to End Sterilization Abuse and the Abortion Action Coalition. I was very aware that my lack of involvement affected my thinking and writing *overall.* Certain perceptions were simply unavailable to me because I no longer was doing that particular kind of ongoing work. And I am referring to missing something much deeper than access to specific information about sterilization and reproductive rights. Activism has spurred me to write the kinds of theory and criticism I have written and has provided the experiences and insights that have shaped the perceptions in my work. Many examples of this vital relationship between activism and theory exist in the work of thinkers such as Ida B. Wells-Barnett, W. E. B. Du Bois, Lillian Smith, Lorraine Hansberry, Frantz Fanon, Barbara Deming, Paolo Freire, and Angela Davis.

A critic's involvement or lack of involvement in activism, specifically in the context of the feminist movement, is often signally revealed by the approach she takes to Lesbianism. If a woman has worked in organizations where Lesbian issues have been raised, where homophobia was unacceptable and struggled with, and where she had the opportunity to meet and work with a variety of Lesbians, her relationship to Lesbians and to her own homophobia would undoubtedly be affected. The types of political organizations in which such dialogue occurs are not, of course, exclusively Lesbian and may focus upon a range of issues, such as women in prison, sterilization abuse, reproductive freedom, health care, domestic violence, and sexual assault.

Black feminist critics who are Lesbians can usually be counted upon to approach Black women's and Black Lesbian writing nonhomophobically. Non-Lesbian Black feminist critics are not as dependable in this regard. I even question at times designating Black women—critics and noncritics alike—as feminists who are actively homophobic in what they write, say, or do, or who are passively homophobic because they ignore Lesbian existence entirely.[7] Yet such critics are obviously capable of analyzing other sexual and political implications of the literature they scrutinize. Political definitions, particularly of feminism, can be difficult to pin down. The one upon which I generally rely states: "Feminism is the political theory and practice that struggles to free *all* women: women of color, working-class women, poor women, disabled women, lesbians, old women—as well as white, economically privileged, heterosexual women. Anything less than this vision of total freedom is not feminism, but merely female self-aggrandizement."[8]

A Black gay college student recently recounted an incident to me that illustrates the kind of consciousness that is grievously lacking among nonfeminist Black women scholars about Black Lesbian existence. His story indicates why a Black feminist approach to literature, criticism, and research in a variety of disciplines is crucial if one is to recognize and understand Black Lesbian experience. While researching a history project, he contacted the archives at a Black institution that has significant holdings on Black women. He spoke to a Black woman archivist and explained that he was looking for materials on Black Lesbians in the 1940s. Her immediate response was to laugh uproariously and then to say that the collection contained very little on women during that period and nothing at all on Lesbians in any of the periods covered by its holdings.

Not only was her reaction appallingly homophobic, not to mention impolite, but it was also inaccurate. One of the major repositories of archival material on Black women in the country of course contains material by and about Black Lesbians. The material, however, is not identified and defined as such and thus remains invisible. This is a classic case of "invisibility [becoming] an unnatural disaster," as feminist poet Mitsuye Yamada observes.[9]

I suggested a number of possible resources to the student and in the course of our conversation I told him I could not help but think of Cheryl Clarke's classic poem "Of Althea and Flaxie." It begins:

> In 1943 Althea was a welder
> very dark
> very butch
> and very proud
> loved to cook, sew, and drive a car
> and did not care who knew she kept company with a woman.[10]

The poem depicts a realistic and positive Black Lesbian relationship which survives Flaxie's pregnancy in 1955, Althea's going to jail for writing numbers in 1958, poverty, racism, and, of course, homophobia. If the archivist's vision had not been so blocked by homophobia, she would have been able to direct this student to documents that corroborate the history embodied in Clarke's poem.

Being divorced from the experience of feminist organizing not only makes it more likely that a woman has not been directly challenged to examine her homophobia, but it can also result in erroneous approaches to Black Lesbian literature, if she does decide to talk or write about it. For example, some critics, instead of simply accepting that Black Lesbians and Black Lesbian writers exist, view the depiction of Lesbianism as a dangerous and unacceptable "theme" or "trend" in Black women's writing. Negative discussions of "themes" and "trends," which may in time fade, do not acknowledge that for survival, Black Lesbians, like any oppressed group, need to see our faces reflected in myriad cultural forms, including literature. Some critics go so far as to see the few Black Lesbian books in existence as a kind of conspiracy and bemoan that there is "so much" of this kind of writing available in print; they put forth the supreme untruth that it is actually an advantage to be a Black Lesbian writer.

For each Lesbian of color in print there are undoubtedly five dozen whose work has never been published and may never be. The publication of Lesbians of color is a "new" literary development, made possible by alternative, primarily Lesbian/feminist presses. The political and aesthetic strength of this writing is indicated by its impact having been far greater than its actual availability. At times its content has had revolutionary implications. But the impact of Black Lesbian feminist writing, to which Calvin Hernton refers, should not be confused with easy access to print, to readers, or to the material perks that help a writer survive economically.

Terms like "heterophobia," used to validate the specious notion that "so many" Black women writers are now depicting loving and sexual relationships between women, to the exclusion of focusing on relationships with men, arise in an academic vacuum, uninfluenced by political reality. "Heterophobia" resembles the concept of "reverse racism." Both are thoroughly reactionary and have nothing to do with the actual dominance of a heterosexual white power structure.

Equating Lesbianism with separatism is another error in terminology, which will probably take a number of years to correct. The title of a workshop at a major Black women writers' conference, for example, was "Separatist Voices in the New Canon." The workshop examined the work of Audre Lorde and Alice Walker, neither of whom defines herself as a separatist, either sexually or racially.

In his introduction to *Confirmation: An Anthology of African American Women*, co-editor Imamu Baraka is critical of feminists who are separatists, but he does not mention that any such thing as a Lesbian exists. In his ambiguous yet inherently homophobic usage, the term "separatist" is made to seem like a mistaken political tendency, which correct thinking could alter. If "separatist" equals Lesbian, Baraka is suggesting that we should change our minds and eradicate ourselves. In both these instances the fact that Lesbians do not have sexual relationships with men is thought to be the same as ideological Lesbian "separatism." Such an equation does not take into account that the majority of Lesbians of color have interactions with men and that those who are activists are quite likely to be politically committed to coalition work as well.

Inaccuracy and distortion seem to be particularly frequent pitfalls when non-Lesbians address Black Lesbian experience because of generalized homophobia and because the very nature of our oppression may cause us to be hidden or "closeted," voluntarily or involuntarily isolated from other communities, and as a result unseen and unknown. In her essay "A Cultural Legacy Denied and Discovered: Black Lesbians in Fiction by Women," Jewelle Gomez asserts the necessity for realistic portrayals of Black Lesbians:

> These Black Lesbian writers . . . have seen into the shadows that hide the existence of Black Lesbians and understand they have to create a universe/home that rings true on all levels. . . . The Black Lesbian writer must throw herself into the arms of her culture by acting as student/teacher/participant/observer, absorbing and synthesizing the meanings of our existence as a people. She must do this despite the fact that both our culture and our sexuality have been severely truncated and distorted.
>
> Nature abhors a vacuum and there is a distinct gap in the picture where the Black Lesbian should be. The Black Lesbian writer must recreate our home, unadulterated, unsanitized, specific and not isolated from the generations that have nurtured us.[11]

This is an excellent statement of what usually has been missing from portrayals of Black Lesbians in fiction. The degree of truthfulness and self-revelation that Gomez calls for encompasses the essential qualities of verisimilitude and authenticity that I look for in depictions of Black Lesbians. By verisimilitude I mean how true to life and realistic a work of literature is. By authenticity I mean something even deeper—a characterization which reflects a relationship to self that is genuine, integrated, and whole. For a Lesbian or a gay man, this kind of emotional and psychological authenticity virtually requires the degree of self-acceptance inherent in being out. This is not a dictum, but an observation. It is not a coincidence, however, that the most vital and useful Black Lesbian feminist writing is being written by Black Lesbians who are not caught in the impossible bind of simultaneously hiding identity yet revealing self through their writing.

Positive and realistic portrayals of Black Lesbians are surely needed, portraits that are, as Gomez states, "unadulterated, unsanitized, specific." By positive I do not mean characters without problems, contradictions, or flaws, mere uplift literature for Lesbians, but instead, writing that is sufficiently sensitive and complex, which places Black Lesbian experience and struggles squarely within the realm of recognizable human experience and concerns.

As African-Americans, our desire for authentic literary images of Black Lesbians has particular cultural and historical resonance, since a desire for authentic images of ourselves as Black people preceded it long ago. After an initial period of racial uplift literature in the nineteenth and early twentieth centuries, Black artists during the Harlem Renaissance of the 1920s began to assert the validity of fully Black portrayals in all art forms including literature. In his pivotal essay of 1926, "The Negro Artist and the Racial Mountain," Langston Hughes asserted:

> We younger Negro artists who create now intend to express our individual dark-skinned selves without fear or shame. If white people are pleased we are glad. If they are not, it doesn't matter. We know we are beautiful. And ugly too. The tom-tom cries and the tom-tom laughs. If colored people are pleased we are glad. If they are not, their displeasure doesn't matter either. We build our temples for tomorrow, strong as we know how, and we stand on top of the mountain, free within ourselves.[12]

Clearly, it was not always popular or safe with either Black or white audiences to depict Black people as we actually are. It still is not. Too many contemporary Blacks seem to have forgotten the universally debased social-political position Black people have occupied during all the centuries we have been here, up until perhaps the Civil Rights Movement of the 1960s. The most racist definition of Black people has been that we were not human.

Undoubtedly every epithet now hurled at Lesbians and gay men—"sinful," "sexually depraved," "criminal," "emotionally maladjusted," "deviant"—has also been applied to Black People. When W. E. B. Du Bois described life "behind the veil," and Paul Laurence Dunbar wrote,

> We wear the mask that grins and lies,
> It hides our cheeks and shades our eyes,—
> This debt we pay to human guile;
> With torn and bleeding hearts we smile,
> And mouth with myriad subtleties.
>
> Why should the world be overwise,
> In counting all our tears and sighs?
> Nay, let them only see us, while
> We wear the mask.[13]

what were they describing but racial closeting? For those who refuse to see the parallels because they view Blackness as irreproachably normal, but persist in defining same-sex love relationships as unnatural, Black Lesbian feminist poet, Audre Lorde, reminds us: "'Oh,' says a voice from the Black community, 'but being Black is NORMAL!' Well, I and many Black people of my age can remember grimly the days when it didn't used to be!"[14] Lorde is not implying that she believes that there was ever anything wrong with being Black, but points out how distorted "majority" consciousness can cruelly affect an oppressed community's actual treatment and sense of self. The history of slavery, segregation, and racism was based upon the assumption by the powers-that-be that Blackness was decidedly neither acceptable nor normal. Unfortunately, despite legal and social change, large numbers of racist whites still believe the same thing to this day.

The existence of Lesbianism and male homosexuality is normal, too, traceable throughout history and across cultures. It is a society's *response* to the ongoing historical fact of homosexuality that determines whether it goes unremarked as nothing out of the ordinary, as it is in some cultures, or if it is instead greeted with violent repression, as it is in ours. At a time when Acquired Immune Deficiency Syndrome (AIDS), a disease associated with an already despised sexual minority, is occasioning mass hysteria among the heterosexual majority (including calls for firings, evictions, quarantine, imprisonment, and even execution), the way in which sexual orientation is viewed is not of mere academic concern. It is mass political organizing that has wrought the most significant changes in the status of Blacks and other people of color and that has altered society's perceptions about us and our images of ourselves. The Black Lesbian feminist movement simply continues that principled tradition of struggle.

A Black woman author's relationship to the politics of Black Lesbian feminism affects how she portrays Black Lesbian characters in fiction. In 1977, in *Toward a Black Feminist Criticism*, I had to rely upon Toni Morrison's *Sula* (1974), which did not explicitly portray a Lesbian relationship, in order to analyze a Black woman's novel with a woman-identified theme. I sought to demonstrate, however, that because of the emotional primacy of Sula and Nel's love for each other, Sula's fierce independence, and the author's critical portrayal of heterosexuality, the novel could be illuminated by a Lesbian feminist reading. Here I will focus upon three more recent works—*The Women of Brewster Place, The Color Purple*, and *Zami: A New Spelling of My Name*—which actually portray Black Lesbians, but which do so with varying degrees of verisimilitude and authenticity, dependent upon the author's relationship to and understanding of the politics of Black Lesbian experience.

Gloria Naylor's *The Women of Brewster Place* (1983) is a novel composed of seven connecting stories. In beautifully resonant language Naylor makes strong sexual political statements about the lives of working poor and working-class Black women and does not hesitate to explore the often problematic nature of their relationships with Black men—lovers, husbands, fathers, sons. Loving and supportive bonds between Black women are central to her characters' survival. However, Naylor's portrayal of a Lesbian relationship in the sixth story, "The Two," runs counter to the positive framework of women bonding she has previously established. In the context of this novel a Lesbian relationship might well embody the culmination of women's capacity to love and be committed to each other. Yet both Lesbian characters are ultimately victims. Although Naylor portrays the community's homophobia toward the lovers as unacceptable, the fate that she designs for the two women is the most brutal and negative of any in the book.

Theresa is a strong-willed individualist, while her lover Lorraine passively yearns for social acceptability. Despite their professional jobs, they have moved to a dead-end slum block because of Lorraine's fears that the residents of their two other middle-class neighborhoods suspected that they were Lesbians. It does not take long for suspicions to arise on Brewster Place, and the two women's differing reactions to the inevitable homophobia they face is a major tension in the work. Theresa accepts the fact that she is an outsider because of her Lesbianism. She does not like being ostracized, but she faces others' opinions with an attitude of defiance. In contrast, Lorraine is obsessed with garnering societal approval and would like nothing more than to blend into the straight world, despite her Lesbianism. Lorraine befriends Ben, the alcoholic building superintendent, because he is the one person on the block who does not reject her. The fact that Ben has lost his daughter and Lorraine has lost her father, because he refused to accept her Lesbianism, cements their friendship. Naylor writes:

> "When I'm with Ben, I don't feel any different from anybody else in the world."
>
> "Then he's doing you an injustice," Theresa snapped, "because we are different. And the sooner you learn that, the better off you'll be."
>
> "See, there you go again. Tee the teacher and Lorraine the student, who just can't get the lesson right. Lorraine who just wants to be a human being—a lousy human being who's somebody's daughter or somebody's friend or even somebody's enemy. But they make me feel like a freak out there, and you try to make me feel like one in here. That only place I've found some peace, Tee, is in that damp ugly basement, where I'm not different."
>
> "Lorraine." Theresa shook her head slowly. "You're a lesbian—do you understand that word?—a butch, a dyke, a lesbo, all those things that kid was shouting. Yes, I heard him! And you can run in all the basements in the world, and it won't change that, so why don't you accept it?"
>
> "I have accepted it!" Lorraine shouted. "I've accepted it all my life, and it's nothing I'm ashamed of. I lost a father because I refused to be ashamed of it—but it doesn't make me any *different* from anyone else in the world."
>
> "It makes you damned different!"
>
> . . . .
>
> "That's right! There go your precious 'theys' again. They wouldn't understand—not in Detroit, not on Brewster Place, not anywhere! And as long as they own the whole damn world, it's them and us, Sister—them and us. And that spells different!"[15]

Many a Lesbian relationship has been threatened or destroyed because of how very differently lovers may view their Lesbianism, for example, how out or closeted one or the other is willing to be. Naylor's discussion of difference represents a pressing Lesbian concern. As Lorraine and Theresa's argument shows, there are complicated elements of truth in both their positions. Lesbians and gay men are objectively different in our sexual orientations from heterosexuals. The society raises sanctions against our sexuality that range from inconvenient to violent, and that render our social status and life experiences different. On the other hand we would like to be recognized and treated as human, to have the basic rights enjoyed by heterosexuals, and, if the society cannot manage to support how we love, to at least leave us alone.

In "The Two," however, Naylor sets up the women's response to their identity as an either/or dichotomy. Lorraine's desire for acceptance, although completely comprehensible, is based upon assimilation and denial, while Naylor depicts Theresa's healthier defiance as an individual stance. In the clearest statement of resistance in the story, Theresa thinks: "If they practiced that way with each other, then they could turn back to back and beat the hell out of the world for trying to invade their territory. But she had found no such sparring partner in Lorraine, and the strain of fighting alone was beginning to show on her" (p. 136). A mediating position between complete assimilation or alienation might well evolve from some sense of connection to a Lesbian/gay community. Involvement with other Lesbians and gay men could provide a reference point and support that would help diffuse some of the straight world's power. Naylor mentions that Theresa socializes with gay men and perhaps Lesbians at a bar, but her interactions with them occur outside the action of the story. The author's decision not to portray other Lesbians and gay men, but only to allude to them, is a significant one. The reader is never given an opportunity to view Theresa or Lorraine in a context in which they are the norm. Naylor instead presents them as "the two" exceptions in an entirely heterosexual world. Both women are extremely isolated and although their relationship is loving, it also feels claustrophobic. Naylor writes:

> Lorraine wanted to be liked by the people around her. She couldn't live the way Tee did, with her head stuck in a book all the time. Tee didn't seem to need anyone. Lorraine often wondered if she even needed her. . . .
> . . . She never wanted to bother with anyone except those weirdos at the club she went to, and Lorraine hated them. They were coarse and bitter, and made fun of people who weren't like them. Well, she wasn't like them either. Why should she feel different from the people she lived around? Black people were all in the same boat—she'd come to realize this even more since they had moved to Brewster—and if they didn't row together, they would sink together. (p. 142)

Lorraine's rejection of other Lesbians and gay men is excruciating, as is the self-hatred that obviously prompts it. It is painfully ironic that she considers herself in the same boat with Black people in the story, who are heterosexual, most of whom ostracize her, but not with Black people who are Lesbian and gay. The one time that Lorraine actually decides to go to the club by herself, ignoring Theresa's warning that she won't have a good time without her, is the night that she is literally destroyed.

Perhaps the most positive element in "The Two" is how accurately Naylor depicts and subtly condemns Black homophobia. Sophie, a neighbor who lives across the airshaft from Lorraine and Theresa, is the "willing carrier" of the rumor about them, though not necessarily its initiator. Naylor writes:

> Sophie had plenty to report that day. Ben had said it was terrible in there. No, she didn't know exactly what he had seen, but you can imagine—and they did. Confronted with the difference that had been thrust into their predictable world, they reached into their imaginations and, using an ancient pattern, weaved themselves a reason for its existence. Out of necessity they stitched all of their secret fears and lingering childhood nightmares into this existence, because even though it was deceptive enough to try and look as they looked, talk as they talked, and do as they did, it had to have some hidden stain to invalidate it—it was impossible for them both to be right. So they leaned back, supported by the sheer weight of their numbers and comforted by the woven barrier that kept them protected from the yellow mist that enshrouded the two as they came and went on Brewster Place. (p. 132)

The fact of difference can be particularly volatile among people whose options are severely limited by racial, class, and sexual oppression, people who are already outsiders themselves.

A conversation between Mattie Michaels, an older Black woman who functions as the work's ethical and spiritual center, and her lifelong friend, Etta, further prods readers to examine their own attitudes about loving women. Etta explains:

> "Yeah, but it's different with them."
>
> "Different how?"
>
> "Well . . . " Etta was beginning to feel uncomfortable. "They love each other like you'd love a man or a man would love you—I guess."
>
> "But I've loved some women deeper than I ever loved any man," Mattie was pondering. "And there been some women who loved me more and did more for me than any man ever did."
>
> "Yeah." Etta thought for a moment. "I can second that but it's still different, Mattie. I can't exactly put my finger on it, but . . . "
>
> "Maybe it's not so different," Mattie said, almost to herself. "Maybe that's why some women get so riled up about it, 'cause they know deep down it's not so different after all." She looked at Etta. "It kinda gives you a funny feeling when you think about it that way, though."
>
> "Yeah, it does," Etta said, unable to meet Mattie's eyes. (pp. 140–41)

Whatever their opinions, it is not the women of the neighborhood who are directly responsible for Lorraine's destruction, but six actively homophobic and woman-hating teenage boys. Earlier that day Lorraine and Kiswana Browne had encountered the toughs who unleashed their sexist and homophobic violence on the two young women. Kiswana verbally bests their leader, C. C. Baker, but he is dissuaded from physically retaliating because one of the other boys reminds him: "That's Abshu's woman, and that big dude don't mind kickin' ass" (p. 163). As a Lesbian, Lorraine does not have any kind of "dude" to stand between her and the violence of other men. Although she is completely silent during the encounter, C. C.'s parting words to her are, "I'm gonna remember this, Butch!" That night when Lorraine returns from the bar alone, she walks into the alley which is the boys' turf. They are waiting for her and gang-rape her in one of the most devastating scenes in literature. Naylor describes the aftermath:

> Lorraine lay pushed up against the wall on the cold ground with her eyes staring straight up into the sky. When the sun began to warm the air and the horizon brightened, she still lay there, her mouth crammed with paper bag, her dress pushed up under her breasts, her bloody pantyhose hanging from her thighs. She would have stayed there forever and have simply died from starvation or exposure if nothing around her had moved. (p. 171)

She glimpses Ben sitting on a garbage can at the other end of the alley sipping wine. In a bizarre twist of an ending Lorraine crawls through the alley and mauls him with a brick she happens to find as she makes her way toward him. Lorraine's supplicating cries of " 'Please. Please.' . . . the only word she was fated to utter again and again for the rest of her life" conclude the story (pp. 171, 173).

I began thinking about "The Two" because of a conversation I had with another Black Lesbian who seldom comes in contact with other Lesbians and who has not been active in the feminist movement. Unlike other women with whom I had discussed the work, she was not angry, disappointed, or disturbed by it, but instead thought it was an effective portrayal of Lesbians and homophobia. I was taken aback because I had found Naylor's depiction of our lives so completely demoralizing and not particularly realistic. I thought about another friend who told me she found the story so upsetting she was never able to finish it. And of another who had actually rewritten the ending so that Mattie hears Lorraine's screams before she is raped and saves her. In this "revised version," Theresa is an undercover cop, who also hears her lover's screams, comes into the alley with a gun, and blows the boys away. I was so mystified and intrigued by the first woman's defense of Naylor's perspective that I went back to examine the work.

According to the criteria I have suggested, although the Lesbian characters in "The Two" lack authenticity, the story possesses a certain level of verisimilitude. The generalized homophobia that the women face, which culminates in retaliatory rape and near murderous decimation, is quite true to life. Gay and Lesbian newspapers provide weekly accounts, which sometimes surface in the mainstream media, of the constant violence leveled at members of our communities. What feels disturbing and inauthentic to me is how utterly hopeless Naylor's view of Lesbian existence is. Lorraine and Theresa are classically unhappy homosexuals of the type who populated white literature during a much earlier era, when the only options for the "deviant" were isolation, loneliness, mental illness, suicide, or death.

In her second novel, *Linden Hills* (1985), Naylor indicates that Black gay men's options are equally grim. In a review of the work, Jewelle Gomez writes:

> One character disavows a liaison with his male lover in order to marry the appropriate woman and inherit the coveted Linden Hills home. . . . We receive so little personal information about him that his motivations are obscure. For a middle-class, educated gay man to be blind to alternative lifestyles in 1985 is not inconceivable but it's still hard to accept the melodrama of his arranged marriage without screaming "dump the girl and buy a ticket to Grand Rapids!" Naylor's earlier novel [*The Women of Brewster Place*] presented a similar limitation. While she admirably attempts to portray black gays as integral to the fabric of black life she seems incapable of imagining black gays functioning as healthy, average people. In her fiction, although they are not at fault, gays must still be made to pay. This makes her books sound like a return to the forties, not a chronicle of the eighties.[16]

Gomez's response speaks to the problems that many Lesbian feminists have with Naylor's versions of our lives, her persistent message that survival is hardly possible. I do not think we simply want "happy endings," although some do occur for Lesbians both in literature and in life, but an indication of the spirit of survival and resistance which has made the continuance of Black Lesbian and gay life possible throughout the ages.

In considering the overall impact of "The Two," I realized that because it is critical of homophobia, it is perhaps an effective story for a heterosexual audience. But because its portrayal of Lesbianism is so negative, its message even to heterosexuals is ambiguous. A semi-sympathetic straight reader's response might well be: "It's a shame something like that had to happen, but I guess that's what you get for being queer." The general public does not want to know that it is possible to be a Lesbian of whatever color and not merely survive, but thrive. And neither does a heterosexual publishing industry want to provide them with this information.

The impact of the story upon Lesbian readers is quite another matter. I imagine what might happen if a Black woman who is grappling with defining her sexuality and who has never had the opportunity to read anything else about Lesbians, particularly Black ones, were to read "The Two" as a severely cautionary tale. Justifiably, she might go no further in her exploration, forever denying her feelings. She might eventually have sexual relationships with other women, but remain extremely closeted. Or she might commit suicide. As a Black Lesbian reader, I find Naylor's dire pessimism about our possibilities to be the crux of my problems with "The Two."

Alice Walker's portrayal of a Lesbian relationship in her novel *The Color Purple* (1982) is as optimistic as Naylor's is despairing. Celie and Shug's love, placed at the center of the work and set in a rural southern community between the World Wars, is unique in the history of African-American fiction. The fact that a book with a Black Lesbian theme by a Black woman writer achieved massive critical acclaim, became a bestseller, and was made into a major Hollywood film is unprecedented in the history of the world. It is *The Color Purple* which homophobes and antifeminists undoubtedly refer to when they talk about how "many" books currently have both Black Lesbian subject matter and an unsparing critique of misogyny in the Black community. For Black Lesbians, however, especially writers, the book has been inspirational. Reading it we think it just may be possible to be a Black Lesbian and live to tell about it. It may be possible for us to write it down and actually have somebody read it as well.

When I first read *The Color Purple* in galleys in the spring of 1982, I believed it was a classic. I become more convinced every time I read it. Besides great storytelling, perfect Black language, killingly subtle Black women's humor, and an unequivocal Black feminist stance, it is also a deeply philosophical and spiritual work. It is marvelously gratifying to read discussions of nature, love, beauty, God, good, evil, and the meaning of life in the language of our people. The book is like a jewel. Any way you hold it to the light you will always see something new reflected.

The facet of the novel under consideration here is Walker's approach to Lesbianism, but before going further with that discussion, it is helpful to understand that the work is also a fable. The complex simplicity with which Walker tells her story, the archetypal and timeless Black southern world in which it is set, the clear-cut conflicts between good and evil, the complete transformations undergone by several of the major characters, and the huge capacity of the book to teach are all signs that *The Color Purple* is not merely a novel, but a visionary tale. That it is a fable may account partially for the depiction of a Lesbian relationship unencumbered by homophobia or fear of it and entirely lacking in self-scrutiny about the implications of Lesbian identity.

It may be Walker's conscious decision to deal with her readers' potentially negative reactions by using the disarming strategy of writing as if women falling in love with each other were quite ordinary, an average occurrence which does not even need to be specifically remarked. In the "real world" the complete ease with which Celie and Shug move as lovers through a totally heterosexual milieu would be improbable, not to say amazing. Their total acceptance is one clue that this is indeed an inspiring fable, a picture of what the world could be if only human beings were ready to create it. A friend told me about a discussion of the book in a Black writers' workshop she conducted. An older Black woman in the class asserted: "When that kind of business happens, like happened between Shug and Celie, you know there's going to be talk." The woman was not reacting to *Purple* as a fable or even as fiction, but as a "real" story, applying her knowledge of what would undoubtedly happen in real life where most people just aren't ready to deal with Lesbianism and don't want to be.

Because the novel is so truthful, particularly in its descriptions of sexual oppression and to a lesser extent racism, the reader understandably might question those aspects of the fable which are not as plausible. Even within the story itself, it is conceivable that a creature as mean-spirited as Mr.—— might have something to say about Shug, the love of his life, and Celie, his wife, sleeping together in his own house. For those of us who experience homophobia on a daily basis and who often live in fear of being discovered by the wrong person(s), like the teenage thugs in "The Two," we naturally wonder how Celie and Shug, who do not hide their relationship, get away with it.

Another fabulous aspect of Celie's and Shug's relationship is that there are no references to how they think about themselves as Lesbian lovers in a situation where they are the only ones. Although Celie is clearly depicted as a woman who at the very least is not attracted to men and who is generally repulsed by them, I am somewhat hesitant to designate her as a Lesbian because it is not a term that she would likely apply to herself and neither, obviously, would the people around her. In a conversation with Mr.—— in the latter part of the book Celie explains how she feels:

> He say, Celie, tell me the truth. You don't like me cause I'm a man?
> I blow my nose. Take off they pants, I say, and men look like frogs to me.
> No matter how you kiss 'em, as far as I'm concern, frogs is what they stay.
> I see, he say.[17]

Shug, on the other hand, is bisexual, another contemporary term that does not necessarily apply within the cultural and social context Walker has established. There is the implication that this is among her first, if not only sexual relationship with another woman. The first and only time within the novel when Shug and Celie make love, Walker writes:

> She say, I love you, Miss Celie. And then she haul off and kiss me on the mouth.
> *Um*, she say, like she surprise. I kiss her back, say, *um*, too. Us kiss and kiss till us can't hardly kiss no more. Then us touch each other.
> I don't know nothing bout it, I say to Shug.
> I don't know much, she say. (p. 109)

Despite her statement of inexperience, Shug is a wonderfully sensual and attractive woman who takes pleasure in all aspects of living from noticing "the color purple in a field" to making love with whomever. When Shug tries to explain to

Celie why she has taken up with a nineteen-year-old boy, the two women's differing perspectives and sexual orientations are obvious. Walker writes:

> But Celie, she say. I have to make you understand. Look, she say. I'm gitting old. I'm fat. Nobody think I'm good looking no more, but you. Or so I thought. He's nineteen. A baby. How long can it last?
> He's a man. I write on the paper.
> Yah, she say. He is. And I know how you feel about men. But I don't feel that way. I would never be fool enough to take any of them seriously, she say, but some mens can be a lots of fun.
> Spare me, I write. (p. 220)

Eventually Shug comes back to Celie and Walker implies that they will live out their later years together. The recouplings and reunions that occur in the novel might also indicate that the story is more fantasy than fact. But in Celie and Shug's case, the longevity of their relationship is certainly a validation of love between women.

The day Shug returns, Celie shows her her new bedroom. Walker writes:

> She go right to the little purple frog on my mantelpiece.
> What this? she ast.
> Oh, I say, a little something Albert carve for me. (p. 248)

Not only is this wickedly amusing after Celie and Mr. ——'s discussion about "frogs," but Mr. ——'s tolerance at being described as such to the point of his making a joke-gift for Celie seems almost too good to be true. Indeed Mr. ——'s transformation from evil no-count to a sensitive human being is one of the most miraculous one could find anywhere. Those critics and readers who condemn the work because they find the depiction of men so "negative" never seem to focus on how nicely most of them turn out in the end. Perhaps these transformations go unnoticed because in Walker's woman-centered world, in order to change, they must relinquish machismo and violence, the very thought of which would be fundamentally disruptive to the nonfeminist reader's world-view. It is no accident that Walker has Celie, who has become a professional seamstress and designer of pants, teach Mr.—— to sew, an ideal way to symbolize just how far he has come. In the real world, where former husbands of Lesbian mothers take their children away with the support of the patriarchal legal system, and in some cases beat or even murder their former wives, very few men would say what Mr.—— says to Celie about Shug: "I'm real sorry she left you, Celie. I remembered how I felt when she left me" (p. 238). But in the world of *The Color Purple* a great deal is possible.

One of the most beautiful and familiar aspects of the novel is the essential and supportive bonds between Black women. The only other person Celie loves before she meets Shug is her long-lost sister, Nettie. Although neither ever gets an answer, the letters they write to each other for decades, and Celie's letters to God before she discovers that Nettie is alive, comprise the entire novel. The work joyously culminates when Nettie, accompanied by Celie's children who were taken away from her in infancy, return home.

Early in the novel Celie "sins against" another woman's spirit and painfully bears the consequences. She tells her stepson, Harpo, to beat his wife, Sofia, if she doesn't mind him. Soon Celie is so upset about what she has done that she is unable to sleep at night. Sofia, one of the most exquisitely defiant characters in Black women's fiction, fights Harpo right back and when she finds out Celie's part in Harpo's changed behavior comes to confront her. When Celie confesses that she advised Harpo to beat Sofia because she was jealous of Sofia's ability to stand up for herself, the weight is lifted from her soul, the women become fast friends, and she "sleeps like a baby."

When Shug decides that Celie needs to leave Mr.——— and go with her to Memphis, accompanied by Mary Agnes (Squeak), Harpo's lover of many years, they make the announcement at a family dinner. Walker writes:

> You was all rotten children, I say. You made my life a hell on earth. And your daddy here ain't dead horse's shit.
>
> Mr.——— reach over to slap me. I jab my case knife in his hand.
>
> You bitch, he say. What will people say, you running off to Memphis like you don't have a house to look after?
>
> Shug say, Albert. Try to think like you got some sense. Why any woman give a shit what people think is a mystery to me.
>
> Well, say Grady, trying to bring light. A woman can't get a man if peoples talk.
>
> Shug look at me and us giggle. Then us laugh sure nuff. Then Squeak start to laugh. Then Sofia. All us laugh and laugh.
>
> Shug say, Ain't they something? Us say um *hum*, and slap the table, wipe the water from our eyes.
>
> Harpo look at Squeak. Shut up Squeak, he say. It bad luck for women to laugh at men.
>
> She say, Okay. She sit up straight, suck in her breath, try to press her face together.
>
> He look at Sofia. She look at him and laugh in his face. I already had my bad luck, she say. I had enough to keep me laughing the rest of my life. (p. 182)

This marvelously hilarious scene is one of countless examples in the novel of Black women's staunch solidarity. As in *The Women of Brewster Place*, women's caring for each other makes life possible; but in *The Color Purple* Celie and Shug's relationship is accepted as an integral part of the continuum of women loving each other, while in the more realistic work, Lorraine and Theresa are portrayed as social pariahs.

If one accepts that *The Color Purple* is a fable or at the very least has fablelike elements, judgments of verisimilitude and authenticity are necessarily affected. Celie and Shug are undeniably authentic as Black women characters—complex, solid, and whole—but they are not necessarily authentic as Lesbians. Their lack of self-consciousness as Lesbians, the lack of scrutiny their relationship receives from the outside world, and their isolation from other Lesbians make *The Color Purple*'s categorization as a Lesbian novel problematic. It does not appear that it was Walker's intent to create a work that could be definitively or solely categorized as such.

The question of categorization becomes even more interesting when one examines critical responses to the work, particularly in the popular media. Reviews seldom mention that Celie and Shug are lovers. Some critics even go so far as to describe them erroneously as good friends. The fact that their relationship is simply "there" in the novel and not explicitly called attention to as Lesbian might also account for a mass heterosexual audience's capacity to accept the work, although the novel has of course also been homophobically attacked.[18] As a Black Lesbian feminist reader, I have questions about how accurate it is to identify Walker's characters as Lesbians at the same time that I am moved by the vision of a world, unlike this one, where Black women are not forced to lose their families, their community, or their lives, because of whom they love.

A realistic depiction of African-American Lesbian experience would neither be a complete idyll nor a total nightmare. Audre Lorde terms *Zami: A New Spelling of My Name* (1982) a "biomythography," a combination of autobiography, history, and myth. I have chosen to discuss it here, because it is the one extended prose work of which I am aware that approaches Black Lesbian experience with *both* verisimilitude and authenticity. *Zami* is an essentially autobiographical work, but the poet's eye, ear, and tongue give the work stylistic richness often associated with well-crafted fiction. At least two other Black women critics, Barbara Christian and Jewelle Gomez, have included *Zami* in their analyses of Black Lesbians in fiction.[19] Because *Zami* spans genres and carves out a unique place in African-American literature as the first full-length autobiographical work by an established Black Lesbian writer, it will undoubtedly continue to be grouped with other creative prose about Black Lesbians.

The fact that *Zami* is autobiographical might be assumed to guarantee its realism. But even when writing autobiographically, an author can pick and choose details, can create a persona that has little or nothing to do with her own particular reality, or she might fabricate an artificial persona with whom the reader cannot possibly identify. A blatant example of this kind of deceptive strategy might be an autobiographical work by a Lesbian that fails to mention that this is indeed who she is; of course there are other less extreme omissions and distortions. Undoubtedly, Lorde has selected the material she includes in the work, and the selectivity of memory is also operative. Yet this work is honest, fully rounded, and authentic. It is not coincidental that of the three works considered here, *Zami* has the most to tell the reader about the texture of Black Lesbian experience and that it is written by an out Black Lesbian feminist. The candor and specificity with which Lorde approaches her life are qualities that would enhance Black Lesbian writing in the future.

Zami is a Carriacou word "for women who work together as friends and lovers."[20] Just as the title implies, *Zami* is woman-identified from the outset and thoroughly suffused with an eroticism focusing on women. Lorde connects her Lesbianism to the model her mother, Linda, provided—her pervasive, often intimidating, strength; her fleeting sensuality when her harsh veneer was lifted—and also to her place of origin, the Grenadian island of Carriacou, where a word already existed to describe who Linda's daughter would become. As in the two novels *The Color Purple* and *The Women of Brewster Place*, in *Zami* relationships between women are at the center of the work. Here they are complex, turbulent, painful, passionate, and essential to the author's survival.

Although Lorde continuously explores the implications of being a Black Lesbian and she has an overt consciousness about her Lesbianism which is missing from Naylor's and Walker's works, she does not define Lesbianism as a problem in and of itself. Despite homophobia, particularly in the left of the McCarthy era; despite isolation from other Black women because she is gay; and despite primal loneliness because of her many levels of difference, Lorde assumes that her Lesbianism, like her Blackness, is a given, a fact of life which she has neither to justify nor explain. This is an extremely strong and open-ended stance from which to write about Black Lesbian experience, since it enables the writer to deal with the complexity of Lesbianism and what being a Black Lesbian means in a specific time and place. Lorde's position allows Black Lesbian experience to be revealed from the inside out. The absence of agonized doubts about her sexual orientation and the revelation of the actual joys of being a Lesbian, including lush and recognizable descriptions of physical passion between women, make *Zami* seem consciously written for a Lesbian reader. This is a significant point because so little is ever written with us in mind, and also because who an author considers her audience to be definitely affects her voice and the levels of authenticity she may be able to achieve. Writing from an avowedly Black Lesbian perspective with Black Lesbian readers in mind does not mean that a work will be inaccessible or inapplicable to non-Black and non-Lesbian readers. Works like *Zami*, which are based in the experiences of writers outside the "mainstream," provide a vitally different perspective on human experience and may even reveal new ways of thinking about supposedly settled questions. Or, as Celie puts it in *The Color Purple*: "If he [God] ever listened to poor colored women the world would be a different place, I can tell you" (p. 175). It would be more different still if "he" also listened to Lesbians.

The fact that *Zami* is written from an unequivocally Black Lesbian and feminist perspective undoubtedly explains why it is the one book of the three under discussion that is published by an alternative press, why it was turned down by at least a dozen trade publishers, including one that specializes in gay titles. The white male editor at that supposedly sympathetic house returned the manuscript saying, "If only you were just one," Black or Lesbian. The combination is obviously too much for the trade publishing establishment to handle. We bring news that others do not want to hear. It is unfortunate that the vast majority of the readers of *The Women of Brewster Place* and *The Color Purple* will never have the opportunity to read *Zami*.

Lorde's description of Black "gay-girl" life in the Greenwich Village of the 1950s is fascinating, if for no other reason than that it reveals a piece of our cultural history. What is even more intriguing is her political activist's sense of how the struggles of women during that era helped shape our contemporary movement and how many of our current issues, especially the desire to build a Black Lesbian community, were very much a concern at that time. The author's search for other Black Lesbians and her lovingly detailed descriptions of the fragments of community she finds give this work an atmosphere of reality missing in "The Two" and *The Color Purple*. Unlike Lorraine and Theresa and Celie and Shug, Lorde is achingly aware of her need for peers. She writes:

> I remember how being young and Black and gay and lonely felt. A lot of
> it was fine, feeling I had the truth and the light and the key, but a lot of it
> was purely hell.

> There were no mothers, no sisters, no heroes. We had to do it alone, like our sister Amazons, the riders on the loneliest outposts of the kingdom of Dahomey. . . . There were not enough of us. But we surely tried. (pp. 176–177)

> Every Black Woman I ever met in the Village in those years had some part in my survival, large or small, if only as a figure in the head-count at the Bag on a Friday night.
>
> Black lesbians in the Bagatelle faced a world only slightly less hostile than the outer world which we had to deal with every day on the outside—that world which defined us as doubly nothing because we were Black and because we were Woman—that world which raised our blood pressures and shaped our furies and our nightmares. . . . All of us who survived those common years have to be a little proud. A lot proud. Keeping ourselves together and on our own tracks, however wobbly, was like trying to play the Dinizulu War Chant or a Beethoven sonata on a tin dog-whistle. (p. 225)

The humor, tenacity, and vulnerability which Lorde brings to her version of being in "the life" are very precious. Here is something to grab hold of, a place to see one's face reflected. Despite the daily grind of racism, homophobia, sexual, and class oppression, compounded by the nonsolutions of alcohol, drugs, suicide, and death at an early age, some women did indeed make it.

Lorde also describes the much more frequent interactions and support available from white Lesbians who were in the numerical majority. Just as they are now, relationships between Black and white women in the 1950s were often undermined by racism, but Lorde documents that some women were at least attempting to deal with their differences. She writes:

> However imperfectly, we tried to build a community of sorts where we could, at the very least, survive within a world we correctly perceived to be hostile to us; we talked endlessly about how best to create that mutual support which twenty years later was being discussed in the women's movement as a brand new concept. Lesbians were probably the only Black and white women in New York City in the fifties who were making any real attempt to communicate with each other; we learned lessons from each other, the values of which were not lessened by what we did not learn. (p. 179)

Lorde approaches the meaning of difference from numerous vantage points in *Zami*. In much of her work prior to *Zami* she has articulated and developed the concept of difference which has gained usage in the women's movement as a whole and in the writing of women of color specifically. From her early childhood, long before she recognizes herself as a Lesbian, the question of difference is *Zami*'s subtext, its ever-present theme. Lorde writes: *"It was in high school that I came to believe that I was different from my white classmates, not because I was Black, but because I was me"* (p. 82). Although Lorde comes of age in an era when little if any tolerance existed for those who did not conform to white male hegemony, her stance and that of her friends is one of rebellion and creative resistance, including political activism, as opposed to conformity and victimization. *Zami* mediates the versions of Lesbianism presented in *The Women of Brewster Place* and *The Color Purple*. It is not a horror story, although it reveals the difficulties of Black

Lesbian experience. It is not a fable, although it reveals the joys of a life committed to women.

Since much of her quest in *Zami* is to connect with women who recognize and share her differences, particularly other Black Lesbians, it seems fitting that the work closes with her account of a loving relationship with another Black woman, Afrekete. Several years before the two women become lovers, Lorde meets Kitty at a Black Lesbian house party in Queens. Lorde writes:

> One of the women I had met at one of these parties was Kitty.
>
> When I saw Kitty again one night years later in the Swing Rendezvous or the Pony Stable or the Page Three—that tour of second-string gay-girl bars that I had taken to making alone that sad lonely spring of 1957—it was easy to recall the St. Alban's smell of green Queens summer-night and plastic couch-covers and liquor and hair oil and women's bodies at the party where we had first met.
>
> In that brick-faced frame house in Queens, the downstairs pine-paneled recreation room was alive and pulsing with loud music, good food, and beautiful Black women in all different combinations of dress. (p. 241)

The women wear fifties dyke-chic, ranging from "skinny straight skirts" to Bermuda and Jamaica shorts. Just as the clothes, the smells, the song lyrics, and food linger in the author's mind, her fully rendered details of Black Lesbian culture resonate within the reader. I recalled this party scene while attending a dinner party at the home of two Black Lesbians in the deep South earlier this year. One of the hostesses arrived dressed impeccably in white Bermuda shorts, black knee-socks, and loafers. Her hair straightened, 1980s style much like that of the 1950s, completed my sense of déjà vu. Contemporary Black Lesbians are a part of a cultural tradition which we are just beginning to discover through interviews with older women such as Mabel Hampton and the writing of authors like Ann Allen Shockley, Anita Cornwell, Pat Parker, and Lorde.

When she meets Afrekete again, their relationship helps to counteract Lorde's loneliness following the break-up of a long-term relationship with a white woman. The bond between the women is stunningly erotic, enriched by the bond they share as Black women. Lorde writes:

> By the beginning of summer the walls of Afrekete's apartment were always warm to the touch from the heat beating down on the roof, and chance breezes through her windows rustled her plants in the window and brushed over our sweat-smooth bodies, at rest after loving.
>
> We talked sometimes about what it meant to love women, and what a relief it was in the eye of the storm, no matter how often we had to bite our tongues and stay silent. . . .
>
> Once we talked about how Black women had been committed without choice to waging our campaigns in the enemies' strongholds, too much and too often, and how our psychic landscapes had been plundered and wearied by those repeated battles and campaigns.
>
> "And don't I have the scars to prove it," she sighed. "Makes you tough though, babe, if you don't go under. And that's what I like about you; you're like me. We're both going to make it because we're both too tough and crazy not to!" And we held each other and laughed and cried about what we had

paid for that toughness, and how hard it was to explain to anyone who didn't already know it that soft and tough had to be one and the same for either to work at all, like our joy and the tears mingling on the one pillow beneath our heads. (p. 250)

The fact that this conversation occurs in 1957 is both amazing and unremarkable. Black Lesbians have a heritage far older than a few decades, a past that dates back to Africa, as Lorde herself documents in the essay "Scratching the Surface: Some Notes on Barriers to Women and Loving."[21] Lorde's authentic portrayal of one segment of that history in *Zami* enables us to see both our pasts and futures more clearly. Her work provides a vision of possibility for Black Lesbians surviving whole, despite all, which is the very least we can demand from our literature, our activism, and our lives.

Despite the homophobic exclusion and silencing of Black Lesbian writers, the creation of complex, accurate, and artistically compelling depictions of Black Lesbians in literature has been and will continue to be essential to the development of African-American women's literature as a whole. The assertion of Black women's right to autonomy and freedom, which is inherent in the lives of Black Lesbians and which is made politically explicit in Black Lesbian feminist theory and practice, has crucial implications for all women's potential liberation. Ultimately, the truth that never hurts is that Black Lesbians and specifically Black Lesbian writers are here to stay. In spite of every effort to erase us, we are committed to living visibly with integrity and courage and to telling our Black women's stories for centuries to come.

NOTES

1. Calvin Hernton, "The Sexual Mountain and Black Women Writers," *The Black Scholar* 16, no. 4 (July/August 1985); 7.

2. Barbara Christian, *Black Feminist Criticism: Perspectives on Black Women Writers* (New York: Pergamon, 1986), p. 188.

3. Audre Lorde and Ann Allen Shockley are two exceptions. They have published with both commercial and independent publishers. It should be noted that Lorde's poetry is currently published by a commercial publisher, but that all of her works of prose have been published by independent women's presses. In conversation with Lorde I have learned that *Zami: A New Spelling of My Name* was rejected by at least a dozen commercial publishers.

4. Christian, *Black Feminist Criticism*, pp. 199–200.

5. Alice Walker, "Breaking Chains and Encouraging Life," in *In Search of Our Mothers' Gardens: Womanist Prose* (New York: Harcourt Brace Jovanovich, 1984), pp. 288–289.

6. In her essay "The Black Lesbian in American Literature: An Overview," Ann Allen Shockley summarizes Jones's negative or inadequate treatment of Lesbian themes in her novels *Corregidora* and *Eva's Man* and in two of her short stories. Ann Allen Shockley, "The Black Lesbian in American Literature: An Overview," in *Home Girls: A Black Feminist Anthology*, ed. Barbara Smith (Latham, N.Y.: Kitchen Table Press, 1982), p. 89.

7. In her essay "The Failure to Transform: Homophobia in the Black Community," Cheryl Clark comments: "The black lesbian is not only absent from the pages of black political analysis, her image as a character in literature and her role as a writer are blotted out from or trivialized in literary criticism written by black women." Clarke also cites

examples of such omissions. In *Home Girls*, ed. Smith, pp. 204–205.

8. Barbara Smith, "Racism and Women's Studies," in *All the Women Are White, All the Blacks Are Men, But Some of Us Are Brave: Black Women's Studies,* ed. Gloria Hull, Patricia Bell Scott, and Barbara Smith (New York: Feminist Press, 1981), p. 49.

9. Mitsuye Yamada, "Invisibility Is an Unnatural Disaster: Reflections of an Asian American Woman," in *This Bridge Called My Back: Writings by Radical Women of Color,* ed. Cherríe Moraga and Gloria Anzaldúa (Latham, N.Y.: Kitchen Table Press, 1984), pp. 35–40.

10. Cheryl Clarke, *Narratives: Poems in the Tradition of Black Women* (Latham, N.Y.: Kitchen Table Press, 1983), p. 15.

11. Jewelle Gomez, in *Home Girls,* ed. Smith, p. 122.

12. Langston Hughes, "The Negro Artist and the Racial Mountain," in *Voices from the Harlem Renaissance*, ed. Nathan Huggins (New York: Oxford, 1976), p. 309. It is interesting to note that recent research has revealed that Hughes and a number of other major figures of the Harlem Renaissance were gay. See Charles Michael Smith, "Bruce Nugent: Bohemian of the Harlem Renaissance," in *In the Life: A Black Gay Anthology,* ed. Joseph F. Beam (Boston: Alyson, 1986), pp. 213–214 and selections by Langston Hughes in *Gay and Lesbian Poetry in Our Time: An Anthology,* ed. Carl Morse and Joan Larkin (New York: St. Martin's, 1988), pp. 204–206.

13. Paul Laurence Dunbar, "We Wear the Mask," in *The Life and Works of Paul Laurence Dunbar,* ed. Wiggins (New York: Kraus, 1971), p. 184.

14. Audre Lorde, "There Is No Hierarchy of Oppressions," in *The Council on Interracial Books for Children Bulletin, Homophobia and Education: How to Deal with Name-Calling,* ed. Leonore Gordon, Vol. 14, nos. 3 & 4 (1983), 9.

15. Gloria Naylor, *The Women of Brewster Place* (New York: Penguin, 1983), pp. 165–166. All subsequent references to this work will be cited in the text.

16. Jewelle Gomez, "Naylor's Inferno," *The Women's Review of Books* 2, no. 11 (August 1985), 8.

17. Alice Walker, *The Color Purple* (New York: Washington Square, 1982), p. 224. All subsequent references to this work will be cited in the text.

18. In his essay "Who's Afraid of Alice Walker?" Calvin Hernton describes the "hordes of . . . black men (and some women)" who condemned both the novel and the film of *The Color Purple* all over the country. He singles out journalist Tony Brown as a highly visible leader of these attacks. Brown both broadcast television shows and wrote columns about a book and movie he admitted neither to have read nor seen. Hernton raises the question, "Can it be that the homophobic, nitpicking screams of denial against *The Color Purple* are motivated out of envy, jealousy and guilt, rather than out of any genuine concern for the well-being of black people?" Calvin Hernton, *The Sexual Mountain and Black Women Writers* (New York: Anchor, 1987), pp. 30–36.

19. Christian, *Black Feminist Criticism,* pp. 187–210. Gomez, in *Home Girls,* ed. Smith, pp. 118–119.

20. Audre Lorde, *Zami: A New Spelling of My Name* (Freedom, Calif.: Crossing, 1983), p. 255. All subsequent references to this work will be cited in the text.

21. Audre Lorde, *Sister Outsider* (Freedom, Calif.: Crossing, 1984), pp. 45–52.

FEMINIST AND ETHNIC LITERARY THEORIES IN ASIAN AMERICAN LITERATURE

(1993)

Johnella Butler notes that women's studies scholars in their "task of changing the world . . . are cast with [Black studies, Asian American studies, Latino studies, and American Indian studies] with whom in many ways we are uneasy." The tensions between women's studies and ethnic studies, according to Butler, rise from the fact that women's studies scholarship, theory, and pedagogy are being radically altered by the scholarship of women of color; that women's studies "is privileged because it is peopled largely by white women who move more freely than men or women of color throughout the academy."[1] Butler's candid account of the contested site within women's studies to accommodate the experiences and scholarship of women of color counters the usual attempts to gloss over the dis-ease that she has characterized in Euro-American feminist responses to ethnic scholarship.

Butler's account recognizes the absence of symmetrical, like-minded relations between the two groups, one concerned with gender issues, especially the imbalance of power and the attempt to rectify these historical imbalances between women and men, and the other concerned with analysis of race and ethnicity, specifically, the imbalance of power between dominant white groups and peoples of color and the attempt to change the unequal sets of relationships. The asymmetrical goals of feminist and ethnic scholars within the same instructional structures have given rise to conflict and hostility.[2] The gender/ethnic split is mirrored, moreover, in *both* communities, among white feminists who, according to some women of color, have been defining feminism in narrow terms privileged by their positions as whites; and among men of color who, "desiring to maintain power over 'the women' at all costs, have been among the most willing reinforcers of the fears and myths about the women's movement, attempting to scare us away from figuring things out for ourselves."[3]

Nevertheless, feminist and ethnic literary discourses, although demonstrating this asymmetry in relation to each other, are often inextricably intertwined. Both practices have led to personally charged readings whose impetus and power relate critically suspect notions such as experience, the subjective, and the local, to ideologies undergirding literary evaluation. Feminist and ethnic literary criticisms resist and interrogate the claim that aesthetic criteria form a dominant, autonomous, objective, privileged position.[4] Both are said to lack a specifying theory. Although feminist literary criticism is seen as more sociopolitically driven than literary by critics such as Ellen Messer-Davidow,[5] other critics such as Hazel V. Carby have questioned the value of an essentially Black theory and practice of criticism, noting of Henry Louis Gates's ethnic-based theory that "the exposition of uniquely black literary strategies is accomplished as much through the work of Geoffrey Hartman, Harold Bloom, Jacques Lacan and others as it is through the insights of a wide range of African-American critics including Houston Baker, Amiri Imamu Baraka and Sterling Brown."[6] Generally, feminist and ethnic critics oppose hegemonic disciplines. Many have presented themselves as cultural pluralists and revisionists, calling attention to, among other things, neglected or omitted texts that, even by established standards, should be admitted into the canon.[7] They operate as interventionists disrupting the totalizing naturalization of white male culture.

These common purposes, however, do not imply that feminist and ethnic criticisms share inherently sympathetic identities or areas of overlap that allow them to synthesize critical orientations. Even when, bound together in a common cause of revising the canon, both feminist and ethnic critics select similar ethnic texts, one cannot assume that they share integral or identical traditions. My essay attempts to unpack textual instances where ethnic and feminist issues have intersected, to analyze how their diverging emphases necessitate an ethnic-cultural nuancing of conventional Euro-American feminist positions on gender/power relations and a feminist critique of ethnic-specific identity. For my argument, I focus on Asian American women's writing. In the analysis of ethnic identity politics and feminist ideological conjunctions, I argue, first, that Asian American (restricted here to Japanese, Chinese, and Korean American) literature has been an active site of masculinist views and feminist resistance, and, second, that these women's texts are symptomatic of the struggle to refigure the subject between the often oppositional demands of ethnic and gender identity. The tension, to my mind, is not merely or wholly over the question of who should be read—female or male writers, whose canon is it, anyway?—but over how representation of the subject is negotiated between ethnic and feminist thematics.

The polarities between feminist and masculinist assertions of identity were already in place in the traditional East Asian patriarchal constructions of society.[8] They were further exacerbated by a history of racism (similar histories apply to Chinese, Japanese, South Asian, and Filipino male immigration and delayed or difficult entry for women) that disempowered Asian males and separated them for long periods from women and families, and by the entry of Asian social norms into a differently restrictive American culture.[9] These polarities can be seen as still operative in the debates over Asian American women marrying out and in the debates that occasionally flare up to illuminate the problems of power relations between Asian American women and men.[10]

In was only in the 1970s that the notion of a body of Asian American literature recognizable as a separate canon became common. This literature can be said to represent the paradoxical phenomenon known as a "new tradition." Even as the texts are self-conscious expressions of "a new political consciousness and identity," their commentaries locate them in a "recovered" ethnic history. Texts like Maxine Hong Kingston's *The Woman Warrior: Memoirs of a Girlhood among Ghosts* and *China Men* are like a slow development of photographs taken years ago; even as their textuality appears for the first time before our eyes, we are reminded that the images were posed in a time already past, that history and textuality form one subject.[11] The commentator observes the coloration of the text as it appears for the first time with a postmodern consciousness of the text's belatedness, an awareness that the images are to be understood in the contexts of a lapidary of discourses on and from the past: memoir, myth, family and community history, folk tales, talk-story.[12] This insistence on past narratives, whether as Old World culture and values, immigrant history, race suffering, communal traditions, or earlier other language traces, is a marked feature of much Asian American literature and criticism, just as the recovery of a woman's culture, woman's language, and neglected women's texts and traditions forms a major feature of feminist criticism.[13]

DEFINING THE FIELD

Three publication events mark the increasing acceptance of an "Asian American" canon: the appearance of three anthologies (*Asian American Authors*, 1972; *Asian-American Heritage: An Anthology of Prose and Poetry*, 1974; *Aiiieeeee!: An Anthology of Asian-American Writers*, 1974) in the early seventies; the first (and still the only) book-length study of the literature, Elaine H. Kim's *Asian American Literature: An Introduction to the Writings and Their Social Context* in 1982; and the 1988 *Asian American Literature: An Annotated Bibliography* (King-kok Cheung and Stan Yogi) which conferred academic legitimacy to the field through its publication by the Modern Language Association Press.[14] These publications relate coherent historiographies of an Asian American literary tradition and of the contesting of that tradition. In doing so, they also provide a grounding for the culture and affect its identity formation for the future.

Like feminist critics, these ethnic-identified critics share the task of identifying stereotypes and countering them. Their criticism in the 1970s, exemplified by the influential introduction of *Aiiieeeee!*, was restricted to a critique of stereotypes of the emasculated Asian American male. These authors modeled their thinking on the militant African American antiacademic rhetoric manifested in Ishmael Reed's work.[15] Unfortunately, they also adopted the sexist stance of Reed's position and the attack on male stereotypes reiterated and reinforced stereotypes of females. In the *Aiiieeeee!* Introduction, the animus against stereotypes appears specially reserved for women writers of Chinese American descent who were accused of collaborating with white supremacists in propagating the stereotypes of the submissive, patriotic, model, and "dual-personality" (a psychological term used by sociologists of the fifties to explain the consequences of biculturality on Japanese Americans) Asian American.[16]

Chinese American women writers were conspicuous for their absence from these anthologies. In the issue of the *Yardbird Reader* (1974) guest edited by Frank Chin and Shawn Wong, only four women writers are represented: two Japanese American short story writers, Hisaye Yamamoto and Wakako Yamauchi; a Filipina poet, Cyn. Zarco; and a Chinese-German American poet, Mei Berssenbrugge; as against eleven men, of whom eight are Chinese Americans. In *Aiiieeeee!*, again only four women writers are included against ten men, and only one of the women was Chinese American as opposed to five Chinese American male writers.

One may be led to conclude from these selections that this ethnic literature up to the 1970s was full of talented male writers and most deficient in women writers. The 1991 *Big Aiiieeeee!*, which despite the title is a completely different anthology from the 1974 anthology, is even more severe in its exclusion of Chinese American women writers, who are entirely unrepresented.[17]

That the 1974 selection is distorted is evident from the editors' introduction, which is replete with references to Chinese American women scholars and writers whose works are critiqued and denigrated. The 1974 anthology can be said to be superseded by the 1991 anthology, but its editorial arguments are still significant today as they helped form a generation of opinion on Asian American cultural identity. The opening sentence of this introduction signals the content of that quarrel—who owns the ground of this ethnic writing: "In the 140-year history of Asian America, fewer than ten works of fiction and poetry have been published by American-born Chinese, Japanese, and Filipino writers." The statement suggests that the anthology will include as Asian American only the work of American-born citizens of Asian descent. Yet the anthology does not bear out this conclusion, as Carlos Bulosan, Louis Chu, Oscar Penaranda, and possibly Sam Tagatac are foreign-born. The preface to the anthology similarly negotiates this categorical ambivalence. The anthology is claimed as "exclusively Asian-American. That means Filipino-, Chinese-, and Japanese-Americans, American born and raised, who got their China and Japan from the radio, off the silver screen, from television, out of comic books." But the editors equivocate later to include the foreign-born, explaining that "between the writer's actual birth and the birth of sensibility, we have used the birth of the sensibility as the measure of being an Asian-American."[18] Although a recognizable ethnicized sensibility is assumed, it is defined negatively, as one that has "no actual memories of life in Asia." Asian American, therefore, is a category reserved only for citizens who are totally grounded in American life and who have received their images of Asia from an American collective and popular imagination.

The facts of Asian immigration to the United States, however, are such that any definition of what an Asian American sensibility is must always be provisional. The first Chinese entered the United States in 1820; by 1882, when the Chinese Exclusion Act was passed by Congress, there were 107,488 Chinese in the United States, less than 0.02 percent of the population; when the act was repealed in 1943, Chinese made up only 0.05 percent of the population.[19] Similar restrictive and repressive legislation kept the numbers of Japanese, Filipino, Korean, and other Asian Americans low. The changes in the immigration laws in 1965 that altered the race quota to a nationality criterion, and the Family Reunification Act of 1968 led to an explosion of the Asian population; "the population of Americans of Asian and Pacific Island descent has more than doubled in the past decade—up from an estimated 3.5 million in 1980 to about 7.3 million in 1990, according to the U.S. Census Bureau. California leads the nation with about 2.8 million people of Asian and Pacific Island descent—up 127% since 1980."[20] In the face of the rapid increase and changing ethnic cultures of non-American-born Asian Americans now resident in the United States, to limit this literature to the writings produced by American-born Asians is indefensibly arbitrary. Indeed, Cheung and Yogi's *Asian American Literature: An Annotated Bibliography* gave the body of Asian American writing a contemporary breadth of references that

Aiiieeeee! and its successor, *The Big Aiiieeeee!* did not even attempt. The bibliography substantiates the recent transformations of the field, particularly in regard to the contributions from the newer Asian immigrant groups—the Korean, Filipino, Vietnamese, South Asian, and Southeast Asian, each of whom is given a separate category. Containing 3,395 items, the bibliography is already in need of a new edition, particularly in order to include a cross-reference to writing by Asians and works by and of Asian American women.

Aiiieeeee! set out to be more than a collection of works by writers of Asian descent. The editors asserted an authority as culture makers and namers, authorizing their version of Asian American sensibility. In their introduction, they assailed the assumption of continuity between Asian American culture and Asian culture. The positive valuation of Asian culture undergirding the American perception of the Asian American, they argued, was "a work of racist art" to keep the Asian American estranged from America. This reified representation insists on an identity as Old World Asian, preventing the perception of dynamism, hybridity, New World vitality, and other more interactive qualities that characterize a burgeoning ethnic culture in the United States. Offering Black American culture as their model, the editors argued that Asian Americans should "invent" their culture, not passively accept the distortions of high Asian cultural elements that white Americans foist on them. Consequently, they certified as authentic only those writers who exhibited "Asian American," rather than an Asian or Euro-American, sensibility. This sensibility, the editors concluded, was specifically constructed through male-centered language and culture: "Language is the medium of culture and the people's sensibility, including the style of manhood. . . . On the simplest level, a man in any culture speaks for himself. Without a language of his own, he is no longer a man."[21] The assumption, therefore, is that Asian American men who assert "manhood" decide, possess, and exhibit the legitimate cultural national sensibility.

Elaine H. Kim's chapter, "Chinatown Cowboys and Warrior Women," in her study *Asian American Literature: An Introduction to the Writings and Their Social Context*, provides an early critique of the masculinism evident in the *Aiiieeeee!* introduction. Analyzing Frank Chin's essays and dramas, Kim concludes that his "sexism, cynicism, and sense of alienation (among other factors) have prevented him from creating protagonists who can overcome the devastating effects of racism on Chinese American men."[22] In a recent essay, Kim revises her critique to render a more harmonious, less oppositional reading of Asian American writing. Agreeing in part with the *Aiiieeeee!* editors, Kim argues that U.S. race and gender hierarchies have objectified Asian Americans as permanent outsiders and sexual deviants: "Asian men have been coded as having no sexuality, while Asian women have nothing else." Although such social realities have resulted in differences between nationalist and feminist concerns, the woman's voice in works such as Kingston's *Tripmaster Monkey*, she asserts, "dissolves binary oppositions of ethnicity and gender."[23]

My own reading of Asian American literature demonstrates less a solution than a continuous negotiation between often conflicting cultural constructions of ethnicity and gender. To my mind, in the last fifteen years, after publication of Kingston's *The Woman Warrior* in 1976, the literature has been the site of conscious and explicit conflict, between *women's* ideas of culture and cultural nationalism as claimed by some males, preeminently presented in the *Aiiieeeee!* introduction, and more curiously elaborated as neo-Confucianist ideology in Frank Chin's essay "Come All Ye Asian American Writers," in *The Big Aiiieeeee!*[24] This gender split was explicitly caused by the intervention of feminist issues and is marked historically by the publication of two anthologies of women's writing in 1989, *The Forbidden Stitch: An Asian American Women's Anthology* and *Making Waves: An Anthology of Writings by and about Asian American Women*. These anthologies, although not directly addressing the masculinist ideology that undergirded the 1970s' literary movement, exhibit a difference from the earlier anthologies in their constituting of ethnic subject and culture. Primarily, they are a stage for women who claim, not the minor representation given in the 1970s' anthologies, but all the attention. Men are present in the work but often appear as aggressors or as ignorant of women's needs: "He beat me with the hem of a kimono"; "Father's belt"; "Men know nothing of sex."[25] Moreover, the works counter stereotypes of Asian American women in Asian and white cultures. *Making Waves* features sociological and historical essays that analyze images of Asian women in the media ("Lotus Blossoms Don't Bleed: Images of Asian Women") and express the dilemma of living biculturally in societies that insist on a hegemonic identity ("Growing Up Asian in America").[26]

More significantly, in contrast to the 1970s' male critique of the concept of "dual personality," the anthologies foreground the instabilities of identity and represent the oscillating and crisscrossing of national, racial, and subjective borders that characterize the experience of biculturalism: "How is one to know and define oneself? From the inside—within a context that is self defined, from a grounding in community and a connection with culture and history that are comfortably accepted? Or from the outside—in terms of messages received from the media and people who are often ignorant?"[27] Kesaya E. Noda's essay, for example, beginning in "confusions and distortions," resolves itself in its construction of "I am racially Japanese," "I am a Japanese American," "I am a Japanese American woman." This tripartite construction of Asian American identity, affirmatively propositional, counters the 1970s' syllogistic construction: "I am not Asian," "I am not white American," "I am Asian American (male)." The feminist intervention in the evolving tradition of this writing has led to a reclamation of mother/other origin, an affirmation of continuity or relation between origin and present tense, and a new foregrounding of gender identity. Paradoxically, the absence of an attempt to illuminate an Asian American sensibility has resulted in the affirmation of sensibilities marked by softened categories, elastic cultural spaces, and a more global antihegemonic construction of identity.

In contrast to the *Aiiieeeee!* anthology, neither women's anthology attempts to explicate an exclusive boundary of ethnic sensibility. In fact, the selection of works that manifest emotional and physical bonds to a non-American homeland indicates an elastic sense of identity to encompass the past of Asian national identity as well as an American writing present. Moreover, no attempt is made to separate the selections into ethnic groups; works by South Asian, Korean, Filipino, Japanese, Chinese, and other Asian American women appear side by side, organized thematically or sequentially. Thus, together with an increased diversity of Asian national representations is a decreased emphasis on categorical national difference. The very multiplicity appears to result in a blurring of national boundaries and an assertion of organizational principles through commonalities of experience rather than differences of attributes.

The 1980s' selections of Asian American women's writing share with the 1970s' anthologies general themes of immigrant concerns and first-generation conflicts, acknowledgement of cultural sources and roots in Asian societies, and thematics of family bond/conflicts. *The Forbidden Stitch* foregrounds new writing that manifests "subjectivity as gendered," inclusive of a "contemporary Asian American culture [that] is not dictated from a central committee."[28] The editors of the 1980s' anthologies worked in collectives, as communities of women. The ethnic culture of these anthologies is nonauthoritative, decentered, nondogmatic, unprogrammatic, uncategorizing, inclusive, qualities that some feminist theoreticians such as Carol Gilligan argue characterize female sensibilities.[29]

The editors avoided propositions that constructed universalist notions of Asian American women's experiences. In the introductory essay to *Making Waves,* for example, Sucheta Mazumdar argues that for Asian Americans whose histories of exclusion, isolation, discrimination, exploitation, and internment result in "severe trauma," "ethnic identity supersedes gender and class. For women of color, concerns arising out of racial identity are an integral aspect of their overall identity." Yet even within this general observation many exceptions exist. As Mazumdar elaborates:

> The impact of gender on Asian women in America varies enormously even within the same class and ethnic group. While the idea that female children are of less value than male children permeates all Asian cultures . . . the effect of this value-system on an American-born woman is quite different than on an immigrant one.

For the Asian-born woman, moving away from a relatively closed patriarchal world into a relatively democratized, egalitarian, interrogative America, immigration can be a liberalizing and freeing experience. Mazumdar cites a national survey of college-educated woman from India living in the United States that showed 33.3 percent of the women working in the technical fields and 50 percent in the academic fields described themselves as feminists.[30] Traditional Asian valuation of authoritarian husbands is frequently subverted by the working woman's growing economic independence and interaction in larger social relations that reflect different, more positive values of the female.

INVENTING NEW PLOTS

For the woman writer whose ethnic community is patriarchal, ethnic and feminist values and identities must inevitably intersect in potentially uneasy, conflicting, or violent ways. In male-centered ethnic societies, the woman usually remains on the margin, invisible, mute, or constrained to limited stereotypical roles of possession—child or mother, domestic worker, or sexual object. Most assertions of female identity of qualities falling outside the subordinate ranks and delineated kinship roles may be read as subversive of male power and, by implication, of one's ethnic community. To be a free woman, such a woman must be at some level a "no name woman," that is, outcast from her ethnic community. Thus, Kingston's aunt, a "no name woman" who carries an illegitimate child, has broken the Chinese patriarchal laws of kinship and descent, has become a non-Chinese, a nonhuman, and drowns herself in the well, an act of retribution for breaking the name of the father, the final patriarchal control over all women. In the intersection of race and gender identity, the woman who represents the urgencies of her gender (her sexuality, her maternality) against a race imperative is in a position to be violently erased. But that is in the traditional master plot of ethnic patriarch as villain and ethnic woman as victim.

Rejecting this race and gender plot (encompassing female infanticide, clitoridectomy, child brides, dowries, brideburning, catalog brides, enforced purdah, suttee—the archetypal patterns of female oppression and male masterhood),[31]Asian American women have been busy inventing new plots that are complicated by race and class issues. One alternative narrative to the representation of woman as a victim to patriarchy is that of the disempowering of the central male figure in the Asian kinship nexus by a racist and classist white American society. Through the eyes of Asian American daughters, the father's humiliations, losses, and pathetic struggles against white social authority are both indictments against racism (and therefore an assertion of ethnic protest) as well as evidence of patriarchal impotence (and therefore a stripping away of ethnic core identity). Jeanne Wakatsuki Houston and James Houston's 1974 *Farewell to Manzanar* constructs this double-edged critique of Asian/American cultures in its portrayal of the gradual emasculation of the powerful Papa figure. Because Papa "didn't want to be labelled or grouped by anyone," the daughter has grown up in an all-white neighborhood. Because he had terrified her with the threat, "I'm going to sell you to the Chinaman," she grows up with "this fear of Oriental faces." "Papa had been the patriarch," she tells us explicitly. The internment process changed him to "a man without a country. . . . He was suddenly a man with no rights who looked exactly like the enemy." The Japanese values that supported his patriarchal role, through the internment, have become erased; he is now "without a country," "the enemy." In the face of the FBI arrest, "all he had left . . . was his tremendous dignity."[32]

Nine months later, Papa returns from North Dakota to join his family in the camp in Manzanar. "He was not the same man. Something had happened to him in North Dakota." The first unforgettable object the young Wakatsuki sees on her father's return is his cane, a symbol both of his weakened physical self and also of his demoralized spirit. For even after his limp goes away, he uses the cane "as a kind of swagger stick, such as military officers use." The humiliation resulting from his imprisonment leads to Papa's distortion of patriarchal values into an abusive and futile machismo: "When he was angry he would wield [the cane] like the flat of a sword, whacking out at his kids or his wife or his hallucinations . . . a sad, homemade version of the samurai sword his great-great-grandfather carried in the land around Hiroshima, at a time when warriors weren't much needed anymore, when their swords were both their virtue and their burden." The father's identity is inextricably bound up with a samurai, a male warrior, genealogy; but in the new country, this identity is superseded and superannuated. "The camp was where our lifelines intersected," Wakatsuki Houston writes.

"That intersection—for me a birthplace," whereas "things finished for him there"[33] is one daughter's ruthless rewriting of the race and gender plot. In the life story, Asian patriarchal identity dies at that very intersection of the birth of feminist consciousness.

When Wakatsuki Houston wrote, "It [the cane symbolizing samurai tradition and Asian patriarchal self-construction] helps me to understand how Papa's life would end in a place like Manzanar," she did not mean his literal and physical death. In fact, his physical presence as alcoholic, abusive husband and father looms large in the daughter's life: "With Papa back our cubicle was filled to overflowing . . . what crowded the room . . . was Papa himself, his dark, bitter, brooding presence." In her proleptic statement, Wakatsuki Houston was representing the antinomies of patriarchal tradition and evolving feminist consciousness in their mutually erasive positions, foreshadowing the death of her ethnic past and its displacement by a feminine discourse. This discourse bears little resemblance to the attitudes associated today with feminists, for hers was a prefeminist world. In her explorations in the camp, the young girl sees an orphan being confirmed in a Catholic ceremony: "She was dressed like a bride, in a white gown, white lace hood, and sheer veil, walking towards the altar" . . . I was pierced with envy . . . that this girl, this orphan, could become such a queen."[34] The self-image the young Japanese American girl desires is the idealized white female future, the girl as bride and queen.

The Japanese father does not passively stand by as his daughter buys into the assimilative code. In an illuminating instance, he resists her baptism into Catholicism on the grounds that "you get baptized now, how are you going to find a good Japanese boy to marry?" He recognizes in his daughter's apparent religious fervor the subversion of his control. The daughter's dreams of being "the white-gowned princess" are obstructed by her father, and in counterresistance she turns to practicing her baton, a complex symbol of male sexual mastery that reappears later to figure her prefeminist discourse: "Angrily I would throw [the baton] into the air and watch him twirl, and catch him, and throw him high, again and again and again."[35]

The chapter "The Double Impulse" spells out the place of gender in the ethnic dilemma. Released from Manzanar, the young girl still carries the trauma of racial hurt with her. She has internalized the internment into "true shame," "some submerged belief that this treatment is deserved." From this shame of ethnic identity come the related impulses—"the urge to disappear and the desperate desire to be acceptable," to assimilate, which is another form of death of ethnicity. Her "birth" as an American is enabled by her other identity as female. As the lead majorette in the Girl Scouts, which she describes as "like a sorority," she finds "intuitively that one resource I had to overcome the war-distorted limitations of my race would be my femininity." "The boys in the band loved having us out there in front of them all the time, bending back and stepping high, in our snug satin outfits and short skirts. Their dads, mostly navy men, loved it too." Wakatsuki tells us, "I was too young to consciously use my sexuality or to understand how an Oriental female can fascinate Caucasian men,"[36] indicating her later adult discomfort with the forms of complicity that women traditionally engage in so as to do well in patriarchal systems.

Yet one should not underestimate her prefeminist understanding that her "feminine" resource can liberate her from ethnic-specific patriarchal control and violence nor the consequent psychic dislocation of her complicity in white patriarchal definitions of the feminine which she seeks as an alternative to her father's "good Japanese-boy husband" paradigm. Her unhappy confusion of identity is plangently represented in the narrative of what should have been the culmination of her white-female dream, her crowning as carnival queen. To win the event, she had dressed as an exotic, "with a flower-print sarong, black hair loose and a hibiscus flower behind my ear." For the ceremony, however, she accepts her parents' version of a respectable and modest image and wears a "frilly ball gown that covered almost everything and buried my legs under layers of ruffles . . . a white-gowned figure out of Gone with the Wind." Caught between a host of possible images, "an odori dancer for Papa," a princess, or "this kind of [Hollywood] heroine," the young woman becomes conscious of the shabby and provisional, the unsatisfactory nature of her self-construction. "It was too late now not to follow this make-believe carpet to its plywood finale, and I did not yet know of any truer destination."[37]

Jeanne Wakatsuki Houston wrote this life story in collaboration with her Anglo writer-husband and has since published only autobiographical essays. For this Asian American woman to give birth to a self outside her traditional Asian patriarchal constructions of dutiful daughter and wife, she had to seek acceptance through exploiting her sexuality and her exoticism in a white patriarchal world, denying the integrity of both her ethnic and her female self. This dilemma posed in the narrative is also manifest in the questions surrounding the text's authorship. Written as an autobiography in the first person, the book's signature is shared with an Anglo male. Thus, even in its Japanese American woman's voice, it is compromised in its very assertion of ethnicity and femininity. The overlap, doubleness, of authorship is not simply a matter of coauthorship, for the text presents itself as a first-person ethnic woman's life story. As Mary V. Dearborn argues in *Pocahontas's Daughters: Gender and Ethnicity in American Culture*, the absence of self-possession, the duplicity of ethnic women's texts, and its appropriation by white males, are noticeable features of ethnic women's literature.[38]

The theme of intergenerational tension and conflict, specifically between an Old World patriarch and a daughter who is attracted to New World culture with all its promise of privileged womanhood, is not peculiar to Asian American literature. Dearborn points out that it forms the major theme of works by earlier ethnic woman writers.[39] Anzia Yezierska's *Bread Givers* narrates the daughter's bitter struggle to break free from an oppressive, exploitative, tradition-bound father to a liberated life.[40] Wakatsuki Houston's narrative, however, differs from this common thematic in that, as Thomas Sowell points out, "The 'generation gap' between first and second generations of Japanese American was . . . greater than in other immigrant groups." Moreover, the internment experience, which functions in Japanese American literature as slavery does in African American writing, provides the major intergenerational coloration. As Sowell describes it, "Life within the internment camps considerably altered traditional Japanese roles and patterns of life. The very low wages paid for performing various tasks in camp were the same for women as for men, for young or old, and so the role of the father as primary breadwinner was completely undermined."[41] The internment experience, as illustrated in Wakatsuki Houston's story, marks the moment in Japanese

American culture, between ethnicity as patriarchal discourse and the emergence of the Japanese American woman as subject, seeking a different constitution of her female self.

A similar intergenerational conflict between Old World patriarch and American daughter is manifested in Chinese American women's writing. For example, the strict patriarch in Jade Snow Wong's *Fifth Chinese Daughter* (although he escapes the emasculation that the Japanese father suffers in *Farewell to Manzanar*) is compelled finally to change his views on the inferior status of his fifth daughter.[42] Wong offers an alternative ethnic/gender plot in which the patriarch retains his position and the daughter represses her female subjectivity in order to succeed in her ethnic identity as her father's *son*.[43]

These two Asian American daughters' narratives demonstrate that their identities form sites of conflict between the different ideological valuations of the individual, the community, and gender that distinguish Asian cultures from U.S. culture. In the process of countersocialization, from Asian and Confucianist values to Euro-American values, inevitable conflicts occur within each woman simultaneously with external difficulties in her roles as obedient daughter and independent individual and professional. The contradictions between Asian and U.S. (that is, Euro-American) socially inscribed positions for women and the internal resistance within the Asian woman to those cultural elements that seemingly would liberate her from patriarchal constraints are evident in the 1984 novel *Clay Walls*, by a second-generation Korean American woman, Kim Ronyoung.[44]

The novel traces the lives of a Korean couple who flee the Japanese imperialists in Korea for a Korean immigrant community in Los Angeles. Haesu, a *Yangban*, or aristocrat, is married against her will to Chun, the third son of a farmer, a landless peasant or *Sangnyom*, a lower-class person. Because a high-ranking American missionary has intervened for Chun, Haesu's parents cannot refuse without losing face. As an object of possession and exchange, Haesu is handed over to Chun to maintain her family's social status. Arriving in California, Haesu attempts to help her husband economically by working as a domestic. We first meet her refusing to scrub the toilet for a wealthy Euro-American woman. As an American immigrant, she has lost her traditional superiority, but adherence to her Korean ethnic identity allows her to maintain her class identity. Her aristocratic ethnic status permits her to resist both a new classist (based on capital) American society as well as her traditionally lower-class husband.

Through Haesu's character, the novel dramatizes the oppression of women within traditional Korean patriarchal society. Although Chun desires his wife physically, he functions within this structure where women are commodified as objects of exchange and as sexual creatures to serve male desire. For example, although Haesu resists his advances, he takes her in an act clearly represented as marital rape: "Pressing his chest against her nipples and jamming his knees against her thighs, he formed a human vise. She wanted to scream herself free. . . . Grunting like a barnyard animal, he collapsed in a heap on top of her." After a bitter quarrel and violation, the narrator tells us, "She did not know the word for what he had done to her. 'That thing' is how she referred to coitus. She didn't know the word for rape." Haesu's ignorance of the word figures her ignorance of her rights as a human in U.S. culture. Her understanding of her marital relations is based on her education in Confucianist society. When Chun tells her,

"Money is a man's affair," the narrator emphasizes that he is speaking for a community: "The terms were clear. They did not originate with Chun. Their roles had been handed down through the centuries, made clear by Confucius centuries ago."[45] These early scenes offer familiar feminist grievances. We are prepared to read Haesu as a feminist heroine, socially and morally superior to the male, whose acculturation in the Euro-American ideology of individual rights will set her on a female identity divergent from the traditional Asian identity.

Instead, the novel offers a complex narrative of female resistance to male domination in more differentiated terms than this prescribed feminist position would allow. Haesu notes the inequity in status between female and male in Korean society: "As long as a man provided for his family, he was beyond criticism. A woman, on the other hand, was measured by how well she served the men in her family, first her father, then her husband and, finally, her son."[46] Yet, although voicing a criticism of this dominant male position, Haesu abandons the critique for a different kind of resistance that does not undermine the traditional role of the female as mother and homemaker. The novel's development falls in line with and supports the very division of gender roles that it explicitly criticizes in its opening. The questioning of the value of gender divisions occurs at a level of social tragedy that obscures it and foregrounds instead issues of race and class. Haesu's choice—to stay home and raise her three children—represents an immigrant Asian woman's perspective that, although critical of aspects of Confucianist values, chooses to remain within that social structure, using its attributes for her own ends. Her ends preclude the feminist objective, "women's sacred duty to herself"; instead, they encompass the welfare of her children, her family's economic security, and her community status. Haesu incorporates material attributes of U.S. culture—for example, less constrained dress and social intercourse, shedding women's enforced physical seclusion—without challenging the overt values of her ethnic society. Indeed, once the children arrive, the novel concentrates on concerns of racial inequality that Haesu fears will prevent her children from achieving success in the United States. The narrative moves from a discourse and critique of gender relations to a discourse and critique of race relations.

The novel's second part focuses on Chun and undermines whatever critique of patriarchy may have been inferred from the first part. Chun is represented as the victim of U.S. racial legislation *and* Asian patriarchal values. Under Confucianist teaching, the husband is identified as the provider. Without social standing and without emotional bonds, this economic function is the only legitimation Chun receives from Haesu. When he loses the business because of corrupt municipal policies, and his savings through a gambling addiction, he loses his tenuous economic function in the family. He leaves Los Angeles for Reno and dies years later without returning to his family. Having no money, the traditional Korean patriarch becomes a "nothing," erased in the matriarchal bonded family. Chun's final annihilation is figured in the safe, "the only thing that belonged to Papa," which the desperate Haesu forces open, only to find "nothing in here."[47]

In the power relation between Chun and Haesu, potentially feminist issues of patriarchal oppression staged in the arranged marriage and of male violence represented in the scenes of marital rape are diffused and dispersed by more pressing representations of the bondage of the male, of female psychosexual punishment of the male, of male frustration, disempowerment, and erasure. *Clay*

Walls reminds us that in U.S. culture, the immigrant Asian male, burdened by racial legislation, is more threatened with dysfunction than the Asian woman. The woman, supported by the presence of her children and the social network of her ethnic community, survives. The novel also demonstrates how, in U.S. culture, certain cultural values are disabling for Asian males, such as the male's primary identity with the economic function of provider and the construction of masculine pride and stoicism. Yet for Haesu, other Korean cultural values help her survive. The traditional seclusion of women in the home offers her the psychic resources to support her children through piecework sewing, and the traditional value of children gives her an overriding motive for economic struggle.

Clay Walls does not provide a Euro-American-style feminist text. Its focus is on the transformation of individuals caught between ethnic cultures rather than between gender roles. Moving from gender to ethnicity, the perspective inevitably moves from women's domestic issues to ethnic social issues. In communities where men appear to be under greater adaptive stress than women, as is generally the case for people of color in the United States, the cultural/social perspective also foregrounds men and their struggles in a race- and class-, as well as gender-, divided society.

That *Clay Walls* is not produced from within a Euro-American feminist agenda is most clearly evidenced in the portrayal of Faye, Haesu's youngest child and only daughter. As a second-generation American-born Korean American, Faye may be expected to display greater sensitivity to the unequal positions of female-male power. Faye's character, however, reproduces the race-class-gender nexus in her immigrant mother's life. Faye rejects the working-class illegitimate Willie who defiantly plays up his low status in the community. She accepts her mother's injunction against finding a profession and works instead, with her mother's permission, as a drill-press operator during the Pacific War, a gesture of patriotism rather than of individual fulfillment. Her future as a worker is figured in the description of her job: "to drill holes in precisely the same place on identical pieces of dull black metal." Like Haesu's, the course of Faye's life is predicated on men; following her mother's example, she waits for and finds a Korean American man, the kind of upper-class man that Haesu had wanted for herself. Her mother educates her in Korean female submissiveness: "In Korea, children do what their parents say. Parents do everything for their children and the children respect them for it." (This homily excludes the sons who had left home earlier for their own adventures.) Haesu arranges a blind date between Faye and Daniel Lee, an assimilated Korean American from an all-white Connecticut town, a Yale graduate and U.S. Army officer, who speaks English "without a trace of an accent." Daniel is the fantasy male rescuer whose figure "solves" the unequal class conflict that troubled the first-generation marriage and reconciles for Haesu/Faye the contradictory desires for preserving the integrity of a Korean ethnic identity and for assimilation into white U.S. society. Daniel as male authority manifests what all the other Korean American characters have been unable to do, the ability to negotiate conflicting ethnic cultural demands without anxiety and stress: "I live among one group of people while my commitments are to another. WASP assumptions require that I be one thing and my ancestry demands another. . . . [B]ut we who live here have something in common. If not physically then intellectually. In many cases, experientially."[48] The careers of the Korean American female protagonists, as delineated in *Clay Walls*, are dependent on men; women do not interrogate male social dominance or transgress traditional female roles.

ASIAN AMERICAN FEMINISM

In the texts discussed, the Asian American female, in order to pursue her interests in a race-conscious society, has to modify her rejection of patriarchal ethnic identity. Mitsuye Yamada asserts that "being a feminist activist is more dangerous for women of color" and that feminist agendas should be accommodated within an affirmation of ethnic culture: "Asian Pacific women need to affirm our culture while working within to change it."[49] Her position assumes an overlapping of categories that will enable the conventional and stereotypical hostility between ethnic cultures, traditionally organized for patriarchal ends, and emerging women's identities, expressed in socially transforming concerns for the rights of women, to be defused, synthesized, or merged into a new sensibility. The construction of gender need not be contingent on the ethnic versions of female roles and experiences, nor need the construction of ethnicity depend on patriarchal constructions of an ethnic group; feminist identity, therefore, should be recoverable inside Asian American culture and history. Yet Kim's *Clay Walls*, Wong's *Fifth Chinese Daughter*, and Jeanne Wakatsuki Houston's career provide a caution against too easily assuming the merger of ethnic and feminist identities.

While Wakatsuki Houston's memoir, *Farewell to Manzanar*, demonstrates her resistance to ethnic-identified patriarchy, her 1985 autobiographical essays in *Beyond Manzanar: Views of Asian American Womanhood*, like the narrative of Faye's growing up, erase that earlier resistance and return as if without a memory to the usual constructions of Japanese cultural values that mute women's voices and concerns. In *Beyond Manzanar*, Wakatsuki Houston recuperates her Japanese roots by recuperating a Japanese mother whose figure integrates the American mode of individualism (she marries for romantic love) and "a prized identity" of peers and community almost exclusively of Japanese descent. Wakatsuki Houston privileges the maternal component in the ethnic community, equates it with "service," and conflates the narrative of maternal service with that of approved female subordination: "My mother, already inherently prepared to subordinate herself in their relationship . . . zealously sought for ways to elevate [the husband's] position in the family." The author's internalized conflict, between aggressive, assertive attitudes identified as "Caucasian" in ethnic culture and submissive passive, receptive characteristics identified as Japanese woman, surfaces in her marital relation to her Caucasian husband. Wakatsuki Houston "solves" this "double identity" by claiming "cultural hybridness," an acceptance of cultural and psychological divergence in her personality. Her resolution, however, can be read as itself a compliance with both racist and sexist constructions of female identity; as she admits in her essay, "The Geisha, the Good Wife, and Me," there are roles that "Westerners, including me, have amalgamated into one stereotype . . . the submissive, docile, self-sacrificing, artlessly perfect Japanese wife."[50] Wakatsuki Houston's later essays move the dilemma of the woman in a patriarchal ethnic community from the problem of patriarchy to the solution of sexist role playing.

Farewell to Manzanar had foregrounded a plot in which the female protagonist seeks and finds a woman's identity, no matter how partial and unsatisfactory, out-side the Japanese father's version, a self-representation that locates content in white America's version of the princess, exotic native, or Hollywood heroine. This ethnically transgressive yet American assimilative mode of self-representation is one common form of the intersection of ethnicity and feminism in much Asian American writing. In two randomly selected poems in the 1986 Asian American Special Edition of *Contact II*, for example, Genny Lim and Karen Tei Yamashita situate their representations of woman in recognizably feminist yet nonethnically identified codes.[51] Treating sexuality with a remarkable candor and explicitness associated with the emphasis on writing the body that feminist literary criticism has privileged, both poems break any stereotypical notions the reader may have concerning Asian American female modesty, submissiveness, and passivity. In-deed, stereotypes aside, they transgress common social rules of female behavior that still pervade middle-class societies of any ethnic camp. Lim's title, "If Sartre Was a Whore," immediately places the poem in a Western cultural orientation; the stanzas describe a larger-than-life female energy principle:

> They call her whore
> because she fucks with pleasure
> They sneer
> because she loves women
> Queen bee
> She sucks life's nectar
> from one-night stands.

This figure of bisexual energy and the pleasure principle contains nothing of stereotypes of Asian American women in its representation.[52] Similarly, Yama-shita's "Midwifs" with its playful uses of jazz rhythms and linguistic registers bor-rows its diction and images from African American blues lyrics:

> Say man lady
> hootche kootche woman
> huddled on you hootche kootche womb
> baring breasts to wet
> lips and tongues of father the son, ghosts
> in dreams caress the nights
> in middle age sing crazy like a loon.[53]

Both poems appear to demonstrate that the construction of female sexual en-ergy need not be ethnic-bound. Yet, although these poems operate outside the context of Asian ethnicity, or at least allude to it chiefly by transgression and ex-clusion, as representations they are no less culture-bound because they displace references to images, ideas, and behavior commonly associated with Asian-ethnic societies and locate their women's content instead in European and African American contexts. The choices of that preeminent European philosopher Sartre and the jazz-influenced diction and rhythms offer a counter-European and Afri-can American ground in these poems, illustrating that when Asian American writ-ers write from non-Asian American centers, they are already situated in another ethnic domain. We should read the poems of Lim and Yamashita as constructed

within a Western tradition of *l'écriture féminine*.[54] In this Western feminist poetics, women's physicality, maternality, sexuality, and eroticism are foregrounded
as a defiant inscription of female experience outside the forms of phallocentric
and logocentric poetics. As Susan Rubin Suleiman suggests, women's writing is
claiming the right to "dirty" words and to subjects long forbidden to women by a
patriarchal discourse that in idealizing women as other than material had deprived
women of the power of the material.[55] In these two poems, their subjects, idioms, jazz syncopations, metaphors, and figures are coded Euro-African American.
These poems construct women's bodies but go outside Asian American culture-
specific codes to do so.

It is generally accepted that one tradition of women's writing in the French-
Anglophone tradition is a writing of the body as reflected in thematics and choice
of diction. A tradition of ethnic immigrant writing is also grounded on a body of
thematics (Old World/New World conflict; alienation/assimilation; intergenerational
tensions rising out of cross-cultural differences, and so forth). In such a contrasting morphology, *Farewell to Manzanar* and *Clay Wall* may be considered more ethnic than feminist texts. But if we also consider that the theme of women's
oppression by patriarchal structures and the representation of women's struggles
to free themselves from these ancient bonds form another tradition of women's
writing, then surely these two books, which unreel the twisted strands of the cultural pressures of descent (being born into an ethnic community) and consent
(attempting to constitute a woman's identity of one's own outside the imprisonment of culture), meet at the intersection of ethnic and feminist traditions.

In contrast, by placing their poems in a European and African American rhetorical context, Lim and Yamashita demonstrate a conscious decision to forgo the
complexities of intersecting Asian American and feminist cultures, choosing instead to position themselves in other cultural contexts in which female sexuality
can be assertively represented without the countering repressions of culture-
specific patriarchal attitudes. Reading the different representations of woman by
these writers, we are reminded of how ethnic and gender identities are continuously negotiated in tension against each other, the very act of naming and representing, that is, of writing, composed of strategies of identity that challenge
each other in a dialogical mode within the texts themselves. The challenge of
pluralism, of an ideology that seeks to include divergent, even conflicting, cultural components, is acutely articulated in such texts, situated in the intersections
of ethnic and feminist identities.

NOTES

1. Johnella E. Butler, *NWSAction* 2 (Winter 1989); 1, 2.
2. Many women of color scholars have written of what Barbara Christian has called the
"conflict of choice and possibility," caused by divergent ethnic and feminist lines of inquiry. See her article, "But Who Do You Really Belong To (Black Studies or Women's Studies?" in *Across Cultures: The Spectrum of Women's Lives*, ed. Emily K. Abel and Marjorie L.
Pearson (New York: Gordon & Breach, 1989), 18. Patricia Zavella indicts "the early feminist criticisms of the nuclear family" and asserts that for some Chicanas "the white, middle-
class focus of American feminism" implied a form of racism (see "The Problematic
Relationship of Feminism and Chicana Studies," in *Across Cultures*, 26).

3. Barbara Smith, Introduction, *Home Girls: A Black Feminist Anthology* (New York: Kitchen Table–Women of Color Press, 1983), xxv.

4. See Donna Perry, "Procne's Song: The Task of Feminist Literary Criticism," in *Gender/Body/Knowledge: Feminist Reconstructions of Being and Knowing*, ed. Alison M. Jaggar and Susan R. Bordo (New Brunswick, N.J.: Rutgers University Press, 1989). Perry nicely summarizes feminist literary criticism's political agenda, pointing out that

> it originates in the critic's recognition that women, whatever their race or color, experience the world differently from men, that their status outside the dominant white male middle-class culture allows (or even compels) them to critique it. . . . The feminist literary critic is committed to changing the world by challenging patriarchal assumptions, judgments, and values, particularly as they affect women (p. 293).

5. Ellen Messer-Davidow argues that the "subject of feminist literary criticisms appears to be not literature but the feminist study of ideas about sex and gender that people express in literary and critical media"; from that premise, she calls for a position of "perspectivity" which assumes the "we as diverse knowers must insert ourselves and our perspectives into the domain of the study and become, self-reflexively, part of the investigation." See "The Philosophical Bases of Feminist Literary Criticisms," *New Literary History* 19 (Autumn 1987): 11, 88.

6. Hazel V. Carby, "Telling Fruit from Roots," *Times Literary Supplement*, 29 Dec. 1989–4 Jan. 1990, 1446.

7. For a critique of the problematics of pluralism raised by feminist literary inquiry, see Annette Kolodny, "Dancing Through the Minefield: Some Observations on the Theory, Practice, and Politics of a Feminist Literary Criticism," *Feminist Studies* 6 (Spring 1980): 1–25; reprinted in *The New Feminist Criticism*, ed. Elaine Showalter (New York: Pantheon Books, 1985), 144–67. Although Kolodny acknowledges that pluralism "seems to threaten a kind of chaos for the future of literary inquiry," she asserts that the task for feminist critics is "to initiate nothing less than a playful pluralism, responsive to the possibilities of multiple critical schools and methods" (p. 161).

8. For discussions of women's positions in traditional Asian patriarchal social structures, see Kay Ann Johnson, *Women, the Family, and Peasant Revolution* (Chicago: Univ. of Chicago Press, 1983); Marilyn Blatt Young, ed., *Women in China: Studies in Social Change and Feminism* (Ann Arbor: Center for Chinese Studies, University of Michigan, 1973); Judith Stacey, *Patriarchy and Socialist Revolution in China* (Berkeley: University of California Press, 1983); Sharon L. Sievers, *Flowers in Salt: The Beginnings of Feminist Consciousness in Modern Japan* (Stanford: Stanford University Press, 1983); Susan Pharr, *Political Women in Japan* (Berkeley: University of California Press, 1981); Takie Sugiyama Lebra, *Japanese Women: Constraint and Fulfillment* (Honolulu: University of Hawaii Press, 1984); Alice Chai, "Korean Women in Hawaii," in *Women in New Worlds, 1903–1945*, ed. Hilah F. Thomas and Rosemary Skinner Keller (Nashville: Abingdon Press, 1981), 77–87; Sheila Rowbotham, *Women, Resistance, and Revolution: A History of Women and Revolution in the Modern World* (1972; rpt. New York: Vintage, 1974), esp. the chapter, "When the Sand-Grouse Flies to Heaven," 170–99; Sylvia A. Chipp and Justin J. Green, eds., *Asian Women in Transition* (University Park: Pennsylvania State University Press, 1980); Judy Chu, "Southeast Asian Women in Transition" (Paper presented at the Immigration Women Project Conference, Long Beach City College, California, Sept. 1984); Beverley Lindsay, ed., *Comparative Perspectives of Third World Women* (New York: Praeger, 1980); and Perdita Huston, *Third World Women Speak Out: Interview in Six Countries on Change, Development, and Basic Needs* (New York: Praeger, 1979). Recent studies of the role of international corporate capital and development in further eroding Asian women's human rights include Rachel Grossman, "Women's Place in the Integrated Circuit," *Southeast Asia Chronicle* 66 (Jan.–Feb. 1979): 2–17/*Pacific Research* 9 (July–Oct. 1978): 2–17; and Marlyn, "The Sale of Sexual Labor in the

Philippines: Marlyn's Story," introduced and translated by Brenda Stoltzfus, *Bulletin of Concerned Asian Scholars* 22, no. 4 (1970): 13–19.

9. Sexual dysfunction and misogyny among Chinese immigrants, resulting from long separations from their womenfolk, a social phenomenon created by the various Asian exclusion acts between 1882 and 1943, are documented, for example, in Paul C. P. Siu's study, *The Chinese Laundryman: A Study of Social Isolation*, ed. John Duo Wei Tchen (New York: New York University Press, 1987), esp. 250–71. Sucheta Mazumdar points out that "for immigrant women arrival in American can be liberating. Societal norms of the majority community frequently provide greater personal freedom than permitted in Asian societies" (p. 15). See "General Introduction: A Woman-Centered Perspective on Asian American History," *Making Waves: An Anthology of Writings by and about Asian American Women*, ed. Asian Women United of California (Boston: Beacon, 1989), 1–22. Psychological studies have posited that "conflicts between traditional Chinese roles and feminist orientations may exist for many Chinese American females." See Stanley Sue and James K. Morishima, "Personality, Sex-Role Conflict, and Ethnic Identity," in *The Mental Health of Asian Americans: Contemporary Issues in Identifying and Treating Mental Problems*, ed. Stanley Sue and James K. Morishima (San Francisco: Jossey-Bass, 1982), 93–125.

10. The hostility roused in Asian American men at Asian American women who date or marry outside their ethnic community has not yet been documented, but various personal writings testify to this phenomenon. See, for example, Tommy S. Kim's "Asian Goils Are Easy," *Tealeaves* (Fall 1989), 24: "oriental sluts with attitudes/ I'm so, special so unique— no/ boy Chinee/ understand me—no / satisfy need. . . . / A race of Wong-/ wanna-be's: Suzie/ feeling sick/ 'cause she needs white dick/ to fix an itch/ in her too-tight twat," and so forth.

11. See Carol Neubauer, "Developing Ties to the Past: Photography and Other Sources of Information on Maxine Hong Kingston's *China Men*," *MELUS* 10, no. 4 (1983): 17–36, for a discussion of how Kingston uses photographs to help develop her strategy of memory in her memoirs.

12. For discussions of Kingston's postmodernist genre collages, see Linda Ching Sledge, "Maxine Hong Kingston's *China Men*: The Family Historian as Epic Poet," *MELUS* 7 (198): 3–22; and Marilyn Yalom's "*The Woman Warrior as Postmodern Autobiography*," in *Approaches to Teaching Kingston's "The Woman Warrior,"* ed. Shirley Geok-lin Lim (New York: Modern Language Association Press, 1991).

13. For examples of historical and archival recoveries, see, for example, Marlon K. Hom, *Songs of Gold Mountain: Cantonese Rhymes from San Francisco Chinatown* (Berkeley: University of California Press, 1987); Him Mark Lai, *A History Reclaimed: An Annotated Bibliography of Chinese-Language Materials on the Chinese of America*, ed. Russell Leong and Jean Pang Yip (Los Angeles: Resource Development and Publications, Asian American Studies Center, University of California, 1986); Mark Him Lai, Genny Lim, and Judy Yung, eds. and trans., *Island: Poetry and History of Chinese Immigrants on Angel Island, 1910–1940* (San Francisco: HOC DOI, 1980); and Sau-Ling Wong, "Tales of Postwar Chinatown: Short Stories of *The Bud, 1947–1948*," *Amerasia* 14 (1988): 61–79.

14. Kai-yu Hsu and Helen Palubinskas, eds. *Asian-American Authors* (1972; rpt., Boston: Houghton Muffin, 1976); David Hsin-Fu Wand, ed., *Asian-American Heritage: An Anthology of Prose and Poetry* (New York: Washington Square Press, 1974); Frank Chin et al., eds., *Aiiieeeee! An Anthology of Asian-American Writers* (1974; rpt., Washington, D.C.: Howard University Press, 1983); Elaine H. Kim, *Asian American Literature: An Introduction to the Writings and Their Social Context* (Philadelphia: Temple University Press, 1982); King-Kok Cheung and Stan Yogi, *Asian American Literature: An Annotated Bibliography* (New York: MLA Press, 1988). Since the essay was written a number of other books have appeared. See *Reading the Literatures of Asian America*, ed. Shirley Geok-lin Lim and Amy Ling (Philadelphia: Temple University Press, 1992); Sau-ling Wong, *Reading Asian American Literature: From*

Necessity to Extravagance (Princeton, N.J.: Princeton University Press, 1993); and King-Kok Cheung, *Articulate Silences: Hisaye Yamamoto, Maxine Hong Kingston, Joy Kogawa* (Ithaca: Cornell University Press, 1993).

15. Ishmael Reed encouraged Frank Chin and Shawn Wong; Chin appeared in *Yardbird Reader*, no. 2 (1973): 21–46; and *Yardbird Reader*, no. 3 (1974): vi–x. Chin and Wong guest edited the special Asian American issue of *Yardbird Reader*, no. 3 (1974). Reed's invective against African American women writers for the feminist critiques of African American male abuse which he claims is a form of scapegoating that plays to racist sentiments is manifest in his polemical satire, *Reckless Eyeballing* (New York: St. Martin's Press, 1988).

16. See *Aiiieeeee!*, 14–15, for a criticism of the stereotype of the demasculinized male in Asian American culture.

17. *The Big Aiiieeeee!*, ed. Jeffery Paul Chan et al. (New York: Meridan, 1991).

18. See Chin et al., 3, ix, xi.

19. Jack Chen, *The Chinese of America* (San Francisco: Harper & Row, 1980), 3.

20. George White, "A Spicy Market," *Los Angeles Times*, 21 Aug. 1991, D2.

21. Chin et al., 35.

22. Kim, 189.

23. Elaine H. Kim, "'Such Opposite Creatures': Men and Women in Asian American Literature," *Michigan Quarterly Review* 29 (Winter 1990): 69, 71.

24. Maxine Hong Kingston, *The Woman Warrior: Memoirs of a Girlhood among Ghosts* (New York: Knopf, 1977); Frank Chin, "Come All Ye Asian American Writers of the Real and the Fake," in *The Big Aiiieeeee!*, 1–92.

25. Shirley Geok-lin Lim and Mayumi Tsutakawa, eds., *The Forbidden Stitch: An Asian American Women's Anthology* (Corvallis, Ore.: Calyx, 1989), 85, 91, 79.

26. *Making Waves*, 308, 243.

27. Kesaya E. Noda, "Growing Up Asian in America," in *Making Waves*, 244.

28. Lim and Tsutakawa, 14.

29. Carol Gilligan, *In a Different Voice: Psychological Theory and Women's Development* (Cambridge: Harvard University Press, 1982).

30. Sucheta Manzumdar, "General Introduction: A Woman-Centered Perspective on Asian American History," in *Making Waves*, 15, 16.

31. Although such a catalog of social phenomena oversimplifies and overgeneralizes Asian women's status as victims of patriarchy, it does point to a history of unequal power relations in Asian societies.

32. Jeanne Wakatsuki Houston and James Houston, *Farewell to Manzanar* (New York: Bantam, 1974), 8, 9, 12, 6.

33. Ibid., 32, 32.

34. Ibid., 47, 83.

35. Ibid., 83, 84.

36. Ibid., 114, 117.

37. Ibid., 124, 128, 130.

38. Mary V. Dearborn, *Pocahontas's Daughters: Gender and Ethnicity in American Culture* (New York: Oxford Press, 1986). See Dearborn's discussion of the ethnic woman's "compromised authorship," 17–30.

39. Dearborn elucidates the thematic of the immigrant daughter's struggle against the Old World patriarch in texts as diverse as Mary Antin's *The Promised Land* and Anzia Yezierska's *Bread Givers*: "If one's own father is renounced, indeed, erased, the bastardized immigrant is free to adopt the founding fathers as her own. Moreover, by this act, she adopts an American identity" (p. 88).

40. Anzia Yezierska, *Bread Givers* (1925; rpt., New York: Persea Books, 1975)

41. Thomas Sowell, *Ethnic America: A History* (New York: Basic Books, 1981), 170, 173. On the disintegration of *issei* families during the internment, see also Ann Umemoto,

"Crisis in the Japanese American Family," *Asian Women* (Berkeley: Asian Women's Journal, 1971), 31–34.

42. Jade Snow Wong, *Fifth Chinese Daughter* (1945; rpt., Seattle: University of Washington Press, 1989).

43. See an expanded discussion of Jade Snow Wong's authbiography in Shirley Geoklin Lim, "The Tradition of Chinese-American Women's Life-Stories: Thematics of Race and Gender in Jade Snow Wong's *Fifth Chinese Daughter* and Maxine Hong Kingston's *The Woman Warrior*," in *American Women's Autobiography,* ed. Margo Culley (Madison: University of Wisconsin Press, 1992).

44. Kim Ronyoung, *Clay Walls* (1984; rpt., Seattle: University of Washington Press, 1990).

45. Ibid., 17, 30, 28.

46. Ibid., 28.

47. Ibid., 188.

48. Ibid., 271, 275, 298.

49. Mitsuye Yamada, "Asian Pacific American Women and Feminism" in *This Bridge Called My Back: Writings by Radical Women of Color,* ed. Cherríe Moraga and Gloria Anzaldúa (Watertown, Mass.: Persephone Press, 1981), 71–75, 74, 35.

50. Jeanne Wakatsuki Houston, *Beyond Manzanar: Views of Asian American Womanhood* (Santa Barbara: Capra Press, 1985), 9, 12, 18, 23, 27.

51. Genny Lim, "If Sartre Was a Whore," *Contact/II* (Winter/Spring 1986): 28; Karen Tei Yamashita, "Midwifs," *Contact/II* (Winter/Spring 1986): 29.

52. For discussions of popular U.S. stereotypes of Asian American women as erotica, see Frank Gibney, "Those Exotic (Erotic) Japanese Women," *Cosmopolitan* (May 1975), 166, 180–81; Elaine Louie, "The Myth of the Erotic Exotic," *Bridge* 2 (April 1973): 19–20; Kay Carter, "Dragon Lady/Geisha Girl: Hollywood's Mythical Asian Female," *Neworld* 2 (Fall 1975): 37–53.

53. Yamashita, 29.

54. For examples of discussions on *l'écriture féminine*, see *New French Feminisms: An Anthology,* ed. Elaine Marks and Isabelle de Courtivron (New York: Schocken Books, 1981), esp. 161–186, which takes up the questions: "In what ways does women's writing call attention to the fact that the writers are women?" and Isn't the final goal of writing to articulate the body?" (see Chantal Chawaf, "Linguistic Flesh," 177)

55. Susan Rubin Suleiman, "Re-Writing the Body: The Politics and Poetics of Female Exoticism," in *The Female Body in Western Culture: Contemporary Perspectives,* ed. Susan Rubin Suleiman (Cambridge: Harvard University Press, 1986), 7–29.

BLACK WRITING, WHITE READING

race and the politics of feminist interpretation

(1993)

I

> I realize that the set of feelings that I used to have about
> French men I now have about African-American women.
> Those are the people I feel inadequate in relation to and try to
> please in my writing. It strikes me that this is not just idiosyncratic.
> —JANE GALLOP, "CRITICIZING FEMINIST CRITICISM"

Twyla opens the narrative of Toni Morrison's provocative story "Recitatif" (1982) by recalling her placement as an eight-year-old child in St. Bonaventure, a shelter for neglected children, and her reaction to Roberta Fisk, the roommate she is assigned: "The minute I walked in . . . I got sick to my stomach. It was one thing to be taken out of your own bed early in the morning—it was something else to be stuck in a strange place with a girl from a whole other race. And Mary, that's my mother, she was right. Every now and then she would stop dancing long enough to tell me something important and one of the things she said was that they never washed their hair and they smelled funny. Roberta sure did. Smell funny, I mean."[1] The racial ambiguity so deftly installed at the narrative's origin through codes that function symmetrically for black women and for white women ("they never washed their hair and they smelled funny") intensifies as the story tracks the encounters of its two female protagonists over approximately thirty years. Unmediated by the sexual triangulations (the predations of white men on black women, the susceptibility of black men to white women) that have dominated black women's narrative representations of women's fraught connections across racial lines, the relationship of Twyla and Roberta discloses the operations of race in the feminine.[2] This is a story about a black woman and a white woman: but which is which?

I was introduced to "Recitatif" by a black feminist critic, Lula Fragd. Lula was certain that Twyla was black; I was equally convinced that she was white; most of the readers we summoned to resolve the dispute divided similarly along racial lines. By replacing the conventional signifiers of racial difference (such as skin color) with radically relativistic ones (such as who smells funny to whom) and by substituting for the racialized body a series of disaggregated cultural parts—pink-scalloped socks, tight green slacks, large hoop earrings, expertise at playing jacks, a taste for Jimi Hendrix or for bottled water and asparagus—the story renders race a contested terrain variously mapped from diverse positions in the social landscape. By forcing us to construct racial categories from highly ambiguous social cues, "Recitatif" elicits and exposes the unarticulated racial codes that operate at the boundaries of consciousness. To underscore the cultural specificity of these codes, Morrison writes into the text a figure of racial undecidability: Maggie, the mute kitchen worker at St. Bonaventure, who occasions the text's only mention of skin color, an explicitly ambiguous sandy color, and who walks through the text with her little kid's hat and her bowed legs "like parentheses," her silent self a blank parenthesis, a floating signifier ("R," p. 245). For both girls a hated reminder of their unresponsive mothers, Maggie is not "raced" to Twyla (that is, she is by default white): to Roberta, she is black. The two girls' readings of Maggie become in turn clues for our readings of them, readings that emanate similarly from our own cultural locations.

My own reading derived in part from Roberta's perception of Maggie as black; Roberta's more finely discriminating gaze ("she wasn't pitch-black, I knew," is all Twyla can summon to defend her assumption that Maggie is white) seemed to me to testify to the firsthand knowledge of discrimination ("R," p. 259). Similarly, Roberta is skeptical about racial harmony. When she and Twyla retrospectively discuss their tense encounter at a Howard Johnson's where Twyla was a waitress in the early 1960s, they read the historical context differently: "'Oh, Twyla, you know how it was in those days: black—white. You know how everything was.' But I didn't know. I thought it was just the opposite. Busloads of blacks and whites came into Howard Johnson's together. They roamed together then: students, musicians, lovers, protesters. You got to see everything at Howard Johnson's and blacks were very friendly with whites in those days" ("R," p. 255). In the civil rights movement that Twyla sees as a common struggle against racial barriers, Roberta sees the distrust of white intervention and the impulse toward a separatist Black Power movement: she has the insider's perspective on power and race relations.

It was a more pervasive asymmetry in authority, however, that secured my construction of race in the text, a construction I recount with considerable embarrassment for its possible usefulness in fleshing out the impulse within contemporary white feminism signalled by the "not just idiosyncratic" confession that stands as this paper's epigraph. As Gallop both wittily acknowledges the force of African-American women's political critique of white academic feminism's seduction by "French men" and, by simply transferring the transference, reenacts the process of idealization that unwittingly obscures more complex social relations, I singled out the power relations of the girls from the broader network of cultural signs.[3] Roberta seemed to be consistently the more sophisticated reader of the social scene, the subject presumed by Twyla to know, the teller of the better (although not necessarily more truthful) stories, the adventurer whose casual mention of an appointment with Jimi Hendrix exposes the depths of Twyla's social ignorance ("'Hendrix? Fantastic,' I said. 'Really fantastic. What's she doing now?'" ["R," p. 250]) From the girls' first meeting at St. Bonaventure, Twyla feels vulnerable to Roberta's judgment and perceives Roberta (despite her anxiety about their differences) as possessing something she lacks and craves: a more acceptably negligent mother (a sick one rather than a dancing one) and, partially as a consequence, a more compelling physical presence that fortifies her cultural authority. Twyla is chronically hungry; Roberta seems to her replete, a daughter who has been adequately fed and thus can disdain the institutional Spam and Jell-O that Twyla devours as a contrast to the popcorn and Yoo-Hoo that had been her customary fare. The difference in maternal stature, linked in the text with nurture, structures Twyla's account of visiting day at St. Bonaventure. Twyla's mother, smiling and waving "like she was the little girl," arrives wearing tight green buttocks-hugging slacks and a ratty fur jacket for the chapel service, and bringing no food for the lunch that Twyla consequently improvises out of fur-covered jelly beans from her Easter basket ("R," p. 246). "Bigger than any man," Roberta's mother arrives bearing a huge cross on her chest, a Bible in the crook of her arm, and a basket of chicken, ham, oranges, and chocolate-covered graham crackers ("R," p. 247). In the subsequent Howard Johnson scene that Twyla's retrospective analysis links with the frustrations of visiting day ("The wrong food is always with the wrong people. Maybe that's why I got into waitress work later—to match up the right people with the right food" ["R," p. 248]) the difference in stature is replayed between the two daughters. Roberta, sitting in a booth with "two guys smothered in head and facial hair," her own hair "so big and wild I could hardly see her face," wearing a "powder-blue halter and shorts outfit and earrings the size of bracelets," rebuffs Twyla, clad in her waitress outfit, her knees rather than her midriff showing, her hair in a net, her legs in thick stockings and sturdy white shoes ("R," p. 249). Although the two bodies are never directly represented, the power of metonymy generates a contrast between the amplitude of the sexualized body and the skimpiness and pallor of the socially harnessed body. Twyla's sense of social and physical inadequacy vis-à-vis Roberta, like her representation of her mother's inferiority to Roberta's, signalled Twyla's whiteness to me by articulating a white woman's fantasy (my own) about black women's potency.[4] This fantasy's tenaciousness is indicated by its persistence in the face of contrary evidence. Roberta's mother, the story strongly implies, is mentally rather than physically ill, her capacity to nurture largely fictional; Roberta, who is never actually represented eating, is more lastingly damaged than Twyla by maternal neglect, more vulnerable as an adult to its memory, a weakness on which Twyla capitalizes during their political conflicts as adults; the tenuousness of the adult Roberta's own maternal status (she acquires stepchildren, rather than biological children, through her marriage to an older man) may also testify figuratively to a lack created by insufficient mothering.

Pivoting not on skin color, but on size, sexuality, and the imagined capacity to nurture and be nurtured, on the construction of embodiedness itself as a symptom and source of cultural authority, my reading installs the (racialized) body at the center of a text that deliberately withholds conventional racial iconography. Even in her reading of this first half of the story, Lula's interpretation differed from mine by emphasizing cultural practices more historically nuanced than my categorical distinctions in body types, degrees of social cool, or modes of mothering. Instead of reading Twyla's body psychologically as white, Lula read Twyla's name as culturally black; and she placed greater emphasis on Roberta's language in the Howard Johnson scene—her primary location being a decidedly white hippie "oh, wow"—than on the image of her body gleaned by reading envy in the narrative gaze and by assigning racial meaning to such cultural accessories as the Afro, hoop earrings, and a passion for Jimi Hendrix that actually circulated independently of race throughout the counterculture of the 1960s; as Lula knew and I did not, Jimi Hendrix appealed more to white than to black audiences.[5] Roberta's coldness in this scene—she barely acknowledges her childhood friend—becomes, in Lula's reading, a case of straightforward white racism, and Twyla's surprise at the rebuff reflects her naivete about the power of personal loyalties and social movements to undo racial hierarchies.

More importantly, however, this scene was not critical for Lula's reading. Instead of the historical locus that was salient for me—not coincidentally, I believe, since the particular aura of (some) black women for (some) white women during the civil rights movement is being recapitulated in contemporary feminism (as I will discuss later)—what was central to her were scenes from the less culturally exceptional 1970s, which disclosed the enduring systems of racism rather than the occasional moments of heightened black cultural prestige. In general, Lula focussed less on cultural than on economic status, and she was less concerned with daughters and their feelings toward their mothers than with these daughters' politics after they were mothers.

When Twyla and Roberta meet in a food emporium twelve years after the Howard Johnson scene, Twyla has married a fireman and has one child and limited income; Roberta has married an IBM executive and lives in luxury in the wealthy part of town with her husband, her four stepchildren, and her Chinese chauffeur. Twyla concludes in a voice of seemingly racial resentment: "Everything is so easy for them. They think they own the world" ("R," p. 252). A short time later the women find themselves on opposite sides of a school integration struggle in which both their children are faced with bussing: Twyla's to the school that Roberta's stepchildren now attend, and Roberta's to a school in a less afflu- ent neighborhood. After Twyla challenges Roberta's opposition to the bussing, Roberta tries to defuse the conflict: "'Well, it is a free country.' 'Not yet, but it will be,'" Twyla responds ("R," p. 256). Twyla's support of bussing, and of social change generally, and Roberta's self-interested resistance to them position the women along the bitter racial lines that split the fraying fabric of feminism in the late 1970s and early 1980s.[6]

Privileging psychology over politics, my reading disintegrates in the story's sec- ond half. Lula's reading succeeds more consistently, yet by constructing the black woman (in her account, Twyla) as the politically correct but politically naive and morally conventional foil to the more socially adventurous, if politically conser- vative, white woman (Roberta), it problematically racializes the moral (op)po- sitions Morrison opens to revaluation in her extended (and in many ways parallel) narrative of female friendship, *Sula*.[7] Neither reading can account adequately for the text's contradictory linguistic evidence, for if Twyla's name is more charac- teristically black than white, it is perhaps best known as the name of a white dancer, Twyla Tharp, whereas Roberta shares her last name, Fisk, with a cel- ebrated black (now integrated) university. The text's heterogeneous inscriptions of race resist a totalizing reading.

Propelled by this irresolution to suspend my commitment to the intentional fallacy, I wrote to Toni Morrison. Her response raised as many questions as it resolved. Morrison explained that her project in this story was to substitute class for racial codes in order to drive a wedge between these typically elided categories.[8] Both eliciting and foiling our assumption that Roberta's middle-class marriage and politics, and Twyla's working-class perspective, are reliable racial clues, Morrison incorporated details about their husbands' occupations that encourage an alternative conclusion. If we are familiar (as I was not) with IBM's efforts to recruit black executives and with the racial exclusiveness of the firemen's union in upstate New York, where the story is set, we read Roberta as middle-class black and Twyla as working-class white. Roberta's resistance to bussing, then, is based on class rather than racial loyalties: she doesn't want her (middle-class black) stepchildren bussed to a school in a (white) working-class neighborhood; Twyla, conversely, wants her (white) working-class child bussed to a middle-class school (regardless of that school's racial composition). What we hear, from this perspective, in Twyla's envy of Roberta, "Everything is so easy for them," and in her challenge to the status quo—it's not a free country "but it will be"—is class rather than (or perhaps compounded by) racial resentment, the adult economic counterpart to Twyla's childhood fantasy of Roberta's plenitude.

By underscoring the class-based evidence for reading Twyla as white, Morrison confirms at once my own conclusion and its fantasmatic basis. Morrison's weighting of social detail, her insistence on the intersections, however constructed, between race and class, are more closely aligned with Lula's political perspective than with my psychological reading, fueled by racially specific investments that the text deliberately solicits and exposes. By both inviting and challenging racialized readings that are either "right" for the "wrong" reasons or "wrong" for the "right" ones, "Recitatif" focusses some questions to address to the massive, asymmetrical crossing of racial boundaries in recent feminist criticism. If white feminist readings of black women's texts disclose white critical fantasies, what (if any) value do these readings have—and for whom?[9] How do white women's readings of black women's biological bodies inform our readings of black women's textual bodies? How do different critical discourses both inflect and inscribe racial fantasies? What rhetorical strategies do these discourses produce, and (how) do these strategies bear on the value of the readings they ostensibly legitimate?

Black feminists have debated the politics and potential of white feminists' critical intervention, but they have not compared or critiqued specific reading strategies, which is perhaps more properly a task of white self-criticism.[10] This essay attempts to contribute to this task by examining signal moments, across a range of discourses, in the white critical texts emerging with such volume and intensity within contemporary feminism. By "contemporary" I mean since 1985, a watershed year that marked the simultaneous emergence of what has been called postfeminism and, not coincidentally, of pervasive white feminist attention to texts by women of color.[11] This new attentiveness was overdetermined: by the sheer brilliance and power of this writing and its escalating status in the literary marketplace and, consequently, the academy; by white feminist restlessness with an already well-mined white female literary tradition; and by internal logic of white feminism's trajectory through theoretical discourses that, by evacuating the referent from the signifier's play, fostered a turn to texts that reassert the authority of experience, that reinstate political agency, and that rearticulate the body and its passions. The end of the most confident and ethnocentric period of the second wave (roughly 1970–1985) has interestingly collapsed postfeminism and prefeminism as the ideological frameworks in which white women turn to black women to articulate a politics and to embody a discursive authority that are either lost or not yet found. Like Frances D. Gage's perception of Sojourner Truth rescuing the faltering 1851 Women's Rights conference in Akron through the power of her physical presence and resounding question, "A'n't I a woman?" which took "us up in her strong arms and carried us safely over the slough of difficulty turning the whole tide in our favor"; or, in one of the generative contexts for the second wave of feminism, like Jane Stembridge's discovery of a miraculously unashamed mode of female speech in Fanny Lou Hamer's proud bearing and voice at a 1964 SNCC rally—"Mrs. Hamer . . . knows that she is good. . . . If she didn't know that . . . she wouldn't stand here, with her head back and sing! She couldn't speak the *way* that she speaks and the way she speaks is this: she announces. I do not announce. I apologize"; the postfeminist turn to black women novelists enacts an anxious transference onto black women's speech.[12]

As Valerie Smith has eloquently argued, the attempt to rematerialize an attenuated white feminism by routing it through black women's texts reproduces in the textual realm white women's historical relation to the black female bodies that have nurtured them.[13] This relation unfolds along a spectrum of materiality. More complex than its prefeminist analogue, contemporary white feminism invokes black women's texts not only to relegitimate the feminist agenda called into question by post-structuralism but also, paradoxically, to relegitimate post-structuralism by finding its prefiguration in black women's texts. Yet whether as a corrective difference or a confirming similarity, as a sanction for a renewed or a resuspended referentiality, black women writers are enlisted to bestow a cultural authority that derives in part from their enforced experience of embodiment.

To attempt to do justice to the spectrum of white feminist approaches, I have organized this study through three case studies that, although far from exhaustive, nevertheless offer a range of influential discourses: deconstruction, psychoanalysis, and cultural criticism. This sequence traces a trajectory from a strategy that seems able to escape my own fantasmatic production of an embodied other to one that unexpectedly reproduces it. My conclusion will turn to the conclusion of "Recitatif" to reopen the question of reading and race.

2

> The nonblack feminist critic / theorist who honestly engages his or her own autobiographical implication in a brutal past is likely to provide nuances such as that of the black feminist critic. What, however, are the preconditions and precautions for the nonblack feminist critic / theorist who dares to undertake such a project?
> —MAE G. HENDERSON, RESPONSE TO HOUSTON A. BAKER, JR., "THERE IS NO MORE BEAUTIFUL WAY"

Through the exchanges between Derrida and Lacan, we have become familiar with the debate between deconstruction and psychoanalysis over the discursive construction of subjectivity. Recent work by two prominent white feminist theorists, Barbara Johnson and Margaret Homans, suggests how this debate plays out in the related question of the discursive construction of race: a question especially urgent for critics reading and writing across racial lines.

Because it directly poses the question of the white reader's relation to the African-American text and because it has widely influenced readings of Zora Neale Hurston in particular, and of race in general, "Thresholds of Difference: Structures of Address in Zora Neale Hurston" is an apt focus for a study of Barbara Johnson's textual strategies.[14] "Thresholds" mounts an enormously complex and brilliant critique of the belief in essential racial differences that for Johnson is the substance of racism. (Arguing that black representations of a black essence always operate within a "specific interlocutionary situation" and are "matters of strategy rather than truth," Johnson brackets the question of a possible black belief in, or desire for belief in, a black identity ["T," p. 285]). Through a reading of three Hurston texts—"How It Feels to Be Colored Me" (1928); "What White Publishers Won't Print" (1950); and *Mules and Men* (1935)—Johnson maps the interlocutionary situations that generate Hurston's ambiguous and contradictory representations of racial identity and difference. Rather than a constant, color (which figures race for both Hurston and Johnson) varies with positions in discursive exchanges whose subversion of the difference between inside and outside, self and other, is detailed in Johnson's reading of Hurston's complex relation as a northern anthropologist to the southern black communities whose folklore (or "lies") she represents in *Mules and Men*. By anticipating and legitimating the project of dereferentializing race, and by relocating differences between the races as internal differences (as in her celebrated figure of resemblances among the heterogeneous contents of differently colored bags), Hurston—or the Hurston represented by these particular texts—is a deconstructive critic's dream.[15]

In the body of the essay, Johnson and Hurston seem to speak in a single voice, but the two voices occasionally diverge, and through their divergence the essay interrogates the politics of interracial reading. Paralleling the "multilayered envelope of address" with which Hurston frames the folktales of *Mules and Men*, Johnson frames her own readings with an analysis of her position as a "white deconstructor" interpreting a "black novelist and anthropologist" ("T," p. 278). As her language indicates, the frame deploys the rhetoric of racial essences the rest of the essay deconstructs. In addressing (as does Hurston's frame) the politics of a discourse on race, the frame also demonstrates their effects: the interlocutory situation of a white reading of a black text demands some acknowledgment of racial differences. The essay thus deploys a schizophrenic discourse, split between a first-person discourse on the politics of discourse across race and a third-person discourse on the discursive (de)construction of race. The discursive position of a "white deconstructor" of race is self-different, embracing both the assertion and the deconstruction of difference, positions the text constructs as white and black, respectively.

These positions, however, are themselves unstable. Through what becomes an excess of politicized rhetoric in the frame, read retrospectively against the text's interior, the differences between outside and inside, first person and third person, white and black, collapse and with them the tension between politics and deconstruction. If the questioning of motive and audience in the frame's opening paragraph are to be taken straight, the response the next paragraph offers is far more problematic: "It was as though I were asking her [Hurston] for answers to questions I did not even know I was unable to formulate. I had a lot to learn, then, from Hurston's way of dealing with multiple agendas and heterogeneous implied readers" ("T," p. 278). The deference to Hurston seems as disingenuous as Hurston's comparably located and requisite expressions of gratitude to her white patron, Mrs. Osgood Mason; for as much as Johnson has to learn from Hurston about strategic discursive constructions of race, she has little to learn from her about strategies of discourse generally: far from a humble student or innocent reader with no anterior agendas of her own, she constitutes Hurston as much in her own deconstructive image as she is herself reconstituted by Hurston's texts.[16] Yet read in the context of Johnson's reading of *Mules and Men*, the dissembling rhetoric of the frame becomes a deliberate imitation of Hurston's imitation of the strategy of "lying" that she learns from the Eatonville residents who, weary of white folks prying into their ways, set verbal "'toy (s)'" "'outside the door[s]'" of their minds to distract and deceive their white investigators ("T," p. 286). If, as Johnson argues, "it is impossible to tell whether Hurston the narrator is *describing* a strategy [of lying] or *employing* one" since "Hurston's very ability to fool us—or to fool us into *thinking* we have been fooled—is itself the only effective way of conveying the rhetoric of the 'lie,'" Johnson's ability to fool us functions analogously as a rhetorical tool that, once we have understood its calculated impact, transports us along with both Hurston and Johnson from the outside to the inside of Eatonville's discursive universe ("T," pp. 286, 289).

The fluidity of this boundary transgression, however, conceals an important difference between Hurston crossing the boundaries between subject and object, North and South, literate and oral communities, and Johnson or her white readers crossing a racial boundary. In the course of Johnson's essay, a discourse on positionality comes to displace, as well as to produce, a discourse on race. As the frame slides into the interior, the questions it raises disappear. There is no further problem about a white deconstructor writing about, or writing as, a black novelist and anthropologist, since position has come to stand for race. This erasure of conflict is clear when the frame briefly returns at the end, merging Johnson's and Hurston's voices in the single conclusion that "the terms 'black' and 'white,' 'inside' and 'outside,' continue to matter" only as diversely inhabited and mutually constitutive positions on a signifying chain ("T," p. 289). By dislocating race from historically accreted differences in power, Johnson's deconstructive reading dovetails with Hurston's libertarian politics.[17]

In Johnson's discourse on gender, by contrast, her feminist politics enforce a distinction, political rather than metaphysical, between the positions inhabited by men and women: "Jacques Derrida may sometimes see himself as *philosophically* positioned as a woman, but he is not *politically* positioned as a woman. Being positioned as a woman is not something that is entirely voluntary." The shift from gender to race in the next sentence—"Or, to put it another way, if you tell a member of the Ku Klux Klan that racism is a repression of self-difference, you are likely to learn a thing or two about repression"—bypasses the racial analogy to the problematic masculine (= white) assumption of a figuratively feminine (= black) position to insinuate the reaction of the racist that places the white deconstructor in a position of vulnerability akin to (rather than politically distinct from) the black person's position.[18] Similarly, Johnson distinguishes more firmly between the figurative and the literal in relation to gender than to race: "the re-valuation of the *figure* of the woman by a male author cannot substitute for the actual participation of women in the literary conversation. Mallarmé may be able to speak from the place of the silenced woman, but as long as *he* is occupying it, the silence that is broken in theory is maintained in reality."[19] Johnson's relent-lessly deconstructive discourse on race subverts the equivalent gestures that would subject her own role as a white deconstructor to her critique of masculine deconstructions of gender. This difference within her practice of deconstruction, the undoing of a counterpart for race to the feminist resistance to deconstruction, facilitates the project of writing across race. The interlocutory situation that re-quires the white critic to acknowledge racial difference also requires her to dis-solve the tension between literal and figurative, political and philosophical, voluntary and involuntary modes of sameness and difference.

Johnson's essay first appeared in the 1985 special issue of *Critical Inquiry* en-titled "'Race,' Writing and Difference," edited by Henry Louis Gates, Jr., whose position on the figurative status of race is signalled by the quotation marks with which he encloses the word; Johnson's essay conforms clearly to that volume's ideology. Gates has been criticized for the politics of his deconstruction of race, and some of the most passionate criticism has been launched by black feminists. Following one of these women, Joyce A. Joyce, Margaret Homans argues com-pellingly in a recent essay, "'Racial Composition': Metaphor and the Body in the Writing of Race," that Gates's, and thus by extension Johnson's, deliteralization of race is effectively a masculinist position.[20] The difference between Johnson and Homans derives to a significant degree from the shift from deconstruction to psychoanalysis and the consequent shift from the inside/outside opposition privi-leged by deconstruction to that between body and language, or the literal and the figurative, which psychoanalysis genders oppositely from deconstruction. Whereas for Johnson, playing primarily off Derrida, figuration enacts an emancipatory feminine displacement of phallogocentric reference, for Homans, playing off Lacan and Chodorow, figuration enacts a masculine displacement of the specifically female (maternal) body whose exclusion founds the symbolic reg-ister. Whereas for Johnson the figurativeness of race is enabling for all races, for Homans it enables only men, since women across race accede to figuration only by devaluing the femaleness that is culturally conflated with the body. Paradoxi-cally, however, both positions serve to legitimate white feminist readings of black women's texts: privileging the figurative enables the white reader to achieve figu-rative blackness: privileging the literal enables the white *woman* reader to forge a gender alliance that outweighs (without negating) both racial differences within gender and racial alliances across gender.

"'Racial Composition'" takes as its starting point the debate on black literary criticism carried out in four texts in a 1987 issue of *New Literary History*: the origi-nal essay by Joyce A. Joyce, "The Black Canon: Reconstructing Black American Literary Criticism," criticizing the deliteralization of race in Gates and Houston A. Baker, Jr.; the responses by Gates and Baker; and Joyce's response to them.[21] Building on her premises that "the position Gates inherits from post-structuralism identifies and celebrates the abstract as masculine and devalues embodiment as female," and that Gates "substitute(s), in the undesirable position of the refer-ent or ground from which language differentiates itself, female for black,"

Homans deftly teases out a gendered subtext in the exchange ("RC," pp. 3–4).[22] In Joyce's critique of the assimilation of black literary criticism to the elite discourse of post-structuralism that, through its esoteric terminology and representation of race as a metaphor, severs its connections with the black reading community, with literary traditions rooted in the lived experience of black people, and with the concrete, sensuous features of black literary language, Homans sees a defense of the "body that is troped as female in post-structuralist theory and whose absence that theory requires" ("RC," p. 7). In the high-handed and patronizing responses by Gates and Baker, she uncovers these critics' sexualized self-representations as the saviors of a feminized black literary body in danger of a retrograde sensualization at the hands of black feminists. Homans then proceeds, via an analysis of the more egalitarian tone and terms of the debate on essentialism within black feminism, to a powerful analysis of the rhetoric of critical scenes in narratives by Alice Walker, Toni Morrison, and Maya Angelou, where the tension between (relatively) literal and figurative language constitutes the "rhetorical form in which the debate over racial and gendered 'essence' is worked out. The use or representation of a relatively literal language corresponds to and puts into practice a belief in the embodiedness of race and of gender . . . while the view that race is figurative coincides with and is performed as a celebration of language as figuration and a tendency to use conspicuous metaphors" ("RC," p. 5). While insisting on the necessity of maintaining, at different times, both positions, Homans calls attention to black women writers' continuing and complex commitment "to the body and to the literal," a commitment that contrasts in both its substance and its ambivalence with Gates's and Baker's unequivocal endorsement of the figurative, and that reiterates, within a different context, Homans's own perspective in *Bearing the Word* ("RC," p. 19).[23] As Johnson extends and reauthorizes deconstruction through Hurston, Homans extends and reauthorizes, primarily through Walker, a revaluation of the literal.

Like Johnson, Homans frames her argument by positioning herself in relation to black women's texts. Both frames incorporate acknowledgments of racial difference; but whereas Johnson becomes, in the course of her argument, figuratively black, Homans becomes more emphatically white: "Neither literally nor figuratively a black feminist, then (nor even figuratively literally), I would prefer, following bell hooks' recommendation, to identify my perspective clearly as that of a white feminist" ("RC," p. 38). Homans's feminist critique of the overvaluation of the figurative demands that, in direct opposition to Johnson, she affirm the literalness of (at least her own) race.

This is a necessary conclusion, in the context of Homans's argument, and also a brave and a problematic one. By embodying her own whiteness, Homans contests the racialization that coexists with the more overt gendering of the symbolic register. In a white feminist counterpart to Gates's strategy of making blackness figurative and figuration black ("figuration is the nigger's occupation"), Homans insistently pinions (female) whiteness to literality, resisting through a different route the dominant culture's splitting of a white symbolic realm from a black materiality.[24] Homans affirms solidarity with black women by asserting a literal difference that is ultimately overridden by the sameness of literality: by the shared association with embodiment.

In resisting white patriarchal culture's dissociation from the body, however,

Homans also implicitly resists a recurrent construction of whiteness by black women writers such as Walker who, in one of the scenes from *The Temple of My Familiar* that Homans analyzes from a different perspective, represents whiteness as the "hideous personal deficiency" of having no skin, of being "a ghost," the quintessence of lack, not only of color, but also of body itself.[25] The occasional and moving alliances between black and white women that Homans analyzes in texts by Walker and Morrison do not necessarily produce or reflect a shared experience of embodiment. Six months pregnant, beaten, "sweating" milk for the eighteen-month-old baby from whom she has been separated, torn between "the fire in her feet and the fire on her back," Sethe hears Amy Denver's "young white voice . . . like a sixteen-year-old boy's" before she sees the scrawny body with its "arms like cane stalks" (*B*, pp. 79, 31, 34, 32). Although she has been "'bleeding for four years,'" Amy "'ain't having nobody's baby'": the carmine velvet that constitutes the goal of *her* escape sublimates the reproductive female body into cloth (*B*, p. 83). As the midwife whose *last* name is conferred on Sethe's baby, Amy is affiliated as closely with the absent (and literate) father (with whom the baby will strongly identify) as with the birthing mother. By "reading" the scar inscribed on Sethe's back, Amy is positioned on the side of figuration vis-à-vis the massively embodied Sethe. By implying that the embodiment black and white women share is weightier than differences in color, Homans proposes a commonality often called into question by black women's texts.

More problematically, however, literalizing whiteness logically entails reliteralizing blackness as well, and an argument for the literalness of race (or sex) can be safely made only from the position of the subordinated race (or sex), which can define and revalue its own distinctiveness. Speaking for the literal from a position of dominance risks reinscribing the position of the dominated. Homans's position on figuration leads her to an impasse: as a woman she can't ally herself with a (masculine) position on the figurativeness of race: as a *white* woman she can't ally herself with black women writers' (ambivalent) adherence to the embodiedness of race without potentially reproducing the structure of dominance she wants to subvert. There are as serious, although very different, problems with revaluing the literalness of race as with asserting its figurativeness.

3

> I began to wonder whether there was any position from which a white middle-class feminist could say anything on the subject [of race] without sounding exactly like [a white middle-class feminist]. . . . The rhetorical predictability of it all. The political correctness. . . . In which case it might be better not to say anything.
> —NANCY K. MILLER, "CRITICIZING FEMINIST CRITICISM"

Different as are their consequences for the reading of race, deconstruction and psychoanalysis are both subjectivist critical ideologies that mandate a high degree of self-reflexiveness. Materialist feminisms, by contrast, which have always had priority within black feminist discourse, emphasize the political objections (and objectivity) of the reading over the question of personality.[26] Designed to disclose systematically (and ultimately to change) the intersecting axes of race, class, gender, and sexuality through which women are multiply and differentially oppressed, materialist feminisms, both black and white, have de-emphasized the reader's racial location. White readers within this discourse have paid only perfunctory (if any) attention to the problem of their own positionality, and black materialists have generally been hospitable to white women's readings of black texts.[27] It is not coincidental that Valerie Smith, who insists on the materialist orientation of black feminist theory, also redefines this theory to "refer not only to theory written (or practiced) by black feminists, but also to a way of reading inscriptions of race (particularly but not exclusively blackness), gender (particularly but not exclusively womanhood), and class in modes of cultural expression"; or that Hazel Carby, writing within the discourse of cultural studies, has become one of the most resolutely antiessentialist and politically exacting black feminist voices, calling into question simultaneously the presumption of interracial sisterhood and the presumption of seamless continuity between racial experience, discourse, and interpretation.[28] The de-essentialization of race among black feminists (in contrast to both white feminists and male Afro-Americans) has occurred primarily through the intervention of material rather than textual differences, and under the aegis of Marxism and cultural studies rather than deconstruction.

Materialist feminism would appear to be the approach through which white critics could write about black women's texts with the least self-consciousness about racial difference and perhaps with the least difference. Yet white investments in some form of black cultural or social specificity, investments exempted from analysis under the banner of an interracial socialist feminist sisterhood, tend to intervene in white readings of black texts, substituting racial for class specificity rather than disrupting each with the other. Racial differences are visibly played out in the critical response to *The Color Purple*. Both black and white feminists from diverse critical schools have celebrated the text's subversive stance toward the narrative and rhetorical conventions of epistolary, sentimental, and realist fiction, and toward the sexual, domestic, and spiritual institutions of patriarchy.[29] But among materialist feminists race has made a difference in the assessment of the novel's politics. For example, bell hooks criticizes the novel for isolating individual quests and transformative private relationships from collective political effort, for celebrating the "ethics of a narcissistic new-age spirituality wherein economic prosperity indicates that one is chosen," and for breaking with the revolutionary impulse of the African-American literary tradition epitomized by the slave narrative; Cora Kaplan, in an essay entitled "Keeping the Color in *The Color Purple*," defends the novel from accusations of bourgeois liberalism by British socialists who, she feels, have "bleached" the text into "an uncontentious, sentimental, harmless piece of international libertarianism" by failing to understand its relation to "a specifically racial set of discourses about the family and femininity." Kaplan revalues the novel through a black cultural context that hooks claims the novel has repudiated.[30] And whereas Hazel Carby criticizes the critics who, through their celebration of *The Color Purple* (and its line of descent from *Their Eyes Were Watching God*), indulge in a romantic vision of rural black culture that enables them to avoid confronting the complex social crises in the urban black community, Susan Willis praises the novel for contesting industrial capitalism by resurrecting the homestead and cottage industry.[31] The representation of black social relations as utopian alternatives to industrial capitalism or to patriarchal nationalism has appealed more to white than to black materialist feminists.[32]

This appeal, and its problems, surface clearly in the work of Willis, who deserves special attention as the only white feminist author of a book on black women novelists and of an essay in Cheryl A. Wall's recent anthology of black feminist criticism, *Changing Our Own Words* (1989).[33] In *Specifying: Black Women Writing the American Experience* (1987), Willis maps the ways that twentieth-century black women novelists record through their narrative strategies and subjects the shift from a southern agrarian to a northern industrial economy. Suffused with nostalgia for an agrarian culture that in Willis's opinion supported a "noncommodified relationship" between an author, her language, and her audience, the book insists that "one of the major problems facing black writers today is how to preserve the black cultural heritage in the face of the homogenizing function of bourgeois society."[34] This romanticization of "the" black cultural heritage, whose truth resides in an uncontaminated past to which these novels' protagonists repeatedly return, becomes apparent through the contrast between Willis's study and Hazel Carby's *Reconstructing Womanhood: The Emergence of the Afro-American Woman Novelist*, published the same year, which situates nineteenth-century black women's cultural discourses in relation to hegemonic ideologies.[35] In her essay "I Shop Therefore I Am: Is There a Place for Afro-American Culture in Commodity Culture?" however, Willis begins to engage this relation by shifting from a strict economic reading of a discrete literary tradition to a more variegated account of African-American participation in the cultural arena produced by commodity capitalism. The essay, more than the book, positions Willis in a relation to Fredrick Jameson analogous to that between Johnson and Derrida, and even more to that between Homans and Lacan, since Willis, like Homans, prioritizes what is unincorporated by a master system. "I Shop Therefore I Am" opens up the third term that Jameson brackets in "Reification and Utopia in Mass Culture," the term representing the possibility of "authentic cultural production" by marginal social groups that inhabit a position outside the dialectic of high culture and mass culture. More committed than Jameson to criticizing mass culture from a position of estrangement that tends in her work to devolve into a place of authenticity, Willis both racializes and genders a cultural exterior, relinquishing black men to an ambiguous dance of subversion and assimilation with mass culture while retaining black women as unambivalent voices of resistance.[36]

Willis answers her central question—whether it is possible for African Americans to participate in commodity culture without being assimilated to it—in gendered terms. The essay plays Toni Morrison, whose Claudia in *The Bluest Eye* represents for Willis "the radical potential inherent in the position of being 'other' to dominant society" by repudiating the white-dominated culture industry epitomized by a Shirley Temple doll, against Michael Jackson, who "states himself as a commodity" through the vertiginous display of self-transformations and imitations that undo the possibility of authenticity ("I," pp. 174, 187). "*Moonwalker* suggests a split between contemporary black women's fiction, which strives to create images of social wholeness based on the rejection of commodity capitalism, and what seems to be a black male position which sees the commodity as something that can be played with and enjoyed or subverted" ("I," p. 195). Although Willis

reluctantly admits the subversive possibilities of parody, represented in her essay by Jackson and by the black film and art critic Kobena Mercer, who argues
that commodity culture heightens the radical potential of artifice, she clearly prefers the authenticity represented for her by Morrison and Walker, with whom the
essay begins and ends. This preference incurs two penalties. First, Willis's analytical inventiveness and subtlety are most impressively released by untangling
the contradictions of mass cultural figures: Michael Jackson and his conservative
antitype Mickey Mouse, on whose genealogical descent from the tradition of
black minstrelsy she brilliantly speculates in an epilogue to a slightly different
version of this essay that was published in *New Formations*. The utopian pressures Willis levies on black women writers, by contrast, simplify her interpretation. Moreover, by pitting black women novelists against black male cultural
critics and performers, Willis sidesteps an encounter with the black feminist critics who have endorsed the position she characterizes as "black male." Although
there is more of an encounter with black feminist criticism in the essay, where
Willis acknowledges her differences from Carby, for example, but doesn't theorize them, than in the book, where she lists black feminists in a general bibliography rather than engaging with them individually, Willis still doesn't interrogate
what fuels her own investment in black women writers' representation of "social
wholeness," "the autonomous subject," and "fullness of . . . humanity" ("I," pp.
195, 174).[37]

The essay, however, does offer clues. In contract to Homans, who invokes black
women's representations of alliances with white women to underscore the prospects of reciprocity and commonality, Willis enlists black women's representations
of white women to suggest women's socially constructed differences. In *The Bluest Eye*'s characterization of "frozen faced white baby dolls" and in *Meridian*'s account of the mummified white female body exhibited for profit by her husband,
Willis finds images of the reification white women suffer through immersion
(both longer and deeper than black women's) in the culture of commodities.
Haunting the white female consumer's version of the cogito, "I shop therefore I
am" (parody is apparently a strategy available to white feminists if not to black),
the specter of the self's mortification as commodity drives the commitment to
the difference of black women's texts, as the title of the other version of this essay indicates: "I Want the Black One: Is There a Place for Afro-American Culture in Commodity Culture?" Overtly, this title replaces the voice of the white
female consumer whose identity is shopping with the voice of the black female
consumer manipulated into buying black replicants of white commodities,
Christie dolls instead of Barbies. Yet this overdetermined referent of the first-person pronoun betrays as well (and this is presumably why this title was not used
for the version of this essay in Wall's anthology) the desire of the white feminist
critic who also wants "the black one"—the text that promises resistance and integrity, the utopian supplement to her own "deconstruction of commoditiess."[38]
White feminists, like the frozen or mummified white women represented in some
black women's texts, seem in Willis's discourse to be corpses finding political energy through the corpus of black women.

Willis's essay brings us back, through a different route, to my reading of
Roberta as a site of authority and plenitude figured as a vital, integrated body. In
contrast to Johnson and Homans, who locate black and white women on the same

(although opposite) sides of the symbolic register's divide, Willis and I operate from a model of difference rather than similarity. The claims for sameness is enabled by, and in turn reauthorizes, belief in a subversive feminine position in language (whether the subversion operates through figuration or literality); the argument for an idealized (biological, social, or literary) difference is fueled by the perception of an increasingly compromised white feminist social position drained by success of oppositionality. But whether argued in terms of sameness or of difference, or in terms of the symbolic or the social domains, these theorizations of reading across race are marked by white desires.

4

> The first thing you do is to forget that i'm Black. Second, you must
> never forget that i'm Black.
> (PAT PARKER, "FOR THE WHITE PERSON WHO WANTS TO KNOW
> HOW TO BE MY FRIEND")

How, then, should we evaluate this critical undertaking? The question incorporates two complexly interwoven ones, a hermeneutic question about difference and a political question about legitimacy, that I wish to (re)open briefly in my conclusion by returning to my starting point: reading "Recitatif."

To produce an allegory about reading and race, I omitted aspects of the story—most importantly, its own conclusion—that complicate the division between the characters and, consequently, between their readers. "Recitatif" ends with parallel recognitions by Twyla and Roberta that each perceived the mute Maggie as her own unresponsive, rejecting mother, and therefore hated and wanted to harm her. After dramatizing the differences produced by race and class, the story concludes with the shared experience of abandoned little girls who, in some strange twist of the oedipal story, discover that they killed (wanted to kill), as well as loved (wanted to love), their mothers (see "R," p. 261).[39] Sameness coexists with difference, psychology with politics. Race enforces no absolute distinctions between either characters or readers, all of whom occupy diverse subject positions, some shared, some antithetical.[40] By concluding with a psychological narrative that crosses differences (indeed, with a variant of *the* universalizing psychological narrative), "Recitatif" complicates, without cancelling, both its narrative of difference and the differences in reading that this narrative provokes.

Race enters complexly into feminist reading. The three case studies examined in this essay do indicate certain pervasive tendencies among white feminists, who have tended to read black women's texts through critical lenses that filter out the texts' embeddedness in black political and cultural traditions and that foreground instead their relation to the agendas of white feminism, which the texts alter, or prefigure, but ultimately reconfirm. For despite Jane Gallop's account of the displacement of French men by African-American women as figures of authority for white feminists, the discourses produced by French (and German and American) men continue to shape the reading habits of white feminists, who are usually better trained in literary theory than in African-American cultural studies. There has been little in white feminism comparable to the detailed reconstructions of black women's literary traditions produced by Barbara Christian, Mary Helen Washington, Deborah E. McDowell, Gloria T. Hull, Nellie Y. McKay, or Margaret B. Wilkerson; or to the mapping of this literature's social and discursive contexts produced by Hazel Carby, Barbara Smith, Valerie Smith, bell hooks, Michele Wallace, Audre Lorde, or June Jordan.[41] Instead, we have tended to focus our readings on the "celebrity" texts—preeminently those by Hurston, Walker, and Morrison—rather than on "thick" descriptions of discursive contexts, and have typically written articles or chapters (rather than books) representing black women's texts as literary and social paradigms for white readers and writers. In these texts we have found alternative family structures, narrative strategies, and constructions of subjectivity: alternative, that is, to the cultural practices of white patriarchy, with which literature by white women has come to seem uncomfortably complicit.[42] The implied audience for this critical venture has been white.

The critical picture is not, however, entirely black and white. As the work of Hortense J. Spillers demonstrates especially well, black feminists draw from, as well as criticize, a range of "high" theoretical discourses, including the psychoanalytic discourses that have functioned more prominently within white feminism.[43] As Deborah E. McDowell has powerfully argued, moreover, white feminist tendencies to construct black feminism as "high" theory's political "other" reinscribe, rather than rework, the theory/politics opposition.[44] White feminist criticism is itself fractured by class and generational differences that partially undo the racial divide. Some still-unpublished essays, particularly those by a new and differently educated generation of graduate students, and some essays that are published less visibly than those analyzed in this paper, more closely approximate the historical and political concerns of black feminist criticism. Yet however interwoven with and ruptured by other differences, race remains a salient source of the fantasies and allegiances that shape our ways of reading.

Difference, however, paradoxically increases the value of crossing racial boundaries in reading. Our inability to avoid inscribing racially inflected investments and agendas limits white feminism's capacity either to impersonate black feminism, and potentially to render it expendable, or to counter its specific credibility. More important, white feminist readings contribute, however inadvertently, to a project many black feminists endorse: the racialization of whiteness.[45] As masculinity takes shape in part through its constructions of femininity, whiteness— that elusive color that seems not to be one—gains materiality through the desires and fantasies played out in its interpretations of blackness, interpretations that, by making the unconscious conscious, supplement articulated ideologies of whiteness with less accessible assumptions. Reading black women's texts, and reading our readings of them, is one (although certainly not the only) strategy for changing our habitual perception that "race is always an issue of Otherness that is not white: it is black, brown, yellow, red, purple even."[46]

Articulating the whiteness implied through the construction of blackness approaches, through a different route, the goal of Toni Morrison's recent critical project: "to avert the critical gaze from the racial object to the racial subject; from the described and imagined to the describers and imaginers; from the serving to the served."[47] There is a significant political difference, of course, between Morrison analyzing European-American texts and white feminist theorists staking critical claims to the African-American texts that constitute a privileged and endangered terrain of black feminist inquiry.[48] The risks of this intervention have been circumscribed, however, by the effectiveness of black feminists in establishing the authority of their own positions and by the failure of "high" theory to secure some unproblematic grounding for white feminists by either resolving or displacing the politics of reading and race. If we produce our readings cautiously and locate them in a self-conscious and self-critical relation to black feminist criticism, these risks, I hope, would be counterbalanced by the benefits of broadening the spectrum of interpretation, illuminating the social determinants of reading, and deepening our recognition of our racial selves and the "others" we fantasmatically construct—and thereby expanding the possibility of dialogue across as well as about racial boundaries.

NOTES

1. Toni Morrison, "Recitatif," in *Confirmation: An Anthology of African American Women*, ed. Amiri Baraka (LeRoi Jones) and Amina Baraka (New York, 1983), p. 243; hereafter abbreviated "R." I am deeply indebted to Lula Fragd for bringing this story to my attention and to Toni Morrison for generously discussing it with me. I am also very grateful to Margaret Homans for sharing with me an early draft of "'Racial Composition': Metaphor and Body in the Writing of Race," which became central to my thinking on writing and race; and to Janet Adelman, John Bishop, Mitchell Breitwieser, Carolyn Dinshaw, Catherine Gallagher, Anne Goldman, Crystal Gromer, Dori Hale, Saidiya Hartman, Marianne Hirsch, Tania Modleski, Helene Moglen, Michael Rogin. Dianne Sadoff, Susan Schweik, Valerie Smith, Hortense Spillers, and Jean Wyatt for their helpful comments on this essay.

2. The intervention of white men in relationships between black and white women is repeatedly represented in slave narratives, best epitomized perhaps by Harriet Jacobs, *Incidents in the Life of a Slave Girl: Written by Herself* (1861); the intervention of white women in black heterosexual relationships is most fully explored in the civil rights fiction typified by Alice Walker, *Meridian* (1976). For a study of American literary representations of the relationships between black an white women in the nineteenth-century South, see Minrose C. Gwin, *Black and White Women of the Old South: The Peculiar Sisterhood in American Literature* (Knoxville, Tenn., 1985); for an optimistic characterization of interracial female friendships in recent American women's fiction, see Elizabeth Schultz, "Out of the Woods and into the World: A Study of Interracial Friendships between Women in American Novels," in *Conjuring: Black Women, Fiction, and Literary Tradition*, ed. Marjorie Pryse and Hortense J. Spillers (Bloomington, Ind., 1985), pp. 67–85.

3. *Transference* is Gallop's own term for her relation to black feminist critics. In her *Around 1981: Academic Feminist Literary Theory* (New York, 1992), esp. pp. 169–70, Gallop critiques the idealization and exoticization of black women, but she limits herself to making the transference conscious rather than positing alternatives to it. In "Transferences: Gender and Race: The Practice of Theory," delivered at the University of California, Berkeley, 3 Apr. 1992, Deborah E. McDowell, who had inadvertently occasioned Gallop's comments about transference, deliberately spoke back from, and thereby exploded, the position of the transferential object.

4. The "not just idiosyncratic" nature of this fantasy is suggested by Gallop's accounts in "Tongue Work" and "The Coloration of Academic Feminism" in *Around 1981*, pp. 143–76 and 67–74, and, by extension through the analogies she draws between constructions of race and class, in "Annie Leclerc Writing a Letter, with Vermeer," in *The Poetics of Gender*, ed. Nancy K. Miller (New York, 1986), pp. 137–56. In her analysis of the black woman's telling role in Joan Micklin Silver's film *Crossing Delancey*, Tania Modleski outlines an

especially exploitative enactment of this fantasy; see Tania Modleski, *Feminism without Women: Culture and Criticism in a "Postfeminist" Age* (New York, 1991), pp. 129–30. In Richard Dyer, "Paul Robeson: Crossing Over," *Heavenly Bodies: Film Stars and Society* (London, 1986), Dyer succinctly summarizes the most pervasive, nongendered version of this fantasy: "Black and white discourses on blackness seem to be valuing the same things—spontaneity, emotion, naturalness—yet giving them a different implication. Black discourses see them as contributions to the development of society, white as enviable qualities that only blacks have" (p. 27).

5. On the general phenomenon of black innovation and white imitation in postwar American culture, see Kobena Mercer, "Black Hair/Style Politics," *New Formations* 3 (Winter 1987): 33–54.

6. For a particularly powerful statement of the disenchantment bred among women of color by white women's opposition to bussing, see Nikki Giovanni, "Why Weren't Our 'Sisters in Liberation' in Boston?" *Encore*, 6 Jan. 1975, p. 20.

7. By tracing the course of a friendship from girlhood through adulthood, "Recitatif" filters the narrative of *Sula* (1973) through the lens of race, replacing the novel's sexual triangulation with the tensions of racial difference. It is hard for me to imagine that the critical question that Sula, Roberta's knowing, transgressive counterpart, poses to Nel— "How do you know? . . . About who was good. How do you know it was you?"—could be translated, in "Recitatif," into a white woman's challenge to a woman of color (Morrison, *Sula* [New York, 1973], p. 146).

8. In this exchange (November 1990), Morrison provided a more detailed account of her intentions than she does in her only (and very recently) published comment on the story, in the preface to her *Playing in the Dark: Whiteness and the Literary Imagination* (Cambridge, Mass., 1992): "The kind of work I have always wanted to do requires me to learn how to maneuver ways to free up the language from its sometimes sinister, frequently lazy, almost always predictable employment of racially informed and determined chains. (The only short story I have ever written, 'Recitatif,' was an experiment in the removal of all racial codes from a narrative about two characters of different races for whom racial identity is crucial)" (p. xi).

9. Although I realize that by isolating white/black dynamics of reading from white feminist readings of texts by other women of color I am reinforcing the unfortunate collapse of "color" and "black," encompassing such a diverse textual field within a single analysis would blur important differences. In contrast, for example, to black feminist complaints about the white feminist misrecognition of the politics and language of black feminism, Norma Alarcón protests the Anglo-American feminist resistance to granting theoretical status to the multiple-voiced subjectivity of women of color; see Norma Alarcón, "The Theoretical Subject(s) of *This Bridge Called My Back* and Anglo-American Feminism," in *Making Face, Making Soul: Haciendo Caras*, ed. Gloria Anzaldúa (San Francisco, 1990), pp. 356–69. For a different perception of white feminism's response to the multiple voicing characterizing texts by women of color, see Teresa de Lauretis, "Eccentric Subjects: Feminist Theory and Historical Consciousness," *Feminist Studies* 16 (Spring 1990): 115–50.

10. The strongest questions about, although not unqualified opposition to, white feminist readings of black women's texts have been posed by bell hooks. See, for example, bell hooks [Gloria Watkins], "Critical Interrogation: Talking Race, Resisting Racism," *Inscriptions* 5 (1989): 159–62, and "Feminism and Racism: The Struggle Continues," *Zeta* (July–Aug. 1990): 41–43; see also Patricia Hill Collins, "The Social Construction of Black Feminist Thought," *Signs* 14 (Summer 1989): 745–73. Or some more positive perspectives, see Valerie Smith, "Black Feminist Theory and the Representation of the 'Other,'" in *Changing Our Own Words: Essays on Criticism, Theory, and Writing by Black Women*, ed. Cheryl A. Wall (New Brunswick, N.J., 1989), pp. 38–57; Hazel V. Carby, *Reconstructing Womanhood: The Emergence of the Afro-American Woman Novelist* (New York, 1987), chap. 1; Michele

Wallace, "Who Owns Zora Neale Houston? Critics Carve Up the Legend," in *Invisibility Blues: From Pop to Theory* (London, 1990), pp. 179–80; Barbara Christian, "But What Do We Think We're Doing Anyway: The State of Black Feminist Criticism(s) or My Version of a Little Bit of History," in *Changing Our Own Words*, pp. 67, 73; and hooks, *Talking Back: Thinking Feminist, Thinking Black* (Boston, 1989), chap. 7. For a trenchant black male critique of the racial privilege concealed behind the self-referential gestures of some white male commentators on African-American texts, see Michael Awkward, "Negotiations of Power: White Critics, Black Texts, and the Self-Referential Impulse," *American Literary History* 2 (Winter 1990): 580–606. See also Kenneth W. Warren, "From under the Superscript: A Response to Michael Awkward," and Awkward, "The Politics of Positionality: A Reply to Kenneth Warren," *American Literary History* 4 (Spring 1992): 97–109.

11. In "Feminism, 'Postfeminism,' and Contemporary Women's Fiction," in *Tradition and the Talents of Women*, ed. Florence Howe (Urbana, Ill., 1991), pp. 268–91, Deborah Silverton Rosenfelt proposes 1985 as the date of postfeminism's emergence and defines the phenomenon succinctly as the "uneven incorporation and revision [of feminism] inside the social and cultural texts of a more conservative era" (p. 269). For a more negative assessment of postfeminism, and a broader location of its origins in the mid-1980s, see Gayle Greene, *Changing the Story: Feminist Fiction and the Tradition* (Bloomington, Ind., 1991), esp. part 3. In selecting 1985 as the watershed year in white feminists' engagement with questions of racial location, I am building on Miller's suggestion in the conversation held between Miller, Marianne Hirsch, and Jane Gallop, published under the title "Criticizing Feminist Criticism," in *Conflicts in Feminism*, ed. Hirsch and Evelyn Fox Keller (New York, 1990), p. 359. In 1985 *Conjuring*, the first anthology of literary criticism coedited by a black woman and a white woman, was published. The same year *The Color Purple* was selected as the focus for a collective presentation at the sixth annual British conference on "Literature/Teaching/Politics"; this presentation culminated in several white feminist essays on the novel. This year also witnessed the first serious white British feminist response to critiques by women of color: see Michèle Barrett and Mary McIntosh, "Ethnocentrism and Socialist-Feminist Theory," *Feminist Review*, no. 20 (June 1985): 23–47; for four different responses to this essay, see Caroline Ramazanoglu, Hamida Kazi, Sue Lees, and Heidi Safia Mirza, "Feedback: Feminism and Racism," *Feminist Review*, no 22 (Feb. 1986): 83–105, and Kum-Kum Bhavnani and Margaret Coulson, "Transforming Socialist-Feminism: The Challenge of Racism," *Feminist Review*, no. 23 (June 1985): 81–92. Another way to mark the shift occurring in 1985 is to contrast the semantic fields of two identical titles: *Between Women: Biographers, Novelists, Critics, Teachers, and Artists Write about Their Work on Women*, ed. Carol Asche, Louise DeSalvo, and Sara Ruddick (Boston, 1984), about the enabling identification between women writers and the women about whom they write, and Judith Rollins, *Between Women: Domestics and Their Employers* (Philadelphia, 1985), about the conflicts between white women and the black women who work for them.

12. I am following Phyllis Marynick Palmer's wonderful reading of Sojourner Truth's role at the Akron Women's Rights convention in "White Women/Black Women: The Dualism of Female Identity and Experience in the United States," *Feminist Studies* 9 (Spring 1983): 151, 153. Palmer quotes from Frances D. Gage, "The Akron Convention," in *The Feminist Papers: From Adams to de Beauvoir*, ed. Alice Rossi (New York, 1974), p. 429. Paula Giddings cites Jane Stembridge's reaction to Fanny Lou Hamer in her *When and Where I Enter: The Impact of Black Women on Race and Sex in America* (New York, 1984), p. 301. For SNCC's complex role in catalyzing the second wave of a white feminist movement, see chap. 17, and Sara Evans, *Personal Politics: The Roots of Women's Liberation in the Civil Rights Movement and the New Life* (New York, 1979). In *Meridian* and in "Advancing Luna—and Ida B. Wells" (1977), Walker offers narrative accounts of white women's predatory relation to a movement that gave them the illusion of purposefulness.

13. See Valerie Smith, "Black Feminist Theory and the Representation of the 'Other.'" in *Changing Our Own Words*, pp. 38–57.

14. See Barbara Johnson, "Thresholds of Difference: Structures of Address in Zora Neale Houston," *Critical Inquiry* 12 (Autumn 1985): 278–89; hereafter abbreviated "T." For evidence of this essay's influence, see Angela P. Harris, "Race and Essentialism in Feminist Legal Theory," *Stanford Law Review* 42 (Feb. 1990): 581–615; Priscilla Wald, "Becoming 'Colored': The Self-Authorized Language of Difference in Zora Neale Hurston," *American Literary History* 2 (Spring 1990): 79–100; Wallace, "Who Owns Zora Neale Hurston?" pp. 172–85; Tamar Katz, "'Show Me How To Do Like You': Didacticism and Epistolary Form in *The Color Purple*," in *Alice Walker*, ed. Harold Bloom (New York, 1989), esp. pp. 191–92. The race of the reader is not an issue in "Thresholds"'s companion piece, published the year before, "Metaphor, Metonymy, and Voice in *Their Eyes Were Watching God*," in *Black Literature and Literary Theory*, ed. Henry Louis Gates, Jr. (New York, 1984), pp. 205–15, in which gender performs a more critical role than race; similarly, in her "Apostrophe, Animation, and Abortion," *A World of Difference* (Baltimore, 1987) pp. 184–99, another outstanding essay on structures of address, differences in gender occlude racial differences, which are theorized for neither the poets nor the critic. In Johnson's other African-American essays, such as "Euphemism, Understatement, and the Passive Voice: A Genealogy of Afro-American Poetry" and "The Re(a)d and the Black," in *Reading Black, Reading Feminist: A Critical Anthology*, ed. Gates (New York, 1990), pp. 204–11 and 145–54, the racial position of the reader is similarly bracketed.

15. The Hurston represented by other texts fulfills other critical dreams. See, for example, Mary Helen Washington, foreword, *Their Eyes Were Watching God* (1937; New York, 1990), pp. vii–xiv, and Walker, "On Refusing to Be Humble by Second Place in a Contest You Did Not Design: A Tradition by Now" and "Looking for Zora," in Zora Neale Hurston, *I Love Myself When I Am Laughing . . . and Then Again When I Am Looking Mean and Impressive: A Zora Neale Hurston Reader*, ed. Walker (New York, 1979), pp. 105, 297–313, and "Foreword: Zora Neale Hurston—A Cautionary Tale and a Partisan View," in Robert E. Hemenway, *Zora Neale Hurston: A Literary Biography* (Urbana, Ill., 1977), pp. xi–xviii. In *I Love Myself When I Am Laughing*, Walker describes "How It Feels to Be Colored Me" as "an excellent example of Zora Neale Hurston at her most exasperating" (p. 151). For a black feminist reading that is closer to Johnson's, but is routed through Bakhtin instead of Derrida, see Mae Gwendolyn Henderson, "Speaking in Tongues: Dialogics, Dialectics, and the Black Woman Writer's Literary Tradition," in *Changing Our Own Words*, pp. 16–37.

16. For a similar critique, see Tzvetan Todorov, "'Race,' Writing, and Culture," in *"Race," Writing, and Difference*, ed. Gates (Chicago, 1986), pp. 379–80.

17. Hurston's resistance to considering race a sociopolitical obstacle to success recurs throughout her writing. For example, she asserts: "I do not belong to the sobbing school of Negrohood who hold that nature somehow has given them a lowdown dirty deal and whose feelings are all hurt about it . . . I have seen that the world is to the strong regardless of a little pigmentation more or less. No, I do not weep at the world—I am too busy sharpening my oyster knife" (Hurston, "How It Feels to Be Colored Me," *I Love Myself When I Am Laughing*, p. 153). Similar claims pervade her autobiography, *Dust Tracks on a Road* (1942). For an analysis of Hurston's racial politics, see Hemenway, *Zora Neale Hurston*, esp. chap. 11. For a different reading of Johnson's position in this essay, see Awkward, "Negotiations of Power," 603–4.

18. Johnson, introduction, *A World of Difference*, pp. 2–3.

19. Johnson, "Les Fleurs du Mal Armé: Some Reflections on Intertexuality," *A World of Difference*, p. 131. As the paragraph continues, Johnson qualifies, but does not undo, the figurative/literal distinction. The pressures created by Johnson's racial position are visible in her differences of emphasis from the Afro-Americanist whose position on race is closest, indeed very close to her own: Henry Louis Gates, Jr.; see , for example, her response

to Gates's "Canon-Formation, Literary History, and the Afro-American Tradition: From the Seen to the Told," in *Afro-American Literary Study in the 1990s*, ed. Houston A. Baker, Jr., and Patricia Redmond (Chicago, 1989), pp. 14–38, 39–44.

20. "'Racial Composition': Metaphor and the Body in the Writing of Race" was first delivered at the conference on "Psychoanalysis in African-American Contexts: Feminist Reconfigurations" at the University of California, Santa Cruz, October 1992; hereafter abbreviated RC. In the revised version in which it will appear in *Female Subjects in Black and White: Race, Psychoanalysis, Feminism*, ed. Elizabeth Abel, Barbara Christian, Helene Moglen (forthcoming from The University of California Press), Homans more explicitly historicizes all the positions taken in the 1987 critical debate among Joyce A. Joyce, Henry Louis Gates, Jr., and Houston A. Baker, Jr., and more strenuously emphasizes the inextricability of figurative and literal constructions of race. By foregrounding the status of the literal in Homans's argument, I hope not to minimize the other side of her argument, but to clarify some of the stakes of the positions assumed by Johnson and Homans, both of whom have in fact been influenced by both deconstruction and psychoanalysis. For some earlier examples of Homans's writing on African-American women's texts, see Margaret Homans, "'Her Very Own Howl': The Ambiguities of Representation in Recent Women's Fiction," *Signs* 9 (Winter 1983): 186–205, which is primarily concerned with negotiating tensions between Anglo-American and French feminist positions on language and women's experience; "The Woman in the Cave: Recent Feminist Fictions and the Classical Underworld," *Contemporary Literature* 29 (Fall 1988): 369–402, which, by reading Gloria Naylor's *Linden Hills* with Luce Irigaray's *Speculum of the Other Woman*, also foregrounds the compatibility of French feminist discourse and fiction by African-American women; and "'Women of Color': Writers and Feminist Theory," *NLH* 25 (Fall 1994): 73–94, which examines white feminist uses of writing by women of color.

21. See Joyce A. Joyce, "The Black Canon: Reconstructing Black American Literary Criticism," *New Literary History* 18 (Winter 1987): 335–44; Gates, "'What's Love Got to Do with It?': Critical Theory, Integrity, and the Black Idiom," *New Literary History* 18 (Winter 1987): 345–62; Baker, "In Dubious Battle," *New Literary History* 18 (Winter 1987): 363–69; and Joyce, "'Who the Cap Fit': Unconsciousness and Unconscionableness in the Criticism of Houston A. Baker, Jr., and Henry Louis Gates, Jr.," *New Literary History* 18 (Winter 1987): 371–84. In a recent interview with Charles H. Rowell ("An Interview with Henry Louis Gates, Jr.," *Callaloo* 14 [1991]: 444–63), Gates qualifies and clarifies the basis for his response to Joyce (pp. 451–52). For a different configuration of race, gender, and reading in the *NLH* (and other) critical debates, see Awkward, "Race, Gender, and the Politics of Reading," *Black American Literature Forum* 22 (Spring 1988): 5–27. Rather than gendering the dispute between Joyce and Baker and Gates, Awkward allies Joyce's position on race with Elaine Showalter's position on feminism as reductively sociopolitical modes of criticism and contrasts both with the more fluid post-structuralist approaches represented by Baker and Gates, on the one hand, and by Mary Jacobus on the other. One uncomfortable consequence of Awkward's construction is that, by using white feminism as his frame of reference, he erases Joyce's participation in the discourse of black feminism. For yet another account of the *NLH* debate, see Diana Fuss's chapter, "'Race' under Erasure? Post-Structuralist Afro-American Literary Theory," *Essentially Speaking: Feminism, Nature and Difference* (New York, 1989), pp. 73–96; Fuss sides primarily with Gates and Baker and mentions the gender implications of the debate only in passing.

22. Homans focusses appropriately on Gates rather than Baker, since the label *post-structuralist* applies far more accurately to Gates. In "Caliban's Triple Play," Baker's response to Gates's special issue of *Critical Inquiry*, for example, Baker sounds at times uncannily like Joyce in criticizing Anthony Appiah, and implicitly Gates as well, for belittling the visible, biological signs of race that function so perniciously in the "real" political world; see Baker, "Caliban's Triple Play," in *"Race," Writing, and Difference*, pp. 381–95. For a

critique of Baker's "essentialism," see Elliott Butler-Evans, "Beyond Essentialism: Rethinking Afro-American Cultural Theory," *Inscriptions* 5 (1989): 121–34. For a defense of Baker's "materialism," see Fuss, *Essentially Speaking*, pp. 86–93. Baker is definitely an "essentialist" when it comes to gender, as is clear in his recent book, *Workings of the Spirit: The Politics of Afro-American Women's Writing* (Chicago, 1991), and from Henderson's response to Baker's essay "There Is No More Beautiful Way: Theory and the Poetics of Afro-American Women's Writing," in *Afro-American Literary Study in the 1990s*, pp. 135–63. In her response to the panel on "Black Feminism" at the Wisconsin Conference on Afro-American Studies in the Twenty-First Century (Apr. 1991), Carby singled out for criticism Baker's idealization of black women writers and erasure of black feminist critics.

23. See Homans, *Bearing the Word: Language and Female Experience in Nineteenth-Century Women's Writing* (Chicago, 1986), especially chap. 1, which juxtaposes Lacan and Chodorow to explore the association of the literal with the feminine.

24. For Gate's revision of the traditional saying "signification is the nigger's occupation" to "figuration is the nigger's occupation," see "Criticism in the Jungle" and "The Blackness of Blackness: A Critique of the Sign and the Signifying Monkey," *Black Literature and Literary Theory*, pp. 1–24, 285–321. For the cultural splitting of a disembodied white femininity from a black female materiality, see Christian, *Black Feminist Criticism: Perspectives on Black Women Writers* (New York, 1985), chap. 1, and Carby, *Reconstructing Womanhood*, chap. 2.

25. Walker, *The Temple of My Familiar* (San Diego, 1989), p. 360. This passage actually describes a white man, but the ghostliness and disembodiedness attributed to whiteness are typically applied to white women as well, not only throughout Walker's fiction, but also in the distinction she draws between (black) "womanist" and (white) "feminist": "Womanist is to feminist as purple to lavender" (Walker, *In Search of Our Mothers' Gardens* [New York, 1983], p. xii). Note the similarity between Walker's account of white people's skinlessness and Morrison's description of "the men without skin" who operate the slave ship in *Beloved* ([New York, 1987], p. 210: hereafter abbreviated *B*); or between Walker's account and, from a different ethnic perspective, the white "ghosts" of Maxine Hong Kingston, *The Woman Warrior: Memoirs of a Girlhood among Ghosts* (New York, 1976).

26. For an especially powerful and influential account of black materialist feminism, see The Combahee River Collective, "A Black Feminist Statement," in *All the Women Are White, All the Blacks are Men, But Some of Us Are Brave: Black Women's Studies*, ed. Gloria T. Hull, Patricia Bell Scott, and Barbara Smith (Old Westbury, N.Y., 1982), pp. 13–22; see also Bonnie Thornton Dill, "Race, Class, and Gender: Prospects for an All-Inclusive Sisterhood," *Feminist Studies* 9 (Spring 1983): 131–50. For a warning against eclipsing the formal and imaginative qualities of literature by privileging sociopolitical analysis, see Christian, "But What Do We Think We're Doing Anyway."

27. Two examples of white materialist feminist criticism that either do not consider the critic's racial position an obstacle, or consider it a readily surmountable obstacle, are Lauren Berlant, "Race, Gender, and Nation in *The Color Purple*," *Critical Inquiry* 14 (Summer 1988): 831–59, and Anne E. Goldman, "'I Made the Ink': (Literary) Production and Reproduction in *Dessa Rose* and *Beloved*," *Feminist Studies* 16 (Summer 1990): 313–30. For some examples of black materialist feminist willingness to entertain readings by white feminists, see Carby, *Reconstructing Womanhood*, chap. 1; Carby's argument that there are no "pure, autonomous cultures that belong to particular groups or classes people" implicitly opens the analysis of cultural struggles and articulations to a diverse materialist readership (Carby, "The Canon: Civil War and Reconstruction" *Michigan Quarterly Review* 28 [Winter 1989]: 442). See also hooks, *Talking Back*, chap. 7, and Valerie Smith, "Black Feminist Theory and the Representation of the 'Other.'"

28. Valerie Smith, "Black Feminist Theory and the Representation of the 'Other,'" p. 39. See Carby, *Reconstructing Womanhood*, chap. 1.

29. See, for example, Deborah E. McDowell, "'The Changing Same': Generation Connections and Black Women Novelists," *New Literary History* 18 (Winter 1987): 281–302; Henderson, *The Color Purple*: Revisions and Redefinitions," *Sage* 2 (Spring 1985): 14–18, repr. in *Alice Walker*, pp. 67–80; Thadious M. Davis, "Alice Walker's Celebration of Self in Southern Generations," *Southern Quarterly* 21 (Summer 1983): 39–53, repr. in *Alice Walker*, pp. 25–37; Christian, "Alice Walker: The Black Woman Artist as Wayward" and "No More Buried Lives: The Theme of Lesbianism in Audre Lorde's *Zami*, Gloria Naylor's *The Women of Brewster Place*, Ntozake Shange's *Sassafras, Cypress and Indigo*, and Alice Walker's *The Color Purple*," in *Black Feminist Criticism: Perspectives on Black Women Writers*, ed. Christian (New York, 1985), pp. 81–102 and 187–204; Katz, "'Show Me How to Do Like You'"; pp. 185–94; Jean Wyatt, "Eros as Creativity: The Extended Family in *The Color Purple*," *Reconstructing Desire: The Role of the Unconscious in Women's Reading and Writing* (Chapel Hill, N.C., 1990), pp. 164–85); Holly Hite, "Romance, Marginality, Matrilineage: *The Color Purple*," *The Other Side of the Story: Structures and Strategies of Contemporary Feminist Narrative* (Ithaca, N.Y., 1989), pp. 103–26. It is interesting to note, nevertheless, a difference in emphasis: some black feminists (preeminently McDowell) have emphasized the novel's subversion of the conventions of characterization and diction governing black literature, whereas most white feminists have located the novel in relation to the dominant traditions of white literature.

30. hooks, "Writing the Subject: Reading *The Color Purple*" in *Alice Walker*, p. 223; Cora Kaplan, "Keeping the Color in *The Color Purple*," *Sea Changes: Essays on Culture and Feminism* (London, 1986), pp. 182, 187. Focusing on twentieth-century black male discourses on gender and the family, Kaplan is foregrounding a different black literary tradition from hooks, yet, as the title of her essay indicates, she insists that the novel's value resides in its relation to specifically black cultural traditions. In Alison Light, "Fear of the Happy Ending: *The Color Purple*, Reading and Racism," in *Plotting Change: Contemporary Women's Fiction*, ed. Linda Anderson (London, 1990). pp. 85–96, the novel's "imaginary resolution of political and personal conflicts" (p. 87), which hooks protests in relation to a black audience, is endorsed in terms of the political importance of utopianism for a (white) feminist audience. Black discursive specificity enables Kaplan's rehabilitation of the text; white reading specificity implicitly enables Light's.

31. See Carby, "It Just Be's Dat Way Sometime: The Sexual Politics of Women's Blues," *Radical America* 20, no. 4 (1986): 11, and Susan Willis, *Specifying: Black Women Writing the American Experience* (Madison, Wis., 1987), chaps. 5 and 7.

32. The tendency toward idealization troubles even the most brilliant materialist reading of the text, Berlant's, "Race, Gender, and Nation in *The Color Purple*." For although Berlant ultimately repudiates the novel's (in her view inadequate) "womanist" alternative to patriarchal nationalism, her struggle to endorse this alternative contrasts with her less ambivalent negative representation of white women's privatized cultural bonds and identifications in her essay "The Female Complaint," *Social Text*, no. 19–20 (Fall 1988): 237–59. Despite her political critique of Walker's text, Berlant is more sympathetic to it than either hooks or Carby.

33. See Willis, "I Shop Therefore I Am: Is There a Place for Afro-American Culture in Commodity Culture?" in *Changing Our Own Words*, pp. 173–95; hereafter abbreviated "I."

34. Willis, *Specifying*, pp. 16, 72.

35. See Carby, "Reinventing History/Imagining the Future," review of *Specifying*, by Willis, *Black American Literature Forum* 23 (Summer 1989): 381–87. In this detailed and largely favorable review, Carby criticizes only the romanticization of rural black folk culture, which for Carby typifies a misleading trend in contemporary Afro-American cultural history. Willis's book has received extensive and largely favorable reviews from black feminists. Although several have decried its arbitrary historical boundaries and selection of texts, they have mostly found her historically grounded readings provocative and illuminating.

See, for example, Christian, "Connections and Distinctions," review of *Specifying*, by Willis, *The Women's Review of Books* 4 (July–Aug. 1987): 25–26; Wall, "Black Women Writers: Journeying along Motherlines," review of *Specifying*, by Willis, *Callaloo* 12 (1989): 419–22; and McDowell, review of *Specifying*, by Willis, *Color, Sex, and Poetry: Three Women Writers of the Harlem Renaissance*, by Hull, and *The Character of the Word*, by Karla Holloway, *Signs* 14 (Summer 1989): 948–52. One critic with nothing good to say about this "odd Marxist colonization (domestication? deflowering?) of black women writers" is Wallace, "Who Owns Zora Neale Hurston?" p. 184.

36. Fredric Jameson, "Reification and Utopia in Mass Culture," *Social Text* 1 (Winter 1979): 140; Jameson devotes only a paragraph to this possibility. In his later essay "Postmodernism, or, The Cultural Logic of Late Capitalism," *New Left Review* 146 (July–Aug. 1984): 53–92, he greatly complicates the position from which might emanate a political art no longer tied to cultural enclaves whose marginality is representable in two-dimensional space; there is no longer any position unincorporated within "the truth of postmodernism, that is, . . . the world space of multinational capital" (p. 92); Willis, however, is responding primarily to "Reification and Utopia in Mass Culture." For Willis, the utopian possibilities of marginal space are available to diverse groups. In her "Gender as Commodity," *South Atlantic Quarterly* 86 (Fall 1987): 403–21, for example, children play the role that black women writers play in "I Shop Therefore I Am"; in Willis, "*Fantasia*: Walt Disney's Los Angeles Suite," *Diacritics* 17 (Summer 1987): 83–96, the nature represented in the "Nutcracker" sequence images the utopian social relations of a space outside of capitalist production. In "*Fantasia*," Willis begins with the perspective of historical estrangement that the film offers for critiques of contemporary mass culture but slides into the utopian position offered by the "Nutcracker" sequence. In her discourse on black women's writing, estrangement is consistently utopian.

37. Willis's footnote to Carby painfully reveals her struggle to agree and disagree simultaneously rather than to analyze the sources of their differences. Carby' position in general is closer to Kobena Mercer's than to Willis's, calling Willis's gender analysis into question. Similarly, although Willis cites Sylvia Wynter's essay on minstrelsy as parody (see Sylvia Wynter, "Sambos and Minstrels," *Social Text* 1 [Winter 1979]: 149–56), she doesn't speculate about why Wynter is so much less ambivalent about the subversive power of parody than Willis is. Wallace's essay on Michael Jackson, "Michael Jackson, Black Modernisms and 'The Ecstasy of Communication'" (1989) (*Invisibility Blues*, pp. 77–90), which appeared about the same time as Willis's, is closer to Wynter's analysis than to Willis's, further problematizing the gender alliance across racial lines. About her resistance to grappling with individual black feminist critics in her book, Willis explains: "Taken as a whole, these [black feminist] books define the critical context for my thinking about the literature. None of these texts is directly cited in my interpretations because I chose not to speak to the criticism. Such a method would have produced a very different book" (p. 183). This "very different book" might have beneficially entailed some dialogue about differences rather than a construction of difference based on the desire for a vision of "transformed human social relationships and the alternative futures these might shape" (p. 159).

38. Willis, "I Want the Black One: Is There a Place for Afro-American Culture in Commodity Culture?" *New Formations*, no. 10 (Spring 1990): 96.

39. I am borrowing, with thanks, Sue Schweik's insights and formulation.

40. For an powerful statement of a similar conclusion about race and reading, see Mary Helen Washington, "How Racial Differences Helped Us Discover Our Common Ground," in *Gendered Subjects: The Dynamics of Feminist Teaching*, ed. Margo Culley and Catherine Portuges (Boston, 1985), pp. 221–29. Washington decides: "I will never again divide a course outline and curriculum along racial lines (as I did in 'Images of Women') so that the controlling purpose is to compare the responses of white women and black women, because I see how much the class imitates the syllabus. I do not want to see black women

in opposition to white women as though that division is primary, universal, absolute, immutable, or even relevant" (pp. 227–28).

41. This is not an inclusive list of black feminist critical projects, practitioners, or texts; it merely calls attention to some influential examples of black feminist writing on, or collections of, black women writers, such as *Black Women Novelists: The Development of a Tradition, 1893–1976*, ed. Christian (Westport, Conn., 1980) and Christian, *Black Feminist Criticism*; Washington, *Black-Eyed Susans: Classic Stories by and about Black Women* (Garden City, N.Y., 1975), *Midnight Birds: Stories by Contemporary Black Women Writers* (Garden City, N.Y., 1980), and *Invented Lives: Narrative of Black Women 1860–1960* (Garden City, N.Y., 1987); McDowell, "New Directions for Black Feminist Criticism," in *The New Feminist Criticism: Essays on Women Literature, and Theory*, ed. Elaine Showalter (New York, 1985), pp. 186–99, and *Slavery and the Literary Imagination*, ed. McDowell and Arnold Rampersad (Baltimore, 1989); the series Black Women Writers (Boston, 1987–••); Hull, *Color, Sex, and Poetry: Three Women Writers of the Harlem Renaissance* (Bloomington, Ind., 1987) and *Give Us Each Day: The Diary of Alice Dunbar-Nelson* (New York, 1984); *Critical Essays on Toni Morrison*, ed. Nellie Y. McKay (Boston, 1988); *Nine Plays by Black Women*, ed. Margaret B. Wilkerson (New York, 1986); Carby, *Reconstructing Womanhood*; Barbara Smith, "Toward a Black Feminist Criticism" (1977), in *All the Women Are White, All the Blacks Are Men, But Some of Us Are Brave*, pp. 157–75; Valerie Smith, "Black Feminist Theory and the Representation of the 'Other,'" and *Self-Discovery and Authority in Afro-American Narrative* (Cambridge, Mass., 1987); hooks, *Ain't I a Woman: Black Women and Feminism* (Boston, 1981), *Feminist Theory from Margin to Center* (Boston, 1984), *Talking Back*, and *Yearning: Race, Gender, and Cultural Politics* (Boston, 1990); Wallace, *Invisibility Blues*; Audre Lorde, *Sister Outsider: Essays and Speeches* (Trumansburg, N.Y., 1984); and June Jordan, *Civil Wars* (Boston, 1981).

42. For some recent white feminist accounts of the alternatives offered by black women's texts, see Elizabeth Abel, "Race, Class, and Psychoanalysis? Opening Questions," in *Conflicts in Feminism*, ed. Marianne Hirsch and Evelyn Fox Keller (New York, 1990), pp. 184–204; Hirsch, *The Mother/Daughter Plot: Narrative, Psychoanalysis, Feminism* (Bloomington, Ind., 1989), esp. pp. 176–99; Hite, *The Other Side of the Story*, pp. 103–26; Elizabeth Meese, *(Ex)Tensions: Re-Figuring Feminist Criticism* (Urbana, Ill., 1990), pp. 129–54 (and for other women of color, chaps. 2 and 5); Roberta Rubenstein, *Boundaries of the Self: Gender, Culture, Fiction* (Urbana, Ill., 1987), pp. 125–63 (and all of part 2 for other women of color); and Wyatt, *Reconstructing Desire*, pp. 164–209.

43. For some examples of Spillers's revisionist use of psychoanalytic theory, see her "Interstices: A Small Drama of Words," in *Pleasure and Danger*, ed. Carol Vance (Boston, 1984), pp. 73–100, and "Mama's Baby, Papa's Maybe: An American Grammar Book," *Diacritics* 17 (Summer 1987): 65–81. Spillers's work productively complicates the distinction Susan Thistlethwaite draws in her *Sex, Race, and God: Christian Feminism in Black and White* (New York, 1989) between the psychological focus of white feminism and the sociopolitical focus of black feminism.

44. McDowell made this argument in a paper called "Residues," delivered at the Wisconsin Conference on Afro-American Studies in the Twenty-First Century.

45. Carby and hooks have both written pervasively and eloquently about this need; for some recent examples, see Carby, "The Politics of Difference," *Ms.* (Sept.–Oct. 1990): 84–85, and hooks, "Critical Interrogation." On whiteness as "the metaphor for the metaphorical production of the Subject as one devoid of properties," see David Lloyd, "Race under Representation," *Oxford Literary Review*, no. 1–2 (1991): 13. On the asymmetry of the system of racial marking, which "inscribes the system of domination on the body of the individual, assigning to the individual his/her place as a dominated person" while not assigning "any place to the dominator," who remains unmarked, see Colette Guillaumin, "Race and Nature: The System of Marks," *Feminist Issues* 8 (Fall 1988): 41.

46. hooks, "Critical Interrogation," p. 162.

47. Morrison, *Playing in the Dark*, p. 90.

48. In "The Race for Theory," *Cultural Critique* 6 (Spring 1987); 51–63, Christian powerfully demonstrates the distorting effects of literary theory's intervention in the reading of black women's texts. Although she does not hold white *feminists* responsible for this intervention, her argument clearly applies to white feminist (as well as masculinist) theoretical discourses.

history

Great deeds of great men; chronological accounts of battles and borders, treaties and territories: this is what "history" connoted through much of the twentieth century, but recently the term has come to embrace much more. Historiography has departed from the diachronic narratives of political and military "events," moving into more synchronic accounts of such matters as courtship conventions, attitudes toward smell and personal hygiene, and even patterns of weather in the past. The "new history" tries, among other things, to scrutinize the experience of those who have inhabited the margins of culture and society, whose voices had previously been silenced because their race, class, gender, or nationality denied them access to power and self-expression in the world of "events."

In literary studies, "new historicism" (epitomized by such journals as *Representations* and *American Literary History*) holds texts up against nonliterary documents from their own historical period, looking at how a culture's discourse on a topic—be it power, sexuality, knowledge, madness, punishment (the subjects associated with Michel Foucault, an important influence upon this movement)—affects our interpretation of literature addressing that same topic. New historicism has been very influential in putting literary texts firmly back into the historical context from which structuralism and its theoretical descendants had tended to alienate them. Arguably, though, history was already playing a significant role in feminist criticism before the rise of new historicism. Such feminist commentators as Judith Lowder Newton (in an essay called "History as Usual? Feminism and the 'New Historicism'") and Linda Boose (in "The Family in Shakespeare Studies; or—Studies in the Family of Shakespeareans; or—the Politics of Politics") assert that feminists have been bringing history to bear on literary criticism long enough to shake the "new" from "historicism's" usual appellation. To be sure, not all feminist criticism treats "history" in a way that "historicists" would approve. The "images of women" movement of the 1970s, along with certain modes of Freudian and Jungian archetypal criticism (neither of which is represented in this volume), tended to locate certain female figures in texts (for example, the "earth mother" or the "bitch goddess") outside of history, pointing to the recurrence of types and of psychological patterns without reference to their specific moments in time. Indeed, in the essay we reprint here, Newton mentions the tendency of gynocriticism (the study of women's literary tradition) "to focus on the presence of unchanging or transhistorical patterns," a focus she identifies as the crucial difference between her project and those of Elaine Showalter, Nina Auerbach, and Sandra M. Gilbert and Susan Gubar. Although these critics arrange their work around historical periods and chronological developments, Newton argues, they do not account for literature's relation to "developing material conditions" or "shifting ideologies." In other words, practitioners of gynocriticism do not usually adopt a Marxist model of explanation for historical change and stasis.

Feminist historicists quite often do adopt a largely Marxist model of historical change, but not in an uncritical way. To a certain extent, all of the essays in this section invoke a vision of history that is based on certain Marxist premises—a focus on class and economics, a questioning of the dominant ideology, capitalism, and struggle. As essays in other sections of *Feminisms* (notably "Class," "Discourse," and "Desire") reveal, Marxism has often provided a vocabulary for feminist analysis of women's social and political status. Perhaps one reason for the seeming compatibility of the two modes is Marxism's insistence that there is such a thing as "the material conditions, the real conditions" (as Newton calls them) operating in the world. Feminists agree that the oppression of women is a reality that ought to be eradicated, and Marxism's grounding in economic evidence provides both reinforcement for that view and an operative model for its analysis. Still, feminists question the invisibility of women in most classical Marxism, and are therefore suspicious of its methods, often invoking other modes of analysis—psychoanalysis, Foucauldian cultural studies, postcolonial criticism—to temper Marxism's role in their discussions. Further, feminists are skeptical about the way that "material conditions" have sometimes been defined, and often turn very different lenses on those conditions, suggesting that previously ignored texts—conduct books, housekeeping manuals, or testimony about sexual harassment, for example—may constitute a different version of the "real relations" than has previously been acknowledged. Feminist historicism, then, is marked not just by an affinity with Marxism, but also by a questioning of certain fundamental issues in the previous writing of history: the importance of the individual, the functioning of power, the separation between the public and the private, the constitution of gender difference itself, and even the existence and importance of a linear chronology.

When Julia Kristeva sets out to write a history of the women's movement, she links it to women's desires. In "Women's Time" (first published in French in 1979; translated into English in 1981), Kristeva connects the large issues of linguistic, political, and historical change to questions of desire. She argues that initially, women wanted political, economic, and reproductive equality, but, more recently, "second generation" feminists have wanted to explore their own difference and the specificity of women's experiences and language. Using both psychoanalytic and socialist frames of reference, Kristeva casts doubt on the whole notion that women's desires are fundamentally different from men's, and pursues what the ramifications of those desires would be if they *were* different. She is troubled by what she sees as an uncritical acceptance of women's difference and questions whether the writings published as *l'écriture féminine* (see "Body" for an elaboration and explanation of this term) are any closer to women's desire than were other forms of writing. She also casts doubt on the notion that women would wield power more positively than men do, citing the recent history of women who have come to power as evidence that there is no difference. Her "history" is therefore specifically marked by issues of psychoanalysis.

Kristeva turns, then, from examining the history of the feminist movement to projecting the future of it. In a move that may strike some as antifeminist, she suggests a model of desire in which gender is not particularly an issue. As she sees it, both men and women suffer from a sense of being unfulfilled and lacking; both men and women suffer the psychic split that Freud called the *Spaltung* and Lacan located at the entry into language. Kristeva therefore hopes for a third generation of feminist thinkers who will develop a "space" where "sexual identity" (because it preserves the fiction of an "identity," rather than a fundamental split, in the subject) would disappear. She closes her essay with thoughts about ethics and aesthetics (especially of women's writing) within this new space, wondering if the time has come to reintroduce deliberately a notion of morality into feminist thought.

The most explicitly Marxist of the selections here, Judith Lowder Newton's, "Power and the Ideology of 'Women's Sphere,'" the Introduction to *Women Power, and Subversion: Social Strategies in British Fiction, 1778–1860* (1981) addresses a central tenet of feminist history, the division in nineteenth-century England and America between the "public sphere"—the world of events, economics, and men—and the "private sphere"—the world of domesticity, morality, and women. The notion of separate spheres grows out of the research of such women's historians as Gerda Lerner, Carroll Smith-Rosenberg, and Mary Ryan, and has provided literary critics with a lens through which to see nineteenth-century women's fiction in the context of the culture (rather than the individual authors) that produced it. Newton's book studies four canonical women's novels, Frances Burney's *Evelina*, Jane Austen's *Pride and Prejudice*, Charlotte Brontë's *Villette*, and George Eliot's *The Mill on the Floss*. Taken outside of historical context, all of these novels could be read as reinforcing a conservative status quo and undermining the potential power of their protofeminist heroines. Seen within the framework of the ideology of separate spheres, however, the novels take on a subversive aspect.

As Newton explains, nineteenth-century women's conduct manuals promoted the idea that women's "power" consisted not of publicly exercised "ability," but rather of "influence" within the domestic realm. The heroines of these novels, however, possess "ability," and their power—though often covertly manifested—undermines the separate sphere ideology that was gradually coming to dominate Anglo-American gender relations between Burney's time and Eliot's. A historical approach that looked to women authors' biographies for evidence of feminist rebellion might yield more evidence of "influence" than of "ability" in these writers' extraliterary lives. But, as Newton insists, "To write subversively is more than a means of exercising influence. It is a form of struggle—and a form of power."

By shifting the focus from the private experience of heroines in novels to the wider arena of empire, and by looking at "first world" texts from an explicitly marginal perspective, Gayatri Chakravorty Spivak adjusts what it means to think about history in connection with feminist criticism. In "Three Women's Texts and a Critique of Imperialism" (1985), Spivak adopts a contentious stance at once: whereas received wisdom would assume that feminism (opposed as it is to the oppression of women) would be "naturally" antithetical to imperialism (the oppression of conquered peoples), Spivak observes that "the emergent perspective of feminist criticism reproduces the axioms of imperialism." She substantiates the charge with reference to feminist readings of *Jane Eyre*, which, Spivak explains, participate in the ideology of individualism that is central to colonizing impulses. To assign a "self" to the "other," to "world" a region or culture (for example, to designate a group of places as "the third world") by enumerating it in a series where the "first" is "ours," is to participate in imperialism. Spivak shows how *Jane Eyre* supports the ideology of individual uniqueness and "soul making," and reads Jean Rhys's *Wide Sargasso Sea* as a "reinscription" of Brontë's text. Her counterexample is Mary Shelley's *Frankenstein*, which—with its complex playing out of issues of sexual reproduction and self-construction—deconstructs the ideology that shapes *Jane Eyre*.

Spivak asserts that feminist criticism that wants to go beyond the limits established by individualist assumptions must "turn to the archives of imperialist governance"; she also concedes that her essay does not do so, though her later work will. Given the absence of those nonliterary documents from this piece, we can see that Spivak's way of bringing "history" to literary studies is quite distinct from Kristeva's or Newton's. Spivak does not trace a chronology of women's writing—*Frankenstein* was published twenty-nine years before the text that it "deconstructs"—nor does she compare a novel's discourse about imperialism with official or nonliterary statements on empire from the period. Instead, Spivak reads the novels with an eye to the history of the long-term, as we can see it from a postcolonial perspective. She is not interested in charting biographies of (or progress through) individual authors; like the Marxist critics from whom she explicitly separates herself, Spivak is more concerned with analyzing the social constitution of the self. "The most I can say," she explains, "is that it is possible to read these texts, within the frame of imperialism and the Kantian ethical moment, in a politically useful way." One of her most politically suggestive conclusions is that "the absolutely Other cannot be selfed," another warning against indulging a Western individualist feminism that would try to name the "Third-World Woman" as a signifier.

In "Some Call It Fiction: On the Politics of Domesticity" (1990), Nancy Armstrong continues the work of historicizing fiction and class-consciousness that she began in her ground-breaking book, *Desire and Domestic Fiction* (1987). In "Some Call It Fiction," Armstrong challenges several ideas that have been central to the writing of history and to the history of feminist criticism: First, she challenges a notion of history that regards "public" events as primary, and places "private" ones, like personal life and literature, in a separate—and secondary—sphere. Second, working through a history that considers sexuality, domestic prescriptions, educational plans for girls, literary texts, and public political practices equally, Armstrong challenges the very sexual differentiation on which so much feminist criticism is based, suggesting that even sexual difference itself can and should be historicized. "Where others have isolated rhetorical strategies that naturalize the subordination of female to male," she writes, "no one has thoroughly examined the figure that differentiates the sexes." Armstrong here demonstrates the way that changes in domestic life, newly differentiated ideas of "male" and "female" spheres, preceded changes in public ideas of factory production and political rule; she challenges Foucault's idea that the clinic and prison represent institutional prototypes for government by surveillance, suggesting instead that the household provided that model. Looking at the history of educational reforms aimed at middle-class women, Armstrong discovers that eighteenth-century prescriptions for the education of young ladies provide a model for nineteenth-century governmental controls, and demonstrates, by closely examining a scene of reading in Charlotte Brontë's *Shirley*, how that educational model works to create a consciousness that is both class and gender specific.

As does Armstrong, Lauren Berlant questions history's division into public and private in "The Queen of America Goes to Washington City: Harriet Jacobs, Frances Harper, Anita Hill" (1993). Berlant examines a point in the history of national politics where body, gender, race, and sexuality meet, a point where the politics of sex reveals the politics of citizenship. Looking at testimony—specifically African-American women testifying about sexual harassment to a national audience—Berlant argues that Jacobs, Harper, and Hill employ a "national pedagogy of failed teaching" to try to educate the public about their private experiences of citizenship and its violation. She examines the way that "[t]hey take their individual losses as exemplary of larger ones, in particular the failure of the law and the nation to protect the sexual dignity of women from the hybrid body of patriarchal official and sexual privilege," and suggests that what they do is to write a history of racially charged sexual power and abuse in which the nation, not an individual, is considered the perpetrator. Berlant links many of the issues important in contemporary historicist debate—the body, the relation between public and private, the disposition of power—to interrogate the limits and possibilities of citizenship and national identity when the body politic denies the individual's experience of her own body and history. Berlant argues that African-American women respond to such a denial by creating texts that "tactically blur [the] line . . . between personal and national tyranny," a performance that she calls "Diva Citizenship," an imagining of a Queen of America who embodies and performs justice. Like other writers in this section, Berlant imagines a history of women that also projects a political future in which women will play a very different role in politics.

—DPH & RRW

WOMEN'S TIME

(1981)

The nation—dream and reality of the nineteenth century—seems to have reached both its apogee and its limits when the 1929 crash and the National-Socialist apocalypse demolished the pillars that, according to Marx, were its essence: economic homogeneity, historical tradition, and linguistic unity.[1] It could indeed be demonstrated that World War II, though fought in the name of national values (in the above sense of the term), brought an end to the nation as a reality: It was turned into a mere illusion which, from that point forward, would be preserved only for ideological or strictly political purposes, its social and philosophical coherence having collapsed. To move quickly toward the specific problematic that will occupy us in this article, let us say that the chimera of economic *homogeneity* gave way to *interdependence* (when not submission to the economic superpowers), while *historical* tradition and *linguistic* unity were recast as a broader and deeper determinant: what might be called a *symbolic denominator*, defined as the cultural and religious memory forged by the interweaving of history and geography. The variants of this memory produce social territories which then redistribute the cutting up into political parties which is still in use but losing strength. At the same time, this memory or symbolic denominator, common to them all, reveals beyond economic globalization and/or uniformization certain characteristics transcending the nation that sometimes embrace an entire continent. A new social ensemble superior to the nation has thus been constituted, within which the nation, far from losing its own traits, rediscovers and accentuates them in a strange temporality, in a kind of "future perfect," where the most deeply repressed past gives a distinctive character to a logical and sociological distribution of the most modern type. For this memory or symbolic common denominator concerns the response that human groupings, united in space and time, have given not to the problems of the *production* of material goods (i.e., the domain of the economy and of the human relationships it implies, politics, etc.) but, rather, to those of *reproduction*, survival of the species, life and death, the body, sex, and symbol. If it is true, for example, that Europe is representative of such a sociocultural ensemble, it seems to me that its existence is based more on this "symbolic denominator," which its art, philosophy, and religions manifest, than on its economic profile, which is certainly interwoven with collective memory but whose traits change rather rapidly under pressure from its partners.

It is clear that a social ensemble thus constituted possesses both a *solidity* rooted in a particular mode of reproduction and its representations through which the biological species is connected to its humanity, which is a tributary of time; as well as a certain *fragility* as a result of the fact that, through its universality, the symbolic common denominator is necessarily echoed in the corresponding symbolic denominator of another sociocultural ensemble. Thus, barely constituted as such, Europe finds itself being asked to compare itself with, or even to recognize itself in, the cultural, artistic, philosophical, and religious constructions belonging to other supranational sociocultural ensembles. This seems natural when the entities involved were linked by history (e.g., Europe and North America, or Europe and Latin America), but the phenomenon also occurs when the universality of this denominator we have called symbolic juxtaposes modes of production and reproduction apparently opposed in both the past and the present (e.g., Europe and India, or Europe and China). In short, with sociocultural ensembles of the European type, we are constantly faced with a double problematic: that of their *identity* constituted by historical sedimentation, and that of their *loss of identity* which is produced by this connection of memories which escape from history only to encounter anthropology. In other words, we confront two temporal dimensions: the time of linear history, of *cursive time* (as Nietzsche called it), and the time of another history, thus another time, *monumental time* (again according to Nietzsche), which englobes these supranational, sociocultural ensembles within even larger entities.

I should like to draw attention to certain formations which seem to me to summarize the dynamics of a sociocultural organism of this type. The question is one of sociocultural groups, that is, groups defined according to their place in production, but especially according to their role in the mode of reproduction and its representations, which, while bearing the specific sociocultural traits of the formation in question, are *diagonal* to it and connect it to other sociocultural formations. I am thinking in particular of sociocultural groups which are usually defined as age groups (e.g., "young people in Europe"), as sexual divisions (e.g., "European women"), and so forth. While it is obvious that "young people" or "women" in Europe have their own particularity, it is nonetheless just as obvious that what defines them as "young people" or as "women" places them in a diagonal relationship to their European "origin" and links them to similar categories in North America or in China, among others. That is, insofar as they also belong to "monumental history," they will not be only European "young people" or "women" of Europe but will echo in a most specific way the universal traits of their structural place in reproduction and its representations.

Consequently, the reader will find in the following pages, first, an attempt to situate the problematic of women in Europe within an inquiry on time: that time which the feminist movement both inherits and modifies. Second, I will attempt to distinguish two phases or two generations of women which, while immediately universalist and cosmopolitan in their demands, can nonetheless be differentiated by the fact that the first generation is more determined by the implications of a national problematic (in the sense suggested above), while the second, more determined by its place within the "symbolic denominator," is European *and* trans-European. Finally, I will try, both through the problems approached and through the type of analysis I propose, to present what I consider a viable stance for a European—or at least a European woman—within a domain which is henceforth worldwide in scope.

WHICH TIME?

"Father's time, mother's species," as Joyce put it; and, indeed, when evoking the name and destiny of women, one thinks more of the *space* generating and forming the human species than of *time*, becoming, or history. The modern sciences of subjectivity, of its genealogy and accidents, confirm in their own way this intuition, which is perhaps itself the result of a sociohistorical conjuncture. Freud, listening to the dreams and fantasies of his patients, thought that "hysteria was linked to place."[2] Subsequent studies on the acquistion of the symbolic function by children show that the permanence and quality of maternal love condition the appearance of the first spatial references which induce the child's laugh and then induce the entire range of symbolic manifestations which lead eventually to sign and syntax.[3] Moreover, antipsychiatry and psychoanalysis as applied to the treatment of psychoses, before attributing the capacity for transference and communication to the patient, proceed to the arrangement of new places, gratifying substitutes that repair old deficiencies in the maternal space. I could go on giving examples. But they all converge on the problematic of space, which innumerable religions of matriarchal (re)appearance attribute to "woman," and which Plato, recapitulating in his own system the atomists of antiquity, designated by the aporia of the *chora*, matrix space, nourishing, unnameable, anterior to the One, to God and, consequently, defying metaphysics.[4]

As for time, female[5] subjectivity would seem to provide a specific measure that essentially retains *repetition* and *eternity* from among the multiple modalities of time known through the history of civilizations. On the one hand, there are cycles, gestation, the eternal recurrence of a biological rhythm which conforms to that of nature and imposes a temporality whose stereotyping may shock, but whose regularity and unison with what is experienced as extrasubjective time, cosmic time, occasion vertiginous visions and unnameable *jouissance*.[6] On the other hand, and perhaps as a consequence, there is the massive presence of a monumental temporality, without cleavage or escape, which has so little to do with linear time (which passes) that the very word "temporality" hardly fits: All-encompassing and infinite like imaginary space, this temporality reminds one of Kronos in Hesiod's mythology, the incestuous son whose massive presence covered all of Gea in order to separate her from Ouranos, the father.[7] Or one is reminded of the various myths of resurrection which, in all religious beliefs, perpetuate the vestige of an anterior or concomitant maternal cult, right up to its most recent elaboration, Christianity, in which the body of the Virgin Mother does not die but moves from one spatiality to another within the same time via dormition (according to the Orthodox faith) or via assumption (the Catholic faith).[8]

The fact that these two types of temporality (cyclical and monumental) are traditionally linked to female subjectivity insofar as the latter is thought of as necessarily maternal should not make us forget that this repetition and this eternity are found to be the fundamental, if not the sole, conceptions of time in numerous civilizations and experiences, particularly mystical ones.[9] The fact that certain currents of modern feminism recognize themselves here does not render them fundamentally incompatible with "masculine" values.

In return, female subjectivity as it gives itself up to intuition becomes a problem with respect to a certain conception of time: time as project, teleology, linear and prospective unfolding; time as departure, progression, and arrival—in other words, the time of history.[10] It has already been abundantly demonstrated that this kind of temporality is inherent in the logical and ontological values of any given civilization, that this temporality renders explicit a rupture, an expectation, or an anguish which other temporalities work to conceal. It might also be added that this linear time is that of language considered as the enunciation of sentences (noun + verb; topic–comment; beginning–ending), and that this time rests on its own stumbling block, which is also the stumbling block of that enunciation—death. A psychoanalyst would call this "obsessional time," recognizing in the mastery of time the true structure of the slave. The hysteric (either male or female) who suffers from reminiscences would, rather, recognize his or her self in the anterior temporal modalities: cyclical or monumental. This antinomy, one perhaps embedded in psychic structures, becomes, nonetheless, within a given civilization, an antinomy among social groups and ideologies in which the radical positions of certain feminists would rejoin the discourse of marginal groups of spiritual or mystical inspiration and, strangely enough, rejoin recent scientific preoccupations. Is it not true that the problematic of a time indissociable from space, of a space-time in infinite expansion, or rhythmed by accidents or catastrophes, preoccupies both space science and genetics? And, at another level, is it not true that the contemporary media revolution, which is manifest in the storage and reproduction of information, implies an idea of time as frozen or exploding according to the vagaries of demand, returning to its source but uncontrollable, utterly bypassing its subject and leaving only two preoccupations to those who approve of it: Who is to have power over the origin (the programming) and over the end (the use)?

It is for two precise reasons, within the framework of this article, that I have allowed myself this rapid excursion into a problematic of unheard of complexity. The reader will undoubtedly have been struck by a fluctuation in the term of reference: mother, woman, hysteric. ... I think that the apparent coherence which the term "woman" assumes in contemporary ideology, apart from its "mass" or "shock" effect for activist purposes, essentially has the negative effect of effacing the differences among the diverse functions or structures which operate beneath this word. Indeed, the time has perhaps come to emphasize the multiplicity of female expressions and preoccupations so that from the intersection of these differences there might arise, more precisely, less commercially, and more truthfully, the *real fundamental difference* between the two sexes: a difference that feminism has had the enormous merit of rendering painful, that is, productive of surprises and of symbolic life in a civilization which, outside the stock exchange and wars, is bored to death.

It is obvious, moreover, that one cannot speak of Europe or of "women in Europe" without suggesting the time in which this sociocultural distribution is situated. If it is true that a female sensibility emerged a century ago, the chances are great that by introducing *its own* notion of time, this sensibility is not in agreement with the idea of an "eternal Europe" and perhaps not even with that of a "modern Europe." Rather, through and with the European past and present, as through and with the ensemble of "Europe," which is the repository of memory, this sensibility seeks its own trans-European temporality. There are, in any case, three attitudes on the part of European feminist movements toward this conception of linear temporality, which is readily labeled masculine and which is at once both civilizational and obessional.

TWO GENERATIONS

In its beginnings, the women's movement, as the struggle of suffragists and of existential feminists, aspired to gain a place in linear time as the time of project and history. In this sense, the movement, while immediately universalist, is also deeply rooted in the sociopolitical life of nations. The political demands of women; the struggles for equal pay for equal work, for taking power in social institutions on an equal footing with men; the rejection, when necessary, of the attributes traditionally considered feminine or maternal insofar as they are deemed incompatible with insertion in that history—all are part of the *logic of identification*[11] with certain values: not with the ideological (these are combated, and rightly so, as reactionary) but, rather, with the logical and ontological values of a rationality dominant in the nation-state. Here it is unnecessary to enumerate the benefits which this logic of identification and the ensuing struggle have achieved and continue to achieve for women (abortion, contraception, equal pay, professional recognition, etc.); these have already had or will soon have effects even more important than those of the Industrial Revolution. Univeralist in its approach, this current in feminism *globalizes* the problems of women of different milieux, ages, civilizations, or simply of varying psychic structures, under the label "Universal Woman." A consideration of *generations* of women can only be conceived of in this global way as a succession, as a progression in the accomplishment of the initial program mapped out by its founders.

In a second phase, linked, on the one hand, to the younger women who came to feminism after May 1968 and, on the other, to women who had an aesthetic or psychoanalytic experience, linear temporality has been almost totally refused, and as a consequence there has arisen an exacerbated distrust of the entire political dimension. If it is true that this more recent current of feminism refers to its predecessors and that the struggle for sociocultural recognition of women is necessarily its main concern, this current seems to think of itself as belonging to another generation—qualitatively different from the first one—in its conception of its own identity and, consequently, of temporality as such. Essentially interested in the specificity of female psychology and its symbolic realizations, these women seek to give a language to the intrasubjective and corporeal experiences left mute by culture in the past. Either as artists or writers, they have undertaken a veritable exploration of the *dynamic of signs*, an exploration which relates this tendency, at least at the level of its aspirations, to all major projects of aesthetic and religious upheaval. Ascribing this experience to a new generation does not only mean that other, more subtle problems have been added to the demands for sociopolitical identification made in the beginning. It also means that, by demanding recognition of an irreducible identity, without equal in the opposite sex and, as such, exploded, plural, fluid, in a certain way nonidentical, this feminism situates itself outside the linear time of identities which communicate through projection and revindication. Such a feminism rejoins, on the one hand, the archaic (mythical) memory and, on the other, the cyclical or monumental temporality of marginal movements. It is certainly not by chance that the European and trans-European problematic has been posited as such at the same time as this new phase of feminism.

Finally, it is the mixture of the two attitudes—*insertion* into history and the radical *refusal* of the subjective limitations imposed by this history's time on an experiment carried out in the name of the irreducible difference—that seems to have broken loose over the past few years in European feminist movements, particularly in France and in Italy.

If we accept this meaning of the expression "a new generation of women," two kinds of questions might then be posed. What sociopolitical processes or events have provoked this mutation? What are its problems: its contributions as well as dangers?

SOCIALISM AND FREUDIANISM

One could hypothesize that if this new generation of women shows itself to be more diffuse and perhaps less conscious in the United States and more massive in Western Europe, this is because of a veritable split in social relations and mentalities, a split produced by socialism and Freudianism. I mean by *socialism* that egalitarian doctrine which is increasingly broadly disseminated and accepted as based on common sense, as well as that social practice adopted by governments and political parties in democratic regimes which are forced to extend the zone of egalitarianism to include the distribution of goods as well as access to culture. By *Freudianism* I mean that lever, inside this egalitarian and socializing field, which once again poses the question of sexual difference and of the difference among subjects who themselves are not reducible one to the other.

Western socialism, shaken in its very beginnings by the egalitarian or differential demands of its women (e.g., Flora Tristan), quickly got rid of those women who aspired to recognition of a specificity of the female role in society and culture, only retaining from them in the egalitarian and universalistic spirit of Enlightenment Humanism, the idea of a necessary identification between the two sexes as the only and unique means for liberating the "second sex." I shall not develop here the fact that this "ideal" is far from being applied in practice by these socialist-inspired movements and parties and that it was in part from the revolt against this situation that the new generation of women in Western Europe was born after May 1968. Let us just say that in theory, and as put into practice in Eastern Europe, socialist ideology, based on a conception of the human being as determined by its place in *production* and the *relations of production*, did not take into consideration this same human being according to its place in *reproduction*, on the one hand, or in the *symbolic order*, on the other. Consequently, the specific character of women could only appear as nonessential or even nonexistent to the totalizing and even totalitarian spirit of this ideology.[12] We begin to see that this same egalitarian and in fact censuring treatment has been imposed, from Enlightenment Humanism through socialism, on religious specificities and, in particular, on Jews.[13]

What has been achieved by this attitude remains nonetheless of capital importance for women, and I shall take as an example the change in the destiny of women in the socialist countries of Eastern Europe. It could be said, with only slight exaggeration, that the demands of the suffragists and existential feminists have, to a great extent, been met in these countries, since three of the main egalitarian demands of early feminism have been or are now being implemented despite vagaries and blunders: economic, political, and professional equality. The fourth, sexual equality, which implies permissiveness in sexual relations (including homosexual relations), abortion, and contraception, remains stricken by taboo in Marxian ethics as well as for reasons of state. It is, then, this fourth equality which is the problem and which therefore appears *essential* in the struggle of a new generation. But simultaneously and as a consequence of these socialist accomplishments—which are in fact a total deception—the struggle is no longer concerned with the quest for equality but, rather, with difference and specificity. It is precisely at this point that the new generation encounters what might be called the *symbolic* question.[14] Sexual difference—which is at once biological, physiological, and relative to reproduction—is translated by and translates a difference in the relationship of subjects to the symbolic contract which is the social contract: a difference, then, in the relationship to power, language, and meaning. The sharpest and most subtle point of feminist subversion brought about by the new generation will henceforth be situated on the terrain of the inseparable conjunction of the sexual and the symbolic, in order to try to discover, first, the specificity of the female, and then, in the end, that of each individual woman.

A certain saturation of socialist ideology, a certain exhaustion of its potential as a program for a new social contract (it is obvious that the effective realization of this program is far from being accomplished, and I am here treating only its system of thought) makes way for . . . Freudianism. I am, of course, aware that this term and this practice are somewhat shocking to the American intellectual consciousness (which rightly reacts to a muddled and normatizing form of psychoanalysis) and, above all, to the feminist consciousness. To restrict my remarks to the latter: Is it not true that Freud has been seen only as a denigrator or even an exploiter of women? as an irritating phallocrat in a Vienna which was at once Puritan and decadent—a man who fantasized women as sub-men, castrated men?

CASTRATED AND/OR SUBJECT TO LANGUAGE

Before going beyond Freud to propose a more just or more modern vision of women, let us try, first, to understand his notion of castration. It is, first of all, a question of an *anguish* or *fear* of castration, or of correlative penis *envy*; a question, therefore, of *imaginary* formations readily perceivable in the *discourse* of neurotics of both sexes, men and women. But, above all, a careful reading of Freud, going beyond his biologism and his mechanism, both characteristic of his time, brings out two things. First, a presupposition for the "primal scene," the castration fantasy and its correlative (penis envy) are hypotheses, a priori suppositions intrinsic to the theory itself, in the sense that these are not the ideological fantasies of their inventor but, rather, logical necessities to be placed at the "origin" in order to explain what unceasingly functions in neurotic discourse. In other words, neurotic discourse, in man and woman, can only be understood in terms of its own logic when its fundamental causes are admitted as the fantasies of the primal scene and castration, even if (as may be the case) nothing renders them present in reality itself. Stated in still other terms, the reality of castration is no more real than the hypothesis of an explosion which, according to modern astrophysics, is at the origin of the universe: Nothing proves it, in a sense it is an article of faith, the only difference being that numerous phenomena of life in this "big-bang" universe are explicable only through this initial hypothesis. But one is infinitely more jolted when this kind of intellectual method concerns inanimate matter than when it is applied to our own subjectivity and thus, perhaps, to the fundamental mechanism of our epistemophilic thought.

Moreover, certain texts written by Freud (*The Interpretation of Dreams,* but especially those of the second topic, in particular the *Metapsychology*) and the recent extensions (notably by Lacan),[15] imply that castration is, in sum, the imaginary construction of a radical operation which constitutes the symbolic field and all beings inscribed therein. This operation constitutes signs and syntax; that is, language, as a *separation* from a presumed state of nature, of pleasure fused with nature so that the introduction of an articulated network of differences, which refers to objects henceforth and only in this way separated from a subject, may constitute *meaning.* This logical operation of separation (confirmed by all psycholinguistic and child psychology) which preconditions the binding of language which is already syntactical, is therefore the common destiny of the two sexes, men and women. That certain biofamilial conditions and relationships cause women (and notably hysterics) to deny this separation and the language which ensues from it, whereas men (notably obsessionals) magnify both and, terrified, attempt to master them—this is what Freud's discovery has to tell us on this issue.

The analytic situation indeed shows that it is the penis which, becoming the major referent in this operation of separation, gives full meaning to the *lack* or to the *desire* which constitutes the subject during his or her insertion into the order of language. I should only like to indicate here that, in order for this operation constitutive of the symbolic and the social to appear in its full truth and for it to be understood by both sexes, it would be just to emphasize its extension to all that is privation of fullfillment and of totality; exclusion of a pleasing, natural, and sound state: in short, the break indispensable to the advent of the symbolic.

It can now be seen how women, starting with this theoretical apparatus, might try to understand their sexual and symbolic difference in the framework of social, cultural, and professional realization, in order to try, by seeing their position therein, either to fulfill their own experience to a maximum or—but always starting from this point—to go further and call into question the very apparatus itself.

LIVING THE SACRIFICE

In any case, and for women in Europe today, whether or not they are conscious of the various mutations (socialist and Freudian) which have produced or simply accompanied their coming into their own, the urgent question on our agenda might be formulated as follows: *What can be our place in the symbolic contract?* If the social contract, far from being that of equal men, is based on an essentially sacrificial relationship of separation and articulation of differences which in this way produces communicable meaning, what is our place in this order of sacrifice and/or of language? No longer wishing to be excluded or no longer content with the function which has always been demanded of us (to maintain, arrange, and perpetuate this sociosymbolic contract as mothers, wives, nurses, doctors, teachers . . .), how can we reveal our place, first as it is bequeathed to us by tradition, and then as we want to transform it?

It is difficult to evaluate what in the relationship of women to the symbolic as it reveals itself now arises from a sociohistorical conjuncture (patriarchal ideology, whether Christian, humanist, socialist or so forth), and what arises from a structure. We can speak only about a structure observed in a sociohistorical context, which is that of Christian, Western civilization and its lay ramifications. In this sense of psychosymbolic structure, women, "we" (is it necessary to recall the warnings we issued at the beginning of this article concerning the totalizing use of this plural?) seem to feel that they are the casualties, that they have been left out of the sociosymbolic contract, of language as the fundamental social bond. They find no affect there, no more than they find the fluid and infinitesimal significations of their relationships with the nature of their own bodies, that of the child, another woman, or a man. This frustration, which to a certain extent belongs to men also, is being voiced today principally by women, to the point of becoming the essence of the new feminist ideology. A therefore difficult, if not impossible, identification with the sacrificial logic of separation and syntactical sequence at the foundation of language and the social code leads to the rejection of the symbolic—lived as the rejection of the paternal function and ultimately generating psychoses.

But this limit, rarely reached as such, produces two types of counterinvestment of what we have termed the sociosymbolic contract. On the one hand, there are attempts to take hold of this contract, to possess it in order to enjoy it as such or to subvert it. How? The answer remains difficult to formulate (since, precisely, any formulation is deemed frustrating, mutilating, sacrificial) or else is in fact formulated using stereotypes taken from extremist and often deadly ideologies. On the other hand, another attitude is more lucid from the beginning, more self-analytical which—without refusing or sidestepping this sociosymbolic order—consists in trying to explore the constitution and functioning of this contract, starting less from the knowledge accumulated about it (anthropology, psychoanalysis, linguistics) than from the very personal affect experienced when facing it as subject and as a woman. This leads to the active research,[16] still rare, undoubtedly hesitant but always dissident, being carried out by women in the human sciences; particularly those attempts, in the wake of contemporary art, to break the code, to shatter language, to find a specific discourse closer to the body and emotions, to the unnameable repressed by the social contract. I am not speaking here of a "woman's language," whose (at least syntactical) existence is highly problematical and whose apparent lexical specificity is perhaps more the product of a social marginality than of a sexual-symbolic difference.[17]

Nor am I speaking of the aesthetic quality of productions by women, most of which—with a few exceptions (but has this not always been the case with both sexes?)—are a reiteration of a more or less euphoric or depressed romanticism and always an explosion of an ego lacking narcissistic gratification.[18] What I should like to retain, nonetheless, as a mark of collective aspiration, as an undoubtedly vague and unimplemented intention, but one which is intense and which has been deeply revealing these past few years, is this: The new generation of women is showing that its major social concern has become the sociosymbolic contract as a sacrificial contract. If anthropologists and psychologists, for at least a century, have not stopped insisting on this in their attention to "savage thought," wars, the discourse of dreams, or writers, women are today affirming—and we consequently face a mass phenomenon—that they are forced to experience this sacrificial contract against their will.[19] Based on this, they are attempting a revolt which they see as a resurrection but which society as a whole understands as murder. This attempt can lead us to a not less and sometimes more deadly violence. Or to a cultural innovation. Probably to both at once. But that is precisely where the stakes are, and they are of epochal significance.

THE TERROR OF POWER OR THE POWER OF TERRORISM

First in socialist countries (such as the U.S.S.R. and China) and increasingly in Western democracies, under pressure from feminist movements, women are being promoted to leadership positions in government, industry, and culture. Inequalities, devalorizations, underestimations, even persecution of women at this level continue to hold sway in vain. The struggle against them is a struggle against archaisms. The cause has nonetheless been understood, the principle has been accepted.[20] What remains is to break down the resistance to change. In this sense, this struggle, while still one of the main concerns of the new generation, is not, strictly speaking, *its* problem. In relationship to *power*, its problem might rather be summarized as follows: What happens when women come into power and identify with it? What happens when, on the contrary, they refuse power and create a parallel society, a counter-power which then takes on aspects ranging from a club of ideas to a group of terrorist commandos?[21]

The assumption by women of executive, industrial, and cultural power has not, up to the present time, radically changed the nature of this power. This can be clearly seen in the East, where women promoted to decision-making positions suddenly obtain the economic as well as the narcissistic advantages refused them for thousands of years and become the pillars of the existing governments, guardians of the status quo, the most zealous protectors of the established order.[22] This identification by women with the very power structures previously considered as frustrating, oppressive, or inaccessible has often been used in modern times by totalitarian regimes: the German National Socialists and the Chilean junta are examples of this.[23] The fact that this is a paranoid type of counterinvestment in an initially denied symbolic order can perhaps explain this troubling phenomenon; but an explanation does not prevent its massive propagation around the globe, perhaps in less dramatic forms than the totalitarian ones mentioned above, but all moving toward leveling, stabilization, conformism, at the cost of crushing exceptions, experiments, chance occurrences.

Some will regret that the rise of a libertarian movement such as feminism ends, in some of its aspects, in the consolidation of conformism; others will rejoice and profit from this fact. Electoral campaigns, the very life of political parties, continue to bet on this latter tendency. Experience proves that too quickly even the protest or innovative initiatives on the part of women inhaled by power systems (when they do not submit to them right off) are soon credited to the system's account; and that the long-awaited democratization of institutions as a result of the entry of women most often comes down to fabricating a few "chiefs" among them. The difficulty presented by this logic of integrating the second sex into a value system experienced as foreign and therefore counterinvested is how to avoid the centralization of power, how to detach women from it, and how then to proceed, through their critical, differential, and autonomous interventions, to render decision-making institutions more flexible.

Then there are the more radical feminist currents which, refusing homologation to any role of identification with existing power no matter what the power may be, make of the second sex a *countersociety*. A "female society" is then constituted as a sort of alter ego of the official society, in which all real or fantasized possibilities for *jouissance* take refuge. Against the sociosymbolic contract, both sacrificial and frustrating, this countersociety is imagined as harmonious, without prohibitions, free and fulfilling. In our modern societies which have no hereafter or, at least, which are caught up in a transcendency either reduced to this side of the world (Protestantism) or crumbling (Catholicism and its current challenges), the countersociety remains the only refuge for fulfillment since it is precisely an a-topia, a place outside the law, utopia's floodgate.

As with any society, the countersociety is based on the expulsion of an excluded element, a scapegoat charged with the evil of which the community duly constituted can then purge itself;[24] a purge which will finally exonerate that community of any future criticism. Modern protest movements have often reiterated this logic, locating the guilty one—in order to fend off criticism—in the foreign, in capital alone, in the other religion, in the other sex. Does not feminism become a kind of inverted sexism when this logic is followed to its conclusion? The various forms of marginalism—according to sex, age, religion, or ideology—represent in the modern world this refuge for *jouissance*, a sort of laicized transcendence. But with women, and insofar as the number of those feeling concerned by this problem has increased, although in less spectacular forms than a few years ago, the problem of the countersociety is becoming massive: It occupies no more and no less than "half of the sky."

It has, therefore, become clear, because of the particular radicalization of the second generation, that these protest movements, including feminism, are not "initially libertarian" movements which only later, through internal deviations or external chance manipulations, fall back into the old ruts of the initially combated archetypes. Rather, the very logic of counterpower and of countersociety necessarily generates, by its very structure, its essence as a simulacrum of the combated society or of power. In this sense and from a viewpoint undoubtedly too Hegelian, modern feminism has only been but a moment in the interminable process of coming to consciousness about the implacable violence (separation, castration, etc.) which constitutes any symbolic contract.

Thus the identification with power in order to consolidate it or the constitution of a fetishist counterpower—restorer of the crises of the self and provider of *jouissance* which is always already a transgression—seem to be the two social forms which the face-off between the new generation of women and the social contract can take. That one also finds the problem of terrorism there is structurally related.

The large number of women in terrorist groups (Palestinian commandos, the Baader-Meinhoff Gang, Red Brigades, etc.) has already been pointed out, either violently or prudently according to the source of information. The exploitation of women is still too great and the traditional prejudices against them too violent for one to be able to envision this phenomenon with sufficient distance. It can, however, be said from now on that this is the inevitable product of what we have called a denial of the sociosymbolic contract and its counterinvestment as the only means of self-defense in the struggle to safeguard an identity. This paranoid-type mechanism is at the base of any political involvement. It may produce different civilizing attitudes in the sense that these attitudes allow a more or less flexible reabsorption of violence and death. But when a subject is too brutally excluded from this sociosymbolic stratum; when, for example, a woman feels her affective life as a woman or her condition as a social being too brutally ignored by existing discourse or power (from her family to social institutions); she may, by counterinvesting the violence she has endured, make of herself a "possessed" agent of this violence in order to combat what was experienced as frustration—with arms which may seem disproportional, but which are not so in comparison with the subjective or more precisely narcissistic suffering from which they originate. Necessarily opposed to the bourgeois democratic regimes in power, this terrorist violence offers as a program of liberation an order which is even more oppressive, more sacrificial than those it combats. Strangely enough, it is not against totalitarian regimes that these terrorist groups with women participants unleash themselves but, rather, against liberal systems, whose essence is, of course, exploitative, but whose expanding democratic legality guarantees relative tolerance. Each time, the mobilization takes place in the name of a nation, of an oppressed group, of a human essence imagined as good and sound; in the name, then, of a kind of fantasy of archaic fulfillment which an arbitrary, abstract, and thus even bad and ultimately discriminatory order has come to disrupt. While that order is accused of being oppressive, is it not actually being reproached with being too weak, with not measuring up to this pure and good, but henceforth lost, substance? Anthropology has shown that the social order is sacrificial, but sacrifice orders violence, binds it, tames it. Refusal of the social order exposes one to the risk that the so-called good substance, once it is unchained, will explode, without curbs, without law or right, to become an absolute arbitrariness.

Following the crisis of monotheism, the revolutions of the past two centuries, and more recently fascism and Stalinism, have tragically set in action this logic of the oppressed goodwill which leads to massacres. Are women more apt than other social categories, notably the exploited classes, to invest in this implacable machine of terrorism? No categorical response, either positive or negative, can currently be given to this question. It must be pointed out, however, that since the dawn of feminism, and certainly before, the political activity of exceptional women, and thus in a certain sense of liberated women, has taken the form of murder, conspiracy, and crime. Finally, there is also the connivance of the young girl with her mother, her greater difficulty than the boy in detaching herself from the mother in order to accede to the order of signs as invested by the absence and separation constitutive of the paternal function. A girl will never be able to reestablish this contact with her mother—a contact which the boy may possibly rediscover through his relationship with the opposite sex—except by becoming a mother herself, through a child, or through a homosexuality which is in itself extremely difficult and judged as suspect by society; and, what is more, why and in the name of what dubious symbolic benefit would she want to make this detachment so as to conform to a symbolic system which remains foreign to her? In sum, all of these considerations—her eternal debt to the woman-mother—make a woman more vulnerable within the symbolic order, more fragile when she suffers within it, more virulent when she protects herself from it. If the archetype of the belief in a good and pure substance, that of utopias, is the belief in the omnipotence of an archaic, full, total, englobing mother with no frustration, no separation, with no break-producing symbolism (with no castration, in other words), then it becomes evident that we will never be able to defuse the violences mobilized through the counterinvestment necessary to carrying out this phantasm, unless one challenges precisely this myth of the archaic mother. It is in this way that we can understand the warnings against the recent invasion of the women's movements by paranoia,[25] as in Lacan's scandalous sentence "There is no such thing as Woman."[26] Indeed, she does *not* exist with a capital "W," possessor of some mythical unity—a supreme power, on which is based the terror of power and terrorism as the desire for power. But what an unbelievable force for subversion in the modern world! And, at the same time, what playing with fire!

CREATURES AND CREATRESSES

The desire to be a mother, considered alienating and even reactionary by the preceding generation of feminists, has obviously not become a standard for the present generation. But we have seen in the past few years an increasing number of women who do not only consider their maternity compatible with their professional life or their feminist involvement (certain improvements in the quality of life are also at the origin of this: an increase in the number of day-care centers and nursery schools, more active participation of men in child care and domestic life, etc.) but also find it indispensable to their discovery, not of the plenitude, but of the complexity of the female experience, with all that this complexity comprises in joy and pain. This tendency has its extreme: in the refusal of the paternal function by lesbian and single mothers can be seen one of the most violent forms taken by the rejection of the symbolic outlined above, as well as one of the most fervent divinizations of maternal power—all of which cannot help but trouble an entire legal and moral order without, however, proposing an alternative to it. Let us remember here that Hegel distinguished between female right (familial and religious) and male law (civil and political). If our societies know well the uses and abuses of male law, it must also be recognized that female right is designated, for the moment, by a blank. And if these practices of maternity, among others, were to be generalized, women themselves would be responsible for elaborating the appropriate legislation to check the violence to which, otherwise, both their children and men would be subject. But are they capable of doing so? This is one of the important questions that the new generation of women encounters, especially when the members of this new generation refuse to ask those questions, seized by the same rage with which the dominant order originally victimized them.

Faced with this situation, it seems obvious—and feminist groups become more aware of this when they attempt to broaden their audience—that the refusal of maternity cannot be a mass policy and that the majority of women today see the possibility for fulfillment, if not entirely at least to a large degree, in bringing a child into the world. What does this desire for motherhood correspond to? This is one of the new questions for the new generation, a question the preceding generation had foreclosed. For want of an answer to this question, feminist ideology leaves the door open to the return of religion, whose discourse, tried and proved over thousands of years, provides the necessary ingredients for satisfying the anguish, the suffering, and the hopes of mothers. If Freud's affirmation—that the desire for a child is the desire for a penis and, in this sense, a substitute for phallic and symbolic dominion—can be only partially accepted, what modern women have to say about this experience should nonetheless be listened to attentively. Pregnancy seems to be experienced as the radical ordeal of the splitting of the subject:[27] redoubling up of the body, separation and coexistence of the self and of an other, of nature and consciousness, of physiology and speech. This fundamental challenge to identity is then accompanied by a fantasy of totality—narcissistic completeness—a sort of instituted, socialized, natural psychosis. The arrival of the child, on the other hand, leads the mother into the labyrinths of an experience that, without the child, she would only rarely encounter: love for an other. Not for herself, nor for an identical being, and still less for another person with whom "I" fuse (love or sexual passion). But the slow, difficult, and delightful apprenticeship in attentiveness, gentleness, forgetting oneself. The ability to succeed in this path without masochism and without annihilating one's affective, intellectual, and professional personality—such would seem to be the stakes to be won through guiltless maternity. It then becomes a creation in the strong sense of the term. For this moment, utopian?

On the other hand, it is in the aspiration toward artistic and, in particular, literary creation that woman's desire for affirmation now manifests itself. Why literature?

Is it because, faced with social norms, literature reveals a certain knowledge and sometimes the truth itself about an otherwise repressed, nocturnal, secret, and unconscious universe? Because it thus redoubles the social contract by exposing the unsaid, the uncanny? And because it makes a game, a space of fantasy and pleasure, out of the abstract and frustrating order of social signs, the words of everyday communication? Flaubert said, "Madame Bovary, c'est moi."

Today many women imagine, "Flaubert, c'est moi." This identification with the potency of the imaginary is not only an identification, an imaginary potency (a fetish, a belief in the maternal penis maintained at all costs), as a far too normative view of the social and symbolic relationship would have it. This identification also bears witness to women's desire to lift the weight of what is sacrificial in the social contract from their shoulders, to nourish our societies with a more flexible and free discourse, one able to name what has thus far never been an object of circulation in the community: the enigmas of the body, the dreams, secret joys, shames, hatreds of the second sex.

It is understandable from this that women's writing has lately attracted the maximum attention of both "specialists" and the media.[28] The pitfalls encountered along the way, however, are not to be minimized: For example, does one not read there a relentless belittling of male writers whose books, nevertheless, often serve as "models" for countless productions by women? Thanks to the feminist label, does one not sell numerous works whose naive whining or market-place romanticism would otherwise have been rejected as anachronistic? And does one not find the pen of many a female writer being devoted to phantasmic attacks against Language and Sign as the ultimate supports of phallocratic power, in the name of a semi-aphonic corporality whose truth can only be found in that which is "gestural" or "tonal"?

And yet, no matter how dubious the results of these recent productions by women, the symptom is there—women are writing, and the air is heavy with expectation: What will they write that is new?

IN THE NAME OF THE FATHER, THE SON ... AND THE WOMAN?

These few elements of the manifestations by the new generation of women in Europe seem to me to demonstrate that, beyond the sociopolitical level where it is generally inscribed (or inscribes itself), the women's movement—in its present stage, less aggressive but more artful—is situated within the very framework of the religious crisis of our civilization.

I call "religion" this phantasmic necessity on the part of speaking beings to provide themselves with a *representation* (animal, female, male, parental, etc.) in place of what constitutes them as such, in other words, symbolization—the double articulation and syntactic sequence of language, as well as its preconditions or substitutes (thoughts, affects, etc.). The elements of the current practice of feminism that we have just brought to light seem precisely to constitute such a representation which makes up for the frustrations imposed on women by the anterior code (Christianity or its lay humanist variant). The fact that this new ideology has affinities, often revindicated by its creators, with so-called matriarchal beliefs (in other words, those beliefs characterizing matrilinear societies) should not overshadow its radical novelty. This ideology seems to me to be part of the broader antisacrificial current which in animating our culture and which, in its protest against the constraints of the sociosymbolic contract, is no less exposed to the risks of violence and terrorism. At this level of radicalism, it is the very principle of sociality which is challenged.

Certain contemporary thinkers consider, as is well known, that modernity is characterized as the first epoch in human history in which human beings attempt to live without religion. In its present form, is not feminism in the process of becoming one?

Or is it, on the contrary and as avant-garde feminists hope, that having started with the idea of difference, feminism will be able to break free of its belief in Woman, Her power, Her writing, so as to channel this demand for difference into each and every element of the female whole, and, finally, to bring out the singularity of each woman, and beyond this, her multiplicities, her plural languages, beyond the horizon, beyond sight, beyond faith itself?

A factor for ultimate mobilization? Or a factor for analysis?

Imaginary support in a technocratic era where all narcissism is frustrated? Or instruments fitted to these times in which the cosmos, atoms, and cells—our true contemporaries—call for the constitution of a fluid and free subjectivity?

The question has been posed. Is to pose it already to answer it?

ANOTHER GENERATION IS ANOTHER SPACE

If the preceding can be *said*—the question whether all this is *true* belongs to a different register—it is undoubtedly because it is now possible to gain some distance on these two preceding generations of women. This implies, of course, that a *third* generation is now forming, at least in Europe. I am not speaking of a new group of young women (though its importance should not be underestimated) or of another "mass feminist movement" taking the torch passed on from the second generation. My usage of the word "generation" implies less a chronology than a *signifying space*, a both corporeal and desiring mental space. So it can be argued that as of now a third attitude is possible, thus a third generation, which does not exclude—quite to the contrary—the *parallel* existence of all three in the same historical time, or even that they be interwoven one with the other.

In this third attitude, which I strongly advocate—which I imagine?—the very dichotomy man/woman as an opposition between two rival entities may be understood as belonging to *metaphysics*. What can "identity," even "sexual identity," mean in a new theoretical and scientific space where the very notion of identity is challenged?[29] I am not simply suggesting a very hypothetical bisexuality which, even if it existed, would only, in fact, be the aspiration toward the totality of one of the sexes and thus an effacing of difference. What I mean is, first of all, the demassification of the problematic of *difference*, which would imply, in a first phase, an apparent de-dramatization of the "fight to the death" between rival groups and thus between the sexes. And this not in the name of some reconciliation—feminism has at least had the merit of showing what is irreducible and even deadly in the social contract—but in order that the struggle, the implacable difference, the violence be conceived in the very place where it operates with the maximum intransigence, in other words, in personal and sexual identity itself, so as to make it disintegrate in its very nucleus.

It necessarily follows that this involves risks not only for what we understand today as "personal equilibrium" but also for social equilibrium itself, made up as it now is of the counterbalancing of aggressive and murderous forces massed in social, national, religious, and political groups. But is it not the insupportable situation of tension and explosive risk that the existing "equilibrium" presupposes which leads some of those who suffer from it to divest it of its economy, to detach themselves from it, and to seek another means of regulating difference?

To restrict myself here to a personal level, as related to the question of women, I see arising, under the cover of a relative indifference toward the militance of the first and second generations, an attitude of retreat from sexism (male as well as female) and, gradually, from any kind of anthropomorphism. The fact that this might quickly become another form of spiritualism turning its back on social problems, or else a form of repression[30] ready to support all status quos, should not hide the radicalness of the process. This process could be summarized as an *interiorization of the founding separation of the sociosymbolic contract,* as an introduction of its cutting edge into the very interior of every identity whether subjective, sexual, ideological, or so forth. This in such a way that the habitual and increasingly explicit attempt to fabricate a scapegoat victim as foundress of a society or a countersociety may be replaced by the analysis of the potentialities of *victim/executioner* which characterize each identity, each subject, each sex.

What discourse, if not that of a religion, would be able to support this adventure which surfaces as a real possibility, after both the achievements and the impasses of the present ideological reworkings, in which feminism has participated? It seems to me that the role of what is usually called "aesthetic practices" must increase not only to counterbalance the storage and uniformity of information by present-day mass media, data-bank systems, and, in particular, modern communications technology, but also to demystify the identity of the symbolic bond itself, to demystify, therefore, the *community* of language as a universal and unifying tool, one which totalizes and equalizes. In order to bring out—along with the *singularity* of each person and, even more, along with the multiplicity of every person's possible identifications (with atoms, e.g., stretching from the family to the stars)—the *relativity of his/her symbolic as well as biological existence,* according to the variation in his/her specific symbolic capacities. And in order to emphasize the *responsibility* which all will immediately face of putting this fluidity into play against the threats of death which are unavoidable whenever an inside and an outside, a self and an other, one group and another, are constituted. At this level of interiorization with its social as well as individual stakes, what I have called "aesthetic practices" are undoubtedly nothing other than the modern reply to the eternal question of morality. At least, this is how we might understand an ethics which, conscious of the fact that its order is sacrificial, reserves part of the burden for each of its adherents, therefore declaring them guilty while immediately affording them the possibility for *jouissance,* for various productions, for a life made up of both challenges and differences.

Spinoza's question can be taken up again here: Are women subject to ethics? If not to that ethics defined by classical philosophy—in relationship to which the ups and downs of feminist generations seem dangerously precarious—are women not already participating in the rapid dismantling that our age is experiencing at various levels (from wars to drugs to artificial insemination) and which poses the *demand* for a new ethics? The answer to Spinoza's question can be affirmative only at the cost of considering feminism as but a *moment* in the thought of that anthropomorphic identity which currently blocks the horizon of the discursive and scientific adventure of our species.

Translated by Alice Jardine and Harry Blake

NOTES

1. The following discussion emphasizes Europe in a way which may seem superfluous to some American readers given the overall emphasis on deterritorialization. It is, however, essential to the movement of an article that is above all devoted to the necessity of paying attention to the place from which we speak.—AJ.

2. Sigmund Freud and Carl G. Jung, *Correspondence* (Paris: Gallimard, 1975), 1:87.

3. R. Spitz, *La Première Année de la vie de l'enfant* [First year of life: a psychoanalytic study of normal and deviant development of object relations] (Paris: PUF, 1958); D. Winnicott, *Jeu et réalité* [Playing and reality] (Paris: Gallimard, 1975); Julia Kristeva, *"Noms de lieu"* in *Polylogue* (Paris: Editions du Seuil, 1977), translated as "Place Names" in Julia Kristeva, *Desire in Language: A Semiotic Approach to Literature and Art*, ed. Leon S. Roudiez, trans. Thomas Gora, Alice Jardine, and Leon Roudiez (New York: Columbia University Press, 1980) (hereafter cited as *Desire in Language*).

4. Plato, *Timeus* 52: "Indefinitely a place; it cannot be destroyed, but provides a ground for all that can come into being; itself being perceptible, outside of all sensation, by means of a sort of bastard reasoning; barely assuming credibility, it is precisely that which makes us dream when we perceive it, and affirm that all that exists must be somewhere, in a determined place. . . . " (author's translation).

5. As most readers of recent French theory in translation know, *la féminin* does not have the same pejorative connotations it has come to have in English. It is a term used to speak about women in general, but, as used most often in this article, it probably comes closest to our "female" as defined by Elaine Showalter in *A Literature of Their Own* (Princeton, N.J.: Princeton University Press, 1977). I have therefore used either "women" or "female" according to the context (cf. also n. 9 in "Introduction to Julia Kristeva's 'Women's Time'" [*Signs* 7 (1981):5–12; hereafter cited as "Introduction"]). "Subjectivity" here refers to the state of being "a thinking, speaking, acting, doing or writing agent" and never, e.g., as opposed to "objectivity" (see the glossary in *Desire in Language*).—AJ.

6. I have retained *jouissance*—that word for pleasure which defies translation—as it is rapidly becoming a "believable neologism" in English (see the glossary in *Desire in Language*).—AJ.

7. This particular mythology has important implications—equal only to those of the oedipal myth—for current French thought.—AJ.

8. See Julia Kristeva, "Hérétique de l'amour," *Tel quel*, no. 74 (1977), pp. 30–49.

9. See H. C. Puech, *La Gnose et la temps* (Paris: Gallimard, 1977).

10. See Alice Jardine, "Introduction to Julia Kristeva's 'Women's Time,'" *Signs* 7 (1981):5–12.

11. The term "identification" belongs to a wide semantic field ranging from everyday language to philosophy and psychoanalysis. While Kristeva is certainly referring in principle to its elaboration in Freudian and Lacanian psychoanalysis, it can be understood here, as a logic, in its most general sense (see the entry on "identification" in Jean LaPlanche and J. B. Pontalis, *Vocabulaire de la psychanalyse* [The language of psychoanalysis] [Paris: Presses Universitaires de France, 1967; rev. ed., 1976]).—AJ.

12. See D. Desanti, "L'Autre Sexe des bolcheviks," *Tel quel*, no. 76 (1978); Julia Kristeva, *Des Chinoises* (Paris: Editions des femmes, 1975), translated as *On Chinese Women*, trans. Anita Barrows (New York: Urizen Press, 1977).

13. See Arthur Hertzberg, *The French Enlightenment and the Jews* (New York: Columbia

University Press, 1968); *Les Juifs et la révolution française*, ed. B. Blumenkranz and A. Seboul (Paris: Édition Privat, 1976).

14. Here, "symbolic" is being more strictly used in terms of that function defined by Kristeva in opposition to the semiotic: "it involves the thetic phase, the identification of subject and its distinction from objects, and the establishment of a sign system" (see the glossary in *Desire in Language*, and Alice Jardine, "Theories of the Feminine: Kristeva," *Enclitic*, in press).—AJ.

15. See, in general, Jacques Lacan, *Écrits* (Paris: Éditions du Seuil, 1966) and in particular, Jacques Lacan, *Le Séminaire XX: Encore* (Paris: Éditions du Seuil, 1975).—AJ.

16. This work is periodically published in various academic women's journals, one of the most prestigious being *Signs: Journal of Women in Culture and Society*, University of Chicago Press. Also of note are the special issues: "Écriture, féminité, féminisme," *La Revue des sciences humaines* (Lillie III), no. 4 (1977); and "Les Femmes et la philosophie," *Le Doctrinal de sapience* (Éditions Solin), no. 3 (1977).

17. See linguistic research on "female language": Robin Lakoff, *Language and Women's Place* (New York: Harper & Row, 1974); Mary R. Key, *Male/Female Language* (Metuchen, N.J.: Scarecrow Press, 1973); A. M. Houdebine, "Les Femmes et la langue," *Tel quel*, no. 74 (1977), pp. 84–95. The contrast between these "empirical" investigations of women's "speech acts" and much of the research in France on the conceptual bases for a "female language" must be emphasized here. It is somewhat helpful, if ultimately inaccurate, to think of the former as an "external" study of language and the latter as an "internal" exploration of the process of signification. For further contrast, see, e.g., "Part II: Contemporary Feminist Thought in France: Translating Difference" in *The Future of Difference*, ed. Hester Eisenstein and Alice Jardine (Boston: G. K. Hall & Co., 1980); the "Introductions" to *New French Feminisms*, ed. Elaine Marks and Isabelle de Courtivron (Amherst: University of Massachusetts Press, 1980); and for a very helpful overview of the problem of "difference and language" in France, see Stephen Heath, "Difference" in *Screen* 19 no. 3 (Autumn 1978):51–112.—AJ.

18. This is one of the more explicit references to the mass marketing of "écriture féminine" in Paris over the last ten years.—AJ.

19. The expression *à leur corps défendant* translates as "against their will," but here the emphasis is on women's bodies: literally, "against their bodies." I have retained the former expression in English, partly because of its obvious intertextuality with Susan Brownmiller's *Against Our Will* (New York: Simon & Schuster, 1975). Women are increasingly describing their experience of the violence of the symbolic contract as a form of rape.—AJ.

20. Many women in the West who are once again finding all doors closed to them above a certain level of employment, especially in the current economic chaos, may find this statement, even qualified, troubling, to say the least. It is accurate, however, *in principle*: whether that of infinite capitalist recuperation or increasing socialist expansion—within both economies, our integration functions as a kind of *operative* illusion.—AJ.

21. The very real existence and autonomous activities of both of these versions of women's groups in Europe may seem a less urgent problem in the United States where feminist groups are often absorbed by the academy and/or are forced to remain financially dependent on para-academic/governmental agencies.—AJ.

22. See *Des Chinoises*.

23. See M. A. Macciocchi, *Éléments pour une analyse du fascisme* (Paris: 10/18, 1976); Michèle Mattelart, "Le Coup d'état au féminin," *Les Temps modernes* (January 1975).

24. The principles of a "sacrificial anthropology" are developed by René Girard in *La Violence et la sacré* [Violence and the sacred] (Paris: Grasset, 1972) and esp. in *Des Choses cachées depuis la fondation du monde* (Paris: Grasset, 1978).

25. Cf. Micheline Enriquez, "Fantasmes paranoïaques: différences des sexes, homosexualité, loi du père," *Topiques,* no. 13 (1974).

26. See Jacques Lacan, "Dieu et la jouissance de la femme" in *Encore* (Paris: Éditions du Seuil, 1975), pp. 61–71, esp. p. 68. This seminar has remained a primary critical and polemical focus for multiple tendencies in the French women's movement. For a brief discussion of the seminar in English, see Heath (n. 17 above).—AJ.

27. The "split subject" (from *Spaltung* as both "splitting" and "cleavage"), as used in Freudian psychoanalysis, here refers directly to Kristeva's "subject in process/in question/on trial" as opposed to the unity of the transcendental ego (see n. 14 in "Introduction").—AJ.

28. Again a reference to *écriture féminine* as generically labeled in France over the past few years and not to women's writing in general.—AJ.

29. See Seminar on *Identity* directed by Lévi-Strauss (Paris: Grasset & Fasquelle, 1977).

30. Repression (*le refoulement* or *Verdrängung*) as distinguished from the foreclosure (*la forclusion* or *Verwerfung*) evoked earlier in the article (see LaPlanche and Pontalis).—AJ.

POWER AND THE IDEOLOGY OF "WOMAN'S SPHERE"

(1981)

> . . . women, in their position in life, must be content to be inferior to men; but as their inferiority consists chiefly in their want of power, this deficiency is abundantly made up to them by their capability of exercising influence.
> —SARAH ELLIS, *THE DAUGHTERS OF ENGLAND*, 1845

> . . . as with work on the lower classes, slave populations, and peasants, work on relations between the sexes makes the location of power a trickier business than when one is looking at governments, parties, factions, and clientage systems. Power can lodge in dangerous nooks and crannies.
> —NATALIE ZEMON DAVIS, "'WOMEN'S HISTORY' IN TRANSITION," 1976

> The powers of the weak are, finally, more powerful than we think and can only be ignored by the powerful at their peril.
> —ELIZABETH JANEWAY, "ON THE POWER OF THE WEAK," 1975

In April of 1850, when Elizabeth Gaskell confessed to Tottie Fox that "the discovery of one's exact work in the world is the puzzle: . . . I am sometimes coward enough to wish we were back in the darkness where obedience was the only seen duty of women,"[1] she was finding words for a private and personally troubling experience of a more general ideological crisis, a crisis of confidence over the status, the proper work, and the power of middle-class women. This crisis of confidence, which emerged in the 1830s and 1840s in Great Britain, took the form of a prolonged debate over the "woman question," a debate so extensive that in 1869 Frances Power Cobbe was provoked to remark that "of all theories concerning women, none is more curious than the theory that it is needful to make a theory about them. . . . We are driven to conclude," she continues, that while men grow like trees "women run in moulds, like candles, and we can make them long-threes or short-sixes, whichever we please."[2]

The debate over the "woman question," in addition to its mass production of theories about women's "mission," "kingdom," or "sphere," gave an emphasis to the subject of women's power, and in particular to their influence, which was historically unprecedented. One has only to take manuals addressed to genteel women in the late eighteenth century and lay them alongside those written for middle-class women some sixty to seventy years later to see a deepening tension over women's power begin to manifest itself like footprints in a flower garden. In 1774, for example, in *A Father's Legacy to His Daughters*, John Gregory makes very few allusions to the power or influence of women. Although women are recognized as having been designed to "soften [the] hearts and polish [the] manners" of men, Gregory is less interested in the power women have to redeem men than charmed by the facility with which they please them. Woman's sphere, therefore, is not conceived of as the locus of a particular influence. Genteel women in Gregory's *Legacy* are "companions and equals" of men, rational beings, and their separate world is recommended not because it affords them power but because it lends them scope in which to be rationally human, in which to exercise "good sense and good taste."[3]

Twenty years later, however, James Fordyce makes many references to women's influence. One of his first *Sermons to Young Women* is "on the Importance of the Female Sex, especially the Younger Part," and in it he reassures women that a "principal source of your importance is the very great and extensive influence which you in general have with our sex." Genteel women have more extensive tasks in Fordyce than to polish manners and instill decency: they are to "promote general reformation" among men. And their separate sphere is important less as a realm in which they may demonstrate good taste than as a dominion in which they exercise a specific potency: "There is an influence, there is an empire which belongs to you . . . I mean that which has the heart as its object."[4]

By 1798 Thomas Gisborne, in *An Enquiry into the Duties of the Female Sex*, feels prompted to remind women not only that they have "influence" but that its effects are "various and momentous" and that this influence, like the power of men, extends to society as a whole. Thus, genteel women are urged to consider "the real and deeply interesting effects which the conduct of their sex will always have on the happiness of society." But the insistence upon women's influence reaches a culmination some thirty years later when Sarah Ellis begins *The Women of England* (1839) by declaring both that women's influence is social in nature and that it is in some ways more socially significant than the power of men: "You have deep responsibilities; you have urgent claims; a nation's moral worth is in your keeping."[5]

This same tension and counterinsistence in relation to women's power leave traces on periodical literature addressed to the "woman question." In 1810, for example, an author for the *Edinburgh Review* makes only one reference to women's influence, giving far more emphasis to the dignity, the delightfulness, and the ornamental quality of women's character and to the importance of their personal happiness. But by 1831, in literature of the same kind, power and influence are frequent subjects of concern, and references to both are accompanied by a sharpening distinction between what is appropriate to women and what to men. Most authors—and it is worth noting that much of this literature was written by men—reject the notion that women have power, but they acknowledge and give value to the fact that women possess "enormous," "immense," or "vast" "influence." This influence, of course, is always reassuringly unobtrusive, "secret," "unobserved," an "undercurrent below the surface."[6]

In 1833 a writer for *Fraser's Magazine*, who is actually defending the female character, is still obliged to doubt the existence of amazons, though he admits that there are many instances of "females acting in a body in defence of their homes." In 1841 an author for the *Edinburgh Review* dismisses the proposition that men and women will ever be equal "in power and influence upon the affairs of the world" and warns, rather ill-naturedly, that if women "be made ostensibly powerful . . . the spirit of chivalry . . . will speedily cease." But women do have "immense influence," he concedes, and that influence must "be allowed to flow in its natural channels, namely domestic ones." In the same year a writer for the *Westminster Review* admits that "power" as encoded in laws seems "permanent and transmittable in nature, while influence dies with the possessor," but women, he concludes hopefully, do not *want* power in the first place: " . . . the peculiar duties of women are guarded by instincts and feelings more powerful than the desire for political power."[7]

This valorization of women's influence, it should be clear, was aimed at devaluing actions and capacities which we can only call other forms of power, and, in this way, the peddling of women's influence, in a sort of ideological marketplace, functioned to sustain unequal power relations between middle-class women and middle-class men. Having influence, in fact, having the ability to persuade others to do or to be something that was in *their* own interest, was made contingent upon the renunciation of such self-advancing forms of power as control or self-definition. To have influence, for example, the middle-class woman was urged to relinquish self-definition; she was urged to become identified by her services to others, in particular to men:

> . . . men in general are more apt than women, to act and think as if they were created to exist of, and by, themselves; and this self-sustained existence a wife can only share, in proportion as she is identified in every thing with her husband.

> It is necessary for her to lay aside all her natural caprice, her love of self-indulgence, her vanity, her indolence—in short, her very *self*—and assuming a new nature, which [is] to spend her mental and moral capabilities in devising means for promoting the happiness of others, while her own derives a remote and secondary existence from theirs.[8]

Having influence also required women to lay aside any desire for the power to achieve, especially outside the domestic sphere, for "it is from an ambitious desire to extend the limits of this sphere, that many have brought trouble upon themselves." And even within the home, achievement must be circumscribed. The possession of talent is "the possession of a dangerous heritage—a jewel which cannot with propriety be worn." Most centrally, of course, the power of control must be renounced, and Sarah Ellis apologizes for suggesting that women "preside" even in the home, being "aware that the word *preside*, used as it is here, may produce a startling effect upon the ear of man." To have influence, in effect, meant doing without self-definition, achievement, and control, meant relinquishing power for effacement of the self in love and sacrifice: "All that has been expected to be enjoyed from the indulgence of selfishness, must then of necessity be left out of our calculations, with all that ministers to the pride of superiority, all that gratifies the love of power, all that converts the woman into the heroine."[9]

The preoccupation with women's power that leaves its mark on nineteenth-century manuals and on other literature addressed to the "woman question" reappears like a bold thread in the texture of the works in this study. But it is significant that the heroines of these works, Evelina, Elizabeth Bennet, Lucy Snowe, and Maggie Tulliver, are generally endowed not with power as influence but with power as ability and that Burney, Austen, Brontë, and Eliot give evidence of that "love of power . . . that converts the woman into the heroine." Indeed, it is one of the characteristic strategies of these authors to subvert masculine control and male domination in their novels by quietly giving emphasis to female capability, as if the pattern in the background of an embroidered piece had been subtly worked into relief.

One form of ability, for example, is autonomy, the power of being one's own person, and being one's own person is multiply and often subtly defined. It may mean having one's private opinions—Evelina's letters are full of unflattering observations about men—or it may take the shape of self-defending actions—Evelina refuses a dance partner against the rules; Elizabeth deftly rejects Darcy's proposal. Women are also made powerful in these novels by being endowed with the capacity to achieve, to perform tasks, to act not merely on other individuals but on situations, and although the scope of achievement is more limited in female characters than in male—Madame Beck makes a success of a school for girls but not of being an industrial capitalist—the emphasis given to achievement as power is used in *Villette*, as in other works, to balance or even to outweigh the power of male characters and so to alter what we *feel* in the course of reading the novel about the traditional divisions of power between women and men. Some women writing fiction, it appears, having found it unthinkable, unrealistic, or unhealthy to give their female characters such traditionally masculine power as the power of control, managed to make women *seem* powerful, nevertheless, by giving emphasis and value to power as capacity.

In choosing to focus on female ability, of course, these writers themselves exercised a form of agency, of resistance to dominant values. In their foregrounding of female ability and in their subversive undercutting of male control, they illustrate what Elizabeth Janeway has maintained: even "a withdrawal of attention . . . a concentration on other areas" are "ways in which the weak exercise their power."[10] The ability of female characters and the power strategies of their creators, however, are difficult at first to see, and part of the difficulty at least lies in our own cultural limitations. Our very definitions of power—like our conceptions of "history" or of "art"—have been deformed by traditions which have systematically excluded women. In all fields of women's studies, therefore, our shift in focus from the limitations of women's situation to the reality of their persisting power has raised questions about what power really is. It has committed us both to broadened definitions of power and to a certain openness, to an acknowledgment of the idea that female power "can lodge in dangerous nooks and crannies."[11]

Berenice Carroll, for example, has reminded us that the definition of power primarily as "control, dominance, and influence" is of recent origin and that the primary meaning of power as late as 1933 was "ability, energy, and strength." Power, according to Carroll, has been defined not just as control but also as "ability," as the capacity to assert "one's will over one's body, one's own organs and functions and over the physical environment—a power which is seen as inherently satisfying and not merely as an instrument to other ends, as neither requiring nor leading to the power to command obedience in other persons."[12] Power as ability, that is, has been defined both as achievement and competence and, by implication, as a form of self-definition or self-rule. It is this power of ability or capability that seams together the fiction I am going to explore.

Of course, power in women's fiction may also be difficult to see because power is a subject and a capacity which make women writers ill at ease, and uneasiness breeds disguise or, at the least, obliqueness. In the eighteenth and nineteenth centuries, in particular, the act of writing in itself appeared to lend women a self-assertiveness which seemed out of keeping with properly feminine aspirations. Elaine Showalter suggests that the ambivalence which many women writers felt toward the self-revelation and assertion necessary to writing fiction prompted a whole spectrum of defensive strategies which ranged from the use of male pseudonyms to the punishment of aspiring heroines to the author's insistence in private life on the conventionality of her own womanhood. More recently, Sandra Gilbert and Susan Gubar have isolated a pervasive "anxiety of authorship—a radical fear that she cannot create, that because she can never become a 'precursor' the act of writing will isolate or destroy her" as a crucial mark of women's literary subculture in the nineteenth century.[13] To write at all and then to write of power, perhaps to perform some transforming action in one's fiction upon traditional power divisions, was surely to multiply defensive strategies, and in *Evelina*, *Pride and Prejudice*, *Villette*, and *The Mill on the Floss* the ability of female characters and the power strategies of their creators are systematically disguised, offset, or explained into moonshine. Evelina's satirical strictures, for example, are excused by her innocence and by her ignorance of city ways, and Elizabeth Bennet's refreshing self-direction is qualified by her defensive ironies. She may speak her mind to Darcy, may finally change him, and the reader is allowed to enjoy her daring, but at the same time we are continually reminded that Elizabeth is wrong about Wickham and wrong about Darcy and that she is controlled by her desire to please both.

Although each of these novels, moreover, is the story of a quest, the story of entry into the world, of education, and of growth, including growth in power, the heroine's power is sometimes renounced and often diminished at the end of the novel, so that it seems that the work has had nothing to do with power at all.[14] For no matter how much force the heroine is granted at the beginning of her story, ideology, as it governed life and as it governed literary form, required that she should marry, and marriage meant relinquishment of power as surely as it meant the purchase of wedding clothes. Thus, Evelina gives up satire in the third volume of the novel in order to weep, faint, and otherwise prepare herself for the princely Orville, and Elizabeth Bennet, though her own woman to the end, still dwindles by degrees into the moral balance required in Darcy's wife. Even in *Villette* and *The Mill on the Floss*, where marriage plots are more totally resisted, resistance appears ultimately to exhaust authorial resources. The quest of Lucy Snowe ends abruptly with the death of Lucy's fiancé, and in *The Mill on the Floss* the unwed heroine drowns at the end of the novel.

As they wrote about quest and entry into the world these authors, it should be clear, felt the pressure of ideologies which required circumscription of power as rigorously as they required marriage (and more loss of power) as a "happy" ending. These are not difficulties with which male writers have had to wrestle, and it is the experience of these pressures, which are at once acceded to and rebelled against, that gives rise to the peculiar dominance in these novels of tension, disguise, and ultimately disjunctions of form. In any work, of course, it is not only what a text does say but what it does not say that reveals its relation to dominant images, ideas, and values. It is in the "significant *silences* of a text, in its gaps and absences, that the presence of ideology can be most positively felt."[15] But in these novels in particular, the very covertness of power, the nature and degree of its disguise, the very omission of overt reference are of the greatest interest, for subversion, indirection, and disguise are natural tactics of the resisting weak, are social strategies for managing the most intense and the most compelling rebellions.

In these specific novels, finally, the tensions created by each author's struggle with conventions—by her insistence on dealing with female power in the first place, her subversion of traditional power relations, her substitution of ability for influence, and her refusal, for the most part, totally to relinquish the heroine's ability at the end of the story—were surely intensified by the fact that each novel had an unusually direct origin in the author's own experience. Each writer, in fact, appears to be working through some painful personal encounter with culturally imposed patterns of male power and female powerlessness. In Burney this is specifically the shock of being reduced to merchandise in the marriage market. In Austen it is more generally the experience of being without money, without carriages, without options, the enduring experience of suffering restrictions upon her autonomy, and in Brontë and Eliot it is the external and internal limitations imposed on their passionate and half-guilty desire to achieve.

Taken together, then, these novels may be said to register a developing tension over women's power, a tension which appears to have been central to that general crisis of consciousness over the role and status of middle-class women which surfaced in the 1830s and 1840s. What is more significant, however, is that in their subversion of traditional power relations and ultimately in their substitution of female ability for feminine influence these novels delineate a line of covert, ambivalent, but finally radical resistance to the ideology of their day. Taken together, they seem to articulate what Raymond Williams has called an emergent "structure of feeling," a development of consciousness which is as yet embryonic, which is tied to dominant ideology, but which is nevertheless alternative or oppositional to dominant values, suggesting that the alternative to "received and produced fixed forms" is "not silence: not the absence, the unconscious, which bourgeois culture has mythicized. It is a kind of feeling and thinking which is indeed social and material, but each in an embryonic phase before it can become fully articulate and defined exchange."[16]

The line of resistance, moreover, grows bolder as the ideology of women's influence takes hold. Between Burney's *Evelina* in 1778 and Eliot's *The Mill on the Floss* in 1860, conceptions of male power in these novels are expanded so that women's power and the unequal power divisions between women and men become increasingly a matter of overt concern. Men's power in Burney almost always takes the form of force or control in social situations—of assault in ballrooms or ravishment in carriages. Power is the ability to impose one's self on another or to defend one's self from imposition. But in Eliot men's power is the ability not only to dominate others but to define the self and to achieve: " . . . you are a man, Tom, and have power, and can do something in the world."[17] That men have more power than women, therefore, is made more significant in *The Mill on the Floss* than in *Evelina*.

Between Burney and Eliot, too, unequal divisions of power are increasingly perceived or conceived of in these novels as imposed by the community rather than as natural or given. The community as a force, therefore, becomes more and more dominant—although its force may be mystified, as in *Villette*—and that development is accompanied by a growing tendency to portray community values as ideology and as ideology unwittingly internalized by the heroine. At the same time, however, the strategy of giving power to the heroine, the power of ability rather than of influence or control, becomes more and more pronounced and is expressed in the increasing emphasis given to quest—the development of the heroine and especially of her desire for power—at the expense of love. In Burney, for example, an incipient quest plot is simply abandoned to the love plot in the third volume, while in Austen love and quest are forced into an uneasy balance.

Taken together, then, these novels suggest more ways in which women's writing may be both the locus of compensating fantasies and the site of protest, actions expressive of the authors' power, and in this respect the following study develops a line of reading which feminist critics have begun to explore. Patricia Spacks, for example, has written of one woman artist that "her own power was the power to imagine what she wished of others . . . to re-create her experience in a way that made it tolerable." Ellen Moers has written of the gothic and of factory novels as the locus of middle-class women's displaced protest of their lot. Elaine Showalter has suggested several ways in which a subculture of female writers was informed by covert ways of dramatizing the inner life, by fantasies of "money, mobility, and power." Nina Auerbach has explored fictional communities of women as the continuing source of female strength. And most recently Sandra Gilbert and Susan Gubar have posited a whole tradition among female writers of creating "submerged meanings, meanings hidden within or behind the more accessible, 'public' content of their works," so that the works "are in some sense palimpsestic, works whose surface designs conceal or obscure deeper, less accessible (and less socially acceptable) levels of meaning." Each of these critics works helpfully and fertilely within the assumption that "art enables men and women both to order, interpret, mythologize or dispose of their own experience."[18]

But most studies of subversive strategies in women's fiction have tended to focus on the presence of unchanging or transhistorical patterns or have tended to isolate the text not just from developing material conditions but from shifting ideologies as well, and this tendency to universalize has led many of us to claim, rather too easily, that art is a transforming action upon history without our having to say in fact what that history has been. Susan Gubar and Sandra Gilbert, for example, while recognizing the reality of "male-dominated society" and of women's attempts to redefine their society along with their art, have focused their study on women's struggle against "patriarchal literary authority" and patriarchal images and conventions. Nina Auerbach, too, although she makes some striking connections between text and historical context, does not give emphasis to the changing ideological and material situations in which the evolution of literary myth takes place. My own work differs in that it attempts to trace the shifting historical situation in which literary redefinitions and evolutions unfolded.

Elaine Showalter, of course, does explore female literary traditions in the context of the "still-evolving relationships between women writers and their society," but where she has given us an overview of a female literary tradition my own aim has been to lay out paradigms of reading in which the complexities and ambiguities of the relation between novel and cultural context are central.[19] Indeed, it is one project of this study to suggest how works of women's fiction might be read in several contexts—in relation to the changing material conditions of women's lives, to the ideological representations and distortions of those conditions, to an author's particular biographical experience of these, and to the ideological content and shaping force of such conventions in women's fiction as the quest and the marriage plot. Following Terry Eagleton (more or less), I have assumed that a work of fiction presents itself to us less as "historical than as a sportive flight from history, a reversal and a resistance of history."[20] Although I make note of the way in which a text might be said to "evoke" historical situations,[21] I have dwelt on the way it relates itself to ideological perceptions or distortions of those situations. I have dwelt, that is, on the way a work of fiction relates itself to ideas, images, and values which insure that the situation in which one class has power over another and in which men have power over women is seen as natural or not seen at all. Specifically, I have asked how these works both support and resist ideologies which have tied middle-class women to the relative powerlessness of their lot and which have prevented them from having a true knowledge of their situation, but I have also tried to consider how ideologies governing middle-class women intersect with and are interdependent upon more general ideologies which sustain and legitimate the power of the male bourgeoisie in relation to society as a whole.

My aim, in this, has been first to read the text more fully, for to locate threads of rebellion in a text without articulating rather specifically what is being rebelled against is to see only part of the pattern in the text itself, and it is not fully to see the transforming significance—and the limitations—of the subversive themes, metaphors, or strategies which, with painstaking labor, have been discovered. To see a text in isolation from its historical conditions is not fully enough to answer the question "So what?"—a question which Lillian Robinson has posed as the hardest we can ask ourselves as critics. A second aim has been to understand the present by coming to better terms with our collective past. Implicit in my focus, for example, are the assumption that ideology has been central to women's oppression and the assumption that literature gives us a peculiarly revealing access to the way in which ideology has been experienced. Studying the relation of literature and ideology allows us to explore one area of what has been called "the emotional texture of life for individuals in the past . . . " "the existential consequences of occupying a particular social location . . . " "the structure of choices" which the situation of women afforded them.[22] In examining both the text's subversion of ideology and its adherence to it, moreover, we may come to some understanding of the degree to which female writers may have acted as agents or as arbiters of change, for works of fiction practice upon their readers, skew the angle of vision from which readers experience their relation to the real, the degree of confidence which they feel in traditional social relations. Most important, finally, it is in exploring the ways in which women have experienced ideology in the past that we may come to understand the outlines of its hold upon us in the present and so move closer to our own delivery from illusion.[23]

But to explore the relation of a text to ideology is to do more than examine its relation to ideas, for "it is not the consciousness of [men and women] that determines their being, but on the contrary, their social being that determines their consciousness."[24] To understand the significance of a text's relation of ideology one must also examine the material conditions, the real relations, the contradictions out of which that ideology emerged. Between 1774 and 1845, for example, the particular historical conditions which gave rise to the ideology of woman's sphere are partially and unreflectingly evoked by manuals addressed to genteel women. Between 1774 and 1845, that is, these manuals are informed by the presence of an interesting conjunction. Mounting references to women's influence are accompanied by more and more frequent allusions to a general discontent among genteel women with the limitations of their role and status and by a deepening consciousness of the fact that men of the middle orders are enjoying economic and social mobility. In 1774 Dr. Gregory betrays little consciousness of any troubling insignificance in women's domestic lot. If the handiwork of upper-middle-class women is of no more than "trifling" value, if its significance lies for the most part in its enabling them "to fill up, in a tolerably agreeable way, some of the many solitary hours you must necessarily pass at home," that is a fact which is to be taken for granted. By 1794, however, James Fordyce is far more conscious than Dr. Gregory of married and single women of the middle- and upper-middle classes who are feeling insignificant or discontent with their sphere. Fordyce, in fact, is apparently surrounded by women with complaints. He hears young women exclaiming that, "though God has given you capacities of intellectual improvement, men have denied you the opportunities of it," and the complaint is "a very common one, and very popular with your sex." Four years later Gisborne begins his *Enquiry* by admitting that the "sphere of domestic life ... admits far less diversity of action, and consequently of temptation, than is found in the widely differing professions and employments" of men, and he suggests that genteel young women in general complain that "the sphere in which women are destined to move, is so humble and so limited, as neither to require nor reward assiduity." By 1839 dissatisfaction with their lot appears so endemic to ordinary women of the middle class, not just to "masculine" grumblers, that Ellis is moved to begin her manual on a note of sweeping disapproval: "the women of England are ... less usefull, and less happy than they were." Domestic usefulness particularly is in decline, and the author complains that it is difficult even to praise such "quiet and unobtrusive virtues" as remain "without exciting a desire to forsake the homely household duties of the family circle to practise such as are more conspicuous, and consequently more productive of an immediate harvest of applause."[25]

Significantly, the growing fear—or the increasing evidence—that middle-class women were discontent with the limitations of their sphere is accompanied in these manuals by a deepening awareness of the fact that middle-class men were making money and enjoying a social significance which they had not enjoyed before. In both Fordyce and Gisborne this emphasis on the discontent of women is accompanied by mounting references to the social significance of money among the middle classes, money earned, of course, by males. And in Ellis women's purported discontent with their lack of status is very frequently juxtaposed with a world in which money is everything, in which men are entirely devoted to efforts and calculations relating to their "pecuniary success."

What this unreflecting conjunction of references to female power, female discontent, and economic contradiction evokes is the causal relation between the "woman question" and what came to be perceived at least about the economic value of middle-class women between 1778 and 1860, a period which spans industrial takeoff and the establishment of bourgeois-class society—for the development of industrial capitalism did change the economic situation of middle-class women relative to that of middle-class men. Eric Hobsbawm, for example, notes that the "crucial achievement" of the industrial and French revolutions was that

> they opened careers to talent [the talent of middle-class men], or at any rate to energy, shrewdness, hard work, and greed. Not all careers, and not to the top rungs of the ladder, except perhaps in the USA. And yet, how extraordinary were the opportunities, how remote from the nineteenth century state hierarchical ideal of the past! . . . in 1750 the son of a book binder would, in all probability, have stuck to his father's trade. Now he no longer had to. Four roads to the stars opened before him: business, education (which in turn led to the three goals of government, service, politics, and the free professions), the arts, and war.[26]

By the mid-nineteenth century the development of industrial capitalism had not led middle-class women along the same four roads. Indeed, although the absence of statistical data makes it difficult to compare women in preindustrial Britain with women of this later time, it has been argued that "industrialization far from emancipating women led to a contraction of some of their traditional functions in the economy—to a degree from which they have yet fully to recover." The nineteenth-century labor force, according to Eric Richards, was increasingly male-dominated, and "apart from domestic service, textiles, stitching, and washing there was little else open to women of any class in England before the final decades of the century."[27] The number of women employed in middle-class occupations, moreover, was even lower, for the trend toward employing women even in such spheres as shops, civil service, and business, all of which were open to men, did not begin until after 1870.[28]

At the same time, the recognized economic status of dependent married middle-class women also suffered a decline relative to the rising economic status of middle-class men, and the causes generally forwarded for what may be seen at least as a *shift in perception* are that, with the development of industrialization, home production of many household products declined; that household industries in which women and children worked alongside husbands and fathers also dwindled;[29] and that, as men's work separated further from the home, new definitions and perceptions of work were further developed, definitions and perceptions which made married women's work in the home less *visible* as work than it had been before.[30]

Literature on the "woman question," for example, makes frequent allusions to a decline in women's domestic labor and economic status, and, without claiming that this literature actually describes the middle-class woman's experience day to day, it is still possible to trace an indication of how women's domestic work was seen.[31] Thus in 1810 an article in the *Edinburgh Review* observes that "the time of women is considered worth nothing at all," and in 1841 the *Westminster Review* remarks that an "attendant effect of luxury and civilization is to procure leisure for the housekeeper as well as everybody else. The greater perfection and division of labor procures for us all the necessities and comforts of life almost ready made."[32] What some literature on the "woman question" also suggests is that this ostensible decline in women's economic activity and the recognized value of their work was linked with a decline in their status as well. In 1869, after remarking that "men have taken away from women the employments which formerly were appropriated to them," such as spinning, sewing, and domestic labors, one author goes on to observe that

> when these and such like avocations were available to women of every rank, they were not only provided with subsistence, but they held that definite place in society and filled those recognized duties which placed them on a footing of substantial dignity, and forbade the raising of any question whether [their] capacities were equal with those of men or not. Not intentionally, but actually, by the progress of science and forms of social existence that position has been taken from women.[33]

Unpaid domestic work lost visibility, then, at a time when it was not yet possible for middle-class women to enter the labor market in any equitable way, and the low status of women's work in the labor market must have enforced the low status of women's work in the home—and vice versa. At the same time, the rising economic and social power of middle-class men gave increasing value to work that was to be done by males, work that was at once public, divorced from the home, and salaried. All this was bound to have an effect on women's status as it also had on their sense of power,[34] and it is largely these economic and social contradictions which gave rise to an ideological crisis in which questions about women's status, power, and influence were central. Indeed, the establishment by the mid-nineteenth century of an ideological emphasis on women's influence was largely an attempt to resolve this economic contradiction and to maintain the subordination of middle-class women to middle-class men, an attempt to keep the lid on middle-class women by assuring them that they *did* have work, power, and status after all.

The ideology of woman's sphere, however, was also established at a time when industrial capitalism was beset both by economic crisis and by working-class unrest. The progress of industrial capitalism, according to Eric Hobsbawm, was far from smooth, and by the 1830s and 1840s it "produced major problems of growth not to mention revolutionary unrest unparalleled in any other period of recent British history." Working-class consciousness, in fact, came into existence between 1815 and 1848, more especially around 1830, shortly before the new ideology of woman's sphere emerged. As in America, the ideology of woman's sphere in Britain may be said to have "enlisted women in their domestic roles to absorb, palliate, and even to redeem the strain of social and economic transformation."[35] Women, in their isolation from competitive economic practices, were to act as the conscience of bourgeois society and through their influence over men mitigate the harshness of an industrial capitalist world. Woman's sphere, therefore, was defined as the "intellectual education of childhood, the moral guidance of youth, the spiritual influence over the home and society, [and] the softening of relations between class and class which bind those together by deeds of love whom the material interests keep apart."[36] In reality, of course, "the canon of domesticity did not directly challenge the modern organization of work and pursuit of wealth. Rather, it accommodated and promised to temper them."[37] The ideology of woman's sphere, that is, served the interests of industrial capitalism by insuring the continuing domination of middle-class women by middle-class men and, through its mitigation of the harshness of economic transition, by insuring the continuing domination of male bourgeoisie in relation to working-class men and women as a whole.

The development of industrial capitalism, then, between *Evelina* and *The Mill on the Floss* empowered middle-class men, economically and socially, while it was *felt* at least to have disempowered middle-class women, and the development of this economic contradiction, of the ideological crisis which it provoked, and the attempts at ideological resolution which accompanied both inform and shape the women's fiction I am going to explore. Indeed, in these novels an emergent and rebellious structure of feeling about inequities of power between women and men is accompanied by a more and more overt evocation—and resentment—of economic inequities as well. Power divisions, for example, are linked with increasing explicitness to differences in economic function. Thus in *Evelina* Burney scorns money consciousness by projecting it onto the vulgar lower classes, but in *Pride and Prejudice* Austen draws attention to a relation between money and power before silently subverting it. In *Villette* access to work that pays is persistently felt to be the most fundamental source of power, although Brontë may be said to present the connection without making it fully articulate, and in *The Mill on the Floss* Eliot analytically evokes what Burney, Austen, and Brontë have either unreflectingly grasped or only partially presented. In *The Mill on the Floss* the division between men's and women's recognized economic functions is the major determinant of their power. And much of the first half of the novel is devoted to analyzing how that relation determines the lives of Tom and Maggie Tulliver.

Protest against power inequities between women and men, moreover, as expressed in the increasing emphasis given to conventional marriage plots, is brought into conjunction with buried protest first against class division and ultimately against capitalist development itself. Indeed the relation of each work to an ideology about women also locates it in relation to general ideologies about class division and ultimately about industrial capitalist relations. Burney, for example, endorses the class power of landed men in order to sustain a courtly ideology about genteel women, while Austen's endorsement of Elizabeth's independence is of a piece with her endorsement of economic individualism in middle-class men. Brontë's bitter resentment of the inequities of money between middle-class women and middle-class men leads to mystified protest on behalf of all those who are "creatures of shadow" rather than "creatures of sunshine," and Eliot's analysis of male and female socialization sees industrial capitalist development as dangerous, if not to the working class, at least to middle-class women.

What might appear at first to be relatively simple resistance to the ideology of woman's sphere therefore takes on, in this larger context, a wider significance; resistance to an ideology governing middle-class women intersects with resistance to ideologies sustaining capitalist relations as a whole, and it is this intersection which helps explain the radical content and finally the radical curtailment of rebellious strategies for women in these novels—an argument if there ever was one for looking at gender in relation to class. For protest of women's powerlessness is disconcerting enough. When it leads—intuitively and half consciously—to resentment of the economic inequities between women and men and to distaste for capitalist ethics and capitalist economic relations as a whole, rebellion becomes far more frightening and much more difficult to sustain, a fact which has its effect on the shape of these novels. What might be seen, that is, as a growth of consciousness that is potentially revolutionary—an emergent feeling on the part of the authors that power divisions are imposed rather than natural and a mounting resistance to those divisions in their fiction—does not in fact find satisfactory expression in their art. In these novels growing resistance produces growing tension, and the tension becomes particularly acute as, historically, the ideology of women's influence and ideologies sustaining industrial capitalism are established. The heroine's, and the author's, rebellion is not abandoned, but it is directed into fantasies of power which are increasingly apparent as fantasies and increasingly difficult to sustain. In Brontë and in Eliot, indeed, the authors themselves seem patently disbelieving.

The thrust of this tension, however, is not toward resignation so much as toward further covertness and further disguise, and this indicates at once the force with which ideology inhibits and the persistence with which women rebelled. Their rebelliousness, moreover, is more than a brand of false consciousness, for if on the one hand subversive writing defuses the desire for power by satisfying the longing for it, on the other subversive writing is itself an action upon one's readers and one's world. It is not only socialist novels which can destroy "conventional illusions" about human relations. Any novel may do so when it "shakes the optimism of the bourgeois world, when it casts doubt on the eternal nature of existing society, even if the author does not propose answers, even though [she] might not openly take sides."[38] To write subversively is more than a means of exercising influence. It is a form of struggle—and a form of power.

NOTES

1. Elizabeth Gaskell, letter to Eliza Fox, [April? 1850], letter 69, in *The Letters of Mrs. Gaskell*, ed. J. A. V. Chapple and Arthur Pollard, p. 109.

2. Frances Power Cobbe, "The Final Cause of Woman," in *Woman's Work and Woman's Culture*, ed. Josephine E. Butler, p. 1.

3. John Gregory, *A Fathers Legacy to His Daughters*, pp. 6–7, 52.

4. James Fordyce, *Sermons to Young Women*, 1: 24, 26, 213.

5. Thomas Gisborne, *An Enquiry into the Duties of the Female Sex*, pp. 8, 6; Sarah Ellis, *The Women of England*, p. 6.

6. "Advice to Young Ladies on the Improvement of the Mind," *Edinburgh Review* 15 (January 1810): 314; Henry Thomas Buckle, "The Influence of Women on the Progress of Knowledge," *Fraser's Magazine* 57 (April 1858): 396, 397; "Rights and Conditions of

Women," *Edinburgh Review* 73 (January 1841): 204; "Spirit of Society in England and France," *Edinburgh Review* 52 (January 1831): 378.

7. "The Female Character," *Fraser's Magazine* 7 (1833): 593; "Rights and Conditions of Women," pp. 192, 204; P.M.Y., "Woman and Her Social Position," *Westminster Review* 35 (January 1841): 22, 25.

8. Sarah Ellis, *The Wives of England*, p. 26; Ellis, *Women of England*, pp. 15–16.

9. Ellis, *Wives of England*, pp. 41, 37, 14, 46.

10. Elizabeth Janeway, "On the Power of the Weak," *Signs* 1 (1975): 105.

11. Natalie Zemon Davis, "'Women's History' in Transition: The European Case," *Feminist Studies* 3 (Spring–Summer 1976): 90.

12. Berenice A. Carroll, "Peace Research: The Cult of Power," *Journal of Conflict Resolution* 16 (December 1972): 585, 588, 589, 591.

13. Showalter, *A Literature of Their Own*, pp. 19, 21, 22, 23; Sandra M. Gilbert and Susan Gubar, *The Madwoman in the Attic*, pp. 49, 51.

14. See Jean E. Kennard, *Victims of Convention*, p. 13. Much of my own thinking about love and quest plots comes from Rachel Blau DuPlessis.

15. Eagleton, *Marxism and Literary Criticism*, p. 35.

16. Raymond Williams, *Marxism and Literature*, pp. 132, 131.

17. George Eliot, *The Mill on the Floss*, ed. Gordon S. Haight, p. 304.

18. Spacks, *The Female Imagination*, p. 219; Showalter, *A Literature of Their Own*, p. 28; Gilbert and Gubar, *The Madwoman in the Attic*, p. 73; Robinson, *Sex, Class, and Culture*, p. 80.

19. Gilbert and Gubar, *The Madwoman in the Attic*, pp. xi, 49; Showalter, *A Literature of Their Own*, p. 12.

20. Terry Eagleton, *Criticism and Ideology*, p. 72.

21. I am perhaps closer here to Pierre Macherey: "The literary work must be studied in a double perspective: in relation to history, and in relation to an ideological version of that history." A text, however, does not "reflect" history for Macherey but "by means of contradictory images . . . represents and evokes the historical contradictions of the period." See *A Theory of Literary Production*, trans. Geoffrey Wall, pp. 115, 126.

22. Charles E. Rosenberg, "Introduction: History and Experience," *The Family in History*, pp. 2, 3.

23. Eagleton, *Criticism and Ideology*, p. 101; Eagleton, *Marxism and Literary Criticism*, p. 18.

24. Karl Marx, "Preface," *A Contribution to the Critique of Political Economy*, quoted in *Dynamics of Social Change*, ed. Howard Selsam, David Goldway, and Harry Martel, p. 52.

25. Gregory, *Legacy*, p. 51; Fordyce, *Sermons*, p. 224; Gisborne, *Enquiry*, pp. 2, 7; Ellis, *Women of England*, pp. 5, 14.

26. Eric J. Hobsbawm, *The Age of Revolution*, pp. 226–227; see also Ivy Pinchbeck, *Women Workers and the Industrial Revolution*, pp. 314–315.

27. Eric Richards, "Women in the British Economy since about 1700: An Interpretation," *History* 59 (October 1974): 337, 349.

28. See Lee Holcombe, *Victorian Ladies at Work*, p. 216.

29. The decline of household industry and the separation of men's work from the home are well documented. See, for example, Alice Clark, *The Working Life of Women in the Seventeenth Century*, p. 269; Pinchbeck, *Women Workers and the Industrial Revolution*, p. 307; Peter Laslett, *The World We Have Lost*, p. 17; Richards, "Women in the British Economy," p. 345; Theresa M. McBride, "The Long Road Home: Women's Work and Industrialization," in *Becoming Visible*, ed. Renate Bridenthal and Claudia Koonz, p. 283.

30. See Lise Vogel, "The Contested Domain: A Note on the Family in the Transition to Capitalism," *Marxist Perspectives* 1 (Spring 1978): 63, 66. See also Nancy F. Cott, *The Bonds of Womanhood*, p. 61.

31. Patricia Branca argues persuasively that middle-class women were not idle, as

women's manuals of the period often suggest, but I think it likely that manuals which were, as Branca maintains, "naggingly critical of middle-class women" reflected a general cultural tension about the recognized economic function of such women and about the status of women's work. See *Silent Sisterhood*, p. 16.

32. "Advice to Young Ladies," p. 300; P. M.Y., "Woman and Her Social Position," p. 15.

33. John Boyd-Kinnear, "The Social Position of Women in the Present Age," in *Woman's Work and Woman's Culture*, ed. Butler, pp. 334–335.

34. See Clark, *Working Life of Women*, p. 302; Pinchbeck, *Women Workers and the Industrial Revolution*, p. 312; Heidi Hartmann, "Capitalism, Patriarchy, and Job Segregation by Sex," *Signs* 1 (1976): 152; Margaret George, "From 'Goodwife' to 'Mistress': The Transformation of the Female in Bourgeois Culture," *Science and Society* 37 (1973): 156.

35. Hobsbawm, *Age of Revolution*, pp. 57, 249; Cott, *Bonds of Womanhood*, p. 70.

36. "Female Labour," *Fraser's Magazine* 61 (March 1860): 371, 370.

37. Cott, *Bonds of Womanhood*, p. 69.

38. Friedrich Engels, quoted in Macherey, *Theory of Literary Production*, p. 119.

WORKS CITED

"Advice to Young Ladies on the Improvement of the Mind." *Edinburgh Review* 15 (January 1810): 299–315.

Auerbach, Nina. *Communities of Women: An Idea in Fiction.* Cambridge, Mass.: Harvard University Press, 1978.

———. "The Power of Hunger: Demonism and Maggie Tulliver. *Nineteenth Century Fiction* 30 (September 1975): 150–171.

Austen, Jane. *Pride and Prejudice.* New York: Holt, Rinehart & Winston, 1949.

Branca, Patricia. *Silent Sisterhood: Middle Class Women in the Victorian Home.* Pittsburgh: Carnegie-Mellon University Press, 1975.

Bridenthal, Renate, and Claudia Koonz, eds. *Becoming Visible: Women in European History.* Boston: Houghton Mifflin, 1977.

Brontë, Charlotte. *Villette.* Ed. Geoffrey Tillotson and Donald Hawes. Boston: Houghton Mifflin, 1971.

Buckle, Henry Thomas. "The Influence of Women on the Progress of Knowledge." *Fraser's Magazine* 57 (April 1858): 395–407.

Burney, Frances. *Evelina: or, The History of a Young Lady's Entrance into the World.* New York: W. W. Norton, 1965.

Carroll, Berenice A. "Peace Research: The Cult of Power." *Journal of Conflict Resolution* 16 (December 1972): 505–616.

Clark, Alice. *The Working Life of Women in the Seventeenth Century.* London: Frank Cass, 1968.

Cobbe, Frances Power. *The Duties of Women: A Course of Lectures.* Boston: Geo. H. Ellis, 1882.

———. "The Final Cause of Woman." In *Woman's Work and Woman's Culture: A Series of Essays,* ed. Josephine E. Butler, pp. 1–25. London: Macmillan, 1869.

Cott, Nancy F. *The Bonds of Womanhood: "Woman's Sphere" in New England, 1780–1835.* New Haven: Yale University Press, 1977.

Davis, Natalie Zemon. "'Women's History' in Transition: The European Case." *Feminist Studies* 3 (Spring–Summer 1976): 83–103.

Eagleton, Terry. *Criticism and Ideology: A Study in Marxist Literary Theory.* London: NLB, 1976.

———. *Marxism and Literary Criticism.* Berkeley & Los Angeles: University of California Press, 1976.

Eliot, George. *The Mill on the Floss.* Ed. Gordon S. Haight. Boston: Houghton Mifflin, 1961.

Ellis, Sarah. *The Daughters of England: Their Position in Society, Character, and Responsibilities,*

1845; *The Wives of England: Their Relative Duties, Domestic Influence, and Social Obligations,* 1843; *The Women of England: Their Social Duties, and Domestic Habits,* 1839; rpt. in *The Family Monitor and Domestic Guide.* New York: E. Walker, n.d.

"The Female Character." *Fraser's Magazine* 7 (1833): 591–601.

"Female Labour." *Fraser's Magazine* 61 (March 1860): 359–371.

Fordyce, James. *Sermons to Young Women.* 2 vols. London: A. Millar, W. Law, & R. Cater, 1794.

Gaskell, Elizabeth. *The Letters of Mrs. Gaskell.* Ed. J. A. V. Chapple and Arthur Pollard. Cambridge, Mass.: Harvard University Press, 1967.

George, Margaret. "From 'Goodwife' to 'Mistress': The Transformation of the Female in Bourgeois Culture." *Science and Society* 37 (1973): 152–177.

Gilbert, Sandra, and Susan Gubar. *The Madwoman in the Attic: The Woman Writer and the Nineteenth-Century Literary Imagination.* New Haven: Yale University Press, 1979.

Gisborne, Thomas. *An Enquiry into the Duties of the Female Sex.* Philadelphia: James Humphreys, 1798.

Gregory, John. *A Father's Legacy to His Daughters.* New York: Garland Publishing, 1974.

Hartmann, Heidi. "Capitalism, Patriarchy, and Job Segregation by Sex." *Signs* 1 (1976): 137–169.

Hobsbawm, Eric J. *The Age of Revolution: 1789–1848.* New York: New American Library, 1962.

Holcombe, Lee. *Victorian Ladies at Work: Middle-Class Working Women in England and Wales, 1850–1914.* Newton Abbot: David & Charles, 1973.

Janeway, Elizabeth. "On the Power of the Weak." *Signs* 1 (1975): 103–109.

Kennard, Jean E. *Victims of Convention.* Hamden, Conn.: Archon Books, 1978.

Kinnear, John Boyd. "The Social Position of Women in the Present Age." In *Woman's Work and Woman's Culture: A Series of Essays,* ed. Josephine E. Butler, pp. 332–366. London: Macmillan, 1869.

Laslett, Peter. *The World We Have Lost.* New York: Charles Scribner's Sons, 1965.

Macherey, Pierre. *A Theory of Literary Production.* Trans. Geoffrey Wall. London: Routledge & Kegan Paul, 1978.

Moers, Ellen. *Literary Women.* Garden City, N.Y.: Doubleday, 1976.

Pinchbeck, Ivy. *Women Workers and the Industrial Revolution: 1750–1850.* New York: Augustus M. Kelley, 1969.

P.M.Y. "Woman and Her Social Position." *Westminster Review* 35 (January 1841): 13–27.

Richards, Eric. "Women in the British Economy since about 1700: An Interpretation." *History* 59 (October 1974): 337–357.

"Rights and Conditions of Women." *Edinburgh Review* 73 (January 1841): 189–209.

Robinson, Lillian S. *Sex, Class, and Culture.* Bloomington: Indiana University Press, 1978.

Rosenberg, Charles E. *The Family in History.* Philadelphia: University of Pennsylvania Press, 1975.

Selsam, Howard, David Goldway, and Harry Martel, eds. *Dynamics of Social Change: A Reader in Marxist Social Science.* New York: International Publishers, 1970.

Showalter, Elaine. *A Literature of Their Own: British Women Novelists from Brontë to Lessing.* Princeton: Princeton University Press, 1977.

Spacks, Patricia. *The Female Imagination.* New York: Avon Books, 1972.

"Spirit of Society in England and France." *Edinburgh Review* 42 (January 1831): 374–387.

Vogel, Lise. "The Contested Domain: A Note on the Family in the Transition to Capitalism." *Marxist Perspectives* 1 (Spring 1978): 50–73.

Williams, Raymond. *Marxism and Literature.* Oxford: Oxford University Press, 1977.

GAYATRI CHAKRAVORTY SPIVAK

THREE WOMEN'S TEXTS AND A CRITIQUE OF IMPERIALISM

(1985)

It should not be possible to read nineteenth-century British literature without re-membering that imperialism, understood as England's social mission, was a cru-cial part of the cultural representation of England to the English. The role of literature in the production of cultural representation should not be ignored. These two obvious "facts" continue to be disregarded in the reading of nineteenth-century British literature. This itself attests to the continuing success of the imperialist project, displaced and dispersed into more modern forms.

If these "facts" were remembered, not only in the study of British literature but in the study of the literatures of the European colonizing cultures of the great age of imperialism, we would produce a narrative, in literary history, of the "worlding" of what is now called "the Third World." To consider the Third World as distant cultures, exploited but with rich intact literary heritages waiting to be recovered, interpreted, and curricularized in English translation fosters the emer-gence of "the Third World" as a signifier that allows us to forget that "worlding," even as it expands the empire of the literary discipline.[1]

It seems particularly unfortunate when the emergent perspective of feminist criticism reproduces the axioms of imperialism. A basically isolationist admira-tion for the literature of the female subject in Europe and Anglo-America establishes the high feminist norm. It is supported and operated by an information-retrieval approach to "Third-World" literature which often employs a deliberately "non-theoretical" methodology with self-conscious rectitude.

In this essay, I will attempt to examine the operation of the "worlding" of what is today "the Third World" by what has become a cult text of feminism: *Jane Eyre*.[2] I plot the novel's reach and grasp, and locate its structural motors. I read *Wide Sargasso Sea* as *Jane Eyre*'s reinscription and *Frankenstein* as an analysis—even a deconstruction—of a "worlding" such as *Jane Eyre*'s.[3]

I need hardly mention that the object of my investigation is the printed book, not its "author." To make such a distinction is, of course, to ignore the lessons of deconstruction. A deconstructive critical approach would loosen the binding of the book, undo the opposition between verbal text and the bio-graphy of the named subject "Charlotte Brontë," and see the two as each other's "scene of writ-ing." In such a reading, the life that writes itself as "my life" is as much a pro-duction in psychosocial space (other names can be found) as the book that is written by the holder of that named life—a book that is then consigned to what *is* most often recognized as genuinely "social": the world of publication and distribution.[4] To touch Brontë's "life" in such a way, however, would be too risky here. We must rather strategically take shelter in an essentialism which, not wishing to lose the important advantages won by U.S. mainstream feminism, will continue to honor the suspect binary oppositions—book and author, individual and history—and start with an assurance of the following sort: my readings here do not seek to undermine the excellence of the individual artist. If even minimally successful, the readings will incite a degree of rage against the imperialist narrativization of history, that it should produce so abject a script for her. I provide these assurances to allow myself some room to situate feminist individualism in its historical determination rather than simply to canonize it as feminism as such.

Sympathetic American feminists have remarked that I do not do justice to Jane Eyre's subjectivity. A word of explanation is perhaps in order. The broad strokes of my presuppositions are that what is at stake, for feminist individualism in the age of imperialism, is precisely the making of human beings, the constitution and "interpellation" of the subject not only as individual but as "individualist."[5] This stake is represented on two registers: childbearing and soul making. The first is domestic-society-through-sexual-reproduction cathected as "companionate love"; the second is the imperialist project cathected as civil-society-through-social-mission. As the female individualist, not-quite/not-male, articulates herself in shifting relationship to what is at stake, the "native female" as such (*within* discourse, *as* a signifier) is excluded from any share in this emerging norm.[6] If we read this account from an isolationist perspective in a "metropolitan" context, we see nothing there but the psychobiography of the militant female subject. In a reading such as mine, in contrast, the effort is to wrench oneself away from the mesmerizing focus of the "subject-constitution" of the female individualist.

To develop further the notion that my stance need not be an accusing one, I will refer to a passage from Roberto Fernández Retamar's "Caliban."[7] José Enrique Rodó had argued in 1900 that the model for the Latin American intellectual in relationship to Europe could be Shakespeare's Ariel.[8] In 1971 Retamar, denying the possibility of an identifiable "Latin American Culture," recast the model as Caliban. Not surprisingly, this powerful exchange still excludes any specific consideration of the civilizations of the Maya, the Aztecs, the Incas, or the smaller nations of what is now called Latin America. Let us note carefully that, at this stage of my argument, this "conversation" between Europe and Latin America (without a specific consideration of the political economy of the "worlding" of the "native") provides a sufficient thematic description of our attempt to confront the ethnocentric and reverse-ethnocentric benevolent double bind (that is, considering the "native" as object for enthusiastic information retrieval and thus denying its own "worlding") that I sketched in my opening paragraphs.

In a moving passage in "Caliban," Retamar locates both Caliban and Ariel in the postcolonial intellectual:

> There is no real Ariel-Caliban polarity: both are slaves in the hands of Prospero, the foreign magician. But Caliban is the rude and unconquerable

> master of the island, while Ariel, a creature of the air, although also a child of the isle, is the intellectual.
>
> The deformed Caliban—enslaved, robbed of his island, and taught the language by Prospero—rebukes him thus: "You taught me language, and my profit on't/ Is, I know how to curse." ["C," pp. 28, 11]

As we attempt to unlearn our so-called privilege as Ariel and "seek from [a certain] Caliban the honor of a place in his rebellious and glorious ranks," we do not ask that our students and colleagues should emulate us but that they should attend to us ("C," p. 72). If, however, we are driven by a nostalgia for lost origins, we too run the risk of effacing the "native" and stepping forth as "the real Caliban," of forgetting that he is a name in a play, an inaccessible blankness circumscribed by an interpretable text.[9] The stagings of Caliban work alongside the narrativization of history: claiming to *be* Caliban legitimizes the very individualism that we must persistently attempt to undermine from within.

Elizabeth Fox-Genovese, in an article on history and women's history, shows us how to define the historical moment of feminism in the West in terms of female access to individualism.[10] The battle for female individualism plays itself out within the larger theater of the establishment of meritocratic individualism indexed in the aesthetic field by the ideology of "the creative imagination." Fox-Genovese's presupposition will guide us into the beautifully orchestrated opening of *Jane Eyre*.

It is a scene of the marginalization and privatization of the protagonist: "There was no possibility of taking a walk that day. . . . Out-door exercise was now out of the question. I was glad of it," Brontë writes (*JE*, p. 9). The movement continues as Jane breaks the rules of the appropriate topography of withdrawal. The family at the center withdraws into the sanctioned architectural space of the withdrawing room or drawing room; Jane inserts herself—"I slipped in"—into the margin—"A small breakfast-room *adjoined* the drawing room" (*JE*, p. 9; my emphasis).

The manipulation of the domestic inscription of space within the upwardly mobilizing currents of the eighteenth- and nineteenth-century bourgeoisie in England and France is well known. It seems fitting that the place to which Jane withdraws is not only not the withdrawing room but also not the dining room, the sanctioned place of family meals. Nor is it the library, the appropriate place for reading. The breakfast room "contained a book-case" (*JE*, p. 9). As Rudolph Ackerman wrote in his *Repository* (1823), one of the many manuals of taste in circulation in nineteenth-century England, these low bookcases and stands were designed to "contain all the books that may be desired for a sitting-room without reference to the library."[11] Even in this already triply off-center place, "having drawn the red moreen curtain nearly close, I [Jane] was shrined in double retirement" (*JE*, pp. 9–10).

Here in Jane's self-marginalized uniqueness, the reader becomes her accomplice: the reader and Jane are united—both are reading. Yet Jane still preserves her odd privilege, for she continues never quite doing the proper thing in its proper place. She cares little for reading what is *meant* to be read: the "letterpress." *She* reads the pictures. The power of this singular hermeneutics is precisely that it can make the outside inside. "At intervals, while turning over the leaves of my book, I studied the aspect of that winter afternoon." Under "the clear panes of glass," the rain no longer penetrates, "the drear November day" is rather a one-dimensional "aspect" to be "studied," not decoded like the "letter-press" but, like pictures, deciphered by the unique creative imagination of the marginal individualist (*JE*, p. 10).

Before following the track of this unique imagination, let us consider the suggestion that the progress of *Jane Eyre* can be charted through a sequential arrangement of the family/counter-family dyad. In the novel, we encounter, first, the Reeds as the legal family and Jane, the late Mr. Reed's sister's daughter, as the representative of a near incestuous counter-family; second, the Brocklehursts, who run the school Jane is sent to, as the legal family and Jane, Miss Temple, and Helen Burns as a counter-family that falls short because it is only a community of women; third, Rochester and the mad Mrs. Rochester as the legal family and Jane and Rochester as the illicit counter-family. Other items may be added to the thematic chain in this sequence: Rochester and Céline Varens as structurally functional counter-family; Rochester and Blanche Ingram as dissimulation of legality—and so on. It is during this sequence that Jane is moved from the counter-family to the family-in-law. In the next sequence, it is Jane who restores full family status to the as-yet-incomplete community of siblings, the Riverses. The final sequence of the book is a *community of families*, with Jane, Rochester, and their children at the center.

In terms of the narrative energy of the novel, how is Jane moved from the place of the counter-family to the family-in-law? It is the active ideology of imperialism that provides the discursive field.

(My working definition of "discursive field" must assume the existence of discrete "systems of signs" at hand in the socius, each based on a specific axiomatics. I am identifying these systems as discursive fields. "Imperialism as social mission" generates the possibility of one such axiomatics. How the individual artist taps the discursive field at hand with a sure touch, if not with transhistorical clairvoyance, in order to make the narrative structure move I hope to demonstrate through the following example. It is crucial that we extend our analysis of this example beyond the minimal diagnosis of "racism.")

Let us consider the figure of Bertha Mason, a figure produced by the axiomatics of imperialism. Through this white Jamaican Creole, Brontë renders the human/animal frontier as acceptably indeterminate, so that a good greater than the letter of the Law can be broached. Here is the celebrated passage, given in the voice of Jane:

> In the deep shade, at the further end of the room, a figure ran backwards and forwards. What it was, whether beast or human being, one could not . . . tell: it grovelled, seemingly, on all fours; it snatched and growled like some strange wild animal: but it was covered with clothing, and a quantity of dark, grizzled hair, wild as a mane, hid its head and face. [*JE*, p. 295]

In a matching passage, given in the voice of Rochester speaking *to* Jane, Brontë presents the imperative for a shift beyond the Law as divine injunction rather than human motive. In the terms of my essay, we might say that this is the register not of mere marriage or sexual reproduction but of Europe and its not-yet-human Other, of soul making. The field of imperial conquest is here inscribed as Hell:

> "One night I had been awakened by her yells . . . it was a fiery West Indian night. . . .
>
> "'This life,' said I at last, 'is hell!—this is the air—those are the sounds of the bottomless pit! *I have a right* to deliver myself from it if I can. . . . Let me break away, and go home to God!' . . .
>
> "A wind fresh from Europe blew over the ocean and rushed through the open casement: the storm broke, streamed, thundered, blazed, and the air grew pure. . . . It was true Wisdom that consoled me in that hour, and showed me the right path. . . .
>
> "The sweet wind from Europe was still whispering in the refreshed leaves, and the Atlantic was thundering in glorious liberty. . . .
>
> "'Go,' said Hope, 'and live again in Europe. . . . You have done all that God and Humanity require of you.'" [*JE*, pp. 310–11; my emphasis]

It is the unquestioned ideology of imperialist axiomatics, then, that conditions Jane's move from the counter-family set to the set of the family-in-law. Marxist critics such as Terry Eagleton have seen this only in terms of the ambiguous *class* position of the governess.[12] Sandra Gilbert and Susan Gubar, on the other hand, have seen Bertha Mason only in psychological terms, as Jane's dark double.[13]

I will not enter the critical debates that offer themselves here. Instead, I will develop the suggestion that nineteenth-century feminist individualism could conceive of a "greater" project than access to the closed circle of the nuclear family. This is the project of soul making beyond "mere" sexual reproduction. Here the native "subject" is not almost an animal but rather the object of what might be termed the terrorism of the categorical imperative.

I am using "Kant" in this essay as a metonym for the most flexible ethical moment in the European eighteenth century. Kant words the categorical imperative, conceived as the universal moral law given by pure reason, in this way: "In all creation every thing one chooses and over which one has any power, may be used *merely as means*; man alone, and with him every rational creature, is an *end in himself*." It is thus a moving displacement of Christian ethics from religion to philosophy. As Kant writes: "With this agrees very well the possibility of such a command as: *Love God above everything, and thy neighbor as thyself.* For as a command it requires respect for a law which *commands love* and does not leave it to our own arbitrary choice to make this our principle."[14]

The "categorical" in Kant cannot be adequately represented in determinately grounded action. The dangerous transformative power of philosophy, however, is that its formal subtlety can be travestied in the service of the state. Such a travesty in the case of the categorical imperative can justify the imperialist project by producing the following formula: *make* the heathen into a human so that he can be treated as an end in himself.[15] This project is presented as a sort of tangent in *Jane Eyre*, a tangent that escapes the closed circle of the *narrative* conclusion. The tangent narrative is the story of St. John Rivers, who is granted the important task of concluding the *text*.

At the novel's end, the *allegorical* language of Christian psychobiography—rather than the textually constituted and seemingly *private* grammar of the creative imagination which we noted in the novel's opening—marks the inaccessibility of the imperialist project as such to the nascent "feminist" scenario. The concluding passage of *Jane Eyre* places St. John Rivers within the fold of *Pilgrim's Progress*. Eagleton pays no attention to this but accepts the novel's ideological lexicon, which establishes St. John Rivers' heroism by identifying a life in Calcutta with an unquestioning choice of death. Gilbert and Gubar, by calling *Jane Eyre* "Plain Jane's Progress," see the novel as simply replacing the male protagonist with the female. They do not notice the distance between sexual reproduction and soul making, both actualized by the unquestioned idiom of imperialist presuppositions evident in the last part of Jane Eyre:

> Firm, faithful, and devoted, full of energy, and zeal, and truth, [St. John Rivers] labours for his race. . . . His is the sternness of the warrior Greatheart, who guards his pilgrim convoy from the onslaught of Apollyon. . . . His is the ambition of the high master-spirit[s] . . . who stand without fault before the throne of God; who share the last mighty victories of the Lamb; who are called, and chosen, and faithful. [*JE*, p. 455]

Earlier in the novel, St. John Rivers himself justifies the project: "My vocation? My great work? . . . My hopes of being numbered in the band who have merged all ambitions in the glorious one of bettering their race—of carrying knowledge into the realms of ignorance—of substituting peace for war—freedom for bondage—religion for superstition—the hope of heaven for the fear of hell?" (*JE*, p. 376). Imperialism and its territorial and subject-constituting project are a violent deconstruction of these oppositions.

When Jean Rhys, born on the Caribbean island of Dominica, read *Jane Eyre* as a child, she was moved by Bertha Mason: "I thought I'd try to write her a life."[16] *Wide Sargasso Sea*, the slim novel published in 1965, at the end of Rhys' long career, is that "life."

I have suggested that Bertha's function in *Jane Eyre* is to render indeterminate the boundary between human and animal and thereby to weaken her entitlement under the spirit if not the letter of the Law. When Rhys rewrites the scene in *Jane Eyre* where Jane hears "a snarling, snatching sound, almost like a dog quarrelling" and then encounters a bleeding Richard Mason (*JE*, p. 210), she keeps Bertha's humanity, indeed her sanity as critic of imperialism, intact. Grace Poole, another character originally in *Jane Eyre*, describes the incident to Bertha in *Wide Sargasso Sea*: "So you don't remember that you attacked this gentleman with a knife? . . . I didn't hear all he said except 'I cannot interfere legally between yourself and your husband.' It was when he said 'legally' that you flew at him" (*WSS*, p. 150). In Rhys' retelling, it is the dissimulation that Bertha discerns in the word "legally"—not an innate bestiality—that prompts her violent *re*action.

In the figure of Antoinette, whom in *Wide Sargasso Sea* Rochester violently renames Bertha, Rhys suggests that so intimate a thing as personal and human identity might be determined by the politics of imperialism. Antoinette, as a white Creole child growing up at the time of emancipation in Jamaica, is caught between the English imperialist and the black native. In recounting Antoinette's development, Rhys reinscribes some thematics of Narcissus.

There are, noticeably, many images of mirroring in the text. I will quote one from the first section. In this passage, Tia is the little black servant girl who is Antoinette's close companion: "We had eaten the same food, slept side by side, bathed in the same river. As I ran, I thought, I will live with Tia and I will be like her. . . . When I was close I saw the jagged stone in her hand but I did not see her throw it. . . . We stared at each other, blood on my face, tears on hers. It was as if I saw myself. Like in a looking glass" (*WSS*, p. 38).

A progressive sequence of dreams reinforces this mirror imagery. In its second occurrence, the dream is partially set in a *hortus conclusus*, or "enclosed garden"— Rhys uses the phrase (*WSS*, p. 50)—a Romance rewriting of the Narcissus topos as the place of encounter with Love.[17] In the enclosed garden, Antoinette encounters not Love but a strange threatening voice that says merely "in here," inviting her into a prison which masquerades as the legalization of love (*WSS*, p. 50).

In Ovid's *Metamorphoses*, Narcissus's madness is disclosed when he recognizes his Other as his self: "Iste ego sum."[18] Rhys makes Antoinette see her *self* as her Other, Brontë's Bertha. In the last section of *Wide Sargasso Sea*, Antoinette acts out *Jane Eyre*'s conclusion and recognizes herself as the so-called ghost in Thornfield Hall: "I went into the hall again with the tall candle in my hand. It was then that I saw her—the ghost. The woman with streaming hair. She was surrounded by a gilt frame but I knew her" (*WSS*, p. 154). The gilt frame encloses a mirror: as Narcissus' pool reflects the selfed Other, so this "pool" reflects the Othered self. Here the dream sequence ends, with an invocation of none other than Tia, the Other that could not be selfed, because the fracture of imperialism rather than the Ovidian pool intervened. (I will return to this difficult point.) "That was the third time I had my dream, and it ended. . . . I called 'Tia' and jumped and woke" (*WSS*, p. 155). It is now, at the very end of the book, that Antoinette/Bertha can say: "Now at last I know why I was brought here and what I have to do" (*WSS*, pp. 155–56). We can read this as her having been brought into the England of Brontë's novel: "This cardboard house"—a book between cardboard covers—"where I walk at night is not England" (*WSS*, p. 148). In this fictive England, she must play out her role, act out the transformation of her "self" into that fictive Other, set fire to the house and kill herself, so that Jane Eyre can become the feminist individualist heroine of British fiction. I must read this as an allegory of the general epistemic violence of imperialism, the construction of a self-immolating colonial subject for the glorification of the social mission of the colonizer. At least Rhys sees to it that the woman from the colonies is not sacrificed as an insane animal for her sister's consolidation.

Critics have remarked that *Wide Sargasso Sea* treats the Rochester character with understanding and sympathy.[19] Indeed, he narrates the entire middle section of the book. Rhys makes it clear that he is a victim of the patriarchal inheritance law of entailment rather than of a father's natural preference for the firstborn: in *Wide Sargasso Sea*, Rochester's situation is clearly that of a younger son dispatched to the colonies to buy an heiress. If in the case of Antoinette and her identity, Rhys utilizes the thematics of Narcissus, in the case of Rochester and his patrimony, she touches on the thematics of Oedipus. (In this she has her finger on our "historical moment." If, in the nineteenth century, subject-constitution is represented as childbearing and soul making, in the twentieth century psychoanalysis allows the West to plot the itinerary of the subject from Narcissus [the "imaginary"] to Oedipus [the "symbolic"]. This subject, however, is the normative male subject. In Rhys' reinscription of these themes, divided between the female and the male protagonist, feminism and a critique of imperialism become complicit.)

In place of the "wind from Europe" scene, Rhys substitutes the scenario of a suppressed letter to a father, a letter which would be the "correct" explanation of the tragedy of the book.[20] "I thought about the letter which should have been written to England a week ago. Dear Father . . ." (*WSS*, p. 57). This is the first instance: the letter not written. Shortly afterward:

> Dear Father. The thirty thousand pounds have been paid to me without question or condition. No provision made for her (that must be seen to). . . . I will never be a disgrace to you or to my dear brother the son you love. No begging letters, no mean requests. None of the furtive shabby manoeuvres of a younger son. I have sold my soul or you have sold it, and after all is it such a bad bargain? The girl is thought to be beautiful, she is beautiful. And yet . . . [*WSS*, p. 59]

This is the second instance: the letter not sent. The formal letter is uninteresting; I will quote only a part of it:

> Dear Father, we have arrived from Jamaica after an uncomfortable few days. This little estate in the Windward Islands is part of the family property and Antoinette is much attached to it. . . . All is well and has gone according to your plans and wishes. I dealt of course with Richard Mason. . . . He seemed to become attached to me and trusted me completely. This place is very beautiful but my illness has left me too exhausted to appreciate it fully. I will write again in a few days' time. [*WSS*, p. 63]

And so on.

Rhys' version of the Oedipal exchange is ironic, not a closed circle. We cannot know if the letter actually reaches its destination. "I wondered how they got their letters posted," the Rochester figure muses. "I folded mine and put it into a drawer of the desk. . . . There are blanks in my mind that cannot be filled up" (*WSS*, p. 64). It is as if the text presses us to note the analogy between letter and mind.

Rhys denies to Brontë's Rochester the one thing that is supposed to be secured in the Oedipal relay: the Name of the Father, or the patronymic. In *Wide Sargasso Sea*, the character corresponding to Rochester has no name. His writing of the final version of the letter to his father is supervised, in fact, by an image of the *loss* of the patronymic: "There was a crude bookshelf made of three shingles strung together over the desk and I looked at the books, Byron's poems, novels by Sir Walter Scott, *Confessions of an Opium Eater* . . . and on the last shelf, *Life and Letters of* . . . The rest was eaten away" (*WSS*, p. 63).

Wide Sargasso Sea marks with uncanny clarity the limits of its own discourse in Christophine, Antoinette's black nurse. We may perhaps surmise the distance between *Jane Eyre* and *Wide Sargasso Sea* by remarking that Christophine's unfinished story is the tangent to the latter narrative, as St. John Rivers' story is to the former. Christophine is not a native of Jamaica; she is from Martinique. Taxonomically, she belongs to the category of the good servant rather than that of the pure native. But within these borders, Rhys creates a powerfully suggestive figure.

Christophine is the first interpreter and named speaking subject in the text. "The Jamaican ladies had never approved of my mother, 'because she pretty like pretty self' Christophine said," we read in the book's opening paragraph (*WSS*, p. 15). I have taught this book five times, once in France, once to students who had worked on the book with the well-known Caribbean novelist Wilson Harris, and once at a prestigious institute where the majority of the students were faculty from other universities. It is part of the political argument I am making that all these students blithely stepped over this paragraph without asking or knowing what Christophine's patois, so-called incorrect English, might mean.

Christophine is, of course, a commodified person. "She was your father's wedding present to me" explains Antoinette's mother, "one of his presents" (*WSS*, p. 18). Yet Rhys assigns her some crucial functions in the text. It is Christophine who judges that black ritual practices are culture-specific and cannot be used by whites as cheap remedies for social evils, such as Rochester's lack of love for Antoinette. Most important, it is Christophine alone whom Rhys allows to offer a hard analysis of Rochester's actions, to challenge him in a face-to-face encounter. The entire extended passage is worthy of comment. I quote a brief extract:

> "She is Creole girl, and she have the sun in her. Tell the truth now. She don't come to your house in this place England they tell me about, she don't come to your beautiful house to beg you to marry with her. No, it's you come all the long way to her house—it's you beg her to marry. And she love you and she give you all she have. Now you say you don't love her and you break her up. What you do with her money, eh?" [And then Rochester, the white man, comments silently to himself] "Her voice was still quiet but with a hiss in it when she said 'money.'" [*WSS*, p. 130]

Her analysis is powerful enough for the white man to be afraid: "I no longer felt dazed, tired, half hypnotized, but alert and wary, ready to defend myself" (*WSS*, p. 130).

Rhys does not, however, romanticize individual heroics on the part of the oppressed. When the Man refers to the forces of Law and Order, Christophine recognizes their power. This exposure of civil inequality is emphasized by the fact that, just before the Man's successful threat, Christophine had invoked the emancipation of slaves in Jamaica by proclaiming: "No chain gang, no tread machine, no dark jail either. This is free country and I am free woman" (*WSS*, p. 131).

As I mentioned above, Christophine is tangential to this narrative. She cannot be contained by a novel which rewrites a canonical English text within the European novelistic tradition in the interest of the white Creole rather than the native. No perspective *critical* of imperialism can turn the Other into a self, because the project of imperialism has always already historically refracted what might have been the absolutely Other into a domesticated Other that consolidates the imperialist self.[21] The Caliban of Retamar, caught between Europe and Latin America, reflects this predicament. We can read Rhys' reinscription of Narcissus as a thematization of the same problematic.

Of course, we cannot know Jean Rhys' feelings in the matter. We can, however, look at the scene of Christophine's inscription in the text. Immediately after the exchange between her and the Man, well before the conclusion, she is simply driven out of the story, with neither narrative nor characterological explanation or justice. "'Read and write I don't know. Other things I know.' She walked away without looking back" (*WSS*, p. 133).

Indeed, if Rhys rewrites the madwoman's attack on the Man by underlining of the misuse of "legality," she cannot deal with the passage that corresponds to St. John Rivers' own justification of his martyrdom, for it has been displaced into the current idiom of modernization and development. Attempts to construct the "Third-World Woman" as a signifier remind us that the hegemonic definition of literature is itself caught within the history of imperialism. A full literary reinscription cannot easily flourish in the imperialist fracture or discontinuity, covered over by an alien legal system masquerading as Law as such, an alien ideology established as only Truth, and a set of human sciences busy establishing the "native" as self-consolidating Other.

In the Indian case at least, it would be difficult to find an ideological clue to the planned epistemic violence of imperialism merely by rearranging curricula or syllabi within existing norms of literary pedagogy. For a later period of imperialism—when the constituted colonial subject has firmly taken hold—straightforward experiments of comparison can be undertaken, say, between the functionally witless India of *Mrs. Dalloway*, on the one hand, and literary texts produced in India in the 1920s, on the other. But the first half of the nineteenth century resists questioning through literature or literary criticism in the narrow sense, because both are implicated in the project of producing Ariel. To reopen the fracture without succumbing to a nostalgia for lost origins, the literary critic must turn to the archives of imperial governance.

In conclusion, I shall look briefly at Mary Shelley's *Frankenstein*, a text of nascent feminism that remains cryptic, I think, simply because it does not speak the language of feminist individualism which we have come to hail as the language of high feminism within English literature. It is interesting that Barbara Johnson's brief study tries to rescue this recalcitrant text for the service of feminist autobiography.[22] Alternatively, George Levine reads *Frankenstein* in the context of the creative imagination and the nature of the hero. He sees the novel as a book about its own writing and about writing itself, a Romantic allegory of reading within which Jane Eyre as unself-conscious critic would fit quite nicely.[23]

I propose to take *Frankenstein* out of this arena and focus on it in terms of that sense of English cultural identity which I invoked at the opening of this essay. Within that focus we are obliged to admit that, although *Frankenstein* is ostensibly about the origin and evolution of man in our society, it does not deploy the axiomatics of imperialism.

Let me say at once that there is plenty of incidental imperialist sentiment in *Frankenstein*. My point, within the argument of this essay, is that the discursive field of imperialism does not produce unquestioned ideological correlatives for the narrative structuring of the book. The discourse of imperialism surfaces in a curiously powerful way in Shelley's novel, and I will later discuss the moment at which it emerges.

Frankenstein is not a battleground of male and female individualism articulated in terms of sexual reproduction (family and female) and social subject-production (race and male). That binary opposition is undone in Victor Frankenstein's laboratory—an artificial womb where both projects are undertaken simultaneously, though the terms are never openly spelled out. Frankenstein's apparent antagonist is God himself as Maker of Man, but his real competitor is also woman as the maker of children. It is not just that his dream of the death of mother and bride and the actual death of his bride are associated with the visit of his monstrous homoerotic "son" to his bed. On a much more overt level, the monster is a bodied "corpse," unnatural because bereft of a determinable childhood: "No father had watched my infant days, no mother had blessed me with smiles and caresses; or if they had, all my past was now a blot, a blind vacancy in which I distinguished nothing" (*F*, pp. 57, 115). It is Frankenstein's own ambiguous and miscued understanding of the real motive for the monster's vengefulness that reveals his own competition with woman as maker:

> I created a rational creature and was bound towards him to assure, as far as was in my power, his happiness and well-being. This was my duty, but there was another still paramount to that. My duties towards the beings of my own species had greater claims to my attention because they included a greater proportion of happiness or misery. Urged by this view, I refused, and I did right in refusing, to create a companion for the first creature. [*F*, p. 206]

It is impossible not to notice the accents of transgression inflecting Frankenstein's demolition of his experiment to create the future Eve. Even in the laboratory, the woman-in-the-making is not a bodied corpse but "a human being." The (il)logic of the metaphor bestows on her a prior existence which Frankenstein aborts, rather than an anterior death which he reembodies: "The remains of the half-finished creature, whom I had destroyed, lay scattered on the floor, and I almost felt as if I had mangled the living flesh of a human being" (*F*, p. 163).

In Shelley's view, man's hubris as soul maker both usurps the place of God and attempts—vainly—to sublate woman's physiological prerogative.[24] Indeed, indulging a Freudian fantasy here, I could urge that, if to give and withhold to/from the mother a phallus is *the* male fetish, then to give and withhold to/from the man a womb might be the female fetish.[25] The icon of the sublimated womb in man is surely his productive brain, the box in the head.

In the judgment of classical psychoanalysis, the phallic mother exists only by virtue of the castration-anxious son; in *Frankenstein*'s judgment, the hysteric father (Victor Frankenstein gifted with his laboratory—the womb of theoretical reason) cannot produce a daughter. Here the language of racism—the dark side of imperialism understood as social mission—combines with the hysteria of masculism into the idiom of (the withdrawal of) sexual reproduction rather than subject-constitution. The roles of masculine and feminine individualists are hence reversed and displaced. Frankenstein cannot produce a "daughter" because "she might become ten thousand times more malignant than her mate . . . [and because] one of the first results of those sympathies for which the demon thirsted would be children, and a race of devils would be propagated upon the earth who might make the very existence of the species of man a condition precarious and full of terror" (*F*, p. 158). This particular narrative strand also launches a thoroughgoing critique of the eighteenth-century European discourses on the origin of society through (Western Christian) man. Should I mention that, much like Jean-Jacques Rousseau's remark in his *Confessions*, Frankenstein declares himself to be "by birth a Genevese" (*F*, p. 31)?

In this overtly didactic text, Shelley's point is that social engineering should not be based on pure, theoretical, or natural-scientific reason alone, which is her implicit critique of the utilitarian vision of an engineered society. To this end, she presents in the first part of her deliberately schematic story three characters, childhood friends, who seem to represent Kant's three-part conception of the human subject: Victor Frankenstein, the forces of theoretical reason or "natural philosophy"; Henry Clerval, the forces of practical reason or "the moral relations of things"; and Elizabeth Lavenza, that aesthetic judgment—"the aerial creation of the poets"—which, according to Kant, is "a suitable mediating link connecting the realm of the concept of nature and that of the concept of freedom . . . (which) promotes . . . *moral* feeling" (*F*, pp. 37, 36).[26]

This three-part subject does not operate harmoniously in *Frankenstein*. That Henry Clerval, associated as he is with practical reason, should have as his "design . . . to visit India, in the belief that he had in his knowledge of its various languages, and in the views he had taken of its society, the means of materially assisting the progress of European colonization and trade" is proof of this, as well as part of the incidental imperialist sentiment that I speak of above (*F*, pp. 151–52). I should perhaps point out that the language here is entrepreneurial rather than missionary:

> He came to the university with the design of making himself complete master of the Oriental languages, as thus he should open a field for the plan of life he had marked out for himself. Resolved to pursue no inglorious career, he turned his eyes towards the East as affording scope for his spirit of enterprise. The Persian, Arabic, and Sanskrit languages engaged his attention. [*F*, pp. 66–67]

But it is of course Victor Frankenstein, with his strange itinerary of obsession with natural philosophy, who offers the strongest demonstration that the multiple perspectives of the three-part Kantian subject cannot cooperate harmoniously. Frankenstein creates a putative human subject out of natural philosophy alone. According to his own miscued summation: "In a fit of enthusiastic madness I created a rational creature" (*F*, p. 206). It is not at all farfetched to say that Kant's categorical imperative can most easily be mistaken for the hypothetical imperative—a command to ground in cognitive comprehension what can be apprehended only by moral will—by putting natural philosophy in the place of practical reason.

I should hasten to add here that just as readings such as this one do not necessarily accuse Charlotte Brontë the named individual of harboring imperialist sentiments, so also they do not necessarily commend Mary Shelley the named individual for writing a successful Kantian allegory. The most I can say is that it is possible to read these texts, within the frame of imperialism and the Kantian ethical moment, in a politically useful way. Such an approach presupposes that a "disinterested" reading attempts to render transparent the interests of the hegemonic readership. (Other "political" readings—for instance, that the monster is the nascent working class—can also be advanced.)

Frankenstein is built in the established epistolary tradition of multiple frames.

At the heart of the multiple frames, the narrative of the monster (as reported by Frankenstein to Robert Walton, who then recounts it in a letter to his sister) is of his almost learning, clandestinely, to be human. It is invariably noticed that the monster reads *Paradise Lost* as true history. What is not so often noticed is that he also reads Plutarch's *Lives*, "the histories of the first founders of the ancient republics," which he compares to "the patriarchal lives of my protectors" (*F,* pp. 123, 124). And his *education* comes through "Volney's *Ruins of Empires,*" which purported to be a prefiguration of the French Revolution, published after the event and after the author had rounded off his theory with practice (*F,* p. 113). It is an attempt at an enlightened universal secular, rather than a Eurocentric Christian, history, written from the perspective of a narrator "from below," somewhat like the attempts of Eric Wolf or Peter Worsley in our own time.[27]

This Caliban's education in (universal secular) humanity takes place through the monster's eavesdropping on the instruction of an Ariel—Safie, the Christianized "Arabian" to whom "a residence in Turkey was abhorrent" (*F,* p. 121). In depicting Safie, Shelley uses some commonplaces of eighteenth-century liberalism that are shared by many today: Safie's Muslim father was a victim of (bad) Christian religious prejudice and yet was himself a wily and ungrateful man not as morally refined as her (good) Christian mother. Having tasted the emancipation of woman, Safie could not go home. The confusion between "Turk" and "Arab" has its counterpart in present-day confusion about Turkey and Iran as "Middle Eastern" but not "Arab."

Although we are a far cry here from the unexamined and covert axiomatics of imperialism in *Jane Eyre,* we will gain nothing by celebrating the time-bound pieties that Shelley, as the daughter of two antievangelicals, produces. It is more interesting for us that Shelley differentiates the Other, works at the Caliban/Ariel distinction, and *cannot* make the monster identical with the proper recipient of these lessons. Although he had "heard of the discovery of the American hemisphere and *wept with Safie* over the helpless fate of its original inhabitants," Safie cannot reciprocate his attachment. When she first catches sight of him, "Safie, unable to attend to her friend [Agatha], rushed out of the cottage" (*F,* pp. 114, [my emphasis], 129).

In the taxonomy of characters, the Muslim-Christian Safie belongs with Rhys' Antoinette/Bertha. And indeed, like Christophine the good servant, the subject created by the fiat of natural philosophy is the tangential unresolved moment in *Frankenstein.* The simple suggestion that the monster is human inside but monstrous outside and only provoked into vengefulness is clearly not enough to bear the burden of so great a historical dilemma.

At one moment, in fact, Shelley's Frankenstein does try to tame the monster, to humanize him by bringing him within the circuit of the Law. He "repair[s] to a criminal judge in the town and . . . relate[s his] history briefly but with firmness"— the first and disinterested version of the narrative of Frankenstein—"marking the dates with accuracy and never deviating into invective or exclamation. . . . When I had concluded my narration I said, 'This is the being whom I accuse and for whose seizure and punishment I call upon you to exert your whole power. It is your duty as a magistrate'" (*F,* pp. 189, 190). The sheer social reasonableness of the mundane voice of Shelley's "Genevan magistrate" reminds us that the absolutely Other cannot be selfed, that the monster has "properties" which will not be contained by "proper" measures:

> "I will exert myself [he says], and if it is in my power to seize the monster, be assured that he shall suffer punishment proportionate to his crimes. But I fear, from what you have yourself described to be his properties, that this will prove impracticable; and thus, while every proper measure is pursued, you should make up your mind to disappointment." [*F*, p. 190]

In the end, as is obvious to most readers, distinctions of human individuality themselves seem to fall away from the novel. Monster, Frankenstein, and Walton seem to become each others' relays. Frankenstein's story comes to an end in death; Walton concludes his own story within the frame of his function as letter writer. In the *narrative* conclusion, he is the natural philosopher who learns from Frankenstein's example. At the end of the *text*, the monster, having confessed his guilt toward his maker and ostensibly intending to immolate himself, is borne away on an ice raft. We do not see the conflagration of his funeral pile—the self-immolation is not consummated in the text: he too cannot be contained by the text. In terms of narrative logic, he is "lost in darkness and distance" (*F*, p. 211)— these are the last words of the novel—into an existential temporality that is co-herent with neither the territorializing individual imagination (as in the opening of *Jane Eyre*) nor the authoritative scenario of Christian psychobiography (as at the end of Brontë's work). The very relationship between sexual reproduction and social subject-production—the dynamic nineteenth-century topos of feminism-in-imperialism—remains problematic within the limits of Shelley's text and, paradoxically, constitutes its strength.

Earlier, I offered a reading of woman as womb holder in *Frankenstein*. I would now suggest that there is a framing woman in the book who is neither tangential, nor encircled, nor yet encircling. "Mrs. Saville," "excellent Margaret," "beloved Sister" are her address and kinship inscriptions (*F*, pp. 15, 16, 22). She is the oc-casion, though not the protagonist, of the novel. She is the feminine *subject* rather than the female individualist: she is the irreducible *recipient*-function of the let-ters that constitute *Frankenstein*. I have commented on the singular appropriative hermeneutics of the reader reading with Jane in the opening pages of *Jane Eyre*. Here the reader must read with Margaret Saville in the crucial sense that she must *intercept* the recipient-function, read the letters *as* recipient, in order for the novel to exist.[28] Margaret Saville does not respond to close the text as frame. The frame is thus simultaneously not a frame, and the monster can step "beyond the text" and be "lost in darkness." Within the allegory of our reading, the place of both the English lady and the unnamable monster are left open by this great flawed text. It is satisfying for a postcolonial reader to consider this a noble reso-lution for a nineteenth-century English novel. This is all the more striking be-cause, on the anecdotal level, Shelley herself abundantly "identifies" with Victor Frankenstein.[29]

I must myself close with an idea that I cannot establish within the limits of this essay. Earlier I contended that *Wide Sargasso Sea* is necessarily bound by the reach of the European novel. I suggested that, in contradistinction, to reopen the epistemic fracture of imperialism without succumbing to a nostalgia for lost origins, the critic must turn to the archives of imperialist governance. I have not turned to those archives in these pages. In my current work, by way of a modest and inexpert "reading" of "archives," I try to extend, outside the reach of the European novelistic tradition, the most powerful suggestion in *Wide Sargasso Sea*: that *Jane Eyre* can be read as the orchestration and staging of the self-immolation of Bertha Mason as "good wife." The power of that suggestion remains unclear if we remain insufficiently knowledgeable about the history of the legal manipulation of widow-sacrifice in the entitlement of the British government in India. I would hope that an informed critique of imperialism, granted some attention from readers in the First World, will at least expand the frontiers of the politics of reading.

NOTES

1. My notion of the "worlding of a world" upon what must be assumed to be uninscribed earth is a vulgarization of Martin Heidegger's idea; see "The Origin of the Work of Art," *Poetry, Language, Thought,* trans. Albert Hofstadter (New York, 1977), pp. 17–87.

2. See Charlotte Brontë, *Jane Eyre* (New York, 1960); all further references to this work, abbreviated *JE*, will be included in the text.

3. See Jean Rhys, *Wide Sargasso Sea* (Harmondsworth, 1966); all further references to this work, abbreviated *WSS*, will be included in the text. And see Mary Shelley, *Frankenstein; or, the Modern Prometheus* (New York, 1965); all further references to this work, abbreviated *F*, will be included in the text.

4. I have tried to do this in my essay "Unmaking and Making in *To the Lighthouse*," in *Women and Language in Literature and Society*, ed. Sally McConnell-Ginet, Ruth Borker, and Nelly Furman (New York, 1980), pp. 310–27.

5. As always, I take my formula from Louis Althusser, "Ideology an Ideological State Apparatuses (Notes towards an Investigation)," *Lenin and Philosophy and Other Essays*, trans. Ben Brewster (New York, 1971), pp. 127–86. For an acute differentiation between the individual and individualism, see V. N. Vološinov, *Marxism and the Philosophy of Language*, trans. Ladislav Matejka, and I. R. Titunik, Studies in Language, vol. 1 (New York, 1973), pp. 93–94 and 152–53. For a "straight" analysis of the roots and ramifications of English "individualism," see C. B. MacPherson, *The Political Theory of Possessive Individualism: Hobbes to Locke* (Oxford, 1962). I am grateful to Jonathan Rée for bringing this book to my attention and for giving a careful reading of all but the very end of the present essay.

6. I am constructing an analogy with Homi Bhabha's powerful notion of "not-quite/not white" in his "Of Mimicry and Man: The Ambiguity of Colonial Discourse," *October* 28 (Spring 1984): 132. I should also add that I use the word "native" here in reaction to the term "Third-World Woman." It cannot, of course, apply with equal historical justice to both the West Indian and the Indian contexts nor to contexts of imperialism by transportation.

7. See Roberto Fernández Retamar, "Caliban: Notes towards a Discussion of Culture in Our America," trans. Lynn Garafola, David Arthur McMurray, and Robert Márquez, *Massachusetts Review* 15 (Winter–Spring 1974): 7–72; all further references to this work, abbreviated "C," will be included in the text.

8. See José Enrique Rodó, *Ariel*, ed. Gordon Brotherston (Cambridge, 1967).

9. For an elaboration of "an inaccessible blankness circumscribed by an interpretable text," see my "Can the Subaltern Speak?" *Interpretation of Culture*, eds. Cary Nelson and Lawrence Grossberg (Urbana, Ill., 1988).

10. See Elizabeth Fox-Genovese, "Placing Women's History in History," *New Left Review* 133 (May–June 1982): 5–29.

11. Rudolph Ackerman, *The Repository of Arts, Literature, Commerce, Manufactures, Fashions, and Politics* (London, 1823), p. 310.

12. See Terry Eagleton, *Myths of Power: A Marxist Study of the Brontës* (London, 1975); this is one of the general presuppositions of his book.

13. See Sandra M. Gilbert and Susan Gubar, *The Madwoman in the Attic: The Woman Writer and the Nineteenth-Century Literary Imagination* (New Haven, Conn., 1979), pp. 360–62.

14. Immanuel Kant, *Critique of Practical Reason, The "Critique of Pure Reason," the "Critique of Practical Reason" and Other Ethical Treatises, the "Critique of Judgement,"* trans. J. M. D. Meiklejohn et al. (Chicago, 1952), pp. 328, 326.

15. I have tried to justify the reduction of sociohistorical problems to formulas or propositions in my essay "Can the Subaltern Speak?" The "travesty" I speak of does not befall the Kantian ethic in its purity as an accident but rather exists within its lineaments as a possible supplement. On the register of the human being as child rather than heathen, my formula can be found, for example, in "What Is Enlightenment?" in Kant, *"Foundations of the Metaphysics of Morals," "What Is Enlightenment?" and a Passage from "The Metaphysics of Morals,"* trans. and ed. Lewis White Beck (Chicago, 1950). I have profited from discussing Kant with Johnathan Rée.

16. Jean Rhys, in an interview with Elizabeth Vreeland, quoted in Nancy Harrison, *An Introduction to the Writing Practice of Jean Rhys: The Novel as Women's Text* (Chapel Hill: Univ. of North Carolina Press, 1988). This is an excellent, detailed study of Rhys.

17. See Louise Vinge, *The Narcissus Theme in Western European Literature Up to the Early Nineteenth Century,* trans. Robert Dewsnap et al. (Lund, 1967), chap. 5.

18. For a detailed study of this text, see John Brenkman, "Narcissus in the Text," *Georgia Review* 30 (Summer 1976): 293–327.

19. See, e.g., Thomas F. Staley, *Jean Rhys: A Critical Study* (Austin, Tex., 1979), pp. 108–16; it is interesting to note Staley's masculist discomfort with this and his consequent dissatisfaction with Rhys' novel.

20. I have tried to relate castration and suppressed letters in my "The Letter As Cutting Edge," in *Literature and Psychoanalysis; The Question of Reading: Otherwise,* ed. Shoshana Felman (New Haven, Conn., 1981), pp. 208–26.

21. This is the main argument of my "Can the Subaltern Speak?"

22. See Barbara Johnson, "My Monster/My Self," *Diacritics* 12 (Summer 1982): 2–10.

23. See George Levine, *The Realistic Imagination: English Fiction from Frankenstein to Lady Chatterley* (Chicago, 1981), pp. 23–35.

24. Consult the publications of the Feminist International Network for the best overview of the current debate on reproductive technology.

25. For the male fetish, see Sigmund Freud, "Fetishism," *The Standard Edition of the Complete Psychological Works of Sigmund Freud,* ed. and trans. James Strachey et al., 24 vols. (London, 1953–74), 21 :152–57. For a more "serious" Freudian study of *Frankenstein,* see Mary Jacobus, "Is There a Woman in This Text?" *New Literary History* 14 (Autumn 1982): 117–41. My "fantasy" would of course be disproved by the "fact" that it is more difficult for a woman to assume the position of fetishist than for a man; see Mary Ann Doane, "Film and the Masquerade: Theorising the Female Spectator," *Screen* 23 (Sept./Oct. 1982): 74–87.

26. Kant, *Critique of Judgement,* trans. J. H. Bernard (New York, 1951), p. 39.

27. See [Constantin François Chasseboeuf de Volney], *The Ruins; or, Meditations on the Revolutions of Empires,* trans. pub. (London, 1811). Johannes Fabian has shown us the manipulation of time in "new" secular histories of a similar kind; see *Time and the Other: How Anthropology Makes Its Object* (New York, 1983). See also Eric R. Wolf, *Europe and the People Without History* (Berkeley and Los Angeles, 1982), and Peter Worsley, *The Third World,* 2d ed. (Chicago, 1973); I am grateful to Dennis Dworkin for bringing the latter book to my attention. The most striking ignoring of the monster's education through Volney is in

Gilbert's otherwise brilliant "Horror's Twin: Mary Shelley's Monstrous Eve," *Feminist Studies* 4 (June 1980): 48–73. Gilbert's essay reflects the absence of race-determinations in a certain sort of feminism. Her present work has most convincingly filled in this gap; see, e.g., her recent piece on H. Rider Haggard's *She* ("Rider Haggard's Heart of Darkness," *Partisan Review* 50, no. 3 [1983]: 444–53).

28. "A letter is always and *a priori* intercepted, . . . the 'subjects' are neither the senders nor the receivers of messages. . . . The letter is constituted . . . by its interception" (Jacques Derrida, "Discussion," after Claude Rabant, "Il n'a aucune chance de l'entendre," in *Affranchissement: Du transfert et de la lettre*, ed. René Major [Paris, 1981], p. 106; my translation). Margaret Saville is not made to appropriate the reader's "subject" into the signature of her own "individuality."

29. The most striking "internal evidence" is the admission in the "Author's Introduction" that, after dreaming of the yet-unnamed Victor Frankenstein figure and being terrified (through, yet not quite through, him) by the monster in a scene she later reproduced in Frankenstein's story, Shelley began her tale "on the morrow . . . with the words 'It was on a dreary night of November'" (*F*, p. xi). Those are the opening words of chapter 5 of the finished book, where Frankenstein begins to recount the actual making of his monster (see *F*, p. 56).

NANCY ARMSTRONG

SOME CALL IT FICTION:
ON THE POLITICS OF DOMESTICITY

(1990)

> It is queer how out of touch with truth women are. They live in a world of their own, and there has never been anything like it, and never can be.
>
> JOSEPH CONRAD, *HEART OF DARKNESS*

For some years now, American scholars have been puzzling out the relationship between literature and history. Apparently the right connections were not made when literary histories were first compiled. Yet in turning to the question of how some of the most famous British novelists were linked to their moment in time, I have found I must begin at step one, with extremely powerful conventions of representation. Though old and utterly familiar, nothing new has taken their place. Their potency has not diminished in this country despite the theory revolution and the calls for a new literary history that came in its wake. The conventions to which I refer are many and various indeed, but all reinforce the assumption that history consists of economic or political events, as if these were essentially different from other cultural events. Some of us—a distinct minority, to be sure—feel that to proceed on this assumption is to brush aside most of the activities composing everyday life and so shrink the category of "the political" down to a very limited set of cultural practices. And then, having classified most of our symbolic activities as "personal," "social," or "cultural" (it is all much the same), traditional histories would have us place them in a secondary relationship either to the economy or to the official institutions of state. This essay is written in opposition to models of history that confine political practices to activities directly concerned with the marketplace, the official institutions of the state, or else resistance to these. I write as one who feels that such models have not provided an adequate basis for understanding the formation of a modern bureaucratic culture or for our place, as intellectuals, within it. More than that, I regard any model that places personal life in a separate sphere and that grants literature a secondary and passive role in political history as unconsciously sexist. I believe such models necessarily fail to account for the formation of a modern bureaucratic culture because they fail to account for the place of women within it.

Some of our best theorizers of fiction's relationship to history—Raymond Williams in England and Edward Said in the United States—have done much to tear down the barrier between culture and state. They demonstrate that the middle-class hegemony succeeded in part because it constructed separate historical narratives for self and society, family and factory, literature and history. They suggest that by maintaining these divisions within culture, liberal intellectuals continue to sanitize certain areas of culture—namely, the personal, domestic, and literary. The practices that go by these names consequently appear to be benignly progressive, in their analyses, to provide a place of escape from the political world, and even to offer forms of resistance. Still, I would argue, such efforts as those of Williams and Said will be only partially successful so long as they continue to ignore *the sexual division of labor* that underwrites and naturalizes the difference between culture and politics.

THE LIMITS OF POLITICAL HISTORY

To put some life into all these abstractions, let me now turn to domestic fiction and the difficulties that scholars encounter when they try to place writing of this kind in history. Ian Watt convincingly describes the socioeconomic character of the new readership for whom Defoe, Richardson, and Fielding wrote, a readership whose rise in turn gave rise to the novel. But Watt has no similar explanation for Austen. Her popularity he ascribes to her talent, and her talent, to nature. And so he concludes that nature must have given Austen a good eye for details.[1] Although Williams moves well beyond such reflection theories in his groundbreaking account of the information revolution, his model of history ultimately serves us no better than Watt's when it comes to explaining domestic fiction. His *Long Revolution* regards intellectual labor as a political force in its own right without which capitalism could not have unfolded as smoothly and completely as it appears to have done. But however much power Williams grants this domain, it belongs to culture and, as such, exists in a secondary relationship with political history. To historicize writing, he feels compelled to give it a source in events outside of and prior to writing. He does not entertain the possibility that the classic unfolding of capitalism was predicated on writing, much less on writing by women or writing that appealed to the interests of a female readership.[2] For Williams as for Watt, historical events take place in the official institutions of state or else through resistance to these institutions, and both forms of power are exercised primarily through men.

I have found Watt and Williams especially helpful for establishing links between the history of fiction and the rise of the new middle classes in England. At the same time, I am perplexed to find that, in establishing a relationship between writing and political history, these otherwise conscientious scholars completely neglect to account for the most obvious fact of all, namely, that sometime during the eighteenth century, in the words of Virginia Woolf, "the middle class woman began to write."[3] If, as Watt and Williams say, the rise of the novel was directly related to the rise of the new middle classes, then some of our best literary evidence suggests that the rise of the novel was related to the emergence of women's writing as well. In drawing this equation, of course, I have doubled the difficulties entailed in historicizing fiction, for I have suggested that to historicize fiction we must politicize not only intellectual labor but female labor as well.

Much of British fiction exists at the intersection of these two definitively modern subsets of culture and is thereby twice removed from the mainstream of political history.

The writing I call domestic fiction is gender-inflected writing. Unlike the work of earlier women of letters, it comes to us as women's writing. In designating certain forms of writing as feminine, it designates other writing as masculine. The enclosure that marks a Jane Austen novel does not simply distinguish her "world" from that of a Shakespeare, a Blake, a Dickens, or a Yeats. The boundaries it constructs between inside and outside are personal in a far more wide-reaching and historically significant way. They mark the difference between the world over which women novelists have authority—the domain of the personal—and that which is ruled by men and their politics. In doing this, Austen makes Richardson the father of the novel, for, like him, she identifies the work of the novelist with the writing of women as well as with other forms of labor that are suitably feminine.[4] To move beyond the impasse that prevents us from situating this work in history, we have it seems to me, to toss out the idea that the gendering of vast areas of culture was a consequence of political events over which men had control. To consider gender itself as a political formation over which modern cultures gave women authority, we will have to invert these priorities. Having done so, one comes face to face with the possibility that a revolution in the home preceded the spread of the factory system and all that hinged upon its becoming the means of distributing the wealth of the nation.[5]

To deal with this possibility, I begin with the proposition Marx put forth in *The German Ideology* and Gramsci later developed into the concept of "hegemony" in his essays on the formation of intellectuals and the organization of culture and education: no political revolution is complete without a cultural revolution. To dominate, the dominant group must offer to one and all a view that makes their form of domination seem true and necessary if not desirable and right. Gramsci developed the contradiction inherent in Marx's notion of labor—that labor was not only a commodity, but also a social practice—into a theory that stressed the double-sidedness of middle-class power: it controlled not only the physical dimension of production but also the social dimension. During the twentieth century, moreover, Gramsci could see that a form of power that worked through spatial location, supervision, and individuals' relationship with machines was giving way to something more ubiquitous—bureaucratic control that divided and hierarchized individuals so as to place their labor on separate social planes. And indeed, as the wage was generalized to include members of this and other bureaucracies, those who performed productive labor shrank in number and importance.

More recently, therefore, a number of us who work in the humanities and social sciences have begun to feel theories of resistance which depend upon an essentialized class or, for that matter, any other essentialized group will no longer do. Once taken up by theory, such essentialisms quickly cease to represent the possibility of power coalescing outside a pluralistic society. Rather, they identify contradictory positions within that system and, in so doing, only supply more differences in a differential system that exists on an abstract plane of ideas. The system to which I refer is no system in the abstract, however, but the disciplinary institution itself. Slouching by way of homology from one cultural site to another, it has achieved the status of a paradigm. In its atomizing structure, political issues get lost. Everything matters. All truths are equivalent—only some are more complex and, in this respect alone, more satisfying than others. In the maze of differences, the difference between positive and negative has all but disappeared, and the paradise of liberalism seems near at hand.[6]

So perceiving *her* historical moment, one can consider in a radically materialist light the Foucauldian propositions that the modern state was called into being in writing, exists mainly as a state of mind, and perpetuates itself through the well-orchestrated collection, regulation, and dissemination of information. The idea of order that Foucault sometimes calls "discourse" or "power" and at other times names "sexuality" or "discipline" is indeed a ruling idea. But in a world that is ruled more surely by ideas than by physical or economic means, one has to be especially careful not to hypothesize some corresponding "reality" as their source. We cannot grant these ideas the autonomy, universality, and mystic interconnection that they have achieved, but neither can we seek out some more primary truth behind or below them. Rather, we must understand them, as Foucault suggests, as the self-conception of a class that has achieved hegemony. And hegemony, in the case of modern post-industrial societies, depends on self-conceptions capable of swallowing up all opposition in a single system of micro-differences.

The power of the system depends upon the production of a particular form of consciousness that is at once unique and standardizing. In place of what he calls the "repressive hypothesis," the assumption that culture either "suppresses" or "imposes itself on" the individual's desire, Foucault offers a productive hypothesis that turns this commonplace on its ear. The first volume of *The History of Sexuality* argues that the very forms of subjectivity we consider most essential to ourselves as selves had no existence prior to their symbolization, that the deepest and most private recesses of our being are culturally produced.[7] His *Discipline and Punish* mounts a detailed historical argument to show that the truth of the modern individual existed first as writing, before she or he was transformed successively into speech, thought, and unconscious desire.[8] Thus Foucault enables us to see the European Enlightenment as a revolution in words, which gave writing a new and awesome power over the world of objects as it shaped the individuals who established a relationship with that world through reading. In England, I would like to suggest, this cultural revolution was the only kind of revolution to occur during the eighteenth century, because in England the revolution in words took a form that prevented popular revolution.[9]

Having torn down the conceptual barrier between writing and political history, we have cleared the way to see the intellectual labor of women as part of the mainstream of political events. Foucault will not help us achieve this particular step, however. His *History of Sexuality* is not concerned with the history of gender. Nor does it deal with the role that writing for, by, and about women played in the history of sexuality, For this reason, his procedures cannot identify the decisive events that detached family life from politics, and these are the very events that tie the formation of a domestic domain to the development of an institutional culture in England. Foucault's *Discipline and Punish* overlooks the fact that the modern household served as the groundbreaking prototype of modern institutions. His *History of Sexuality* neglects to theorize the power of that prototype as it spills over from this account of modern personal life into his account of institutional power to saturate and make intelligible the theory of discipline. Despite the anti-Cartesian thrust of his work, Foucault does not finally break through the barrier that separates his position as theorizer of the sexual subject in *The History of Sexuality* from the one he takes up in order to theorize the political subject in *Discipline and Punish*. Yet not only does he use the same figure to think out the two; he also gives the strategies producing the sexual subject (those organizing the home) priority in his thinking over the strategies that subject the individual to the state (those of disciplinary institutions).

Central to the central chapter on "Panopticism" in *Discipline and Punish* is Foucault's figure of the city under plague. In contrast with leprosy, which calls for exclusionary strategies more consistent with the aristocratic imagination of power, the plague, as he plays with the figure, seems to require inclusion and enclosure as preconditions for a modern system of surveillance. The division of the population into progressively smaller subdivisions of which the household is the basic module, is followed by the ritual purification of each and every household:

> Five or six days after the beginning of the quarantine, the process of purifying the houses one by one is begun. All the inhabitants are made to leave; in each room "the furniture and goods" are raised from the ground or suspended from the air; perfume is poured around the room; after carefully sealing the windows, doors and even the keyholes with wax, the perfume is set alight. Finally, the entire house is closed while the perfume is consumed; those who have carried out the work are searched, as they were on entry, "in the presence of the residents of the house, to see that they did not have something on their persons as they left that they did not have on entering." Four hours later, the residents are allowed to re-enter their homes. (p. 197)

Such enclosure and purification of the house produces a new household free from the taint of any unregulated intercourse with the world, its membrane permeable only to certain kinds of information. Reading this account of the plague, I am struck by the difference between its place in the modern imagination and its use by Boccaccio, who imagined a small aristocratic community safely ensconced in the country to pass the time free from the infection of the city. In this early modern world, those who remain in the city are to be regarded as a different social body altogether, behaving much like the riotous and grotesquely permeable body celebrated by Bakhtin. How significant, then, that Foucault, in contrast with Bakhtin, imagines a city purified from the inside out by the production of hygienically pure domestic spaces within the body politic! In this attempt to fantasize the present from the position of the past, households serve as magical spaces where people go to die in order that they may be reborn as modern individuals—enclosed and self-regulating.

Having pursued the internal logic of his figure thus far, Foucault extends it outward from the newly enclosed domestic world—as from a new source of power—into the cultural and political domains, and from there into history. First, he notes how a "whole literary fiction of the festival grew up around the plague: suspended laws, lifted prohibitions, the frenzy of passing time, bodies mingling together without respect, individuals unmasked, abandoning their statutory identity and the figure under which they had been recognized, allowing a quite different truth to appear. But," he continues, "there was also a political dream of the plague, which was exactly its reverse: not the collective festival, but strict divisions; not laws transgressed, but the penetration of regulation into even the smallest details of everyday life . . . ; not masks that were put on and taken off, but the assignment to each individual of his 'true' name, his 'true' place, his 'true' disease" (pp. 197–198). On the metaphor of the city under plague thus rests Foucault's entire theory of the development of modern institutions: "If it is true that the leper gave rise to rituals of exclusion, which to a certain extent provided the model for and general form of the Great Confinement, then the plague gave rise to disciplinary projects" (p. 198). Metaphorical use of disease allows him to declare the eighteenth-century hospital with its anatomy theater as the historical prototype for the modern prison.

And to be sure, I *like* Foucault for transgressing the boundary between the therapeutic and the punitive to demonstrate how much they have in common. But this, to my mind, is also a way of avoiding the full implications of his chosen metaphor, the city under plague, implications that would destroy the differences between sexual subject and political subject, and between these and the subject's material body, all of which rest upon preserving the line that divvies up cultural information according to gender. This is the line between inside and outside that is implanted in his metaphor from the beginning to distinguish personal from political life. This is the first division of the conceptual zygote, the line without which the fantasy of an entire political world cannot develop its inexorable symmetry, a symmetry that cuts beneath and through particular features that culture manifests at one site rather than another. While he opens the category of political power considerably by including institutions other than those officially charged to distribute wealth and power, Foucault extends the cultural scope of discipline only so far as institutions that, in becoming institutions, came to be dominated by men. Thus if power does not originate in the minds of individual men or in the bodies of men collectively, it arises from the cultural patterns that make men think of themselves as certain kinds of men and exercise power accordingly.

But if one pursues the implications of Foucault's chosen metaphor for modern power, his city under plague, in contrast with a Boccaccian remedy, contains a certain form of household that is the perfect and obvious answer to the indiscriminate mingling of bodies spreading the infection. When we expand our concept of the political further even than Foucault's, we discover grounds on which to argue that the modern household rather than the clinic provided the proto-institutional setting where government through relentless supervision first appeared, and appeared in its most benevolent guise. Foucault never takes note of these continuities between home and state even though they are as plain as the words on his page. More curious still is his failure to acknowledge the fact that a home espoused by various subgroups aspiring for the status of "respectability," a home overseen by a woman, actually preceded the formation of other social institutions by at least fifty years. There is little to suggest this household took root in practice much before the beginning of the nineteenth century, even though it frequently appeared in the literature and political argumentation of the previous century. From writing, it can be argued, the new family passed into the realm of common sense, where it came to justify the distribution of national wealth through wages paid to men. Indeed, it remains extremely powerful to this day as both metaphor and metonymy, the unacknowledged model and source of middle-class power.[10]

THE POWER OF DOMESTICITY

It is at this point in my argument that a feminist perspective must be invoked, but it cannot be a feminism that sinks comfortably into the rhetoric of victimization. It has to be thoroughly politicized. By this I mean we must be willing to accept the idea that, as middle-class women, we are empowered, although we are not empowered in traditionally masculine ways. We have to acknowledge that as middle-class intellectuals we are not critical mirrors of a separate and more primary process orchestrated by others—be they politicians, bureaucrats, captains of industry, or simply men. As women intellectuals we are doubly implicated in the process of reproducing the state of mind upon which other openly and avowedly political institutions depend. It is on this basis that I reject the notion that women's writing exists in a domain of experience outside of political history. I can no longer accept what conventional histories assume—that such writing occupies the secondary status of a "reflection" or "consequence" of changes within more primary social institutions—the army, hospital, prison, or factory. To the contrary, my evidence reveals domestic fiction actively disentangled the language of sexual relations from that of political economy. The rhetoric of this fiction (in Wayne Booth's sense of the term) laid out a new cultural logic that would eventually become common sense, sensibility, and public opinion. In this way, female knowledge successfully combatted one kind of power, based on title, wealth, and physical force, with another, based on the control of literacy. By equating good reading with what was good for women readers, a new standard for reading laid down the semantic ground for common sense and established the narrative conventions structuring public opinion. The new standard of literacy helped to bring a new class of people into existence. This class laid claim to the right to privacy on behalf of each individual. Yet this class set in motion the systematic invasion of private life by surveillance, observation, evaluation, and remediation. In a word, it ruled, still rules, through countless microtechniques of socialization, all of which may be lumped together under the heading of education.[11] During the second half of the nineteenth century, institutions were created to perform these operations upon masses of people in much the same way as domestic fiction did upon characters.

Those of us who have grown up within an institutional culture consequently carry around a voice much like that of a fictional narrator in his or her head. Sensitive to the least sign of disorder—a foul word, a piece of clothing undone, some food sliding off one's fork, or, worse still, some loss of control over bodily functions—the presence of this voice, now nearly two hundred years old, more surely keeps us in line than fear of the police or the military. For the unofficial forms of power have a terrible advantage over those which are openly and avowedly regulatory. They make us afraid of ourselves. They operate on the supposition that we harbor desires dangerous to the general good. Believing in the presence of a self that is essentially subversive, we keep watch over ourselves—in mirrors, on clocks, on scales, through medical exams, and by means of any number of other such practices. Thus we internalize a state that is founded on the conflict between self and state interests, and we feel perfectly justified in enacting its power—which is, after all, only good for oneself—upon others.

Convinced that power exerted in and through the female domain is at least as powerful as the more conventional forms of power associated with the male, I want to sketch out the relationship between the two during the modern period. I will suggest that modern institutional cultures depend upon the separation of "the political" from "the personal" and that they produce and maintain this separation on the basis of gender—the formation of masculine and feminine domains of culture. For, I will argue, even as certain forms of cultural information were separated into these two opposing fields, they were brought together as an intricate set of pressures that operated on the subject's body and mind to induce self-regulation. We can observe this peculiarly effective collaboration of the official and unofficial forms of power perhaps most clearly in the formation of a national education system during the Victorian period and in the whole constellation of efforts that went on simultaneously to appropriate leisure time.[12] British fiction participates in both efforts and therefore demonstrates the modes of collaboration between them.

To introduce their highly influential *Practical Education* in 1801, Maria Edgeworth and her father announce their break with the curriculum that reinforced traditional political distinctions: "On religion and politics we have been silent because we have no ambition to gain partisans, or to make proselytes, and because we do not address ourselves to any sect or party."[13] In virtually the same breath, they assure readers, "With respect to what is commonly called the education of the heart, we have endeavored to suggest the easiest means of inducing useful and agreeable habits, well regulated sympathy and benevolent affections" (p. viii). Their program substitutes abstract terms of emotion and behavior for those of one's specific socioeconomic identity. Rooting identity in the very subjective qualities that earlier curricula had sought to inculcate in young women alone, the Edgeworths' program gives priority to the schoolroom and parlor over the church and courts for purposes of regulating human behavior. In doing this, their educational program promises to suppress the political signs of human identity (which is of course a powerful political gesture in its own right). Perfectly aware of the power to be exercised through education, the Edgeworths justify their curriculum for cultivating the heart on grounds that it offered a new and more effective method of policing. In their words, "It is the business of education to prevent crimes, and to prevent all those habitual propensities which necessarily lead to their commission" (p. 354).

To accomplish their ambitious political goal, the Edgeworths invoke an economy of pleasure which cannot in fact be understood apart from the novel and the criticism that was produced both to censor and to foster it. First, the Edgeworths accept the view prevailing during the eighteenth century which said that fiction was sure to mislead female desire:

> With respect to sentimental stories, and books of mere entertainment, we must remark, that they should be sparingly used, especially in the education of girls. This species of reading cultivates what is called the heart prematurely,

lowers the tone of the mind, and induces indifference for those common pleasures and occupations which . . . constitute by far the greatest portion of our
daily happiness. (p. 105)

But the same turn of mind could as easily recognize the practical value of pleasure when it is harnessed and aimed at the right goals. Convinced that "the pleasures of literature" acted upon the reader in much the same way as a child's "taste
for sugarplums" (p. 80), forward-thinking educators began to endorse the reading of fiction, so long as it was governed by principles that made conformity seem
desirable.

In formulating a theory of mass education in which fiction had a deceptively
marginal role to play, the Edgeworths and their colleagues were adopting a rhetoric which earlier reformers had used to level charges of violence and corruption
against the old aristocracy. They placed themselves in the tradition of radical Protestant dissent going back to the sixteenth century, a tradition which had always
argued that political authority should be based on moral superiority. Sexual relations so often provided the terms for making this claim that no representation of
the household could be considered politically neutral. To contest that notion of
the state which depended upon inherited power, puritan treatises on marriage
and household governance represented the family as a self-enclosed social unit
into whose affairs the state had no right to intervene. Against genealogy they posited domesticity. But in claiming sovereignty for the natural father over his household, these treatises were not proposing a new distribution of political power.
They were simply trying to limit the monarch's power. To understand the social
transformation that was achieved by the English Revolution (according to Christopher Hill, not achieved until more than a century later), we have to turn away
from what we consider to be the political themes of the puritan argument and
consider instead what happens to gender.[14]

According to Kathleen M. Davis, the puritan doctrine of equality insisted upon
the difference of sexual roles, in which the female was certainly subordinate to
the male, and not upon the equality of the woman in kind. "The result of this
partnership," she explains, "was a definition of mutual and complementary duties and characteristics." Gender was so clearly understood in these oppositional
terms that it could be graphically represented:[15]

HUSBAND	WIFE
Get goods	Gather them together and save them
Travel, seek a living	Keep the house
Get money and provisions	Do not vainly spend it
Deal with many men	Talk with few
Be "entertaining"	Be solitary and withdrawn
Be skillful in talk	Boast of silence
Be a giver	Be a saver
Apparel yourself as you may	Apparel yourself as it becomes you
Dispatch all things outdoors	Oversee and give order within

In so representing the household as the opposition of complementary genders,
the authors of countless puritan tracts asked readers to imagine the household as

a self-enclosed social unit. But if these authors wanted to define the family as an independent source of authority, their moment did not arrive. The puritan household consisted of a male and a female who were structurally identical, positive and negative versions of the same thing. The authority of the housewife described above could not yet be imagined as a positive thing in its own right. Until she took up her vigil and began to order personal life, a single understanding of power reigned, and men fought to determine the balance among its various parts.

Unlike the authors of seventeenth-century marriage manuals and domestic economies, the educational reformers of nineteenth-century England could look back on a substantial body of writing whose main purpose was to produce a historically new woman. During the centuries between the English Revolution and the present day, this woman was inscribed with values which appealed to a whole range of competing interest groups, and, through her, these groups seized authority over domestic relations and personal life. In this way, I believe, they created a need for the kind of surveillance which modern institutions provide. Indeed, the last two decades of the seventeenth century saw an explosion of writing aimed at educating the daughters of the numerous aspiring social groups. The new curriculum promised to educate these women in such a way as to make them more desirable than women who had only their own rank and fortune to recommend them. This curriculum exalted a woman whose value resided chiefly in her femaleness rather than in the traditional signs of status, a woman who possessed emotional depth rather than a physically stimulating surface, one who, in other words, excelled in the very qualities that differentiated her from the male. As gender was redefined in these terms, the woman exalted by an aristocratic tradition of letters ceased to appear so desirable. In becoming the other side of this new sexual coin, she represented surface rather than depth, embodied material as opposed to moral value, and displayed idle sensuality instead of unflagging concern for the well-being of others. So conceived, the aristocratic woman no longer defined what was truly and most desirably female.

But it was not until the mid-nineteenth century that the project of defining people on the basis of gender began to acquire some of the immense political influence it still exercises today. Around the 1830s, one can see the discourse of sexuality relax its critical gaze on the aristocracy as the newly forming working classes became a more obvious target of moral reform. Authors suddenly took notice of social elements who had hardly mattered before. These reformers and men of letters discovered that rebellious artisans and urban laborers, for example, lacked the kind of motivation that supposedly characterized normal individuals. Numerous writers sought out the source of poverty, illiteracy, and demographic change in these underdeveloped individuals, whose behavior was generally found to be not only promiscuous but also ambiguously gendered. Once they succeeded in translating an overwhelming economic problem into a sexual scandal, middle-class intellectuals could step forward and offer themselves, their technology, their supervisory skills, and their institutions of education and social welfare as the appropriate remedy for growing political resistance.

In all fairness, as Foucault notes, the middle classes rarely applied institutional procedures to others without first trying them out on themselves. When putting together a national curriculum, the government officials and educators in charge adopted one modeled on the educational theory that grew up around the Edgeworths and their intellectual circle, the heirs of the dissenting tradition.[16] This was basically the same as the curriculum proposed by eighteenth-century pedagogues and reformers as the best way of producing a marriageable daughter. By the end of the eighteenth century, the Edgeworths were among those who had already determined that the program aimed at producing the ideal woman could be applied to boys just as well as to girls. And by the mid-nineteenth century, one can see the government figuring out how to administer much the same program on a mass basis. In providing the conceptual foundation for a national curriculum, a particular idea of the self thus became commonplace, and as gendered forms of identity determined how people thought of themselves as well as others, that self became the dominant social reality.

Such an abbreviated history cannot do justice to the fierce controversies punctuating the institution of a national education system in England. I simply call attention to this material as a site where political history obviously converged with the history of sexuality as well as with that of the novel to produce a specific kind of individual. I do this to suggest the political implications of representing these as separate narratives. As it began to deny its political and religious bias and to present itself instead as a moral and psychological truth, the rhetoric of reform obviously severed its ties with an aristocratic past and took up a new role in history. It no longer constituted a form of resistance but enclosed a specialized domain of culture apart from political relations where apolitical truths could be told. The novel's literary status hinged upon this event. Henceforth fiction would deny the political basis for its meaning and refer instead to the private regions of the self or to the specialized world of art but never to the use of words that created and still maintains these distinctions so basic to our culture. Favored among kinds of fiction were novels that best performed the rhetorical operations of division and self-containment and thus turned existing political information into the discourse of sexuality. These works of fiction gave novels a good name, a name free of politics, and often the name of a woman such as Pamela, Evelina, Emma, or Jane Eyre. Then, with the translation of human identity into sexual identity came widespread repression of the political literacy characterizing an earlier culture, and with it, too, mass forgetting that there was a history of sexuality to tell.

THE POLITICS OF DOMESTIC FICTION

Let me offer a detailed example of the exchange between reader and literary text to provide a sense of how the power of domesticity works through such an exchange. Charlotte Brontë flaunted this very power in writing her novel *Shirley*. The novel contains an otherwise gratuitous scene where Shakespeare's *Coriolanus* is read aloud and critiqued, as if to give the reader precise rules for reading, rules that should fascinate literary historians. They are not Brontë's own but rules developed during the preceding century by countless authors of ladies' conduct books and educational treatises. These authors proposed the first curriculum to include native British literature. Around the time Brontë sat down to write *Shirley*, a new generation of writers had taken up the question of how to distinguish good reading from bad. Their efforts swelled the growing number of Victorian magazines.

Whether or not girls should read novels was the concern that shaped the debates over a curriculum for women during the eighteenth century, then nineteenth-century pedagogical theory developed around the question of how to make fiction useful for teaching foreigners and working-class people as well as women and children. Rules for reading developed along with the national standard curriculum that extended a curriculum originally meant only for girls of the literate classes to young Englishmen and women at various levels and their counterparts throughout the colonies. It is much the same theory of education that informs our educational system today. By using this example from *Shirley* to illustrate the rationale and procedures by which Victorian intellectuals extended what had been regarded as a female form of literacy to male education, I also want to mark an important difference between Charlotte Brontë's understanding of this process and our own. She was, I believe, far more aware of the politics of literary interpretation than we are.

One of her least colorful heroines, Caroline Helstone, uses Shakespeare to while away an evening of leisure with her beloved cousin and future husband, Robert Moore, a surly manufacturer, whose authoritarian way of dealing with factory hands is earning him threats of Luddite reprisals. During this, their one intimate moment together until the end of the novel, they reject all the pastimes available to lovers in an Austen novel in favor of reading Shakespeare's *Coriolanus*. Far more detailed than any such exchange in earlier fiction, this act of reading spells out the procedures by which reading literature was thought to produce a form of knowledge that was also a form of social control. Robert Moore is half Belgian, half English. It is through reading Shakespeare that, according to Caroline, he "shall be entirely English."[17] For, as she patiently explains to him, "Your French forefathers don't speak so sweetly, nor so solemnly, nor so impressively as your English ancestors, Robert." But being English does not identify a set of political affiliations—as it would in Shakespeare's time. It refers instead to essential qualities of human mind. Caroline has selected a part for Robert to read aloud that, in her words, "is toned with something in you. It shall waken your nature, fill your mind with music, it shall pass like a skillful hand over your heart. . . . Let glorious William come near and touch it; you will see how he will draw the English power and melody out of its chords."

I have called this relationship between reader and text an exchange in order to stress the fact that writing cannot be turned to the task of constituting readers without giving up old features and acquiring new ones of its own; to dwell on the reader is to explain but one half of the transformational logic of this exchange. Just as Robert, the rude Belgian, becomes a gentle Englishman by reading Shakespeare, so, too, the Jacobean playwright is transformed by the domestic setting in which he is read. Caroline urges Robert to receive the English of another historical moment as the voice of an ancestor speaking to him across time and cultural boundaries. To no one's surprise, the written Shakespeare, thus resurrected, has acquired the yearnings and anxieties of an early nineteenth-century factory owner. And as we observe the Bard becoming the nineteenth-century man, we also witness an early version of our own literary training. Here, extending through the educated middle-class female to the male and, through him, acquiring universal application, we can see how voices that speak from positions vastly different in social space and time quickly translate into aspects of modern consciousness.

Thus Shakespeare becomes the means of reproducing specifically modern states of mind within the reader. Reading Shakespeare is supposed "to stir you," Caroline explains, "to give you new sensations. It is to make you feel your life strongly, not only your virtues, but your vicious, perverse points. Discover by the feeling the reading will give you at once how high and how low you are" (p. 115). If Shakespeare loses the very turns of mind that would identify him with his moment in history, then Robert loses features of a similar kind in Brontë's representation of the scene of reading. And this, of course, is the point. Reading Shakespeare translates Robert's political attitudes into essential features of mind. It simultaneously objectifies those features and subjects them to evaluation. The "English power" that Robert acquires by reading literature is simply the power of observing himself through the lens of liberal humanism—as a self flushed with the grandiosity of an ordinariness that has been totally liberated from historical bias and political commitment. For it is through this lens that the novel has us perceive the transformations that come over Robert as he reads *Coriolanus* under the gentle tutelage of Caroline Helstone: "stepping out of the narrow line of private prejudices, he began to revel in the large picture of human nature, to feel the reality stamped upon the characters who were speaking from that page before him" (p. 116).

Her tutoring induces Robert to renounce one mode of power—which Caroline associates with the imperiously patriarchal nature of Coriolanus—and to adopt another—which she identifies as a benevolent form of paternalism. As it is administered by a woman and used to mediate a sexual exchange, *Coriolanus* becomes the means for effecting historical change: *Coriolanus* becomes Caroline. Performed as writing and reading, that is, the play becomes the means of internalizing a form of authority identified with the female. The political implications of feminizing the reader are clear as Caroline gives Robert a moral to "tack to the play: . . . you must not be proud to your workpeople; you must not neglect chances of soothing them, and you must not be of an inflexible nature, uttering a request as austerely as if it were a command" (p. 114). Brontë is less than subtle in dramatizing the process by which reading rids Robert of the foreign devil. She seems to know exactly what political objective is fulfilled as he fills the mold of the Englishman and benevolent father. Brontë also puts the woman in charge of this process even though she gives her heroine the less imperious passages to read. Retiring, feminine, and thoroughly benign, Caroline's power is hardly visible as such. Yet she is clearly the one who declares that reading has the power "to stir you; to give you new sensations. It is to make you feel your life strongly, not only your virtues, but your vicious, perverse points" (p. 115). And when Robert has finished reading, she is the one to ask, "Now, have you felt Shakespeare?" (p. 117). She suppresses all that belongs to the past as so much noise in her effort to bring under examination the grand currents of emotion that run straight from Shakespeare to the modern day reader, a reader who is thoroughly English. In thus guiding his reading with her smiles and admonitions, Caroline executes a set of delicate procedures capable of translating any and all cultural information into shades of modern middle-class consciousness and the substance of a literary text. Although its setting—during the Luddite rebellions—makes *Shirley* anachronistic by about thirty years, the solution it proposes for the problem of political resistance, through the production of a new ruling-class mentality, mark this novel as utterly Victorian—perhaps even ahead of its time.

As similar textualizing strategies were deployed here and elsewhere throughout Victorian culture, an intricate system of psychological differences completely triumphed over a long-standing tradition of overtly political signs to usher in a new form of state power. This power—the power of representation over the thing represented—wrested authority from the old aristocracy on grounds that a government was morally obliged to rehabilitate deviant individuals rather than subdue them by force. The Peterloo Massacre of 1819 made it clear that the state's capacity for violence had become a source of embarrassment to the state. Overt displays of force worked against legitimate authority just as they did against subversive factions.[18] If acts of open rebellion had justified intervention in areas of society that government had not had to deal with before, then the government's use of force gave credence to the workers' charges of government oppression. The power of surveillance came into dominance at precisely this moment in English history, displacing traditional displays of violence. Remarkably like the form of vigilance that insured an orderly household, this power did not create equality so much as trivialize the material signs of difference by translating all such signs into differences in the quality, intensity, direction, and self-regulatory capability of an individual's desire.

In saying this, I am not suggesting that we should use British fiction to identify forms of repression or to perform acts of liberation, although my project has a definite political goal. I simply want to represent the discourse of sexuality as deeply implicated in—if not directly responsible for—the shape of the novel, and to show the novel's implication, at the same time, in producing a subject who knew herself and saw that self in relation to others according to the same feminizing strategies that had shaped fiction. I regard fiction, in other words, both as a document and as an agency of cultural history. I believe it helped to formulate the ordered space we now recognize as the household, that it made that space totally functional and used it as the context for representing normal behavior. In doing all this, fiction contested alternative bases for human relationships. As the history of this female domain is figured into political history, then, it will outline boldly the telling cultural move upon which, I believe, the supremacy of middle-class culture ultimately hinged. That is, it will reenact the moment when writing invaded, revised, and contained the household according to strategies that distinguished private from social life and thus detached sexuality from political history.

Where others have isolated rhetorical strategies that naturalize the subordination of female to male, no one has thoroughly examined the figure that differentiates the sexes as it links them together by sexual desire. And if no one asks why, how, and when gender differentiation became the root of human identity, no degree of theoretical sophistication can help us understand the totalizing power of this figure and the very real interests such power inevitably serves. So basic are the terms "male" and "female" to the semiotics of modern life that no one can use them without to some degree performing the very reifying gesture whose operations we need to understand and whose power we want to historicize.

Whenever we cast our political lot in the dyadic formation of gender, we place ourselves in a classic double bind, which confines us to alternatives that are not really alternatives at all. That is to say, any political position founded primarily on sexual identity ultimately confirms the limited choices offered by such a dyadic model. Once one thinks within such a structure, sexual relationships appear as the model for all power relationships. This makes it possible to see the female as representative of all subjection and to use her subjectivity as if it were a form of resistance. Having inscribed social conflict within a domestic configuration, however, one loses sight of all the various and contrary political affiliations for which any given individual provides the site. This power of sexuality to appropriate the voice of the victim works as surely through inversion, of course, as by strict adherence to the internal organization of the model.

Still, there is a way in which I owe everything to the very academic feminism I seem to critique, for unless it were now acceptable to read women's texts as women's texts, there would be no call to historicize this area of culture. In view of the fact that women writers have been taken up by the Norton Anthology as part of the standard survey of British literature and also as a collection all of their own, and in view of the fact that we now have male feminists straining to hop on the bandwagon, I feel it is simply time to take stock. It is time to consider why literary criticism presently feels so comfortable with a kind of criticism that began as a critique both of the traditional canon and of the interpretive procedures the canon called forth. This should tell us that by carving out a separate domain for women within literary criticism, feminist criticism has yet to destabilize the reigning metaphysics of sexuality. Literary historians continue to remain aloof from but still firmly anchored in a narrow masculinist notion of politics as more and more areas within literary studies have given ground to the thematics of sexuality promoted by academic feminism. Indeed, a sexual division of labor threatens to reproduce itself within the academy whereby women scholars interpret literature as the expression of the sexual subject while male scholars attend to matters of history and politics. To subvert this process, I believe we must read fiction not as literature but as the history of gender differences and a means by which we have reproduced a class and culture specific form of consciousness.

NOTES

1. Ian Watt, *The Rise of the Novel* (Berkeley: University of California Press, 1957), p. 57.

2. In *The Long Revolution* (New York: Columbia University Press, 1961), Williams sets out to show how the "creative" or cultural dimension of social experience opposed existing forms of political authority during the seventeenth and eighteenth centuries and won. Part one of his book indeed gives culture priority over the official institutions of state (as it must during the eighteenth century), claiming that cultural history "is more than a department, a special area of change. In this creative area the changes and conflicts of the whole way of life are necessarily involved" (p. 122). But latent in this promise to extend the category of "the political" broadly to include "the whole way of life" is the contradictory suggestion that political practices are also a special category of "the whole." The second notion of politics emerges in part two, where Williams describes such historical processes as the growth of the reading public, of the popular press, and of standard English through which the new middle classes converted the power of language into economic

power. Here the narrow definition of political events, as those which take place in the houses of government, the courts, and the marketplace, assumes control over the "creative" cultural dimension of social experience. For example, Williams writes, "as 1688 is a significant political date, so 1695 is significant in the history of the press. For in that year Parliament declined to renew the 1662 Licensing Act, and the stage for expansion was now fully set" (p. 180). Had Williams actually gathered data that would compose the record of "the whole" of life, he might have broken out of this circle. But, in producing cultural histories, he invariably bows to tradition and stops before entering into the female domain.

3. Virginia Woolf, *A Room of One's Own* (New York: Harcourt, Brace and World, 1975), p. 69.

4. For an account of the early eighteenth-century tradition that links the novel to criminal culture, see Lennard Davis, *Factual Fictions: The Origins of the English Novel* (New York: Columbia University Press,1983), pp.123–137. For the objection to novels because of their quasi-erotic appeal, see John Richetti, *Popular Fiction Before Richardson's Narrative Patterns 1700–1734* (Oxford: Clarendon, 1969). In an issue of Addison's *Spectator*, for example, Mr. Spectator warns readers about the perils of May, advising that women "be in a particular Manner how they meddle with Romances, Chocolates, Novels, and the like inflamers, which I look upon to be very dangerous to be made use of during this great Carnival of Nature," quoted in *Four Before Richardson: Selected English Novels 1720–1727*, William H. McBurney, ed. (Lincoln: University of Nebraska Press, 1963), p. ix. Toward the end of the eighteenth century, however, one discovers a good number of pedagogical treatises echo Austen's *Northanger Abbey* in advocating certain works of fiction as the fitting way to occupy leisure time. The fiction that was supposed to have a salutory effect on young women was either produced by lady novelists that gained currency during the age of Burney and the other lady novelists or else by earlier novelists who celebrated the same domestic virtues and saw the same form of domestic happiness as the ultimate reward for demonstrating these virtues. It was during this time, as Homer O. Brown explains, that certain novels were published under the editorship of Scott and Barbauld and marked as polite reading, and on the basis of this limited and anomalous body of works, a history of the novel was constructed backward in time (from his book in progress, *Institutions of the English Novel in the Eighteenth Century*).

5. A number of social historians have suggested that the factory system, and with it the economic domination of the new middle classes, was stalled until the beginning of the nineteenth century. In *The Making of the English Working Class* (New York: Random House, 1966) p. 198, E. P. Thompson suggests that fear of Jacobinism produced a new alignment between landowners and industrialists that divided the traditional resistance to industrustrialization. In *The Machinery Question and the Making of Political Economy* (Cambridge: Cambridge University Press, 1980), Maxine Berg explains how the development of political economy as a problem-solving logic at the end of the eighteenth century helped to make industrialization seem like an answer rather than a problem to be avoided at all costs. It was under such conditions that various authors first saw how many people had economic interests in common with the industrialists and described them as a class. In *Desire and Domestic Fiction: A Political History of the Novel* (New York: Oxford University Press, 1987), I carry this argument further by suggesting that well before they felt they had economic interests in common, numerous social groups ranging between the lower gentry and skilled workers were persuaded, in large part by authors unknown to us today, to buy into a single notion of personal life that centered around the kind of woman one desired to marry and the sort of happiness she would provide (pp. 59–95).

6. In discussing Feuerbach, Marx not only stresses that the "ruling ideas" of an epoch are the ideas of a ruling class who "regulate the production and distribution of ideas of their age" (p. 64). He also speculates that during the modern epoch, the production and distribution of ideas (i.e., the production of consciousness) will become increasingly im-

portant to the preservation of the bourgeois "state" and to its eventual disintegration or overthrow, *The German Ideology*, Part One, C. J. Arthur, ed. (New York: International Publishers, 1985). Without sliding back into the idealist philosophy from which Marx sought to rescue "the production of ideas," Gramsci applies the contradiction inherent in Marx's notion of labor to intellectual labor. The intellectual does not necessarily identify with the ruling class by reproducing the ideas inherited from the past but at certain moments may expand their political horizon by lending unity and coherence to the view of an emergent group, *The Modern Prince and Other Writings* (New York: International Publishers, 1957). In *Hegemony and Socialist Strategy*, Winston Moore and Paul Cammack, trs. (London: Verso, 1985), Ernesto Laclau and Chantal Mouffe update this principle for a postmodern society by broadening Gramsci's notions of both power and resistance. Where the difference between production in the traditional sense and the production of information has virtually disappeared, the antagonism between worker and owner is likewise dispersed. Where such polarities could once be taken for granted, then, it becomes extremely difficult to create polarities along political lines. Laclau and Mouffe find it necessary to depart from Gramsci's reliance on the emergence of labor in conflict with capital and to turn instead to the intellectual labor of negativities and positivities out of the contemporary swamp of equivalences. For another important analysis of power in postmodern society, see Bonaventura de Sousa Santos, "Law and Community: The Changing Nature of State Power in Late Capitalism," *International Journal of the Sociology of the Law* (1980), 8: 379–397.

7. Michel Foucault, *The History of Sexuality*, vol. 1, *An Introduction*, Robert Hurley, tr. (New York: Pantheon, 1978).

8. *Discipline and Punish: The Birth of the Prison*, Alan Sheridan, tr. (New York: Vintage, 1979). All citations are to this edition.

9. In *The Imaginary Puritan: Literature and the Origins of Personal Life* (Berkeley: Univ. of California Press, 1992), Leonard Tennenhouse and I explain at length how the English Revolution failed to produce the base transformations that mark political revolution. We argue for a more adequate definition of the political, showing that while political change, in the narrow sense of the term, failed to occur, cultural change was profound and lasting. Before the modern middle classes gained economic control, and well before they gained control of the Houses of Parliament, a new class of intellectuals gained hegemony over aristocratic culture as it translated puritanism into the secular practices composing modern domesticity and personal life.

10. I have argued this at length in *Desire and Domestic Fiction*. This essay began as an early version of the introduction and later developed into a theoretical investigation of my argument with literature, history, and academic feminism. I refer readers to the book for evidence supporting the necessarily brief outline of the events in the history of modern sexuality which composes part of this essay.

11. In "'The Mother Made Conscious': The Historical Development of a Primary School Pedagogy," *History Workshop* (1985), vol. 20, Carolyn Steedman has researched the rationale and analyzed the process by which the techniques of mothering were extended beyond the household and, through the establishment of a national educational system, became the gentle but unyielding girders of a new institutional culture.

12. See, for example, Peter Stallybrass and Allon White, *The Politics and Poetics of Transgression* (London: Methuen, 1986); Peter Clark, *The English Alehouse: A Social History 1200–1830* (London: Longman, 1983); Thomas Walter Laqueur, *Religion and Respectability: Sunday Schools and Working Class Culture 1780–1850* (New Haven: Yale University Press, 1976).

13. Maria Edgeworth and Robert L. Edgeworth, *Practical Education* (London, 1801), 2: ix. Citations in the text are to this edition.

14. For a discussion of the paternalism that emerged in opposition to patriarchy in seventeenth-century puritan writing, see Leonard Tennenhouse, *Power on Display: the Politics of Shakespeare's Genres* (New York: Methuen, 1986), especially the chapter entitled

"Family Rites." In describing the alternative to patriarchy that arose at the end of the seventeenth and beginning of the eighteenth century in aristocratic families, Randolph Trumbach opposes the term "patriarchal" to the term "domesticity," by which he refers to the modern household. This social formation is authorized by internal relations of gender and generation rather than by way of analogy to external power relations between monarch and subject or between God and man, *The Rise of the Egalitarian Family* (New York: Academic Press, 1978), pp. 119–163.

15. Kathleen M. Davis, "The Sacred Condition of Equality—How Original were Puritan Doctrines of Marriage?" *Social History* (1977), 5: 570. Davis quotes this list from John Dod and Robert Cleaver, *A Godly Forme of Householde Gouernment* (London, 1614).

16. See Brian Simon, *Studies in the History of Education 1780–1870* (London: Lawrence and Wishart. 1960), pp. 1–62.

17. Charlotte Brontë, *Shirley*, Andrew and Judith Hock, eds. (Harmondsworth: Penguin, 1974), p. 114. Citations of the text are to this edition.

18. E. P. Thompson, pp. 680–685.

LAUREN BERLANT

THE QUEEN OF AMERICA
GOES TO WASHINGTON CITY

harriet jacobs, frances harper, anita hill

(1993)

For many readers of Harriet Jacobs, the political uncanniness of Anita Hill has been a somber and illuminating experience. These two "cases" intersect at several points: at the experience of being sexually violated by powerful men in their places of work; at the experience of feeling shame and physical pain from living with humiliation; at the use of "going public" to refuse their reduction to sexual meaning, even after the "fact" of such reduction; at being African American women whose most organized community of support treated gender as the sign and structure of all subordinations to rank in America, such that other considerations—of race, class, and political ideology—became both tacit and insubordinate.[1] In these cases, and in their public reception, claims for justice against racism and claims for justice against both patriarchal and heterosexual privileges were made to compete with each other: this competition among harmed collectivities remains one of the major spectator sports of the American public sphere. It says volumes about the continued and linked virulence of racism, misogyny, heterosexism, economic privilege, and politics in America.

In addition to what we might call these strangely non-anachronistic structural echoes and political continuities, the cases of Hill and Jacobs expose the unsettled and unsettling relations of sexuality and American citizenship—two complexly related sites of subjectivity, sensation, affect, law, and agency. The following are excerpts from Frances Harper's 1892 novel *Iola Leroy*, Jacobs's narrative, and Hill's testimony. Although interpretive norms of production, consumption, and style differ among these texts, each author went public in the most national medium available to her. For this and other reasons, the rhetorical gestures that rhyme among these passages provide material for linking the politics of sex and the public sphere in America to the history of nationality itself, now read as a domain of sensation and sensationalism, and of a yet unrealized potential for fashioning "the poetry of the future" from the domains where citizens register citizenship, along with other feelings:[2]

> [Iola Leroy:] "I was sold from State to State as an article of merchandise. I had outrages heaped on me which might well crimson the cheek of honest womanhood with shame, but I never fell into the clutches of an owner for whom I did not feel the utmost loathing and intensest horror." . . .

[Dr. Gresham:] "But, Iola, you must not blame all for what a few have done." [Iola:] "A few have done? Did not the whole nation consent to our abasement?" (Frances E. W. Harper, *Iola Leroy* [1892])[3]

I have not written my experiences in order to attract attention to myself, on the contrary, it would have been more pleasant to me to have been silent about my own history. Neither do I care to excite sympathy for my own sufferings. But I do earnestly desire to arouse the women of the North to a realizing sense of the condition of two million of women at the South, still in bondage, suffering what I suffered, and most of them far worse. . . . [My] bill of sale is on record, and future generations will learn from it that women were articles of traffic in New York, late in the nineteenth century of the Christian religion. It may hereafter prove a useful document to antiquaries, who are seeking to measure the progress of civilization in the United States. (Harriet A. Jacobs, *Incidents in the Life of a Slave Girl* [1861])[4]

It is only after a great deal of agonizing consideration, and sleepless—number of—great number of sleepless nights, that I am able to talk of these unpleasant matters to anyone but my close friends. . . . As I've said before, these last few days have been very trying and very hard for me and it hasn't just been the last few days this week.

It has actually been over a month now that I have been under the strain of this issue. Telling the world is the most difficult experience of my life, but it is very close to having to live through the experience that occasioned this meeting. . . .

The only personal benefit that I have received from this experience is that I have had an opportunity to serve my country. I was raised to do what is right and can now explain to my students first hand that despite the high costs that may be involved, it is worth having the truth emerge. (Anita Hill, *New York Times*, 12 October 1991; 15 October 1991)[5]

ON THE SUBJECT OF PERSONAL TESTIMONY AND THE PEDAGOGY OF FAILED TEACHING

When Anita Hill, Harriet Jacobs, and Frances Harper's Iola Leroy speak in public about the national scandal of their private shame, they bring incommensurate fields of identity into explosive conjunction. Speaking as private subjects about sexual activities that transpired within the politically charged spaces of everyday life, their testimony remains itself personal, specifically about them, their sensations and subjectivity. We hear about "my experiences," "my own suffering," "unpleasant matters"; we hear of desires to return to silence, and of longings to be relieved of the drive to consign this material to public life, which requires the speaker to reexperience on her body what her rhetoric describes. But since their speech turns "incidents" of sexuality into opportunities for reconstructing what counts as national data—that is, since these sexual autobiographies all aim to attain the status of a *finding*, an official expert narrative about national protocols— the authors must make themselves representative and must make the specific sensational details of their violation exemplary of collective life. It is always the autobiographer's task to negotiate her specificity into a spectacular interiority worthy of public notice. But the minority subject who circulates in a majoritarian public sphere occupies a specific contradiction: insofar as she is exemplary, she has distinguished herself from the collective stereotype; and at the same time, she is also read as a kind of foreign national, an exotic representative of her alien "people" who reports to the dominant culture about collective life in the crevices of national existence. This warp in the circulation of identity is central to the public history of African American women, for whom coerced sexualization has been a constitutive relay between national experience and particular bodies.

Hence the specifically juridical inflection of "personal testimony." This hybrid form demarcates a collectively experienced set of strains and contradictions in the meaning of sexual knowledge in America: sexual knowledge derives from private experiences on the body and yet operates as a register for systemic relations of power; sexual knowledge stands for a kind of political counterintelligence, a challenge to the norms of credibility. rationality, and expertise that generally organize political culture; and yet, as an archive of injury and of private sensation, sexual knowledge can have the paradoxical effect of *delegitimating* the very experts who can represent it as a form of experience. As the opening passages show, these three women produced vital public testimony about the conditions of sexuality and citizenship in America. Their representations of how nationality became embodied and intimate to them involve fantasies of what America is, where it is, and how it reaches individuals. This requires them to develop a national pedagogy of failed teaching: emerging from the pseudo-private spaces where many kinds of power are condensed into personal relations, they detail how they were forced to deploy persuasion to fight for sexual dignity, and how they lost that fight. They take their individual losses as exemplary of larger ones, in particular the failure of the law and the nation to protect the sexual dignity of women from the hybrid body of patriarchal official and sexual privilege. They insist on representing the continuous shifting of perspectives that constitutes the incommensurate experience of power where national and sexual affect meet. They resist, in sum, further submission to a national sexuality that blurs the line between the disembodied entitlements of liberal citizenship and the places where bodies experience the sensation of being dominated. For all these verbs of resistance, the women represent their deployment of publicity as an act made under duress, an act thus representing and performing unfreedom in America. These three narrators represent their previous rhetorical failures to secure sexual jurisdiction over their bodies, challenging America to take up politically what the strongest individualities could not achieve.

Anita Hill is the most recent in a tradition of American women who have sought to make the nation listen to them, to transform the horizons and the terms of authority that mark both personal and national life in America by speaking about sexuality as the fundamental and fundamentally repressed horizon of national identity, legitimacy, and affective experience. That these are African American women reflects the specific sexual malignity black women have been forced to experience in public as a form of white pleasure and a register of white power in America. In this sense the imagination of sexual privacy these women express is a privacy they have never experienced, except as a space of impossibility. Anita Hill situated her own testimony not as a counter to the sexual economy of white erotics but in the professional discourse of an abused worker. Therefore, in Hill's testimony, two histories of corporeal identity converge. In both domains of experience, before sexual harassment became illegal, it was a widespread social practice protected by law. Invented as a technical legal category when middle-class white women started experiencing everyday violations of sexual dignity in the workplace, it has provided a way to link the banality and ordinariness of female sexualization to other hard-won protections against worker exploitation and personal injury.[6] It has also contributed to vital theoretical and policy reconsiderations of what constitutes the conditions of "consent" in the public sphere, a space which is no longer considered "free," even under the aegis of national-democratic protections.

What would it mean to write a genealogy of sexual harassment in which not an individual but a nation was considered the agent of unjust sexual power? Such an account of these complaints would provide an incisive critique of the modes of erotic and political dominance that have marked gender, race, and citizenship in America. It would register the sexual specificity of African American women's experience of white culture; it would link experiences of violated sexual privacy to the doctrine of abstract national "personhood," making America accountable for the private sexual transgressions of its privileged men and radically transforming the history of the "public" and the "private" in America; it would show how vital the existence of official sexual underclasses has been to producing national symbolic and political coherence; finally, and more happily, it would provide an archive of tactics that have made it possible to reoccupy both the sexual body and America by turning the constraints of privacy into information about national identity. I take the texts which I have quoted—Harriet Jacobs's slave narrative *Incidents in the Life of a Slave Girl*, Frances E. W. Harper's novel *Iola Leroy*, and the testimony of Anita Hill—as my sensorium of citizenship. The women in these texts each determine, under what they perceive to be the pressure or the necessity of history, to behave as native informants to an imperial power, that is, to mime the privileges of citizenship in the context of a particular national emergency. These national emergencies are, in chronological order, slavery, reconstruction, and the nomination of Clarence Thomas to the Supreme Court. They respond to these emergencies, these experiences of national sexuality, by producing what might be read as a counter-pornography of citizenship. For the next two sections I will locate the history of gesture and sense that characterizes this genre in readings of the nineteenth-century texts, and then shift historical perspective to Anita Hill in section four. Senators without pants, lawyers without scruples, and a national fantasy of corporeal dignity will characterize this story.

A MEDITATION ON NATIONAL FANTASY, IN WHICH WOMEN MAKE NO DIFFERENCE

These texts provide evidence that American citizenship has been profoundly organized around the distribution and coding of sensations. Two distinct moments in the nineteenth-century texts crystalize the conditions and fantasies of power motivating this affective domination, and so represent the negative space of political existence for American women in the last century. It may not appear that the sexual and affective encounters I will describe are indeed national, for they take place intimately between persons, in what look like private domains. The women's enslavement within the sensational regime of a privileged heterosexuality leads, by many different paths, to their transposition of these acts into the context of nationality. Even if sexual relations directly forced on these women mark individuals as corrupted by power, the women's narratives refuse to affirm the private horizon of personal entitlement as the cause of their suffering. America becomes explicitly, in this context, accountable for the sexual exploitation it authorizes in the guise of the white male citizen's domestic and erotic privilege.

Incidents in the Life of a Slave Girl registers many moments of intense corporeal stress, but one particular transitional gesture measures precisely on Harriet Jacobs's body the politics of her situation: hers is a hybrid experience of intimacy and alienation of a kind fundamental to African American women's experience of national sexuality under slavery. A mulatta, she was thought by some whites to be beautiful, a condition (as she says) that doubles the afflictions of race. She writes that the smallest female slave child will learn that "If God has bestowed beauty upon her, it will prove her greatest curse. That which commands admiration in the white woman only hastens the degradation of the female slave" (28). Racial logic gave America a fantasy image of its own personal underclass, with European-style beauty in the slave population justifying by nature a specific kind of exploitation by whites, who could mask their corporeal domination of all slaves in fantasies of masculine sexual entrapment by the slave women's availability and allure. For dark-skinned "black" women this form of exploitation involved rape and forced reproduction. These conditions applied to mulatta women too, but the lightness of these women also provided material for white men's parodic and perverse fantasies of masking domination as love and conjugal decorum.[7] Theatrically they set up a parallel universe of sexual and racial domestic bliss and heterosexual entitlement: this involved dressing up the beautiful mulatta and playing white-lady-of-the-house with her, building her a little house that parodied the big one, giving her the kinds of things that white married ladies received, only in this instance without the protections of law. Jacobs herself was constantly threatened with this fancy life, if only she would consent to it.

This relation of privilege, which brought together sexual fantasy and the law, disguised enslavement as a kind of courtship, and as caricature was entirely a production of the intentions and whims of the master. Harriet Jacobs was involved in an especially intricate and perverse game of mulatta sexual guerilla theater. One of *her* moves in this game was to become sexually involved with a white man other than her owner, Dr. Flint. (This man's *nom de théâtre* is "Mr. Sands," but his real name was Samuel Tredwell Sawyer and he was a United States Congressman, a status to which I will return in the next section.) Jacobs reports that Mr. Sands seemed especially sympathetic to her plight and that of their two children, and when he is introduced in the narrative's first half he seems to represent the promise of a humane relation between the sexes in the South—despite the fractures of race and in contrast to the sexual and rhetorical repertoire of violences with which Dr. Flint tortures Jacobs and her family. But the bulk of *Incidents* finds Jacobs in constant psychic torture about Sands himself. Her anxiety about whether he will remember her when she is gone, and remember his promises to free their children, makes her risk life and limb several times to seek him out: "There was one person there, who ought to have had some sympathy with [my] anxiety; but the links of such relations as he had formed with me, are easily broken and cast away as rubbish. Yet how protectingly and persuasively he once talked to the poor, helpless, slave girl! And how entirely I trusted him! But now suspicions darkened my mind" (142). No longer believing that Sands is a man of his word, Jacobs at length decides to escape—not at first from the South, but from Dr. Flint, following an intricately twisted path through the swamps, the hollow kitchen floors, and the other covert spaces of safety semi-secured by the slave community.[8] This spatial improvisation for survival culminates in a move to her grandmother's attic, where she spends seven years of so-called freedom, the price of which was lifelong nervous and muscular disruptions of her body. On the last day of her transition from enslavement, which was also the end of her freedom of movement, Jacobs's final act was to walk the public streets of her home town (Edenton, North Carolina) in disguise, one that required perverse elaborations of the already twisted epidermal schema of slavery. In her traveling clothes she does not assume white "lady's" apparel but hides her body in men's "sailor's clothes" and mimes the anonymity of a tourist, someone who is passing through; second, in this last appearance in her native town she appears in blackface, her skin darkened with charcoal. A juridically black woman whose experience of slavery as a mulatta parodies the sexual and domestic inscription of whiteness moves away from slavery by recrossing the bar of race and assuming the corporeal shroud of masculinity. This engagement with the visible body fashions her as absolutely invisible on the street. Moving toward escape, she passes "several people whom [she] knew," but they do not recognize her. Then "the father of my children came so near that I brushed against his arm; but he had no idea who it was" (113).

When Mr. Sands does not recognize Jacobs, though he sees her and touches her body, it becomes prophetically clear how specific his interest in her was. He desired a mulatta, a woman who signifies white but provides white men a different access to sexuality. Dressed as a man, she is invisible to him. With a black face, she is invisible to him, no longer an incitement to his desire. Touching him she thinks about other kinds of intimacy they have had—she calls him the father of their children—but in a certain sense her body registers what is numb to his *because* he is privileged. He has the right to forget and to not feel, while sensation and its memory are all she owns. This is the feeling of what we might call the slave's two bodies: sensual and public on the one hand; vulnerable, invisible, forgettable on the other. It is not surprising in this context that until Jean Fagan Yellin performed her research, the scholarly wisdom was that Harriet Jacobs could not have produced such a credible narrative. Her articulate representation of her sensational experience seemed itself evidence for the fraudulence of her authorship claims.[9]

If Jacobs experiences as a fact of life the political meaninglessness of her own sensations, Harper represents the process whereby Iola is disenfranchised of her sensations. In the following passage Iola discovers that she is a slave, politically meaningful but, like Jacobs, sensually irrelevant. Harper meticulously narrates Iola's sustained resistance to the theft of her senses by the corporeal fantasies of the slave system.[10] This resistance is a privilege Iola possesses because of the peculiar logic of racial identity in America, which draws legal lines that disregard the data of subjectivity when determining the identity of "race." Iola is a mulatta raised in isolated ignorance of her mother's racial history. Her mother, Marie, was a Creole slave of Eugene Leroy's, manumitted and educated by him before their marriage. Against Marie's wishes, the father insists that the children grow up in ignorance of their racial complexity, the "cross" in their blood. He does this to preserve their self-esteem, which is founded on racial unself-consciousness and a sense of innate freedom (84). When the father dies, an unscrupulous cousin tampers with Marie's manumission papers and convinces a judge to negate them. He then sends a lawyer to trick Iola into returning South and thus to slavery. Her transition between lexicons, laws, privileges, and races takes place, appropriately, as a transition from dreaming to waking. She rides on the train with the lawyer who will transport her "home" to the slave system, but she is as yet unknowing, dreaming of her previous domestic felicity:

> In her dreams she was at home, encircled in the warm clasp of her father's arms, feeling her mother's kisses lingering on her lips, and hearing the joyous greetings of the servants and Mammy Liza's glad welcome as she folded her to her heart. From this dream of bliss she was awakened by a burning kiss pressed on her lips, and a strong arm encircling her. Gazing around and taking in the whole situation, she sprang from her seat, her eyes flashing with rage and scorn, her face flushed to the roots of her hair, her voice shaken with excitement, and every nerve trembling with angry emotion. (103)

When, like the Prince in a debauched *Sleeping Beauty*, the lawyer kisses Iola, he awakens her and all of her senses to a new embodiment. At first Iola dreams of life in the white family, with its regulated sexualities and the pleasure of its physical routine. Feeling her father's arms, kissing her mother, hearing the servants, snuggling with mammy: these are the idealized domestic sensations of white feminine plantation privilege, which provides a sensual system that is safe and seems natural. This is why Iola does not understand the lawyer's violation of her body. Since he already sees her as public property, authorized by a national slave system, he feels free to act without her prior knowledge, while she still feels protected by white sexual gentility. Thus the irony of her flashing-eyed, pulsating response: to Iola this is the response of legitimate self-protectiveness, but to the lawyer the passion of her resistance actually increases her value on the slave market. Her seduction and submission to the master's sexuality would reflect the victory of his economic power, which is a given. Her sensations make no sense to the slave system; therefore they are no longer credible. Her relation to them makes no difference. This is the most powerful index of powerlessness under the law of the nation.

SLAVERY, CITIZENSHIP, AND UTOPIA: SOME QUESTIONS ABOUT AMERICA

I have described the political space where nothing follows from the experience of private sensation as a founding condition of slave subjectivity, a supernumerary nervous system here inscribed specifically and sexually on the bodies and minds of slave women. We see, in the narratives of Jacobs and Iola Leroy, that the process of interpellating this affective regime was ongoing, and that no rhetoric could protect them from what seemed most perverse about it, the permission it seemed to give slave owners to create sexual fantasies, narratives, masquerades of domesticity within which they could pretend *not* to dominate women, or to mediate their domination with displays of expenditure and chivalry.

But if this blurring of the lines between domination and play, between rhetorical and physical contact, and between political and sexual license always worked to reinforce the entitled relation to sensation and power the master culture enjoyed, both *Incidents* and *Iola Leroy* tactically blur another line—between personal and national tyranny. In the last section I described the incommensurate experiences of intimacy under slavery. Here I want to focus on how these intimate encounters with power structure Jacobs's and Harper's handling of the abstract problem of *nationality* as it is experienced—not as an idea, but as a force in social life, in experiences that mark the everyday. For Jacobs, writing before Emancipation, the nation as a category of experience is an archive of painful anecdotes, bitter feelings, and precise measurements of civic failure. She derives no strength from thinking about the possibilities of imagined community: hers is an antiutopian discourse of amelioration. In contrast, Harper writes after the war and enfranchisement. These conditions for a postdiasporic national fantasy provide the structure for her re-imagination of social value and civic decorum in a radically reconstructed America. The felt need to transform painful sexual encounters into a politics of nationality drove both of these women to revise radically the lexicon and the narratives by which the nation appears as a horizon both of dread and of fantasy.

Jacobs's *Incidents* was written for and distributed by white abolitionists whose purpose was to demonstrate not just how scandalous slavery was but how central sexuality was in regulating the life of the slave. Yet the reign of the master was not secured simply through the corporeal logics of patriarchy and racism. Jacobs shows a variety of other ways her body was erotically dominated in slavery—control over movement and sexuality, over time and space, over information and capital, and over the details of personal history that govern familial identity—and links these scandals up to a powerful critique of America, of the promises for democracy and personal mastery it offers to and withholds from the powerless.

Jacobs's particular point of entry to nationality was reproductive. The slave mother was the "country" into which the slave child was born, a realm unto herself whose foundational rules constituted a parody of the birthright properties of national citizenship. Jacobs repeatedly recites the phrase "follow the condition of the mother," framed in quotation marks, to demonstrate her only positive representation in the law, a representation that has no entitlement, a parodically American mantra as fundamental as another phrase about following she had no right to use, "life, liberty and the pursuit of happiness."

But the technicalities of freedom were not enough to satisfy Jacobs that America had the potential to fulfill its stated mission to be a Christian country. To gain free, unencumbered motherhood would be to experience the inversion of the sexual slavery she has undergone as a condition of her noncitizenship: at the end of the text, her freedom legally secured, she considers herself still unfree in the absence of a secure domestic space for her children.[11] But if Jacobs's relation to citizenship in the abstract is bitter and despairing, her most painful nationally authorized contact was intimate, a relation of frustrating ironic proximity.

I have characterized her sexual and reproductive relation with Mr. Sands, the United States Congressman Samuel Tredwell Sawyer. A truly sentimental fiction would no doubt reveal something generous about Congressman Sawyer, about a distinguished political career that might have included, somehow, traces of the influence Jacobs had on Sawyer's consciousness, revealed in a commitment to securing legal consensus on the humanity of slaves; and it would be simply trivial to note that issues of the *Congressional Globe* from 1838 reveal him in another universe of political consciousness, entirely undistinguished (he seems concerned with laws regulating duelling). More important, *Incidents* establishes that his rise to national office directly correlated with his increasing disregard for his promises to emancipate their children and her brother, both of whom he had bought from Flint in isolated acts of real empathy for Jacobs. Like many liberal tyrants, Sawyer so believes that his relative personal integrity and good intentions place him above moral culpability that he has no need to act morally within the law. Indeed, the law is the bar to empathy. When Harriet's brother William escapes from him, Sawyer says petulantly, "I trusted him as if he were my own brother, and treated him as kindly. . . . but he wanted to be a free man. . . . I intended to give him his freedom in five years. He might have trusted me. He has shown himself ungrateful; but I shall not go for him, or send for him. I feel confident that he will soon return to me" (135–36).

Later, Jacobs hears a quite different account from her brother, but what's crucial here is that the congressman whose sexual pleasure and sense of self-worth have been secured by the institution of slavery is corrupted by his proximity to national power. Yet Jacobs speaks the language of power, while Sawyer speaks the language of personal ethics; she looks to political solutions, while his privilege under the law makes its specific constraints irrelevant to him. Under these conditions Jacobs concludes three things about the politics of national sexuality. One is borne out by the performative history of her own book: "If the secret memoirs of many members of Congress should be published, curious details [about the sexual immorality of official men] would be unfolded" (142). The second she discovers as she returns from a trip to England where she has found political, sexual, racial, and spiritual peace and regeneration: "We had a tedious winter passage, and from the distance spectres seemed to rise up on the shores of the United States. It is a sad feeling to be afraid of one's native country" (186). Third, and finally, having established America as a negative space, a massive space of darkness, ghosts, shame, and barbarism, Jacobs sees no possibility that political solutions will ameliorate the memory and the ongoing pain of African American existence—as long as law marks a border between abstract and practical ethics. By the end of *Incidents* national discourse itself has become a mode of memorial rhetoric, an archive of dead promises.

I have identified thus two kinds of experience of the national for Jacobs: the actual pain of its practical betrayals through the many conscriptions of her body that I am associating with national sexuality and a psychic rage at America for not even trying to live up to the conditions of citizenship it promises in law and in spirit. After emancipation, in 1892 when Frances Harper is writing *Iola Leroy,* speaking at suffrage conferences at the National Congress of Negro Women, and at the Columbian Exposition, she imagines that citizenship might provide a model of identity that ameliorates the experience of corporeal mortification that has sustained American racisms and misogyny.[12] Harper argues that "more than the changing of institutions we need the development of a national conscience, and the upbuilding of national character," but she imagines this project of reconstruction more subtly and more radically than this kind of nationalistic rhetoric might suggest.[13] She refuses the lure of believing that the discourse of disembodied democratic citizenship applies to black Americans: she says, "You white women speak here of rights. I speak of wrongs. I, as a colored woman, have had in this country an education which has made me feel as if I were in the situation of Ishmael, my hand against every man, and every man's hand against me."[14] But Jacobs's solution to the enigma of social life under racism and misogyny—to privatize social relations—was not the only solution to this violent touching of hands. In contrast to Jacobs's narrative, Harper's *Iola Leroy* seizes the scene of citizenship from white America and rebuilds it, in the classic sense, imagining a liberal public sphere located within the black community.[15] More than a critical irritant to the white "people," the text subverts the racially dominant national polity by rendering it irrelevant to the fulfillment of its own national imaginary. Harper's civic and Christian black American nationality depends not only on eliding the horizon of white pseudo-democracy; she also imagines that African American nationalism will provide a model of dignity and justice that white American citizens will be obliged to follow.

A double movement of negation and theorization transforms the condition of citizenship as the novel imagines it. Harper's critical tactic banishes white Americans from the utopian political imaginary activity of this text. The initial loss of white status is performed, however, not as an effect of African American rage but rather as an act of white political rationality. A general in the Northern Army, encountering the tragedy of Iola's specific history and the detritus of the war, disavows his own identification as an American: he thinks, "Could it be possible that this young and beautiful girl had been a chattel, with no power to protect herself from the highest insults that lawless brutality could inflict upon innocent and defenseless womanhood? Could he ever again glory in his American citizenship, when any white man, no matter how coarse, cruel, or brutal could buy or sell her for the basest purposes? Was it not true that the cause of a hapless people had become entangled with the lightnings of heaven, and dragged down retribution upon the land?" (39). This repudiation envelops national, racial, and gendered self-disenfranchisement, and clears the way for a postpatriarchal, postracist, Christian commonwealth. Its ethical aura hovers over the novel's postwar narrative as well: Iola's experience of racism and misogyny in the metropolitian and commercial spaces of the North induces more pronouncements by whites about the unworthiness of white people to lead America in official and everyday life, since it is white national culture that has transformed the country from a space of enlightenment to a place of what she calls shadows and foreshadowing.

Such political self-impeachments by whites make it possible for Harper to reinvent a truly African American–centered *American* citizenship. In this sense, race in *Iola Leroy* is not solely a negative disciplinary category of national culture but becomes an archive of speech and life activities recast as a political arsenal. The originary form for African American insurgent community building derives from the subversive vernacular practices of slave life—from, as the first chapter title suggests, "The Mystery of Market Speech and Prayer Meetings." The narrative opens in the marketplace, where the slaves are shown to use an allegorical language to communicate and to gossip illegally about the progress of freedom during the Civil War. Just as the white masters travel, "talking politics in . . . State and National capitals" (7), slaves converse about the freshness of butter, eggs, and fish: but these ordinary words turn out to contain covert communication from the battlefield (7–8). In addition to exploiting the commercial space, the slave community performs its political identity at prayer meetings, where more illegal communication about the war and everyday life under slavery also transpires in allegory and secrecy.

The internal communications and interpretations of the community become public and instrumental in a different way after the war, when the place where the community met to pray to God and for freedom is transformed into a site where families dispersed by slavery might recombine: "They had come to break bread with each other, relate their experiences, and tell of their hopes of heaven. In that meeting were remnants of broken families—mothers who had been separated from their children before the war, husbands who had not met their wives for years" (179). These stories demonstrating kinship locate it not, however, in memories of shared lives or blood genealogies but rather in common memories of the violence of familial separation and dispersal. Under the conditions of legal impersonality which had governed slave personhood, the repetition of personal narratives of loss is the only currency of identity the slaves can exchange. The collective tactic here after slavery is to circulate self-descriptions in the hope that they will be repeated as gossip and heard by relatives, who will then come to the next convention and recite their own autobiographies in the hope that the rumor was true, that their story had an echo in someone else's life.

The collective storytelling about the diasporic forces of slavery is reinvented after the migration north, in salons where what Harper calls *conversazione* take place. Habermas and Landes have described the central role of the salon in building a public sphere.[16] Its function was to make the public sphere performatively democratic: more permeable by women and the ethnic and class subjects who had been left out of aristocratic privilege and who learned there to construct a personal and collective identity through the oral sharing of a diversity of written ideas. Harper explains at great length how conventions and *conversazione* transformed what counted as "personal" testimony in the black community: the chapter "Friends in Council," for example, details papers and contentious conversations about them entitled "Negro Emigration," "Patriotism," "Education of Mothers," and "Moral Progress of the Race," and a poem written by Harper herself entitled "Rallying Cry." All of these speeches and the conversations about them focus on uplifting the race and rethinking history; and the conditions of uplifting require imagining a just America, an America where neither race nor sexuality exists as a mode of domination. As Iola's friend, Miss Delaney, says, "I want my pupils to do all in their power to make this country worthy of their deepest devotion and loftiest patriotism" (251). Finally, after these face-to-face communities of African Americans seeking to transform their enslaved identities into powerful cultural and political coalitions are established, a literary tradition becomes possible: Iola herself is asked to serve the race by writing the story of her life that is this novel. Harper, in the afterword to the novel, imagines a new African American literature, "glowing with the fervor of the tropics and enriched by the luxuriance of the Orient." This revisionary aesthetic will, in her view, fill the African American "quota of good citizenship" and thus "add to the solution of our unsolved American problem" (282). In sum, the transmission of personal narrative, inscribed into the interiority of a community, becomes a vehicle for social transformation in *Iola Leroy*, recombining into a multicultural, though not multiracial, public sphere of collective knowledge. In so reconstructing through mass-circulated literature the meaning of collective personhood, and in so insisting on a "quota system" of good citizenship based not on racial assimilation but on a national ethics, the African American community Harper imagines solves the problem of America for itself.

DIVA CITIZENSHIP

When you are born into a national symbolic order that explicitly marks your person as illegitimate, far beyond the horizon of proper citizenship, and when your body also becomes a site of privileged fantasy property and of sexual contact that the law explicitly proscribes but privately entitles, you inhabit the mulatta's genealogy, a genealogy of national experience. The national body is ambiguous because its norms of privilege require a universalizing logic of disembodiment, while its local, corporeal practices are simultaneously informed by that legal privilege and—when considered personal, if not private—are protected by the law's general proximity. The African American women of this narrative understood that only a perversely "un-American" but nationally addressed text written from the history of a national subculture could shock white citizens into knowing how compromised citizenship has been as a category of experience and fantasy, not least for the chastised American classes.

This question of sexual harassment is thus not just a "woman's" question. A charged repertoire of private domination and erotic theatricality was licensed by American law and custom to encounter the African American women of whom I have written here, and many others, whose locations in hierarchies of racism, homophobia, and misogyny will require precisely and passionately written counterhistories. In twentieth-century America, anyone coded as "low," embodied, or subculturally "specific" continues to experience, with banal regularity, the corporeal sensation of nationality as a sensation over which she/he has no control. This, in the broadest sense, is sexual harassment. These texts break the sanitizing silences of sexual privacy in order to create national publics trained to think, and thus to think differently, about the corporeal conditions of citizenship. One of these conditions was the evacuation of erotic or sexual or even sensational life itself as a possible ground of personal dignity for African American women in America. As the rational, anti-passional logic of *Incidents* and *Iola Leroy* shows, the desire to become national seems to call for a *release* from sensuality—this is the cost, indeed the promise, of citizenship.

But the possibility of a revitalized national identity flickers in traces of peculiar identification within these texts. I call this possibility Diva Citizenship, but can only describe, at this point, the imaginable conditions of its emergence as an unrealized form of political activity. Diva Citizenship has a genealogy too, a dynastic, dignified, and pleasuring one. It courses through a variety of media forms and public spheres—from the Old Testament through CNN, through the works of bell hooks, Donna Haraway, Wayne Koestenbaum, and others.[17] For Haraway, cyborg citizenship replaces the "public/private" distinction as a paradigm for political subjectivity; hooks similarly derives the potential politics of the "third world diva girl" from the everyday forms of assertive and contesting speech she absorbed among "Southern black folk." These forms of speech are lived as breaches of class decorum between and among white, Third World, and African American feminists who discipline the ways women take, hold, use, respect, or demonize public authority: hooks sees the transgression of these decorums as central to liberation politics. For Koestenbaum, the Diva's public merging of "ordinariness touched by sublimity" has already been crucial to the emergence of a "collective gay subcultural imagination," where the public grandiosity of survival, the bitter banality of negotiating everyday life, generates subversive gossip about icons that actually works to create counterculture. "Where there is fever," he writes, "the need for police arises." Crossing police barricades and the civilizing standards of public life, Diva Citizenship takes on as a national project redefining the scale, the volume, and the erotics of "what you can [sincerely] do for your country."

One strategy of slave literature has been its royalist strain.[18] In *Iola Leroy*, Harper locates the promise of Diva Citizenship in the Biblical story of Queen Esther. Marie, Iola Leroy's mother, makes an abolitionist speech, executing a performance of refracting ironies. Marie speaks as a Creole slave woman to a free white audience on the day she graduates from the "finishing" school that will enable her to pass as the white wife of Albert Leroy: "Like Esther pleading for the lives of her people in the Oriental courts of a despotic king, she stood before the audience, pleading for those whose lips were sealed, but whose condition appealed to the mercy and justice of the Nation" (75). The analogies between Marie and Esther are myriad: forced to pass as a Persian in the court of Ahasuerus the King and her husband, Esther speaks as a Jew to save her people from genocide. She mobilizes her contradictions to unsettle the representational and political machinery of a dominant culture that desires her. It is not only in the gesture of special pleading that Marie absorbs Esther, but in the analogy between the mulatta woman and the assimilated Jew. Esther's capacity to pass likewise not only made her erotic masquerade the default activity of her everyday embodiment but also gave her sexual access to power—which she used not in a prevaricating way but under the pressure of a diasporic ethics. Purim, Queen Esther's holiday, is offered as a day of masquerade, revelry, and rage at tyranny—although as a story additionally about a wronged Queen (Vashti) and a holocaust, its status as an origin tale of domestic and imperial violence cannot be glossed over.[19] But Queen Esther stands in Harper's text as another foreign national separated at birth from the privileges of nationality, and also as a slave to masterly fantasies of sexual hierarchy and sensational excess who learned to countertheatricalize her identity and to wield it against injustice.

Jacobs's contribution to this monarchical fantasy politics deploys the Queen not as a figure of tactical self-distortion and instrumental sexual intimacy but as a figure of superior power who remakes the relations between politics and the body in America. She represents the "state of civilization in the late nineteenth century of the United States" by showing a variety of indirect and noncoherent ways the nation came into deliberate contact with slaves—through scandalous and petty torture. In turn, Jacobs shows how the slaves misrecognize, in potentially and sometimes strategically radical ways, what constitutes the nation. This passage takes place in an extraordinary chapter titled "What Slaves Are Taught to Think of the North." Jacobs describes at great rageful length the relation between the sexual brutality of masters to slaves and their lies, what she calls "the pains" masters take to construct false scenarios about "the hard kind of freedom" that awaited freed or escaped slaves in the North. She argues that these slaves, so demoralized by the impossibility of imagining political freedom, become actively complicit in the local scene of sexual savagery—actually sneaking "out of the way to give their masters free access to their wives and daughters" (44)— because sexuality is the only exchange value the slaves pseudo-possess. Jacobs takes the example of these relations of misrecognition and affective distortion and turns them back on the nation:

> One woman begged me to get a newspaper and read it over. She said her husband told her that the black people had sent word to the queen of 'Merica that they were all slaves; that she didn't believe it, and went to Washington city to see the president about it. They quarrelled, she drew her sword upon him, and swore that he should help her to make them all free.
> That poor ignorant woman thought that America was governed by a Queen, to whom the President was subordinate. I wish the President was subordinate to Queen Justice. (45)

Let us suppose it were true that the Queen of America came down to Washington and put the knife to the President's throat. Her strategy would be to refute his privilege, and that of citizens like him, to be above the sensational constraints of citizenship. The Queen of America educates him about his own body's boundaries with a cold tip of steel, and he emancipates the slaves. But Jacobs, never one to give the nation credit for even potentially recognizing its excesses, closes this anecdote not advocating violence on this individual President but subversively transferring the horizon of national identity to its illiterate citizens. She does this in order to counter what Donna Haraway has called "the informatics of domination":[20] using the misrecognitions of everyday life as the base of her national archive, Jacobs shows how national consciousness truly cuts a path through gossip, deliberate lies of the masters, the national press, the President of the United States who lives in Washington, the Queen of America who is dislocated from any specific capital, and the Queen of Justice who rules, perhaps in a universe parallel to that of the other Queen, and who has no national boundaries. In so creating this genealogy, this flow chart of power whose boundaries expand with every sentence written about America, Jacobs dislocates the nation from its intelligible forms. She opens up a space in which the national politics of corporeal identity becomes displayed on the monarchical body, and thus interferes with the fantasy norms of democratic abstraction; in so doing, she creates an American history so riddled with the misrecognitions of mass nationality that it is unthinkable in its typical form, as a narrative about sovereign subjects and their rational political representation. For no American president could be subordinate to any Queen—of America or of Justice. Bracketing that horizon of possibility, it becomes imperative to take up the scandalous promise of Jacobs's strategy, which is to exploit a fantasy of cutting across the space that doesn't exist, where abstract and corporeal citizenship come into contact not on the minoritized body but on *the body of the nation.*

It is this phantasmatic body that the Anita Hill/Clarence Thomas hearings brought to us in the delusional week before the vote. It was alluded to in the corporeality of Thomas himself: in his alleged exploitation of personal collegiality in federal workspaces; in the racist fantasies that he evoked to account for his victimization by Hill and on the Hill; in the aura of the minority stereotype black authority represents as a "token" on the Supreme Court. The national body is signified in Hill's own body as well, which displayed all of the decorums of bourgeois national polity while transgressing the veil between official and private behavior that grounds the erotic power of the state. Finally, the body of the nation was configured in the images of senators sitting in judgment and in the experts they brought in to testify to the law and to issues of "character" and "appearance."[21]

What I want to focus on is a displaced mediation of the national embodiment Hill and Thomas produced, in a television sitcom about the activities of a white and female-owned Southern business: the episode of *Designing Women* entitled "The Strange Case of Clarence and Anita" that aired shortly after the vote. In many ways, this episode reproduces the legitimacy of masculine speech over feminine embodiment in the political public sphere, most notably by contrasting news clips of speaking powerful men to clips that represent Hill only in tableau moments of demure silence before the Senate Judiciary Committee. Thus in one light the show's stifling of Hill reproduces a version of the imperial fantasy Gayatri Chakravorty Spivak describes, in which white women "heroically" save brown women from brown *and* white men. But while Hill herself demonstrated respect for national decorums and conservative ideologies of authority, her *case* substantially disrupted norms of embodiment of the national space and, indeed, revealed and produced disturbances in what counts as the national space itself.[22]

In this episode, the characters share private opinions about Thomas and Hill, along with painful personal memories of sexual harassment; but under the pressure of historical circumstance, the ordinary space of intimacy they share comes into contact with a media frenzy: tee shirts they buy at the mall that say "He did it" or "She lied" turn their bodies into billboards, which they flash angrily at each other; opinion polls that register the micro-fluctuations of "public sentiment" generate conversation about linguistic bias and motivate assertions of their own superiority to the numerically represented "people"; CNN, reinstated as the source of national identity, transforms the undifferentiated stream of opinions from all over the country into national data as "official" as that emanating from Washington itself; the television set focuses the collective gaze, such that domestic and public spheres become merged, as do news and entertainment (the character Julia Sugarbaker, for example, suggests that Thomas belongs not on the Supreme Court, but in the National Repertory Theatre); and, in the climactic moment, a local television reporter tapes an interview with Suzanne Sugarbaker, a Thomas supporter, and Mary Jo Shively, a self-described "feminist," right in their living room. What's striking about the condensation of these media forms and forms of embodied political intimacy is how close so many different and over-lapping American publics become—and in the context not of a soap opera but of a situation comedy that refuses, this time, to contain the "situation" within the frame of its half-hour. Judge Thomas and Professor Hill turn into "Clarence" and "Anita" in this situation, like TV neighbors having a domestic row; and the di-verse, incorrect, passionate, and cynical range of opinions that flow in the room take on the status of personal and political gossip. Not just gossip about judges or senators without pants but about the intimate details of national identity.

At one point Mary Jo explodes in rage at Senator John Danforth's claim, shown on CNN, that Anita Hill suffered from a delusional disease in which she con-fused her own desire for power with the power of Thomas's sexual desire. Hear-ing Danforth's pleasure in this pop-psych diagnosis rouses Mary Jo to call his office in Washington. But she is frustrated in this desire because the line is busy. I myself wanted to call Washington during Hill's testimony or to testify in any way to my own banal/expert knowledge of the nonconsensual erotics of power we code as "harassment." The desire for contact sometimes took the phantas-matic form of a private letter to a senator, or one to a newspaper, sometimes a phone encounter, sometimes a fantasy that a reporter from the national news or "Nightline" would accost me randomly on the street and that my impromptu elo-quence would instantly transport me to the televisual realm of a Robert Bork, where my voice and body would be loud, personal, national, and valorized.

In my view this ache to be an American diva was not about persuasion. It de-rived from a desire to enter a senator's body and to dominate it through an ori-fice he was incapable of fully closing, an ear or an eye. This intimate fantasy communication aimed to provoke sensations in him for which he was unprepared, those in that perverse space between empathy and pornography that Karen Sánchez-Eppler has isolated as constitutive of white Americans' interest in slaves, slave narratives, and other testimonials of the oppressed.[23] And in so appealing to a senator's authority over the terms in which I experience my (theoretically impossible) sexualized national being, I imagined making him so full and so sick with knowledge of what he has never experienced officially that he would lose, perhaps gratefully, his sensual innocence about—not the power of his own sexual-ity—but the sexuality of his own power, and . . .

This is where my fantasy of swearing out a female complaint would falter, stop knowing itself and what it wanted. The desire to go public, to exploit the dispersed media of national life, became my way of approximating the power of official nationality to dominate bodies—a motive which, in a relation of overiden-tification, I and many others had mapped onto Hill's majestic and courageous citi-zenship. It also suggested to me that the fantasy of addressing the nation directly, of violating the citizen's proper silence about the sensations of citizenship, is a fantasy that many Americans live.[24]

The horizon of critical possibility lies, however, not in orchestrating mass cul-ture and mass nationality through the pseudo-immediacy of "electronic town halls," currently offered as a solution to the problem of recovering representa-tional politics as a kind of collective decision making in the United States. Diva Citizenship reminds us that the legal tender of contemporary politics is no longer calibrated according to a gold standard of immediacy, authenticity, and rationality; the bodily distortions and sensual intimacy of national media degrade representations of political agency and therefore bleed into a space of surprise where political experiments in re-imagining agency and critical practice itself can be located, perhaps among the kinds of queenly gestures and impulses toward freedom I have recorded here.

To close: the final narrative image of *Designing Women*, which merges a radical embodied female citizenship with the aura of the star system. Annie Potts, who plays Mary Jo Shively, wears Bette Davis drag. Dixie Carter, who plays Julia Sugarbaker, masquerades as Joan Crawford. Having come directly from a dress rehearsal of a local theatrical adaptation of *What Ever Happened to Baby Jane?* they sit on the couch, exhausted. They are not exhausted from the rehearsal, but from the rage they have expended on what they call this "day of [national] infamy." Meanwhile, their friends slow dance the night away, like pre-adolescents at a slumber party. Bette asks Joan to dance with her. They get up and look at each other. "Who should lead?" asks Bette Davis. "Well, Bette," says Joan Crawford, "considering who we are, I think we both should." And who are they? As Joan says to Bette in an earlier moment, "two of the toughest talking big-shouldered broads ever to live in this country."

NOTES

Special thanks to Gordon Hutner, Miriam Hansen, and audiences at Rutgers, the University of North Carolina, Chicago State, and the MLA for insightful and impassioned critical responses.

1. The most incisive overview of the feminist, as opposed to class- and race-based, interpretations of the Hill-Thomas events is by Nancy Fraser, in "Sex, Lies, and the Public Sphere: Some Reflections on the Confirmation of Clarence Thomas," *Critical Inquiry* 18 (Spring 1992): 595–612. Fraser sees this event as a symptom of transformations of and contestations over definitions of public and private, publicity and privacy. See also Rosemary L. Bray, "Taking Sides Against Ourselves," *The New York Times Magazine,* 17 November 1991, 56–97. Two volumes have recently emerged that perform repeatedly the adjustments between gender, race, class, and ideological identity categories I am describing here, with much emphasis on the "problem" of articulating "gender" not only with "race" but also with the political movements that make these categories contested and unstable ones in the political public sphere. *The Black Scholar* has assembled *Court of Appeal: The Black Community Speaks Out on the Racial and Sexual Politics of Thomas vs. Hill,* ed. Robert Chrisman and Robert L. Allen (New York: Ballantine, 1992), from which the following essays are directly germane: Calvin Hernton, "Breaking Silences," 86–91; June Jordan, "Can I Get a Witness," 120–24; Barbara Smith, "Ain't Gonna Let Nobody Turn Me Around," 185–89; Rebecca Walker, "Becoming the Third Wave," 211–13. In Toni Morrison's edited volume, *Race-ing Justice, En-gendering Power: Essays on Anita Hill, Clarence Thomas, and the Construction of Social Reality* (New York: Pantheon, 1992), see especially Kimberlé Crenshaw, "Whose Story Is It Anyway? Feminist and Antiracist Appropriations of Anita Hill," 402–40; Christine Stansell, "White Feminists and Black Realities: The Politics of Authenticity," 251–68; Cornel West, "Black Leadership and the Pitfalls of Racial Reasoning," 390–401.

2. The word "experience" is important in the texts I am addressing and in the one I am writing here, and requires some explication. The category "experience" is not meant

to refer to self-evident autobiographical data over which the experiencing person has control: the experience of being dominated, for example, is subjective, and therefore incompatible descriptions of it might engender legitimate contestation. But I take experience here more fundamentally to be something produced in the moment when an activity becomes framed as an event, such that the subject enters the empire of quotation marks, anecdote, self-reflection, memory. More than a category of authenticity, "experience" in this context refers to something someone "has," in aggregate moments of self-estrangement. Jacobs, Harper, and Hill are aware of the unreliability of experience as data both in their own perceptions and in their drive to produce convincing evidence to buttress their arguments for social change or informed consciousness. For a strong summary of the current historicist argument over the evidentiary use of experience, see Joan W. Scott, "The Evidence of Experience," *Critical Inquiry* 17 (Summer 1991) 773–97; and, more critically, Mas'ud Zavarzadeh and Donald Morton, "Theory Pedagogy Politics: The Crisis of 'The Subject' in the Humanities," in their collection *Theory/Pedagogy/Politics: Texts for Change* (Urbana: Univ. of Illinois Press, 1991), 1–32; and Chris Weedon, "Post-Structuralist Feminist Practice," in the same volume, 47–63. The phrase "the poetry of the future" comes, famously, from Karl Marx, *The 18th Brumaire of Napoleon Bonaparte.*

3. Frances E W. Harper, *Iola Leroy; or, Shadows Uplifted* (1892; rpt., College Park, Md.: McGrath, 1969), 115–16. All further references will be contained in the text.

4. Harriet A. Jacobs, *Incidents in the Life of a Slave Girl: Written by Herself* (edited by Lydia Maria Child), ed. Jean Fagan Yellin (Cambridge: Harvard Univ. Press, 1987).

5. Anita Hill, *New York Times*, 12 October 1991, sec. 1; 15 October 1991, sec. 1.

6. For the myriad transformations in legal theory and practical juridical norms regulating what counts as "injury" and "harm" to women, see *At the Boundaries of Law: Feminism and Legal Theory*, ed. Martha Albertson Fineman and Nancy Sweet Thomadsen (New York: Routledge, 1991); and *Feminist Legal Theory: Readings in Law and Gender*, ed. Katharine T. Bartlett and Roseanne Kennedy (Boulder: Westview, 1991).

7. There is a large outstanding bibliography on this subject. It includes Hazel Carby, *Reconstructing Womanhood* (New York: Oxford Univ. Press, 1987); P. Gabrielle Foreman, "The Spoken and the Silenced in *Incidents in the Life of* a *Slave Girl* and *Our Nig*," *Callaloo* 13 (Spring 1990): 313–24; Jane Gaines, "White Privilege and Looking Relations: Race and Gender in Feminist Film Theory," *Screen* 8 (Autumn 1988): 12–27; Hortense J. Spillers, "Notes on an Alternative Model—Neither/Nor," in *The Difference Within: Feminism and Critical Theory*, ed. Elizabeth Meese and Alice Parker (Philadelphia: John Benjamins, 1989), 165–87 and "Mama's Baby, Papa's Maybe: An American Grammar Book," *Diacritics* 17 (Summer 1987): 65–81.

8. See Valerie Smith, "'Loopholes of Retreat': Architecture and Ideology in Harriet Jacobs's *Incidents in the Life of a Slave Girl*," in *Reading Black Reading Feminist*, ed. Henry Louis Gates Jr. (New York: Meridian, 1990), 212–26.

9. See Jean Fagan Yellin, "*Written by Herself*: Harriet Jacob's Slave Narrative," *American Literature* 53 (1981): 479–86.

10. I adapt this notion of "theft" from Harryette Mullen's work on orality and writing in *Incidents in the Life of a Slave Girl*. See "Runaway Tongue: Resistant Orality in *Uncle Tom's Cabin, Our Nig, Incidents in the Life of a Slave Girl*, and *Beloved*," in *The Culture of Sentiment: Race, Gender, and Sentimentality in Nineteenth-Century America*, ed. Shirley Samuels (New York: Oxford Univ. Press, 1992), 244–64.

11. On the counternational politics of gender and kinship in *Incidents*, see Spillers, "Mama's Baby, Papa's Maybe."

12. To place *Iola Leroy* in the context of Harper's complex political activities, see Carby, *Reconstructing Womanhood*, 63–94. Carby's chapter on Harper emphasizes the race/gender axis of her concerns, and provides crucial support to my thinking about nationality. See also Frances Smith Foster's Introduction to Frances Ellen Watkins Harper, *A Brighter Coming Day: A Frances Harper Reader* (New York: Feminist Press, 1990), 3–40.

13. Frances Ellen Watkins Harper, "Duty to Dependent Races," in *Black Women in Nineteenth-Century American Life: Their Words, Their Thoughts, Their Feelings*, ed. Bert James Loewenberg and Ruth Bogin (1891; rpt., University Park: Pennsylvania State Univ. Press, 1976), 245.

14. Harper, *A Brighter Coming Day*, 218.

15. The argument that nationality can overcome the fractures of race operates throughout Harper's speeches and poems as well. Perhaps the most condensed and eloquent of these was delivered at the Columbian Exposition. See "Woman's Political Future," in *The World's Congress of Representative Women*, ed. May Wright Sewall (Chicago: Rand, McNally, 1894), 433–38.

16. Jürgen Habermas, *The Structural Transformation of the Public Sphere: An Inquiry into a Category of Bourgeois Society*, trans. Thomas Burger (Cambridge: Harvard Univ. Press, 1989), 31–43; Joan B. Landes, *Women and the Public Sphere in the Age of the French Revolution* (Ithaca Cornell Univ. Press, 1988), 22–31.

17. Donna Haraway, "A Manifesto for Cyborgs," in *Simians, Cyborgs, and Women: The Reinvention of Nature* (New York: Routledge, 1991), 162; bell hooks, "Third World Diva Girls," in *Yearning: Race, Gender, and Cultural Politics* (Boston: South End, 1990), 89–102; Wayne Koestenbaum, "The Codes of Diva Conflict," chap. 3 of *The Queen's Throat: Opera, Homosexuality, and the Mystery of Desire* (New York: Poseidon, 1993). See also Laura Kipnis, "(Male) Desire and (Female) Disgust: Reading *Hustler*," in *Cultural Studies*, ed. Lawrence Grossberg, Cary Nelson, and Paula Treichler (New York: Routledge, 1992), 373–91; Miriam Hansen, "The Return of Babylon: Rudolph Valentino and Female Spectatorship (1921–1926)," part 3 of *Babel and Babylon: Spectatorship in American Silent Film* (Cambridge: Harvard Univ. Press, 1991); Andrew Ross, *No Respect* (New York: Routledge, 1989); Carole-Anne Tyler, "Boys Will Be Girls: The Politics of Gay Drag," in *Inside/Out: Lesbian Theories, Gay Theories* (New York: Routledge, 1991), 32–71; and Patricia J. Williams, "A Rare Case Study of Muleheadedness and Men," in Morrison, *Race-ing Justice, En-gendering Power*, 159–71.

18. Barry Weller, "The Royal Slave and the Prestige of Origins," *Kenyon Review* 14 (Summer 1992): 65–78.

19. I focus here on the analogy Harper seems to make between Esther's complicated ethnic masquerade and Marie's racial one, and on the conditions for political speech that ensued. The *Book of Esther* as a whole tells a far more complex story. On the one hand, it might have provided Harper, and us, with a less patriarchalized model of feminine power: Queen Vashti, whose refusal to display her royal beauty to a banquet of drunken courtiers provoked Elizabeth Cady Stanton's *The Woman's Bible* to name her "the first woman recorded whose self-respect and courage enabled her to act contrary to the will of her husband. . . . [in] the first exhibition of individual sovereignty of woman on record. . . . true to the Divine aspirations of her nature" (86–88). On the other hand, the *Book of Esther* is a story about holocausts, a Jewish one averted and a Macedonian one revengefully executed by the Jews themselves (Elizabeth Cady Stanton and the Revising Committee, *The Woman's Bible* [1898; rpt., Seattle: Coalition Task Force on Women and Religion, 1974]).

20. Haraway, 161.

21. See especially Wahneema Lubiano, "Black Ladies, Welfare Queens, and State Minstrels: Ideological War by Narrative Means," in Morrison, 321–63.

22. The original sentence, describing the mentality of "imperialist subject-production," is "White men are saving brown women from brown men" (Gayatri Chakravorty Spivak, "Can the Subaltern Speak?" in *Marxism and the Interpretation of Culture* [Urbana: Univ. of Illinois Press, 1988], 296).

23. Karen Sánchez-Eppler, "Bodily Bonds: The Intersecting Rhetorics of Feminism and Abolition," *Representations* 24 (Fall 1988): 28–59.

24. The fantasy of diminishing the scale of America to make the nation a place one

might encounter has a long history in American letters. See Lauren Berlant, *The Anatomy of National Fantasy: Hawthorne, Utopia, and Everyday Life* (Chicago: Univ. of Chicago Press, 1991); Jody Berland, "Angels Dancing: Cultural Technologies and the Production of Space," in Grossberg, Nelson, and Treichler, 39–55; and John Caughie, "Playing at Being American," *Logics of Television: Essays in Cultural Criticism*, ed. Patricia Mellencamp (Bloomington: Indiana Univ. Press, 1990), 44–58.

class

Difference—the exploration of differences between men and women—has been one of the chief concerns of feminist criticism. Recently, though, feminist theorists have become interested in the differences between women, insisting that to categorize women as just "women" is to reinscribe a sexist ideology that sees all women as interchangeable. Differences exist among women in many aspects, including race, age, sexual preference, and social class, but class difference often gets erased under dominant American ideology. The myth of democracy is based on an ideal of classlessness; part of feminism's task is to consider the implications of that myth for women. The essays in this section explore not only what the differences of social class might mean, but where they come from, and how they have been—and continue to be—part of the oppression of women. They also take on a critical question for late-twentieth-century progressive politics by considering how differences of class and gender overlap with questions of ethnicity and race.

Many feminists have long felt that not all women share the same struggle, that working women have very different lives and different concerns from those of middle- and upper-class women. Yet when they turn to the most fully theorized analysis of class, Marxist critique, they find that it devotes almost all its attention to men and traditionally male institutions. As Heidi Hartmann asserts in her essay "The Unhappy Marriage of Marxism and Feminism" (quoted as an epigraph to Cora Kaplan's essay below), "The 'Marriage' of marxism and feminism has been like the marriage of husband and wife depicted in English common law: marxism and feminism are one, and that is marxism." Much of the criticism that unites a feminist analysis with attention to issues of social class was born of an uneasiness with feminist and Marxist critiques, a sense that the two had not yet really met on common ground. The essays in this section attempt to bring analyses of gender and class oppression together in a way that demeans neither, but instead complicates both.

These essays also try to work through the question of the place in literary studies of what has been traditionally the academic domain of the social sciences. How do gender and class issues become literary questions? Although each essay answers this problem differently, they all share one assumption: literature has a definite function in society beyond simple aesthetic pleasure. Aesthetic pleasure itself, they argue, is clearly tied to the way literature acts as a social agent (for more on this viewpoint, see "Institutions," "Canon," and "History"). Literature does not exist in a realm that is somehow independent of social and political questions, but is intricately involved in our understanding of culture and the shaping of society.

Cora Kaplan's "Pandora's Box: Subjectivity, Class and Sexuality in Socialist Feminist Criticism" (first published in 1985, reprinted here from her book *Sea Changes* [1986]) addresses the theoretical problems of a socialist feminist criticism. Too often, she argues, feminism ignores its roots in a liberal humanism that, at its inception in the Romantic period, was sexist and racist (she uses Mary Wollstonecraft's early writings as examples here). The acceptance of the concepts of the "individual self" and the "moral psyche" lead one away from political analysis of the collective. On the other hand, she argues, socialist feminism too often ignores the power of women's psychic lives, treating them as mere products of a social system, indistinguishable from men's. Kaplan urges that feminist critique avoid such polarization and "come to grips with the relationship between female subjectivity and class identity." Recognizing the difficulty in even defining what we mean by "class" in literary analysis, Kaplan develops a working definition and turns to an analysis of nineteenth-century fiction (here *Jane Eyre*) and our readings of it (represented by Virginia Woolf's interpretation) to examine the ways that class and sexual identities became "welded together" in the nineteenth century and thereby became "sinister." We need a theory of both class and sexual desire to unpack this complex symbolization, she argues, and to understand the history behind both the literary representation and our own reactions to it.

In "Romance in the Age of Electronics: Harlequin Enterprises" (1985), Leslie Rabine asks how Harlequin romances appeal to the women who read them, usually women who work in clerical positions. Her answer is that these novels appeal to the needs of working women by "focusing on the juncture between their sexual, emotional needs on the one hand and their needs concerning work relations on the other." Noting that more and more Harlequin heroines have jobs, react to a negative work world, and fall in love with their bosses, Rabine suggests that this eroticization of a problematic work world signifies a desire for a "different social structure . . . [where there is] an end to the division between the domestic world of love and sentiment and the public world of work and business." She argues that we cannot isolate the reading of romance novels from the context in which they are read, from the women who read them, or from the production and marketing of the novels (Janice Radway elaborates a similar argument in "The Readers and Their Romances," reprinted here in "Reading"). The novels represent for these women fantasies of escape from their positions of relative powerlessness in an automated business world, but the form and production of the romances themselves—standardized as they are—neutralize any threat the novels could offer to patriarchal ideology.

In "I Shop Therefore I Am: Is There a Place for Afro-American Culture in Commodity Culture?" (1989), Susan Willis turns from the production of mass culture texts for white working women to the consumption of mass culture commodities by African Americans. Willis contrasts the hostility toward commodity culture in novels by Toni Morrison and Alice Walker to the production of it in videos by Michael Jackson, to raise the question of whether black women and black men have different relations to a world of production and consumption that seeks to define and control them. Willis examines the way that Morrison and Walker condemn commodity culture as a form of white domination, a means to erase racial, sexual, and cultural difference through a forced assimilation to a white ideal. Willis describes this as a "black mimicry of a white cultural model," which she sees as an attempt to create a dehumanized race of "black replicants" of white culture. In contrast to this model, Willis reads Michael Jackson's series of physical transformations as a race- and gender-heterogeneous form of blackface. Willis employs critical analyses that read blackface as both capitulating to commodity culture and subverting it, as both participating in the racial and sexual stereotyping of blacks and resisting the enforcement of white bourgeois culture. Willis suggests that Jackson's *Moonwalker* video "defines the commodity form in the tradition of blackface as the nexus of a struggle," but also outlines the difference between black men's and women's relation to commodity culture. Whereas black men can see the commodity as something available for play and subversion, Willis argues, black women strive "to create images of social wholeness based on the rejection of commodity capitalism."

Rosaura Sánchez, in "Discourses of Gender, Ethnicity, and Class in Chicano Literature" (1992), looks at Chicano literature by placing it in dialogue with history and critical theory. Sánchez show how explicitly ideological readings of Chicano literature can help frame important questions about the relation between social and political battles, history, literature, and about who is speaking and for whom they are speaking in a literary text. Sánchez sees subjectivity as determined by an individual's participation in many different "collectivities"—like a nation, gender, ethnic group, social class, or family—and as constructed amid powerful ideological discourses. Within this framework, she argues, we must "consider both agency and system" in reading literature, and we must realize that "identity with any particular collectivity does not automatically trigger one political position or another." In her examination of texts by Américo Paredes, Rolando Hinojosa, Arturo Islas, and Roberta Fernández Intaglio, Sánchez suggests that discourses of ethnicity, gender, class, and political affiliation are layered; she provides an analysis of the intersection of class contradiction, political domination, and gender and ethnic differences, showing that texts cannot be explained by their connection to just one collectivity. Like other writers in this section, Sánchez points to the need to articulate not just one kind of difference, but the way that multiple differences overlap and compete.

—DPH

PANDORA'S BOX

subjectivity, class, and sexuality in socialist feminist criticism

(1 9 8 5)

Feminist criticism, as its name implies, is criticism with a Cause, engaged criticism. But the critical model presented to us so far is merely engaged to be married. It is about to contract what can only be a *mésalliance* with bourgeois modes of thought and the critical categories they inform. To be effective, feminist criticism cannot become simply bourgeois criticism in drag. It must be ideological and moral criticism; it must be revolutionary.
LILLIAN ROBINSON, 'DWELLING IN DECENCIES' (1978)

The 'Marriage' of marxism and feminism has been like the marriage of husband and wife depicted in English common law: marxism and feminism are one, and that is marxism . . . we need a healthier marriage or we need a divorce.
HEIDI HARTMANN, 'THE UNHAPPY MARRIAGE
OF MARXISM AND FEMINISM' (1981)

I

In spite of the attraction of matrimonial metaphor, reports of feminist nuptials with either mild-mannered bourgeois criticism or macho mustachioed Marxism have been greatly exaggerated. Neither liberal feminist criticism decorously draped in traditional humanism, nor her red-ragged rebellious sister, socialist feminist criticism, has yet found a place within androcentric literary criticism, which wishes to embrace feminism through a legitimate public alliance. Nor can feminist criticism today be plausibly evoked as a young deb looking for protection or, even more problematically, as a male 'mole' in transvestite masquerade. Feminist criticism now marks out a broad area of literary studies, eclectic, original and provocative. Independent still, through a combination of choice and default, it has come of age without giving up its name. Yet Lillian Robinson's astute pessimistic prediction is worth remembering. With maturity, the most visible, well-defined and extensive tendency within feminist criticism has undoubtedly bought into the white, middle-class, heterosexist values of traditional literary criticism, and threatens to settle down on her own in its cultural suburbs. For, as I see it, the present danger is not that feminist criticism will enter an unequal dependent alliance with any of the varieties of male-centered criticism. It does not need to, for it has produced an all too persuasive autonomous analysis which is in many ways radical in its discussion of gender, but implicitly conservative in its assumptions about social hierarchy and female subjectivity, the Pandora's box for all feminist theory.

This reactionary effect must be interrogated and resisted from within feminism and in relation to the wider socialist feminist project. For, without the class and race perspectives which socialist feminist critics bring to the analysis both of the literary texts and of their conditions of production, liberal feminist criticism, with its emphasis on the unified female subject, will unintentionally reproduce the ideological values of mass-market romance. In that fictional landscape the other structuring relations of society fade and disappear, leaving us with the naked drama of sexual difference as the only scenario that matters. Mass-market romance tends to represent sexual difference as natural and fixed—a constant, transhistorical femininity in libidinized struggle with an equally 'given' universal masculinity. Even where class difference divides lovers, it is there as narrative backdrop or minor stumbling-block to the inevitable heterosexual resolution. Without overstraining the comparison, a feminist literary criticism which privileges gender in isolation from other forms of social determination offers us a similarly partial reading of the role played by sexual difference in literary discourse, a reading bled dry of its most troubling and contradictory meanings.

The appropriation of modern critical theory—semiotic with an emphasis on the psychoanalytic—can be of great use in arguing against concepts of natural, essential and unified identity: against a static femininity and masculinity. But these theories about the production of meaning in culture must engage fully with the effects of other systems of difference than the sexual, or they too will produce no more than an anti-humanist avant-garde version of romance. Masculinity and femininity do not appear in cultural discourse, any more than they do in mental life, as pure binary forms at play. They are always, already, ordered and broken up through other social and cultural terms, other categories of difference. Our fantasies of sexual transgression as much as our obedience to sexual regulation are expressed through these structuring hierarchies. Class and race ideologies are, conversely, steeped in and spoken through the language of sexual differentiation. Class and race meanings are not metaphors for the sexual, or vice versa. It is better though not exact, to see them as reciprocally constituting each other through a kind of narrative invocation, a set of associative terms in a chain of meaning. To understand how gender and class—to take two categories only—are articulated together transforms our analysis of each of them.

The literary text too often figures in feminist criticism as a gripping spectacle in which sexual difference appears somewhat abstracted from the muddy social world in which it is elsewhere embedded. Yet novels, poetry and drama are, on the contrary, peculiarly rich discourses in which the fused languages of class, race and gender are both produced and re-represented through the incorporation of other discourses. The focus of feminist analysis ought to be on that heterogeneity within the literary, on the intimate relation there expressed between all the categories that order social and psychic meaning. This does not imply an attention to content only or primarily, but also entails a consideration of the linguistic processes of the text as they construct and position subjectivity within these terms.

For without doubt literary texts do centre the individual as object and subject of their discourse. Literature has been a traditional space for the exploration of gender relations and sexual difference, and one in which women themselves have been formidably present. The problem for socialist feminists is not the focus on the individual that is special to the literary, but rather the romantic theory of the subject so firmly entrenched within the discourse. Humanist feminist criticism does not object to the idea of an immanent, transcendent subject but only to the exclusion of women from these definitions which it takes as an accurate account of subjectivity rather than as a historically constructed ideology. The repair and reconstitution of female subjectivity through a rereading of literature becomes, therefore, a major part, often unacknowledged, of its critical project. Psychoanalytic and semiotically oriented feminist criticism has argued well against this aspect of feminist humanism, emphasizing the important structural relation between writing and sexuality in the construction of the subject. But both tendencies have been correctly criticized from a socialist feminist position for the neglect of class and race as factors in their analysis. If feminist criticism is to make a central contribution to the understanding of sexual difference, instead of serving as a conservative refuge from its more disturbing social and psychic implications, the inclusion of class and race must transform its terms and objectives.

II

The critique of feminist humanism needs more historical explication than it has so far received. Its sources are complex, and are rooted in that moment almost 200 years ago when modern feminism and Romantic cultural theory emerged as separate but linked responses to the transforming events of the French Revolution. In the heat and light of the revolutionary decade 1790–1800, social, political and aesthetic ideas already maturing underwent a kind of forced ripening. As the progressive British intelligentsia contemplated the immediate possibility of social change, their thoughts turned urgently to the present capacity of subjects to exercise republican freedoms—to rule themselves as well as each other if the corrupt structures of aristocratic privilege were to be suddenly razed. Both feminism as set out in its most influential text, Mary Wollstonecraft's *A Vindication of the Rights of Woman* (1792), and Romanticism as argued most forcefully in Wordsworth's introduction to *Lyrical Ballads* (1800) stood in intimate, dynamic and contradictory relationship to democratic politcs. In all three discourses the social and psychic character of the individual was centred and elaborated. The public and private implications of sexual difference as well as of the imagination and its products were both strongly linked to the optimistic, speculative construction of a virtuous citizen subject for a brave new egalitarian world. Theories of reading and writing—Wollstonecraft's and Jane Austen's as well as those of male Romantic authors—were explicitly related to contemporary politics as expressed in debate by such figures as Tom Paine, Edmund Burke and William Godwin.

The new categories of independent subjectivity, however, were marked from the beginning by exclusions of gender, race and class. Jean-Jacques Rousseau, writing in the 1750s, specifically exempted women for his definition; Thomas Jefferson, some twenty years later, excluded blacks. Far from being invisible ideological aspects of the new subject, these exclusions occasioned debate and polemic on both sides of the Atlantic. The autonomy of inner life, the dynamic psyche whose moral triumph was to be the foundation of republican government, was considered absolutely essential as an element of progressive political thought.

However, as the concept of the inner self and the moral psyche was used to denigrate whole classes, races and genders, late-nineteenth-century socialism began to de-emphasize the political importance of the psychic self, and redefine political morality and the adequate citizen subject in primarily social terms. Because of this shift in emphasis, a collective moralism has developed in socialist thought which, instead of criticizing the reactionary interpretation of psychic life, stigmatizes sensibility itself, interpreting the excess of feeling as regressive, bourgeois and non-political.

Needless to say, this strand of socialist thought poses a problem for feminism, which has favoured three main strategies to deal with it. In the first, women's psychic life is seen as being essentially identical to men's, but distorted through vicious and systematic patriarchal inscription. In this view, which is effectively Wollstonecraft's, social reform would prevent women from becoming regressively obsessed with sexuality and feeling. The second strategy wholly vindicates women's psyche, but sees it as quite separate from men's, often in direct opposition. This is frequently the terrain on which radical feminism defends female sexuality as independent and virtuous between women, but degrading in a heterosexual context. It is certainly a radical reworking of essentialist sexual ideology, shifting the ground from glib assertions of gender complementarity to the logic of separatism. The third strategy has been to refuse the issue's relevance altogether—to see any focus on psychic difference as itself an ideological one.

Instead of choosing any one of these options, socialist feminist criticism must come to grips with the relationship between female subjectivity and class identity. This project, even in its present early stages, poses major problems for the tendency. While socialist feminists have been deeply concerned with the social construction of femininity and sexual difference, they have been uneasy about integrating social and political determinations with an analysis of the psychic ordering of gender. Within socialist feminism, a fierce and unresolved debate continues about the value of using psychoanalytic theory, because of the supposedly ahistorical character of its paradigms. For those who are hostile to psychoanalysis, the meaning of mental life, fantasy and desire—those obsessive themes of the novel and poetry for the last two centuries—seems particularly intractable to interpretation. They are reluctant to grant much autonomy to the psychic level, and often most attentive to feeling expressed in the work of non-bourgeois writers, which can more easily be read as political statement. Socialist feminism still finds unlocated, unsocialized psychic expression in women's writing hard to discuss in non-moralizing terms.

On the other hand, for liberal humanism, feminist versions included, the possibility of a unified self and an integrated consciousness that can transcend material circumstance is represented as the fulfilment of desire, the happy closure at the end of the story. The psychic fragmentation expressed through female characters in women's writing is seen as the most important sign of their sexual

subordination, more interesting and ultimately more meaningful than their social oppression. As a result, the struggle for an integrated female subjectivity in
nineteenth-century texts is never interrogated as ideology or fantasy, but seen as
a demand that can actually be met, if not in 1848, then later.

In contrast, socialist feminist criticism tends to foreground the social and economic elements of the narrative and socialize what it can of its psychic portions.
Women's anger and anguish, it is assumed, should be amenable to repair through
social change. A positive emphasis on the psychic level is viewed as a valorization of the anarchic and regressive, a way of returning women to their subordinate ideological place within the dominant culture, as unreasoning social beings.
Psychoanalytic theory, which is by and large morally neutral about the desires expressed by the psyche, is criticized as a confirmation and justification of them.

Thus semiotic or psychoanalytic perspectives have yet to be integrated with
social, economic and political analysis. Critics tend to privilege one element or
the other, even when they acknowledge the importance of both and the need to
relate them. A comparison of two admirable recent essays on Charlotte Brontë's
Villette, one by Mary Jacobus and the other by Judith Lowder Newton, both informed by socialist feminist concerns, can illustrate this difficulty.

Jacobus uses the psychoanalytic and linguistic theory of Jacques Lacan to explore the split representations of subjectivity that haunt *Villette*, and calls attention to its anti-realist gothic elements. She relates Brontë's feminized defence of
the imagination, and the novel's unreliable narrator-heroine, to the tension between femininity and feminism that reaches back to the eighteenth-century debates of Rousseau and Wollstonecraft. Reading the ruptures and gaps of the text
as a psychic narrative, she also places it historically in relationship to nineteenth-
century social and political ideas. Yet the social meanings of *Villette* fade and all
but disappear before 'the powerful presence of fantasy,' which 'energizes *Villette*
and satisfies that part of the reader which also desires constantly to reject reality
for the sake of an obedient, controllable, narcissistically pleasurable image of self
and its relation to the world' (Jacobus 1979, p. 51). In Jacobus's interpretation,
the psyche, desire and fantasy stand for repressed, largely positive elements of a
forgotten feminism, while the social stands for a daytime world of Victorian social regulation. These social meanings are referred to rather than explored in the
essay, a strategy which renders them both static and unproblematically unified.
It is as if, in order to examine how *Villette* represents psychic reality, the dynamism of social discourses of gender and identity must be repressed, forming the
text's new 'unconscious.'

Judith Lowder Newton's chapter on *Villette* in her impressive study of nineteenth-
century British fiction, *Women, Power, and Subversion* (1981), is also concerned with
conflicts between the novel's feminism and its evocation of female desire. Her
interpretation privileges the social meanings of the novel, its search for a possible
détente between the dominant ideologies of bourgeois femininity and progressive
definitions of female autonomy. For Newton, 'the internalized ideology of
women's sphere' includes sexual and romantic longings—which for Jacobus are
potentially radical and disruptive of mid-Victorian gender ideologies. The psychic level as Newton describes it is mainly the repository for the worst and most
regressive elements of female subjectivity: longing for love, dependency, the material and emotional comfort of fixed class identity. These desires which have 'got

inside' are predictably in conflict with the rebellious, autonomy-seeking feminist impulses, whose source is a rational understanding of class and gender subordination. Her reading centres on the realist text, locating meaning in its critique of class society and the constraints of bourgeois femininity.

The quotations and narrative elements cited and explored by Jacobus and Newton are so different that even a reader familiar with *Villette* may find it hard to believe that each critic is reading the same text. The psychic level exists in Newton's interpretation, to be sure, but as a negative discourse, the dead weight of ideology on the mind. For her, the words 'hidden,' 'private' and 'longing' are stigmatized, just as they are celebrated by Jacobus. For both critics, female subjectivity is the site where the opposing forces of femininity and feminism clash by night, but they locate these elements in different parts of the text's divided selves. Neither Newton nor Jacobus argues for the utopian possibility of a unified subjectivity. But the *longing* to close the splits that characterize femininity—splits between reason and desire, autonomy and dependent security, psychic and social identity—is evident in the way each critic denies the opposing element.

III

My comments on the difficulties of reading *Villette* from a materialist feminist stance are meant to suggest that there is more at issue in the polarization of social and psychic explanation than the problem of articulating two different forms of explanation. Moral and political questions specific to feminism are at stake as well. In order to understand why female subjectivity is so fraught with *Angst* and difficulty for feminism, we must go back to the first full discussion of the psychological expression of femininity, in Mary Wollstonecraft's *A Vindication of the Rights of Woman*. The briefest look will show that an interest in the psychic life of women as a crucial element in their subordination and liberation is not a modern post-Freudian preoccupation. On the contrary, its long and fascinating history in 'left' feminist writing starts with Wollstonecraft, who set the terms for a debate that is still in progress. Her writing is central for socialist feminism today, because she based her interest in the emancipation of women as individuals in revolutionary politics.

Like so many eighteenth-century revolutionaries, she saw her own class, the rising bourgeoise, as the vanguard of the revolution, and it was to the women of her own class that she directed her arguments. Her explicit focus on the middle class, and her concentration on the nature of female subjectivity, speaks directly to the source of anxiety within socialist feminism today. For it is at the point when women are released from profound social and economic oppression into greater autonomy and potential political choice that their social and psychic expression becomes an issue, and their literary texts become sites of ambivalence. In their pages, for the last 200 years and more, women characters seemingly more confined by social regulation than women readers today speak as desiring subjects. These texts express the politically 'retrogade' desires for comfort, dependence and love as well as more acceptable demands for autonomy and independence.

It is Mary Wollstonecraft who first offered women this fateful choice between the opposed and moralized bastions of reason and feeling, which continues to determine much feminist thinking. The structures through which she developed her ideas, however, were set for her by her mentor Jean-Jacques Rousseau, whose writing influenced the political and social perspectives of many eighteenth-century English radicals. His ideas were fundamental to her thinking about gender as well as about revolutionary politics. In 1792, that highly charged moment of romantic political optimism between the fall of the Bastille and the Terror when *A Vindication* was written, it must have seemed crucial that Rousseau's crippling judgement of female nature be refuted. How else could women freely and equally participate in the new world being made across the Channel? Rousseau's ideas about subjectivity were already immanent in Wollstonecraft's earlier book *Mary: A Fiction* (1788). Now she set out to challenge directly his offensive description of sexual difference which would leave women in post-revolutionary society exactly where they were in unreformed Britain, 'immured in their families, groping in the dark' (Wollstonecraft 1975a, p. 5).

Rousseau had set the terms of the debate in his *Emile* (1762), which describes the growth and education of the new man, progressive and bourgeois, who would be capable of exercising the republican freedoms of a reformed society. In Book V, Rousseau invents 'Sophie' as a mate for his eponymous hero, and here he outlines his theory of sexual asymmetry as it occurs in nature. In all human beings passion was natural and necessary, but in women it was not controlled by reason, an attribute of the male sex only. Women, therefore,

> must be subject all their lives, to the most constant and severe restraint, which is that of decorum; it is therefore necessary to accustom them early to such confinement that it may not afterwards cost them too dear. . . . we should teach them above all things to lay a due restraint on themselves. (Rousseau 1974, p. 332)

To justify this restraint, Rousseau allowed enormous symbolic power to the supposed anarchic, destructive force of untrammelled female desire. As objects of desire Rousseau made women alone responsible for male 'suffering.' If they were free agents of desire, there would be no end to the 'evils' they could cause. Therefore the family, and women's maternal role within it, were, he said, basic to the structure of the new society. Betrayal of the family was thus as subversive as betrayal of the state; adultery in *Emile* is literally equated with treason. Furthermore, in Rousseau's regime of regulation and restraint for bourgeois women, their 'decorum'—the social expression of modesty—would act as an additional safeguard against unbridled, excessive male lust, should its natural guardian, reason, fail. In proscribing the free exercise of female desire, Rousseau disarms a supposed serious threat to the new political as well as social order. To read the fate of a class through the sexual behaviour of its women was not a new political strategy. What is modern in Rousseau's formulation is the harnessing of these sexual ideologies to the fate of a new progressive bourgeoisie, whose individual male members were endowed with radical, autonomous identity.

In many ways, Mary Wollstonecraft, writing thirty years after *Emile*, shared with many others the political vision of her master. Her immediate contemporary Thomas Paine thought Rousseau's work expressed 'a loveliness of sentiment in favour of liberty,' and it is in the spirit of Rousseau's celebration of liberty that Wollstonecraft wrote *A Vindication*. Her strategy was to accept Rousseau's description of adult women as suffused in sensuality, but to ascribe this unhappy state of things to culture rather than nature. It was, she thought, the vicious and damaging result of Rousseau's punitive theories of sexual difference and female education when put into practice. Excessive sensuality was for Wollstonecraft, in 1792 at least, as dangerous if not more so than Rousseau had suggested, but she saw the damage and danger first of all to women themselves, whose potential and independence were initially stifled and broken by an apprenticeship to pleasure, which induced psychic and social dependency. Because Wollstonecraft saw prepubescent children in their natural state as mentally and emotionally unsexed as well as untainted by corrupting desire, she bitterly refuted Rousseau's description of innate infantile female sexuality. Rather, the debased femininity she describes is constructed through a set of social practices which by constant reinforcement become internalized parts of the self. Her description of this process is acute:

> Every thing they see or hear serves to fix impressions, call forth emotions, and associate ideas, that give a sexual character to the mind. . . . This cruel association of ideas, which every thing conspires to twist into all their habits of thinking, or, to speak with more precision of feeling, receives new force when they begin to act a little for themselves. (Wollstonecraft 1975a, p. 177)

For Wollstonecraft, female desire was a contagion caught from the projection of male lust, an ensnaring and enslaving infection that made women into dependent and degenerate creatures, who nevertheless had the illusion that they acted independently. An education which changed women from potentially rational autonomous beings into 'significant objects of desire' was, moreover, rarely reversible. Once a corrupt subjectivity was constructed, only a most extraordinary individual could transform it, for 'so ductile is the understanding and yet so stubborn, that the association which depends on adventitious circumstances, during the period that the body takes to arrive at maturity, can seldom be disentangled by reason' (p. 116).

What is disturbingly peculiar to *A Vindication* is the undifferentiated and central place that sexuality as passion plays in the corruption and degradation of the female self. The overlapping Enlightenment and Romantic discourses on psychic economy all posed a major division between the rational and the irrational, between sense and sensibility. But they hold sensibility *in men* to be only in part an antisocial sexual drive. Lust for power and the propensity to physical violence were also, for men, negative components of all that lay on the other side of reason. Thus sensibility in men included a strong positive element too, for the power of the imagination depended on it, and in the 1790s the Romantic aesthetic and the political imagination were closely allied. Sexual passion controlled and mediated by reason, Wordsworth's 'emotion recollected in tranquility,' could also be put to productive use in art—by men. The appropriate egalitarian subjects of Wordsworth's art were 'moral sentiments and animal sensations' as they appeared in everyday life (Wordsworth and Coleridge 1971, p. 261). No woman of the time could offer such an artistic manifesto. In women the irrational, the sensible, even the imaginative are all drenched in an overpowering and subordinating sexuality. And in Wollstonecraft's writing, especially in her last, unfinished novel *Maria, or the Wrongs of Woman* (1798), which is considerably less punitive about women's sexuality in general than *A Vindication*, only maternal feeling survives as a positively realized element of the passionate side of the psyche. By defending women against Rousseau's denial of their reason, Wollstonecraft unwittingly assents to his negative, eroticized sketch of their emotional lives. At various points in *A Vindication* she interjects a wish that 'after some future revolution in time' women might be able to live out a less narcissistic and harmful sexuality. Until then they must demand an education whose central task is to cultivate their neglected 'understanding.'

It is interesting and somewhat tragic that Wollstonecraft's paradigm of women's psychic economy still profoundly shapes modern feminist consciousness. How often are the maternal, romantic-sexual and intellectual capacity of women presented by feminism as in competition for a fixed psychic space. Men seem to have a roomier and more accommodating psychic home, one which can, as Wordsworth and other Romantics insisted, situate all the varieties of passion and reason in creative tension. This gendered eighteenth-century psychic economy has been out of date for a long time, but its ideological inscription still shadows feminist attitudes towards the mental life of women.

The implications of eighteenth-century theories of subjectivity were important for early feminist ideas about women as readers and writers. In the final pages of *A Vindication*, decrying female sentimentality as one more effect of women's psychic degradation, Wollstonecraft criticizes the sentimental fictions increasingly written by and for women, which were often their only education. 'Novels' encouraged in their mainly young, mainly female audience 'a romantic twist of the mind.' Readers would 'only be taught to look for happiness in love, refine on sensual feelings and adopt metaphysical notions respecting that passion.' At their very worst the 'stale tales' and 'meretricious scenes' would by degrees induce more than passive fantasy. The captive, addicted reader might, while the balance of her mind was disturbed by these erotic evocations, turn fiction into fact and 'plump into actual vice' (p. 183). A reciprocal relationship between the patriarchal socialization of women and the literature that supports and incites them to become 'rakes at heart' is developed in this passage. While Wollstonecraft adds that she would rather women read novels than nothing at all, she sets up a peculiarly gendered and sexualized interaction between women and the narrative imaginative text, one in which women become the ultimately receptive readers easily moved into amoral activity by the fictional representation of sexual intrigue.

The political resonance of these questions about reader response was, at the time, highly charged. An enormous expansion of literacy in general, and of the middle-class reading public in particular, swelled by literate women, made the act of reading in the last quarter of the eighteenth century an important practice through which the common sense and innate virtue of a society of autonomous subject-citizens could be reached and moulded. An uncensored press, cheap and available reading matter and a reading public free to engage with the flood of popular literature, from political broadsheets to sensational fiction, was part of the agenda and strategy of British republicanism. 'It is dangerous,' Tom Paine warned the government in the mid-1790s after his own writing had been politically censored, 'to tell a whole people that they should not read.' Reading was a civil right that supported and illustrated the radical vision of personal independence. Political and sexual conservatives, Jane Austen and Hannah More, as well as the republican and feminist left, saw reading as an active, not a passive function of the self, a critical link between the psychic play of reason and passion and its social expression. New social categories of readers, women of all classes, skilled and unskilled working-class males, are described in this period by contemporaries. Depending on their political sympathies, observers saw these actively literate groups as an optimistic symptom of social and intellectual progress or a dire warning of imminent social decay and threatened rebellion.

Wollstonecraft saw sentiment and the sensual as reinforcing an already dominant, approved and enslaving sexual norm, which led women to choose a subordinate social and subjective place in culture. The damage done by 'vice' and 'adultery,' to which sentimental fiction was an incitement, was a blow to women first and to society second. Slavish legitimate sexuality was almost as bad for women in Wollstonecraft's view as unlicensed behaviour. A more liberal regime for women was both the goal and the cure of sentimental and erotic malaise. In *A Vindication* women's subjection is repeatedly compared to all illegitimate hierarchies of power, but especially to existing aristocratic hegemony. At every possible point in her text, Wollstonecraft links the liberation of women from the sensual into the rational literally and symbolically to the egalitarian transformation of the whole society.

'Passionlessness,' as Nancy Cott has suggested (Cott 1978), was a strategy adopted both by feminists and by social conservatives. Through the assertion that women were not innately or excessively sexual, that on the contrary their 'feelings' were largely filial and maternal, the imputation of a degraded subjectivity could be resisted. This alternative psychic organization was represented as both strength and weakness in nineteenth-century debates about sexual difference. In these debates, which were conducted across a wide range of public discourses, the absence of an independent, self-generating female sexuality is used by some men and women to argue for women's right to participate equally in an undifferentiated public sphere. It is used by others to argue for the power and value of the separate sphere allotted to women. And it is used more nakedly to support cruder justifications of patriarchal right. The idea of passionlessness as either a natural or a cultural effect acquires no simple ascendancy in Victorian sexual ideology, even as applied to the ruling bourgeoisie.

As either conservative or radical sexual ideology, asexual femininity was a fragile, unstable concept. It was constructed through a permanently threatened transgression, which fictional narrative obsessively documented and punished. It is a gross historical error to infer from the regulatory sexual discourses in the novel the actual 'fate' of Victorian adulteresses, for novels operated through a set of highly punitive conventions in relation to female sexuality that almost certainly did not correspond to lived social relations. However, novels do call attention to the difficulty of fixing such a sexual ideology, precisely because they construct a world in which there is no alternative to it.

IV

One of the central weaknesses of humanist criticism is that it accepts the idea advanced by classical realism that the function of literature is mimetic or realistic representation. The humanist critic identifies with the author's claim that the text represents reality, and acts as a sympathetic reader who will test the authenticity of the claim through the evidence of the text. The Marxist critic, on the other hand, assumes that author and text speak from a position within ideology—that claims about fictional truth and authenticity are, in themselves, to be understood in relation to a particular historical view of culture and art which evolved in the Romantic period. Semiotic and psychoanalytic theories of representation go even further in rejecting the possibility of authentic mimetic art. They see the literary text as a system of signs that constructs meaning rather than reflecting it, inscribing simultaneously the subjectivity of speaker and reader. Fiction by bourgeois women writers is spoken from the position of a class-specific femininity. It constructs us as readers in relation to that subjectivity through the linguistic strategies and processes of the text. It also takes us on a tour, so to speak, of a waxworks of other subjects-in-process—the characters of the text. These fictional characters are there as figures in a dream, as constituent structures of the narrative of the dreamer, not as correct reflections of the socially real.

It is hard for feminism to accept the implications of this virtual refusal of textual realism, if only because literature was one of the few public discourses in which women were allowed to speak themselves, where they were not the imaginary representations of men. None the less, the subjectivity of women of other classes and races and with different sexual orientations can never be 'objectively' or 'authentically' represented in literary texts by the white, heterosexual, middle-class woman writer, however sympathetically she invents or describes such women in her narrative. The nature of fiction and the eccentric relation of female subjectivity itself both to culture and to psychic identity, as understood from a psychoanalytic perspective, defeats that aim. We can, however, learn a great deal from women's writing about the cultural meanings produced from the splitting of women's subjectivity, especially her sexuality, into class and race categories. But before we say more about this way of reading women's writing we need a more precise working definition of 'class.'

Unlike subjectivity, 'class' has been a central category for socialist feminist criticism, but remains somewhat inert within it, if not within socialist feminist theory as a whole. Socialist critics hesitate to identify their own object of study, the literary text, as a central productive site of class meaning, because it seems too far away from 'real' economic and political determinations. The same worry, conversely, can induce a compensatory claim that *all* the material relations of class can be discovered within the discourse: indeed, that they are most fully represented there, because language is itself material. These positions, which I confess I have parodied a little, remain unresolved in current debate, although efforts at *détente* have been made. They indicate the uneasy relationship between the political and the literary in the Marxist critical project, an unease shared by socialist feminists too.

Among socialist historians in the last few years the understanding of the history of class has undergone vigorous reappraisal in response to debates about the changing composition and politics of the working class in modern capitalist societies. In a recent collection of essays, *The Languages of Class*, the British historian of the nineteenth century Gareth Stedman Jones proposes some radical approaches to that history which have an immediate relevance for the analysis of representation. First of all, Stedman Jones asks for a more informed and theoretical attention by historians to the linguistic construction of class. '"Class" is a word embedded in language and should be analysed in terms of its linguistic content,' he states. In the second place, 'class' as a concept needs to be unpacked, and its differential construction in discourse recognized and given a certain autonomy:

> because there are different languages of class, one should not proceed upon the assumption that 'class' as an elementary counter of official social description, 'class' as an effect of theoretical discourse about distribution or productive relations, 'class' as the summary of a cluster of culturally signifying practices or 'class' as a species of political or ideological self-definition, share a single reference point in anterior social reality. (Stedman Jones 1983, pp. 7–8)

While 'anterior social reality' hangs slightly loose in this formulation, the oppressively unitary character of class as a concept is usefully broken down. Class can be seen as defined in different terms at different levels of analysis, as well as being 'made' and 'lived' through a variety of languages at any given point in history.

How can this pulling apart of the languages of class help socialist feminist critics to put class and gender, social and psychic together in a non-reductive way? First of all, these distinctions put a useful space between the economic overview of class—the Marxist or socialist analysis—and the actual rhetoric of class as it appears in a novel. The class language of a nineteenth-century novel is not only or even primarily characterized by reference to the material circumstances of the protagonists, though that may be part of its representation there. The language of class in the novel foregrounds the language of the self, the inner discourse of the subject *as* class language, framing that discourse through the dissonant chorus of class voices that it appropriates and invents. In the novel, class discourse *is* gendered discourse; the positions of 'Emile' and 'Sophie' are given dramatic form. Class is embodied in fiction in a way that it never is either in bourgeois economic discourse or in Marxist economic analysis. In those discourses of class, gender is mystified, presented in ideological form. In fiction, though difference may be presented through sexual ideologies, its immanent, crucial presence in the social relations of class, as well as its psychic effects, is strongly asserted. Fiction refuses the notion of a genderless class subjectivity, and resists any simple reduction of class meaning and class identity to productive forces. This refusal and resistance cannot be written off, or reduced to the humanist ideologies of transcendence which those fictions may also enunciate, for the presence of gendered subjectivity in nineteenth-century fiction is always 'in struggle' with the Romantic ideologies of unified identity.

Within socialist feminist cultural analysis it has been easier to describe the visual or linguistic fusion of class and gender meanings in representation than it has been to assess the role such fusion plays in the construction of either category. Let us assume that in these signifying practices class is powerfully defined through sexual difference, and vice versa, and that these representations are constitutive of certain class meanings, not merely a distorted or mendacious reflection of other languages. 'Class' needs to be read through an ensemble of these languages, often contradictory, as well as in terms of an economic overview. The overpowering presence of gender in some languages of class and its virtual absence in others needs to be related not to a single anterior definition of class reality, but to the heterogeneous and contradictory nature of that reality.

Literature is itself a heterogeneous discourse, which appropriates, contextualizes and comments on other 'languages' of class and gender. This process of intertextuality—the dialogic, as the Russian critic Bakhtin called it (Bakhtin 1981)—undermines the aspirations of the text towards a unifying definition. The language of class in the nineteenth-century novel obsessively inscribes a class system whose divisions and boundaries are at once absolute and impregnable and in constant danger of dissolution. Often in these narratives it is a woman whose class identity is at risk or problematic; the woman and her sexuality are a condensed and displaced representation of the dangerous instabilities of class and gender identity for both sexes. The loss and recuperation of female identity within the story—a favourite lost-and-found theme from *Mansfield Park* to *Tess*—provides an imaginary though temporary solution to the crisis of both femininity and class. Neither category—class or gender—was ever as stable as the ideologies that support them must continually insist. The many-layered, compacted representations of class and gender found in imaginative literature are not generic metaphors, peculiar to fiction, drama and poetry, though in them they are given great scope. They occur in many other nineteenth-century discourses—metonymic, associative tropes which are linked by incomparable similarities, through a threat to identity and status that inheres to both sets of hierarchies, both structures of difference.

The class subjectivity of women and their sexual identity thus became welded together in nineteenth-century discourses and took on new and sinister dimensions of meaning. Ruling groups had traditionally used the sexual and domestic virtue of their women as a way of valorizing their moral authority. By focusing on the issue and image of female sexual conduct, questions about the economic and political integrity of dominant groups could be displaced. When the citizen subject became the crucial integer of political discourse and practice, this type of symbolization, which was always 'about' sexual difference as well as 'about' the political, took on new substantive, material meaning. The moral autonomy of individuals and the moral behaviour of social groups now converged in a political practice and theory—liberal, constitutional and legitimated through an expanding franchise—in which the individual voter was the common denominator of the political. Women, as we have seen, were explicitly excluded from these political practices, but, as we have also seen, attempts to naturalize that exclusion were never wholly successful. Feminism inserted itself into the debate just at the point where theories of innate difference attempted to deny women access to a full political identity. The debate about women's mental life signalled, as I have suggested, a more general anxiety about non-rational, unsocial behaviour. Female subjectivity, or its synecdotal reference, female sexuality, became the displaced and condensed site for the general anxiety about individual behaviour which republican and liberal political philosophy stirred up. It is not too surprising that the morality of the class as a whole was better represented by those who exercised the least political power within it, or that the punishment for female sexual transgression was fictionally represented as the *immediate* loss of social status.

The ways in which class is lived by men and women, like the ways in which sexual difference is lived, are only partly open to voluntary, self-conscious political negotiation. The unconscious processes that construct subjective identity are also the structures through which class is lived and understood, through which political subjection and rebellion are organized. Arguing for the usefulness of psychoanalysis in historical analysis, Sally Alexander emphasizes that its theories do not imply a universal human nature. Rather,

> Subjectivity in this account is neither universal or ahistorical. First structured through relations of absence and loss, pleasure and unpleasure, difference and division, these are simultaneous with the social naming and placing among kin, community, school, class which are always historically specific. (Alexander 1984, p. 134)

Literary texts give these simultaneous inscriptions narrative form, pointing towards and opening up the fragmentary nature of social and psychic identity, drawing out the ways in which social meaning is psychically represented. It is this symbolic shaping of class that we should examine in fiction. Literary texts tell us more about the intersection of class and gender than we can learn from duly noting the material circumstances and social constraints of characters and authors.

However mimetic or realistic the aspirations of fiction, it always tells us less about the purely social rituals of a class society organized around the sexual division of labour than about the powerful symbolic force of class and gender in ordering our social and political imagination. The doubled inscription of sexual and social difference is the most common, characteristic trope of nineteenth-century fictions. In these texts, the difference between women is at least as important an element as the difference between the sexes, as a way of representing both class and gender. This salient fact often goes unnoticed in the emphasis of bourgeois criticism on male/female division and opposition. In turn, this emphasis on heterosexual antagonisms and resolutions effaces the punitive construction of alternative femininities in women's writing. If texts by women reveal a 'hidden' sympathy between women, as radical feminist critics often assert, they equally express positive femininity through hostile and denigrating representations of women. Imperilled bourgeois femininity takes meaning in relation to other female identities, and to the feminized identities of other social groups which the novel constructs and dialogizes. The unfavourable symbiosis of reason and passion ascribed to women is also used to characterize both men and women in the labouring classes and in other races and cultures. The line between the primitive and the degraded feminine is a thin one, habitually elided in dominant discourse and practically used to limit the civil and political rights of all three subordinated categories: blacks, women and the working class.

Through that chain of colonial associations, whole cultures became 'feminized,' 'blackened' and 'impoverished'—each denigrating construction implying and invoking the others. 'True womanhood' had to be protected from this threatened linguistic contamination, not only from the debased subjectivity and dangerous sexuality of the lower-class prostitute, but from all other similarly inscribed subordinate subjectivities. The difference between men and women in the ruling class had to be written so that a slippage into categories reserved for lesser humanities could be averted. These fragmented definitions of female subjectivity were not only a mode through which the moral virtue of the ruling class was represented in the sexual character of its women; they also shaped, and were shaped by, the ways in which women of the middle and upper classes understood and represented their own being. It led them towards projecting and displacing on to women of lower social standing and women of colour, as well as on to the 'traditionally' corrupt aristocracy, all that was deemed vicious and regressive in women as a sex.

It is deeply troubling to find these projected and displaced representations in the writing of sexual and social radicals, and in the work of feminists from Wollstonecraft to Woolf, as well as in conservative sexual and social discourses. They are especially marked in those texts and writers who accept in whole or in part the description of mental life and libidinal economy of the Enlightenment and the moral value attached to it. In *A Vindication*, working-class women are quite unself-consciously constructed as prostitutes and dirty-minded servants corrupting bourgeois innocence. Turn the page over and you will also find them positioned in a more radical sense as the most brutalized victims of aristocratic and patriarchal despotism. Note the bestial descriptions of the female poor in Elizabeth Barrett Browning's *Aurora Leigh*. Remember the unhappy, ambivalent and contradictory relationship to black subjectivity, male and female, of many mid-nineteenth-century American feminists and abolitionists. Most distressing of all, because nearer to us in time, think about the contrast between Woolf's public polemical support of working-class women and the contempt with which the feelings and interests of her female servants are treated in her diaries, where they exist as lesser beings. These representations are neither natural nor inevitable. They are the historic effects of determinate social divisions and ideologies worked through psychic structures, worked into sexual and social identity. If they are understood they can be changed.

In Ann Radcliffe's *Mysteries of Udolpho*, one of the most popular of the Enlightenment gothic novels of the 1790s, the heroine, Emily, flees from the sinister importunities of her titled foreign host. The scene is rural Italy, as far away as possible from genteel British society. Emily's flight from the castle is precipitous, and in her terror and haste she forgets her hat. Within the world of the text, Emily's bare head threatens her identity as pure woman, as surely as do the violent, lascivious attentions of her pursuer. Both the narrative and her flight are interrupted while Emily restores her identity by purchasing 'a little straw hat' from a peasant girl. A woman without a hat was, in specular terms, a whore; the contemporary readership understood the necessary pause in the story. They understood too that the hat, passed from peasant to lady, securing the class and sexual status of the latter, was not only a fragment of domestic realism set against gothic fantasy. Hat and flight are part of a perfectly coherent psychic narrative in which aristocratic seducer, innocent bourgeois victim, peasant girl and straw hat play out the linked meanings of class and sexuality.

Stories of seduction and betrayal, of orphaned, impoverished heroines of uncertain class origin, provided a narrative structure through which the instabilities of class and gender categories were both stabilized and undermined. Across the body and mind of 'woman' as sign, through her multiple representations, bourgeois anxiety about identity is traced and retraced. A favourite plot, of which *Jane*

Eyre is now the best-known example, sets the genteel heroine at sexual risk as semi-servant in a grand patriarchal household. This narrative theme allowed the crisis of middle-class femininity to be mapped on to the structural sexual vulnerability of all working-class servants in bourgeois employment. Such dramas were full of condensed meanings in excess of the representation of sexuality and sexual difference. A doubled scenario, in which the ideological and material difference between working-class and bourgeois women is blurred through condensation, it was popular as a plot for melodrama with both 'genteel' and 'vulgar' audiences.

We do not know very much so far about how that fictional narrative of threatened femininity was understood by working-class women, although it appeared in the cheap fiction written for servant girls as well as in popular theatre. Nineteenth-century bourgeois novels like *Jane Eyre* tell us almost nothing about the self-defined subjectivity of the poor, male or female. For, although they are both rich sources for the construction of dominant definitions *of* the inner lives of the working classes, they cannot tell us anything about how even these ideological inscriptions were lived *by* them. For an analysis of the subjectivity of working-class women we need to turn to non-literary sources, to the discourses in which they themselves spoke. That analysis lies outside the project of this paper but is, of course, related to it.

I want to end this chapter with an example of the kind of interpretative integration that I have been demanding of feminist critics. No text has proved more productive of meaning from the critic's point of view than Charlotte Brontë's *Jane Eyre*. I have referred to the condensation of class meanings through the characterization and narrative of its heroine, but now I want to turn to that disturbing didactic moment in volume 1, chapter 12, which immediately precedes the entry of Rochester into the text. It is a passage marked out by Virginia Woolf in *A Room of One's Own*, where it is used to illustrate the negative effect of anger and inequality on the female literary imagination. Prefaced defensively—'Anybody may blame me who likes'—it is a passage about need, demand and desire that exceed social possibility and challenge social prejudice. In Jane's soliloquy, inspired by a view reached through raising the 'trap-door of the attic,' the Romantic aesthetic is reasserted for women, together with a passionate refusal of the terms of feminine difference. Moved by a 'restlessness' in her 'nature' that 'agitated me to pain sometimes,' Jane paces the top floor of Thornfield and allows her 'mind's eye to dwell on whatever bright visions rose before it':

> to let my heart be heaved by the exultant movement which, while it swelled it in trouble, expanded it with life; and, best of all, to open my inward ear to a tale that was never ended—a tale my imagination created, and narrated continuously; quickened with all of incident, life, fire, feeling, that I desired and had not in my actual existence. (Brontë 1976, p. 110)

This reverie is only partly quoted by Woolf, who omits the 'visionary' section, moving straight from 'pain . . . ' to the paragraph most familiar to us through her citation of it:

> It is in vain to say that human beings ought to be satisfied with tranquillity; they must have action; and they will make it if they cannot find it. Millions are condemned to a stiller doom than mine, and millions are in silent revolt

against their lot. Nobody knows how many rebellions besides political rebellions ferment in the masses of life which people earth. Women are supposed to be very calm generally: but women feel just as men feel; they need exercise for their faculties, and a field for their efforts as much as their brothers do; they suffer from too rigid a restraint, too absolute a stagnation, precisely as men would suffer; and it is narrow-minded in their more privileged fellow-creatures to say that they ought to confine themselves to making puddings and knitting stockings, to playing on the piano and embroidering bags. It is thoughtless to condemn them, or laugh at them, if they seek to do more or learn more than custom has pronounced necessary for their sex.

When thus alone I not unfrequently heard Grace Poole's laugh. . . .

This shift from feminist polemic to the laugh of Grace Poole is the 'jerk,' the 'awkward break' of 'continuity' that Woolf criticizes. The writer of such a flawed passage

will never get her genius expressed whole and entire. Her books will be deformed and twisted. She will write in a rage where she should write calmly. She will write foolishly where she should write wisely. She will write of herself when she should write of her characters. She is at war with her lot. How could she help but die young, cramped and thwarted? (Woolf 1973, p. 70)

It is a devastating, controlled, yet somehow uncontrolled indictment. What elements in this digression, hardly a formal innovation in nineteenth-century fiction, can have prompted Woolf to such excess? Elaine Showalter analyses this passage and others as part of Woolf's 'flight into androgyny,' that aesthetic chamber where masculine and feminine minds meet and marry. Showalter's analysis focuses on Woolf's aesthetic as an effect of her inability to come to terms with her sexuality, with sexual difference itself. Showalter's analysis is persuasive in individual terms, but it does not deal with all of the questions thrown up by Brontë's challenge and Woolf's violent response to it. In the sentences that Woolf omits in her own citation, Brontë insists that even the confined and restless state could produce 'many and glowing' visions. Art, the passage maintains, can be produced through the endless narration of the self, through the mixed incoherence of subjectivity spoken from subordinate and rebellious positions within culture. It was this aesthetic that Woolf as critic explicitly rejected.

However, the passage deals with more than sexual difference. In the references to 'human beings' and to unspecified 'millions,' Brontë deliberately and defiantly associates political and sexual rebellion even as she distinguishes between them. In the passage the generic status of 'men' is made truly trans-class and transcultural when linked to 'masses,' 'millions' and 'human beings,' those larger inclusive terms. In 1847, on the eve of the second great wave of modern revolution, it was a dangerous rhetoric to use.

Its meaningful associations were quickly recognized by contemporary reviewers, who deplored the contiguous relationship between revolution and feminism. Lady Eastlake's comments in the *Quarterly Review* of 1849 are those most often quoted:

We do not hesitate to say, that the tone of mind and thought which has overthrown authority and violated every code human and divine abroad, and fostered chartism and rebellion at home is the same which has also written *Jane Eyre.*

Yet Charlotte Brontë was no political radical. She is pulled towards the positive linking of class rebellion and women's revolt in this passage through her anger at the misrepresentation and suppression of women's identity, not via an already held sympathy with the other masses and millions. It is a tentative, partial movement in spite of its defiant rhetoric, and it is checked in a moment by the mad, mocking female laughter, and turned from its course a few pages later by the introduction of Rochester into the narrative. For Woolf, Jane's soliloquy spoils the continuity of the narrative with its 'anger and rebellion.' Woolf turns away, refuses to comprehend the logical sequence of the narration at the symbolic level of the novel.

Jane's revolutionary manifesto of the subject, which has its own slightly manic register, invokes that sliding negative signification of women that we have described. At this point in the story the 'low, slow ha'ha!' and the 'eccentric murmurs' which 'thrilled' Jane are ascribed to Grace Poole, the hard-featured servant. But Grace is only the laugh's minder, and the laugh later becomes 'correctly' ascribed to Rochester's insane wife, Bertha Mason. The uncertain source of the laughter, the narrator's inability to predict its recurrence—'There were days when she was quite silent; but there were others when I could not account for the sounds she made'—both mark out the 'sounds' as the dark side of Romantic female subjectivity.

Retroactively, in the narratives the laughter becomes a threat to all that Jane had desired and demanded in her roof-top reverie. Mad servant, mad mistress, foreigner, nymphomaniac, syphilitic, half-breed, aristocrat, Bertha turns violently on keeper, brother, husband and, finally, rival. She and her noises become the condensed and displaced site of unreason and anarchy as it is metonymically figured through dangerous femininity in all its class, race and cultural projections. Bertha must be killed off, narratively speaking, so that a moral, Protestant femininity, licensed sexuality and a qualified, socialized feminism may survive. Yet the text cannot close off or recuperate that moment of radical association between political rebellion and gender rebellion, cannot shut down the possibility of a positive alliance between reason, passion and feminism. Nor can it disperse the terror that speaking those connections immediately stirs up—for Woolf in any case.

Woolf was at her most vehement and most contradictory about these issues, which brought together for her, as for many other feminists before and after, a number of deeply connected anxieties about subjectivity, class, sexuality and culture. Over and over again in her critical writing, Woolf tries to find ways of placing the questions inside an aesthetic that disallows anger, unreason and passion as productive emotions. Like Wollstonecraft before her, she cannot quite shake off the moral and libidinal economies of the Enlightenment. In 'Women and Fiction' (1929) she frames the question another way:

> In *Middlemarch* and in *Jane Eyre* we are conscious not merely of the writer's character, as we are conscious of the character of Charles Dickens, but we are conscious of a woman's presence—of someone resenting the treatment of

> her sex and pleading for its rights. This brings into women's writing an ele-
> ment which is entirely absent from a man's, unless, indeed, he happens to
> be a working man, a Negro, or one who for some other reason is conscious of
> disability. It introduces a distortion and is frequently the cause of weakness.
> The desire to plead some personal cause or to make a character the mouth-
> piece of personal discontent or grievance always has a distressing effect, as if
> the spot at which the reader's attention is directed were suddenly two-fold
> instead of single. (Woolf 1979, p. 47)

Note how the plea for a sex, a class, a race becomes reduced to individual, personal grievance, how subordinate position in a group becomes immediately
pathologized as private disability, weakness. Note too how 'man' in this passage
loses its universal connotation, so that it only refers normatively to men of the
ruling class. In this passage, as in *Jane Eyre*, the metonymic evocation of degraded
subjectivities is expressed as an effect of subordination, not its rationale nor its
cause. But the result is still a negative one. For the power to resist through fictional language, the language of sociality and self; the power to move and en-
lighten, rather than blur and distress through the double focus, is denied. Instead,
Woolf announces the death of the feminist text, by proclaiming, somewhat pre-
maturely, the triumph of feminism.

> The woman writer is no longer bitter. She is no longer angry. She is no longer
> pleading and protesting as she writes. . . . She will be able to concentrate upon
> her vision without distraction from outside. (Woolf 1979, p. 48)

This too is a cry from the roof-tops of a desire still unmet by social and psychic
experience.

Although the meanings attached to race, class and sexuality have undergone
fundamental shifts from Wollstonecraft's (and Woolf's) time to our own, we do
not live in a post-class society any more than a post-feminist one. Our identities
are still constructed through social hierarchy and cultural differentiation, as well
as through those processes of division and fragmentation described in psychoanalytic theory. The identities arrived at through these structures will always be precarious and unstable, though *how* they will be so in the future we do not know.
For the moment, women still have a problematic place in both social and psychic representation. The problem for women of woman-as-sign has made the self-
definition of women a resonant issue within feminism. It has also determined the
restless inability of feminism to settle for humanist definitions of the subject, or
for materialism's relegation of the problem to determinations of class only. I have
emphasized in this chapter some of the more negative ways in which the Enlightenment and Romantic paradigms of subjectivity gave hostage to the making
of subordinate identities, of which femininity is the structuring instance. Although psychoanalytic theories of the construction of gendered subjectivity stress
difficulty, antagonism and contradiction as necessary parts of the production of
identity, the concept of the unconscious and the psychoanalytic view of sexuality dissolve in great part the binary divide between reason and passion that dominates earlier concepts of subjectivity. They break down as well the moralism
attached to those libidinal and psychic economies. Seen from this perspective,
'individualism' has a different and more contentious history within feminism than
it does in androcentric debates.

It is that history which we must uncover and consider, in both its positive and its negative effects, so that we can argue convincingly for a feminist rehabilitation of the female psyche in non-moralized terms. Perhaps we can come to see it as neither sexual outlaw, social bigot nor dark hiding-place for treasonable regressive femininity waiting to stab progressive feminism in the back. We must redefine the psyche as a structure, not as a content. To do so is not to move away from a feminist politics which takes race and class into account, but to move towards a fuller understanding of how these social divisions and the inscription of gender are mutually secured and given meaning. Through that analysis we can work towards change.

WORKS CITED

Alexander, Sally (1984) 'Women, Class and Sexual Difference,' *History Workshop*, 17, pp. 125–49.

Bakhtin, M. M. (1981) *The Diologic Imagination: Four Essays*, ed. Michael Holquist. Austin, Texas: University of Texas Press.

Brontë, Charlotte (1976) *Jane Eyre* (1847) ed. Margaret Smith. London: Oxford University Press.

Cott, Nancy F. (1978) 'Passionlessness: An Interpretation of Victorian Sexual Ideology, 1790–1850,' *Signs*, 2, 2, pp. 219–33.

Hartmann, Heidi (1981) 'The Unhappy Marriage of Marxism and Feminism: Towards a More Progressive Union.' In Lydia Sargent (ed.), *The Unhappy Marriage of Marxism and Feminism: A Debate on Class and Patriarchy*, pp. 1–42. London: Pluto Press.

Jacobus, Mary (1979) 'The Buried Letter: Feminism and Romanticism in *Villette*.' In Mary Jacobus (ed.), *Women Writing and Writing about Women*, pp. 42–60. London: Croom Helm.

Marxist-Feminist Literature Collective (1978) 'Women's Writing: *Jane Eyre, Shirley, Villette, Aurora Leigh*.' In *1848: The Sociology of Literature*, proceedings of the Essex conference on the Sociology of Literature (July 1977), pp. 185–206.

Newton, Judith Lowder (1981) *Women, Power, and Subversion: Social Strategies in British Fiction 1778–1860*. Athens, Ga.: University of Georgia Press.

Radcliffe, Ann (1966) *The Mysteries of Udolpho* (1794). London: Oxford University Press.

Robinson, Lillian S. (1978) 'Dwelling in Decencies: Radical Criticism and the Feminist Perspective.' In *Sex, Class, and Culture*, pp. 3–21. Bloomington, Ind.: Indiana University Press.

Rousseau, Jean-Jacques (1974) *Emile* (1762). London: Dent.

Said, Edward W. (1978) *Orientalism*. London: Routledge & Kegan Paul.

Stedman Jones, Gareth (1983) *Languages of Class: Studies in English Working Class History 1832–1982*. Cambridge: Cambridge University Press.

Wollstonecraft, Mary (1975a) *A Vindication of the Rights of Woman* (1792). New York: Norton.

Wollstonecraft, Mary (1975b) *Maria, or The Wrongs of Woman* (1798). New York: Norton.

Woolf, Virginia (1973) *A Room of One's Own* (1929). Harmondsworth: Penguin.

Woolf, Virginia (1979) 'Women and Fiction.' In Michele Barrett (ed.), *Women and Writing*, pp. 44–52. London: Women's Press.

Wordsworth, William, and Coleridge, Samuel Taylor (1971) *Lyrical Ballads* (1798, 1800), ed. R. L. Brett and A. R. Jones. London: Methuen.

ROMANCE IN THE AGE OF ELECTRONICS HARLEQUIN ENTERPRISES

(1985)

Harlequin, as it advertises itself, is the "world's no. 1 publisher of romance fiction!" Like its imitators and rivals, Dell's Candlelight Romances, Bantam's Loveswept, and Simon and Schuster's Silhouette Romances, Harlequin turns out on its giant, computerized printing presses an ever-increasing number of uniformly jacketed and uniformly written romantic narratives per month.[1] Formerly a moderately successful Canadian publishing house, in 1971 it hired Lawrence Heisley, a Procter and Gamble marketing man, as its new president. He turned feminine romantic love into superprofits for his then all-male board of directors by transferring to the sale of books the techniques used to sell detergent to housewives. By turning love into a consumer product, Harlequin increased its net earnings from $110,000 in 1970 to over $21 million by 1980.

But packaging alone cannot account for the loyalty of 14 million readers. The novels' flyleaf assures readers that "no one touches the heart of a woman quite like Harlequin," and marketing statistics—188 million books sold in 1980, sales accounting for 30 percent of all mass market paperbooks in a major bookstore chain—support this claim.[2] What exactly is the secret to a woman's heart that Harlequin and its rivals have learned, and how have they turned this knowledge into profits for themselves?

SECRETS OF A WOMAN'S HEART

Harlequin may owe its dramatic growth in popularity to the fact that the romances now respond to specific needs of working women. Focusing on the juncture between their sexual, emotional needs on the one hand and their needs concerning work relations on the other, it involves both their deepest, most private, most intimate feelings, and at the same time their very broad relations to the process of social history. Impressive analyses by Tania Modleski, Ann Barr Snitow, and Janice A. Radway[3] have explained the popularity of mass market romances by examining how they respond to women's deep yearnings, but have not talked about why these romances have gained their phenomenal popularity just in the last ten to fifteen years. Moreover, in the past couple of years, since Snitow and Modleski wrote their studies, the romance industry has been undergoing an accelerated process of change. Given the fact that their heroines' stories increasingly join the personal, sexual relations of private life to the work relations of the marketplace, we might ask what in the Harlequin formula responds to new needs of women as a result of recent profound changes in both their domestic and paid labor situations, and how that formula might change in the future.

As Harlequin Romances have become more popular, more and more of their heroines have jobs. Yet these working heroines have more subversive desires than simply to join the labor force: they are reacting to the limits of a sterile, harsh, alienating, fragmented work world itself. In spite of some fairly glamorous jobs, the working Harlequin heroines, melodramatically engaged in defiant struggles with their heroes—who are usually their bosses—demand from them and their world two additional changes in their situation. First, as the heroine struggles against the irresistible power of her hero, she also struggles *for* something, which she calls "love," but beyond that does not define any further. What she wants from the hero is recognition of herself as a unique, exceptional individual. In addition to acknowledging her sexual attraction and her professional competence, he must also recognize her as a subject, or recognize her from her own point of view.

Second, the heroines seek more than simply to succeed in the man's world. An analysis of the romances will show that on an implicit level they seek not so much an improved life within the possibilities of the existing social structure, but a different social structure. The very facts that the hero is both boss and lover, that the world of work and business is romanticized and eroticized, and that in it love flourishes suggest that the Harlequin heroines seek an end to the division between the domestic world of love and sentiment and the public world of work and business.

Since in Harlequin the struggle to gain recognition for a deep feminine self merges with the struggle—however implicit or utopian—to create a new, more integrated world, a reading of these romances uncovers a certain power possessed by even formulaic narratives. Because they cannot help but recount a woman's life all of a piece, they may be able to reveal certain insights about women's lives and women's desires that escape empirical science. These romance narratives show us that an individual woman's need to be recognized in her own sense of self and the need to change a more global social structure are interdependent.

In *Loving with a Vengeance: Mass-Produced Fantasies for Women*, Tania Modleski says that "in Harlequin Romances, the need of women to find meaning and pleasure in activities which are not wholly male-centered such as work or artistic creation is generally scoffed at."[4] But in the past few years that has changed. Although in the mid-seventies, the average Harlequin heroine was either just emerging from home, or was a secretary or nurse who quit her unrewarding job at marriage, by the late seventies, many Harlequin heroines had unusual and interesting, if not bizarre careers. More and more frequently both hero and heroine started taking the heroine's job or creative activity seriously.

Almost never images of passive femininity, the heroines of the late seventies are active, intelligent, and capable of at least economic independence. Nicole, in *Across the Great Divide*, is a dedicated and competent swimming coach; Anna, in *Battle with Desire*, is an internationally known violinist at the age of twenty-two; Kerry, in *The Dividing Line*, also twenty-two, is on the board of directors of a prestigious department store. Furthermore, the hero often gives moral support to the heroine in her career, and intends to continue supporting her career aspirations after their marriage.[5]

By the early eighties, the heroines' careers go beyond the wildest dreams of the most ardent National Organization for Women member and often become the selling point that distinguishes one romance from another. As one example, Danni in *Race for Revenge* is about to "succeed triumphantly in the male dominated world of motor racing,"[6] and Karla Mortley in Candlelight Romance's *Game Plan* "joins the rugged New York Flyers as a ballet trainer" only to find that "the womanizing quarterback MacGregor proves hard to tackle."[7] In 1984 Harlequin added to its line a new, more sophisticated series, Harlequin Temptations, where the hero worries that the heroine will place her career before him. In the romances of the mid-eighties the careers range from the banal, like movie actresses and famous pop singers, to the unique, like engineering Ph.D. Frankie Warburton in *Love Circuit*, who falls in love with the electronics heir that contracts for her services as a computer consultant. More than one heroine is an advertising executive who falls in love with her client. University editorial assistant Liza Manchester in *Public Affair* is an "outspoken member of Graham University's feminist community" who falls in love with Professor Scott Harburton. And— inevitably—Gabriella Constant in *By Any Other Name* is a best-selling romance writer who falls in love with her publisher.[8]

Although the hero of these romances is not always the heroine's boss, he most often either is the boss or holds a position of economic or professional power over the heroine. More important, as the advertising brochure for the new Harlequin Temptation series demonstrates, the boss figure remains the prototype for the Harlequin hero. Promising to let us experience "The passionate torment of a woman torn between two loves . . . the siren call of a career . . . the magnetic advances of an impetuous employer . . . ," it advertises its flagship novel of the new series, *First Impressions*, by saying: "Tracy Dexter couldn't deny her attraction to her new boss."[9]

Because in Harlequin Romances, plot, characters, style, and erotic scenes have been set by formula, freedom to vary the heroine's job gives an author one of the few avenues for bringing originality, individuality, and creative freedom into a romance. An unusual job offers compositional opportunities for an unusual setting and unusual conflicts between the hero and heroine. But the job situation also serves a deeper purpose. Beyond showing the uncanny ability of mass culture to ingest any kind of social, economic, or cultural historic change in women's lives, these heroines with their fabulous jobs might help to explain why women respond to romance so much more massively than to other mass market reading. New Right how-to books exhort their readers to be "real" women by staying home to protect the family; liberal how-to books, such as *The Cinderella Complex*, urge women to cease wanting to "be *part* of somebody else" and "to get into the driver's seat" of "the man's world";[10] and women's magazines claim to show readers how to excel in each separate segment—sex, work, family, emotion—of their madly disarticulated, schizophrenic lives. Supermarket romances, alone among mass market literature, focus on the conflictive relations among these segments.

WOMEN'S WORK/WOMEN'S CULTURE

The same socioeconomic changes of the 1960s and 1970s, which created a new kind of working woman, also created the conditions for Harlequin's commercial success. These are, according to Harry Braverman in *Labor and Monopoly Capital*, the restructuring of business into huge international conglomerates; the "extraordinary growth of commercial concerns" (like Harlequin) in comparison with production; and along with this the extraordinary explosion of bureaucracy and office work with its systems management, computerization, and assembly-line processing of paper.[11] These conditions include new categories of work, and, occurring around 1960, "the creation of a new class of workers," low-paid clerical workers, overwhelmingly female. According to Roslyn L. Feldbert and Evelyn Nakano Glenn, between 1960 and 1980, employment in clerical and kindred occupations doubled. They cite dramatic growth in work categories created by the new technology, and also by the business expansion that Braverman describes.[12]

The women who work for these huge conglomerates and bureaucracies, in clerical positions, in service positions, and as assemblers of the new electronic machinery, as well as the women whose shopping, banking, education, medical care, and welfare payments have been changed by these new developments, constitute a large part of the readership of Harlequin Romances. And the musicians, painters, poets, coaches, car racers, Olympic athletes, photographers, and female executives of the romances, with their glamorous jobs, are these readers' idealized alter egos. Although readers are well aware that the romances are unreal fantasies, their passionate attachment to the genre could not be explained without an intense identification with the heroine on the level of ego ideal.

Between 40 and 60 percent of the mass market romance readership works outside the home.[13] The assumption has been that these romances contain housewifely fantasies, but if that is so, then why do so many of them revolve around work situations, however glamorized? Among the many possible reasons for this, the most obvious is that as countless statistics show, almost all these readers can expect to work sometime in their lives, moving in and out of the labor market. Moreover, a good number of them can expect to be single mothers, for at least part of their lives. But these fantasies involving work situations suggest that feminists, and especially feminist organizers, might do away with this categorization of women into working women on the one hand and housewives on the other. The content of Harlequins suggests that the readers, like the heroines, do not compartmentalize their lives in this way, becoming different people when they go to work. Although the immediate concerns caused by workplace or home may be different, our deeper abiding concerns remain the same, whether at home or on the job. To draw a strong division between working women and housewives comes perhaps from applying to women a male model. For the average man, work and home really are very different. At work the man must accept the power of his employer, while at home he is master of his family and finds relaxation. The average woman, on the other hand, finds herself contending with a masculine power both at home and at work. By combining the sexual domination of a lover and the economic domination of an employer in the same masculine figure, Harlequins draw attention to the specificity of the contemporary feminine situation.

In a sensitive study that explains the popularity of mass market romances by interviewing a group of readers from one bookstore, Janice Radway says that women report they read the romances for relaxation and escape. "When asked to specify what they are fleeing from," she says, "they invariably mention the 'pressures' and 'tensions' they experience as wives and mothers."[14] A group of working women I spoke to also said they read the romances to escape. But the escape portrayed in the working heroine's romances is somewhat more precise about the pressures and tensions it aims to soothe.

The heroine's fantasy dilemmas compensate exactly for those elements of women's work in the clerical factories—and for that matter in any factories—that critics of job automation find most oppressive. A reading of Harlequin Romances in the context of these critiques yields insights into the heroine's (and perhaps the author's and readers') conflicts; their grievances against their living, working, and sexual situations; and the intensity with which they feel these grievances, but also into the extent to which the romances and their authors have adopted the basic corporate structure of present work relations as the invisible and unchallenged framework of their romantic vision.

Two themes of revolt and fantasy escape that run most strongly through the romances concern the depersonalization of the cybernetic world and the powerlessness of the feminine individual within it. Surprisingly enough, the heroine's lack of power and freedom corresponds rather closely to what sociologists have found out about the worker's lack of power and freedom in the computerized and bureaucritized workplace. According to Braverman, contemporary clerical workers and low-paid factory workers suffer from a lack of control over the work process, over the social use to which products will be put, over their own mental processes, and even over their own bodies. The assembly line structuring of clerical work, says Braverman, results from applying to office work the techniques of Taylorism, which factory owners began using in the 1920s and 1930s to gain maximum efficiency by breaking down the unity of the labor process into its smallest discrete elements. While Taylorization yields greater productivity, its effects on the worker, whose tasks and bodily movements are also broken down to their smallest elements, are devastating.

With every movement of the office worker or lower paid assembler controlled for maximum efficiency, and every moment of her day accounted for, she has lost all decision-making power not only over the products she is making, but also even over her own bodily movements and minutest scheduling of her own time. Braverman talks about clerical workers feeling "shackled" and quotes a vice-president of an insurance company as saying of a room full of key punchers: "'All they lack is a chain!'"[15] Ida Russakoff Hoos, in *Automation in the Office*, reports interviewing a supervisor who described key punchers keeping supplies of tranquilizers in their desks and feeling "frozen."[16] And Ellen Cantarow cites findings of "appalling rates of coronary heart disease in women clerical workers"[17] as a result of lack of control.

The force of Harlequin comes from its ability to combine, often in the same image, the heroine's fantasy escape from these restraints and her idealized, romanticized, and eroticized compliance with them. It does this through diverse types of story elements, which are remarkably consistent from romance to romance. At first and most simple compensation of the readers' situation is that by contrast to the jobs most working readers have, the jobs of Harlequin heroines, while greatly varied, almost always have in common that the work is meaningful in itself, challenging, has a direct effect on the well-being of other people, is a craft that requires skill or talent, and is one that gains recognition for a job well done. A second, slightly more complex compensatory fantasy is that Harlequin heroines do fight for, and win, control over their jobs and a great deal of freedom.

A central, and one of the most attractive, compensations offered by Harlequin is that the romances respond to the depersonalization of the Harlequin reader's life, not only in her workplace, but also in her shopping, her banking, in her relations to government, to school, and to all the services she now obtains from giant, faceless bureaucracies, which make her feel, as Tessa in *The Enchanted Island* thinks, "like a small, impersonal cog in a machine."[18] The relations between the heroines and their bosses may be love/hate relations, but they are intensely intimate. Although decisions about how the reader spends her time in the corporate workplace are made by real men, she never sees them. In the conglomerate, the real decision makers may be in another state or another country, and in terms of the corporate hierarchy, they are in another universe. They are so removed from the secretary or assembler as to seem disembodied gods. In the world of Harlequin, the god descends from the executive suite and comes to her.

But in addition to this direct compensation for the depersonalized relations of the corporate world, the working heroines also idealize the reader's sense that she herself has been reduced to one more interchangeable part of the office's "integrated systems." In *Battle with Desire* Gareth the hero, who is also violinist Anna's conductor, tells her: "You and I together, Anna, will give them a performance they'll never forget. . . . The music will be a prelude to our love" (p. 157). Yet Anna is hurt and asks herself: "But was it love for herself, or because she had been the instrument of such superb music?" Although Anna's position is a highly idealized fantasy, it raises the same conflict experienced by those women in Hoos's study who feel their bosses regard them (if at all!) as an instrument or a part of the machinery.

A fourth and still more complex compensation concerns directly the theme of power. In the romances, the heroine fights ardently against the power the hero has over her. Because the power figure represents both her lover and her boss, this relation between one man and one woman reverberates on a larger network of social relations, all structured according to inequality of power. Thus the boss-lover can become an analogy for other men in the reader's life, such as her husband. The heroines reject the dependence or submissiveness that is most often forced upon their resisting spirit: Nicole in *Across the Great Divide* finds in her new boss Lang "something too suggestive of a rugged relentlessness . . . that she just couldn't bring herself to suffer meekly and which set her on the offensive." In her own mind, she rejects arrogant hierarchies, and when the board of the swim club threatens to fire her, "she was determined not to submit tamely. If she was going down, she would be going down fighting!" (pp. 30, 165).

In the most complex and contradictory of story elements, the romances combine in one image an escape from the "frozen" feeling of working readers and an eroticized acquiescence to it. The heroine's struggle-filled, stormy relationship with the hero involves a strange combination of tempestuous physical movement and physical restraint by the hero. In one of dozens of examples, Nicole, in *Across the Great Divide*, struggles with Lang.

> "I hate the lot of you!" she sobbed brokenly. "And don't touch me!" trying to jerk out of his hold. "You're all a load of two faced liars, only interested in your own egotistical aims." Then, when he didn't release her, "I said don't *touch* me!" as she began pummelling violently at his broad chest.
> "For God's sake, Nicky!" Lange gripped her wrists grimly in one hand and wrenched open the car door with the other. "Get in," he muttered, and bundled her flailing figure on to the back seat. Slamming the door behind them, he pinned her helplessly to his muscular form until she had exhausted her struggles and consented to stay there, crying quietly. (p. 140)

The "shackles" of the office or factory job are on the one hand compensated for by vigorous movement; on the other hand they are romanticized and eroticized. The hero restrains the heroine not out of an impersonal desire for efficiency, but out of a very personal desire to have her respond to him. He restrains her in an attempt to control her anger, to arouse her sexually, to fulfill his burning desire to have her confess her feelings for him, or all three. The heroine's anxiety no longer has its source in the cold, nagging, unpleasant fear that her boss will fire her if she rebels (or that her husband will reject her or worse) but in the warm, seductive, obsessive fear that she will not be able to resist his potent sexual magnetism, especially since he goes to considerable effort to create intimate situations where he can exert it. Transformed by the romances, the heroine's restraint becomes on the one hand intermittent, and on the other hand emotionally and sexually gratifying. Instead of having to take tranquilizers to repress her internalized rage, like the office workers in Hoos's study and Cantarow's article, the Harlequin heroine is privileged to vent it violently and directly against her restrainer, even while this restraint takes an idealized form.

This strange mingling of protest and acquiescence to the situation of many contemporary women makes the Harlequin Romances so seductive and so contradictory. On the one hand, the heroine is empowered to revolt without risking masculine rejection because the hero desires her more the angrier she becomes, but on the other hand, the romances also sexualize her impotence. This particular combination of elements intensifies our emotional involvement with a story that both arouses and nullifies the very subversive impulses that attracted us to it in the first place.

CHANGING TIME, CHANGING CONFLICT

Harlequin's double message is all the more potent in that the heroine's conflict is also double. At stake for her in the romances that put the work situation at the center of the plot is both her social identity and the deepest core of her feminine self. A surprising number of Harlequins employ the same vocabulary to describe the inner conflict of the heroine as she struggles against the hero on his own grounds where he has all the weapons. His main weapon in this idealized world is his powerful sexual attraction; her main weakness is her susceptibility to that attraction, which quickly becomes total love. Her struggle aims to prevent the hero from exploiting her love for his own sexual desires, and the conflict this struggle awakens in her is described by the key words "humiliation" and "pride." Nicole finds that

> the most galling part of the whole episode had been her unqualified surrender to Lang's lovemaking. That she should have so readily submitted—no, welcomed it was far more honest, she confessed painfully—was something she found impossible to accept. The only thought left to salvage at least some of her *pride* being the knowledge that Lang wasn't aware how deeply her feelings were involved. Her *humiliation* was bad enough now, but it would have known no bounds if she had inadvertently revealed how she really felt about him. (p. 144, italics mine.)

In *Stormy Affair* Amber faces the same problem: "She could not say: 'I would love to live here and marry you but only if you say you love me. . . . ' At least she still had sufficient *pride* to avoid the *humiliation* such a statement would cause."[19]

Through the heroine's impossible choice between two painful and destructive alternatives, summed up by the terms "humiliation" and "pride," Harlequin Romances call attention to a feminine character structure that differs from the masculine one. Both Radway and Snitow have discussed this feminine character structure in the Harlequin heroine, and both have relied on Nancy Chodorow's theory to analyze it.[20] According to Chodorow, capitalist-patriarchal family structure and childrearing practices produce in boys more strongly defined and closed-off ego boundaries, and in girls more fluid ego boundaries, so that men tend to define themselves as a separate, self-sufficient entity, while women tend to define themselves in terms of their relation to other people. Unable to adopt a rock-like, closed, thinglike self, such as the one the hero seems to possess, the Harlequin heroine's self alternates until the end of the romance between two forms of destruction: "humiliation," which signals a dissolution of her self into the masculine self, and "pride," a self-control that shrivels up her self by denying its needs and desires. Solution: the hero must recognize and adopt the relational, feminine form of the self.

This difference in character structure between women and men, which Harlequins emphasize as the cause of the heroine's problems, is inherited from the industrial revolution. With the separation of work from home, women were socialized to immerse themselves in the intense emotional world of the domestic sphere. Self-perpetuating family practices made that socialization seem like a "natural" feminine character. Now with the cybernetic revolution, women must also, like men, make their way in the rationalistic world of business, but they take with them the emotional makeup they have inherited from the past. They do not have, and in many cases do not want to have, the harder, more competitive, success-oriented emotional equipment with which men have been socialized in order to succeed, or even simply to survive.

If Harlequin heroines' character structure is inherited from the industrial revolution, their narrative structure is also inherited from one of the most prominent literary genres of the industrial revolution, the romantic novel. Although Sally Mitchell and Tania Modleski have traced the genealogy of Harlequin romances back to forms of nineteenth-century popular fiction, such as seduction novels, historical romances, penny magazine aristocratic romances, and gothic novels,[21] the quest for self-fulfillment carried out by the heroes and heroines of nineteenth-century high romanticism has also found a twentieth-century refuge in contemporary mass market romances. As writer Louella Nelson told me of her romance *Freedom's Fortune*: "This book is about a woman's quest for courage and self-worth."[22]

The inner conflict of the Harlequin heroines is a more explicitly sexualized version of feminine conflicts analyzed by authors writing during the industrial revolution, such as the Brontë sisters. Problems of sexual difference that beset the Harlequin heroines also confront the heroines of Brontë's *Shirley*, where Caroline Helstone says: "Shirley, men and women are so different: they are in such a different position. Women have so few things to think about—men so many: you may have a friendship with a man while he is almost indifferent to you. Much of what cheers your life may be dependent on him, while not a feeling or interest of moment in his eyes may have reference to you." Shirley answers: "Caroline . . . don't you wish you had a profession—a trade?"[23]

The Harlequin heroines do have a trade—and a lot of things to think about—but they still resemble the Brontëan heroines in that for them sexual sensation, feelings of love, and rational thought are all intimately connected. They cannot be compartmentalized and sealed off from each other. When these heroines fall in love, they think about love and their lover all the time. The heroes of Harlequin Romances, like the heroes of *Jane Eyre* and *Shirley*, are emotionally divided between the world of love and the world of business and public affairs, and therefore fragmented in their psychic structure. For them, or so it seems to the heroine, sex is divorced from other feelings, and love from other areas of their life. It seems that whenever he wills it, the hero can simply shut her image off and think about other things.

From this fragmentation, the Harlequin heroes, like their nineteenth-century brothers, M. Emanuel in *Villette* or Robert Moore in *Shirley*, draw their strengths for success in the world. But since the Harlequin heroines must now also survive alone in that world, they can only, as Nicole says, attempt to conceal their feelings, try to pretend to be like the hero. But the heroine's wholeness, which is also her weakness, means that her outer appearance and actions cannot but reflect her inner emotions. The heroines are transparent where the heroes are opaque.

In fact the heroine frequently suspects until the end of the novel that the hero has no tender feelings under his harsh surface, and that therefore he does not have to exhaust all his energy in the fight for self-control the way she does. In *Stormy Affair*, for instance, Amber thinks that "she must pull herself together and not let Hamed Ben Slouma see that he in any way affected her" (p. 25). But "Hamed with his keen perception knew exactly what was going on in her mind. . . . 'Perhaps your desires were greater than mine, or do you think it could be that I have more self-control? You're very *transparent*, my charming one'" (p. 100, italics mine). The effect of all these differences between the hero and heroine is to increase the hero's power over this outsider in his world. But even this conflict contains within it wish-fulfilling compensations. If Ben Slouma finds Amber transparent, at least he cares enough to observe her transparency and is interested enough in her to notice what goes on inside her. If the heroine's anger is impotent, at least she has the chance to vent it with great rage at its rightful target, and at least he stays around to listen to it, even, as in the case of Tessa's boss Andrew, "with interest" (*The Enchanted Island*, p. 157).

Utopian and formulaic as they are, in Harlequin Romances the heroine's struggle and conflict serve to overcome something more than a merely psychological passivity or a role that a woman could simply choose to play or not to play. Although its roots in a total social situation are not so clearly shown as in the novels of the Brontës, the Harlequin heroine's conflict is shown to be a very real lack of power to be herself in relations controlled by others. Her very activity and anger are signs of her impotence in the face of the more powerful male. Thus Nicole "seethed impotently" (*Across the Great Divide*, p. 99), and Debra "tried to control the rage and humiliation she was feeling," while Jordan's "composure wasn't disturbed by [Kathleen's] burst of anger."[24]

Like their nineteenth-century predecessors, Jane Eyre, Caroline Helstone, and Lucy Snowe, the Harlequin heroines seek recognition as a subject in their own right from their own point of view. And also like these earlier heroines, Harlequin heroines find that this recognition must take a different form than that sought by romantic heroes. A hero like St. John Rivers in *Jane Eyre* becomes closed in on himself, static, and self-sufficient as an absolute totality when he achieves this recognition. Brontë rejects this form of the self and the narcissistic form of love it demands, and seeks fulfillment for a form of the self which is essentially fluid, essentially changing, and essentially involved in a dynamic, living network of intimate relations with others.

Like the Brontë heroines, although in a less reflective and more narcissistic way,[25] the Harlequin heroines find that women in our soceity are already endowed with this relational form of the self, but that it never achieves recognition or fulfillment. The cause of pain and obscurity rather than success, it in fact tends to get lost altogether in a relation with the hero's harder, closed self, and to merge into his. This is what Anna finds in *Battle with Desire*: "Anna knew she mustn't give in. . . . And it wasn't getting any easier to resist, the urge to fight was melting away, so she made one final attempt at self-respect" (p. 19). What really melts here are the boundaries of the heroine's personhood and her sense of individuality as she loses herself in the other. Harlequins, unlike "real life," provide a solution: the hero adopts the feminine form of the self, recognizes it as valid, and gives the heroine the same tender devotion she gives to him.

The genius of the Harlequin Romances is to combine the struggle for the recognition of feminine selfhood and the struggle to make the work world a home for that self. As the cover blurb of *The Dividing Line* tells us of Kerry and Ross, who have inherited interests in a department store: "She liked old fashioned friendliness and service. He was all for modern impersonal efficiency. Between them, Sinclairs was becoming a battle ground." Even the idealized form of Kerry's angry struggle against Ross, and violinist Anna's questioning resentment against Gareth, suggest a need to go beyond an analysis like that in *Hearth and Home: Images of Women in the Mass-Media*, edited by Gaye Tuchman, Arlene Kaplan-Daniels, and James Benet. The book criticizes the mass media image of women for implying that "her fate and her happiness rest with a man, not with participation in the labor force,"[26] but it would be impoverishing even the impoverished romances to say that their heroines really want both. They want so much more besides. Not content with Helen Gurley Brown's rationalistic advice to "have it all," they don't want it the way it is now; they want the world of labor to change so that women can find happiness there, and they want men to change so that men will just as much find *their* happiness with women.

Hearth and Home sees hope for equality in "economically productive women who insist on the abandonment of old prejudices and discriminatory behaviors."[27] But Harlequin Romances suggest women who abandon the present structures of economic production because those structures force women to give up their values, their ethos, and even their particular sense of self for success, or, more likely, for mere survival. The vastly popular Harlequin Romances implicitly and potentially pose a demand for profound structural transformations of the total social world we inhabit. And like their romantic forebears, the heroines desire that this new world be not just our same old world improved, but a different, better world. The problem is that Harlequin Enterprises, having learned these secrets to a woman's heart, exploited them by turning them into marketable formulas, which divorced the conflicts from their causes and cut off the path toward reflecting upon any realistic solutions.

ROMANTIC ASPIRATIONS—RATIONALIZED FORM

In her analysis of women readers, Radway has pointed out that "we would do well not to condescend to romance readers as hopeless traditionalists who are recalcitrant in their refusal to acknowledge the emotional costs of patriarchy. We must begin to recognize that romance reading is fueled by dissatisfaction and disaffection."[28] Yet there is a crucial distinction to be made between dismissing the very justifiable fantasies and desires of Harlequin readers or the undoubted achievements of romance writers, and criticizing a multinational publishing corporation that exploits those fantasies and achievements. Modleski is probably closer to the mark when she says of Harlequin that "their enormous and continuing popularity . . . suggests that they speak to very real problems and tensions in women's lives," but that the texts arouse subversive anxieties and desires, and then "work to neutralize them."[29]

The methods of editing, producing, marketing, and distributing Harlequin Romances are part and parcel of the depersonalized, standardized, mechanistic conglomerate system that the Harlequin heroines oppose. Harlequin heroines seek interconnectedness in the social, sexual, and economic world as a whole. Yet their very search is contained in a static, thinglike, literary structure, which denies their quest and turns it into its opposite.

Radway reports that the readers she interviewed understand very well that "the characters and events . . . of the typical romance do not resemble the people and occurrences they must deal with in their lives."[30] At issue in the case of Harlequin, however, is not the illusion that the events in the romances are real, but the illusion that reading a romance constitutes only a relation to a text and to an author: To see the act of reading a romance as simply a relation between the reader and the printed page is to isolate this act from its larger context.

We are used to thinking of a publisher as a mediator between the readers and a book written by an individual author, but Harlequin has changed this. Although Harlequin is studied in few university literary classes, it is referred to in management classes as a sterling example of successful business practices that students should learn to emulate. According to business professor Peter Killing, Harlequin's success is due precisely to its doing away with the reader–text and reader–author relation:

> Harlequin's formula was fundamentally different from that of traditional publishers: content, length, artwork, size, basic formats, and print, were all standardized. Each book was not a new product, but rather an addition to a clearly defined product line. The consequences of this uniformity were significant. The reader was buying a *Harlequin novel*, rather than a book of a certain title by a particular author.... There was no need to make decisions about layouts, artwork, or cover design. The standardized size made warehousing and distribution more efficient. Employees hired from mass-marketing companies such as Procter and Gamble had skills and aptitudes which led them to do well at Harlequin.[31]

Harlequin thought of everything—except the readers, the authors, and the creative freedom which has traditionally been the cornerstone of literature in Western culture. This publishing giant molded romantic aspirations into super-rationalist forms of communication, the very antithesis of the readers' desires.

It is not the idealization of marriage in the romances, nor any specific content, that neutralizes their challenges to patriarchal ideology, but rather the form of the romances, and the form of communication Harlequin sets up between the corporate giant and the readers. Like the Brontëan heroes and heroines, whose desires for sublime sexual communion were a protest against the rationalizing forces of the industrial revolution, the Harlequin romances both protest against and compensate for their readers' dissatisfaction with the Taylorization of their lives as workers and consumers of goods and services. But when Harlequin instituted its new methods, the romantic quest and the sublime sexual communion were themselves Taylorized, so that the apparent escape from a depersonalized, coldly compartmentalized world led the reader right back into it.

Harlequin reduced romantic aspirations to the rational distillation of a formula. The General Editorial Guidelines of 1982 for *Worldwide Library Superromances*, in its directions to writers, broke down the fluid process of the romantic quest into its component set of static categories—"structure," "characters," "plot," "subplots," "romance," "sex," "viewpoint," and "writing style"—and in the past even set forth each step in the plot.

> —Introduction of hero and heroine, their meeting.
> —Initial attraction or conflict between them.
> —Romantic conflicts or heroine's qualms about hero.
> —Counterbalance to developing romance (i.e., sensual scenes, getting to know each other, growth of love vs. conflicts).
> —Hero's role in creating conflict.
> —Resolution of conflicts and happy ending, leading to marriage.
> —The development of the romance should be the primary concern of the author, with other story elements integrated into the romance.[32]

Sex (always of course coupled with "shared feeling rather than pure male domi-nation" [General Editorial Guidelines]) is meted out in measured amounts and in measured doses of "sensuality" at measured intervals of the plot. As a further rationalization, the romantic quest can even be broken down numerically and quantified, so that, as the 1982 Guidelines for Writing Harlequin's *New* Ameri-can Romances tell us, "parts of the plot can take place anywhere in the world provided that at least 80% of the novel takes place in the United States."[33]

But in 1984, with changes in readers' tastes and the growth of the authors' pro-fessional association Romance Writers of America, the Editorial Guidelines deny there is a formula: "Every aspiring Harlequin writer has a very clear picture of what makes these lines so successful, to the extent that some people have even tried to reduce it to a formula."[34]

A CHANGING GENRE: THE AUTHOR AS HEROINE

Yet so much has changed and continues to change since 1980, when growth in the industry led authors to organize Romance Writers of America as a support group, that it is impossible to tell what will happen in the future. Present devel-opments could lead not only to changes in the texts of the romances, but also to changes in the romance industry. Harlequin's very success could open up the po-tential contradictions inherent in the corporation's methods. The same kinds of struggles against rationalizing power its themes portray could be turned against it. When Romance Writers of America held its first national convention in 1981, the organization saw as its main opponent a literary establishment and vaguely defined public that did not recognize the value of romance as "women's litera-ture."[35] But as conditions governing author–corporate relations change, the in-dustry itself might become another opponent.

Harlequin has responded to declining sales in face of competition by the clas-sic strategy of buying out its major competitor (Silhouette Romances). But au-thors have had a quite different response to growth in the romance industry. Although Harlequin's monopolizing strategy should work to make even more im-personal the author–publisher relation, authors have been seeking (as if in imita-tion of their own heroines) more affirming relations with the publisher and greater job satisfaction.

In her study of Harlequin Romances, Margaret Ann Jensen reports that the ex-perience of becoming writers has caused many romance authors to "identify themselves as feminists," to become self-assertive, and to become more aware of themselves as working women who have succeeded in a profession quite diffi-cult to break into. In addition to combating "the negative image of romance in the literary world," romance writers, she says, have two new concerns. They "are attempting to organize to improve the standards within their field"; they are also engaging in "an increasing outspokenness about the romantic fiction industry" and making "critical responses to it."[36] At a Romance Writers of America meet-ing in Southern California, one candidate for office in the organization raised these same two issues. She spoke first of the need to "raise the standards of writing" and prevent "mediocre" writing. Then, after mentioning other writers' organizations that are more "militant," she spoke of the need to "increase our clout with publishers" and "improve the deal we're getting on contracts."[37]

Although authors still speak with indignation of the scorn that they face, saying that romances deserve the same respect as mysteries and science fiction, they also raise the above-mentioned other issues concerning the romance industry itself. Authors find themselves disadvantaged by the very marketing practice of Harlequin to which Peter Killing attributes Harlequin's economic success: Harlequin promotes its lines but rarely its authors. And Silhouette has followed suit. In a 1980 interview, Silhouette president P. J. Fennel said: "We're out to get brand name loyalty, so we're not selling individual titles."[38] Because of this practice, and because a romance is on the market for only a month, romance authors have to hustle their own books and find their own markets. They can also, they report, have a difficult time getting royalties from the publisher, with waits of up to two years.[39]

Although this kind of issue is just beginning to be addressed, the issues concerning quality of writing and personal creativity have already begun to be acted upon. Each product line in the romance industry has its own formula, and as the formulas have multiplied, they have also loosened. As a result, an author can pick the line that gives her or him the most freedom. More important, through Romance Writers of America, authors have formed their own critique groups, so that influences on their writing now also come from their peers and not only from the publishing institutions. Romances are beginning to be better and more carefully written, with more variety in the formulas, and with more attention to detail. Although some romances repeat a mechanical version of the formula, other romances like Leigh Roberts's *Love Circuits* are different. Roberts's work, where the hero, tender and loving from the beginning, wears a Charlotte Brontë T-shirt, and where the heroine has a witty sense of humor, brings some surprising transformations to the formula. Like any kind of formula writing—or any kind of writing—romance writing requires skill and talent.

As the corporation follows its destiny of expansion, conglomeration, and product diversification, differences between the mass production needs of the corporation and authors' needs may prove to be potential cracks in the Harlequin machine. The authors' own quest for creative individuality, for economic independence, and for recognition may make them the heroines of their own "real life" romance, with conflicts and adventures outside the text just as gripping as those inside.

NOTES

1. Catering to an exclusively feminine audience, mass market romances are an international phenomenon, with single romances or whole romance series being translated into as many as fourteen languages. Harlequin Enterprises, the best-selling and most successful publisher of this genre, has been imitated by many competitors both in America and in Europe. Harlequin publishes a set number of romances per month, categorized into different series according to a carefully measured degree of explicit sex, known as "sensuality" in the trade. Harlequin publishes Harlequin Romances, Harlequin Presents, and Harlequin Temptations, as well as a mystery-romance series, a gothic romance series, a

longer series called Superromances, and an American romance series. Like any corporate consumer product, Harlequin and its competitors are constantly "diversifying" their line, proliferating into a dizzying array of series.

Other publishers now have romance series for more mature and/or divorced women, like Berkeley-Jove's Second Chance at Love, or for adolescent girls, like Simon & Schuster's First Love. This series shares the teen-romance shelves with the Sweet Dream series from Bantam; Young Love from Dell; Caprice from Grosset & Dunlap; and two series from Scholastic, whose Wishing Star and Wild Fire sold 2.25 million copies in 1982.

Information taken from Brett Harvey, "Boy Crazy," *Village Voice* 27 (10–16 Feb. 1982): 48–49; Stanley Meisler, "Harlequins: The Romance of Escapism," *Los Angeles Times,* 15 Nov. 1980, pt. 1, 7–8; Rosemary Nightingale, "True Romances," *Miami Herald,* 5 Jan. 1983; J. D. Reed, "From Bedroom to Boardroom: Romance Novels Court Changing Fancies and Adorable Profits," *Time,* 13 Apr. 1981, 101–4; interview with Jany Saint-Marcoux, editor of Collections sentimentales, Éditions Tallandier; "Romantic Novels Find Receptive Market," *Santa Ana Register,* 26 July 1979, sec. E, 1; *Standard and Poors Corporation Records* 43 (New York: May 1982), 8475.

2. See Reed. According to Margaret Ann Jensen, the very success of Harlequin has caused these figures to decline drastically. Because so many publishers are now imitating Harlequin and competing with it, Harlequin's "share of the market has dropped to 45 percent. . . . All signs indicate that Harlequin is a financially distressed corporation." See Jensen, *Love's $weet Return: The Harlequin Story* (Toronto: Women's Educational Press, 1984). In order to offset this decline, Harlequin is purchasing Silhouette Romances.

3. Tania Modleski, *Loving with a Vengeance: Mass-Produced Fantasies for Women* (Hamden: Archon Books, 1982); Ann Barr Snitow, "Mass Market Romance: Pornography for Women is Different," *Radical History Review* 20 (Spring–Summer 1979): 141–61, reprinted in *Powers of Desire: The Politics of Sexuality,* ed. Ann Snitow, Christine Stansell, and Sharon Thomas (New York: Monthly Review Press, 1983); Janice A. Radway, "Women Read the Romance: The Interaction of Text and Context," *Feminist Studies* 9 (Spring 1983): 53–78.

4. Modleski, 113.

5. Kerry Allyne, *Across the Great Divide* (1980); Ann Cooper, *Battle with Desire* (1980); Kay Thorpe, *The Dividing Line* (1980). All books published by Harlequin Books, Toronto, London, New York, Amsterdam, Sydney, Hamburg, Paris, Stockholm. Page numbers appear in parentheses in the text.

6. Lynsey Stevens, *Race for Revenge* (Toronto: Harlequin, 1981), Back Cover.

7. Advertisement for Sara Jennings, *Game Plan* (Garden City, N.Y.: Candlelight Ecstasy Romances, 1984), Back Cover.

8. Leigh Roberts, *Love Circuits* (Harlequin Temptations, 1984); Sarah James, *Public Affair* (Harlequin American Romance, 1984); Marion Smith Collins, *By Any Other Name* (Harlequin Temptations, 1984). All books published by Harlequin Enterprises, Toronto. Page numbers appear in parentheses in the text.

9. Advertisement for Harlequin Temptations, found in Harlequin books of July 1984 (Toronto: Harlequin Enterprises, 1984).

10. Colette Dowling, *The Cinderella Complex: Women's Hidden Fear of Independence* (New York: Simon & Schuster Pocket Books, 1981), 2, 54.

11. Harry Braverman, *Labor and Monopoly Capital: The Degradation of Work in the Twentieth Century,* Special Abridged Edition (Special Issue of *Monthly Review,* 26 [July–August 1974]), 50.

According to Braverman, by 1970 in the United States, clerical work was one of the fastest growing occupations and had become one of the lowest paid, its pay "lower than that of every type of so-called blue collar work" (51). Of its 10 million members, by 1978, 79.6 percent were women. In 1970, clerical work included 18 percent of all gainfully employed persons in the United States, a percentage equal to that of production work of all sorts.

12. Roslyn L. Feldberg and Evelyn Nakano Glenn, "Technology and Work Degradation: Effects of Office Automation on Women Clerical Workers," in *Machina ex Dea*, ed. Joan Rothschild (New York: Pergamon Press. 1983), 62.

13. Radway (57) reports that 42 percent of the women in her study work outside the home, and says that Harlequin claims that 49 percent of its audience works outside the home. A 1984 Waldenbooks survey found that 63 percent of its romance readers held jobs outside the home. (Doug Brown, "Research Dissects the Romantic Novel," *L.A. Times*, Sept. 19, 1984, V, 8).

14. Ibid., 60.

15. Braverman, 61.

16. Ida Russakoff Hoos, *Automation in the Office* (Washington, 1961), 53, cited in Braverman.

17. Ellen Cantarow, "Working Can Be Dangerous to Your Health," *Mademoiselle*, August 1982, 114–16.

18. Eleanor Farnes, *The Enchanted Island* (Toronto: Harlequin Enterprises, 1971). Page numbers appear in parentheses in the text.

19. Margaret Mayo, *Stormy Affair* (Toronto: Harlequin Enterprises, 1980). Page numbers appear in parentheses in the text.

20. Radway; Snitow; and Nancy Chodorow, *The Reproduction of Mothering: Psychoanalysis and the Sociology of Gender* (Berkeley: University of California Press, 1978).

21. Sally Mitchell, *The Fallen Angel: Chastity, Class, and Women's Reading, 1835–1880* (Bowling Green, Ohio: Bowling Green University Press, 1981); and Modleski.

22. Personal communication from Louella Nelson, author of *Freedom's Fortune*, Harlequin Superromance (Toronto: Harlequin Books, 1984).

23. Charlotte Brontë, *Shirley* (Baltimore: Penguin Books, 1974), 234–35.

24. Janet Dailey, *The Matchmakers* (Toronto: Harlequin Enterprises, 1978); Elizabeth Graham, *Come Next Spring* (Toronto: Harlequin Enterprises, 1980).

25. For the role of narcissism in the Harlequin Romances, see Modleski.

26. Gaye Tuchman, Arlene Kaplan Daniels, and James Benet, eds., *Hearth and Home: Images of Women in the Mass Media* (New York: Oxford University Press, 1978), 18.

27. Ibid., 4.

28. Radway, 68.

29. Modleski, 14, 30.

30. Radway, 59.

31. Peter Killing, *Harlequin Enterprises Limited: Case Material of the Western School of Business Administration* (London, Ontario: University of Western Ontario, 1978), 3.

32. General Editorial Guidelines, *Worldwide Library Superromances* (Toronto: Harlequin Enterprises, 1982), 2.

33. Guidelines for Writing Harlequin's *New* American Romances (Toronto: Harlequin Enterprises, 1982), 3.

34. *Harlequin Romance and Harlequin Presents Editorial Guidelines* (Ontario: Harlequin Books, 1984), 1.

35. George Christian, "Romance Writers, Going to the Heart of the Matter (and the Market), Call for Recognition," *Publisher's Weekly*, 24 July 1980. The first national conference of Romance Writers of America was held in Houston, in June 1981, with 800 participants, mostly women.

36. Jensen, 73–74.

37. Speech given at a meeting of Romance Writers of America, Orange County Chapter.

38. Vivien Lee Jennings, "The Romance Wars," *Publisher's Weekly*, 24 Aug. 1984, 50–55.

39. Information gathered from conversations with authors at meeting. See note 37.

SUSAN WILLIS

I SHOP THEREFORE I AM

is there a place for afro-american culture in commodity culture?

(1989)

〜〜〜〜〜〜〜〜〜〜〜〜〜〜〜〜〜〜〜〜〜〜〜〜〜〜〜〜〜〜

> Adults, older girls, shops, magazines, newspapers, window signs—all the world had agreed that a blue-eyed, yellow-haired, pink-skinned doll was what every girl child treasured.
>
> —TONI MORRISON, *THE BLUEST EYE*

In her powerfully compressed first novel, *The Bluest Eye*, Toni Morrison scrutinizes the influence of the white-dominated culture industry on the lives and identities of black Americans. She tells the story of three young girls: Claudia and Frieda, who are sisters, and Pecola, who comes to stay with them during a period when her own brawling parents are cast out of their storefront home. The book's setting is a working-class urban black neighborhood during the 1930s and 1940s, a time when it is already clear that American culture means white culture, and this in turn is synonymous with mass media culture. Morrison singles out the apparently innocuous—or as Frieda and Pecola put it, "cu-ute"[1]—Shirley Temple, her dimpled face reproduced on cups, saucers, and baby dolls, to show how the icons of mass culture subtly and insidiously intervene in the daily lives of Afro-Americans.

Of the three girls, Claudia is the renegade. She hates Shirley Temple and seethes with anger when she sees the blue-eyed, curly haired child actress dancing alongside the culture hero that Claudia claims for herself—Bojangles. As she sees it, "Bojangles is [her] friend, [her] uncle, [her] daddy, [and he] ought to have been soft-shoeing it and chuckling with [her]" (19). Claudia's intractable hostility toward Shirley Temple originates in her realization that in our society, she, like all racial "others," participates in dominant culture as a consumer, but not as a producer. In rejecting Shirley Temple and wanting to be the one dancing with Bojangles, Claudia refuses the two modes of accommodation that white culture holds out to black consumers. She neither accepts that white is somehow superior, which would enable her to see Shirley Temple as a proper dancing partner for Bojangles; nor does she imagine herself miraculously translated into the body of Shirley Temple so as to vicariously live white experience as a negation of blackness. Instead, Claudia questions the basis for white cultural domination. This she does most dramatically by dismembering and tearing open the vapid blue-eyed baby dolls her parents and relatives give her for Christmas presents. Claudia's hostility is not blind, but motivated by the keen desire to get at the roots of white domination, "to see of what it was made, to discover the dearness, to find the beauty, the desirability that had escaped [her], but only [her]" (20).

Claudia's unmitigated rage against white culture, its dolls and movie stars, is equaled only by her realization that she could ax little white girls made of flesh and blood as readily as she rips open their plaster and sawdust replicas. The only thing that restrains Claudia from committing mayhem is her recognition that the acts of violence she imagines would be "disinterested violence" (22). This is an important point in Morrison's development of Claudia as the representation of a stance that Afro-Americans in general might take against white domination. By demonstrating that violence against whites runs the risk of being "disinterested violence," Morrison suggests that white people are little more than abstractions. As the living embodiments of their culture, all white people partake of the Shirley Temple icon. To some extent, all are reified subjects, against whom it is impossible for blacks to mount passionate, self-affirming resistance or retaliation. In defining Claudia as someone who learns "how repulsive disinterested violence [is]" (22), Morrison affirms the fullness of her character's humanity.

BEING DIFFERENT

Morrison's treatment of Claudia explores the radical potential inherent in the position of being "other" to dominant society. The critical nature of *The Bluest Eye* may be best appreciated when apprehended in relation to efforts by Edward Said and Frantz Fanon to expose the emotionally crippling aspects of colonialism. Morrison's genius as a writer of fiction is to develop the experience of "otherness" and its denunciation in ways that were not open to either Said in *Orientalism* or Fanon in *Black Skin White Masks*. This is because Morrison's fictional characters, while they articulate history, are not themselves bound by historical events and social structures as were Fanon's patients whose case histories are the narrative raw material of his book. Morrison's portrayal of Pecola is the most horrifying example of the mental distortion produced by being "other" to white culture. She transforms the Fanonian model of a little black girl caught behind a white mask into a little black girl whose white mask becomes her face. Pecola's dialectical antithesis is, then, Claudia who tears to shreds the white mask society wants her to wear.

However, Claudia's critical reversal of "otherness" is short lived. Indeed, she later learned to "worship" Shirley Temple, knowing even as she did "that the change was adjustment without improvement" (22). In this, Morrison suggests that white cultural domination is far too complex to be addressed only in a retaliatory manner. A simple, straightforward response to cultural domination cannot be mounted, let alone imagined, because domination is bound up with the media, and this with commodity gratification. Claudia's desire to dance with Bojangles raises a question so crucial as to put all of American culture to the test. That is, can we conceive of mass culture as black culture? Or is mass culture by its very definition white culture with a few blacks in it? Can we even begin to imagine the media as a form capable of expressing Afro-American cultural identity?

Morrison addresses these questions by way of a parable. She tells the story of how Claudia and her sister plant a bed of marigolds and believe that the health and vigor of their seeds will ensure the health and vigor of their friend's incestuously conceived child. Morrison makes the parallel explicit; "We had dropped our seeds in our own little plot of black dirt just as Pecola's father had dropped his seeds in his own plot of black dirt" (9). But there were no marigolds. The seeds "shriveled and died" (9) as did Pecola's baby. The parable of the flower garden resonates with more meaning than the mere procreation and survival of black people. In its fullest sense, the parable asks if we can conceive of an Afro-American cultural garden capable of bringing all its people to fruition. In the absence of a whole and sustaining Afro-American culture, Morrison shows black people making "adjustments" to mass white culture. Claudia preserves more integrity than her sister, Frieda, but both finally learn to love the white icon. Pecola magically attains the bluest eyes and with them the madness of assimilation to the white icon. Maureen, the "high-yellow dream child with long brown hair," mimics the white icon with rich displays of fashion: "patent-leather shoes with buckles," "colored knee socks," and a "brown velvet coat trimmed in white rabbit fur and a matching muff" (52–53). Taken together, the four young girls represent varying degrees of distortion and denial of self produced in relation to a culture they and their parents do not make, but cannot help but consume. Can we, then, conceive of Afro-American culture capable of sustaining all four young girls, individually and collectively? And can such a culture take a mass form? To open up these questions, I move into the present, out of literature and into advertising, where mass media culture has made black its "other" most frequently viewed population as compared to the less visible Asian Americans and all but invisible Hispanics.

SHOP TILL YOU DROP

> I don't want to know! I just want that magical moment when I go into a store and get what I want with my credit card. I don't even want to know I'll have to pay for it.—Comment made by a white male student when I explained that commodity fetishism denies knowledge of the work that goes into the things we buy.

There is a photograph by Barbara Kruger that devastatingly sums up the abstraction of self and reality in consumer society. The photo shows no more than a white hand whose thumb and forefinger grasp a red credit-card-like card, whose motto reads "I Shop Therefore I Am."[2] Kruger's photo captures the double nature of commodity fetishism as it informs both self and activity. The reduction of being to consumption coincides with the abstraction of shopping as well. This is because "using plastic" represents a deepening of the already abstract character of exchange based on money as the general equivalent.

If shopping equals mere existence, then the purchase of brand names is the individual's means for designating a specific identity. Consumer society has produced a population of wearers of such corporate logos as Esprit, Benetton, Calvin Klein, Jordache, and the latest on the fashion scene, McDonald's McKids. The stitched or printed logo is a visible detail of fashion not unlike the stickers on a banana peel. In the eyes of the corporate fashion industry, our function is to bring advertising into our daily lives. We may well ask if we are any different from the old-time sandwich board advertisers who once patrolled city streets with signs recommending "Eat at Joe's."

Until recently it was clear in the way fashion featured white models that buying a brand name designer label meant buying a white identity. The workers who produce brand name clothing today are predominantly Chinese, Filipino, and Mexican; or, closer to home, they are Hispanics and Asian Americans, but the corporations are as white as the interests and culture of the ruling class they maintain. The introduction of black fashion models in major fashion magazines like *Vogue, Harper's Bazaar,* and *Glamour* may have at one time represented a potential loosening of white cultural hegemony. But this was never fully realized because high fashion circumscribes ethnic and racial identity by portraying people of color as exotic. Today, blacks appear in all forms of advertising, most often as deracinated, deculturated black integers in a white equation. This is even true in many of the ads one finds in such black magazines as *Ebony* and *Essence,* where the format, models, and slogans are black mirror images of the same ads one sees month by month in the white magazines. For instance, in February 1988, Virginia Slims ran a magazine and billboard ad that featured a white model in a red and black flamenco dancing dress. Black magazines and billboards in black neighborhoods ran the same ad, same dress. The only difference was the black model inside the dress.

Whether black people can affirm identity by way of a brand name is nowhere more acutely posed than by Michael Jordan's association with Air Nike. Michael Jordan *is* Air Nike. He is not just shown wearing the shoes like some other champion might be shown eating "the breakfast of champions." Rather, his name and the brand form a single unified logo-refrain. No other sports star, white or black, has ever attained such an intimate relationship between self and commodity. However, the personal connection between product and star does not suggest a more personalized product, rather it speaks for the commodification of Jordan himself. Moreover, the intimate oneness between the black basketball player and the white sneaker does not represent an inroad on the white corporation, but it does ensure that thousands of black youths from sixteen to twenty-five will have a good reason for wanting hundred-dollar shoes.

A decade before Michael Jordan made black synonymous with a brand name, Toni Morrison used another of her novels to demonstrate the futility of affirming blackness with a white label. In *Song of Solomon,* Morrison depicts the anguish of Hagar, who wakes one morning to the realization that the reason for her boyfriend's lack of interest is her looks. "Look at how I look. I look awful. No wonder he didn't want me. I look terrible."[3] Hagar's "look" is black urban, northern, working class, with a still strong attachment to the rural South. What little connection she has to the larger white culture has been fashioned out of her mother's sweepstakes prizes and her grandmother's impulse purchases. There is nothing contrived or premeditated about Hagar and the way she spontaneously defines herself and her love for Milkman. Her boyfriend, on the other hand, is the progeny of the urban black middle class whose forbears conquered the professions and gained access to private property. Not as fully assimilated to the brand name as Michael Jordan, Milkman nevertheless is a walking collection of commodities from his "cordovan leather" shoes (255) to his "good cut of suit" (256).

In rationalizing her boyfriend's rejection of her as a fault of her "looks," Hagar assimilates race to style. She had previously been devastated by Milkman's flirtation with a woman with "penny-colored hair" and "lemon-colored skin" (319), and decides that in order to hold on to her boyfriend she must make herself into a less-black woman. What Hagar does not grasp is that Milkman's uncaring regard for her is an expression of his primary sexism as well as his internalized acceptance of the larger society's racist measure of blacks in terms of how closely an individual's skin and hair approximate the white model. Hagar lives her rejection as a personal affront and turns to the only means our society holds out to individuals to improve their lot and solve their problems: consumption. Hagar embodies all the pain and anxiety produced when racism and sexism permeate an intimate relationship; she is the living articulation of consumer society's solution to racism and sexism. This is, buy a new you. Transform yourself by piling on as many brand name styles and scents as your pocketbook will allow. The solution to a racist society is a "pretty little black skinned girl" (310) "who dresses herself up in the white-with-a-band-of-color skirt and matching bolero, the Maidenform brassiere, the Fruit of the Loom panties, the no color hose, the Playtex garter belt and the Joyce con brios" (318); who does her face in "sunny glow" and "mango tango"; and who puts "baby clear sky light to outwit the day light on her eyelids" (318).

Morrison reveals her sensitive understanding of how commodity consumption mutilates black personhood when she has Hagar appear before her mother and grandmother newly decked out in the clothes and cosmetics she hauled home through a driving rainstorm: her "wet ripped hose, the soiled white dress, the sticky, lumpy face powder, the streaked rouge, and the wild wet shoals of hair" (318). If Hagar had indeed achieved the "look" she so desperately sought, she would only have been a black mimicry of a white cultural model. Instead, as the sodden, pitiful child who finally sees how grotesque she has made herself look, Hagar is the sublime manifestation of the contradiction between the ideology of consumer society that would have everyone believe we all trade equally in commodities, and the reality of all marginalized people for whom translation into the dominant white model is impossible.

Morrison's condemnation of commodity consumption as a hollow solution to the problems of race, class, and gender is as final and absolute as are Hagar's subsequent delirium and death. Unable to find let alone affirm herself, unable to bridge the contradiction in her life by way of a shopping spree and a Cinderella transformation, Hagar falls into a fever and eventually perishes.

If consumer society were to erect a tombstone for Hagar, it would read "Shop till you drop." This is clearly the ugliest expression ever coined by shopping mall publicity people. Yet it is currently proclaimed with pride and glee by compulsive shoppers from coast to coast. Emblazoned on T-shirts, bumper stickers, and flashy advertising layouts, "shop till you drop" attests the ultimate degradation of the consumer. How often have you heard a young woman remark, such as the one I saw on the "Newlywed Game," "Whenever I feel low, I just shop till I drop!"? This is exactly what Hagar did. The difference between Morrison's por-

trayal of Hagar and the relish with which the "Newlywed" contestant characterizes her shopping orgies is Morrison's incisive revelation of the victimization and
dehumanization inherent in mass consumption "Shop till you drop" is a message
aimed at and accepted largely by women. (I have yet to hear a male shopper characterize himself in such a way.) The extreme sexism of the retail and advertising
industries could not be more abusively stated. However, the victimization, the
sexism, the degradation and dehumanization—all go unnoticed because the notion of consumption is synonymous with gratification. To demonstrate the fundamental impossibility of realizing gratification in commodity consumption, we
have only to shift the focus from consumption to production. Now I ask you,
would anyone wear a T-shirt proclaiming "Work till you drop"? The cold fact of
capitalism is that much of the work force is expendable. Are we to assume that a
fair number of consumers are also expendable provided they set high consumption standards on the way out?

FROM BLACK REPLICANTS TO MICHAEL JACKSON

Toni Morrison's blatant condemnation of the fetishizing quality of white-dominated
commodity culture is by no means unique to the tradition of black women writers. In her novel *Meridian*, Alice Walker creates a caricature of the reification of
white society that is even more grotesque than Morrison's frozen-faced white
baby dolls. This is the dead white woman whose mummified body is carted about
from town to town and displayed as a side-show attraction by her money-grubbing
husband. In death, as was probably the case in her life, the white woman's labor
power is the basis for her husband's livelihood. As a dead body, she is literally
the embodiment of the congealed labor that exemplifies the commodity form.
What Morrison and Walker are documenting in their portrayals of reified white
characters is the consequence of the longer and deeper association with the commodity form that whites in our society have had as opposed to racial minorities.
In reacting so strongly against the fetishizing power of the commodity, contemporary black women's fiction stands aghast at the level of commodity consumption that Hagar attempts in *Song of Solomon*, and suggests that total immersion in
commodities is a fairly recent historical phenomenon for the broad mass of Afro-
Americans. Indeed, one way to read *Song of Solomon* is as a parable of black
peoples' integration with the commodity form that is depicted across the book's
three female generations, from Pilate who trades and barters for daily needs and
very seldom makes a commodity purchase, to her daughter, Reba, who gets and
gives a vast array of commodities that she wins rather than purchases, to Hagar,
who desperately yearns for and dies because of commodities. The larger implications of Morrison's parable suggest that while the commodity form has been
dominant throughout the twentieth century, daily-life economics may have been
only partially commodified owing to the many social groups that, until recently,
did not fully participate as consumers.

While Morrison rejects out of hand the possibility of creating a positive, affirming black cultural identity out of "sunny glow" and "mango tango," Kobena Mercer, the British film and art critic, dramatically affirms the contrary. In considering
the politics of black hairstyles, Mercer defines an approach to consumer society

that sees commodities giving new forms of access to black people's self-expression.[4] Mercer contrasts the social meanings associated with the Afro, a hairstyle popular among black radicals in the sixties and the general cultural movement that promoted "black is beautiful" on into the seventies, with the conk, a hairstyle contrived during the late thirties and early forties by urban black males. Mercer sees the popular interpretation of these two hairstyles wholly influenced by the way Western culture has, ever since romanticism, validated the natural as opposed to the artificial. The "Fro" was read culturally as making a strong positive statement because it was taken to represent the natural. Then, because Western mythology equates the natural with the primitive—and primitive with Africa—the "Fro" was seen as truly African, hence, the most valid form of Afro-American cultural expression. Mercer deflates all the myths by pointing out that the "Fro" was not natural but had to be specially cut and combed with a pik to produce the uniform rounded look. Moreover, the cultural map of African hairstyles reveals a complex geography of complicated plaits and cuts that are anything but natural. Mercer's final point is that if the "Fro" was seen as natural, it was defined as such by dominant white society for whom the longer hairstyles of the late sixties meant hippies and their version of a communal back-to-nature movement. In this way, dominant white culture assimilated the "Fro" to its meanings, including its countercultural meanings.

By comparison, Mercer sees the conk allowing a form of Afro-American cultural expression that was not possible with the "Fro" precisely because the conk was seen as artificial. At the time of its popularity and even on into the present, the conk has been condemned as an attempt by black men to "whiten" their appearance. Mercer gives the prevailing line of thought by citing Malcolm X on his own first conk: "on top of my head was this thick, smooth sheen of red hair—real red—as straight as any white man's. . . . [The conk was] my first really big step towards self-degradation." In contrast, Mercer's opinion of the conk is very different. As he sees it, if black men were trying to make themselves look more white and more acceptable to white ideals of style, they would not have chosen the conk. The hair was straightened by what he calls a "violent technology" and treated to produce a tight cap of glistening red to orange hair. For its artificiality, the conk made a radical cultural statement that cannot be inscribed in dominant racialized interpretations of culture.

> Far from an attempted simulation of whiteness I think the dye was used as a stylized means of defying the "natural" colour codes of conventionality in order to highlight artificiality and hence exaggerate a sense of difference. Like the purple and green wigs worn by the black women, which Malcolm mentions in disgust, the use of red dye seems trivial: but by flouting convention with varying degrees of artifice such techniques of black stylization participated in a defiant "dandyism," fronting-out oppression by the artful manipulation of appearances.[5]

Mercer's point is finally that black culture has at its disposal and can manipulate all the signs and artifacts produced by the larger culture. The fact that these are already inscribed with meanings inherited through centuries of domination does not inhibit the production of viable culture statements, even though it influences the way such statements are read. The readings may vary depending on the historical period as well as the class, race, and gender of the reader. Mercer's own reading of the conk is facilitated by current theories in popular culture that see the commodity form as the raw material for the meanings that people produce. From this point of view, the most recognizable commodity (what is seen as wholly "artificial") is somehow freer of past associations and more capable of giving access to alternative meanings.

There is, however, an important consideration that is not addressed either by Morrison in her condemnation of commodity culture or by Mercer in his delight over the possibilities of manipulating cultural meanings. This is the way the dominant white culture industry produces consumable images of blacks. Considerable effort in Afro-American criticism has been devoted toward revealing racism in the images of blacks on television and in film, but little has been written about more mundane areas such as advertising and the mass toy market. I suggest a hypothesis that will help us understand consumer society in a more complex way than to simply point out its racism. That is, in mass culture many of the social contradictions of capitalism appear to us as if those very contradictions had been resolved. The mass cultural object articulates the contradiction and its imaginary resolution. Witness the way mass culture suggests the resolution of racism.

In contrast to Morrison's Claudia, who circa 1940 was made to play with white baby dolls, black mothers in the late sixties could buy their little girls Barbie's black equivalent: Christie. Mattel marketed Christie as Barbie's friend, and in so doing, cashed in on the civil rights movement and black upward social mobility. With Christie, Mattel also set an important precedent in the toy industry for the creation of black replicants of white cultural models. The invention of Christie is not wholly unlike the inception of a black Shirley Temple doll. If the notion of a black simulacrum of Shirley Temple is difficult to imagine, this is because only recent trends in mass marketing have taught us to accept black replicants as "separate but equal" expressions of the white world. In the 1930s a black Shirley Temple would not have been possible, but if she were a five-year-old dancing princess today, Mattel would make a doll of her in black and white and no one would consider it strange. I say this because as soon as we started to see those grotesque, sunken-chinned white Cabbage Patch dolls, we started to see black ones as well. Similarly, the more appealing, but curiously furry-skinned My Child dolls are now available in black or white and boy or girl models. Clearly, in the 1980s, race and gender have become equal integers on the toy store shelf. I know many white girls who own mass-marketed black baby dolls such as these, but I have yet to see a single little black girl with a black Cabbage Patch doll. What these dolls mean to little girls, both black and white, is a problem no adult should presume to fully understand, particularly as the dolls raise questions of mothering and adoption along with race. I mention these dolls because they sum up for me the crucial question of whether it is possible to give egalitarian expression to cultural diversity in a society where the white middle class is the norm against which all else is judged. This is another way to focus the problem I raised earlier when I asked whether it is possible for Afro-American culture to find expression in a mass cultural form.

In an essay inaugurating her participation in the new magazine *Zeta*, bell hooks develops the important distinction between white supremacy and older forms of racism. Hooks sees white supremacy as "the most useful term to denote exploitation of people of color in this society"[6] both in relation to liberal politics and liberal feminism. I would add that white supremacy is the only way to begin to understand the exploitation of black people as consumers. In contrast to racism which bars people of color from dominant modes of production and consumption, white supremacy suggests the equalization of the races at the level of consumption. This is possible only because all the models are white. As replicants, black versions of white cultural models are of necessity secondary and devoid of cultural integrity. The black replicant ensures, rather than subverts, domination. The notion of "otherness," or unassimilable marginality, is in the replicant attenuated by its mirroring of the white model. Finally the proliferation of black replicants, in toys, fashion, and advertising smothers the possibility for creating black cultural alternatives.

While the production of blacks as replicants of whites has been the dominant mass-market strategy for some twenty years, there are indications that this formula is itself in the process of being replaced by a newer mode of representation that in turn suggests a different approach to racism in society. I am referring to the look of racial homogeneity that is currently prevalent in high-fashion marketing. Such a look depicts race as no more meaningful than a blend of paint. For example, the March 1988 issue of *Elle* magazine featured a beige woman on its cover. Many more fashion magazines have since followed suit in marketing what is now called "the new ethnicity." The ethnic model who appeared on *Elle* is clearly not "a high yellow dream child," Morrison's version of a black approximation to whiteness circa 1940. Rather, she is a woman whose features, skin tone, and hair suggest no one race, or even the fusion of social contraries. She is, instead, all races in one. A skimming perusal of *Elle*'s fashion pages reveals more beige women and a great number of white women who have been photographed in beige tones. The use of beige fashion models is the industry's metaphor for the magical erasure of race as a problem in our society. It underscores white supremacy without directly invoking the dominant race. To understand how this is achieved we have only to compare the look of racial homogeneity to the look of gender homogeneity. For some time now the fashion industry has suggested that all women, whether they are photographed in Maidenform or denim, whether they are twelve years old or forty-five, are equally gendered. Dominant male-defined notions about female gender, such as appear in fashion advertising, have inured many women to the possibility of gender heterogeneity. Now the suggestion is that women with the proper "look" are equally "raced." Such a look denies the possibility for articulating cultural diversity precisely because it demonstrates that difference is only a matter of fashion. It is the new fall colors, the latest style, and the corporate logo or label—a discrete emblematic representation of the otherwise invisible white corporate godfather.

I mention *Elle*'s beige women because the fashion industry's portrayal of racial homogeneity provides an initial means for interpreting Michael Jackson who in this context emerges as the quintessential mass cultural commodity.[7] Nowhere do we see so many apparent resolutions of social contradiction as we apprehend in Michael Jackson. If youth culture and expanding youth markets belie a society whose senior members are growing more numerous, more impoverished, more marginal every day, then Michael Jackson as the ageless child of thirty represents a solution to aging. If ours is a sexist society, then Michael Jackson, who expresses both femininity and masculinity but fails to generate the threat or fear generally associated with androgeny, supplies a resolution to society's sexual inequality. If ours is a racist society, then Michael Jackson, who articulates whiteness and blackness as surgical rather than cultural identities, offers an easy solution to racial conflict.

Recently I was struck when Benson on the television show by the same name remarked that Michael Jackson looked like Diana Ross. The show confirmed what popular opinion has been saying for some time. The comparison of Michael Jackson to Diana Ross is particularly astute when we see Jackson as both a "look" and a music statement. Rather than defining Michael Jackson in relation to the black male music tradition, I think it makes more sense to evaluate his music with respect to black women singers—and to go much further back than Diana Ross to the great blues singers like "Ma" Rainey, Bessie Smith, and Ethel Waters. Diana Ross and the Motown sound is in many ways the mass cultural cancellation of the threatening remembrance of "ladies who really did sing the blues." In a path-breaking essay on the sexual politics of the blues, Hazel Carby shows how the black women blues singers attacked patriarchy by affirming women's right to mobility and sexual independence.[8] Getting out of town and out from under a misbehaving man, refusing to be cooped up in the house, and taking the initiative in sexual relations—these are the oft-repeated themes of the black female blues tradition. By comparison, the incessant chant style developed by Diana Ross and the Supremes features refrains aimed at the containment of women's desire and the acceptance of victimization. Background percussion that delivers a chainlike sound reminiscent of slavery is an apt instrumental metaphor for lyrics such as "My world is empty without you, Babe," "I need your love, oh, how I need your love." By physically transforming himself into a Diana Ross look-alike, Michael Jackson situates himself in the tradition of black women's blues. The thematic concerns of his music often take up the question and consequences of being sexually a renegade, that is, "bad"; however, Jackson ultimately represents the black male reversal of all that was threatening to patriarchy in black women's blues music. Where the black women singers affirmed the right to self-determination, both economically and sexually, Jackson taunts that he is "bad" but asks for punishment. Jackson toys with the hostility associated with sexual oppression, but rather than unleashing it, he calls for the reassertion of a patriarchal form of authority .

This does not, however, exhaust the question of Michael Jackson. As the most successful Afro-American in the mass culture industry, Jackson begs us to consider whether he represents a successful expression of Afro-American culture in mass form. To begin to answer this question we need to go back to the notion of the commodity and recognize that above all else Michael Jackson is the consummate expression of the commodity form. Fredric Jameson offers one way of understanding Michael Jackson as a commodity when he defines the contradictory function of repetition. On the one hand, repetition evokes the endlessly reproducible and degraded commodity form itself. Jameson demonstrates how mass culture, through the production of numerous genres, forms, and styles, attempts to create the notion of newness, uniqueness, or originality. What is contradictory about repetition is that while we shun it for the haunting reminder of commodity seriality, we also seek it out. This, Jameson sees, is especially the case in popular music, where a single piece of music hardly means anything to us the first time we hear it, but comes to be associated with enjoyment and to take on personal meanings through subsequent listenings. This is because "the pop single, by means of repetition, insensibly becomes part of the existential fabric of our own lives, so that what we listen to is ourselves, our own previous auditions."[9]

From this point of view, we might be tempted to interpret Michael Jackson's numerous physical transformations as analogous to Ford's yearly production of its "new" models. Jackson produces a new version of himself for each concert tour or album release. The notion of a new identity is certainly not original with Jackson. However, the mode of his transformations and its implications define a striking difference between Michael Jackson and any previous performer's use of identity change. This is particularly true with respect to David Bowie, whose transformation from Ziggy Stardust to The Thin White Duke were enacted as artifice. Concocted out of makeup and fashion, Bowie's identities enjoyed the precarious reality of mask and costume. The inconcrete nature of Bowie's identities, coupled with their theatricality, were, then, the bases for generating disconcerting social commentary. For Jackson, on the other hand, each new identity is the result of surgical technology. Rather than a progressively developing and maturing public figure who erupts into the social fabric newly made up to make a new statement, Jackson produces each new Jackson as a simulacrum of himself whose moment of appearance signals the immediate denial of the previous Michael Jackson. Rather than making a social statement, Jackson states himself as a commodity. As a final observation, and this is in line with Jameson's thoughts on repetition, I would say that the "original" Michael Jackson, the small boy who sang with the Jackson Five, also becomes a commodified identity with respect to the subsequent Michael Jacksons. In Jameson's words, "the first time event is by definition not a repetition of anything: it is then reconverted into repetition the second time around."[10] The Michael Jackson of the Jackson Five becomes "retroactively" a simulacrum once the chain of Jackson simulacra comes into being. Such a reading is a devastating cancellation of the desire for black expression in mass culture which Toni Morrison set in motion when she asked us to imagine Claudia dancing in the movies with Bojangles. This interpretation sees the commodity form as the denial of difference. All moments and modes are merely incorporated in its infinite seriality.

Commodity seriality negates the explosive potential inherent in transformation, but transformation, as it is represented culturally, need not only be seen as an expression of commodity seriality. In the black American entertainment tradition, the original metaphor for transformation, which is also a source for Michael Jackson's use of identity change, is the blackface worn by nineteenth-century minstrel performers. When, in 1829, Thomas Dartmouth Rice, a white man, blackened his face and jumped "Jim Crow" for the first time, he set in motion one of the most popular entertainment forms of the nineteenth century. By the late 1840s, the Christy Minstrels had defined many of the standard routines and characters, including the cakewalk and the Sambo and Bones figures that are synonymous with minstrelsy. In the 1850s and 1860s, hundreds of minstrel troupes were touring the states, generally on a New York–Ohio axis. Some even journeyed to London where they were equally successful. By the 1880s and 1890s there were far fewer troupes, but the shows put on by the few remaining companies expanded into mammoth extravaganzas, such as those mounted by the Mastodon Minstrels.

Broadly speaking, the minstrel shows portrayed blacks as the "folk," a population wholly formed under a paternalistic southern plantation system. They were shown to be backward and downright simpleminded; they were lazy, fun loving, and foolish, given to philandering, gambling, and dancing; they were victimized, made the brunt of slapstick humor and lewd jokes. The men were "pussy whipped" and the women were liars, cheats, and flirts. No wonder the minstrel shows have been so roundly condemned by Afro-American intellectuals, including Nathan Huggins, for whom the most crippling aspect of minstrelsy is the way its popularity prevented the formation of an alternative "Negro ethnic theater."[11] Nevertheless, a few critics have advanced the notion that minstrelsy represents a nascent form of people's culture, whose oblique—albeit distorted—reference to real plantation culture cannot be denied.[12] What is interesting is that neither position in this debate seems adequate to explain why blacks performed in minstrel shows, and why, when they did so, they too blackened their faces with burnt cork and exaggerated the shape of their lips and eyes. If the shows promoted the debasement of blacks, can black participation in them be explained by their immense popularity, or the opportunity the shows provided to blacks in entertainment, or the money a performer might make? If the shows were an early form of people's theater, was it, then, necessary for blacks in them to reiterate the racist stereotyping that blackface signified?

An initial response to those questions is provided by Bert Williams, one of the most famous black actors of this century, who joined the Ziegfield Follies against the protests of the entire white cast. Williams proved incredibly successful, earning up to $2,500 a week. Nevertheless, he chose throughout his career to perform in blackface. In their anthology of black theater, James Hatch and Ted Shine suggest that blackface was for Bert Williams "a badge of his trade, a disguise from which to work, and a positive reminder to his audience that he was a black man."[13] These explanations get at the motives behind Bert Williams's choice, but I suggest we consider blackface as something more than a disguise or mask and apprehend it, instead, as a metaphor that functions in two systems of meanings. On the one hand, it is the overt embodiment of the southern racist stereotyping of blacks; but as a theatrical form, blackface is a metaphor for the commodity. It is the sign of what people paid to see. It is the image consumed, and it is the site of the actor's estrangement from self into role. Blackface is a trademark, and as such it can be either full or empty of meaning.

In his comprehensive study on minstrelsy, Eric Lott interprets blackface in terms of race and gender relations. He describes it as the site where all sorts of dissimulations and transformations take place that have their origin in social tensions. In blackface, white men portrayed black men; black men portrayed white men portraying black men, and men, both black and white, became female impersonators and acted the "wench." Audiences enjoyed flirting with the notion of actually seeing a black man perform on stage, when such was generally not allowed. And they enjoyed the implications of seeing men put themselves in the bodies of women so as to enact sexual affairs with other men. Blackface allowed the transgression of sexual roles and gender definition even while it disavowed its occurrence. As Eric Lott points out, minstrelsy was highly inflected with the desire to assume the power of the "other," even while such power was being denigrated and denied. As he puts it, minstrelsy was "a derisive celebration of the power of blacks"[14] (and I would add, of women, too) which is contained within the authority of the white male performer. So, on the one hand, blackface is heavily laden with overt racist and sexist messages; on the other hand, it is hollowed of social meanings and restraints. This makes blackface a site where the fear of miscegenation can be both expressed and managed, where misogyny can be affirmed and denied, and where race and gender can be stereotyped and transgressed.

The contradictory meanings of minstrelsy offer another way of looking at Michael Jackson, who from this perspective emerges as the embodiment of blackface. His physical transformations are his trademark—a means for bringing all the sexual tensions and social contradictions present in blackface into a contemporary form. From this perspective, Jackson's artistic antecedent is not Diana Ross or even Bert Williams, but the great black dancer Juba, who electrified white audiences with his kinetic skill which had people seeing his body turned back to front, his legs turned left to right. While Juba performed in blackface, his body was for him yet a more personal means of generating parody and ironic self-dissimulation. Juba's "Imitation Dance" offered his highly perfected rendition of each of the blackfaced white actors who had defined a particular breakdown dance, as well as an imitation of himself dancing his own consummate version of breakdown. This is the tradition that best defines Michael Jackson's 1989 feature-length video, *Moonwalker*. Here, Jackson includes video versions of himself as a child singing and dancing the Motown equivalent of breakdown, then ricochets this "real" image of himself off the image of a contemporary child impersonator who imitates Jackson in dress, face, song, and dance, and finally, bounces these versions off a dozen or so other memorable Jackson images—his teen years, Captain EO—which are preserved on video and appear like so many Jackson personae or masks. In fading from one version of Jackson to the next or splicing one Jackson against another, *Moonwalker* represents transformation as formalized content. Not surprisingly, most of the stories on the video are about transformation—a theme stunningly aided by the magic of every cinematic special effect currently available.

In opening her analysis of the sambo and minstrel figures, Sylvia Wynter states that the "imperative task" of black culture is "transformation." Wynter's optimistic account of the power of stigmatized black and popular culture to create a system of subversive countermeanings leads her to see minstrelsy as the place where black culture "began the cultural subversion of the normative bourgeois American reality."[15] Michael Jackson's *Moonwalker* opens with the desire for equally sweeping social change. The initial piece, "Man in the Mirror," surveys the faces of the world's disinherited, vanquished, and famished people, along with their often martyrized benefactors—Gandhi, Mother Teresa, the Kennedy brothers, Martin Luther King, Jr.—against whom are counterposed the images of fascist oppressors from Hitler to the Klan. The message of the song, hammered home to the beat of the refrain, is that if you want to change the world, begin with the Man in the Mirror. That the desire for social change is deflected into multitudinous self-transformations is to varying degrees the substance of all the video narratives assembled in *Moonwalker*. Two of these specifically demonstrate how blackface is redefined in the rubric of contemporary commodity culture.

In "Smooth Criminal," the grease and burnt cork that turned the minstrel artist into Jim Crow or Zip Coon are replaced by the metallic shell and electronic circuitry that turn Michael Jackson into a larger-than-life transformer robot. The story has Michael Jackson pitted against a depraved white drug lord bent on taking over the world by turning all young children (white and black; boys and girls) into addicts. The drug lord is aided by an army of gestapo troops, reminiscent of the stormtroopers from *Star Wars*. At the story's climactic moment, the army encircles Jackson, trapping him in the depths of their drug factory hideaway. Writhing on the floor under a relentless spotlight, completely surrounded by the faceless army, Michael Jackson is caught in a setting that dramatically summons up a parallel image: the rock star, alone on the stage in an stadium where he is besieged by a wall of faceless fans. The emblematic similarity between the story of persecution and subjugation and the experience of rock stardom establishes a connection to the minstrel tradition where the theater was the site for enacting the forms of domination and their potential transformation.

Jackson's submission to the forces of domination is broken when the drug lord begins to beat a little girl whom he has kidnapped and whose cries push Jackson to the brink of superhuman action. Suddenly, Jackson's face, already tightly stretched over surgically sculpted bones, becomes even more taut—indeed, metallic. His eyes lose their pupils, glow, and become lasers. Jackson rises, and a control box pops out of his stomach. His feet and arms sprout weapons. Michael Jackson is a robot. The transformation makes a stunning commentary on all Jackson's real-life physical transformations that *Moonwalker* cites and suggests that robotics is the logical next step in medical technology's reshaping of the human body.

However, the most powerful implication of Jackson's transformation—one that every child will grasp—is that Michael Jackson has made himself into a commodity. He is not a generic robot, but specifically a transformer. This Jackson demonstrates when he subsequently transforms himself from robot warrior into an armed space vehicle. In this shape, he ultimately vanquishes the drug lord. In another essay, I developed the significance of transformers as metaphors of gendering under capitalism.[16] Jackson's assimilation to transformer includes the erasure of gender traits simultaneous with the assumption of absolute male sexual potency. The transformer represents industrial technology in commodity form. If in this country, industry and the market are controlled by a largely white male hierarchy, then Jackson's transformation figurally raises the question of social power relationships. The question is whether Jackson, in becoming a transformer, appropriates an image associated with white male economic and sexual domination or whether he has been assimilated to the image. Is this a case of usurping power, or has Jackson, as "other," merely been absorbed? Another way to look at this question is to ask if the appropriation of the commodity form is in any way analogous to previous instances where blacks have appropriated white cultural forms. We might substitute religion for the commodity and ask some of the same questions. Has religion, commencing with colonization and the slave trade, functioned as an ideological arm of white domination, or does the appropriation of religion by the black church represent the reverse of colonization, where blacks denied salvation claimed God for their own? We are back to the dilemma I initially posed with reference to Toni Morrison, who might well argue that the transformer represents a form of colonization even more dehumanizing than that embodied by the blue-eyed Pecola because in it race and gender are wholly erased. In contrast, Kobena Mercer might be tempted to see the transformer as today's equivalent of the conk.

As if in response, and to consider the commodity from yet another angle, Michael Jackson enacts another parable of transformation. In "Speed Demon," the video wizards employ the magic of claymation to turn Michael Jackson into a Brer Rabbit figure, whose invisible popular culture referent is, of course, Gumby. "He was once a little green blob of clay, but you should see what Gumby can do today." This is a refrain familiar to children's television audiences of the early seventies. The song is about transformation from blob of clay to boy, making Gumby a proto-transformer. Indeed, Gumby's boyish de-gendering corresponds with the erasure of gender traits that we see in the transformers. His body absolutely smooth and malleable, Gumby's only noticeable features are his big eyes and rubbery mouth. If gender is de-emphasized, Gumby's green hue suggests possible racial otherness. This is not a farfetched interpretation, as Gumby coincides with the advent of "Sesame Street," where multiracial and multicultural neighborhoods are depicted by collections of multicolored humans, monsters, and animals. Purple, yellow, green, and blue are the colors of "Sesame Street's" Rainbow Coalition.

"Speed Demon" reworks the themes of pursuit and entrapment in a theatrical setting that parallels, although in a more lighthearted way, the portrayal of these themes in the transformer script. In this case Michael Jackson is pursued by overly zealous fans, who, during the course of a movie studio tour, recognize Michael Jackson and chase him through various lots and sound stages. The fans are grotesquely depicted as clay animations with horribly gesticulating faces and lumpy bodies. At one point Jackson appears to be cornered by a host of frenzied fans, but manages to slip into a vast wardrobe building where he discovers a full head mask of a rather goofy, but sly-looking rabbit. At this point, Jackson undergoes claymation transformation. This completely redefines the terms of his relationship to his pursuers. Claymation turns Michael Jackson into a motorcycle-riding Brer Rabbit, the trickster of the Afro-American folk tradition who toys with the oppressors, outsmarts them, outmaneuvers them—and with glee! The Speed Demon is Gumby, he is Brer Rabbit, and he is also most definitely Michael Jackson, whose "wet curl" look caps the clay head of the rabbit, and whose trademark dance, the moonwalk, is the rabbit's particular forte.

At the tale's conclusion, Michael, having eluded his pursuers, greets the sunrise in the California desert. Here he removes the rabbit disguise, which at this point is not the claymation body double but a simple mask and costume that Jackson unzips and steps out of. But lo and behold, the discarded costume takes on a life of its own and becomes a man-sized moonwalking rabbit who challenges Jackson to a dancing duel. In a video rife with transformations and doublings, this is the defining instance. In dance, the vernacular of black cultural expression, the conflict between the artist and his exaggerated, folksy, blackface alter ego is enacted.[17] Like Juba dancing an imitation of himself, Michael Jackson separates himself from his blackface and outmoonwalks the commodity form of himself.

In posing transformation as the site where the desire for black cultural autonomy coincides with the fetishization of commodity capitalism, *Moonwalker* denies commodity serialty. Instead, it defines the commodity form in the tradition of blackface as the nexus of struggle. The cultural commodity is not neutral, but instead defines a zone of contention where the terms of cultural definition have been largely determined by the white male-dominated system of capitalist production and reified by the fetishizing nature of the commodity itself.

In my accounts of "Smooth Criminal" and "Speed Demon," I suggest that some commodity manifestations provide more room for counterstatements than others. The transformers are so closely associated with high-tech capitalism that they offer little opening other than the ambiguity over appropriation versus assimilation. By comparison, the complex relationship between Gumby, Brer Rabbit, and Michael Jackson creates a space where the collision between black vernacular and mass media forms suggests the subversion of domination. "Speed Demon" deconstructs the commodity form, and with it, Michael Jackson as well, who, by the end of the video, emerges as a multiple subject reflected back from a dozen commodified mirror images. *Moonwalker* engages commodity fetishism and opens up the commodity form, but does it provide a platform for the emergence of what Stuart Hall calls the "concrete historical subject"?[18] Is there a Meridian in this text, capable of discovering a self out of the social fragments and conflicts? Can anything approaching the autonomous subject be discerned in this text? *Moonwalker* suggests a split between contemporary black women's fiction, which strives to create images of social wholeness based on the rejection of commodity capitalism, and what seems to be a black male position which sees the commodity as something that can be played with and enjoyed or subverted. Where Michael Jackson tricks the commodity form, and is able to do so precisely because its meanings are fetishized and therefore not culturally specific, Alice Walker refuses commodity fetishism and, in *The Color Purple*, imagines a form of cottage industry that has Celie organizing the collective production of customized pants for her extended community of family and friends. Jackson reaches back into the culture industry to minstrelsy and seizes blackface, updates it in contemporary forms, and unites himself with the history of black male actors who were made and unmade by their relationship to the commodity. Contrariwise, Alice Walker looks back upon commodity production, sees its earliest manifestation in the "slops" produced for slaves,[19] its continuation in the fashion industry that destroyed Morrison's Hagar, and summarily denies the possibility of the mass-produced commodity as having anything to offer Afro-Americans.

NOTES

1. Toni Morrison, *The Bluest Eye* (New York: Washington Square Press, 1979), 19. All references are to this edition and are given in the text.
2. Barbara Kruger, "Untitled," 1987.
3. Toni Morrison, *Song of Solomon* (New York: New American Library, 1977), 312. All references are to this edition and are given in the text.

4. Kobena Mercer, "Black Hair/Style Politics," *New Formations* 3 (Winter 1987): 33–54.

5. Ibid., 46, 47–49.

6. bell hooks, "Overcoming White Supremacy," *Zeta*, January 1988, p. 24.

7. In embarking on this by no means complete interpretation of Michael Jackson, I draw on many conversations with Deborah Chay of the Graduate Program in Literature, Duke University.

8. Hazel Carby, *Radical America* 20, 4 (June/July 1986): 9–22. Carby specifically defines the blues singers as "part of a larger history of the production of Afro-American culture within the North American culture industry." In conceptualizing Afro-American culture as somehow autonomous with respect to dominant mass culture, Carby takes a very different position from my own. Her claim for the vitality of Afro-American cultural production has validity given the boldly racial nature of the blues singers and their music and given that the mass media culture in the 1920s was less developed than it had become by the late 1930s, the period Morrison documented in *The Bluest Eye* and certainly less homogenized than it is today.

9. Fredric Jameson, "Reification and Utopia in Mass Culture," *Social Text* 1 (Winter 1979): 135–148; quotation on p. 138.

10. Ibid., 137.

11. Nathan Irvin Huggins, *Harlem Renaissance* (New York: Oxford University Press, 1971), 286.

12. For a summary of the critical debate surrounding minstrelsy, see Eric Lott, "Blackface and Blackness: Politics of Early Minstrelsy," paper delivered to the American Studies Convention, Miami, October 1988.

13. James V. Hatch, ed., and Ted Shine, consultant, *Black Theater USA* (New York: Macmillan, 1974), 618.

14. Lott, "Blackface and Blackness."

15. Sylvia Wynter, "Sambos and Minstrels," *Social Text* 1 (Winter 1979): 149–156; quotation on p. 155.

16. Susan Willis, "Gender as Commodity," *South Atlantic Quarterly* 86, 4 (Fall 1987): 403–421.

17. Cultural critics have traced the challenge, the calling out, the duel motif to African tribal tradition. It is seen in Caribbean stick fighting, later makes its way into the challenges hurled by sound system DJs during the early years of reggae, and now may be found in rap music and breakdance competition. See Dick Hebdige, *Cut 'n' Mix* (London: Methuen, 1987).

18. Stuart Hall, "On Postmodernism and Articulation," *Journal of Communication Inquiry* 10, 2 (Summer 1986): 45–60. In a theoretical climate dominated by the notion of a postmodern subject, interpolated from many fragmented social positions, Hall recommends that in the final instance, marginalized peoples must and will function as concrete historical subjects, whose political engagement binds together multiple subject positions.

19. Stuart Ewen and Elizabeth Ewen, *Channels of Desire* (New York: McGraw-Hill, 1982), 167.

ROSAURA SÁNCHEZ

DISCOURSES OF GENDER, ETHNICITY AND CLASS IN CHICANO LITERATURE

(1 9 9 2)

I am honored to have been invited to present this lecture in honor of one of our distinguished Chicano scholars, Dr. Américo Paredes, who, along with the late George Sánchez, was one of the first Chicano professors to be hired at the University of Texas at Austin. Today, fortunately, there are several Chicano professors on this campus, among them several distinguished scholars and writers, like Ricardo Romo, Rolando Hinojosa, Ramón Saldívar, David Montejano, Gilberto Cárdenas, and José Limón, to name just a few. It would be important to recall that just 20 years ago we were not highly visible on this campus, nor for that matter at other universities in the Southwest. It bears keeping in mind that even today, despite the fact that we are fast becoming one of the largest ethnic minorities in this country, our undergraduate and graduate enrollments in universities across the nation have in fact decreased and we continue to face low levels of recruitment and retention of Chicano students and faculty.

The numbers game however is not our only problem. Your own ongoing controversy here at U.T. Austin concerning a freshman writing course dealing with "difference" is similar to that found on other campuses where conservatives have rallied against any attempt to challenge the traditional curriculum emphasizing Eurocentric male scholarship. Reactions against a curriculum seeking to incorporate ethnic, feminist and Third World cultural production, much like reactions against Affirmative Action, have only sought to stifle the discourses of the exploited, oppressed and marginalized in this society. Even among minority scholars there is today, seemingly, a call for retreat from contestatory discourses. Their advice is that minority scholars accept their role in academia and learn to "converse" with mainstream literature and culture. For Henry Louis Gates and other multicultural scholars, "oppositional criticism" is partisan, divisive, and "tends to draw barriers between the oppressed and the oppressor, between the center and the margins of culture" (Winkler 8). This line of commentary ignores the fact that these barriers are always already there and are not the result of minority discourses and that, for the most part, those involved in minority studies today have in fact been weaned on mainstream culture. Thus, while the dialogue with mainstream culture has been long, it has also been one-sided. We have for too long been the audience; for dominant discourses have served to train the majority of minority professionals and academics and we have had to demonstrate competence

in these hegemonic discourses to earn our degrees. In fact, most Chicano literature professors and writers, for example, have received their university degrees
in Latin American/Spanish or English/American literature from traditional Spanish and English departments. For many of us research in Chicano history and literature has been a relatively new area of study that we have had to develop once
out in the field. No, the problem has not been our failure to participate, howso-
ever marginally, in the dialogue, but rather, our failure, for the most part, to get a
turn to speak, to be recognized and taken seriously.

Calls for reevaluating our concern with institutional failure to include the works
of minorities and women in the literary canon ignore the fact that this exclusion
is not a problem separate from the "social and political battles outside academe"
(Winkler 8), but rather an extension of the same social conditions in which non-
academic members of minority groups and women in general struggle. The exclusion of minority and women's work from mainstream university literature
classes points, in fact, to the multiple constraints within which most of these texts
are historically produced and the many barriers that minority writers must overcome to appear in print. This exclusion does not however negate the institutionalization of minority literature, so that we consequently often find ourselves
within academia but segregated. We do however agree with Cornel West that cultural critics need to analyze "the problems of women and minority groups in the
world outside academe" (Winkler 8–9). In fact we would insist that an adequate
analysis of cultural production, whether minority or mainstream, is impossible
without an analysis of the outside world, of history and society. This perhaps explains why one of the salient characteristics of Chicano literature is its dialogue
with history and its focus on collective subjectivity.

My remarks today on the discourses of gender, class and ethnicity in Chicano
literature are, in fact, a dialogue with a number of texts in Chicano literature, with
critical theory, and with Chicano history. The groundwork for this dialogue began here at U.T. in the 60s, when I did my undergraduate and graduate work in
Spanish Literature and Romance Linguistics. There were then over three hundred Chicano students on this campus, and by the time I left in 1972, many more,
but in 1961 when I first came, Chicano students were not highly visible. Back
then I would often stop after class at the Black women's co-op to see my friend
Jolene Scott, who had also come to the university from San Angelo; at that time
dorms, skating rinks and many other places around campus were still segregated.
That co-op and the Benson Latin American Collection where I worked as a student were places of refuge for me. That the segregation and blatant racism of
that period is still very much with us was made evident in the T.V. showing of
Los Angeles policemen beating Rodney King. But, then, police brutality is not
unfamiliar to Chicanos in Texas, even when perpetrated by our own kind in the
Texas Valley.

In truth, my preparation for this talk began many years ago, after many years
of training in the state of Texas. A native of the state, I had the equivalent of
thousands of academic units in the exploration of racism, through observation and
participation, albeit on the receiving end, of ethnic, cultural and linguistic discriminatory practices. As a person of working-class origin I also learned a good
deal about exploitation, though I then thought it simply an extension of racism
and had to wait several years to discover there were already constructs—class and

labor exploitation—to explain our oppression. Experience in itself, of course, does not guarantee insight or understanding; it is not, as Spivak indicates, "the final arbiter" (Spivak 281) but it can certainly set the stage for response to interpellation by particular discourses of analysis. It is perhaps this general marginalization in society, on the basis of class, ethnicity and gender, that Chicano literature has reconstructed textually, sometimes to counter mainstream representation, sometimes in collusion with these same stereotypical representations, but more often in an effort to recuperate oral texts, memories and recollections of past events that have long been ignored, erased, denied and dismissed.

History, as historians are wont to tell us, is a slippery beast. Attempts to reconstruct the past always lead to questions on the relation between texts and history and, particularly as regards Chicano Literature, to questions as to the dominant voices in marginalized cultural production. One may ask: "Does the subaltern group speak through its own production, or is it voiceless even here as Spivak finds in colonialist historiography and literature?" (Spivak 287). Do Chicano writers speak for the marginalized minority or do they constitute a sort of indigenous elite, voicing only hegemonic ideological discourses? Is there a subaltern subjectivity, and if so, what are its traits? The problem of course has no easy answers, but I will pose it here in terms of a historical and materialist framework that attempts to grapple with some of these questions.

Let us begin by noting that a literary text is composed of a multiplicity of discourses from a variety of social spheres. These discourses are social products in the sense that they are produced in society and precede the actual writing or reading of a text. Discourses are ideological and they offer perspectives on the world through the constructs they constitute. These discursive constructs are powerful tools because they are the basis for our analysis of reality. They are, in fact, sites of struggle, for discourses serve as much to distort and conceal as to demystify and disarticulate other constructs; they can serve as well to contest ideological discourses in order to resist particular practices. In effect, we relate to reality through discourses, through texts, although reality is not reducible to discourse or text. History, for example, is not reducible to historiography, yet our perspective on the past is, to a large extent, the product of texts, of theoretical and documentary texts, whether oral or written. In the same way, discourses on race, for example, affect the way we think about members of different races. In fact, discourses on race have served to legitimate slavery, oppression, lynching, rape, Jim Crow laws, segregation and a myriad of less blatant racist policies. Racist practices are of course not reducible to discourses on race, but the latter allow us to see how meanings and concepts have been deployed in the social field to condone or give rise to the former. Discourses are, thus, powerful practices and, in a restricted sense, "material," even though they are not economic but rather ideological in nature.

Allow me to pursue this further. Discursive constructs can be used to naturalize phenomena, to make certain practices appear as natural. There is nothing "natural" for example about distinguishing people on the basis of race. They could as easily be distinguished on the basis of being left or right-handed, tall or short, blue or brown eyed, by blood type or some other trait. What is clear is that particular constructs serve particular interests in society; thus, Europeans used this construct back in the sixteenth century to justify the enslavement of Africans or to question the "humanity" of the native peoples of the New World. One can speak then of hegemonic discourses, those discourses that serve the interests of the dominant classes. Marxists used to speak of the dominant ideology as that of the bourgeoisie in a capitalist system, but today we speak of hegemonic ideological discourses, following Gramsci, to refer to the ideologies generated by dominant class fractions which ally and are able "to coerce subordinate classes to conform to hegemonic interests," securing in this way their consent to their own subordination (Hall 332). Hegemony, as Stuart Hall indicates, "is accomplished through the agencies of the superstructure—the family, education systems, the church, the media and cultural institutions, as well as the coercive side of the state—the law, police, army," etc. (Hall 333). In recognizing this, we are not reducing individuals to the level of mere puppets to be dangled about by hegemonic ideologies and structural constraints, for as Marx indicated, human beings also have the capacity to change the world. Men and women can resist and counter oppressive practices or for that matter, accommodate to them and even be complicit and consent to their own subordination. It is through this consent that hegemonic forces attain consensus.

The response of the individual to hegemonic and nonhegemonic discourses can be seen as a response to a call, "un llamado," un "sentirse aludido" as we would say in Spanish, to an interpellation. It is this interpellation by ideological discourses that determines identity or subjectivity. If in the past critics viewed subjectivity in essentialist terms, as if every individual were a subject characterized by some essential feature, today subjectivity is increasingly seen as decentered, as fragmented, as not fixed. In fact, critics today speak of a variety of subject positions that individuals assume in response to a variety of discourses. In my analysis of Chicano literature, I am concerned fundamentally with the various discourses which interpellate characters in novels and short stories and with the subject positions generated within these texts, for, just as discourses serve for social construction, they also serve for the literary reconstruction of economic, political and cultural spaces within the literary text.

I have found recent works in feminist theory quite useful in the analysis of subjectivity, especially those which are beginning to note the importance of analyzing gender in relation to other discourses and practices of marginalization and domination, namely those generated with respect to the intersection of class, race, ethnicity, sexuality and nation. This orientation allows feminists to finally focus on differences among women and to view subjectivity within various overlapping, intersecting and competing spaces marked by the conjunctures of these very discourses (de Lauretis 134–135). Feminist notions of a layered space or template are akin to constructs within the model proposed by Goran Therborn that I have used elsewhere. Therborn for example, analyzes competing, overlapping and intersecting ideological discourses within material and historical matrices, while allowing for the positing of Althusser's structures in dominance. This framework permits the consideration of a number of interconnecting social practices and discourses and not only makes us aware of the contingency of these practices but also allows us to bear in mind that at given historical junctures, one of the practices or discourses may be dominant. Therborn's model, thus, enables us to view the interpellation of individuals by discourses of ethnicity, gender, class, nation, religion, family, sexuality, and even region, generation, etc. An individual, then, can identify in terms of several subject positions: as, for example, a male Chicano of the working class, Catholic, heterosexual, member of a large extended family, second generation, Texas Valley resident, eldest son, etc. In looking at the model a bit closer, however, one has to note that identity or subjectivity is defined in terms of discourses of collectivities or agencies, like family, ethnic group, class. What becomes clear, and this bears stressing, is that despite emphasis to the contrary, subjectivity is generated by discourses of collectivity, that is, an individual identifies as a member of a set of collectivities. This, of course, requires that we view discourses in terms of competing interests within collectivities, This concept of centering subjectivity in collectivities is an important cultural and political construct in Chicano literature.

One individuates, then, as a member of various collectivities, of what have been called "imagined communities" (Anderson 15) like nation, family, gender, religion. In their very discursive construction, these collectivities or agencies form closures with strategies of exclusion and usurpation (Mouzelis 59). One cannot, however, focus only on cultural agency nor on the formation of a collective awareness of common interests, without noting the specific location of these agencies in terms of their structural positions, that is, their location within the economic, political and cultural spheres. Only a consideration of structural constraints allows us to understand a collectivity's capacity to maintain or transform its structural position. Agencies, of course, cannot be reduced to their structural position, but neither can they be analyzed outside of their socio-structural location.

The approach must be balanced, therefore, and consider both agency and system, for collective actors also form part of particular classes and politically, are either dominant or dominated. Class antagonisms cannot however be reduced to conflicts of "difference" (Mouzelis 62). In fact "difference" and "class" constantly compete for the position of dominance as social constructs. We know all too well that collectivities uniting in terms of difference (for example, along ethnic or racial lines) may fragment along class lines. Differences of race, ethnicity, nation, gender, family, religion, region or sexuality, by the same token, may fragment class alliances. Perhaps the best way to view these social sites is as a cluster of features, all contingent and all potentially determinant at any given moment in time. Given that all these discourses generated within these various structural and collective spaces are ideological, they may be further analyzed as hegemonic or counter-hegemonic. The distinction is crucial as it determines whether one consents to the dominant ideological discourses or dissents. Of course, the dominant strategy is to contain all discourses within the hegemonic framework. Thus, hegemonic discourses, for example, often function to erase potential interpellations; for example, they often seek to efface awareness of class position by interpellating the population as members of an ambiguous grouping called "the middle class," a position which brackets social distinctions and calls for consent rather than class consciousness; so too does interpellation as "Americans" serve to efface the diverse and hierarchical ethnic composition of this country. Thus, discourses of ethnicity and race or nation or gender or of any other collectivity may likewise be contained within the hegemonic framework and generate strategies of accommodation. Of course, resistance to the framework will by the same token be enabled by counter-discourses generated within the same social sites. In other words, given that no individual occupies only one position within the social formation and within various collectivities, the situation is always contradictory, with the various spheres reinforcing or contradicting each other. Thus, identity with any particular collectivity does not automatically trigger one political position or another.

For purposes of situating representations of Chicanos in literary texts, we will need to conceptualize collective actors in terms of their relation to economic structures, as well as to institutions of domination, like the army, police, government, or even cultural or ideological institutions, like media, the church, and educational apparatuses (Mouzelis 56). Not all cultural or economic agencies are institutionalized, however. Families, for example, have legal recognition as social and economic units within society and so do labor unions and political parties. But collectivities, like "class," do not exist as concrete organizations, nor are ethnic minorities, like Chicanos, organized bodies. The latter are emergent "imagined communities" (Anderson) and rely for the most part on unofficial identification, not with a foreign nation, like Mexico, but with a subordinated national minority within this country. Individuals are interpellated then by discourses generated at a structural level as well as within cultural spheres, with power relations within one sphere off-setting, countering or re-affirming those within another sphere. If cultural agencies allow us to account for difference, structural constraints and positionality allow us to account for exploitation and domination. Although the articulation of all these various discourses must be considered within a particular moment, we can never disregard historical conditions, nor the fact that when discussing Chicanos we are dealing with the cultural production of a conquered, geographically deterritorialized, displaced and subordinated population. Nor, moreover, can we forget that human beings are both products and producers of the society they inhabit.

It is to these antagonistic relationships and collectivities that various Chicano writers have addressed themselves in their novels and short stories by representing a diversity of individuals within given historical conditions, interpellated principally by discourses of ethnicity, class and gender. In some Chicano texts individual subjectivity is often presented in conflict with collective subjectivity, especially that of family or ethnicity, as we shall see. Overall, in the texts on which I will now comment, one finds a layered discursive space constituted by discourses which intersect and allow for a deconstruction of either contradiction (at a class level), domination (at a political level), or difference (at the level of gender, ethnicity, family or generation).

The interaction of discourses of ethnicity, gender and class is highly evident in the novel by Américo Paredes, *George Washington Gómez*, published in 1990 but written between 1936 and 1940 (Hinojosa intro 5). All the spheres alluded to previously, the economic, the political and the cultural are represented here and specific structural constraints and contradictions are seen to articulate with institutions of domination. Within this configuration we find a set of actors, Texas Mexicanos who have lost control of the means of production, who are dominated at the political level, excluded from dominant Anglo circles and denied opportunities on the basis of national origin and language The complex interrelationship between these various spheres is well represented in this novel of a Steinbeckian bent. In fact, the discourses of nation and national origin overlap with discourses of class, and generate collective actors who are constantly the victims of political repression.

Allow me for a moment to restate the all too well known facts: After the United States invaded and took half of the Mexican territory during the middle of last century, the ruling landowning Mexican class residing in the Southwest faced not only loss of land and disempowerment but harassment and violence at the hands of Anglos, particularly at the hands of the infamous Texas Rangers. This ethnic conflict has been documented, among others, by Cárdenas, who, in an essay dealing with immigration policies in this country reviews racist arguments in Congress against Mexican immigration on grounds that "Mexicans posed racial threats to the homogeneity of the American people because of their biological inferior status" and were therefore undesirable as settlers (Cárdenas 69, 71). Montejano's history of Anglo-Mexican relations in Texas and the economic development of the state likewise provides extensive analysis of this economic and ethnic conflict, particularly of the narrated armed insurrection of Texas Mexicans in the Valley during the period of 1915–1917, its brutal suppression by Texas Rangers and the cessation of hostilities with the resolution of the Mexican Revolution (125). The rebels, under the Plan de San Diego (Texas), called for independence of the Southwest from "Yankee tyranny" and the creation of an independent republic (Montejano 117). Montejano indicates that the rebellion, which left hundreds dead and thousands displaced, was initiated by Texas Mexicans who were threatened by commercial agriculture—"rancheros and vaqueros, shopkeepers and artisans and some sharecroppers" and by those who sought to regain land lost by their families in the Valley.

It is this historical space and its aftermath that Paredes reterritorializes in *George Washington Gómez*. The emphasis of the novel is on agency, rather than on system, and its focus is oriented toward micro-politics, rather than toward macrostructures. It is the failure, at the level of the ethnic collectivity, of Feliciano García that we follow throughout the novel as he tries to live up to another man's dream. After joining his brother Lupe in the seditious Texas Mexican insurrection, Feliciano finds himself having to choose between fleeing into Mexico or returning to care for his sister's family after the death of her husband Gumersindo at the hands of the Texas Rangers, los Rinches, this in order to realize Gumersindo's dream that his newly born son become a great man; it was for this reason that he named him George Washington Gómez. Gumersindo's dying words to Feliciano, as he lies wounded and abandoned on a dirt road, are a plea for an upbringing without hate and violence for his son. But the violence represented here does not end with Gumersindo's death and the suppression of the insurrection. As the novel reveals, the political domination of the Mexicanos in areas where they are the majority population has violent repercussions in the schools as well, where Mexican children suffer a different type of violence, social and academic. In the particular case of Gualinto, as George Washington is called, he is abused by a teacher of Mexican origin. The ethnic collectivity is, thus, seen to be divided not only on the basis of particular attributes, like educational attainment, but also on the basis of class; here upwardly mobile Mexicanos are not averse to exploiting their own.

In the novel, when Feliciano returns to care for his family, he is forced to leave his hometown where his participation in the insurrection might become known. With his sister María and her children in tow, Feliciano moves to another town on the Rio Grande and to a different type of employment. This occupational shift, necessary given his family's loss of ranch land and his inability to leave his family to become a vaquero on someone else's ranch, has the effect of improving his lot somewhat, since being a bartender in a cantina and the political lackey of the Blue Party in town has its advantages, among these the ability to buy a house from the owner of the cantina and later rent the site of the cantina to set up a grocery store. In his dealings with the dominant structures, Feliciano learns to hide his hate and distrust of the Gringo but he is ultimately unprepared for Gualinto's later transformation.

Gender positioning is also crucial in the novel. The text establishes that Gualinto, from birth, was favored in a family that included two other children, female, and was expected to do well, economically and socially, to live up to his namesake. The girls, on the other hand, were taken out of school and expected to become housewives. At one point, cultural taboos against out-of-wedlock pregnancy are transgressed by one of Gualinto's sisters, for which reason she is severely beaten by her mother. Here Maruca's escapade points not to changes in female subordination after occupational mobility but to changing patterns of supervision and intercultural interaction. Ethnic and class exclusion, however, persists, as is evident in the father of her Anglo boyfriend's refusal to allow his son's marriage to a working-class Mexican; instead he prefers to marry his son to the also pregnant daughter of the well-to-do and fair-skinned Osuna family. We can see here that exclusion is primarily class-based, but involves as well racist considerations.

George Washington Goméz might be considered to be a 1940s version of a Richard Rodríguez. In both cases it is apparently the university experience away from home that provides the finishing touches on the process of acculturation. Paredes's novel ultimately reveals the pitfalls of assimilation, for far from articulating his uncle's counter-discourses, Gualinto returns to the Valley a most pliable subject, spouting discourses of accommodation to hegemonic institutions, as a lieutenant in the Army's counter-intelligence service, married to a blonde Anglo woman, and full of disdain for his own family and ethnic collectivity. His uncle Feliciano's cynical comment, "The leader of his people," as he listens to Gualinto from the porch out on his farm expresses his disgust with his nephew's self-importance and contempt for local efforts by former classmates to organize Mexicans politically. In effect the contradictions were always there, for we recall that the boy who was once bothered by racism and discrimination against Mexicans was also the boy who was ashamed of his working-class home. The boy who hated the Gringo while "admiring his literature, his music, his material goods" was also the boy who loved Mexicans "with a blind fierceness" while "almost despising [them] for [their] slow progress in the world" (150). The novel in effect demystifies the reader's expectations of the scholarship boy from the poor Dos Veintidós barrio. By the time he returns from Washington, Gualinto, now "George," the liminal character who once straddled two worlds, has made new alliances and broken with his Mexican collectivity. In fact, Feliciano's nephew has become a Ranger or "Rinche" of sorts, a new national ranger back to spy on his Mexican friends on the border, more sophisticated in his tactics perhaps, but equally dangerous, and more so for his willingness to betray his own kind.

Paredes's novel is, thus, one of acculturation, betrayal and dislocation, that is, displacement from one class and ethnic location to another. It is important to note that the second is possible here because of the character's fair skin. He can pass for white.

Paredes's novel is an important work that fills a void in our Chicano literary history; it is the story not only of intercultural and inter-class conflict and political domination, but also of the fragmentation of the Mexican collectivity, a community which, although always divided along class lines, even before Texas independence or the Mexican War, had formed a collective awareness of common interests and common enemies in the face of hostilities against Mexicans. As the work traces the changes taking place in Texas Valley communities, we see how by the time of the Depression and later during World War II, these collective discourses of the national minority are drastically diluted, although not erased, by economic and political processes taking place in this country. The discourses of social mobility and a new patriotism to the larger national "imagined community" soon outweigh the other discourses of collectivity and resistance, at least in the mind of Gualinto, but obviously not in the case of his high school friends, who stayed in the Valley and still see themselves first and foremost as Texas Mexicans.

This uneasy interplay between the collective and the individual within the social matrix appears as a constant in Chicano literature, as we have found in several of the Klail City Death Trip Series novels by Rolando Hinojosa. In his latest work, *Becky and Her Friends*, the main character reformulates her location within the Chicano collectivity and abandons her participation within the Anglo closure. In this particular novel, it is the social practices of a female character which are observed, praised or critiqued by a variety of informants interviewed by a male narrator. The voices are supportive or critical, depending on the individual's allegiances to one of the two Valley Mexican families: the Buenrostro-Malacara clan or the Leguizamón-Leyva-Escobar family. References to Becky's class and cultural location also allow us to view relationships within classes and between ethnic groups in what is best described as a bicultural but highly segmented space. In fact, in this novel we find the character Becky plotting new maps for herself and reterritorializing the social space (abandoned by her own mother) by re-creating a sense of community with Jehú Malacara and his Mexican friends.

Given the fragmented structure of the novel, there are striking gaps and discontinuities which do not allow the reader to trace the "overnight" transformation of what was formerly a rather opportunistic, assimilated, social climber. Yet the transformation of Becky, to be fair, is only partial and limited, for the most part, to the cultural sphere. The Becky we now find is a business woman. Her space is the market place, in which her mentor Viola Barragán buys and sells business ventures with the help of Becky, who administers some of her companies. As such, both Viola Barragán and Becky Malacara participate in exploitation like any capitalist entrepreneur, although paternalistically or rather, maternalistically, in relation to the Texas Mexican community by looking out for Chicano contractors, in a way like a Chicana "Mamá Grande." But Becky is involved in another power struggle that is not primarily economic in nature, but rather defined by gender and family. It is through the use of multiple voices and perspectives that the novel traces not only the community's pettiness but also Becky's decision to break with particular cultural and family closures that restrict her: specifically, with family taboos against divorce and against separating from the politically and socially mobile Escobar in order to strike out on her own, as a single working mother with two children. Up until now, her cultural allegiances have been with the dominant Anglo circles in the Texas Valley, but her independence, her divorce from the Bank-manipulated Ira Escobar, spurs her on to reject inclusion in the dominant Anglo enclave. In the process she assumes a new ethnic and family identity but her class location is not really affected as she not only acquires a good-paying job, but comes into family property herself, even while ensuring the Escobar property rights of her children. What is particularly aggravating to her pushy mother, however, is the loss of ties to the powerful Escobar-Leguizamón family. The nuclear family disintegration is but temporary, however, for shortly thereafter she joins a new collectivity, that of the Malacaras-Buenrostros, long-time enemies of the Leguizamón family, a clan described throughout the Klail City Death Trip Series as an opportunistic family with economic rather than ethnic priorities. As Becky establishes new family ties with Jehú Malacara, she relearns her Spanish and reenters the Mexican ethnic fold. The novel, thus, posits the discursive nature of cultural identity as Becky opts for an alternative cultural construct to define her life. Here again we find that cultural agencies are the sites of ethnic mobility and difference, for it is only at this level that alternatives are posed. In the end, Becky remains ultimately locked into the constraints of love and marriage.

Arturo Islas's last novel, *Migrant Souls*, also focuses on family discourses. As in his first novel, *The Rain God*, social contradictions, cultural difference and interpersonal conflicts all crystallize within the domestic space of the Angel family which resides in the fictitious city of Del Sapo, by all indications much like El Paso, Texas. It is most fitting that the first part of this second novel be entitled "Flight into Egypt," for that is the irony of the tale. Attempts at either geographical or ideological flight from what the younger generations consider "the medieval atmosphere of Del Sapo" (said to be "enough to drive any intelligent, sensitive person quite mad") inevitably lead to a return to the family fold. In Islas's novel, the Angel family, like the Chicano population at large, is heterogeneous; it consists of first-generation immigrants, second-generation working-class sons and daughters, and some professional grandchildren. The landowning status of the family back in Mexico before immigration has led to pretentious airs among the first and second generations. In fact, the Angel family pretends to be what it is not. Its imaginary representation of itself is an attempt to conceal the mestizaje of the family, its intolerance for any deviation from the norm, and its many contradictions. Yet the skeletons in the family's closet of the last two generations include divorce, homosexuality, illegitimate children, religious fanaticism, public scandals and snobbishness. A continuation of the author's first novel, this narrative focuses on Josie and Serena, two of Eduviges Angel's three children who dare to challenge the norm established by their mother and grandmother. Josie, in particular, wants nothing more than to go far away from the family and after her marriage to Harold Newman, she does indeed escape to California; but when her ten-year marriage ends, she returns to Del Sapo. Her "flight into Egypt" is thus a return to ideological bondage and the tight closure of the family collectivity, which both defines family members' roles and castigates them, especially women, for not fulfilling them. Men in the Angel family may stray, but for a woman to be left by her husband because of her affair with another man is unforgivable. Josie's divorce only serves to heighten the antagonism between herself and her mother. In the face of the contradictory inclusion/exclusion trap, Miguel Chico, who has his own conflictive relationship with the family, discovers a romantic solution: acceptance of loss and love. Thus, within the Islas novel, the family closure, like ethnic collectivity itself, is demystified to a certain extent, but then remystified, for although the novel disarticulates the family's contradictions, in the end these are reconstructed not as contradictions but as differences, which can be neutralized through enduring organic family ties.

Family-centered narratives in Chicano literature are not limited to the private domestic sites of one household, for not only is the concept of family broader, but it often includes the outside community. The "family" functions then as a microcosm of the ethnic community or of the region, as in the case of the Texas Valley. This allegorical dimension in part explains why the family in many of these works is male-centered; increasingly, however, as the literary production of Chicana women has increased, the family space has been feminized. The gendering of the family is an important construct in the works of Helena María Viramontes, Mary Helen Ponce, Sandra Cisneros, Denise Chávez, Irene Beltrán Hernández, Margarita Cota Cárdenas, and Roberta Fernández, to name just a few. These and other writers have gone beyond the representation of feminine subjectivity in essentialist terms and have chosen to focus on the diversity of subjectivities and on the collective experiences of women in Chicano/Mexicano/Latino communities.

Although some works continue to represent women as burdened by the fatum of the past experiences of mothers and grandmothers, as if time were cyclical and repetitive, for the most part new works by Chicanas account nicely for differences among women. Chicano literature has been criticized for offering formulaic images of Chicano/Mexicano women, as for example that of the older woman or *curandera* who displays unusual skills in the use of herbs and healing or in the reading of cards, images which have appeared and reappeared in fiction by both Chicano men and women. But in the work of another Texan, Roberta Fernández's *Intaglio*, we find that alongside traditional representations like that of Zulema, the story-telling woman or Leonor, the witch or card-reading woman, new images are constructed, like that of Andrea, the dancer, Amanda, the fabulous seamstress, or Filomena, the domestic worker. Here feminine gender discourses are intersected by family's economic and political discourses, and the subjectivities interpellated run counter to the narrator's expectations, as in the case of Aura who turns her back on her family to serve the economic and political interests of her husband, or Isla, who puts up with an abusive husband, or Consuelo, who resents her sister's special upbringing and career, or Filomena, the Army widow who faces life alone without her children, who have been sent to Mexico to reside with relatives because of her economic constraints. Despite the representation of economic conditions which serve as the backdrop for these subjectivities, it is not the material conditions that are foregrounded in these short stories but rather the subjective pain or cultural difference which fixes them in time and space as images of resignation.

Within this tapestry of set, almost static, figures there are a few representations in the Fernández text of women that, as in Arturo Islas's novel, seek liberation by escaping from the family space which constrains and limits them. The fact that discourses of individualism are central to many Chicana narratives is not difficult to understand, since individualism is the dominant ideological discourse, offering liberation from the immediate constraints of the collectivity. Thus often an individualist response is posited as a solution to counter oppressive family and communal practices. In the Fernández work, individualist economic interpellations are critiqued, to the extent that they are shown to be detrimental to family interests. In the case of Aura, the profit motive is stronger than any allegiance to the old folks and their welfare and so their house is sold by the granddaughter. In the case of Andrea, her career is placed above the needs or resentments of her sister. All too often the solutions forged are merely a continuation of oppressive patterns, as is set forth in the case of Verónica, who after being raped is married off to a young man who does not suspect that he is not the father of the child to come. Female characters are thus presented as contradictory figures, with no single function, role, or trait to define them; all are situated, however, within their capacity to affirm or counter the dominant practices and values of the ethnic collectivity.

This awareness of the diversity of subjectivities is evident not only in the works of Hinojosa, Paredes, Islas and Fernández, but also in that of Sergio Elizondo. During the decade of the 60s when I was a graduate student and a Teaching Assistant here, my supervisor was Professor Sergio Elizondo, who at that time was also the faculty adviser of the Mexican American Youth Organization. That decade, like those since, witnessed not only student activism against the Vietnam War and social struggle for civil rights but also a number of local cases of police brutality and abuse. It was, some of you may remember, during that decade that two Chicano Job Corps trainees who came to Austin for the weekend and took a joy ride in a "borrowed" car were shot to death by the police. A little later, in Dallas, a policeman playing Russian roulette with a youth picked up for questioning shot him to death, and here in Austin proper another child running from a convenience store with some stolen baloney was also killed. These episodes of police brutality have been, and continue to be, all too common episodes not only in Texas but throughout the nation, for as you know if you watch T.V., policemen are rather more likely to be quick on the trigger when the suspects are Black or Latino. Carlos Morton, for one, has given voice to the discourse of community outrage against this violence in his play *The many muertes de Richard Morales*, as has Elizondo in his novel *Muerte en una estrella*, which reconstructs the dying discourses of two Job Corps teenagers shot by the police on the streets of Austin. In Elizondo's innovative novel, it is the multiple subjectivities of Oscar Balboa, age 16, and his short life of memories that we witness within a narrative that traces the structural constraints of the period, the class position of the two Chicano youths, and the struggles initiated by farmworkers and Chicano students throughout the Southwest in the late 60s.

Elizondo's latest novel, *Suruma*, focusses on another problematic, that of immigration and political alienation, a constant, like conquest and family conflict, in Chicano literature, especially that by Helena María Viramontes, Miguel Méndez, Irene Beltrán Hernández and Genaro González. The space of the immigrant, like that of the exile, becomes a counter-site of sorts, an imaginary heterotopia of displacement in opposition to the real sites of work and home (Foucault 24). Within this imaginary site, individuals feel displaced between two different locations and part of neither. Everything serves to remind the individuals either of streets, places, people left behind or of the "foreignness" of the spaces in which they reside. This displacement is the lot of several immigrant families represented in Elizondo's highly fragmented novel, be they from Mexico, Poland, or Germany. In a way, this heterotopia serves as allegory for those of us who never lose our sense of displacement (even though we were born here) and who never find Suruma, the parodied utopia, land of immigrants, surumatos, children and lovers of the sun. Note however that displacement, like difference, fails to consider exploitation and structural constraints which are integral to the experience of Third World immigrants, as well as to working-class minorities who are born here.

Chicano novelists and short story writers have used many literary strategies to call attention to the cultural, political, and economic constraints within which Chicanos live and work, constraints formative of discourses used to construct Chicano subjectivities. In all of the literary examples commented upon here, and in a good many published works, it is clear that ethnic discourses are paramount, even when articulated within family, gender and class discursive spaces. In addition to a marked sense of collectivity, we have noted a common thread of dissent running through these various texts, all of which have been written by Texas Chicano and Chicana writers and published during the last two years. This representation of cultural agencies and collective subjectivity has become an important problematic within Ethnic Studies as critics and theorists alike posit the need for a new politics of representation. Hall, for example, argues not only for a recognition of diversity of subjective positions and cultural identities but also for the recognition that ethnicity can only be analyzed in its articulation with class and gender. The intersection of these often competing discourses of gender, ethnicity and class, as has been noted, is central to all the Chicano narratives that we have briefly discussed today. Clearly, as long as Chicano men and women continue to be contained within social spaces marked by subordination, marginality and exploitation, Chicano literature will also be intersected by counter discourses and retain a strong historical perspective. And yes, the subaltern does have a voice; it is the voice of the collectivity.

WORKS CITED

Anderson, Benedict. 1987. *Imagined Communities*. London: Verso, 1987.

Beltrán Heredia, Irene. 1989. *Across the Great River*. Houston, Texas: Arte Público Press.

Cárdenas, Gilberto. 1975. "United States Immigration Policy toward Mexico: an historical perspective," in *Chicano Law Review*, v. 11, 66–91.

de Lauretis, Teresa. 1988. "Displacing Hegemonic Discourses: Reflections on Feminist Theory in the 1980's," in *Inscriptions*, Nos. 3–4, 127–152.

Elizondo, Sergio. 1984. *Muerte en una estrella*. México: Tinta Negra Editores.

Elizondo, Sergio. 1984. *Suruma*. El Paso: Dos Pasos Editores.

Fernández, Roberta. 1990. *Intaglio. A Novel in Six Stories*. Houston: Arte Público Press.

Foucault, Michel. 1986. "Of Other Spaces," in *Diacritics*, v. 16, no. 1, 22–27.

González, Genaro. 1988. *Rainbow's End*. Houston: Arte Público Press.

Hall, Stuart. 1977. "Culture, the Media and the 'Ideological Effect,'" in J. Curran *et al.* (eds), *Mass Communication and Society*. London: Arnold.

Hinojosa, Rolando. 1990. *Becky and Her Friends*. Houston: Arte Público Press.

Hinojosa, Rolando. 1990. "Introduction" to Américo Paredes. *George Washington Goméz*. Houston: Arte Público Press, 5–6.

Islas, Arturo. 1990. *Migrant Souls*. New York: W. Morrow and Co.

Islas, Arturo. 1984. *The Rain God*. Palo Alto: Alexandrian Press.

Montejano, David. 1987. *Anglos and Mexicans in the Making of Texas, 1836–1986*. Austin: University of Texas Press.

Mouzelis, Nicos P. 1990. *Post-Marxist Alternatives*. London: Macmillian.

Paredes, Américo. 1990. *George Washington Goméz*. Houston: Arte Público Press.

Spivak, Gayatri Chakravorty. 1988. "Can the Subaltern Speak?" in Cary Nelson and Lawrence Grossberg, *Marxism and the Interpretation of Culture*. Chicago: University of Illinois Press.

Therborn, Goran. 1980. *The Ideology of Power and the Power of Ideology*. London: Verso.

Winkler, Karen J. 1990. "Proponents of 'Multicultural' Humanities Research Call for a Critical Look at Its Achievements," in *The Chronicle of Higher Education*, 11-28-90, A5, A8 and A9.

men

"**M**en" may well be the most controversial subject heading in this anthology. Some readers may feel that, after all, a book called *Feminisms* should not even concern itself with "men." What does "Men" have to do with feminism(s)? The semantic difficulties of even asking this question are illustrative. Does it mean "What place do male critics have in feminism" or "What place do men as subjects have in feminism"? Or could it mean "What does feminism have to offer toward coming to a clearer understanding of men?" Here, we take it to mean all three.

Mary Jacobus addresses the first sense of that question. She is responding to, among other things, an influential essay by Elaine Showalter, "Critical Cross-Dressing: Male Feminists and the Woman of the Year," an essay that characterizes male feminist literary critics as in some sense "academic Tootsies." Showalter expresses an anxiety shared by many that the movement of male critics into feminist criticism is less alliance than colonization, that, like the title character of the Dustin Hoffman film *Tootsie*, these men are "wearing women's clothes" just to advance their own personal careers, a move that will exclude women from the one refuge they have found in the academy.

Jacobus refutes this position in "Reading Woman (Reading)" (1987) by addressing directly the question of what difference the sex of the reader makes to literary criticism, in particular, and to reading at large. In this chapter from her book *Reading Woman*, she critiques three essays that focus on cross-dressing and gender: Showalter's, an essay by Sandra Gilbert called "Costumes of the Mind: Transvestism as Metaphor in Modern Literature," and one by Shoshana Felman, "Rereading Femininity" (none of these essays is reprinted in this volume, but other essays by all three authors do appear here). Jacobus argues that the theory of reading should be grounded in a psychoanalytic theory of subjectivity that recognizes that gender is constructed through language. Psychoanalysis, she argues, does not try to *define* gender, but to describe where it comes from; it is therefore necessary, she argues, to any feminist explanation of women's relation to discourse. By the same token, though, she argues that feminism, with its focus on the importance of gender in culture, is necessary to any use of psychoanalysis. Jacobus critiques Showalter and Gilbert because they do not adopt this model of gender, but praises Felman's essay because it urges a theory of reading that recognizes fluid sexual identities.

Susan Jeffords and Joseph Boone address the second sense of the question this section raises: "What place do men as subjects have in feminism?" Of course, men were a chief subject of much early feminist literary criticism. Kate Millett's *Sexual Politics* (1970), one of the first expressly feminist works of literary criticism, addressed the patriarchal abuses of male authors, male characters, and male readers. But after Elaine Showalter proposed the idea of gynocriticism (the study of female-authored texts and women-centered issues), work on male-authored texts and male-centered issues almost disappeared from feminist criticism. In the last few years, though (as Showalter explains in "A Criticism of Our Own," in "Practice"), we have seen the beginnings of "gender theory," an analysis that, working from feminist criticism, takes gender to be a, if not *the*, decisive factor in literary meaning. Since feminist critics have argued convincingly that gender differences are constructed differences, the reasoning goes, shouldn't that mean stereotypical masculinity is as constructed—and as deforming—as stereotypical femininity? The result is a new way of examining texts, a way of looking at "masculinity" as a product of patriarchy that is potentially as damaging to those subjected to it as is "femininity." "Gender theory" does not see men as simply perpetrators of sexual oppression, but as themselves victims of it; it takes the onus of historical abuses off men per se, and assigns the blame instead to patriarchy as a system.

There is, of course, much disagreement as to whether gender theory is a good thing. Skeptical feminist critics ask whether gender studies are not just a way to relegitimate traditionally male-dominated literary studies, a way to exploit feminist critique against its own best interests. Proponents argue that it is an expansion of feminist criticism that genuinely recognizes the discursive, constructed nature of patriarchal gender norms, a necessary step if we are ever to realign oppressive gender politics. This is, of course, a debate that cannot be resolved here—if at all—but it is a useful dialogue to keep in mind while reading the essays that follow.

Susan Jeffords examines the extremely male-dominated world of war (or, rather, war films) in "Masculinity as Excess in Vietnam Films: The Father/Son Dynamic" (1988). Jeffords's particular focus in this essay, like her work in the book *The Remasculinization of America: Gender and Representations of the Vietnam War,* is the combat scene and its relation to the stabilization of a masculine identity. Using *Platoon* and the Rambo film series as her examples, she argues that these films are not so much about war as about the destabilization of masculinity in American culture, about the confusion of a young man as to which of several father figures he should emulate; "*this* is the fear, the anxiety, the threat, the violence that underlies [the] combat sequence . . . in Vietnam film—not a battle with NVA soldiers." The real focal points of the films are not war itself but the linear movement of power from a (white) father to a (white) son; the narrative tension arises from the threat that someone inappropriate—a woman or a man of color—will usurp that power. The resolutions of the films, she points out, are not the resolution of the war, but of the reconstruction and stabilization of a particular masculine identity. Within these films, the combat scenes function as "excess" in a number of ways: as warnings about the results of such gender destabilization, as distractions from the crisis of masculine identity, and as the means to reestablish that threatened identity. Jeffords reads these films not as simple maturation stories, but as powerful narratives that attempt to reconstruct a patriarchal notion of masculinity at a particular point in social history—the 1970s and 1980s—when feminism had offered a strong challenge to it.

Like Susan Jeffords, Joseph A. Boone examines father-son relationships in "Creation by the Father's Fiat: Paternal Narrative, Sexual Anxiety, and the Deauthorizing Designs of *Absalom, Absalom!*" (1989), but unlike Jeffords, Boone examines father-son relationships that go wrong, relationships in which power is not successfully transferred from the white father to the white son. Boone takes as his starting point the suggestion that all narrative is, finally, oedipal narrative—that is, narrative that is about the successful accession to power of the son. Instead, he asks, "Might there be ways in which even paternal fictions deauthorize their proclaimed originary power?" Using William Faulkner's *Absalom, Absalom!*

as a model, Boone suggests that paternal fictions may well be manifestations of anxieties about masculinity itself—about masculine sexuality, about procreative (and creative) power, about race and gender, and about the always metaphorical status of paternity—and may also be self-subverting, as Thomas Sutpen's attempt to "plot" his family proves to be. The things that Sutpen wants most to contain, Boone shows, those things that symbolize "otherness" and "nonmaleness"—femininity, blackness, homosexuality, daughters—are the very things that escape his plotting and take on a life of their own. Even what Sutpen most desires—sons to carry on his name—he ends up disowning because of his fear of otherness.

Boone turns to the role of incest in the novel and points out that the relationships between men in the novel conform exactly to the paradigm of male homosocial bonding that Eve Kosofsky Sedgwick develops (in "Desire"). Those homosocial bonds, though, reveal their origin in deep anxieties about homoeroticism and male identity development. The homosocial male bonds in the novel also reveal the deeply problematic relation to women in the novel, especially to mothers, who are almost entirely absent, and to daughters who keep the story alive, only to subvert and "de-oedipalize" it. Boone concludes that *Absalom, Absalom!* reveals the real anxiety behind the surface story of Oedipus: "Oedipus, however empowered by our society or its myth-making processes, is finally and nonetheless a vulnerable man caught in the middle of a story that he has indeed helped create but cannot control—caught, as it were, with his pants down, his fallacies exposed, his repressive efforts showing for the ineffectual cover-up they are." Narrative, he argues, finally escapes and transgresses the Law of the Father.

The final essay in this section, Joseph Litvak's "Pedagogy and Sexuality" (1995), addresses two issues important to feminist criticism, but not much discussed in this volume: pedagogy and male (heterosexual) privilege. Pedagogy has long been of interest to feminist critics from both inside and outside the institution of literary criticism; feminist critics argue for a different relation between students and professors, a different attitude toward expertise and classroom order, and even a different relation to knowledge itself (some good starting points for work in feminist pedagogy are: *Gender in the Classroom: Power and Pedagogy*, edited by Susan L. Gabriel and Isaiah Smithson [1990], *Feminisms and Critical Pedagogy*, edited by Carmen Luke and Jennifer Gore [1992], and essays by Dale Bauer [1990] and Laurie Finke [1993] in *College English*, or in the journal *Feminist Teacher*).

Litvak extends the feminist interest in pedagogy specifically to include the issue of sexuality in the classroom; that is, in what ways does the teacher's sexual orientation—whether explicit, or acted on, or acknowledged, or not—influence not just pedagogy, but also the way students perceive that teacher and what is taught? Litvak moves from three of his own experiences—with his junior-high French teacher, Mr. Boyer, with Paul de Man in graduate school, and with his own teaching—to the question of how pedagogy is linked to heterosexual male privilege. The ideal of the professor "empt[ied] . . . of all sexual desire," he argues, is a "trick . . . more available to straight men than to anyone else. [Because] . . . it already constitutes a large part of their social construction *as* straight men." On the other hand, he shows, teaching as a sexual, desiring being is not always a successful pedagogical strategy, either. Litvak concludes that "the opposition between teaching as opposition and teaching as seduction is no less deconstructible than any other," and that there is a way to occupy a pedagogical position in between self-censorship and mystique. His essay also shows, as do the other essays in this section, that there is a relation, if not an easy and uncomplicated one, between "Men" and feminism.

—DPH

READING WOMAN (READING)

(1987)

> It was a change in Orlando herself that dictated her choice of a woman's dress and of a woman's sex. And perhaps in this she was only expressing rather more openly than usual . . . something that happens to most people without being thus plainly expressed. For here again, we come to a dilemma. Different though the sexes are, they intermix. In every human being a vacillation from one sex to the other takes place, and often it is only the clothes that keep the male or female likeness, while underneath the sex is the very opposite of what it is above. Of the complications and confusions which thus result every one has had experience.
>
> VIRGINIA WOOLF, *ORLANDO*[1]

Or, "it is clothes that wear us and not we them"; Woolf's *Orlando* (1928) again. Can we say the same of language—that words speak us and not we them—and hence of reading too? What would "reading woman" mean if the object of our reading (woman as text) and the reading subject (reader as already read) were gendered only as the result of the reading process? What if, to put it another way, there were no gender identity except as constituted by clothes, or by language— just as there is no "literal" meaning to oppose to metaphor, but only metaphors of literalness. As Shoshana Felman puts it,

> if it is clothes alone, i.e., a cultural sign, an institution, which determine our reading of the sexes, which determine masculine and feminine and insure sexual opposition as an orderly, hierarchical polarity; if indeed clothes make the *man*—or the woman—are not sex roles as such, inherently, but travesties?[2]

In Woolf's novel, Orlando's transvestism is not simply a travesty which mimics or exaggerates the signs by which gender identity is culturally instituted and maintained; rather, Orlando might be said to dress up at (cross-)dressing, exposing the dilemma ("here again, we come to a dilemma") or impossible choice of gender; as the *OED* has it, "A choice between two . . . alternatives, which are or appear equally unfavorable; a position of doubt or perplexity, a 'fix.'" In Felman's words, transvestite roles become "transvesties of a travesty," since there is no unequivocal gender identity to render ambiguous in the first place, but only the masquerade of masculine and feminine.

If there is no literal referent to start with, no identity or essence, the production of sexual difference can be viewed as textual, like the production of meaning. Once we cease to see the origin of gender identity as biological or anatomical— as given—but rather as instituted by and in language, "reading woman" can be posed as a process of differentiation for which psychoanalysis provides a model. In Freudian terms, the subject acquires both gender and subjectivity by its passage through the Oedipus and castration complexes; in Lacanian terms, the subject's entry into the symbolic order, and hence the subject's gender, are determined by relation to the phallus and (it amounts to the same thing) by taking up a predetermined position within language.[3] In order to read as women, we have to be positioned as already-read (and hence gendered); by the same token, what reads us is a signifying system that simultaneously produces difference (meaning) and sexual difference (gender). We might go further and say that in constituting woman as our object when we read, we not only read in gender, but constitute ourselves as readers. The stabilizing, specular image of woman in the text makes reading possible by assuring us that we have women's faces too—or men's, for that matter, since "woman" serves also as a figure for or reflection of "man."[4] Reading woman becomes a form of autobiography or self-constitution that is finally indistinguishable from writing (woman). Putting a face on the text and putting a gender in it "keeps the male or female likeness" (in Woolf's words) while concealing that "vacillation from one sex to another" which both women and men must keep, or keep at bay, in order to recognize themselves as subjects at all. The monster in the text is not woman, or the woman writer; rather, it is this repressed vacillation of gender or the instability of identity—the ambiguity of subjectivity itself which returns to wreak havoc on consciousness, on hierarchy, and on unitary schemes designed to repress the otherness of femininity.

Feminist critics have traditionally concerned themselves with the woman writer, and especially with what Woolf calls "the difference of view, the difference of standard."[5] Women's writing occupies an unchallenged place in the politics of feminist criticism and in the classroom; yet the category itself remains problematic (defined by authorship? by style or by language? by refusal of the very categories "masculine" or "feminine"?). More recently, feminist criticism has concerned itself with the woman reader—with woman as the producer of her own system of meanings; meanings that may challenge or subvert patriarchal readings and undo the traditional hierarchy of gender.[6] So much so that Jonathan Culler can make the question of "Reading as a Woman" an exemplary instance for his discussion of readers and reading in *On Deconstruction* (1982). "For a woman to read as a woman," he concludes, paraphrasing Peggy Kamuf's "Writing Like a Woman," "is not to repeat an identity or an experience that is given but to play a role she constructs with reference to her identity as a woman, which is also a construct, so that the series can continue: a woman reading as a woman reading as a woman."[7] The appeal to "experience," whether reader's or writer's, short-circuits this process and creates an illusory wholeness or identity, denying the internal division which simultaneously produces the gendered subject and the reading subject. Since "reading woman" necessarily entails both a theory of reading and a theory of woman—a theory of subjectivity and a theory of gender—I want to look at the double question of reading woman (reading) or woman reading (woman) from the perspective of three feminist essays which raise these theoretical issues by way of the metaphor of transvestism ("the clothes that wear us"). The first is Sandra Gilbert's "Costumes of the Mind: Transvestism as Metaphor in Modern Literature"; the second is a review article by Elaine Showalter, "Critical Cross-Dressing: Male Feminists and the Woman of the Year"; and the third is Shoshana Felman's "Rereading Femininity."[8] Each of these three feminist critics has been highly influential in defining what "reading woman" might mean, whether for Anglo-American readers or, in the case of Felman, in a Franco-American context; yet they reveal strikingly different assumptions about both gender and textuality—so much so that the first two essays deploy the metaphor of transvestism in the context of a theory of gender identity which the third essay, Felman's, sets out to deconstruct. Perhaps this difference can be attributed to the fact that while Gilbert and Showalter have attempted to construct a feminist literary and critical "herstory," Felman situates herself at the intersection of literature and psychoanalysis. Significantly, for my purposes at least, Felman's essay takes as its point of departure a rereading of Freud's 1932 lecture "On Femininity." The intervention of psychoanalysis in the context of feminist criticism and theory, I shall argue, makes all the (sexual) difference. Read as a history of the way in which "the difference of view" is produced, rather than an attempt to describe what it consists of, psychoanalysis frees women's writing from the determinism of origin or essence while providing feminist criticism with a way to refuse the institutionalization of sexual and textual difference as gender identity and hence as questions that cannot be posed at all.

Sandra Gilbert's "Costumes of the Mind" is an "argumentative history" (Gilbert's own phrase) designed to rewrite literary history in feminist terms. A speculative account of twentieth-century modernism based on differing uses of the transvestism metaphor by men and women, her essay champions the (female) opponents of sexual hierarchy. Whereas Joyce in the Nighttown episode of *Ulysses*, Lawrence in "The Fox," and Eliot in *The Wasteland* all portray gender disorder or the blurring of sexual distinctions either as a means of endorsing conservative views of male dominance, or as nightmare (Gilbert argues), feminist transvestism becomes a means to subvert and repudiate the hierarchical views of the male modernists. Woolf's *Orlando*, for instance, portrays gender identity as fluid, multiple, and interchangeable; in Gilbert's phrase, "insouciant shiftings" (Woolf's "vacillation from one sex to the other") replace the fixity of gender identity. Gilbert clearly privileges this vision of the happily multiform self or genderless identity beyond sexual divisions which she sees in the "utopian" androgyny of writing by Djuna Barnes and H.D. The culminating metaphor of her essay, fittingly, is the gesture by which the heroines in writing by Atwood, Chopin, and Plath all discard their clothes in order to "shatter the established paradigms of dominance and submission associated with the hierarchy of gender and restore the primordial chaos of transvestism or genderlessness."[9] Although Gilbert does not ask whether this fantasy of utopian androgyny or primordial genderlessness could ever be realized, she does ask what might account for the differing gender ideologies of male and female modernists. In the last resort, however, her inquiry is limited by a theory of gender in which the relation between body and subject remains unmediated by either the unconscious or language. The answers she provides—psychobiography on one hand, literary history on the other—reveal the unquestioned argument that underpins her "argumentative history." For all her sympathy with Woolf's transvestite metaphor, her assumptions about both identity and history are ones that finally reproduce the very fixities which *Orlando is* supposed to unsettle.

To take identity first. In order to account for the specifically male anxieties which Gilbert sees as energizing the "nightmare fantasies" of the male modernists, she invokes Joyce's ambivalent relation to mother, church, and country; Lawrence's mother-dominated childhood; and Eliot's clouded first marriage. But if psychobiography fixes gender identity thus, what price the "insouciant shiftings" of *Orlando?* And what factors in the formative years and relationships of female modernists might account for their differing view of gender arrangements? Are men constituted by their object relations, while women remain somehow immune to such identity fixes and fixations? What the answer to these questions might be we never learn, since for Gilbert the modernist writer is already unambiguously gendered, either male (hierarchical, conservative) or female (insouciantly shifting, feminist). Significantly, Gilbert quotes extensively from Robert Stoller's *Sex and Gender* (1975) on the subject of male transvestism; in Stoller's terms, gender identity is either male or female, a "core identity" that is only rendered equivocal by unsatisfactory object relations and that may in fact uncannily correspond to biological and genetic factors even where it appears anomalous, as in the case of the boy raised as a girl who effortlessly adapts to his "new" gender ("Although he would seem to fit into the category of those rare people who have no difficulty in shifting their gender identity. . . . He never did shift his identity. He always felt . . . that he was a male").[10] Like Nancy Chodorow in *The Reproduction of Mothering* (1978), which also draws on Stoller's work, Gilbert ultimately assumes (by implication at least) the possibility of what Chodorow calls "the establishment of an unambiguous and unquestioned gender identity."[11] For Stoller, in fact, there is really no shifting at all, but only mistaken identity.

Gilbert, however, is primarily a revisionary literary herstorian and interpreter rather than a theorist (or even a psychoanalytic reader); and so it is no surprise that her account of twentieth-century modernism turns on what is often seen as its crucially determining (his)torical event—the differing implications for men and women of World War I. While the war years left men figuratively and literally shattered, Gilbert argues, they offered women the chance to redress their previously disinherited state. Every white feather given to a young man thereby dispatched to the trenches might mean another job for a woman; every angel in the house—every Red Cross nurse—became an avenging angel of death. The figure of the female angel of destruction, familiar from Gilbert and Gubar's *The Madwoman in the Attic* (1979), gives Gilbert's account of literary modernism a mythic dimension which itself derives from the myths of male modernists such as Yeats (Herodias' castrating daughters in "Nineteen Hundred and Nineteen," for instance). Why should the turn to history give birth to this vision of avenging female monstrosity? Is it possible that where the text of history is concerned, women can only be monsters or aberrations, since history itself (as Gilbert duly notes) is a conspiracy to marginalize or repress them? Hence the view of history offered in Woolf's *Between the Acts* (1941) by Miss La Trobe, who seems, in

Gilbert's words, "to want to fragment history in order to ruin it" rather than "shoring up fragments of history against her ruin."[12] On the face of it, Gilbert endorses Woolf's modernist and feminist theory of history both here and in *Orlando*, where "shifts in literary style, shifts in historical styles, changing modalities of all kinds . . . remind us that . . . all is in flux." Yet in the last resort her own position turns out to be closer to that of the male modernist who, in her own words, "insists that the ultimate reality underlying history . . . is and must be the Truth of Gender"[13] than to the view that the ultimate reality underlying gender is history. Perhaps it is not so much the monster, woman, to which history gives birth, as the monster flux. Like identity, the very notion of (literary) history attempts to repress ambiguity and division; and what is repressed necessarily returns, in the language of the unconscious, as an avenging monster.

If Gilbert can be seen as falling back on the disorders of history to fix the still more threatening disorders of gender identity, what of Elaine Showalter's unsettling juxtaposition of recent forays into feminist criticism by male critics, on one hand, and Dustin Hoffman's 1982 film, *Tootsie*, on the other? "Critical Cross-Dressing" asks, shrewdly and wittily, whether the conversion to feminist criticism by male theorists such as Jonathan Culler in *On Deconstruction* and Terry Eagleton in *The Rape of Clarissa* (1982) is merely a form of transvestism akin to female impersonation—an appropriation which, like cross-dressing in *Tootsie*, can be viewed as a way of promoting masculine power while ostensibly masking it. Showalter's initial question ("Is male feminism a form of critical cross-dressing, a fashion risk of the 1980s that is both radical chic and power play?")[14] leads to others that are especially germane to feminist criticism; questions such as: is reading learned, and can men learn to read as feminists? Is "reading as a woman" fundamentally differentiated from "reading as a man," and if so, by what (political, sociological, or ideological) differences? Showalter persuasively unmasks *Tootsie* as not so much a feminist film but rather a film that reveals Hoffman's sense of the actor's career as feminine—passive, vulnerable, and physically exposed. Accordingly she diagnoses its transvestism, as Gilbert diagnoses that of the male modernists, in terms once more derived from Robert Stoller's *Sex and Gender*. For Stoller, the transvestite man sets out to prove that he is better than a biological woman because he is a woman with a penis.[15] *Tootsie*, Showalter argues, has it both ways. Michael Dorsey becomes a female star while still being able to lift heavy suitcases and grab taxis. But, while this is acute and apt, what has it to do with reading? Has Showalter allowed two different questions, that of female impersonation and that of reading as a woman, to become elided? Are they really the same (or at least analogous) questions, as she implies, or are they questions whose very conflation reveals an underlying contradiction in her theory of gender?

Contrasting Eagleton and Culler, Showalter represents the first as the Dustin Hoffman of literary theory—the Marxist critic who fears (like Lovelace himself in Richardson's novel) that he is effeminized by writing, and whose appropriation of feminist criticism attempts to recuperate its "phallic" power, just as Lovelace in Eagleton's own analysis attempts to recover Clarissa's imaginary phallic power by raping her. This "phallic criticism" is for Showalter simply "another raid on the resources of the feminine in order to modernize male dominance."[16] The effect, she observes, is to silence or marginalize feminist criticism by speaking for it, while simultaneously silencing the "something equivocal and personal in [Eagleton's] own polemic" which she sees as motivating his criticism. What is this "something equivocal"? Showalter's phrase occurs in the context of what is arguably her central thesis about reading and writing as a woman:

> Like other kinds of criticism . . . feminist criticism is both reading and writing, both the interpretation of a text and the independent production of meaning. It is through the autonomous act of writing, and the confrontation with the anxiety that it generates, that feminist criticism is both reading and writing, both the interpretation of a text and the independent production of meaning. It is through the autonomous act of writing, and the confrontation with the anxiety that it generates, that feminist critics have developed theories of women's writing, *theories proved on our own pulses.* (p. 147; my italics)

Just as *Tootsie* reveals Hoffman's sense of the actor's career as feminine, and just as *Clarissa* reveals Richardson's anxiety about the feminizing effects of writing, so for the Marxist critic (Showalter suggests) there may be something effeminate about literary criticism as opposed to revolutionary action. But if one sees writing itself as feminine—and here Showalter's view is unclear—then there can be no specifically feminist theory of women's writing as opposed to men's, and no way in which such theories can be proved experientially on the pulses of women. Showalter comes close to glimpsing that textuality at once produces gender and simultaneously produces equivocation, only to repress that insight with the language of the body ("proved on our own pulses"). By invoking the experience of being biologically female, she closes the very question which she opens in her discussion of Eagleton.

Culler's argument, as Showalter accurately recapitulates it, is precisely to "demonstrate some difficulties in the feminist appeal to the woman reader's experience, an experience and an identity which is always constructed rather than given." For Culler, "'reading as a woman' is always a paradoxical act, in that the identity as 'Woman' must always be deferred" (pp. 139, 141). With apparent approval, Showalter summarizes Culler's analysis of feminist theories of reading, including his insistence that the appeal to female experience as a source of authority is always a double or divided request since the condition of being a woman is simultaneously seen as given and as created. She then proceeds to her own question, apropos of Culler's work: namely, "can a *man* read as a woman?" Noting that while Culler never presents himself as a feminist critic, he does offer a feminist reading of Freud's *Moses and Monotheism* (1939), she asks further "whether a male feminist is in fact a man reading as a woman reading as a woman?" Showalter is ready to concede that Culler has avoided the pitfall of female impersonation by reading "not as a *woman*, but as a man and a feminist" (p. 142). But one might well ask why it matters. If reading as a woman is a paradoxical act, reading as a man must involve a similarly double or divided demand. Showalter comes close to implying that while reading as a woman may (if she accepts Culler's view of the matter) involve constructing a gender identity, reading as a man does not. In other words, her theory of gender identity remains ultimately untouched by Culler's argument. Though ostensibly careful to distinguish between the essentialist "woman" reader and the "feminist" reader (a reader who may be male or female), Showalter chooses to emphasize what she calls feminist reading because "it has the important aspect of offering male readers a way to produce feminist criticism that avoids female impersonation" (p. 143). But again, if criticism—like reading and writing—can be viewed as all a matter of cross-dressing anyway, Culler's avoidance of female impersonation is neither here nor there. Ironically, Culler's "feminist" reading of *Moses and Monotheism* is designed to show why "the promotion of the paternal" should produce patriarchal criticism's characteristic concern with legitimacy of meaning and with the prevention of illegitimate interpretations. This very preoccupation with legitimacy and illegitimacy, this very preference for unambiguous meanings and stable origins, is precisely what underlies Showalter's unease about the shiftiness of critical cross-dressing in the academy.

Showalter's energetic polemic is fueled by understandable professional anxiety about preserving an area in criticism that is specific to women. This anxiety is played out most clearly in her final paragraph, which culminates in a comic apocalyptic fantasy. "Without closing the door on male feminists," she writes, "I think that Franco-American theory has gone much too far in discounting the importance of signature and gender in authorship."[17] Though she warns against essentialist simplicities ("Culler's deconstructive priorities lead him to overstate the essentialist dilemma of defining the *woman* reader"), it is surely essentialism—whether theoretical or professional—that we glimpse here, for without essentialism identity itself comes into question, and with it "the importance of signature and gender in authorship" (what one might call the *Moses and Monotheism* principle, or the insistence on legitimate origin). "Going much too far" for Showalter means the cover of the *Diacritics* special issue of summer 1982, enigmatically entitled "*Cherchez la Femme: feminist critique/feminine text.*" Here is her description:

> On a white background is a figure in a black tuxedo and high heels, resting one knee on a bentwood chair à la Marlene Dietrich. The figure has no hands or head. On the back cover, a dress, hat, gloves, and shoes arrange themselves in a graceful bodiless tableau in space. No "vulgar" feminist, the chic Diacritical covergirl hints at the ephemera of gender identities, of gender signatures.[18]

To invoke *Orlando* once more, the cover says: "it is clothes that wear us and not we them." For Showalter this graphic display of the metaphoricity of clothes risks dispersing gender identity altogether, leaving only the headless (i.e., silent) woman, the *corps morcelé* of nightmare.

Hence the form taken by Showalter's dream of the feminist literary conference of the future: the demonic woman rises to speak, but mutates into a column of fire; the Diacritical woman rises to speak, but she is headless; and finally the third panelist, a transvestite male, takes the podium: "He is forceful, he is articulate; he is talking about Heidegger or Derrida or Lévi-Strauss or Brecht. He is wearing a dress." The phallic critic, or rather, the deconstructive or Marxist critic, has successfully usurped the feminist. Showalter is surely right to be canny about the appropriative moves of the masculine critical establishment vis-à-vis feminist criticism. But the very uncanniness of this final vision should alert the reader to what has been elided by her argument—namely, woman and text, body and subject. Showalter comes dangerously close to endorsing a position she has earlier derided, that of Lewis Lapham opposing the admission of women to the Century Club ("The clarity of gender makes possible the human dialectic"); in her own text the reemergence of gender hierarchy necessarily brings with it the accompanying specter of gender disorder. But in the last resort, her fantasy reveals what is troubling about the fashion for female impersonation—the uneasy recognition that when the text takes off its clothes, it is indeed disembodied, uncanny, and silent. In other words, the very discontinuity of (female) body and (feminine) text is the scandal that experientially based theories of the woman reader displace onto the scandal of critical cross-dressing in the 1980s.

Showalter views critical cross-dressers with all the suspicion that Joyce, Lawrence, and Eliot bring to transvestism. What theoretical argument might provide a less residually conservative theory of gender, a more revisionary reading of woman? Shoshana Felman's "Rereading Feminity" approaches the question of the woman reader (woman as other) "otherwise"; that is, in the light of psychoanalytic theory.[19] Freud's question, "What is femininity?" asks, Felman points out, "what is femininity—*for men?*" As she elaborates it, the question is rather, "what does the question—'what is femininity—*for men?*' mean *for women?*" A short answer to this longer question might be: the silencing or elimination of woman. Felman's reading of a story by Balzac, "The Girl with the Golden Eyes," in the light of Freud's lecture "On Femininity" poses, in her own words, "the double question of the reading of sexual difference and of the intervention of sexual difference in the very act of reading." Read as the story of a triangular relationship (the interference of an affair between a man and a woman in an existing affair between two women), Balzac's text, Felman argues, "at once explores and puts in question the very structure of opposition between the sexes, as well as the respective definitions of masculinity and femininity."[20] Her analysis of the way in which class struggle and gender struggle both spring from a *division* which is institutionalized as an authoritative *order* by *hierarchy* (her terms) neatly deconstructs the conservative ideology of Gilbert's male modernists. Like Eagleton's Lovelace or Showalter's Eagleton, the rake in Balzac's story can be viewed as a man in search of his own phallus—a man for whom the girl with the golden eyes is only a narcissistic reflection of his desire. In this conventional polarity of masculine and feminine, woman serves only as a metaphor for man; he alone has a proper identity, since woman is always a figurative substitute for man. Hence her final reduction to the *corps morcelé*—in Balzac's story, literally a bloody and mutilated corpse—of Showalter's nightmare. In this scheme of things, woman's only function is to mediate desire or to serve as a medium of exchange. Deprived of her function, she is expendable.

Felman's reading of "The Girl with the Golden Eyes" is also designed as a lesson in how not to read—"how to *stop reading* through the exclusive blind reference to a masculine signified" (p. 27). But just as the rake, Henri, reads Paquita (the girl with the golden eyes) in terms of a masculine signified, so Paquita herself can only read "in the feminine." Bound erotically to a Marquise whom we later learn is Henri's half-sister, Paquita loves Henri for his ambiguous resemblance to a woman. In the famous transvestite scene from Balzac's story, she dresses Henri in the Marquise's clothes so that he may better resemble her beloved. For Felman, in fact,

> Balzac's text could be viewed . . . as a rhetorical dramatization and a philo-
> sophical reflection on the constitutive relationship between transvestism and
> sexuality, i.e., on the constitutive relationship between sex roles and cloth-
> ing. If it is clothes, the text seems to suggest, if it is clothes alone, i.e., a cul-
> tural sign, an institution, which determine masculine and feminine and insure
> sexual opposition as an orderly, hierarchical polarity; if indeed clothes make
> the *man*—or the woman—are not sex roles as such, inherently, but travesties?
> Are not sex roles but travesties of the ambiguous complexity of real sexual-
> ity, of real sexual difference? (p 28)

Henri and Paquita, Felman concludes, "are thus but transvestisms of the other
sex's deceptively unequivocal identity; that is, they are travesties of a travesty."
Like words, gender identity can be travestied or exchanged; there is no "proper"
referent, male or female, only the masquerade of masculinity and femininity. At
the climax of her ecstatic sexual intercourse with Henri, Paquita cries out: "Oh!
Mariquita"—as Felman points out, a name which links that of Henri (de Marsay),
Paquita herself, and the Marquise, thereby subverting the conventional opposition of masculine and feminine and staging "the ambiguous complexity of real
sexuality." In addition, the name "Mariquita" means in Spanish, according to
Felman, "an effeminate man"; we are told that Paquita's ecstatic cry pierces
Henri's heart. The challenge here is not just to sexual hierarchy (Henri finds a
woman installed in his place) but, Felman argues, to the smooth functioning of
representation. Where Henri had previously found his ideal self—an imaginary,
unequivocal sexual identity—reflected in Paquita's golden eyes, he now finds
only division and the evidence of ironic misrecognition. The betrayer that must
be cast out is the principle of difference, here redefined as femininity itself. Although the jealous Marquise forestalls Henri's revenge on Paquita, brother and
sister come face to face over her dead body with the principle of ambiguity which
each embodies for the other. Henri's discovery, that his rival is not other, but the
same, installs his double as feminine. In Felman's words, "Since Henri himself
has a woman's face, the feminine, Henri discovers, is not *outside* the masculine,
its reassuring canny *opposite*, it is *inside* the masculine, its uncanny *difference from
itself*" (p. 41). Inside every transvestite man, a woman is struggling to get out (a
view of transvestism radically opposed to that of Stoller).

Femininity, in Felman's terms, "*inhabits* masculinity" as otherness or disruption; it is the uncanny of repression itself. Another name for it, though Felman
does not invoke it, might be "bisexuality"—a bisexuality that necessarily returns
as monstrosity. Henri first describes the girl with the golden eyes as "the woman
of [his] dreams":

> She is the original of that ravishing picture called *La Femme Caressant sa
> Chimère,* the warmest, the most infernal inspiration of the genius of antiquity;
> a holy poem prostituted by those who have copied it for frescoes and mosa-
> ics; for a heap of bourgeois who see in this gem nothing more than a gewgaw
> and hang it on their watch-chains—whereas, it is the whole woman, an abyss
> of pleasure into which one plunges and finds no end. . . . And here I am to-
> day waiting for this girl whose chimera I am, asking nothing better than to
> pose as the monster in the fresco.[21]

What can we make of this strange allusion to *La Femme Caressant sa Chimère*, seemingly an antique Pompeian fresco? Balzac apparently has in mind a passage from Henri Latouche's Neapolitan novel, *Fragoletta* (1829) where, during a visit to the Palazzo Studii, Latouche's characters discuss this and other paintings:

> "Et cette femme caressant une Chimère . . . c'est donc là une idée de tous les temps? Ce monstre aux ailes de colombe et aux nageoires de poisson est un bien bizarre objet d'affection; mais que de grâces dans l'attitude et particulièrement dans les bras de cette femme!" "Et que d'amour dans son regard. . . . On sent que rien de réel n'obtiendra jamais un tel culte de sa part."[22]

Balzac himself described the central character of Latouche's novel as "cet être inexprimable, qui n'a pas de sexe complet, et dans le coeur duquel luttent la timidité d'une femme et l'énergie d'un homme, qui aime la soeur, est aimé du frère, et ne peut rien rendre à l'un ni à l'autre. . . . "; "comme *l'Hermaphrodite*," he concludes, "*Fragoletta* restera monument."[23] The reference here is to Polyclitus's hermaphroditic statue, a discussion of which follows closely after that of the fresco and provides the centerpiece for Latouche's representation of the bisexual as an emblem of love. Elsewhere in Balzac's writing, "ce monstre" is, of course, the bisexual;[24] and the monster whom Henri views in his imagination as the object of Paquita's desire is himself—monstrous not by contrast with her ideality, but because, as we duly discover, his own gender identity is ambiguous. When Henri vows vengeance on Paquita for daring to love a woman in the guise of a man, he attempts to destroy the monster of bisexuality that always lurks within. Ironically, her death confronts him more surely with what she screens, the woman who is his monstrous or ambiguous double—with the femininity which he must deny if he is to maintain the illusion of unequivocal gender identity on which his masculinity depends.

Balzac's rake and his half-sister are alike in seeing Paquita as an object of exchange to be possessed or discarded at will (like her mother, "She comes from a country where women are not beings, but things—chattels, with which one does as one wills, which one buys, sells, and slays").[25] Whether viewed as an object of exchange or as the mediator of desire, Paquita transgresses the system in which she is inscribed by daring to be a desiring subject in her own right, and one whose desire disrupts the hierarchical opposition of masculine and feminine. As she intervenes in Balzac's story to reveal the scandalous interchangeability of man and woman—each standing for the other—so Felman herself, she points out, intervenes in Freud's lecture "On Femininity." Felman disrupts Freud's text as Paquita ruins representation in Balzac's story by daring to be at once a desiring and a speaking subject. Freud had posed the problem of femininity as a problem for men; the question *of* women is opened in a manner which closes it *for* them. As Felman writes,

> In assuming here my place as a speaking subject, I have then *interfered*, through female utterance and reading, in Freud's male writing. I have *enacted* sexual difference in the very act of reading Freud's interrogation of it; enacted it as precisely difference, with the purpose not of rejecting Freud's interrogation, but of displacing it, of carrying it beyond its *stated* question, by

disrupting the transparency and misleadingly self-evident universality of its male enunciation.[26]

But—one might ask—is Freud's text so misleadingly, so self-evidently and universalizingly "male" after all? Doesn't textuality itself (like Eagleton's writing) always contain "something equivocal"?

Freud's fictive "lecture" actually starts a paragraph earlier than Felman's opening quotation implies ("Today's lecture . . . may serve to give you an example of a detailed piece of analytic work"). It begins conventionally enough, at first sight, with the time-honored words, "Ladies and Gentlemen"—only to announce a problem: "All the while I am preparing to talk to you I am struggling with an internal difficulty" (*SE* 22:112). What is this "internal difficulty"? Surely nothing else but the recognition by Freud of his own ambiguous relation to discourse (Felman's "enunciation"), and hence to gender as well. He is, he confesses, "uncertain . . . of the extent of [his] license"; how far can he go? (Like Franco-American theory in Showalter's polemic, could he go "much too far"?) Should an introduction to psychoanalysis such as these *New Introductory Lectures* have been left "without alteration or supplement" (*SE* 22:112)? he asks. One might ask, in turn, why a lecture "On Femininity" should take the appearance of "alteration or supplement." *Alteration* (an everyday euphemism for the neutering of domestic pets) and *supplement* (*après* Derrida, an academic euphemism for writing-as-masturbation) are terms that suggest unmanning effects, as if both theory and writing reenact the internal division by means of which sexual identity is constituted (or should I say, "fixed"?).

Freud proposes, he tells his imaginary audience, to bring forward "nothing but observed facts." But it is precisely the evidence of observation—the empiricism of scientific inquiry—that his lecture dismantles at the outset:

> When you meet a human being, the first distinction you make is "male or female?" and you are accustomed to make the distinction with unhesitating certainty. Anatomical science shares your certainty at one point and not much further. The male sexual product, the spermatozoon, and its vehicle are male; the ovum and the organism that harbours it are female. . . . [But] Science next tells you something that runs counter to your expectations and is probably calculated to confuse your feelings. It draws your attention to the fact that portions of the male sexual apparatus also appear in women's bodies, though in an atrophied state, and vice versa in the alternative case. It regards their occurrence as indications of *bisexuality*, as though an individual is not a man or a woman but always both. (*SE* 22:113–14)

If anatomical science can provide only an ambiguous answer to the riddle of gender, then, Freud writes "you are bound to . . . conclude that what constitutes masculinity or femininity is an unknown characteristic which anatomy cannot lay hold of" (*SE* 22:114). Could "psychology" provide an answer, perhaps? No, since it merely reinscribes in the realm of mental life either anatomy or conventional attributions of gender to qualities such as activity or passivity. If "psychology too is unable to solve the riddle of femininity" (*SE* 22:116), what of psychoanalysis? For Freud, psychoanalytic inquiry would take the form of an aporia, refusing the idea of a secret or "essence" altogether. Instead of demanding an answer to the riddle against which so many heads have knocked—"Heads in hieroglyphic bonnets, / Heads in turbans and black birettas . . . " (*SE* 22:113n.)[27]—psychoanalysis asks how differentiation itself comes about: "In conformity with its peculiar nature, psychoanalysis does not try to describe what a woman is—that would be a task it could scarcely perform—but sets about enquiring how she comes into being" (*SE* 22:116). The "peculiar nature" of psychoanalysis, Freud suggests, is not to describe what is, knocking its head against the opaque reality of observation or representation, but rather to uncover the process by which that reality or set of representations is constructed.

The outlines of what Freud calls "the prehistory of women"—a process of sexual differentiation founded on the differing operations on boy and girl of the Oedipus and castration complexes—forms (in Gilbert's phrase) an "argumentative history" with which feminists in turn have argued; arguing, that is, both with Freud and among themselves.[28] Rather than rehearsing here that (pre)history or the debate which surrounds "On Femininity," I want simply to invoke the crucial but problematic thesis of bisexuality put forward in Freud's lecture. Though he at first thought of bisexuality in terms of an undifferentiated sexual nature prior to the institution of sexual difference, Freud came to see bisexuality, in the words of Juliet Mitchell and Jacqueline Rose—whose *Feminine Sexuality* (1983) contains the most sustained account of a revised, Lacanian Freud—as standing for "the very uncertainty of sexual division itself" and as inseparable from "the division and precariousness of human subjectivity."[29] This Lacanian reading of sexual difference would emphasize in particular what Rose calls "the availability to all subjects of both positions in relation to that difference itself." Lacan and language simultaneously install the subject in sexual difference, and sexual difference in the subject: "For Lacan, men and women are only ever in language. . . . All speaking beings must line themselves up on one side or the other of this division, but anyone can cross over and inscribe themselves on the opposite side from that to which they are anatomically destined."[30] But as Stephen Heath points out in *The Sexual Fix* (1984), bisexuality works both ways in theoretical arguments, functioning "as the beginning of an alternative representation, as an insistence against the one position, the fixed sexual order, man and woman"; but also returning "as a confirmation of that fixity, a strategy in which differences . . . are neutralized into the given system of identity."[31] On one hand, bisexuality as crossing over or shifting: on the other, bisexuality as the old fix. Though he seems to start by dissolving the opposition between masculine and feminine, Freud ends by reaffirming the old order; masculinity provides the measure for the feminine. For Sarah Kofman in *The Enigma of Woman* (1985), Freud first masters sexual difference by positing an original masculinity in women, making the girl's bisexuality more pronounced than the boy's, and then establishes a norm of bisexuality which predisposes women to hysteria; the sign of feminine sexual difference becomes the sign of feminine neurosis.[32] The binary opposition returns to obliterate sexual difference while restoring sexual hierarchy.

Yet a resourceful reading of Freud's "On Femininity" (such as Kofman provides) might reveal that the very bisexuality posited for women makes them, not a derivative of man, but rather, in their complexity, a model for sexuality in general. As Culler puts it, "the moves by which psychoanalysis establishes a hierarchical opposition between man and woman rely on premises that reverse this hierarchy."[33] Reversal becomes the first and necessary step, the point of lever-age for dismantling a theoretical structure in which the feminine is produced only as a negative term: as lack. If, from a Lacanian point of view, "masquerade" (cross-dressing?) "is the very definition of 'femininity' precisely because it is con-structed with reference to a male sign,"[34] that definition, in turn, is itself clearly a form of masquerade, an imposture. Freud's account of the "peculiar nature" of psychoanalysis ("psycho-analysis does not try to describe what a woman is . . . but sets about enquiring how she comes into being," *SE* 22:116) could well be re-phrased as Rose's Lacanian account of the "peculiar nature" of femininity: "Psy-choanalysis does not produce that definition. It gives an account of how that definition is produced."[35] Hence the importance of psychoanalysis for any ac-count of women's relation to, and constitution by, discourse. But there is another side to it. Reread, not as given, but as produced, "femininity"—woman—also de-mands a rereading of the text of psychoanalysis. Hence the importance of femi-nist criticism for any account of the constitution of psychoanalytic discourse. The theoretical reversal reveals the role played by woman in sustaining Freud's theory of gender. But it also reveals how that theory can be reread to produce a theo-retical formulation in which the emphasis shifts from "woman" to "reading."

Orlando too might be called an "argumentative history"—the history of a woman writer. Orlando's gender shift from masculine to feminine occurs during the reign of Charles I at approximately the moment when (according to Woolf's literary-historical scheme) it was possible for the first time to become a woman writer and not the suicidal Judith Shakespeare of A *Room of One's Own* (1929). Though at once lover and beloved, Orlando is also a poet whose writing provides history of literary possibilities from 1500 to Woolf's own age. Indeed, like A *Room of One's Own, Orlando* can be read as the history of its own writing. Though she lighteart-edly takes issue with essentialist notions of gender—such as "(1) that Orlando had always been a woman, (2) that Orlando is at this moment a man"[36]—Woolf's underlying concern is with questions of writing. The convergence of Orlando and authorial concerns, or gender and writing, is most clearly marked when Orlando, having married and so met the requirements of the spirit of her age (at this point, the Victorian age) "could write, and write she did. She wrote. She wrote. She wrote." With this, Orlando's biographer, and text, break off for a long digression on the mind of the writer at work. The life of a writer refuses to be written. Woolf as biographer can only invoke processes that are at once Orlando's and her own: "this mere woolgathering; this thinking; this sitting in a chair day in, day out, with a cigarette and a sheet of paper and a pen and an ink pot."[37] Writing and think-ing, Orlando neither thinks of a gamekeeper (like Lady Chatterley) nor pens him a note (the only forms of thinking and writing nobody objects to in a woman); she is, Woolf observes, "one of those monsters of iniquity who do not love." This monster who will neither love nor (like Henri de Marsay) kill, is "no better than a corpse," a mere body: "if . . . the subject of one's biography will neither love nor kill, but will only think and imagine, we may conclude that he or she is no better than a corpse and so leave her."[38] Looking out of the window, the only resource left, the biographer searches for other signs of life; returning from her year's imaginative absorption, Orlando-as-writer similarly pushes aside her pen, comes to the window with her completed manuscript, and exclaims: "Done!"

Life is most fully present when the life of the writer and the writing of the life merge, breaking down the distinction between subject and object; between woman as writer or woman as written, woman as reader or woman as read. Orlando and her biographer, in other words, create each other by mutual substitution; the masquerade—Orlando's transvestite progress through the literary ages—is that of writing, where fictive and multiple selves are the only self, the only truth, the writer knows.

What Gilbert calls "a revisionary biography"[39] can be seen as autobiography; specifically, as female autobiography. Woolf wrote to Vita Sackville-West apropos of *Orlando*, "it sprung upon me how I could revolutionise biography in a night."[40] In a review of Harold Nicolson's biography, *Some People* (1927), written while she was at work on *Orlando*, Woolf described "the new biography" as one in which we realize that "the figure which has been most completely and most subtly displayed is that of the author"; one in which we realize that "Truth of fact and truth of fiction are incompatible" and "the life which is increasingly real to us is the fictive life."[41] *Orlando* culminates—or rather, fails to culminate—with a mock peroration in which the (auto)biographical subject meditates inconclusively on herself as woman writer; on the "true self" that is "a woman. Yes, but a million other things as well." In the face of such irrepressible diversity, such multiplicity of shifting selves, the biographer throws in her hand:

> But (here another self came skipping over the top of her mind like the beam from a lighthouse). Fame! (She laughed.) Fame! Seven editions. A prize. Photographs in the evening papers (. . . we must here snatch time to remark how discomposing it is for her biographer that this culmination and peroration should be dashed from us on a laugh casually like this; but the truth is that when we write of a woman, everything is out of place—culminations and perorations; the accent never falls where it does with a man).[42]

"When we write of a woman, everything is out of place." Or, as Barbara Johnson has written apropos of women and autobiography, "the monstrousness of selfhood is intimately embedded within the question of female autobiography. Yet how could it be otherwise, since the very notion of a self, the very shape of human life stories, has always, from St. Augustine to Freud, been modeled on the man."[43]

Orlando "discomposes" or undoes her (auto)biographer because the displaced accent also displaces the writing subject. "When we write of a woman everything is out of place"; displacement, not hierarchy, becomes the order of the day. These multiple displacements—from one self to another, from masculine to feminine, from biography to autobiography, from reader to writer—constitute the "insouciant shiftings" of writerly non-identity or otherness which simultaneously preclude both closure (culminations and perorations) and certainty (truth). "If you want to know more about femininity," Freud inconclusively concludes his lecture, "enquire from your own experience of life, or turn to the poets" (*SE* 22: 135). When literature turns from experience to psychoanalysis for an answer to the riddle of femininity, psychoanalysis turns the question back to literature, since it is in language—in reading and in writing woman—that femininity at once discloses and discomposes itself, endlessly displacing the fixity of gender identity by the play of difference and division which simultaneously creates and uncreates gender, identity, and meaning. "The difference (of view)" which we look for in reading woman (reading) is surely nothing other than this disclosure, this discomposition, which puts the institution of difference in question without erasing the question of difference itself.

NOTES

1. Virginia Woolf, *Orlando, A Biography* (New York and London: Harcourt Brace Jovanovich, 1928), pp. 188–89.

2. Shoshana Felman, "Rereading Femininity," *Yale French Studies* (1981), 62:28.

3. Juliet Mitchell and Jacqueline Rose, eds., *Feminine Sexuality: Jacques Lacan and the école freudienne* (London and New York: Norton, 1989). See the introductions, pp. 1–57 *passim* for the evolution of Freudian and Lacanian theories of the gendered subject.

4. "Defined by man, the conventional polarity of masculine and feminine names woman as a *metaphor of man*. Sexuality . . . functions . . . as the sign of a rhetorical convention, of which woman is the *signifier* and man the *signified*. Man alone has thus the privilege of proper meaning"; Felman, "Rereading Femininity," p. 25.

5. Virginia Woolf, "George Eliot," *Collected Essays of Virginia Woolf*, 4 vols. Leonard Woolf, ed. (London: Hogarth Press, 1966–67), 1:204.

6. See, for instance, Annette Kolodny, "A Map for Rereading: Or, Gender and the Interpretation of Literary Texts," *New Literary History* (Spring 1980), 11(3):451–67, and Jean E. Kennard, "Convention Coverage or How to Read Your Own Life," *New Literary History* (Autumn 1981), 13(1):69–88, as well as Judith Fetterley, *The Resisting Reader: A Feminist Approach to American Fiction* (Bloomington: Indiana University Press, 1978).

7. Jonathan Culler, *On Deconstruction: Theory and Criticism after Structuralism* (Ithaca: Cornell University Press, 1982), p. 64, and in this volume in "Reading"; cf. Peggy Kamuf, "Writing Like a Woman," in Sally McConnell-Ginet, Ruth Borker, and Nelly Furman, eds., *Women and Language in Literature and Society*, p. 298 (New York: Praeger, 1980).

8. Sandra Gilbert's essay was first published in *Critical Inquiry* (Winter 1980), 7(2):391–417 and republished in Abel, ed., *Writing and Sexual Difference*, pp. 193–219; Elaine Showalter's review article appeared in *Raritan* (Fall 1983), 3(2):130–49; and Shoshana Felman's essay appeared in *Yale French Studies* (1981), 62:19–44.

9. Gilbert, "Costumes of the Mind," p. 218.

10. Robert J. Stoller, "A Contribution to the Study of Gender Identity," *International Journal of Psycho-Analysis* (April–July 1964), 45(2–3):223. Stoller's concept of "core gender identity" is also elaborated in "Facts and Fancies: An Examination of Freud's Concept of Bisexuality," in Jean Strouse, ed., *Woman and Analysis*, pp. 343–64 (New York: Grossman, 1974). Cf. Gilbert, "Costumes of the Mind," pp. 199–200 and *n.* for citation of Stoller's work on transvestism.

11. See Nancy Chodorow, *The Reproduction of Mothering: Psychoanalysis and the Sociology of Gender* (Berkeley: University of California Press, 1978), p. 158, and cf. Mitchell and Rose, *Feminine Sexuality*, p. 37*n.* for a brief analysis of Chodorow's displacement of "the concepts of the unconscious and bisexuality in favour of a notion of gender imprinting . . . which is compatible with a sociological conception of role."

12. Gilbert, "Costumes of the Mind," p. 214.

13. *Ibid.*, pp. 207, 214.

14. Showalter, "Critical Cross-Dressing," p. 134.

15. See Robert J. Stoller, *Sex and Gender,* 2 vols. (New York: Jason Aronson, 1975), 1:177, and cf. Showalter, "Critical Cross-Dressing," p. 138, and Gilbert, "Costumes of the Mind," p. 199.

16. Showalter, "Critical Cross-Dressing," p. 146.

17. *Ibid.*, p. 149; cf. the debate between Peggy Kamuf, "Replacing Feminist Criticism," and Nancy Miller, "The Text's Heroine: A Feminist Critic and Her Fictions," in *Diacritics* (Summer 1982), 12(2):42–47, 48–53.

18. Showalter, "Critical Cross-Dressing," p. 149.

19. Cf. the subtitle of Felman's "Literature and Psychoanalysis," special issue of *Yale French Studies* (1977), 55/56, "The Question of Reading: Otherwise."

20. Felman, "Rereading Femininity," pp. 21, 22.

21. Honoré de Balzac, "The Girl with the Golden Eyes," *The Thirteen*, Ellen Marriage and Ernest Dowson, trans. (London: Society of English Bibliophiles, 1901), pp. 308–9.

22. "And this woman caressing a Chimera . . . is this, then, an idea for all time? This monster with the wings of a dove and with the fins of a fish is a rather bizarre object of affection; but such grace in the attitude and particularly in the arms of this woman!" "And such love in her look . . . one senses that nothing of reality will ever be reached by such worship on her part." Henri Latouche, *Fragoletta: Naples et Paris en 1789* (Paris: Pour la Société des Médecins Bibliophiles, 1929), p. 42.

23. "This inexpressible being, who does not have a complete sex, and in whose heart the timidity of a woman and the energy of a man are in conflict, who loves the sister, and is loved by the brother, and can return nothing to one or to the other. . . . "; like "*The Hermaphrodite*," "*Fragoletta* will remain a monument." Honoré de Balzac, "Du roman historique et de *Fragoletta* (1831)," *Oeuvres Complètes de Honoré de Balzac: Oeuvres Diverses*, 3 vols., Marcel Bouteron and Henri Longnon, eds. (Paris: Louis Conard, 1935–40); 1:207.

24. See, for instance, Honoré de Balzac, *Peau de chagrin* (Paris: Éditions Gallimard, 1974), p. 204, and for another chimera in Balzac's *Sarrasin*, cf. Roland Barthes, *S/Z*, Richard Miller, trans. (New York: Hill and Wang, 1974), pp. 63–64.

25. Honoré de Balzac, "The Girl with the Golden Eyes," p. 356.

26. Felman, "Rereading Femininity," p. 21.

27. See Jane Gallop, *The Daughter's Seduction: Feminism and Psychoanalysis* (Ithaca: Cornell University Press, 1982), pp. 59–62, for a reading of the role played by these lines in Freud's text.

28. See, for instance, Luce Irigaray, *Speculum of the Other Woman*, Gillian C. Gill, trans. (Ithaca: Cornell University Press, 1985), pp. 13–129, for an extended reading of "On Femininity"; cf. Jane Gallop's reading of Irigaray in *The Daughter's Seduction*, pp. 56–79, and reprinted in this volume, pp. 411–29; and Part Two of Sarah Kofman's, *The Enigma of Woman: Woman in Freud's Writings*, Catherine Porter, trans. (Ithaca: Cornell University Press, 1985), pp. 101–225; Kofman's reading of Freud also takes issue with Irigaray's.

29. Mitchell and Rose, *Feminine Sexuality*, pp. 12, 29. Mitchell and Rose's book should also be read in the context of Gallop's less sanitized, more diacritical reading of Lacan on femininity; see in *The Daughter's Seduction*, pp. 1–42, where Gallop's point of departure is Mitchell's earlier reading of Freud in her *Psychoanalysis and Feminism* (Harmondsworth: Penguin, 1974).

30. Mitchell and Rose, *Feminine Sexuality*, p. 49 and note. Cf. also the discussion in Parveen Adams and Elizabeth Cowie, "Feminine Sexuality: Interview with Juliet Mitchell and Jacqueline Rose," *m/f* (1983), 8:13.

31. Stephen Heath, *The Sexual Fix* (New York: Schocken Books, 1984), p. 142.

32. See Sarah Kofman, *The Enigma of Woman: Woman in Freud's Writings*, trans. Catherine Porter (Ithaca: Cornell University Press, 1985), pp. 122–42, 202–10.

33. See Culler, *On Deconstruction*, p. 171.

34. Mitchell and Rose, *Feminine Sexuality*, p. 43.

35. *Ibid.*, p. 57.

36. Woolf, *Orlando*, p. 139.

37. *Ibid.*, pp. 226, 267.

38. *Ibid.*, p. 269.

39. Gilbert, "Costumes of the Mind," p. 208.

40. Nigel Nicholson and Joanne Trautman, eds., *The Letters of Virginia Woolf*, 4 vols. (New York and London: Harcourt Brace Jovanovich, 1975–79), 3:429.

41. Virginia Woolf, "The New Biography," *Collected Essays*, 4: 233–34.

42. Woolf, *Orlando*, pp. 310, 312. Cf. the later, more explicit text, with its reference to "this culmination to which the whole book moved, this peroration with which the book was to end"; *Orlando: A Biography* (Harmondsworth: Penguin, 1963), p. 220.

43. Barbara Johnson, "My Monster/My Self," *Diacritics* (Summer 1982), 12(2):10.

MASCULINITY AS EXCESS IN VIETNAM FILMS

the father/son dynamic of american culture

(1988)

American filmic representations of the Vietnam War narrate the exchange, transference, or continuation of power between father and son, the defining parameters for the definitions and determination of the masculine subject in American social relations. From *The Green Berets* (1966), in which a primary subplot tells the story of a marine "adopting" a Vietnamese boy, to *Uncommon Valor* (1983), in which an Army Colonel returns to Vietnam to rescue his son from a POW camp; to *Rambo III*, in which Rambo is befriended by an orphaned Afghani boy—these narratives record as their primary tension the stabilization of relations between figures who are positioned as "father" and "son."[1] Whether those relations are failed, as in *The Deer Hunter*, corrupted, as in *Apocalypse Now*, or fulfilling, as in the Rambo series, the dynamic and intention of the father/son relation remains the same: to define and determine power as existing only in and through the exchange between father and son, and to insure that alternate sources and forms of power—in Vietnam films, women, Vietnamese, and blacks; feminism, communism, and revolution—are denied and defeated. This is what American wars—whether fought "at home" or "in country"—are about.

Moments of exchange and transfer of power are clouded and deferred by scenes of violence in Vietnam narration, scenes that function to distract from recognitions that power is not absolute (i.e. is situational) or that it can be "stolen" by someone other than a "son" (i.e. by the "enemy"). For example, in *First Blood*, Rambo begins the film alone, drifting, and powerless; he is easily apprehended and jailed by Sheriff Teasle and his deputies. At the film's close, after multiple scenes of violence against both men and property, Rambo has disrupted an entire town and has demonstrated his ability to kill or maim at will. Though handcuffed and subdued in the last scene, surrounded by police cars and expectant rifles, we know that his power is only controlled, not absent. He could, and as subsequent films will show, does, strike again at any moment.

Presentations of violence like these perform two simultaneous functions: first, to distract from recognition that power is being exchanged—importantly, not gained or lost—here, between Teasle and Trautman/Rambo; second, to suggest to the viewer that a consequence of power disconnected from the apparently stable subject positions of father/son is destruction, death, and confusion, and that without the narrational reinstatement of the son/father's control/identity, that destruction would continue. Finally, scenes of violence serve as intimidation/entertainment for the viewer. Intimidation in suggesting that "war" is a game we as viewers are unable to play and, more importantly, win (Rambo would catch us too); entertainment in that, as we identify with the hero, we repress our own helplessness before that hero (here recall the significance of Claudia Springer's recognition [in "Anti-war Film as Spectacle: Contradictions of the Combat Sequence," *Genre* 21.4 (1988): 479–86] that in these scenes "we could die; we do not die"). I will refer to these scenes of violence as moments of excess, not of power, but of the father/son dynamic.

The specific point I want to argue in this essay is that scenes of violence—combat sequences in war films—are products of a destabilization of the father/son dynamic, moments when the masculine subject being constituted in the film is made ambiguous or contradictory *as* and *by* its movement along the father/son continuum, i.e. as power is transferred—from father to son (who becomes father) or from one father to another—it is not connected to a stable identity. It is important to recognize that these moments of destabilization are *not* moments when either the masculine subject or the father/son dynamic are being directly challenged for their sufficiency, but instead are necessary disruptions that occur in the process of exchanging power. Consequently, to interpret Vietnam films, or, as I will later suggest, any dominant cultural representations of violence, through their "political" positions—as in the numerous discussions of whether *Platoon is* "liberal" or "conservative"—is to accept as significant a specific location along that continuum—one can overturn the father, one can imitate the father—and not examine the fact of the paradigm itself, i.e. that "liberal" and "conservative" are defined by and have meaning only within the father/son dynamic. By examining moments of excess—points of exchange—I believe we can best read the operation of that dynamic and propose possibilities for its negation.

Jeanine Basinger, in her definitive study of the World War II combat film as a genre, remarks, "The best antiwar film has always been the war film,"[2] and later, "a film which says 'war is hell,' but makes it thrilling to watch, denies its own message" (95). The contradictions embedded in such arguments underscore the necessity of Claudia Springer's astute comments on combat sequences as excess. As she concludes, "Combat sequences have to be analyzed in relation to their narrative frameworks" (12) in order to determine how their "excess" will be read by viewers, as pro- or antiwar, for example, in the case of *Platoon*, or as conservatively militaristic or subversive in the case of the Rambo films. While it can be stated that combat sequences *can* be interpreted in multiple ways due to their narrative position as excess, it is clear that they are not generally so interpreted, due to general cultural codes that influence how we view violence, as well as to the specific narrative context established by the film for understanding the significance of the combat sequence as a particular occasion. I will argue in this essay that the narrative context within which those sequences are controlled and interpreted is the father/son dynamic.

The combat film is, first and foremost, a film not simply about men but about the construction of the masculine subject, and the combat sequence—or, more generally, scenes of violence in combat films, whether as fighting in battle, torture, prison escapes, or explosions—is the point of excess, not only for the filmic narrative, but for masculine subjectivity. Because the continuous progression of (social) narrative depends upon the stable positioning of power as affiliated with the father, exchanges of power between fathers and sons or transferences of power in which the son becomes the father cannot be openly articulated. As breaks in that narrative continuity through productions of excess as spectacle, combat sequences provide deferring arenas from such exchanges and allow transferences of power to occur, at the close of which power relations, though altered, appear continuous and stable. Combat sequences are produced by and relieve moments of crisis in the construction of the masculine subject, and function narratively to enable exchanges of power within and between the father/son dynamic that stabilizes that subject.

There are two films that exhibit these points most clearly and that will be the focus for my discussions here: Oliver Stone's *Platoon* (1987) and the Rambo series, particularly *Rambo: First Blood, Part II*. I choose them not only for their combat displays, but for their openly political positions: Stone's film as a type of antiwar statement from the point of view of the man in battle, and Stallone's as a pro-vet/antigovernment bureaucracy statement that asks for social recognition of the Vietnam veteran's strength and achievements; in other words, both are films that do not take as their proposed messages the promotion of combat or warfare but have in both cases clearly foregrounded political issues. But as Basinger says of the World War II combat film: "The combat film pieces can be put together as a propaganda machine or as an anti-propaganda machine, as an 'America is beautiful' or an 'America is an imperialist dog' message. 'War is necessary' or 'war is never necessary'" (16). Such confusions of political "message" should not be attributed, as they are by Basinger, to the "flexibilities" of the genre, or, as they are by Richard Corliss, *Time*'s reviewer of *Platoon*, to the "cunning" and "complexity"[3] of the directors. Instead, they should be recognized as indications that these films are not chiefly *about* their stated political messages or historical reviews or revisions, but about something altogether different, something that discussion of combat films as political statements functions only to cloud and defer: the constructions, reproductions, and reshapings of the masculine subject within the father/son dynamic that structures patriarchy.

Because Kristin Thompson's definitive essay on cinematic excess insists so emphatically upon the *materiality* of filmic elements as excess, I want to pause briefly to discuss how I intend to use the concept of "excess" to delineate a cultural and not a filmic formation, specifically, to refer to the construction of "masculinity" as excess.

In her study of the materiality of filmic narrative, Kristen Thompson defines excess: "A film can be seen as a struggle of opposing forces. Some of these forces strive to unify a work, to hold it together sufficiently that we may perceive and follow its structures. Outside any such structures lie those aspects of the work which are not contained by its unifying forces—the 'excess.'"[4] Specifically, Thompson identifies material elements such as sound, textures of costumes, acting style, unclear items, etc., as providing "a perceptual play by inviting the spectator to linger over devices longer than their structured function would seem to warrant" (133). Functioning as they do in the narrative structure, such elements "may serve at once to contribute to the narrative and to distract our perception from it" (134). Consequently, excess "is precisely those elements which escape unifying impulses" (141).

Elsewhere,[5] I have argued that this notion of "excess" depicts the production of gender itself, as the production and enforcement of gender relations requires a constant reaffirmation and enactment of its structures in order to maintain its "existence." This argument stems from statements like those by Susan Brownmiller, who says of "femininity" that "it always demands more. It must constantly reassure its audience by a willing demonstration of difference."[6] How can these two forms of excess—one referring to the materiality of filmic narratives and the other to the ideological enactments of gender relations—be compared and combined?

In her essay, Thompson turns to the Russian Formalist concept of "motivation" to explain how excessive elements may be noticed in some narratives and not others: "Strong realistic or compositional motivation will tend to make excessive elements less noticeable. . . . But at other times, a lack of these kinds of motivations may direct our attention to excess. More precisely, excess implies a gap or lag in motivation" (134). Motivation would here apply to the "unifying structures" (134) of a filmic narrative function of the individual elements within a film in their relation to the overall "motivation" that links those elements together to create the appearance of a unified structure.

"Motivation" and "demand" are, as I am using them here, equivalent. It is, for example, the demand for the illusion that cinema depict "reality"—a demand that, to use Brownmiller's words, "must constantly reassure its audience"—that sets up the motivation for cinematic "realism,"[7] the inclusion of the very material elements that Thompson identifies as incidents of excess. The textures of costumes, the appearance of unexplained items, the pressures of sound—all participate in the overdetermination of realism that marks classic Hollywood cinema and the productions of dominant culture. Thompson's material analysis identifies the ways in which these "demands" become visually identifiable.

As I want to use these terms here, the "unifying structures" of cultural narratives are the primary arguments of a patriarchal system—the father/son dynamic; the "motivation," to make that system appear coherent, and, in Thompson's words, "reasonable"; the "demand," constantly to reaffirm the sufficiency of that system and its exhaustion of that motivation; the "excess," the multiple ways in which that demand can never be met.

It is the presence of excess that "motivates"—requires—the constant reproduction of narrative. At the same time, such excess is a necessary product of narrativization as an attempt to reconcile contradictions and oppositions within the social network, disjunctions that can never be fully reconciled or "explained" by or through representational productions. In this way, the excess of masculinity—finally of gender itself—as I am using it here is the point at which we can be "distracted," in quite the way Thompson suggested for material aspects of film, from the "unifying structure" of patriarchal narratives, a version of what Antony Easthope calls making masculinity "visible": "Social change is necessary and a precondition of such change is an attempt to *understand* masculinity, to make it visible."[8] In different terms, the excess of masculinity can lead to what Paul Smith has posed as the concept of "resistance," not simply conscious resistance to inadequate positions of identification offered by narrative, but resistance as a structural feature of representational productions, "a notion of resistance which would be able to recognize it as, in fact, a veritable *product* of ideological interpretation."[9]

In the terms I am suggesting here, the father/son dynamic that formulates and is one of the primary mechanisms for reproducing patriarchal systems simultaneously offers a "unifying narrative" to explain the processes of social relations *and* produces excess that distracts us from accepting that narrative as wholly "our" story. It is out of *both* of these processes that the tensions surrounding the exchange of power between fathers and sons arises: on the one hand, showing the linear and stable passage of power as "unifying," and, on the other, because power is being exchanged at all, revealing that exchange as possibly unstable and vulnerable to failures and mistakes. The father/son dynamic then identifies one of the principal locations for "resistance" to patriarchal systems in the very definition of its narrative process, i.e. though the son may replace the father, the son is not the father. It is in response to and as a deterrence of this contradiction that narrational violence is produced.

To say that masculinity is excess is then to argue that the gender system of American culture cannot fulfill the motivation of a patriarchal system to establish itself as exhaustive.[10] Because gender has no material existence, must enact itself through and upon bodies, it can only be *affiliated* with material elements, and because this affiliation can never be a complete identification, there is a constant slippage between gender and materiality in subject experience. Consequently, any attempt to enact gender through material formations—and gender can be *only* so enacted—must produce excess, moments during which the materiality of those formations asserts itself as separate from gender (think here of the extreme close-ups of Rambo's arm, shots that are unidentifiable until we can place them in the larger context of Rambo's body). The reproduction of gender through material formations is both a consequence and a denial of this separation.

There are several consequences of defining "excess" in gender terms, specifically in this argument, as masculinity. Let me list a few of them:

> It will be assumed that there will be no dominant narrative in a patriarchal system that does not include gender as excess, or, more typically, masculinity as excess.

> Though Thompson's definition of excess stems from her analysis of cinema, and I will be discussing filmic narratives here, these arguments apply equally to any dominant cultural production, any articulation of cultural narrative that participates in a patriarchal system.

> In order to fulfill the "constant demand" of patriarchy to insist upon its materiality, gender must constantly be reproduced and renegotiated to fit the specific terms of a particular culture and historical moments. As I will argue in this essay, those terms are now ones that depict the resurgence of power in and through the father, or in which the son willingly (if sometimes perversely) adopts the father's role and position. These are the most visible articulations of the reproduction of gender relations, suggesting in the interplay between constructions of the father and the son that such positions exhaust simultaneously the subject relations of masculinity and of gender.

> That such dominant structures are constructed to deny what Smith calls the "multiple interpolations" of subjects and, therefore, the resistance that rises

from contradictions between these positions. That the goal of such analyses is, like that of Thompson's analysis of cinematic excess, to offer "an awareness of excess [that] may help change the status of narrative in general for the viewer."[11]

In the following pages, I will offer an analysis of the combat sequences in two dominant narratives in which the constructions of productions of masculinity are key aspects of the filmic "motivation"—Oliver Stone's *Platoon* and the *Rambo* sequence—in an effort to delineate the operation of masculinity as excess. As I hope to show, it is at the point of the narration of combat sequences that we can best recognize the excess of masculinity, primarily because it is there that the father/son relations that form the motivation for dominant narratives are transferred and negotiated. It is also there that the tensions aroused by the excess of the production of the masculine subject are relieved and deferred through the spectacle of combat (i.e. "this is not what we are fighting about").

There are three combat sequences in *Platoon*: the first, while Chris Taylor (Charlie Sheen) is still a "cherry," a battle in which he receives his first injury, a superficial neck wound; the second, when the platoon is ambushed by the NVA, a battle during which Taylor exhibits bravery and competence as a soldier and after which Sergeant Elias is killed by Sergeant Barnes; and the third, the final and longest battle scene of the film, in which the battalion's position is overrun by NVA and Taylor is wounded, and after which Taylor kills Barnes. Preceding each of these scenes is dialogue that shows Taylor's uncertainty about his identity and purpose; as that uncertainty increases, and *in direct response to it*, the combat scenes become increasingly longer and more violent. Following each scene is a reshaping of the depiction of masculinity, specifically, of paternal father/son relations, until at the film's conclusion, Taylor takes over the father's position as a way of stabilizing that identity and controlling the excess of its production or the resistance to it.

Before the first battle, Taylor has his initial exposure to Vietnam and the war. There is confusion, and the camera during the first patrol is placed in such a way that we never see Taylor's face clearly, are unable to establish firm connections with him as a focus for our identification; the camera positions thus exemplify the ways in which we are positioned as viewers to experience as our own these crises in subjectivity, and then to instill in us a desire for a return to stability, for a stable and distant camera. He speaks of "Hell [as] the impossibility of Reason" and admits in a letter to his grandmother that he "made a big mistake coming here." He then claims that he "just want[s] to be anonymous. Like everybody else," and then hopes that "maybe from down here I can start up again and be something I can be proud of, without having to fake it, maybe . . . I can see something I don't yet see, learn something I don't yet know." He wakes Junior for his watch, goes to sleep himself, and is awakened by the sound of approaching NVA.

Stone wants us to see this character as someone confused, disoriented, beginning to question his reasons for being in Vietnam. These are all overt political impressions that are translated into the visual and verbal narrative of the film. But more than this, Taylor's monologue, coming as it does immediately before the first combat sequence, can be read as an increasing deterioration of his sense of himself as subject, in which he is "anonymous," has no individuality, and is seeking for an identity that he "can be proud of," someone he can become "without having to fake it," i.e. an "authentic" subject position. In the midst of this ambiguity of identity, Taylor finds that his paternal connections—his grandfather fighting in WWI and his father in WWII—are no longer meaningful as a means of solidifying that identity. Instead, he must start all over again, "way down here in the mud," and produce a "new" personality that will not depend upon theirs. More specifically, he must discover a "new" father in relation to whom he can establish his own identity, i.e. a father who, unlike his own, has power: "[my parents] wanted me to be just like them—respectable, hardworking, making $200 a week, a little house, a family. . . . I didn't want my whole life to be predetermined by them." Though Taylor speaks here of his parents, it is clear he is speaking only of his father, who, in 1967, would most likely be the one who is "hard-working, making $200 a week." In addition, by writing to his grandmother, he severs any connections to any male line in his family. His last words before the combat scene are to his mother, not his father: "tell Mom I miss her too," an affinity that will be completely denied by the film's close.

The ensuing combat scene is a product of this disjunction between continuous father/son identities. Abandoning both his grandfather and father, Taylor maintains connections only to the women in his family, and instead chooses to immerse himself into the "anonymity"[12] of the male community that is the combat situation in American culture.[13] Because those new ties are insecure—Taylor is still a "cherry," i.e. a son[14]—and the old ones intact through women, Taylor's wound is a surface one, i.e. the damage to his subjectivity is superficial because he has not wholly severed himself from his previous masculine identity.

Before the second combat scene, Taylor's confusion increases. Following the near-massacre of the Vietnamese village, during which Taylor finds his own limits for behavior brought into question as he taunts a retarded Vietnamese boy, Taylor voices more ambiguity: "It's a struggle to maintain my sanity—it's all a blur. I don't know what's right and what's wrong anymore. There's a civil war in the platoon. . . . " Not only has he lost his previous social identity by rejecting his father's lifestyle and seeking for "anonymity," he now is forced to abandon all prior notions of moral valuation, even the very "reason" upon which he was able to judge that war is like hell, "the loss of reason." In his anonymity, "it's all a blur."

Taylor recites these lines in a voiceover as the platoon wades through a waist-high stream during monsoon rains. Big Harold, angry that he didn't get his assignment to a laundry detail that would take him out of combat, says, "Shit, got to paint myself white get one of dem jobs. Get ma request in for a circumcision." Taylor then pulls a leech off of his cheek.

Importantly, Stone eliminates several lines from the screenplay here. The scene begins with Big Harold pulling a leech "out of his open crotch area," saying, "Shit, lookit this little fucker trying to get up ma glory hole." After his remark about the circumcision, Francis says to Harold, "Gonna cut your pecker down to size huh Big Harold?" who answers, "Dat's okay wid me, better to have a small one den no one at all," to which King replies, "Your girlfriends gonna look for new lovers, man. Best thing a bro's got's his flap."[15]

While the film's juxtaposition of Big Harold's comments on circumcision and Taylor's leech seems merely coincidental, the screenplay shows these scenes to be intimately linked through an imagery of castration. The leech that is trying to enter Big Harold's penis prefaces circumcision as literal castration—"Gonna cut your pecker down to size"—and ties this to a fear of/for women—"Your girlfriends gonna look for new lovers." At the close of this discussion, Taylor's apparently blithe move to pick a leech off of his cheek takes on a greater meaning as a hint at his own pending castration, both at the hands of the war and the powerful father.

Such scenes enable us to read how the structure of the father/son dynamic and the masculine subject it stablizes are intimately linked to racial difference in Vietnam films. Stone's screenplay shows how the threat of castration that underlies the exchange of power between father and son (i.e. that the son could not become the father) is more readily articulated in relation to black rather than white men: the leech that is in Big Harold's penis is only on Taylor's cheek. The white penis is here both mythified as unseeable and made unavailable for comparison with the mythically larger black penis.[16] As in other Vietnam films, this threat is translated through a fear of the responses of women, not men, in an effort to suppress the tensions of racial difference between men.[17]

Big Harold's line about circumcision must, I think, also be read in relation to an earlier joke of the film. The lieutenant, whom Stone's screenplay describes as having a "false masculinity" (53), i.e. cannot be a father, declines playing poker with Barnes and his group by saying, "Nah, I wouldn't want to get raped by you guys. . . . " (53). O'Neill replies, "What are you saving up to be Lieutenant—Jewish?" (53). There are complex racisms voiced here—only white men get out of combat, white men are circumcised, Jews are circumcised, Jews are virgins/feminine, "false masculinity" belongs to Jews and those like them who can't play poker with men like Barnes, Jews hoard money, etc.—that overlap race, class, and gender issues. Without trying to unwind these knotted articulations of difference, it is clear that Big Harold's brief comment refers to this complex set of prejudices that are otherwise denied by the camaraderie of scenes like those in the "Underworld," where men bond together regardless of backgrounds. Big Harold's single line here hints at the explosion of that collective image as dictated in its most threatening terms—castration ("Get ma request in for a circumcision"). Taylor's leech makes him vulnerable to this threat.

Racial difference as constructed in *Platoon* insures that the father/son dynamic will have meaning only for white men.[18] As these scenes show, Jews and blacks are argued as "non-men," not simply "feminized," but men who *willingly* castrate themselves—Big Harold requests circumcision, Lt. Wolfe chooses not to play poker for fear of being "raped," and later, at the end of the final battle scene, Francis, who has survived the battle unharmed, stabs himself in the leg rather than face more combat. Much of this argument is directed against reading, as Clyde Taylor suggests, King as "actually more of a father-figure to Charlie than Elias." Taylor explains that, "deprived of the moral authority that neither the film nor its primary audience will grant him, [King's] characterization tips toward the familiar role of black male mammy to innocent white youth. . . . Where Elias' affirmation is an activist, apocalyptic salvationism, King's is a brotherly accommodationism."[19] King's relationship to Taylor is structured in such a way that he *cannot* be seen as a father, must be seen as at best a "brother," racially neutralized through self-castration. The black soldiers in *Platoon* are negated as well as possible enemies through their companionship with Taylor and their relative separation, both physically and emotionally, from the interests and concerns of white soldiers. Denied both the possibility of being fathers or sons-who-could-become-fathers, black soldiers in *Platoon* are situated to insure their non-participation in the father/son dynamic that defines these films and therefore their non-participation in the exchange of power.

The second combat sequence of the film occurs immediately after this scene. As the platoon walks through a wooded area, they are ambushed, the enactment of castration in combat.[20] Unlike the first combat scene, where the American patrol was staging an ambush of the Vietnamese, here the Americans are vulnerable, they are being killed, and they may soon be trapped. As Elias describes it, "Flank's wide open, dinks get 3–4 snipers in these holds, when Third Platoon comes up, they'll get us in a crossfire with 'em. We'll shoot each other to shit, then they'll hit us with everything they got. It'll be a massacre!" (87). Previously being attacked by the Vietnamese, here men are in danger of killing themselves.

Such scenes fit in with popular interpretations of the film like Richard Corliss's "Americans were fighting themselves, and both sides lost"[21] and are very much part of how Stone wants to portray the Vietnam War as a battle within America, between Americans like Barnes and Elias, who fight wars differently and who both die in the film. But these scenes also exemplify a masculinity in peril, led into an ambush by a clever and unseen "feminine" enemy to "massacre" itself. Men like Big Harold are "requesting" their own circumcisions. Men like Wolfe are in charge. Men like Barnes are killing men like Elias, and men like Taylor are confused and "in a blur." *This* is the fear, the anxiety, the threat, the violence that underlies this combat sequence and others in Vietnam film—not a battle with NVA soldiers.

The last combat scene, the longest and most elaborate of the film, is the final explosion of masculinity in *Platoon*. With Elias, Taylor's positive role model—one of his "fathers"—now dead at Barnes's hands, and Taylor unable to act on his desires for revenge, the film is in its most complete state of disorder and confusion. Soldiers who had seemed hardened before are crying now; both O'Neill and Junior are frightened that they will die in a battle in which they know they are outnumbered, merely "bait" to draw out the NVA. Even Barnes says, "everybody gotta die sometime."[22] Taylor's despair is at its lowest: "People like Elias get wasted and people like Barnes just go on making up rules any way they want and what do we do, we just sit around in the middle and suck on it!" (106). And Taylor, whose only link to a secured identity before Vietnam was through his letters to his grandmother, has stopped writing.

King: What's the matter wid you? . . . How come you ain't writing no more? You was always writing something home. Looks like youse half a bubble off, Taylor.

> What about your folks? That grandma you was telling me about? . . .
> (Chris shakes his head.)
> Girl?
> (Chris' eyes answer negatively.)
> Must be somebody?
> Chris: . . . there's nobody. (105)

Now completely cut off from his past, Taylor's identity is entirely dependent upon his immediate surroundings, the war he is in and the men he is fighting with. It is at this point that we can see how the masculine subject as traditionally defined by American culture has been deteriorating (though never disappearing) throughout the film—moving from the initial confusion and disorientation of arriving in Vietnam to do this final silence of disconnection. Taylor has finally found that bottom, that spot "way down here in the mud," from which he "can start up again," the point from which the masculine subject can be reconstructed, no longer in relation to "the world," but now only in relation to the interconnected subjectivity of masculinity in Vietnam. Out of this confusion, the final battle scene occurs, in which their position is overrun and Taylor proves himself to be a rabid combat soldier, able to sense danger, to kill, and to survive.

At the peak of the battle, Barnes, red-eyed and in a fury of killing—what Stone calls "the essence of evil" (123)—is about to attack Taylor with a trenching tool when an American plane drops a bomb on their position and the screen blacks out. When the scene returns at dawn of the next day, Stone's camera signifies that a change has occurred. Shot in black and white, not color, the camera pans across the multiple bodies of soldiers and the decimated jungle, turning slowly to color again. While filmically this is meant to show Taylor's gradual return to consciousness, this single use of black-and-white film in an otherwise intensely colored and closely-shot cinema signifies more than Taylor's physical awakening. It also marks the "dawn" of a different masculine subject, Taylor's appearance as a father. During the battle, Taylor emerged from his confusion and loss of identity as a "warrior,"[23] a man who no longer knew fear. On his first patrol, he was paralyzed by the sight of the enemy, unable to act, unprepared to fight, sitting draped in a blanket and separated from his gun and Claymore ignitors. Here, he is not only prepared, but he abandons his protected foxhole and charges the enemy straight on, killing with fury and skill. No longer afraid to act, no longer threatened, Taylor emerges during this battle with a different identity. It is finally only Barnes that seems able to stop him.

Why? Let me digress for a moment to discuss *Platoon*'s portrayal of the enemy before returning to Taylor's final battle with Barnes. As the combat scenes become longer and more violent, as Taylor himself kills more and more people, as Taylor's distance from his previous identity increases, the enemy becomes more and more distinct. Only shadows against a misty night in the first combat scene, and then fleeting and hidden figures in the battle in the woods, the enemy in this final combat scene has become identifiable. We see NVA soldiers preparing booby traps, selecting weapons, examining maps. Taylor hears their voices beyond his foxhole. We see in slow-motion the firing of an RPG (rocket-propelled grenade) that explodes Taylor's abandoned foxhole. We see NVA soldiers killing Bunny point blank in his chest, and wounding Barnes and Taylor. And then finally, at the height of the battle, we see Barnes.

The increasing specificity of the enemy has now become fixed, not on the NVA soldiers whom Taylor is able to kill and who finally die from the bomb explosion, but upon Barnes. It is Barnes whom Taylor must fight in order to establish his own identity. The Vietnamese become merely a backdrop for the display of American masculinity struggling to stabilize itself in a revised environment.[24] But the increasing specificity of the Vietnamese as enemy works both to focus our attention upon perceiving the enemy, an attention that culminates in seeing

Barnes as enemy, and at the same time to distract us from seeing other American men—specifically, other white American men—as enemies. Stone wants us to conclude finally that *only* Barnes is the enemy, so that while battles against the NVA will go on, Barnes's death marks a significant ending to one particular struggle, that for Taylor's masculine identity. As a "two-timer" (soldiers who have been wounded twice), Taylor leaves this battlefield for good. In the simplest of terms, his war is over.

By focusing entirely upon Barnes as the "enemy," the film has succeeded in negating fears that power might be taken by someone outside the father/son dynamic, in this case by the Vietnamese. As Taylor's distance from his biological father grows, and his relation to his "new" fathers, Elias and Barnes, becomes more defined—in other words, as his identification of positions of power increases—the enemy becomes clearer, until we learn that the "real" enemy is the evil and powerful father, the one Taylor must defeat in order to secure his own power, to become a father himself. In telling the story in this way, *Platoon* shows why the father/son dynamic is the logic of patriarchy: by declaring that power exists only within the framework of the masculine arena—the war—and only by identifying and affiliating with a strong father, alternate forms of power are denied; according to *Platoon*, one can only gain power—what Stone chooses to call "experience"—by acknowledging and accepting this system as exhaustive and determinative. Consequently, that Barnes should finally be identified as the enemy does not challenge but instead confirms the father/son dynamic as system. All meaning stems from and acquires "truth" only as it becomes a character in this narration.

At the film's close, the confusion that has so haunted Taylor has disappeared. Because the war itself is not resolved, seems, at the close of this film, to have the possibility of going on forever, any sense of resolution the film offers must stem, not from a change in the war, but from a change in Taylor. The film's resolution rests then not upon the war but upon the stabilization of masculinity through acquisition of the power of the father. As the last words of the film declare, Taylor is now quietly confident that he has a knowledge to impart, a message to deliver: "those of us who did make it have an obligation to build again, to teach others what we know and to try with what's left of our lives to find a goodness and meaning to this life."[25] While the film would like us to see this change as a product of Taylor's experience in war and discovery of a part of himself that he could not know while still in college, I find another explanation more convincing.

The change in Taylor is a product of a reconstruction and stabilization of his masculine identity through his testing and rejection of various masculine models—his father and grandfather, Elias and Barnes—until in the end he establishes an identity that is separate from theirs but still part of them, "the child born of those two fathers" (129). This might sound at first like a simple maturation narrative, in which a young man struggles to separate himself from his father or father-figure. What distinguishes *Platoon* from such narratives and marks it as a product of contemporary gender concerns in American culture is Taylor's relationship to multiple fathers,[26] each of whom represents a different aspect of previously denied notions of manhood: Taylor's father, the middle-class breadwinner; his grandfather and father, the dutiful patriots who served their country and could fulfill their commitment to the *polis*; Elias, the peace-loving, compassionate, and sensuous man; and Barnes, the ruthless, law-breaking renegade who kills to survive. Taylor tests himself as each of these heroes—goes to college, enlists in the Army, rescues young girls from rape, and kills lustfully in battle—and accepts none of them as satisfactory. But instead of offering a "new" and alternate model, Taylor integrates these into a single character: he will return home having fulfilled his commitment as a "patriot" and having become a "warrior"; he maintains his compassion as he shows concern for Francis's wounds; and he has established his own law in killing Barnes and suffering no recrimination for it. His is not a "new" masculinity but a revised version of the old ones. What knowledge has he gained? That none of these masculine characters can continue independently in American culture, but that joined together in a revised character, they can "survive."[27] This is the coalescence of a masculinity that had become dispersed; by gathering itself under the umbrella of the "god/father," it can achieve a restabilized position of power.

With all other fathers dead or neutralized in the film, Taylor becomes the "new" father at its close, able "to teach to others what we know" and to "build again." Stone's screenplay is especially instructive here, as he describes Taylor's departing helicopter as "now rising to meet God" (128). Through his experiences in war, Taylor has gained a perspective that enables him to see what others cannot, a perspective that is "god-like," authoritative, and powerful. As the closing position of the film from which Taylor narrates his new goals of "teaching" and "building," it can be described as nothing less than paternal.

The combat scenes of *Platoon* have led emphatically to this point. The increasing violence of the combat sequences can be seen as a direct result of the increasing ambivalence of the masculine character as it is severed from previous forms of stability and identification. The combat sequences are eruptions of the anxiety about this ambivalence as well as forums within which the tension of that anxiety can be dispelled and "new" masculine roles can be tried on. That anxiety decreases and is arrested as the masculine subject becomes stabilized through the adoption of the position of father. The resolution of the father/son tension is not then coincidentally but structurally tied to combat scenes because it is through combat sequences that the son is enabled (often through the literal death of the father) to adopt an altered paternal role. The deterioration of the masculine subject is halted only by the son becoming the father; only through restabilization of the position of the father is violence arrested.

It is here that Springer's discussion of the spectatorial security in viewing death becomes again relevant. Identifying as we do with Taylor, a character who we know will not die in the film, we share that security of witnessing and causing death, being twice wounded, and yet not being vulnerable to death. It is as well the "security" of the masculine character within patriarchy, enabling experimentation with the "death" of previous masculinities along with "wounds" to present ones, and yet not being vulnerable to the "death" of masculinity itself.[28] By inviting the viewer to take Taylor's character at its point of identification, we are being asked to share, not simply this conclusion, but the system that enabled its production.

This is the cultural appeal of the combat film, explains its rise, as now, during periods when cultural conceptions of masculinity are being brought under examination. In American culture, such periods have often coincided with postwar years during which men who have been in combat must return to a society that has altered its gender roles during their absence,[29] but it is not necessarily the case that combat films are linked to actual wars or combat scenarios.[30] To make this kind of gender/genre elision is to misperceive the operation of violence in culture. Combat narratives are linked to efforts to produce restabilized images of masculinity during historical moments when gender roles are being renegotiated, but they are only the most apparent and not the exclusive means by which such renegotiation occurs. In representations of the Vietnam War, those images are most generally oriented toward producing and promoting a paternal masculinity.[31]

The Rambo films show how this promotion takes place historically, shifting its relations and representations during the past decade. The three films, *First Blood* (Kotcheff, 1982), *Rambo: First Blood, Part II* (Cosmatos, 1985), and *Rambo III* (Macdonald, 1988), display different stages in the historical development of a reconstructed American masculinity that has occurred in recent years. First, these films sequentially display the rejection of various forms of masculine identification, progressively triumphing over traditional middle-class roles (*First Blood*), institutionalized forms of paternity (*Rambo: First Blood, Part II*), and finally global/international political authorities (*Rambo III*). But more importantly, in addition to distancing its own presentations of masculinity from these positions, the Rambo films reinscribe masculine relations within a revised father/son dynamic that confirms masculinity as the relevant framework for subjective and social relations in American culture. The Rambo films offer this paternity in its most compact forms, not only in Rambo's rejected relationships to the American government and the military as paternal figures, but in relationship to Rambo's mentor and teacher, Colonel Trautman.

First Blood shows Rambo struggling unwillingly against a town sheriff who is a Korean War veteran. This is the fairly straightforward battle with a traditional father figure that Chris Taylor is able, five years later, to dismiss so readily in his epistolary rejection of his father's way of life. Sheriff Teasle is shown to have middle-class concerns and prejudices, judging Rambo a hippie, and wanting only to keep his town of Hope, Oregon, a quiet and safe place for its citizens. The ease with which Rambo disrupts that quiet and destroys that town are only the most superficial evidences that Teasle's masculinity and the middle-class ethic he represents are no longer sufficient in a post-Vietnam world. But in spite of this easy rejection of Teasle, Rambo's character at the close of the film is firmly subordinated to that of Colonel Trautman, Rambo's leader and teacher in the Army. When Rambo walks away from a final pending gun battle (the fact that this kind of full-scale combat scene is *avoided* in *First Blood* marks its early participation in masculine revision; anxieties about masculinity are here repressed rather than explored and exploded), it is under Trautman's protective arm. It is clear that Trautman still has control over Rambo, is, in fact, the only man—the only type of masculinity—that can stop him. Rambo does not, in this first film, gain the kind of "god-like" independence that Chris Taylor inhabits at the end of *Platoon*.

In the second film, *Rambo: First Blood, Part II*, Rambo has a distinctively different paternal figure to react against. Not the conservative middle-class figure of Sheriff Teasle, Rambo here must work against Marshall Murdock, government representative in charge of a POW rescue mission that can gain Rambo a pardon from the jail sentence he is serving as a result of his actions in *First Blood*. Murdock's is a technologically sophisticated, bureaucratized, professional, and powerful paternal figure whose influence and abilities far surpass those of Sheriff Teasle. Also a World War II veteran, but one who has moved beyond that time into a corporate era, Murdock is politically wise and economically clever. His power as paternal authority figure is made most clear at the moment when he singly decides to abandon Rambo and a rescued POW to a pursuing Vietnamese patrol by declaring to the helicopter pilots who could rescue Rambo, "Abort the mission!"

But again, as in *First Blood*, Rambo triumphs over this adversary, returning with the POWs Murdock said did not exist, destroying Murdock's computers (the source of his virility), and threatening to return and "find" him if Murdock fails to find other POWs (this threat is visually articulated as castration, when Rambo, laying Murdock across a desktop, stabs his foot-long knife into the table by Murdock's ear). As in the first film, *Rambo* closes with his relation to Trautman, though here Rambo is moving out of the subordinate position that confined him in *First Blood*. Instead of accepting Trautman's offer to "come home," Rambo walks deliberately away from Trautman and off into the jungles of Thailand. Though it is still clear that Trautman is the only man who retains any link to Rambo, the only one to whom he will speak, there is a decided distance between them as Rambo separates himself from Trautman.

In *Rambo III*, Rambo's entire mission is defined by a now clearly altered paternal relationship with Trautman. The early advertisements for *Rambo III* make this shift clear. On subsequent pages of film sections of newspapers, Rambo's motivations are declared, in bold print, without context or ascription (as if everyone understands the context for their meaning): "The first time was for himself/ The second was for his country/ This time is for a friend." Naming Trautman as Rambo's "friend" suggests the distance traveled between this film and *First Blood*, where it is clear that Rambo and Trautman are not on a level to be "friends." Here, though Rambo refuses to accompany Trautman on a mission to help Afghan rebels, he quickly offers to rescue Trautman when he is captured by Russian soldiers. The incentive for action here is straightforwardly linked to this paternal tie, with masculine roles reversed; now Rambo must save the "father" who first saved him. The authority figure of the film is a Russian colonel renowned for his torture techniques and ruthlessness. This is the "evil" father-figure that was Barnes in *Platoon*, a man who survives by making his own rules and eliminating all who disrupt his power. But instead of the moral evil that formed the center of Stone's concerns, Colonel Zaysen's is the multinational corporate power that does not respect national boundaries, is interested not in justice or political position but careerist maneuvering (he excels at his job so that he can be promoted out of Afghanistan), and is focused upon destroying the family unit and traditional way of life that "subvert" his enforcement of power.

To mark the clear shift in paternal relations that has taken place in representations of the 1980s, Rambo not only succeeds in rescuing his "father" but then proceeds to fight beside and outdo him on the battlefield. The close of *Rambo III* shows its distance from *First Blood*: instead of walking out to a waiting police force under the protection of Trautman's raincoat and sheltering arm, Rambo and Trautman drive away from the celebrating Afghan tribes, exchanging quips about their military successes. They are no longer father and son but buddies.[32] Rambo has taken the place of the father (he is "adopted" by a small Afghan boy as evidence of his own ability to stand as father) and the father has been "wounded," infantilized, and had to depend upon the son for his own survival.

What a look at the combat sequences of the Rambo films reveals is that these multiple battles with successively more powerful and threatening father-figures are *not* the focus of the narrative force in these films; instead, these plot strains are diversions to distract us from recognizing the actual source of tension and intensity in these narratives—the restructuring of the father-son relation and the production of the masculine subject within that frame.

Rambo—a film about the rescue of American POWs, of "lost men"—records the story of the son's recognition that the father is not all-powerful, and of the son's exchange of power with and in support of the father. Trautman, who taught Rambo how to survive in war, who rescued Rambo from his first "battle" at home, and who promises Rambo a pardon for volunteering for this mission, is shown in this film not to be in charge. Instead, his power is subordinated to that of Murdock, the man who heads the rescue mission. During successive scenes of the film, Trautman's remaining power is increasingly cut away by Murdock, until he finally is unable to help Rambo at all. When Rambo and a POW are unexpectedly sighted by the rescue helicopter, Murdock aborts the mission and recalls the ship. Though Trautman orders, "We're going down," the doorgunner, one of Murdock's assistants, points a gun at Trautman and replies, "You're not going anywhere." When Trautman screams, "There's men down there! Our men!" the gunner answers coolly, "No. *Your* men. Don't be a hero." As the helicopter flies away, Rambo calls out, "Colonel! Don't leave!"

The violence of the film's combat scenes increases in direct proportion to the decline of Trautman's power. More specifically, the most extended and violent scenes of the film—Rambo's single-handed defeat of his numerous Russian and Vietnamese pursuers—occur *immediately* following Murdock's emasculation of Trautman, when he tells him, "I'm in charge here. You're just a tool." The film's narration is set up in such a way that we are to see the death of Co Bao, Rambo's Vietnamese female guide, at the hands of a Vietnamese officer as Rambo's motivation for this rampage (while with Co, he had earlier agreed that they were heading to Thailand, not back to get the POWs). But there is not a continuous line between Co's death and Rambo's rampage. Instead, the death and burial are interrupted by a scene of Trautman's demanding that Murdock gather a rescue team to help Rambo. It is here that Murdock declares that he, not Trautman, is in charge. The film then cuts to Rambo's hands on Co's grave and his return to exact revenge upon his pursuers.

Framing the final emasculation of the father, Co's death and burial become diversions for the film's narration of the reconstruction of masculine identity. The immediacy of the physical and emotional ties between Rambo and Co seems to outweigh the bond between Trautman and Rambo. And the brevity and inaction of the intervening scene between Trautman and Murdock would make it appear incidental in comparison to the lengthy and action-filled scenes with Co. But the placement of these scenes reveals where the weight of the film's tension lies, as it is Trautman's "death," not Co's, that precedes the celebrated combat sequence that follows. The grave at which Rambo kneels could just as well be the grave in which Trautman's father-image has been laid to rest. It is finally the tension of Trautman's emasculation, not Co's death, that must be relieved and reoriented by the elaborate violence that follows.

Co functions as well to siphon off the tension of the homoerotic overtones in the Trautman/Rambo bond. It is immediately prior to Trautman's final displacement as father-figure that Co kisses Rambo and asks him to take her to America. (Is it perhaps this kiss that marks Trautman's downfall, as he is here rejected by the son? Such questions hint at the degree to which all events in these narrations are diversions from the tensions involved in restructuring the father/son dynamic as the focus for masculine identification.) Co's impersonation of the prostitute echoes in this kiss to confirm her as heterosexual and feminine, something her role as Rambo's guide seemed to deny ("You didn't expect a woman?"). When the father is released from his elevated and thereby nonerotic position (nonerotic because fully sexed, completely in possession of the power of castration), the possibility of homoerotic links between men comes into play. As Rambo and Trautman are exchanging power in these scenes, passing through each other's identities (Trautman held at gunpoint in the helicopter is Rambo at the end of *First Blood*; Rambo, knowing that Trautman has either betrayed him or been made helpless to assist him, must "save" himself, must become his own mentor/father; etc.), they must guard this exchange and restructuring of masculine power from recognition of the homoerotic. Co's presence serves this purpose; when the exchange is released, she must be eliminated.

Co must die in this film because her death mediates between Trautman's failure as a father and Rambo's resuscitation of Trautman's power and his own elevation as masculine strength. When Trautman is prevented from rescuing Rambo by Murdock's bureaucracy, it is Co who saves him. Her entrance into the camp as a disguised prostitute underscores her position as feminine, making Trautman's helplessness all the more demeaning. It is thus not accidental that Co's death would be linked so intimately to the final negation of Trautman's power by Murdock. It is as if, abandoned by the father, she has taken his place while Rambo is in the camp, i.e. taken over the power of the father in rescuing the son. In order for Rambo to revive his own masculinity as well as that of Trautman, Co, as reminder of that substitution, must be eliminated in order for the bond between father and son to be reaffirmed and restructured, to be reintroduced into a world outside the imagery of failure and loss associated with the POW camp. This is the strongest anxiety that the ensuing combat sequence must dispel—that a woman could take the place of the father in rescuing the son from his tormentors.

After the combat scene, when Rambo has defeated the Russians and the Vietnamese, Rambo announces over a helicopter radio that he is returning with POWs. As the men in the receiving room begin to cheer, they halt and look questioningly at Murdock, waiting for his response. When Murdock leaves the room in silence (supposedly from Rambo's threat to come back and "get" him), Trautman takes over, saying "You heard him! Let's go!" Though again in charge and in a position superior to Murdock's, it is only through Rambo that Trautman has regained his power, to the point that his "orders" are only references to Rambo's own orders to prepare for their arrival. And when Rambo returns to the base, Trautman only follows him as he first destroys the computers, threatens

Murdock, and then walks off toward Thailand. Though Trautman is still the significant figure in relation to whom we are to view Rambo, he is no longer the powerful mentor of *First Blood*, but is now a product of Rambo's own strength and activity.

The most spectacular combat sequence in *Rambo III* (a film that is almost entirely combat scenes of various kinds, a result of the father's kidnapping—the threat of his disappearance and death, and of the final and most complete exchange of power) is the culmination of this exchange of power between father and son, and the confirmation of Rambo's reconstruction as father-figure. As the film's most celebrated dialogue indicates, this paternal imagery, like Chris Taylor's, is god-like: When Zaysen hears that Rambo is coming to rescue Trautman, he asks, "Who do you think this man is? God?" and Trautman replies, "No, God would have mercy. He won't." After having rescued Trautman from his Soviet torturers and apparently evaded their pursuers, Rambo and Trautman find themselves surrounded by a large and technologically sophisticated Soviet force. When they are told to surrender, and Trautman asks Rambo what they should do, Rambo replies, "Fuck 'em," and they decide to fight. When it seems that they will be easily killed, Afghan rebels ride to their rescue on horseback, and they collectively defeat the Russian soldiers.

The triumph of Rambo and the Afghan rebels in the ensuing scenes validates the value of the personal versus the impersonal, the individual versus the corporate, and the paternal versus the bureaucratic[33] line. Rambo's valiant but hopeless desire to fight the Russian army is evidence of his commitment to the paternal and masculine characters that define him. Having gone to such lengths to rescue the father—to insure the father's "survival"—Rambo would rather die than relinquish that image. More to the point, without the figure that represents and insures that system, without that system itself, Rambo would himself be powerless, "defeated." What saves him is his own portrayal as father-figure to the Afghan soldiers, emblematically shown in the boy who is drawn to Rambo as his mentor and father-image. It is finally as if the Afghan rebels are fighting—not for political, national or religious independence from the Soviet occupation forces (there is no discussion in the film of reasons for rebellion other than to protect wives and children from Soviet torture and murder, again constructing the Afghan characters in a solely patriarchal vocabulary)—but for the possibility of confirming that a father-figure—a "savior"—continues to exist. As in *Rambo*, before this final threat to the father's power, the rebels were prepared to leave the area and seek safety elsewhere. But the threat of emasculation, here so much stronger because *both* white father-figures will be eliminated, brings the "rebels" back to the battlefield and to victory.

The Rambo sequence shows then the gradual progression and translation of power from father to son, as the son is reconstructed as father and the production of masculinity is, momentarily, assured. Clearly, there are displayed shifts in the purported values and "beliefs" of father and son, so that Rambo's apparent independence and rejection of the military institution that Trautman still participates in seems a radical change, along with Rambo's altered definition of patriotism and individual responsibility to national demands. Because the son does not replicate the father in any of these cases, significant change in power relations and definitions seems to have occurred. But such issues function only to distract our attention from the repetition, not of the father himself, but of the father's position and significance as stabilizer for social meaning. Such repetition serves to maintain the structural features of subject construction in patriarchy while altering its specific characteristics.

The elaborate and distracting displays of combat sequences help to suggest that actual change has occurred, as we visualize the literal destruction of the very landscape of previous meaning production and must, as we are visually instructed to do, "start over again." It is here that we recognize the spectatorial value of overhead shots like that at the end of *Platoon*, which function to convince us of the destruction of the "old order" and the apparent start of a "new." And while the spectacular display of combat scenes may yield a kind of exhilaration and euphoria of power not linked to a subject position and available for assumption by the spectator, we are clearly instructed as to the consequences of such exhilaration—death and destruction. As *Platoon* shows most emphatically, by the end of a lengthy combat scene, we are, designedly, exhausted by uncontrolled displays of power and are positioned to *desire* a return to order, a reinstallation of ourselves as stable subjects in relation to a stabilized subject order. This may then be *the* key function of the combat sequence in narrative: to encourage our desire for a return of the father and the stable order he represents.

The importance of films like *Platoon* and the Rambo narratives is then that they provide an arena within which it appears that *only* the father/son dynamic determines meaning and that masculinity is the only arena for the definition and recognition of the subject. The only relevant question of these and films like them is not *if* the father/son dynamic is significant, but of *how* it will be played out. In such terms, the masculine subject is presented as moving only between these two poles, being either father or son, but not daring to be neither (this position is relegated to the feminine in all of these films). The cultural function of these narratives is to display at large the tensions surrounding masculine subjectivity and to resolve them through the depiction of active and powerful father figures.

Combat sequences thus function in this project in two ways: First, to relieve tensions aroused by the filmic narration or brought to the film by the audience about the stability, place, and power of the masculine subject. Second, to provide a means by which the masculine subjectivities portrayed in the film can change, shift emphasis, and exchange roles without having to reveal those roles as themselves suspect or in peril. To portray a masculine subject in transition would suggest that this subject is neither stable nor sufficient; combat scenes distract us from seeing these exchanges occur. The increasingly spectacular nature of these scenes in contemporary film is evidence of how risky such sights would be as well as of how unstable that subjectivity is felt to have become.

Combat sequences reveal that the structural excess of contemporary American culture is the construction of the masculine subject within the frame of the father/son dynamic. The comments made here about combat sequences can be applied to various aspects of contemporary American culture, in fact, to the structure of that culture itself. The recent resurgence of the popularity of action films is only one indication of how this structure is being enacted. Films like *Lethal Weapon*, *The Big Easy*, *Road Warrior* and *Mad Max*, *Star Wars*, and *The Empire Strikes Back*, and many others show how scenes of violence are resolved by the stabilization of a father-figure at the end of the film. Much of the popularity of the issue of "male-bashing" (discussed in such forums as "The Oprah Winfrey Show," "Donahue," "Geraldo," and the television special "Of Macho and Men") stems, I suspect, not only from a backlash to feminism, but from an anxiety that too much criticism and alteration of masculine roles may lead, not to a replacement of the father with a "new" man, but with the disappearance of the father and the stable subject positions he designates altogether (in such ways, the father/son dynamic dovetails with terrorism). And certainly political fears about having a woman or a black man as vice-president are linked to this logic.

The question that must be asked is this: Is the apparent resurgence of cultural violence, both on film and in social relations, an indication that the father/son dynamic has suffered from challenges to its sufficiency and needs to be reaffirmed, or simply that it is, as is said of the Death Star in *The Empire Strikes Back* (the ultimate emblem of phallic destructive power), "fully operational"? Though a detailed answer to this question would require more space than I can take here, and obviously neither of these situations would be absolutely applicable at any single moment, let me suggest a general rule for reading the historical stability of the father/son dynamic and the patriarchal structure it enacts: that during periods in which the father/son dynamic and its confirmation and definition of the masculine subject are being challenged and altered, dominant representations focus on narrations of the son; during periods when those challenges have been addressed and constructions of the masculine subject have been restabilized in relation to those challenges, dominant representations offer the narration of the father. For example, during the 1970s, a period when constructions of masculinity were being challenged and reshaped, films focused on sons rather than fathers: *Easy Rider, Butch Cassidy and the Sundance Kid, Midnight Cowboy, The Graduate*, etc. Though shown primarily battling and being defeated by insurmountable external and indifferent social forces (the Father)—the military, corporations—these sons were shown to be rejecting positions as fathers, sharing and altering power relations rather than confirming them. Neither necessarily more "progressive" nor "subversive" than films of the 1980s, these narratives indicate how the father/son dynamic is able to respond to local historical conditions while maintaining its determination of the structure of social relations and, at the same time, reformulating those structures to adapt to different social circumstances.

Finally, it is excess that enables alterations in the construction of the masculine subject in particular historical settings. What this suggests, to return to Thompson's argument, is that excess is *both* the moment at which the narrative structure, the "unifying system," can be read *and* the point at which that structure alters itself. This is the problem presented by Thompson's insistence on reading excess within individual films; by expanding the concept to see its function *between* films, as in the Rambo series, we can recognize that the excess of one narrative provides material for a subsequent narratives's renegotiation of gender relations. What is overdetermined as "style" in one setting can be incorporated as coherent "character" in another. The "son" of one film is adopted as "father" in the next. Thus, while the concept of excess enables us to read individual narrative arrangements, it enables us to see as well how cultural narratives are negotiated, reformulated, and "adopted."

NOTES

As so often, I would like to thank Robyn Wiegman for a helpful reading of an early draft of this essay.

1. I choose to describe these relations through "positions" rather than depictions or imagery to emphasize that the same character can, and in many cases does, occupy both positions during a single narrative, moving from son to father or vice versa.

2. Jeanine Basinger, *The World War II Combat Film: Anatomy of a Genre* (New York: Columbia University Press, 1986), xi.

3. Richard Corliss, "Platoon: Viet Nam, The Way it Really Was, On Film," *Time* 129.4 (January 26, 1987):59.

4. Kristen Thompson, "The Concept of Cinematic Excess," in *Narrative, Apparatus, Ideology: A Film Theory Reader*, ed. Philip Rosen (New York: Columbia University Press, 1986), 130.

5. *The Remasculinization of America: Gender and Representations of the Vietnam War* (Bloomington: Indiana University Press, 1989).

6. Susan Brownmiller, *Femininity* (New York: Fawcett Columbine, 1984), 15.

7. Anthony Easthope defines succinctly how realism functions in cultural representations: "Realism aims to naturalise ideology. That is, it seeks to change the effect and force of constructed meanings so that they do not appear constructed but rather as obvious, inevitable and part of how things really are" ("Realism and Its Subversion: Hollywood and Vietnam," in *Tell Me Lies About Vietnam: Cultural Battles for the Meaning of the War*, eds. Alf Louvre and Jeffrey Walsh [Milton Keynes, England: Open University Press, 1988]).

8. Anthony Easthope, *What a Man's Gotta Do: The Masculine Myth in Popular Culture* (London: Paladin, 1986), 7.

9. Paul Smith, *Discerning the Subject* (Minneapolis: University of Minnesota Press, 1988), xxxi.

10. Gender and the patriarchal system are not to be seen as equivalent or interchangeable. Gender relations are one of the primary ways in which patriarchal structures are enacted, but they are not the only way. Delineations of other forms of difference—particularly race, class, age and sexuality—are historically varied and foregrounded in relation to gender as mechanisms for the specification of patriarchies.

11. Thompson, 140.

12. Where masculinity was previously assumed to be equivalent to the universal, it is now marked as equivalent to the "anonymous," a strategy that is designed to take away an aura of privilege from the masculine position by rephrasing it as non-position.

13. In spite of the increasing numbers of women in the American military, all services still adhere to the rule that women are to be excluded from combat situations (though many women medical veterans of the Vietnam War point out the hypocrisy of this position, as women were frequently exposed to shellings, mortar barrages, and direct attacks while working in field hospitals).

14. Because "cherry" is a gendered term derived from female sexuality, it might seem that I am undermining my own argument here. At this point in time, Taylor, as occupying the position of the son, is, in relation to the father (who is fully masculine), affiliated by difference with the non-masculine, i.e., the feminine, and therefore can be likened to the female body. Significantly, such likening applies only to a part of that body that can "change" and "disappear," the hymen, suggesting that the son's potential ascendancy to the position of the father via "experience" will enable him to leave any and all affiliations with the female body and the feminine. As Jacques Derrida has shown (*Spurs: Nietzsche's Styles*, trans. Barbara Harlow [Chicago: University of Chicago Press, 1979], 1), this is not the case, and the hymen will leave its "trace," posing another site for resistance.

15. Oliver Stone, *Platoon* (New York: Vintage, 1987), 82.

16. Stanley Kubrick's *Full Metal Jacket* (1987) is even more explicit about this threat of racial comparison of the male penis. As the other squad members look on, a Vietnamese prostitute who had first said she would not have sex with Eightball because he was "too beaucoup" changes her mind when he actually shows her his penis. Through a non-white woman's eyes, the black man's penis can be seen and judged as like that of the white man. For a discussion of white male anxieties about the black penis see Trudier Harris's *Exorcising Blackness: Historical and Literary Lynching and Burning Rituals* (Bloomington: Indiana University Press, 1984).

17. For a fuller discussion of race and gender in American culture, see Robyn Wiegman's *Negotiating the Masculine: Configurations of Race and Gender in American Culture* (doctoral dissertation, University of Washington, 1988).

18. *Platoon* has been charged with racism by numerous critics. Acel Moore says, for example that "the black characters in the film are all peripheral. All the main characters are white" ("Vietnam Film Deserves Another 'Award': For Racism," *Seattle Times,* February 18, 1987:A8). It is what Richard Corliss calls a "passive racism. The black soldiers are occasionally patronized and sentimentalized; they stand to the side while the white soldiers grab all the big emotions" (58). Clyde Taylor identifies it most concisely when he asks, "What kind of rupture would have been made if Charlie had been cast as black . . . ?" and answers, "[I]f Charlie were black, his blowing away of Barnes would burst the repressive limits of colonialist mythmaking. . . . [W]hen a black infantryman in *A Soldier's Story* kills a black sergeant as fascist as Barnes, the film's text condemns him" ("The Colonialist Subtext in Platoon," *Cineaste* 15.4:9).

19. Taylor, 9.

20. In Donald Pfarrer's *Neverlight* Katherine Vail tells her husband, Richard, whose platoon was ambushed in Vietnam, "I have never been ambushed, thank god, and you, thank god, have never had a miscarriage at five months" (New York: Laurel, 1982:74). The sustained linkage in Vietnam representation between combat actions and reproduction makes a reading of ambush as castration all the more feasible: the loss of a foetus for the female is, in this logic, the equivalent of castration for the male. In such ways the female subject is presumed to be constructed in similar manners and terms as the male.

21. Corliss, 55.

22. Stone, 109.

23. As Judith Hicks Stiehm insightfully reminds us, the "only unique role men have had in society is a social one—that of warrior—a role that is risky, unpleasant, and often short in duration. During peacetime modern men lack a specific way of proving that they are men" (*Bring Me Men and Women: Mandated Change at the U.S. Air Force Academy* [Berkeley: University of California Press, 1981], 296).

24. Richard Corliss makes explicit the racism of this thinking in *Platoon*: "The nearly 1 million Vietnamese casualties are deemed trivial compared with America's loss of innocence, of allies, of geopolitical race. And the tragedy of Viet Nam is seen as this: not that they died, but that we debased ourselves by killing them" (58).

25. Stone, 129.

26. If we think, for example, of earlier English and American novels that narrate the son's development—*Tom Jones, Humphrey Clinker, For Whom the Bell Tolls, Catcher in the Rye*—none shows this multiple depiction of fathers nor the full ascendence of the son to the father's role through an integration and adoption of the paternal position. It is at this juncture that class issues would become most relevant to arguments about the constructions of masculinity.

27. Though there is not a space to discuss this here, it is in such positionings of sons taking the positions of several fathers that we can see the link between patriarchy and capi-

talism, as the imagery of multiple fathers combining to form a single more unified and pow-erful figure ties in with contemporary corporate structures and multinational corporations.

28. James G. Frazer's *The Golden Bough* (New York: Macmillan, 1984) explains the ways in which "primitive" societies sustained the myths of an immortal masculinity through kill-ing kings who showed any signs of weakness, wounds, or aging, so that their kings would have the illusion of perpetual youth, strength, and virility (265–274). Though space does not permit, it is easy to see how such needs are met in contemporary culture through the "immortality" of the filmic image on the one hand and the invulnerability of the charac-ters within the film on the other. Rambo is the most obvious case in point.

29. Though many have discussed the effects of the soldier's return on women's posi-tion in American and British society, Peter G. Filene in particular discusses these effects on the construction off a masculine character in *Him/Her/Self: Sex Roles in Modern America* (Baltimore: Johns Hopkins University Press, 2nd ed., 1986).

30. Though Jeanine Basinger suggests that combat films are adapted to address differ-ent interests during non-combat periods, in particular the maintenance of military readi-ness (107), and the revisionary treatment of previous wars (99), her dependent definition of the combat film as generated by World War II prevents recognition of the extent to which these films are merely part of an overall argument to negotiate and reproduce mas-culine imagery in patriarchal interests.

31. For a fuller discussion of those presentations of fathering and fathers in Vietnam representation, see my "Reproducing Fathers: Gender and the Vietnam War in American Culture" (in *The Cultural Legacy of Vietnam: Uses of the Past in the Present*, ed. Peter Ehrenhaus and Richard Morris [1990]).

32. Robin Wood identifies what he calls the "male duo" film, such as *Butch Cassidy and the Sundance Kid, Easy Rider*, and *Thunderbolt and Lightfoot*, of the 70s, explaining their ap-pearance as "a response to certain social developments centered on the emancipation of women and the resultant undermining of the home," in which the films' "implicit atti-tude is 'You see, we can get along pretty well without you'" (*Hollywood From Vietnam to Reagan* [New York: Columbia University Press, 1986], 24). Such examples show the his-torical shift that has taken place from the 70s to the 80s in relation to alterations in gender positions. Whereas the characters in these films are invariably "pals," with both sharing flaws and heroic qualities, the father/son films of the 80s are much more oriented toward discrepant relations between men; where "buddy" films relate exchanges of power be-tween these men and the society they oppose, inevitably in such a way that the society, however malevolently displayed, retains power through the elimination of the duo, the fa-ther/son films show how that exchange has been internalized so that power is exactly a relation between men and not between marginalized men and society-at-large. Though power relations may be briefly destabilized in 80s films, it is always clear in what terms those relations are to be restabilizied, i.e. only within the terms of masculine relations.

33. In "The New Vietnam Films: Is the Movie Over" (*Journal of Popular Film and Tele-vision* 13.4 [1986]:186–95), I describe how the U.S. government is depicted in recent Viet-nam representation as "feminine," not only being represented by women, but being as well weak, interested in negotiation rather than action, indecisive, and passive. In similar ways, the bureaucratic is opposed to the paternal as an almost maternal organization: Rambo must cut himself free from the technological equipment that threatens to kill him as he dangles from the plane that is to drop him in Vietnam in *Rambo*, a clear metaphor of severing an umbilical cord that attempts to kill its foetus. That Rambo cuts his own "cord" is signifi-cant of the portrayed self-sufficiency of the masculine subject in this film.

CREATION BY THE FATHER'S FIAT

paternal narrative, sexual anxiety, and the deauthorizing designs of absalom, absalom!

(1989)

> Death of the Father would deprive literature of many of its pleasures.
> If there is no longer a Father, why tell stories? Doesn't every narra-
> tive lead back to Oedipus?
>
> Roland Barthes, *The Pleasure of the Text*

> You do not do, you do not do
> Any more, black shoe
> . . .
> Daddy, Daddy, you bastard, I'm through
>
> SYLVIA PLATH, "DADDY"

> There was an old woman who lived in a shoe
> She had so many children she didn't know what to do
>
> MOTHER GOOSE RHYME

Is the Oedipus story, the doomed plot of fathers and their progeny, really paradigmatic of all narrative? Is every story, as Roland Barthes suggests, a "staging of
the (absent, hidden, hypostatized) father" calculated to whet our appetite "to
know, to learn the origin and end," after the manner of Oedipus? Much recent
and influential theorizing about narrative has assumed as much, from Peter
Brooks's psychoanalytically based analysis of narrative authority in terms of failed
fathers to Teresa de Lauretis's feminist argument that all stories construct their
acting subjects as masculine—that is, as mirrors of Oedipus questing for answers
to riddles through a text-space inexorably gendered feminine.[1] It seems to me
that we should not only begin questioning the assumed universality of the oedipal scenario as the basis of all narrative, but also pause to ask whether any "origin," be it Oedipus or other, is really descriptive of the possible desires that
fictions may engender. Might not it be, as Susan Stanford Friedman has recently
suggested, that "the concept of all narrative as necessarily Oedipal is a plot *against*
narrative," perhaps a plot of the father himself? Some feminist critics have indeed begun to propose alternatives to the father's plot by turning to lyric modes
of structuration, Chodorovian theories of preoedipal bonding between mother and
daughter, and female morphological models to describe a female-based textual
erotics distinguishing women writers from Madame de Lafayette and George

Eliot to Kate Chopin and Virginia Woolf.[2] But what would happen, I keep wondering, were we to scrutinize father-centered fictions in the same way, scratching the surface of Oedipus to see what lies beneath? Might there be ways in which even paternal fictions deauthorize their proclaimed originary power? And how absolute is the assertion (pace de Lauretis) that the female position in such plots can never serve as their motive desire or shaping force but only as a marker of their limits?

These are questions I should like to begin exploring by turning to William Faulkner's *Absalom, Absalom!* (1936), a modernist classic in which the power of the father—as lawgiver, as namer, as literal and figurative "author" of being—is immediate and near to overwhelming. Set in the strife-torn American South in the decades surrounding the Civil War, the legend of Thomas Sutpen emerging from the text's multiple narrative voices would seem, at first glance, to raise to the status of heroic myth the will-to-power of a father whose driving obsession is that of generation, of *producing* generations, as an exercise of his patriarchal privilege as name-bearer and at the expense—or neglect—of the women who actually bear his namesakes. Sutpen's determined effort to produce a male dynasty that will immortalize his name and confirm his status, however, hides a much more pressing psychological imperative, one related to his society's construction of manhood: for Sutpen uses his children as a means of imposing his ego on the external world, re-creating its otherness in his own image. He thus unconsciously practices what Luce Irigaray has identified as a specular "logic of the same,"[3] striving to confirm his autonomy, power, and superiority as a man by creating sons who will mirror his desires back to him.

By envisioning himself as the autonomous creator of his own dynasty, moreover, Sutpen effectually treats his family as a text, subject to his authorial whims and control. What interests me is the fact that this family text, this paternal design, proves inherently self-subverting; it not only unravels itself, but it does so in ways that exceed the generational rebelliousness (especially of sons against fathers) that critics like Peter Brooks have taught us to expect in examples of "oedipally plotted" narrative. In fact, the frayed designs of the father in *Absalom, Absalom!* should begin to make us suspicious of the way in which our cultural institutions have forced a duplicitous, indeed disastrous, link between the materials of male procreativity and our metaphors of narrativity. For the story that Faulkner finally tells, once we read through and into the various lacunae punctuating this multilayered text, ends up being less a demonstration of the ubiquity of the father than of the threats to paternal ubiquity that make the father's story an impossibility from its very inception. Indeed, Sutpen's self-proclaimed authority reveals itself to be less an abstract universal and more a highly ambiguous construction, one founded on a profound anxiety about the meaning of masculinity itself—an anxiety suffusing his all-too-tangible identity as a man, as a sexual being, and as a father for whom the status of paternity must always be ambivalent rather than assured.

And this is an anxious narrative, indeed, if the sheer frustration that it provokes in many of its readers is any reliable indication. However much one may praise Faulkner's achievement, one can hardly deny the extreme perversity, the downright irritability at times, of his narrative method: readers inevitably find themselves trapped in a labyrinth of repeating stories and proliferating interpretations that remain frustratingly incomplete, unresolvable, and partial. Admittedly, all stories by definition provoke some degree of anxiety, temporarily frustrating us with detours and digressions in order to heighten our anticipation of their resolutions. *Absalom, Absalom!,* however, plays out this tendency to an extreme that points us back to the anxieties and frustrations embedded in its specific representation of paternal authority. And the primary source of Sutpen's anxiety involves precisely the repressed elements of his plot, all those visible signifiers of otherness, of nonmaleness—female sexuality, racial difference, latent homosexuality, daughter-texts—that his dynastic scheme has been constructed to subdue and contain. But despite such efforts at containment, these subversive elements *do* escape the father's plotting, threatening to wreck its transcendent designs and thus call the invisible, hypostatized authority upon which Sutpen's male identity rests into question.

For the critic in search of Oedipus, for the reader interested in issues of race and gender, the result is profoundly important. For these "escaped" strands of narrative reconstitute, reorder, our perception of where we have been and what we (might mistakenly think we) have been reading: that which confronts us is no longer "simply" an oedipal retelling, for Sutpen's paternal design has been deauthorized, shown to be illusive even in its origin. Out of such rereadings, of not only this but other novels, a much more real and vulnerable father, stripped of his guises and abstractions, his powerful absences and preordained plots, may hopefully emerge—one whose material presence immediately problematizes the cultural ethos that constructs fatherhood as a doomed heroic narrative, and one whose story, always "other" than his self-representation would have us believe, calls forth our sympathy rather than fear.

Those readers of *Absalom, Absalom!* left frustrated by Faulkner's elliptical narration may take some comfort in the fact that the novel's narrators find themselves left in equal states of frustration, seemingly fated to repeat a story that refuses to die. This makes for a particularly masochistic erotics of the text, as it were, both in regard to the tellers and to the sexually anxious narrative that is the subject of their protracted telling. But what, exactly, are the investments of Rosa Coldfield, Mr. Compson, and his son Quentin (abetted by his Harvard roommate Shreve) in retelling this already-told legend, and what can their proliferating interpretations of Sutpen's life tell us, in turn, about the self-subverting "plot of the father" being enacted in this novel? Quite a bit, I should like to suggest, once we look at their urge to narrate in light of Freud's conjectures about the human compulsion to repeat repressed or traumatic psychic materials as a means of exorcizing the tyranny of the past. For at least to Rosa, Mr. Compson, and Quentin, the myth of Sutpen is not simply a fascinating source of endless speculation but a specific threat to be expunged. Thus each of their retellings becomes, in a real sense, a fight to master a story that threatens to master them. For Sutpen represents to these narrators, as he does within his own plot, an authority figure whose interdiction, like that of all fathers, appears irrevocable. In the psychodrama of narrative transference that ensues, therefore, Rosa, Mr. Compson, and Quentin weave their tales to ward off what they intuitively sense to be the castrating power of this demonic, now absent, but still ever-powerful father.

On the other hand, their narrations simultaneously reveal an investment in *not* mastering this story, in letting it continue without end. At least subconsciously, that is, all three tellers repeat (and listen to and then repeat again) Sutpen's story as a way of putting their own lives on hold, of postponing a confrontation with present-day reality. Examining their compulsion to repeat in this light, we can see how intimately their roles as narrators are linked to the psychosexual anxieties that motor Faulkner's entire enterprise. The example of Rosa is the most complex, a point to which I will return, but in terms of Faulkner's initial representation of her "lonely thwarted old female flesh embattled for forty-three years in the old insult"[4] of virginity, her narration is presented as the garrulous outpouring of a spinster's "impotent yet indomitable frustration" (7); talk has become the only way of wreaking vengeance upon the "long-dead object" (7) of her hatred, Sutpen, for having jilted her those forty-three years before, as well as an erotic substitute for the life that she claims has ended in that past moment. The world-weary Mr. Compson, on the other hand, uses the saga of Sutpen's dynasty as a pretext for indulging in decadent fantasies of desire that allow him to avoid the reality of his own dynasty's decline and his impotence to do anything about it. For Quentin, too, the sexual and textual are inextricably, and masochistically, linked: relaying the incestuous triangle formed by Sutpen's progeny to Shreve allows him to participate verbally in the very desires that he also harbors yet fears to initiate.[5] Internalizing his inaction as a failure of manhood, Quentin, like Rosa and his father, turns to the erotics of narrating as a substitute for the erotic fulfillment that is missing in life.

What are the anxieties hidden within Sutpen's story, then, that so powerfully summon forth the thwarted, indeed doomed, narrative desires of these storytellers? To begin to answer this question, we need to look more closely at Sutpen's desire to be the omniscient, omnipotent author of his personal history, for he often treats his life as if it were a plot-in-progress, a narrative design that already exists as a Platonic whole in his mind: "You see, I had a design in my mind" (263), he will repeatedly explain to General Compson, his one confidant and Quentin's grandfather, in the two episodes in chapter 7 when we get the story in his own words. And as far as this self-nominated maker of "designs" is concerned, the plan or blueprint he has conceived merely awaits physical realization or consummation. The operative words here, however, are "physical" and "consummation," since Sutpen's plan depends on issuing forth a dynasty of sons who will immortalize his name. He wishes to become the author, that is, of nothing less than a paternal plot, an explanatory myth of origins and endings that will at once give his identity retrospective significance and proleptic authority. "You see, I had a design," his confession to General Compson continues, "To accomplish it I should require money, a house, a family, slaves . . . [and] incidentally, of course, a wife" (263).

Likewise, the Sutpen legend inherited and embellished by Jefferson's community of tellers powerfully attests to the stakes involved in Sutpen's self-assumed status as sole author of his familial design. In Rosa's estimation, for example, Sutpen is a consummate if demonic master artist who orchestrates his godlike arrival into Jefferson as high mythic drama, willing the plantation Sutpen's Hundred out of swampland, marrying into respectability, begetting his family. The biblical allusions that Rosa uses to describe Sutpen's enterprise only accentuate his self-appointed role as archetypal, disembodied Father-Creator; not only does he summon a world into being "out of the soundless Nothing . . . like the olden-time *Be Light*" (9), but he remains, like the unspeakable divinity of Jehovah, "not articulated in this world" (171), and, like the original patriarch Adam, the sole "namer" of his progeny and possessions: "He named them all himself: all his own get and all the get of his wild niggers . . . naming with his own mouth his own ironic fecundity" (61–62).

Underlying the authorial control that Sutpen exerts over his design is the wish "to make his position impregnable" (15), and, ironically, the only means to the abstract ideal of impregnability is by the very *real* sexual act of impregnation. Hence Sutpen's creative enterprise—even before it involves marriage to Ellen Coldfield—is repeatedly embued in phallic imagery. Hyperbolically described as a "thunderclap" orgiastically "abrupt[ing]" upon the scene (8), he claims his "virgin" land (40) in an act of archetypally masculine aggression, "overrun[ning] the astonished earth" in a "conquest" that is as violent as it is an act of possession (8). Analogously, he penetrates the Coldfield sanctum to claim his virgin bride "with the abruptness of a tornado" that wreaks "irrevocable and incalculable damage" (23) and is gone. Always "project[ing] himself ahead," as if "in some fierce dynamic rigidity of impatience" (159) to consummate his design, Sutpen effectually masquerades as the phallus; even the terms of his decline and death remain recalcitrantly phallic. Repudiated by his one legitimate son, Henry, he sets out to father an illegitimate one, his attitude likened to "an old worn-out cannon which realizes that it can deliver just one more fierce shot" (181), and that "next time there might not be enough powder for . . . a full-sized load" (279).

As all this exaggerated phallicism would seem to indicate, the male act of impregnation is fraught with more anxiety and uncertainty than Sutpen would care to acknowledge; until the symbolic father proves he also has a body, that the word can indeed be made flesh, he leaves his dream of an "impregnable" position open to challenge. Thus, when his final plot to sire a male heir by Milly Jones misfires, as it were, it is appropriate that Sutpen meets his death in an act of symbolic castration, felled by the scythe that Milly's incensed grandfather raises against him: one thwarted Bearer of the Phallus topples another in an act of now meaningless conquest.

Plainly, it is neither old-fashioned lust nor dewy-eyed sentimentality that prompts Sutpen's phallic aggressiveness. A much more abstract, narcissistic desire motivates his monomaniacal urge to procreate. For Sutpen primarily, essentially, conceives of his "family plot" as an extension of his own ego, a blueprint for imposing and imprinting his identity on all his surroundings. Paternity, like the godly power of naming, becomes a way of subsuming one's anxieties about authority by rendering one's possessions miniature, hence inferior and less threatening versions of oneself. Given such an overwhelming narcissistic imperative, the authority of fatherhood inevitably becomes sadistic, for Sutpen's entire sense of himself rests on the psychic, when not physical, violation and penetration of the identities of all his dependents—whether his wife, children, slaves, or, on a textual level, the narrators and readers who inherit his story. Sutpen's anxious desire for complete mastery over his story, his paternal text, however, turns on a very ambiguous relation to the Southern caste system he purports to uphold. Only at the novel's midpoint do we learn, via his retrospective explanation to General Compson, that Sutpen's entire design springs from humiliations undergone as an adolescent, turned away from the front door of *his* master's plantation as poor white trash by a "monkey-dressed butler nigger" (231). In effect, the rest of Sutpen's life is "spent"—and here sexual, social, and psychological levels of meaning interpenetrate—in a series of violent entries to make up for this one barred threshold; class, race, and gender come together in a devastating illumination of the anxieties underpinning this father's desire for an identity based on disembodied authority rather than the all-too-embodied inferiority he has felt as a youth. Designed to cover over the vulnerability briefly exposed in this incident, Sutpen's paternal plot thus turns out to be in large part a compensatory narrative, one that tries not merely to explain his origins, but to explain *away* his origins by means of his more successful ends.[6]

All this may have begun to sound like the stuff of a classically oedipal narrative—the father who was once an ashamed son begets sons who in turn rebel against him—until we look more closely at the narratological implications of Sutpen's attempt to give shape to the plot of his own life. For as an artist, Sutpen is so fixated on the final product—establishing a genealogy that will immortalize his single-handed rise to an "impregnable" position of authority—that he forgets the necessary "middle" that constitutes the very substance of narrative plot, the living "middle" that is always, necessarily, transgressive, a deviation from the straight line that in linking the beginning and end would obviate the need for "story." In narrative terms, that is, Sutpen neglects metonymy, the flow of event that is the means to an end, in favor of metaphor, the illumination conferred by the end itself. And this oversight critically dooms Sutpen's esthetic design, precisely because, like all plots of the father, life is not, in the final measure, a written text, however much patriarchy may treat it as such; Sutpen's story will have no final illumination until it is over, leaving him quite literally unable to predict its "meaning."[7]

Hence, by definition lacking the retrospective vision of a completed whole, Sutpen is actually too involved in the making of his history to be either the removed, omniscient author he impersonates or the all-powerful abstraction whose disembodied law he would have his subjects obey without question. Nor is Sutpen's premature determination of his "ends" his only oversight. He also fails to see that the very goal, the fixed metaphor, toward which he drives is itself contrary to the stasis he desires. For the very achievement of a genealogy of Sutpens-in-perpetuity, far from being final, must necessarily remain metonymic, depending on a continuing line of generations that must occur *in*, not out of, time. Sutpen's desire to summon into creative being the "fixed goal in his mind" (53), whose static meaning he has already determined, will always escape his impositions since he, a living man, cannot freeze life into a final shape before it has ended.

Most obvious among the transgressive elements disturbing the synchronic reading of the "end" that Sutpen attempts to impose on the narrative "middle" of his paternal plot are, of course, his children. Male and female, black and white—the straight and pure line of patronymic descent that Sutpen means to create deviates rather wildly from his Platonic intentions. The case of his two sons is particularly telling in this regard. Sutpen's legitimate heir, Henry, quite simply repudiates his birthright, choosing fraternity with his illegitimate half brother, Charles Bon, over fealty to his father. Forcing a break in Sutpen's design by depriving him of his heir, Henry effectually abandons the family text, and he returns only to die and bring the House of Sutpen to an apocalyptic close more final than any of Sutpen's projected ends. However, as the very fact of Henry's return home at the end of his life suggests, his revolt against Sutpen's command has really never ceased, nor have his acts of defiance entirely escaped the Law of the Father. Eventually murdering Charles, the beloved brother for whom he has repudiated his inheritance, Henry in fact executes "the office of the outraged father's pistol-hand" (179), perversely fulfilling Sutpen's desire while thwarting his own. In the vicious circle of patriarchal logic in which Henry finds himself trapped (doomed to rebel against, yet serve, his father), we have the most unadulterated evidence of a strand of oedipal narrative at work in Faulkner's text: according to classic Freudian theory, sons wish to replace the father but do so by acceding to the father's law, learning to wield the same phallic power. Yet the fact is that Henry does not *simply* become Sutpen or, for that matter, the phallus. Self-exiled to an unknown plot, a figurative no-man's-land outside the text where he exists as a non-Sutpen, he comes to emblematize an element of difference, or indifference, that Sutpen's design cannot control; refusing the rules of male procreativity (as far as we know he sires no heirs) *and* creativity (by becoming a creative absence in Faulkner's text), Henry in his small way reveals the "outraged father's pistol-hand" to be no more than an "outrage": a victimizing authority whose only law is violent coercion of the self.

If the son Henry repudiates his father, in a chiasmic reversal the father Sutpen has already repudiated his firstborn son, Charles Bon, for "not [being] adjunctive or incremental to the design which I had in mind" (240)—the consequence of Sutpen's belated discovery that Eulalia Bon, his first wife, is partially black. As the taint that Sutpen's plot attempts to void, Bon thus represents a kind of return of the "textually repressed" when he appears at the door of Sutpen's Hundred as Henry's best friend. And the repressed in Sutpen's design, the already written that cannot be erased, is not only this son's blackness. It is also Sutpen's own unconscious, governed, as we have already seen, by a pathology of lack and need that reaches back to that fateful day when he was denied access to his master's plantation and made so painfully aware of his own economic and social inferiority in a white man's world of power. Thus, it is ironically appropriate that the specter of the "boy symbol . . . on the outside of a white door" (261) makes its return in the very body of Sutpen's illegitimate son, knocking (as Sutpen once did) at a plantation door that is now Sutpen's; and this event, significantly, introduces an element of repetition into the father's fiction of progress that subverts its desired linearity. The successful transcendence of origins for which Sutpen has plotted so long and hard cannot, after all, cover over its narrative beginnings in a boy's specific, anxiety-stricken crisis of identity.

The self-defeating nature of authority derived from such ambiguous origins is exposed by Sutpen's reaction to this unwonted reminder of the past; for in refusing to acknowledge his kinship to Bon, the mirror-image of his youth, Sutpen denies, in a literal as well as figurative sense, his own flesh and blood. As such, Bon's return begins to disrupt Sutpen's plot. But at the same time, Sutpen's threatening presence deprives Bon's life of any narrative shape other than that of inactive passivity. For Bon desperately *needs* that very acknowledgment of origins that his father's plot attempts to suppress; as long as Sutpen withholds his recognition, Bon lacks the retrospective ordering perspective that would allow the rest of his life to assume an intentional or meaningful pattern.

Sutpen thus exerts a stultifying, castrating effect on both his sons. He has "unmanned" Henry by condemning him to serve as his unwilling "pistol-hand," and he condemns Charles Bon to a life of hopelessly masochistic waiting, textually evoked in the "feminine" imagery used to describe him.[8] But in so victimizing his sons, Sutpen also dooms his own plot, which, as we have seen, depends on male heirs, and thereby provides a clue to the self-subverting nature of his sexual and paternal authority. For, ultimately, the stymied desires of Henry for autonomy and of Bon for recognition stand less as proof of Sutpen's incontrovertible power than as signifiers of the profound anxieties underlying his phallic identity—anxieties given narrative figuration as plot excrescences, "castrations" or "feminizations" of the parent plot, formed by sons whose sin is only imperfectly to reflect the father's image.

While the conflict of sons and fathers in our culture will always be oedipal to some degree, I have begun to suggest how the "deviant" narrative energies generated by this conflict—which I have just described as plot excrescences—begin to deauthorize the story of the father in its very origin. If we turn from a consideration of Henry and Bon as sons to their role as siblings, linked with their sister, Judith, in an incestuous triangle, the text reveals an even more powerfully transgressive permutation of antipaternal narrative. The intense affinity of Henry and Judith early establishes incest as a brother-sister attraction. But it is the introduction of Bon (not yet known to be their half brother) into the Henry-Judith dyad that makes possible "the pure and perfect incest" (96) that Mr. Compson attributes to Henry in one of the novel's most famous passages. For by plotting the engagement of his best friend Bon to his sister, Henry makes possible a doubly satisfying displacement of his own incestuous desire. Not only does it allow him to possess Judith "in the person of the brother-in-law, the man whom he would be if he could become, metamorphose into, the lover, the husband"; but it also allows him the homoerotic satisfaction, via Judith's mediation, of uniting with the object of his worshipful infatuation, Bon, "by whom he would be despoiled, choose for despoiler, if he could become, metamorphose into the sister, the mistress, the bride" (96). The incestuous parameters of this configuration are not confined to Henry and Judith, once we become aware that Bon is also Sutpen's son: the subsequent engagement of Bon and Judith, as well as the attraction between the half brothers, also become literally incestuous possibilities.

Which is to say that the incestuous, as nearly all of Faulkner's critics have acknowledged, forms an extremely powerful undertow in Sutpen's paternal plot. To what degree the structure of incest supports an oedipal reading of this novel is another question. John Irwin has most prominently linked the two patterns as refractions of the same wish, a move facilitated by his Freudian reading of the oedipal triangle of mother-son-father, wherein the brother's desire for the sister becomes a displacement of an original desire for the mother.[9] But in the world of *Absalom, Absalom!*, Ellen Coldfield, Henry's mother, is strikingly absent as an object of desire, for Henry or anyone else, and Charles's mother, Eulalia Bon, only has textual life insofar as she is a projection of the narrators' fantasies of her. What Henry and Bon seek in incestuous union with Judith has very little to do with a return to the maternal womb and much more to do with their ambivalent relations to their father and to each other.

In fact, all three of the incestuous variations formed by these siblings covertly work to block Sutpen's design. For example, if we turn to the violation of the incest taboo incipient in Henry and Judith's closeness, and look at it from an anthropological rather than psychoanalytic perspective, it becomes clear that their endogamic exclusivity undermines Sutpen's need for those external family alliances (such as he has sought by marrying into Coldfield respectability) that will strengthen his dynasty and better its chances for survival. The incestuous union of Bon and Judith, on the other hand, threatens to adulterate the racial purity of the central family line with the impermissable taint of negro blood.[10] And, third, the pairing of Henry and Bon would strike the biggest blow of all to Sutpen's design by its nonreproductive nature; their union threatens no line of descent at all. As a thematic element of this text, then, sibling incest stands in direct opposition to the plot of the father. It is also worth observing that one of the threats of incest, structurally speaking, is that it augurs a continual return of the same, hence a break in temporal and genealogical progression. Thus, what I earlier called the narrative perversity of this novel—its nonchronological ordering, its doublings of character and narrative levels, its repetitions and continual loopings back in time—can be seen as a structural analogue of this thematically represented incestuous impulse, working equally to frustrate the straightforward progress upon which Sutpen's dynastic narrative model depends.[11] What, then, does it finally mean that Sutpen's design depends on progeny whose desires subvert that plan? Most simply put, all of these children become tangible emblems of Sutpen's worst fears about otherness: whether in the form of femaleness (as in Judith's case), blackness (as in Bon's), or latent homosexuality (as in Henry's), these siblings in their myriad incestuous alignments return to the surface of Sutpen's text precisely those repressions upon which its construction of masculine power, racial superiority, and (hetero)sexual procreativity have depended.

The anxieties that gender, race, and sexuality create for Sutpen's phallic identity become all the clearer once we recognize the extent to which the world of this novel is structured by a complex network of male bonding. Designed to confirm men's power through their exchange of women, the male homosocial bond, as Eve Kosofsky Sedgwick has shown, simultaneously generates men's deepest anxieties about their manhood precisely at that point where culturally fostered camaraderie between men becomes barely distinguishable from sexual intimacy.[12] Male identity within patriarchy—no less Southern patriarchy—depends, that is, on a very fine, often ambiguous line separating the acceptable from the unacceptable, the "real" man from the sexual suspect. And this is the very boundary on which Henry and Bon's relationship dangerously hovers. There are the obvious explanations, of course, including blood-affinity, for their bonding—Henry sees in Bon the sophisticated and worldly mentor figure he would like to become, Bon sees in Henry confirmation of his paternal origins (*"He has my brow my skull my jaw my hands"* [314]). But "love" is the quality that Faulkner's narrators continually invoke to describe the youths' mutual attraction; and, as we have seen above, one of the functions, perhaps *the* primary function, of the sibling incest triangle is to bond Henry and Bon over the body of Judith, in a homoerotic union whose structure is also ineluctably homosocial: "it was not Judith who was the object of Bon's love or of Henry's solicitude. She was just the blank shape, the empty vessel in which each of them strove to preserve . . . what each conceived the other to believe him to be—the man and the youth, seducer and seduced, who had known one another, seduced and been seduced, victimized in turn each by the other" (120). Given the novel's title, critics have understandably made much of Faulkner's use of the Absalom-Tamar-Ammon biblical analogue to elucidate its incest triangles.[13] But if we dig behind this analogue to the preceding generation of Absalom's father, David, we will uncover another, almost equally applicable, archetype—"the love that passeth understanding" shared by the youthful David and Jonathan. And this archetype, presenting homoerotic male comradeship in its most idealized and disembodied form, can be seen at work in the way the various narrators (especially the men) re-create Henry's love for Bon, poeticizing the tragic division that comes between the two youths while relegating Judith, the "blank" page on which the story of their division is written, to the background.

The tragedy, however, is not simply that Henry and Bon fall out in the end. It is that from the very beginning of their friendship they are only able to conceive of their mutual desires within the homosocial and consequently heterosexual terms provided by the father's law, in which "the similarity of gender" looms as an "insurmountable barrier" (95), a final and hopeless intervention, to realized love. Given this cultural repression of the homoerotic, along with the paternal anxieties about masculinity that it inevitably reproduces, it is ironically fitting that the act of murder serves as their final, and only, consummation. The gunshot that Henry fires at Bon, "heard only by its echo" (153), becomes an ironically apt metaphor for a sexual climax that never occurs, itself only "heard" in the narrative via its reverberating absence. With this image, we return, circuitously, to the militaristic metaphor—the nearly exhausted "cannon" with its one good last load—used to describe Sutpen's procreative imperialism. But whereas the father's rusty weapon invoked the act of sexual intercourse as unfeeling violence, the firing of Henry the son's pistol connotes an act of anguished violence deprived even of the sex: all that is left is an empty, unanswered erotic charge.

The homosocial structure that turns love into murder also suffuses and disturbs the historical, psychological, and narrative levels of Sutpen's dynastic plot. Historically speaking, if Henry and Bon can be seen as fraternal soul mates at war, so too the Civil War from its inception was viewed in familial terms as the struggle of brother against brother—a struggle, moreover, fought over the figuratively female body of the mother country herself. Second, in psychological terms, *Absalom, Absalom!* includes a terrifyingly visceral primal scene in which the act of parental copulation to which the young child is exposed is replaced, significantly, by an emblem of the homosocial, exclusively male, network of power that governs Sutpen's world. For I would argue that the set piece serving as the climax of the very first chapter, the wrestling spectacle that Ellen discovers her children furtively watching from the barn loft, forms this text's most authentic equivalent of Freud's famed "two-backed" beast—only this vision is not of mother and father, but of two naked men locked in an embrace, a public display, that is actually a deadly struggle for "supremacy, domination" (29). Nor are the wrestlers "the two black beasts she had expected to see but instead a white one and a black one . . . her husband and the father of her children standing there naked and panting and bloody and the negro just fallen evidently" (29).

Here, finally, is the father's uncovered, carnal body. And here, too, is the David and Jonathan archetype stripped of its ideality, caught in a violent embrace that not only embodies the underlying structure and fate of men's relationships in patriarchal society but that also encodes, quite visibly, the ugly truth of hierarchical relations in the American South: white triumphing over black. That the father *forces* Henry to watch this overtly public display of male competition, that the mother's entrance into the tableau virtually makes no difference ("I don't expect you to understand it . . . because you are a woman" [30]), powerfully suggests that exposure to the homosocial paradigm—not simply heterosexual coitus—has become *the* affective experience in the formation of male identity in the world of this novel, as well as in the creation of its oedipal plots.[14]

The same might also be said of the oedipal myth itself, once we look at the story of the father that precedes, in narrative time, the drama of discovery that Sophocles records. For the fact is that the curse leading King Laius to abandon his son Oedipus in the first place originates in a crime that is at once homosocial *and* homosexual in nature: it is none other than Laius's violation of his brotherly bond with a neighboring king (Pelops) by raping that ruler's son (Chrysipus) that precipitates the curse of the House of Laius, a curse carried out by *his* son's enactment of the "oedipal drama" of incest and patricide. Faulkner's text may thus be said unconsciously to supplement Freud's paradigmatic scenario of male identity development by restoring to the oedipal myth its hidden pre-text, its suppressed origin, in homosocial violence.

The complicities of male bonding infiltrate *Absalom, Absalom!* on yet a third level, that of its narrative retelling. For Quentin and his roommate Shreve, the novel's final narrators, participate in a creative intercourse of words that intimately bonds them, via Sutpen's story, in a "marriage of speaking and hearing . . . in order to overpass to love" (316): an act of imaginative union that nonetheless, as we shall see, also becomes a shouting match, a battle for mastery not only over this story but over each other, a frustrated dialogue that ends in an ejaculation of love-hate ("*I dont hate it*, he thought, panting in the cold air . . . *I dont. I dont!*" [378]) as abrupt as the gunshot at the gate of Sutpen's Hundred beyond which Henry and Bon, unable to "pass" (133), stop forever.

As all these instances of male bonding begin to indicate, the place allotted to women in Sutpen's construction of his family text, even more than that of wayward or unclaimed sons, is extremely peripheral.[15] Yet the very inconsequentiality of the roles accorded women in Sutpen's plan, like its other suppressed elements, becomes a potent sign and symptom of those very anxieties that fuel the plot of the father in the first place. For beneath the flowery encomiums adorning ante- and postbellum rhetoric about women, its representations of the Southern belle reveal a profound misogyny and fear of female sexuality. A case in point is the fundamentally contradictory attitude underlying the eroticized images that Mr. Compson, for one, uses to describe women—on the one hand, as empty "vessels" (108, 119–20) waiting to be filled, on the other, as parasitic "vampires" (67, 86) actively draining life from others: he who bases his power on the phallus as an instrument of penetration stands, in his worst nightmares, to be penetrated, sucked dry. And if men like Mr. Compson or Sutpen—and perhaps Faulkner himself—see women as endangering their own potency, it is precisely because female sexuality harbors the one element—the bodily ability to reproduce—that men's ostensible power and designs can never completely control. Women's sexuality has an authority, a creative fiat, to which all the father's fictions of authority in the world can only presume, can only possess by way of metaphor.

The most striking textual manifestation of the male anxieties engendered by female sexuality in *Absalom, Absalom!*, I would suggest, involves the absence of mothers throughout the *entire* novel. Both in Sutpen's plot and in the text as a whole, motherhood is by and large an invisible state. Those mothers represented in any depth are literally disembodied male projections (such as Mr. Compson's evocation of Ellen or Shreve's fiction of Eulalia Bon). Other mothers—Sutpen's, Clytie's, Ellen and Rosa's, Milly Jones's, Jim Bond's, even Quentin's—are simply stricken from the text, often without explanation. Two such revealing lacunae involve Mrs. Coldfield, who literally drops out of the picture during her daughter Ellen's wedding in chapter 2, and the "coal black and ape-like woman" (205) that Bon's son Charles Etienne brings home as his wife, who disappears from the postwar narration without a trace once she has served her primary function in the plot by giving birth to a son, Jim Bond.[16]

As the example of Charles Etienne's wife also indicates, the lack of mothers in this text is complemented by the quite visible, disruptive rise of black sons. For the one realized dynasty in the novel, the legacy of all Sutpen's procreative efforts, is the genealogy that stretches from his repudiated son, Charles Bon, to his great-grandson Jim Bond, a genealogy that is at once male (which, after all, is Sutpen's dream) *and* characterized by an exponential rise in degree of blackness (the nightmarish opposite of his dream). Once again, an aspect of the otherness—here, the taint of racial otherness—that Sutpen has attempted to exclude from his design redounds upon his authorial control, and, once again, the outcome points to the unresolved anxieties of identity that work to unravel this father's plot from its inception. For Sutpen's greatest fear has always been an adulteration of the family plot by those extraneous narratives—the story of mothers and daughters, half-caste sons, "unmanly" men—that stand outside, hence threaten the hegemony, of his desired identity as all-powerful, white patriarch. It is fitting, then, that a woman—Eulalia Bon—is made the culprit responsible for introducing the strain of negro blood that upsets Sutpen's projected ends by "defiling" the family line; in the novel's complex symbology, femaleness, and particularly female sexuality, is often equated with an equatorial darkness personified by the black races.[17]

Indeed, the specific challenge that the pairing of fecundity and racial otherness poses to white male identity, thus to the sanctity of Sutpen's plan, forms the novel's closing statement, as Shreve taunts Quentin about the horror that the very idea of Sutpen's black heirs hold for the Southern imagination: "I think that in time the Jim Bonds are going to conquer the western hemisphere. Of course it won't be quite in our time and of course as they spread toward the poles they will *bleach out again* like the rabbits and the birds do, so they won't show up so sharp against the snow. But it will still be Bond; and so in a few thousand years, I who regard you will also have sprung from the loins of African kings" (378, emphasis added). Shreve's vision is not simply that the black race (like metonymy run wild) will conquer the world, but more precisely that whiteness will cease to be a marker of difference, the absolute metaphor of achieved ends, once the various races eventually mix *under the guise of* whiteness. For the Southern aristocracy, then, the great fear is the threat of nondifferentiation, of the collapse of the boundaries and polarities that allow for the repression and subjugation of otherness constitutive of (in this case) white male identity. And these boundaries, as the psychoanalyst Jessica Benjamin has shown, have everything to do with the male child's desire to repudiate the powerful maternal connection in order to establish his separate sense of self.[18]

If Sutpen's paternal masterplot cannot successfully do away with his black descendants, neither can it totally neutralize the covertly transgressive presence of his two daughters, Judith and Clytie. Unlike their white and black counterparts in Henry and Bon, these half sisters seem doomed to inhabit the background of Sutpen's family text, ever-present but useless in furthering his patronymic designs (both remain childless) except as the dutiful keepers of his house. Their joint impassivity, however, should not be construed as unconditional passivity: they may keep his house, but they do not necessarily keep to his plot.[19] Judith, for instance, at first glance appears totally identified with her father, yet of all the Sutpens it is she who most actively concerns herself with preserving a written record that will allow for the handing down, even to strangers, of the suppressed stories underlying the official history of the family's rise and fall. Thus, Judith passes Bon's crucial letter to her on to General Compson's wife, in an act of female-to-female transmission that makes possible Mr. Compson's retelling of these events to his son Quentin forty-five years later: the transmission of father-to-son, the ostensible basis for this (and all oedipal) narrative, depends on at least one prior transaction that is an exchange between women rather than men.[20]

Like Judith, Clytie also proves a covertly destabilizing force in Sutpen's design. "Free yet incapable of freedom," she is the embodiment of the "perverse and inscrutable paradox" (156) of slavery: at once too proud to think of herself as chattel yet never questioning the fact that Sutpen is her absolute master. Yet this unacknowledged daughter is also "the presiding augur of [Sutpen's] disaster" (256), who with the murderous fury of her classical namesake, Clytemnestra, brings destruction onto the House of her father, setting fire to Sutpen's Hundred rather than cede to Rosa her guardianship of the dying Henry. As in Judith's passing on to Mrs. Compson of Bon's letter, it is once again an act of transmission between women—what one might call Rosa's telepathic decoding of the secret Clytie has kept hidden at Sutpen's Hundred—that has enabled this story from its beginnings. Authorial fiat, it would seem, does not lie entirely in the hands of the father.

Which returns us, at long last, to Rosa Coldfield—a surrogate "daughter" of Sutpen's text—and to a reconsideration of the role she plays in the making and unmaking of the father's story. I have already mentioned how Rosa's "outraged recapitulation" (8) of the Sutpen legend may initially strike one as a spinster's "impotent" act of revenge, the perverted child, as it were, of her years of sexual frustration and emotional sterility. But there is another, much more actively subversive side to Rosa's role as narrator that I should like us to consider—one that is productive, indeed potent, rather than powerless or self-defeating. Established at the very beginning of chapter 1 as Yoknapatawpha County's "poetess laureate," Rosa is the only published writer, however open to question the quality of her writings may be, among the novel's narrators, "issuing . . . poems, ode, eulogy, and epitaph, out of some . . . implacable unreserve of undefeat" (11). One might also take note of the fact that she begins writing only when her neurotic, Yankee-sympathizing father nails himself in the attic during the war—becoming, as indeed, Henry Sutpen hidden in *his* attic will also become a half century later, a *male* version of the madwoman in the attic, Gilbert and Gubar's figure for the woman writer's angry double. Even more importantly, Rosa's authorial status is reflected in the fact that she is the narrator who initiates this text by summoning Quentin to her house, first to listen to her tale and then to serve as her witness on the revelatory night-trip to Sutpen's Hundred where Henry is discovered: without Rosa, there would be, to put it simply, no novel for us to read.[21]

Nor is Rosa's garrulous narrative style, elongated by seemingly endless and frustrating repetitions, only an emblem of the speaker's sexual unfulfillment or her passive entrapment in a long-dead past, however much both may be contributing factors. Rather, I would suggest, the technique of deferral and postponement that marks her retelling may be a sign of her subversive if partial power *over* Sutpen's text and its desired climaxes. At the beginning of this discussion, I suggested that Sutpen's story itself refuses to die, exacting its revenge on its auditors by dooming them to perpetual frustration. But in Rosa's case, we can also reverse this proposition to state that it is *she* who refuses to let Sutpen's story die. In effect, by using her role as narrator to keep the unruly plot-in-process, the transgressive narrative "middle" that Sutpen would rather ignore, alive and anxiously disruptive, Rosa rebels against what I have already characterized as his compulsive desire for metaphor, for the completed goal or design. If oedipal narrative is an explanatory myth of beginnings and endings, the search for the "proper" narrative death that will bestow retrospective meaning on the irregularities and deviations of the individual's life-career, then Rosa's refusal to lay the myth of Sutpen to rest de-oedipalizes, in a real sense, its power; rewriting Sutpen's deeds as undying and communal legend, she "unstrings"—to use Susan Winnett's memorable metaphor—the oedipal logic of a "masterplot that wants to have told us in advance where it is that we should take our pleasures and what must inevitably come of them."[22] Rosa emphatically takes her pleasures elsewhere, as we can see in the metonymic play of the "middle" to which her "outraged recapitulation" of "undefeat" gives vent, and in so doing her narrative retelling clears space for our illuminated rereading of the self-subverting forces, the plot excrescences, generated by Sutpen's textual enterprise. In the war between Sutpen's formidable will-to-power and her own authorial stratagems, Rosa finally succeeds in turning the castrating power of the father against itself: the psychic wounds he has inflicted on his progeny redound posthumously to rend his own suddenly vulnerable narrative.[23]

The primary recipient of the narrative transmission that Rosa initiates and at least symbolically closes, of course, is Quentin Compson. "Maybe someday you will remember this," she tells him, "and write about it" (10). The fictional improvisation that he and his college roommate Shreve weave from the "rag-tag and bob-ends of old tales and talking" (303), forming the reader's most immediate link to the recorded events of the novel, becomes another retelling that, like

Rosa's, will not let Sutpen's story die easily. Yet if Rosa's habits of deferral amount to a covert counterplot against the father, the boys' obsessive reliving of his history indicates that what cannot "die" for each of them primarily involves the unresolved anxieties of masculine identity that have driven Sutpen to his doom. For Quentin especially, the anxieties of sexual and creative generation that have beset Sutpen's design now become his own personal nightmare: *"Yes, we are both Father. Or maybe Father and I are both Shreve, maybe it took Father and me both to make Shreve or Shreve and me both to make Father or maybe Thomas Sutpen to make all of us"* (261–62). In other words, because both Quentin and Shreve *are* sons, the Harvard-bred, male inheritors of the dominant culture (and not dispossessed daughters like Rosa, Judith, or Clytie), they cannot escape the crises of authority and conflicts of identity embedded in the story that they retell.

One can see this truth, first of all, in the way their creative dialogue begins to repeat the pattern—and contradictions—of homosocial bonding characterizing the world of Sutpen and his progeny, as their "marriage" of words is transformed into a struggle for mastery ("Wait, I tell you! . . . I am telling [it]" [277]); their very intimacy has become the grounds for an increasingly anxious contest of male one-upmanship. Second, at least for Quentin, storytelling only enmeshes him more disastrously in the self-subverting struggle of fathers and sons, as he attempts to make himself the primary narrator of the events that his father has told him, indeed to become his father's superior in knowledge by telling the story better than his progenitor.[24] Finally, even the lacunae in Quentin and Shreve's fiction refer us back to tremendous anxieties of identity motivating Sutpen's desire to establish a dynasty in his own image. For the questions that remain unanswered in *Absalom, Absalom!*—Is miscegenation really the key to Sutpen's repudiation of Bon? How does Bon learn (if ever) that he is black? What does the dying Henry reveal to Quentin?—all turn on questions of white male identity, of which the only explanations are those *created* by the boys. The fundamental uncertainty of the status of such "fictionalized" explanations—upon which not only the novel's "mystery" but Sutpen's otherwise inexplicable repudiation of his sons rests—thus self-reflexively points to the uncertainties lying at the core of phallic identity itself.

An emblem for the anxiety produced by such uncertainties exists in the climactic moments of the novel. When Quentin finally confronts the dying Henry at Sutpen's Hundred, a much-discussed gap in narration occurs, as the two engage in a surreal, italicized dialogue consisting of a short series of repetitive phrases that eventually move full circle without confirming anything; this elliptical conversation, as Peter Brooks has noted, "seems to constitute a kind of hollow structure, a concave mirror or black hole at the center of the narrative."[25] And this fear of empty centers, of dark "holes" and gaps into which all meanings tumble and out of which nothing certain emerges—imagery powerfully evocative of female sexuality in our culture—is very much, and on very many levels, what the anxieties haunting *Absalom, Absalom!* (and often its critics) are all about.

For years critics have pointed out how Faulkner's foregrounding of issues of intelligibility within this text have made it a quintessential example of novelistic self-reflexivity; the fundamental uninterpretability of this anxiety-producing text, I would add, has everything to do with its interrogation of the grounds on which all plots of the father erect their dubious beginnings. For underneath those masterful designs, *Absalom, Absalom!* reveals a story not of the power of the father, but of how one man's sexual anxieties dismantle the very notion of his transcendent, abstract authority. Oedipus, however empowered by our society or its myth-making processes, is finally and nonetheless a vulnerable man caught in the middle of a story that he has indeed helped create but cannot control—caught, as it were, with his pants down, his fallacies exposed, his repressive efforts showing for the ineffectual cover-up they are. Moreover, as Shreve's prophecies on the last page warn of Sutpen's dynastic dreams, there is always the nigger who gets away: all those fractious, marginal excrescences of plot, all those emblems of "nonmaleness," of otherness, that refuse to mirror the father or confine their desires to his preformulated masterplot. Thus Shreve says of any and all attempts to give a balanced, tidy explanation of Sutpen's failure: "Which is all right, it's fine; it clears the whole ledger, you can tear all the pages out and burn them, except for one thing. And do you know what that is? . . . You've got one nigger left" (378). Escaping the shapers of dynastic and narrative designs by their very exclusion, these trangressive elements remain, then, to unravel the ends whereby the father would explain his origins and to return the reader to the obsessions that remain in play, despite the paternal effort to repress difference, in the midst of a story doomed by its very premises never to end.

NOTES

I should like to acknowledge a debt of gratitude to the students in the graduate course, "The Psychology of Sex and Self," where I first taught this novel in 1985. I am particularly grateful for the contributions of Deirdre d'Albertis and Elizabeth Young, whose seminar papers I cite below.

1. Barthes, *The Pleasure of the Text*, trans. Richard Miller (New York: Hill and Wang, 1975), 10, 47; Brooks, *Reading for the Plot: Design and Intention in Narrative* (New York: Knopf, 1984), esp. chap. 3; Teresa de Lauretis, *Alice Doesn't: Feminism, Semiotics, Cinema* (Bloomington: Indiana University Press, 1984), esp. chap. 5.

2. Friedman, "Lyric Subversions of Narrative in Women's Writing: Virginia Woolf and the Tyranny of Plot," in *Reading Narrative: Form, Ethics and Ideology*, ed. James Phelan (Columbus: Ohio State University Press, 1989). In what is perhaps the most important feminist reworking of oedipal models since de Lauretis, Susan B. Winnett extracts a female-based morphological model of narrative desire from Mary Shelley's *Frankenstein* and George Eliot's *Romola* in order to counter the male assumptions of sexual pleasure and response girding traditional Freudian-based structures, in "Coming Unstrung: Women, Men, Narrative, and (the) Principles of Pleasure," *PMLA* 105 (May 1990): 505–518. For alternative narrative models based on the mother-daughter relations, see, among many others, Marianne Hirsch, "A Mother's Discourse: Incorporation and Repetition in *La Princesse de Clèves*," Yale French Studies 62 (1982): 63–87, and Elizabeth Abel, "(E)merging Identities: The Dynamics of Female Friendship in Contemporary Fiction by Women," *Signs: A Journal of Women in Culture and Society* 6 (1981): 413–35.

3. Irigaray, *Speculum de l'autre femme* (Paris: Minuit, 1974).

4. Faulkner, *Absalom, Absalom!* (1936; repr. New York: Vintage, 1972), 14. All further references to this work appear in the text.

5. Quentin's unmentioned incestuous feelings for his sister Caddy can be derived from an intertextual reading of *Absalom, Absalom!* with *The Sound and the Fury* (1929). See John

T. Irwin's influential reading of the two novels as companion texts in *Doubling and Incest/ Repetition and Revenge: A Speculative Reading of Faulkner* (Baltimore: Johns Hopkins University Press, 1975).

6. Brooks, *Reading for the Plot*, 300, also uses the phrase "compensatory plot" to describe Sutpen's design; what I find fascinating about so many of Brooks's insightful points, as my frequent citations begin to indicate, is the degree to which, if taken another step, these very arguments could be used to deauthorize the fairly exclusively masculine oedipal model that his reading attempts to establish for the novel.

7. Brooks, *Reading*, 301, puts it well when he notes that "Sutpen attempts to write the history of the House of Sutpen prospectively, whereas history is evidently always retrospective. . . . One cannot postulate the authority and outcome of a genealogy in its origin." Or, as one of my students, Deirdre d'Albertis, noted in a seminar paper, Sutpen is "doomed to fail" because one cannot demand "an end in the midst of [one's] middle. . . . The violation of time which enables Sutpen to impose narrative selection on his life can be sustained only in such moments of isolated telling, not in the organization of his own 'work in progress' or unfinished existence" (in " 'The Web of the Text': Narrative Strategies in Faulkner's *Absalom, Absalom!*" [1985]).

8. Bon's worldly sophistication and sensuality, as filtered through Mr. Compson's jaded fin-de-siècle projections, becomes "a little femininely flamboyant" (110), the seductive charm of an "indolent esoteric hothouse bloom" (97). His feminized sexuality is repeatedly evoked in Mr. Compson's mental image of the student lounging around his quarters in flowered dressing gowns and "the outlandish and almost feminine garments of his sybaritic privacy" (96).

9. Irwin, *Doubling*, 43 (here Irwin is reading Freud through Otto Rank) and 88–90.

10. Sutpen, of course, is not bothered by issues of racial purity when he beds any of his slaves, such as Clytie's mother.

11. See also Patricia Tobin's discussion of incest and narrative repetition in *Time and the Novel: The Genealogical Perspective* (Princeton: Princeton University Press, 1978),107–32, and Brooks, *Reading*, 109, on literary incest as the threat of a narrative "short circuit."

12. Sedgwick, *Between Men: English Literature and Male Homosocial Desire* (New York: Columbia University Press, 1985), 1–5.

13. See 2 Samuel 13. Absalom, son of King David, kills his brother Ammon for raping their sister Tamar.

14. It should be added that this exposure to the homosocial paradigm may be primary in female development as well; unknown to Sutpen, Judith and Clytie also witness the scene and, unlike the sickened Henry, remain ominously unmoved.

15. Lévi-Strauss's observation in *The Elementary Structures of Kinship* (Boston: Beacon, 1969), 115, that women serve as items of exchange between men, thereby solidifying a male network of power, is reflected in the mediating function of women in this novel: Sutpen accepts Eulalia Bon from her father in exchange for saving his plantation on Haiti during the slave uprising; Ellen Coldfield is the prize of his demonic dealings with her father ("whose daughters he might even have won at cards" [20]); Milly is the understood price her grandfather Wash Jones pays for the privilege of drinking scuppernong wine with the master. "So it was no story about women," Mr. Compson says of the life-story Sutpen confesses to his father the general, "and certainly not about love" (248).

16. Sutpen's mother, for instance, is accorded only one sentence, where she is described as "a fine wearying woman" who died in her son's youth (223); Clytie's mother is presumably one of the two nameless slave women Sutpen has brought with him from Haiti; Milly's mother is mentioned for the first time in the chronology that ends in novel. In the chapter of a work-in-progress of which this article is a much reduced and edited part, I examine in greater depth the case of Mrs. Coldfield (Ellen and Rosa's mother) and of Jim Bond's mother. The disappearance of both women provides a glaring example of a degree of tex-

tual repression so extreme that it creates outright inconsistencies and "loose ends" in Faulkner's otherwise scrupulously woven narrative design.

17. The equation of gender and race implicit in Freud's (in)famous characterization of female sexuality as a dark continent is echoed in Faulkner's text. For Sutpen describes the island of Haiti, where he encounters female sexuality for the first time in the form of Eulalia Bon, with her shadowy racial heritage, as "a dark inscrutable continent from which the black blood, the black bones and flesh and thinking and remembering and hopes and desires, was ravished by violence" (250). I am grateful to Elizabeth Young for bringing this connection to light in her seminar paper "Gender and Anxiety in William Faulkner's *Absalom, Absalom!*" (1985).

18. Benjamin persuasively argues that sons who have passed through the oedipal crisis into an awareness of gender difference experience a need for separation and differentiation from the mother much more extreme than that experienced by daughters. To establish a separate sense of their maleness, men are propelled to embrace an ethos of solipsistic individuality, based on such absolute ego-boundaries that a profound sense of inner alienation ensues. This in turn leads to violent attempts to break out of egoistic enclosure through domination, possession, and control of other selves—the very methods by which Sutpen attempts to effect his plot and impose his identity on the world around him. See "Master and Slave: The Fantasy of Erotic Domination," in *Powers of Desire: The Politics of Sexuality*, eds. Snitow, Stansell, and Thompson (New York: Monthly Review, 1983), 281–82.

19. In this light, it is worth noting that Judith and Clytie, along with Rosa, form an all-female "triumvirate" whose combined strength keeps Sutpen's plantation running throughout the last months of the war. Without men ("No, it did not even require the first day of the life we were to lead together to show us we did not need [Sutpen], had not the need for any man" [154]), the three women weave a narrative for their lives shaped to *their own desires*—"we now existed in an apathy which was almost peace" (155). This is, significantly, a story without designs, or what Rosa identities as the "furious desire" and "mad intention" (154) fueling Sutpen's monomaniacal impulse to climax and completion.

20. This is not to ignore the importance of the complementary "man-to-man" transmissions between Sutpen and General Compson (whose subject, appropriately, is a father-son narrative), passed on to Mr. Compson and thence to Quentin; my point is that this male chain of narrative transactions often depends on unrecognized female exchanges, which not only make possible the father-son story that the men want to tell, but keep alive the counteroedipal strands of plot I am interested in excavating. Moreover, Judith's effort to make a mark, a protesting counterstatement, does not stop with her passing on of Bon's letter to General Compson's wife. For, as Deirdre d'Albertis, "The Web of the Text," has brilliantly shown, Judith constructs her own textual equivalent of Sutpen's family plot, and even hides it out in the open, in her arrangement of the family graveplot upon the successive deaths of Ellen, Sutpen, Bon, and Charles Etienne. Within this demarcated plot of land, Judith places the various tombstones so that Sutpen is surrounded with the denied, disruptive elements of *his* plot; then, to complete *her* counterplot, she orders her headstone from her deathbed, which is tellingly placed "at the opposite end of the enclosure, *as far from the other four* as the enclosure could permit" (210, emphasis added). Symbolically fulfilling the role of her biblical namesake, the Judith who beheads, castrates, the patriarchal oppressor, by so encompassing Sutpen's grave, Judith thus also leaves behind a silent testimonial to the marginal position that, as an expendable daughter, she has always occupied in his plot.

21. On the subversive centrality of Rosa's narrative role, see Linda Kauffman, "A Lover's Discourse in *Absalom, Absalom!*," *Modern Fiction Studies* 29 (1983): 183–200, and Robert Con Davis, "The Symbolic Father in Yoknapatawpha County," *The Journal of Narrative Technique* 10 (1980): 39–55. Davis sees Rosa as the Lacanian "Other" of the symbolic

father, attesting to "the repressed experience that lies within paternal structures"—namely, the "feminine"; Rosa thus "emerges as the dominant figure in this paternal fiction, over and above . . . the males the novel seems to be about" (39).

22. Winnett, "Coming Unstrung," 38. What Winnett says apropos Eliot's *Romola* about the communal genesis of legend as a counter to the intentions of oedipal plotting has equal significance for the counternarratives established by *Absalom*'s community of tellers: "legend tells a story that is over. Its significance has been established not by its protagonist, but by the community whose retelling of the story has become the sole measure of its importance. . . . The narrative significance of a life history lies ultimately in the hands (ears, mouths, pens) of others; however we attempt to shape this plot in terms of our sense of its retrospective significance, the retelling of the tale is always beyond our control" (32–33).

23. Given the fact that hidden origins and proleptic endings are the essential cornerstones of Sutpen's masterplot, it is fascinating to note how Rosa usurps control over both the beginning and end of the novel that tells his story. Not only does she regulate the text's opening—without her summons to Quentin, as we have seen, there would be no novel per se—but by making Quentin her companion, her witness, on the revelatory night-trip to Sutpen's Hundred, where Henry is discovered, she also summons into being the final event of the Sutpen family plot—the fire, set by Clytie, that burns down the house, destroys its last white descendant, and sends Rosa "to bed because it was finished now, there was nothing left. . . . And so she died" (376). These are simultaneously the penultimate events narrated by the two boys, and within a page of the mention of her death, the novel ends. It is as if the literal "story" must cease when Rosa is no longer alive to keep it going. Thus, even in death Rosa continues to usurp Sutpen's desire for metaphoric finality, preempting his "proper" end by "breaking off" the account of *his* story where and when *she* desires.

24. I am indebted to Michele Whelan for making a similar point in class. Much of Irwin's argument also has to do with Quentin's contradiction-ridden attempts to master his father through the fantasy of a reversal of generations (*Doubling*, 68–76).

25. Brooks, *Reading*, 306.

PEDAGOGY AND SEXUALITY

(1995)

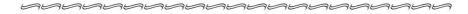

THE FRENCH LESSON

Near the end of my career in junior high school, I heard a mildly titillating story about a certain teacher—a French teacher—at the high school I was to attend in the fall.[1] (Why, as in Eve Sedgwick's "A Poem Is Being Written"—an important model for this essay, by the way—is it always a French teacher! If French teachers didn't exist, American culture would no doubt have to invent them. Come to think of it, it sort of *did* invent them.) It seemed that if you took French, as I planned to do, you might well end up in the classroom of a certain Mr. Boyer. And it seemed—here's the titillating part—that Mr. Boyer, whose name was almost too good to be true, was famous at the high school for "liking boys." Though it's been a long time, I'm pretty sure my gleeful informant managed to embellish his tale with suitably lurid images of lechery and molestation.

I think the reason this memory has stayed with me for so long is not that the conversation in question revealed to me something scandalously new but, rather, that it confirmed an intuition that I had been forming ever since who knows when. In other words, while the story about Mr. Boyer had as its salient theme the *abuse* of pedagogical power, it actually illuminated something about the *normal* functioning of teachers in relation to students. In its sensationalistic way, the story emphasized that the classroom—any classroom—is a highly eroticized space: eroticized in different ways and with different effects, depending on the gender and sexuality of the teacher and the gender and sexuality of the students, but eroticized nonetheless—even or especially when the teacher goes strictly by the book and when nothing recognizably erotic takes place in that classroom.

I won't deny that a large part of my interest in this story amounted to sheer prurient curiosity about Mr. Boyer and his alleged advances: If Mr. Boyer likes boys, I undoubtedly asked myself, will he like me? And if he likes me, will he do to me what he does to the others? Yet what was ultimately more compelling about the story was its dramatization of the insight that "liking boys" and, for that matter, "liking girls"—where those euphemisms designate homosexuality and heterosexuality in general—were not merely extracurricular activities. Rather, they were ways of being that our teachers carried into their classrooms and communicated to us, whether or not they wanted to, as much as if not more than they did the authorized subject matter of algebra, American history, English, and, of course, French. Ostensibly, sexuality was the most "personal" thing about a person, not just a private matter but in some sense the very essence of privacy, that which is by definition "nobody else's business." It was becoming clear to me, however, that acquiring *cultural* literacy—as one is supposed to do in school—meant, to no small degree, acquiring *sexual* literacy, not learning how to exclude the private from the public but learning how to read the private as it is everywhere obliged to manifest itself *in* public.

My point is that, if you grow up in this culture, you become remarkably sophisticated, well before college age, about the sexuality of your teachers—more sophisticated, perhaps, than about your own sexuality, which, as they say, is another story. This sophistication doesn't consist primarily in an explicit trading of information about sexual organs and practices, though it usually includes plenty of that kind of exchange. What defines it best is an acute, often merciless receptivity to the ways in which the sexual "truth" about a person spreads out to suffuse everything he or she says and does, especially at the level of apparently nonsexual words and deeds and especially when he or she is unconscious of their "true" significance.

I am drawing, of course, on Michel Foucault's distinction between sexuality and sex. For Foucault, sexuality is not reducible to what you do in bed; unlike sex, which is a biological category, sexuality is a cultural, a discursive, category—perhaps *the* category whereby we learn, in this culture, to make sense of the world. Sexuality, as Foucault formulates it, is the "putting into discourse of sex" (12). Being sophisticated about sexuality thus means being able to pick up on the innumerable ways in which our culture makes sex speak. It is this sophistication, I take it, that was at work not only in my friend's story about Mr. Boyer but also, for example, in all the endless little jokes that—like lots of students—my classmates and I would make about our teachers, not always behind their suggestively vulnerable and vulnerably suggestive backs.

I suppose I should come out at this point as, among other things, a compulsive mimic. By the ninth grade I'd built up a repertoire of (more or less cruel) imitations of almost all the teachers in the school. (Becoming a certain kind of class clown—everybody loves a clown—is of course one of the strategies a lot of gay or protogay kids adopt to survive in the intensely homophobic worlds of junior high and high school.) I think I realized even then that my imitations—of both female and male teachers—got a lot of their bite from an insistent playing up of whatever was most uncomfortably indicative of a given teacher's erotic specificity. Whatever little verbal or gestural tic seemed most decisively to betray the secret of his or her desire, that was what I would zero in on to the delight of my peers. Not surprisingly, however, the imitations that were most in demand were those of teachers thought to be gay. (And by *gay* here, I mean "gay men." Significantly, it almost never seemed to occur to me or my "friends" that any of our teachers might be lesbians; in this respect, we were no doubt obeying the cultural imperative to misrecognize—or simply *not* to recognize—lesbian lives and meanings, even when they're staring us in the face.) If apparently straight teachers had to be worked up into figures of fun, then apparently gay male teachers (needless to say, none of our teachers ever came out to us) seemed "naturally" hilarious. That is, if our sophistication about the sexuality of straight teachers was largely subliminal, what we "knew" about our gay teachers, we "knew" consciously, ostentatiously, aggressively.

In "Tearooms and Sympathy," Lee Edelman examines heterosexist culture's "insistence on the presentation of the gay male body as public spectacle" (*Homographesis* 154). As Edelman argues, this spectacle primarily serves not to satisfy some voyeuristic urge of the straight spectator but, rather, to "shore up 'masculinity' by policing the borders at which sexual difference is definitionally produced" (159). As a junior impressionist, I was more than happy, I'm afraid, to serve as a rookie cop—to assist, that is, in this enforcement of sexual boundaries, whereby the increasing visibility and problematicality of the gay man promotes the increasing invisibility and unproblematicality of straight society as a whole, but especially of the straight man. It wasn't long, then, before I was regaling my classmates with my wickedly acute rendition of Mr. Boyer—but of a Mr. Boyer who, despite my junior high school friend's ominous assurances, spent most of his time trying to pass rather than making passes. So what my routine consisted of, essentially, was a florid amplification of all the little ways in which the notorious French teacher revealed not so much his homosexuality as his closetedness; it was a question, in short, of ruthlessly bringing out his techniques for not coming out, techniques that were thereby seen repeatedly and delectably to backfire. If I was thus performing the cultural work of presenting the gay male body as public spectacle, I was presenting it the way straight society likes most to see it—as hiding ashamedly from a supervisory agency that it can never really elude, so knowing, so expert is that agency in detecting that body's every ruse, in exposing all the ironic accidents whereby it predictably puts itself into discourse.

In doing Mr. Boyer, as I remember all too well, one of my favorite shticks was to ape his recitation of what seemed to be one of *his* favorite shticks, about how "just because two men love each other, society assumes they're homosexuals." The joke, you see, was that he wasn't fooling anyone; eventually, with some egging on from my friends, the line was expanded into "just because two men live in the same house, just because they sleep in the same bed, just because they like to fondle each other's genitals. . . . " But while I thought that the joke was on Mr. Boyer, it turned out, of course, that the joke was on me. I congratulated myself at the time for what I took to be the sophisticated truth telling implicit in my unmasking of this necessarily cautious gay teacher, who seemed every inch the less than gay, pre-Stonewall stereotype of "the homosexual," of the queer in the old, untransvalued sense of the term, with all its abjective violence. But in my wittiness I was unwittingly locking myself into the very double bind that he was enacting—into the tight paradoxical space of closeted homosexuality, whose emblem, as D. A. Miller has suggested in *The Novel and the Police*, is the open secret.

As a version of the open secret, Mr. Boyer's line about what society erroneously assumes wasn't just part of a cover-up, although that was certainly one of its functions: it was also, as now seems painfully obvious, the only means he had, in that homophobic time and at that homophobic place, for claiming a modicum of pedagogical control over the interpretation of his own sexuality—for letting us know that he *had* a secret and for clueing us in on what that secret might be. If, on the one hand, we recognized something depressingly dishonest and banal in the "just because x, it doesn't mean y" logic of his formulation, on the other hand, we chose not to recognize that he was also, through the same formulation, holding open the possibility that two men might love each other and that it *might* mean that they *were* gay. Or, rather, *I* chose not to recognize that. I chose, that is, to close the closet door on myself if not on Mr. Boyer. And for the next eight years, I, too, would be inhabiting the constrictive, attenuated realm of compulsory ambiguity typified by "just because two men love each other, society assumes they're homosexuals."

Did anything ever "happen" between Mr. Boyer and me? Well, yes, sort of. Somehow it came about that I needed to stay after class one day and go over some *explication de texte.* Sitting next to Mr. Boyer at his desk, I suddenly felt his hand on my thigh, which is where it stayed, decorously and discreetly, for the next half hour, until it was time for me to leave. Along with a sense of relief that nothing more had happened, there was probably something in my response equivalent to the line in the old Peggy Lee song "Is that all there is?" But I can't have been all that disappointed, since, long before this hands-on instruction, I had already learned the sad lesson that Mr. Boyer had to teach me: that decorousness and discretion, rigorously maintained as a system of furtive, halting, or merely half-hearted words and gestures, of thighs and whispers, were indeed all there was to a certain socially constructed model of male homosexuality, the only model, I might add, available to a gay—or, rather, extremely unavowedly protogay—high school student in Richard Nixon's middle America of 1971.

THE LESSON OF PAUL DE MAN

Let me elide my college years, which, like many gay undergraduates, I spent in a painful sort of sexual fugue, and fast-forward to New Haven, Connecticut, and the year 1978, when I found myself enrolled in the comparative literature department at Yale—more specifically, in Paul de Man's graduate seminar. (Since you could still do French in comp. lit., the French connection—along with everything it stood for—wasn't exactly severed; moreover, although de Man himself was from Belgium, that status could seem at the time a sufficient metonymy for Frenchness *tout court.*)

Admittedly, to talk about this particular pedagogue under the rubric of pedagogy and sexuality may seem not so much novel as simply beside the point. Since the discovery of de Man's wartime writings, the relevant terms of discussion would appear to be, shall we say, pedagogy and politics or pedagogy and anti-Semitism. My aim is hardly to dismiss those issues: they're very much on the scene of what I want to say; but I want to focus for a minute on a somewhat different (though inextricably related) kind of politics and ideology—the politics and ideology of gender and sexuality. A memory of de Man that keeps coming back to me, along with the more obviously resonant ones, is of a class on Yeats, in which de Man, slipping into the apparently digressive mode that was one of his pedagogical hallmarks, began to relate a rather funny—if probably apocryphal—anecdote about Yeats's private life. I can't reconstruct it very well anymore, nor would it seem particularly funny even if I were to do so, since the point is that I'm no longer willing to sell it as a piece of humor. It took off from some casual remarks about the symbolism of the tower in Yeats, which led to a story about how Yeats insisted on living in a tower on the outskirts of town. In case we were interested in buying a tower, de Man continued, we should know that there wasn't any shopping nearby, which meant that poor Mrs. Yeats had to ride her bicycle into town three times a week to get groceries for her husband, for which he finally rewarded her—here's the punch line— by referring to her in "The Circus Animals' Desertion" as "that raving slut/ Who keeps the till" (336).

A lot of people in that intensely cultish class clearly got a kick out of this disarmingly loose-jointed story, which seemed to epitomize the cool irony for which de Man was famous. (You have to realize that this was still prefeminist Yale.) I, for one, thought both the story and de Man were pretty cool, which is why, as soon as I got a chance to teach Yeats myself, I recycled the bicycle story as though it were my own. And for several years, that routine played as well in my classroom as it had in de Man's, though it probably would have gone over even better if I had done it in a Belgian accent. But although I wasn't doing the accent, I was still, of course, engaged in a process of imitation—this time, imitation of a heterosexually identified male mentor, whose pedagogical style virtually defined, for me, what might be referred to as "teaching as a straight man." By 1982, when I arrived at Bowdoin as an assistant professor and started playing de Man (whose name, especially in contrast with Mr. Boyer's, has an obvious allegorical resonance), I had already acknowledged to myself that I was gay and had been living for some time with my lover, the aforementioned Lee Edelman. Yet while the mask was therefore off in my "private" life, I was still trying to keep it on in the classroom, not so much through a conscious policy of deception as through the largely unconscious ideological programming that constitutes what it means to become a teacher in this culture.

If becoming a teacher means, for many people, becoming a straight male teacher, a role for which de Man was my model, what does his Yeats anecdote tell us about that role? For one thing, insofar as it is an anecdote, it tells us that teaching as a straight man is no more nonnarrative than teaching as a gay man is nontheoretical. But it does say something about a certain straight male strategy of using narrative to overcome narrative. In relating his story, and in relating it as he did, de Man, I would argue, was giving us a lesson in how to ascend from narrative into theory.

Nothing could have been more seductive, at the time, than the way in which he appeared to be telling us something about himself even as he kept us at a calculated distance or in which he appeared to be giving himself up to the pleasures of free association even as he subjected his discourse to the strictest possible discipline. Nothing could have been more seductive, as I say, unless it was his enactment of a certain bored, urbane knowingness vis-à-vis the dreary realities of marital politics. Now, it might have seemed that de Man was thus offering a feminist or even a potentially lesbian and gay critique of patriarchal, heterosexist domesticity, but it didn't seem that way at all, not just because of his identification as heterosexual but also because of the grimly totalizing force of his irony itself. If, that is, the humor of the story seemed to consist in its equal opportunity cynicism, if the joke was as much at Yeats's expense as it was at his wife's, its ultimate effect was to install de Man in the tower, catapulting de Man to the supreme position of the normative, disembodied consciousness that, not controlled by the discourse of sexuality but controlling it, sees everything, knows everything, and remains blankly indifferent to everything. Staging his own evacuation as a desiring subject, de Man stunningly transformed himself into something like a transcendental ego.

As Miller has argued, it may not finally be that much fun to perform this kind of "theoretical" self-abstraction: it can recall "the professional deformation that positively requires such alienation for efficient job performance—and not just, of course, from those who aren't white, male, or heterosexual-identified, but also (even more, of course) from those who . . . are so entitled" ("Black Veil" 52). Whatever its costs to the performer, however, the performance, as I've said, had an extremely seductive effect on at least one member of the audience, and I'd wager that similar performances in similar classrooms seduce a lot of people into becoming professors themselves. But if there's something undeniably sexy about appearing to empty yourself of all sexual desire, this paradoxical trick is more available to those whose social entitlement most requires it: it is more available to straight men than to anyone else. What allows straight men to bring it off convincingly is that it already constitutes a large part of their social construction *as* straight men. From Ernest Hemingway to Kevin Costner, from Dick Tracy to Dick Cheney, the strong, silent type has been the dream of masculinist American culture, where acting like a man means acting like you're not acting at all, since the ones who make sexual spectacles of themselves are women and gay men. As performed by gay men and by both lesbians and straight women, the straight male disappearing act may not, therefore, be a surefire hit.

However much the paradoxicality of the act seems to resemble that of, say, the open secret, the two techniques have different consequences for classroom politics: where the straight male power play registers as a tour de force, the closeted gay or lesbian teacher's compulsory ambiguity seems, like all compulsions, forced on him or her; the difference, if you will, is as great as that between Mr. Boyer and de Man. As for my own reception, I have no idea how many of my students took my teaching as a straight man for the real thing and how many of them read my act as I had read my high school French teacher's; when you're in the closet, as Sedgwick reminds us, you never really know what people think. After several years at Bowdoin, at any rate, it started to become harder for me to tell the difference between being in the tower with de Man and being in the closet with Mr. Boyer; the mask of male heterosexual privilege began to seem oppressively indistinguishable from the mask of homosexual constraint. And that's what takes us to our third and final story.

GOODBYE, MR. CHIPS

Even if I hadn't stopped teaching Yeats a few years ago, I would still have stopped telling de Man's story in class. As my teaching, along with my scholarship, became increasingly feminist, the idea of getting comic mileage out of Mrs. Yeats's exploitation came to seem increasingly grotesque. But if feminism itself was becoming my new pedagogical vehicle, it, too, served partially to dissimulate: although I was perfectly sincere in my critique of patriarchy, my male feminism tended to serve as a way of teaching against heterosexism and homophobia without actually having to come out. In other words, I believed in what I was telling my students, but I wasn't telling them the whole story. And while this reticence seemed pragmatically defensible at the time, it had some rather disturbing practical consequences.

For example, the semester before the one in which I wrote the first version of this essay, I was teaching a seminar called Literary Theory. One of the tenets for the course was Terry Eagleton's book of the same name. Somewhere around Columbus Day, we were discussing his chapter on poststructuralism, whose alleged political impotence Eagleton asserts through a parodic rehearsal of the writings of the gay French critic Roland Barthes—there's that French connection again. Things were going relatively well until I decided to point out the strains of francophobia, erotophobia, and homophobia in Eagleton's prose. Incorrigible ham that I am, I chose to mock Eagleton's mockery of Barthes by enacting my own parody of the virile, salt-of-the-earth political activism that Eagleton privileges over Barthes's ostensibly effete, apolitical, all too Parisian autoeroticism. After miming with fist and palm the pounding phallic thrust of Eagleton's macho Marxism as it goes to inseminate an implicitly feminized social reality, I proceeded to figure, by contrast and with even greater brio, the various masturbatory pleasures of the nonreferential textual play that Barthes celebrates.

Though this bit seemed at first to be going over fairly well, I began to suspect that something was wrong when one of the women in the class, looking rather unamused, turned to another woman and started a conversation I couldn't hear. And sure enough, about a week later the first student came to my office to tell me that something had indeed been wrong: that while the five men in the class had obviously been enjoying my routine, she and both the other women in the class had been feeling acutely alienated, as though the classroom had suddenly been transformed into the men's locker room. Now, when this student confirmed my suspicions, my response was one of considerable chagrin: I felt, to be perhaps dangerously candid, as though I had been caught with my pants down, in the full criminal sense of that cliché.

I tried to cover, or recover, myself by explaining to the student, and subsequently to the class as a whole, that I had intended my little performance as a feminist debunking of Eagleton's phallocentrism. I talked about how, in attempting to deconstruct the locker room, only to reconstruct it on some level, I had inadvertently illustrated one of the acknowledged predicaments of deconstruction in general. And this explanation was all true, as far as it went. Yet the problem was that it didn't go far enough. For the students who thought I was straight, my profession of good faith may have seemed a little abstract, not to say downright unconvincing. But for the students who thought I was gay, the open secret of my sexuality may have seemed even more discrediting. For as long as I let that sexuality remain an open secret, as I'm pretty sure it was for some if not all of the students, my professions of solidarity with the women in the class could always be called into question; that is, it could always be inferred that, while pretending to support the female students, I was far more interested in trying to charm the male students—that my apparent subversion of the phallus constituted an excuse for trying to get a rise out of it.

In another text that we read in the Literary Theory seminar, a critic named Gerald M. MacLean, who comes out unmistakably as a married heterosexual man, writes: "I don't think anyone has begun to examine fully the range of erotic interactions between students and teachers. In class I flirt, consciously and consistently. But I play for laughs and flirt with the men too" (149). A straight male teacher can say that and get away with it: if it's understood that when he's "flirting with the men" he's just "playing for laughs," it goes without saying that when he's playing it straight—flirting normally and normatively—the "students" interpellated as the objects of that flirtation are all female students. I don't know too many straight female teachers who would say the equivalent of what MacLean says, but if they did, chances are they'd seem to be asking for trouble. Were a lesbian teacher publicly to acknowledge sexual interest in her students, she'd most likely open herself up to the charge of using her classroom as a recruitment center. And in a culture perpetually haunted (and thrilled) by the possibility that pedagogy might turn into pederasty, such a statement by a gay male teacher still has to be made with a certain circumspection. So in trying (as I was indeed doing) to win my male students over to feminism, was I also flirting with them? At Bowdoin, I answered, "Maybe I was." Here I can say, more bluntly and with a certain air of insouciance, "Of course I was." But the flirtation depended crucially on my closetedness: if I wanted the male students to "like me," I wanted them to like me not as a teacher who "liked boys" but as one of the boys, as what our culture, in all its strong, silent eloquence, calls a regular guy.

I've mentioned, of course, my suspicion that this masquerade was being perceived as such. But I still wanted to have it both ways: not so differently from Mr. Boyer (who had even better reasons for playing it safe), I was trying to speak out of both sides of my mouth at once, obliquely making certain gay-affirmative points while counting on a vague presumption of my heterosexuality to legitimate them—and not only to legitimate them but also, frankly, to make *me*, well, more desirable as their purveyor. At the same time, however, I was beginning to find the contradictions of this double bind intellectually and politically untenable, emotionally enervating, and just generally not worth it. Under such circumstances, how could the masquerade not begin to wear thin to the point of transparency? The masturbation episode, as I came to call it, seemed to exemplify everything that was inauthentic and off target and uncomfortable-making about the seminar in which it occurred, and it forced me to do some rethinking about the kind of teacher I wanted to be.

CODA

As a result of that rethinking, I came out to one of my classes the following semester. The coming-out story is supposed to have a happy ending, but my experience with that class was less than happy. Too many of the comments on the end of the semester course evaluation forms boiled down to some version of "the teacher emphasizes sex too much" or of the less guarded "the teacher emphasizes homosexuality too much" If the actual discourse of the class hadn't quite prepared me for the formulaic dismissiveness of these parting shots, it may simply have been because a lot of the students had made the cynical decision that the best way to get through the course was by treating my gay pedagogy as the particular orthodoxy to which they would have to pay lip service until a more palatable alternative came along. In effect, they ended up trying to reconstruct the gay male teacher as the straight male teacher they wished he had been in the first place.

Of course, they couldn't quite succeed, less because of any conscious resistance I may have offered than because of the irrepressible interference of an older model of the homosexual teacher, a model that, for all its apparent obsolescence, our culture just won't give up: the model of—who else?—Mr. Boyer. Hoping to transcend the opposition between teaching as a straight man and teaching as a pathetic closet case, I wound up reinscribing that opposition in my own person, back in the familiar territory of the pedagogical double bind. For if I took on some of the straight man's power—without any of the seductiveness that goes with it— I found myself stereotyped at the same time as the bearer of a sexuality popularly conceived either as a surrender of power or as an abuse of it.

In no way do I claim to speak as the representative gay pedagogue. But from my own nonuniversal vantage point, it seems that, no matter how knowing and sophisticated a gay male teacher is in his management of his own pedagogical-sexual performance, he remains susceptible to the following interpretations: For many straight male students, he's both contemptible (he wants to be treated "like a woman") and threatening (he wants to treat you like one). For many straight female students, his homosexuality means either that he's misogynistic (he doesn't like women) or that he's merely indifferent (he won't play his prescribed role in the academic version of *Father Knows Best*). For many closeted lesbian, gay, and bisexual students, he's someone who might blow your cover. And even for many out lesbian, gay, and bisexual students, he's less a role model than, given the pervasive ageism of the culture, well, both contemptible and threatening again.

This isn't to say that there haven't been some good moments in classes where I've come out. But I've come to realize that when you teach gay, just as when you try to teach straight, certain discomforts may be irreducible as well as inevitable for all concerned. If you like to think of yourself as an oppositional critic, and as someone who carries his or her critical activity into the classroom, then maybe you have to accept the fact that you can't simultaneously *épater les bourgeois* and charm their pants off.

As the lesson of Paul de Man might go to show, of course, the opposition between teaching as opposition and teaching as seduction is no less deconstructible than any other. But as that lesson also shows, not all oppositional pedagogies are equally seductive. Professing a relatively unseductive oppositionality can seem like another form of self-censorship, a de Manian ascesis without any of the mystique such a pose so successfully confers. Moreover, if you're gay, the position of pain in the institutional ass is never entirely voluntary. Yet if it chooses you as much as you choose it, you *can* figure out your own way of occupying it, of playing with and against it, and in the process you can both have some fun and teach people some lessons for which they may not thank you but that may not feel merely like discipline and punishment either.

NOTE

This essay is the abbreviated text of a lecture I first presented at my home institution, Bowdoin College, in the spring of 1990. Readers will quickly recognize that, in addition to being about pedagogy, it is a pedagogical exercise; it was originally written for a specific undergraduate audience, and it retains the traces of that specificity. I presented a revised version of the essay at the Homotextualities conference at the State University of New York, Buffalo, in October 1991. In recasting the essay for that occasion, I framed and modified the original structure with remarks designed for a more professional audience; some of those changes have also been preserved here, especially in the coda. Thus, though my title might suggest a certain global reach, the essay is the condensed record of two quite local performances, for two quite different audiences. It of course addresses a third audience as well—the audience of its current readers, who, I assume, might appreciate this brief account of its history.

WORKS CITED

Eagleton, Terry. *Literary Theory: An Introduction*. Minneapolis: U of Minnesota P, 1983.

Edelman, Lee. "Tearooms and Sympathy; or, The Epistemology of the Water Closet." *Nationalisms and Sexualities*. Ed. Andrew Parker et al. New York Routledge, 1992. 263–84. Rev. and rpt. in *Homographesis: Essays in Gay Literary and Cultural Theory*. New York: Routledge, 1994. 148–70.

Foucault, Michel. *An Introduction*. Trans. Robert Hurley. New York: Vintage, 1980. Vol. 1 of *A History of Sexuality*.

MacLean, Gerald M. "Citing the Subject." *Gender and Theory: Dialogues on Feminist Criticism*. Ed. Linda Kauffman. Oxford: Blackwell, 1989. 140–57.

Miller, D. A. "The Administrator's Black Veil: A Response to J. Hillis Miller." *ADE Bulletin* 88 (1987): 49–53.

———. *The Novel and the Police*. Berkeley: U of California P, 1988.

Sedgwick, Eve Kosofsky. *Epistemology of the Closet*. Berkeley: U of California P, 1990.

———. "A Poem Is Being Written." *Representations* 17 (1987): 110–43.

Yeats, W. B. *The Collected Poems of W. B. Yeats*. New York: Macmillan, 1974.

autobiography

Autobiography is ubiquitous in feminist literary criticism. As subject matter, autobiography seems specially suited to the study of women's literature in Western culture, since so many women have written (though not always published) letters, journals, diaries, or stories of their lives. Two women writers in particular, Virginia Woolf and Maxine Hong Kingston, have recently come into prominence as authors of texts that take the writer's "self" as subject matter. In this section of *Feminisms* we include essays focusing on Woolf's and Kingston's autobiographical works as illustrations of new theories about ways a writer's gender can affect her writing of this genre.

In addition to being a popular subject area, autobiography touches on "subject" in another sense in feminist scholarship: Feminist theorists and critics—breaking with the conventions of objectivity that dominate traditional Anglo-American criticism—often evoke themselves as the "speaking subjects" of their own writing. When the writer's presence seems to tear through the fabric of the academic text—revealing glimmers of the lived experience that forms the context for scholarly writing—"confessional" moments occur in otherwise conventional prose. The confessional mode can also govern an entire essay, as it does here in the selections by Jane Tompkins and—in an ironic mode—Linda Kauffman, or in Rachel Blau DuPlessis's essay "Washing Blood," reprinted in *The Pink Guitar* (1990), an influential precedent for this kind of feminist work. In this new form of academic writing, autobiography merges with scholarship, and a personal voice begins—if only tentatively—to take shape in expository prose.

Whether their focus is autobiography-as-subject-matter or the essayist's own subjective experience of living and writing about life, the four essays in this section circle around themes that have become central to much feminist literary criticism: the controversial relation between authorship and authority, and the related quest for a "voice"; the bonds and divisions between the individual woman and the family, community, and culture around her; and the sense of a double or divided self, common in postmodern writing but especially problematic for women. As essays in the "Institutions" and "Discourse" sections of *Feminisms* indicate, the "self" poses a set of vexed questions for feminist theory: if a "self" is always a social or institutional construct, if it is indeed (as Gayatri Spivak argues in "History" and Paula Gunn Allen explains in "Ethnicity") an instrument of patriarchal and imperialist oppression, how can a feminist writer come to terms with looking for a "self" in another woman's writing, or constituting a "self" in her own? Feminist theories of autobiography resort to various strategies—from psychoanalytic models to personal anecdotes—to confront these difficulties.

In academic writing as in autobiography, finding a voice is a challenge for women, as Jane Tompkins demonstrates in her 1987 essay "Me and My Shadow." As conscious of doubleness as any autobiographer, Tompkins represents her writing self as split between two voices, that of an academic critic who knows how to use all the critical terminology, all the moves, and that of "a Person who wants to write about her feelings." Oscillating fearlessly between the public side of her working life (as in her direct scholarly response to the Ellen Messer-Davidow essay that inspired this piece) and the private side (as in allusions to her stockinged feet, her childhood conflicts, her anger at men, her present need to go to the bathroom), Tompkins goes as far as any academic feminist has dared to go in pushing out the boundaries of academically appropriate writing. As she explains, the public/private split is a fiction anyway, perpetuated by a system that assigns the private realm of emotions to women in order simultaneously to devalue both females and feelings (for an explanation of the historical context in which this split occurred, see the introduction to "History"). In her call for "love," not "anger," as a dominant academic mode (and her recognition that such a call is embarrassing because it is "mushy" and "sentimental"), in her evocation of the voices of poststructuralist theorists alongside her "own" voice's questioning, musing, even humming, Tompkins is redefining the way autobiography might inform the feminist theory and criticism of the future: the way it might have its effect—like some of its sources—in the world of experience outside texts.

The subject of Sidonie Smith's *A Poetics of Women's Autobiography* (1987) is the textual representation of women's own life experiences over the past five hundred years, since Margery Kempe wrote her life story. Identifying patterns in women's writing about their lives, Smith holds those patterns up against androcentric histories and theories of autobiography to show how that scholarly field has overlooked female-written texts. Smith's study culminates in her analysis of Kingston's *The Woman Warrior,* reprinted here. "Maxine Hong Kingston's *Woman Warrior,* Filiality and Woman's Autobiographical Storytelling," as Smith observes, complicates the already marginal position of the female autobiography by adding ethnicity (Chinese American) and social position (working class) to the mix. According to Smith, Kingston's book is "meta-autobiography," as much "about" its own process of being written as it is "about" its writer's life. Kingston intertwines stories of her own memories with legends her mother told her, so that her "self" gets represented always within the context of her familial and cultural heritages.

As Smith sees it, Kingston's book is full of doublings: The author's voice intertwines dialogically (that is, in dialogue) with her mother's; The daughter's experience is contrasted with that of the older women in her family; the daughter sees herself mirrored in a "dumb" Chinese-American girl at school who will not speak. In the end, says Smith, Kingston overcomes familial and minority/majority-cultural bans on women's speaking, reaching "total identification" with her storytelling mother as "woman poet." The mother's stories served initially to induct the daughter into her filial role in an oppressive family structure, but they function ultimately to empower her to find a voice.

Shari Benstock, in "Authorizing the Autobiographical" (1988), looks to psychoanalysis for a way to address the doubleness of self at the heart of autobiographical writing. Benstock elucidates Jacques Lacan's model of the "mirror stage" to explain the complexities involved in writing autobiography, especially for women. Contrasting the Lacanian idea of the self with the version of selfhood that dominates androcentric theories of autobiography, Benstock shows how helpful psychoanalysis can be to the study of women's autobiography, through the example of Virginia Woolf. Instead of seeing the self as a unified entity whose depths can be plumbed and whose essence could be transmitted through carefully crafted prose, as traditional autobiographical theory sees it, Lacan views the self as fundamentally split between the "I" that one holds to be an ideal and the "I" that one sees reflected back from others. As Benstock explains, Lacan locates the individual's awareness of this split at "the mirror stage," the moment when the child first recognizes its own reflection, and realizes that "I" is—from another perspective—also an "other." Not coincidentally, this developmental moment occurs during the stage in which the child also acquires language.

Written and spoken words, then, come to represent (or to occupy) the slippage, the gap between the two selves, for—as Benstock explains—language is "both internal and external." To the autobiographer, language is "the . . . symbolic system that both constructs and is constructed by the writing subject." Benstock builds upon Lacan's abstract and universalizing theory to think in terms of individual social development and lived experience. Using Virginia Woolf's most "personal" and most informal writing—her diaries and fragments of memoir—Benstock shows how a woman autobiographer can explore the unconscious. She is looking at Woolf's earliest memories of mirror reflections, sexual abuse, and family members (especially her mother), focusing on Woolf's feminine awareness of her own "otherness," even from herself. For Benstock, Woolf's earnest endeavor to avoid shaping, censoring, or editing her journal-writing leads the texts into the realm of the unconscious. Rather than choosing significant contextual details to re-create in language, Woolf tries to include "everything that forms the background of perception and action," everything traditionally left out of autobiography. In this light, Woolf becomes a model for feminist autobiographers, having reconfigured "authority" in a way that allows for a split subjectivity.

Linda Kauffman's "The Long Goodbye: Against Personal Testimony, or An Infant Grifter Grows Up" (1992) is a tour de force that places the other essays in this section—indeed, the "confessional" aspects of all feminist criticism—in an ironic light. The irony is that the "infant grifter" is, of course, Kauffman herself, as she reveals in the catchy narrative passage that opens the piece. Although Kauffman's autobiographical details figure so prominently in her essay, she provides them to demonstrate her point "against personal testimony," which is primarily that it is open to interpretation, that it tends to feed into oppressive master-narratives and that it allies feminist criticism—however unconsciously—with individualism. Excessive focus on the self, she argues, carries "the implicit message . . . that you cannot change society, only yourself. Such interpretations," she maintains, "perpetuate narcissism and personal passivity instead of inspiring political action and social change."

Kauffman rejects the arguments of Jane Tompkins and of Barbara Christian (in "Institutions") against using "male" theoretical discourse in academic feminist writing. Kauffman's spirited defense of "theory" points out that to reject theory is to "discourage investigation of any complicating factors that may weaken the stance of victimization or moral superiority. It avoids the complicated question of collusion and complicity either in one's own oppression, or with institutions." Kauffman is acutely aware of feminism's interdependency with institutions, particularly academia, and of the relative privilege of academic feminists in the context of the larger social world. "While we are being exhorted to focus on our feelings," she remarks, "a lot of people are falling through the cracks in our society." She advocates keeping the lines of "self-critique" open within feminism, and (like Gayatri Chakravorty Spivak in "History") challenges the idea that feminism's goal is individual self-fulfillment. "I never thought feminism was about happiness. I thought it was about justice." The reader of Kauffman's essay learns a lot about Kauffman's "self": the personal voice behind the "I" of her essay is as vivid as that in Tompkins's work. But Kauffman exemplifies how a feminist scholar can write in the first person without making herself the ultimate subject of her writing, for—as she puts it—"writing about yourself does not liberate you, it just shows how ingrained the ideology of freedom through self-expression is in our thinking." Kauffman's essay brings *Feminisms* full circle, as it reopens the questions about the relationships between the self and institutions with which this anthology begins. The dialogue here between Tompkins and Kauffman is a fitting emblem for the open-endedness of the conversation that literary feminisms continue to carry on.

—RRW

ME AND MY SHADOW

(1987)

I wrote this essay in answer to Ellen Messer-Davidow's 'The Philosophical Bases of Feminist Literary Criticisms,' which appeared in the Fall 1987 issue of *New Literary History* along with several replies, including a shorter version of this one. As if it weren't distraction enough that my essay depends on someone else's, I want, before you've even read it, to defend it from an accusation. Believing that my reply, which turns its back on theory, constituted a return to the 'rhetoric of presence,' to an 'earlier, naive, untheoretical feminism,' someone, whom I'll call the unfriendly reader, complained that I was making the 'old patriarchal gesture of representation' whose effect had been to marginalize women, thus 'reinforcing the very stereotypes women and minorities have fought so hard to overcome.' I want to reply to this objection because I think it is mistaken and because it reproduces exactly the way I used to feel about feminist criticism when it first appeared in the late 1960s.

I wanted nothing to do with it. It was embarrassing to see women, with whom one was necessarily identified, insisting in print on the differences between men's and women's experience, focusing obsessively on women authors, women characters, women's issues. How pathetic, I thought, to have to call attention to yourself in that way. And in such bad taste. It was the worst kind of special pleading, an admission of weakness so blatant it made me ashamed. What I felt then, and what I think my unfriendly reader feels now, is a version of what women who are new to feminism often feel: that if we don't call attention to ourselves *as* women, but just shut up about it and do our work, no one will notice the difference and everything will be OK.

Women who adopt this line are, understandably, afraid. Afraid of being confused with the weaker sex, the sex that goes around whining and talking about itself in an unseemly way, that can't or won't do what the big boys do ('tough it out') and so won't ever be allowed to play in the big boys' games. I am sympathetic with this position. Not long ago, as organizer of an MLA session entitled 'Professional Politics: Women and the Institution,' I urged a large roomful of women to 'get theory' because I thought that doing theory would admit us to the big leagues and enable us at the same time to argue a feminist case in the most unimpeachable terms—those that men had supplied. I busily took my own advice, which was good as far as it went. But I now see that there has been a price for this, at least there has been for me; it is the subject of my reply to Ellen. I now tend to think that theory itself, at least as it is usually practiced, may be one of the patriarchal gestures women *and* men ought to avoid.

There are two voices inside me answering, answering to, Ellen's essay. One is the voice of a critic who wants to correct a mistake in the essay's view of epistemology. The other is the voice of a person who wants to write about her feelings (I have wanted to do this for a long time but have felt too embarrassed). This person feels it is wrong to criticize the essay philosophically, and even beside the point: because a critique of the kind the critic has in mind only insulates academic discourse further from the issues that make feminism matter. That make *her* matter. The critic, meanwhile, believes such feelings, and the attitudes that inform them, are soft-minded, self-indulgent, and unprofessional.

These beings exist separately but not apart. One writes for professional journals, the other in diaries, late at night. One uses words like 'context' and 'intelligibility,' likes to win arguments, see her name in print, and give graduate students hardheaded advice. The other has hardly ever been heard from. She had a short story published once in a university literary magazine, but her works exist chiefly in notebooks and manila folders labelled 'Journal' and 'Private.' This person talks on the telephone a lot to her friends, has seen psychiatrists, likes cappuccino, worries about the state of her soul. Her father is ill right now, and one of her friends recently committed suicide.

The dichotomy drawn here is false—and not false. I mean in reality there's no split. It's the same person who feels and who discourses about epistemology. The problem is that you can't talk about your private life in the course of doing your professional work. You have to pretend that epistemology, or whatever you're writing about, has nothing to do with your life, that it's more exalted, more important, because it (supposedly) *transcends* the merely personal. Well, I'm tired of the conventions that keep discussions of epistemology, or James Joyce, segregated from meditations on what is happening outside my window or inside my heart. The public-private dichotomy, which is to say, the public-private *hierarchy*, is a founding condition of female oppression. I say to hell with it. The reason I feel embarrassed at my own attempts to speak personally in a professional context is that I have been conditioned to feel that way. That's all there is to it.

I think people are scared to talk about themselves, that they haven't got the guts to do it. I think readers want to know about each other. Sometimes, when a writer introduces some personal bit of story into an essay, I can hardly contain my pleasure. I love writers who write about their own experience. I feel I'm being nourished by them, that I'm being allowed to enter into a personal relationship with them. That I can match my own experience up with theirs, feel cousin to them, and say, yes, that's how it is.

> When he casts his leaves forth upon the wind [said Hawthorne], the author addresses, not the many who will fling aside his volume, or never take it up, but the few who will understand him. . . . As if the printed book, thrown at large on the wide world, were certain to find out the divided segment of the writer's own nature, and complete his circle of existence by bringing him into communion with it. . . . And so as thoughts are frozen and utterance, benumbed unless the speaker stand in some true relation with this audience—

it may be pardonable to imagine that a friend, a kind and apprehensive, though not the closest friend, is listening to our talk. (Nathaniel Hawthorne, 'The Custom-House,' *The Scarlet Letter*, pp. 5–6)

Hawthorne's sensitivity to the relationship that writing implies is rare in academic prose, even when the subject would seem to make awareness of the reader inevitable. Alison Jaggar gave a lecture recently that crystallized the problem. Western epistemology, she argued, is shaped by the belief that emotion should be excluded from the process of attaining knowledge. Because women in our culture are not simply encouraged but *required* to be the bearers of emotion, which men are culturally conditioned to repress, an epistemology which excludes emotions from the process of attaining knowledge radically undercuts women's epistemic authority. The idea that the conventions defining legitimate sources of knowledge overlapped with the conventions defining appropriate gender behavior (male) came to me as a blinding insight. I saw that I had been socialized from birth to feel and act in ways that automatically excluded me from participating in the culture's most valued activities. No wonder I felt so uncomfortable in the postures academic prose forced me to assume; it was like wearing men's jeans.

Ellen Messer-Davidow's essay participates—as Jaggar's lecture and my précis of it did—in the conventions of Western rationalism. It adopts the impersonal, technical vocabulary of the epistemic ideology it seeks to dislocate. The political problem posed by my need to reply to the essay is this: to adhere to the conventions is to uphold a male standard of rationality that militates against women's being recognized as culturally legitimate sources of knowledge. To break with the convention is to risk not being heard at all.

This is how I would reply to Ellen's essay if I were to do it in the professionally sanctioned way.

The essay provides feminist critics with an overarching framework for thinking about what they do, both in relation to mainstream criticism and in relation to feminist work in other fields. It allows the reader to see women's studies as a whole, furnishing useful categories for organizing a confusing and miscellaneous array of materials. It also provides excellent summaries of a wide variety of books and essays that readers might not otherwise encounter. The enterprise is carried out without pointed attacks on other theorists, without creating a cumbersome new vocabulary, without exhibitionistic displays of intellect or esoteric learning. Its practical aim—to define a field within which debate can take place—is fulfilled by *New Literary History*'s decision to publish it, and to do so in a format which includes replies.

(Very nice, Jane. You sound so reasonable and generous. But, as anybody can tell, this is just the obligatory pat on the back before the stab in the entrails.)

The difficulty with the essay from a philosophical, as opposed to a practical, point of view is that the theory it offers as a basis for future work stems from a confused notion of what an epistemology is. The author says: 'An epistemology . . . consists of assumptions that knowers make about the entities and processes in a domain of study, the relations that obtain among them, and the proper methods for investigating them' (p. 87). I want to quarrel with this definition.

Epistemology, strictly speaking, is a *theory* about the origins and nature of knowledge. As such, it is a set of ideas explicitly held and consciously elaborated, and thus belongs to the practice of a sub-category of philosophy called epistemology. The fact that there is a branch of philosophy given over to the study of what knowledge is and how it is acquired is important, because it means that such theories are generated not in relation to this or that 'domain of study' but in relation to one another: that is, within the context of already existing epistemological theories. They are rarely based upon a study of the practices of investigators within a particular field.

An epistemology does not consist of 'assumptions that knowers make' in a particular field; it is a theory about how knowledge is acquired which makes sense, chiefly, in relation to other such theories. What Messer-Davidow offers as the 'epistemology' of traditional literary critics is not *their* epistemology, if in fact they have one, but her description of what she assumes their assumptions are, a description which may or may not be correct. Moreover, if literary critics should indeed elaborate a theory of how they got their beliefs, that theory would have no privileged position in relation to their actual assumptions. It would simply be another theory. This distinction—between actual assumptions and an observer's description of them (even when one is observing one's own practice)—is crucial because it points to an all-important fact about the relation of epistemology to what really gets done in a given domain of study, namely this: that epistemology, a theory about how one gets one's knowledge, in no way determines the particular knowledge that one has.

This fact is important because Messer-Davidow assumes that if we change our epistemology, our practice as critics will change, too. Specifically, she wants us to give up the subject-object theory, in which 'knowledge is an abstract representation of objective existence,' for a theory which says that what counts as knowledge is a function of situation and perspective. She believes that it follows from this latter theory that knowledge will become more equitable, more self-aware, and more humane.

I disagree. Knowing that my knowledge is perspectival, language-based, culturally constructed, or what have you, does not change in the slightest the things I believe to be true. All that it changes is what I think about how we get knowledge. The insight that my ideas are all products of the situation I occupy in the world applies to all of my ideas equally (including the idea that knowledge is culturally based); and to all of everybody else's ideas as well. So where does this get us? Right back to where we were before, mainly. I still believe what I believe and, if you differ with me, think that you are wrong. If I want to change your mind I still have to persuade you that I am right by using evidence, reasons, chains of inference, citations of authority, analogies, illustrations, and so on. Believing that what I believe comes from my being in a particular cultural framework does not change my relation to my beliefs. I still believe them just as much as if I thought they came from God, or the laws of nature, or my autonomous self.

Here endeth the epistle.

But while I think Ellen is wrong in thinking that a change of epistemology can mean a change in the kinds of things we think, I am in sympathy with the ends she has in view. This sympathy prompts me to say that my professionally correct reply is not on target. Because the target, the goal, rather, is not to be fighting over these questions, trying to beat the other person down. (What the goal is, it is harder to say.) Intellectual debate, if it were in the right spirit, would be wonderful. But I don't know how to be in the right spirit, exactly, can't make points without sounding rather superior and smug. Most of all, I don't know how to enter the debate without leaving everything else behind—the birds outside my window, my grief over Janice, just myself as a person sitting here in stockinged feet, a little bit chilly because the windows are open, and thinking about going to the bathroom. But not going yet.

I find that when I try to write in my 'other' voice, I am immediately critical of it. It wobbles, vacillates back and forth, is neither this nor that. The voice in which I write about epistemology is familiar, I know how it ought to sound. This voice, though, I hardly know. I don't even know if it has anything to say. But if I never write in it, it never will. So I have to try. (That is why, you see, this doesn't sound too good. It isn't a practiced performance, it hasn't got a surface. I'm asking you to bear with me while I try, hoping that this, what I write, will express something you yourself have felt or will help you find a part of yourself that you would like to express.)

The thing I want to say is that I've been hiding a part of myself for a long time. I've known it was there but I couldn't listen because there was no place for this person in literary criticism. The criticism I would like to write would always take off from personal experience. Would always be in some way a chronicle of my hours and days. Would speak in a voice which can talk about everything, would reach out to a reader like me and touch me where I want to be touched. Susan Griffin's voice in 'The Way of All Ideology.' I want to speak in what Ursula LeGuin, at the Bryn Mawr College commencement in 1986, called the 'mother tongue.' This is LeGuin speaking:

> The dialect of the father tongue that you and I learned best in college . . . only lectures. . . . Many believe this dialect—the expository and particularly scientific discourse—is the *highest* form of language, the true language, of which all other uses of words are primitive vestiges. . . . And it is indeed a High Language . . . Newton's *Principia* was written in it in Latin . . . and Kant wrote German in it, and Marx, Darwin, Freud, Boas, Foucault, all the great scientists and social thinkers wrote it. It is the language of thought that seeks objectivity.
>
> . . . The essential gesture of the father tongue is not reasoning, but distancing—making a gap, a space, between the subject or self and the object or other. . . . Everywhere now everybody speaks [this] language in laboratories and government buildings and headquarters and offices of business. . . . The father tongue is spoken from above. It goes one way. No answer is expected, or heard.
>
> . . . The mother tongue, spoken or written, expects an answer. It is conversation, a word the root of which means 'turning together.' The mother tongue is language not as mere communication, but as relation, relationship. It connects. . . . Its power is not in dividing but in binding. . . . We all know it by heart. John have you got your umbrella I think it's going to rain. Can you come play with me? If I told you once I told you a hundred times. . . . O what am I going to do? . . . Pass the soy sauce please. Oh, shit . . . You look like what the cat dragged in. (pp. 3–4)

Much of what I'm saying elaborates or circles around these quotes from LeGuin. I find that having released myself from the duty to say things I'm not interested in, in a language I resist, I feel free to entertain other people's voices. Quoting them becomes a pleasure of appreciation rather than the obligatory giving of credit, because when I write in a voice that is not struggling to be heard through the screen of a forced language, I no longer feel that it is not I who am speaking, and so, there is more room for what others have said.

One sentence in Ellen's essay stuck out for me the first time I read it and the second and the third: 'In time we can build a synchronous account of our subject matters as we glissade among them and turn upon ourselves' (p. 79).

What attracted me to the sentence was the 'glissade.' Fluidity, flexibility, versatility, mobility. Moving from one thing to another without embarrassment. It is a tenet of feminist rhetoric that the personal is political, but who in the academy acts on this where language is concerned? We all speak the father tongue, which is impersonal, while decrying the fathers' ideas. All of what I have written so far is in a kind of watered-down expository prose. Not much imagery. No description of concrete things. Only that one word, 'glissade.'

> Like black swallows swooping and gliding
> in a flurry of entangled loops and curves . . .

Two lines of a poem I memorized in high school are what the word 'glissade' called to mind. Turning upon ourselves. Turning, weaving, bending, unbending, moving in loops and curves.

I don't believe we can ever turn upon ourselves in the sense Ellen intends. You can't get behind the thing that casts the shadow. *You* cast the shadow. As soon as you turn, the shadow falls in another place. Is still your shadow. You have not got 'behind' yourself. That is why self-consciousness is not the way to make ourselves better than we are.

Just me and my shadow, walkin' down the avenue.

It is a beautiful day here in North Carolina. The first day that is both cool and sunny all summer. After a terrible summer, first drought, then heat-wave, then torrential rain, trees down, flooding. Now, finally, beautiful weather. A tree outside my window just brushed by red, with one fully red leaf. (This is what I want you to see. A person sitting in stockinged feet looking out of her window—a floor to ceiling rectangle filled with green, with one red leaf. The season poised, sunny and chill, ready to rush down the incline into autumn. But perfect, and still. Not going yet.)

My response to this essay is not a response to something Ellen Messer-Davidow has written; it is a response to something within myself. As I reread the opening pages I feel myself being squeezed into a straitjacket; I wriggle, I will not go in. As I read the list 'subject matters, methods of reasoning, and epistemology,' the words will not go down. They belong to a debate whose susurrus hardly reaches my ears.

The liberation Ellen promises from the straitjacket of a subject–object epistemology is one I experienced some time ago. Mine didn't take the form she outlines, but it was close enough. I discovered, or thought I discovered, that the post-structuralist way of understanding language and knowledge enabled me to say what I wanted about the world. It enabled me to do this because it pointed out that the world I knew was a construct of ways of thinking about it, and as such, had no privileged claim on the truth. Truth in fact would always be just such a construction, and so, one could offer another, competing, description and so help to change the world that was.

The catch was that anything I might say or imagine was itself the product of an already existing discourse. Not something 'I' had made up but a way of constructing things I had absorbed from the intellectual surround. Post-structuralism's proposition about the constructed nature of things held good, but that did not mean that the world could be changed by an act of will. For, as we are looking at this or that phenomenon and re-seeing it, re-thinking it, the rest of the world, that part from which we do the seeing, is still there, in place, real, irrefragable as a whole, and making visible what we see, though changed by it, too.

This little lecture pretends to something I no longer want to claim. The pretense is in the tone and level of the language, not in what it says about post-structuralism. The claim being made by the language is analogous to what Barthes calls the 'reality effect' of historical writing, whose real message is not that this or that happened but that reality exists. So the claim of this language I've been using (and am using right now) lies in its implicit deification of the speaker Let's call it the 'authority effect.' I cannot describe the pretense except to talk about what it ignores: the human frailty of the speaker, his body, his emotions, his history; the moment of intercourse with the reader—acknowledgment of the other person's presence, feelings, needs. This 'authoritative' language speaks as though the other person weren't there. Or perhaps more accurately, it doesn't bother to imagine who, as Hawthorne said, is listening to our talk.

How can we speak personally to one another and yet not be self-centered? How can we be part of the great world and yet remain loyal to ourselves?

It seems to me that I am trying to write out of my experience without acknowledging any discontinuity between this and the subject matter of the profession I work in. And at the same time find that I no longer want to write about that subject matter, as it appears in Ellen's essay. I am, on the one hand, demanding a connection between literary theory and my own life, and asserting, on the other, that there is no connection.

But here is a connection. I learned what epistemology I know from my husband. I think of it as more his game than mine. It's a game I enjoy playing but which I no longer need or want to play. I want to declare my independence of it, of him. (Part of what is going on here has to do with a need I have to make sure I'm not being absorbed in someone else's personality.) What I am breaking away from is both my conformity to the conventions of a male professional practice and my intellectual dependence on my husband. How can I talk about such things in public? How can I *not*.

Looking for something to read this morning, I took three books down from my literary theory shelf, in order to prove a point. The first book was Félix Guattari's *Molecular Revolution*. I find it difficult to read, and therefore have read very little of it, but according to a student who is a disciple of of Deleuze and Guattari, 'molecular revolution' has to do with getting away from ideology and enacting revolution within daily life. It is specific, not programmed—that is, it does not have a 'method,' nor 'steps,' and is neither psychoanalytic nor marxist, although its discourse seems shaped by those discourses, antithetically. From this kind of revolution, said I to myself, disingenuously, one would expect some recognition of the personal. A revolution that started with daily life would have to begin, or at least would have sometimes to reside, at home. So I open at a section entitled 'Towards a New Vocabulary,' looking for something in the mother tongue, and this is what I find:

> The distinction I am proposing between machine and structure is based solely on the way we use the words; we may consider that we are merely dealing with a 'written device' of the kind one has to invent for dealing with a mathematical problem, or with an axiom that may have to be reconsidered at a particular stage of development, or again with the kind of machine we shall be talking about here.

> I want therefore to make it clear that I am putting into parentheses the fact that, in reality, a machine is inseparable from its structural articulations and conversely, that each contingent structure is dominated (and this is what I want to demonstrate) by a system of machines, or at the very least by one logic machine. (p. 111)

At this point, I start to skip, reading only the first sentence of each paragraph.

> 'We may say of structure that it positions its elements. . . .'
> 'The agent of action, whose definition here does not extend beyond this principle of reciprocal determination. . . .'
> 'The machine, on the other hand remains essentially remote. . . .'
> 'The history of technology is dated. . . .'
> 'Yesterday's machine, today's and tomorrow's, are not related in their structural determinations. . . .'

I find this langugae incredibly alienating. In fact, the paragraph after the one I stopped at begins: 'The individual's relation to the machine has been described by sociologists following Friedmann as one of fundamental alienation.' I will return to this essay some day and read it. I sense that it will have something interesting to say. But the effort is too great now. What strikes me now is the incredibly distancing effect of this language. It is totally abstract and impersonal. Though the author uses the first person ('The distinction I am proposing,' 'I want therefore to make it clear'), it quickly became clear to me that he had no interest whatsoever in the personal, or in concrete situations as I understand them—a specific person, at a specific machine, somewhere in time and space, with something on his/her mind, real noises, smells, aches and pains. He has no interest in his own experience of machines, or in explaining why he is writing about them, what they mean to him personally. I take down the next book: *Poetry and Repression* by Harold Bloom.

This book should contain some reference to the self, to the author's self, to ourselves, to how people feel, to how the author feels, since its subject is psychological: repression. I open the book at page I and read:

> Jacques Derrida asks a central question in his essay on 'Freud and the Scene of Writing': 'What is a text, and what must the psyche be if it can be repre-

sented by a text?' My narrow concern with poetry prompts the contrary question: 'What is a psyche, and what must a text be if it can be represented by a psyche?' Both Derrida's question and my own require exploration of three terms: 'psyche,' 'text,' 'represented.'

'Psyche is ultimately from the Indo-European root.' (p. 1)—and I stop reading.

The subject of poetry and repression will involve the asking and answering of questions about 'a text'—a generalized, non-particular object that has been the subject of endless discussion for the past twenty years,—and about an equally disembodied 'psyche' in relation to the thing called 'a text'—not, to my mind, or rather in view of my desires, a very promising relation in which to consider it. Answering these questions, moreover, will 'require' (on whose part, I wonder?) the 'exploration' of 'three terms.' Before we get to the things themselves—psyches, texts—we shall have to spend a lot of time looking at them *as words*. With the beginning of the next paragraph, we get down to the etymology of 'psyche.' With my agenda, I get off the bus here.

But first I look through the book. Bloom is arguing against canonical readings (of some very canonical poems) and for readings that are not exactly personal, but in which the drama of a self is constantly being played out on a cosmic stage—lots of references to God, kingdom, Paradise, the fall, the eternal—a biblical stage on which, apparently, only men are players (God, Freud, Christ, Nietzsche, and the poets). It is a drama that, although I can see how gripping Bloom can make it, will pall for me because it isn't *my* drama.

Book number three, Michel Foucault's *History of Sexuality,* is more promising. Section One is entitled 'We "other Victorians."' So Foucault is acknowledging his and our implication in the object of the study. This book will in some way be about 'ourselves,' which is what I want. It begins:

> For a long time, the story goes, we supported a Victorian regime, and we continue to be dominated by it even today. Thus the image of the imperial prude is emblazoned on our restrained, mute, and hypocritical sexuality. (p. 3)

Who, exactly, are 'we'? Foucault is using the convention in which the author establishes common ground with his reader by using the first person plural—a presumptuous, though usually successful, move. Presumptuous because it presumes that we are really like him, and successful because, especially when an author is famous, and even when he isn't, 'our' instinct (I criticize the practice and engage in it too) is to want to cooperate, to be included in the circle and the author is drawing so cosily around 'us.' It is chummy, this 'we.' It feels good, for a little while, until it starts to feel coercive, until 'we' are subscribing to things that 'I' don't believe.

There is no specific reference to the author's self, no attempt to specify himself. It continues:

> At the beginning of the seventeenth century . . .

I know now where we are going. We are going to history. 'At the beginning of the seventeenth century a certain frankness was still common, it would seem.' Generalizations about the past, though pleasantly qualified ('a certain frankness,' 'it would seem'), are nevertheless disappointingly magisterial. Things continue in a generalizing vein—'It was a time of direct gestures, shameless discourse, and open transgressions.' It's not so much that I don't believe him as that I am uncomfortable with the level or the mode of discourse. It is everything that, I thought, Foucault was trying to get away from, in *The Archaeology of Knowledge*. The primacy of the subject as the point of view from which history could be written, the bland assumption of authority, the taking over of time, of substance, of event, the imperialism of description from a unified perspective. Even though the subject matter interests me—sex, hypocrisy, whether or not our view of Victorianism and of ourselves in relation to it is correct—I am not eager to read on. The point of view is discouraging. It will march along giving orders, barking out commands. I'm not willing to go along for the march, not even on Foucault's say-so (I am, or have been, an extravagant admirer of his).

So I turn to 'my' books. To the women's section of my shelves. I take down, unerringly, an anthology called *The Powers of Desire* edited by Christine Stansell, Ann Snitow, and Sharon Thompson. I turn, almost as unerringly, to an essay by Jessica Benjamin entitled 'Master and Slave: The Fantasy of Erotic Domination,' and begin to read:

> This essay is concerned with the violence of erotic domination. It is about the strange union of rationality and violence that is made in the secret heart of our culture and sometimes enacted in the body. This union has inspired some of the holiest imagery of religious transcendence and now comes to light at the porno newsstands, where women are regularly depicted in the bonds of love. But the slave of love is not always a woman, not always a heterosexual; the fantasy of erotic domination permeates all sexual imagery in our culture. (p. 281)

I am completely hooked, I am going to read this essay from beginning to end and proceed to do so. It gets better, much better, as it goes along. In fact, it gets so good, I find myself putting it down and straying from it because the subject is *so* close to home, and therefore so threatening, that I need relief from it, little breathers, before I can go on. I underline vigorously and often. Think of people I should give it to to read (my husband, this colleague, that colleague).

But wait a minute. There is no personal reference here. The author deals, like Foucault, in generalities. In even bigger ones than his: hers aren't limited to the seventeenth century or the Victorian era. She generalizes about religion, rationality, violence. Why am I not turned off by this as I was in Foucault's case? Why don't I reject this as a grand drama in the style of Bloom? Why don't I bridle at the abstractions as I did when reading Guattari? Well?

The answer is, I see the abstractions as concrete and the issues as personal. They are already personal for me without being personal*ized* because they concern things I've been thinking about for some time, struggling with, trying to figure out for myself. I don't need the author to identify her own involvement, I don't need her to concretize, because these things are already personal and concrete for me. The erotic is already eroticized.

Probably, when Guattari picks up an article whose first sentence has the words 'machine,' 'structure,' and 'determination,' he cathects it immediately. Great stuff. Juicy, terrific. The same would go for Bloom on encountering multiple references to Nietzsche, representation, God the father, and the Sublime. But isn't

erotic domination, as a subject, surer to arouse strong feeling than systems of machines or the psyche that can be represented as a text? Clearly, the answer depends on the readership. The people at the convenience store where I stop to
get gas and buy milk would find all these passages equally baffling. Though they
might have uneasy stirrings when they read Jessica Benjamin. 'Erotic domination,'
especially when coupled with 'porno newsstands,' does call some feelings into
play almost no matter who you are in this culture.

But I will concede the point. What is personal is completely a function of what
is perceived as personal. And what is perceived as personal by men, or rather,
what is gripping, significant, 'juicy,' is different from what is felt to be that way
by women. For what we are really talking about is not the personal as such, what
we are talking about is what is important, answers one's needs, strikes one as immediately *interesting*. For women, the personal is such a category.

In literary criticism, we have moved from the New Criticism, which was anti-
personal and declared the personal off-limits at every turn—the intentional fallacy, the affective fallacy—to structuralism, which does away with the self
altogether—at least as something unique and important to consider—to
deconstruction, which subsumes everything in language and makes the self non-
self-consistent, ungraspable, a floating signifier, and finally to new historicism
which re-institutes the discourse of the object—'In the seventeenth century'—
with occasional side glances at how the author's 'situatedness' affects his writing.

The female subject *par excellence*, which is her self and her experiences, has
once more been elided by literary criticism.

The question is, why did this happen? One might have imagined a different
outcome. The 1960s paved the way for a new personalism in literary discourse
by opening literary discussion up to politics, to psychology, to the 'reader,' to the
effects of style. What happened to deflect criticism into the impersonal labyrinths
of 'language,' 'discourse,' 'system,' 'network,' and now, with Guattari, 'machine'?

I met Ellen Messer-Davidow last summer at the School of Criticism and Theory
where she was the undoubted leader of the women who were there. She organized them, led them (I might as well say us, since, although I was on the faculty as a visiting lecturer, she led me, too). At the end of the summer we put on
a symposium, a kind of teach-in on feminist criticism and theory, of which none
was being offered that summer. I thought it really worked. Some people, eager
to advertise their intellectual superiority, murmured disappointment at the 'level'
of discussion (code for, 'my mind is finer and more rigorous than yours'). One
person who spoke out at the closing session said he felt bulldozed: a more honest and useful response. The point is that Ellen's leadership affected the experience of everyone at the School that summer. What she offered was not an
intellectual performance calculated to draw attention to the quality of her mind,
but a sustained effort of practical courage that changed the situation we were in.
I think that the kind of thing Ellen did should be included in our concept of
criticism: analysis that is not an end in itself but pressure brought to bear on a
situation.

Now it's time to talk about something that's central to everything I've been
saying so far, although it doesn't *show*, as we used to say about the slips we used
to wear. If I had to bet on it I would say that Ellen Messer-Davidow was

motivated last summer, and probably in her essay, by anger (forgive me, Ellen, if I am wrong) anger at her, our, exclusion from what was being studied at the School, our exclusion from the discourse of 'Western man.' I interpret her behavior this way because anger is what fuels my engagement with feminist issues; an absolute fury that has never even been tapped, relatively speaking. It's time to talk about this now, because it's so central, at least for me. I hate men for the way they treat women, and pretending that women aren't there is one of the ways I hate most.

Last night I saw a movie called *Gunfight at the OK Corral*, starring Burt Lancaster and Kirk Douglas. The movie is patently about the love-relationship between the characters these men play—Wyatt Earp and Doc Holliday. The women in the movie are merely pawns that serve in various ways to reflect the characters of the men, and to advance the story of their relationship to one another. There is a particularly humiliating part, played by Jo Van Fleet, the part of Doc Holliday's mistress—Kate Fisher—whom he treats abominably (everybody in the movie acknowledges this, it's not just me saying so). This woman is degraded over and over again. She is a whore, she is a drunkard, she is a clinging woman, she betrays the life of Wyatt Earp in order to get Doc Holliday back, she is *no longer young* (perhaps this is her chief sin). And her words are always in vain, they are chaff, less than nothing, another sign of her degradation.

Now Doc Holliday is a similarly degraded character. He used to be a dentist and is now a gambler, who lives to get other people's money away from them; he is a drunk, and he abuses the woman who loves him. But his weaknesses, in the perspective of the movie, are glamorous. He is irresistible, charming, seductive, handsome, witty, commanding; it's no wonder Wyatt Earp falls for him, who wouldn't? The degradation doesn't stick to Kirk Douglas; it is all absorbed by his female counterpart, the 'slut,' Jo Van Fleet. We are embarrassed every time she appears on the screen, because every time, she is humiliated further.

What enrages me is the way women are used as extensions of men, mirrors of men, devices for showing men off, devices for helping men get what they want. They are never there in their own right, or rarely. The world of the Western contains no women.

Sometimes I think *the world* contains no women.

Why am I so angry?

My anger is partly the result of having been an only child who caved in to authority very early on. As a result I've built up a huge storehouse of hatred and resentment against people in authority over me (mostly male). Hatred and resentment and attraction.

Why should poor men be made the object of this old pent-up anger? (Old anger is the best anger, the meanest, the truest, the most intense. Old anger is pure because it's been dislocated from its source for so long, has had the chance to ferment, to feed on itself for so many years, so that it is nothing but anger. All cause, all relation to the outside world, long since sloughed off, withered away. The rage I feel inside me now is the distillation of forty-six years. It has had a long time to simmer, to harden, to become adamantine, a black slab that glows in the dark.)

Are all feminists fueled by such rage? Is the molten lava of millennia of hatred boiling below the surface of every essay, every book, every syllabus, every newsletter, every little magazine? I imagine that I can open the front of my stomach like a door, reach in, and pluck from memory the rooted sorrow, pull it out, root and branch. But where, or rather, who, would I be then? I am attached to this rage. It is a source of identity for me. It is a motivator, an explainer, a justifier, a no-need-to-say-more greeter at the door. If I were to eradicate this anger somehow, what would I do? Volunteer work all day long?

A therapist once suggested to me that I blamed on sexism a lot of stuff that really had to do with my own childhood. Her view was basically the one articulated in Alice Miller's *The Drama of the Gifted Child*, in which the good child has been made to develop a false self by parents who cathect the child narcissistically. My therapist meant that if I worked out some of my problems—as she understood them, on a psychological level—my feminist rage would subside.

Maybe it would, but that wouldn't touch the issue of female oppression. Here is what Miller says about this:

> Political action can be fed by the unconscious anger of children who have been . . . misused, imprisoned, exploited, cramped, and drilled. . . . If, however, disillusionment and the resultant mourning can be lived through. . . . then social and political disengagement do not usually follow, but the patient's actions are freed from the compulsion to repeat. (p. 101)

According to Miller's theory, the critical voice inside me, the voice I noticed butting in, belittling, doubting, being wise, is 'the contemptuous introject.' The introjection of authorities who manipulated me, without necessarily meaning to. I think that if you can come to terms with your 'contemptuous introjects,' learn to forgive and understand them, your anger will go away. But if you're not angry, can you still act? Will you still care enough to write the letters, make the phone calls, attend the meetings? You need to find another center within yourself from which to act. A center of outgoing, outflowing, giving feelings. Love instead of anger. I'm embarrassed to say words like this because I've been taught they are mushy and sentimental and smack of cheap popular psychology. I've been taught to look down on people who read M. Scott Peck and Leo Buscaglia and Harold Kushner, because they're people who haven't very much education, and because they're mostly women. Or if not women, then people who take responsibility for learning how to deal with their feelings, who take responsibility for marriages that are going bad, for children who are in trouble, for friends who need help, for themselves. The disdain for popular psychology and for words like 'love' and 'giving' is part of the police action that academic intellectuals wage ceaselessly against feeling, against women, against what is personal. The ridiculing of the 'touchy-feely,' of the 'Mickey Mouse,' of the sentimental (often associated with teaching that takes students' concerns into account), belongs to the tradition Alison Jaggar rightly characterized as founding knowledge in the denial of emotion. It is looking down on women, with whom feelings are associated, and on the activities with which women are identified: mother, nurse, teacher, social worker, volunteer.

So for a while I can't talk about epistemology. I can't deal with the philosophical bases of feminist literary criticisms. I can't strap myself psychically into an apparatus that will produce the right gestures when I begin to move. I have to deal with the trashing of emotion, and with my anger against it.

This one time I've taken off the straitjacket, and it feels so good.

NOTE

Parts of this essay are reprinted from *New Literary History* 19 (Autumn 1987), by kind permission.

WORKS CITED

Benjamin, Jessica 1983. 'Master and Slave: the Fantasy of Erotic Domination,' in *The Powers of Desire: The Politics of Sexuality*, ed. Ann Snitow, Christine Stansell, and Sharon Thompson. New York: Monthly Review Press: 280–9.

Bloom, Harold 1976. *Poetry and Repression: Revision from Blake to Stevens*. New Haven, Conn.: Yale University Press.

Foucault, Michel 1980. *The History of Sexuality, Volume I: An Introduction*. Trans. Robert Hurley. New York: Vintage Books. Copyright 1978 by Random House, Inc. [Originally published in French as *La Volonté de savoir*. Paris: Éditions Gaillimard, 1976.]

Griffin, Susan 1982. 'The way of all ideology,' in *Made from the Earth: an Anthology of Writings*. New York: Harper and Row: 161–82.

Guattari, Félix 1984. *Molecular Revolution: Psychiatry and Politics*. Trans. Rosemary Sheed, intro. David Cooper. New York: Penguin Books. [First published as *Psychanalyse et transversalité* (1972), and *La Révolution moléculaire* (1977).]

Hawthorne, Nathaniel 1960–1. *The Scarlet Letter and Other Tales of the Puritans*. Ed. with an intro. and notes by Harry Levin. Boston, Mass.: Houghton Mifflin Co.

LeGuin, Ursula 1986. 'The Mother Tongue,' *Bryn Mawr Alumnae Bulletin* (Summer): 3–4.

Miller, Alice 1983. *The Drama of the Gifted Child*. New York: Basic Books.

MAXINE HONG KINGSTON'S WOMAN WARRIOR

filiality and woman's autobiographical storytelling

(1 9 8 7)

〜〜〜〜〜〜〜〜〜〜〜〜〜〜〜〜〜〜〜〜〜〜〜〜〜〜〜〜〜

> It is hard to write about my own mother. Whatever I do write, it is
> my story I am telling, my version of the past. If she were to tell her
> own story other landscapes would be revealed. But in my landscape
> or hers, there would be old, smoldering patches of deep-burning
> anger.
>
> —ADRIENNE RICH, *OF WOMAN BORN*

Since Harriet Martineau wrote her autobiography in 1856, many hundreds of
women have contributed the story of their lives to the cultural heritage. Writers,
artists, political figures, intellectuals, businesswomen, actors, athletes—all these
and more have marked history in their own way, both as they lived their lives
and as they wrote about them. A tradition so rich and various presents a challenge to the critic of twentieth-century autobiography. There is much to be written about the works; indeed, studies of twentieth-century autobiography are
beginning to emerge. Articles now abound. I do not want to conclude this study
of women's autobiographies without attention to a contemporary work; but I also
realize that there are many choices that would have served my critical purposes.
Nonetheless, for me at least, no single work captures so powerfully the relationship of gender to genre in twentieth-century autobiography as Maxine Hong
Kingston's *Woman Warrior.*

And so it is fitting to conclude this discussion of women's autobiography with
The Woman Warrior: Memoirs of a Girlhood among Ghosts, which is, quite complexly,
an autobiography about women's autobiographical storytelling. A postmodern
work, it exemplifies the potential for works from the marginalized to challenge
the ideology of individualism and with it the ideology of gender. Recognizing the
inextricable relationship between an individual's sense of "self" and the
community's stories of selfhood, Kingston self-consciously reads herself into existence through the stories her culture tells about women. Using autobiography
to create identity, she breaks down the hegemony of formal "autobiography" and
breaks out of the silence that has bound her culturally to discover a resonant voice
of her own. Furthermore, as a work coming from an ethnic subculture, *The Woman
Warrior* offers the occasion to consider the complex imbroglios of cultural fictions
that surround the autobiographer who is engaging two sets of stories: those of the

dominant culture and those of an ethnic subculture with its own traditions, its own unique stories. As a Chinese American from the working class, Kingston brings to her autobiographical project complicating perspectives on the relationship of woman to language and to narrative.

Considered by some a "novel" and by others an "autobiography," the five narratives conjoined under the title *The Woman Warrior* are decidedly five confrontations with the fictions of self-representation and with the autobiographical possibilities embedded in cultural fictions, specifically as they interpenetrate one another in the autobiography a woman would write.[1] For Kingston, then, as for the woman autobiographer generally, the hermeneutics of self-representation can never be divorced from cultural representations of woman that delimit the nature of her access to the word and the articulation of her own desire. Nor can interpretation be divorced from her orientation toward the mother, who, as her point of origin, commands the tenuous negotiation of identity and difference in a drama of filiality that reaches through the daughter's subjectivity to her textual self-authoring.

Preserving the traditions that authorize the old way of life and enable her to reconstitute the circle of the immigrant community amidst an alien environment, Kingston's mother dominates the life, the landscape, and the language of the text as she dominates the subjectivity of the daughter who writes that text. It is Brave Orchid's voice, commanding, as Kingston notes, "great power," that continually reiterates the discourses of the communty in maxims, talk-story, legends, family histories. As the instrument naming filial identities and commanding filial obligations, that voice enforces the authority and legitimacy of the old culture to name and thus control the place of woman within the patrilineage and thereby to establish the erasure of female desire and the denial of female self-representation as the basis on which the perpetuation of patrilineal descent rests. Yet that same voice gives shape to other possibilities, tales of female power and authority that seem to create a space of cultural significance for the daughter; and the very strength and authority of the maternal voice fascinates the daughter because it "speaks" of the power of woman to enunciate her own representations. Hence storytelling becomes the means through which Brave Orchid passes on to her daughter all the complexities of and the ambivalences about both mother's and daughter's identity as woman in patriarchal culture.[2]

Storytelling also becomes the means through which Kingston confronts those complexities and ambivalences. In dialogic engagement with her mother's word, she struggles to constitute the voice of her own subjectivity, to emerge from a past dominated by stories told to her, ones that inscribe the fictional possibilities of female selfhood, into a present articulated by her own storytelling. Her text reveals the intensity of that struggle throughout childhood and adolescence and the persistence of those conflicts inherent in self-authoring well into adulthood; for, not only is that effort the subject in the text; it is also dramatized by the text. In the first two narratives she re-creates the stories about women and their autobiographical possibilities passed on to her by her mother: first the biographical story of no-name aunt, an apparent victim and thus a negative model of female life scripts, and then the legendary chant of the warrior woman Fa Mu Lan, an apparent heroine and positive model. But as she explores their fates, Kingston questions the very basis on which such distinctions are predicated. Uncovering layer by layer the dynamics and the consequences of her mother's interpretations as they resonate with the memories of her past, the daughter, as she too passes them on to posterity, circles around them, critiquing them, making them her own. Next she reconstructs out of the autobiographical fragments of Brave Orchid's own Chinese experience a biography of her mother, discovering by the way the efficacies of powerful storytelling for the woman who has fallen in status with her translation to another culture. In the fourth piece, an elaborate fabrication played on actual events, she becomes even more keenly attentive to all autobiographical and biographical representations, including her own. Looking back to the beginnings of her own struggle to take a voice, she traces in the final narrative the origins of her own hermeneutics. The apparent line of progress, which as it ends returns us to the beginning, becomes effectively a circle of sorts, a textual alternative to the constricting patriarchal circle Kingston has had to transgress.

"'You must not tell anyone,' my mother said, 'what I am about to tell you. In China your father had a sister who killed herself. She jumped into the family well. We say that your father has all brothers because it is as if she had never been born.'"[3] With that interdiction of female speech, uttered in the name of the father, Kingston's mother succinctly elaborates the circumstances of the sister's suicide. The concise maternal narrative concludes with forceful injunctions and powerful maxims inscribing the filial obligations of daughters in the patriarchal order: "'Don't let your father know that I told you. He denies her. Now that you have started to menstruate, what happened to her could happen to you. Don't humiliate us. You wouldn't like to be forgotten as if you had never been born. The villagers are watchful'" (5). Kingston thus situates the origins of her autobiography in her recollection of the story her mother used to contextualize the moment of transition ineradicably marking female identity and desire. That event, as it proclaims woman's sexual potency, proclaims also woman's problematic placement within the body social, economic, politic, and symbolic.[4] While her body, the locus of patrilineal preservation, will be contracted out to male authority to serve as the carrier of legitimate sons and of the order those sons perpetuate, it will always remain a potential source of disruption and disintegration in the community: It may provide no sons for the line of descent; or it may entertain strangers and thus introduce illegitimate children and an alternative genealogy into the order.[5] Should a daughter opt for the latter (unfilial) alternative, warns the mother, the patriarchal order will work efficiently to punish her transgression of the contract, eliminating her body and name from the world of things and of discourse. Kingston's aunt has suffered this fate: Her family, like the villagers, has enacted its own cleansing ritual; and Kingston's mother has perpetuated the ritual in the very way she tells the story. The aunt's name remains unuttered; and her interpretation of events is sacrificed, within the mother's text, to concern for the villagers' actions. Only her body assumes significance as it reveals the sign of its transgression, as it plugs up the family well.

   The mother's cautionary tale at once affirms and seeks to cut off the daughter's kinship with a transgressive female relative and her unrepressed sexuality.[6] Kingston acknowledges the effectiveness of that strategy by revealing later in the narrative that for a long time she accepted her mother's interpretation and kept her counsel, thereby colluding in the perpetuation of both her own silencing and the erasure of her aunt's name:

> I have believed that sex was unspeakable and words so strong and fathers so frail that "aunt" would do my father mysterious harm. I have thought that my family, having settled among immigrants who had also been their neighbors in the ancestral land, needed to clean their name, and a wrong word would incite the kinspeople even here. But there is more to this silence: they want me to participate in her punishment. And I have. (18)

Now, however, at the moment of autobiographical writing, Kingston resists identification with mother and father by breaking the silence, returning to the story that marked her entrance into sexual difference and constituting her own interpretation of events. She comes to tell another story, seeking to name the formerly unnamed—the subjectivity of her aunt. As she does so, she imagines her aunt in a series of postures toward that excess of sexuality signified by the growth of her womb. Initially dismissing the probability that "people who hatch their own chicks and eat embryos and the heads for delicacies and boil the feet in vinegar for party food, leaving only the gravel, eating even the gizzard lining— could . . . engender a prodigal aunt" (7), she imagines her aunt the victim of rape, fearful, silent, and vulnerable before her victimizer. But she suspends that narrative line, apparently dissatisfied with its unmitigated emphasis on female powerlessness and will-lessness. Beginning again, Kingston enters her aunt's subjectivity from another perspective, preferring to see her as a willful woman after "subtle enjoyment." Contemplating this posture, she finds herself increasingly aware of the gaps in her mother's tale, which motivate her to ask further questions of the story and to piece together an alternative textual genealogy.[7]

Instead of imagining her aunt as one of "the heavy, deep-rooted women" who "were to maintain the past against the flood, safe for returning" (9), and thus as victim, she imagines her as a woman attuned to "a secret voice, a separate attentiveness" (13), truly transgressive and subversive. The fruit of her womb becomes the mark exposing the priority of her desire for sexuality and autobiographical inscription. Indeed, the expansion of her very body and of her sense of her own authority to define herself ultimately challenges the ontological roots of her culture—"the real"; for publicized female subjectivity points to the fundamental vulnerability of the patrilineage by exposing it as a sustained fiction.[8] The alternative genealogy thus engendered breaks the descent line, subverting the legitimacy of male succession that determines all lines in patriarchy—descent lines, property lines, and lines of texts.[9] "The frightened villagers, who depended on one another to maintain the real," writes Kingston, "went to my aunt to show her a personal, physical representation of the break she had made in the 'roundness.' Misallying couples snapped off the future, which was to be embodied in true offspring. The villagers punished her for acting as if she could have a private life, secret and apart from them" (14).

While her journey across the boundaries that circumscribe the patriarchal order takes the aunt into the unbounded spaces of self-representation, Kingston acknowledges also that this "rare urge west" (9) leads her into the vast spaces of alienation, fearfulness, and death. Expelled from the family circle, her aunt becomes "one of the stars, a bright dot in blackness, without home, without a companion, in eternal cold and silence" (16). While the endless night proposes limitless identities beyond the confining borders of repetitive patriarchal representations, it promotes the "agoraphobia" attending any move beyond the carefully prescribed boundaries of ancestral, familial, and community paradigms of female self-representation. Overwhelmed by the vast spaces of possibility, the aunt returns to the genealogical source, reestablishing her cultural "responsibility" by giving birth in the pigsty—"to fool the jealous, pain-dealing gods, who do not switch piglets" (16)—and then by killing herself and her child—"a child with no descent line would not soften her life but only trail after her, ghostlike, begging her to give it purpose" (17). From one point of view, then, the aunt enacts on her own body and her own alternative genealogical text the punishment of the tribe, fulfilling her filial responsibilities to her circle by eliminating the source of contamination from its center and thereby restoring it to its unbroken configuration. She thus returns to the silence that defines her condition and her identity. From another point of view, however, the aunt's suicide continues her rebellion in a congeries of ways.[10] First, she brings back with her to the center of her natal circle the two loci of greatest pollution in Chinese culture—the moments of birth and death.[11] Second, by jumping back into the circle—the family well—she contaminates, in a recapitulated gesture of disruption, the water that literally and symbolically promises the continuance of patrilineal descent and the symbolic order it nourishes. Third, she takes with her the secret of paternal origins, never revealing the name of the father. Saving the father's face, she paradoxically erases the paternal trace, betraying in yet another way the fundamental fragility of undisputed paternal authority. Finally, by withholding from her natal family the name of the offender whose actions have caused such disgrace, she denies them the means to recover face by enacting their own revenge on the violator.[12] Thus, while she seems to capitulate before the monolithic power of the order against which she has transgressed, Kingston envisions her as a "spite suicide," an antiheroine whose actions subvert the stability of an order that rests on the moral imperatives of filial obligations, including sexual repression. Her very silence becomes a powerful presence, a female weapon of vengeance. Toward the end of this imaginative portrait, Kingston returns once again to her mother's tale by repeating the earlier refrain: "'Don't tell anyone you had an aunt. Your father does not want to hear her name. She has never been born'" (18). Yet while Kingston repeats her mother's words, she does so with a critical difference. Unlike her mother, she engenders a story for her aunt, fleshing out the narrative and incorporating the subjectivity previously denied that woman. Individualizing her mother's cautionary and impersonal tale, she transforms in the process both her aunt's text and her aunt's body from a maxim (a mere vessel to hold patriarchal signifiers) into a "life." Moreover, she ensures that she herself becomes more than a mere vessel preserving her mother's maxims, however deeply they may be embedded in her consciousness. For the story of this "forerunner," her "urge west" and her agoraphobia, becomes a piece in the puzzle of her own erased and erasable identity: "Unless I see her life branching into mine, she gives me no ancestral help" (10). And so, the filiations of her own story stretch backward to her aunt's, and the filiations of her aunt's story stretch forward to her own, as the two lives interpenetrate, crossing narrative boundaries in the text as Kingston interweaves her childhood experiences in the immigrant community encircling her with the imaginative biography of her aunt.

Kingston retrieves her aunt from the oblivion of sexuality repressed and textuality erased by placing her in an alternative narrative: the line of matrilineal descent to which she traces her origins and through which she gives voice to her subjectivity. Like her aunt's before her, this transgression of the injunction to filial silence challenges the priority of patrilineal descent. Allowing her imagination to give voice to the body of her aunt's text, Kingston expresses in her own way the excess of narrative (textuality) that links her intimately to that earlier excess of sexuality she identifies in her aunt. Indeed, her aunt becomes her textual "child," product of the fictions through which Kingston gives "birth" to her, and, by the way, to herself. Her story thus functions as a sign, like her aunt's enlarging belly, publicizing the potentially disruptive force of female textuality and the matrilineal descent of texts.

On the level of her mother's tale, then, the originating story of Kingston's autobiography testifies to the power of the patriarchy to command through mothers the silence of daughters, to name and to unname them, and thereby to control their meaning in discourse itself. On another level the opening piece displaces the mother's myth with the daughter's, thereby subverting the interpretations on which patrilineal descent and filial responsibilities are predicated and establishing a space in which female desire and self-representation can emerge. Yet Kingston concludes with a word of caution:

> My aunt haunts me—her ghost drawn to me because now, after fifty years of neglect, I alone devote pages of paper to her, though not origamied into houses and clothes. I do not think she always means me well. I am telling on her, and she was a spite suicide, drowning herself in the drinking water. The Chinese are always very frightened of the drowned one, whose weeping ghost, wet hair hanging and skin bloated, waits silently by the water to pull down a substitute. (19)

As the final sentence suggests, the identification may not be fortuitous, for autobiographical journeys and public self-representations are problematic adventures for daughters to pursue. Kingston does not yet know her aunt's name; and the subjectivity she has created for her remains only another interpretation, a fiction. Nor, by implication, can she be sure that she will ever know the truth about her own past. Her name is never uttered in the text; and her memories and stories may only be fictions too. This maternal trace, disruptive of the patriarchal order, may be potentially as threatening to Kingston as it was to her aunt. Indeed, she may be the child—"it was probably a girl; there is some hope of forgiveness for boys" (18)—that her aunt takes with her to the grave. Ultimately, the full, the "real" story of woman may lead to madness and to self-destruction rather than to legitimate self-representation.

Kingston in the second piece engages another of her mother's representations of female autobiography, a story from which she learned that Chinese girls "failed if we grew up to be but wives and slaves." Here she does not distinguish in quotation marks the words of her mother; rather, she moves directly to her own elaboration of Fa Mu Lan's chant.[13] But she goes further, appropriating not only the chant but also the very body of that legendary woman warrior: The identities of *Woman Warrior* and of woman narrator interpenetrate until biography becomes autobiography, until Kingston and Fa Mu Lan are one.[14] Through this fantasy of mythic identification, the adult daughter inscribes an autobiography of "perfect filiality" through which she fulfills her mother's expectations and garners her mother's unqualified love. Simultaneously, this "life" enables her to escape confinement in conventional female scripts and to enter the realm of heroic masculine pursuits—of education, adventure, public accomplishment, and fame. Ironically, however, Kingston's mythical autobiography betrays the ontological bases on which that love, power, and compliance with perfect filiality rest.

The woman warrior gains her education beyond the engendered circle of community and family in a magical, otherworldly place where male and female difference remains undelineated. Her educators are a hermaphroditic couple beyond childbearing age whose relationship appears to be one of relative equality; and the education they offer encourages her to forge an identity, not through conventional formulations of woman's selfhood, but through a close identification with the creatures of nature and the secrets of natural space.[15] In such a space female sexuality, signaled by the onslaught of puberty, remains a "natural" event rather than a cultural phenomenon situating the girl in a constellation of attitudes toward female pollution and contamination. Nonetheless, that education, while it appears to be liberating, presupposes Fa Mu Lan's total identification with the desires of her family, ubiquitously present even in its absence. For instance, she passively watches in the gourd as her own wedding ceremony takes place despite her absence, the choice of husband entirely her parents' prerogative. Ultimately, woman can be trained as warrior only in a space separate from family; but she can enter that space only because her sacrifice to the circle is the basis on which her education takes place at all. Consequently, her empowerment does not threaten to disrupt the representations of the patriarchal circle; on the contrary, it serves both the family and the discourse of gender.

When she returns home, Fa Mu Lan takes her place, not as "woman," but as extraordinary woman—as, that is, man: "My parents killed a chicken and steamed it whole, as if they were welcoming home a son" (40). As surrogate son, she replaces her father in battle, eventually freeing her community from the exploitation and terrorization of the barons. Yet she must do more than enact the scenario of male selfhood. She must erase her sexual difference and publicly represent herself as male, a "female avenger" masquerading in men's clothes and hair styles. And while her sexual desire is not repressed altogether, as in the case of the virginal Joan of Arc to whom Kingston alludes, it must remain publicly unacknowledged. Hidden inside her armor and her tent, her "body" remains suppressed in the larger community.[16] It also bears the marks of her textual and sexual appropriation by man: "Now when I was naked, I was a strange human being indeed—words carved on my back and the baby large in front" (47). The lines of text on her back are not her own creation: They are the words by which the father has inscribed his law on her body, wounding her in the process. And her belly is full of a male heir whose birth will ensure the continuance of the patrilineage she serves in her heroism.[17] Finally, and most telling, the narrative's closure asserts the ultimate limitations of the warrior woman's autobiographical possibilities. Fa Mu Lan's story breaks roughly into two parts: the narratives of preparation and public action. It thus reinscribes the traditional structure of androcentric self-representation, driven by a linear-causal progression. Once the revenge carved on her back has been enacted, however, both her life as woman warrior and her autobiography end. Having returned home to unmask herself and to be recuperated as publicly silenced wife and slave, she kneels before her parents-in-law: "'Now my public duties are finished. . . . I will stay with you, doing farmwork and housework, and giving you more sons'" (53–54). There is nothing more to be said by her and of her.

Fa Mu Lan's name, unlike the name of no-name aunt, is passed on from generation to generation, precisely because the lines of her story as woman warrior and the lines of her text as woman autobiographer reproduce an androcentric paradigm of identity and selfhood and thereby serve the symbolic order in "perfect filiality." Since both life and text mask her sexual difference and thereby secure her recuperation in the phallic order by inscribing her subjectivity and her selfhood in the law of the same representation, they legitimate the very structures man creates to define himself, including those structures that silence women.[18]

The heroic figure of Fa Mu Lan thus represents a certain kind of woman warrior, a culturally privileged "female avenger." Embedded in Kingston's fantasy autobiography, however, lies a truly subversive "story" of female empowerment. Imaged as tiny, foot-bound, squeaky-voiced women dependent on male authority for their continued existence, the wives of warriors, barons, and emperors who haunt the interstices of the textual landscape are, in one sense, conventional ghosts. Yet those apparently erased ciphers become, in another sense, the real female avengers:

> Later, it would be said, they turned into the band of swordswomen who were a mercenary army. They did not wear men's clothes like me, but rode as women in black and red dresses. They bought up girl babies so that many poor families welcomed their visitations. When slave girls and daughters-in-law ran away, people would say they joined these witch amazons. They killed men and boys. I myself never encountered such women and could not vouch for their reality. (53)

Such "witch amazons" are figures of all that is unrepressed and violent in ways both sexual and textual, in the narrator herself as well as in the social order. Wielding unauthorized power, they do not avenge the wrongs of fathers and brothers; they lead daughters against fathers and sons, slaying the source of the phallic order itself.[19] Moreover, they do so, not by masking, but by aggressively revealing their sexual difference. Paradoxically, Fa Mu Lan has liberated the women who subvert the order she serves, just as Kingston the narrator has released the rumor that subverts the story she tells.

Kingston's memories of the real, rather than mythical, childhood also subvert the fiction she has created out of her mother's expectations. Juxtaposing to this autobiography of androcentric selfhood another self-representation that undermines the priority of the fantasy of "perfect filiality," Kingston betrays Fa Mu Lan's story as a fragile fiction only coterminous with the words that inscribe it as myth. And the jarring texture of her recollected experience—its nervous, disjointed, unpoetic, frustrated prose—calls into question the basis for the seamless elegance and almost mystical lyricism of Fa Mu Lan's poetic autobiography.

Kingston recalls the repetition of commonplace maxims that deny female significance ("Feeding girls is feeding cowbirds"; "When you raise girls, you're raising children for strangers"; "Girls are maggots in the rice"); the pressures of a language that conflates the ideographs representing the female "I" and "slave"; the images "of poor people snagging their neighbors' flotage with long flood hooks and pushing the girl babies on down the river" (62). All these signs and stories of her culture equate her identity as "girl" with failed filiality and engender in her a profound sense of vulnerability and lack. Thus she remembers how she tried to fulfill her filial obligations in the only way imaginable to her: She works at being a "bad" girl—for, as she asks, "Isn't a bad girl almost a boy?" (56). She rejects the traditional occupations of femininity: refusing to cook, breaking dishes, screaming impolitely as maxims are mouthed, defiantly telling her parents' friends that she wants to become a lumberjack, bringing home straight As, those signs from another culture of her extraordinary public achievements. She adopts, that is, the cultural postures of a "son" by generating signs imitative of male selfhood. But her efforts to be the phallic woman do not earn the love and acceptance of her mother and community, as they do Fa Mu Lan. And so her experience gives the lie to that other autobiography: Everywhere the legend is betrayed as a misleading fiction.[20]

In the end, there remains only one residual locus of identity between Kingston and Fa Mu Lan: "What we have in common are the words at our backs. The ideographs for revenge are 'report a crime' and 'report to five families.' The reporting is the vengeance—not the beheading, not the gutting, but the words. And I have so many words—'chink' words and 'gook' words too—that they do not fit on my skin" (63). Her appropriation of the pen, that surrogate sword, and her public inscription of the story of her own childhood among ghosts become the reporting of a crime—the crime of a culture that would make nothing of her by colonizing her and, in so doing, steal her authority and her autobiography from her as her mother's legend would do. In the tale the forces of exploitation remain external to her family; but in her own experience they remain internal, endemic to the patriarchal family whose existence is founded on the colonization and erasure of women in service to the selfhood of men and boys and whose perpetuation is secured through the mother's word. By simultaneously enacting and critiquing that legendary story of female power, Kingston manages to shatter the complacencies of cultural myths, problematic heroines, and the illusory autobiographical possibilities they sanction. By "slaying" the stories of men and boys and phallic women warriors, she allies herself with the true female avengers of her tale. Fa Mu Lan may have denied her identity with such women; Kingston does not.

Whereas the first two narratives explore the consequences of Kingston's appropriation of her mother's stories, the third goes through the stories to the storyteller herself. Three scrolls from China serve as the originating locus of this biography of her mother pieced together with "autobiographical" fragments. Texts that legitimate her mother's professional identity as doctor, the scrolls stimulate biography because they announce public achievements, a life text readable by culture. They also announce to the daughter another mother, a mythic figure resident in China who resisted the erasure of her own desire and who pursued her own signifying selfhood. In her daughter's text, Brave Orchid becomes a kind of "woman warrior," whose story resonates with the Fa Mu Lan legend: both women leave the circle of the family to be educated for their mission and both return to serve their community, freeing it through many adventures from those forces that would destroy it. Both are fearless, successful, admired.

Kingston's biography accretes all varieties of evidence testifying to her mother's bravery and extraordinariness. Portrayed as one of the "new women, scientists who changed the rituals" (88), Brave Orchid bears the "horizontal name of one generation" that truly names her rather than the patronym signifying woman's identity as cipher silently bonding the patrilineage. Thus Kingston's awe-filled narration of her mother's confrontation with the Sitting Ghost takes on such synecdochic proportions in the text: "My mother may have been afraid, but she would be a dragoness ('my totem, your totem'). She could make herself not weak. During danger she fanned out her dragon claws and riffled her red sequin scales and unfolded her coiling green stripes. Danger was a good time for showing off. Like the dragons living in temple eaves, my mother looked down on plain people who were lonely and afraid" (79). The ensuing battle between woman and ghost unfolds as a primal struggle with the dynamics and the rhythms of an attempted rape. A physically powerless victim of the palpably masculine presence who "rolled over her and landed bodily on her chest" (81), Brave Orchid is initially unable to challenge his strength. But she ultimately prevails against the Boulder, defeating him with the boldness of her word and the power of the images she voices to taunt him into submission and cowardice. Such fearlessness and verbal cunning characterize subsequent adventures the daughter invokes: the coexistence with ghosts and strange monsters populating the countryside through which she travels on her way to administer to the sick; the bargain she drives with the slave dealer; her response to the birth of monster babies; and her bold orientation toward food.[21]

Embedded in the daughter's representation of her mother's extraordinariness, however, lies another, a palimpsest that tells of her mother's preoccupation with autobiographical interpretation. Even more important than the story of Brave Orchid's confrontation with the Sitting Ghost is the re-creation of her narrative of the encounter. Skillful in creating compelling stories of her experience, Brave Orchid makes of the ghost a vividly ominous antagonist, thereby authoring herself as powerful protagonist. Such imaging ensures the emboldening of her presence in the eyes and imaginations of the other women (and of her daughter): "'I am brave and good. Also I have bodily strength and control. Good people do not lose to ghosts'" (86). Kingston also suggests that her mother secured the same admiration in other ways. By studying in secret, "she quickly built a reputation for being brilliant, a natural scholar who could glance at a book and know it" (75). Returning to her village, she "wore a silk robe and western shoes with big heels"; thereafter she maintained that posture by never dressing "less elegantly than when she stepped out of the sedan chair" (90). By avoiding treatment of the terminally ill, she ensured that her powers as doctor were magnified. In linguistic and behavioral postures, Brave Orchid orchestrates her public image, inscribes, that is, her own autobiography as extraordinary woman.

The mother's mode of self-authoring complicates the daughter's effort to reconstruct her mother's biography. Brave Orchid's stories about China become the only archival material out of which Kingston can create that "life"; and yet the stories are already "representations" or "fictions" of her experiences before she reaches an America where she is no doctor, where she works daily washing other people's laundry or picking fruit and vegetables in the fields, where she is no longer woman alone but a wife and mother, where she is no woman warrior dressed elegantly in silk. "You have no idea how much I have fallen" (90), she confesses and therein suggests the efficacy of stories and storytelling as means to preserve her extraordinariness. Significantly, the dynamics of the mother's fate recall those of Fa Mu Lan's: Adventures concluded, both return to the home of the husband as wife and slave, there to become the subject of wonderful tales of an earlier glory in a faraway place.

Kingston's narrative, as it interpenetrates her autobiography with her mother's biography, reveals how problematic such stories can become for the next generation. From one point of view, they can be exhilarating, creating in children the admiration that is so apparent in Kingston's text. But from another, they generate confusions and ambiguities, since as a child Kingston inflected the narratives with her own subjectivity, attending to another story within the text of female heroism. For Brave Orchid's tales of bravery and exoticism are underwritten by an alternative text of female vulnerability and victimization. The story elaborating the purchase of the slave girl reaffirms the servile status of women and actually gives legitimacy to Kingston's fears her parents will sell her when they return to China. The stories of babies identify femaleness with deformity and suggest to the daughter the haunting possibility that her mother might actually have practiced female infanticide. The story of the crazy lady, scurrying directionless on bound feet, encased in the mirror-studded headdress, caught in her own self-destructive capitulations, dramatizes communal fear of the anomalous woman who embodies the threat of uncontrolled female sexuality and subversive alliances between women—always strangers within the community—and the enemy outside.

All these tales from her mother's past, by reinforcing the representation of women as expendable, resonate with Kingston's sense of displacement in her family and in the immigrant community in America, her confusion about her sexuality, and her fears of her own "deformities" and "madnesses." They leave her with food that suffocates her, a voice that squeaks on her, and nightmares that haunt the long nights of childhood. They also complicate Kingston's sense of identification with her mother by betraying the basis on which her tales of extraordinariness are founded, that is, the powerlessness of ordinary women and children and their cruel and insensitive victimization, even at the hands of Brave Orchid herself. In fact, in her self-representation Kingston identifies herself with the "lonely and afraid," a victim of her mother's stories, and thus no true heroine after her mother's model. Paradoxically, her mother, the shaman with the power of word and food, has, instead of inspiring her daughter to health and heroism, made the daughter, sick, hungry, vulnerable, fearful.

In the closing passage of this third narrative, Kingston re-creates her most recent encounter with her mother and, through it, her continuing resistance to her mother's victimizing presence. Ironically, the scene recapitulates the earlier scene of her mother's biography. The dark bedroom, the late hour recall the haunted room at the medical school. Here Brave Orchid is herself the ghost who would continue to haunt her daughter: "My mother would sometimes be a large animal, barely real in the dark; then she would become a mother again" (118). Like Brave Orchid before her, Kingston grasps the only weapon effective in overcoming that ghost—the words with which she resists her. In the syncopated rhythm of statement and rebuttal, she answers her mother's vision of things with her own, challenging unremittingly the power of her mother to control interpretations. She also offers an alternative representation of her mother in this closing scene, portraying her as an old woman, tired, prosaic, lonely, a woman whose illusions of returning to China have vanished, whose stories have become peevish, repetitious. In creating a portrait of her mother as neither fearless nor exotic, the daughter demystifies Brave Orchid's presence and diffuses the power of her word.

For all the apparent rejection of her mother as ghost, the final passage points to a locus of identification between mother and daughter and a momentary rapprochement between the two. In saying goodnight, Kingston's mother calls her Little Dog, a name of endearment unuttered for many years, and, in that gesture of affection, releases her daughter to be who she will. As a result, Kingston experiences the freedom to identify with her; for, as the daughter makes evident in her biography, her mother before her had strayed from filial obligations, leaving her parents behind in pursuit of her own desire: "I am really a Dragon, as she is a Dragon, both of us born in dragon years. I am practically a first daughter of a first daughter" (127). At this moment of closure, Kingston affectionately traces her genealogy as woman and writer to and through her mother in a sincere gesture of filiality, acknowledging as she does so that her autobiography cannot be inscribed outside the biography of her mother, just as the biography of her mother cannot be inscribed outside her own interpretations. Mother and daughter are allied in the interpenetration of stories and storytelling, an alliance captured in the ambiguous reference of the final sentence: "She sends me on my way, working always and now old, dreaming the dreams about shrinking babies and the sky covered with airplanes and a Chinatown bigger than the ones here" (127). As the motifs of the final pages suggest, both mother and daughter are working always and now old.

In the fourth narrative Kingston does not take the word of her mother as her point of narrative origin. She will reveal at the inception of the next piece that the only information she received about the events narrated in the fourth piece came from her brother through her sister in the form of an abrupt, spare bone of a story: "What my brother actually said was, 'I drove Mom and Second Aunt to Los Angeles to see Aunt's husband who's got the other wife'" (189). Out of a single factual sentence, Kingston creates a complex story of the two sisters, Brave Orchid and Moon Orchid. She admits that "his version of the story may be better than mine because of its bareness, not twisted into designs" (189); but the "designs" to which she alludes have become integral to her autobiographical interpretations.

In Kingston's designs Moon Orchid, like Brave Orchid in "Shaman," embodies her name: She is a flower of the moon, a decorative satellite that revolves around and takes its definition from another body, the absent husband. Mute to her own desire, attendant always on the word of her husband she represents the traditional Chinese wife, a woman without autobiographical possibilities. "For thirty years," comments her niece, "she had been receiving money from him from America. But she had never told him that she wanted to come to the United States. She waited for him to suggest it, but he never did" (144). Unlike Brave Orchid, she is neither clever nor shrewd, skilled nor quick, sturdy nor lasting. Demure, self-effacing, decorative, tidy, refined—she is as gracefully useless and as elegantly civilized as bound feet, as decoratively insubstantial as the paper cut-outs she brings her nieces and nephews from the old country. Having little sub-jectivity of her own, she can only appropriate as her own the subjectivity of others, spending her days following nieces and nephews through the house, de-scribing what they do, repeating what they say, asking what their words mean. While there is something delightfully childlike, curious, and naive about that nar-ration of other people's lives, there is a more profound sadness that a woman in her sixties, unformed and infantile, has no autobiography of her own.

When her husband rejects her, giving his allegiance to his Chinese American wife, who can speak English and aid him in his work, he denies the very onto-logical basis on which Moon Orchid's selfhood is predicated and effectually erases her from the lines of descent. He also undermines with his negation of her role what autobiographical representations she has managed to create for herself. "'You became people in a book I read a long time ago'" (179), he tells the two sisters, dramatically betraying the elusiveness of the "fictions" on which Moon Orchid has sustained her identity as first wife. Once having been turned into a fairy-tale figure from a long time past, this woman loses the core of her subjec-tivity and literally begins to vanish: She appears "small in the corner of the seat" (174); she stops speaking because the grounds for her authority to speak have been undermined—"All she did was open and shut her mouth without any words coming out" (176); later she stops eating, returning to Brave Orchid's home "shrunken to the bone." Ultimately, she vanishes into a world of madness where she creates repetitive fictions, variations on a story about vanishing without a trace. Thus she fantasizes that Mexican "ghosts" are plotting to snatch her life from her, that "'they' would take us in airplanes and fly us to Washington, D.C., where they'd turn us into ashes . . . drop the ashes in the wind, leaving no evi-dence" (184). The tenuousness, evanescence, and elusiveness of identity press on her so that everywhere she sees signs (sees, that is, evidence of the legitimacy of her own interpretations) that alien males threaten to erase her from the world, leaving no trace of her body as her husband has left no trace of her patrilineal existence. To protect herself she withdraws into the "house" of her sister, that edifice that has supported her construction of an identity as first wife. There she literally makes of the house what it has always been metaphorically—a living coffin—windows shut and darkened, "no air, no light," and she makes of storytelling itself a living coffin. As Brave Orchid tells her children, "'The differ-ence between mad people and sane people . . . is that sane people have variety when they talk-story. Mad people have only one story that they talk over and over'" (184). Only after Brave Orchid commits her to a mental institution does she find a new fiction to replace the old one, a renewed identity as "mother" to the other women ("daughters") who can never vanish. In the end the story of vanishing without leaving a trace becomes the only trace that is left of her, an impoverished autobiographical absence.

Her mother Kingston now represents, not as the "new woman" of "Shaman," but as a traditional woman intent on preserving her family from harm by main-taining the old traditions against the erosions of American culture. Through the conventions of speaking (Chinese), eating, greeting, chanting, storytelling, she keeps China drawn around her family in a linguistic and gustatory circle. More particularly, she seeks to preserve the old family constellation and, with it, the identity of woman. Thus, from Brave Orchid's "Chinese" perspective, her sister is a first wife, entitled to certain privileges and rights, even in America. Yet, in her allegiance to the old traditions of filial and affinal obligations, Brave Orchid becomes shortsighted, insensitive, and destructive. She succeeds only in making other women (her niece, who remains trapped in a loveless marriage; her sister, who dies in a mental institution) unhappy, sick, even mad; and she does so be-cause, failing to anticipate just how misplaced the traditions and myths have be-come in the new world, she trusts her word too well. The stories she tells create illusions that fail of reference to any reality.

The story of the Empress of the Western Palace is a case in point. "'A long time ago,'" Brave Orchid tells her sister on the drive to Los Angeles,

> "the emperors had four wives, one at each point of the compass, and they lived in four palaces. The Empress of the West would connive for power, but the Empress of the East was good and kind and full of light. You are the Em-press of the East, and the Empress of the West has imprisoned the Earth's Emperor in the Western Palace. And you, the good Empress of the East, come out of the dawn to invade her land and free the Emperor. You must break the strong spell she has cast on him that has lost him the East." (166)

The myth, however, is an inappropriate text through which to interpret Moon Orchid's experience. The Empress of the West is not conniving; the Emperor does not want freeing; and the Empress of the East cannot break the spell. More-over, for all Brave Orchid's forceful narratives of the projected meeting among Moon Orchid, the husband, and the second wife, the actual scene is pitifully hu-morous, squeezed as it is in the backseat of the car. "'What scenes I could make'" (146), she tells her sister; but the only scenes she makes are in her fantasies of them (and her daughter the storyteller is the one who actually makes the scene). Though she is not entirely speechless when they confront Moon Orchid's hus-band, she is obviously awed by the wealthy, successful, and much younger man, and by the pressure of his young, efficient wife. Kingston creates a Brave Orchid bested in the game of fictionalizations. The husband has turned the two sisters into characters from a book read long ago, a devastating recapitulation of their efforts to turn him into the fictional Emperor. While the power of her myths to help define and situate identities has been eroded by another cultural tradition, Brave Orchid herself has not been destroyed because, unlike Moon Orchid, she is willful, hardworking, clever, intelligent, shrewd, stubborn, "brave"—all those qualities that have enabled her to cope with and to survive in her translation to another cultural landscape. Moreover, she can always fabricate another story, as she does when she urges her children to sabotage any plans her husband, now in his seventies, might have to marry a second wife. Nonetheless, other women are victimized by her words, their autobiographical possibilities cut off.

Through the "designs" in "At the Western Palace," Kingston confronts explic-itly the problematics of autobiographical "fictions." Both Moon Orchid and Brave

Orchid serve as powerful negative models for the perils of autobiography. Moon Orchid, bereft of the husband who defines her place and who sets the limits of her subjectivity within the structures of the patrilineage, succumbs to an imagination anchored in no-place, an imaginative rootlessness threatening Kingston herself. Overwhelmed by repetitious fantasies, her aunt vanishes into a world where alien males continually plot to erase her from existence, a preoccupation that resonates with Kingston's childhood fears of leaving no culturally significant autobiographical trace. A woman of no autobiography, Moon Orchid cannot find a voice of her own, or, rather, the only subjectivity that she finally voices is the subjectivity of madness. Brave Orchid, too, serves as a powerful negative model. She would write a certain biography of her sister, patterned after traditional interpretations of the identity of a first wife. In preserving her interpretations, however, she victimizes other women by failing to make a space in her story for female subjectivity in unfamiliar landscapes, by remaining insensitive to her sister's fears and desires, as she remains insensitive to her daughter's desires. Giving her unquestioning allegiance to language, she fails to recognize the danger in words, the perils inherent in the fictions that bind.

In the end Kingston, too, has created only a fiction, an elaborate story out of the one sentence passed by her brother through her sister; and she, too, must beware the danger in words as she constructs her stories of those other women, more particularly her mother. To a certain extent she seems to do so in this fourth narrative. For all the negative, even horrifying, aspects of Brave Orchid's fierce preservation and Moon Orchid's repetitious fantasies, both women come across in this section as fully human. Her mother, especially, does so; and that is because, releasing her mother to be her own character, under her own name "Brave Orchid," rather than as "my mother," the daughter penetrates her mother's subjectivity with tender ironies and gentle mercies. In doing so, she effaces her own presence in the text as character, her presence implied only in the reference to Brave Orchid's "children." Unlike her mother, then, who does not imagine the contours of her sister's subjectivity, Kingston here tries to think like her mother and her aunt. Yet even as she creates the fullness of her mother out of her word, she recognizes the very fictionality of her tale—its "designs" that serve her own hermeneutical purposes. She, too, like her mother within her story, negotiates the world by means of the fictions that sustain interpretations and preserve identities. In the persistent reciprocities that characterize Kingston's storytelling, her mother becomes the product of her fictions, as she has been the product of her mother's.

Kingston represents in the final piece, "A Song for a Barbarian Reed Pipe," her adolescent struggle to discover her own speaking voice and autobiographical authority. This drama originates in the memory of her mother's literally cutting the voice out of her: "She pushed my tongue up and sliced the frenum. Or maybe she snipped it with a pair of nail scissors. I don't remember her doing it, only her telling me about it, but all during childhood I felt sorry for the baby whose mother waited with scissors or knife in hand for it to cry—and then, when its mouth was wide open like a baby bird's, cut" (190). Notably, Kingston remembers, not the actual event, but the reconstruction of the event in language, a phenomenon testifying to the power of the mother's word to constitute the daughter's history, in this case her continuing sense of confusion, horror, deprivation, and violation. Her mother passes on a tale of female castration, a rite of passage analogous to a clitoridectomy, that wounding of the female body in service to the community, performed and thereby perpetuated by the mother.[22] It is a ritual that results in the denial to woman of the pleasure of giving voice to her body and body to her voice, the pleasure of autobiographical legitimacy and authority.

In her re-creation of the confrontation with the Chinese American girl in the bathroom of the Chinese school, Kingston evokes her childhood confusion about speechlessness: "Most of us," she comments, "eventually found some voice, however faltering. We invented an American-feminine speaking personality, except for that one girl who could not speak up even in Chinese school" (200). A kind of surrogate home, the Chinese school functions as the repository of old traditions and conventional identities within the immigrant community; and the bathroom is that most private of female spaces—only for girls, only for certain activities, which, as it locates the elimination of matter from the body, ultimately becomes associated with female pollution and shame. In that space, Kingston responds cruelly, even violently, to the female image before her, abhorring the girl's useless fragility: her neat, pastel clothes; her China-doll haircut; her tiny, white teeth; her baby-soft, fleshy skin—"like squid out of which the glassy blades of bones had been pulled," "like tracing paper, onion paper" (206). Most of all, she abhors her "dumbness," for this girl, who cannot even speak her name aloud, is ultimately without body or text. "'You're such a nothing,'" Kingston remembers yelling at her. "'You are a plant. Do you know that? That's all you are if you don't talk. If you don't talk, you can't have a personality. You'll have no personality and no hair. You've got to let, people know you have a personality and a brain. You think somebody is going to take care of you all your stupid life?'" (210).

Yet, while the girl stands mute before the screaming Kingston, they both weep profusely, wiping their snot on their sleeves as the seemingly frozen scene wraps them both in its embrace. Kingston remembers feeling some comfort in establishing her difference from the girl, taking pride in her dirty fingernails, calloused hands, yellow teeth, her desire to wear black. But the fierceness with which she articulates her desire for difference only accentuates her actual identity with the nameless girl: Both are the last ones chosen by teams; both are silent and "dumb" in the American school. An exaggerated representation of the perfect Chinese girl, this girl becomes a mirror image of Kingston herself, reflecting her own fears of insubstantiality and dumbness (symbolized for her in the zero intelligence quotient that marks her first-grade record). In the pulling of the hair, the poking of the flesh, Kingston captures the violence of her childhood insecurity and self-hatred. Striking the Chinese American girl, she strikes violently at her own failure to take a voice and at all her mother's prior narratives of female voicelessness. Tellingly, her aggressive attack on that mirror image eventuates, not in the girl's utterance of her name, but in Kingston's eighteen-month illness, which ensures that she indeed does become like the other girl. Confined to bed, isolated inside the house, she is literally silenced in the public space, a fragile and useless girl. Attended always by her family, she too becomes a plant, a nothing. Ironically, she says of that time: "It was the best year and a half of my life. Nothing happened" (212). The admission betrays the tremendous relief of not having to prove to people she has "a personality and a brain," the powerful enticement of succumbing to the implications of her mother's narratives and her culture's maxims, the confusing attractiveness of not having to find a public voice, of not struggling with shame.

For, as her narrative recollection reveals, taking a voice becomes complicated by her sense of guilt. She is ashamed to speak in public with a voice like those of the immigrant women—loud, inelegant, unsubtle. She is ashamed to speak the words her mother demands she say to the druggist ghost because she considers her mother's words, as they exact compliance with traditional beliefs, to be outdated. She is ashamed to keep the same kind of silences and secrets her mother would keep because such secrets command her duplicity before the teachers she respects. For all these reasons she would not speak like her mother (and Chinese women) in her American environment; but her own efforts to take the appropriate American-feminine voice fail, and that failure too gives her cause for shame. In public her voice becomes "a crippled animal running on broken legs" (196), a duck voice; her throat "cut[s]" off the word; her mouth appears "permanently crooked with effort, turned down on the left side and straight on the right" (199). Her face and vocal cords continue to show the signs of her prior castration, the physical mutilation and discomfort that mark her relationship to language and to any public enunciation of subjectivity.

The landscape of her childhood, as she reconstructs it, reveals the underlying logic in Kingston's failure to overcome her symbolic disability. Seeing around her the humiliating representations of woman, hearing words such as "maggots" become synonyms for "girls," suspecting that her mother seeks to contract her out as the wife and slave of some young man, perhaps even the retarded boy who follows her around with his box full of pornographic pictures, she negotiates a nightmare of female victimization by adopting the postures of an unattractive girl, the better to foil her mother's efforts and to forestall her weary capitulation. Cultivating that autobiographical signature, she represents herself publicly as the obverse of her mother's image of the charming, attractive, practical young girl by becoming clumsy, vulgar, bad-tempered, lazy, impractical, irreverent, and stupid "from reading too much" (226). She becomes, that is, a kind of fiction; and the psychic price she pays for orchestrating such a public posture is high. Publicly appearing as the "dumb" and awkward girl, she does not earn the affection and respect of her family and community. Moreover, she must convince herself of the reality of her mind by constantly attending to the grades she earns in the American school, those signs, unrecognized in her Chinese culture, that signal her access to other discourses. She remains "dumb" in another sense, for she recognizes even in childhood that "talking and not talking made the difference between sanity and insanity," in that "insane people were the ones who couldn't explain themselves" (216). Since she cannot give voice to her subjectivity except by indirection and dissimulation, externalizing in an awkward masquerade the text of publicly unexpressed desires, she finds commonality with the anomalous women such as Pee-A-Nah and Crazy Mary, who retreat into imaginary worlds, there to haunt the outskirts of the immigrant community and the imaginations of its children.

The culmination of this struggle with voice comes when Kingston finally attempts to "explain" her silenced guilts, the text of which lengthens daily, and to represent her repressed desires to her mother, believing that by doing so she will establish some grounds for identification and overcome her profound isolation and dumbness: "If only I could let my mother know the list, she—and the world—would become more like me, and I would never be alone again" (230). Recapitulating the earlier castration, her mother cuts her tongue by refusing to acknowledge the daughter's stories as legitimate: "'I can't stand this whispering,' she said looking right at me, stopping her squeezing. 'Senseless grabbings every night. I wish you would stop. Go away and work. Whispering, whispering, making no sense. Madness. I don't feel like hearing your craziness'" (233). In response, Kingston swallows her words, but only temporarily. The tautness of her vocal cords increasing to a breaking point, she later bursts the silence, uttering in a cathartic moment the text of her inner life before her mother. Finally, this girl takes on a voice, albeit in great confusion, and thereby authors a vision, textualizes her subjectivity, and legitimizes her own desires. She embarks, that is, on the autobiographical enterprise, articulating her interpretations against her mother's.

In this battle of words, mother and daughter, products of different cultural experiences, systems of signs, and modes of interpretation, speak two different "languages" and inscribe two different stories—graphically imaged in the sets of quotation marks that delimit their separate visions and betray the gap in the matrilineage as the circle of identity, of place and desire, is disrupted. Unable to understand the mother, unwilling to identify with her, the daughter would, in ironic reciprocity, cut off her mother's word: "'I don't want to listen to any more of your stories; they have no logic. They scramble me up. You lie with stories. You won't tell me a story and then say, 'This is a true story,' or 'This is just a story'" (235). But her mother's reluctant admission—"'We like to say the opposite'" (237)—forces Kingston to question, at the moment of their origin, her own interpretations and thus the "truth" or "fictiveness" of the autobiography she would inscribe through her memories of the past. As a result, the young Kingston comes to recognize the relativity of truth, the very elusiveness of self-representation that drives the autobiographical enterprise. "Ho Chi Kuai" her mother calls her; and, even to the moment in her adult life when she writes her autobiography, she cannot specify, can only guess, the meaning of the name her mother gave her from that culture she would leave behind. In the end she can only try to decipher the meaning of her past, her subjectivity, her desire, her own name: "I continue to sort out what's just my childhood, just my imagination, just my family, just the village, just movies, just living" (239).

Kingston closes *The Woman Warrior* with a coda, returning it to silence after telling two brief stories, one her mother's, one hers. She starts with the former: "Here is a story my mother told me, not when I was young, but recently, when I told her I also talk-story. The beginning is hers, the ending, mine" (240). Notably, her mother's story is now a gift. Passed from one storyteller to another, it signals the mother's genuine identification with the daughter. Yet the two-part story also functions as a testament to difference, the simple juxtaposition of two words rather than the privileging of one before the other. Here, at last, Kingston lets her mother's word stand without resisting it.

Her mother's story, set in the China of the previous generation, presents Kingston's grandmother as a willful and powerful woman who, convinced "that our family was immune to harm as long as they went to plays" (241), loves to attend theater performances. Unfolding in the ironies of the unexpected, the contingencies of opposites, the absence of linear logic, the story is emblematic of Brave Orchid's individual narrative style and vision, of the kinds of stories she tells. It speaks both of the horrifying vulnerability of women and of their fierce and commanding power; and it tells of the power of art to sustain the continuity of life and the power of interpretations to turn adversity and victimization to triumph. Through her "gift," mother places daughter in the line of powerful "Chinese" women whose source of inspiration and whose very survival in the midst of vulnerability lie in the word of the creative imagination.

Kingston follows her mother's words with what she imagines might be the story on the stage at one of those performances. Turning toward rather than resisting her Chinese roots, she takes as her protagonist a Chinese poet who lived in the second century.[23] Forced to live among barbarians for twelve years, during which time she bears two children who cannot speak Chinese, Ts'ai Yen remains isolated beyond the boundaries that sustain her sense of place and identity. Nonetheless, she eventually discovers that even barbarians make music of life and longing, reflecting civilized, rather than merely primitive, sensibilities. In the midst of cultural difference, the poet finds a commonality of experience and subjectivity through the language of art, which enables her to give voice to her own desire for self-representation and, in doing so, to join the circle of humanity. Eventually, Ts'ai Yen is ransomed, returning to her home "so that her father would have Han descendants" (243); but the more momentous "birth" she contributes to posterity is the song of sadness, anger, and wandering created out of her experience in the alien land. Speaking of human yearning, it "translates well" through the generations and across communal boundaries. Ultimately, the story of Ts'ai Yen, the woman of words, is the tale of Brave Orchid, who finds herself hostage in the barbarian land of America where even her children, born like Ts'ai Yen's among the aliens, cannot "speak" her native language, cannot understand her. Yet the tale is simultaneously that of Kingston herself, whose sense of alienation is doubly complicated, since, as a product of two cultures, she remains outside the circle of both. Mother and daughter sing the songs of sadness, loneliness, and displacement, finding their common sustenance in the word. Thus through her storytelling Kingston can create the total identification of mother and daughter as they both become Ts'ai Yen, woman poet.

In that final juxtaposition of two stories, Kingston asserts the grounds of identification with her mother, affirming continuities rather than disjunctions in the line.[24] She is her mother's daughter, however much she may distance herself geographically and psychologically, learning from her the power and authority that enable her to originate her own storytelling. Carrying on the matrilineal trace, she becomes like her mother a mistress of the word in a culture that would privilege only the lines, textual and genealogical, of patrilineal descent.[25] With her text she gives historical "birth" to Brave Orchid, creating for her a textual space in the genealogical record, and she gives "birth" to herself as the daughter who has passed through the body and the word of the mother.

1136 SIDONIE SMITH

NOTES

1. Albert E. Stone comments that Kingston's autobiography joins others in "this terrain of contemporary autobiography which abuts the continent of fiction" (Albert E. Stone, *Autobiographical Occasions and Original Acts* [Philadelphia: Univ. of Pennsylvania Press, 1982], p. 25).

2. For a review article on recent literature on mothers and daughters, see Marianne Hirsch, "Mothers and Daughters," *Signs: Journal of Women in Culture and Society* 7 (Summer 1981): 200–22. See also Adrienne Rich, *Of Woman Born* (New York: Norton, 1976), esp. ch. 9.

3. Maxine Hong Kingston, *The Woman Warrior: Memoirs of a Girlhood among Ghosts* (New York: Random House, 1977), p. 3. Subsequent citations appear in the text.

4. At this moment the female body, emitting the menstrual flow and promising the subsequent discharge of childbirth portended in the blood, becomes one powerful and primary source of pollution in the community: The blood emitted reaffirms the association of woman with the dangerous powers of life and death, those two events that bring into play the processes of disintegration and integration within the patrilineal group and the forces of disorder and order in the community. See Emily M. Ahern, "The Power and Pollution of Chinese Women," in *Women in Chinese Society*, ed. Margery Wolf and Roxane Witke (Stanford: Stanford University Press, 1975), pp. 193–214. See also Mary Douglas, *Parity and Danger: An Analysis of Concepts of Pollution and Taboo* (New York: Praeger, 1966), esp. pp. 114–28.

5. For a discussion of the subversive power of woman's womb, see Susan Hardy Aiken, "Dinesen's 'Sorrow-acre': Tracing the Woman's Line," *Contemporary Literature* 25 (Summer 1984): 165–71.

6. For a discussion of *The Woman Warrior* with an attention to certain dynamics in the work that is similar to my own, see Paul John Eakin, *Fictions in Autobiography: Studies in the Art of Self-invention* (Princeton: Princeton Univ. Press, 1985), pp. 255–75. As Eakin comments on this first "cautionary" tale, he focuses on the relation of woman to her community. I find Eakin's analysis throughout stimulating. Although we read the work in similar ways, we often give different emphases to the details.

7. Margery Wolf, "Women and Suicide in China," in *Women in Chinese Society*, ed. Wolf and Witke, p. 112. Why, for instance, was this married aunt living with her own parents rather than with her in-laws? And who had been the stranger, or was he a stranger, who had entered her house/womb? Kingston notes that a woman pregnant by someone near to, perhaps even in, her natal family would lay bare the vulnerability of the patrilineage to violations by incest.

8. Aiken, p. 167. See also Gayle Rubin, "The Traffic in Women: Notes on the 'Political Economy' of Sex," in *Toward an Anthropology of Women*, ed. Rayna R. Reiter (New York: Monthly Review Press, 1975), pp. 157–210; and Tony Tanner, *Adultery in the Novel: Contract and Transgression* (Baltimore: Johns Hopkins Univ. Press, 1979), pp. 58–66.

9. See Ahern, pp. 199–202.

10. See Wolf, pp. 113–14.

11. See Ahern, p. 198.

12. See ibid., p. 113.

13. Florence Ayscough, *Chinese Women: Yesterday and Today* (Boston: Houghton Mifflin, 1937), pp. 214–22.

14. Suzanne Juhasz makes this point also in her essay, "Towards a Theory of Form in Feminist Autobiography: Kate Millet's *Flying* and *Sita*; Maxine Hong Kingston's *The Woman Warrior*," in *Women's Autobiography: Essays in Criticism*, ed. Estelle C. Jelinek (Bloomington: Indiana Univ. Press, 1980), p. 234.

15. She does not succumb to the agoraphobia that presses so heavily upon her no-name aunt. Indeed, despite cold and hunger, she prospers in the midst of illimitable space and possibilities.

16. Kingston/Fa Mu Lan recognizes that her very life depends on this successful erasure of her true identity: "Chinese executed women who disguised themselves as soldiers or students, no matter how bravely they fought or how high they scored on the examination" (46). In that way traditional Chinese culture effectively denied women access to the power signified by the sword and the power signified by the surrogate sword, the pen and the knowledge it inscribed.

17. In the original legend Fa Mu Lan remains chaste during her years as the woman warrior. Kingston does make a space in her interpretation and her text for female sexuality, but, as I note above, it remains suppressed in the larger community.

18. Josette Féral, "Antigone or the Irony of the Tribe," *Diacritics* 8 (Fall 1978): 4.

19. The baron whom Kingston/Fa Mu Lan finally slays mistakes her for this kind of warrior. In response to his query about her identity, she tells him she is "a female avenger." His response—"'Oh, come now. Everyone takes the girls when he can. The families are glad to be rid of them'" (51)—suggests that he understands her to be an avenger of the wrongs of woman. Kingston/Fa Mu Lan specifies that the crime she seeks to avenge is, however, his impressment of her brother.

20. Her heroic space is far larger than that which provided the canvas for Fa Mu Lan's adventures: "Nobody in history has conquered and united both North America and Asia" (58). The public gestures of heroism she attempts are not uttered in a dazzling display of swordsmanship but in a self-effacing, tentative, "squeaky" voice that identifies her, not with the woman warrior, but with the "wives and slaves" tucked into the interstices of the mythical narrative. In her modern American space, the martial arts are not the grandiose gestures of heroic action; they are merely exercises "for unsure little boys kicking away under fluorescent lights" (62). Moreover, in Communist China her relatives, instead of being identified with the exploited peasants, are identified as exploiting landowners and punished as the barons in the myth.

21. As the daughter knows, "all heroes are bold toward food" (104). They demonstrate by their gustatory feats their power over the natural world, their high degree of aristocratic cultivation, and their association with the sacred. See Claude Lévi-Strauss, *The Raw and the Cooked*, trans. John and Doreen Weightman (New York: Harper & Row, 1969).

22. See Mary Daly, *Gyn/Ecology: The Metaethics of Radical Feminism* (Boston: Beacon Press, 1978), pp. 153–77.

23. For a brief biography of Ts'ai Yen, see Wu-chi Liu and Irving Yucheng Lo, eds., *Sunflower Splendor: Three Thousand Years of Chinese Poetry* (Garden City: Anchor, 1975), pp. 537–58.

24. For a discussion of the narrative rhythms of identification and differentiation in *The Woman Warrior* and *China Men*, see Suzanne Juhasz, "Maxine Hong Kingston: Narrative Technique and Female Identity," in *Contemporary American Women Writers*, ed. Catherine Rainwater and William J. Scheik (Lexington: Univ. Press of Kentucky, 1985), pp. 173–89.

25. See Aiken, pp. 175–84.

AUTHORIZING THE AUTOBIOGRAPHICAL

(1988)

> I suggest that one could understand the life around which autobiography forms itself in a number of other ways besides the perfectly legitimate one of "individual history and narrative": we can understand it as the vital impulse—the impulse of life—that is transformed by being lived through the *unique medium of the individual and the individual's special, peculiar psychic configuration*; we can understand it as *consciousness, pure and simple, consciousness referring to no objects outside itself, to no events, and to no other lives*; we can understand it as *participation in an absolute existence* far transcending the shifting, changing unrealities of mundane life; we can understand it as the *moral tenor of the individual's being.* Life in all these latter senses does not stretch back across time but extends down to the roots of individual being; *it is atemporal, committed to a vertical thrust from consciousness down into the unconscious rather than to a horizontal thrust from the present into the past.*
>
> JAMES OLNEY, "SOME VERSIONS OF MEMORY" (EMPHASIS ADDED)

In this extended definition of "the life around which autobiography forms itself," James Olney has accounted for nearly all the concerns addressed by the essays in this book. In one way or another each contributor has taken up the issues enumerated here: the assertion that autobiography is "transformed by being lived through the unique medium of the individual"; the assumption that the individual bears a "special, peculiar psychic configuration"; the belief that autobiography represents "consciousness, pure and simple . . . referring to no objects outside itself, to no events, and to no others" and that it transcends "the shifting, changing unrealities of mundane life"; the supposition that "life . . . does not stretch back across time but extends down to the roots of individual being," moving in "a vertical thrust from consciousness down into the unconscious rather than to a horizontal thrust from the present to the past." These essays take up such premises in order to revise them, to rethink the very coincidence of "ontology" and "autobiography." That each of these premises should prove an "issue" in the essays that follow derives, I think, from the primary contexts of their writing—the concerns with gender, race, class, and historical and political conditions in the theory and practice of women's autobiographical writings.

How does writing mediate the space between "self" and "life" that the autobiography would traverse and transgress? One definition of autobiography suggests that it is an effort to recapture the self—in Hegel's claim, to know the self through "consciousness" (Gusdorf 38). Such a claim presumes that there is such a thing as the "self" and that it is "knowable." This coming-to-knowledge of the self constitutes both the desire that initiates the autobiographical act and the goal toward which autobiography directs itself. By means of writing, such desire presumably can be fulfilled. Thus the place to begin our investigation of autobiography might be at the crossroads of "writing" and "selfhood."[1]

INITIATING AUTOBIOGRAPHY

> The autobiographical perspective has . . . to do with taking oneself up and bringing oneself to language.
> —JANET VARNER GUNN, *AUTOBIOGRAPHY*

If the autobiographical moment prepares for a meeting of "writing" and "selfhood," a coming together of method and subject matter, this destiny—like the retrospective glance that presumably initiates autobiography—is always deferred. Autobiography reveals gaps, and not only gaps in time and space or between the individual and the social, but also a widening divergence between the manner and matter of its discourse. That is, autobiography reveals the impossibility of its own dream: what begins on the presumption of self-knowledge ends in the creation of a fiction that covers over the premises of its construction. Georges Gusdorf has argued that "the appearance of autobiography implies a new spiritual revolution: the artist and model coincide, the historian tackles himself as object" (31). But in point of fact, the "coincidence" of artist and model is an illusion. As Jacques Lacan has noted, the "mirror stage" of psychic development that initiates the child into the social community and brings it under the law of the Symbolic (the law of language as constituted through society) serves up a false image of the child's unified "self." This unity is imposed from the outside (in the mirror reflection) and is in Ellie Ragland-Sullivan's words, "asymmetrical, fictional, and artificial." As Ragland-Sullivan continues, the "mirror stage must, therefore, be understood as a metaphor for the vision of harmony of a subject essentially in discord" (26–27). The "discord" that gives the lie to a unified, identifiable, coterminous self has been built up out of the images, sounds, and sensory responses available to the child during the first six months or so of its life; it is called the unconscious, or that which derives from an experience of "self" as fragmented, partial, segmented, and different. The developing child drives toward fusion and homogeneity in the construction of a "self" (the *moi* of Lacan's terminology) against the effects of division and dissolution. The unconscious is thus not the lower depths of the conscious (as in Olney's description of it) but rather an inner seam, a space between "inside" and "outside"—it is the space of difference, the gap that the drive toward unity of self can never entirely close. It is also the space of writing, which bears the marks and registers the alienating effects of the false symmetry of the mirror stage.

[Here I bracket some considerations about a developing self with particular reference to divisions between the soma and psyche and to mirrors.

In Virginia Woolf's "A Sketch of the Past," her effort at writing her own memoirs, she comments at length on her relation to mirrors, remembering crucial events from her childhood in which mirrors played some part:

> There was a small looking-glass in the hall at Talland House. It had, I remember, a ledge with a brush on it. By standing on tiptoe I could see my face in the glass. When I was six or seven perhaps, I got into the habit of looking at my face in the glass. But I only did this if I was sure that I was alone. I was ashamed of it. A strong feeling of guilt seemed naturally attached to it. (*Moments of Being* 67–68)

Woolf lists various reasons for this shame—that she and Vanessa were "tomboys" and that "to have been found looking in the glass would have been against our tomboy code" (68); or that she inherited "a streak of the puritan," which made her feel shame at self-regard or narcissistic behavior. From a readerly perspective, neither of these reasons seems adequate to the kind of shame she clearly felt before the looking glass, a shame that lasted her entire life. Further on in this memoir, she continues her commentary on female beauty: "My mother's beauty, Stella's beauty, gave me as early as I can remember, pride and pleasure" (68). She declares that her "natural love for beauty was checked by some ancestral dread," then clarifies and qualifies her perceptions: "Yet this did not prevent me from feeling ecstasies and raptures spontaneously and intensely and without any shame or the least sense of guilt, so long as they *were disconnected with my own body*" (68; emphasis added).

Slowly, as though with dread, Woolf comes to "another element in the shame which I had in being caught looking at myself in the glass in the hall" (68). She declares that she was "ashamed or afraid" of her own body. The memory of the hallway with its looking glass is overlaid by another memory of that same hallway, a scene that may well have been reflected for her in the very looking glass of which she speaks. This memory is of George Duckworth raising her onto the slab outside the dining room and "there he began to explore my body":

> I can remember the feel of his hand going under my clothes; going firmly and steadily lower and lower. I remember how I hoped that he would stop; how I stiffened and wriggled as his hand approached my private parts. But it did not stop. His hand explored my private parts too. I remember resenting, disliking it—what is the word for so dumb and mixed a feeling? It must have been strong, since I still recall it. This seems to show that a feeling about certain parts of the body; how they must not be touched; how it is wrong to allow them to be touched; must be instinctive. (69)

Sexual abuse adds itself to the shame of looking at the face in the mirror. Or perhaps sexual abuse actually preceded the shame of looking in the glass. Woolf's memories, we shall see, do not announce their sequence; their timing always contradicts the logical sequence of conscious thought and action, escaping the dating of calendars and clocks. In recounting the scene with George Duckworth, Woolf does not claim to have discovered the reason for her shame at looking at her own face, she admits to having "only been able to discover some possible reasons; there may be others; I do not suppose that I have got at the truth; yet this is a simple incident; and it happened to me personally; and I have no motive for lying about it" (69). The layers of conscious recall and justification overlap each other, their movement inexorably marked by the semicolons of these clauses that march her back to the moment in the hallway, just as her circuitous "tunnel-ing" method of finding her way back to the past had brought her to the scene with George Duckworth from another direction—from the reflection of her own face in the mirror.

Woolf has one more comment on the "mirror stage" of her own sexual and psy-chic development:

> Let me add a dream; for it may refer to the incident of the looking-glass. I dreamt that I was looking in a glass when a horrible face—the face of an ani-mal—suddenly showed over my shoulder. I cannot be sure if this was a dream, or if it happened. Was I looking in the glass one day when something in the background moved, and seemed to me alive? I cannot be sure. But I have always remembered the other face in the glass, whether it was a dream or a fact, and that it frightened me. (69)

Two things presumably occur at the mirror stage: a realization (even if it cannot yet be verbalized) of wholeness, completeness, in an image that contradicts the intuited understanding that the child is still fragmented, uncoordinated, and not yet experiencing bodily reactions through a kind of psychic "wholeness"; and a shock of awareness that the image (which may be seen not in a mirror, but rather in a parent's or a sibling's face) is that of an *other*—someone or something unlike and unconnected to the infant. The mirror stage marks a differentiation that is potentially frightening, a moment that cannot be recaptured through memory as such, a moment that hangs in a space that is neither dream nor fact, but both. The mirror stage marks both the exceptional and the common; it is a stage com-mon to us all, but within our experience—and this experience exists outside and beyond memory—this stage marks us as exceptional, differentiated. What should be communicated in this moment is a wholeness, an integration that is present in the image but not yet apparent in experience. For Woolf such an experience—really an aftershock of trauma—recorded both differentiation and a psychic/so-matic split. A mysterious, frightening, unknown shame clouds the mirror; the other face in the mirror marks dread.]

In a definition of the autobiographical act that strikingly recapitulates the ef-fects of Lacan's mirror stage, Georges Gusdorf has written: "Autobiography . . . requires a man to take a distance with regard to himself in order to reconstitute himself in the focus of his special unity and identity across time" (35). The ef-fect of such a distancing and reconstituting is precisely the effect of the mirror stage: a recognition of the alienating force within the specular (the "regard") that leads to the desperate shoring-up of the reflected image against disintegration and division. What is reinforced in this effort is the *moi*, the ego; what is pushed aside (or driven into the darkened realms of the repressed) is the split in the sub-ject (who both "is" and "is not" the reflected image) that language effects and cannot deny. Man enforces a "unity and identity across time" by "reconstitut-ing" the ego as a bulwark against disintegration; that is, man denies the very ef-fects of having internalized the alienating world order. One such "denial" is autobiography itself, at least as it is defined by Gusdorf, who would place random reflections on self and society, such as diaries, journals, and letters, in a category separate from (and prior to—the sources for) the *self-conscious* autobiography in which the writer "calls himself as witness for himself" (29).

For Gusdorf, autobiography "is the mirror in which the individual reflects his own image" (33); in such a mirror the "self" and the "reflection" coincide. But this definition of autobiography overlooks what might be the most interesting aspect of the autobiographical; the measure to which "self" and "self-image" might not coincide, can never coincide in language—not because certain forms of self-writing are not self-conscious enough but because they have no investment in creating a cohesive self over time. Indeed, they seem to exploit difference and change over sameness and identity: their writing follows the "seam" of the conscious/unconscious where boundaries between internal and external overlap. Such writing puts into question the whole notion of "genre" as outlined by the exclusionary methods of Gusdorf's rather narrow definition of the autobiographical. And it is not surprising that the question of "genre" often rides on the question of gender.[2]

Psychic health is measured in the degree to which the "self" is constructed in separateness, the boundaries between "self" and "other" carefully circumscribed. From a Gusdorfian perspective, autobiography is a re-erecting of these psychic walls, the building of a linguistic fortress between the autobiographical subject and his interested readers: "The autobiography that is thus devoted exclusively to the defence and glorification of a man, a career, a political cause, or a skillful strategy . . . is limited almost entirely to the public sector of existence" (36). Gusdorf acknowledges that "the question changes utterly when the private face of existence assumes more importance" (37), but he suggests that "the writer who recalls his earliest years is thus exploring an enchanted realm that belongs to him alone" (37). In either kind of autobiography, the writing subject is the one presumed to *know* (himself), and this process of knowing is a process of differentiating himself from others.[3] The chain-link fence that circumscribes his unique contributions is language, representative of the very laws to which this writing subject has been subjected; that is, language is neither an external force nor a "tool" of expression, but the very symbolic system that both constructs and is constructed by the writing subject. As such, language is both internal and external, and the walls that defend the *moi* are never an entirely adequate defense network against the multiple forms of the *je*.

If the linguistic defense networks of male autobiographers more successfully keep at bay the discordant *je*, it may be because female autobiographers are more aware of their "otherness." Like men, we are subjected to the phallic law, but our experience of its social and political effects comes under the terms of another law—that of gender. Ragland-Sullivan comments that "the early mother is internalized as the source of one's own narcissism, prior to the acquisition of individual boundaries, while the father's subsequent, symbolic role is that of teaching these boundaries—he is a limit-setter. As a result, the father is later both feared and emulated, since his presence has taught the infant about laws and taboos" (42). Language itself, as Lacan has shown, is a defense against unconscious knowledge (179). But it is not an altogether successful defense network, punctuated as it is by messages from the unconscious, messages that attempt to defeat this "fencing-off" mechanism; indeed, there is no clearly defined barrier between the conscious and the unconscious. Fenced in by language, the speaking subject is primordially divided.[4]

This division is apparent as well in writing, and especially in autobiographical writing. Denial of the division on the part of some theoreticians of autobiography, however, is itself a symptom of autobiographical writing—a repeated but untranslated, unconscious message. This message is directed at the culture from the position of the Other, by those who occupy positions of internal exclusion within the culture—that is, by women, blacks, Jews, homosexuals, and others who exist on the margins of society. A frequent spokesperson for those who have been denied full rights within the society on the grounds of gender, Virginia Woolf also questioned the limits of genre, with particular regard to autobiography. In 1919, at age thirty-seven, she was particularly concerned with these issues, thinking to what use she might put her diary and at what point in her life she would begin writing her memoirs. She begins by suggesting that "this diary does not count as writing, since I have just re-read my year's diary and am much struck by the rapid haphazard gallop at which it swings along, sometimes indeed jerking almost intolerably over the cobbles" (20 January 1919). But the next sentence justifies this fast-paced method as preserving that which "if I stopped and took thought . . . would never be written at all," that which "sweeps up accidentally several stray matters which I would exclude if I hesitated, but which are the diamonds of the dustheap." Thinking of her future self at age fifty, Woolf conjures up on the diary page an image of herself, wearing reading glasses, poring over the pages of the past in preparation for the writing of her memoirs. Many years later, when Woolf was fifty-eight, she placed her memoir writing even further in the future, commenting in her diary: "I may as well make a note I say to myself: thinking sometimes who's going to read all this scribble? I think one day I may brew a tiny ingot out of it—in my memoirs" (19 February 1940). The "brewing" method would seem to be reductive—to eliminate the dross and save the gold.

Woolf did not live to write her memoirs, and the bulk of the autobiographical Virginia Woolf exists in her diary and letters, forms whose generic boundaries she extended and reconstructed. The diary, for instance, was constantly reexamined as a cultural artifact, as a living presence, as a necessary exercise for her fatigued mind, as a secret place (she found it impossible to write in it, for instance, if anyone else were in the room). She used the diary to pose theoretical and practical questions of writing, a place where the very definitions of writing might be reexamined:

> There looms ahead of me the shadow of some kind of form which a diary might attain to. I might in the course of time learn what it is that one can make of this *loose, drifting material of life*; finding another use for it than the use I put it to, so much more consciously and scrupulously, in fiction. What sort of diary should I like mine to be? Something loose knit and yet not slovenly, *so elastic that it will embrace anything, solemn, slight or beautiful that comes into my mind*. I should like it *to resemble some deep old desk, or capacious hold-all*, in which one flings a mass of odds and ends without looking them through. I should like to come back, after a year or two, and *find that the collection had sorted itself and refined itself and coalesced*, as such deposits so mysteriously do, into a mould, transparent enough to reflect the light of our life, and yet steady,

> tranquil compounds with the aloofness of a work of art. The main requisite, I think on re-reading my old volumes, *is not to play the part of censor*, but to write as the mood comes or of anything whatever; since I was curious to find how I went for things put in haphazard, and found the significance to lie *where I never saw it at the time*. (20 April 1919; emphasis added)

Setting aside momentarily the question of what Woolf might have done with the materials she later rediscovered in the "hold-all" of the diary, we can readily see that her efforts at defining the diary's form in the broadest terms possible ("so elastic that it will embrace anything, solemn, slight or beautiful that comes into my mind") and assigning the sorting, refining, and coalescing of such deposits into "a mould, transparent enough to reflect the light of our life," radically redefine the whole autobiographical project. Woolf does not conceive of such an undertaking in terms that Augustine, Rousseau, Montaigne, Proust, or Sir Leslie Stephen would recognize. She removes herself—that is, herself conceived as a censor—from this enterprise, discredits the notion of "self-consciousness"—indeed, she argues for the importance of the thoughtless, the loose, the unrestrained, the unconscious, and refrains from all efforts to shape, sort, or subordinate this material to her will. She rather systematically cuts out from under herself the props that hold up her authority as an *author*, turning authority back to the matter that constitutes her "subject"—and that subject is not necessarily the "self" of traditional autobiography. Woolf gives power to conscious artifice through fiction, a creation that also bears a relation to the "loose, drifting material of life." But for the purposes of memoir writing, she wishes to conceive of a different form and purpose—a conception that is infinitely deferred, as her own death puts an end to the project. That such a project would have followed the unconscious, would have followed the seam of writing itself, is undeniable, as the sections from *Moments of Being* discussed in the second part of this essay demonstrate.

> It took me a year's groping to discover what I call my tunnelling process, by which I tell the past by installments as I have need of it. This is my prime discovery so far; and the fact that I've been so long finding it proves, I think, how false Percy Lubbock's doctrine is—that you can do this sort of thing consciously. (*Diary*, 15 October 1923)

Later she comments, "as far as I know, as a writer I am only now writing out my mind" (20 March 1926), in a turn of phrase that suggests multiple relations between "mind" and "writing." In 1933, she notes "how tremendously important unconsciousness is when one writes" (29 October 1933). Such commentaries on the workings of the mind ally themselves with others that address questions of narrative method and artistic systems. On 25 September 1929, she writes in the diary: "Yesterday morning I made another start on *The Moths* [later retitled *The Waves*] . . . and several problems cry out at once to be solved. Who thinks it? And am I outside the thinker? One wants some device which is not a trick." And on 2 October 1932, in an entirely different context, she writes in irritation at reading D. H. Lawrence's published letters of what she calls his "preaching" and "systematizing": "His ruler coming down and measuring them. Why all this criticism of other people? Why not some system that includes the good? What a discovery that would be—a system that did not shut out." The relation of the conscious to the unconscious, of the mind to writing, of the inside to the outside of political and narrative systems, indicate not only a problematizing of social and literary conventions—a questioning of the Symbolic law—but also the need to reconceptualize form itself.

In other words, where does one place the "I" of the autobiographical account? Where does the Subject locate itself? In definitions of autobiography that stress self-disclosure and narrative account, that posit a self called to witness (as an authority) to "his" own being, that propose a double referent for the first-person narrative (the present "I" and the past "I"), or that conceive of autobiography as "recapitulation and recall" (Olney 252), the Subject is made an Object of investigation (the first-person actually masks the third person) and is further divided between the present moment of the narration and the past on which the narration is focused. These gaps in the temporal and spatial dimensions of the text itself are often successfully hidden from reader and writer, so that the fabric of the narrative appears seamless, spun of whole cloth. The effect is magical—the self appears organic, the present the sum total of the past, the past an accurate predictor of the future. This conception of the autobiographical rests on a firm belief in the *conscious* control of artist over subject matter; this view of the life history is grounded in authority. It is perhaps not surprising that those who cling to such a definition are those whose assignment under the Symbolic law is to *represent* authority, to represent the phallic power that drives inexorably toward unity, identity, sameness. And it is not surprising that those who question such authority are those who are expected to submit to it, those who line up on the other side of the sexual divide—that is, women.[5] The self that would reside at the center of the text is decentered—and often is absent altogether—in women's autobiographical texts. The very requirements of the genre are put into question by the limits of gender—which is to say, because these two terms are etymologically linked, genre itself raises questions about gender.[6]

FISSURES OF FEMALE DISCONTINUITY

> Alas, my brothers
> Helen did not walk
> upon the ramparts,
> she whom you cursed
> was but the phantom and the shadow thrown
> of a reflection
>
> —H.D., *HELEN IN EGYPT*

How do the fissures of female discontinuity display themselves, and what are their identifying features? On what authority can we ascribe certain forms of discontinuity to the female rather than to the male, assigning them as functions of gender rather than of social class, race, or sexual preference? One might remark that such issues are not raised—either directly or indirectly—by those texts that form the tradition of autobiographical writings in Western culture. The confessions of an Augustine or a Rousseau, the *Autobiography of Thomas Jefferson*, or the

Education of Henry Adams do not admit internal cracks and disjunctures, rifts and ruptures. The whole thrust of such works is to seal up and cover over gaps in memory, dislocations in time and space, insecurities, hesitations, and blind spots. The consciousness behind the narrative "I" develops over time, encompassing more and more of the external landscape and becoming increasingly aware of the implications of action and events, but this consciousness—and the "I" it supports—remains stable. The dissection of self-analysis premises the cohesion of a restructured self. Any hint of the disparate, the disassociated, is overlooked or enfolded into a narrative of synthesis. This "model" of autobiography, a product of the metaphysic that has structured Western thinking since Plato, repeated itself with unsurprising frequency until the early twentieth century—until the advent of what we now term Modernism put into question the organic, unifying principles of artistic creation that had reasserted themselves with such force in the nineteenth century.

The influence of Freud's discovery of the unconscious cannot be discounted in the unsettling of the "I" that had heretofore stood at the center of narrative discourse. (In accounting for this "unsettling" of self-unity, one must also consider the political and social effects of World War I, the advent of industrial mechanization, the loss of belief in God, the fall of colonial empires, and the changing status of women and minorities, all of which altered the cultural landscape against which literature was produced in the early years of the twentieth century. We live today in a world that has been constructed out of these changes; nearly all the changes that discomposed the complacent world of 1910 have been culturally assimilated, except perhaps the full force of Freud's discoveries. Predictably, its effects are most tenaciously resisted precisely where they are most evident: in language—in speech and writing.) The instability of this subject is nowhere more apparent than in women's writing of this period, in texts by Djuna Barnes, Isak Dinesen, H.D., Mina Loy, Anaïs Nin, Jean Rhys, Gertrude Stein, and Virginia Woolf, writing that puts into question the most essential component of the autobiographical—the relation between "self" and "consciousness." The simultaneous exploration of the autobiographical and probing of self-consciousness in works by each of these writers suggests not that they knew their Freud better than T. S. Eliot, James Joyce, Ezra Pound, or W. B. Yeats, but that as women they felt the effects of the psychic reality Freud described more fully than did men. Gender became a determining issue at the point at which culture (broadly defined in both its psychic and social terms) met aesthetic principles.

As I have argued elsewhere, female Modernism challenged the white, male, heterosexual ethic underlying the Modernist aesthetic of "impersonality" (e.g., the transformation of the textual "I" from the personal to the cultural).[7] It is this white, male, heterosexual ethic that poststructuralist critics have exposed behind the facade of a supposedly apolitical artistic practice.[8] Poststructuralism has taught us to read the politics of every element in narrative strategy: representation; tone; perspective; figures of speech; even the shift between first-, second-, and third-person pronouns. In identifying the "fissures of female discontinuity" in a text, for example, we also point toward a relation between the psychic and the political, the personal and the social, in the linguistic fabric.[9]

Although Virginia Woolf did not publish her memoirs, she did leave behind fragments of a memoir collected under the title *Moments of Being*. These five pieces ("Reminiscences," "A Sketch of the Past," and three readings done for the Memoir Club—"22 Hyde Park Gate," "Old Bloomsbury," and "Am I a Snob?") retrace the same material: that portion of her young adulthood between the deaths of her mother in 1895 and her father in 1904. In addition, much of this material is incorporated into two of her novels, *To the Lighthouse* and *The Years*. While the "content" of the fictions and the reminiscences is strikingly similar, the variations of perspective, through a shift of prounouns both between texts and within texts, signal discontinuities. In the memoirs in particular, these discontinuities are striking. They suggest that the entire project is poised over an abyss of selflessness, or, to put it differently, that the entire project is posed on the question of self and its relation to language and storytelling strategies.

She begins with "the first memory" of "red and purple flowers on a black ground—my mother's dress." The flowers, seen close up (she is on her mother's lap), are assumed to be anemones; the conveyance is either a train or an omnibus; the light suggests that it is evening and "we were coming back to London" (*Moments of Being* 64). As soon as this scene is suggested, however, it reverses itself, giving life to a second scene:

> But it is more convenient *artistically* to suppose that we were going to St. Ives, for that will lead to my other memory, which also seems to be my first memory, and in fact it is the most important of all my memories. If life has a base it stands upon, if it is a bowl that one fills and fills and fills—then my bowl without a doubt stands upon this memory. (64; emphasis added)

This second memory diverges both in time and place from the first. Comprised of sound rather than sight, it translates the former memory into a different medium:

> It is of lying half asleep, half awake, in bed at the nursery at St. Ives. It is of hearing the waves breaking, one, two, one, two, and sending a splash of water over the beach; and then breaking, one, two, one, two, behind a yellow blind. It is of hearing the blind draw its little acorn across the floor as the wind blew the blind out. It is of lying and hearing this splash and seeing this light, and feeling, it is almost impossible that I should be here; of feeling the purest ecstasy I can conceive. (64–65)

We know that the unconscious is comprised of just such "memories"—of images and sounds—and that later identity reflects these first sensory experiences.[10] Virginia Woolf's writing is characterized by the recurrence of such experiences; indeed, *The Waves* reflects the images and repeats the rhythms of precisely these two moments: "The sun sharpened the walls of the house, made a blue fingerprint of shadow under the leaf by the bedroom window. The blind stirred slightly, but all within was dim and unsubstantial" (*The Waves* 8). As a writer, Woolf knew how to make such experiences work toward aesthetic coherence; as critics, we know how to read such textual effects, working sound against image to make the metonymic metaphoric. But what is most striking from the "Sketch" itself is not the self-reinforcing aspect of the two memories, but the disparity between them: juxtaposed to each other within the same paragraph, they mark not only different psychic moments, but difference itself. Later in the text Woolf herself comments on this discovery of difference, but not before she has discussed artistic considerations, the place of the self in memoir writing, and the peculiarities of her social education.

The "first memory"—which is not a memory at all, strictly speaking—is displaced by an "other memory, which also seems to be my first memory." This displacement is effected for "artistic convenience," a change that reverses the narrative direction—toward St. Ives rather than toward London. But this change enforces another: although the first memory is conditioned by the light (which seems to be evening), the second memory can be reached by reversing not only the direction of the train but by inverting evening and morning: if they are leaving London for St. Ives, then the scene is lit by morning rather than evening light. Although the second memory is not dependent on light—as its "focus" is sound—the "yellow blind" of the room suggests visibility. The time of day in this second memory is unclear from an initial reading (it could be either morning or evening), and the confusion is cleared up only later, when Woolf apparently realizes the "connection" between the two scenes. Both are occasioned by displacement, and they shadow forth a doubling and displacement of "self."

Having remarked on the "pure ecstasy" that the second memory conveys, Woolf stops the narrative to comment on autobiography itself:

> I could spend hours trying to write that [the scene of the second memory] as it should be written, in order to give the feeling which is even at this moment very strong in me. But I should fail (unless I had some wonderful luck); I dare say I should only succeed in having the luck if I had begun by describing Virginia herself. (65)

The writer's "luck" becomes dependent on conventional literary forms—here the requirement that the autobiographical begin with a description of the central character. Woolf sets aside the evidence that her method, adopted at random, "without stopping to choose my way, in the sure and certain knowledge that it will find itself" (64), has already provided crucial elements not of the *self* but of the elements out of which the unconscious is constructed. She has tapped the unconscious, and the effect has been to split the "subject" that her autobiography struggles to delineate. She has stumbled against "one of the memoir writer's difficulties—one of the reasons why, though I read so many, so many are failures. They leave out the person to whom things happened" (65). At this juncture, "Adeline Virginia Stephen, the second daughter of Leslie and Julia Prinsip Stephen, born on the 25th January 1882" is inserted into the text. But this historical Virginia Stephen is of little help to Virginia Woolf the memoirist, as neither knows how history and lineage "made them," or—more important—"what part of this" history "made me feel what I felt in the nursery at St. Ives." Woolf confesses to not knowing "how far I differ from other people." A crucial factor in this "not knowing" has been her social and educational conditioning: "Owing partly to the fact that I was never at school, never competed in any way with children of my own age, I have never been able to compare my gifts and defects with other people's" (65). Elsewhere—in her diaries and letters, in *A Room of One's Own*, in *Three Guineas*—Virginia Woolf wrote at length, with passion and anger, against the strictures of her Victorian upbringing, against its isolation, against the intellectual and emotional hardships of its expectations for women. Of whatever else this social setting deprived her, its cruelest denial was a community in which she could learn and against which she could measure herself.

Two sentences in this paragraph from "A Sketch of the Past" are linked, and they lead to an explanation for the second memory. The first sentence is the one on which the paragraph is premised ("They [memoirs] leave out the person to whom things happened"); the second is the realization that because of the circumstances of her upbringing Woolf does not know "how far I differ from other people." That is, she has been absent in her own memoir—thus committing the sin of so many memoirs—because she cannot measure her own *difference* from others. And it is precisely this difference, this individuality, on which the traditional memoir premises itself. This problem of difference suggests to Woolf "another memoir writer's difficulty." Unlike others, she has no standard of comparison, and it is this lack that leads to a rationale for the kinds of reminiscences she has already delineated:

> But of course there was one external reason for the intensity of this first impression: the impression of the waves and the acorn on the blind; the feeling, as I describe it sometimes to myself of lying in a grape and seeing through a film of semi-transparent yellow—it was due partly to the many months we spent in London. The *change of nursery was a great change*. And there was the long train journey; and the excitement. I remember the dark; the lights; the stir of the going up to bed. (65; emphasis added)[11]

The memory of the waves at St. Ives is specifically marked here as "this first impression," perhaps blotting out, or at least circumventing, that prior "first memory" of the flowers on the "black ground" of the mother's dress. The explanation for the feeling that results from this impression uses elements from both memories: although the impression of the waves and the acorn on the blind reside in hearing ("It is of hearing the blind draw its little acorn across the floor as the wind blew the blind out"), Woolf's description relies on sight ("the feeling . . . of lying in a grape and seeing through a film of semi-transparent yellow"). The two impressions belong to different sensory orders, and their coincidence (one explained in terms of the other) is the result of "a great change"—a registering of difference between the London and St. Ives nurseries. It is significant that this registration occurs in a section of the text in which individual difference is denied and made the excuse for the failure of memoir writing: "I do not know how far I differ from other people." The "I" in this sentence is absent precisely to the extent that it is doubled ("I . . . I"): selfhood registered in difference from others is demonstrated on *social* grounds to be nonexistent; coexistent selfhood across time and space is shown to be nonexistent even under the auspices of memory. These impressions displace hierarchies (first, second), refuse synthesis, and resist distinctions between external and internal, conscious and unconscious.

In these fragments from what would have become her memoirs, Woolf attempts to come to terms with the notion of "memoirs" itself. She examines carefully the two presumed essential ingredients ("personal history and narrative"), posing difficult theoretical questions through her own autobiographical practice. Despite the claim that the "subject of the memoir" must be central to it—must provide not only the "I" but the "eye" of its telling—she finds it impossible to place

herself in that position. Indeed, she finds it nearly impossible to name herself;
"Adeline Virginia Stephen" was never a name she was known by, and in the late
1930s, when she began constructing her reminiscences, her name—the one by
which she was called and by which she called herself, the name that provided
the signature to her texts, including this one—was something different. The central figure of the early years of her development was her mother, the woman
who—until after the writing of *To the Lighthouse*—"obsessed" Virginia Woolf.

> I could hear her voice, see her, imagine what she would do or say as I went
> about my day's doings. She was one of the invisible presences who after all
> play so important a part in every life. This influence, by which I mean the
> consciousness of other groups impinging upon ourselves; public opinion; what
> other people say and think; all those magnets which attract us this way to be
> like that; or repel us the other and make us different from that; has never
> been analyzed in any of those Lives which I so much enjoy reading, or very
> superficially. (80)

Such "invisible presences" keep "the subject of this memoir" in place, according to Woolf. And it is the question of place—of space—that absorbs the autobiographical writer's attention as much as the proverbial issue of time. The
mother, who occupied "the very centre of that great Cathedral space which was
childhood" (81), becomes an "invisible presence" in Woolf's later life. Indeed, it
is her removal from temporal and spacial existence that provides the central
trauma of Woolf's narrative, an absence over which scar tissue knots this narrative and refuses to let the story unwind itself over the years. Like Gertrude
Stein's obsession with the year 1907 (the year Alice B. Toklas entered her life,
changing its contours and directions), Virginia Woolf's continual return to the
morning of her mother's death, the morning she awoke to news of this loss and
was led to her mother's bedroom to kiss her goodbye, constitutes a symptom of
the writing, or a scab that is picked until it bleeds and forms again. Significantly,
this scene is repeated twice in the memoir fragments, is reconstructed in *The
Years*, and marks the moment of temporal absence ("Time Passes") in *To the Lighthouse*. For Virginia, Julia Stephen was "the creator of that crowded merry world
which spun so gaily in the centre of my childhood. . . . She was the centre; it was
herself. This was proved on May 5, 1895. For after that day there was nothing
left of it" (84).

The centrality of the mother to this lost world of childhood, the nearness of
her presence, prevents Woolf from describing her "in the present" of the past.
All that becomes available are "those descriptions and anecdotes which after she
was dead imposed themselves upon my view of her" (83). That is, the action of
memory has been translated through narrative (description and anecdote), leaving a hole where once there was a center: "Of course she was central. I suspect
the word 'central' gets closest to the general feeling I had of living so completely
in her atmosphere that one never got far enough away from her to see her as a
person" (83). A first memory of this mother centers on the flowers on the black
ground of her dress: "I . . . saw the flowers she was wearing very close" (64). The
point is not that Woolf's mother became an "invisible presence" after her death,
but that she was always an invisible presence—too central, too close, to be observed: "If we cannot analyze these invisible presences, we know very little of

the subject of the memoir; and again how futile life-writing becomes. I see myself as a fish in a stream; deflected; held in place; but cannot describe the stream" (80).

Thus the workings of memory, crucial to the recollection implicit in life writing, are found to be suspect. They slip beyond the borders of the conscious world; they are traversed and transgressed by the unconscious. Every exercise in memory recall that Woolf tries in these autobiographical efforts demonstrates the futility and failure of life writing. What is directly gazed upon in the memory remains absent; what is "revealed" comes by side glances and hints, in the effects of sound, light, smell, touch. Returning to the peculiar power of the "two strong memories" that initiate "A Sketch of the Past," Woolf comments, "I am hardly aware of myself, but only of the sensation. I am only the container of the feeling of ecstasy, of the feeling of rapture" (67). She wonders whether "things we have felt with great intensity have an existence independent of our minds" and whether "some device will be invented by which we can tap them" (67). She believes that "strong emotion must leave its trace" (67). Finding a way to tap these resources, to rediscover these traces, becomes both the overriding desire in her memoir writing and the cause of its failure. She is forced to discount memories: "As an account of my life they are misleading, because the things one does not remember are as important; perhaps they are more important" (69). Woolf attempts to explain away the intellectual difficulties posed by the problem of remembering and not remembering by dividing life into "moments of being" and "moments of non-being." She constructs a tapestry in which there is "hidden a pattern" that connects both the being and nonbeing of everyday life. She tries to find a means by which to include in the "life" that which is excluded in life writing: everything that forms the background of perception and action.

Woolf's effort leads to the construction of a series of metaphors by which to image the relation of present to past, of perception to action, of writing to living. She first builds a platform, a base on which to stand in recollecting the past, and decides to "include the present—at least enough of the present to serve as a platform to stand upon. It would be interesting to make the two people, I now, I then, come out in contrast" (75). There is no intention of reconciling these two people seen from the platform of the present ("I now, I then"). Woolf's project is nothing like the one James Olney describes for Richard Wright in *Black Boy*: "This double-reference 'I' delivers up a twofold *bios*—here and now, there and then, both the perpetual present and the historic past—and it is the tenuous yet tensile thread of memory that joins the two 'I's, that holds together the two *bioi*, and that successfully redeems the time of (and for) Richard Wright" (248).

Redemption and the action of recollection (in the sense of "gathering again") by which it claims to be achieved are shown by Woolf to be the deadly temptations of the autobiographical. On 25 October 1920 she had admitted to her diary the happiness that writing gave her: "and with it all how happy I am—if it weren't for my feeling that it's a strip of pavement over an abyss." Her fictional narratives (all of which could be termed "autobiographical" to some degree) were the strip of pavement over the abyss of self. While these fictions were in some sense a pretense against the primordial split subject (and were created "out of" that split), the memoir posed the question of selfhood directly; it forced Virginia Woolf to look into the abyss—something she could not do. Using a metaphor that explores surface and depth, the "experience" of present and past, along narrative movement, Woolf writes: "The past only comes back when the present runs so smoothly that it is like the sliding surface of a deep river. Then one sees through the surface to the depth" (98). This "sliding surface" is not available to conscious thought and practice; indeed, it demands an *unconsciousness* of the present. The present cannot call attention to itself (the "pavement" or the "platform" of the present must be invisible). That is, "to feel the present sliding over the depths of the past, peace is necessary. The present must be smooth, habitual." Later in the same paragraph, Woolf reverses this process in an effort to restore a "sense of the present": "I write this partly in order to recover my sense of the present by getting the past to shadow this broken surface" (98).

Woolf concludes her contemplation of the autobiographical act and its relation to writing, memory, and self-consciousness by returning to its initial impetus— what she calls "scene-making":

> But, whatever the reason may be, I find that scene-making is my natural way of marking the past. Always a sense of scene has arranged itself; representative; enduring. This confirms me in my instinctive notion: (it will not bear arguing about; it is irrational) the sensation that we are sealed vessels afloat on what is convenient to call reality; and at some moments, the sealing matter cracks; in floods reality; that is, these scenes—for why do they survive undamaged year after year unless they are made of something comparatively permanent? (122)

It is the very admission of "irrationality" that interests here. Woolf views the past not as a "subject matter"—a content as such—but rather as a method, a scene making. Such scenes arrange themselves (much as the matter in the "hold all" composed itself) in moments when the "sealing matter" of identity and selfhood cracks. Unable to argue logically the ontology of autobiography by means of self-consciousness, Woolf moves toward an "instinctive notion" that the "sealed vessel" of selfhood is an artificial construct, that it "cracks" and floods, allowing access to that which in conscious moments is considered wholly separate and different from self—"what it is convenient to call reality."

But Woolf's notion of reality would share little with T.S. Eliot's. Hers is not a shock of recognition in the mirror but rather a linguistic space (a "scene") that conceals—and tries to seal itself against—the gap (the "crack") of the unconscious. Language, which operates according to a principle of division and separation, is the medium by which and through which the "self" is constructed. "Writing the self" is therefore a process of simultaneous sealing and splitting that can only trace fissures of discontinuity. This process may take place through "the individual's special, peculiar psychic configuration," but it is never an act of "consciousness, pure and simple"; it always refers to "objects outside itself, to . . . events, and to . . . other lives"; it always participates in "the shifting, changing unrealities of mundane life"; it is never "atemporal" (Olney 239). There is no grid whose horizontal axis represents a "thrust from the present into the past" and whose vertical axis constitutes a "thrust from consciousness down into the unconscious" (Olney 239). Instead, this scene forms itself as a kind of writing:

> so it seemed to me
> that I had watched

as a careful craftsman,

the pattern shape,
Achilles' history,
that I had seen him like the very scenes

on his famous shield,
outlined with the graver's gold;
true, I had met him, the New Mortal,

baffled and lost,
but I was a phantom Helen
and he was Achilles' ghost.
(*Helen in Egypt*, 262–63)

NOTES

1. Olney's "Some Versions of Memory" examines the *bios* at the center of this word without attention to the terms that enclose it—auto/graphy. In particular, this essay fails to mention that without *graphé* autobiography would not exist—that is, it is known only through the writing.

2. Gusdorf's essay "Conditions and Limits of Autobiography" opens with the declaration: "Autobiography is a solidly established literary genre" (28). James Olney's later essay in the same volume suggests "the impossibility of making any prescriptive definition for autobiography or placing any generic limitations on it at all" (237). Indeed, whether autobiography can be circumscribed within generic definitions is an important issue in autobiography studies. To date, however, there has been no rigorous investigation of the question of genre in relation to autobiography.

It is important to note that for Gusdorf autobiography is a genre that belongs to men, whose public lives it traces. Women are denied entrance to this writing for reasons examined in Susan Friedman's essay in Benstock, ed., *The Private Self*.

3. The "subject presumed to know" is a Lacanian construction belonging not, as one might expect, to the conscious realm of thinking (as "the one consciously in control") but to the unconscious. This subject is "supposed" precisely because the speaking (or writing) subject senses a lack in itself, and supposes, in Ellie Ragland-Sullivan's terms, that "'something' somewhere knows more than he or she. That 'something' furnishes the speaker with the authority for a given opinion" (172). The sense of an internal division, the claim of an authority from "elsewhere" (in the Other residing in the unconscious), problematizes the assigning of authority in the speaking/writing situation. Both meanings of "suppose" are at work here: to believe, especially on uncertain or tentative grounds; to expect or require, to presume.

4. This division cannot be "healed"; identity itself rests in this division, the effects of the working of the unconscious. Ragland-Sullivan comments: "Humans have an unconscious because they speak; animals have no unconscious because they do not speak. Since Lacan views repression and verbal symbolization as concurrent processes, which both mark the end of the mirror stage and create a secondary unconscious, we can look for answers to the self/ontology riddle in the transformational processes that mark repression" (173). For a particularly cogent reading of the effects of this division in women's writing, see Buck.

5. Not only women are included in this group, but all humans who—for whatever reasons—are not seen to represent authority. Psychosexual identity often does not coincide with biological sexuality, and thus male homosexuals fall into this grouping (and female

homosexuals resist its effects), as do all others considered powerless and marginal—blacks, Jews, the economically deprived, and so on.

6. For an exhaustive analysis of the relation of *genre* and gender, see Jacques Derrida, "La Loi du Genre/The Law of Genre," which traces the etymological transferences of the two terms, and my essay "From Letters to Literature," which traces the effects of this law on one literary *genre*.

7. See Benstock, "Beyond the Reaches of Feminist Criticism" and *Women of the Left Bank*; DeKoven, A *Different Language*; DuPlessis, *Writing Beyond the Ending*; Friedman, "Modernism of the Scattered Remnant" and *Psyche Reborn*; Friedman and DuPlessis, "'I Had Two Loves Separate'"; Gubar, "Blessings in Disguise" and "Sapphistries"; Kolodny, "Some Notes on Defining a 'Feminist Literary Criticism'"; Marcus, "Laughing at Leviticus" and "Liberty, Sorority, Misogyny"; and Stimpson, "Gertrice/Altrude."

8. Special reference needs to be made to the work of Roland Barthes, Hélène Cixous, Jacques Derrida, Jacques Lacan, Michel Foucault, and Julia Kristeva. Interestingly, each of these people is excluded in one way or another from the dominant national discourse (French, white, male heterosexual); each sees himself or herself as (or is seen as being) an "outsider." This outsidership—which takes various forms and exerts varying effects over the "subjects" that these writers choose to discuss and the ways in which they discuss them—has been overlooked entirely by those critics who claim that collectively these people constitute a hegemonic power.

9. Lacan's reading of Freud teaches us that the social constructs the personal: "In 'The Agency of the Letter' (1957) Lacan says that there is no original or instinctual unconscious. Everything in the unconscious gets there from the outside world via symbolization and its effects" (Ragland-Sullivan 99). This discovery by Freud and its patient explication by Lacan have been systematically disregarded by most American interpreters of this work, especially by American feminists who ground their objections to Lacan's reading on the presumption that it separates the unconscious and the social or that it gives the unconscious the power (through the phallic signifier) to construct the external environment.

10. The unconscious is composed of these initial perceptions. Because of its physical helplessness and dependency, the child spends much of its early months listening and looking, taking in the environment around itself. Although it cannot use language, it assimilates sounds and rhythms. Ellie Ragland-Sullivan writes: "earliest perception is inseparable from the effects of the outside world, both linguistic and visual. . . . Since the primordial subject of unconsciousness is formed by identification with its first images and sensory experiences, it will thereafter reflect the essence of these images and objects in identity" (18).

11. The first summer that the Stephen family spent at St. Ives was 1882, the summer following Virgina's birth on January 25. She would have been six or seven months old that summer, and it is possible that the memories she "recalls" here are not memories at all but initial impressions of her environment—impressions that preceded use of language.

WORKS CITED

Benstock, Shari. "Beyond the Reaches of Feminist Criticism: A Letter from Paris." *Tulsa Studies in Women's Literature* 3 (1984): 5–7. Rpt. in *Feminist Issues in Literary Scholarship*. Ed. Shari Benstock. Bloomington: Indiana University Press, 1987. 7–29.

———. "From Letters to Literature: *La Carte Postale* in the Epistolary *Genre*." *Genre* 18 (Fall 1985): 257–95.

THE LONG GOODBYE

against personal testimony,
or an infant grifter grows up

(1 9 9 2)

> We lived as usual. Everyone does, most of the time. Whatever is go-
> ing on is as usual. Even this is as usual, now. We lived, as usual, by
> ignoring. Ignoring isn't the same as ignorance, you have to work at it.
> Nothing changes instantaneously: in a gradually heating bathtub
> you'd be boiled to death before you knew it.
> MARGARET ATWOOD, *THE HANDMAID'S TALE*

Since this is essay is written against the grain of individualism, novelistic discourse,[1] and personal testimony, let's dispense with the personal immediately: for
400 years, every male Kauffman was a Protestant minister and missionary. Rack-
ing his brain to invent the occupation that would be most rebellious and least
remunerative, my father became a Bible salesman. I was his sidekick: together
we sold Bibles and religious paraphernalia to servicemen in bus stations up and
down the Southern California coast, pitching piety and scoring sales, though privately we scorned the suckers. My job: to "look innocent." I was five. (One item
I remember vividly: a trippy 3-D color picture of Jesus that lit up when you
plugged it in; to my infant eyes, Jesus looked like a psychedelic cartoon, "turned
on" in both senses of the word.) Since he had the IQ of a genius, my father disdained bosses and nine-to-five routines: instead, he worked successively in various kinds of sales, and as our fortunes declined, as a milkman, cab driver, and
grifter. My most vivid childhood memories: the glittering marquees on the strip
in Vegas, especially the huge cowboy tipping his hat at the Golden Nugget, who
reminded me of Howdy Doody, and the Silver Slipper, which reminded me of
Cinderella. Another sublime memory is the Long Beach Pike, a pretty seedy
scene in those days; my antics amused the carneys while Dad conned the sailors,
all of us grifting according to our gifts.

From the age of eleven, I worked nights in his janitor business, cleaning banks,
offices, and the model homes spreading over Orange County, California, in the
1960s like mould on cheese. Although legitimate, this job was the most humiliating: how dare the morons traipsing through these houses look at *me* with pity,
while I cleaned around them? While polishing the tellers' windows in banks, I
cultivated murderous fantasies, malevolently sizing up the huge fortress-like safes
and thinking, *"Let's blow this sucker up, Dad!"* Once he began to drink and gamble

in earnest, we successively lost the furniture, the car, finally the only house we'd ever own. My mother and I waitressed for $1.25 per hour each to raise my college money, and ate at the restaurant, since the only staple in steady supply at home was vodka. Once the newspapers and telephone were cut off, we lived in virtual seclusion. Long before Reagan invented the rhetoric of a "safety net" for the "truly needy," we had fallen right through.

Depending on my mood, my past strikes me as having all the makings of an Arthur Miller tragedy or Beckettian comedy. I developed a chameleon-like ability to move up and down the socioeconomic ladder, for I was raised to imitate the gentility of my reverend ancestors, despite our chronic lack of cash. In the 1950s, I remember literally being homeless (I was so young, I thought we were "camping"); but eventually we managed to "pass" in the middle class, living largely on credit. No wonder my doctoral dissertation was on Dickens and Faulkner: my family alternately resembled the Micawbers and the Pockets, the Compsons and the Snopeses.

As the last sentence indicates, I clearly believe that our intellectual work as feminists is directly related to our personal histories; that our subjective experiences influence our politics, that our psychic traumas affect our teaching and writing.

So what's my beef?

First, I dislike the "our" in the previous paragraph; among many other assumptions it takes for granted, the one that is probably most accurate is therefore most troubling: "we" all do the same kind of labor, i.e., feminist work in higher education in America. Are "we" feminist scholars solipsistically talking only to ourselves?

Second, it's too easy to validate my credentials. My checkered past is too easy to transform into a Nixonian Checkers speech of bathos. By insisting on the authority of my personal experience, I effectively muzzle dissent and muffle your investigation into my motives. "I've suffered more than you" is a false (albeit fashionable) piety, as if we needed to (or could) distance ourselves from bourgeois banalities. It elicits a phony competition to prove that "I was poorer than you." (My mother used to joke, "I was so poor, I didn't have a mother.")

Third, the facts of "my life and hard times" rearrange themselves generically into one of several novelistic lines, including, but not limited to, the following:

• The nobility of suffering. That's the first lie: suffering never ennobles, it only humiliates, and—if you're lucky—enrages.

• Ms. Horatio Alger: anybody in America can rise to the top with hard work, and fulfill the American dream.

That lie disguises the randomness of existence: it is only by chance that I am not a welfare mother, a stripper, or a waitress. In this light, the fact that I am white and was at least able to forage in the middle class considerably outweighs the fact that I am female. The lie's corollary: I raised myself by my bootstraps; so better had you—what we might currently call "the Clarence Thomas syndrome."

• Revolutionary impulses led me to the university.

In fact, I sought the university precisely because I saw it as a haven from the chaos and craziness of "real life"; far from scorning "the ivory tower," I was, I smugly thought, fleeing into one. Unfortunately, carrying on the Kauffman trait of exquisite bad timing, shortly after I arrived at the University of California, Santa Barbara, in 1967, police and National Guard patrols put the university under siege: classes were suspended, curfews imposed, students were beaten and arrested. As the Bank of America burned down, the National Guard murdered a student who was trying to *protect* the bank's precious property. Kevin Moran perished, but the bank rose from the ashes with a new fortress-like design within weeks.

- The anti-war movement radicalized me.

I have no nostalgia for those years (1967–1971). They were as close as I ever want to come to total chaos: one couldn't depend either upon the students, the police, or the National Guard for rationality, much less protection. Incredibly, scarcely 20 years ago some Americans found it normal to be murdering students on campuses, from Kent State to Jackson State, from Augusta to Santa Barbara. Not only did I learn how quickly a police state can become the norm, but I discovered how many Americans would avidly support one.

- Out of the impassioned radical evolved an impassioned feminist.

I owe to my mother whatever semblance of normality my childhood had; I owe my feminism to her fierce insistence that I escape the traps that thwarted her, and to the model my older sister provided of an escape route: studying English literature.

At the time, that solution did not seem nearly so quixotic as it does in retrospect: in 1972 we naively believed that the university was the most egalitarian of institutions, the one most receptive to social change and justice. Instead, it turned out to be among the most reactionary and entrenched. In contrast to law school and medical school, which at least rely on quantitative measurements in evaluation, English departments in those days relied on the vaguely F. R. Leavisite criteria of qualitative response to "felt life." Leavisite standards still dominated English departments in the 1960s and 1970s, and—make no mistake—they still dominate in the evaluations of many full professors to this day.

My sister, Kay Austen, is now an ex-English professor. While tenured at the University of Hawaii, she fell ill. The University seized the opportunity and terminated her in retaliation for her affirmative action work. For the past ten years she has battled paralyzing illness while waging a sex discrimination case of *Bleak House* proportions against the University. Court testimony revealed that University officials conspired to deny her health care when her condition was "gravely life-endangering." Testimony also revealed that they considered putting her under surveillance when she was living 6,000 miles away. Whether she ever finally "wins" this case or not, the University remains the victor—precisely by forcing each individual victim of discrimination to go through the long, arduous process over and over again.[2] I want feminist scholarship to reach an audience that transcends the academy, but that doesn't prevent me from mourning the decimation (I use that word literally) of a generation of feminist scholars who have been exiled from academic life by sexual harassment, retaliation, and discrimination in the past twenty-five years.

Is it even possible to write against the grain of individualism? When you read my opening gambit, didn't it make you (whether you know me personally or not) want to know more? That is precisely my point: there is something fatally alluring about personal testimony. Even theoretical texts can be co-opted by critics who insist on interpreting in the same old way. It happens to feminists, materialists, post-structuralists alike. One reason I devoted the past decade to writing about love and epistolary fiction was to see whether it was possible to wrest signification away from representation by demonstrating that even love—the emotion that's supposed to be the most private, the most authentic, the most inviolate—is artifice, a construct. The French have known this for a long time: "Some people would never have been in love, had they never heard love talked about," said La Rochefoucauld. Consider Roland Barthes's *Fragments d'un discours amoureux*: Barthes's aim was to emphasize the fragmentary and discursive aspects of the text, rather than to create the lover-as-hero, because:

> If you put the lover in a love story, you reconcile him with society because telling stories is a coded activity. Society tames the lover through the love story. I took Draconian measures so the book would not be a love story, so the lover would be left in his nakedness, a being inaccessible to the usual forms of social recuperation, the novel in particular. (Barthes, 1985: 302–03)

But (here's the grifter's voice again): Americans are hooked on authenticity and sincerity. Ironically, in the English translation, Barthes's "Draconian measures" are co-opted from the title forward: *A Lover's Discourse: Fragments* makes the lover, not discourse, primary; it reduces his analysis to psychology, when his aims were figural and structural. It suggests that we are reading the real sentiments of a lover named Roland Barthes, as if he were merely a lovelorn columnist, some French version of Ann Landers or Dr. Ruth Westheimer.

Imagine substituting the word *feminist* for *lover* in the passage above: you reconcile the feminist to society because telling stories is a coded activity, as I tried to demonstrate by highlighting the implied narrative lines in my own history. Society tames the feminist through the story in particular, the allure of personal testimony in general. Are feminists succeeding in finding ways to make their work inaccessible to the usual forms of social "recuperation"—a word that in French simultaneously connotes co-option? Lest you accuse me of setting up a minor strain in feminist criticism as a "straw woman," I am arguing that such recuperation infects not just feminist criticism, but reader-response criticism, psychoanalytic criticism, materialist criticism, *and even post-structuralism*. Let me take another improbable example: at a conference, when Jacques Derrida hears the rumor that he is in analysis, he asks,

> Who am I and what have I done so that this might be the truth of their desire? . . . This must signify something not negligible in the air of their times and the state of their relation to what they read, write, do, say, live, etc. (Derrida, 1980: 203)

I have purposely seized upon Barthes and Derrida because post-structuralist strategies are supposed to *preclude* the kinds of responses I am describing. Even if "we" (and here my presumption is glaring) are post-structuralist, postmodernist, anti-humanist feminists, "we" are avid consumers of true confessions, suckers for sentimentality. (As you'll see below, I am not in the least exempt from these lapses myself.) How can I as a feminist describe and account for "the air of [our] times and the state of [our] relation to what we read, write, do, say, live, etc." more precisely? A few symptomatic reflections follow.

One can obviously use the personal voice without forgetting history, society, politics. More difficult to resist is the temptation to view the personal as inherently paradigmatic, the individual life story as coherent, unified, orally inspiring. It makes us see similarity where in fact there are only differences—irresolvable, irreconcilable differences at that. Invocations to personal experience are appealing because they imply that one can surmount injustice and triumph over adversity. In fact, most disappointments last a lifetime, and many injuries are irremediable. The older I get, the less I'm able to construct a moral even to my own story that doesn't lie with every word. As Laurie Anderson says about New Yorkers, "There are ten million stories in New York City, and no one knows which is theirs." The air of our times and the state of our relation to what we read, write, do, say, live, involves our saturation in images and in the cult of personality, which reduce protests, movements, ideas to *People* magazine or "Entertainment Tonight" sound bites; one projects an image to be tagged, marketed, commodified. (*Look what happened to Jesus!*) In the eighteenth century the quintessential medium was the essay; today it is the celebrity interview. We live in a society that no longer nourishes itself with beliefs but with images; the image always has the last word (Debord, 1970; Barthes, 1985). Have feminists defused the power of the image? Hardly. Can they do so? Probably not. But many have been engaged for the past decade in deconstructing the images in advertising, cinema, literature, and popular culture through which femininity is constructed. Other feminists, however, reduce "Theory" to a passing fad, philosophy to a season's fashion.

Right now, I'm haunted by one particularly audacious image, publicizing a new magazine called *Allure*. It features a Chinese woman in Maoist dress in a grainy black and white photograph. One spot of vivid color relieves her (primitive, totalitarian) drabness: her lips are a vivid red. The copy reads:

> Why 6,000,000 women who used to carry a little red book now carry a little red lipstick. Beauty makes a statement. And when nail polish becomes political, and fashion becomes philosophy, Allure magazine will be there. With reporting about fragrance and fitness, cosmetics and culture, travel and trends. Allure: the revolutionary beauty.

How are we going to confront the fact that feminism has become another product, and that we are implicated in its commodification? That's one thing I hoped *Feminisms and Institutions* would do: front the facts of complicity with social institutions, examine the complexities of shifting allegiances and conflicting commitments by engaging men and women in dialogue (Kauffman, 1989b). Complicity is not a pleasant topic. One of the sobering discoveries I've made as a feminist is that institutions shape us more than we shape them. No one in 1972 could have predicted that feminism would make such remarkable inroads in our educational, legal, civil institutions. Nor did anyone dream that the Equal Rights Amendment would fail, that the nation would so passionately embrace neo-conservatism, that the world would be gripped again by the fervor of fundamentalism. Despite our desire to believe in the myth of (Enlightenment) progress, such are the facts. One of the profound paradoxes confronting feminists in the 1990s is that, despite the massive transformations feminism has wrought, we are facing increasingly intransigent conservative powers that will remain in force far into the next century. (If he lasts as long as Thurgood Marshall, Clarence Thomas will be on the bench until 2031.) I wanted to see if it was possible to protest against feminism's commodification *and* to attack the premises of bourgeois individualism—the cornerstone supporting the American mythology of the individual as a unique, coherent, unified self.

One of the ways that feminism obviously cooperates in promoting that ideology is through literature. The case of Doris Lessing's *The Golden Notebook* is illustrative. The novel, published in 1962, is usually heralded as one of the first manifestos of the modern women's liberation movement. Anna Wulf is represented as suffering a schizophrenic "breakdown" at the hands of sexist society; since her "illness" results in a paralysis of the will and a writing block, evidence of her "cure" is that the novel commences with her novella "Free Women." Fiction is thus reduced to a tragic representation of life: "life" is reduced to a tale of individual malaise. The implicit message is that you cannot change society, only yourself. Such interpretations perpetuate narcissism and personal passivity instead of inspiring political action and social change (Ohmann, 1983; Newton and Rosenfelt, 1985). In fact, the novel is a sustained critique of subjectivity and of the individual's obsession with the personal. Ella (one of Anna Wulf's multiple "selves") reflects, "How boring these emotions are that we're caught in and can't get free of, no matter how much we want to" (Lessing, 1962: 318).[3] Far from focusing on the individual, the novel disassembles the history of the twentieth century, ranging from Stalinist Russia to Algeria, Korea, China, Africa, America, and Indochina. Lessing insists that what we call the psyche is influenced as much by social, political, and economic traumas as by the personal. Here's an antidote to individualism from Lessing herself:

> When *The Golden Notebook* came out, I was astonished that people got so emotional about that book, one way or another. They didn't bother to see, even to look at, how it was shaped. . . . What I'm trying to say is that it was a detached book. It was a failure, of course, for if it had been a success, then people wouldn't get so damned emotional when I didn't want them to be. (Howe, 1967: 311–13)

Lessing's only failure, in my view, was to underestimate readers' and reviewers' capacity to fold all attempts to go beyond what is now known as "the representational fallacy" back into the criteria of bourgeois realism—the view of literature as a reflection of individual experience. Elaine Showalter, for example, insists that Lessing "will have to face the limits of her own fiction very soon if civilization survives. . . . Either she will have to revise her apocalyptical prophecies (like other millenarians), or confront, once again, the struggling individual" (Showalter, 1976: 313). But in Lessing's view, it is precisely the ideology Showalter endorses that may lead to apocalypse, for the individual cannot be confronted in isolation, separated from a complex matrix of international politics, environmental issues, multinational economics, and global military conflict. Margaret Atwood chillingly depicts the consequences of that ideology in *The Handmaid's Tale*: apocalypse is inevitable if we continue to be sunk in subjectivity. Atwood almost seems to take Showalter's ideas to their absurd but logical conclusion; the novel is a sustained parody of the theory of gynocriticism: "You wanted a women's culture. Well, now there is one. It isn't what you meant" (Atwood, 1986: 127). In many ways, the same prophecies Lessing made in 1962 are reaccentuated and defamiliarized by Atwood 24 years later: organizing military coups, destabilizing governments, re-settling "undesirables" and repressing civil liberties have all come to seem "nor-mal." When *The Handmaid's Tale* appeared in 1986, few of us were aware of the extent to which her dystopia was already a reality in some parts of the world: Nicolae Ceausescu forced women to bear up to five children to increase the nation's power, and women were subjected to forced gynecological examinations every three months to make sure they hadn't had abortions. The enormity of these crimes has only come to the world's attention since the Romanian revolu-tion in 1989, although Atwood explicitly describes these horrors in the novel's historical note:

> Rumania ... had anticipate Gilead in the eighties by banning all forms of birth control, imposing compulsory pregnancy tests on the female population, and linking promotion and wage increases to fertility. (Atwood, 1985: 305)

Lessing and Atwood wonder what drives people collectively to embrace their own repression. What vicissitudes of psychic life account for the appeal of fas-cism? Experimental novelists have been trying to lead us away from the ideol-ogy of individualism and toward avant-garde conceptualizations for the past 75 years, but academic critics have frequently recuperated and reprocessed them like American cheese—bland, but familiar. As a feminist literary critic I want texts to challenge the boundaries of realism, of genre, of narrative, not to subordinate the (anti-representational anti-bourgeois, anti-narrative) other into the same—the same old story.

In the past decade, many feminists have either challenged or surmounted the dichotomy described above between Anglo-American New Criticism and French post-structuralism. Many more (myself included) have practically re-tooled in or-der to incorporate materialist analyses. Didn't we say goodbye to personal testi-mony, with its valorization of the power and autonomy of individual psyche, a long time ago? As Teresa de Lauretis observed in 1984,

> What we call "Experience" should instead be defined as a process shaped co-equally by the relation of the inside and the outside: Experience has a mo-bile relation to the reality it encounters, the subjectivity it assumes, and the discursive practices within which it unfolds. Subjectivity is constructed from experience, but what one comprehends as subjective are in fact material, economic, and interpersonal social and historical relations. (de Lauretis, 1984: 150)

In fact, however, the appeal to the personal and the concomitant repudiation of "theory" seems to be making a pretty snappy comeback, presaged in 1983 by Elaine Showalter's "Critical Cross-Dressing: Male Feminists and the Woman of the Year," which warns feminists of the "seductions" of "male Theory" in general and post-structuralism in particular (Showalter, 1983). The notion that feminists are being "seduced" by so-called "male Theory" has persisted throughout the decade. Barbara Christian reinforces Showalter's view that "Theory" is a passing fashion when she argues that literature has been taken over by Western philosophers who are intimidating people of color, feminists, radical critics, and creative writers with a language "which mystifies rather than clarifies our condition, making it possible for a few people who know that particular language to control the critical scene" (Christian, 1989: 229).[4]

In my view, the languages of critical theory are difficult because of their foundations in disciplines that were long isolated from literary studies. That the New Critics actively sought such isolation for ideological purposes has been well documented.[5] But the sentiment is nonetheless representative of a current *strain* (in both senses of the word) in feminism. Seduced by "male Theory," we have lost touch, so the argument goes, with the revolutionary fervor of the first wave of feminism, and only by once again focusing on our own consciousness can we recapture the spirit of an earlier age.

But isn't it at least possible that rather than blaming ("male") Theory, we must confront a totally transformed economic and historical moment? The only sure thing about all idyllic epochs, as Raymond Williams once observed, is that they are always gone. Let's face it: that's true of feminist idylls too. Perhaps we should recall some of our mistakes in the idyllic old days, like Patricia Spacks's disclaimer that she did not discuss the work of black women in *The Female Imagination* because she was "reluctant and unable to construct theories about the experience [she hasn't] had" (Spacks, 1975: 5). Remember the searing question Alice Walker asked? "Spacks never lived in the 19th century Yorkshire, so why theorize about the Brontës?" (Walker, 1983: 372). Walker attacked the theoretical weakness and unexamined assumptions of bourgeois individualism in (white) feminist literary criticism. (Below, I discuss some mistakes in my own earlier scholarship.)

In "Me and My Shadow," Jane Tompkins similarly warns that theory is "one of the patriarchal gestures women and men ought to avoid." She argues that "the female subject par excellence, which is her self and her experiences, has once more been elided by literary criticism" (Tompkins, 1989: 122).[6] To Tompkins, feminism's function is to facilitate self-discovery about one's victimage at the hands of patriarchy, to idealize woman's superior moral sense, her "Sentimental Power" (Tompkins, 1985).[7]

The cumulative effect of this approach is to discourage investigation of any complicating factors that may weaken the stance of victimization or moral superiority. It avoids the complicated question of collusion and complicity either in one's own oppression, or with institutions. The underlying premise is that writing reflects a world already bathed in the emotional light that the solitary woman projects. This strain of feminism thus resurrects the mirror and the lamp of Romanticism, the movement most closely aligned with the expressive theory of art. The criteria of value are sincerity and authenticity, which inevitably lock us back into the very dichotomies (male intellect versus female institution; head versus body, etc.) that so many other feminists have spent so much time trying to dismantle. Ironically, the argument that women can only write about themselves has been the cornerstone of *sexist* criticism of women writers since Sappho (Kauffman, 1986). This hyperbolically sexualized rhetoric nonetheless persists, refiguring the feminist as Clarissa, virtuous victim who must vigilantly ward off the masculine seductions of loveless, disembodied "Theory." Nancy Miller confesses, "Barthes has seduced me"; she also refers to "the appeal of a headier (sexier . . .) destabilization from deconstructive, psychoanalytic, and neo-Marxist perspectives. . . . The chapters of this book all testify to my awareness of their seductions" (Miller, 1988: 3, 17).[8] If we keep perpetuating this tired rhetoric, feminist criticism *will*—like Clarissa—end up starving itself to death.

What "male Theory" is hurting most, such critics agree, is women's *feelings*. Says Tompkins: "I'm tired of the conventions that keep discussions of epistemology . . . segregated from meditations on what is happening . . . inside my heart . . . I have to deal with the trashing of emotion, and with my anger against it" (Tompkins, 1989: 122–23, 138). Christian's words are almost identical: she yearns for the integration "between feeling/knowledge, rather than the split between the abstract and the emotional" (Christian, 1989: 229). This integration, she argues, would allow the black woman to "pursue herself as subject" (Christian, 1989: 235). Such protests belie a nostalgia for a clear, transparent language that never did exist. Self-division does not result from some plot by theorists to persecute writers. Instead, the vicissitudes of psychic life are far more complex, as is language's mastery over us, with all its internal tensions and contradictions. The yearnings for integration and unity fly in the face of the discoveries in linguistics, psychoanalysis, and post-structuralism about the construction of the subject—namely that (like Anna Wulf), we are always *beside ourselves* in multiple senses. Striving for integration through self-expression can only be viewed as a quixotic enterprise when one considers the structure of the unconscious. The political efficacy of such self-regard (in both senses of the word) is also questionable. Moreover, what is happening "inside our hearts" is subject to convention as much as discussions of epistemology are, as my discussion of love made clear earlier. The ideology informing such yearnings for integration is seldom made explicit, nor is it clear how such integration could advance the collective cause of social justice for women, African-Americans, or African-American women.

To return to my discomfort with the use of the collective "we": how can "we" overcome the tendency to be hermetically sealed, like Clarissa in her coffin, in academic obsessions? The last thing I want is for feminism to embalm itself by becoming the new orthodoxy. On the one hand, we maintain that the university is a microcosm of society; that the work we do in academia is political work. I think that is true. Nevertheless, social injustice and racial inequality cannot be conflated with a contest of faculties—a distinction Tompkins, Christian, and Miller all blithely ignore. Tompkins confesses that she once told a panel at the Modern Language Association Convention to "'get theory' because I thought that doing theory would admit us to the big leagues" (Tompkins, 1989: 122). Nancy Miller's concept of politics is bounded in a nutshell: the seminar table and fellowship panel: she broods over "problems between 'us' and 'them' [which] loomed large in institutional terms—tenure, promotions, journals, fellowships, etc." We can't do political work within the university unless we constantly remind ourselves that it is a sphere of relative privilege and entitlement—a reminder that makes it difficult to sympathize with Miller's unabashed confession that "To the extent that I was vividly untenured, I of course worried at all times about everyone" (Miller, 1988: 13). Beyond the politics of the profession—ranging from Christian's indictment of those whom she perceives as controlling the "critical scene" to MLA panels and academic "big leagues"—lies a vaster political arena and a harsher national mood. The allure of personal testimony makes it easy to conflate the *feminist* with the *academic* perspective. Like looking through the wrong end of a telescope, all one sees is in miniature.

Radical work goes on in universities, but only if one turns the telescope around. One of the advantages of the theoretical project of dismantling traditional disciplines and of undoing the traditional divisions—the *disciplining* of academics—is that the interrelations between culture and society, power and ideology can no longer masquerade as innocent or invisible. Whereas Christian protests that "there has been a takeover in the literary world of Western philosophers from the old literary elite, the neutral humanists" (Christian, 1989: 225), she does not seem aware that "neutral humanists" is a non sequitur, if not an oxymoron. Christian is dedicated to offering new readings to promote a black female literary tradition, but new readings alone will not insure the preservation of that tradition. Ironically, Marxists, feminist theorists, African-American scholars, and students of popular culture have all contributed to exposing what is at stake in the production of literary texts and movements. One of the most exhilarating facets of reconceptualizing academic study today is the opportunity to help students comprehend this process and to demystify its operation. Continually exposing and undermining the construction of knowledge is vital to every project of redefining feminism. That project is perpetual—and perpetually threatened by co-option and commodification.

One strain of feminism that has been commodified most successfully is the therapeutic model. Tompkins chides those who see pop psychologists like M. Scott Peck and Leo Buscaglia as "mushy" and "sentimental" (Tompkins, 1989: 138), but she fails to see how by endorsing them she uncritically perpetuates individualism. What cannot be ignored is how such books promote that ideology: the individual—removed from history, economics, *and even from the unconscious*—is depicted as someone who always has choices, and whose choices are always "free." Adversity is merely the product of a "bad attitude, negative thinking, or low self-esteem." To be a subject (to recognize oneself as a free and unique being) is itself an effect of subjection to ideology. In this light, it is clearly a delusion that by throwing off the straitjacket of formal expository prose, anyone will be revealing her "true," unique self. Writing about yourself does not liberate you, it just shows how ingrained the ideology of freedom through self-expression is in our thinking.

It's worth mentioning the other best-sellers that have proliferated recently, disseminating similar messages: *Men Who Hate Women and Women Who Love Them*; *The Dance-Away Lover*; *The Peter Pan Principle*; *Smart Women, Foolish Choices*; *Men Who Can't Love*; and *Women Who Love Too Much*. One cannot ignore the ways in which these books exploit feminism as a commodity, complete with sophisticated and expensive marketing research campaigns to target consumers. Indeed, the audience for such books seems to be insatiable. Not only are these books targeted for an exclusively female audience, but they are relentless in their insistence on "normality"—not to mention heterosexuality. In the guise of teaching women how to deal with their feelings, these books feed on the media hype about the so-called man-shortage. They assiduously avoid analysis of historical and socioeconomic factors, reproducing instead the tired stereotypes of Woman as Victim, as masochist, as "Love Junkie" who needs to be "cured" of her "addiction" to love through a strict regimen of group therapy and confession. Femininity as disease: where have we heard that before? These are the books that are seriously engaged in reproducing femininity for mass-market consumption.

What is not negligible in "the air of our times and the state of our relation to what we read, write, do, say, live, etc." is how resilient individualism is, and how relentlessly it co-opts feminism. While we are being exhorted to focus on our feelings, a lot of people are falling through the cracks in our society. It is no accident that the hysterical hyperbole about "family values" reached its apex just as the actual kinship system began to recede (Mitchell, 1975: 227–31). The same anomaly applied to individualism: the hyperbole about the individual masks an alarming erosion of civil liberties in the United States. The bathtub has been gradually heating for some time now:

• September 1989: The U.S. Court of Appeals overturns a lower court order to shut down the "High Security Unit" (HSU) at the Federal Correctional Institution in Lexington, Kentucky. Designed specifically to control women convicted of politically motivated crimes, the HSU has been denounced by the American Civil Liberties Union as a "living tomb"; by Amnesty International as "deliberately and gratuitously oppressive"; and by the Soviet Union as a U.S. human rights violation. Gilda Zwerman's extensive research on women in American prisons reveals that this High Security Unit

> utilizes and manipulates the "terrorist" label in order to justify the "special" treatment of political prisoners [and represents] an expansion in the use of incapacitation, surveillance, and deterrence as mechanisms for social control and repression to a degree heretofore unprecedented in the U.S. correctional system.[9]

Along with Alejandrina Torres, a Puerto Rican nationalist, Susan Rosenberg was HSU's first inmate, and remained there for nearly two years. Convicted of carrying weapons and explosives for a radical group, Rosenberg is serving 58 years for a crime that—had she "merely" been a terrorist at an abortion clinic—would have garnered her a suspended sentence.

• October 7, 1989: The Senate passes a House-approved amendment, sponsored by Senator Jesse Helms, preventing federal funding of "obscene" art and requiring all recipients of National Endowment for the Arts and National Endowment for the Humanities grants to sign an affidavit certifying that the monies will not be used to produce works that contain "depictions of sadomasochism, homoeroticism, the sexual exploitations of children or individuals engaged in sex acts and which, when taken as a whole, do not have serious literary, artistic, political or scientific merit." Reminiscent of the loyalty oaths of the 1950s, the three categories are presented as if they were synonymous "perversions"; who will define "serious merit" remains unspecified. The cumulative effect is to force artists to steer clear of what they think the public might find indecent, which is a far broader category than obscenity.[10] Playwright Arthur Miller observes that self-censorship is already so widespread that it has allowed freedom to be "killed without a trace."[11]

• February 6, 1990: A bill introduced in the Washington State legislature, sponsored by Republican Jim West, would make it a crime for people under the age of 18 to engage in sex, including "heavy petting." The fine: 90 days in jail and five thousand dollars, unless they decide to marry.

• April 21, 1990: The Reverend Donald Wildmon and the American Family Association target photographer David Wojnarowicz's work by taking two homosexual images out of context from a larger collage and mailing the enlarged images to every member of Congress, as well as 178,000 pastors on the American Family Association's mailing list. Wojnarowicz, now dead from AIDS, filed suit and won a Pyrrhic legal victory.[12]

• September 1990–January 1991: 11 out of 15 fund-raising letters from three leading Religious Right groups targeted homosexuality as the most dangerous menace in America today.[13]

I am not implying that these incidents are unproblematic. They are not equivalent to one another. They may not even be among the worst examples of the current state of affairs. I've purposely included injustices that might not normally be regarded as specifically *feminist* concerns, because it is precisely the interconnection of feminist issues with other injustices that urgently needs our attention in the 1990s. My examples are symptoms of other dilemmas facing the nation: how far are we willing to go in suspending the Constitution to combat drug trafficking, pornography, health epidemics, crime? Wherever we turn, the most vulnerable institutions and individuals are under attack: not just the arts and humanities, but women, children, immigrants, the aged, the poor, the infirm. The aim is to widen the net of surveillance, to create language and action that transforms police campaigns into a "'war' on ____" fill in the blank). We no longer question either the desirability or the necessity of surveillance and punishment. What does it say about our society that we can only conceive of social problems and solutions in terms of crime and disease? When the infrastructure of our cities is collapsing, when millions are hungry and homeless, when our financial institutions are imploding, how do we still find the means to siphon off enormous resources to fund preposterous pornography commissions, to put rap singers on trial, to demand urine samples from employees, to persecute those with AIDS? The Right has replaced the specter of communism with enemies from within— within the body politic and the body: leftists and feminists within the university, microbiological bogeys, viruses in the immune system, in computers, in the womb (Haraway, 1989; Petchesky, 1987; Treichler, 1988). Under the banner of "normative health," repression is proliferating at a prodigious pace.

I'm conscious of the paradox involved in engaging in a critique of individualism on the one hand and arguing for the preservation of civil rights on the other hand. The mythology of individual freedom and choice is inflated in direct proportion to the erosion of civil liberties, which are undergoing the most massive assault since the McCarthy era. That assault is intricately interwoven with an assault on the poor, the disenfranchised, the intellectually, politically, and sexually suspect. The Right has turned the rhetoric of equality against its citizens: "equal rights for unborn women" and "crime victims' rights," like the "pro-life" anti-abortion campaign, cunningly disguise the repression which is actually being pro-moted. To offer one more example: the Senate Judiciary Committee, whose wisdom and good judgment is so fresh in our minds since the Clarence Thomas–Anita Hill travesty, will soon vote on a "pornography victims' compensation act," which would allow the so-called "victims" of pornography to sue producers and distributors of films, books, etc. *The Accused* is one type of film that could be re-moved from shelves, since it depicts a gang-rape.[14] For the first time in history, the logic of civil rights is turned *away* from its traditional support of expression: censorship would mean a *furthering* of civil rights (Downs, 1989: 60). Feminists can protest against these repressions without necessarily endorsing the ideology of individualism. We can agree that the individual is the product of power, and still recognize that, today in America, that power is becoming increasingly con-centrated among fundamentalists and conservatives, whether one turns to edu-cation, politics, religion, media, advertising, economics, or the law.

What can I as a feminist literary critic do? I can address the misapprehensions of representation: What has led us to view symbols and representations as dan-gerous menaces, the dissemination of which must be controlled? I can use my own personal history to critique the underlying assumptions about person and story, as I have tried to do here. Moreover, I'm the perfect candidate to critique "women's ways of knowing" and "sentimental power" because my first book, *Dis-courses of Desire*, was at some points an implicit endorsement. In one passage, I remark:

> I have tried to expose the devaluation of the sentimental as another form of repression, with ramifications as serious at the end of the twentieth century as sexual repression was at the end of the nineteenth. (Kauffman, 1986: 316)

I now see that such an approach to sentimentality has led in directions I couldn't have predicted—although I now think I should have been able to predict them. Feminism's greatest strength has always been its capacity for self-critique, and it would be a great pity to see that capacity muted by the insistence on consensus. Feminist criticism has confronted numerous dilemmas in the past decade: how to engage in post-structuralist theory without losing sight of the material body? What does it mean to be constituted as a subject in and of language? Which texts (and which ideologies) survive and why? I think we still have the most to learn from the ruptures, limitations, and contradictions in our thinking. In *Special De-livery*, I propose and enact a conscious strategy of what I call "infidelity": one can show how one's own arguments may subsequently become inadequate; one can even confess how one's desires may be in conflict with the theoretical stances one endorses. One can highlight rather than blithely eliding the paradoxes that are irreconcilable, the consequences that are irremediable. As *Special Delivery* went to press, I discovered a similar argument in Sandra Harding's *Whose Science? Whose Knowledge?* In a chapter entitled "Reinventing Ourselves as Other," she ex-horts us to provide "traitorous" identities and social locations, and to engage in traitorous readings of the assumptions we make in and about texts (Harding, 1991: 288–95). Such assumptions include racist, regional, heterosexist, and sexist as-sumptions. I would add that sexism infects both genders; as a discursive con-struct, can't we finally put to rest that *bête noire*, "the white male"?

As a feminist, I have not everything to do, but something. Even while endorsing post-structuralist strategies, I cannot wait for the revolution that has no model to come before I act. (But I *can* continue to deconstruct the terms in which the arguments are framed, and the assumed ideology underlying them.) Rather than contributing to the successful working of the machinery of society, I want my work to be a counterfriction to the machine. Despite the fact that my family were the black sheep of generations of Protestants, I wholeheartedly endorse the word's etymology in *protest*.

We are living in a politically exhausted culture, and still responding to it with exhausted genres. Personal testimony can sometimes be eloquent, but it is not an infinitely inexhaustible genre. Too often it reinforces the blind belief that we are all intrinsically interesting, unique, that we deserve to be happy. My happiness, frankly, is not very important in the grand scheme of things. I never thought feminism was about happiness. I thought it was about justice. The times demand a frontal attack on the complex political alliances—civil, legal, economic, educational, religious—that are acting in conspiracy, explicitly and implicitly, to boil us alive. Atwood is right; it takes effort to ignore, and a united front ill serves feminism at this particular historical moment. While some warn against betraying "mothers," or trashing the "sisterhood," this merely reveals the relentless rhetoric of familialism (another staple of bourgeois ideology) in yet another guise. Meanwhile, far more serious betrayals are unfolding before our eyes. When I began this essay, the Helms debate was just heating up; it already seems long ago and far away. In fact, as you read them, didn't the dates I mentioned seem antiquated? Have they already ceased to alarm us? Now, in September 1991, it is abundantly apparent just how cheap and easy personal testimony is: Clarence Thomas is relying on the same maudlin strategy to silence dissent at the confirmation hearings for his appointment to the Supreme Court. Deflecting every political challenge, every question of intentionality, and every issue of constitutional interpretation, he invokes the supreme authority of personal experience: nobody knows the troubles he's seen because he's from Pinpoint, Georgia, son of a sharecropper. His invocation to personal authority disguises his opportunism, his indebtedness to the civil rights movement he now repudiates, his cynicism. Today's grifters aren't in Vegas; they are testifying in a circus-like atsmosphere[15] on Capitol Hill.

Feminism is far more than the effort to "express" "women's personal experience," and its "territory" extends far beyond the bonds of family, beyond the lecture hall, beyond academia. Growing up among grifters, I learned early how illusions are fabricated, how false piety smells. That doesn't mean I have no illusions, no hopes, dreams, etc. It does mean that I want continually to cast doubt on the status of knowledge—*even as we are in the process of constructing it*—a perpetual project. By resisting the flattering temptation to talk solely to and about ourselves, we can concentrate on defying repressions that have already come to seem "normal." The pace of contemporary events is like a speeding convertible; we can ill afford to be enchanted by the rear-view mirror. Rather than mythologizing ourselves or the past, can't we total those disabled vehicles and—at long last—wave goodbye to all that?

NOTES

1. The connections between the ideology of bourgeois individualism and the novel as a genre have been made by Nancy Armstrong, *Desire and Domestic Fiction: A Political History of the Novel* (Oxford: Oxford University Press, 1987); Lennard J. Davis, *Resisting Novels: Ideology and Fiction* (New York: Methuen, 1987); and Linda Kauffman, *Special Delivery: Epistolary Modes in Modern Fiction* (Chicago: University of Chicago Press, 1992), among many other recent studies.

2. In March 1991, Kay Austen won 10 years' back pay and 10 years' front pay in the first court ruling to find the university liable for sex discrimination. Federal Judge Samuel P. King ruled that Austen was subjected to "harassment, retaliation and discrimination": "the record is clear that the University of Hawaii administration closed ranks to support him against her."

3. My views of *The Golden Notebook* and *The Handmaid's Tale* are developed in greater depth in *Special Delivery: Epistolary Modes in Modern Fiction* (Chicago: University of Chicago Press, 1992).

4. *Gender and Theory* is structure dialogically so that each essay is followed by a critique: see Michael Awkward's "Appropriative Gestures: Theory and Afro-American Literary Criticism," in response to Christian, and Gerald M. MacLean's "Citing the Subject," in response to Tompkins.

5. In addition to Ohmann, op. cit., see Terry Eagleton, *Literary Theory: An Introduction* (Minneapolis: University of Minnesota Press, 1983); Frank Lentricchia, *Criticism and Social Change* (Chicago: University of Chicago Press, 1983); and Janet Batsleer, Tony Davies, Rebecca O'Rourke, and Chris Weedom, *Rewriting English: Cultural Politics of Gender and Class* (London: Methuen, 1985).

6. I suspect (and sincerely hope) that I am the "unfriendly reader" to whom Tompkins refers in her essay, because critique is an invaluable aspect of engagement between women who are friends as well as feminists; conversely, by generously playing the role of "unfriendly reader" of *Special Delivery,* Jane immeasurably improved my book.

7. See also Mary Field Belencky, Blythe McVicker Clinchy, Nancy Rule Goldberger, Jill Mattuck Tarule, *Women's Ways of Knowing: The Development of Self, Voice, and Mind* (New York: Basic Books, 1986). Carol Gilligan's work has also been instrumental in promoting this view; in addition to *In A Different Voice* (Cambridge, Mass.: Harvard University Press, 1982), see "Joining the Resistance: Psychology, Politics, Girls and Women," *Michigan Quarterly Review* 29: 4 (Fall 1990): 501–36.

8. In *Getting Personal*, Miller recycles the same rhetoric to defend Tompkins and attack Gerald MacLean in their exchange in *Gender and Theory*. For an alternative interpretation, see Mary Poovey's review article in *Modern Philology* (May 1991): 415–420.

9. Cited by Patricia Golan, "America's Most Dangerous Woman?" *On the Issues* 13 (1989): 15–21.

10. *The New York Times*, November 10, 1990.

11. *The Washington Post*, November 13, 1990. *The New York Times* reported on September 18, 1991, that government documents were released that show that the National Endowment for the Arts bowed to political pressure in rescinding the grants it had initially recommended for Karen Finley, John Fleck, Holly Hughes, and Tim Miller (*New York Times,* p. B1, 3). The next day, the Senate voted 68 to 28 to prohibit the NEA from awarding grants that would promote materials that depict "sexual or excretory activities or organs" in an "offensive way" (*New York Times,* September 20, 1991, p. B2).

12. Wojnarowicz's lawsuit was settled in August 1990. Reverend Wildmon was asked to send a "corrective letter" to subscribers on the American Family Association's mailing list, and Wojnarowicz was awarded one dollar.

13. *Right-Wing Watch* 1:4 (February 1991): 2.

14. *The New York Times*, November 7, 1991.

15. Or should I say *peep*-show atmosphere? After this essay went to press, the Senate Judiciary Committee was forced to postpone the Senate vote in order to give the appearance of taking sexual harassment seriously: law professor Anita Hill testified that Thomas sexually harassed her when she worked for him in the Department of Education and the Equal Employment Opportunity Commission—the very agency that is supposed to investigate such abuses. On October 15, 1991, the Senate confirmed Clarence Thomas's nomination by a vote of 52–48. The same senators who glossed over Thomas's credibility when he insisted that he never discussed *Roe v. Wade* felt no compunction about trying to destroy the credibility of Professor Hill, labelling her a "perjurer," a "fantasist," and alluding repeatedly to her "proclivities." Ironically, in the kangaroo court of the media, Clarence Thomas "won" because his testimony was passionate and personal: as if suddenly remembering that he was black, he compared the Senate hearings to a "high-tech lynching." Anita Hill was deemed too cool, dispassionate, impersonal. Few spectacles so vividly demonstrate the abuses of personal testimony; with this one, I rest my case.

WORKS CITED

Atwood, Margaret, 1986. *The Handmaid's Tale.* Boston: Houston Mifflin.

Barthes, Roland, 1985. *The Grain of the Voice: Interviews. 1962–1980.* trans. Linda Coverdale. New York: Hill and Wang.

Christian, Barbara, 1989. "The Race for Theory," in *Gender and Theory: Dialogues on Feminist Criticism*, ed. Linda Kauffman. Oxford: Basil Blackwell, pp. 225–37.

de Lauretis, Teresa, 1980. *Alice Doesn't: Feminism, Semiotics, Cinema.* Bloomington: Indiana University Press.

Debord, Guy, 1970. *Society of Spectacle.* Detroit: Black and Red Press.

Derrida, Jacques, 1980. *The Post Card: From Socrates to Freud and Beyond,* trans. Alan Bass. Chicago: University of Chicago Press.

Downs, Donald Alexander, 1989. *The New Politics of Pornography.* Chicago: University of Chicago Press.

Haraway, Donna, 1989. "The Biopolitics of Postmodern Bodies: Determinations of Self in Immune System Discourse," *Differences* 1:1:3–43.

Harding, Sandra, 1991. *Whose Science? Whose Knowledge?* Ithaca: Cornell University Press.

Howe, Florence, 1967. "A Talk with Doris Lessing," *Nation* 6 March: 311–13.

Kauffman, Linda S., 1992. *Special Delivery: Epistolary Modes in Modern Fiction.* Chicago: University of Chicago Press.

———, 1986. *Discourses of Desire: Gender, Genre, and Epistolary Fictions.* Ithaca: Cornell University Press.

———, ed. 1989a. *Gender and Theory: Dialogues on Feminist Criticism.* Oxford: Basil Blackwell.

———, ed. 1989b. *Feminism and Institutions: Dialogues on Feminist Theory.* Oxford: Basil Blackwell.

Lessing, Doris, 1962. *The Golden Notebook.* New York: Simon and Schuster, reprinted Bantam Books, 1991.

Miller, Nancy K., 1991. *Getting Personal: Feminist Occasions and Other Autobiographical Acts.* New York: Routledge.

———, 1988. *Subject to Change: Reading Feminist Writing.* New York: Columbia University Press.

Mitchell, Juliet, 1975. *Psychoanalysis and Feminism: Freud, Reich, Laing and Women.* New York: Vintage.

Newton, Judith and Deborah Rosenfelt, eds. 1985. *Feminist Criticism and Social Change: Sex, Class and Race in Literature and Culture.* New York: Methuen.

Ohmann, Richard, 1983. "The Shaping of the Canon of U.S. Fiction, 1960–75" *Critical Inquiry* 10: 199–223.

Petchesky, Rosalind, 1987. "Fetal Images: The Power of Visual Culture in the Politics of Reproduction," *Feminist Studies* 13:2: 263–92.

Showalter, Elaine, 1976. *A Literature of Their Own: British Women Novelists from Brontë to Lessing.* Princeton: Princeton University Press.

———, 1983. "Critical Cross-Dressing: Male Feminists and the Woman of the Year," *Raritan Review* 3: 130–49.

Spacks, Patricia Meyer, 1975. *The Female Imagination.* New York: Knopf.

Tompkins, Jane, 1985. *Sensational Designs: The Cultural Work of American Fiction 1790–1860.* Oxford: Oxford University Press.

———, 1989. "Me and My Shadow," in *Gender and Theory,* ed. Linda S. Kauffman. Oxford: Blackwell.

Treichler, Paula, 1988. "AIDS, Homophobia, and Biomedical Discourse: An Epidemic of Signification," in *AIDS: Cultural Analysis, Cultural Activism,* ed. Dougles Crimp. Cambridge: MIT Press.

Walker, Alice, 1983. *In Search of Our Mothers' Gardens.* San Diego: Harcourt Brace Jovanovich.

ABOUT THE AUTHORS

Elizabeth Abel, Associate Professor of English at the University of California at Berkeley, is the author of *Virginia Woolf and the Fictions of Psychoanalysis* (1989), as well as several studies of women novelists, and of race, gender, and cultural politics. She is also the editor of *Writing and Sexual Difference* (1982), and the co-editor of *The Voyage In: Fictions of Female Development* (1983), *The Signs Reader: Women, Gender, and Scholarship* (1983), and *Female Subjects in Black and White: Race, Psychoanalysis, Feminism* (1997).

Paula Gunn Allen is Professor of English at the University of California at Los Angeles. Her books include *The Sacred Hoop: Recovering the Feminine in American Indian Traditions* (1986), *Grandmothers of the Light: A Medicine Woman's Sourcebook* (1991); and *Voice of the Turtle: American Indian Literature* (1994), as well as the edited collection *Spider Woman's Granddaughters: Traditional Tales and Contemporary Writing by Native American Women* (1989). Among her more recent essays are "'Border Studies: The Intersection of Gender and Color" (1992) and "Sky Woman and Her Sisters" (1992). She is also the author of several volumes of poetry and fiction.

Gloria Anzaldúa is the author of *Borderlands: The New Mestiza = La Frontera* (1987) and two bilingual children's picture books, as well as the recent essays "Chicana Artists: Exploring Nepantla, el lugar de la frontera" (1993) and "Theorizing Lesbian Experience" (1993). She is also the editor of *Making Face, Making Soul: Haciendo Caras: Creative and Critical Perspectives by Feminists-of-Color* (1990) and co-editor of *This Bridge Called My Back* (1981). She is currently completing doctoral studies at the University of California at Santa Cruz.

Nancy Armstrong is Professor of Comparative Literature at Brown University and the author of *Desire and Domestic Fiction: A Political History of the Novel* (1987) and, with Leonard Tennenhouse, co-author of *The Imaginary Puritan: Literature, Intellectual Labor, and the Origins of Personal Life* (1992) and "History, Poststructuralism, and the Question of the Narrative" (1993). Armstrong and Tennenhouse have also co-edited *The Ideology of Conduct: Essays on Literature and the History of Sexuality* (1987) and *The Violence of Representation: Literature and the History of Violence* (1989).

Dale Bauer is Professor of English and Women's Studies at the University of Wisconsin, Madison. She is the author of *Feminist Dialogics: A Theory of Failed Community* (1988), and *Edith Wharton's Brave New Politics* (1994) and co-editor, with Susan Jaret McKinstry, of *Feminism, Bakhtin, and the Dialogic* (1991). Among her recent publications are "The Other 'F' Word: The Feminist in the Classroom" (1990) and "The Meanings and Metaphors of Student Resistance" (1994).

Nina Baym is Professor of English and Jubilee Professor of Liberal Arts and Sciences at the University of Illinois, Urbana-Champaign. Professor Baym has written extensively about Hawthorne as well as nineteenth-century American women's literature. She recently published *American Women Writers and the Work of History, 1790–1860* (1995); other books include *Feminism and American Literary History: Essays* (1992), *Woman's Fiction: A Guide to Novels by and about Women in America, 1820–70* (1978; second edition, 1993), and *Novels, Readers, and Reviewers: Responses to Fiction in Antebellum America* (1984).

Catherine Belsey, Professor of English at the University of Wales College of Cardiff, is the chair of the Centre for Critical and Cultural Theory. Her publications include *John Milton: Language, Gender, Power* (1988), *The Subject of Tragedy: Identity and Difference in Renaissance Drama* (1985), and *Desire: Love stories in Western culture* (1994). Among her recent articles are "Love in Venice" (1992), "The Name of the Rose in *Romeo and Juliet*" (1993), and "Postmodern Love: Questioning the Metaphysics of Desire" (1994).

Shari Benstock is the author of articles ranging in topic from Modernism to feminist scholarship. Her critical works include *Women of the Left Bank: Paris, 1900–1940* (1986), *Textualizing the Feminine: On the Limits of Genre* (1991), *No Gifts from Chance: A Biography of Edith Wharton* (1994), and *On Fashion* (1994). She is the editor of *Feminist Issues in Literary Scholarship* (1987), *The Private Self: Theory and Practice of Women's Autobiographical Writings* (1988), and *Coping with Joyce* (1989). She is Professor of English at the University of Miami.

Lauren Berlant is Professor of English at the University of Chicago. The author of several studies of utopia, nationality, and the body, she has published *The Anatomy of National Fantasy: Hawthorne, Utopia, and Everyday Life* (1991). Her recent shorter works include "National Brands/National Body: *Imitation of Life*" (1991), "Queer Nationality" (1992), "America, 'Fat,' the Fetus" (1994), and "'68, or Something" (1994).

Joseph A. Boone, Associate Professor of English at the University of Southern California, Los Angeles, is the author of numerous studies examining male desire, male feminist criticism, and nineteenth- and twentieth-century fiction. He is the author of *Tradition Counter Tradition: Love and the Form of Fiction* (1987) and co-editor of *Engendering Men: The Question of Male Feminist Criticism* (1990). His recent publications include "Staging Sexuality: Repression, Representation, and 'Interior' States in *Ulysses*" (1993), "Rubbing Aladdin's Lamp" (1994), and "Vacation Cruises: Or, the Homoerotics of Orientalism" (1995).

Cordelia Chávez Candelaria, Professor of English and Chicano Studies at Arizona State University, is the editor of a special edition of *Frontiers* dedicated to Mexican-American women writers. She is also the author of *Chicano Poetry: An Introduction* (1986), and "Code-Switching as Metaphor in Chicano Poetry" (1988), as well as a collection of poetry.

Terry Castle is Professor of English at Stanford University and has published extensively on eighteenth-century English literature. She is the author of *Clarissa's Ciphers: Meaning and Disruption in Richardson's* Clarissa (1982), *Masquerade and Civilization: The Carnivalesque in Eighteenth-Century English Culture and Fiction* (1986), *The Apparitional Lesbian: Female Homosexuality and Modern Culture* (1993), and *The Female Thermometer: Eighteenth-Century Culture and the Invention of the Uncanny* (1995).

Barbara Christian is Professor of Afro-American Studies at the University of California. Berkeley, where she was the first black woman to have received tenure. Her critical works include the widely known article "The Race for Theory" (1988) and "But Who Do You Really Belong To—Black Studies or Women's Studies?" (1989), as well as several recent articles on the fiction of Afro-American women including Gwendolyn Brooks, Paule Marshall, and Toni Morrison. She is also the author of *Black Women Novelists: The Development of a Tradition 1892–1976* (1980) and *Black Feminist Criticism: Perspectives on Black Women Writers* (1985).

Hélène Cixous is a novelist, dramatist, essayist, and founding theorist of contemporary French feminism. She is the author of numerous articles and books, including *Entre l'Écriture* (1986), *The Newly Born Woman* (with Catherine Clement, 1986), *L'Heure de Clarice Lispector* (1989), *"Coming to Writing" and Other Essays* (1991), *Three Steps on the Ladder of Writing* (1993), and *The Hélène Cixous Reader* (1994). She is the Head of the Centre d'Études Féminines and Professor of English Literature at the Université de Paris VIII.

Teresa de Lauretis is Professor of History of Consciousness at the University of California, Santa Cruz. The author of several books including *Alice Doesn't: Feminism, Semiotics, Cinema* (1984), *Technologies of Gender: Essays on Theory, Film, and Fiction* (1987), and *The Practice of Love: Lesbian Sexuality and Perverse Desire* (1994), as well as numerous articles, she is also the editor of *Feminist Studies: Critical Studies* (1986). She is currently working on a book of essays on film and psychoanalysis.

Wai-Chee Dimock is Professor of English at Brandeis University and the author of *Empire for Liberty: Melville and the Poetics of Individualism* (1989), as well as the co-editor of *Rethinking Class: Literary Studies and Social Formations* (1994). Her new book, *Residues of Justice* (1996), explores law and political philosophy from the qualifying perspectives of literary studies and feminist theory.

Shoshana Felman, the Thomas E. Donnelly Professor of French and Comparative Studies at Yale University, is the author of *Writing and Madness: (Literature/Philosophy/Psychoanalysis)* (1985), *Jacques Lacan and the Adventure of Insight:*

Psychoanalysis in Contemporary Culture (1987), and *What Does a Woman Want?: Reading and Sexual Difference* (1993). She is the co-author, with Dori Laub, of *Testimony: Crises of Witnessing in Literature, Psychoanalysis, and History* (1992), and the editor of *Literature and Psychoanalysis: The Question of Reading: Otherwise* (1982).

Judith Fetterley, Professor of English at the State University of New York, Albany, is the author of *The Resisting Reader: A Feminist Approach to American Fiction* (1978), *Provisions: A Reader from Nineteenth-Century American Women* (1985), and co-editor of *American Women Regionalists 1850–1910: A Norton Anthology* (1991). Among her extensive work on gender and sexual politics in American literature are "*My Antonía*, Jim Burden, and the Dilemma of the Lesbian Writer" (1986) and "Reading about Reading: 'A Jury of Her Peers,' 'The Murders in the Rue Morgue,' and 'The Yellow Wallpaper'" (1986). Among her recent work is "'Not in the Least American': Nineteenth-Century Literary Regionalism" (1994).

Susan Stanford Friedman, Professor of English and Women's Studies at the University of Wisconsin, Madison, is the author of *Psyche Reborn: The Emergence of H.D.* (1981), *Penelope's Web: Gender, Modernity, H.D.'s Fiction* (1990), and articles on modernism, women's poetry, feminist theory, psychoanalysis, narrative theory, and academic feminism. She is the co-editor of *Signets: Reading H. D.* (1991) and the editor of *Joyce: The Return of the Repressed* (1993). Recent essays include "Beyond White and Other: Relationality and the Narratives of Race in Feminine Discourse" and "'Beyond' Gynocriticism and Gynesis: The New Geography of Identity and the Futuure of Feminist Criticism."

Jane Gallop is Professor of English and Comparative Literature and teaches in the Modern Studies Program at the University of Wisconsin, Milwaukee. She has published widely on feminist, literary, and psychoanalytic theory. Her books include *The Daughter's Seduction: Feminism and Psychoanalysis* (1982), *Reading Lacan* (1985), *Thinking Through the Body* (1988), and *Around 1981: Academic Feminist Literary Theory* (1992). Forthcoming is *Feminist Accused of Sexual Harassment* (1997).

Sandra M. Gilbert is Professor of English at the University of California, Davis. In addition to several volumes of her own poetry, Professor Gilbert has written *Acts of Attention: The Poems of D.H. Lawrence* (2nd ed., 1990) and studies of women poets such as Dickinson, Levertov, Plath, Millay, Sarton, and Nin. She is widely known for her collaborative works with Susan Gubar, which include *The Madwoman in the Attic: The Woman Writer and the Nineteenth-Century Literary Imagination* (1979), *The Female Imagination and the Modernist Aesthetic* (1986), *No Man's Land: The Place of the Woman Writer in the Twentieth Century* (3 vols. 1987–1994), and *Masterpiece Theater: An Academic Melodrama* (1995). She and Gubar have also co-edited *Shakespeare's Sisters: Women Poets, Feminist Critics* (1979), *The Norton Anthology of Literature by Women: The Tradition in English* (1985), and *Mothersongs: Poems For, By, and About Mothers* (1995).

Susan Gubar, Professor of English and Women's Studies at Indiana University, is the co-editor, with Jonathan Kamholtz, of *English Inside and Out: The Places of Literary Criticism* (1993). She has also recently published the essay "Feminist Misogyny: Mary Wollstonecraft and the Paradox of 'It Takes One to Know One'" (1994). She is widely known for her collaborative works with Sandra Gilbert, which include *The Madwoman in the Attic: The Woman Writer and the Nineteenth-Century Literary Imagination* (1979), *The Female Imagination and the Modernist Aesthetic* (1986), *No Man's Land: The Place of the Woman Writer in the Twentieth Century* (3 vols. 1987–1994), and *Masterpiece Theater: An Academic Melodrama* (1995). She and Gilbert have also co-edited *Shakespeare's Sisters: Women Poets, Feminist Critics* (1979), *The Norton Anthology of Literature by Women: The Tradition in English* (1985), and *Mothersongs: Poems For, By, and About Mothers* (1995).

Margaret Homans is Professor of English at Yale University. She is the author of numerous studies of women's writing in the Victorian period, as well as in contemporary fiction, including *Women Writers and Poetic Identity: Dorothy Wordsworth, Emily Brontë, and Emily Dickinson* (1980) and *Bearing the Word: Language and Female Experience in Nineteenth-Century Women's Writing* (1986). Her recent articles include "Dinah's Blush, Maggie's Arm: Class, Gender, and Sexuality in George Eliot's Early Novels" (1993) and "Feminist Fictions and Feminist Theories of Narrative" (1994); she is the editor of *Virginia Woolf: A Collection of Critical Essays* (1993).

bell hooks is the name under which Gloria Watkins writes extensively concerning such topics as the relation of mothering, violence, and writing to African-Americans. Her books include *Ain't I a Woman: Black Women and Feminism* (1981), *Feminist Theory from Margin to Center* (1984), *Talking Back: Thinking Feminist, Thinking Black* (1989), *Yearning: Race, Gender, and Cultural Politics* (1990), *Breaking Bread: Insurgent Black Intellectual Life* (1991), *Black Looks: Race and Representation* (1992), *Sisters of the Yam: Black Women and Self-Recovery* (1993), *Outlaw Culture: Resisting Representations* (1994), *Teaching to Transgress: Education as the Practice of Freedom* (1994), and *Killing Rage: Ending Racism* (1995). She is currently Distinguished Professor of English at City College in New York.

Luce Irigaray practices psychoanalysis at École des Hautes Études en Sciences Sociales in Paris. Her writing examines issues of language, the female body, psychoanalysis, and sexual difference. English translations of her books include *Speculum of the Other Woman* (trans. 1985), *This Sex Which Is Not One* (trans. 1985), *Elemental Passions* (trans. 1992), *An Ethics of Sexual Difference* (trans. 1993), *Sexes and Genealogies* (trans. 1993), and *Thinking the Difference: For a Peaceful Revolution* (trans. 1994).

Mary Jacobus, the Anderson Professor of English at Cornell University, is the author of *Women Writing and Writing about Women* (1979), *Reading Woman: Essays in Feminist Criticism* (1986), and *Romanticism, Writing and Sexual Difference: Essays on The Prelude (1989)*. She has also published the essays "'The Third Stroke': Reading Woolf with Freud" (1988) and "Madonna: Like a Virgin, or, Freud, Kristeva, and the Case of the Missing Mother" (1986), as well as co-editing, with Evelyn Fox Keller and Sally Shuttleworth, *Body Politics: Women and the Discourses of Science* (1990).

Susan Jeffords is Professor of English and Women's Studies at the University of Washington and Dean of the Social Sciences. The author of numerous studies that examine war, gender, and nationalism, she has published *The Remasculini-zation of America: Gender and the Vietnam War* (1989), *Hard Bodies: Hollywood Masculinity in the Reagan Era* (1994), and *Seeing Through the Media: The Persian Gulf War* (1994). She is co-founder of the journal *Genders*.

Myra Jehlen is Board of Governors Professor of Literature at Rutgers University. She has written, among other works, *American Incarnation: The Individual, the Nation, and the Continent* (1986) and the *Literature of Colonization: 1580–1800* in *The Cambridge Literary History of the United States*, Volume I (1994); she is also the co-editor of *The English Literatures of America* (1996).

Barbara Johnson is Professor of English and Comparative Literature, as well as the Chair of Comparative Literature, at Harvard University. She is the author of *The Critical Difference: Essays in the Contemporary Rhetoric of Reading* (1980), *A World of Difference* (1987), *The Postmodern in Feminism* (1992), and *Freedom and Interpretation* (1993); she is the co-editor, with Jonathan Arac, of *Consequences of Theory* (1991). In addition to translating *La Dissemination* by Jacques Derrida, she has published numerous other works that range in topic from Mallarmé to African-American women's fiction. Her most recent essays include "'Aesthetic' and 'Rapport' in Morrison's *Sula*" (1993) and "Lesbian Spectacles: Reading *Sula, Passing, Thelma and Louise*, and *The Accused*" (1993).

Ann Rosalind Jones, Professor of Comparative Literature at Smith College, is the author of *The Currency of Eros: Women's Love Lyric in Europe 1540–1620* (1990), as well as numerous essays examining sixteenth-century literature. Among her other works are examinations of French feminism and the essay "Enabling Sites and Gender Difference: Reading City Women with Men" (1991).

Cora Kaplan is Professor of English, as well as Director of the Institute for Research on Women, at Rutgers University. The author of numerous studies of women's nineteenth-century literature, she has published *Sea Changes: Culture and Feminism* (1986) as well as the recent essays "Fictions and Feminism: Figuring the Material" (1993) and "The Professional Fix: Anglophone Feminist Criticism in National Contexts" (1993). She has edited the anthology *Salt and Bitter and Good: Three Centuries of English and American Women Poets* (1975) and co-edited, with Victor Burgin and James Donald, *Formations of Fantasy* (1986).

Linda S. Kauffman is Professor of English at the University of Maryland. She is the author of *Discourses of Desire: Gender, Genre, and Epistolary Fictions* (1986) and *Special Delivery: Epistolary Modes in Modern Fiction* (1992), and editor of several volumes of feminist criticism and theory, including *Feminism and Institutions: Dialogues on Feminist Theory* (1989), *Gender and Theory: Dialogues on Feminist Criticism* (1989), and *American Feminist Thought at Century's End* (1993). She is also the author of numerous articles including "Special Delivery: Twenty-First-Century Epistolarity in *The Handmaid's Tale*" (1989), which won the Florence Howe prize as the best feminist essay of the year in 1988, and "Framing *Lolita*: Is There a Woman in the Text?" (1993).

Annette Kolodny is Professor of Comparative Cultural and Literary Studies at the University of Arizona and the author of *The Lay of the Land: Metaphor as Experience* and *History in American Life and Letters* (1975) and *The Land Before Her: Fantasy and Experience of the American Frontiers. 1630–1860* (1984), as well as numerous explorations of feminist theory, including a follow-up to her essay "Dancing Through the Minefield," called "Dancing between Left and Right: Feminism and the Academic Minefield in the 1980s" (1988). Among her most recent articles is "Inventing a Feminist Discourse: Rhetoric and Resistance in Margaret Fuller's *Woman in the Nineteenth Century*" (1994).

Julia Kristeva, Professor at the Université de Paris VII, is also a psychoanalyst and writer. Her works cover a wide breadth of topics, including clinical depression, narratology, semiotics, political philosophy, and Chinese women. Her books include *Language: The Unknown* (1990), *Desire in Language: A Semiotic Approach to Literature and Art* (1980), *Tales of Horror: An Essay on Abjection* (1982), *Revolution in Poetic Language* (1984), *Nations Without Nationalism* (1993), *Proust and the Sense of Time* (1993), and *New Maladies of the Soul* (1995).

Susan S. Lanser is Professor of English and Director of Comparative Literature at the University of Maryland. She is the author of numerous articles dealing with feminism and narratology. Her work includes *The Narrative Act: Point of View in Fiction* (1981), and *Fictions of Authority: Women Writers and Narrative Voice* (1992), as well as "Burning Dinners: Feminist Subversion of Domesticity" (1993) and "Compared to What? Global Feminism, Comparatism, and the Master's Tools" (1994).

Paul Lauter is the A. K. and G. M. Smith Professor of Literature at Trinity College, Connecticut and the general editor of the *Heath Anthology of American Literature*. He recently served as the president of the American Studies Association. He writes about canon formation (*Canons and Contexts*, 1991), working-class literature, women and professionalism, and Cold War culture.

Shirley Geok-lin Lim is Professor of English and Women's Studies at the University of California at Santa Barbara, as well as an editor for the journal *Feminist Studies*. She is the co-editor, with Amy Ling, of *Reading the Literatures of Asian America* (1992), and editor of *Approaches to Teaching Kingston's* The Woman Warrior (1991), and *The Forbidden Stitch: An Asian American Women's Anthology* (1989). She is the author of two critical studies, and has published four books of poems, two collections of short stories, and a book of memoirs, *Among the White Moon Faces* (1996).

Amy Ling is Professor of English and Director of Asian American Studies at the University of Wisconsin, Madison. She is the author of numerous critical articles, among them "Maxine Hong Kingston and the Dialogic Dilemmas of Asian American

Writers" (1995), "Chinese American Women Writers: The Tradition Behind Maxine Hong Kingston" (1990), "Asian-American Literature: A Brief Introduction and Bibliography" (1985). She is the author of *Between Worlds: Women Writers of Chinese Ancestry* (1990) and *Chinamerican Reflections* (1987), a chapbook of her poems and paintings, and co-editor of seven critical literary anthologies.

Joseph Litvak is Associate Professor of English at Bowdoin College and the author of numerous studies of contemporary literary theory and nineteenth-century fiction. Among his publications are "Back to the Future: A Review-Article on the New Historicism, Deconstruction, and Nineteenth-Century Fiction" (1988) and *Caught in the Act: Theatricality in the Nineteenth-Century English Novel* (1992); *Strange Gourmets: Sophistication, Theory, and the Novel* is forthcoming.

Jane Marcus is Distinguished Professor of English at City University of New York and City College of New York. Author of *Virginia Woolf and the Languages of Patriarchy* (1987), and *Art & Anger: Reading Like a Woman* (1988), she is also the editor of three volumes of Woolf criticism and *The Young Rebecca West*. She has written Afterwords to Feminist Press reprints of women's World War I novels and June Arnold's *Sister Gin*. She is a socialist feminist critic, whose recent work includes "Corpus/Corps/Corpse: Writing the Body in/at War" (1989), "Britannia Rules *The Waves*," "Race in a Room of One's Own," and a project on Nancy Cunnard.

Biddy Martin is Assistant Professor of German and Women's Studies at Cornell University. She is the author of *Woman and Modernity: The (Life)Styles of Lou Andreas-Salomé* (1991), as well as articles on German literature and art nouveau, and sexual difference and feminist criticism. She has published works such as "Feminism, Criticism and Foucault" (1982) and "The Hobo, the Fairy, and the Quarterback" (1994).

Deborah E. McDowell is Associate Professor of English at the University of Virginia. She is the author of *"The Changing Same": Black Women's Literature, Criticism, and Theory* (1995); the co-editor, with Arnold Rampersad, of *Slavery and the Literary Imagination* (1989); and the editor of the Beacon Black Women Writers Series. She has published several studies about black women novelists, including "'That Nameless . . . Shameful Impulse': Sexuality in Nella Larsen's *Quicksand* and *Passing*" (1988), "'The Self and the Other': Reading Toni Morrison's *Sula* and the Black Female Text" (1988), and "Boundaries: Or, Distant Relations and Close Kin" (1989).

Nellie McKay is Professor of Afro-American and American Literature at the University of Wisconsin, Madison, and is widely published on issues of Afro-American writing, including black theater, autobiography, and the canon. She is the editor of *Critical Essays on Toni Morrison* (1988), co-editor of the *Norton Anthology of Afro-American Literature* (forthcoming), and Associate Editor of *African American Review*. Her publications include *Jean Toomer, Artist: A Study of his Literary Life and Work 1894–1936* (1984) and the recent essays "Alice Walker's 'Advancing Luna—and Ida B. Wells' A Struggle toward Sisterhood" (1991), "Beyond the Story: Reading Black Women's Lives in Madison, WI" (1993), and "The Journals of Charlotte L. Forten-Grimké: *Les Lieux de Memoire* in African-American Women's Autobiography" (1994).

Elizabeth Meese, Professor of English at the University of Alabama, is the author of works examining feminist criticism, lesbianism, and canonicity. Among others, her works include *Crossing the Double-Cross: The Practice of Feminist Criticism* (1986), *E(x)tensions: Re-figuring Feminist Criticism* (1990), and *(Sem)Erotics: Theorizing Lesbian: Writing* (1992). She is the co-editor of *The Difference Within* (1989) and *Feminist Critical Negotiations* (1992).

Helena Michie, Professor of English at Rice University, is the author of *The Flesh Made Word: Female Figures and Women's Bodies* (1987) and *Sororophobia: Differences Among Women in Literature and Culture* (1992) and co-author of *Confinements: Fertility and Infertility in Contemporary Culture* (1997). She has also published articles exploring the nineteenth century, women's identity, psychoanalysis, and sisterhood, including "Mother, Sister, Other: The 'Other Woman' in Feminist Theory" (1986) and "'Dying between Two Laws': Girl Heroines, Their Gods, and Their Fathers in *Uncle Tom's Cabin* and the Elsie Dinsmore Series" (1989).

Chandra Talpade Mohanty, Professor of Women's Studies at Hamilton College, New York, has research interests that include antiracist pedagogy and postcolonial feminism. She is the co-editor, with Ann Russo and Lourdes Torres, of *Third World Women and the Politics of Feminism* (1991), and with Jaqui Alexander, of *Feminist Genealogies, Colonial Legacies, Democratic Futures* (1996).

Laura Mulvey is Postgraduate Programme Tutor at the British Film Institute. Her work includes *Visual and Other Pleasures* (1989), "Some Thoughts on Theories of Fetishism in the Context of Contemporary Culture" (1989), "British Feminist Film Theory's Female Spectators: Presence and Absence" (1989), "Afterthoughts on 'Visual Pleasure and Narrative Cinema' Inspired by *Duel in the Sun*" (1990), and *Fetishism and Curiosity* (1996).

Beth Newman is Associate Professor of English at Southern Methodist University in Dallas. Professor Newman's publications examine speakers, seduction, and the gaze in nineteenth-century literature. Among her works are the essays "Getting Fixed: Feminine Identity and Scopic Crisis in *The Turn of the Screw*" (1992) and "*The Heart of Midlothian* and the Masculinization of Fiction" (1994).

Judith Newton is Professor and Director of Women's Studies at the University of California, Davis. She is the author of *Women, Power, and Subversion: Social Strategies in British Fiction 1778–1860* (1981) and *Starting Over: Feminism and the Politics of Cultural Critique* (1994). She is co-editor of *Sex and Class in Women's History* (1983) and *Feminist Criticism and Social Change: Sex, Class, and Race in Literature and Culture* (1985). Recent articles explore post-1960s masculinities including "Family/Value: Reflections on a Long Revolution" (1994) and, with Judith Stacey, "Ms.Representations: Reflections on Studying Academic Men" (1995).

Diane Price Herndl is Associate Professor of English at New Mexico State University. She is the author of *Invalid Women: Figuring Feminine Illness in American Fiction and Culture, 1840–1940* (1993) as well as essays on Bakhtin and feminist theory, and psychoanalysis and feminism. Her recent work includes "The Invisible (Invalid) Woman: African-American Women, Illness, and Nineteenth-Century Narrative" (1995).

Leslie Rabine, Professor of French at the University of California, Irvine, is author of *Reading the Romantic Heroine: Text, History, Ideology* (1985), co-author of *Feminism, Socialism, and French Romanticism* (1993), and co-editor of *Rebel Daughters: Women and the French Revolution* (1992). Her current research concerns the global circulation of African fashion.

Janice Radway is Professor of English at Duke University and the author of numerous studies of romance literature, especially in relation to gender, class, and readership. She is the author of *Reading the Romance: Women, Patriarchy, and Popular Literature* (1984; revised 1991) and has also published widely on book clubs, including the essay "The Scandal of the Middlebrow: The Book-of-the-Month Club, Class Fracture, and Cultural Authority" (1990).

Lillian S. Robinson is Garvin Professor of English at Virginia Polytechnic Institute and State University. She has written *Sex, Class, and Culture* (1978) and *Monstrous Regiment: The Lady Knight in Sixteenth-Century Epic* (1985) and is co-author of *Feminist Scholarship: Kindling in the Groves of Academe* (1985). She is also co-editor of *Revealing Lines: Autobiography, Biography and Gender* (1990). Recent articles include "The Practice of Theories: An Immodest Proposal" (1994) and "'The Great Unexamined': Silence, Speech, and Class" (1994).

Joanna Russ, Professor of English at the University of Washington, is the author of feminist science fiction and of critical studies, both of which often explore the concept of utopia. Her books include *How to Suppress Women's Writing* (1983) and *To Write Like a Woman: Essays in Feminism and Science Fiction* (1995), and her recent articles include "The Autobiography of My Mother" (1991) and "The Counterdiscourse of the Feminine" (1992).

Rosaura Sánchez is Professor of Spanish at the University of California, San Diego. Her publications include examinations of the work of Rolando Hinojosa, Chicano discourse, and Chicano literature and its relation to postmodernism. Her publications include *Telling Identities: The Californio Testimonios* (1995), "Subjectivity in Chicano Literature" (1990), and "Ideological Discourses in Arturo Islas's *The Rain God*" (1991).

Patrocinio P. Schweickart, Professor of English at the University of New Hampshire is widely published in the area of feminist theory, as well as feminist literary criticism. She is co-editor, with Elizabeth A. Flynn, of *Gender and Reading: Essays on Readers, Texts, and Contexts* (1986), and her publications include "Engendering Critical Discourse" (1987), "Reading Teaching, and the Ethic of Care" (1990), and "What Are We Doing? What Do We Want? Who Are We? Comprehending the Subject of Feminism" (1995). Her essay "Reading Ourselves: Toward a Feminist Theory of Reading" won the Florence Howe Award in 1984. She is editor of *NWSA Journal.*

Eve Kosofsky Sedgwick, Professor of English at Duke University, is the author of *Between Men: English Literature and Male Homosocial Desire* (1985); *Epistemology of the Closet* (1990); *Tendencies* (1993), and numerous articles examining homosexuality, including the essay "Socratic Raptures, Socratic Ruptures: Notes Toward Queer Performativity" (1993). She also has published explorations of gender relations in authors such as Henry James, Walt Whitman, Laurence Sterne, and Willa Cather.

Elaine Showalter, Chair and Professor of English at Princeton University, is a founding theorist in Anglo-American feminist criticism. In addition to editing several feminist criticism anthologies, including *Speaking of Gender* (1989), she is the author of *A Literature of Their Own: British Women Novelists from Brontë to Lessing* (1977), *The Female Malady: Women, Madness, and Culture in England 1830–1980* (1985), *Sexual Anarchy: Gender and Culture at the Fin de Siècle* (1990), *Sister's Choice: Tradition and Change in American Women's Writing* (1991) and *Daughters of Decadence: Women Writers of the Fin de Siècle* (1993). Her recent articles include "On Hysterical Narrative" (1993) and "American Gynocriticism" (1993).

Barbara Smith is a black feminist, writer, activist, and co-founder of Kitchen Table Press; she is the co-editor of *Conditions: Five, The Black Women's Issue* (1979), *Home Girls: A Black Feminist Anthology* (1983), and *All the Women are White, and All the Blacks are Men, But Some of Us Are Brave: Black Women's Studies* (1982) as well as the co-author of *Yours in Struggle: Three Feminist Perspectives on Anti-Semitism and Racism* (1984). Her essays examine issues of racism, sexuality, and writing and include "A Press of Our Own: Kitchen Table: Women of Color Press" (1989) and "Packing Boxes and Editing Manuscripts: Women of Color in Feminist Publishing" (1993).

Sidonie Smith, Professor of English and Director of Women's Studies at the University of Michigan, is the author of *Where I'm Bound: Patterns of Slavery and Freedom in Black American Autobiography* (1974), *A Poetics of Women's Autobiography: Marginality and the Fictions of Self-Representation* (1987), and *Subjectivity, Identity, and the Body: Women's Autobiographical Practices in the Twentieth Century* (1993). She is the co-editor of *De/colonizing the Subject: The Politics of Gender in Women's Autobiography* (1992) and *Getting a Life: Uses of Autobiography* (1996), and the author of essays including "The Autobiographical Manifesto: Identities, Temporalities, Politics" (1992) and "'Who's Talking/Who's Talking Back?: The Subject of Personal Narrative" (1993).

Valerie Smith, Professor of English at the University of California, Los Angeles, is the editor of *African American Writers* (1991) and *New Essays on* Song of Solomon (1995) and co-editor of *The Columbia History of the American Novel* (1991), as well as the author of *Self-Discovery and Authority in Afro-American Narrative* (1987). She is also the author of several articles on Afro-American literature and black women film-makers as well as "Gender and Afro-Americanist Literary Theory and Criticism" (1989) and "Reading the Intersection of Race and Gender in Narratives of Passing" (1994).

James J. Sosnoski is Professor of English at the University of Illinois, Chicago, as well as the Executive Director of Alternative Educational Environments. He is the author of *Token Professionals and Master Critics: A Critique of Orthodoxy in Literary Studies* (1994) and *Modern Skeletons in Postmodern Closets: A Cultural Studies Alternative* (1995); his recent essays range from students and computers in the classroom to literary studies and postmodernity, and include "What Does It Mean to Work at Reading Narratives" (1992).

Hortense Spillers is the editor of *Comparative American Identities: Race, Sex, and Nationality in the Modern Text* (1991) and is author of many essays on women and African-American literature, including "'The Permanent Obliquity of an In(pha)llibly Straight': In the Time of the Daughters and the Fathers" (1989); she is the co-editor, with Majorie Pryse, of *Conjuring: Black Women Fiction and Literary Tradition* (1985). She is currently Professor of English at Cornell University.

Gayatri Chakravorty Spivak is Avalon Foundation Professor in the Humanities at Columbia University and the author of *In Other Worlds: Essays in Cultural Politics* (1987), *Outside in the Teaching Machine* (1993), and *The Spivak Reader* (1995). Spivak is the author of several studies of Yeats, and the translator of Jacques Derrida's *Of Grammatology* and the fiction of Mahasweta Devi. Her publications, which explore (among other issues) colonization, internationalization, and French feminism, include, "French Feminism Revisited: Ethics and Politics" (1992), "Echo" (1993), "The Burden of English" (1993), and "Examples to Fit the Title" (1994).

Jane Tompkins, Professor of English at Duke University, is a teacher, writer, and workshop leader. She is the author of *Sensational Designs: The Cultural Work of American Fiction, 1790–1860* (1985) and *West of Everything* (1991), as well as the editor of *Reader-Response Criticism: From Formalism to Post-Structuralism* (1981). Her latest book, *A Life in School: What the Teacher Learned* (1996), is an autobiographical critique of classroom practice and the culture of academic institutions.

Robyn R. Warhol is Professor of English and Director of Women's Studies at the University of Vermont. Author of *Gendered Interventions: Narrative Discourse in the Victorian Novel* (1989) and co-editor of *Women's Work* (1991), she has published essays on feminist narratology, narrative strategies in nineteenth-century prose, and nineteenth-century British and American women authors. Her recent essays include "'Reader, Can You Imagine? No, You Cannot': The Narratee as Other in Harriet Jacobs's Text" (1995) and "Narrating the Unnarratable: Gender and Metonymy in the Victorian Novel " (1994). She is currently working on a poetics of serial fiction and soap opera.

Susan Willis is the author of *Specifying: Black Women Writing the American Experience* (1987), *A Primer for Daily Life* (1991), and *Inside the Mouse: Work and Play at*

Disney World (1995), as well as essays on American popular culture and Caribbean literatures. Her recent works include "Hardcore: Subculture American Style" (1993) and *Play for Profit* (1996). She is Associate Professor of English at Duke University.

Bonnie Zimmerman is Professor of Women's Studies at San Diego State University. Her critical studies include *The Safe Sea of Women: Lesbian Fiction, 1969–1989* (1990), "Lesbians Like This and That: Some Notes on Lesbian Criticism for the 90s" (1992), "Perverse Reading: The Lesbian Appropriation of Literature" (1993), and "George Eliot's Sacred Chest of Language" (1993).

ALTERNATIVE ARRANGEMENTS FOR *FEMINISMS*

As our introduction explains, the arrangement of *Feminisms* is meant to be neither prescriptive nor definitive. We offer this index as a set of suggestions toward other ways of organizing the material. We include references to a few literary authors and works that appear repeatedly in these essays, to help instructors select primary texts they might teach with this book.

ACADEMIA

ACTIVISM

AFRICAN-AMERICAN FEMINIST THEORY

DISCOURSE

DOMESTICITY/HOME/FAMILY

ETHNICITY/RACE

WRITING
NANCY ARMSTRONG, "Some Call It Fiction,"
SHARI BENSTOCK, "Authorizing the Autobiographical,"
HÉLÈNE CIXOUS, "The Laugh of the Medusa,"
SUSAN STANFORD FRIEDMAN, "When a 'Long' Poem Is a 'Big' Poem,"
SANDRA M. GILBERT, and SUSAN GUBAR, "Infection in the Sentence,"
MARY JACOBUS, "Reading Women (Reading),"
ANN ROSALIND JONES, "Writing the Body,"
ELIZABETH MEESE, "When Virginia Looked at Vita,"
LESLIE RABINE, "Romance in the Age of Electronics,"
JOANNA RUSS, "Anomalousness" and "Aesthetics,"
JANE TOMPKINS, "Me and My Shadow,"

EIGHTEENTH-CENTURY WOMEN'S LITERATURE
NANCY ARMSTRONG, "Some Call It Fiction,"
CORA KAPLAN, "Pandora's Box,"
HELENA MICHIE, "Confinements,"
BETH NEWMAN, "'The Situation of the Looker-On,'"
GAYATRI CHAKRAVORTY SPIVAK, "Three Women's Texts,"

NINETEENTH-CENTURY WOMEN'S LITERATURE
NANCY ARMSTRONG, "Some Call It Fiction,"
NINA BAYM, "The Madwoman and Her Languages,"
LAUREN BERLANT, "The Queen of America Goes to Washington City,"
TERRY CASTLE, "Sylvia Townsend Warner,"
WAI-CHEE DIMOCK, "Feminism, New Historicism, and the Reader,"
SANDRA M. GILBERT, and SUSAN GUBAR, "Infection in the Sentence,"
NELLIE McKAY, "Reflections on Black Women Writers,"
JUDITH LOWDER NEWTON, "Power and Ideology of 'Women's Sphere,'"
LESLIE RABINE, "Romance in the Age of Electronics,"
PATROCINIO P. SCHWEICKART, "Reading Ourselves,"
GAYATRI CHAKRAVORTY SPIVAK, "Three Women's Texts,"

TWENTIETH-CENTURY WOMEN'S LITERATURE
TERRY CASTLE, "Sylvia Townsend Warner,"
SUSAN STANFORD FRIEDMAN, "When a 'Long' Poem Is a 'Big' Poem,"
BARBARA JOHNSON, "Apostrophe, Animation, and Abortion,"
NELLIE McKAY, "Reflections on Black Women Writers,"
ELIZABETH MEESE, "When Virginia Looked at Vita,"
LESLIE RABINE, "Romance in the Age of Electronics,"
JANICE RADWAY, "Readers and Their Romances,"
BARBARA SMITH, "The Truth That Never Hurts,"
SIDONIE SMITH, "Maxine Hong Kingston's *Woman Warrior*,"
VALERIE SMITH, "Black Feminist Theory,"
GAYATRI CHAKRAVORTY SPIVAK, "Three Women's Texts,"
SUSAN WILLIS, "I Shop Therefore I Am,"

AUTHOR/TITLE INDEX

TEXT PERMISSIONS

The editors gratefully acknowledge permission to reprint essays from the following sources:

Institutions: Shoshana Felman, "Women and Madness: The Critical Phallacy," *Diacritics* (Winter 1975): 2–10. Sandra M. Gilbert and Susan Gubar, "Infection in the Sentence: The Woman Writer and the Anxiety of Authorship," from *The Madwoman in the Attic: The Woman Writer and the Nineteenth-Century Literary Imagination* (New Haven: Yale University Press, 1979); copyright © 1979 by Yale University Press; reprinted by permission. James J. Sosnoski, "A Mindless Man-driven Theory Machine: Intellectuality, Sexuality, and the Institution of Criticism," in *Feminism and Institutions: Dialogues on Feminist Theory,* ed. Linda Kauffman (Oxford: Basil Blackwell, 1989). Barbara Christian, "The Highs and Lows of Black Feminist Criticism," (1990). Helena Michie, "Confinements: The Domestic in the Discourses of Upper-Middle-Class Pregnancy," (New Brunswick, N.J.: Rutgers University Press, 1996); copyright © 1996 by Helena Michie.

Canon: Bonnie Zimmerman, "What Has Never Been: An Overview of Lesbian Feminist Literary Criticism," *Feminist Studies* 7: 3 (Fall 1981): 451–475; reprinted by permission of the publisher, Feminist Studies Inc., c/o Women's Studies Program, University of Maryland, College Park, MD 20742. Joanna Russ, "Anomalousness" and "Aesthetics" from *How to Supress Women's Writing* (Austin: University of Texas Press, 1983); copyright © 1983 by Joanna Russ; reprinted by permission of the author and the University of Texas Press. Lillian S. Robinson, "Treason Our Text: Feminist Challenges to the Literary Canon," *Tulsa Studies in Women's Literature* 2 : 1 (Spring 1983); copyright © 1983 by the University of Tulsa; reprinted by permission of the publisher. Paul Lauter, "Caste, Class, and Canon," in *A Gift of Tongues: Critical Challenges in Contemporary American Poetry,* ed. Marie Harris and Kathleen Aguero (Athens: University of George Press, 1987); copyright © 1987 by Paul Lauter. Nellie McKay, "Reflections on Black Women Writers: Revising the Literary Canon," in *The Impact of Feminist Research in the Academy,* ed. Christie Farnham (Bloomington: Indiana University Press, 1987).

right © 1985 by Cornell University; used by permission of the publisher, Cornell University Press. Laura Mulvey, "Visual Pleasure and Narrative Cinema," *Screen* 16: 3 (Autumn 1975). Beth Newman, "'The Situation of the Looker-On': Gender, Narration, and Gaze in *Wuthering Heights*," *PMLA* 105 (1990): 1029–1041; reprinted by permission of the Modern Langauge Association of America. Elizabeth Meese, "When Virginia Looked at Vita, What Did She See; or, Lesbian: Feminist: Woman—What's the Differ(e/a)nce?," *Feminist Studies* 18 : 1 (Spring 1992) 99–117; reprinted by permission of the publisher, Feminist Studies Inc., c/o Women's Studies Program, University of Maryland, College Park, MD 20742.

Desire: Jane Gallop, "The Father's Seduction" from *The Daughter's Seduction* (Ithaca, N.Y.: Cornell University Press, 1982); copyright © 1982 by Jane Gallop; used by permission of the publisher, Cornell University Press. Eve Kosofsky Sedgwick, "Introduction" and "Gender Asymmetry and Erotic Triangles," from *Between Men: English Literature and Male Homosexual Desire* (New York: Columbia University Press, 1985). Terry Castle, "Sylvia Townsend Warner and the Counterplot of Lesbian Fiction," from *The Apparitional Lesbian* (New York: Columbia University Press, 1993); copyright © 1993; reprinted with permission of the publisher. bell hooks, "Male Heroes and Female Sex Objects: Sexism in Spike Lee's *Malcolm X*," *Cineaste* 19:4 (1993).

Reading: Judith Fetterley, "Introduction: On the Politics of Literature," from *The Resisting Reader: A Feminist Approach to American Fiction* (Bloomington: Indiana University Press, 1977). Janice Radway, "The Readers and Their Romances," from *Reading the Romance: Women, Patriarchy, and Popular Literature* (Chapel Hill: University of North Carolina Press, 1984); copyright © 1984 by the University of North Carolina Press; reprinted by permission. Patrocinio P. Schweickart, "Reading Ourselves: Toward a Feminist Theory of Reading," in *Gender and Reading: Essays on Readers, Texts, and Contexts*, ed. Elizabeth A. Flynn and Patrocinio P. Schweickart (Baltimore: Johns Hopkins University Press, 1986). Wai-Chee Dimock, "Feminism, New Historicism, and the Reader" (1991).

Discourse: Catherine Belsey, "Constructing the Subject: Deconstructing the Text," in *Feminist Criticism and Social Change*, ed. J. Newton and D. Rosenfelt (London: Methuen, 1985). Susan S. Lanser, "Toward a Feminist Narratology," *Style* 20 : 3 (Fall 1986): 341–363. Barbara Johnson, "Apostrophe, Animation, and Abortion," *Diacritics* 16 : 1 (Spring 1986): 29–39. Dale Bauer, "Gender in Bakhtin's Carnival," from *Feminine Dialogics: A Theory of Failed Community* (Albany: State University of New York Press, 1988). Susan Stanford Friedman, "When a 'Long' Poem is a 'Big' Poem: Self-Authorizing Strategies in Women's Twentieth-Century 'Long Poems'," *LIT* 2 (l990): 9–25.

Ethnicity: Paula Gunn Allen, "Kochinnenako in Academe: Three Approaches to Interpreting a Keres Indian Tale," from *The Sacred Hoop: Recovering the Feminine in American Indian Traditions* (Boston: Beacon Press, 1986); copyright © 1986 by Paula Gunn Allen; reprinted by permission of Beacon Press. Gloria Anzaldúa, "La conciencia de la mestiza: Towards a New Consciousness," from *Borderlands/La*